PRODUCTION RESOURCE • VOL. 11 2009-2010 EDITION

WWW.NEWYORK411.COM

THE TRI-STATE AREA'S PROFESSIONAL REFERENCE GUIDE FOR FILM, TELEVISION, COMMERCIAL AND MUSIC VIDEO PRODUCTION

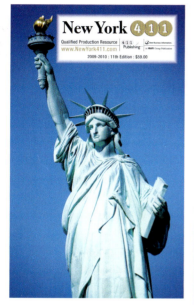

Cover photo by John Hutchinson
ALSAM (Association of Location Scouts & Managers)

Publisher: **Sean Killebrew**

Senior Editor: **Steve Atinsky**
Assistant Editor: **Bryan Cuprill**
Assistant Editor: **Marjorie Galas**
Editorial Assistant: **Tom Wilson**

Advertising Director, New York: **Jeffry Gitter**
Account Executive: **Spencer Aaronson**
Online Account Executive: **Aaron Biberstein**
Account Executive: **Annmarie LaRocca**
Sales Coordinator: **Jane Hur**

Group Production Director: **Mary Bradley**
Production Director: **Carlos Lopez**
Group Art Director: **Jennifer Rzepka**
Graphic Designer: **Andrea Wynnyk**

Senior Manager of Operations: **Joni Ballinger**
Business Manager: **Juliette Nichols**

Manager of Online Services: **Apul Bhalani**
Client Service Manager: **James Dennis**

Tad Smith
CEO

Neil Stiles
President, Publisher
Variety Entertainment Group

Jim Guttridge
Vice President, Finance

Linda Buckley-Bruno
Group Publisher
Home Entertainment Group

The Publisher has taken all reasonable measures to ensure the accuracy of the information in this edition of New York 411® but cannot accept responsibility for any errors or omissions or any liability resulting from the use or misuse of any such information. The entire contents of the 2009-10 edition of New York 411® by 411 Publishing Company may not be reproduced or transmitted in any form or by any graphic, digital, electronic, mechanical or other means including photocopying, recording, taping or information storage and retrieval systems of any nature without the prior written permission of the Publisher. All rights reserved. 411 Publishing reserves the right to remove and/or requalify listings at any time. Address all correspondence to: 411 Publishing Company, 5900 Wilshire Boulevard, 31st Floor, Los Angeles, California 90036, USA.

411 Publishing Book Sales
(323) 617-9400
411 Publishing Editorial and Administration:
(800) 545-2411
411 Publishing Advertising Sales:
(800) 545-2411 FAX (323) 617-9535
www.LA411.com www.NewYork411.com www.Variety411.com

A *Variety* Group Publication

Letter From The Publisher and Editorial Staff

In April of 2008 New York Governor David Paterson tripled the state tax credit for below-the-line expenses to 30% resulting in an explosion of film and television production. Within ten months more than 125 film and television projects had taken advantage of the expanded state credits. Together with an additional 5% credit provided by New York City, the incentives helped create and retain an estimated 19,000 jobs. However, due to the success of program, funds that had been orginally designed to last through 2013, were exhausted within a year of its inception.

New York 411, in support of the New York Production Alliance's efforts to re-new the incentives, placed a roadblock on our website for several weeks linking to the NYPA wesbsite, which spearheaded a letter writing campaign to extend the credits through 2009 and beyond. In April the Governor included funds for the 30% state tax incentive for 2009-10 in the state budget.

We've added some new categories for this year's directory in response to calls from users. These include: Nautical Film Services, Aerial Picture Vehicles, Steadicam Operators and Budgeting & Scheduling.

For our tabs this year we've gone with an "unseen New York" theme—hidden gems and places that are off the beaten path but great filming locations for features, TV and commercials. A big thank you to the photograhers at the Association of Location Scouts & Managers (ALSAM) for their great work.

Thanks also goes out to our allies at the New York State Film Commission and the NYC Mayor's office, New York's unions and guilds and the film offices in Connecticut, New Jersey and Philadelphia for their assistance.

Please know that we are here to support the New York production community. If you have suggestions, comments, general feedback, etc. please feel free to call us directly: (323) 617-9410.

Sean Killebrew
Publisher

Steve Atinsky
Senior Editor

How To Use New York 411

New York 411 is divided into ten sections, and each section is divided into categories. There are over 200 specific categories in New York 411 for all your production needs, from the first day of pre-production, to the last day of post.

You can find exactly what you need quickly with our detailed indexes, found at the front of the book. The Company/Crew Index will help you find a specific company or individual by name, while the General Index lists over 3,000 specific products and services and tells you where in the book they may be found. Please note that the General Index points to the first page of a category, while the description item may be found throughout the category.

New York 411 is proud to include listings from Local 52, Local 161, Local 600, Local 764, Local 798, Local 829, and the DGA for the New York area. The lists containing the names and phone numbers of union members were provided directly from these unions and only feature members in the New York area (LA union members who work in New York would not be included in these lists). The Crew section contains Union Listings as well as our Qualified Listings. For example, you will see a category titled "Camera Assistants (Local 600 NY)" and another just called "Camera Assistants." The first contains names provided by the unions, the latter is made up of our New York 411 Qualified Listings.

For those who already have a Qualified Listing with us and whose names appeared on the union list, we have used the contact information that was originally provided to us by that individual on their New York 411 listing application. In most cases these listees use our online updating system to give us their current information.

As with all of our listings, every reasonable effort has been made to insure that all listing information is current and accurate. Please refer to the next page for information on how to update your listing at any time.

How To Advertise In New York 411

411 Publishing offers a variety of advertising packages in our print and online directories.

Because we strive to maintain a balance of editorial content and advertising in our print directories, ad space is limited. Additionally, since key spots, including tabs, go quickly, we recommend that you reserve space early for the 2010-2011 edition.

Among the options that will increase your company's prominence in our online directory are:

Impact Listing (IPL): Puts you in the blue section at the top of all searches. Also includes 10 search terms.

Enhanced Dedicated Page (EDP): A listing page on which you can provide expanded copy about your company, as well as downloadable images and documents. This also includes a red arrow next to your name on the list.

Premium IPL: This is a combination of the IPL and EDP options.

411 Features: Have you produced a video showcasing your products and/or services? 411 Features will give you the opportunity to display that video exclusively in your category, on your listing page and on the Home Page (in rotation with other videos). This is a new product for 411, and as a result, you will gain added exposure in your run-of-site campaign.

To become an online advertiser or to learn more about our print and online advertising programs, please call us at (800) 545-2411.

How To Update Your Current Listing

New York 411 sends every listee an e-mail in the winter prompting you to confirm or update your existing listing for the next print edition of the directory.

You can, however, update your listing at any time by going to **www.NewYork411.com**, and clicking on the "Edit Your Listing" button at the top of the page, where you will be prompted to enter your user name and password for verification. Your user name is the e-mail address which you provided us for contacting you. If you are unsure as to what your user name may be, or if you need to be issued one, please e-mail us at 411update@reedbusiness.com.

If you are unsure as to what your password may be, use the "Forgot Password" link and we'll send that information to your contact e-mail address. Please note: the e-mail address you enter to request your password MUST match your user name e-mail address.

If you have further questions regarding adding our amending a listing, please send an e-mail to 411update@reedbusiness.com.

Unless you are applying for a new category, please do not fill out a new application, as you will be charged for something you already have. There is no charge for changes to existing listings. You may also download an apllication or apply online at **www.newyork411.com**.

How To Get Listed In New York 411

Since our first edition in 1980, 411's editorial staff has meticulously researched and verified that every listing is qualified to be included in our directories and on our Web sites. We reserve the right to remove and/or requalify listings at any time.

Listing Requirements:

1. For New York 411: Applicants must be located in the Tri State (New York, New Jersey and Connecticut) or Philadelphia areas. For the majority of our categories, work must be performed in the aforementioned areas.

    For LA 411: Applicants must be located in Southern California (Los Angeles, Orange, Riverside, Santa Barbara, San Bernardino, San Diego or Ventura counties). For the majority of our categories, work must be performed in the aforementioned areas.

2. You are allowed to apply for up to five (5) categories.

3. All applicants must include a current resume or letter on company letterhead OR you may create a text version in our online application process.

4. You must complete the application in full including three (3) local references for each category for which you believe you are qualified and in which you would like to appear. References will be called by our applications editor. Call sheets, contracts or pay stubs are also acceptable.

5. 411 reserves the right to ask for additional references if those given are not verifiable or do not meet our professional guidelines.

6. References must be for film, television or commercials:
    - Films must have a minimum two-week theatrical release.
    - TV & commercials must be for Broadcast or Cable Networks. Local cable credits are not acceptable.

    Internet credits are only acceptable when produced for AMPTP affiliated companies—Studios, Broadcast
    Networks, certain Cable Networks and Independent Producers.
    - Film & TV references are preferred but not required for a limited number of Location & Production Support categories such as Car Rentals, Travel Agencies, Notaries, etc.

7. All applicants must pay an application fee of $200 for a new application and $50 for each additional category. Applicants can pay by credit card or business check. **All application fees are non-refundable regardless of whether an application is eventually accepted or not**. Listings are editorial content and have no monetary value.

8. A separate application must be submitted for each 411 directory you wish to be listed in.

9. Advertising with 411 has no bearing on listing approvals. As you do not have to be a qualified listee to advertise, advertisers do not automatically qualify for listings.

10. No special provisions—such as additional text—can be provided in listings. No exceptions.

11. We only list companies by their actual business name. You may be asked to provide a copy of your state/city business license to confirm your name.

12. You may apply at any time. However, to be included in the next book, completed applications must be received prior to the advertised deadline. 411 will process your application as fast as possible. During season, this may take upwards of several weeks. Please be patient.

13. Applicants may be required to complete an interview with our editors.

14. The 411 Publishing editorial staff has final say in all matters regarding what goes into our directories and our Web sites. 411 Publishing reserves the right to review, confirm, edit and or omit any listing or Enhanced Dedicated Page in whole or in part at our discretion.

15. NOT ALL APPLICANTS WILL QUALIFY.

16. You must provide at least three references per category AND pay your application fee BEFORE we can begin processing your application.

Submit Your Completed Application and any additional materials you need to send for verification to:
Application Dept.
LA 411 Publishing Co.
5900 Wilshire Blvd., 31st Fl.
Los Angeles, CA 90036
Fax: (323) 917-9535

Application For New York 411 Freelance or Business Listing

SUBMITTING AN APPLICATION DOES NOT GUARANTEE A LISTING.
PRINT BOOK DEADLINE: FRIDAY FEBRUARY 12, 2010

The application fee for NY411 is $200 for the first category and $50 for each additional category*. **The fee is non-refundable. Submitting an application does not guarantee a listing.** Listings have no monetary value. You are allowed to apply for up to five categories. You may apply at any time, however to be considered for the next printed book we must have your completed materials by Friday, February 12, 2010. Listings will appear both in print and online. *Application fee waived for advertisers (for ad rates, please call 646-746-6891 or email jeffry.gitter@reedbusiness.com).

☐ Enclosed is my application fee for $_____ for my listing(s) ($200 First/$50 ea. addl.)   Number of Listings:_____ (Limit 5)

☐ Please send me _____ copies of the 2009-10 NY411 for $49 plus 8.375% sales tax & s/h ($6 per copy) $_____
(This is a special rate that is $10 off the regular price)

Payment Info   (Check or credit card only. No cash.)   Total:_____

☐Visa ☐MC ☐Amex Card#_____   Expires_____   Name on Card_____

Cardholder Signature_____   or Check# _____

(make checks payable to 411 Publishing)
☐ Please contact me regarding display advertising or enhanced listing advertising

General Information Required

First Name _____   Last Name _____

Company Name _____   Type of Business _____

Street Address _____   Apt./Suite Number _____

   Print This Address? Yes ☐ or No ☐

City _____   ZIP Code _____

( ) _____   ( ) _____   ( ) _____
Local Phone Number   Additional Phone   Fax Number

@ _____   http:// _____
E-mail Address (To be published)   Web Address

@ _____
E-mail Address (For our contact purposes)

All information contained in every listing appears in print and online without exception

Requirements for Listing With New York 411

Three Recent Project References Required per Category

- Advertising with 411 has no bearing on listing approvals. You do not have to be a qualified listee to advertise. Advertisers do not automatically qualify for listings. Listings are editorial content and have no monetary value.

- You must complete this application—**ONLY COMPLETE APPLICATIONS WITH PAYMENT WILL BE CONSIDERED**—and **mail** it to: Application Dept., LA 411 Publishing Co., 5900 Wilshire Blvd., 31st Fl., Los Angeles, CA 90036.

- You must be located in New York, New Jersey, Connecticut or the Philadephia area or regularly provide services in that area. (Production Companies and Post Production Companies must be physically located in the area.)

- Please enclose a current resume and/or a letter written on your company letterhead explaining who you are, the services your company provides, why you belong in the categories you are applying for and how long you've been in business.

- **References are required** and must be from a variety of local advertising agencies, film, TV, commercial production companies or music video production companies for work you we hired to perform in the past twelve months. References will be contacted by phone. Call sheets, contracts, invoices or pay stubs are also acceptable.

- **You must submit three references for each category that you are applying for.** References may be repeated if you performed more than one service for a particular company.

- Applicants may be required to complete an interview with our editors. 411 editorial staff has final say in all matters regarding what goes into our directories and on our Web sites. **Not all applicants will qualify.** For a complete list of application requirements go to www.la411.com and click on the Listing Info tab.

List categories for which you are applying: _____

NEW YORK 411® CATEGORY LIST BY TAB SECTION

AD AGENCIES & PROD. COMPANIES
Advertising Agencies
Advertising Agency Freelance Producers
Animation Production Companies
Commercial Directors
Commercial Production Companies
Corporate & Video Production Companies
Independent Directors Reps
Infomercial Production Companies
Motion Picture Production Companies
Music Video Directors
Music Video Production Companies
Production Offices
Promo Production Companies
Public Relations
Storyboard Artists
Television Production Companies
Trailer Production Companies

POST PRODUCTION
Audio Post Facilities
Commercial Editorial Houses
Composers & Sound Designers
Computer Graphics & Visual FX
Digital Intermediates
Duplication
DVD, Authoring & Replication
Editing Equipment Rentals & Sales
Editors
Film & Tape Storage
Film Laboratories—Motion Picture
Film Laboratories—Still Photography
Mobile Video Units, Satellite & Transmission Services
Music Libraries & Publishing
Music Production & Sound Design
Opticals
Post Houses
Post Production Supervisors
Screening Rooms
Stock Footage & Photos
Titling, Captioning & Broadcast Design
Visual FX Artists
Visual FX Supervisors & Producers

SETS & STAGES
Backings & Scenic Artists (Local 829)
Backings & Scenic Aricsts (Local 52)
Backings & Scenic Artists
Set Design, Construction & Rentals
Set Sketchers
Still Photography Studios & Lofts
Stages
Stages—Portable
TV Studios

LOCATION SERVICES & EQUIPMENT
Air Charters
Air Freight & Courier Services
Airlines
Airports
Bus Charters
Car Rentals
Cargo & Passenger Vans
Caterers
Communications Equipment
Consulates General
Crating & Packing
Custom Brokers & Carnets
Film Commissions—International
Film Commissions—North America
Hotels & Short-Term Housing
Limousine & Car Services
Location Libraries, Management & Scouts
Locations
Motorhomes & Portable Dressing Rooms
Moving, Storage & Transportation
Parking Services
Portable Restrooms
Production Services—International
Production Services—North America
Security & Bodyguards
Travel Agencies
Water Trucks
Weather

PRODUCTION SUPPORT
Acting/Dialect Coaches
Animals & Trainers
Budgeting & Scheduling
Casting Directors
Casting Facilities
Choreographers

Computers, Office Equipment & Supplies
Computer Consultants & Software
Digital Casting & Video Conferencing
Directories & Trade Publications
Entertainment Attorneys
Extras Casting Agencies
Hand & Leg Models
Insurance Brokers & Guarantors
Janitorial & Strike Services
Large Scale Event Planning
Libraries, Research & Clearance
Massage Therapists
Messenger Services
Nautical Film Services & Coordination
Notaries
Payroll & Production Accountants (Local 161 NY)
Payroll & Production Accountants
Promotional Products
Transcription & Secretarial Services
Talent & Modeling Agencies
Technical Advisors
Translation & Interpretation Services
Wrap Party Locations

CAMERA & SOUND EQUIPMENT
Aerial Equipment
Aerial—Fixed Wing & Helicopter Pilots
Camera Cars & Tracking Vehicles
Camera Rentals—Motion Picture
Camera Rentals—Still Photography
Motion Control
Raw Stock
Sound Equipment Rentals & Sales
Teleprompting Services & Cue Cards
Video Assist Services
Video Cameras & Equipment
Video Display, Playback & Projection

HIGH DEF
HD Cameras & Equipment
HD Duplication
HD Editing Equipment
HD Equipment Manufacturers
HD Post Houses
HD Screening Rooms
HD Stock Footage
HD Tape Stock

GRIP & LIGHTING EQUIPMENT
Booms, Cranes & Camera Support
Hoisting & Lift Equipment/Cherry Pickers
Climate Control Systems
Construction & Yard Equipment Rentals
Grip & Lighting Expendables
Grip Equipment
Lighting Equipment & Generators
Production Equipment & Accessories
Trucks & Vans

PROPS & WARDROBE
Aerial Picture Vehicles
Animatronics, Puppets & Makeup FX
Architectural Elements
Art Fabrication, Licensing & Rentals
Arts & Crafts Supplies
Atmospheric/Lighting Special FX & Pyrotechnics
Boats & Nautical Props
Building/Surface Materials & Hardware
Canopies & Tents
Car Prep, Rigging & Prototypes
Color-Correct Props
Costume Makers & Rentals
Draperies & Window Treatments
Dry Cleaners
Eyewear & Jewelry
Fabrics
Firearms & Weapons
Flags, Graphics & Signage
Flowers, Greens & Plants
Foam
Furnishings—Antique & Vintage
Furnishings—Contemporary
Games, Toys & Amusements
Glass
Hair, Makeup & Wardrobe Supplies
Ice
Lamps & Lighting Fixtures
Medical & Scientific Props
Memorabilia & Collectibles
Metals & Foils
Musical Instrument Rentals
Neon
Photo, Video & Electronic Props

Picture Vehicles
Plastics, Plexiglas & Fiberglass
Product Placement
Prop Fabrication & Mechanical FX
Prop Houses
Restaurant & Kitchen Equipment
Specialty Props
Sporting Goods
Studio Services
Tailoring & Alterations
Uniforms & Surplus
Vintage Clothing & Accessories

CREW
Agents, Reps & Job Referral Services
Ambulance/Paramedics & Nurses (Local 52 NY)
Ambulance/Paramedics & Nurses
Art Directors/Production Designers (Local 829 NY)
Art Directors/Production Designers
Camera Assistants (Local 600 NY)
Camera Assistants
Camera Operators (Local 600 NY)
Camera Operators
Camera Operators - Aerial (Local 600 NY)
Camera Operators - Steadicam (Local 600 NY)
Camera Operators - Steadicam
Camera Operators - Underwater (Local 600 NY)
Carpenters/Shop Craft (Local 52 NY)
Craft Service (Local 52)
Craft Service
Digital Imaging Technicians (Local 600 NY)
Digital Imaging Technicians
Directors of Photography (Local 600 NY)
Directors of Photography
First Assistant Directors (DGA NY)
First Assistant Directors
Food Stylists & Home Economists
Gaffers & Electricians (Local 52 NY)
Gaffers & Electricians
Grips (Local 52 NY)
Grips
Hair & Makeup Artists (Local 798 NY)
Hair & Makeup Artists
Lighting Directors
Producers
Production Coordinators (Local 161)
Production Coordinators
Production Managers
Production Stills Photographers (Local 600 NY)
Production Stills Photographers
Props Department (Local 52 NY)
Props Department
Script Supervisors (Local 161 NY)
Script Supervisors
Second Assistant Directors (DGA NY)
Second Assistant Directors
Set Decorators
Sound Mixers (Local 52 NY)
Sound Mixers
Stage Managers (DGA NY)
Studio Teachers/Welfare Workers
Stunt Coordinators & Performance Drivers
Trade Associations/Unions
Training Centers
Underwater Technicians
Unit Production Managers (DGA NY)
VTR Operators (Local 52 NY)
VTR Operators
Wardrobe Stylists/Costume Designers (Local 829)
Wardrobe Stylists/Costume Designers
Wardrobe Supervisors (Local 764 NY)

CITY GUIDE (ONLINE ONLY)
Bars
Bookstores
Broadway, Concerts & Sports Ticketing
Car Rentals
Clubs
Gift Services & Florists
Hotels
Limousine & Car Services
Movie Theaters
Museum & Art Galleries
Online Rental & Purchase Resources
Party Resources
Real Estate Agents and Agencies
Restaurant Delivery Services
Restaurant Roundup
Short-Term Furnished & Corporate Housing
Taxicabs
Tours & Attractions

For detailed information about reference requirements please call: (800) 545-2411 or go to www.LA411.com & click on the Apply to Be Listed tab.

Ordering Information

Complete this form and send with your payment to:
Attn: Book Sales Dept., 411 Publishing, 5900 Wilshire Blvd., 31st Fl.
Los Angeles, CA 90036
or order through our online store at www.NewYork411.com

For credit card orders, air and international shipments or questions call: (800) 545-2411, x79400 or (323) 617-9400 or contact Juliette Nichols at jnichols@reedbusiness.com. Credit card orders received by 12:00 noon PST will be shipped via Fed-Ex that day. Please allow five working days for delivery on all orders.

Quantity	Item		Price	Tax	Shipping	Total
	LA 411 2009	(CA or NY orders)	$79.00	$7.30	$7.00	
		(Elsewhere)		$0.00	$7.00	
	New York 411 2010/2011	(CA or NY orders)	$59.00	$4.94	$6.00	
		(Elsewhere)		$0.00	$6.00	

Make checks payable to 411 Publishing Company

_____
Name/Title

_____
Company/Profession

_____
Address (No P.O. Boxes Please)   City

_____
State   Zip Code   Telephone

Filming In New York State

New York State Governor's Office for Motion Picture & Television Development

State Tax Incentives
The New York State Governor's Office for Motion Picture and Television Development offers you Four Ways to Save:
- **30%** New York State Film Production Credit
- Empire State Commercial Production Credit
- Sales Tax Exemptions
- Investment Tax Credit

Location Assistance
The NY State Governor's Office for Motion Picture & TV Development offers the following free resources and services:
- Preliminary location research and scouting, as well as extensive location contacts.
- A comprehensive location library with over 200,000 images available for research.
- A liaison to the following:
    - State Agencies such as the Port Authority (for airports, bridges and tunnels in NYC) and the Metropolitan Transit Authority (for NYC subways, buses, Metro North & Long Island Railroad).
    - State-owned facilities such as prisons, hospitals and armories.
    - Federally-owned sites such as the Statue of Liberty and Fire Island National Seashore.
    - State-wide network of film-friendly contacts and services that will facilitate your production.

Call our office when planning to film in or outside of New York City, and when using state-owned facilities, buildings, State Parks anywhere in New York State and New York City. State-owned facilities within NYC include the Port Authority (buses and airports) and the Metropolitan Transit Authority (trains and subways), bridges, tunnels, piers, etc.

Child Performer Permits:
- Parents/Guardians are required to get permits for their child performers from the New York Sate Department of Labor.
- Employers of child performers are required to get certificates from the Department of Labor.
- Parents/Guardians are required to provide evidence of the establishment of a trust account for their child performer.
- Part of every child performer's earnings is required to be withheld by their employers for placement into a trust account.
- Child Performers must provide evidence of satisfactory academic performance from their schools of enrollment.

If you need more information visit www.labor.state.ny.us or contact: (800)-HIRE-992; CPinfo@labor-state.ny.us

For further assistance, call the NY Governor's Office for Motion Picture & Television Development at (212) 803-2330.

Permits
Each individual town, village or city regulates its own permits and sets its own schedule of fees. The Governor's Office for Motion Picture and Television Development can provide assistance with permits for localities throughout New York State, including local contacts in the New York City region.

The Governor's Office for Motion Picture and Television Development supplies applications for filming permits for the State Parks on Long Island. However, when completed they should be returned to the Long Island State Parks office by fax or mail. Referrals and contacts are available through the Governor's Office for all other State Parks.

Insurance
There is no statewide insurance requirement policy in New York State. Requirements are set by each local jurisdiction. If required, be prepared to provide a signed Certificate of Insurance naming the local town, village or city as the "Additional Insured." The amount required, which may differ between jurisdictions, is generally $1,000,000.

Other Assistance
The Governor's Office for Motion Picture and Television Development provides information on union rates, work rules and the most current labor laws, and supplies copies of the Guide to Sales Tax Breaks for the Film Industry, a publication that details tax breaks available for filmmakers. The Office also provides information on federal, state and local regulations affecting trucking, aviation, use of wild and domesticated animals, and child performer labor laws.

Whether your production is a feature film or a student project, the Governor's Office for Motion Picture and Television Development is available to help with your production and make your script a reality.

Remember: If it's in the script, it's in New York State!

Pat Swinney Kaufman
New York State Governor's Office for Motion Picture & Television Development
633 Third Ave., 33rd Floor
New York, NY 10017
(212) 803-2330
(212) 803-2339 Fax
www.nylovesfilm.com

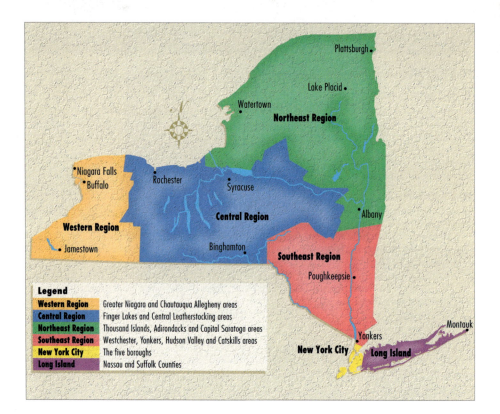

Where To Shoot In New York State

I. New York City

The birthplace of film production in the U.S., and home base for many of the most creative minds in filmmaking, New York City has enjoyed a boom in film and television production in recent years. More than 60 sound stages are available for production, as well as the most famous urban landscape in the world for location shooting. A center for broadcast and cable television as well as feature filmmaking, New York City, with its top ad agencies and record labels, is also a hub of commercial and music video production. At every stage of production, from pre-production to post, New York City offers state-of-the-art facilities, world-class talent, and an unmatched level of creative energy.

II. Long Island Region

NASSAU COUNTY
Nassau County is known for the grand mansions of the 'Gold Coast' as well as picturesque villages, ponds, beaches and parks. Only 45 minutes from Manhattan, Nassau County also features a wide variety of residential areas and office parks.

SUFFOLK COUNTY
Home to the mansions and beaches of the Hamptons as well as blue-collar communities and all-American suburbs, Suffolk County can provide looks from New England villages to Midwest towns. Agricultural landscapes and stunning oceanfront vistas can all be found here.

III. Southeast Region

CITY OF YONKERS
Yonkers is Westchester County's largest municipality, with 19 square miles and nearly four miles of waterfront. Just 10 miles from New York City, Yonkers features distinctive neighborhoods ranging from urban to suburban settings, including Grecian gardens, a 40-acre wildlife sanctuary overlooking the Hudson River, and a stately City Hall. Yonkers also features over 100 parks and playgrounds, 34 public schools, three hospitals and nearly 20 shopping centers.

WESTCHESTER COUNTY
Westchester County is the busiest production area outside of New York City, providing a diversity of locations only minutes from Manhattan. Westchester County's mansions and estates, vineyards, indoor ice rinks, prisons and office parks, as well as miles of Hudson River shoreline to the west and acres of beaches on the east, offer an unsurpassed diversity of locations while minimizing costs.

UNIQUE INCENTIVES FOR FILM PRODUCTION IN NYC

0% sales tax

production tax credit

free outdoor advertising

free permits, police, public locations

free promotional broadcast on NYC TV and radio

world-class concierge service from script to screen

online, searchable photo library of public locations

discounts for NYC productions at participating vendors

MICHAEL R. BLOOMBERG MAYOR
KATHERINE L. OLIVER COMMISSIONER
DIAL 311 OR OUTSIDE NYC DIAL (212) NEW-YORK
WWW.NYC.GOV/FILM

THE CITY OF NEW YORK
MAYOR'S OFFICE
OF FILM, THEATRE
AND BROADCASTING

HUDSON VALLEY
The Hudson Valley corridor is an area encompassing seven counties from 30 minutes to three hours from New York City. The area is full of small towns, suburban looks, college campuses, farms and historic buildings dating back 300 years. It is renowned for its rivers, valleys, and stately mansions. The area is easy to access and offers a talented labor pool of industry professionals.

CATSKILLS
Only 90 miles from New York City, the Catskill region offers spectacular mountains, lush river valleys, and crystal clear lakes and streams. You will also find wineries, covered bridges, antique railroads and quaint country inns.

IV. Northeast Region

CAPITOL-SARATOGA
In addition to the State Capitol, this region boasts architecture from Victorian and Georgian to Gothic and Greek Revival. It also is home to the historic city neighborhoods of Troy and Saratoga as well as gracious resorts, a National Battlefield, and the 2,100-acre Spa State Park.

ADIRONDACKS
Situated less than five hours from New York City, the rugged high peaks of the Adirondacks are a six million-acre natural sanctuary—the largest wilderness preserve outside of Alaska. The abundance of water flowing through the awe-inspiring mountains and forests contributes to nearly 2,500 lakes and ponds and more than 30,000 miles of rivers and streams. Lake Placid, site of the 1932 and 1980 Winter Olympics, is one of many scenic villages nestled in this breathtaking landscape. The region also contains 18th-century revolutionary forts and historic great camps.

THOUSAND ISLANDS
The unique geography of the Thousand Islands offers locations such as the St. Lawrence Seaway—200 miles of forested coastline with endless islands, picturesque small towns and historic sites such as Boldt Castle and Sackets Harbor, made famous in the War of 1812. The 3,300-foot Robert Moses Power Dam is one of the biggest in the Northeast.

V. Central Region

ROCHESTER-FINGER LAKES
Rochester, home to Eastman Kodak, is home to one of the largest production communities in the East, with numerous resources available for filming from grip rentals and production companies to a large and experienced crew base. Rochester is also one of the snowiest cities in the U.S., while the Finger Lakes region boasts gorgeous scenery—waterfalls, dramatic canyons, picturesque small towns, forests and wilderness, and spectacular fall foliage.

CENTRAL LEATHERSTOCKING
The heartland of New York State's Native American experience, this region is home to the fabled Erie Canal, Howe Caverns and the Baseball Hall of Fame. The cities of Binghamton and Syracuse offer great mid-20th century looks and historic turn-of-the-century architecture.

VI. Western Region

BUFFALO-NIAGRA
This region offers filmmakers unique and diverse locations, from Niagra Falls to the shores of Lake Erie. Locations in Buffalo, New York's second largest city, range from gritty urban neighborhoods to beautiful art deco skyscrapers and 19th century architecture.

CHAUTAUQUA ALLEGHENY
From the small towns of the Allegheny foothills, to verdant Amish farmland, this area features an 1891 opera house, and the Victorian village of the Chautauqua Institute.

For information on filming in New York State, contact the New York Governor's Office of Film and Television Production at (212) 803-2330 for assistance with location scouting, local liaisons, and permit assistance.

New York State Tax Exemption For The Film Industry

Below is an excerpt from New York State's "A Guide to Sales Tax for the Film Industry." For the complete guide, contact the New York State Governor's Office for Motion Picture and Television Development at (212) 803-2330, or visit www.nylovesfilm.com.

Producers as Manufacturers

The production of a film is considered a manufacturing activity when the production results in the creation of a film for sale. When making a film for sale, the producer is entitled to all of the exemptions available to manufacturers. However, the producer must register as a New York State sales tax vendor to exercise a right to exemptions. Once registered, the producer may issue the appropriate exemption certificates to its suppliers.

Producers who are not registered as sales tax vendors should request A Guide to Sales Tax in New York State, Publication 28, which contains a registration application form.

Exclusions and Exemptions

Property Used or Consumed in Production

Machinery or equipment, as well as parts, tools and supplies, used or consumed directly or predominantly in the production of a film for sale may be purchased or leased exempt from all sales and use tax. Machinery or equipment is used predominantly in production if more than 50 percent of its use is directly in the production phase of a process.

The exemptions provided above for machinery predominantly used or consumed in production do not apply to the purchase of property used for administrative purposes. Administration includes such activities as sales promotions, general office work, ordering and receiving materials, making travel arrangements, the preparation of shooting schedules, and the preparation of work and payroll records.

Property and Services Purchased for Resale

A manufacturer registered as a New York State sales tax vendor may make certain purchases for resale. Materials and services on these materials that will become a component of the product sold (e.g., original negative) may be purchased exempt from tax, if a properly completed Resale Certificate, Form ST-120, is issued to the supplier.

Installing, Repairing, Maintaining and Servicing

Charges to install, repair, maintain or service production equipment, parts, tools and supplies are exempt from New York State and New York City taxes.

Utilities Used in Production

Utilities used or consumed directly and exclusively in the production of a film for sale are exempt from tax. However, this exemption does not apply to the New York City tax.

Motor Fuels Used in Production

Motor fuel (e.g., gasoline) or diesel motor fuel used or consumed directly and exclusively in the production of a film for sale is exempt from tax. However, this exemption does not apply to the New York City tax.

New York State and local taxes must be paid on all motor fuel and diesel motor fuel when purchased. However, if the motor fuel or diesel motor fuel is used directly and exclusively in production, the purchaser may claim a refund by filing the appropriate refund application. Application for Refund of Sales on Automotive Fuels, Form FT-500, should be used to claim a refund of sales tax paid on motor fuel (gasoline) and/or diesel motor fuel.

New York City Sales and Use Tax

All of the exemptions described above also apply to the New York City tax, with the following exceptions: The purchase of utilities and fuel used in the production of a film for sale is not exempt from the New York City tax. However, a producer is entitled to claim a credit for the amount of New York City tax paid on electricity and electric service used in the production of a film for sale. The credit is allowed against the New York City General Corporation Tax or Unincorporated Business Tax. In addition, the exemption described above for motor fuel does not apply to the New York City sales and use tax.

Exemption Certificates

Film producers must furnish a properly completed Exempt Use Certificate, Form ST-121, to their suppliers to exempt their purchases of qualifying production machinery, equipment, parts, tools or supplies for use or consumption directly and predominantly in the production of a film for sale. This certificate must also be furnished to those who install, repair, maintain or service the exempt machinery, equipment, parts, tools or supplies.

Producers who purchase tangible personal property that becomes a physical component part of the film and is actually transferred to the consumer must issue a properly completed Resale Certificate, Form ST-120, to their supplier.

A properly-completed exemption certificate must be furnished, and accepted in good faith, no later than 90 days after delivery of the property or service or the sale will be considered a taxable sale. These exemption certificates may only be issued by a person registered as a New York vendor.

Filming In New York City

The Mayor's Office of Film, Theatre and Broadcasting:

For more than forty years, the Mayor's Office of Film, Theatre & Broadcasting (MOFTB) has been the one-stop shop for the international production center here, which provides 100,000 New York entertainment professionals with employment and generates over $5 billion dollars annually. This office is an advocate for all kinds of productions, from major feature films and television series to commercials, music videos, documentaries, student films and red carpet premieres. We provide a free permit and services to assist your project. We have a reputation for finding a way to say yes.

In 2005, the MOFTB unveiled the "Made in NY" incentive program, which includes a tax credit for qualified film and television productions, a one percent marketing credit which provides free advertising on City bus shelters and NYC TV to "Made in NY" productions, a discount card which provides reductions of at least 10 percent at more than 850 local vendors, and the "Made in NY" logo, a mark of distinction awarded to projects which shoot 75 percent or more in New York City.

The MOFTB Permit:

Our permit forms are available for downloading from our website: www.nyc.gov/film
Please visit the site for permit forms as well as current information about production in New York City.

HOW SHOOTING WITH OUR PERMIT WORKS:

The permit we issue to your production provides access to public locations and location parking for essential production vehicles throughout 300 square miles of public settings in the city's five boroughs, including 27,000 acres of city parks. When your project is shooting at an exterior location and requires traffic control, re-routing, work in the street, or a scene with guns or uniformed police, you must have the special NYPD Movie and Television Unit on the location. The police unit will assign its officers at no charge to you. All decisions with respect to what is permitted are made by MOFTB, working in close consultation with the NYPD Movie & TV Unit, and other key city agencies as necessary. Since August 2008, rules have been adopted by the MOFTB which determine when a permit is and is not required when shooting on City property.

When a Permit Is Required:

Under the adopted rules, a permit is required for filming if equipment or vehicles are used or if the person filming asserts exclusive use of City property. Equipment does not include hand-held devices (such as hand-held film, still, or television cameras or videocameras) or tripods used to support such cameras, but a permit is required in certain situations when the person filming asserts exclusive use of City property while using a hand-held device.

When a Permit Is Not Required

A permit is not required for filming that uses hand-held cameras or tripods and does not assert exclusive use of City property. Standing on a street, walkway of a bridge, sidewalk, or other pedestrian passageway while using a hand-held device and not otherwise asserting exclusive use of City property is not an activity that requires a permit.

Optional Permits

When a permit is not required, it is possible to apply for an optional permit. A person wishing to apply for an optional permit would present much of the same documentation as someone seeking a required permit (i.e. request for dates, times and locations and contact information). Liability insurance is not required in connection with an optional permit. Sometimes there has been confusion as to whether or not a permit is required. As a result, and as an accommodation to filmmakers, MOFTB has routinely issued permits in those instances where a permit is not required. The rules are consistent with this longstanding practice.

Liability Insurance

Liability insurance is needed for those who obtain a required permit. However, when an applicant can demonstrate that obtaining the required insurance would impose an unreasonable hardship, MOFTB may waive the need for liability insurance. In addition, student filmmakers can meet their liability insurance obligations through coverage under their school's insurance program.

INSURANCE:

In order for you or your organization to be eligible for a Motion Picture or Television Permit (a required permit), you must present to MOFTB an original certificate of insurance, which is signed by the Broker's Authorized Representative. Please see our website for the exact language that must be on the certificate, and for other insurance requirements and guidelines.

PRE-PRODUCTION:
Very simple shoots of one or two days, or shoots of longer duration, which are walk-and-talk, and are not working in the street do not require police assistance. It is possible to get a permit for this type of project within 24 hours before shooting, providing the insurance certificate and permit application are presented in good order before noon of the day before shooting.

Pre-Production Meeting:
All feature films, television movies, series or specials, elaborate exterior commercial shoots and music videos doing exteriors with celebrities, multiple locations and/or playback, must have a pre-production meeting with the MOFTB. It is recommended that this meeting be scheduled with the MOFTB about three weeks before shooting, but must be scheduled no later than five business days before the shoot begins.

After your main pre-production meeting at the MOFTB where the entire schedule is discussed, a permit which contains a listing of location activities can usually be issued quickly for feature films and TV projects. Longer and more complex productions customarily send along several location requests at least three to four days before the shoot dates, which helps the NYPD Movie & TV Unit to plan coverage. The outside deadline for all permit issuance in all cases, is by noon of the day before any shoot on a Tuesday through Friday, and by 4:00 pm on the Thursday before a shoot on Saturday, Sunday and/or Monday.

PARKING FEATURES OF THE PERMIT:
The permit provides for special parking privileges at working locations for vehicles essential to your shoot, defined as equipment trucks, lifts, cranes, campers and honeywagons. Crew or personal cars are not covered by the permit.

SPECIAL PERMISSIONS:
The NY State Department of Labor issues and administers child performer permits. Visit their website at www.labor.state.ny.us and click on the Child Performer Center icon in lower right hand corner. If you have further questions, contact the NY State Governor's Office for Motion Picture and TV Development at (212) 803-2330.

Special Effects:
Pyrotechnics, fire effects and explosions, including simulated and other smoke effects using a substance with a flash point of less than 400 degrees Fahrenheit, at both exterior and interior locations, require a prior inspection and supervision at the shoot by the New York City Fire Department. Exceptional requests (e.g. removing a lamppost, building a stage) may require additional permits from another city agency. MOFTB will advise you as to who to contact in these cases.

SPECIAL JURISDICTIONS:
There are a few frequently requested locations within the city which are under the jurisdiction of other governmental bodies and are not available on the MOFTB permit, and require special permits. Here are two major exceptions:

In order to film scenes involving the use of subway stations, trains or buses, you must make arrangements well in advance, from one to five weeks or more, with the Metropolitan Transit Authority (MTA). The MTA's Special Events Unit will provide you with an estimated cost for your request. Other divisions of the MTA provide access to Grand Central Station and the Metro North and Long Island train lines.

The Port Authority arranges shoots at all airports, the PATH trains to New Jersey, certain piers and the Lincoln and Holland Tunnels to New Jersey.

GENERAL LOCATION ASSISTANCE:
For any location sites not directly available through our permit, the MOFTB production unit has extensive contacts and will support your requests. This includes the MTA, the Port Authority, government buildings, parks and landmarks under state or federal jurisdiction, as well as many privately owned locations such as Rockefeller Center and most non-profit institutions, which have relationships to city government such as the American Museum of Natural History and Lincoln Center. When you start pre-production, we will provide additional details, and we will work with you to anticipate and resolve any problems that may arise.

Mayor's Office of Film, Theatre & Broadcasting
Michael R. Bloomberg, Mayor
Katherine Oliver, Commissioner
1697 Broadway, New York, NY 10019
(212) 489-6710
(212) 307-6237 Fax
www.nyc.gov/film

Michael R. Bloomberg,
Mayor
Katherine L. Oliver,
Commissioner

THE CITY OF NEW YORK
MAYOR'S OFFICE
OF FILM, THEATRE,
AND BROADCASTING

1697 Broadway
New York, NY 10019
tel: (212) 489-6710
fax: (212) 262-7677

OFFICIAL
MOTION PICTURE -
TELEVISION PERMIT

PERMIT NO. _____

This permit is issued to the applicant to film or televise on streets or property subject to the jurisdiction of the City of New York at the times and locations designated below. The permit must be in the possession of the applicant at all times while on location. For additional assistance call the Permit Division: (212) 489-6710 Ext. 250. Police Unit: (212) 489-6710, x219.

NOT VALID UNLESS SIGNED BY MAYOR'S OFFICE FILM COORDINATOR. PERMIT FORMS MUST BE TYPED. HANDWRITTEN FORMS ARE NOT ACCEPTED.

Date Of Application: _____

1. Company: _____ Production Contact: _____

2. Street: _____ City: _____ State: ____ Zip: _____

Telephone #:: _____ Fax #: _____ 3. Permit Type (choose one): _____

Complete this application. If a shooting or rigging permit, all locations should be requested on the "Schedule A" form.

Dates: Shooting (mm/dd/yy) - From: _____ To: _____ Rigging (mm/dd/yy) - From: _____ To: _____

Scouting (mm/dd/yy) - From: _____ To: _____ Times From: _____ To: _____

4. Animals, firearms, special effects or unusual scenes: _____

5. Child Performers (16 years or under): No ☐ Yes ☐ If yes, specify child's age and activity on "Schedule A" form

6. Equipment format (choose one): _____ #in cast & crew: _____

No. of Trucks 24' and above: _____ No. of Trucks below 24': _____ No. of Autos: _____

List all production vehicle plate numbers on the Drop/Add list

7. ☐ Feature Film ☐ TV Movie ☐ TV Series/Special ☐ Commercial ☐ Industrial ☐ Other - Identify: _____

Title: _____ Publicist: _____

Director: _____ Producer(s): _____

Prod. Mgr.: _____ Location Mgr./ Cell Phone: _____

8. If TV commercial name product: _____

Permits are not issued until the insurance requirements are fulfilled. An original certificate must be on file. Click here for information.

9. Insurance Broker: _____ Phone: _____

Policy #: _____ Amount: _____ Expiration Date: _____

The applicant agrees to indemnify The City of New York and to be solely and absolutely liable upon any and all claims, suits and judgments against the City and/or the applicant for personal injuries and property damages arising out of or occurring during the activities of the applicant, his (its) employees or otherwise. The applicant further agrees to comply with all pertinent provisions of New York laws, rules and regulations. This permit may be revoked at anytime.

FOR PARKING REGULATIONS, REFER TO FACT SHEET

Date	Signature of Representative	Title

DO NOT WRITE BELOW THIS LINE
The Mayor's Office Seal must be embossed on original copy

Dated _____
(Rev. 7/94)

_____
Film Coordinator, Mayor's Office of Film, Theatre and Broadcasting

XVI

Filming In New York City

Shooting in New York?
Need a Great Production Assistant?

Call BWI to hire experienced, reliable "Made in NY" PAs

- Every "Made in NY" PA is a valid licensed driver
- Graduates are pre-screened, trained and fully vetted
- Placements for advance shoots, next morning or same day

Our service is FREE.

Call our Hotline day or night:
718-757-5816
Email: kfinch@bwiny.org
www.bwiny.org

The "Made in NY" PA Training Program is a collaboration between Brooklyn Workforce Innovations and the NYC Mayor's Office of Film, Theatre and Broadcasting

Where To Shoot In New York City

2008 was a another go-go production year in the Big Apple—but down from 28,594 shooting days in 2007 in the five boroughs to 27,251. This was wholly attributable to the aftermath of the WGA strike, the unresolved SAG stand-off, and the wounded economy. It is nonetheless the fourth highest total in the nearly 42 years of the Mayor's Office of Film Theater and Broadcasting.

Manhattan, the core of the Apple, is most often the star of the show. The smallest borough—23 square miles of the full city's 301—contains a vast diversity of architecture, moods, cultures and milieus squeezed on, above and below its surface.

The Upper West Side—from W. 72nd to W. 96th St (some maps set 106th), and Riverside Drive along the Hudson to Central Park West—is always popular. Grand, pre-war doorman apartment blocks rule on Riverside Drive and West End Avenue, and an east-west grid of tree-lined streets enclose a vast array of vintage brownstones. Restaurants, shops, bistros and bars line Columbus and Amsterdam Avenues and two-way four-lane Broadway. The Greco facade of the Museum of Natural History dominates W. 77th to 81st streets opposite Central Park. The green belt of Riverside Park from 72nd St. to 121st, offers swirling pathways, river and sunset views, the 79th Street Boat Basin, basketball and tennis courts, baseball and soccer fields, a skateboard arena, the Soldiers and Sailors Monument, and a massive stone block wall along much of its length that girds the steep pitch to the park beside and below the Drive. Brownstone families, single apartment dwellers, private schools and classic residential architecture define much of the Upper West Side.

The renaissance of Harlem—110th to 145th St., from St. Nicholas Avenue to Madison Avenue—continues, but vestiges of its remarkable history remain. The Apollo Theater (near Frederick Douglas Boulevard) has been hosting concerts of megastars since 1913. Malcolm X Boulevard (a/k/a/ Lenox Ave.) and Adam Clayton Powell Boulevard retain numerous facades with original detail even as most of iconic 125th St. has been chain-stored and multiplexed. Sylvia's and Lenox Lounge are local and tourist destinations. Urban blight has yielded to high rises, but productions seeking funky period or retro environs can still find them (as did big-feature Vietnam-era American Gangster in '06). Stately beauty and historic gems will be found on Strivers' Row, W. 138th and 139th Sts. off Frederick Douglas; at Graham Court, a century-old palace of large apartments at Adam Clayton Powell and W. 117th; and near the many restored brownstones west of Marcus Garvey Park. Whatever the project, Harlem—and northward to Hamilton Heights and Sugar Hill—has abundant grace and grit.

The villages of West, Greenwich, and East span nearly river to river, 11th Avenue to Avenue D, from 14th Street and the beginning of the midtown grid, to Houston Street on the southern edge. In between productions will find brownstone, bohemian and barrio. Period homes (Victorian, colonial, etc.) line narrow streets of cobblestone, not far from new glass-tower condos on 11th Avenue/West Side Highway, or the bistros and clubs in the diminished and modernized meatpacking district just below far W. 14th St. Hotel Gansevoort, Pastis, Soho House, Florent and Lotus, for starters, are moments from Hogs & Heifers, the oasis of bikers, beer, and celebrity bras on trophy antlers. The old High Line (elevated railway) across Washington Street is becoming a unique park, and a new Andre Balasz hotel straddles it on 14th at Washington St. and 10th Ave. Moving east four or five avenues, Greenwich Village spans from 6th Ave. to Broadway and W. 14th St. to W. Houston. The central campus of New York University is gathered around Washington Square Park and The Arch. Echoes of the '50s to '70s can be found between Macdougal St. and LaGuardia Place, 8th and Houston. The East Village begins at Cooper Union on Astor Place and St. Marks Place (E. 8th), reaches Tompkins Square Park at Avenue A and so-called Alphabet City, and ends at Avenue D. Vivid murals adorns walls near bars, boutiques, bodegas, clubs and cafes; gardens bloom between tenements where community organizations and extended families rule. Though evermore gentrified, the vibrant or brooding East Village is a most interesting and popular production locale.

Years and decades before the early '00 boom years, many mid-to-late 19th century textile warehouses in SoHo (South of Houston Street, once called South Village, or the Cast Iron District) were zoned for the work and residence of artists. They have been converted to luxury lofts above furniture showrooms, fashion boutiques and art galleries. The Belgian block (cobblestone) streets of Mercer, Greene and Crosby are picturesque artifacts of ages past. Droves of cosmopolitans visit long-established and new restaurants and global-brand shops along Prince and Spring Streets, Broadway and West Broadway. SoHo's southern boundary is the multi-block bazaar of Canal Street. A residential/industrial area runs west past 6th Avenue, from Varick to Washington Streets. On West Houston near Varick is the blue neon marquee Film Forum, a key venue for independent, topical and classic cinema. The distinctive domain of SoHo is always a popular location.

TriBeCa—Triangle Below Canal—passes south from Canal to Vesey Streets (at Ground Zero), and west from Broadway to the Hudson River. In a past era, TriBeCa was a center of shipping and industry, but now is well known as a mainstay of the NYC production machine where stars and producers live and/or work. Families, too (hence the handle of "Triburbia").

Hungry indies, well-fed studio films and small companies work prep to post on brick and cobblestone blocks like Duane or Vestry Streets. Because of its hybrid beauty and pedigree vitality, TriBeCa is often a backlot. A once small annual film festival of the same name has become a showcase for domestic and international productions.

Also notable in Manhattan: Chelsea; Clinton (a/k/a Hell's Kitchen); the buzzing Lower East Side; the gardens of Fort Tryon Park; the fabled Upper East Side, and the campuses of City University New York near W. 135th and Amsterdam Avenue.

Consider the unique former Coast Guard post of Governor's Island off the tip of Manhattan and Red Hook, Brooklyn. Its 172 acres—92 of them are both a National Historic Landmark District and a New York City Historic District—include grand promenades, regal trees, a 14-acre Great Lawn, and nearly 225 structures, from 18th- 19th century fortifications and pre-Civil War arsenal buildings to Victorian and Romanesque Revival housing, a movie theatre and a former military hospital. A 2.2-mile esplanade with dramatic Manhattan, Brooklyn and harbor views rings the island.

Some years ago NYC endured a shortage of studio space that limited productions even as location shooting thrived. Since then, many facilities have been upgraded or expanded (www.nyc.gov/html/film/html/resources/studios.shtml) and projects can now play in the pool of studio, location and metro talent from prep to post. Since 2004, for instance, the 300-acre Brooklyn Navy Yard has been more than a former shipbuilding landmark and industrial park (with many locations of its own). Inside the fence, Steiner Studios is a complex of five stages totaling nearly 100,000 square feet, as well as offices, design shops and post facilities. Productions needing "college campus," industry or waterfront can shoot in the Yard. Steiner and other stages around the city combine with the legendary energy of local crews to host shoots from all over the world.

For well over a century, a dynamo of American industry was the Brooklyn riverfront sections of Williamsburg and Greenpoint. In recent decades, as pioneer tenants and savvy developers repurposed many underused or derelict building, 'Billburg' became a hot shooting destination, but some of its 'bohemian' nature has been changed by high-rise residencies. The bridge roughly bisects the area, but more accurately Southside is Navy Yard to S. 1st St, and Northside from Grand St. to N. 15th at McCarren Park. Commerce and culture live in push-pull, especially in the Northside, where lofts, clubs, galleries and trendy restaurants share buildings or blocks with workshops and warehouses. Here, Bedford Avenue has been dubbed the "new Greenwich Village." Apartment towers and a green state park sprout on formerly industrial Kent Avenue along the river, and further changes to this classic cityscape are imminent.

Greenpoint begins at McCarren Park and ends at Newtown Creek. Like Williamsburg, many blocks of this mixed-use middle- and working-class area are remnants from eras of foundries and shipping. Industry is now adjacent to renovated loft buildings or vinyl-sided apartment or family walk-ups. Production and lighting rental houses occupy former warehouses on streets that can seem sullen or alien. West or Java Streets are eerily deserted in daytime, while nearby Manhattan and Greenpoint Avenues buzz with commerce. Broadway Stages and Cinema World are well-established stages here.

Directly north in Queens is Long Island City, an industrial, commuters, museum, and production hub. Silvercup Studios, a former bakery, and Silvercup East, which opened in 1999, comprise 18 stages and 400,000 square feet. Beyond LIC, in the global crossroads of Astoria, is Kaufman Astoria Studios, a pioneer film factory where Edward G. Robinson, the Marx Brothers, and Paramount Studios began. Reborn in the late 1970s, KAS is six stages plus production offices, lighting rental and recording facilities. Astoria itself is a multi-national nexus. Grand Avenue, for instance, offers a full spectrum of cuisine and cultures. Just to the north, passing above Astoria Park are the impressive trestles of Rte. 278/Triborough Bridge, and the Hell Gate Bridge that bears trains above the swift, tidal East River. These areas are readily accessible via subways, the Queensboro Bridge, the Midtown Tunnel and Long Island Expressway.

Also in Queens: the tranquility of affluent Douglaston/Douglas Manor, close to Nassau County, and nearby Fort Totten with the former homes of military families and a superb vista of the Throgs Neck Bridge; semi-suburban Kew Gardens; Flushing Meadows Park near Shea Stadium; a picturesque elevated subway along 31st St. in Astoria; the industrial core of Maspeth; the long boardwalk at Rockaway Beach; and the magnificent views of midtown and Upper East Manhattan from Gantry State Park in Hunters Point.

Park Slope, Brooklyn is a fraternal twin of Manhattan's Upper West Side. Adjacent to the 526 acres of Prospect Park, a large tract of the "Slope"—dubbed "the Gold Coast" when turn-of-the-20th financiers built brownstones and townhouses here—is a National Historic District on gently inclined tall-tree streets such as Carroll and 1st, and Garfield and Montgomery Places. Flatbush Avenue, Grand Army Plaza and the main Brooklyn Library anchor the northern end of Prospect Park, which extends down Prospect Park West to 15th Street. Within the hilly landscape designed by Olmstead and Vaux—the masters of Central Park—is one of the largest urban meadows in the U.S., stands of old forest, a lake, and many secluded paths. The Battle of Long Island, the largest clash of the American Revolution, was fought here on August 27, 1776, and for some hours was focused at Battle Pass on the park's East Drive, near Flatbush Ave. The main arteries of 7th Avenue, from President to 15th Streets, and 5th Ave. from 3rd Street to Sterling Place, are screen-worthy "urban village" strips of shops, food and cafes.

A portion of Prospect Park South is a Landmark Historic District of fine Victorian, Italian Renaissance and other style homes circa the late 19th and early 20th centuries, with lawns and wide porches on streets under big trees. Productions seeking a magical suburbia find the spacious graces here a world away from tight high-rise streets, but are still in New York City. The section is of a piece with Ditmas Park, Flatbush and Midwood, and all are set between Ocean and Coney Island Avenues, and Church and Foster Avenues. Also nearby, between Flatbush and Ocean Avenues, is the small but classic CUNY campus of Brooklyn College, replete with lawns, brick halls and a bell tower.

Also in Brooklyn: the waterside homes of Mill Island; old industrial Bushwick and revitalized Red Hook; tiny, lonesome Vinegar Hill; tony DUMBO (Down Under Manhattan Bridge Overpass); historic brownstone Fort Greene; and beloved Brooklyn Heights with a stunning view of Manhattan from the Promenade.

Riverdale, Bronx seems far from NYC. Wave Hill House is an 1843 mansion and gallery on 28 acres. A former residence of Mark Twain, Teddy Roosevelt and other notables, it boasts lawns and gardens with spectacular views of the Jersey Palisades across the wide Hudson. Eastward in Fieldston, a fabulous hamlet of Tudor and Colonial homes and lawns under majestic trees, is Manhattan College. Fieldston and the campus border huge Van Cortlandt Park and Route 9—known south of the Bronx as Broadway.

Also in the Bronx: the grand apartment block rows along Grand Concourse; the classic elevated subway on White Plains Road; the literary Hall of Fame and picturesque quad at Bronx Community College that was an early incarnation of NYU; the bustling commerce of The Hub; the splendors of New York Botanical Gardens and the Bronx Zoo near Fordham University; the junk-yard and industrial zone of Hunts Point; the seaside village City Island; and the bay-view mansions of Country Club and Spencer Estates.

The western rim of Staten Island, the most "suburban" borough—the third largest but least populated—almost kisses New Jersey. It has four golf courses, dozens of areas with single homes, large wooded tracts like Fresh Kills Park, and a long boardwalk beginning at Fort Wadsworth Gateway National Recreation Area beside Lower New York Bay. The Botanical Gardens and Snug Harbor Cultural Center, once a sailors' retirement home, are nestled in quiet middle-class Livingston and Randall Manor. Todt Hill, near Richmond County Country Club, and Grymes Hill, adjacent to Saint John's University, are upscale communities. The Historical Society of Richmondtown maintains old homes and a very old (1695) schoolhouse. The College of Staten Island and Wagner Memorial College are shoot-friendly. A Yankees' minor league team plays in St. George, near the Landmark Historic District and the Ferry terminal across the harbor from Manhattan.

New York City has countless faces—and many neighborhoods, parks and properties to scout in addition to those sampled here. Call or visit the Mayor's Office of Film, Theatre and Broadcasting, 1697 Broadway at 53rd St., (212) 489-6710, to learn what production areas are on the Hot Spot List (and therefore temporarily off-limits). As always, permits and police assistance are free. Blank permits, insurance information, films in production, available city-owned locations at the Hot Shots Photo Library, and much more are at www.nyc.gov/html/film/html/index/index.shtml. In addition to enabling crews to get on the street, several years ago MOFTB issued the Made in NY Discount Card. This entitles qualifying productions to reduced costs of vital goods and services, Accounting to Wardrobe, at over 800 citywide vendors. Producers and Production Managers take note: MOFTB has partnered with Brooklyn Workforce Innovation (BWI) to recruit and train essential production assistants. To quote the Mission Statement from the MOFTB website: "To provide individuals from diverse communities with training for entry-level positions in film production and access to employers in New York City's production industry, and to teach production assistants how to work collaboratively with local communities when they shoot on location throughout the five boroughs."

Lastly, productions, New Rule: henceforth, all lighting generators will be required to use Ultra Low Sulfur Diesel (ULSD) fuel.

MOFTB was founded in 1967, so applause to a team that has long helped to make it happen, and works harder every year to keep pace with the production industry.

New York City remains the world's greatest and safest big city for productions. Come join the thousands of other television episodes, commercials, feature films and photo shoots that have fallen in love with this vast set. Action!

Mark D. McKennon
The Location Station
Brooklyn NY 11215
(718) 768-5539 / (917) 744-8730
scoutman12001@yahoo.com
www.scoutman.com

Filming In New Jersey

Interest in filming in New Jersey is at an all-time high for many reasons, including the state's location diversity, its proximity to New York and the professional support you'll receive from the New Jersey Motion Picture and Television Commission.

The New Jersey Motion Picture & Television Commission is staffed by industry professionals, and enjoys the full support of the Governor's Office and state and local governments. Whether you are still considering New Jersey or have already decided to shoot in the state, you'll get red carpet treatment.

PERMITS AND INSURANCE

New Jersey contains 21 counties and 566 municipalities. Each city and town has its own unique regulations pertaining to film production. The New Jersey Motion Picture and Television Commission should be consulted before specific communities are approached.

Some cities and towns in the state have formal permit procedures, others do not. However, permits are generally required for filming such locations as county, state and national parks and historic sites, state and county highways, railroad and airport terminals and military posts.

As a rule, filmmakers working in New Jersey are required to carry general liability insurance in the amount of $1 million ($2 million in the City of Newark). Additional insurance may be required of crews using pyrotechnic effects or performing stunts. Typically, production companies are asked to present certificates of insurance naming property owners as "additional insured." Further, property owners must be relieved of all liability in connection with production work taking place on their respective locations.

CHILD LABOR LAWS

There is no minimum age requirement for children working in motion pictures and television programs. However, minors under the age of 16 must procure a Special Theatrical Permit from the local issuing officer in the district in which a production is being filmed. Said minors can work no longer than five hours daily, 24 hours weekly, six days a week. Combined hours of school and work must not exceed eight hours daily. Minors under 16 are prohibited from working before 7 a.m. or after 11:30 p.m. unless special permission has been granted by the Department of Labor. Minors under 16 must be accompanied at all times by an adult who is a parent, guardian or representative of the employer.

Minors between the ages of 16 and 18 can work as long as eight hours daily, 40 hours weekly, six days a week. They must obtain an Employment Certificate from the local issuing officer in the district in which a production is being filmed. Minors between the ages of 16 and 18 are prohibited from working before 6 a.m. or after 11:30 p.m. unless special permission has been granted by the Department of Labor.

FIREARMS

Although working automatic and semi-automatic weapons is illegal in New Jersey, provision has been made for the use of theatrical firearms of every variety. A permit must be obtained from the New Jersey State Police in order to use or transport such theatrical firearms in the state. Out-of-state permits are not valid. In addition, specific information about the firearms and the parties responsible for them must be provided both to the New Jersey State Police and to the local police in the jurisdiction where said weapons will be used.

EXPLOSIVES

Special effects sequences, depending on their nature and scop, may require specific permits and/or permissions from the state, its counties or municipalities. Effects using explosives must be performed by an effects coordinator who is licensed to use explosives in the state of New Jersey. Advance inspection of a given site by the local utility companies may also be necessary in some cases.

Pyrotechnical effects must be performed in cooperation with local fire department officials, who may inspect designated location sites and materials to be used. In certain instances, permission from the New Jersey Department of Environmental Protection must also be granted.

TAXES IN NEW JERSEY

EXEMPTION FROM NEW JERSEY'S 7% SALES TAX
Certain tangible property used directly and primarily in the production of films and television programs is exempt from New Jersey's 7% sales tax. This tangible property includes the purchase of replacement parts for machinery, tools and other supplies, the purchase of lumber and hardware to build sets, the rental of picture cars, the purchase or rental of other types of props, and costs related to the repair of camera and lighting equipment.

For specific information about New Jersey tax laws, contact the New Jersey Division of Taxation at (609) 588-2200.

INCENTIVES
20% Tax Credit Program
New Jersey offers a tax credit in an amount equal to 20% of qualified production expenses, available to production companies meeting certain criteria, chiefly:

(1) At least 60% of the total expenses of a project, exclusive of post-production costs, will be incurred for services performed and goods used or consumed in New Jersey.

(2) Principal photography of a project commences within 150 days after the approval of the application for the credit.

The tax credit is saleable and transferable. The program has an annual cap of $30 million.

New Jersey Film Production Assistance Program
This program allows producers of film projects made in the state to be eligible for loan guarantees through the New Jersey Economic Development Authority. Guaranteeing a portion of loans made by other lenders encourages these lenders to finance projects they might not ordinarily finance on their own. Loan guarantees cannot exceed 30% of the bank financing cost of the project, or $1.5 million, whichever is less.

Important criteria for eligibility are as follows:
1. At least one-half of material and production costs must be spent in New Jersey.
2. At least 70% of shooting days must take place in the state.
3. Prevailing wage must be paid to workers employed in the project to be financed.
4. The project must possess performance bonds.

Application forms and additional details about the program are available at www.njeda.com.

UNIONS
Most of New Jersey falls under the jurisdiction of the unions and guilds based in New York City. (See the "Crew" section of this book for listings of New York union locals.)

Steven Gorelick, Executive Director
New Jersey Motion Picture and Television Commission
153 Halsey St., 5th Floor
P.O. Box 47023
Newark, New Jersey 07101
(973) 648-6279
(973) 648-7350 Fax
www.njfilm.org

LA 411 VARIETY411.com New York 411

GO GREEN!

Interested in learning what you or your company can do to go green?

411 Publishing has partnered with Reel Green Media in an effort to assist you in transforming your business practices into green business practices.

Reel Green Media helps companies, productions and individuals in the entertainment industry develop and use more sustainable methods. The team of green consultants at Reel Green Media will help you develop a plan that works for your company and your objectives.

The first step on the path to adopting green practices is just a click away.

Visit www.reelgreenmedia.com to see what you can do to go green.

Has your company already gone green? If so, we want to know about it!

411 now features a dedicated online section promoting listees who have incorporated green standards into their organization and consumer output. Visit our Green Section to see if you qualify as a "Green Listee" – if you do, your listing will be designated with the ♻ symbol.

Visit www.resource411.com/Green for more information.

Where To Shoot In New Jersey

New Jersey boasts an outstanding variety of locations, which have been used to simulate many different periods and settings.

Hudson and Essex Counties are urban, industrial areas in close proximity to New York City. Hudson County offers factories, apartment and row housing, and period bridgework. Jersey City, the second largest city in New Jersey, has a highly built-up downtown, with older and contemporary office buildings and retail shops. Its Journal Square area is New Jersey's version of Times Square.

Essex County is home to Newark, the largest city in the state, that is undergoing a dramatic economic and cultural renaissance. Some of the most modern and prestigious office towers have sprung up near Newark Bay, and the recently opened New Jersey Performing Arts Center rivals major concert halls throughout the world. The busy Newark International Airport serves the entire metropolitan area. Essex County also contains many attractive suburban communities including Montclair, a highly popular film location.

Bergen, Middlesex, Union and Passaic Counties are predominantly suburban, offering a wide variety of wealthy homes and estates, middle and lower-middle-class housing, tree-lined streets, shopping malls, parks and scattered industrial locales. The Meadowlands Sports Complex in East Rutherford (Bergen County) is comprised of Giants Stadium, the Continental Airlines Arena, and the Meadowlands Racetrack. Rutgers, the State University, is located in New Brunswick and Piscataway (Middlesex County). Cities and towns of note include Eaglewood and Hackensack in Bergen County; Paterson, Passaic and Wayne in Passaic County, Elizabeth, Plainfield and Westfield in Union County; Perth Amboy, Woodbridge and New Brunswick in Middlesex County.

Morris County is notable for its county seat, Morristown, and the many charming small towns along Route 24. The county has historical significance dating back to Revolutionary times and George Washington's encampment in what is now Morristown National Park. The Great Swamp National Wildlife Refuge is a large wilderness area in the midst of the suburbs.

Warren and Sussex Counties fall within the mountain and lake regions of New Jersey. They are predominantly rural, dotted with small towns, quaint shops, older homes, country estates, and cabins. High Point, in Sussex County, is the point of highest elevation in New Jersey. The Delaware Water Gap, with its huge cliffs and rushing waters, is spectacularly scenic. Vernon, in Sussex County, is home to the state's largest ski resort. Towns of note include Newton in Sussex County and Phillipsburg and Hackettstown in Warren County.

Somerset and Hunterdon Counties consist of rolling farmland, quaint, rural towns, suburban communities and some very large and extravagant estate homes. Somerset County is in the heart of New Jersey's horse country, Hunterdon contains the state's only covered bridge and some of the most picturesque farmland available. Major towns include Flemington and Lambertville in Hunterdon County and Somerville and Bernardsville in Somerset County.

Mercer County is part suburban, part rural. Princeton, with its Tudor architecture and ivy-covered walls, is reminiscent of Oxford, England. It is home to the prestigious Princeton University as well as some of the country's foremost research facilities. Cities and Towns of Interest include Trenton (the state capital) and Hopewell.

Monmouth, Ocean and Atlantic Counties constitute most of the New Jersey shore region, containing miles of beachfront and boardwalk, amusement areas, harbors, marinas and lighthouses. Many beach communities, cottages and bungalows can be found in these coastal areas. Monmouth County contains many large, elegant homes, a commercial fishery, and the PNC Arts Center, the large amphitheater that has been one of New Jersey's most successful concert venues. Atlantic City in Atlantic County is the foremost tourist destination in New Jersey, offering glitzy hotel/casinos and world-class entertainment. Notable Cities and Towns: Freehold, Asbury Park, Spring Lake and Ocean Grove in Monmouth County; Point Pleasant, Seaside Heights and Toms River in Ocean County; Atlantic City in Atlantic County.

Burlington County is in the heart of The Pine Barrens, a huge wilderness area with dense forest, scenic rivers, and swampland. This region contains very small, rural communities whose native inhabitants have a unique, Ozark-like culture and folklore. Burlington County also has an industrial section located in and around Burlington City.

Camden County offers a variety of sites just minutes from Philadelphia. The city of Camden is the county seat and its urban center. The revitalized waterfront area is home to the New Jersey State Aquarium and the Blockbuster Entertainment Center, South Jersey's premiere concert venue. Cherry Hill is a wealthy suburban community with large, expensive homes.

Salem, Gloucester and Cumberland Counties are predominantly rural in nature. Farms and small communities abound. Gloucester County has suburban areas as well. Interesting Cities and Towns: Salem in Salem County, Bridgeton and Vineland in Cumberland County, Glassboro in Gloucester County.

Cape May County is the southernmost county in New Jersey, part of which is located below the Mason-Dixon line. It contains popular shore resort communities such as Wildwood and Ocean City, laden with boardwalk style shops, amusements and rides. Cape May City is a quaint Victorian paradise, featuring architecturally magnificent bed-and-breakfast establishments and charming shopping areas.

SIGN UP TODAY

INPRODUCTION
NEWSLETTERS

POWERED BY: **VARIETY** LA 411 New York 411

For the first time, *Variety* & *411 Publishing* are partnering to produce the most comprehensive weekly production email updates in the entertainment industry. Available for free upon registration.

Reach thousands of entertainment professionals vested in the current status of television and film production projects. **IN PRODUCTION** newsletters will provide abbreviated listings of the entire slate of Los Angeles and New York-based film and television projects in pre- (film only), current and post-production status updated on a weekly basis.

SIGN UP TODAY: www.NewYork411.com

For additional questions, please call: Sean Killebrew
323.965.2038 • skillebrew@reedbusiness.com

Filming In Connecticut

Connecticut Commission on Culture & Tourism Film Division

The right location is key to making (or breaking) a film. Connecticut's got rolling hills, high energy cities, peaceful pastoral grounds and nearly 100 miles of coastline.

Add in non-stop casinos, historic architecture and thriving nightlife and you've got 5009 square miles of versatile indoor and outdoor space—the ideal backdrop for nearly any scene.

Our Connecticut film team can lead you through the ins and outs of our state. We've got a Locations Manager who can tell you exactly where to find the ideal location, a Project Manager who will guide you through the procedures, permits and approvals, and an experienced Director who understands the dynamics of productions and what it takes to make it happen.

Connecticut lawmakers have taken action to bring your productions to Connecticut. In 2006, Connecticut passed legislation for a 30% digital media and motion picture tax credit.

One of the most aggressive tax credits in the nation, it welcomes filmmakers and production companies to draw upon everything Connecticut—and invites you to come back for more.

Call (860) 256-2800 to start your next blockbuster in Connecticut.
www.ctfilm.com

Connecticut Film Division
George Norfleet, Film Division Director
Connecticut Commission on Culture and Tourism
One Constitution Plaza Street, Hartford, CT 06103
(860) 256-2800 Phone, (860) 256-2811 Fax
George.Norfleet@ct.gov

For Location Information:
Mark Dixon, Locations Manager
(860) 256-2778 Phone, (860) 256-2763 Fax
Mark.Dixon@ct.gov

For Production Services:
Ellen Woolf, Project Manager
(860) 256-2770 Phone, (860) 256-2763 Fax
Ellen.Woolf@ct.gov

For Tax Credit Information:
Ed Ruggiero, Tax Credit Administrator
(860) 256-2790 Phone, (860) 256-2763 Fax
Ed.Ruggiero@ct.gov

Where To Shoot In Connecticut

THE SOUTHWEST

COASTAL FAIRFIELD COUNTY
The Gold Coast, mansions, industrial cities, high-tech sites, upscale neighborhoods, urban sprawl, working class & inner city neighborhoods, harbor yards, stadium, the Beardsley Zoo.

GREATER NEW HAVEN
Yale University's gothic and Georgian architecture, upscale suburbs, gritty working class and inner city communities, architecturally and ethnically diverse neighborhoods such as Wooster Square, Lighthouse Point Park & Carousel, and the industrial towns and cities of the Naugatuck River Valley.

THE SOUTHEAST

RIVER VALLEY & SHORELINE
Essex Steam Train & Riverboat, Johnsonville Victorian village, the Thimble Islands, Shoreline Trolley Museum, colonial and Victorian villages on the Connecticut River, sandy & rocky coastline, tidal estuaries, streams & waterfalls, and farms & forests.

MYSTIC COAST & COUNTRY
Seacoast villages, fishing fleet, lighthouses, tall ships, historic Mystic Seaport, two world-class casinos, Sonalysts Studios, river mill towns, the Harkness Mansion, historic forts, farmlands, vineyards, and scenic country roads.

THE NORTHWEST

LITCHFIELD HILLS
Quintessential Connecticut, horse country, rustic scenery, classic white steeple churches, upscale farms, lakes, covered bridges, town greens, and estates.

Housatonic Valley
River mill towns, classic New England villages, colonial taverns, vineyards, artist enclave, and rolling farmlands.

WATERBURY REGION
Yankee country, industrial city, mills, working class neighborhoods, the Naugatuck Valley Railroad, historic opera house, clock towers, amusement parks, industrial towns locked in time.

CENTRAL
Blue collar neighborhoods, sprawling suburbs, baseball stadium, orchards, cliffs, and woodlands.

THE NORTHEAST

GREATER HARTFORD
Historic city surrounded by diverse suburbs, turrets and towers, museums, the Old State House, river views, city skylines, and turn-of-the-century opulent homes.

HERITAGE VALLEY
Tobacco fields, trolleys and tracks, colonial prison and copper mines, Connecticut Freedom Trail, international airport and New England Air Museum, Native American trails, and neoclassical architecture.

QUIET CORNER
Connecticut farms, agricultural fairs, small town New England, historic mill towns, gardens, and vineyards.

Filming In Philadelphia

The Greater Philadelphia Film Office

The Greater Philadelphia Film Office serves to attract film and video production to the region, including everything from feature films to TV commercials to music videos and industrial films. It also provides the producer free assistance with parking, permits, hotels, labor, locations and generally acts as liaison between the production and the local community in order to cut red tape where necessary. The Philadelphia film office is also dedicated to growing local film and video production, recognizing its economic impact on job creation and its public relations effects for the region.

Services Available

- Free production guides for all qualified filmmakers
- Daily Web updates, visit www.film.org
- One-stop service for all city department requests
- Location scouting and photo files for the entire region
- Electronic Hotline with job opportunities and industry news
- Complete database of locations and resources
- Referrals and negotiations with businesses
- Coordination with neighborhoods and owners of private property
- Legislative representation to increase incentives that promote film industry growth
- Assistance with government permit or license requirements
- Ongoing dialogue with organized labor
- Philadelphia film crew hats, T-shirts and umbrellas
- Film Office internship program for qualified college students
- State-owned forests, parks, and buildings—We own it, you shoot on it for free
- "Set in Philadelphia" screenwriting competition
- Invitation to premieres of films made in Philadelphia
- Support and promotion of local film festivals
- Greater Philadelphia Filmmakers, a service program of the Greater Philadelphia Film Office, dedicated to the growth of local media artists

Incentives

Pennsylvania has a Film Production Tax Credit program. The state provides up to a 25 percent Film Production Tax Credit for film production expenses incurred in the Commonwealth. The tax credit is available for feature films, television films, television pilots or each episode of a television series. In order to qualify for the tax credit, 60 percent of the total production expenses must be incurred in Pennsylvania.

No more than $75 million per year in total tax credits can be awarded, which is prioritized based on application date. However, productions must start principal photography within 120 days of their application date.

Production expenses that are eligible for a tax credit include wages and salaries under a million dollars, construction, operations, editing, photography, sound synchronization, lighting, wardrobe and accessories, and the cost of rental of facilities and equipment. Marketing and advertising costs, development costs, story rights and music rights cannot be applied toward the tax credit.

The tax credits are fully transferable to a qualified Pennsylvania taxpayer. Contact the Greater Philadelphia Film Office for a current list of brokers. All productions are treated equally regardless of the home state or country of origin.

Hotel occupancy tax is exempt for hotel stays in excess of 30 days.

Philadelphia currently offers qualified productions the use of the Navy Yard Soundstage, the only municipally owned sound stage in the country. It is roughly six miles from center city.

Permits and Parking
As a general rule, no permits are required to shoot on the streets of Philadelphia. GPFO can assist you with obtaining any other permits or licenses that you may need for your production.

The city of Philadelphia may provide up to two free police officers for traffic control and security as needed for filming activity, subject, however, to the discretion of the Greater Philadelphia Film Office and the Philadelphia Police Department.

Filmmakers may be able to use Pennsylvania- and Philadelphia-owned property for location filming fee-free if the property can be made available during the period that the filmmaker requires. Costs incurred and liability insurance coverage, however, will be the responsibility of the production.

Weather
Spring greening begins around the first of April and continues through May. By May 1st the deciduous trees have leaves and the grass is very green. Fall foliage usually peaks after October 15th and before November 1st. Most trees are bare by December.

Child Labor Law
For information about Pennsylvania child labor law,
please visit the following Web site: http://www.dli.state.pa.us/landi/CWP/view.asp?a=185&Q=58124

Sharon Pinkenson, Executive Director
Greater Philadelphia Film Office
100 S. Broad Street, Ste. 600
Philadelphia, PA 19110
(215) 686-2668
(215) 686-3659 Fax
(215) 686-3663 Hot Line (24 Hours)
mail@film.org
www.film.org

Children's Employment Guidelines—New York State

The New York Child Performer Education and Trust Act of 2003 went into effect on March 28, 2004. It established minimal guidelines for the protection of child performers working throughout the entertainment industry in New York State. It is similar to the California "Coogan Law".

All minor performers (under 18 years of age) working in NY State, whether residents of NY State or not are subject to this law. It also applies to all work by NY State Resident Minors working in other states. This law is administered and enforced by the New York State Department of Labor. Additional information on the law can be found at their website: www.labor.state.ny.us/workerprotection/laborstandards/secure/child_index.shtm.

Key Elements of This Law:

1. Permits:
   A. All employers of child performers are required to have a valid Certificate of Eligibility to Employ Child Performers
   B. All child performers must have a valid Employment Permit for a Child Performer.

2. Trust Accounts:
   A. Parents are required to open Trust Accounts for minor performers. They must notify employers of the establishment of these accounts within 15 days of employment. Employers are required to deposit at least 15% of the minor performer's earnings in their Trust Account within 30 days of the last day of employment if the minor is working 30 days or less, or at the end of each payroll period if work is for more than 30 days.
   B. If parents do not open Trust accounts, employers are required to deposit the monies with the NY State Controller's Office.

3. Academic Performance:
   A. Whenever a child performer is not receiving school instruction due to his/her employment schedule, employers must provide a teacher, who either is certified or has credentials recognized by the State of New York. Generally, this means that a teacher is only required if the child will miss more than two consecutive days of school.

Certificate of Eligibility to Employ Child Performers: Even though a payroll service will be the employer of record, the DOL has determined that it requires the employer in control of the talent to obtain the Permit to Employ. So, in general, the Production Company must obtain the Certificate of Eligibility to Employ Child Performers. The application for the "Certificate" can be downloaded from www.labor.state.ny.us/child/index.htm. The certificate costs $350.00 and is vailid for three years. Renewals cost $200.00.

Proof of Worker's Compensation and Disability Insurance must be submitted along with the "Certificate" application.

Agency Pays Talent: In TV commercial production, it often occurs that the advertising agency will pay the actors. In this case, not only the production company, but the advertising agency will need to obtain the Certificate of Eligibility to Employ Child Performers. They would need to provide Proof of Worker's Compensation and Disability Insurance from the advertising agency's talent payment service. In fact, the NYS DOL feels that the advertising agency should obtain the "Certificate" whether or not they are paying the talent.

New York
Steve Bizenov
(646) 829-0702
steve@media-services.com

MEDIA SERVICES
ENTERTAINMENT ACCOUNTING, PAYROLL & SOFTWARE

Los Angeles
Tina Bassir
(310) 471-9369
tina@media-services.com

New York Charities

This is just a small sampling of groups that offer assistance to those in need in the New York area. Some of these organizations work to get excess food to the area's hungry. With the help of this list, if there is more food on set than your crew could eat, you can give one of these organizations a call.

American Cancer Society
(800) 227-2345
www.cancer.org
Cancer prevention, research, education, advocacy and service.

American Humane Association
(818) 501-0123
(800) 677-3420
www.ahafilm.org
The American Humane Association has regulated the safety of animals on movie sets since 1940 and is designated by the Screen Actors Guild as the only animal welfare organization with on-set jurisdiction. They are also responsible for awarding the "No Animals Were Harmed®" end credit to a production that has complied with all animal safety guidelines.

American Red Cross
(800) Help Now
(800) 435-7669
www.redcross.org
Each year, the American Red Cross responds immediately to more than 70,000 disasters, providing relief to those affected, support to the rescue and emergency teams, handles inquiries from family members outside the disaster area, and provides blood and blood products as well as other services to those in need.

The ASPCA (The American Society for the Prevention of Cruelty to Animals)
(212) 876-7700
www.aspca.org
Provides a variety of programs to shelters and individuals, promotes legislation to protect all animals.

Children's Network International
(877) 264-2243
www.childrensnetworkinternational.org
Canned, cooked or uncooked food, and clothes.
Pick-up with 24 hours notice.

Dress for Success New York
32 East 31st Street
Suite 602
New York, New York 10016
(212) 684-3611
www.dressforsuccess.org
Advances low-income women's economic and social development and encourages self-sufficiency through career development and employment retention.

Entertainment Industry Foundation
(213) 240-3900
www.eifoundation.org
Contributes funding and volunteering to a variety of charities.

Food Bank for New York City
39 Broadway
New York, NY 10006
(212) 566-7855
www.foodbanknyc.org

Habitat for Humanity
(800) 422-4828
www.habitat.org

Henry Street Settlement
265 Henry Street
New York, NY 10002
(212) 766-9200
www.henrystreet.org
Henry Street Settlement delivers a wide range of social service and arts programming to more than 100,000 New Yorkers each year.

The Humane Society of the United States
(800) 486-2631
www.hsus.org
Promoting the protection of all animals through a variety of programs and legislation. The producers of the Genesis Awards, which pay tribute to major news and entertainment media for producing outstanding works that raise public awareness of animal issues.

Long Island Cares Inc.
10 Davids Drive
Hauppauge, NY 11788
(631) 582-FOOD
www.licares.org
Long Island Cares provides emergency food where and when it is needed and sponsors programs that help families achieve self-sufficiency.

The Partnership for the Homeless, Inc.
305 Seventh Avenue, 13th Floor
New York, NY 10001
(212) 645-3444
www.partnershipforthehomeless.org

Regional Food Bank of Northeastern New York
965 Albany-Shaker Road
Latham, NY 12110
(518) 786-3691
www.regionalfoodbank.net

Urban Pathways
575 8th Avenue, 9th Floor
New York, NY 10018
(212) 736-7385
www.urbanpathways.org

United Way of New York City
2 Park Avenue
New York, NY 10016
(212) 251-2500
www.unitedwaynyc.org

World Stunt Awards Foundation
(323) 468-4011
www.worldstuntawards.com
Provides support for injured stunt men and women.

Weather Data

New York City

Climatic Averages	Jan	Feb	Mar	Apr	May	Jun	Jul	Aug	Sep	Oct	Nov	Dec
Daily Maximum	38	40	49	61	72	80	85	84	76	66	54	42
Daily Minimum	26	27	34	44	53	63	68	67	60	50	41	30
Monthy Precipitation	3.2	3.1	4.2	3.8	3.8	3.2	3.8	4.0	3.7	3.4	4.1	3.8
Days with >.01" Precipitation	11	10	11	11	11	10	11	10	8	8	9	10
Days with Snow, Ice Pellets > .01"	2	2	2	0	0	0	0	0	0	0	0	2
Days with Thunderstorms	0	0	1	1	3	4	4	4	1	1	0	0
Days with Fog 1/4 mile or less	0	0	0	0	0	0	0	0	0	0	0	0
Clear Days	8	8	9	8	8	8	9	9	11	12	9	9
Partially Cloudy Days	9	9	10	11	12	12	13	12	10	10	10	9
Cloudy Days	14	11	12	12	11	10	10	10	9	10	12	13

Capitol/Saratoga

Climatic Averages	Jan	Feb	Mar	Apr	May	Jun	Jul	Aug	Sep	Oct	Nov	Dec
Daily Maximum	30	33	43	58	70	78	83	81	73	62	48	35
Daily Minimum	12	14	25	36	45	55	60	58	50	39	31	18
Monthy Precipitation	2.4	2.3	3.0	2.9	3.3	3.3	3.0	3.3	3.2	2.9	3.0	3.0
Days with >.01" Precipitation	12	11	12	12	13	11	10	10	10	9	12	12
Days with Snow, Ice Pellets > .01"	4	3	3	1	0	0	0	0	0	0	1	4
Days with Thunderstorms	0	0	1	1	3	5	7	5	2	1	0	0
Days with Fog 1/4 mile or less	1	1	1	1	1	1	2	3	4	4	2	2
Clear Days	6	6	6	6	5	5	6	7	8	8	4	5
Partially Cloudy Days	8	7	8	8	9	11	13	12	10	9	8	7
Cloudy Days	17	15	17	16	17	14	12	13	13	14	19	19

Buffalo/Niagara

Climatic Averages	Jan	Feb	Mar	Apr	May	Jun	Jul	Aug	Sep	Oct	Nov	Dec
Daily Maximum	30	31	40	54	66	76	80	78	71	60	47	35
Daily Minimum	17	18	26	36	46	56	61	60	53	43	34	23
Monthy Precipitation	3.0	2.4	3.0	3.1	2.9	2.7	3.0	4.2	3.4	2.9	3.6	3.4
Days with >.01" Precipitation	20	17	16	14	12	11	10	11	11	12	16	20
Days with Snow, Ice Pellets > .01"	7	6	4	1	0	0	0	0	0	0	3	6
Days with Thunderstorms	0	0	1	2	3	5	6	6	4	2	1	1
Days with Fog 1/4 mile or less	2	2	3	2	2	1	1	1	1	1	1	1
Clear Days	1	2	4	5	6	6	7	7	6	6	2	1
Partially Cloudy Days	6	6	8	8	10	12	13	12	10	8	6	6
Cloudy Days	23	21	20	17	16	12	11	12	14	16	23	23

Finger Lakes

Climatic Averages	Jan	Feb	Mar	Apr	May	Jun	Jul	Aug	Sep	Oct	Nov	Dec
Daily Maximum	31	32	41	56	68	77	82	80	72	61	48	35
Daily Minimum	15	16	25	36	46	55	60	59	52	42	33	21
Monthy Precipitation	2.6	2.7	3.1	3.3	3.2	3.6	3.8	3.8	3.3	3.1	3.5	3.2
Days with >.01" Precipitation	19	16	17	14	13	11	11	11	11	12	16	19
Days with Snow, Ice Pellets > .01"	9	8	5	1	0	0	0	0	0	0	3	8
Days with Thunderstorms	0	0	1	2	3	5	6	6	3	1	1	0
Days with Fog 1/4 mile or less	1	1	1	1	1	1	1	1	1	1	1	1
Clear Days	3	3	5	6	6	7	8	7	7	6	2	2
Partially Cloudy Days	7	6	7	7	10	10	12	11	10	8	6	5
Cloudy Days	22	19	19	17	15	13	11	13	13	18	17	24

Adirondacks

Climatic Averages	Jan	Feb	Mar	Apr	May	Jun	Jul	Aug	Sep	Oct	Nov	Dec
Daily Maximum	25	27	37	50	64	73	77	74	67	56	42	29
Daily Minimum	3	4	16	28	40	49	53	51	44	34	25	10
Monthy Precipitation	2.5	2.4	2.6	3.1	3.6	3.5	3.9	4.4	3.5	3.1	3.1	3.0
Days with >.01" Precipitation	14	12	13	12	14	13	12	13	12	12	14	15
Days with Snow, Ice Pellets > .01"	5	5	4	1	0	0	0	0	0	0	2	5
Days with Thunderstorms	0	0	0	1	3	5	6	5	2	1	0	0
Days with Fog 1/4 mile or less	1	1	1	1	1	1	1	1	2	2	1	1
Clear Days	4	4	6	5	5	5	5	6	6	6	3	3
Partially Cloudy Days	7	7	7	8	9	11	13	12	10	8	5	6
Cloudy Days	20	17	18	17	17	15	13	13	14	17	22	22

Weather Data

Westchester Co./Yonkers

Climatic Averages	Jan	Feb	Mar	Apr	May	Jun	Jul	Aug	Sep	Oct	Nov	Dec
Daily Maximum	37	39	48	62	72	80	85	83	75	64	53	41
Daily Minimum	23	24	32	41	51	60	66	64	58	47	38	28
Monthy Precipitation	3.8	3.6	4.9	4.4	3.9	3.8	4.0	4.5	4.2	4.0	4.7	4.5
Days with >.01" Precipitation	11	10	11	11	11	10	11	10	8	8	9	10
Days with Snow, Ice Pellets > .01"	2	2	2	0	0	0	0	0	0	0	0	2
Days with Thunderstorms	0	0	1	1	3	4	4	4	1	1	0	0
Days with Fog 1/4 mile or less	0	0	0	0	0	0	0	0	0	0	0	0
Clear Days	8	8	9	8	8	8	9	9	11	12	9	9
Partially Cloudy Days	9	9	10	11	12	12	13	12	10	10	10	9
Cloudy Days	14	11	12	12	11	10	10	10	10	10	12	13

Long Island

Climatic Averages	Jan	Feb	Mar	Apr	May	Jun	Jul	Aug	Sep	Oct	Nov	Dec
Daily Maximum	38	40	47	58	68	77	82	81	75	65	54	43
Daily Minimum	21	22	29	37	47	57	63	62	55	44	35	26
Monthy Precipitation	3.8	3.6	4.3	4.0	3.7	2.9	3.3	4.5	3.4	3.9	4.0	4.4
Days with >.01" Precipitation	11	10	11	11	11	10	9	9	8	8	10	11
Days with Snow, Ice Pellets > .01"	2	2	1	0	0	0	0	0	0	0	0	1
Days with Thunderstorms	0	0	1	2	3	4	5	5	2	1	1	0
Days with Fog 1/4 mile or less	2	2	2	2	3	3	2	1	1	2	1	2
Clear Days	8	8	8	8	7	7	7	8	10	11	8	8
Partially Cloudy Days	8	7	9	9	11	11	13	13	9	9	9	9
Cloudy Days	15	13	14	13	13	12	11	11	11	11	14	15

Hudson Valley

Climatic Averages	Jan	Feb	Mar	Apr	May	Jun	Jul	Aug	Sep	Oct	Nov	Dec
Daily Maximum	34	37	46	60	71	79	84	82	74	63	51	38
Daily Minimum	15	17	26	36	46	56	61	59	51	40	31	20
Monthy Precipitation	2.8	2.4	3.3	3.7	3.6	3.4	3.5	3.8	3.7	3.3	3.6	3.2
Days with >.01" Precipitation	12	10	12	12	13	11	9	10	10	9	12	12
Days with Snow, Ice Pellets > .01"	3	3	2	0	0	0	0	0	0	0	1	4
Days with Thunderstorms	0	0	1	2	3	6	7	5	2	1	0	0
Days with Fog 1/4 mile or less	1	1	1	1	1	1	2	3	3	4	2	2
Clear Days	6	6	6	6	5	5	6	7	8	8	4	5
Partially Cloudy Days	8	7	8	8	9	11	13	11	10	9	9	7
Cloudy Days	17	15	17	16	17	14	12	13	12	14	18	19

Coastal Connecticut

Climatic Averages	Jan	Feb	Mar	Apr	May	Jun	Jul	Aug	Sep	Oct	Nov	Dec
Daily Maximum	37	38	46	57	67	76	82	81	75	65	53	41
Daily Minimum	23	23	31	4.	50	59	66	65	58	47	38	27
Monthy Precipitation	3.3	3.0	3.9	3.7	3.4	2.9	3.5	3.7	3.3	3.3	3.8	3.8
Days with >.01" Precipitation	11	10	11	11	11	10	9	9	9	7	10	11
Days with Snow, Ice Pellets > .01"	2	2	1	0	0	0	0	0	0	0	0	2
Days with Thunderstorms	0	0	1	2	3	4	5	4	2	1	0	0
Days with Fog 1/4 mile or less	3	3	3	3	4	4	2	1	1	2	2	2
Clear Days	8	8	8	7	7	8	7	9	10	11	8	8
Partially Cloudy Days	8	7	9	9	10	10	12	11	9	8	8	8
Cloudy Days	15	13	14	14	14	12	12	12	12	12	14	15

Weather Data

Interior Connecticut

Climatic Averages	Jan	Feb	Mar	Apr	May	Jun	Jul	Aug	Sep	Oct	Nov	Dec
Daily Maximum	34	36	46	60	71	80	85	83	75	64	51	37
Daily Minimum	17	19	28	38	47	57	62	60	52	41	33	21
Monthy Precipitation	3.5	3.2	4.2	4.0	3.4	3.4	3.1	4.0	3.9	3.5	4.1	4.2
Days with >.01" Precipitation	11	10	11	11	12	11	10	10	9	8	11	12
Days with Snow, Ice Pellets > .01"	3	3	2	1	0	0	0	0	0	0	1	3
Days with Thunderstorms	0	0	1	1	2	4	5	4	2	1	0	0
Days with Fog 1/4 mile or less	2	2	2	1	2	2	2	2	3	4	2	3
Clear Days	8	7	7	6	5	6	6	7	8	9	6	7
Partially Cloudy Days	8	8	9	8	10	10	12	11	9	9	8	8
Cloudy Days	15	14	16	15	16	14	13	14	13	13	16	17

Northern New Jersey

Climatic Averages	Jan	Feb	Mar	Apr	May	Jun	Jul	Aug	Sep	Oct	Nov	Dec
Daily Maximum	38	40	49	61	72	81	86	84	77	66	54	42
Daily Minimum	24	25	33	43	53	62	68	67	59	48	39	29
Monthy Precipitation	3.1	3.1	4.2	3.6	3.6	2.9	3.9	4.3	3.7	3.1	3.6	3.4
Days with >.01" Precipitation	11	10	11	11	12	10	10	9	8	8	10	11
Days with Snow, Ice Pellets > .01"	2	2	1	0	0	0	0	0	0	0	0	1
Days with Thunderstorms	0	0	1	2	4	5	6	5	2	1	1	0
Days with Fog 1/4 mile or less	2	2	1	1	2	1	1	1	1	2	2	2
Clear Days	8	7	8	7	6	7	7	8	10	11	8	8
Partially Cloudy Days	8	8	9	9	11	11	12	12	9	9	8	8
Cloudy Days	16	13	14	14	14	12	12	12	12	12	14	15

Southern New Jersey

Climatic Averages	Jan	Feb	Mar	Apr	May	Jun	Jul	Aug	Sep	Oct	Nov	Dec
Daily Maximum	41	42	50	62	71	80	84	83	77	66	55	45
Daily Minimum	23	24	32	40	50	59	65	64	56	45	36	27
Monthy Precipitation	3.5	3.3	4.0	3.2	3.1	2.8	4.0	4.7	2.9	3.1	3.7	3.6
Days with >.01" Precipitation	11	10	11	11	10	9	9	9	8	7	9	10
Days with Snow, Ice Pellets > .01"	2	1	1	0	0	0	0	0	0	0	0	1
Days with Thunderstorms	0	0	1	2	3	5	6	5	2	1	1	0
Days with Fog 1/4 mile or less	3	3	3	4	4	4	4	4	3	5	3	3
Clear Days	8	8	8	7	6	7	7	7	10	11	8	8
Partially Cloudy Days	8	7	8	9	10	11	11	11	8	9	9	8
Cloudy Days	15	14	15	14	14	12	13	12	12	12	13	15

Weather Data courtesy of Metro Weather Service.
www.metroweather.com
Brett Zweiback: (800) 488-7866

2009-2010 Sunrises & Sunsets/Eastern Standard Time

This table is based on sunrise and sunset times for New York, New York

	JULY		AUGUST		SEPTEMBER		OCTOBER		NOVEMBER		DECEMBER	
	Rise A.M.	Set P.M.	Rise A.M.	Set P.M.	Rise A.M.	Set P.M.	Rise A.M.	Set P.M.	Rise A.M.	Set P.M.	Rise A.M.	Set P.M.
1	5:28	8:31	5:52	8:11	6:23	7:28	6:52	6:37	6:26	4:52	7:01	4:29
2	5:29	8:31	5:53	8:10	6:24	7:26	6:53	6:36	6:27	4:51	7:02	4:29
3	5:29	8:30	5:54	8:09	6:25	7:24	6:54	6:34	6:29	4:49	7:03	4:28
4	5:30	8:30	5:55	8:07	6:26	7:23	6:55	6:32	6:30	4:48	7:04	4:28
5	5:30	8:30	5:56	8:06	6:27	7:21	6:56	6:31	6:31	4:47	7:05	4:28
6	5:31	8:30	5:57	8:05	6:28	7:19	6:58	6:29	6:32	4:46	7:05	4:28
7	5:32	8:29	5:58	8:04	6:29	7:18	6:59	6:28	6:33	4:45	7:06	4:28
8	5:32	8:29	5:59	8:03	6:30	7:16	7:00	6:26	6:35	4:44	7:07	4:28
9	5:33	8:29	6:00	8:01	6:31	7:14	7:01	6:24	6:36	4:43	7:08	4:28
10	5:34	8:28	6:01	8:00	6:32	7:13	7:02	6:23	6:37	4:42	7:09	4:28
11	5:34	8:28	6:02	7:59	6:33	7:11	7:03	6:21	6:38	4:41	7:10	4:28
12	5:35	8:27	6:03	7:57	6:34	7:09	7:04	6:20	6:39	4:40	7:11	4:28
13	5:36	8:27	6:04	7:56	6:35	7:08	7:05	6:18	6:40	4:39	7:11	4:29
14	5:37	8:26	6:05	7:55	6:36	7:06	7:06	6:17	6:42	4:38	7:12	4:29
15	5:37	8:26	6:06	7:53	6:36	7:04	7:07	6:15	6:43	4:37	7:13	4:29
16	5:38	8:25	6:07	7:52	6:37	7:03	7:08	6:12	6:44	4:37	7:13	4:29
17	5:39	8:24	6:08	7:51	6:38	7:01	7:09	6:12	6:45	4:36	7:14	4:30
18	5:40	8:24	6:09	7:49	6:39	6:59	7:10	6:11	6:46	4:35	7:15	4:30
19	5:41	8:23	6:10	7:48	6:40	6:58	7:11	6:09	6:47	4:34	7:15	4:31
20	5:42	8:22	6:11	7:46	6:41	6:56	7:13	6:08	6:49	4:34	7:16	4:31
21	5:42	8:21	6:12	7:45	6:42	6:54	7:14	6:06	6:50	4:33	7:16	4:31
22	5:43	8:21	6:13	7:43	6:43	6:52	7:15	6:05	6:51	4:33	7:17	4:32
23	5:44	8:20	6:14	7:42	6:44	6:51	7:16	6:03	6:52	4:32	7:17	4:33
24	5:45	8:19	6:15	7:40	6:45	6:49	7:17	6:02	6:53	4:31	7:18	4:33
25	5:46	8:18	6:16	7:39	6:46	6:47	7:18	6:01	6:54	4:31	7:18	4:34
26	5:47	8:17	6:17	7:37	6:47	6:46	7:19	5:59	6:55	4:31	7:18	4:34
27	5:48	8:16	6:18	7:36	6:48	6:44	7:21	5:58	6:56	4:30	7:19	4:35
28	5:49	8:15	6:19	7:34	6:49	6:42	7:22	5:57	6:57	4:30	7:19	4:36
29	5:50	8:14	6:20	7:32	6:50	6:41	7:23	5:55	6:59	4:29	7:19	4:37
30	5:51	8:13	6:21	7:31	6:51	6:39	7:24	5:54	7:00	4:29	7:20	4:37
31	5:52	8:12	6:22	7:29			7:25	5:53			7:20	4:38

2009-2010 Sunrises & Sunsets/Eastern Standard Time

This table is based on sunrise and sunset times for New York, New York

	JANUARY Rise A.M.	JANUARY Set P.M.	FEBRUARY Rise A.M.	FEBRUARY Set P.M.	MARCH Rise A.M.	MARCH Set P.M.	APRIL Rise A.M.	APRIL Set P.M.	MAY Rise A.M.	MAY Set P.M.	JUNE Rise A.M.	JUNE Set P.M.
1	7:20	4:39	7:06	5:13	6:30	5:47	6:39	7:20	5:54	7:52	5:27	8:21
2	7:20	4:40	7:05	5:14	6:28	5:48	6:38	7:21	5:53	7:53	5:26	8:21
3	7:20	4:41	7:04	5:16	6:27	5:49	6:36	7:22	5:52	7:54	5:26	8:22
4	7:20	4:42	7:03	5:17	6:25	5:50	6:34	7:24	5:51	7:55	5:26	8:23
5	7:20	4:43	7:02	5:18	6:23	5:51	6:33	7:25	5:49	7:56	5:25	8:23
6	7:20	4:43	7:01	5:19	6:22	5:52	6:31	7:26	5:48	7:57	5:25	8:24
7	7:20	4:44	6:59	5:21	6:20	5:54	6:30	7:27	5:47	7:58	5:25	8:25
8	7:20	4:45	6:58	5:22	6:19	5:55	6:28	7:28	5:46	7:59	5:24	8:25
9	7:19	4:46	6:57	5:23	6:17	5:56	6:26	7:29	5:45	8:00	5:24	8:26
10	7:19	4:47	6:56	5:24	6:16	5:57	6:25	7:30	5:44	8:01	5:24	8:26
11	7:19	4:49	6:55	5:26	6:14	5:58	6:23	7:31	5:43	8:02	5:24	8:27
12	7:19	4:50	6:53	5:27	6:12	5:59	6:22	7:32	5:42	8:03	5:24	8:27
13	7:18	4:51	6:52	5:28	6:11	6:00	6:20	7:33	5:41	8:04	5:24	8:28
14	7:18	4:52	6:51	5:29	7:09	7:01	6:19	7:34	5:40	8:05	5:24	8:28
15	7:18	4:53	6:50	5:30	7:07	7:02	6:17	7:35	5:39	8:06	5:24	8:29
16	7:17	4:54	6:48	5:32	7:06	7:03	6:15	7:36	5:38	8:07	5:24	8:29
17	7:17	4:55	6:47	5:33	7:04	7:05	6:14	7:37	5:37	8:08	5:24	8:29
18	7:16	4:56	6:46	5:34	7:02	7:06	6:12	7:38	5:36	8:09	5:24	8:30
19	7:16	4:57	6:44	5:35	7:01	7:07	6:11	7:39	5:35	8:10	5:24	8:30
20	7:15	4:59	6:43	5:36	6:59	7:08	6:10	7:40	5:34	8:11	5:24	8:30
21	7:15	5:00	6:42	5:38	6:58	7:09	6:08	7:41	5:33	8:12	5:25	8:30
22	7:14	5:01	6:40	5:39	6:56	7:10	6:07	7:42	5:33	8:13	5:25	8:31
23	7:13	5:02	6:39	5:40	6:54	7:11	6:05	7:43	5:32	8:13	5:25	8:31
24	7:13	5:03	6:37	5:41	6:53	7:12	6:04	7:45	5:31	8:14	5:25	8:31
25	7:12	5:05	6:36	5:42	6:51	7:13	6:02	7:46	5:31	8:15	5:26	8:31
26	7:11	5:06	6:34	5:43	6:49	7:14	6:01	7:47	5:30	8:16	5:26	8:31
27	7:10	5:07	6:33	5:45	6:48	7:15	6:00	7:48	5:29	8:17	5:26	8:31
28	7:09	5:08	6:31	5:46	6:46	7:16	5:58	7:49	5:29	8:18	5:27	8:31
29	7:09	5:10			6:44	7:17	5:57	7:50	5:28	8:18	5:27	8:31
30	7:08	5:11			6:43	7:18	5:56	7:51	5:28	8:19	5:28	8:31
31	7:07	5:12			6:41	7:19			5:27	8:20		

Awards, Expos & Festivals

Academy Awards (310) 247-3000
Academy of Motion Picture FAX (310) 859-9619
Arts & Sciences www.oscars.org/academyawards
8949 Wilshire Blvd.
Beverly Hills, CA 90211
March 7, 2010

AFCI Locations Trade Show 2009 (307) 367-4424 / (323) 461-2324
Association of Film FAX (413) 375-2903
Commissioners Int'l www.afci.org
109 E. 17th St., Ste. 18
Cheyenne, WY 82001
April, 2010 Santa Monica

AFI Los Angeles Int'l Film Festival (323) 856-7600
The American Film Institute FAX (323) 467-4578
2021 N. Western Ave. www.afifest.com
Los Angeles, CA 90027
November, 2009

AICP Shows (323) 960-4763
National LA FAX (323) 960-4766
650 N. Bronson Ave., Ste. 223B www.aicp.com
Los Angeles, CA 90004
Check Web site for dates

American Film Market (310) 446-1000
c/o IFTA FAX (310) 446-1600
10850 Wilshire Blvd., Ninth Fl. www.ifta-online.org/afm
Los Angeles, CA 90024
Managing Director: Jonathan Wolf
November 4-11, 2009

Ann Arbor Film Festival (734) 995-5356
208 ½ S. State St., Ste. 31 FAX (734) 995-5396
Ann Arbor, MI 48104 www.aafilmfest.org
March, 2010

Annie Awards (818) 842-8330
ASIFA-Hollywood FAX (818) 842-5645
2114 Burbank Blvd. www.annieawards.org
Burbank, CA 91502
January, 2010

Artios Awards 323-463-1925
Castin Society of America FAX (323)463-5753
606 N. Larchmont Blvd. www.castingsociety.com
Ste. 4-B
Los Angeles, CA 90004
November 2, 2009 NYC

ASC Awards (323) 969-4333
c/o American Society FAX (323) 882-6391
of Cinematographers www.theasc.com/awards
P.O. Box 2230
Los Angeles, CA 90078
February, 2010

Aspen ShortFest (970) 925-6882
Aspen FilmFest FAX (970) 925-1967
10 E. Hallam St., Ste. 102 www.aspenfilm.org
Aspen, CO 81611
April, 2010

BAFTA/ LA Britannia Awards 44 20 7734 0022
British Academy of Film & TV Arts FAX 44 20 7734 1792
195 Piccadilly www.bafta.org/awards
London, W1J 9LN
United Kingdom
November, 2009

Berlinale/ Berlin Int'l Film Festival 49 30 259 20 0
Potsdamer Strabe 5 FAX 49 30 259 20 299
10785 Berlin www.berlinale.de
Germany
February 11-21, 2010

The Black Maria Film & Video Festival (201) 200-2043
c/o Media Arts Department FAX (201) 200-3490
Fries Hall www.blackmariafilmfestival.org
New Jersey City University
2039 Kennedy Blvd.
Jersey City, NJ 07305
February, 2010

Cannes Film Festival 33 1 53 59 61 00
3, rue Amélie FAX 33 1 53 59 61 10
Paris, F-75007 France www.festival-cannes.org
May, 2010

Cannes Lions Int'l Advertising Festival 44 20 7728 4040
Greater London House FAX 44 20 7728 4030
Hampstead Rd. www.canneslions.com
London, NW17EJ
United Kingdom
June, 2010

Chicago Int'l Children's Film Festival (773) 281-9075
c/o Facets Multi-Media FAX (773) 929-0266
1517 W. Fullerton Ave. www.cicff.org
Chicago, IL 60614
October 22–November 1, 2009

Cine Gear Expo (310) 472-0809
P.O. Box 492296 FAX (310) 471-8973
Los Angeles, CA 90049 www.cinegearexpo.com
June, 2010 Los Angeles

CineQuest (408) 295-3378
P.O. Box 720040 FAX (408) 995-5713
San Jose, CA 95172 www.cinequest.org
February, 2010

CineVegas Film Festival (702) 952-5555
170 S. Green Valley Pkwy., Ste. 120 FAX (702) 952-5556
Henderson, NV 89012 www.clioawards.com
June, 2010

Clio Awards (212) 683-4300
770 Broadway, Sixth Fl. FAX (212) 683-4796
New York, NY 10003 www.clioawards.com
May, 2010

Comic-Con (619) 491-2475
P.O. Box 128458 FAX (619) 414-1022
San Diego, CA 92118 www.comic-con.org
May, 2010

Creative Arts Emmy Awards (818) 754-2800
Academy of Television FAX (818) 761-2827
Arts & Sciences www.emmys.org
5220 Lankershim Blvd.
North Hollywood, CA 91601
September 12, 2009

Directors Guild of America Awards (310) 289-2000
7920 Sunset Blvd. FAX (310) 289-2029
Los Angeles, CA 90046 www.dga.org
July 23-26, 2009

DV Expo, West (212) 378-0400
c/o NewBay Media www.dvexpo.com
810 Seventh Ave., 27th Fl.
New York, NY 10019
October 20-22, 2009 Pasadena Convention Center

Emmy Awards (818) 754-2800
Academy of Television FAX (818) 761-2827
Arts & Sciences www.emmys.org
5220 Lankershim Blvd.
North Hollywood, CA 91601
September 20, 2009

Emmy Awards
New York Chapter (212) 459-3630
Nat'l Academy of Television FAX (212) 459-9772
Arts and Sciences www.nynatas.org
1375 Broadway, Ste. 2103
New York, NY 10018
March, 2010

Film Independent's Spirit Awards (310) 432-1240
Film Independent/Los Angeles FAX (310) 432-1234
9911 W. Pico Blvd., 11th Fl. www.filmindependent.org
Los Angeles, CA 90035
February, 2010

Florida Media Market (305) 372-4563
25 SE Second Ave., Ste. 1148 FAX (305) 372-4564
Miami, FL 33131 www.floridamediamarket.com
October, 2009

Golden Globes (310) 657-1731
c/o Hollywood Foreign FAX (310) 657-5576
Press Association www.goldenglobes.org
646 N. Robertson Blvd.
West Hollywood, CA 90069
January 17, 2010

The Gotham Awards (212) 465-8200
IFP/ New York FAX (212) 465-8525
104 W. 29th St., 12th Fl. www.ifp.org
New York, NY 10001
December, 2009

GRAMMY Awards (310) 392-3777
The Recording Academy FAX (310) 392-2306
3402 Pico Blvd. www.grammy.com
Santa Monica, CA 90405
February, 2010

The Hamptons Int'l Film Festival (631) 324-4600
Three Newtown Mews FAX (631) 324-5116
East Hampton, NY 11937 www.hamptonsfilmfest.org
October 8-12, 2009

Heartland Film Festival (317) 464-9405
200 S. Meridian St., Ste. 220 FAX (317) 464-8409
Indianapolis, IN 46225 www.heartlandfilmfestival.org
October 16-24, 2009

High Def Expo - Beverly Hills (818) 842-6611
3727 W. Magnolia Blvd., Ste. 729 FAX (818) 842-6624
Burbank, CA 91505 www.hdexpo.net
March, 2010

Hollywood Film Festival (310) 288-1882
433 N. Camden Dr., Ste. 600 FAX (310)-288-0060
Beverly Hills, CA 90210 www.hollywoodfestival.com
October 21-26, 2009

Independent Film Week (212) 465-8200
IFP/New York FAX (212) 465-8525
104 W. 29th St., 12th Fl. www.ifp.org
New York, NY 10001
September, 2009

Int'l CINDY Competition (469) 464-4180
3824 Trogden Court FAX (469) 464-4170
Mound, TX 75022 www.cindys.com
Check Web site for dates

Just for Laughs (514) 845-3155
2101 St-Laurent Blvd. FAX (514) 845-4140
Montreal, Quebec www.hahaha.com
Canada H2X 2T5
Summer, 2009

Long Island Int'l Film Expo (516) 783-3199
c/o Bellmore Movies www.liifilmexpo.org
222 Petit Ave., Side Enterence
Bellmore, NY 11710
July 13-19, 2009

Method Fest (310) 535-9230
840 Apollo St., Ste. 314 FAX (310) 535-9128
El Segundo, CA 90245 www.methodfest.com
March, 2010

Miami International Film Festival (305) 237-3456
Miami Dade College FAX (305) 257-7344
25 NE Second St. www.miamifilmfestival.com
Ste. 5501-5
Miami, FL 33132
March, 2010

Mill Valley Film Festival (415) 383-5256
1001 Lootens Pl., Ste. 220 FAX (415) 383-8606
San Rafael, CA 94901 www.mvff.com
October 8-18, 2010

MTV Movie Awards (212) 258-8000 / (310) 752-8000
1515 Broadway FAX (212) 846-1804
New York, NY 10036 www.mtv.com
June, 2010

MTV Video Music Awards (212) 258-8000 / (310) 752-8000
1515 Broadway FAX (212) 846-1804
New York, NY 10036 www.mtv.com
September, 2009

NABSHOW/ National Association of Broadcasters (202) 429-5300 / (800) 342-2460
1771 N St. NW FAX (202) 429-5493
Washington, DC 20036 www.nab.org/conventions/
April, 2010

NATPE Market & Conference (310) 453-4440
770 Broadway, Sixth Fl. FAX (310) 453-5258
Penthouse 10 www.natpe.org
Los Angeles, CA 90036
January 25-28, 2010

Nashville Film Festival (615) 742-2500
P.O. Box 24330 FAX (615) 742-1004
Nashville, TN 37202 www.nashvillefilmfestival.org
April, 2010

New Directors/New Films (212) 875-5367
The Film Society @ Lincoln Center www.filmlinc.com
70 Lincloln Center Plaza
New York, NY 10023
March, 2010

New York Festivals Int'l Film & Video Awards (212) 643-4800
260 W. 39th St., Tenth Fl. FAX (212) 643-0170
New York, NY 10018 www.newyorkfestivals.com
January, 2010

New York Festivals Int'l Advertising In All Media Awards (212) 643-4800
260 W. 39th St., Tenth Fl. FAX (212) 643-0170
New York, NY 10018 www.newyorkfestivals.com
May, 2010

New York Festivals Int'l Television Broadcasting Awards (212) 643-4800
260 W. 39th St., Tenth Fl. FAX (212) 643-0170
New York, NY 10018 www.newyorkfestivals.com
January, 2010

New York Film Festival (212) 875-5600
The Film Society of Lincoln Center www.filmlinc.com
70 Lincoln Center Plaza
New York, NY 10023
Sept. 26-Oct. 12, 2009

The One Show Festival (212) 979-1900
The One Club For Art & Copy FAX (212) 979-5006
21 E. 26th St., Fifth Fl. www.oneclub.com
New York, NY 10010
Check Web site for dates

Palm Springs Int'l Film Festival (760) 322-2930
1700 E. Tahquitz Canyon Way, Ste. 3 FAX (760) 322-4087
Palm Springs, CA 92262 www.psfilmfest.org
January, 2010

Producers Guild Awards (310) 358-9020
8530 Wilshire Blvd., Ste. 450 FAX (310) 358-9520
Beverly Hills, CA 90211 www.producersguild.org
January, 2010

Rhode Island Int'l Film Festival (401) 861-4445
P.O. Box 162   FAX (401) 490-6735
Newport, RI 02840   www.film-festival.org
August 4-9, 2009

Rocky Mountain VidExpo (303) 771-2000
8002 S. Oneida Court   www.vidxpo.com
Centennial, CO 80112
October 21-22, 2009

San Francisco Int'l Film Festival (415) 561-5020
39 Mesa St., Ste. 110   www.sffs.org/sfiff
The Presido
San Francisco, CA 94129
April, 2010

Santa Barbara Int'l Film Festival (805) 963-0023
1528 Chapala St., Ste. 203   FAX (805) 962-2524
Santa Barbara, CA 93101   www.sbfilmfestival.org
January, 2010

Santa Monica Film Festival (310) 264-4274
P.O. Box 5236   FAX (310) 264-4220
Santa Monica, CA 90409   www.smfilmfestival.com
Nov. 6-8, 2009

Seattle Int'l Film Festival (206) 464-5830
400 Ninth Ave. North   FAX (206) 264-7919
Seattle, WA 98109   www.siff.net
May, 2010

Shobiz Expo (212) 404-2345
440 Ninth Ave., 8th Fl.   FAX (212) 253-4123
New York, NY 10001   www.theshobizexpo.com
March, 2010

ShoWest (646) 654-7680
Bally's & Paris Las Vegas   FAX (646) 654-7694
770 Braodway, Fifth Fl.   www.showest.com
New York, NY 10003
March 15-18, 2010

Slamdance Int'l Film Festival (323) 466-1786
5634 Melrose Ave.   FAX (323) 466-1784
Los Angeles, CA 90038   www.slamdance.com
January, 2010

South By Southwest Music & Media Conference (512) 467-7979
SXSW Headquarters, Box 4999   FAX (512) 451-0754
Austin, TX 78765   www.sxsw.com
March, 2010

Sundance Film Festival (435) 658-3456
P.O. Box 684429   (310) 360-1981
Salt Lake City, UT 84068   FAX (801) 575-5175
January, 2010   www.sundance.org

Telluride Film Festival (501) 665-9494
800 Jones St.   FAX (501) 665-9589
Berkeley, CA 94710   www.telluridefilmfestival.org
Sept. 4-7, 2009

Toronto Int'l Film Festival (416) 967-7371
Two Carlton St.   (877) 968-3456
Toronto, ON M5B 1J3   www.tiffg.ca
September 10-19, 2009

Tribeca Film Festival (212) 941-2400
375 Greenwich St.   FAX (212) 941-3939
New York, NY 10013   www.tribecafilm.com/festival
April, 2010

UNAFF—United Nations Association Film Festival (650) 724-5544
P.O. Box 19369   www.unaff.org
Stanford, CA 94309
October 17-25, 2009

U.S. Int'l Film & Video Festival (310) 540-0959
713 S. Pacific Coast Hwy, Ste. A   FAX (310) 316-8905
Redondo Beach, CA 90277   www.filmfestawards.com
June, 2010

Visual Effects Society (VES) Awards (818) 981-7861
5535 Balboa Blvd., Ste. 205   FAX (818) 981-0179
Encino, CA 91316   www.vesawards.com
February, 2010

Woods Hole Film Festival (508) 495-3456
87B Water St.   FAX (508) 495-3456
Woods Hole, MA 02543   www.woodsholefilmfestival.org
July 25-August 1, 2009

WorldFest/ Houston Int'l Film & Video Fest. (713) 965-9955
9898 Bissonet, Ste., 650   FAX (713) 965-9960
Houston, TX 77036   www.worldfest.org
April, 2010

Advertiser Index

Covers & Tabs

Hula Post Production..................Inside Front Cover
New York Production Alliance (NYPA)....Inside Back Cover
New York Governor's Office for Film & TV.......Back Cover

ALSAM/Association of Location Scouts & Mgrs ... Crew Tab
Arenson Prop Center................Props & Wardrobe Tab
Camera Copters, Inc......Camera & Sound Equipment Tab
CECO International..................Sets & Stages Tab
Chelsea Piers................Company/Crew Index Tab
Digital Arts......................Post Production Tab
Directors Film Company....Ad Agencies & Prod. Co.'s Tab
Expressjet........................Advertiser Index Tab
Lauren Berger Collection....Location Services & Equip. Tab
Silvertrucks Lighting........Grip & Lighting Equipment Tab
Top of the Rock Weather Room........General Index Tab
Westprint.......................Production Support Tab
Zeitbyte..............................High Def Tab

Inserts

NYC Mayor's Office of Film, Theatre & Broadcasting.....XI
Brooklyn Workforce Innovations....................XVII

1887 Townhouse......................................190
4-D Creative Media....................................22
7NY..200
A Plus Recording & Transcribing......................247
A-Prompt...270
A.G.E. Services, Inc. - Mobile Air Conditioning......302
AA Executive Town Car & Limousine...................181
AAA Communications...................................163
Abel Cine Tech, Inc..................................251
Able Equipment Rental, Inc...........................308
ABS Payroll & Production Accounting Services.........243
Action Camera Cars, Inc..............................258
Action Footage/Warren Miller Entertainment............94
Aerialexposures.com, LLC.............................252
Aero Mock-Ups, Inc...................................373
Aggreko Event Services...............................315
Airpower Aviation Resources, Inc.....................255
All Access Staging & Productions.....................126
All Creatures Great & Small..........................213
All Mobile Video.........................79, 131, 281
All Star Animals.....................................210
All-Star Locations...................................184
All-Tame Animals.....................................210
ALSAM/Association of Location Scouts and Managers ..184
American Copy Machines...............................223
American Humane Association..........................212
American Residuals & Talent, Inc.....................244
American Sports Medical Equipment....................351
Amy Gossels Casting..................................216
Animal Actors, Inc...................................207
Animals for Advertising, Inc.........................212
Anthony Augliera Inc.................................319
Aqua Effects...205
The Art Department, LLC..............................115
Artificial Reality...................................113
Atlantic Cine Equipment........................256, 297
Auto Props......................................205, 358
Available Teleprompting..............................271
Baby Wranglers Casting, Inc..........................218
Barbizon...304
Barn Truck Rental....................................157
Beauty Props...349
Big Shot, Inc..195
Birds & Animals Unlimited East.......................209
Black Dog Jib Productions, Inc.......................300
Bluebird Express Courier, LLC........................151
Branching Out Productions, Inc.......................497
Bridge Furniture & Props.............................369
Bufalo Niagara Film Commission.......................171
Bulbtronics..305
BuyerZone..147
C&C Studios..134
Call-A-Head Corporation..............................199
Cars On Location.....................................359
Cassone Leasing, Inc.................................194
CDM Sound Studios.....................................42
CECO International..............................31, 313
Celebrity Helicopters................................254
Central Casting......................................219
Chapman/Leonard Studio Equipment, Inc................299
Chelrae Carting LLC..................................231

Cinematicstunts.com/John-Eric Schuman.............545
Cine Magic Stages..........................120, 264
Cinema-Vision.....................................260
City Knickerbocker, Inc...........................350
City Stage..........................117, 118-119
Clearance Domain LLC..............................233
Leslie Collins....................................383
Computer Rent.....................................371
Cooper Film Cars..................................357
Richard Coppola/Motion Control....................264
Corinne's Concepts In Catering....................160
Courier Car Rental................................157
Creative Film Cars................................355
David Dreishpoon's Gourmet........................159
Dawn Animal Agency, Inc...........................211
Dazian Fabrics....................................340
Debbie Regan Locations, Ltd.......................183
Deluxe New York....................................74
DG FastChannel....................................288
Directors' Catering...............................161
Donald Case Casting...............................217
Doubletime Productions.............................95
Drape Kings.......................................337
Dream Cuisine Fine Catering, LLC..................161
Drew Jiritano Special Effects.....................326
Drivers East......................................543
East Coast Digital, Inc............................60
East Coast Lighting, Inc..........................312
Eastern Effects, Inc..............................311
Eclectic-Encore Props, Inc........................368
eEmerge Production Suites..........................32
Empress Media, Inc................................266
Entertainment Services............................314
EPIC Security Corp................................203
Everything Events & Entertainment, LLC............542
Feature Systems/Kits and Expendables/Kitstrucks...295
Firestarter Rentals................................62
Flat Washer.......................................114
Flatotel..179
Foy Inventerprises, Inc...........................542
Frederick P. Rose Hall
  Home of Jazz at Lincoln Center..............91, 187
Gear + Rose Motion Control........................265
The Gemini Co., Inc...............................365
Geppetto Studios, Inc.............................323
Giordano FX.......................................364
Gizmo Special Effects.............................263
Don Glenn...415
Global ImageWorks, LLC.............................94
Globus Studios....................................120
Go Studios..129
Goblin Lighting Services, Inc.....................312
Gotham Scenic, LLC................................114
Graphics for Industry, Inc........................333
Greater Miami Convention & Visitors Bureau........169
GripAndElectric.com...............................316
GRS Systems, Inc..................................280
Guardian Entertainment, LTD........................27
GZ Entertainment & Stunts.........................544
H & B Super Express, Inc..........................155
Hall Associates Flying Effects....................545
Hamptons Locations................................149
Heidi's Fabulous Fatigue Fighters Worldwide.......234
Helinet Aviation Services.........................254
Brian Heller/Aerial Cinematography................256
Hello World....................86, 164, 275, 281
Hero Props..364
Historic Films.....................................93
Lee Hopp..554
Hover-Views Unlimited, Inc./Al Cerullo............253
HPC Productions...................................272
Hula Post Production...............................63
Hunter Ambulance,Inc..............................384
Ichabod Crane, Inc................................300
Infiniti Handling Systems.........................308
Innovative Artists................................381
Intaboro..181
Intelliprompt Inc.................................272
InterNation, Inc..................................248
J & M Effects.....................................326
Jacob K. Javits Convention Center.................189
Jerry Berg Computer Computer Prompting............272
Jewel Street Studios..............................127
Joseph C. Hansen Company, Inc.....................336
K.P. Pro Video, Inc...............................281
K2imaging, Inc....................................277
Ken Lazer Casting.................................216
Kevoo Catering....................................160
Kipperman Casting, Inc............................215

Konduit Inc.	114
LA Digital Post, Inc.	61
Lapietra Machinery & Equipment, Inc.	309
LeNoble Lumber Co., Inc.	329
Lentini Communications	163, 268
Liberty Helicopters	252
LIC Film Studios	125
Lightbox-NY LLC	188
Light Foot Grip & Lighting	315
Location Control, Inc./Coneheads	183
The Location Station/Mark McKennon	184
The Log Cabin Location	188
Lost Soul Picture Cars	358
Majestic Light	296
Manhattan Center Studios	132-133
Manhattan Penthouse	190
Manhattan Propane	372
Mansfield's Executive Transportation	181
Lionel A. Marks	553
Media Services/Showbiz Software	222, 241, 244
MediaMix	123
Metro Film Cars, Inc.	356
Metropolis Studios, Inc.	137
Midwood Ambulance & Oxygen Service, Inc.	384
Miller's Launch	237
Minerva Cleaners	338
Mobile Film & Video Productions	200
Modprop.com	370
Louis J. Morledge, MD	386
Motion Picture Studio Mechanics (IA Local 52)	547
Movie Time Cars, Inc.	358
Mr. John, Inc.	198
National Aerospace Training & Research Center/NASTAR	190
National Flag & Display Co., Inc.	342
NBC News Archives	95
Ncyclomedia, Inc.	278
Nevada Film Office	167
New York Jib	298
New York Ladder & Scaffold Corporation	303, 309
New York Speech Improvement Services	208
NewYork-Presbiterian Emergency Medical Services	385
Next Millenium Productions, Ltd.	85, 136
NPI Production Services, Inc.	242
NYC Mayor's Office	XI
Oliphant Studio	109
On Location Education	541
On Point Resources, Inc.	202
On Time Elite, Inc.	192
PAL Stage	122
PAL Television East	259
Park Avenue Post, Inc.	41, 279
PAWS & Co., LLC	263
PES Payroll	242
Picture Cars East, Inc.	356
Pink Hippo Production Motorhomes	195
Portable Storm	327
PrimaLux Video	21, 274
Ronald A. Primas, M.D., FACP, FACPM, CTH	387
Prince Lumber Co., Inc.	329
Production Central	122
Professional Sound Services, Inc.	269
Props for Today	371
Props NYC	368
Provost Displays	112, 361
QTV Prompting Services	270
Rennert Translation Group	248
Reuters Television International	135
RGH Lighting LLC	314
Riggin Design, Inc.	300
Sam Rohn	507
Royal Buses	192
Royal Production Services	349
Safety First Divers, Inc.	549
David A. (Austin) Salisbury Jr.	552
San Antonio Film Commission	168
Mark Sasahara	433
Scenic Corporation of N.Y.	115
Scott Powers Studios, Inc.	218
Shooting Stars Catering	162
Shooting Star Coaches, Inc.	193
Silvercup Studios	116
Adam Smelin	553
Star Struck Catering	159
Stark Naked Productions, Inc./Elsie Stark Casting	215
State Supply	370
Steeldeck N.Y. Inc.	126
Steiner Studios	121
Stiegelbauer Associates	111
Studio Instrument Rentals (S.I.R.)	353
Stunt Dept., Inc./Chris Barnes	545
Superior Location Van Service, Ltd.	194
Suzanne Couture Modelmaking	363
TDN Artists/The Directors Network	380
Teleprompting.com	271
That Cat Camera Support, LLC	298
Theatrical Stage Employees (IA Local 1)	546
Travel Auto Bag Co., Inc.	348
Tribeca Screening Room	92
truTV Studios	130
TV Prompt	270
United Scenic Artists (IA Local 829)	547
Ventura Insurance Brokerage, Inc.	230
Video Equipment Rentals	274
VIP Prompting Corporation	272
Visual Alchemy, LLC	277
Walton Hauling & Warehouse Corporation	319
Weapons Specialists, Ltd.	341
Wheels for Reels	358
York Scaffolding Equipment Corp.	303, 309
ZFX, Inc.	544
Andy Zuch	552

THE MOST WELL-RESPECTED QUALIFIED DIRECTORY OF ITS KIND!

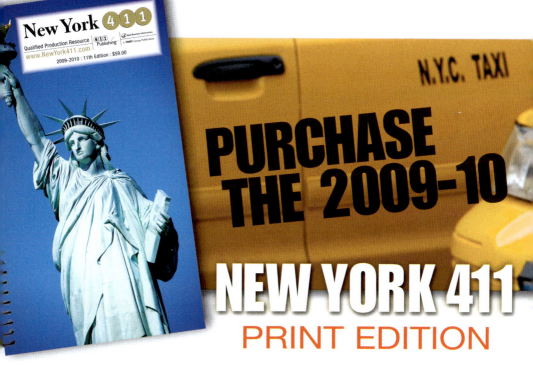

PURCHASE THE 2009-10 NEW YORK 411 PRINT EDITION

BROWSE FROM THOUSANDS OF
COMPANIES, PROFESSIONALS, SERVICES AND LOCATIONS
IN THE NEW YORK TRI-SATE AREA

TO PURCHASE VISIT:
www.NewYork411.com

OR CALL:
323/617-9400

New York 411

NOTES:

EXPERIENCE ROCKEFELLER CENTER® AT EVERY ANGLE.

For details and availability, please contact our Film and Photo Shoot Department at 212-588-8634 or visit rockefellercenter.com and fill out a film/photo request form.

TOP OF THE ROCK™
OBSERVATION DECK
at Rockefeller Center®

620 LOFT & GARDEN
AT ROCKEFELLER CENTER®

Sections & Categories

Ad Agencies & Production Companies
Advertising Agencies
Advertising Agency Freelance Producers
Animation Production Companies
Commercial Directors
Commercial Production Companies
Corporate & Video Production Cos.
Independent Directors' Reps
Infomercial Production Companies
Motion Picture Production Companies
Music Video Directors
Music Video Production Companies
Production Offices
Promo Production Companies
Public Relations
Storyboard Artists
Television Production Companies
Trailer Production Houses

Post Production
Audio Post Facilities
Commercial Editorial Houses
Composers & Sound Designers
Computer Graphics & Visual FX
Digital Intermediates
Duplication
DVD Authoring & Replication
Editing Equipment Rentals & Sales
Editors
Film & Tape Storage
Film Laboratories—Motion Picture
Film Laboratories—Still Photography
Mobile Video Units, Satellite & Transmission Services
Music Libraries & Publishing
Music Production & Sound Design
Opticals
Post Houses
Post Production Supervisors
Screening Rooms
Stock Footage & Photos
Titling, Captioning & Broadcast Design
Visual FX Artists
Visual FX Supervisors & Producers

Sets & Stages
Backings & Scenic Artists (Local 52 NY)
Backings & Scenic Artists (Local 829 NY)
Backings & Scenic Artists
Set Design, Construction & Rentals
Set Sketchers
Stages
Stages—Portable
Still Photography Studios & Lofts
TV Studios

Location Services & Equipment
Air Charters
Air Freight & Courier Services
Airlines
Airports
Bus Charters
Car Rentals
Cargo & Passenger Vans
Caterers
Communications Equipment
Consulates General
Crating and Packing
Customs Brokers & Carnets
Film Commissions—North America
Film Commissions—International
Hotels & Short-Term Housing
Limousine & Car Services
Location Libraries, Management & Scouts
Locations
Motorhomes & Portable Dressing Rooms
Moving, Storage & Transportation
Portable Restrooms
Production Services—North America
Production Services—International
Security & Bodyguards
Travel Agencies
Water Trucks
Weather

Production Support
Acting & Dialect Coaches
Animals & Trainers
Casting Directors
Casting Facilities
Choreographers
Computer Consultants & Software
Computers, Office Equip. & Supplies
Digital Casting & Video Conferencing
Directories & Trade Publications
Entertainment Attorneys
Extras Casting Agencies
Hand & Leg Models
Insurance Brokers & Guarantors
Janitorial & Strike Services
Large Scale Event Planning
Libraries, Research & Clearance
Massage Therapists
Messenger Services
Nautical Film Services & Coord.
Notaries
Payroll & Production Accountants (Local 161 NY)
Payroll & Production Accountants
Promotional Products
Talent & Modeling Agencies
Technical Advisors
Transcription & Secretarial Services
Translation & Interpretation Services
Wrap Party Locations

Camera & Sound Equipment
Aerial Equipment
Aerial—Fixed Wing & Helicopter Pilots
Camera Cars & Tracking Vehicles
Camera Rentals—Motion Picture
Camera Rentals—Still Photography
Motion Control
Raw Stock—Film & Video
Sound Equipment Rentals & Sales
Teleprompting & Cue Card Services
Video Assist Services
Video Cameras & Equipment
Video Display Playback & Projection

High Def
HD Cameras & Equipment
HD Duplication
HD Editing Equipment
HD Equipment Manufacturers
HD Post Houses
HD Screening Rooms
HD Stock Footage
HD Tape Stock

Grip & Lighting Equipment
Booms, Cranes & Camera Support
Climate Control Systems
Construction & Yard Equipment Rentals
Grip & Lighting Expendables
Grip Equipment
Hoisting & Lift Equipment/Cherry Pickers
Lighting Equipment & Generators
Production Equipment & Accessories
Trucks & Vans

Props & Wardrobe
Aerial Picture Vehicles
Animatronics, Puppets & Makeup FX
Architectural Elements
Art Fabrication, Licensing & Rentals
Arts & Crafts Supplies
Atmospheric/Lighting Special FX & Pyrotechnics
Boats & Nautical Props
Building/Surface Materials & Hardware
Canopies & Tents
Car Prep, Rigging & Prototypes
Color-Correct Props
Costume Makers & Rentals
Draperies & Window Treatments
Dry Cleaners
Eyewear & Jewelry
Fabrics
Firearms & Weapons
Flags, Graphics & Signage
Flowers, Greens & Plants
Foam
Furnishings—Antique & Vintage
Furnishings—Contemporary
Games, Toys & Amusements
Glass
Hair, Makeup & Wardrobe Supplies
Ice
Lamps & Lighting Fixtures
Medical & Scientific Props
Memorabilia & Collectibles
Metals & Foils
Musical Instrument Rentals
Neon
Photo, Video & Electronic Props
Picture Vehicles
Plastics, Plexiglas & Fiberglass
Product Placement
Prop Fabrication & Mechanical FX
Prop Houses
Restaurant & Kitchen Equipment
Specialty Props
Sporting Goods
Studio Services
Tailoring & Alterations
Uniforms & Surplus
Vintage Clothing & Accessories

Crew
Agents, Reps & Job Referral Services
Ambulance/Paramedics & Nurses (Local 52 NY)
Ambulance/Paramedics & Nurses
Art Directors/Production Designers (Local 829 NY)
Art Directors/Production Designers
Camera Assistants (Local 600 NY)
Camera Assistants
Camera Operators (Local 600 NY)
Camera Operators
Camera Operators—Aerial (Local 600 NY)
Camera Operators—Steadicam (Local 600 NY)
Camera Operators—Steadicam
Camera Operators—Underwater (Local 600 NY)
Carpenters/Shop Craft (Local 52 NY)
Craft Service (Local 52 NY)
Craft Service
Digital Imaging Techs. (Local 600 NY)
Digital Imaging Technicians
Directors of Photography (Local 600 NY)
Directors of Photography
First Assistant Directors (DGA NY)
First Assistant Directors
Food Stylists & Home Economists
Gaffers & Electricians (Local 52 NY)
Gaffers & Electricians
Grips (Local 52 NY)
Grips
Hair & Makeup Artists (Local 798 NY)
Hair & Makeup Artists
Lighting Directors
Producers
Production Coords. (Local 161 NY)
Production Coordinators
Production Managers
Production Stills Photographers (Local 600 NY)
Production Stills Photographers
Props Department (Local 52 NY)
Props Department
Script Supervisors (Local 161 NY)
Script Supervisors
Second Assistant Directors (DGA NY)
Second Assistant Directors
Set Decorators
Sound Mixers (Local 52 NY)
Sound Mixers
Stage Managers (DGA NY)
Studio Teachers/Welfare Workers
Stunt Coords. & Performance Drivers
Trade Associations/Unions
Training Centers
Underwater Technicians
Unit Production Managers (DGA NY)
VTR Operators (Local 52 NY)
VTR Operators
Wardrobe Stylists/Costume Designers (Local 829 NY)
Wardrobe Stylists/Costume Designers
Wardrobe Supervisors (Local 764 NY)

General Index

16mm Camera Equipment	259
16mm Color Processing	76
16mm Editing Equipment	60
16mm Laboratories	74
16mm Projection Equipment	91
24P HD	280
24P Video Cameras	274
2-Track Mixing	42
2D/3D Animation	5, 53
2D/3D Computer Graphics	53
35mm Camera Equipment	259
35mm Color Processing	76
35mm Editing Equipment	60
35mm Laboratories	74
35mm Projection Equipment	91
4-Wheel Drive Vehicle Rentals	355
4K Cameras	280
5.1 – 7.1 Surround Sound Mixing	42
65mm Camera Equipment	259
70mm Projection Equipment	91
8mm Camera Equipment	259
8mm Laboratories	74

A

Accent Advisors	246
Accent Training	208, 548
Accessories, Camera	259, 296, 318
Accessories, Furniture Rentals	346, 368
Accessories, Production Equipment	318
Accounting Software	222
Accounting, Production	222, 239, 241
Acoustic Coupler Systems	163
Acrylics	361
Acting Coaches	208
Action Props	363
Action Sports Footage	93, 292
Actor Climate Systems	334
Actors & Actresses	215, 246
Actualizing Software	222
Adhesives	304, 325, 348
ADR	42
Advertising Agencies	2
Advertising Agency Freelance Producers	4
Advertising in New York 411, How to	IV
Advisors, Technical	246
Aerial—Fixed Wing & Helicopter Pilots	257
Aerial Camera Mounts	252
Aerial Equipment	252
Aerial Equipment, Camera	252, 259
Aerial Operators	408, 413, 414
Aerial Photography	252, 257
Aerial Picture Vehicles	322
Aerial Production Coordination	252, 257, 542
Aerial Stunt Coordinators	257, 542
African Art	373
African Artifacts, Props	368
Agencies, Travel	204
Agency Producers	4
Agents	380
AICP Computer Software	222
Air Charters	150, 204
Air Cleaners	302
Air Conditioning Units	302
Air Freight & Couriers	151
Air Terminals	151, 154
Airbrushing	76, 106, 107, 109
Airbrushing, Makeup	477, 488
Aircraft	252, 322
Airlines	153
Airplane Mock-Ups	111, 373
Airplanes	150, 252, 322
Airplanes, Radio-Controlled	363, 373
Airports	154
Airstrips	154
Alligators	209
Alterations	334, 377
Aluminum & Steel Furniture	346
Aluminum	352
Ambulance Standby	383, 384
Ambulances, Picture Vehicles	355
American History Research	233
American Indian Props	368
Americana Footage	93, 292
Americana	368
Amphibians	209
Anamorphic Lenses	259
Anamorphic Projection	91
Anchors	328
Animal Bones	373
Animal Skins	373
Animal Walkaround Costumes	334
Animals	209
Animals, Artificial/Mounted	373
Animated Logos	102
Animated Props	363
Animatics	5, 53
Animation	5, 53
Animation Production Companies	5
Animatronics	323
Answering Machines	223
Antique Automobiles	355
Antique Bathroom Fixtures	329
Antique Clothing	334, 378
Antique Crystal	368
Antique Eyeglasses	339, 378
Antique Firearms and Weapons	341
Antique Furniture	345, 368
Antique Hardware	329, 368
Antique Jewelry	339, 378
Antique Prop Houses	345, 368
Antique Rugs	345, 368
Apollo Trailers	258
Apparel, Promotional	245
Appliance Rentals	368
Aquariums	373
Arboretums	187
Archaeological Research	233
Arches, Floral	344
Architectural Details, Antiques & Props	329
Architectural Elements	324
Architectural Models, Prop Fabrication	363
Architecture Books	233
Archival Stock Footage	93, 292
Armor	378
Arms, Camera	296
Army and Navy Surplus	378
Army Vehicles	355
Art Deco Furniture	345, 368
Art Deco Jewelry	339, 378
Art Deco Props	345, 368
Art Directors	380, 388, 391
Art Fabrication	106, 107, 109, 324
Art Furniture	345, 346, 368
Art Licensing and Rentals	324
Art Rentals	368
Art Supplies	325
Articulated Mannequins	323, 363
Artificial Animals	363, 373
Artificial Florals	344, 368
Artificial Food	363, 368, 373
Artists, Storyboards	35, 380
Assemble Editing	47, 85
Associations, Trade	546
Athletic Apparel & Equipment	375
Atmosphere Crowds	229
Atmospheric FX	326
Attorneys, Entertainment	228
Attorneys, Immigration	228
Attractions	249
ATV Camera Cars	258
ATV Camera Mounts	296, 332
ATVs	258, 355
Audio Equipment Rentals	268
Audio Laybacks	42

Audio Post Facilities 42
Audio Services—Film & Video. 42
Audio Sweetening 42
Audio Transfers 42
Audiovisual Equipment 223, 274, 280
Audition Facilities. 221
Autographs 352
Automobiles, Antique to Present 355
Automotive Display Stands 332
Automotive Lighting. 332
Automotive Paint 332
Automotive Prep and Rigging 332
Average Rainfall, Snowfall & Temperatures XXXIII
Aviation History and Research 233
Avid Editing 47, 64
Avids, Rentals & Sales 60, 284
Awards, Expos & Festivals XXXVIII

B

Baby Booms 296, 308
Baby Buggies 368
Baby Casting 215
Baby Wranglers. 380, 383, 384, 541
Backdrops. 106, 107, 109
Backdrops, Custom 106, 107, 109
Backdrops, Rental 106, 107, 109
Background Casting 229
Backings & Scenic Artists 106, 107, 109
Badges 378
Bagpipes 353
Bags, Makeup 348
Bags, Production 318
Bakery Equipment 372
Balloons 232
Balloons, Hot Air 252
Ballroom Dancing Technical Advisors 246
Ballrooms 249
Banners 342
Bar Equipment and Props 368, 372
Barber Shop Equipment & Props 368, 373
Barnyard Animals 209
Barricades 183, 318
Barstools 368, 372
BASE Jumping 246, 542
Base Stations 163
Baskets 368
Baskets, Camera 296
Baskets, Hoisting 308
Bathroom Fixtures 329, 368
Batteries, Camera 262
Beads 325
Bears 209
Beauty Shop Equipment 368, 373
Beauty Supplies 348
Beepers 163
Beer Taps 372
Bees 209
Beta Editing 60, 85
Betacam Video Camera Systems 274
Bicycles 375
Bidders 4
Bidding Software 222
Bikes, Camera 258
Billiard Tables and Props 368, 375
Birds 209
Black and White Processing, Stills 76
Black and White Reversals, Film 74
Blackboards 373
Blacklights 311, 326
Bleachers 126
Blinds 336
Block Ice 350
Blue/Green Screen Facilities 53, 117
Blue/Green Screen Lighting 53, 311
Boats 328
Body Language Technical Advisors 246
Body Painting 477, 488
Body Parts Models 229
Bodyguards 202
Bonding 230
Book Search Service 233
Bookkeepers, Production 239, 241
Boomlifts 308
Booms, Camera 296
Booms, Hoisting 308
Booms, Microphones 268, 296
Boots, Cowboy 334, 378
Bowling Supplies 375
Boxes 73, 166
Boxing Rings and Equipment 375
Brass 352
Breakaway Barricades 183, 318
Breakaway Glass 347
Breakaway Props 347, 363
Breakfast Caterers 159
Bric-a-brac 368
Brick 329
British Taxis 355
Broadcast Design 53, 102
Broadcast Video Equipment 274, 280
Broadcast Video Facilities & Systems 78, 117, 274
Bubble Jet Printers 223
Budgeting Software 222
Bugs, Living 209
Bugs, Artificial & Preserved 373
Building Supplies 329
Bulk Ice 350
Bullhorns 318
Bungee Jumping 542
Bus Charters 155, 157
Bus Signs 342
Buses, Picture Vehicles 355
Butterflies, Living 209
Butterflies, Artificial & Preserved 373
Buttons 340

C

Cable ID Packages 53
Cable-Suspended Camera Mounts 296
Cabs 355
Cakes, Artificial 363, 368, 373
Call Sheet Software 222
Calligraphy 342
Camels 209
Camera Accessories 259, 296, 318
Camera Assistants 380, 398, 407
Camera Baskets 296
Camera Boats 328
Camera Cars 258
Camera Carts 318
Camera Cases 318
Camera Cranes 296
Camera Equipment 259, 274
Camera Expendables 304
Camera Housings, Underwater 259
Camera Mounts 252, 259, 296
Camera Operators 380, 408, 413, 414, 415, 416, 417
Camera Rentals, Motion Picture 259
Camera Rentals, Still Photography 262
Camera Rentals, Video 274
Camera Stores 259, 262
Camera Support 296
Camera Systems, Aerial 252
Camera Systems, Gyro-Stabilized 252
Camera Systems, Motion Control 263
Camera Systems, Remote 259, 296
Camera Trucks and Vans 319
Cameras, Props 354
Cameras, Stunt 259
Cameras, Underwater 259
Camping Equipment 375
Canadian Film Commissions 167
Candelabras 368
Candles 368, 373
Canines 209
Cannons 341

Canoes	328
Canopies	232, 318, 331
Canvas Backings	106, 107, 109
Canvas Manufacturing, Promotional	245
Canvas	336, 340
Caps, Baseball	245, 375
Captions	53, 85, 288
Car Mounts	259, 296, 332
Car Prep, Rigging & Prototypes	332, 355
Car Rentals	156, 355
Car Services	181, 355
Cargo Buckles	196
Cargo Containers	151
Cargo Services	151, 166
Cargo Vans	157
Carnets	166
Carnival and Circus Posters	342
Carnival Equipment	232
Carpenters/Shop Craft (Local 52 NY)	418
Carpeting	329
Carriages	355
Cars, Picture	355
Carts	232, 303
Cases, Camera	318
Cash Registers	368, 372
Casino Equipment	347
Caskets	368
Casting Directors	215
Casting Facilities	221
Casting, Celebrities	215
Casting, Extras	229
Casting, Foreign Language	215
Casting, Non-Union	215
Casting, Real People	229
Castings, Molds	363
Caterers, Production	159
Caterers, Special Events	232
Cathode Lighting	354
Cats	209
Cattle	209
Cel Animation	5
Celebrity Brokering	215
Celebrity Photos	93, 233, 292, 352
Cellular Fax Machines	163
Cellular Modem Interfaces	163, 223
Cellular Phones	163
Ceramic Tile	329
Ceramics	363
Ceremonial Props	373
CGI Animation	53
Chain Hoists	308
Chain Link	329
Chair Risers	126
Chairs	232
Chairs, Antique & Vintage	345
Chairs, Contemporary	346
Chalkboards	368, 373
Chandeliers	350
Character Animation	5
Character Design	5, 53
Charities	XXXI
Charter Buses	155, 157
Chase Cars	258
Chemical Agents	329
Cherry Pickers	303, 308
Chess Sets	347
Child Actors and Models	246
Child-Sized Hands	229
Children's Employment Guidelines	XXX
Chilled Air	302
Chimps	209
China, Props	368, 372
Choir Risers	126
Choreographers	221
Christmas Decorations	232
Christmas Florals & Greens	344
Chrome	352
Church Goods	373
Cibachrome	76
Cinematographers	380, 426, 433
Cinematography Equipment, Aerial	252
Circus & Variety Acts	246
Classroom Equipment	368
Clay Animation	5
Clear Ice Blocks & Cubes	350
Clearance	233
Cliff Rigging	363
Climate Control Systems	302
Climate Information	XXXIII
Clocks	368
Clocks, Antique and Vintage	345
Clocks, Contemporary	346
Closed Captioning	85, 288
Clothing Rentals	334, 376, 378
Coating & Laminating	329
Coffee Services	159, 223, 423, 424
Collectibles	352, 368
Color-Correct Props	333
Color Correction, Tape to Tape	85, 288
Color Film Processing, Stills	76
Color Matching, Paint	329
Colorist, Hair	477, 488
Colorization, Digital	53, 85, 288
Comedy Consultants	246
Commercial Directors	7, 15, 380
Commercial Editors	47, 64
Commercial Production Companies	15
Commercials	15, 102
Communications Equipment	163
Completion Bonds	230
Composers	51, 82
Composite Photography Backings	106, 107, 109
Compositing, Digital	53
Compositing, Optical	84
Computer Animation	5, 53
Computer Consultants	222
Computer Display Terminals	223
Computer Equipment Rentals	223
Computer Graphics & Visual FX	53
Computer Playback	277
Computer Projectors	223
Computer Props	354, 368
Computer Rentals	223
Computer Software	222
Cones, Traffic	183, 318
Confetti FX & Cannons	326
Confetti	232
Connecticut, Filming In	XXVI
Connecticut, Where to Shoot	XXVII
Construction & Yard Equipment Rentals	303
Construction Coordinators	418
Construction Supplies	329
Construction, Set	111
Consulates General	165
Contact Lenses	339
Contemporary Furniture	346, 368
Continuing Education	548
Continuity	525, 526
Contracts Software	222
Control Cables	363
Conversions, International Standards	56, 85, 288
Convertibles, Picture Vehicles	355
Cooking Supplies	372
Coordinators, Production	380, 501, 503
Coordinators, Stunt	380, 542
Copiers	223
Copper	352
Copyright Licensing	233
Copyright Research	233
Corporate Video Production Companies	21
Cosmetics	348
Costume Designers	380, 555, 558
Costume Jewelry	339, 378
Costume Rentals	334
Costume Management Software	222
Couriers, Air	151
Couriers, In-City	235
Cowboy Boots, Vintage – Present	334, 378

General Index

Crackle Tubes 354
Craft Service 423, 424
Craft Supplies 325
Cranes, Camera 296
Cranes, Hoisting 296, 308
Cranes, Truck 296, 308
Crash Housings 259
Crates 196
Crating 166
Creature FX 323
Crew Cabs 319
Crew Jackets 245
Crew Payroll 239, 241
Crew Referrals 380
Crew Training 548
Crew Union Rules 567
Criminology Advisors 246
Crocodiles 209
Crowd Control Barricades 318
Crowds, Atmosphere 229
Crushed Ice 350
Crystal Sync Cameras 259
Crystal, Antique to Present 368
Cubed Ice 350
Cue Cards 270
Cultured Marble 329
Curios 368
Curtains 336, 340
Curtains, Fiber Optic 336
Custom Backings 106, 107, 109
Custom Fabrication, Props 363
Custom Artwork 324
Customs Brokers & Carnets 166
Cut-Aways 355
Cycloramas 106, 107, 109

D

D-5 HD 280
Daggers 341
Dailies, Print 74
Dance Instruction 221
Dance Sport Advisors 246
Dance, Talent Agencies 246
Dancewear 334
DAT Recorders and Supplies 268
Database Consultants 222
Datasets 53
Deadlines, Listings in New York 411 . . . . V, VI
Decorating Materials 232, 329
Decorators, Set 380, 532
Dedo Lighting 311
Dental Props 351
Department Stores, Studio Services 376
Design, Logo 53, 342
Designer Fabrics 340
Designer Furniture, Contemporary 346
Desktop Publishing 342
Detailing, Auto 332
Detective Cars 355
Developing, Still Film 76
DGA First Assistant Directors 447
DGA Rules 590
DGA Second Assistant Directors 527
DGA Work Rules 590
Diagnostic Medical Equipment 351
Dialect Coaches 208, 548
Digital Casting 225
Digital Compositing 53, 85, 288
Digital Film Mixing Theater 42
Digital Film Processing 74
Digital FX 53
Digital FX Supervisors 104
Digital Imaging Technicians 425
Digital Ink 5, 53
Digital Intermediates 56
Digital Media Training 548
Digital Media Transfers 85
Digital Mural Prints 76

Digital Online Editing 47, 64, 85, 288
Digital Optical Compositing 53, 85, 288
Digital Sound Editing 42
Digital Tape Transfers 85, 288
Digital Telecine 53, 85, 288
Digital Versatile Disc Authoring & Replication 58
Digital Video Camera Systems 274
Digitally Fabricated Props and Sculpture 363
Dimensional Lettering 342
Diner Equipment 368, 372
Dinettes 368
Dinnerware 368, 372
Directories 226
Directors Chairs 318
Directors of Photography 380, 426, 433
Directors, Commercial 7, 15, 380
Directors, Music Video 28, 30, 380
Dirt Bikes 375
Disabled Persons Lifts and Ramps 126, 318
Display Clocks 375
Display Fixtures 368
DITs 380, 425
Ditty Belts 318
Diving Advisors 246
Dog Costumes 334
Dogs 209
Dolby Stereo 42, 91, 291
Dolby Surround 42
Dollies, Camera 258, 296
Dolls & Dollhouses 347, 368
Dolly Tracks 258, 296
Domestic Animals 209
Double-Decker Buses 355
Draft Animals 209
Draft Beer Equipment 372
Draperies, Custom & Rental 336
Drapery Dyeing 336, 340
Dress Forms 368, 377
Dressing Rooms, Portable 192
Drivers, Performance 542
Drum Scanning 76
Drums 353
Dry Cleaners 338
Dry Ice 350
DTS Digital Sound 42, 91, 291
Dubbing, Sound 42
Dubbing, Video 56
Duct Tape 304
Duplication, Still Photography 76
Duplication, Video 56, 283
DVD Authoring 58
DVD Replication 58
Dye Sublimation 245
Dyeing 245, 340
Dynamometer Equipment 332

E

Earth Design 111
Eclectic Furniture 368
Edge Coding 74, 85, 288
Edge Numbering 74, 85
Edged Weapons 341
Editing Equipment Rentals & Sales 60, 284
Editing Facilities, Offline & Online 47, 60, 85, 288
Editing Supplies 60, 284
Editing, Film 47, 60, 64
Editing, HD 47, 60, 64, 284, 288
Editing, Sound 42
Editors, Freelance 64, 380
Educational Resources 548
Electrical Equipment & Supplies 303, 304
Electricians 380, 453, 464
Electronic Film Conforming 85, 288
Electronic Props 354, 363, 368
Elephants 209
Embossing 245
Embroidery 245, 334
Emergency Medical Services 383, 384

Employment Agencies . . . 247
Engraving . . . 245
Entertainment Attorneys . . . 228
Ephemera . . . 352
Epoxy . . . 329, 361
Errors & Omissions . . . 233
Espresso Bars and Carts, Mobile . . . 159
Establishing Shots, Stock Footage . . . 93, 292
Estates . . . 187
Etched Glass . . . 347
Ethnic Jewelry . . . 339
Ethnic Props . . . 373
Evening Wear . . . 334, 376, 378
Event Planning . . . 232
Event Staffing . . . 232
Exabyte Transfers . . . 53
Exhibit Props . . . 368
Exotic Animals . . . 209
Exotic Automobiles . . . 355
Expendables, Grip & Lighting . . . 304
Explosives . . . 326
Expos, Awards & Festivals . . . XXXVIII
Extras Casting Agencies . . . 229
Eyewear . . . 339

F

Fabric Design, Treating & Dyeing . . . 340
Fabrics . . . 340
Facilities, Post Production . . . 85, 288
Fake Food . . . 363, 368, 373, 452
Fans . . . 302
Farm Animals . . . 209
Farm Vehicles . . . 355
Fashion Jewelry . . . 339
Fast Photo Labs . . . 76
Faux Finishes . . . 106, 107, 109
Faux Trees . . . 344
Fax Machines . . . 163, 223
Feathers . . . 340
Feature Film Production Companies . . . 27
Feature Film Titles . . . 102
Ferrellels . . . 126
Festivals/Festival Dates . . . XXXVIII
Festoon Lighting . . . 232
Fiber Optic Curtains . . . 336
Fiber Optic FX & Lighting . . . 311, 326
Fiber Optic Network . . . 78, 163
Fiberboard Forms . . . 329
Fiberglass . . . 329, 361
File Management . . . 222
Film & Tape Storage . . . 73
Film and Video Resolution, Output . . . 53, 85, 288
Film Archives . . . 93, 233, 292
Film Commissions—International . . . 176
Film Commissions—North American . . . 167
Film Conforming . . . 85, 288
Film, Developing . . . 74, 76
Film Directories . . . 226
Film Edge Coding . . . 74, 85
Film Editing and Equipment . . . 47, 60, 85, 288
Film Editors . . . 47, 64
Film Laboratories—Motion Picture . . . 74
Film Laboratories—Still Photography . . . 76
Film Liaisons, International . . . 165, 201
Film Mixing Theater . . . 42
Film Offices . . . 167
Film Output . . . 53, 74, 76
Film Permit, New York City, Sample . . . XVI
Film Permits . . . 167
Film Preservation . . . 73, 74
Film Processing, Motion Picture . . . 74
Film Processing, Stills . . . 76
Film Production Equipment . . . 318
Film Production Research . . . 233
Film Production Software . . . 222
Film Projectors & Projection . . . 60, 91
Film, Raw Stock . . . 266
Film Recording . . . 53, 74, 85
Film Reels . . . 60
Film Scanning . . . 53, 85, 288
Film Services, Nautical . . . 236
Film, Still Photography . . . 76, 262
Film Trailers . . . 40, 93, 102, 292
Film Transfers . . . 85, 288
Film/Video Synchronizing Control . . . 277
Filming in Connecticut . . . XXVI
Filming in New Jersey . . . XXI
Filming in New York City . . . XIV
Filming in New York State . . . IX
Filming in Philadelphia . . . XXVIII
Filming Locations . . . 187
Filmmaking Workshops . . . 548
Filters, Photographic . . . 259, 262
Fine Art Papers . . . 325
Fine Art Rentals . . . 324
Fire Trucks . . . 205, 355
Firearms Advisors . . . 246
Firearms . . . 341
Fireplace Mantels . . . 329
Fireworks . . . 326
First Aid, Crew . . . 383, 384
First Assistant Cameramen . . . 398, 407
First Assistant Directors . . . 380, 447, 450
Fish, Living . . . 209
Fitness Equipment . . . 375
Fixed Wing Aircraft . . . 252
Fixed Wing Pilots . . . 257
Fixtures, Bathroom & Plumbing . . . 329, 368
Flags & Banners . . . 342
Flame Artists . . . 104
Flameproofing, Fabric . . . 340
Flares . . . 318
Flats, Sets & Stages . . . 111, 117, 126
Flatscreens . . . 277
Flight Gear . . . 252
Flooring . . . 329
Flowers, Artificial . . . 344
Fluorescent Lighting . . . 311
Fluorescent Materials . . . 340
Flutes . . . 353
Flyfishing Equipment . . . 375
Flying Camera Platforms . . . 252, 296
Flying FX . . . 363
Foam . . . 53, 345
Foam Sculpting and Props . . . 53, 345, 363
Fog FX/Machines . . . 326
Foil Paper . . . 352
Foils . . . 352
Foley . . . 42
Folk Art . . . 373
Food Stylists . . . 380, 452
Food, Artificial . . . 373, 452
Food, Edible . . . 159, 423, 424
Footage Clearance . . . 93, 233, 292
Footage, Stock . . . 93, 292
Footwear . . . 334, 375, 376
Footwear, Military . . . 378
Footwear, Vintage . . . 378
Forecasts, Weather . . . 206
Foreign Language Translators . . . 248
Forklifts . . . 303, 308
Formal Wear . . . 334, 376, 378
Format Conversions, Video . . . 56, 85, 288
Formica . . . 329
Forms, Production . . . 222
Fountains & Statues . . . 363
Frames, Eyeglasses . . . 339
Freight, Air . . . 151
Frogs . . . 209
Front Screen Projection . . . 53, 277
Furniture Rentals—Contemporary . . . 346
Furniture Rentals, Antique and Vintage . . . 345
Furniture, Breakaway . . . 363
Furniture, Fabrication . . . 363
Furs . . . 334, 340, 378
Futuristic Picture Vehicles . . . 355
Futuristic Prop Makers . . . 363

General Index

Futuristic Prop Rentals 368, 373
FX Animation 53
FX Artists 53, 104
FX Props 363
FX, Music & Sound 42
FX, Optical 84

G

Gaffers 380, 453, 464
Gaffers Tape 304
Games 347
Garment Racks 348
Gaslamps 350
Gauze 340
Gauze Backings 106, 107, 109
Gels 304
Gels, Hair 348
Generators 303, 311
Generic Labels and Packages 333, 342
Gilding 106, 107, 109
Glass 347
Glass Painting 106, 107, 109
Glass Tinting, Automotive 332
Gloves 334, 378
Gold Leafing 106, 107, 109
Golf Carts 258, 296
Gourmet Cooking Supplies 372
Granite 329
Graphic Design 245, 342
Graphic Props & Displays 342
Graphics, Color Corrected 333
Graphics, High Definition 47, 53, 85, 288
Graphics, Signage 342
Green/Blue Screen Facilities 53, 117
Green/Blue Screen Lighting 53, 311
Greensmen 344
Grip Equipment 306
Grip Expendables 304
Grips 380, 465, 476
Grizzly Bears 209
Groomers 477, 488
Guarantors 230
Guards, Security 202
Guides, Production 226
Guilds & Unions 546
Guitars 353
Guns 341, 368
Gymnastic Equipment 375
Gyroplane Pilot 257
Gyro-Stabilized Camera Mounts and Systems 252, 259

H

Hair and Fur Fabrics 340
Hair Stylists 380, 477, 488
Hair, Makeup & Wardrobe Supplies 348
Hairpieces 348
Halloween Costumes 334
Hand & Leg Models 229
Hand Embroidery 334
Hand Props 368
Handbags 334, 376, 378
Hand-Held Cameras & Cameramen 259, 426, 433
Hand-Woven Textiles 340
Hang Gliders 252
Hang Gliding Stunt Coordinators 542
Hangars 154
Hard Drive Rentals, Computer 223
Hard Drive Rentals, Non-Linear Editing 60, 284
Hardware, Paint & Lumber 329
Hardware, Vintage 368
Harley-Davidsons 355
Harps 353
Hats 334, 376, 378
Haute Couture 334, 376, 377
HD Camera Operators 408, 413, 414, 415, 416, 417
HD Cameras 280
HD Digital Imaging Technicians 425

HD Directors of Photography 380, 426, 433
HD Duplication 283
HD Equipment Manufacturers 285
HD Equipment Rentals 280
HD Projectors & Projection 60, 91, 280, 291
HD Screening Rooms 91, 291
HD Tape Stock 294
HDTV 85, 288
HDTV Camcorders 280
Heads 296
Hearses 355
Heaters 302, 318
Helicopter Camera Mounts 252, 296
Helicopter Camera Systems 252, 259
Helicopter Mock-Ups 111, 373
Helicopter Pilots 257
Helicopters 252, 322
Heliports 154
Helium Balloons 232
Helium Tank Rentals 232, 318
Helmet Cameras, POV 252
Henry Artists 104
Hero Props, Color Correction 333
Heroes, Ceramic 363
Hi-8 Video 274
High Def Camera Operators . . . 408, 413, 414, 415, 416, 417
High Def Cameras 259, 280
High Def Digital Imaging Technicians 425
High Def Directors of Photography 380, 426, 433
High Def Duplication 283
High Def Equipment Manufacturers 285
High Def Equipment Rentals 280
High Def Projectors & Projection 60, 91, 280, 291
High Def Screening Rooms 91, 291
High Performance Picture Vehicles 355
High Speed Camera Cars 258
Highway Safety Equipment 183, 318, 342
Hi-Speed Photography 53, 93, 292
Historical Re-enactments 246
HMI Lighting 311
Hoisting Equipment 308
Hold Harmless Agreements 228, 230
Hollowware 368
Home Economists 380, 452
Home Electronics, Props 354
Home Furnishings and Accessories, Antique & Vintage . . 345
Home Furnishings and Accessories, Contemporary 346
Homes, Private 187
Homicide Advisors 246
Honeywagons 192
Horse-Drawn Carriages 209
Horses 209
Hospital Props 351, 368
Hot Air Balloons 150, 252
Hot Heads 296
Hot Rods 355
Hotels 177
Hotels, Extended Stay 177
Housewares 368, 372
Housing, Short-Term 177
Hovercrafts 328
How to Advertise in New York 411 IV
How to Get Listed in New York 411 . . . . V, VI
How to Order New York 411 VIII
How to Update Your Listing in New York 411 IV
How to Use New York 411 III
Humidity-Controlled Security Vaults 73
HumVees, Picture Vehicles 355
Hydraulic Cranes 296, 308
Hydraulic Props 363

I

IATSE Guidelines, Commercial Contracts 571
IATSE Locals 546
IBM Computer Rentals 223
IBM Consultants and Software 223
Ice 350
Ice Carving and Sculpture 350

General Index

Ice Chests	232
Ice Skating Surfaces, Portable	350
Image Compositing	47, 53, 85, 288
Image Processing	53, 85, 288
Imaging Supplies	259, 262
Immigration Attorneys	228
Independent Directors Reps	26
Independent Sales Rep Software	222
Industrial Production Companies	21
Industrial Signs	342
Infomercial Production Companies	26
Ink Jet Printers	223
Insects, Living	209
Insects, Artificial & Preserved	373
Insert Stages	117, 138
Insurance Brokers	230
Intercom Systems	163
Interior Design, Contemporary	346
Interior Plants	344
International Film Liaisons	165, 201
International Production Services	201
Internet Directories	226
Interpreters	248
Invisible Wire Rigging	363

J

Janitorial & Strike Services	231
Jeeps, Picture Vehicles	355
Jet Fighter Mock-Ups	111, 373
Jewelry	339
Jewelry, Vintage	378
Jewish Items	373
Jewish Religious Garments	334
Jib Arms	296
Jimmy Jibs	296
Jingles	80, 82
Job Referral Services	380
Journals, Trade	226
Jukeboxes	368

K

Kangaroos	209
Kayaks & Equipment	328, 375
Kem Bays	60, 85
Key Grips	465, 476
Kinescope Transfers	85, 288
Kitchen Equipment	223, 368, 372
Kitchen Facilities, Mobile	159
Kitchen Fixtures & Prop Dressing	368, 372
Kitchen Stages, Prep	117, 138
Kites	375
Knitting Supplies	340
Knitting	334

L

Label Printing	245, 342
Laboratories, Motion Picture	74
Laboratories, Still Photos	76
Laboratory Props	351
Laminates	329
Laminating	342
Lamps	350, 368
Lampshades	350
Land Lines, Temporary	163
Land Models	363
Land Yachts	192, 355
Landscape Materials	329, 344
Laptop Computers	223
Laser Animation FX	53
Laser Cutting	363
Laser FX	326
Laser Printers	223
Latex Balloons	232
Latex Props	363
Laundry Services	338
Law Enforcement Officers	202
Law Offices	228
Lawyers, Immigration	228
Laybacks	42
Layout Boards, Grip	304
Learning Centers	548
Leather Dry Cleaners	338
Leather Fabrication, Props	363
Leather	340
Leatherworking	334
LCD Screens	277
LED Screens	277
Leg Models	229
Legal Advice	228
Legal Research	233
Lenses, Motion Picture	259
Letterpress Printing	342
Levitation FX	363
Liability Insurance	230
Liaisons, International	165, 201
Libraries, Music	42, 80
Libraries, Public	233
Libraries, Research	233
Libraries, Sound FX	42, 80
License Plates, Vintage & Contemporary	373
Licensing, Copyright	233
Lifeguards	383, 384
Lift Equipment	308
Light Towers	311
Lighting Balloons	311
Lighting Crane Trucks	311
Lighting Directors	380, 496
Lighting Equipment & Generators	311
Lighting Expendables	304
Lighting Fixtures	350
Lighting FX, Atmospheric	326
Lighting, Automotive	332
Lighting, Festoon	232, 318
Lighting, Fiber Optic	311, 326
Lighting, Fluorescent	311, 326
Lighting, Strobe	311, 326
Lightning FX	326
Lights, Underwater	311
Limousines	181, 355
Line Producers	380, 497
Linear Editing, Offline & Online	47, 60, 85, 284
Linens	340
Lingerie	334, 376, 378
Linoleum	329
Lipstick Cameras	274
Listing Updates, New York 411	IV
Live Action Integration	53
Live Action Motion Control	263
Livestock	209
Local 600 E. Commercial Work Rules	567
Location Libraries	183
Location Management	183
Location Police	202
Location Scouts	183, 380
Location Security	202
Locations, Shooting	187
Locations, Wrap Party	249
Lofts	127
Logo Design	53, 342
Logos	102
Long Form Commercials, Production	26
Long-Range Forecasts	206
Low Riders	355
Lucite	361
Lumber	329

M

Machinery Props	368
Macintosh Consultants & Software	222
Macintosh Rentals	223
Magazine Search Service	233
Magazines, Period	352
Magazines, Trade	226
Magic Props	347, 368

General Index

Magical Illusions	363
Makeup Artists	380, 477, 488
Makeup Bags	348
Makeup Tables	348
Makeup, Prosthetics	380, 477, 488
Makeup, Special FX	348, 477, 488
Makeup, Supplies	348
Makeup, Theatrical & Stage	348
Man Baskets	308
Management, Locations	183
Manicurists	380, 477, 488
Manlifts	308
Mannequins	363, 368
Manufacturers, High Def Equipment	285
Marble	329
Marble Finishes	106, 107, 109
Marine Advisors and Coordinators	246
Marine Equipment	328, 375
Marine Forecasts	206
Marine Locations	183
Marine Props	328, 368
Marine Technicians	549
Marionettes	363
Martial Arts Advisors	246
Masks	323, 334
Masonry	329
Massage Therapists	234
Material Backings	106, 107, 109
Matte Painting	106, 107, 109
Matte Painting, Digital	53
Matte Photography	53, 104
Mechanical FX	363
Mechanical Props	363
Mechanical Puppets	323
Mechanical Rigging	363
Mechanical Vehicle Modification	332
Medical Advisors	351, 383, 384
Medical Displays, Antique	351
Medical Equipment and Supplies	351
Medical Props	351, 368
Medical Uniforms	351
Medics	380, 383, 384
Memorabilia	352, 368, 378
Men's Grooming	380, 477, 488
Merchandising, Promotional	245
Messenger Services	235
Metals	329, 352
Metalwork	352, 363
Meteorologists	206
Mexican Film Commissions	167
Micro Cameras	274
Microphone Booms	268, 296
Microphones	268
Microphones, Wireless	163
Microscope Props	351
Military Advisors	246
Military Aircraft	252
Military Props	341, 368, 378
Military Research	233
Military Uniforms and Surplus	334, 378
Military Vehicles and Tanks	355
Millinery	334, 376, 378
Mini DV Cameras	274, 280
Mini DV Recorders	274, 280
Mini Ice Cubes	350
Mini Jib	296
Miniature Photography	53
Miniatures, Prop Makers	363
Mini-Blinds	336
Mirrors	347, 348
Mixing Theater, Film	42
Mixing, Audio	42
Mobile Editing Facilities	60, 284
Mobile Espresso Service	159
Mobile Kitchen Facilities	159, 423, 424
Mobile Production Offices	192
Mobile Radios	163
Mobile Refueling	319, 332
Mock-Ups	111, 363, 373

Model Makers, Props	363
Model Trains	347, 368
Modeling Agencies	246
Models, Hand & Leg	229
Models, Radio-Controlled	363
Modems	223
Modular Cranes	296
Modular Office Furniture	223, 346
Mold-Making & Molds	361, 363
Monitors, Computer	223
Monitors, Video	274, 277
Monkeys	209
Monthly Rentals	196
Mopeds	355
Morphing	53
MOS Stages	117, 127
Motion Capture	53
Motion Capture, Animation	53
Motion Control	263
Motion Control Camera Assistants	398, 407
Motion Control Camera Operators	408, 413, 414, 415, 416, 417
Motion Control Camera Systems	259, 263
Motion Control Grips	465, 476
Motion Control Photography	53, 93, 263, 292, 408, 413, 414, 415, 416, 417
Motion Control, Slide & Transparency	85, 288
Motion Graphics	53
Motion Picture Camera Rentals	259
Motion Picture Contracts	228
Motion Picture Contracts Software	222
Motion Picture Production Companies	27
Motion Picture Props Cameras, Antique to Present	354
Motorcycle Rentals	355
Motorcycle Sidecar Platforms	258
Motorhomes & Portable Dressing Rooms	192
Motorized Backings	106, 107, 109
Motorscooters	355
Mountain Bikes	375
Mountaineering Equipment	375
Mounted Animal Props	373
Mounts, Camera	252, 259, 296
Moustaches	348
Movie Posters	352
Movie Trailers	40
Moving, Storage & Transportation	196
Mules	209
Multi-Lingual Services	248
Multimedia Authoring Software	222
Multimedia Computer Consultants & Software	222
Mural Prints	76
Murals	106, 107, 109
Muscle Cars	355
Music and Sound FX	42
Music Boxes	368
Music Clearance and Supervision	233
Music Editing	42
Music Libraries	42, 80
Music Licensing	233
Music Playback Equipment	268
Music Production Companies	82
Music Publishing	80
Music Recording Studios	42
Music Research	233
Music Scoring	42, 82
Music Supervisors	51
Music Video Directors	28, 30, 380
Music Video Editors	47, 64
Music Video Production Companies	30
Musical Equipment, Storage & Transportation	196
Musical Instrument Rentals	353
Musical Instruments and Props	353
Musicians	82, 215
Muslin	106, 107, 109, 340
Mylar	361

General Index

N

Native American Furniture and Rugs 368
Native American Jewelry 373
Native American Nations, Film Commissions 167
Natural Light Studios 127
Nautical Film Coordination 236
Nautical Film Services 236
Nautical Props 328
Negative Cutting 47, 85
Neon 354
Neoprene 304
Nets, Fabric 106, 107, 109, 340
Network ID Packages 53
New Jersey, Filming in XXI
New Jersey, Where to Shoot XXIV
New Listings Deadline for New York 411 . . . . V, VI
New York 411, Application for Freelance or Business Listing VI
New York 411, How to Advertise IV
New York 411, How to Get Listed . . . . V, VI
New York 411, How to Order VIII
New York 411, How to Update Your Listing IV
New York 411, How to Use III
New York City Sample Film Permit XVI
New York City, Filming in XIV
New York City, Where to Shoot XVIII
New York State Tax Exemptions for Film Industry XIII
New York State, Filming in IX
New York State, Where to Shoot X
Newspapers, Fabrication 342
Newspapers, Period 352
Newsreels 93, 292
Non-Linear Editing, Offline & Online 47, 60, 85, 284, 288
Non-Union Casting 215
Notaries 238
Notions 336, 340
Novelties 347, 368
Novelty Acts 246
NTSC & PAL Conversions 85, 288
Nurseries, Plants & Greens 344
Nurses 380, 383, 384

O

Objets D'Art 368
Off-Duty Police Officers 202
Office Equipment Rentals 223
Office Furniture 346
Office Phone Systems and Installation 163, 223
Office Space, Temporary 31
Offline Editing, Linear & Non-Linear 47, 60, 85, 284, 288
Off-Road Camera Cars 258
Off-Road Vehicles 355
On-Camera Handwriting 229
Online Directories 226
Online Editing, Analog & Digital 47, 60, 85, 284, 288
Online Real Estate Resources 196
On-Set Massage 234
Onyx 329
Opera Glasses 339, 378
Optical Compositing 53, 84
Optical Office Props 351
Opticals 84
Orchestral Instruments 353
Organizations, Trade 546
Oriental Costumes and Fabrics 334, 340
Outdoor Clothing 375, 378
Overheads, Grip 304
Overnight Dry Cleaning 338
Overscale Hair and Makeup Artists 380, 477, 488
Oversized Glass 347
Oversized Models and Props, Fabrication 363

P

Packing 166
Pagers 163
Paint 325, 329
Paintbox, Visual FX 53
Painted Backdrops & Scenics 106, 107, 109
Painted Bodies 477, 488
Painted Signs 342
Painting, Matte 53, 106, 107, 109
PAL & NTSC Conversions 85, 288
Pallet Racks 196
Palomino Horses 209
Panoramic Photography 259, 262
Paper, Fine Art 325
Parachutes 252, 378
Parallels 126
Paramedics 380, 383, 384
Parrots 209
Party Costumes 232, 334, 378
Party Ice 350
Party Locations 249
Party Planners 232
Party Props 232, 368
Party Supplies & Equipment 232
Passenger Vans 157
Passports, American 165
Pasties 334, 348
Patinas 106, 107, 109
Payroll & Production Accountants 239, 241
Payroll Software 222
PC Computer Rentals 223
PC Consultants & Software 222
Pea Ice 350
Pedestals 296
Performance Drivers 542
Period Costumes 334, 378
Period Furniture and Accessories 345, 368
Period Jewelry 378
Period Props 368, 373
Period Signage 342
Periodicals, Trade 226
Permissions 233
Permit, New York City, Sample XVI
Philadelphia, Filming in XXVIII
Phone Props 354, 368
Phone Systems 223
Phones, Cellular 163
Phonograph Machines 368
Photo Backings 106, 107, 109
Photo Cut-Outs 76
Photo Ice 350
Photo Labs, Custom 76
Photo Props 354
Photo Research 233
Photoboards 76
Photographers, Stills 380, 505, 507
Photographic Filters 259
Photographic Props 354, 368
Photography, Hi-Speed 53
Photography, Miniature 53
Photography, Time-Lapse 53, 93, 259
Photos, Stock 93, 292
Physicians, On Set 383, 384
Piano Movers 196
Pianos 353
Picture Boats 328
Picture Cars 355
Picture Libraries 233
Picture Vehicles 355
Pilots 257
Piñatas 232
Pinball Machines 347
Pins 245, 340
Planes 150, 252, 322
Planners, Party 232
Planters 344
Plants & Greens 344
Plasma Displays 223, 277
Plasma Globes 354
Plaster Bandages 348, 351
Plastibackings 106, 107, 109
Plastic Foods 368, 373
Plastic Props 368, 373
Plastic Signs 342

General Index

Plastic, Vacuum-Forming............................361
Plastics & Self-Adhering Vinyls.....................361
Plastics, Plexiglas & Fiberglass....................361
Platforms, Camera......................252, 259, 296
Platforms, Stage...................................126
Playback Equipment, Audio.........................268
Playback Equipment, Video.........................274
Plexiglas..361
Plywood...329
Police Cars and Motorcycles.......................355
Police Officers, Off-Duty...........................202
Police Technical Advisors..........................246
Police Uniforms............................334, 378
Polymer Clay Jewelry..............................373
Ponies..209
Porcelain....................................368, 372
Porcupines..209
Portable Air Conditioning Units....................302
Portable Dressing Rooms..........................192
Portable Editing Systems.....................60, 284
Portable Ice Skating Surfaces.....................350
Portable Offices..................................192
Portable Restrooms...............................198
Portable Stages..................................126
Portable Toilets..................................198
Post Houses.................................85, 288
Post Production, Audio.............................42
Post Production, Commercial Editorial..............47
Post Production, Editing Equipment Rentals...60, 284
Post Production Supervisors........................90
Post Production Training Centers..................548
Post Supervision.....................85, 90, 288
Poster Printing...................................342
Posters...352
Pottery Making...................................363
POV Aircraft Camera Systems.....................252
POV Cameras..............................252, 259
POV Helmet Cameras............................252
Power Pods................................259, 296
Powerboats......................................328
PR Firms..34
Practical Lighting.................................350
Precision Drivers.................................542
Preserved Insects................................373
Preserved Plants.................................344
Primates...209
Print Services, Video..............................56
Printed Inserts............................245, 342
Printers, Computer...............................223
Printing, Color Corrected.........................333
Private Homes...................................187
Private Investigators.............................202
Process Photography..............................53
Process Trailers..................................258
Processing, Film Stills.............................76
Processing, Motion Picture Film...................74
Producers..................................380, 497
Producers, Advertising Agency Freelance............4
Product Placement...............................362
Product Pours...................................363
Product Props, Oversized.........................363
Production Accessories...........................318
Production Accountants.....................239, 241
Production Accounting Software..................222
Production Bags..................................318
Production Board Strips..........................222
Production Companies, Commercial.................15
Production Companies, Corporate...................21
Production Companies, Industrial...................21
Production Companies, Infomercial..................26
Production Companies, Motion Picture..............27
Production Companies, Music & Sound Design......82
Production Companies, Music Video.................30
Production Companies, Promo......................33
Production Companies, Television..................38
Production Companies, Trailer.....................40
Production Coordinators..............380, 501, 503
Production Designers...................380, 388, 391
Production Forms Software.......................222

Production Guides................................226
Production Managers........................380, 504
Production Offices.............................31, 138
Production Offices, Mobile........................192
Production Services..........................200, 201
Production Sound Mixers..............380, 534, 539
Production Stills Photographers.......380, 505, 507
Production Tool Bags..............................318
Production Trailers................................192
Production Training Centers......................548
Professional Associations........................546
Programmers, Computer..........................222
Projection, Front & Rear Screen...................277
Projections......................................326
Projectors, Computer.............................223
Projectors, Overhead.............................223
Projectors, Video.................................223
Promo Production Companies......................33
Promos...102
Promotional Products............................245
Prop Food..........................363, 373, 452
Prop Houses.....................................368
Prop Makers, Fabrication.........................363
Prop Masters..............380, 388, 391, 508, 523
Prop Rentals, Furniture – Antique & Vintage.......345
Prop Rentals, Furniture – Contemporary...........346
Prop Rentals, Specialty...........................373
Propane..232
Props and Rigging................................363
Props Department Personnel...........380, 508, 523
Props, Mechanical & Electronic...............363, 368
Props, Mechanical FX and Rigging.................363
Props, Oversized & Miniature.....................363
Props, Storage & Transportation..................196
Prototypes.......................................363
Public Display Fireworks..........................326
Public Domain, Motion Pictures........93, 233, 292
Public Libraries..................................233
Public Relations...................................34
Promotional Products............................245
Publications, Directory & Trade...................226
Publicists...34
Publishing, Music..................................80
Puppeteers & Puppets...........................323
Purses, Vintage..................................378
Pyrotechnics....................................326

Q

Quality Control....................................85
Quantity Duplication, Still Photos..................76

R

Race Cars.......................................355
Radio Archives..................................233
Radio-Controlled Models.........................363
Radio-Controlled Puppets........................323
Radios, 2-Way..................................163
Radios, Props...................................354
Rail Runner.....................................296
Rails, Camera...................................296
Rain Covers, Camera............................318
Rain FX/Machines..........................205, 326
Rainfall, Average..............................XXXIII
Rare and Vintage Cars..........................355
Raw Space, Studios.............................127
Raw Stock, Film & Video........................266
Real People, Talent..............................215
Real Time Motion Control...................53, 263
Rear Screen Projection..........................277
Record Players, Props...........................354
Recording Studios................................42
RED Cameras..............................259, 280
Reenactments, Historical........................246
Referrals, Crew..................................380
Refrigerators, Vintage to Present............368, 372
Refueling Systems, Mobile.................319, 332
Rehearsal Studios..........................117, 138

General Index

Relayers	163
Religious Articles	368, 373
Religious Garments	334, 373
Remote Arms	296
Remote Camera Systems	252, 259, 296
Remote Communications, Audio	42, 163
Remote Heads	259, 296
Remote Sessions	42
Remote-Controlled FX Props	363
Remote-Controlled Robots	363
Remote Heads	259
Rental Art	324
Repeaters	163
Replica Food	363, 373
Replica Signage	342
Replication, DVD	58
Reps, Crew	380
Reps, Independent Sales	26
Reptiles	209
Rescue Vehicles	355
Research Libraries and Services	233
Residuals Software	222
Restaurant & Kitchen Equipment	372
Restoration & Retouching, Film	74
Restoration & Retouching, Still Photos	76
Restrooms, Portable	198
Reversal Prints, Still Photos	76
Reversals, Film	74
Revolving Platforms and Stages	126, 363
Ribbons	245, 340
Riding Gear	373
Rig Runner Dollies	296
Rigging, Car Prep	332
Rigging, Mechanical FX & Props	363
Rights Licensing Software	222
Rings	339
Risers	126
Road Signs	342
Robot Props	373
Robotics	323, 363
Rodents	209
Roll Cages	363
Rotoscoping	53
Routing, Digitized	342, 363
Royalties Software	222
Rubber Props	363
Rugs, Antique to Present	345, 368

S

Sabers	341
Saddles	373
Safety Advisors, Underwater	246
Safety Divers	246, 383, 384
Safety Equipment & Supplies	183, 318
SAG Casting	215
SAG Extras	229
Sailboards, Windsurfing	375
Sailboats	328
Sales Rep Software	222
Salvage, Architectural	324
Satellite Links and Systems	78, 163
Satellite Phones	163
Satellite Services	78
Saxophones	353
Scaffolding	303, 308
Scanning, Digital Imaging	53, 76, 85, 288
Scanning, Film	53, 85, 288
Scene Docks	111
Scenic Artists	106, 107, 109
Scenic Flats	111
Scenic Painting	106, 107, 109
Science Fiction Props	363, 368, 373
Scientific Equipment and Props	351, 368
Scissorlifts	303, 308
Scooters	355
Scoring Stages	42
Scoring, Music	42, 82
Scorpions	209

Scouts, Location	183
Screen Printing	245, 334
Screening Rooms	91, 291
Screens, Blue & Green	106, 107, 109
Screenwriting Software	222
Scrims	106, 107, 109, 311, 336
Script Breakdown Software	222
Script Supervisors	380, 525, 526
Scriptwriting Software	222
Scuba Diving Advisors	246
Scuba Gear	375
Sculpted Props	363
Sculpting, Foam	345, 363
SDDS	42, 91, 291
Search Services, Books & Magazines	233
Searchlights	232
Seasonal Props	373
Second Assistant Cameramen	398, 407
Second Assistant Directors	527, 531
Second Meals	159, 423, 424
Second Unit Directors of Photography	380, 426, 433
Secretarial Services	247
Security & Bodyguards	202
Security Vaults	73
Self-Help Items	373
Semi Trucks	303, 355
Sequins	340
Sessions, Remote	42
Set Decorators	380, 532
Set Design, Construction & Rentals	111
Set Dressing, Props	368
Set Rentals	111
Set Sketches	53, 116, 380
Sets, Permanent	111
Sewing Machines & Props	368
Shades, Window	336
Shaved Ice	350
Shoemakers	334
Shoes	334, 376, 378
Short-Term Housing	177
Shop Craft (Local 52 NY)	418
Show Props	368
Shower Trailers	192
Shuttle Buses	157
Sidecar Platforms, Motorcycles	258
Sign Language Interpreters	248
Signage, Neon	342, 354
Signage, Props & Fabrication	342
Signs, Traffic	183, 318, 342, 368
Silicone	363
Silk Flowers and Plants	344
Silkscreening	245, 334
Silver, Antique	345, 368
Silverware	372
Skeleton and Skull Replications	363
Sketches, Set	53, 116, 380
Skin Care	348
Skin Diving Equipment	375
Skis	375
Sky Backings	106, 107, 109
Sky Surfing Stunt Coordinators	542
Skydiving Advisors	246
Skydiving Equipment	252
Skydiving Stunt Coordinators	542
Sleighs	368, 375
Slide Duplication	76
Slide Transfers	76, 85, 288
Sliders	296
Slipcovers	340
Small Generators	303, 311
Small Package Express	151
Small Wildlife	209
Smoke FX/Machines	326
Snakes	209
Snorkeling Equipment	375
Snow FX/Machines	326
Snowboarding Advisors	246
Snowboarding Equipment	375
Snowdomes	245

General Index

Snowfall, Average . . . XXXIII
Soccer Equipment . . . 375
Social Dance Advisors . . . 246
Soda Equipment . . . 372
Soft Props . . . 363
Software, Computer . . . 222
Soilless Grass . . . 344
Sony HDCam . . . 280
Sound Archives . . . 80, 233
Sound Design . . . 82
Sound Designers . . . 51, 82
Sound Editing, Analog & Digital . . . 42
Sound Equipment . . . 268
Sound FX Libraries . . . 42, 80
Sound Mixers, Production . . . 534, 539
Sound Mixing . . . 42
Sound Stages . . . 117, 138
Sound Stages, Dimensions & Specifications . . . 138
Sound Transfers . . . 42, 74
Space Suits . . . 334, 363
Special FX, Computer Generated . . . 53
Special FX Costumes . . . 334, 363
Special FX Lighting . . . 326
Special FX Makeup . . . 348, 477, 488
Special FX Props . . . 323, 363
Special FX, Visual . . . 53
Special Mechanical FX . . . 363
Specialty Acts . . . 246
Specialty Props . . . 373
Speech Advisors . . . 208, 246
Speech Training Centers . . . 548
Spiders, Living . . . 209
Spiders, Preserved . . . 373
Sport Vehicle Rentals . . . 355
Sporting Goods . . . 375
Sports, Stock Footage . . . 93, 292
Sportswear . . . 375, 376
Spot Coolers . . . 302
Spray Urethane Foam . . . 53, 345
Stabilized Systems . . . 296
Stage Chart . . . 138
Stage Curtains . . . 336
Stage Managers . . . 540
Stages . . . 117, 138
Stages, Dimensions & Specifications . . . 138
Stages, Insert . . . 117, 138
Stages, Portable . . . 126
Stages, Sound . . . 117, 138
Stained Glass . . . 347
Stake Beds . . . 319
Stanchions . . . 318
Standards Conversions . . . 85, 288
Stand-Ins . . . 229
State Film Commissions . . . 167
State Information . . . 167
Station ID Packages . . . 102
Statues . . . 368
Steadicam Assistants . . . 398, 407
Steadicam ATV . . . 296
Steadicam Directors of Photography . . . 380, 426, 433
Steadicam Equipment . . . 259, 296
Steadicam Operators . . . 408, 413, 415, 416
Steel Fabrication . . . 111, 363
Steel . . . 352
Stenciling . . . 106, 107, 109
Step Units . . . 126
Stereo Equipment Props . . . 354
Stereoscopic Cameras . . . 259
Still Photo Labs . . . 76
Still Photo Lofts . . . 127
Still Photo Studios . . . 127
Stills Photographers . . . 380, 505, 507
Stock Footage & Photos . . . 93, 292
Stock Footage Research . . . 93, 233, 292
Stock Units, Scenery . . . 106, 107, 109, 111
Stock, Film . . . 266
Stop Motion . . . 5, 53
Storage & Transportation . . . 196
Storage Tanks, Portable . . . 196
Storage, Film & Tape . . . 73
Store Display Props . . . 373
Store Displays and Interiors . . . 368
Storyboard Artists . . . 35, 380
Storyboarding Software . . . 222
Stoves, Antique to Present . . . 368, 372
Street Closures . . . 183
Street Dressing and Props . . . 368
Street Signs . . . 342
Street Vehicles . . . 355
Stretch Limos . . . 355
Strike Services . . . 231
Strobe Lighting . . . 311, 326
Studio Services . . . 376
Studio Teachers/Welfare Workers . . . 380, 541
Studio, Still Photo . . . 127
Stuffed Animals . . . 368, 373
Stunt Associations . . . 546
Stunt Cameras . . . 259
Stunt Coordinators . . . 542
Stunt Mannequins, Articulated . . . 363
Stunt Vehicles . . . 355
Stylists, Wardrobe . . . 380, 555, 558
Subtitles . . . 53, 85, 102, 288
Succulents . . . 344
Suede Dry Cleaning . . . 338
Suitcases . . . 368, 378
Suits, Walkaround . . . 334
Sunglasses . . . 339
Sunrise & Sunset Chart . . . XXXVI
Super 8 Cameras & Equipment . . . 259
Super 16 Cameras & Equipment . . . 259
Supermarket Props . . . 368, 372
Supervisors, Visual FX . . . 104
Supervisors, Wardrobe . . . 380, 563
Surface Materials . . . 329
Surfaces . . . 106, 107, 109
Surplus, Military . . . 378
Surveillance . . . 202
Survival Equipment Surplus . . . 378
SWAT Tactics Advisors . . . 246
Sweetening, Audio . . . 42
Swiftwater Rescue Technicians . . . 246
Swords . . . 341
Symbolics System . . . 53
Synching . . . 42, 85, 288
Synthesizers . . . 353
Synthetic Animals . . . 373

T

Table Rentals . . . 232, 318, 346
Table Top, Props . . . 106, 107, 109, 346, 368
Tables, Makeup . . . 348
Tableware . . . 372
Tailoring & Alterations . . . 377
Talent & Modeling Agencies . . . 246
Talent Clearance . . . 233
Talent Payments . . . 239, 241
Tanks, Helium . . . 232, 318
Tanks, Military . . . 355
Tanks, Portable Storage . . . 196
Tape Distribution, Video . . . 56
Tape Stock, HD . . . 294
Tape Storage . . . 73
Tape to Film Transfers . . . 85, 288
Tape to Slide Transfers . . . 85, 288
Tape to Still Film Transfers . . . 85, 288
Tape to Tape Color Corrections . . . 85, 288
Tape to Tape Film Simulation . . . 85, 288
Tape, Adhesive . . . 304
Taps, Camera . . . 259
Tassels . . . 340
Tax Exemptions for Film Industry, New York State . . . XIII
Taxi Meters . . . 373
Taxicabs . . . 355
Taxidermy . . . 373
Teachers . . . 380, 541
Technical Advisors . . . 246

General Index

Technical Support, Computer . . . 222
Technical Training . . . 548
Telecine . . . 53, 85, 288
Telecommunication Equipment . . . 163
Telephone Equipment and Supplies . . . 163, 223
Telephoto Lenses . . . 259
Teleprompters . . . 270
Television Production Companies . . . 38
Television, Props . . . 354, 368
Temp Agencies . . . 247
Temp Mixes . . . 42
Temperature-Controlled Storage . . . 73
Temperatures, Average . . . XXXIII
Temporary Automotive Paint . . . 332
Temporary Land Lines . . . 163
Temporary Office Space . . . 31
Tents . . . 232, 318, 331, 375, 378
Textile Manufacturing . . . 340
Theatrical Draperies & Rigging . . . 336
Theatrical Fabrics . . . 340
Theatrical Lighting . . . 311, 326
Theatrical Props . . . 368
Theatrical Sound Systems . . . 268
Theme Parties . . . 232
Theme Props . . . 363
Thermal Protected Sportswear . . . 375
Thread . . . 340
THX Sound . . . 42, 91, 291
Tie and Scarf Cleaning . . . 338
Tie-Dye . . . 245, 378
Tile . . . 329
Time Manipulation Imaging Systems . . . 53
Time-Lapse Photography . . . 53, 93, 292
Tinting, Glass . . . 332, 347
Tires, Truck . . . 332
Title Design . . . 53, 102
Titles, Optical . . . 84
Titling . . . 102
Toilets, Portable . . . 192, 198
Tools . . . 329
Topiaries . . . 344
Torchieres . . . 350
Toupées . . . 348
Tours . . . 249
Tow Dollies . . . 258
Towing, Picture Vehicles . . . 332, 355
Toys . . . 347
Track and Field Equipment . . . 375
Tracking Vehicles . . . 258
Tractions, Medical . . . 351
Tractors . . . 303, 355
Trade Associations . . . 546
Trade Publications . . . 226
Trade Show Expos . . . XXXVIII
Traffic Control and Plans . . . 183
Traffic Safety Equipment . . . 183, 318
Traffic Signals . . . 368
Traffic Signs . . . 183, 318, 342
Trailer Production Companies . . . 40
Trailers . . . 192, 355
Trailers, Movie . . . 40, 102
Trainers, Animal . . . 209
Training Centers . . . 548
Training Video Production . . . 21
Trains, Toy . . . 368
Trampolines . . . 375
Transcription Services . . . 247
Transfers, Digital Tape . . . 42, 85, 288
Transfers, Film to Tape . . . 85, 288
Transfers, Sound . . . 42
Transfers, Tape to Film . . . 85, 288
Transfers, Tape to Slide . . . 85, 288
Transfers, Tape to Still Film . . . 76, 85
Translation . . . 248
Transmission Services . . . 78
Transportation & Storage . . . 196
Transportation, Picture Vehicle . . . 355
Transportation, Trucks & Vans . . . 319
Trash Removal . . . 231
Travel Accessories . . . 318, 376
Travel Agencies . . . 204
Travel Medicine . . . 383, 384
Traveling Notaries . . . 238
Trees, Artificial & Living . . . 344
Tribal Artifacts . . . 368
Trick Horses . . . 209
Tripods . . . 296
Trompe L'Oeil . . . 106, 107, 109
Troop Carriers . . . 355
Trophies . . . 245
Truck Cranes . . . 296, 308
Trucks . . . 319
Trucks, Fire . . . 205, 355
Trucks, Water . . . 205
Trunks . . . 368, 373, 378
Truss Systems for Scaffolding . . . 308
T-Shirts, Promotional . . . 245
Tugboats . . . 328
Turnstiles . . . 318
Turntables . . . 308, 363
Turtles . . . 209
Tutors . . . 380, 541
Tuxedos . . . 334, 376, 378
TV Network/Cable ID Packages . . . 102
TV Props . . . 368
TV Show Opens and Closes . . . 53, 102
TV Studios . . . 130, 138
Typesetting . . . 342
Typewriters . . . 223

U

U.S. History Research . . . 233
Ultimatte . . . 53, 85, 288
Ultralight Aircraft . . . 252
Ultralight Coordination and Consulting . . . 246, 542
Ultrasound Equipment . . . 351
Underwater Advisors . . . 246
Underwater Camera Assistants . . . 380, 398, 407
Underwater Camera Equipment . . . 259
Underwater Directors of Photography . . . 380, 426, 433
Underwater Grips . . . 465, 476
Underwater Housings . . . 259, 296
Underwater Lighting Systems . . . 311
Underwater Operators . . . 408, 413, 417
Underwater P.A. Systems . . . 268
Underwater Systems, Video . . . 274
Underwater Technicians, Crew . . . 549
Uniforms . . . 245, 334, 378
Union Locals . . . 546
Union Rules . . . 567
Unit Production Managers (DGA NY) . . . 550
UNIX Software . . . 222
Unmarked Police Cars . . . 355
Updating Listing, New York 411 . . . IV
Upholstery . . . 340
UPM's . . . 380, 550
Urethane . . . 345, 361, 363
Utility Carts . . . 318

V

Vacuum-Forming . . . 323, 361
Vans . . . 319
Vans, Cargo & Passenger . . . 157
Vice Patrol Advisors . . . 246
Video Assist Services . . . 273
Video Camera Systems . . . 280
Video Conferencing . . . 225
Video Display playback . . . 277
Video Production . . . 21
Video Projection . . . 277
Video Projectors . . . 223, 274
Video Props . . . 354
Video Walls . . . 277
Videotape . . . 266
Vintage Accessories . . . 378
Vintage Barber and Beauty Shop Equipment . . . 373

Vintage Cameras	354
Vintage Clothing	378
Vintage Firearms and Weapons	341
Vintage Furniture	345
Vinyl Sheeting	361
Vinyl Signage	342
Vinyls	329, 340
Visas, Travel	165, 204
Visual FX Artists	104, 380
Visual FX Producers	104, 380
Visual FX Supervisors	104, 380
Voice Advisors	246
Voice Training	208, 548
Voiceover Recording	42, 215
Voiceover Talent	246
VTR Operators	380, 552, 554

W

Wage Rates – IATSE	576
Wagons, Honey	192
Walkaround Costumes	334
Walkie Talkies	163
Wall Glazing	106, 107, 109
Wallpaper/Wallcoverings	106, 107, 109, 329
Wardrobe Rentals	334, 376
Wardrobe Stylists	380, 555, 558
Wardrobe Supervisors	380, 563
Wardrobe Supplies	348
Wardrobe Trailers	192
Wasps	209
Watches, Antique – Present	339, 378
Water Safety Advisors	246
Water Trucks	205
Water Works, Sculpture	363
Wax Sculpture	363
Weapons	341
Weapons Advisors	246
Weather Data	XXXIII
Weather FX	326
Weather Information & Services	206
Wedding Gowns	334, 376, 378
Wedding Rings	339
Welding	363
Welfare Workers	380, 541
Western Costumes	334
Western Jewelry	339
Western Props	368, 373
Western Technical Advisors	246
Western Wear, Vintage	378
Wet Weather Clothing	375, 378
Wheelchairs, Props	351
Where to Shoot in Connecticut	XXVII
Where to Shoot in New Jersey	XXIV
Where to Shoot in New York City	XVIII
Where to Shoot in New York State	X
White Tigers	209
White Water Advisors	246
White Water Rafts	328, 375
Wigs	334, 348, 477, 488
Wild Animals	209
Wind FX/Machines	326
Window Dubbing	85, 288
Window Shades	336
Window Tinting	332, 347
Window Treatments	336
Windsocks	342
Winery Props	372
Wire & Wire Cloth	352
Wire Removal	53
Wire Rigging	363
Wireless Microphones	163
Wireless Systems	163
Women's Wear	334, 376, 378
Wood Paneling & Veneers	329
Wood Supplies	329
Woodies	355
Woolens & Worsteds	340
Word Processing	247
Work Rules – IATSE-AICP	574
Work Rules – IATSE-AICP NE Corridor	580
Workstation Rentals	223
Wrap Party Locations	249
Wrought Iron	352, 363

X

Xenon Lighting	311
Xerox Copiers	223
X-Ray Machines, Props	351

Y

Yachts	328, 355

Z

Zoom Lenses	259

NOTES:

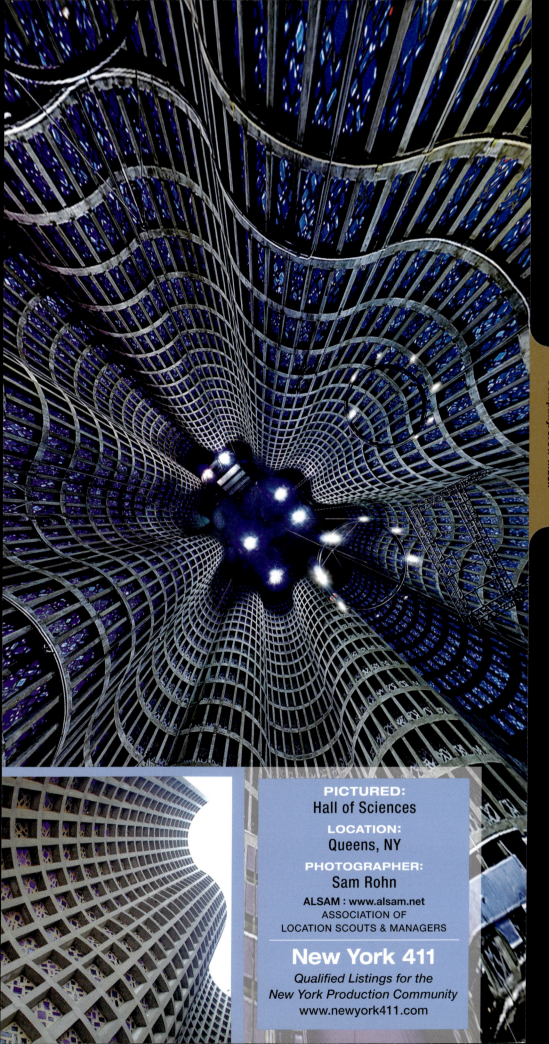

CHELSEA PIERS: ON LOCATION

Film & Television Shoots | Photoshoots | Media Events
Studio Space Available for Lease (3,500 - 8,000 sq. ft.)

KEY FEATURES INCLUDE:
Ground-floor Loading, On-site Parking
Dedicated Staff to Assist, On-site A/V & Catering

23d Street & Hudson River Park
212.336.6777
chelseapiers.com/eventsales

Company/Crew Index

Numbers

1 A Allstar Picture Cars	355
1-800-Translate	248
101 River Views	187
1887 Townhouse	187
1896, The	117, 187
20 Greene Gallery	187
21st Century Security, Inc.	202
24fps Productions, Inc.	280, 283
2StopsBrighter	127
3 Rings Media	58
300 Monks	82
300ml	7
320 Studios NYC	249
3D Training Institute	548
4-D Creative Media	15, 21, 53, 58
57 Screening Room	91
60 Thompson	177
620 Loft & Garden	187
(718)music	80
76 Carriage Company	209, 355
7NY	21, 30
7th Avenue Stationers	325
8 Hats High Animation & Production, Inc.	53
903Films	15, 47, 56, 85, 200, 288
91 East	42, 47

A

A A Amcar	156
A Plus Recording & Transcribing	247
A to Z Couriers	151, 235
A to Z Media	58
A. van Hoek Ltd.	192, 355
A&A Group	2
A&E Television Networks	38
A.G.E. Services, Inc. - Mobile Air Conditioning	302
A.I. Friedman, Inc.	325
a.k.a. films	200
A-Prompt	270
AA Armato & Son	350
AA Executive Town Car & Limousine	155, 355
AAA Acme Discount Film Works	15, 21, 30, 200
AAA American Flag Decorating Co., Inc.	342
AAA Communications	163
AAA Event Services	302, 311, 318, 331
Aab, Alexander	527
Aaron, Fanae	391
Aaron, Mary	477, 488
Aaron, Pamela L.	563
Aartist Loft	380, 488, 558
Abad III, Manuel	465
Abbatecola, Joseph F.	465
Abbott, Brian	477
Abbott, Ray	542
ABC Entertainment	38
ABC Office Essentials Co., Inc.	223
ABC Rental Center	308, 311
ABC WordExpress Worldwide Language Services	248
ABCNews VideoSource	93
Abel Cine Tech, Inc.	259, 274, 280
Abel, Doug	64
Abergel, Adir	488
Abich, Nasar	433
Abingdon Theatre Arts Complex	117, 221
Able Equipment Rental, Inc.	308, 311
Abma, Marie	555
Above & Beyond Artists Agency	35, 116, 380, 391
Abraham, Jacob	550
Abraham, Peter	426
Abraham, Phil	426
Abrams, Brad	447
Abramson, Olga	398
Abramson, Richard Seth	534
Abroms, Edward R.	64
ABS Payroll & Production Accounting Services	241
Abseck, Arlynn	563
Academy Bus Tours	155
Acadia Scenic	111
Accardi, Vincent	418
Accomplished Office Service	247
Accredited Accommodations Inc.	177
AccuWeather, Inc.	53, 206
Ace Banner Flag & Graphics	342
Ace Party Rental	331
Acevedo, Damian	433
Acevedo, Michael	418
Achziger, Lowell B.	453
Acker, Brett	508
Ackerman, Robert	508
Ackerman, Susan	527
Ackerman, Tom	433
Acme Marble Co., Inc.	329
Acme Special Effects	326
Acme Stimuli Design & Production	111
Acne	28
Acocella Group	177
Acord, Lance	433
Acrodyne Industries (Ai)	285
ACS/Aerial Camera Support	296
Acting Management, Inc.	221
Action ATV	258
Action Camera Cars, Inc.	258, 296
Action Footage/Warren Miller Entertainment	93, 292
Action Sports/Scott Dittrich Films	93, 292
Acton, Amy	563
Adam Smelin Enterprises	273
Adams, Heidi	391
Adams, Keith	527
Adams Rents	309
Adar, Nir	452
Addison, Greg	453
Addiss Pat Enterprises, Inc.	245
Adebonojo, Henry	408
Adecco	247
Adee, Troy R.	508
Adee, Walter A.	508
Adee, William C.	508
Adele Recklies Co.	334
Adelman, Tevin	550
Adirondack Rents	346
Adkins, Michael	563
Adler, Gilbert	497
Adler, Sherri	508
Adler, Tony	450
ADM Productions	21, 200
ADM Tronics Unlimited, Inc.	348
Admiral Metals	352
Adorama Rentals	262
Adorno, Jeff	407
Advanced Express, Inc.	151
Advantage Movers	196
Adventure Pictures	93
Advertisers Workshop	2
Advertising Age	226
Advertising Photographers of America/New York	546
Adweek	226
Adweek Directories	226
Adzima, Nanzi	563
Aegean Imports	334
Aerial Focus/Tom Sanders	246, 252, 542
Aerialexposures.com, LLC	252
Aero California	153
Aero Mock-Ups, Inc.	111, 373
Aerolineas Argentinas	153
Aeromexico	153
Aerts, Toon	7
Affair to Remember, An	159
Affleck, Casey	7
Aggreko Event Services	302, 311
Aggressive	7
Agliata, Peter	426
Agnello Films	296
Agnello, Tom	433
Agnes, Mark	563
Agnew, Brian	433
Agostino, Vincent	450, 497
Agredo, Robert A.	465
Agustsson, Magni	433
Aharoni, Gary M.	508
Aharoni, Gregg A.	508
Aharoni, Michael B.	508
Ahern Rentals, Inc.	309
Ahlgren, Martin	426
Ahmad, Maher	391
Ahrens, Bill	433
AIM Productions, Inc.	362
Aimes, Inc.	351
Air Canada	153
Air Conditioner Rental and Leasing	302, 311
Air France	153
Air Jamaica	153
Air Metro Helicopters, Inc.	253
Air New Zealand	153
Air Pegasus Heliport	154
Air Power Video & Film Stock Library	93
Air Royale International	150
Air Sea Land Productions, Inc.	15, 30, 93, 200, 280, 284, 288, 292
Air-Tech	204
AIRCAM Aerial Video and Photography	253
Airpower Aviation Resources, Inc.	253, 322

Entry	Page
AJA Video	285
Aji, Mark	497
AKA Locations	183
Akay, Tet	407
Akdag, Irfan	388, 508
Akerlund, Bill	408
Åkerlund, Jonas	28
Al Giddings Images, Inc.	93
Alabama	167
Alabama-Mobile	167
Alamo	156
Alan Benoit Photography	93
Alan Weiss Productions	21
Alaska	167
Alaska Airlines	153
Alba, Eric	104
Albanese, Andrew	552
Albanese, Julie	508
Albanese, Kenneth J.	418
Albanese, Nicholas	418
Albano, Amy	398
Albano, Joe	51
Albany International Airport	154
Albee, Floyd	391
Albertell, Robert	447
Albert, Martin	426, 465
Alberti, Maryse	426
Alberts, Jonathan	64
Alberts, Timothy	563
Albor, Michael	488
Albright, Brett	408
Albright, Irene	558
Albritton, Ernie	398
Alcantara, Blake	398
Alcantara, Eddy	523
Alcebo, Christy	523
Alcone NYC	348
Alden, Mike	35
Alejandra	488
Aleman, Michel	488
Alemi, Patrick	477
Aleski, Jim	504
Alex Nickason, Jennifer	508
Alexander, Jason	7
Alexander, Jill	508
Alexandre, Maxime	433
Alexeev, Peter	465
Alfieri, Joseph Anthony	418
Alfieri, Joseph S.	418
Alfieri, Michael	465
Alford, Derrick J.	418
Alfredo III, John	508
Alfredo, Richard	523
Alger House	187
Algonquin, The	177
Alio, Sonia M.	388
Alitalia	153
Alkaysi, Ramsey	398
Alkit Pro Camera	76
All Access Staging & Productions	111, 126
All Affairs	331
All Creatures Great & Small	209
All Crew Agency	64, 380, 426, 433, 488, 558
All In One Customhouse Brokers	166
All Mobile Video	56, 60, 78, 274, 280, 283, 284
All Occasions/PartyBuster.com	331
All Reel Design	35
All Seasons Marine Corp.	328
All Star Animals	209
All Star Radios	163
All State Auto Rental	156
All Suffolk Flag Rental Company	342
All Terrain Power Co., Inc.	311
All-Most New Rentals/Vans-to-Go	156, 157
All-Star Locations	183
All-Stock	93, 292
All-Tame Animals, Inc.	209
Alburn, Peter	107, 388
AllCell Rentals	164
Allen, Aleksandr	398
Allen, Andrea	497
Allen, Benita	450
Allen, David H.	508, 523
Allen, Glenn	104
Allen, James C.	418
Allen, Kevin	388
Allen, Shirlena	488
Allen, Stuart	398
Allen, Thomas C.	523
Allencrest Associates	183
Aller, Michel	64
Allix, Nick	64
Allstate Glass Corp.	336, 347
Almeida, Sebastian	398
Almeida, William	453
Alper, Gary	534
Alpha Business Machine Corporation	223
Alpha Engraving Co.	245
ALSAM/Association of Location Scouts and Managers	183, 546
Alston, Loretta	488
Alston, Rico Omega	552
Altamura, Lorraine	488
Alter, Marleen	477
Alternative Pick, The	226
Altizio, Deborah	488
Altman Building, The	127, 187
Altman Rentals, Inc.	306, 311
Altomare, S. Dana	408
Alton, Elizabeth	501
Altschul, Fernando	450
Alufoil Products	352
Alvarado III, Pastor	508
Alvarez, Jose	447
Alvarez, Monserra	477
Alvarez, Shea	555
Alverson, Timothy	64
Alz Productions	53
AM Stock-Cameo Film Library	93
Amadie, Daniel	453
Aman, Brian C.	453
Amanuel, Lawrence	344, 508, 532
Amat, Gonzalo	433
Amateau, Todd	450
Ambadjes, Jacque	384
Ambient Images	93
Ambitious Entertainment	380, 391, 433
Ambrosoni, Margaret	447
Ambu-Care	384
America by Air Stock Footage Library	93, 292
American Airlines	153
American Airlines Cargo	151
American Association of Advertising Agencies (AAAA)	546
American Cinematographer	226
American Classic Limousines	181
American Copy Machines	223
American Federation of TV & Radio Artists (AFTRA)	546
American Foliage & Design Group, Inc.	344
American Folk Art Museum Research Library	233
American Ground Transportation	155, 181
American Heritage Magazine Picture Library	233
American Humane Association	209
American Montage, Inc.	21, 47, 60
American Movie Co.	21, 117, 127, 200
American Museum of Natural History Library	233
American Playback Images	93
American Residuals & Talent, Inc.	241
American Resource Medical Equipment	351
American Society of Composers, Authors & Publishers (ASCAP)	233
American Stock Photography	93
American Taximeters & Communications, Inc.	373
Americh, Georgina	64
Amerifilm Casting, Inc.	215
Ameritania Hotel	177
Ametron Audio Video	266, 294
Amhalise Casting	215
Amico, Roxanne T.	107
Amondson, Nathan	391
Amor, Jose	418
Amphibico	285
Amphibious Medics	384
Amrita	488
Amron, Alison	64
Amsterdam Court Hotel	177
Amtrak	187
Amundsen, Mitch	433
Amusicom	80
Amy Gossels Casting	215
Amzallag, Manuela	558
ANA All Nippon Airways	153
Analog Digital International, Inc.	47, 60
Anania, Michael S.	388
Anastasia, Tricia	453
Anchor Archives	94
Ancona, Amy	391
Andersen, Chris	539
Andersen, Matthew J.	552
Anderson, Belinda	477
Anderson, Bert	477
Anderson, Beth	398
Anderson, Cameron	388
Anderson, David T.	453
Anderson, Erik	416
Anderson, Ethan Lee	527
Anderson, Frederick C.	464
Anderson, Jennifer	563
Anderson, Jill	563

Company/Crew Index

Name	Page
Anderson, Joshua	534
Anderson, Lara	563
Anderson, Monica	7, 28
Anderson Productions	21, 38, 60, 78
Anderson, Ric	540
Anderson, Scott G.	418
Anderson, Shawn Patrick	523
Anderson, Tarin	433
Anderson, Thomas M.	453
Anderson, Wes	7
Andersson, Helene	488
Andraca, Francisco	418
Andracke, Gregory	433
Andre, Philippe	7
Andres, Alexander	398
Andres, Bob	465
Andres, Denise	563
Andrew, Felix	534
Andrew Kolb & Son, Ltd.	324
Andrew Tedesco Studios, Inc.	109
Andrews, Amelia	563
Andrews Catering	159
Andrus, Tara Noel	239
Anetka Enterprises	215
Ang, Stephen	523
Angel Aerial Corporation	157, 205, 303, 309, 311, 319
Angel, Stephanie	525
Angelicola, Rand F.	107
Angelika Entertainment Corporation	27
Angenieux	285
Animal Actors, Inc.	209
Animals Animals/Earth Scenes	94
Animals for Advertising, Inc.	209
Animal Works	209
Animated Arts	53
Animation Entertainment	94, 292
Animatus Studio	5, 53
Animotion, Inc.	5, 53
Anna Samuel & Associates, Inc.	34
Annapolis Mobile Power Services, Inc.	311
Anoff, Matiki A.	477
Anouk	7
ANP Transcriptions	247, 248
ANS International Video	56
Ansbro, James	508
Ansel, Peter	508
Ansin, Mikki	505
Antalocy, Robert J.	418
Anthology Film Archives	233
Anthony Augliera Inc.	196
Anthony, Mark	488
Antonacchio, Henry	418
Antonacchio, John	383
Anton, Jenna	488
Anx, The	42, 47, 85
Anything But Costumes	345, 351, 368, 372
Anzalone, Michael	555, 563
Anziano, James M.	508
Apache Rental Group	164
Aparo's Little John	198
Apex Stock	94
Aphrodite French Cleaners	338
Apicelli, Arianne	527
Apletchef, Dimitri	508
Apollo Theater Foundation	117
Apostol, George	508
Appelle, Lynn	503
Appelson, David	183, 450, 527
Applefeld, Alex	408
Applied Information Management, Inc.	222
Aqua-Effects	205
Aquarium Design	373
Aquavisions	209, 373
Araki, David	465
Arango, Natalie	563
Aranyo, Daniel	433
Arason, Atli	391
ARC Science Simulations	94
Arcenas, Loy	388
Archer, James L.	508
Archer-Telecine Stock Footage Libraries	94
Architectural Antiques Exchange	324, 329
Archival Film Research	233
Archive Films by Getty Images	94
Arcidiacono, Joe	426
Arctic Glacier	350
Ardilley, Daniel	433
Ardoff, Christopher	488
Area 4	58, 288
Arena, Janet	477, 488
Arencibia, Lazaro	477
Arenson Prop Center	346
Arf & Co.	15
Argan, Johanna	558
Argo, Neil	51
Argosy Book Stores, Inc.	352
Arguello, Sergio	433
Argueta, Luis	7
Arilang Travel	204
Arisohn, Michael	453
Arista Flag Corporation	342
Arizona	167
Arizona-Cochise County	167
Arizona-Cottonwood	167
Arizona-Globe	167
Arizona-Page-Lake Powell	167
Arizona-Phoenix	167
Arizona-Prescott	167
Arizona-Sedona	167
Arizona-Tucson	167
Arizona-Wickenburg	167
Arizona-Yuma	167
Arkansas	168
Arkin, Jonathan	388
Arkin, Zachary	453
Arkle, Dave	35
Armitage, Todd	408
Armstrong, Ann	508
Armstrong, Brian D.	508
Armstrong, David A.	433
Armstrong, Douglas H.	465
Armstrong, Kandy L.	534
Armstrong, Miguel	408
Armstrong, Robin	7
Armstrong, Stephanie	508
Armstrong, Willie (Cody)	477
Arnaud, Tony	465
Arndt, Rebecca	398
Arni and Kinski	7
Arni, Stefan	7
Arnold, Alexis	501
Arnold, Jennifer	563
Arnold, Jim	408
Arnold, Randy	433
Arnold, Steve	391
Arnold, Wayne	398
Arnold Worldwide	2
Arnold-Pallad, Jill	563
Arnone, Lisa	525
Arnone, Pamela	477
Arnot, William S.	465
Arnow, Todd	497
Aronoff, Eli	398
Aronowitz, Myles	505
Aronson, Adam	527
Aronson, Daniel	508
Aronson, John	433
Arrangements, Inc. Marine Division	324, 373
Arri CSC	259, 296, 304, 306, 311, 326
Arron, Robert	51
Arroyo, Antonio L.	534
Art & Industry/Doctor Proper, Ltd.	187, 324, 345, 368
Art Department	380, 488, 558
Art Department, LLC, The	111, 368
Art Dept.	363
Art Dept./Brian Kelly	116
Art Flag Co., Inc.	342
Art for Film, LLC	324
ART: ASAP	324
Artamus Restaurant Equipment	372
Artbeats	94, 292
Arteca, Vincent	465
Arthur Brown & Brother Co., Inc.	325
Artificial Reality	111, 363
Artistic F/X, Inc./Don Geyra	107
Artists by Timothy Priano	380, 488, 532, 558
Artists Company, The	15, 30
Artists@Work, Inc.	111
Artkraft Strauss Sign Corporation	354
ArtMix Photography	380, 507
Artmont, Nicole	488
Arts & Entertainment Insurance Brokerage	230
Arvanitis, Yorgos	433
Arvan, Marlene	447
As You Like It Craft Service	424
ASAP Caterers/FoodThoughts	159
Asbury, Richard E.	453
Ascent Media Management East	42, 47, 56, 58, 73, 85, 283, 288
Asch, Jane	107
Ascher, Diana Marie	239
Aselton, Matt	7, 28
Ashley, Michelle	391
Ashton, John	508
Asia Society	249
Asiana Airlines	153
Askew, Charlie	64
ASL Productions, Inc.	296

Company/Crew Index

Entry	Page
Associated Press Television News	78
Association of Film Commissioners International	168
Association of Independent Commercial Producers (AICP)	546
Association of Independent Creative Editors (AICE)	546
Association of the Bar of the City of New York	187, 249
Assured Protection, LLC	384
asterisk	5, 53, 102
Astmann, Jill	477, 488
Astor Travel, Inc.	204
Astoria Films	27
Astro Systems, Inc.	285
Atelier 34 Studio	127
Atherton, Howard	433
Athletic Style Custom Merchants	245
Atkins, Edwin	550
Atlantic Aviation Services	150
Atlantic Cine Equipment, Inc.	253, 259, 280, 296
Atlantic City International Airport	154
Atlantic Coast Catering	159
Atlantic Express Transportation Group	155
Atlantic Motion Pictures	5, 15, 53, 58, 60, 102, 127, 263
Atlantic Television, Inc.	200, 274, 280, 380, 413, 433
Atomic Image	85, 288
Atomic Image Creative Media, Inc.	53
atomic torpedo.com.	183
Attitude New York, Inc.	181
Atwater, Bruce A.	465
Atwood, Jo Ann	508
Au, Theodore	239
Audick, Michael	408
Audience Associates/Big Crowds	229
Audino, Michael	453
audioEngine	42
Audio Mixers, Inc.	42
Auerbach, Simona M.	388
Augenblick Studios, Inc.	5
August, Rafael	453
Auld, Stuart E.	107
Aurnhammer, Donald	465
Aurora Productions International, Inc.	21, 26, 38
Auroux, Bernard	433
Austin, Andre	558
Austin Salisbury Productions.	273
Austin, Stephanie	497
Australia-Melbourne	176
Australia-New South Wales	176
Australia-Queensland	176
Australian Consulate General	165
Austria	176
Austria-Cine Tirol	176
Austrian Consulate General	165
Auszura, Michael	388
Auth, Victoria	558
Auto Props	205, 355
Autodesk	285
Automatic Productions	21, 38
Automobile Film Club of America, Inc.	254, 322, 328, 332, 355
Available Art	324
Available Light	311
Available Teleprompting	270
Avallone, Angelina	477
Avalon Hotel	177
Avdyushko, Varya	558
Avery, Paul	391
Avianca	153
Avid Productions Transcription Services	247
Avid Technology, Inc.	285
Aviles, J. Lourdes	107
Aviles, Juan Enrique V.	418
Avis	156
Avrett, Free & Ginsberg, Inc.	2
Axel Protection Systems, Inc.	202
Axelrad, John	64
Axilrod, Ian	398
Axis Global Systems	151
Ayoub, Jimmy	184, 505
Ayrton, Donald (Lee)	453
Ayson, Steve	7
Azoto, Dominic	426
AzRa Historical Resources/USHist	246
Aztec Video Productions	21

B

Entry	Page
B.	558
B. Rodwin & Co.	232
B&H Photo Video Pro Audio	266, 280, 294, 304
B-hive Stages	127
B-Rave Studio	47
B-Train Films	38
Baan, Maria	383
Baboo Color Labs, Inc.	76
Baby Wranglers Casting, Inc.	215
Baca-Asay, Joaquin	426
Baccari, Joseph M.	453
Bache, Dee	540
Bachik, Tom	488
Back Pocket Recording Studios	42
Back Stage	226
Background, Inc.	229
Backus, David	447
Badalucco Jr., Joseph	508
Badalucco, Michael J.	508
Badger, Matt	7, 28
Badie, Brian	477
Badura, Jorg	7
Baehler, Rebecca	433
Baer, John	505
Baez, Elaine Casillo	488
Baffa, Christopher	433
Bahamas	168
Bailey, Brian W.	534
Bailey, John	426
Bailey, K C	505
Bailey, Mary	525
Baird, Campbell	107, 388, 523, 555
Bakal, Gerald C.	508
Baker Botts, LLP	228
Baker, Ian	433
Baker, Jeffrey	398
Baker, Leah Katherine	501
Baker, Mark	550
Baker, Melanie J.	508
Baker, Phyllis Evans	523
Baker, Robert	477
Baker, Stephen A.	465
Baker, Steven N.	453
Baker, Vivian	477
Baker, William C.	527
Baker, Zene	64
Baklarz, Edward R.	465
Baklarz, Joseph R.	465
Baklarz, Richard	465
Baklarz, Robert	465
Bakr, Tamu-ra	453
Baksic, Amela	558
Bakula, Susan	563
Baldasare, Anthony	508
Balderrama, Tony	433
Baldi, Christian	453
Baldoni, Gail	555
Balducci, Sirad	497
Balducci's	159
Baldwin, Whit	257
Balfour, Cynthia	525
Baliski, Joseph W.	453
Ball, James	408
Ball, Justin	104
Ballantine, Jason	64
Ballard, Karen	505
Balletto, Linda	477
Ballhaus, Florian	426
Ballhaus, Jan	447
Ballou, Bill	418
Ballou, Jasmine	508
Balsmeyer, Randall	426
Baltarzuk, Alexandra	534
Balton, Bruce	408, 465
Balton, Robert	408
Balzarini, Matthew	398
Balzarini, Steven J.	534
Bambini Casting & Wrangling/Michele Avantario	215, 386, 541
Band Pro Film & Digital, Inc.	285
Bandolier, Inc.	363
Baney, David G.	453
Bang Music	82
Bang, Paul F.	534
Banks Jr., Joseph J.	453
Banks, Larry	426
Banks, Raphael (Andre)	453
Baptista, Cesar S.	465
Baptiste-Cummins, Joane	501
Barangan, Hernan	64
Barasch, Mark	51
Baratta, Gene	465
Baratta, James	465
Baratta, Richard	504, 550
Barbalat, Yosef	418
Barbara McNamara Casting, LLC	215, 229
Barbara's Animal People	209
Barber, Alex	433
Barbera, Peter	447
Barbizon	304, 311, 318
Barbosa, Daniela	527
Barbosa, Pattie	563

Company/Crew Index

Name	Page
Barclay Church Supply	334, 373
Barclay, Shelley	508
Barco, Inc.	285
Bardach, Moshe	550
Bardo, Britt	558
Bardolf, Scott	534
Bardunias, Caryn	477
Bari Restaurant Equipment	372
Barish, Geoff	7
Barker, Mia	433
Barker, Nicholas	7
Barker, Phillip	391
Barklage, Jeff	433
Barkley Kalpak Associates	232
Barn Truck Rental	156, 157, 319
Barnable, Lisa	64
BarnDoor Lighting Outfitters	311
Barnes, Brigette	552
Barnes, David	523, 532
Barnes, Emily	558
Barnes, George	64, 413, 433
Barnes, Gilly	7
Barnes, Guy	391
Barnes, James P.	465
Barnes, Kenneth W.	508
Barnes, Michael	465
Barnes, Michael C.	423
Barnes, Patricia A.	423
Barnes Russell	388
Barnes, Scott	488
Barocci, Robert	426
Baron, Caroline	550
Baron, David	398
Baron, Fabien	7
Baron, Junior	534
Barone, Carole	477, 488
Barose, Nick	488
Barosky, Michael A.	534
Barouh, Benoit	391
Barr, Brenda	523, 558
Barr, John	433
Barr, Stephanie	477
Barratt, David	51
Barraza, Monica D.	501
Barrer, Jane	184, 450, 527
Barreto, John T.	508
Barrett Jr., Gerald A.	465
Barrett, Joshua	488
Barrett, K.K.	391
Barrett, Michael	433
Barrios-Smith, Monica	398
Barron, Lynn	488
Barrow, Clayton	453
Barrow, Michael F.	426, 453
Barrow, Peter	426
Barrow, Stephen C.	464
Barry, Michael	426
Barry, Michael Wiliam	534
Barry, Mitch	488
Bartell, Philip	64
Bartelme, Jane	497
Bartle Bogle Hegarty	2
Bartlett, Poppy	391
Bartley, John S.	433
Bartok, Tiffany	488
Barton, Alison C.	465
Barton, Shawn	558
Barton, Will	64
Bartossik, Nikolai	107
Baseline, Inc.	226
Baseman, Andrew	508, 532
Basile, John M.	508
Basinski, Laurence	534
Baskin, Jonathan	64
Bass, Gita	488
Bass, Linda	558
Bastille, Ned	64
Bateaux New York	249
Bateman, June	391, 508, 532
Batey, Shawn	508
Bathhouse Studios	127
Battaglia, Robert	508
Battaglio, Amelia	391
Battat, Stacey	555
Batteau, Robin	51
Battersby-Green, Donna	477
Battistoni, Mario	15
Battle, Wesley S.	465
Battlegrounds	94
Batwin & Robin Productions	21
Bauer, Robert G.	465
Bauer, Rodney	465
Bauer, Sam	64
Bauer-Espinosa, Cynthia	527
Bauers, John	51
Baumann, Axel	408
Baumgartner, Robert A.	453
Baumwell Graphics, Inc.	342
Bautista, Steve	540
Baxter & Liebchen	345
Baxter, Alayne D.	508
Baxter, Richard W.	453
Bayersdorfer, Grady J.	453
Baylin, Zachary	508
Bayo, Guy	477
Bayron, Wylda	408
Bazelli, Bojan	434
BBC Motion Gallery, Los Angeles	95, 292
BBC Motion Gallery, New York	95, 292
BBC Motion Gallery, Toronto	95, 292
BBDO New York	2
BBL Mobile, Inc.	192
BBP, Inc.	38
BC Video, Inc.	38
Be Seated, Inc.	340, 373
Beacon Theatre, The	187
Beall, Thomas	563
Beaman, Daniel	465
Bean, Chris	426
Bean, Christopher	7
Bean, Kevan	7, 426
Bean, Monique	558
Bear Locations	184
Bear, Rhet	434
BearCom	164
Bearden, Adrienne	477
Bearden, Ashley	501
Beasley, Bill	497
Beast TV	47
Beaton, Kelly	453
Beatstreet Productions	42, 82
Beattie, Christopher	465
Beaucarne, Christophe	434
Beauchamp, Eric	391
Beaudoin, Jocelyne	508
Beauman, Nicholas	64
Beauty Props	348, 373
Beavan, Jenny	558
Becchio, Robert	398
Bechini, Gustavo	453
Beck, Jonathan	398
Beck, Joseph	453
Beck, Michelle	477
Beck, Philip	508
Beck, Richard	453
Becker, Brian A.	418
Becker, Judy	391
Becker, Melvin M.	534
Becker, Regis	426
Beckman, Adam	426
Beckerman, Jeff	64
Bed & Breakfast Network of New York	177
Bedard, Michael A.	534
Bederman, Michael	550
Bedford Hotel	177
Bedi, Charles	408
Bednark, Michael	391
Bednark Studio	111
Bee Harris Productions, Inc.	21, 60
Beehive, Inc.	47, 102
Beekman Tower	177
Beer, Steven C.	228
Beers, Sarah	558
Beeson-de Havenon Susan	391, 508, 532
Beethoven Pianos	353
Begin, Julie	488
Begley, John J.	453
Behan, Ruark	465
Behar, Robert	558
Behind the Scenes	151
Behrle, Keith	434
Beier, Evan	501
Beitler, R.N. Maureen	383
Bek, Young	488
Beket, J. R.	453
BeKiaris, James J.	453
Belanger, Christopher P.	465
Belcher, Dana	507
Beld, David	540
Belefant, Brian	7
Beletic, Brian	7, 28
Belgian Consulate General	165
Belinski, Jonathan	434
Bell, Alan	64
Bell, Bruce	383
Bell, Deborah	477
Bell, Fifi	558
Bell III, George	453

Company/Crew Index

Name	Page
Bell, Joshua	239
Bell, Martin	7
Bell, Patty	477
Bella, Teri	388, 508, 532
Bellafiore, Charles	508
Bellair Express	151
Bellairs, Bob	408
Bellamy, Eric Robert	239
Bellanca, Todd	7, 28
Bellavia, Carl	185
Belle, Alycia	558
Belletier, James	398
Bellhouse, Max	391
Bellisio, Angela	398
Bellitto, Jason	398
Bellizzi's Broadway Catering	159
Belluschi, Cat	391, 523
Belmond, Charlene	477
Belmonte, Braden	398
Belous, Anna-Alisa	555
Belschner, Joseph	465
Beltrandi, Nancy	488
Ben Dolphin Productions	15
Ben Hillman & Company, Inc.	102
Ben Kahn Furs	334
Benach, Erin	558
Benas, Hilary	398
Benay's Bird & Animal Source, Inc.	209
Bender, Charly	64
Bender/Helper Impact	34
Bender, Samuel	453
Benedetti, Robert	398
Benedict, Bruce	434
Beneke, Stacy	488
Benevento, Anthony J.	508
Beng, Sng Tong	7
Benham, Christopher	51
Benison, Peter	434
Benizzi, Nicola	398
Benjamin, Jason	534
Benjamin, Mark	7, 426
Benjamin Productions, Inc.	15
Benjamin, The	177
Benner, Dyne	452
Bennett, Elise	109, 388
Bennett, Joan	497, 526
Bennett, Joseph	391
Bennett, Juanita	477
Bennett, Kevin	477
Bennett, Laurence	391
Bennett, Mark Raymon	7
Bennett, Richard	418
Bennett, Robert	418
Bennhoff, Brian	527
Benninghoff, David S	508, 523
Benning, Jeremy	434
Beno, Howie	51
Bens Luxury Car & Limousine Service, Inc.	181
Benson, Laura	501, 550
Benson, Terence	540
Bentjen, Rebecca	558
Bentley, The	177
Benzinger, Suzy	555
Berdan, Brian	64
Berg, Michael	408, 417, 434, 453
Berg, Nancy	488
Berg, Peter	7
Berg, Richard	391
Berg, Russell J.	508
Berg, Timothy	453
Bergbom, Brad	534
Bergdorf Goodman	376
Berger, Alan	447
Berger, Andreas	434
Berger, Barry	477
Berger, Maria	488
Berger, Richard	398
BERGFX	326
Bergh, Jeb	413, 417
Berghoff, Julie	391
Bergin, Tom	534
Berkal, Eric	450
Berkelbach, Mary Frances	383
Berkeley, Pamela	109
Berliner, Roshelle	388
Berman, Audrey	488
Berman, Robert	550
Berman, Shari	7
Bermuda Limousine International	181
Bermudez, Carlos	426
Bernard, Adam	527
Bernard, Andrew	388, 508
Bernard, Evan	7
Bernard, Michael D.	434
Bernardini, Ken	7
Bernberg, Lana	434
Berndt, Wiebke	7
Berner, Bernard	426
Berner, Kim	525
Berner, Paul	434
Bernfeld, Win	408
Bernhard-Link Theatrical LLC	126
Bernknopf, Ronald A.	552
Bernkopf, David	426
Bernstein, Eileen	497
Bernstein, Jeffrey	447
Bernstein, Kristin	527
Bernstein, Martin	418
Bero, Mark	326, 508
Berona, Barry	434
Berritto, Simone	477
Berry, John	453
Berry, Kathy	35
Bertini, Pamela Joan	501
Bertolotti, Gina	488
Bertolozzi, Sonya	477, 488
Bertoni, Stephanie A.	525
Bertrand, Bruce	64, 104
Best III, Alexander	534
Best, Kate	477
Best Shot	95
Beste, Christopher J.	453
Bestway Coach Express	155
Beth Melsky Casting	216
Beth Melsky Satellite Casting	78, 225
Betrancourt, Alain	434
Betsy Davis Backdrops	109
Betty Rankin Locations Unlimited	185
Betulia, Peter A.	465
Betzag, Michael J.	465
Beukes, Avril	64
Bevan Sound	42
Bevenger, Rob	558
Bewley, Lois	558
Bexel	274, 280
Beyda, Kent	64
Beyer, Charles	398
Beymer, John	434
Beyond Our Reality Productions, Inc.	85, 200, 280, 288
Bezahler, Alysse	550
Bialer, Donald M.	465
Bianchi, Adam	465
Bianchini, George	408, 415
Bianco, Annette	477
Bianco, Teresa	477
Bicknell, Michael	453
Biddle, Adam	434
Biear, Stephanie	563
Biebel, Tom	534
Bierlein, Christopher	434
Biernacki, Henry T.	418
Big Apple Car, Inc.	181
Big Apple Visual Group	342
Big Chair Creative Group	2
Big Film Design	53, 102
Big Foot Productions, Inc.	275, 280
Big House Production Group, The	85
Big Mo Pro, Inc.	268
Big Shot, Inc.	192
Big Sky Editorial	47
Big Wave Music	82
Big Yellow Duck	42, 82
Biggs, Janice	497
Bigwood, James	550
Bill Bachmann Studios	95
Bill Dance Casting	229
Bill Quinn Productions	15, 21
Billard, Katri	525
Billboard	226
Billeci, J.B.	453
Billeter, Manuel	408
Billig, Michael	447, 508
Billin, Beverly	501
Billow, Brette	501
Billow, Brian	7
Billups, Scott	425
Bilotti, Wayne	477
Bilous DiBucci Music/Helium Vault Music Library	82
Bilous, Edward	51
Bilz, James	508
Bimmy's Caterers	159
Binasiewicz, Stephen J.	508
Bingemann, Anna	558
Bingham, Chris	477
Binghamton Regional Airport	154
Binkley, Paul	35
Binney, Nixon	426
Bionic	42, 47, 85, 288

Name	Page
Bird, Ivan	434
Bird, Jaimie	509
Bird, Joseph L.	509
Bird, Joseph R.	509
Bird, Kevin	388
Bird, Michael	509
Bird, Timothy	447
Birds & Animals Unlimited East	209
Birkett-Foa, Gioia	534
Birnbaum, R.N. Debra	383
Biscaino, Vincent J.	465
Biscoe, Kate	488
Biscoe, Katherine	477
Biscoe, Max	391
Bishop, Dan	391
Bishop, Maceo	408, 415
Bishop, Stephen	477, 488
Bishop, William J.	509
Bisogna, Joseph A.	418
Bissell, Jim	391
Bivens, Heidi	558
Black Book, The	226
Black Dog Films (RSA Films)	30
Black Dog Jib Productions, Inc.	296
Black, Heidi	64
Black, Kevin A.	239
Black, Marc	51
Black Market Music	82
Black, Sarah E.	453
Black, Taylor L.	501
Black Watch Editorial	47, 85
Black Watch Productions	15, 21, 30, 200
Blackburn, Ray	465
BlackLight Films	96, 292
Blackmagic Design	285
Blackman, Stephen	434
Blackstone Stock Footage	96
Blackwell, Deanna	488
Blades, Matt	465
Blagg, Alan	465
Blaho, Steven A.	465
Blahut, Peter J.	453
Blainey, Sue	64
Blair, Robert G.	453
Blake, Deborah	383
Blake, Kevin E.	509
Blake, Walter E.	418
Blakeslee, Joshua	398
Blakley Equipment	205, 309
Blancato, Tom	453
Blanchette, Laurent	465
Blanchette, Marina	465
Blanck, Peter	426
Blandi, Luca	488
Blandi, Oscar	488
Blandori, Marc	426
Blankenhorn, Craig	505
Blank, Lyda	527
Blaschke, Jarin	434
Blatt Billiards Supply Corp.	375
Blatte, Marc	51
Blechman, Peter	418
Bleecker Prompting, Inc.	271
Bleier, Daniel M.	509
Bleier, Douglas A.	418
Bleier, Gena	64
Bleifeld, Neil	534
Blicker, Erik	51
BLINK Digital	58
Blinking Eye Media	47, 53, 102
Blischok, Troy	398
Blitz, Irv	7
Bloch, Catherine	527
Block, Jean	477, 489
Block, Richard	107
Block, Susan	509
Blomkamp, Neill	7
Bloodwell, Ben	398
Bloom, Donna	550
Bloom, Julie A.	447
Bloomingdale's	376
Blount, Cynthia	527
BLS Limo	181
Bluck, Nigel	434
Blue Bell Lumber & Moulding Co., Inc.	329
Blue Fier Photography/Blue Fier	96
Blue Sky Stock Footage/Bill Mitchell	96, 292
Blue Sky Studios, Inc.	5, 53
Blue Star Jets	150
Bluebird Express Courier, LLC	151
Blum, Arthur	465
Blum, Bill	504
Blum, Joanne	525
Blum, Pamela	453
Blume, Susan	107, 109
Blumenthal, Andy	64
Blunt, Kristi	523
Boak, Michael	109, 391
Boardwalk Entertainment/Alan Wagner Productions	38
Bobick, John T.	465
Bobin, Chris	324, 334, 363
Bobonis, Lisa	526
bobsyouruncle	15, 33, 47
Bocce Club Pictures, LLC	15, 30, 200
Boccia, Frank A.	418
Boccia, Margot	477
Boccia, Tara Joy	509
Bock, Larry	64
Bock, Sheila	509
Bocquet, Gavin	391
Bode-Tyson, Susan S.	509
Bodner Josh	64
Boehling, Garrett	465
Boehm, Cyndie	477
Boeing	187
Boeing Image Licensing	96
Boesch, Gary E.	418
Boesch, John	465
Bogdahn, Kip	426
Bogen, Bob	408
Bogen Imaging, Inc.	311
Boguski, Doc	501
Bokelberg, Oliver	426
Bokor Jr., James C.	465
Bokor, Keith Robert	465
Boland, Jodie	489
Boland/Eggmann Casting	216
Boles III, Thomas J.	465
Bolesta, Joseph J.	453
Bollinger, Frank	391
Bollywood Hollywood Production, Inc.	200
Bolte Medical Urgent Care Center NYC	386
Bolton, Michael	391
Bolz, John	534
Bolz, John H.	465
Bolz, Teresa Ann	509
Bomba, David	391
Bombay Couriers	235
Bonacorda, Joseph P.	453
Bonafina Films	21
Bonanni-Castorino, Laura	477
Bonanno, Chris	7
Bonanno, John	434
Boncher, Eric A.	453
BOND	47, 102
BOND Audio	43
BOND Edit	53
Bonded Services	73
Bongarbiz	246
Bongirne, Chris	550
Boni, Dennis	408, 414
Boniece, James	465
Bonilla, Hugo	453
Bonney, Norman	434
Bonnie Ott Promotions, Inc.	245
Bonny, Jan	7
Bono, James	509
Boome, Adam	64
Boonstra, Michael	501
Boorman, James W.	453
Booth, John Earl	391
Booth, Stephen Lawrence	531
Bordas, Arle	447, 527
Borden, Craig	450
Borel, Erin	501
Borge, Vebe	447
Borgo, Karen	477
Boritt, Beowulf	388
Boritz, Margaret	106
Borman, Rebecca	477
Born, Eli	434
Bornstein, Carrie	497, 504
Bornstein, Charles	64
Borowiak, Patrick	398
Borsen, Teddy	7
Borsetto, Marissa	558
Borsuk, Ethan	398
Bortner, Robert	465
Bortner, Rolf H.	465
Bosco, Anna	239
Bosko, Dan	64
Bosmajian, Harlan	434
Bosma, Karen	501
Bostock, Billy	391
Boston Camera Rental Co.	259, 275, 280
Boston Road Equipment Rentals, Inc.	303
Bostwick, Joan G.	527
Boswell, Merideth	391

Name	Page
Botticelli, Michelle	64
Botula, Brett	504, 527
Bouadana, Ghilaine	563
Boucher, Michael	509
Boudet, Frederic	489
Bouklas, Penelope	558
Bourassa, Frank	398
Bourbonnais, Marissa	489
Boushell, Lorraine	477
Bowe, Kevin	534
Bowen, Douglas M.	418
Bowen, Kim	558
Bowen, Shannon R.	509
Bowen, Thomas F.	418
Bower, Christopher	453
Bower, Stephen	426
Bowers, David	465
Bowery Ballroom, The	249
Bowes, Michael	503
Bow Wow Productions	209
Bowman, Chase	434
Bowman, Paul	509
Boxer, Daniel	509
BOXX Technologies, Inc.	285
Boyce Jr., Timothy R. (T.R.)	534
Boyd, Cassandra	388
Boyd, Coburn	509
Boyd, John	434
Boyd, Michael T.	558
Boyd, Paul	465
Boyd, Russell	434
Boyd, Scott	64
Boyer, Tommy	563
Boylan, Brown, Code, Vigdor & Wilson	228
Boyle, Geoff	434
Boyle, Stephen M.	239
Boynton, Peter	453
Boytos, Nancy	509
Bozman, Ron	497, 550
Bra*Tenders	334, 348, 376, 378
Brabaw, Janice	239
Brackett, Wayne T.	509
Bracone, Ian	398
Bracone, Tom	398, 434
Braden, Mike	434
Bradford Entertainment	38
Bradford, Molly	90, 497
Bradford, Oliver	7
Bradley International Airport	154
Bradshaw, Amy C	555
Bradshaw, Joseph J.	509
Brady, Mathew	426
Brady, Rik	465
Brainstorm Digital	53
Braisin, Kimberly	477
Brait, Nicole	453
Bramberg, Darianne	477
Branca, Salvatore R.	453
Branching Out Productions, Inc.	497, 503, 558
Brandes, Caroline	434
Brandes, Daniel	418
Brandofino, Ralph	398
Brandon, Avery	107, 109
Brandon, David W.	453
Brandon, Maryann	64
Brandt, Jack	509
Brandt, Richard L.	509
Brandt, Stephen	527
Brandwein, Jacqueline	383
Branigan, James	509, 532
Branstetter, Brian	391
Brant, Scott Franklin	239
Braswell Galleries	345, 346, 347, 350, 353
Brause, Richard	534
Bravo, Barbara	398
Bravo Studios	117, 130
Braxton, Sheridan R.	466
Brayman, Veronica	477
Brazil-Amazon	176
Brazilian Consulate General	165
Breakaway Courier Systems	235
Breakdown Services, Ltd.	226
Breard, M. Blair	504, 550
Brearton, Kristoffer	407
Breckel, Rebecca	525
Breen, Charles	391
Breen, James M.	344, 509
Breen, John	466
Breen, Theodore P.	534
Breindel, Scott M.	534
Brennan, Deirdre	509
Brennan, Martin W.	476
Brennan, Michael	466
Brennan, Michael W.	453
Brennan, Steven	509
Brennan, Thomas	418
Brenner, Ira	408, 414, 417, 434
Breschel, Lynn	453
Brian McMillan's Hollywood Animals	209
Briante, Steven	398
Brice, Christina	477
Bricker, Sarah	509
Bridge Furniture & Props	345, 346, 350, 368
Bridgeman Art Library, The	96
Bridges, James	505
Bridges, Laurel Ann	534
Bridges, Mark	558
BridgeStreet Corporate Housing Worldwide	177
Brigante, Gerard	408, 414, 415, 417
Briggs, Edward E.	509
Briggs, Jack	450, 504
Brigham, Chris	550
Bright, Kevin	466
Brignola, Jason	398
Brill, Steve	426, 434, 496
Brillant, Robert	408
Brink Jr., Conrad V.	509
Brink Sr., Conrad F.	509
Brinkmann, Robert	434
Brinster, Mark	7, 434
Brislin, Raymond	426
Brisson, Geraud	64
Brister, Ian	447
British Airways	153
British Consulate General	165
British Virgin Islands	168
Britt, Kelly J.	453
Britt, Mark	408, 417
Britton, Thomas R.	509
Britton, Tobi	489
Brixton, David	64
Broad Street	21
Broad Street Ballroom	187, 249
Broadcast Business Consultants	241
Broadcast Store	266, 294
Broaddus, Michael	391
Broadway Bound	151
Broadway Sound	43, 82
Broadway Stages	117, 127, 249
Broadway Video	38, 85
Broadway Video Duplication	56
Broadway Video Editorial	47
Brocco, Dawn	489
Brockett's Film Fauna, Inc.	210
Brockschmidt, Joan	509
Broder, Robert S.	383
Broecker, Tom	558
Brokenshire, Earle	466
Brolsma, Patricia	534
Bromberg, David M.	466
Bromelmeier, Martha Louise	555
Bronchtein, Henry	550
Brongniart, Bernard X.	466
Brooklyn College Television Center	130
Brooklyn Films	30, 47
Brooklyn Fire Proof	117
Brooklyn Independent Studios	200
Brooklyn Model Works, Inc.	363
Brooklyn Museum of Art	187, 233
Brooklyn Studios	127, 130, 187
Brooks, Faith	501
Brooks, Ira	450, 497, 550
Brook, Sydney	466
Broome Lampshades, Inc.	350
Brosnan, Justen	478
Brotherhood, Nathanael	509
Brouard, Thomas	454
Broughton, John	398
Brouillard	2
Brous, Nancy	555
Broussard, Dawn	489
Brousseau, Bryan	434
Brown, Craig	239
Brown, David	478
Brown, G. Mac	550
Brown, James	7, 28, 426
Brown, Jason A.	509
Brown, Jeffrey T.	434
Brown, Jim L.	466
Brown, Katt	64
Brown, Kenneth	447
Brown, Lauren	398
Brown, Micheline	563
Brown, Stephen	558
Brown, Tom	391
Brown, Zack	555
Brownell, Dale	478
Brozina, Deborah	398

Company/Crew Index

Name	Page
Brozinsky, Mitchell	185
Bruce, Douglas	447
Bruce-Baron, Robin	540
Bruck, Jerry	534
Bruck, Richard	466
Bruck, Rick	466
Brucker, Astrid	555
Bruel, Nicolaj	434
Brugge, Pieter Jan	497
Bruhwiler, Tanya	478
Bruinsma-Gort, Erin Daye	478
Brundage, Lauren	239
Brunetto-Lipman, Adriana	398
Bruning, Melissa	558
Brunner, Joseph	383
Bruno, Michelle	478
Brush, John	466
Brush, Paul	418
Brushfire	2
Bruzenas, Susan	478
Bryan Bantry	246, 380, 489
Bryan, Jennifer	563
Bryan, Robert	534
Bryant, Adam	489
Bryant, D. Eric	509
Bryant, Katherine Jane	558
Bryant Park Hotel	177
Bryen, David	64
Bryl, Nicole	478
Bryld, Eigil	434
Bryn, Norman	323, 478, 489
Brzozowski, Kenneth	418
Buccellato, Francesco	478
Buccellato, Peter	534
Buchanan, Jeff	64
Bucher, John M.	534
Buchholz, Fred	326, 509
Buchman, Timothy H.	418
Buchner, Alan	552
Buck, David H.	418
Buck, Michael	408, 466
Buckland IV Charles E.	466
Buckle, Kristofer	489
Buckley, Martina	391
Buckner, Jacqueline	452
Buckner, Jamie	501
BUDCO Enterprises, Inc.	296, 309
Budd Enterprises, Ltd.	319
Budde, John	426, 454
Buddee, Kim	391
Budelmann, Sven	64
Budget Films, Inc.	96, 292
Budget/Sears	156
Budget Truck Rental	157, 158, 319
Bue, Cima	398
Buehler, Laurie	563
Buffalo-Niagara International Airport	154
Bug Music Publishing	80
Bukowski, Bobby	426
Bukowski, Nicole	239
Bulavinetz, Peter	466
Bulbtronics	304, 311, 312
Buli, Charles	418
Bull, Catherine	64
Bullard, Gabrielle	7
Bullard, Robert	398
Bulldog Service	202
Bundrick, Peter	418
Bundrick, Ryan	418
Bunting Jr., Keith	466
Buonanno, Gary	450, 497
Buono, Alexander	434
Buonsanto, Danny	413
Buras, Milton	478
Burchard, Tiffany	64
Burcksen, Edgar	64
Burdick, John	408, 414
Burgard, Tim	35
Burger Design/Visions Media	21
Burgess, Don	434
Burgess, Janice	398
Burgos, Jorge P.	454
Burhop, Elizabeth/ART department TV, Inc.	391
Burke, Bill	426
Burke, Gary	51
Burke, Glynis J.	454
Burke, James P.	466
Burke, Kenneth J.	466
Burke, Matthew	398
Burke, Michael	398
Burke, Michael F.	454
Burke, Renee Foley	525
Burke, Terrence	408
Burke, Terrence C.	466
Burke, Terrence Laron	466
Burke, William	454
Burkhart, Dennis/Encounter Video	96
Burnett, James (Jamie)	454
Burnham, Alexander (Zan)	509
Burnham, Cornelia	504, 527
Burns, Paul	413, 416
Burns, Scott	7
Burnworth, Michelle	418
Burr, David	434
Burrell, F. Joseph	466
Burrell, Sam	466
Burstein, Jessica	505
Burstein, Nanette	7
Burt, Amy	563
Burt, Don	391
Burt, Graham	398
Burt, Sarah Jackson	509
Burton, Diana E.	509
Burton, Jenny	388
Burton, Linda	391
Burton, Liz	65
Burton-Akdag, Jennifer	509
Burum, Stephen H.	434
Busch, Nathan	478
Buschow, Rob	509
Bush, Jacqueline	489
Business Equipment Rentals	223
Business Methods, Inc.	223
Bussant, Jamie	398
Butcher, Jeff	509
Buteau, Brian	509
Butler, Bill	434
Butler, Kate	399
Butler, Richard W.	388
Butler, Rick	388
Butler-Dougherty, Lauren	501
Buttons Sound, Inc.	43
Butts, Kenneth	399
Butwell, Anna	509
Buzz, Inc.	43, 85, 288
Buzzco Associates, Inc.	5
BVR, Ltd.	259, 275, 280, 296
Byer, Allan	534
Byers, George	399
Bylander, Sheri	65
Byrd, Jeffrey	408
Byrne, Damien	392
Byrne, Erin	563
Byrne, Gifford	563
Byrne, Michael P.	466
BZ/Rights & Permissions, Inc.	233

C

Name	Page
C & S Int'l Insurance Brokers Inc.	230
C&C Studios	78, 117, 130, 268
C-TRL Labs, Inc.	53
Caballero, Eugenio	392
Caban, Edwin	509
Caban, Wilfred	509
Cabana, Rob	65
Cabbages and Kings	160, 424
CableTrak Systems, Inc.	296
Cablecam International, Inc.	280, 296
Cabrera, Eva Z.	525
Cacioli, Laurie	478
Cadalzo, Travis	399
Cadd, Ray	35
Cade, Paul	7
Cado, Ljiljana	478
Cadorette-Acehan, Danielle	563
Cady, Patrick	434
Cager, Donald	504
Caglione Jr., John	478
Cahill, Gregory	466
Cahill, John F.	509
Cahill, Kevin	466
Cailliarec, Pierre	447
Caimi, Paolo	426
Cain, Lance	65
Caio, Tony	7
Cal James Entertainment, Inc.	232
Calabrese, Chris	478
Calas, Leni	509
Caldwell, Ellen	392
Caldwell, Peter C.	454
Caldwell, Robert	454
Caldwell, Stephen	107, 388
Califano, Alfred	447
Califano, Greg	434
Califano, Keith	466
Califano, Kevin	466
California	168
Calitri, Steven C.	408, 454

Company/Crew Index

Name	Page
Call Cuisine Caterers	160
Call the Cops	246
Call-A-Head Corporation	198
Callaghan, Colleen	478
Callaghan Kymbra	478
Callahan, Ryan J.	466
Callahan, William J.	454
Callanan, James	426
Callaway, Thomas	434
Callegari, Victor	478
Calumet Photographic Pro Center	262
Calvaruso, Maria	399
Calzone Case Company	318
Camarda, George	525
Camarro, Paul	509, 532
Camart Studio	127
Cambria, David	454
Cambria, Michael	399
Cambridge Cleaners	338
Cambridge Security Services Corp.	202
Camden County Airport	154
Camelot Catering	160
Camelot Communications Group	15
Camera Cars Unlimited, Inc.	258
Camera Copters, Inc.	254
Camera Moves	296
Camera Obscura, Ltd.	259
Camera One	96, 292
CameraOne Video Production	21
Cameron, Allan	392
Cameron, David	7
Cameron, Dennis	540
Cameron, Don	8
Cameron, Paul	434
Cameron, Susan	208
Camp, J. Eric	425
Campayno, Joseph	478
Campbell, Carol	478
Campbell, Casey	454
Campbell, Dana	558
Campbell, Lynn	478
Campbell, Malcolm	65
Campbell, Matthew Vose	447
Campbell, Murdoch	426
Campbell, William	563
Campe, Brian	527
Campenni, Tony	466
Camping Station	331
Campolo, James F.	466
Campolo Jr., Carmen M.	509
Campus Coach Lines	155
Camuto, Vincent C.	534
Camuto, Vincent P.	534
Canada-Alberta	168
Canada-Argenteuil Laurentians	168
Canada-British Columbia	168
Canada-Calgary	168
Canada-Columbia Shuswap	168
Canada-Edmonton	168
Canada-Manitoba	168
Canada-Montreal	168
Canada-Nanaimo	168
Canada-New Brunswick	170
Canada-Newfoundland	170
Canada-Northwest Territories	170
Canada-Nova Scotia	170
Canada-Nunavut Territory	170
Canada-Okanagan	170
Canada-Ontario	170
Canada-Prince Edward Island	170
Canada-Quebec City	170
Canada-Saskatchewan	170
Canada-Thompson-Nicola	170
Canada-Toronto	170
Canada-Yukon	170
Canadian Press Images, The	96
Canal Street Studio	111
Canavan, Jeff	65
Cancel, Jerry	408
Candle Business Systems, Inc.	223
Candreva, James	399
Candreva, Nick	399
Candrilli, Paul	466
Canelos, Damian E.	534
Canfield, Deborah N.	509
Canfield, Don	399, 413
Canfield, Jeffrey	399
Canfield, Kelly T.	509
Canfield, Philip C.	509
Canfield, Scott	509
Canfield, Shannon	509
Canfield-Longo, Patrice	509
Canfield-Mahon, Jacqueline	509
Cange, Brian David	497
Canicio, Greg	466
Caniglia, Valentina	434
Canino Jr., Clement	552
Cannava, Nancy	497
Canney, Paul	8
Cannold, Jay	504, 550
Cannon, Bruce	65
Canon	285
Cantaldi, Brian	239
Cantarella, Luke	388
Canto, Jacqueline	509
Canton, Daniel B.	454
Cantrell, Christine	478
Cap 21 Studios	221
Cape, Yves	8
Capital Scenic, Inc.	111, 245, 363
Capitol Fishing Tackle	375
Capitol Glass & Sash Co., Inc.	347
Caplan, Dan	35
Capone, Patrick	426
Cappa, Michael	466
Cappello, James	418
Cappelluti, Rose Marie	563
CAPS Universal	241
Capsule Studio	127
Captain Mike's Diving/Michael Carew	236, 375, 549
CaptionMax	102
Captiv 8 Hats	245
Capuano, Andrew C.	534
Capucilli, Bill	418
Caracciola, Lisa L.	383
Caracciolo Jr., Joseph M.	509
Caracciolo, Michael	408, 415
Caravan West Productions	246
Carballar, Luis	65
Carbone, Franco	392
Cardenas, Charisse	392
Cardoni, John	454
Carell, Candace	478
Carella, Candice	558
Carey, Gordon	65
Carey-Perazzo, Patty	527
Carhart, John	65
Caribbean Images	96
Carino, Salvatore	239
Cariot, James P.	418
Carizma Lighting	181
Carl Barth Images	96
Carl Michaels Catering	160
Carl Paolino Studios, Inc.	5, 323, 363
Carl Posey Catering	160
Carl Waltzer Digital Service	342
Carlesimo, Gregg	550
Carleton, Mary (Mickey)	563
Carlino, James	418
Carlson, Eric	65
Carlson, Rey	8, 28
Carlton on Madison Avenue, The	177
Carlyle, The	177
Carman, James	434
Carmel	182
Carmichael, Brian	552
Carmine, Michael	426
Carmody, Christian	399
Carmody, Ian	399
Carnahan, Joe	8
Carner, Mitchell	466
Carney, Jean	478
Carol Hanzel Casting	216
Carole Stupell, Ltd.	372, 373
Carollo, Joyce	478
Carolyn Wade Productions, Inc.	21
Caron, Charles Jefferson	527
Caron, Dominique	454
Caronia, Tony	8
Carovillano, Vincenza	478
Carp, Dan	426
Carp, Jean-Philippe	392
Carpel Video	266, 294
Carpenter, Peter	35
Carpenter, Rhys	273, 454, 554
Carpenter, Robert W.	532
Carpenter, Russell	435
Carr, David M.	466
Carr, Julie	65
Carrafa, John	221
Carranza, Andrew	435
Carraro, William	550
Carriker-Thayer, Teresa M.	388
Carrillo, Will	489
Carroll, Anne	527
Carroll, Chris	450
Carroll, Joe	51
Carroll, Shawn	392

Company/Crew Index

Name	Page
Carroll, Stephanie	388, 532
Carroll, Thomas	399, 534
Cars for Films	355
Cars on Location	158, 192, 319, 332, 355
Carsch, Ruth Gayle	478
Carson, Anne	399
Carter, Craig	478
Carter, Jonathan J.	509
Carter, Roderick	478
Carter, Ruth	558
Carter, Stephen	388
Carter, Yolanda	563
Cartwright, Carolyn	509, 532
Cartwright, Lori	478
Carucci, Joel F.	466
Caruso, Joe	418, 435
Caruso, Phillip	505
Carvalho, Lula	435
Cary, Oliver	408
Casablanca Hotel	177
Casablanca Promotions, Inc.	245
Casala, Ltd.	541
Casanas, Cristina	509
Cascarelli, Stephen	509
Casey, Daniel	399
Casey, James A.	466
Casillo, Charles	466
Casillo, Joseph	466
Casillo-Baez, Elaine	478
Caso, Guy M.	454
Cassavetes, Nick	8
Cassel, Matthew	65
Cassidy, Dan	466
Cassidy, Janet	478, 489
Cassidy, Jay	65
Cassidy, Michael C.	466
Cassidy, Sean	466
Cassidy, William	466
Cassone Leasing, Inc.	192
Casswood Insurance Agency, Ltd.	230
Cast & Crew Entertainment Services	241
Castaldo, Eric	466
Castellano, Gina	239
Castelli Models & Effects	323, 361, 363
Castillo, David C.	426
Casting Society of America	546
Casting Solutions	216
Castle & Pierpont	232, 344
Castro, Jose	408
Castro, Pedro	435
Cat, Ivan	35
Catalano, David	527
Catalano, Francis L.	466
Catania, Mark	466
Catcherelli, Alex	554
Cates, Rachel	501
Cathay Pacific	153
Cathedral Church of St. John the Divine	249
Caton, Matthew	435
Catsikeas, Ellen Athena	527
Caulk, Matthew	399
Cavagnet, Andrew	552
Cavagrotti, Michael	447
Cavallo Jr., Arthur J.	552
Cavanaugh, Ann D.	454
Cavanaugh, Deborah	399
Cawley, Sarah	435
Caydem, Alexis	478
CBS Coverage Group, Inc.	230
CBS News Archives/BBC Motion Gallery	96
CBS Television Design & Set Construction	111
CDM Sound Studios	43
Cecil, Charles	418
Cecil, David Wade	454
CECO International	31, 117, 304, 306, 312
Cederquist, Pamela	527
Celada, Benedett	478
Celada, Valentin	478
CELCO	285
CelebrityFootage	96, 292
Celefex	53
Celimli, Evren	51
Cella, Stefania	392
Cellary, Christopher	454
Celsius Films	15
Cenatiempo, Christopher	399
Center for Design, Digital Arts and Film - NYU	548
Center Line Studios, Inc.	111
Center Stage/NY	221
Centoducati, Benjamin	407
Central Casting	229
Central Jersey Regional Airport	154
Centre Firearms Co., Inc.	341
Cerbone, Anthony J.	504
Cernjul, Vanja	427
Cerny, Michael	8
Cerria, Drew	399
Cerrone, Donald J.	466
Cerullo, Michael J.	466
Cesana, Andrew	525
Cesario, Michael J.	555, 558
Cespedes, Henry	510
Cestare, Suzanne E.	510
Chalakov, Kamen	35
Chamberlain, Doug	435
Chambers	177
Chambers, David	527
Chambers, Jenn	65
Chambliss, Scott	392
Chamma, Giselle	427
Champagne, Michelle	478
Champignon	160
Champion, Bonnie	447
Chan-Shue, Duane	454
Chandler, Mark	523
Chandy, Kay	478
Chanfrault, Francois Eudes	51
Chang, Bernard	35
Chang, Derek	8
Channelbass	268
Chantiles Vigneault Casting, Inc.	216
Chapman, David	392
Chapman, Kimberli Lynne	510
Chapman, Michael	435
Chappel, Tim	558
Chappell, Bob	8
Chappell, Robert	427
Character Translations, Inc.	334
Charged, LLC	5
Charlemagne, Sasha	501
Charles, Allan	427
Charles Banfield Productions	232
Charles, Christian	8
Charles, Cliff	408, 435
Charles Lubin Company, Inc.	344
Charlex, Inc.	53, 288
Charrette	325
Chase, Samuel	454
Chase, Steve	8
Chase, William Robert	550
Chasing Locations	185
Chateau Theatrical Animals & Chateau Stable	210
Chatman-Royce, April	489
Chatterton, Rose	478
Chautauqua County Airport	154
Chavez, Chuy	435
Chea, Claudio	435
Cheatham, Justin T.	454
Chebac, Mihai	427
Chedd, David G.	454
Chediak, Enrique	435
Cheleden, Noreen	527
Chelrae Carting LLC	231
Chelsea Broadcast Services, Inc.	117, 130
Chelsea Garden Center	344
Chelsea Inn	177
Chelsea Motor Rental	158, 320
Chelsea Pictures	15
Chelsea Piers	187, 249
Chelsea Post	56, 85, 283, 288
Chemical Music	82
Chemtob, Robert	185
Chen, LeRoy	399
Chen, Lulu	558
Chenel, Christopher	510
Cheng, Kai Wai	466
Chennault, Tony (Ty)	454
Cheponis, Paul	510
Cheripka, Eric	510
Chernichaw, Limor	478
Cherry Lane Music Publishing	80
Cherry, Larry	478
Cherry, Peter	8
Chertok Associates Inc. - Jazz On Film	96
Cheryl Quarantiello	550
Cheshire Jr., John	454
Cheshire, Molly	454
Chess Forum	347
Chesterman, Frederick	466
Chestnut, Scott	392
Cheung, Andrew	466
Cheung, Radium L.	454
Chevalier, Justine	563
Cheverie, Suzanne	523
Chevillot, Patrick M.	555
Chew, Richard	65
Cheyenne	489
Chiate, Debra	65

Company/Crew Index

Name	Page(s)
Chibnall, Jonathan	65
Chicagoland News Footage	96
Chichester, John	392
Chief Equipment, Inc.	303
Chien, Jean	527
Chien, Nina	399
Childs, Ziska	109, 116
Chiment, Marie Anne	555, 558
Chimples, John	8, 65, 408, 414, 417
Chin, Betty	501
Chin, Judy	478
China Airlines	153
China Club, The	249
Chinagraph	47
Chinlund, James	392
Chinnery, Michelle	478
Chinoy, Spencer	8
Chirrone, Shannon	65
Chisolm, Richard	427
Chiu, Kim	489
Chiu, Robert	478
Chloe Productions, Inc.	216, 241
Cho, Sung Rae	399
Choi, Jane	478
Choi, Jiye	35
Choice Courier	235
Choices: The Recovery Bookstore	373
Chomet Editing	85
Chomyn, Christopher	435
Chosed, Scott	65
Chosen Pictures	47, 60
Choudhury, Gautam K.	534
Chressanthis, James	435
Chris French Cleaners	338
Chris Scalf Illustrations Inc.	35
Christensen, Pernille Bech	65
Christiano, Jeffrey	510
Christie, Neil	454
Christin, Leslie	478
Christmas and Holiday Music	80
Christodoulou, Jon M.	534
Christofori, Joseph	399
Christopher Films	200
Christopher, Samuel	8
Christou, Andrew	8
Chromavision	47, 56, 84, 102, 283
Chu, Eddy	8
Chuck, Wendy	558
Chung, Chunghoon	435
Churchill Corporate Services	177
Churchill Residence Suites	177
Church Street Boxing Gym	187, 375
Chusid, Barry	392
Chyron Corporation	285
Ciampa, Daniel	107
Cianchetta, Frank M.	534
Ciardiello, Dominick	408
Ciccimarro, John J.	418
Cicerchi, Danajean	563
Cicero, Angelo P.	454
Cichon, Mariusz	425
Cicio, Justeen	399
Cieslinski, Carol	497
Cifelli, Andrew	435
Ciganek-Bernini, Lois H.	510
Cimmelli, Hugo J.	510
Cimmelli, Inc.	363
Cimmelli, Leah	510
Cine 60	306, 312
Cine Magic Stages	117, 259, 263
Cine Magnetics Digital & Video Laboratories	56, 58
Cine South de Mexico	201
Cine-Com Payroll	222
Cine/drsa International	15, 201
Cine-Med	386
Cinema Drivers/Tom Anthony's Driving Team	542
Cinema Rentals, Inc.	236, 246, 259, 275
Cinema World Medical Division	386
Cinema World Studios	117, 351
Cinema-Vision	259, 280
CineMarine Team - Cinema Rentals, Inc.	328
Cinematicstunts.com/John-Eric Schuman	246, 341, 542
Cinergy Pictures, Inc.	200
Cinetrax	80
Cinram	58
Ciocca, Stefano	558
Cioccio, Thomas	399
Ciotti, Archangelo V.	466
Cirabisi, John	104
Cirbes, Jeffrey	425
Circle Line Cruises	328
Circle Visual, Inc.	336, 340, 342
Circuit Lighting, Inc.	126, 312
Cirella, Daniel	408
Ciric, Katharine	527
Cirigliano, Charles	418
Citarella, Mary C.	107
Citi Furnished	177
CitiCam Film & Video Services, Inc.	22, 38, 200
CitiCam Video Services, Inc.	86, 275
Citigate Albert Frank	2
CitiVans	192
Citrano, Thomas David	540
Citrone, Richard J.	454
City Expeditor, Inc.	235
City Hall	249
City Intercoms, Inc.	378
City Knickerbocker, Inc.	350
City Lights fx	53
City Lights Home Entertainment	58
City Lights Media Group	56, 86
City Lights Pictures	27
City Lights Post	43, 47, 288
City Lights Productions	15, 22, 30, 33, 200
City Lights Television	38
City Sound Productions	43
City Stage	31, 117, 221, 249
Ciurea, Marcel	466
Cizmazia, Sonja	563
CK Security Group, Inc.	202
Claessen, David	435
Claflin, Brandon	478
Clancy, Michael	555
Clapp, Nathan	399
Claps, Luann	478
Claravall, Sandra	478
Clare, Peter J.	454
Clark, Amanda (Amy)	555
Clark, AmyJoy	501
Clark, Chris	478
Clark, Curtis	8, 435
Clark, Greg	489
Clark, Harry	399
Clark, Joshua	510
Clark, Laurence	418
Clark, Matthew	427
Clark Media	275, 280
Clark, Phil	466
Clark, Rodney	418
Clark, Thomas	466
Clarke, Andrew	454
Clarke, Bill	109
Claro, Manuel Alberto	435
Class Act Location Service	192
Classic Cars	355
Classic Model & Talent, Inc.	246
Claxton, William R.	466
Clay Lacy Aviation, Inc.	96
Claybourne, Doug	550
Clayton, Damion	65
Clayton, Len X.	388
Clayton, Magdalene	563
Clayton, Pashelle	563
Claywell, Mark	8
Clear Talent Group/CTG	221, 246, 380
Clearance Domain LLC	233, 362
Cleary, Angeline	423
Cleary, Keith	418
Clemens, John	399
Clendaniel, Cameron	65
Cleri Model Management	246
Clevergreen Cleaners	338
Cliff Freeman & Partners	2
Cliff, Jonathan	435
Clifford, John	505
Clip Joint for Film, The	96
Clipboard Productions	22
Clock Wise Productions	22, 200
Clockwork Apple, Inc.	363
Cloud Tours	204
Clubfone, Inc.	249
Cmylo, Nile	563
CNN ImageSource	96
Coapman, Thomas	510
Coates, Anne V.	65
Coatney, Jeff	35
Coatsworth, David	497
Cobalt Digital, Inc.	285
Cobalt Studios	109
Coburn, Toni	478
Cochet, Patrice Lucien	435
Coco, Edward	388
Cocuzza-Offenhartz, Joanne	478, 489
Cocuzzo, Dominick	466
Cocuzzo, Pat A.	466
Coda, John	418
Codron, David	65
Coen Brothers, The	8

Company/Crew Index

Name	Page
Coffen, John (Jack)	454
Cohen, Audrey S.	450, 497
Cohen, Donald	8
Cohen, Edward A.	454
Cohen, Elizabeth	478
Cohen, Fred	454
Cohen, Ian D.	454
Cohen, Isaac J.	418
Cohen, Jeri	185
Cohen, Lester	388
Cohen, Paula	527
Cohen, Paul Ira	534
Cohen, Phil	399
Cohen, Trevor	408
Cohl	489
Cohn + Company	15
Cohn, Richard	454
Cohn, Rob Michael	8
Cohn, Tamar	107
Cokeliss, Barney	8
Cola, James	489
Cola, Joseph	478
Colangelo, Joseph	435
Colangelo, Paul	399
Colavito, Peter Thomas	454
Colbeck, Chris	489
Colby-Grauer, Cathy Jo	107
Cole, Charlie	8, 427
Cole, Daniel James	555
Cole, Jennifer	107
Cole, Todd Ian	510
Coleman, Chester	383
Coleman, Douglas E.	510
Coleman, William	427
Coletta, Hallie	107, 109
Collaborations In Communications, Inc.	22
Collegiate Images	96, 233, 292
Colley, Alisa	399
Collins, Chris	501
Collins, Diana	563
Collins, EMT-P C.K.	383
Collins, Jim	8
Collins, Jodi	216
Collins, Joseph	408
Collins, R.N. Leslie	383, 541
Collins, Raymond	408, 415
Collister, Peter L.	435
Collot, Phillipe	35
Collyns, Eddy	527
Colomba, Elizabeth	35
Colombian Consulate General	165
Colombo, Elena	8
Colon, Charles J.	466
Colon, Edgar	408
Colon, Luis	466
Colonna, Pierrot	435
Color Edge	76
Color Reflections, Inc.	342
Colorado	170
Colorado-Boulder	170
Colorado-Clear Creek County	170
Colorado-Colorado Springs	170
Colorado-Fremont/Custer County	170
Colorado-Southwest	170
Colorado-Telluride	170
Colorlab NYC	74, 86, 266
Colossalvision	22, 86, 281, 288
Colour Correction People, Inc.	333
Colston, Caroline	523
Comacho, William	510
Comedy Central	38
Comesky, Steven J.	454
Comitini, Mariela	447
Communications Group, Inc., The	96, 292
Communications Plus Digital	86
Comp 24	333, 342
Company	15
Company 3 NY	86, 289
Compleat Sculptor, The	325
Compleat Strategist	347
Composition Workshop	112, 127
Compositions	82
Compro Productions, Inc.	96
Compulsive Pictures, Inc.	16
Computer Rent	223, 277, 354, 373
CompuWeather	206
Comstock, Amy S.	239
Conable, Benjamin	388
Concepts TV Productions, Inc.	26
Concordia, Thomas	505
Condit, Garth	558
Confer, Jeffrey	427
Conill Advertising, Inc.	2
Conly, Sarah	107, 523, 555
Connecticut	170
Connecticut Film Center Norwalk	117
Connelly, Jonathan	489
Conner, Andrew	454
Conners, Kelly	454
Conners, Tracy	454
Connolly, Sarah	501
Connors, Rachel	525
Conod, Keith	399
Conover, R. B.	408
Consentino, Joseph	435
Consentino, Stephen	408, 415
Constantine, Carolyn	435
Constructive Display, Inc.	112, 364, 373
Consulate	47
Contaldi, Gina	497
Conte, Mike	392
Contemporary Photography Services	507
Contessa, Lorenzo	35, 107
Context Studios	117, 130, 221
Continental Airlines	153
Contreras, Claudio	392
Contreras, Luis	454
Conway, Jeremy	388
Conway, John K.	510
Conway, Joseph T.	510
Conway, Thomas O.	510
Cook, Addison P.	466
Cook, Brandon	510
Cook, Daniel	399
Cook, Mary	479, 489
Cook, Susan	563
Cook, Virginia	555
Cooke, Andrew	527
Cooke, R. Caswell	466
Cooke, Timothy	527
Cooke, Tricia	65
Cookson, Jacqueline	489
Coombs, Stephen	408
Cooney, David	35, 116
Cooney, Jeffrey	8
Cooney, Michael J.	510
Cooper, Douglas	427
Cooper Film Cars	355
Cooper Film Company, Inc., The	306
Cooper, James G.	467
Cooper, Sloane	4
Coots, John	454
Cop Call Consulting, Inc.	246
Copacabana	249
Copans, Seth	525
Copeland, Cory M.	510
Coplan, Caron	559
Coppin, Lorraine	563
Coppola, Joseph A.	510
Coppola, Richard/Motion Control	263
Corapi, Anthony	454
Corbett, John E.	467
Corbis	96
Corbis Motion	96, 292
Corbis Stock Market	97
Corbo, John	563
Corder, Alan	399
Cordice, Sharon	479
Core, Ericson	435
Core, Tobias S.	418
Corenblith, Michael	392
Corgan, Kathleen	399
Corinne's Concepts In Catering	160
Cornerstone Pictures	16
Cornett, Donald	399
Corneville, Martial	479
Cornman, David	65
Corona, Ivan	435
Corporate Image Unlimited, The	245
Corra Films, Inc.	16
Corra, Henry	8
Corrado, Susan	479
Correia, Adrian	435
Correira, John	408
Corrigan, Blaise	542
Corrigan, Lucy	555
Corrubia, Lucas	534
Corry, James	559
Cortazzo, Jason	467
Cortosi, Anthony J.	454
Corwin, Hank	65
Cory, Michael	510
Cosby, Janette	239
Cosgrove, Howard A.	467
Cosimo	8
Cosimo and Company	16
Cossette Communications	2
Cossio, Peter	527

Name	Page
Cossu, Kathy	383
Costa, Damian F.	467
Costa, Damian J.	510
Costabile, Thomas	418
Costain, Michael	489
Costain, Tom	65
Costas, Celia	550
Costea, Monica	479
Costumer, Inc., The	334
Cote, Paul	534
Cothren, Tim	417
Cottle, Rachel	563
Cotugno, Edward	510
Cougar	375
Coughlan, Michelle	399
Coughlan, Tim	399
Coughlin, Cari	65
Coughlin, John	399
Coull, Simon	427
Coulter, Mick	435
Coumarbatch, John	552
Courier Car Rental	158, 320
Cournoyer, Daniel R.	467
Cournoyer, Howard	454
Cousins, Erin	510
Cousins, Patrick	454
Coutroulis, Pauline	479, 489
Coutte, Olivier Bugge	65
Couture, Douglas	563
Covelman, Robert	510, 532
Covington, Ashly	229
Cowan, DeBaets, Abrahams & Sheppard	228
Cowley, Tony	392
Cowperthwaite, Claire	525
Cox, Anthony	467
Cox, Betsy	559
Cox, Brandon	435
Cox, David	447
Cox, Divine T.	467
Cox, Jeffrey A.	510
Cox, Jen	239
Cox, Jerry	534
Cox, Tom	435
Coyle, Jack	418
Coyne, Thomas P.	454
Coyne-Babich, Eileen M	510
Coyne-De Luca Karen	510
Coyne-Rader, Patricia A.	510
CP Communications, Inc.	164
CPT Rental, Inc.	260
Crabill, Justin	413
Crabtree, Ane	559
Cragg, Nelson	435
Craig, Kumi	489
Craig, Lisa Marzolf	563
Craig, Matthew	454
Craig, Stuart	392
Craig, Wayne	8
Craigmile, John	239
Crain, Michael	413, 416, 435
Cramer, Bill	65
Crammer, Jennifer	501
Crane, Jeremy	503
Crank! It! Out!, Inc.	5
Cranzano, Joseph	479
Crawford, Anita	479
Crawford, Gerald	563
Craycroft, Jacob	65
Creative Arts Television	97
Creative Bubble	54, 58, 78, 86, 102, 289
Creative Bubble Sound	43, 82
Creative Business Communications, Inc.	22
Creative Costume Company	334
Creative Engineering	112, 364, 373
Creative Entertainment Connections	380
Creative Film Cars	355
Creative Film Management International, Inc.	16
Creative Group, Inc.	47, 86, 289
Creative Media Communications	22
Creative Production Group	97
Creativity	226
Creators, The	22
Creighton	489
Crenshaw, John	51
Crespo, Ana	479
Cress Photo	262, 304, 326, 354
Crew 1 TV, Inc.	380
Crew Connection	380, 435, 504
Crew Cuts Film & Tape, Inc.	48
crewHD.com	281, 380
CrewStar, Inc.	241, 380
Cribben, Mik	413, 534
Cripe, Jamaine	527
Criscuolo, Gregory	418
Crise, Douglas	65
Crisostomo, Scotch James	239
Cristante, Ivo	392
Cristiano, Anthony	489
Croci, Ron	35
Crockett, David	497
Cronenweth, Jeff	8, 435
Cronenweth, Tim	8
Cronin, Kelly	525
Cronin, W	399
Cronin-Souza, Andrea	454
Cronk, Larry B.	418
Crook, Lisa	28
Crooks, Patrick C.	454
Crosby, Catriona (Cat)	510
Cross, Paul	392
Crosseyed Studio	127, 188
Crossroads Films	16
Crouser, Gregory	552
Crout, Rene	399
Crow, Laura	555
Crowe, Cameron	8
Crowell, Jamie	550
Crowley, Nathan	392
Crowley, Ralph F.S.	454
Crowley, Webb & Associates	2
Crown Limousine	182
Crudo, Richard	435
Crumrine, Rick	399
Crushing Music	82
Crutchfield, Charles	563
Crystal, Tracy	489
Csatlos, Michael	399
CSI Rentals	262, 312
CSI/William Steinberg	372
CSS Music/Dawn Music	80
CTV Archives Sales	97
Cubine, Stephen	497
Cucciarre, Michael S.	418
Cuddy, Carol	550
Cue & A Productions	22
Cuervo, Joseph	479
Cuesta, Michael	8
Cugno, David	552
Culbertson, Keith	534
Culen, Peter	418
Culinary Loft LLC, The	127, 188, 249
Culjak, Abariss	510
Cullen, Lawrence	408
Cullen, Melissa	479
Cullnan, Jay	185
Culver Pictures	97
Cumberbatch, Colin	501
Cumming, Alan	8, 28
Cummings, Howard	392
Cummins, Aleksandra	479
Cuneo Jr., John	467
Cunningham, Jeffrey	435
Cunningham, Lee	510
Cunningham, Michael	399
Cupkovic, Nick	454
Curbean, Daisy	479
Curich, Christine	479
Curious Pictures Corporation	54
Curran, Gavin	454
Curren, William Danial	447
Currie, Robert J.	510
Curry Jr., Michael P.	418
Curry Sr., Michael	418
Curtin, David B.	534
Curtin, John	479
Curtis, Bruce	392
Curtis, Lynne	555, 563
Cushman, Alex	539
Custer, Joel	510
Custom Creations	112, 323, 342, 364
Custom Medical Stock Photo, Inc.	97
Custom Video Productions, Inc.	22
Cutler, Alan	479, 489
Cutler, Gavin	65
Cutler, Michelle	479, 489
Cutshall, Carol	559
Cutting Room, The	188
Cvecich, Lillian	479
Cybulski, Mary	525
Cyc-O-Builders/Re-Cyc Co.	109
Cycan, Michael	418
cYclops productions	16
Cyrus, Kellie	525
Czaja, Jeffrey	107
Czapsky, Stefan	427
Czar Productions	22
Czarnecki, James	527
Czekanski, Cara	563

Company/Crew Index

D

D, John ... 489
D.R. Reiff & Associates ... 230
D's Craft Service ... 424
Daboub, Charlie ... 392
Dabrowski, David A. ... 467
Dachler, Niels ... 408, 414, 415
Daddi, Richard A. ... 419
Daddy-O Productions, Inc. ... 112
Dagort, Philip ... 392
D'Agostino, Diane ... 479
Dahl, John ... 8, 28
Dailey, Benjamin ... 399
Daily Transcripts, Inc. ... 247
Dakota Studio ... 120, 127, 188
D'Alessandro, Federico ... 35
D'Alessandro, Joseph ... 408, 435
Daley, Paul ... 435, 454
Dalglish, Gabriel Camilo S. ... 510
Dalisera, Douglas A. ... 454
Dallis, Amelia ... 497, 504
Dalton, Jeremiah Jay ... 467
Dalton, John T. ... 534
Daly, Bill ... 534
Daly, James ... 399
Daly, Neil ... 447
Daly, Shane ... 435
Damage Studios/Andrea Purcigliotti ... 112
Damast, Boris ... 8
Damiano, Joseph ... 467
Damico, Natalie Marie ... 501
D'Amico, Skip ... 8
Damoiseaux, Lars ... 8
Dan Snyder Locations ... 185
Dana Communications, Inc. ... 2
Dana, Michael ... 435
Danchik, Roger ... 510
Dancing Waters ... 326
Dancy, Peter ... 510
Dandrea, Benjamin A. ... 467
D'Angelo-Hedrick, Mary A. ... 479
D'Angerio, Alan ... 489
Daniel, Lee ... 435
Daniel, Tony ... 35
Danieli, Steve ... 454
Daniels, Greg ... 435
Danielson, Jeffrey A. ... 454
Danis & Danis ... 232
Danny Goldman & Associates ... 216
dantasticfood ... 452
Danziger, Neil ... 534
Danziger, Patricia ... 447, 497
Daraio, Robert ... 425, 552
Darby, David ... 435
Darby, Jerome ... 559
Dardis, John ... 455
Daroma Restaurant Equipment Corp. ... 372
Darrell, Philip ... 455
Darrett, Renoir ... 525
Dart, David ... 427
Datafaction, Inc. ... 222
date with sunrise design..., A. ... 343
Dattner Dispoto & Associates ... 380, 427, 435
Daubeach, Didier ... 435
Davenport, Danelle ... 35
Davenport, David ... 563
Davenport, Kristy Victoria ... 383
Davi-Coppers, Crista ... 479
Daviau, Allen ... 435
David Dreishpoon's Gourmet ... 160, 424
David Forman Music ... 82
David, Jonathan ... 8
David Scharf Photography ... 97
David, Vic ... 65, 413
David Weller Design ... 392
David Zema, Inc./Voice of Success Programs ... 246, 548
Davidson, Michael ... 419
Davidson, Patrice Andrew ... 388
Davies, Ian ... 65
Davies, James (Bear) ... 510
Davies, Timothy A. ... 467
da Vinci Systems, Inc. ... 285
Davis, Alison ... 501
Davis, Andrea ... 4
Davis, Betsy ... 503
Davis, Catherine ... 510
Davis, Chrissie ... 501
Davis, Dan ... 388, 413, 416
Davis, David ... 325
Davis, Don ... 427
Davis, Elliot ... 435
Davis, Glenn ... 455
Davis, Jeff J. ... 423
Davis, Jennifer A. ... 392
Davis, John F. ... 35, 116, 388, 392
Davis, Joseph E. ... 510
Davis, Lisa ... 386, 489
Davis, Scott ... 427
Davis, Vicki R. ... 555
Davis-Godley, Lisa ... 479
Davison, JD ... 497
D'Avolio, Judie ... 525
Dawid, Marek ... 8
Dawley, Aaron ... 467
Dawn Animal Agency, Inc. ... 212
Dawn to Dusk Agency ... 380, 489, 559
Dawn Wolfe's Pawsitively Famous Animal Actors ... 212
Dawson, April ... 479
Day, Andrew J. ... 455
Day, Charlotte ... 489
Day, Robin ... 479, 489
Dazian Fabrics ... 109, 329, 340, 343
Dazian Rentals ... 336
DB Production Services ... 22
DDB Worldwide ... 2
Dea, Joe ... 497
Deanes, James ... 563
De Angelis, Angelina ... 479
De Angelo, Rena ... 510
Dean, Jamie ... 392
Dean, Jason ... 501
Dean, Richard ... 479
Dease, Joshua ... 239
Debbie Regan Locations, Ltd. ... 185
Deberson, Sherry ... 479
de Besche, Austin ... 427
DeBetta, Darlene ... 489
Debie, Benoit ... 435
De Blau, Christopher ... 455
DeBlau, Jerry W. ... 455
De Blau III, John W. ... 455
De Bonis, Joe ... 408, 414, 417, 415
DeBonrepos, Stephen ... 35
De Camp Bus Lines ... 155
De Candia, Vito ... 65
Decca, Anghel ... 435
Decelle, Daniel R. ... 510
Decelle Jr., William E. ... 510
DeClerque, David Stevens ... 550
Decorators Walk/Schumacher ... 340, 345
De Cosmo, Matteo ... 388
De Curtis, Frank ... 510
De Curtis Jr., Frank ... 510
De Curtis, Guido ... 510, 523
De Curtis, Louise ... 510
De Curtis, Peter ... 510
Dedivanovic, Mario ... 489
Deeg, Nicholas ... 399
Deep Hollow Ranch ... 188, 214
Defender Industries, Inc. ... 328
De Filippo, Paul D. ... 510
DeFina, Barbara ... 501, 550
Defonzo, Anthony ... 399
Defrancesco, Anthony ... 399
Deghan, Jennifer ... 392
DeGovia, Jackson ... 392
DeGuzman, Gus ... 35
Dehghan, Jennifer E. ... 388
DeHuff, Bill ... 413
Deitchman, Daniel ... 447, 498
De Jesus, Frank ... 489
De Jesus, Katherine ... 239
Dekart Video ... 48
Delacruz, Julian ... 399
Delahanty, James F. ... 467
Delaney, Kane C. ... 455
Delaney, Maggie ... 455
Delaney, Michael J. ... 455
Delaney Jr., Michael J. ... 455
Delaney, Tracie ... 559
Delaney, Vincent P. ... 455
De Lara, Dana ... 523
Delaware ... 170
Delbonnel, Bruno ... 436
De Leon, Ruth Ann ... 510
Delgado, Jon ... 408
Delgado, Jon M. ... 455
Delgado, Monica ... 239
Del Giudice, Ilysa R. ... 383
Del Giudice, Sal ... 498
DeLigter, Richard ... 8
De Lillo Thomas A. ... 510
Della, Phyllis ... 479
Della Rosa Ricardo ... 436
Dell' Orto, Silvia ... 489
Del Rio, Mildred ... 563
Del Russo, Robert ... 408

Name	Page
Del Sordo, Christopher	399
Delta Airlines	153
Delta Cargo	151
Delta Dash	151
Deluca, Christine	540
De Luca Joseph	510
Delury, Janna	525
Deluxe New York	56, 74, 86, 289
De Maar, Henri	8
DeMaio, Vincent	399
De Mar, Robert A.	510
DeMarco, Frank	427
Demas, Nick	399
DeMato, John	408
De Meglio, Edward	467
De Meo Brothers, Inc.	348
Demers, Francis R.	467
Demeskey, Mandie	510
DeMirjian, Michael	65
Demitri, Melanie	479
Demos, Moira	455
De Nicola, Matthew J.	419
De Nicola, Victor	479
De Nicola Jr., Victor	489
Denier Jr., Thomas L.	479
Denisov, Antoine	436
DeNitto, Daniel	408, 467
D'Enjoy, Claudia	65
Denk, Margaret M.	450, 498
Denmark, Kay	534
Dennett, Darcy	436
Dennis, Elizabeth Ann	501
Dennis, Emily	65
Dennis, Margina	479
Dennis, Patrick	489
Dennis Powers Productions, Inc.	22
Dennis, Sarah	510
Denny, Jim	427, 455
Denoi, Tony	455
Dentsu America	2
Depalma, Denise M.	383
Departure Films	31, 38, 60
De Pasquale III, Eugene C.	467
De Pass, Paul	388
De Paula, Patricia	501
Dependable Transport & Messenger	196, 235, 320
de Rakoff, Sophie	559
Dera, Roslan & Campion	34
Derlig, Olaf	489
De Rogatis, Jerry	510
De Rosa, Anthony	455
De Rosa, Michael A.	455
DeSalvo, Joe	427
Desantis, Christopher	8
de Sa Rego, Sarah	559
DeScenna, Linda	392
Deschanel, Caleb	436
Descoteau, Lynn	498
de Segonzac, Jean	427
De Siena, John J.	467
Design to Deceive/Joshua Turi	323
Design TV	38
Design@Chelsea Post	54, 102
Designomotion	5, 54, 102, 104, 289
De Simone, John	501
DeSimone, Suzanne	323, 479, 489
Des Marais Christopher P.	510
Desmond, Frank	511
Desnouee, Jennifer M.	106
De Sousa, Carolyn	525
Despenzero, Joey	540
Des Rosiers, Melissa	559
D'Este, Roberto	507
de Stefano, Cece	392
De Stefano Joseph V.	510
De Thame, Gerard	8
De Thelismond, Yvens	563
De Titta, Beth Ann	510
De Titta, Christopher J.	510
De Titta, Daniel	510
De Titta Jr., George M.	510, 532
De Titta, Gerald A.	510
De Titta, Nicholas	510
De Titta, Patrice	510
De Titta Di Meo, Anna	510
De Toro, Alberto	65
De Toth, Nicolas	65
Deutsch, Alan	427
Deutsch, Inc.	2
Deutsch, Liz	555
Deutsch, Stuart C.	534
Deveau, Marie-Sylvie	559
Devere, Tracy	563
De Verna, Peter J.	534
De Villa, Debbie	392
DeVilla, Joan	239
Devine, Richard	511
Devine, Thomas F.	455
Devlin, Alex	419
Devlin, John	447
Devlin, Keith J.	455
Devlin Video Intl.	56, 58, 86, 283, 289
DEVLINHAIR Productions, Inc.	22
DeVonish, Kerwin	408
Devonshire, Philip J.	455
DeWinter, Marque	400
Dewitt Stern Group	230
De Wolf, James N.	467
Dey, Tom	8
DG FastChannel	56, 283
DG Systems, Inc.	78
DGA Directory of Members	226
DGA Quarterly	226
DGA Theater	91
DHL	151
Dial 7	182
Dial Car	182
Diamond, Felice	479
Diamond Ice	350
Diamond, Monty	185
Diamond Time, Ltd.	233
Diaz, Alfonso	400
Diaz, Juan	35
Diaz, Jun	65
Dibe, Charlie	501
DiBona, Craig	427
DiBucci, Michelle	51
Dicarlo, Angela	489
di Cesare, Michael	479
dick clark productions Media Archives	97
Dickbauer, Othmar	425
Dickenson, Karen	479
Dickersin, Ged	550
Dickinson, Ben	8, 28
Dickman, Michael T.	511
Didier, Paul	35
Di Dio, Frank R.	419, 467
Dierickx, Arno	8
Dietrich, Daniel P.	419
Dietrichson, Ketil	436
Dieu Donné	188
Diez, Pedro	467
DiFeo, Mike	400
DiFonzo, Michael	563
DiFranco, Naima	559
Dig It Audio, Inc.	43
Di Gennaro, Joe	436
DiGiacomo, Angelo	400
DiGiacomo, Robert	400
Digioia, John	479
Digital Art Video, Inc.	86
Digital Arts	43, 48, 56, 60, 82, 86, 102, 120, 127, 281, 283, 284, 289
Digital Cinema, LLC	43
Digital Content Producer	226
Digital Laundry	120
Digital Magic Animation, LLC	5, 54
Digital Projection, Inc.	285
Digital Vision, Inc.	285
DiGregorio, Richard	427
Di Grigoli, Robert	419
Dileo, Chris	392
Dilks, Victoria	383
Dilley, Leslie	392
Dillinger Jr., James F.	455
Dillon, Kat	498
Dillon, Phil	427
Dillon, Robert	419
DiMaccio, Marco Belli	392
Dimaki, Sylvia	489
DiMartino Jr., E. Paul	200, 503
Di Maulo, Frank	535
Di Meo, Andrew J.	511
Dimeo, Anthony J.	511
Dimirco, Joanne	479
Dingler, Jake	489
Dintenfass, Andrew	427
Dion Peronneau Agency	381, 490, 559
Di Pasquale, Ruth	511
Di Persio, Jane	479, 490
Dipietro, Hugo	35
Directors' Catering	160
Directors Film Company	16, 200, 201
Directors Guild of America (DGA)	546
Directors Network, The	8, 381
Di Rienzo, Gabriel D.	467
Dirk, John J. (Jack)	511
Disador, Stephen	467

Company/Crew Index

Name	Page
Disc Makers	56, 58
Dister, Michael	527
Distribution by Air, Inc./DBA	151
District of Columbia	170
Di Tolla, Daniel E.	511
Ditommaso, Luke	104
Diva	249
Diva Edit	48, 60
Diva Limousine, Ltd.	182
Divincenzo-River, Andrea	479
Divine Moving and Storage	196
Divine Studio	127, 188, 221
Divone, Paul George	419
Dix, Abby	8
Dixon, Cathy	559
Dixon, Chris	455
Dixon, Diane	479
Dixon, Eric	392, 511
Dixon, Scott R.	419
Dixon, Tripp	8
DJM Post Production	86, 289
Djurkovic, Maria	392
DM News	226
dM works	22, 58
DMA Animation	5, 54, 102
DMJ Productions & Digital Media	22
DMP Productions	22
Do, Kim	490
Doak Jr., Allen G.	511
Dobbin, Simon	392
Dobbs, Richard	427
Dobkin, Anna Jane	501
Dobkin, David	8
Documentary Educational Resources	97
Dodd, Kenneth R.	455
Dodge, Norm.	388, 523, 532
Doernberg, David	388
Doggicam, Inc.	285
Doherty, Charles D.	419
Doherty, George	501
Doherty, James T.	419
Doherty, Kara	527
Dolack, Tara	503
Dolan, Christopher E.	455
Dolan, Dede P.	455
Dolan, Edward	535
Dolan, James A. (Peaches)	455
Dolan, James P.	455
Dolan, John (Douglas)	467
Dolan, John P.	467
Dolan, Kathleen M.	511, 532
Dolan, Patrick Michael	436
Dolan, Phelim	8
Dolan, Richard N.	455
Dolan, Ronald P.	455
Dolan, Thomas W.	455
Dolan-Cote, Justine M.	511
Dolby Laboratories, Inc.	285
Doliner, John	392
Dolkart, Lawrence	436
Doll, Matthew	408
Dollar Rent A Car	156
Dolphin, Ben	9, 427
Domanic-Riccio, Jodi	525
Domaniecki, Christine	479, 490
Dombrow, Mark	436
Dominican Republic	170
Dominik, Andrew	9
Domorski Jr., James	552
Donaghy, John J.	467
Donahue, James F.	107
Donahue, Peter	427
Donahue, Tom	65
Donald Case Casting	218
Donegan, Devin	552
Donelian, Dicran (Deke)	427
Donian, Mitchell	455
Donna DeSeta Casting	218
Donna Grossman Casting	218
Donne, Naomi	479, 490
Donnelly, Brian	65
Donnelly, Candice	555
Donnelly, Jack	427
Donnelly, Patrick	427
Donnelly, Sean	400
Donohue, Christopher	467
Donohue, Damien	467
Donohue, George	419
Donohue, John (JD)	467
Donohue Jr., Joseph G.	467
Donohue III, Joseph G.	467
Donohue, Peter G.	467
Donohue, Timothy	447
Donohue-Pace, Christine M.	511
Donovan, Anne	106
Donovan, Melissa	400
Donovan, Sean M.	467
Donovan, S. Patrick	467
Don's Location Vans	192
Doreen Frumkin Casting	218
Doremi Labs, Inc.	285
Doremus & Company	2
Dorf, Paula	479, 490
Dorfman, Pat	447, 498
Dorman, Andrea	407
Dorn, Dody	65
Dorothy Palmer Talent Agency, Inc.	246
Dorrance, Daniel	392
Dorset, Natalie N.	511
Doskey, Janice	498, 527
Dosunmu, Andrew	28
D'Ottillie, Brian	527
Doty, Steven	400
Douaihy, Antoine	527
Doubletime Productions	97
Doughan, Joe	467
Dougherty, Greg	65
Dougherty, Kevin	467
Douglas, Harry	65
Douglas House, Inc.	188
Douglas, Lori	550
Douglas, Richard Bryan	419
Douglass, Jorjee	479
Doumbia, Katherine	479
Dour, Daniel	467
Dovetail Group, Inc., The	22, 38
Dow, Mary J.	501
Dowgin, Richard	467
Dowley, Brian	409, 414
Downing, Laura	563
Downing, Peter	540
Downs, Tom	65
Downtown Manhattan Heliport	154
Doyle, Patrick	400
Doyle, Tanya	501
Doyle, Tomm	419
Doyle, Tracy A.	511
Drago, Robert F.	511
Dragoti, Stan	9
Drape Kings	336
Draper, Inc.	285
Draper, Mynka	559
Draper, Robert	427
Draves, J. Kevin	563
Drazen-Difulvio, Katherine	479
Dream Cuisine Fine Catering, LLC	161
Dreamhire, LLC	268
Drechsler, Ana K.	511
Drechsler, Christian G.	455
Drees, Annette Maria	525
Drellich, Steve	409, 436
Drennan, Harry	511
Drescher, Adam	498
Dressel, Gregory M.	467
Drew Jiritano Special Effects	326
Dreyer, Dianne	525
Dreyfuss, David	447
Drez, Dave	436
Driftwood RV Center/Atlantic City	194
Driscoll, Dan	9
Driscoll Jr., Neil	511
Driscoll, Meredith	563
Driver, Thom	532
Drivers East	542
Drivers Inc.	542
DriveSavers Data Recovery	222
Drobka, Joseph J.	419
Drobot, Lena	423
Drohan IV, Edward A.	511
Drohan, George	511
Drotar, Thomas	392
Drucklieb, William P.	535
Drum Rentals/Vintage Drums	353
Drummond, Blake	501
Dryburgh, Stuart	427
DSC Laboratories	285
Du Art Film and Video	43, 54, 58, 60, 74, 84, 87, 102, 284, 289
Du-All Camera Corp.	260
Dualoy Leather	325
Dublanica, Jesse C.	455
Dubois, David	436
Dubravcic, Predrag	409, 414, 417, 436
Dubway Studios	43
Ducharme, Bruno	9
Duckworth, Shane	400
Ducsay, Bob	65
Duer, Charles E.	467

Name	Page
Duff, Michael	436
Duff, Mike	436
Duff, Skip	65
Duffield, Tom	392
Duffin, Philip	392
Duffy, James	65
Duffy, Robert	66
Duggal Color Projects, Inc.	76
Duggal Underground	76
Duggan, Simon	436
Duhaime, Peter T.	419
Duke, Steven Todd	511
Dukes, Frank P.	106
Dumais, David	564
Dumas, Ray	436
Dummitt, George D.	419
Dumonceau, Stephane	66
Dunaj, Gregory	400
Dunbar, Kellen C.	511
Dunbar, Maryellen	511
Dunbar, Peter K.	511
Duncan Jr., John G.	455
Duncan Sr., John G.	467
Duncan, Julie	511
Duncan, Matt	392, 511
Duncan, Tere	559
Duncklee, William	383
Dunham, Duwayne R.	66
Dunlap, David M.	427
Dunmore, Laurence	9
Dunn, Andrew	436
Dunn, John	555
Dunn, Luisa	51
Dunn, Russell	400
Dunn-Lee, Ionia	559
Dunning, Giles	436
Dunnington, Bartholow & Miller LLP	228
Du Perrieu, Debbe	564
Duplass Brothers	9
Duplication Depot, Inc.	56
Dupont, Phil	450
Du Press, Warren	9
Duran, Colin	400
Durand, Marjorie	479
Durant, Diane	526
Durham, Brian	511
Durian, Marcos	436
Durnin, Joseph M.	511
Durnin Jr., William J.	511
Duroux, Patrick	436
Durst, Marcelo	436
Dusty Promotions, LLC	214
Dutemple, Jeff	400
Duthie, Diann E.	388
Dutton, Philip	400
Duvall, John W.	467
Duys, Henry	419
dv Depot	275
DV Magazine	226
DV/HDcuts	97, 292
Dvideo Multimedia Productions	87
DVS Digital Video, Inc.	285
Dweller By The Stream Bindery	343
DWJ Television	22, 48, 78
Dworin, Arthur	107
Dwyer, John E.	511
Dyas, Guy Hendrix	392
Dye-Namix, Inc.	340
Dyer, James R.	498
Dynamex	235
Dzlewior, Chad	392
Dzurillay, Lawrence	498

E

Name	Page
E.C. Professional Video	275
E.S., Inc.	194, 424
Eagles Nest Studio	127
Eakin, Autumn	400
Ealer, John	436
Eanes, Kent	505
Earl, Don	455
Early Halloween	334, 378
Early, Nancy	447
Earth Video	60
Earth2mars	48
East Coast Digital, Inc.	56, 60, 87
East Coast Lighting, Inc.	306, 314
East Hampton Airlines	150
East Hampton Studios	120
East of Hollywood NY	120
East Point-Waterfront Peninsula Estate	188
East Side Bagels	424
Eastern Effects, Inc.	31, 296, 304, 306, 314, 320
Eastern Mountain Sports	375
Eastern Script Service, Inc.	233
Eastgate Tower Suite Hotel	177
Eastway Aviation	150
EatCatering by Danielle Wilson	424
Eaton, Timothy	436
Eberle, Mark	436
Eberle, Scott	467
Ebneth, Tim	532
Eccles, Charles (Chip)	419
Echard, Debra	392
Echelon Productions, Inc.	200
Echevarria, Alex	35
Echigo, Tomoki	35
Eckardt, Jay	400
Eckert, Terry R.	467
Eclectic • Encore Props, Inc.	343, 345, 346, 370, 373, 375
Eclipse	306, 314
Economy Novelty & Printing	245
Edge Auto & Truck Rental	158
Edge Films/Ken Nahoum Productions	16, 22
Edgewise Media Services, Inc.	266, 294
Edgeworth, Ann L.	511
Edick, Steven D.	455
Edit On Hudson	48
Editors' Hideaway, Inc.	48, 56, 58, 87
Edmiston, James	467
Edmonds, Jason	392
Edmondson, Leighton S.	455
Edwards, Davion	479
Edwards, Eric	436
Edwards, Gregory	273, 552
Edwards, Kate	564
Edwards, Marjorie Gayle	383
eEmerge Production Suites	31
EFEX Rentals, Inc.	326, 332, 347, 364
Effrein, Edwin	400
eFootage, Inc.	97
Egads Computer Corporation	223
Egan III, Edward J.	467
Egan III, John J.	527
Egan, Kevin	409
Egan, Kevin M.	467
Egan, William T.	467
EGC Group, Inc.	2
Eger, Dennis	479
Eggby, David	436
Egozi, Ron	436
Egypt Air	153
Egyud, Mark	455
Ehrenbard, Daniel R.	455
Ehrlich, Jon	51
Eiben, Patricia	564
Eichengreen, Laurie	447
Eichenstein, Eileen	501, 504
Eichner, Michael	467
Eiger, Janet	559, 564
Eilenberg, Carol	447
Einhorn, Peter	51
Eisele, Eileen	559
Eisemann, Kate	450, 498, 527
Eisen, Andrew	66
Eisenberg, Lauri	559
Eisenmann, Micah	455
Eisner, Breck	9
Ekstrand, Linda T.	511
Elaine Gordon Management	229
El Al Israel Airlines	153
Elassad, Christopher	467
Elder, Timothy Raul	535
Eldridge Textile Co.	336, 340
Electrosonic	285
Elefant Films	306, 320
Element	249
Element Productions	16
Eliano, Richard	413
Elias, George	467
Eliopoulos, Steven	400
Elite Coaches	198
Elizabeth Bardsley & Associates, Inc.	233
Elkind, Paulette	479, 490
Elkins, David E.	409, 413
Ellen Rixford Studio	323, 364
Ellensohn, Mark	436
Elliot, Michael	66
Elliot, Peter	400
Elliot, Robert	427
Elliot, Sam	400
Elliot Jr., Stephen	447
Elliott Film Transcription Service	247
Elliott, William A.	392
Ellis, Anita	564
Ellis, Arthur	400
Ellis, Jonathan	383

Ellis, Sean . . . 9
Ellsworth Productions . . . 38
El Mansouri, Mona . . . 9
Elmes, Frederick . . . 427
Elmfors, Osa . . . 400
El Punto Productions . . . 23
Elrom Inc. . . . 58, 102, 247, 248, 283
Else, Marc Laliberté . . . 436
Elswit, Robert . . . 436
Elter, Meredith . . . 511
Eluto, Ken . . . 66
Elvir, Rod . . . 504
Elwell, David . . . 455
Ely, Mitchell . . . 479
Emami, Massoumeh . . . 525
Embriano, Gregory . . . 511
Emem, Ukeme . . . 527
Emerson Machione Lisa . . . 564
Emery, Ross . . . 436
EMI Music Publishing-Film Soundtrack Div. . . . 80
Emil Norsic & Son, Inc. . . . 198
Emmons, Kevin . . . 436
Emmy (ATAS Magazine) . . . 226
Empire Entertainment, Inc. . . . 232
Empire Promotional Products . . . 245
Empress Media, Inc. . . . 266, 294
Empson, Gay Morris . . . 559
EMS, Inc. . . . 241
Endeavor Agency, The . . . 246, 381
Engel, Jack . . . 479
Engelhardt, Margaret . . . 501
Engels, Dayson . . . 467
Engels, Eugene W. . . . 455
Engels, Gene . . . 427
Engels, Glen K. . . . 467
Engels, Jay M. . . . 455
Engels, Kenneth . . . 467
Engels, Russell W. . . . 455
Engels, Ryan . . . 455
Engels, Wade S. . . . 455
Engler, Eric . . . 436
Englezos, George . . . 66
English, Gary . . . 480
English Motion Media . . . 23
Englis, Sunday . . . 480
Engrassia, Gerard . . . 511
Ennis, Inc. . . . 381, 490
Enos, Kris . . . 400
Enterprise . . . 156
Entertainment Partners . . . 241
Entertainment Partners/
Vista Production Accounting Software . . . 222
Entertainment Publishers . . . 222, 226
Entertainment Services . . . 314
Entertainment Travel, Inc. . . . 204
Envision Studios . . . 78, 225
epandmedia/Flashframe Films . . . 16, 30
EPIC Security Corp. . . . 202
Eplett, Jeffrey A. . . . 455
Epoch Films, Inc. . . . 16, 30
Epps, Christian L. . . . 455
Epstein, Peter . . . 447
Epstein, Vadim . . . 527
Epstein's Paint Center . . . 329, 336
Equitable Production Group . . . 87
Erasmus, Nicholas . . . 66
Erb, Geoffrey . . . 427
Erbes-Chan, Johnny . . . 467
Ercole, Jonathan . . . 400
Ercole, Nicoletta . . . 559
Ercolessi, Sergio . . . 450
Erector Sets, Inc. . . . 112
Eric Mower & Associates, Inc. . . . 2
Eric Silvey Entertainment . . . 232
Erne, Ted . . . 409, 414
Ernest Winzer Theatrical & Leather Cleaner . . . 338, 377
Errair, Kendall . . . 564
Escott, Adam . . . 447
Eshelman, Steve . . . 9
Espinosa, Axuve . . . 66
Espinosa, Michael . . . 527
Esposito, Michael A. . . . 419
Esposito, Richard . . . 480
Esposito, Robert A. . . . 535
Estern, Evan . . . 427
Estes, Eldo Ray . . . 480
Estrada-Carrasquillo, Wilfredo . . . 400
Estus, Boyd . . . 427
Etheredge, Paul . . . 450
Etienne, Luc . . . 450
Euro-Pacific Film & Video Productions, Inc. . . . 23, 201
Evangelista, Anton . . . 35
Evangelista-Pollini, Nicole . . . 564
Evangelisto, Robert . . . 511
Evans, Deborah . . . 393
Evans, Gerald . . . 455
Evans, Leesa . . . 559
Evans Jr., Nicholas M. . . . 511
Evans, Wendy . . . 480
Evans, William . . . 400
Eve, Jennifer . . . 559
Event Designs New York . . . 232
Event Radio Rentals, Inc. . . . 164
Everest Production Corp. . . . 43, 48
Evergreen Antiques . . . 345
Everlast Sporting Goods Mfg. . . . 375
Evertz . . . 285
Every Thing Goes . . . 334, 339, 345, 378
Everything Events &
Entertainment, LLC . . . 218, 232, 246, 436, 542
Evolution Music Partners, LLC . . . 80
Evolving Image . . . 109, 346
EVS/Express Video Supply, Inc. . . . 266, 294
EVTV . . . 43
Ewen Industries, Inc. . . . 48, 54
Ewen, Paul . . . 66
Ex Eggs, Inc. . . . 127
Exchange Communications . . . 164, 223
Exclusive Artists Management . . . 381, 490, 559
Executive Charm . . . 161
Executive Fliteways, Inc. . . . 150
Executive Yacht Management, Inc. . . . 328
Exotics Unlimited . . . 214
Expendables Plus, Inc. . . . 304, 318
Extra Connection . . . 229
Extra Talent Agency . . . 229
Extreme Production Music . . . 80
Extreme Skills Productions . . . 218
Eye Shop, The . . . 339
EyeballNYC . . . 102
eyeon Software, Inc. . . . 285

F

Fabbri Mansion (House of the Redeemer) . . . 249
Fabiano, Michael J. . . . 467
Fabor Jallo . . . 436
Fabulous Wallcoverings . . . 329
Fagan, Brant . . . 427
Faggioni, Lauri . . . 9
Fagin, Leslye . . . 540
Fagin-Tuttman, Tina . . . 555
Faherty, John . . . 455
Faherty, Kevin P. . . . 564
Fahrer, Martin D. . . . 388
Fain, Cindy Anita . . . 107, 511
Fairweather, Andrea . . . 480
Faithfull, David . . . 393
Fajen, Kimberly . . . 501
Falcone, Robert A. . . . 455
Falconer, Lynn . . . 555
Falk, Andrew . . . 455
Falkenstein, Andrea . . . 504
Fallon, James . . . 455
Falzarano, Kathryn . . . 511
Fama, Robert . . . 480
Family Jewels, The . . . 339, 340, 378
Famous Frames, Inc. . . . 35, 381
Fancy Cleaners . . . 338
Fancy R&S Leather Cleaners . . . 338
Fanelli Antique Timepieces . . . 339, 345
Fanelli, Michael . . . 455
Fanelli, Peter . . . 455
Fantini, Luca . . . 436
Faraday Technology, Ltd. . . . 285
Farber, William . . . 455
Farbrother, Bernard A. . . . 419
Fares, George . . . 447, 498
Farese III, Michael . . . 467
Farfel Roy/Stunts East . . . 544
Farhood, Jennifer . . . 490
Farid, Amy . . . 490
Farina, John . . . 467
Farkas, Gabriella . . . 35
Farkas, Wendi . . . 559
Farley, Kristin . . . 564
Farley, Scott . . . 480
Farm Boy Films . . . 315
Farm, The . . . 23, 33
Farmer, Chris . . . 393
Farmer, Jim . . . 51
Farmer, Thomas . . . 467
Faro, Michele . . . 523
Farol, Julie . . . 66
Farolfi, Fulvia . . . 490
Farr, David . . . 239
Farraday, John W. . . . 511
Farrar, Jason . . . 527

Company/Crew Index

Name	Page
Farrell, Gregory	455
Farrell, John B.	419
Farrell, Kevin	35
Farrell, Matthew	467
Farrell, Victoria	555
Farulla, Joseph	480
Fashion Award Cleaners	338
Fass, Adele	480
Fass, Brian	427
FastLights	298, 304, 306, 315
Fastuca, Deborah	400
Fatone, Tom	447
Fauci, Jerome	409
Fauer, Jon	9, 427
Faulkenberry Jr., Wes	419
Faxon, Ann	4
Fay, Walter J.	511
Faye, Cynthia	480, 490
FDG	33, 102
Fealy, Jim	427
Fear No Ice	350
Fearon, Millacent	511
Feather, Jay	400
Feature Systems	298, 304, 306, 315, 320
Feature Video Systems, Inc./Joel Holland	273
Featured	185
Febres, Anna	480
Fecht, Douglas	511
Fedeli, Richard	467
Fedeli, Robert J.	455
Fedeli, Ronald M.	455
Federal Express	151
Feder, Nicole	527
Feder, Shari	51
FedEx Custom Critical	151
Fedigan, Sean P.	455
Fedynich, John	185, 527
Fee, Rick	400
Feeley, Erin	501
Feighery, Danny	400
Feigin, Andrew	540
Feil, Gerald	427
Feinberg, Erin	505
Feiner, Harry	107
Feingold, Gregg H.	535
Feith, Daniel W.	455
Fekete, Martha	490
Feldbauer, Elizabeth	564
Feldbauer, George C.	467
Feldbauer, Irene	564
Feldman, Dave	496
Feldman, Lindsay	501
Feldman, Stuart	447, 527
Feldmann, Robert	468
Fellegara, Rich	383
Fellegara, R.N. Kathy	383
Feller, Fern	480
Fellows, Mary E.	511
Fellows, Susan	527
Feltman, Robert	511
Felton, Caitlin	9
Femina, Della/Rothschild Jeary and Partners	2
Fennell, Christine	480
Fennell, Joy	490
Fenske, Roderick	9
Fenton, Andrea M.	511
Fenton, Kate	107
Ferallo, Kerin	501
Ferguson, H. Roxanne	480
Ferguson, Jane	527
Ferguson, Judith	527
Ferguson, Scott	504
Ferguson, Scott King	550
Fernandez, Danny	527
Fernandez, Gavin	400
Fernandez, Stanley	400
Fernbach, Alex	9, 427
Fernberger, Peter	427
Ferone, Joseph Donato	447
Ferraer, Timothy J.	468
Ferrante, Enrico	480
Ferrante, Evan	498
Ferrara, Carl	511
Ferrara, Jay	480
Ferrara, Nicholas	511
Ferraro, Christopher	511
Ferraro, Edward	419
Ferraro, Paul	480
Ferreira, Paolo	490
Ferri, Bruce	496
Ferri, Elisa	490
Ferris, James J.	455
Ferris, Kenneth	427
Ferrucci, Raffaello	455
Ferry, April	559
Fersobe, Sorangel	388
Fertik, Greta	511
Feuer, Todd	66
Ficalora, John	447, 498
Fideler, James	409
Field, The	48, 54
Field, Trayce G.	555
Fiedler, Jeanene K.	423
Fiedler, Mark John	456
Fiedler, William	456
Fields, Charles A.	456
Fields, Robin	564
Fierberg, Steven	436
Fierce Release Designs Corp.	109
Figler, Chris	66
Figueroa, Edwin M.	468
Figueroa, Sandi	564
Filepp, Victor	535
Filley, Jonathan	550
Film & Video Magazine	226
Film & Video Stock Shots, Inc.	97
FILM Archives, Inc.	97
Film Art LA	233, 324
Film Bank, Inc./Corbis Motion	97
Film Collective, The	31
Film Emporium	230, 266, 294
Film Source LA	266, 294
Film, TV & Music Directory	226
Film-to-Tape Transfer Service	87
Film/Video Arts, Inc.	87, 289
Filmcars and Vintage Checker Taxicabs	355
FilmCore Editorial	48
Filmmaker Magazine	226
Final Draft, Inc.	222
Finaldi & Associates	2
Finamore, Michael	535
Finan, Tom	66
Fine, Russell	427
Finerty, Tom	9
Finestone, Steven	436
Finfer, David	66
Finger Lakes Regional Airport	154
Fink, Michael	104
Finkel, Gregory	400
Finkel, Lynn	540
Finkin, Seth	511
Finkin, Stephen	511
Finlay, Joan E.	511
Finlay, Kenneth P.	456
Finley-Holiday Film Corporation	97
Finn, Bruce L.	436
Finn, Daniel M.	468
Finn, Dianne Rossetti	110
Finn, John	239
Finn, Kenneth H.	511
Finnair	153
Finnerty, James M.	468
Finnerty, Jill D.	511
Finnerty, John	468
Finnerty, John M.	468
Finnerty, Joseph A.	468
Finnerty Jr., James W.	476
Fiore, Gerard J.	468
Fiore, Robert J.	468
Firestarter Rentals	60, 284
Firestone, Tina Whitney	559
Firm, The	16
FirstCom Music	80
FirstImage, LLC	26
Fischer, Hulda	511
Fischer, Lorri	527
Fischer, Max	409, 414
Fischetto, Donna	480
Fish Films Footage World	97, 292
Fishel, Glenn	468
Fisher, Dan	66
Fisher, Daniel W.	511
Fisher, Dick	436
Fisher, Elliott	535
Fisher, Eric	409
Fisher Light	315
Fisher, Linda	555, 559
Fisher, Raymond A.	511
Fisher, Robert	447
Fisher, Yolan	511
Fishkin, Martha	511
Fishman, Andrew	468
Fishman, Bettiann	447
Fisichella, Mark	393
Fittipaldi, Joseph Edward	456
Fitzgerald, David	185
Fitzgerald, Kevin	9
Fitzgibbons, Gail	564

Name	Page
Fitzgibbons, Mark	107
Fitzmaurice, Michael	436
Fitzpatrick, David	393
Fitzpatrick, Jamieson	400
Fitzpatrick, Kevin G.	456
Fitzpatrick Jr., Kevin G.	456
Fitzpatrick Manhattan, The	177
Fitzsimmons, Mc Cord	552
Fitzsimons, Brian J.	468
Five Foot Five Productions, Inc.	23, 58
FJC Security Services	202
Fjotland, Glenn	468
Flack, Jan Peter	393
Flack, Sarah	66
Flaherty, Therese	490
Flaiz, David	419
Flam, Mo	436
Flam, Morris	456
Flanagan, Jack	393
Flanagan, John L.	456
Flanagan, Peter Devaney	66
Flandreau, Teddy	409
Flanegin, Molly	393
Flanigan, David	400
Flannery, Matthew	400
Flashcards/Liz Forsyth	271
Flat Rate Cleaners	338
Flat Rate Movers	196
Flat Washer	112
Flatiron Color Lab	76
Flatotel	177
Fleitell, Neil	428
Fleming, Frank	555
Fleming, Joseph	468
Fleming, Tim	436
Fleming-Shon, Amber	107
Flexitoon	323
Flickerlab	54
Flight 9 Group, The	78
Flinn, John C.	436
Flinn, Lewis	51
Flohr, Jeff	425
Flora, Janet	480
Florentine Films/Sherman Pictures	23, 38
Floresca, John	400
Florida	170
Florida-Cape Canaveral	170
Florida-Central Florida	170
Florida-Collier County	170
Florida-Emerald Coast	172
Florida-Fort Lauderdale	172
Florida-Jacksonville	172
Florida-Key West	172
Florida-Miami Beach	172
Florida-Miami-Dade	172
Florida-Orlando	172
Florida-Palm Beach County	172
Florida-Tampa Bay	172
Flowers, Cynthia	564
Flowers, David	456
Flowers, Jill	564
Flow Motion Inc.	56, 58
Floyd, Ricky	393
Floyd, Roxanna	490
Floyd, William	400
Fluid	54, 82
Flynn, Kevin W.	468
Flynn, Michael	498
Flynn, Patrick	66
Flynn, Raymond	535
Flynn, Timothy J.	468
FMP Visual Communications	56
Focus Features	27
Foden, Tom	393
Foerschner, Charles	400
Fogel, Douglas	540
Fogel, Richard	456
Foglia Jr., Robert	525
Foley, Bill	507
Foley Power Systems	302, 315
Foley, Ray	498
Foley, Stephen	511
Folger, Claire	505
Fonda, Peter C.	535
Fondulas, Christopher	535
Fondulas, Maryann	239
Fong, Larry	436
Fonkalsrud, Jeong	480
Font, Marta	564
Fontaine, Andrea	525
Fontaine, Stephane	436
Fontana, Lindsay Ann	550
Fontana, Patrick B.	456
FoodPix	97
Foody, Edward	456
Footage Hollywood	97
Footage Store, The	97, 292
FootageFinder	97
Foote, Cone & Belding	2
Foote, Doug	400
Foote, Gary	51
FOR-A Corporation of America	285
Foraker, Brett	9
Forbes Brothers Production Vehicles	194
Forbes, Doug	66
Forbes, Stefan	428
Ford, Amrita-Diane	480
Ford, Casey J.	456
Ford, C. Romani	480
Ford, John R.	511
Ford, M. Alison	388
Ford, Matthew	456
Ford, Michael	539
Ford Models, Inc.	229, 246
Ford, Richard J.	456
Ford, Roger	393
Ford, Rusty	498
Ford, Thomas M.	456
Ford Wheeler	390
Forensic Films	27
Forma, Anthony	436
Forman, David	51
Forman, Filis	490
Forman, Janet	511
Forman, Mark	437
FormDecor, Inc.	346
Fornes, Steven C.	468
Forns-Escude, Marta	527
Forsberg, Crille	437
Forsberg, Herbert O.	428
Forste, Aaron	527
Forste, Megan	400
Forsyte, Joey	428
Forsyth, Ian	437
Fort Gates Films Unlimited	306, 315
Fort, Mary Jane	559
Forte' Sound	268
Fortier, Damon	393
Fortino, David	468
Fortunato, Jon	400
Fortunato, Joseph	468
Fortunato, Michael A.	535
Fortunato, Pyare	400
Fortunato, Ron	428
Fortune, Jay	456
Fortune, Raymond	456
Foster, Charlie	527
Foster, Eric	437
Foster, Ernest M.	511
Foster, John	428
Foster, Katherine	511
Foster, Kristen	480
Foster, Michael	512
Foster, William J.	512
Foto Care, Ltd.	262
Fountain, Edward A.	512
Four Seasons, The	177
Fournier, Janna	512
Fowles, Careen	564
Fox, John	35
Fox, Richard	450
Fox, Robert	393
Fox-Lerner, Avra	456
Foxtrot Production Services	271
Foy Inventerprises, Inc.	544
Fraasa, Steve	437
Fradianni, Michael	456
Fragapane, Christopher	507
Fraguada, Rafael M.	512
Fraisse, Robert	437
Framepool Inc.	97, 292
Framerunner, Inc.	87, 289
Frameworks Storyboards	35, 381
Framing For Movies	324
France	176
Francine Tint Costume Design/Soft Sculpture	334
Franciosa Jr., Stephen	66
Francis, Donna	523
Francis, Jo	66
Francis, Marcus	490
Francis-Bruce, Richard	66
Francisco, Michelle	452
Franco, Avenol A.	498, 504
Franco, Joe	51
Francois, Fritzgerald	535
Francone, Armond	388
Francovilla, Peter	51
Frank Bee Stores	334

Name	Page
Frank Spadaro Customhouse Brokers	166
Frankel, Reba	456
Frankel, Roberta N.	512
Frankfurt, Kurnit, Klein & Selz	228
Frankham, David	9
Frankie Steinz Costume	334
Franklin, Chris	66
Franklin, Sergei	428
Franklin, Weinrib, Rudell & Vassallo, P.C.	228
Franks, Michael	437
Frank's Sport Shop	331
Frankston, Max E.	552
Frantz, Lisa	388
Franzoni, David	456
Franzoni, Henry Thomas	456
Fraser, Greig	437
Fraser, Patrick	437
Fraser, Walt	437
Fratianni, Ralph	468
Fratianni, Steven	468
Frato, Richard J.	512
Frazen, Robert	66
Frazier, Chad K.	388
Freakfilms, Inc./Merle Becker	66
Frechette, Michael	512
Fred Berner Films	27
Fred Weinberg Music and Sounds	43, 82
Fredenburg, Jacci	555
Frederick, David J.	437
Frederick P. Rose Hall Home of Jazz at Lincoln Center	91, 188
Fredericks, Sarah	512
Frederickson, Mary	388
Fredette, Richard	400
Fredriksz, Robin	490
Free, Adam K.	447
Free Advertising, Inc.	245
Free, Audrey	525
Freed, Jennifer	239
Freed, Robbie	393
Freedman, Jon-David	456
Freedman, Peter W.	535
Freedman, Richard S.	413
Freeman, Christopher H.	388
Freeman, Jackie	564
Freeman, Jonathan	428
Freestyle Collective	54, 102
Freewheelin' Films Stock Footage	98
Freilich, Christopher	437
Fremar, Leslie	559
French Consulate General	165
Frenchway Travel, Inc.	204
Fresh Air Flicks	277
Freund, Kathryn	512
Frey, Larry	9
Frick Art Reference Library	233
Fricke, Walter	456
Fried, Kenneth	4
Friedberg, Mark	388
Friedberg, Rick	9
Friedewald, Eric	419
Friedlander, Richard	104
Friedman, Marvin	9
Friedman, Nancy A.	512
Friedman, Robert E.	535
Friedman, Samuel G.	456
Friedman-Norton, Amy	447, 498
Friedman-Palmieri, Betsy	527
Frings, Michael	9
Fritche, Rob	400
Fritz, Pete	66
Fritzsching, Werner	51
Friz, Joshua	400
Frogley, Louise	559
Frohna, Jim	437
Froling, Alison	512
Frommer, Daniel	383
Frucht, Lisa	564
Fruchtman, Lisa	66
Frumkes, Christopher H.	456
Fryer, James W.	456
FTC/Orlando	260
Fucci, Michael	527
Fuentes, Paul	9
Fuhrmann, Kristi	480
Fujifilm USA, Inc. Motion Picture Divison	266, 294
Fujimoto, Tak	437
Fujinon, Inc.	285
Full Circle Studios	58
Full Glass Films, LLC	16, 27, 200
Full House Productions	43
Fulleda, Frank	535
Fuller, Brad	66
Fuller, Gail	107
Fuller, Leslie	490
Fuller, Matt	35
Fuller, Trish	66
Fullerton, Carl	323, 480, 490
FullMind, LLC.	23, 54
Fulton, Larry	393
Fundus, John K.	535
Fundus, Kathryn G.	512
Fundus, Kenneth J.	468
Fungrai, Anthony	468
Furey, Charles	419
Furey, Gerard J.	419
Furgang & Adwar, LLP	228
Furino, Jimmy	229
Furman Roth Advertising	2
Furmanski, Jonathan	400
Furner, Guy	437
Furr, Daryl D.	456
Fusco-Wickham, Toni	559
Futo, Andy	464
Future Express	151
Future Lighting	326
FX	326
Fymat, Alex	393

G

Name	Page
G & E Music	82
Gabaeff, Isaac	512
Gable, Jordan	468
Gabriel, Joe	409
Gabriele, John	468
Gabriels, Ed	452
Gagliano, William	535
Gagnon, D. Scott	512
Gaily, Paul S.	512
Gair, Joanne	480
Gajwani, Amit	559
Galante, Jason	468
Galante Jr., Richard	468
Galante Sr., Richard A.	476
Galaxy Global Eatery, The	161
Galdo, Daniel	468
Galiardi, Daniel	400
Galindez, Vincent	437
Galinsky, Scott	437
Galione, Joseph	535
Gallacher, Tracey	393
Gallagher, Angela	480
Gallagher, Helen M.	480
Gallagher, Jamie	456
Gallagher, Joe	437
Gallagher, John S.	419
Gallagher, Patrick	66
Gallagher, Randall	468
Gallart, Michael J.	456
Gallegos, Kristin	490
Gallo, Christopher	437
Gallo, Fred J.	419
Gallo, Leah	505
Gallo, Renee	512
Gallo, Steven	468
Galt, Nigel	66
Galthon, Beth	9
Galuppo Jr., John J.	468
Galus, Mara	400
Galvin, Jim E.	456
Galvin, Michael T.	512
Galvin, Timothy	388, 512
Gambardella, Mary	525
Gambardella, Robert	456
Gamiello, Anthony F.	468
Gamiello Jr., Anthony S.	512
Gamiello, Christopher	468
Gamiello, Dennis	468
Gamiello Jr., Dennis	468
Gamiello, Matthew	512
Gamiello, Steven R.	512
Gana, Roger	35
Ganai, Omer	437
Gandy, Sue	555
Ganem, Mitch	185
Gannon, Ellen	501
Ganon, Joan	525
Gant, Julie A.	456
Gantz, Robert	428
Ganz, Robert E.	468
Gara, Marisa	464
Garces, Rosa	239
Garcia, Carlos	400
Garcia, Fabian	480
Garcia, Regina	388
Garcia-Vlasits, David	409
Gardell, Randy	555

Company/Crew Index

Name	Page
Gardenier, John	468
Garden State Limo	182
Gardner, Arthur C.	456
Gardner, Cindy	480
Gardner, James	437
Gardner, Keith J.	535
Gardner, Nick	409
Gardner-Patsos, Julia M.	468
Gardyasz, Christine	512, 532
Garfield, Brad	450
Gargoyle Films, Inc.	16
Garite, Matt	409
Garland, Glenn	66
Garland, Marc	527
Garland, Rebecca	239
Garlitos, Marcial	419
Garner, Steven	456
Garofalo, Michael	400
Garrett, Mark	437
Garrison, Julia	107
Garruba, Peter	185
Gartland, George B.	468
Gartland, James B.	468
Gartland, James V.	468
Garuda-Indonesia	153
Garvey, Brian S.	512, 532
Garvey, Justin T.	468
Garvey, William F.	468
Gary's Loft, Inc.	127, 188
Gaslight Advertising Archives, Inc.	352
Gasparovic, Walter	450
Gasper, Mark	23
Gates, John	428
Gatewood, Thomas	540
Gatland, John	468
Gatto-Cimmelli, Ann	512
Gaudio, Kate	564
Gaunt, Emily	107
Gautier, Eric	437
Gay, Paul	9
Gayan, Nacho	9
Gayesky, Fernando	400
Gayraud, Pierre-Yves	559
Gazal, Christian	66
GDR Equipment Co.	306
Gear + Rose Motion Control	263
Gear For Hire HD	275, 281
Gearity, Eric	468
Geary, Daniel P.	419
Geary, Rachel	480
Gebbia, Paul	480
Gebert, Chris.	535
Geddes, David	437
Gee, Christine M.	525
Gee, Hubert	419
Gefen, Inc.	80
Geiger, Adam	437, 549
Geiger, Pam	490
Geiger, Stephen	107
Geiger, William J.	419
Geisler, John	409, 414
Geissbühler, Luke	428
Geisz, John E.	419
Gelber, Charlie	66
Gelbord, Kay	490
Geldof, Matthew	539
Gelernter, Melissa	501
Geller Agency, The	66, 381, 393, 428, 437, 447, 450, 544, 559
Geller, Edward R.	476
Geller, Jay	476
Gemini Co., Inc., The	323, 364, 373
Gendron, Matthew	66
Gendzier, Nathan	528
General Mayhem	323
Genet, Darren	437
Genser, Abbot	505, 507
Genser, Leslie	393
Gentile Sr., Anthony	512
Geoff Green Photography	507
George, Alenalsa	480
George, Catherine	564
George P. Clarke Advertising, Inc.	2
Georgevich, Dejan	428
Georgia	172
Georgia-Savannah	172
Georgiou, Kay	480
Geppetto Studios, Inc.	323, 334, 364
Gerbson, Steve	498
Gerchberg, Heather G.	490
Geren	559
Gerike, Theo	185
Gering, Jenny	555
German Consulate General	165
Germany-Bavaria	176
Germany-Berlin	176
Gerred, Karyn	107
Gerriets International	318, 336, 340
Gerry Cosby & Co., Inc.	375
Gersh Agency, The	66, 381, 393, 428, 437, 559
Gershenson, M.D. Peter M.	383
Gershenson, R.N. Carolyn A.	383
Gersh, Michael	9
Gersman, Lana	480
Gertsen, Ezra K.	419
Gertsen, Gilbert H.	512
Gertsen, Glenn H.	419
Gertsen, Gordon H.	512
Gertsen, Jesse H.	419
Gertsen, K. Scott	419
Gertsen, Ryan M.	419
Gerull, Helge	437
Gervai, David	51
Gesinski, Jonathan	35
Geto & Demilly, Inc.	34
Getty Images	98, 292
Getz, Deren	185
Getzinger, Scott	512
Geyer, Lawrence	501
Ghertler, Caroline	512, 532
Ghiraldini, Robert	535
Giammalvo, Chris	393
Giammarese, Linda	564
Gianettino & Meredith, Inc.	2
Giannillo, Gregg	480
Giannini, A. Christina	555
Giaquinto III, Daniel P.	512
Giaronomo Productions	40
Gibbons, Anika	501
Gibilisco, Paul	400
Gibson, Anita	480
Gibson, Rachel A.	239
Gibson, Rachelle	525
Gibson, Richard	9
Giegerich, Arthur N.	456
Gierczak, Mary C.	564
Giesbrecht, David	505
Gifford, Felicity	564
Giffune, Gary	512
Gigante Vaz & Partners Advertising, Inc.	2
Gigantic Pictures	31
Giglia, Kim	468
Giguere, Edi	559
Gilbert, John	66
Gilbert, Shaun C.	456
Gilbert, Steve	447
Gilbuena, Kley	512
Gilford, Darren	393
Gilgar Jr., John	456
Gill, Charles	476
Gill, Chris	66
Gill, Megan	66
Gilleran, Billy	468
Gilleran, Charles	468
Gillham, Dan	428
Gilliar, Kathryn	512
Gilligan, Kerri	512
Gilligan, Kevin Casey	468
Gilligan Jr., Thomas D.	512
Gilliland, Jeanne L.	535
Gillis, Doreen	480, 490
Gillis, Spencer	401
Gilly, Paul S.	456
Gilman, Gregory	528
Gilmartin, Gregg	419
Gilmartin, Jim	107
Gilmour, Thomas	425
Gilroy, Daniel	512
Gilroy, John J.	419
Gilroy Jr., James P.	419
Gimenez, Xavi	437
Gimeno, Marissa	523
Ginsberg, Carl	9
Ginsberg, Hildie	480
Ginsberg, Susan	480
Ginsburg, Michael	507
Gioia, Rick	401
Gioiella, David	66
Giordano FX	323, 332, 334, 356, 364, 373
Giorgio Armani	376
Giorgio's of Gramercy Park	161
Giovanniello, Danielle	512
Giovanniello, Neil A.	512
Giovingo, Michael	437
Gipson, Terry	388
Giraldi Productions	16
Giraldi, Robert	9
Girolami, Anthony D.	456

Name	Page
Girolami, Peter R.	456
Girolami, Richard J.	456
Girolami Jr., Richard J.	456
Girouard, Stephen.	468
Gisone, Louis	456
Gitter, Jeffry S.	447, 540
Giudice, Gary	504
Giuliano, Peter	447, 498
Givens, Michael	428
Gizmo Special Effects	264
Gladstone, Steven	437
Gladstone, Valerie	480
Glanzrock, Stephen Andrew	447, 504
Glaser, John (Woody)	401
Glaser, Robyn L.	512
Glass, Chad	35
Glass House New York	188
Glass Restorations	347
Glass, Ted	512
Glassman, Adam	559
Glassman, Paulette	498, 550
Glauberman, Dana	66
Glazer, Tg	528
Glazman, Steven	389
Gleason, Debbie	4
Gleason, Philip G.	535
Gleason's Gym, Inc.	188, 246, 375
Gleaton, Christopher	401
Gleeson, Lisa Marie	456
Glenn, Don	409, 415, 417
Glenwood NYC	177
Glew, Rebecca	239
Glickman, Adam	528
Glisson, Lane	107, 512, 532
Glisson, Steven	107, 110
Global Antiques & Fine Reproductions	364
Global ImageWorks, LLC	98, 233, 293
Global Media Resources, Inc.	266, 294
Global Production Network	201
Global Scenic Studios, Ltd.	112
Global Security Services	202
Global Vision Images	98
Globerson, Sharon	555, 559
Globus Studios	120
Gluck, Lewis	512
Go Film	16
Go Studios	127
Gobbi, Franco	490
Goblin Lighting Services, Inc.	298, 304, 306, 316
Goddard, Preston L.	498, 528
Godek, Brent T.	512
Godfrey, Jinx	66
Godfrey, Lorraine	480
Godfrey, Niko Dee	239
Godlove & Company, Inc.	218
Godwin, Frank	409
Goelz, Anne	389
Goffman, Aaron	393
Goforth, Fritz	428
Gogniat, Georgette	564
Goh, Eileen	564
Gold Shield Executive Services	202
Gold, Steven	51
Goldberg, Ben	51
Goldberg, Harvey	512
Goldblatt, Mark	66
Goldblatt, Stephen	437
Goldcrest Post Production	43, 60, 87, 91, 284, 289, 291
Goldcrest Post Production/Pixel Monkeys	54
Golden, James Edward	447
Golden, Joanne	447, 498
Golden Touch Transportation, Inc.	155
Goldenberg, William	66
Goldfarb, Alan	540
Goldfarb, Erika	501
Goldman, Dina	389
Goldman, Joseph	428, 456
Goldman, Mia	66
Goldmark, Sandra	389
Goldsmith, James	401
Goldsmith, Paul	437
Goldstein, Adam	9
Goldstein, Ali	505
Goldstein, Ari	407
Goldstein, Howard	512
Goldstein, Jess	555
Goldstein, Lionel	9
Goldstein, Michael	419
Gomez, Chuck	401
Gomez, Jackie	490
Gomez, Susan	564
Goncalves, Affonso	66
Gonchor, Jess	389
Gonzales, Damian	456
Gonzales, Dana	437
Gonzales, Thom	480
Gonzalez, Conrad	66
Gonzalez, Ginger	540
Gonzalez, J. Anthony	512
Gonzalez, Joseph J.	501
Gonzalez, Joseph L.	525
Gonzalez, Marcos	528
Gonzalez, Mari Keiko	66
Gonzalez Model and Talent Agency	246
Gonzalez, Robert F.	456
Gooch, John D.	535
Good, Timothy A.	66
Goode, Christopher Giles	550
Goodenough, Gabriel	401
Goodermote, Mark A.	535
Goodkind, Elisa	559
Goodman, Charles	468
Goodman, Gregory E.	498
Goodman, Julie	504
Goodman, Martin	51
Goodmanson, Chris	393
Goodnoff-Cernese, Adam B.	512
Goodridge, George	393
Goodrum, Elizabeth	564
Goodstein, Kenneth	512
Goodwin, Gregory W.	419
Goodwin, Rachel	490
Goon, Charles	503
Gordon, Damon Michael	528
Gordon, Dick	66
Gordon, Elke	490
Gordon, Glenn E.	419
Gordon, Katherine	564
Gore, Catherine	525
Gore-Reeves, Sarah	559
Gori, Robert	239
Gorka, Magdalena	437
Gorman, Anne	564
Gorman, C. Scott	67
Gorman, Katherine D.	512
Gorman, Timothy P.	419
Goroff, Paul V.	468
Gorskaya, Yana	67
Goss, Bradley J.	468
Goss, Dylan	9
Goss, Fred	9
Goss, Kirk	468
Gotham Bike Shop	188
Gotham Digital FX, Inc.	54
Gotham Music, Inc.	43
Gotham Pictures	23
Gotham Scenic, LLC	112
Gotham Sound and Communications, Inc.	164, 268
Goto, Joji	532
Gott, Lauren	490
Goude, Jean-Paul	9
Goulder, Susan M.	512
Gould, Nicholas C.	552
Gould, Thomas W.	535
Gourmet To U, LLC	161
Govan, Deirdra	564
Govoni, Patricia	428
Gozzo, Ron	51
GPI	23
Grace, Coco	490
Grace, Mollie Vera	239
Grace, Peter	552
Grady, James M.	468
Graef, Susan	67
Graf Air Freight	151
Graf, Anthony D.	468
Graf, Jon E.	419
Graf, Robert	498
Graham, Hilmer	67
Graham, Jason Matthew	528
Graham, Jonathan	468
Graham, Stuart	437
Gramaglia, John	67
Gramercy Broadcast Center	120
Gramercy Office Equipment	223
Gramercy Park Hotel	177
Grammer, John H.	419
Grana-Mena, Milton	437
Granaderos, Alyson	490
Grand Brass Lamp Parts	352
Grand Hyatt	177
Grande, Patricia	480
Grandon, Travis	452
Grandview Island Productions	16, 23
Graneto, Christopher F.	468
Granger, Martin	9
Grano, Christopher	512
Granof, Victoria	452

Company/Crew Index

Name	Page
Grant, Afton	409, 415
Grant, Bradley	401
Grant, George E.	468
Grant, Gloria	480, 490
Grant, John	51
Grant, Lyle	35
Grant, Robert (Crow)	419
Grant, Schuyler	67
Grant Wilfley Casting	218, 229
Grantham, Marshall	51
Grantland, Michael	401
Graphics for Industry, Inc.	333
Grasley, Michael	393
Grasso, Francis C.	468
Grasso, James	450
Grasso, Joe	437
Grasso, John	535
Grasso, Mark	468
Grassy Hill	246
Gravatt, Justin	456
Graves, Jill	564
Graves, Kevin	437
Graves, Regina	512
Gravett, Jacques	67
Gray, Deba Jean	512
Gray, F. Gary	9
Gray, Justin	535
Gray, Roger	419
Gray, Scott	67
Gray, William	401
Grayson, Bobby	480
Graziadei, Frank J.	535
Great American Catering	161
Great Voice Co., The	218
Greaves, Katie	401
Greco	512
Greco, Thomas	401
Greek 101.com	245, 334, 373
Greek Consulate General	165
Green, Arthur	428
Green, Bruce	67
Green, Charlie	490
Green, Christopher	401
Green Jr., Daniel	480
Green, David Gordon	9
Green, Dennis T.	535
Green, Gareth	490
Green, Jack	437
Green, Jesse	437
Green, Michael	428
Green, Michael N.	456
Green, Ronald	401
Green, Steph	9, 28
Green, Susanna	234
Greenbaum, Nicole	564
Greenberg, Adam	437
Greenberg, Jerry	67
Greenberg, Marc	528
Greenberg, Robbie	437
Greenberg, Sarah	452
Greenberg, Sherry	550
Greenberg, Steven	456
Greencard Pictures	16
Greene, Callum	498
Greene, Deborah	512
Greene, Meredith	480
Greene, Rachel	564
Greene, Rhonney	564
Greene, Robert	490
Greene, Shawn	456
Greenestreet Films, Inc.	31, 200
Greenfield, Bruce H.	447
Greenfield, Lauren	9
Greenfield-Sanders, Timothy	9
Greenholz, Don	447
Greenpoint Reformed Church	188
Greenpoint Terminal	188
Greenpoint Tool Rentals Corporation	303
Greenroom	346
Greenwell, Mary	490
Greenwood, Jane	555
Greenwood, Sarah	393
Greer, Andrea	525
Greer, Keith	540
Greer, Randy	409
Greer, Randy	414
Greg Hensley Productions	98, 293
Gregoire, Scott	456
Gregorio, Italo	490
Gregory, Glen A.	419
Gregory, James	456
Gregory, Thomas J.	419
Gregory, Wanda	480
Gregory, William R.	419
Gregson, Kelly	564
Greif, Paula	9
Grella, Jamison	456
Greller, Roman	512
Gresham, Gloria	559
Gressis, Joe	67
Greto, Sam	419
Greve, Andrew	456
Grewal, Arv	393
Grey, Joaquin	393
Gribble, David	437
Grieco, Nicole	480
Grief, Paula	28
Grieg, Gary	428
Gries, Phil	437
Grieve, Andy	67
Griffenkranz, Arthur J.	512
Griffin, Marlon	9
Griffin, Zulema	555
Griffith, Clay	393
Griffith, Nancy	512
Griffiths, David	428
Griffon Jr., Robert J.	512
Griffon, Russ J.	513
Grill, David	456
Grill, Gary	419
Grimaldi, Joseph L.	456
Grimes, Linda	480, 490
Grimes, Timothy M.	513
Grimm, Peter	540
Grimolizzi, John	419
GripAndElectric.com	316
Grites, Jeremy S.	468
Grizzly Bear	51
Grobet, Xavier Perez	437
Groody, Thomas M.	513
Groomes, Ronald James	523
Groove Addicts Production Music Catalog	80
Gropman, David	393
Gross, Bruce L.	513
Gross, Laurie	447
Grossman, Zack	35
Grosso, Daniel K.	513
Groth, Jeff	67
Grousset, Sebastien	9
Groves, Rodney	490
GRS Systems, Inc.	48, 58, 87, 268, 275, 277, 281, 283, 284, 289
Grubb, Nate	528
Grubbs, Charles	456
Gruebel, James P.	469
Gruet, Charlie	437
Grunberg, Slawomir	438
Grunke, Ian	469
Grunke, Paul	469
Grupo Taca	153
Gruszynski, Alexander	438
GTN Pictures, LLC	38
GTV, Inc.	48, 54, 87, 102, 289
Guachione, Daniel Glenn	535
Guadarrama, Thomas	425
Guard Brothers, The	9, 28
Guardian Entertainment, LTD	16, 27, 87, 200, 289
Guariello, Victoria	513
Guarneri, Nicola	464
Guarriello, Matthew L.	469
Guarriello, Vincent J.	469
Guava	54
Gucciardo, James	428
Gudnason, Ottar	438
Gueli, Anthony	480
Guerra, Carlos	409, 415
Guerra, Louis J.	447
Guerra Paint & Pigment	325
Guest, Christopher	9
Guest, Joe	528
Guevara, Lisa	401
Guichard, Eric	438
Guilbaud, Steve	239
Guimaraes, Melissa	469
Guindo, Anguibe	535
Guinness Jr. Richard J.	469
Guirard, Jean-Paul	513
Gulick, David W.	513
Gullane Entertainment	38
Gumb, Nzingha	480
Gunn, Sam	67
Gunning, Lisa	67
Gunning, Mark	409
Gunshor, Emily	555
Gunter, Chat	535
Gupta, Sanji F.	438
Gurevich, Eli	239
Gurgo, Robert	456

Company/Crew Index

Name	Page
Gurin, Robin	481, 490
Gurney, David	456
Gurr, Judith	513
Guss, John Walker	528
Gustafson, Grant	67
Gutierrez, John	535
Gutierrez, Manuel	409
Gutin, Vanessa	502
Gutman, Ruth	4
Gutowitz, Michael	67
Gyllenhaal, Kate	221
Gym Source	375
Gyron Systems International, A Division of Wolfe Air Aviation, Ltd.	285
Gyson, Leslie	502
GZ Entertainment & Stunts	327, 364, 544

H

Name	Page
H & B Super Express, Inc.	155
H5	9, 28
Haag, Ulrika	564
Haagensen, Craig	428
Haas, Stephan B.	535
Haase, Eric J.	438
Habacker, Amy	564
Habana Avenue	17
Haber, Franklin R.	535
Haber, Lauren	401
Haberberg, Ari	438
Haberman, Stephanie	504
Hackenberg, Kevin	469
Hackett, Christine Marie	513
Hackler, Chip	409
Hackman, Peter G.	107, 324
Hadco Metal Trading Co., LLC	352
Haddad, Emily	553
Haddad's	194
Hadjadj, Bruno	393
Hafela, Grosvenor Miles	438
Hafitz, Andrew	67
Hafner, Stephanie	67
Haft, Cathy	528
Haft, Craig	401
Haftel, Linda	525
Hagerman, Mark	502
Hagler, Gregory V.	419
Hahn, Karl	438
Hahn, Nicholas	401
Hahn, Rob	428
Haines-Stiles, Nicholas	469
Hair, James	401
Haire, Jennifer	502
Haitian Consulate General	165
Hale, Mitchell	481
Haley, Robert	428
Hall, Adam M.	469
Hall, Alexander	67
Hall, Amy	409, 417
Hall, Cai	401
Hall, Christopher	409
Hall, Conrad	438
Hall, Dennis S.	438
Hall, Geoffrey	438
Hall, Haines	67
Hall, Jeff	393
Hall, Jerome	457
Hall Jr., John	481
Hall, Stanley	481
Hallak Cleaners	338
Hallberg, Jonas	559
Hallenborg, Neil	447, 498
Halley Resources	381, 452, 490, 523, 559
Hallick, Ned	457
Halliday, Jimm	555
Halliday, Justine	67
Halligan, H. Jay	469
Halligan, John J.	469
Halligan, Paul J.	469
Halligan, Thomas	564
Halligan Jr., Thomas E.	469
Hallowell, Todd	498
Halmi Jr., Robert Allen	550
Halpern, Jennifer	555
Halpern, Jennifer Ann	513, 532
Halsey, Richard	67
Ham, Scott	67
Hamburger Woolen Co., Inc.	340
Hamdi, Souraya	481
Hamed, Amir	438
Hamill, Brian	505
Hamilton, Andrew	401
Hamilton, Donna F.	513
Hamilton, James	505
Hamilton, John	401, 528
Hamilton, Kenneth	564
Hamilton, Marcia	490
Hamilton, Sandy	513
Hamilton, Steve	67
Hamilton II, Thomas B.	457
Hamilton, Tim	9
Hamilton, Vanuel Deshawn	239
Hamilton Jr., William	423
Hamilton-Grobler, Kristina	67
Hammadi, Jamal	490
Hammer, Kenneth	419
Hammond, Christopher M.	457
Hammond, Danny	491
Hammond Jr., Kevin J.	513
Hammond, Mark	540
Hammond, Nicholas	535
Hampton, John A.	535
Hampton, Peter J.	393
Hamptons Locations	185
Hamroff, Steven M.	535
Hanania, Barbara	401
Hanania, Caroline	393
Hand Held Films, Inc.	260, 275, 281, 306, 316
Hand, William	401
Handel, Gary	185
Handloser, Sandra	513, 532
Hanessian, Daniel	419
Hanft, Byrne, Raboy & Partners	2
Hank, Daniel	498, 504, 550
Hanken, Eric	513
Hanken, Michele	513
Hankey, Leslie	409, 414, 417
Hankins, Richard C.	393
Hanlon, Matthew L.	469
Hanna, Robert	428
Hannafey, Eugene P.	469
Hannan, Peter	438
Hanousek, Jonathan Joseph	491
Hanozet, Massimo	438
Hansel, Matthew C.	107
Hansen, Andrew	457
Hansen, Edward A.	513
Hansen, Henrik	9
Hansen, John	393
Hansen, Steve	51
Hansen, Warren	438
Hanson, Janet	452
Hanson, Lina	491
Happy	9, 28
Hapsas, Alex	450, 504
Harari, Justine	67
Haraszti, Zsolt	401
Harbick, James	513
Harbron, Patrick	505
Hardinge, Maya	481
Harding, Marlus C.	239
Hardstaff, Johnny	9, 28
Hardwick, Anthony	438
Hardy, Rob	438
Hardy, Tamika	491
Harford, Sacha	491
Harges, David Lee	457
Hargreaves, Sean	393
Harithas, Thalia	502
Harker, James J.	457
Harkins, Shaun	409, 414, 417
Harkness, Leslie	535
Harlem Brownstone Location	188
Harlow, Robert	469
Harmonic Ranch	43
Harrell, Lisa	481
Harrell, Michael D.	513
Harrer, Damien S.	513
Harrer Jr., William	469
Harriet Bass Casting	218
Harrington, George W.	457
Harrington, Mark C.	513
Harrington, Mary Jeanete	481
Harrington, Shane	457
Harrington Talents	200
Harrington, Valerie	525
Harrington-Hughes, Sheila	457
Harriot, Lucien J.	104
Harris, Dierdre	481
Harris, Enid	559
Harris, Gabe	419
Harris, James	469
Harris, Kevin Mark	564
Harris, Neil	10
Harris, Stan	393
Harrison, Cheryl A.	513
Harrison, Chris	67
Harrison, Christopher	67, 221, 481

Company/Crew Index

Harrison, David L. . . . 457
Harrow, Bruce . . . 555
Harry Poster Vintage TVs . . . 354
Hart, Douglas . . . 401, 469
Hart, Robb . . . 51
Hart, Will . . . 505
Hartell, Joanna . . . 513
Hartis, Paul . . . 564
Hartman, Richard . . . 419
Hartman, Tom . . . 393
Hartmann, Peter . . . 438
Hartnett, Christopher . . . 535
Hartnett, Dallas . . . 481, 491
Hartney, Michael H. . . . 513
Harton, Herb . . . 401
Harvey, Jason . . . 409, 417, 438
Harvey, Kelly A. . . . 513
Harvey, Linda Lee . . . 420
Harvey, Marilyn A. . . . 498, 504
Harvey, Timothy . . . 535
Hasbourne, Tiffany . . . 559
Haskell, Michael . . . 457, 496
Haskins, Gahan . . . 185
Hat/Cap Exchange . . . 334
Hau, Alfred . . . 10
Haun, Kim Mitchell . . . 438
Hause, Barbara J. . . . 564
Hausen, David . . . 438
Hausman, Michael Paul . . . 550
Haussman, Michael . . . 10
HAVE, Inc. . . . 56, 58
Havens, Stacy . . . 564
Haverty, Kevin . . . 401
Haviland, Helene . . . 409
Hawaii . . . 172
Hawaii-Big Island . . . 172
Hawaii-Honolulu . . . 172
Hawaii-Kauai . . . 172
Hawaii-Maui . . . 172
Hawaiian Airlines . . . 153
Hawken, Simon . . . 438
Hawkins, Tim . . . 107
Hawrylak, Michael . . . 553
Haxan . . . 10
Hayash, Edward (Ted) . . . 457
Hayash, Ted . . . 464
Hayes, Chris . . . 409, 413
Hayes, Christopher . . . 457
Hayes, Jason . . . 481
Hayes, Jeffrey . . . 550
Hayes, Josh . . . 35
Hayes, Kerry . . . 505
Hayes, Timothy . . . 448
Hayfield, Ernest . . . 505
Haygood, James . . . 67
Hayne, Jacinta Elizabeth . . . 528
Haynes, Dawn . . . 491, 559
Haynes, Jamie . . . 498, 531
Haynie, J. Michael . . . 450
Hays, Holbrook . . . 513
Hays, Sandy . . . 413, 416
Hays, Sanja . . . 560
Hays, William . . . 409, 415
Hayward, Adrian . . . 10
Haywood, Brent . . . 420
Hazirjian, Deke . . . 496
HB Group, Inc. . . . 275, 277, 281
HBO Archives . . . 98
HBO Films (NY) . . . 38
HBO Studio Productions . . . 43, 54, 78, 87, 120, 289
HBR Productions . . . 23
Headroom . . . 82
Headroom Digital Audio . . . 43
Healer, Chris . . . 104
Healy, Marc . . . 51
Healy, Timothy D. . . . 457
Healy, Tom . . . 540
Heaps, Christopher J. . . . 513
Heaps, Steven C. . . . 513
Heaps, Thomas J. . . . 513
Heart, Sherry . . . 481
Heartland Brewery . . . 249
HeavyLight . . . 84
Hebel, Christopher . . . 107
Hebrank, Richard J. . . . 469
Hechanova, Anthony . . . 401
Hecht, Gail Cooper . . . 555
Hedges, Elizabeth . . . 401
Heerdegen, James . . . 469
Heide, Ryan . . . 425
Heidi's Fabulous Fatigue Fighters Worldwide . . . 234
Heiferman, Ryan . . . 51
Heikkila, Andrew . . . 513
Heilweil, Samantha L. . . . 535
Heimann, Betsy . . . 560
Heinemann, Frank . . . 513
Heirloom Biography . . . 54
Heiss, Sonja . . . 10
Heitin, Eli . . . 498
Heitker, Norbert . . . 10
Held, Wolfgang . . . 428
Heldman, Michael . . . 67
Helen Mills Theater . . . 91, 190
Helen Uffner Vintage Clothing LLC . . . 334, 339, 340, 378
Helfand, Jonathan . . . 51
Helicopter Flight Services . . . 150
Helinet Aviation Services . . . 254, 322
Heller, Barbara . . . 528
Heller, Becki . . . 401
Heller, Brian . . . 428
Heller, Dianne . . . 481
Heller, Susan . . . 457
Hellman, Chris . . . 67
Hellman, David . . . 438
Hellman, Ron . . . 393
Hellmund, Mariana . . . 525
Hello World Communications . . . 23, 56, 58, 87, 164, 268, 275, 277, 282, 283, 289, 316
Hells Kitchen Music . . . 80, 82
Helmer, Frank . . . 560
HeloAir, Inc. . . . 254
Hemesath, Brian . . . 564
Hemion, Michelle . . . 401
Hemmert, Clayton . . . 67
Hemming, Lindy . . . 560
Henderson Jr., James . . . 540
Henderson, Jeff . . . 35
Henderson, Zachary . . . 469
Hendra Agency Inc., The . . . 34
Hendrick, Sarah . . . 401
Heneghan, John . . . 401
Henkels, Richard . . . 438
Hennessy, Michael Sean . . . 457
Hennessy, William F. . . . 513
Henning, Erin . . . 401
Hennings, David . . . 438
Henriksen, Scott . . . 438
Henriques, Samuel . . . 407, 409
Henriquez, Eric . . . 448
Henry, Jean . . . 481
Henry, Justin . . . 491
Henry, Marco . . . 498
Henry's International Cuisine . . . 161
Henschel, Paul . . . 10
Hensel, Christopher L. . . . 469
Henselmann, Xavier . . . 457
Hensler, Brad . . . 491
Hensley, Darwin . . . 481
Herlihy, Michael . . . 420
Herman & Lipson Casting, Inc. . . . 220
Herman, Amy . . . 550
Herman, Totie . . . 67
Hernandez, Christopher . . . 469
Hernandez, Gary . . . 67
Hernandez, Pedro . . . 469
Hernandez, Sandra . . . 555
Hernandez, Tony . . . 550
Herndon, Chad . . . 51
Hero Props . . . 366
Herrick, Rosanna . . . 90
Herron, John James . . . 469
Herron, Jonathan . . . 409, 415, 417, 438
Hersey, Daniel . . . 401
Hersey, Ron . . . 438
Hershcopf, Jane . . . 525
Hertz . . . 156
Hertz Equipment Rental Corporation . 298, 303, 309, 316, 320
Hertz Truck & Van . . . 158
Herzog, Yahel . . . 409
Heslep, Liz . . . 401
Hess, Brian T. . . . 513
Hess, Jared . . . 10
Hess, Joshua . . . 438
Hester, Neire . . . 469
Hevessy, William . . . 448
Hewes, William Earl . . . 550
Hewitt, Don . . . 513, 544
Hewitt, Jery . . . 513
Hewitt, Paul . . . 420
Heyer, Thomas Brian . . . 555
Heyman, Regina . . . 528
Hi-Top Productions . . . 82
Hibbard, Julian . . . 507
Hickox, Emma E. . . . 67
Hicks, Dan . . . 564
Hicks, Erin . . . 481
Hicks, Lori . . . 481, 491
Hidden Talents Casting . . . 220

Company/Crew Index

Name	Page
Higgins, Anton F.	535
Higgins, Samantha	513
High Output, Inc.	298, 304, 306, 316, 318
Higham, Matthew	457
Highbridge Car Service	182
Hildebrand, Gary D.	457
Hill, Charles	409
Hill, David	420
Hill, Jeremy K.	457
Hill, Nicholas	513
Hill, Shawnique	560, 564
Hill Studio & Scenic	120, 205, 327
Hill, Thomas J.	469
Hillman Arts	35
Hillygus, Marc	401
Hindle, Jeremy	393
Hinds, Tracey	528
Hines, George	457
Hines, William	457
Hinkel Equipment Rental	303, 310
Hintermeier, Thomas	491
Hinton, James	239
Hionis, Chryss	513
Hippisley Coxe Mei Lai	564
Hiramoto, Keiko	491
Hirn, Brent P.	469
Hirschfeld, Alec	428
Hirschfeld, Marc	401
Hirsch, John	555
Hirsch, Julien	438
Hirschorn, Jack	401
Hirschorn, Jeffrey	413, 416, 428
Hirschorn, Leslie	498
Hirsch, Paul	67
Hirsh, Erin	560
Hirshfield, B. Gray	498
Historic Films	98
History Channel, The	38
Hit & Run Productions	260, 316, 341
Hitchcock, Dennis	10
Hlinomaz, Bonnie	550
Hlinomaz, Petr	428, 457
Hobart, Charlett	560
Hobbie, John	389
Hobbs, R. Richard	185
Hobby	10
Hobo Audio Company	44
Hochstrasser, Alfred	51
Hockenberry Jr., John S.	457
Hocking, Thomas J.	469
Hodgdon, Marilinda	452
Hodges, Jeffrey	409
Hodges, Wesley	401
Hoebel, Petra	504
Hoff, Lawrence	535
Hoffman, Arlo	513
Hoffman, Constance	555
Hoffman, Lynn	564
Hoffman, Nicholas	428
Hoffman, Samuel	448, 550
Hoffman, Vanessa	528
Hofmann, Ruedi	10
Hogan, Mary Ann	491
Hogan, Sean	239
Hohndorf, Julian	438
Holden, Sarah J.	555
Holender, Adam	428
HolidayWorld Productions	38
Holland, Joel	535, 553
Holland, Richard	393
Hollander, Steven	540
Holliday, Andrew	457
Hollister, Ashley	513
Holloman, Tanika Fame	502
Hollyer, Christian	401
Hollywood Edge, The	80
Hollywood Film Registry, The	98, 293
Hollywood Licensing, LLC	98
Hollywood Reporter, The	226
Hollywood Reporter Blu-Book, The	226
Hollywood-Madison Group, The	220
Holman, Douglas	535
Holman, Thomas	535
Holmes, Gavin	420
Holt, Gudrun	481
Holt, James	10
Holt, Paul	393
Holton, Hank	438
Holtzman, Robert	513
Holtzman-Kenny, Linda S.	513
Holway, Jerome	428
Holy Land Art Company, Inc.	373
Holzer, Craig	67
Holzman, Ira	401, 457
Home Planet Productions	185, 293
Home Studios, Inc.	128, 190
home.work.people.	31, 381
Homefront Hardware	303
Homestead Editorial	48
Honess, Peter	67
Honey	491
Hong, Barrett	564
Hong-Man Tung, Amy	502
Hook, Dana S.	469
Hoole, Mary M.	457
Hope, Nathan	438
Hopkins, Dylan	448
Hopkins, Jon	401, 535
Hopp, Lee	554
Hoppe, Margaret E.	513
Hoppe, Richard Kenneth	513
Hoppus, Cliff	560
Hopson, Maury	491
Horak, Steven	481
Horan, Thomas (TJ)	513
Horgan, Deirdre	525
Horlick, Rich	4
Horn, Harold	420
Hornet, Inc.	5, 54, 102
Hornung, Lori	502
Horodner, Larry	185
Horowitz, Eric	67
Horse Drawn Affair, A	214, 356
Horstmann, Mark	420
Horvath & Associates Studios, Ltd.	120
Hostetter, Alan	464
Hostetter, Doug	438
Hot Shots/Corbis Motion	98
Hotchkiss, Ralph	401
Hotel Beacon	177
Hotel Elysée	177
Hotel Metro	177
Hotel Wales	177
Hotlights, Inc.	304, 306, 316, 327
Houghtalen, Claire	535
Houghton, Chris	67
Houghton, Nicholas	513
Houghton, Tom	428
Hould-Ward, Ann Marie	555
Houlle, David E.	464
Houllevigue, Jan	393
Hounsell, Diane	525
Hourie, Troy	389
Hourihan, Chip	185, 450, 498
House, John	469
House Production & Casting	220, 225
Housel, Timothy	428
Houston, Charles	457
Houtman, John	438
Hover-Views Unlimited, Inc./Al Cerullo	255
Howard, Angela	393
Howard Hall Productions	293
Howard, Lee	513
Howard, Matt	457
Howard, Morgan	239
Howard, Seth	560
Howard, Stephen	448
Howard, Tisa	481
Howe, Jason	67
Howell, Daniel	491
Howell, Judy Ruskin	560
Howell-Thornhil, Rosa	535
Howes, Thomas	502
Howie, Daniel	457
Hoy, Maysie	67
HPC Productions	271
HSBC Bank, USA N.A.	230
hscusa.tv.	23, 33, 38, 87, 102
HSI Productions, Inc.	17, 30
HSR/NY	44, 82, 220
Hubbard, Brian Rigney	428
Hubbert, Sean	67
Hudnut, David	36
Hudock, Laura	401
Hudson, Amanda	401
Hudson, Angus	438
Hudson, Bill	10
Hudson, Denise	393
Hudson Hotel	177
Hudson, Kenneth	401
Hudson, Steve	10
Hudson Theatre At Millenium Broadway	190
Hudson, Tim	438
Hudson Valley Locations, Inc.	161, 185
Huey, Victor W.	469
Huff, Angela	491
Huffman, Joshua	502
Hufford, Jay	409

Name	Page
Huggins, Jonathan	513
Hughes, Amanda	67
Hughes, Michael	469
Huidobro, Paula	438
Huitron, Robert	491
Huizinga, Elizabeth	239
Hula Post Production	60
Hulbert, John	469
Hum	80
Hum, Susan	560
Humble TV	5, 17
Hummel, Herbert	535
Humphreys, Rob	438
Hungry Man	17
Hunold, Michael	457
Hunt, Charles	535
Hunter Ambulance, Inc.	356, 386
Hunter, Clark	393
Hunter, Jim	438
Hunter, John	407, 428, 438
Hunter, Paul	10
Huntley, Charles	409
Hupfel, Mott	428
Hurlbut, Shane	438
Hurley, J.M.	425
Hurtado, Mark	36
Hurwitt, Bruce	10
Hurwitz, Tom	428
Huskey, Tonya	564
Huss, Michael	428
Huston, Larry	401
Hutchings, Jack	67
Hutchins, Samuel William	528
Hutchinson, John	185
Hutchinson, Peter	239
Huth, Joni	564
Hutman, Mark	393
Hutson, Jack	535
Huttick, Ross	513
Huynh, Syndey	502
Hyde, Beverley	560
Hyman, Laura	513

I

Name	Page
I.C.B.A., Inc./Bargsten	366
I.M.A./International Military Antiques, Inc.	341, 378
I. Weiss and Sons, Inc.	329, 336, 340, 366
Iadeluca, Fabio	401
Iannelli, Nikki	491
IASCO-TESCO	361
IATSE	546
IBC Digital	5, 54
Iberia Airlines	153
Ibero-American Productions, Inc.	44
Iberti, Elissa T.	555
Iberti, Joseph	550
Ice Tea Productions	5
Icelandic Consulate General	165
Ichabod Crane, Inc.	298, 306
Icke, Russell	67
Iconix	286
Idaho	172
Idris, Sarra	67
Idupuganti, Anura	498, 528
Idziak, Slawomir	438
Iervolino, Sebastian	401
Ifergan, Antoine	491
IGS Video Services, LLC	273
Ihara, Akeo	513
Ihre, Jakob	438
IKA Collective	17
Ikegami Electronics (USA), Inc.	286
Ikon New York, Inc.	246
Ikushima, Nobuhiro	498
Ilardi, Peter A.	535
Iler, Laura	513
Iles, Wendy	491
Illinois	172
Illinois-Chicago	172
Illumination Dynamics	316
Illusion Studio	122
Illusions Management	381, 491, 560
Illy, Richard	457
Ilnseher, Francois	491
Ilson-Burke, Sharon	481
Image Bank Films and Archive Films by Getty Images	98, 293
Image Maintenance	17, 48
IMAGICA Corp. of America	286
Imbarrato, Donna	528
Imgrund, Mark	67
Impact Product Placement	362
Impossible Casting	220
In Record Time, Inc.	245
Independent Aerial Equip.	310
Independent Artists, Inc.	17
Independent Film and Video Monthly	226
Indiana	172
IndiePay, Inc.	241
Indonesian Consulate General	165
Indursky, Michael	401
Industrial Contacts, Inc.	245
Industrial Plastics	345
Industria Super Studio.	122
Infinite Scenarios	17, 23, 27
Infiniti Handling Systems	310
Ingber, Michael	448
Inge, Scott	401
Inglese, Anthony R.	535
Ingram, Jennifer	564
Inn At Irving Place	178
Innovative Artists	381, 393, 428, 438, 560
Ins & Outs, Inc.	268
Inskeep, Thomas	428
Insley, David	428
Instant Karma Films	17
Instructivision, Inc.	23, 60, 275
Intaboro	182
Integrated Studios	5, 44, 87, 122
Integrity Movers	196
Intelliprompt Inc.	271
Inter Video	98, 293
InterContinental Barclay	178
Interface Arts	5, 84, 102
Intermediapost	23, 44, 57, 58
International Cinematographers Guild (IA Local 600)	546
International Cinematographer's Guild Magazine	226
International Creative Management - ICM	381
International Duplication Centre/ International Digital Centre, Inc.	57, 58, 87, 283, 289
International Protective Service Agency	202
International Travel Exchange	204
International Travel Films	98
InterNation, Inc.	102, 220, 248
Intervale Group, LLC, The	87
Inverse Media	5, 54
Inwood, John	438
Iowa-Cedar Rapids	172
Iowa-Des Moines	172
Ipcar, Robert	428
Ippoliti, Colby	513
iProbe Multilingual Solutions, Inc.	44, 56, 87, 103, 220, 247, 248
Ireland	176
Irene, Danielle	491
Irion, Bradley	491
Irish Consulate General	165
Irish Desarno, Lindsay	481
Iritano, Keira	481
Irola, Judy	438
Iron Mountain Film & Sound Archives	73
Ironik Design and Post	48, 87
Irving, Matthew	438
Irwin, Toby	438
Isaacks, Levie	439
Isaacs, Gary	425
Isabella, Catherine	553
Isambert, Anthony	491
Isern, Dave	413, 416, 439
Ishibashi, Matthew	457
Ishii, Ken	535
Iskander, Mai	407, 409, 439
Isla, Demian	481
Israel, Matthew	535
Israel, Nancy Lee	550
Israeli Consulate General	165
Issermann, Dominique	10
Isyomin, David	104
Italy-Campania	176
ITN Source	98
Itri, Anthony J.	469
Itri, Frank	469
It's In The Works, Inc.	333
Itskovich, Anka	560
Itzhak, Milly	401
Iulo, Anthony R.	469
Ivanoff, Peter	36
Iversen, Will	402
Iverson, Abigail	457
Ives, Tim	429
Ivey, Jason	528
Ivey, Jennifer	481
Ivgi, Yossi	491
Ivison, Robert	67
Iwanski, F. Lee	457
IWC Media Services, Inc.	73
Izner-Preston, Ann Marie	481
Izzo, Gregory M.	513
Izzo, Robert (Bob)	469

J

J. Levine Books & Judaica . . . 334, 373
J & M Effects . . . 327, 341, 347, 366
J.M. Salaun, Inc. . . . 82
J.Q. Locations . . . 185
J. Walter Thompson USA, Inc. . . . 2
Jabara, Edward R. . . . 469
Jack-Of-All-Trades Productions . . . 23, 232
Jackiewicz, Gary P. . . . 469
Jackness, Andrew . . . 389
Jackson, Bear . . . 528
Jackson, Darlene . . . 564
Jackson, Gemma . . . 393
Jackson, Glen . . . 491
Jackson, John C. . . . 420
Jackson, Jonathan . . . 539
Jackson, Kevin . . . 513
Jackson, Kim . . . 503
Jackson, Michael A. . . . 457
Jackson, Peter . . . 448
Jackson, Regan . . . 394
Jackson, Robert A. . . . 469
Jackson, Robert B. . . . 448, 450
Jackson, Rory A. . . . 469
Jackson, Tim . . . 513
Jacob & Kole Agency, The . . . 381, 394, 429, 439
Jacob, Abe . . . 535
Jacob, Askia . . . 564
Jacob, James P. . . . 469
Jacob, Susan . . . 402
Jacob K. Javits Convention Center . . . 190
Jacob, Richard . . . 535
Jacobi, Frederik . . . 439
Jacobs, Brian . . . 540
Jacobs, Keith Linwood . . . 239
Jacobs, Todd . . . 535
Jacobs, Michael . . . 540
Jacobsen, Jake . . . 67
Jacobson, Alicia M. . . . 106
Jacobson & Colfin, P.C. . . . 228
Jacobson Group, The . . . 241
Jacobson, Jacqueline . . . 513, 532
Jacobson, Jamie . . . 429
Jacoby Jr., Frank . . . 469
Jacoby Sr., Frank . . . 457
Jacques, Anthony . . . 409
Jacques Carcanagues, Inc. . . . 345
Jaczko, Caroline . . . 550
Jadue-Lillo, Igo . . . 439
Jaffe, David . . . 10
Jaffe, Meryl . . . 540
Jake Films, Inc. . . . 23
Jalbert Productions, Inc. . . . 17, 23, 38, 98
Jamaica-Kingston . . . 172
Jamaican Consulate General . . . 165
James, Bernard . . . 457
James Jr., Isiah . . . 528
James, John . . . 481
James, Patrick . . . 36
James, Peter . . . 439
James, Sheran . . . 4
James, Stanley F. . . . 553
Jamison-Tanchuck, Francine . . . 560
Janas, J. Jared . . . 481
Jane Peterer Music Corporation . . . 80
Janicelli, Kevin . . . 457
Janik, Lukasz . . . 535
Janke, Mary Anne . . . 402
Janks, Christopher D. . . . 420
Jannelli, Anthony . . . 429
Janocko, Malchus . . . 389
Janocko, Rachel Short . . . 389
Jan's Hobby Shop . . . 347, 366
Jansen, Tracy . . . 481
Janssen, Daniel J. . . . 420
Jansson, Mikael . . . 10
Japan Airlines . . . 153
Japanese Consulate General . . . 165
Jarnagin, Alec . . . 409, 415, 439
Jarnagin, Jendra . . . 439
Jasie, Zachary . . . 513
Jason, Julia . . . 10
Jasper, Bradley . . . 502
Javitch, Daphne E. . . . 555
Jean-Baptiste, Lazarus . . . 491
JECO . . . 82
Jeffrey Meyer Turntables . . . 366
Jenkins, Andrews . . . 10
Jennings, Steve . . . 51
Jenny Landey Productions, Inc. . . . 185
Jensen, Angela . . . 540
Jensen, Chuck . . . 491
Jensen, Deborah . . . 389
Jensen, Johnny E. . . . 439
Jensen, Kris . . . 523
Jerard Studio, Inc. . . . 5, 110, 112, 323, 366
Jerry Berg Computer Prompting . . . 271
Jerry Ohlinger's Movie Material Store, Inc. . . . 352
Jess, Stephen . . . 67
Jet Air Service, Inc. . . . 166
Jet Aviation Business Jets . . . 150
Jet Productions . . . 150, 255, 322
jetBlue . . . 153
Jets.com . . . 150
Jeung, Kathy . . . 491
Jew, E.W. . . . 402
Jewel Street Studios . . . 122, 128
JFA, Inc. . . . 241
JFK Terminal 4 . . . 190
JHD Productions, Ltd. . . . 23
Jim Farmer Music . . . 82
Jim Houston Productions, Inc. . . . 23, 38
Jimenez, Roberto . . . 457
Jiminez, Rafael . . . 491
Jirgal, Jeffrey C. . . . 469
Jirgal, Thomas . . . 469
Jiritano, Drew . . . 513
Jiritano, Gregory . . . 513
Jitzmark, Robert . . . 10
Jkobie Music . . . 82
JLS Wheels . . . 195
Joan Kramer & Associates, Inc. . . . 98
Joan Pearce Research Associates . . . 233
joe's production & grille, inc. . . . 260
Jogalla, Lukasz . . . 429
John Bauers Music Productions . . . 82
John Creech Design & Production . . . 112, 366
John E. Allen, Inc. . . . 98
John F. Kennedy International Airport . . . 154
John Sandy Productions, Inc. . . . 98
John Shields Security . . . 202
Johns, Anne . . . 503
Johnson, Adam . . . 402
Johnson, Al . . . 36
Johnson, Allyson . . . 67
Johnson, Angela . . . 481
Johnson, Anne K. . . . 239
Johnson, April . . . 560
Johnson, Christophe . . . 402
Johnson, Dale . . . 513
Johnson, Daniel . . . 535
Johnson, David . . . 439, 448
Johnson, D Michell . . . 481
Johnson, Edward J. . . . 420
Johnson, Florence . . . 481
Johnson, Hugh . . . 10, 439
Johnson, Jamie . . . 10
Johnson III, Jasper Lee . . . 469
Johnson, Jennifer . . . 481
Johnson, Jeremy C. . . . 457
Johnson, Leigh A. . . . 514
Johnson, Lisa . . . 481
Johnson, Michael . . . 491
Johnson, Nils . . . 553
Johnson, Patrick G. . . . 469
Johnson, Peter . . . 67
Johnson, Robert . . . 481
Johnson, Rolf . . . 457
Johnson, Salvatore J. . . . 469
Johnson, Shelly . . . 439
Johnson, Thomas . . . 469
Johnson Jr., Thomas L. . . . 469
Johnson, Zeke . . . 36
Johnson-Guirard, Lori . . . 514, 532
Johnston, Charlie . . . 68
Johnston, John R. . . . 420
Johnston, Kati . . . 550
Johnston, Nina . . . 564
Johnston, Thomas . . . 525
Johnstone, David . . . 481
Johnstone, Miles . . . 448
Joliat, Timothy J. . . . 514
Jonathan Helfand Music & Post . . . 44, 83
Jones, Alexander . . . 402
Jones, Beverly . . . 457
Jones, Brian P. . . . 514
Jones, Carlton . . . 560
Jones, Carolyn . . . 10
Jones, Chris . . . 394
Jones, Dan . . . 402
Jones Jr., Edward . . . 469
Jones, Gary . . . 555
Jones, Glenn W. . . . 514
Jones, Herita . . . 481
Jones, Jeffrey . . . 514
Jones, Kevin . . . 429
Jones, Michael D. . . . 498

Company/Crew Index

Jones, Quenell . . . 402
Jones, Stephen . . . 498
Jones, Tory . . . 389
Jones, William P. . . . 469
Jones-Evans, Steven . . . 394
Jones-Malewich, Patricia A. . . . 383
Jordaan, Francois . . . 394
Jordan, Alaster . . . 68
Jordan, Brian M. . . . 553
Jordan, Bruce R. . . . 469
Jordan, Chris M. . . . 514, 532
Jordan, Gerard J. . . . 420
Jordan, Michael. . . . 450, 504
Jordan, Michael L. . . . 535
Jordan, Steven A. . . . 469
Jordan, Steven J. . . . 514
Jordan, Thomas . . . 535
Jorgenson, Warren . . . 107
Jortner, Michael. . . . 514
Josefczyk, Jeanne . . . 481
Joseph C. Hansen Company, Inc. . . . 336
Joseph, John. . . . 498
Joseph, Rand . . . 540
Joseph, Rochelle . . . 564
Joseph, Vlada J. . . . 514
Joshi, Meera . . . 239
Joyce, Anne . . . 505
Joyce, Edward . . . 429
Joyce, Steven . . . 553
Joy, Michael . . . 10
JRT Music. . . . 80
JSM Music . . . 83
JSterling . . . 491
Judson, Todd. . . . 502
Judy Henderson & Associates Casting . . . 220
Judy Keller Casting, Inc. . . . 220
Juhasz, Imre . . . 439
Juhmeirah Essex House . . . 178
Julien, Don Hollis . . . 528
July, Miranda. . . . 10, 28
Jump . . . 48
June Bateman Fine Art . . . 324
June, Sherri . . . 491
Junge, Val . . . 68
Jupiter Ltg. Co, Inc. . . . 316
Jurkovac, Mike . . . 550
Jurkowski, Bernadette. . . . 564
Just Add Water, Inc. . . . 48
Just, Cecile . . . 540
Just Plastics . . . 361
Just Shades, Inc. . . . 350
Justian, Eric . . . 555
Justin Justin . . . 334, 336, 377
JVC Professional Products . . . 286

K

K/A/S Lighting . . . 306, 316
K.A.S. Music & Sound. . . . 44
K.P. Pro Video, Inc. . . . 275, 282
K-F/X, Inc. . . . 327, 366
K&M Camera . . . 262
K2imaging, Inc. . . . 23, 277, 282
Kachadurian, Zoya . . . 540
Kachikis, Kristian. . . . 439
Kachougian, Kimberly . . . 514
Kaczenski, Chester . . . 394
Kadane, Bubba . . . 51
Kadane, Matt. . . . 51
Kadar, Jerry . . . 514
Kadosh, Emmanuel. . . . 439
Kaehler, Daedra . . . 481
Kagan, Adam . . . 450, 498
Kahanov, Learan. . . . 429, 457
Kahler, Mary . . . 481
Kahn, Joseph . . . 10
Kahn, Mark . . . 457, 496
Kahn, Miles . . . 10, 504
Kahn, Steve . . . 68
Kaimowitz, Nancy . . . 526
Kaiser, Robin. . . . 481
Kalafut, Robert . . . 36
Kalas, Dain . . . 564
Kalas, Janet . . . 110
Kalas, Janet Lee . . . 107
Kalbfus-Paliocha, Melissa . . . 525
Kalfus Ehrlich . . . 560
Kalfus, Renee A. . . . 555
Kall, Michael . . . 420
Kalman, Shane Nathan . . . 528
Kalmanowicz, Max . . . 536
Kalohelani, Keith. . . . 457
Kamen Entertainment Group. . . . 44, 83
Kamfor Jr., Joseph P. . . . 420
Kamin, Brandon . . . 469
Kamin, Richard S. . . . 420
Kamine, Mark . . . 550
Kaminski, Suzette . . . 452
Kammel, Marcie . . . 448
Kammerer, Kenneth . . . 514
Kammerer, Michael J. . . . 469
Kammerer Jr., Michael J. . . . 469
Kander, Nadav . . . 10
Kane, Dierdre L. . . . 514
Kane, Heather D. . . . 514
Kane, Jenny . . . 457
Kane, Jon . . . 10
Kane, Karen . . . 528
Kansas . . . 172
Kansas-Wichita . . . 172
Kantor, Chaim . . . 429
Kantor, Jeff . . . 409, 414, 425
Kantor, Peter. . . . 469
Kaos . . . 10
Kaplan, Glenn . . . 402
Kaplan, Henry . . . 514
Kaplan, Lance . . . 439
Kaplan, Lisa . . . 4
Kaplan, Michael . . . 560
Kappes, David. . . . 550
Karady, Ondine . . . 514
Karakosta, Persefon . . . 481
Karan, Josh. . . . 185, 457
Karas, Michael . . . 536
Karasawa, Chiemi. . . . 525
Karins, J. Fry. . . . 107
Karlin, Keira . . . 481
Karlok, Daniel F. . . . 457
Karlyn, Bethany. . . . 491
Karp, Daniel . . . 439
Karpeles, Ernie . . . 185
Karr, Ian . . . 10
Kasarda, Kevin . . . 402
Kastner, Barbara A. . . . 514
Kastner, Frederick D. . . . 514
Kastner, Keith F. . . . 469
Katagas, Anthony . . . 550
Katcher, Lisa . . . 526
Kates, Karen . . . 514
Kathrens, Philip. . . . 457
Kathy's Medical Production Company, Inc./
Kathy Cossu, R.N. . . . 386
Kathy Wickline Casting . . . 220
Katsoulogiannakis, Theodora . . . 481
Katz, Dochtermann & Epstein . . . 2
Katz, Erika S. . . . 514
Katz, Robin . . . 68
Kauble, John C. . . . 536
Kaufman Astoria Studios. . . . 122, 130
Kaufman, Joan . . . 556
Kaufman, Susan . . . 389, 514, 532
Kaufman, Thomas. . . . 429
Kaufmann, Mark William . . . 528
Kaupas, Algis J. . . . 536
Kavaliauskas, Maryte-Murphy . . . 536
Kavanagh Productions, Inc. . . . 23
Kavanaugh, Kevin. . . . 394
Kawakami, Takahide . . . 528
Kay, Christopher . . . 107
Kay, Erica . . . 502
Kay, Nicholas . . . 425
Kaya, Bilgi. . . . 481
Kaye Lites, Inc. . . . 23, 304, 306, 316
Kaye, Sandye . . . 481
Kaye, Stephen . . . 464
Kaye, Tony . . . 10
Kayeriley, Sanna. . . . 481
Kayon, Renee K. . . . 457
Kays, Daniell. . . . 560
Kazista, Lee . . . 402
Kazmierski, Stephen. . . . 429
Kealey, Jonathan P. . . . 457
Kearns, Michael T. . . . 420
Kearns, Michelle . . . 481
Kearse, Kirsten . . . 525
Keating, Cassandra. . . . 481
Keating, John . . . 409, 469
Keaton, Jeffery W. . . . 457
Keck, Dan . . . 402
Keech, Colin T. . . . 420
Keeling, Michael . . . 394
Keen, Cindy . . . 423
Keenan, Glen . . . 439
Keenan, Mike . . . 539
Keene, Robert. . . . 457
Keep in Touch Communications, Inc. . . . 164
Keeshan, Richard . . . 502
Kehoe, Casey . . . 470

Company/Crew Index

Name	Page
Kehoe, Hilary	502
Keil, Tad	560
Keiser, Michelle	528
Keith, Adam	413, 416
Keith Sherman & Associates	34
Keith-Roach, Steve	439
Keitt, Stan	402, 407
Kell, Linda	560
Keller, Ken	429
Keller, Merle	36
Keller, Robert	420
Kellett, Chris	536
Kelley, Stephen	481
Kelli Lerner Casting	220
Kelly, Barbara	481, 498
Kelly, Christian	532
Kelly, Deanna	528
Kelly, Edward T.	457
Kelly, Gavin	439
Kelly, Greg	429
Kelly, Harold Reid	470
Kelly, James	457
Kelly Jr., John J.	457
Kelly, Joseph W.	470
Kelly, Kate	502
Kelly, R.N., Kathleen M.	383
Kelly, Martin G.M.	539
Kelly, Mary	525
Kelly, Patrick	402
Kelly, Paul D.	389
Kelly, Paula	481
Kelly, Renee	481
Kelly, Robert	482
Kelly, Suzanne	564
Kelly, Timothy J.	470
Kelman, Jacqueline	550
Kelner's Rentals, Inc.	195
Kelsch, Ken	439
Kelsey, Ralph	51
Kelsey, Todd	420
Kelton, John	514
Kelusak, Richard	470
Kempf, Thomas	470
Kemps Film, TV & Video Handbook	226
Kempster, Victor H.	514
Ken Horowitz Photographic Services	76
Ken Lazer Casting	220
Kendall, Shanah-Ann	482
Kendra, Eric	409, 415
Kendrick, Christian	504
Keneally, Kenneth G.	470
Kennedy, Daniel P.	470
Kennedy, John D. (Jack)	470
Kennedy Jr., John T.	470
Kennedy, Kate	514, 532
Kennedy, Kim	528
Kennedy, Morgan	394
Kennedy, Patrick J.	470
Kennedy, Phillip	107
Kennedy, Steve C.	536
Kennedy, Thomas G.	470
Kennedy Travel	204
Kennedy-Jebrane, Eileen M.	514
Kenney, Anne	556
Kenney, Daniel B.	514
Kenny, Francis	439
Kenny, Philip J.	457
Kent, Billy	10
Kent, Debra Susan	550
Kent, James (Jim)	514
Kent, Lisa N.	514
Kent, Suzanne	107
Kentucky	172
Kenyon, Brian	528
Keogh, Timothy	470
Kerekes, Richard C.	470
Kern, Janet	525
Kershaw, Glenn	429
Kerstein, Myron	68
Kerwick Jr., Edward T.	470
Kerwick, Kevin	470
Kerwick, Thomas	470
Kerwick Jr., Thomas E.	470
Kerwick, William V.	470
Keslow Television, Inc. (KTV)	275, 282
Kettell, Meg	402
Kevan, Scott	439
Kevoo Catering	162, 424
Key Digital Systems	286
KeyFrame Editing	48
Keymer, Robert	514
KeywestFilms.com	98
Keywest Technology	286
Khalevich, L. Mila	514
Khan, Giles P.	536
Khorigan, Richard J.	470
Kibbe, Kyle	429
Kibrik, Dmitry	470
Kick, Rachel	482
Kidney, Ric	498
Kids, The	560
Kienhuis, Ronald	413
Kiesser, Jan	439
Kiester, Shane	51
Kilbourne-Kimpton, Cheryl	564
Kilcher, Kevin	402
Kildow, Renee	107
Kilduff, Chris C.	470
Kileen, Jason	68
Kilgore III, John E.	536
Killer Films	27
Killer Tracks	80
Killian, Mark	402
Kim, Jeannette	389
Kim, Jon	514
Kim, Shawn	439
Kim, Tyler H.	514
Kima Travel Group, The	204
Kimball, Jeffrey	439
Kimberg, Yossi	68
Kimelman, David	409, 415, 429
Kimmel, Adam	429
Kimmel, Steve	394
Kimpton, Roger	470
Kimura, Jim	439
Kincaid, Scott	457
Kinery, Devra	491
Kinetic Trailers	40
King, Harry	491
King, Kathleen	536
Kinion, Dina	491
Kinski, Siggi	10
Kinsley, Karen Hummel	556
Kinslow, William	51
Kipperman Casting, Inc.	220
Kirby, Aaron	402
Kirby, Paul	394
Kirby, Sean	439
Kirchoff, Martin	420
Kirkby, Mat	10, 28
Kirkham, Steven	482
Kirkpatrick, Jamie	68
Kirsch, Daniel D.	470
Kirsch, Michael	470
Kirshoff, David	514
Kirshoff, Jack	514
Kirshoff, Steve	514
Kisberg, Ed	68
Kissack, Eric	68
Kissinger Li David L.	457
Kitano, The	178
Kitchen, The	91
Kits and Expendables	302, 304, 318, 331, 348
Kitstrucks	302, 304, 318, 329, 331, 348
Kivilo, Alar	439
Kizer, Ed	536
KJ Films, LLC	306, 316
KL Lighting	316
KLAD	112
Klarenbeck, Justin	10
Klatt, Clifford F.	514
Klatt, Graham	470
Klausen, Raymond	389
Klayer, James	402
Klayer, William	429, 458
Kleban, Johnna	448
Klein, Anthony	470
Klein, Lori	482
Klein, Mark	10
Klein, Mark A.	470
Klein, Maxine Willi	107
Klein, Peter	439
Klein, Saar	68
Klein, Sarit	482
Klein, Todd S.	470
Kleinstein, David	514
Kleiser, Jeff	10
Kleitsch, Todd	482, 491
Kliber, Jill A.	560
Kliman, Rachael	402
Kling, Elizabeth	68
Klingman, Lynzee	68
Klipp, Bradley	514
Klompus, Betsy	389, 514, 532
Kloss, Thomas	439
Klotsas, James	514
Klotz, Joe	68
Kluga, Ray	389

Klusmann, J. Dorothea . . . 514
Knaggs, Jeffrey . . . 482
Knaster, Jeremy . . . 458
Knee, Steven . . . 185
Knickerbocker Plate Glass Company . . . 347
Knief, Rick . . . 10
Kniest, James . . . 439
Knight, David . . . 409, 414
Knight, Keith . . . 528
Knight Security . . . 202
Knoop, Jon W. . . . 448, 514
Knorr, Chad . . . 544
Knott III, Edward J. . . . 470
Knowledge, The . . . 226
Knox, David . . . 429
Knue, Michael N. . . . 68
Ko Karting . . . 231
Kobie, Jawanza . . . 51
Koch, Douglas . . . 439
Koch, Rob . . . 402
Kodak . . . 266
Koenig, Robin . . . 514
Koenigsberg, Scott . . . 402
Koenigswieser, Matthias . . . 439
Koestler, Jennifer . . . 402
Koff, Stacey . . . 525
Kofsky, Doug . . . 402
Kohler Rental . . . 198, 302, 303, 316, 331
Koide, Michina . . . 491
Kolar, Frances . . . 482
Kolins, Howard . . . 540
Kolpin, William J. . . . 514
Kolsby, Marion S. . . . 389
Koltai, Lajos . . . 439
Konczal, Peter . . . 439
Kondor Music . . . 83
Kondor, Robbie . . . 51
Konduit Inc. . . . 112
Koola, Peter . . . 458
Koons, Brian . . . 36
Kordish, Scott . . . 502
Korean Air . . . 153
Korean Consulate General . . . 165
Korelich, Dylan . . . 36
Korey, Kay & Partners . . . 2
Korfine, Amanda . . . 491
Korins, David . . . 389
Korker Sr., Russ . . . 458
Korn, Morton . . . 470
Korner, Petra . . . 439
Koronkiewicz, Dianne . . . 402
Koronkiewicz, Paul . . . 536
Kortze, Denny . . . 402
Koseki, Yuko . . . 68
Kosnac Equipment Rental, Inc. . . . 328
Kostic, Isabelle . . . 185
Kotright, Toussaint . . . 536
Kourtessis, Karen . . . 68
Kousoulas, Gus . . . 504
Kouthoofd, Jesper . . . 10, 28
Kouzoujian Jr., George . . . 420
Kovacs, Mark . . . 448
Koval, Michael . . . 514
Koval, Paul C. . . . 514
Koval, Ronald P. . . . 470
Kover, Gabor . . . 413, 429
Kowalczyk, Paula . . . 556
Kowalski, Peter . . . 429
Koza, Dave . . . 68
Koza III, Edward . . . 470
Kozlowski, Stephen . . . 402
Kozma, Donald . . . 482
Kozmo . . . 491
Kozy, William . . . 536
KPI/Kralyevich Productions, Inc. . . . 39
Kraemer Jr., Fred . . . 514
Krallman, Randy . . . 10
Kramer, Erwin . . . 450, 498
Kramer, Johan . . . 10
Kramer, Liz . . . 498
Kraner, Doug . . . 394
Krantz, Linda . . . 514
Krantz, Michael . . . 394
Krasnakevich, Victoria . . . 514
Kraus & Sons, Inc. . . . 110, 343
Kraus, Liz . . . 498
Krause, Gordon . . . 420
Krause, John M. . . . 470
Kravetz, Carole . . . 68
Kravetz, Ryan . . . 389
Kravitz, Barbra . . . 556
Krebs, Michael . . . 402
Kremer, Peter . . . 273, 554
Kresge, Ken . . . 68
Kretchmar, Sam . . . 425
Kriaris, Michael . . . 185
Krieger, Steven R. . . . 514
Krimbel, Keith . . . 68
Krinsky, Tamah . . . 482
Kriston, Michael . . . 482
Krivobok, Georges N. . . . 389, 514
Kroliczak, Mary . . . 502
Kroll, Kenneth M. . . . 239
Krommydas, Anna . . . 482
Kronen, Jeff . . . 36
Krueger, Thomas . . . 429, 439
Kruglinski, Anne Yung . . . 482
Krumper, Mark . . . 450, 498
Krupa, Howard . . . 439, 476
KSK Studios . . . 17
Kubicek, Christopher . . . 470
Kubicek, Daniel . . . 458
Kubicka, Meg . . . 68
Kuchler, Alwin . . . 439
Kucmeroski, Michael . . . 560
Kudlek, Thomas . . . 470
Kudrowitz, Dave . . . 402
Kuegel, John W. . . . 458
Kugle, Liz . . . 502
Kuhn Jr., Bernard J. . . . 420
Kuhn, Christine . . . 565
Kuhn, Nina . . . 458
Kukkonen, Dan . . . 239
Kulick, Jay . . . 409
Kulow, Heidi . . . 482
Kulzer, Edward . . . 68
Kummert, Robert . . . 470
Kunin, Andrew (Drew) . . . 536
Kunin, Rachel Sage . . . 560
Kunz, Johann . . . 514
Kunz, Peter . . . 523
Kupferberg, Amy . . . 458
Kupferwasser, Ronnie . . . 528
Kuras, Ellen . . . 429
Kurland, Jeffrey . . . 560
Kurland, Peter F. . . . 536
Kuros, Zbigniew . . . 470
Kuse, Richard C. . . . 536
Kushner, Brian . . . 68
Kushner, Don . . . 420
Kushner, June . . . 565
Kushnick, Beth . . . 514, 532
Kutlug, Suad . . . 402
Kuznetzkoff, Dana . . . 448
Kyles, Whitney . . . 556

L

L.A. Bruell, Inc. . . . 23
L.A. Express Charter Service . . . 155
LA 411 . . . 226
La Bonne Cusine Catering . . . 162
La Cuisine . . . 162
LA Digital Post, Inc. . . . 60, 87, 284, 289
La Paloma Films . . . 39
Lab-Link, Inc./Magno Sound & Video . . . 74
Labarthe, Francois-Renaud . . . 394
Labarthe, Jules . . . 439
Labeau, Philippe R. . . . 553
Labiano, Flavio . . . 439
Laborie, Laurent . . . 560
Lacey Costume Wigs . . . 348
LaChapelle, David . . . 10
Lachman, Ed . . . 439
La Corte, Joseph . . . 565
LaCrasia Gloves . . . 334, 378
Ladas, George . . . 36
Laden, Bob . . . 482
Ladin, Terry . . . 502, 503
Ladson, Kevin C. . . . 514
La Farge, James . . . 536
La Ferla, Sandro . . . 110
LaFontaine, Marie Josee . . . 491
LaForce & Stevens . . . 34
Lageoles, Simone . . . 525
Lagerroos, Kjell . . . 439
Lagransky, Vladimir . . . 107
LaGuardia Airport . . . 154
Lahiff, Dominic . . . 10
Lairson, Thomas . . . 402
Lake, Karl . . . 514
Lake, Michael Minard . . . 51
Lakoseljac, Mary Ann . . . 491
Lale For Home . . . 346
Lalino, Charles . . . 458
Lalino, Jeffrey . . . 458
Lalino, Stephen J. . . . 458
Lallas-Brusilovsky, Julia . . . 482

Company/Crew Index

Name	Page
Lamarque, Alex	439
Lamb, Matthew	528
Lambe, Eoin Vincent	514
Lambert, Robert K.	68
Lambert, Sarah	389
Lambert-Andrusko Laura	514, 532
Lambie, Jansen	536
Lamborn, Rod	409, 417, 439
Lamelza, Barbara	491
Lamont, Neil	394
Lamont, Peter	394
Lampel, Alan	458
Lamu Industries	346
LanChile Airlines	153
Lanci, Jason A.	458
Lanci-Leseur, April	402
Landau, David	458
Landau, Natasha	556
Landecho, Edward	514
Landesman, Lloyd	52
Landi, Carl J.	470
Landi, John	439, 458
Landi, Thomas J.	458
Landis, Jane	536
Landolfi, Joseph	514
Landress, Ilene	528
Lane, Clifford	52
Lane, Sara	239
Lane, Sheri	507
Lane Jr., Wallace G. (Woody)	560
Laneuville, Eric	10
Lang, Alison	560
Lang, Calen	409, 417
Lang, Roger P.	420
Langdon, Barbara	409
Langensteiner, Stöps	439
Langley, Marc	68
Langston, Ciiauntel	482
Lanni, Dennis	491
LaNoce's Fine Food For Film, LLC	162, 424
Lantz, Ronnie	536
Lantz, Sylvia	560
Lanza, Sal J.	470
Lanza, Vincent M.	470
Lanzenberg, Christophe	439
Lanzenberg, David	439
LaPatin, Melanie	221, 246
Lapietra Machinery & Equipment, Inc.	303
Laplanche, Jean Pierre	458
Lappin, Thomas	409
Lara, Jose	402
Largent, Kevin	389
Largent Studios, Ltd.	112, 366
Larkin, Edward	470
Larkin Jr., Edward M.	470
Larks, David	36
Larlarb, Suttirat	389, 556
Laroche, Spencer	402
LaRosa, Kevin	255, 257
Larose, Kate	402
Larrea, Robert	536
Larro, Daniel	470
Larsen, Bernie	52
Larsen, Stan	10
La Rue, David John	470
Lascaris, Andre	439
Lasers by Technological Artisans	327
Lask, JJ	68
Laskas, John	68
Lasky, Spencer	429
Lasowitz, Martin	514
La Spina, Tina	482
Lassalle, Richard	389
Lassman, Andy	524
Lasting, Gabrielle	502
La Terra, Ross	514, 532
Latini, Todd	514
Latino, Michael	409
Latonero, Tina	560
Latvis, Mary	402
Lau, Robert	402
Laubscher, Axel	10
Laucella, Ralph	550
Laudati, Michael	482
Laughlin, Bill	524
Lauren Berger Collection	178
Laurence-Berman, Sherri	482
Laurens, Paul	448
Laurenzi, Richard	107
Lavar, Ellin	482, 491
LaVasseur, Chris	409, 414, 440
La Vecchia, Thomas John	515
Lavenziano, Andrew	482
LaVerdiere, Julian	389
Law Offices of Mark Litwak	228
Law Offices of Rosalind Lichter	228
Lawbook Exchange, Ltd., The	374
Lawler, Steven E.	420
Lawley, Rick	68
Lawn, Charles (Buddy)	470
Lawrence, Champagne	482
Lawrence, Christopher	560
Lawrence, David	482
Lawrence, Steve	394
Lawrence, Steven	482, 491
Lawson, Daniel L.	556
Lax, Jennifer	565
Lazan, David	394
Lazar, Jeffrey	448
Lazar, Linda	482
La Zaro Margo	565
Lazarus, Ashley	429
LDI Color Toolbox	223
Le Cirque 2000	249
Le Parker Meridien	178, 249
Leach, Adam	239
Leach, Francis (Bosko)	470
Le Saux Yorick	440
Le Sourd, Philippe	440
Leacock, Robert	10, 429
Leader Instruments Corporation	286
Learoyd, Richard	68
Leather, Michael	515
Lebanese Consulate General	165
LeBlanc, Jim	440
Leblanc, Lance	36
Le Blanc, Paul	491
Lebow, Alan	10, 429, 536
Lebow, Anya N.	515
Lebrecht, John	515
Lechterman, Robert	429
Lecoultre, Francine	560
Lederman, Diane	515
Lederman, Keri Lynn	515
Ledermann, Nicki	482
Lederway, Greg	409, 415
Ledger, Karen	556
Lee, Ahnna	402
Lee, Angela	502
Lee, Charles	394
Lee, David	505
Lee, James D.	528
Lee, Jonathan B.	515
Lee, Kai	389
Lee, Kate	491
Lee, Kristina	502
Lee, Mia	502
Lee, Michael	36
Lee, Sonia	491
Lee, Thomas	528
Lee, Tia	482
Lee, Wing	389
Leech, Ian	10
Lee's Art Shop, Inc.	325
Le Fande ,Richard	553
Lefevre Jr., Edmund (Ted)	389
LeFrak Productions	39
Legacy Recording Studios	44
Leggiere, Joseph	470
Le Goff, Tom	505
Leguizamo, John	10
Lehane, Edward R. (Ted)	470
Lehel, Jason	440
Lehman, Tatyana	239
Lehne, Bret	420
Lehne, William	420
Le, Hoang Anh	420
Lehtonen, Catherine	491
Leiba, Freddie	560
Leiber & Stoller Music Publishing	80
Leibler-Bronfman & Lubalin	2
Leibowitz, Cindy	4
Leibowitz, David Scott	553
Leibowitz, Phyllis	560
Leigh, Carrie	502
Leigh, Eric A.	458
Leigh, Jonathon	458
Leigh, Maggie	110
Leighton, Robert	68
Leining, Mark E.	420
Leiter, Christine	482, 492
LeMay, Damon	402
Leme, Gustavo	11
Lemos, Iris Horta	565
Lempire, Stephane	482
Lenau, Pamela	107
Lenihan, Joseph M.	536
Lenkin, Elysha	560

Company/Crew Index

Name	Page
Lennig, Kurt	458
Lennox, Kevin	560
LeNoble Lumber Co., Inc.	329
Lenoir, Denis	440
Lens & Repro Equipment Corporation, The	262, 354
Lenski, Matt	11, 28
Lentini Communications	164, 223, 266, 268, 276, 305, 318
Lenzer, Donald	429
Leo, Joseph	458
Leo, Michael	458
Leonard, Christopher	470
Leonard, James M.	470
Leonard, Michael	402
Leonard, Sammy	402
Leonard, Wayne T.	524
Leone, Janelle	482
Leone, Talia Helena	502
Leone-Ferraro, Kathleen	515
Leonetti, Gina	528
Leonetti, John R.	440
Leong, George	536
Leonidas, Kevin	515
Lerner, Dan	11
Lesnie, Andrew	440
Lesser, Felice	221
Lesser, Michael	11, 429, 458
Let There Be Neon, Inc.	343, 354
Lettini, Lucia	565
Level 3 Communications	73
Levenstein, Martin	68
Levey, Chuck	440
Levi, Robert	440
Levie, Jordan	402
Levin, David	11
Levine, Abby	425
LeVine, David	458
Levine, Edmund	515
Levine, Joey	52
Levine, Lark	448
Levine, Michael A.	52
Levine, Rachael	409
Levine, Randy	470
Levine, Richard	448
Levinson, Dan	11
Levinson, Sasha	11, 28
Levinson/Fontana Company, The	39
Leviton, Robert H.	246
Levitsky, Gary W.	515
Levitsky, Peter L	515
Levy, Adam	383
Levy, Daniel H.	458
Levy, Jonathan	68
Levy, Jordan	440
Levy, Loren H.	515
Levy, Peter	440
Levy, Rosemarie M.	515
Levy, Samuel	407, 429
Levy, Steven	450, 498, 504
Levy, Stuart	68
Lewallen, Shawn	402
Lewandowski, Theodore J.	515
Lew, Charlie	402
Lew, Darren	429
Lew-Goucher, Mary	531
Lewin, Elyse	11
Lewin, Eric E.	515
Lewin, Nick	11
Lewis, Arthur	540
Lewis, Demetrius	553
Lewis Flinn Music	83
Lewis, Franziska	402
Lewis, Lynn	525
Lewis, Paul	550
Ley, William	470
Li, Alexis	402, 528
Li, Rain	440
Lian-Williams, Anette	482, 492
Libatique, Matthew	440
Liberatore, Anthony	36
Liberatore-Ciardi, Christina	482
Liberty Electrical Supply Co., Inc.	305, 330
Liberty Helicopters	255
Liberty Lighting Limited	306, 316
Libin, Charles	429
Library of Moving Images, The	98
Librizzi-Williams, Linda	482
LIC Film Studios	122
Licata International Productions	200, 201
Liccio Jr., Robert J.	470
Licht, Jason	496
Lichtenstein, Todd	458
Lichtman, Jules	450
Lichtner, Jessica	525
Liddle, George	394, 560
Liddy, Colleen	482
Lieber, Kimberley	515
Lieberman, Elizabeth	107
Lieberman, Joyce	515
Liebgold, Richard	515
Liebler, Todd	402
Liebowitz, Eric	505
Liebowitz, Steven	409
LifeHouse Productions, LLC	5, 54
LifeStockPhotos.com	98
Lifestyle Resources	202, 541
Ligget, Craig	458
Light Foot Grip & Lighting	306, 316
Light House, Inc., The	114, 122, 305, 306, 316
Lightbox-NY LLC	190, 249
Lighting by Gregory, Inc.	350
Lightnin' Rentals	195
Like Dat Music	80
Lilien, Andy	429
Lillian, Mitchell	470
Lillis, James	515
Limberis, Gus	402
Limo Tour, The	182
LimoRes.net	182
Limosner, Pilar	556
Lin, Amy	492
Lin, Jong	440
Lin, Sophia	550
Lincoln Business Machines	223
Lincoln Terrace Cleaners	338
Lindberg, Craig	482, 492
Lindbergh, Peter	11
Lindblom, David	68
Linden Travel Bureau, Inc.	204
Lindenlaub, Karl Walter	440
Lindley, John	11
Line By Line Productions	23, 39, 201
Linear Cycle Productions	98
Linett & Harrison	2
Lineweaver, Stephen	394
Ling, Barbara	394
Link Entertainment	17
Linke, Robert C.	458
Linter, Sandy	492
Lipkowitz, Scott	402
Lipman, Deborah	402
Lipman, Richmond, Greene	3
Lipman, Tina	492
Lippman, Andrew	4
Lippross, Stephen	239
Lipsey, Jeanne	429
Lisa-Raquel	492
Liscinsky, Christopher	458
Liset, Kit	499, 528
Lisi, Gaetano	448
Liska, Peter	540
Liss, Rick	515
Listenik, Barbara	452
Lite Brite Neon	354
Litecky, Bruce	536
Litecky, Steve	458
Lithuanian Consulate General	165
Littee, Ludovic	409
Litten, Jim	458
Little, George L.	560
Little Minx	17, 30
LITTLE x	11
Littlejohn, Victor	515
Littleton, Carol	68
Littman, Mark	68
Litwack, Claudia	423
Livesey, Dennis A.	410
Livesey, Jeffrey	536
Livesey, Nick	11
Livingston, Celeste	334, 377, 565
Livingston, Jarett	539
Livolsi, Joe	440
Liz Lewis Casting Partners	220
Lizzio, John	410, 415, 417
Lloyd, Walt	440
Lo, Amy	502
Lobell, Jeanine	492
Location 05	190
Location Camera, Ltd.	261
Location City, Inc.	195
Location Control, Inc./Coneheads	185, 198
Location Lighting, Ltd.	305, 306, 316
Location Power Source, Ltd.	316
Location Station, The/Mark McKennon	185
Locations Extrordinaire, Inc.	185
Locationview	78
Locke, Rebecca	502
Locksley Productions	201
Lockwood, Henry A.	515

Lodes, Paul	420
Loeb & Loeb, LLP	228
Loeb, Matthew D.	515
Loeb, Maury	68
Loeffler, Heather	515
Loewinger, Lawrence	536
L'Official, Francky	492
Loftin Productions	44
Log Cabin Location, The	190
Log In Productions	39
Lohrer Jr., Richard B.	420
Lois Lane Travel	204
Lokensgard, Michael	515
Lolita	492
Lo Maglio, Jeffrey M.	470
Lombardi, Joseph	239
Lombard, Kerry A.	458
Lombard, Rosemary	502
Lombardo, Ana	515
Lombardo, Tony	68
Lombardozzi, Chris	458
Lomofsky, Sharon	389
London, Gregg	68
London, Melody	68
London, Nick	482
Londoner, Marco	448
Londono, Mateo	440
Long, Bob	410, 414, 415
Long, Deborah	482
Long Island Locations/Lee Davis	186
Long, Lanier	482
Long, Mike	11, 28
Long, Renate	482
Long, William Ivey	556
Longo, Carlo	492
Longo, Patricia	492
Longo, Vincent	492
Longtin, Victor	410
Longyear, Hamilton	402
Lonsdale, Dane	536
Lonsdale, Gordon	440
Lonsdale, R. Michael	536
Lopas, Robert D.	515
Lopes Picture Company, Inc., The	17, 26
Lopes, Rob	11
Lopez, Arturo	554
Lopez, Leslie	492
Lopez, Nathan	402
Lopez, P. J.	429
Lopez, Rick	440
Lopez, Roberto J.	470
Lorberfeld, Cari	540
Lorcott Productions, Inc.	23
Lorenzen, Cory	394
Lorenzo, Angie	482
Loret, Paul	470
Lorino Jr., Pietro	239
Lorms, Lisa	107
Lorraine's Food Factory	162
Los Angeles Post Music, Inc.	80
Loscalzo, Michael	410, 417
Losick, Vic.	440
Lost and Found Props	374
Lost City Arts	345, 346, 350
Lost Highway Films	17
Lost Planet Editorial, Inc.	48
Lost Soul Picture Cars	356
LOT Polish Airlines	153
Lots of Yachts/Lots of Spots	328
Loughran Marie	383
Louie, Tommy	536
Louie, Wes	36
Louis Wolfson II Florida Moving Image Archive	98
Louis-Marie, Franck	36
Louisiana-New Orleans	172
Loungway, Patrick	440
Louthe, William P.	458
Love Jr., Edward F.	458
Love, Frank	402, 420
Love, Reiko	492
Lovelace, Byron	524
Lovell, Emma	492
Lovell, Karen	482
Loven, Ulf	420
Lovett, Cheryl	565
Lovett Productions, Inc.	23, 39, 60
Lovin, Jennifer	239
Lowe, Andrew	458
Lowe, David William	470
Lowe, John	448
Lowe New York	3
Lowell, The	178
Lowe, Ran	540
Lowe, Richard	68
Lowenstein, Carlos	68
Lowry, Brendan	470
Lowry, David F.	470
Lowry III, David F.	470
Lowry, Edward W.	470
Lowry, Gerard J.	471
Lowry, Kevin	471
Lowry, Martin	471
Lowry, Patrick J.	471
Lowry, Shaun	471
Lowry, Thomas E.	471
Lowry Jr., William	471
Lowy-Wright, Marcie S.	515
LSI	286
LTU	153
Lu, Henry	11
Luberda, Matthew J.	471
Luberda, Neil	471
Lubezki, Emmanuel	440
Lucak, Tom	429
Lucas, Deborah	565
Lucas, Ellen	452
Luchsinger, Logan	504
Lucido, Salvatore	36
Luczyc-Wyhowski, Hugo	394
Ludlow, Kimberly A.	525
Luiken, Carol	556
Lukeris, Peter	420
Lulla, Claus	482
Lum, Charles	186, 528
Lumb, Patrick	394
Lumet, Sidney	11
Lumley, Jonathan	458
Lumpkin, Donald	448
Luna Lighting	306, 316
Luna Llena Management, Inc.	381, 492
Luna Luna Zoraida	402
Lunarola, Peter	471
Lundell, Erik R.	515
Lundy, Nicholas	389
Lupi, Daniel	499
Lupu, Veronica	525
Luskey, Francis	515
Lustig, Franz	440
Luton, Jonathan	458
LVM Group	34
LVR/Liman Video Rental Company	32, 62, 78, 268, 276, 282, 284, 316
LVT Laser Subtitling	103
Lyde, Aimée	68
Lyman, Craig	323, 482, 492
Lyn, Diana	505
Lynch, Eugene	458
Lynch, Fionnuala	565
Lynch, Joan	515
Lynch, John	440
Lynch, Matthew	471
Lynch, Stephen	471
Lynch, Thomas	389
Lynch, William	458
Lynn, Judanna	556
Lyons, Amy	107
Lyons, Mandy	482

M

M. Gordon Novelty, Inc.	347
Maalouf, Elie	492
Maas, Liz	525
Maayan, Yehuda	536
Mabin, Robert T.	458
Mably, Chris	440
Mabry, John D.	458
Mabus, Inc.	30
Macat, Julio	440
MacCallum, Bruce	413, 429
MacCarthy, Matthew	440
Macchia, Joseph	482
MacDonald, Alex	407
MacDonald, Jason	68
MacDonald, John	402
MacDonald, Kevin	11
Macdougall, Lorne J.	458
Mac Dougall, Maureen P.	515
MacGhee, William	458
MacGillivray Freeman Films	98
MacGregor, Ian	528
MacGuffin Films, Ltd.	17
Machhausen, Tyron	492
Mack Agency, The	381, 394, 429, 440
Mack, Steve	507
Mackay, Peter	440
MacKenzie Cutler	48, 83
MacKenzie, Ian	68

Company/Crew Index

Name	Page
Mackiewicz Jr., Ronald	482
MacLean, Eduardo	11
MacLean, Jeff	186
Macleod, Dylan	440
Macleod, Kenneth Raymond	389
MacLeod, Stuart	11
Mac Nicholl, Todd	471
MacPherson, Glen	440
Mad River Post, Inc.	48
mad.house, inc.	49
Madden Jr., Thomas	458
Maddi, Mike	482
Maddison, Eric	440
Madeloff, Jennifer	502
Mader, Allan E.	458
Mader, Michelle	536
Maderich, David	492
Madigan, Dennis	420
Madison, Brian P.	515
Madison, Michael	515
Madison Square Garden	190
Madoff, Jeff	11
Madoff Productions	17
Madonna, Enrico	68
Madrid, James	402
Magalios, Constantine Gus	471
Magee, Chris	440
Magee, Kate	11
Magee, Paul	413, 416, 429
Magennis-Hale, Cherish	515
Maggi, Michael R.	515
Maggie Klein & Co.	26
Maggio, Devin	515
Maggio, Vince	448
Maggiore, Janine	560
Maginnis, Molly	560
Magliozzo, Chris	68
Magnet NY	381, 394, 492, 560
Magnetic Image Video	49
Magno Sound & Video	44, 87, 91, 130, 289, 291
Magnum Group, Inc.	248
Magruder, Laura	505
Maguire, Scott	403, 413, 440
Mah, James	458
Maher, John	186, 458
Mahler, Tinayn	482
Mahlke, Ellen	565
Mahon, Brian R.	420
Mahon, Daniel	515
Mahon, Gabrielle	502
Mahon, Kevin	515
Mahoney, Dan	471
Mahoney, Sheila	448
Maiello, James	420
Maiello, Paul	420
Maimone, Kasia Walicka	556
Main Attractions	126, 302, 318, 330, 331
Main, Tim	420
Maine	173
Maine Media Workshops	548
Maine, Sarah A.	515
Maio, Maria	482
Maisner, Bernard	229, 342
Maitland II, Dennis L.	536
Maitland, Kim H.	536
Maitland, Tod A.	536
Majestic Light	298
Major, Grant	394
Major, Tre	492
Majour, Renee	492
Make Believe TV, LLC	23
Make-Up Artists & Hair Stylists (IA Local 798)	546
Makris, Constantine	429
Malasek, Filip	68
Malat, Cheryl	526
Malatino, Donna	492
Malaysia Airlines	153
Malecki, Lee B.	515
Malenda, Andrew	68
Malige, Didier	492
Maliszewski, Jan	429
Malkames, Rick	429
Mallamo, Peter	403
Mallick, Paul E.	458
Malloys, The	28
Malone, Brendon	471
Malone, Dennis	458
Malone, James	458
Malone, Sean	471
Malone, Vern	565
Maloney, Denis	440
Maloney, Donna	565
Malpica, Mitch	403
Mamaril, Ruth	68
Mamet, Allen R.	515
Mammoth Production Packages	261, 268, 298, 306, 316
Mancusi, Joe	403
Mancuso, Jodi	482
Mancuso, Kevin	492
Mancuso, Richard	239
Mancuso, Robert	403
Mandler, Anthony	507
Mandy, A. Domonic	448
Maneche, Daria	560
Manfredi, Tina Marie	389
Manganaro's Hero-Boy	162
Manganelli, Derek	403
Mangan, Patrick	528
Manger, Alan R.	536
Mangravite, Tom	429
Manhattan Center Studios	44, 83, 87, 130
Manhattan Center Studios - Ballrooms	249
Manhattan Dollhouse Shop	347
Manhattan Edit Workshop	548
Manhattan Model Shop	366
Manhattan Motorcars	356
Manhattan Neon Sign Corporation	343, 354
Manhattan Penthouse	190
Manhattan Place Entertainment	276
Manhattan Production Music	80
Manhattan Propane	372
Manhattan Wardrobe Supply	348
Maniaci, Teodoro	429
Mania, John	425
Mania, Peter S.	107
Manic	83
Manic Moose Music	83
Maniolas, James	550
Manion, Randy	528
Manley, Chris	440
Mann, Ann	448, 499
Mann, Aran	394
Mann, Woody	515
Mannain, Brian	515
Manning, Ed	104
Mannix, Bobbie	560
Mannix, Francesca	502
Manor Moving and Storage	197
Manos, Christopher G.	471
Manowitz, Sarah	565
Manser, Janice E.	515
Mansfield, David	440, 549
Mansfield, The	178
Mansfield's Executive Transportation	182
Manwaring, Gareth	403
Manz, Jason	528, 550
Manzione, James J.	458
Manzione, Sean	458
MAPS/Mobile Arts Production Services	195, 201
Mar, Suk Yi	528
Marandi, Sara	11
Marble and Clay	17, 88
Marburger Surgical	351
Marbury, Roger	458
Marcellino, David	499
Marcel, The	178
Marcel, Michael D.	515
March of Time Newsreels and Documentaries	98
Marchetti, Jeffrey	515
Marchetti, Maryann	482
Marco, Phil	11, 429
Marcotte, John	471
Marcus, Charles	410
Marcus, Gary	450
Marcus, Keira	240
Margetson, Andy	11
Margulies, Sherri	68
Maria-Stefania	560
Mariani, Chantal	483
Mariani, Roger	492
Marie, Christine	483
Marie, Estella	565
Marinakis, Eva	483
Marinelli, Marc.	403
Marini, Maria A.	240
Marino, Michael	483
Marino, Rich	440
Marino, William M.	553
Marion's A Go-Go	162
Mario's Express Service, Inc.	197
Mariotti, Enrico	492
Marjoram, Ernie	36
Mark, The	178
Mark Edward, Inc.	382, 492
Mark Forman Productions Corp.	92, 258, 291
Mark Haefeli Productions	23, 88
Mark Ross Films	17, 23
Mark, Stephen	68

Company/Crew Index

Name	Page
Markoe-Byrne, Andie	492
Markopoulos, Rob	11
Markowitz, Barry	429
Markowitz, Jeffrey	540
Marks, David	499
Marks, Dick	11
Marks, Lionel A.	553
Marks, Lydia	532
Marks, Nancy	499
Marks-OMalley, Lydia	515
Markunas, Christopher G.	420
Markus, Robert	471
Marmara - Manhattan, The	178
Maronna, Michael	458
Marquardt, Roche & Partners	3
Marquardt, Stephanie Ann	525
Marquette, Gregory	11
Marquette, Josh	483
Marquinez, Horacio	430
Marra Siliceo Theresa	483
Marriott ExecuStay	178
Marritz, Edward	430
Marro & Associates/SMP	17
Marro, Stephen	11, 440
Marroquin, Charles	471
Marroquin, Rick L.	471
Marrs, Karol	499
Marsala, John	389
Marsden, Adam	440
Marsetti, Albino	410
Marsh, Loretta	383
Marsh, Nicola	440
Marshad Technology Group	24, 39
Marshall, Adam	68
Marshall, Bill	11
Marshall, Carmia	565
Marshall, Cathy	394, 515, 532
Marshall Jr., Clinton W.	515
Marshall, Keith	471
Marshall, Rob	11
Marshall, Tarsha	483
Marti, Pascal	440
Martial Arts, Inc.	246
Martin, Adrian	504, 528
Martin, Alexander	403
Martin, Annie	483
Martin, Edgar	471
Martin, Frank R.	515
Martin, Glenn	11
Martin, Greg	410, 471
Martin, Gregory	240
Martin, Gwyn	565
Martin, Joseph	515
Martin, Keegan	104
Martin, Marjorie	483, 492
Martin, Pam	69
Martin, Paul	394
Martinair-Holland	153
Martinek, Kevin	403
Martinelli, Elaine	240
Martines, Douglas	536
Martinez, Adolfo	36
Martinez, Alejandro	440
Martinez Eydie	483
Martinez, Neida	553
Martinez, Nicole	403
Martinez, Philip	410, 415
Martinez, Rosealee	560
Martinez, Steven	36
Martini, Chris	69
Martini, Michelle	560
Martinovic, Igor	430
Martone, Gary	471
Martorano, Jeanette	458
Martorano Jr., Salvatore (Sal)	458
Martori, Gary	483
Martyn, Gary	502
Marullo, Glen M.	536
Marvco Corporation	340
Marvel, Thomas	440
Maryland	173
Maryland-Baltimore	173
Marzouk, Frida	459
Marzovilla, Michael	430, 459
Marzulli, Chris N.	471
Marzulli, Peter	459
Marzulli, Thomas	471
Mase, James	536
Mask Arts Co./Stanley Allan Sherman	334
Maslansky, Stephanie	556, 560
Maslin, Bryan	440
Maslow Media Group	201, 241
Maslow, Renny	11
Mason, Evelyn	560
Mason, Linda	492
Mason, Matthew	528
Mason, Steve	440
Massa, Louis M.	471
Massachusetts-Boston	173
Massena International Airport	154
Massey, Adam	11
Massimo, Donna	556
Massingham, Damien	69
Masson, Jacqui	394
Masterdisk Studios	58
Masterfile	98
Masters, Dorothy	565
Masterson, Peter	430
Maszkiewicz, Agata	560
Mataya, Geri	483
Matejczyk, Peter	420
Mathison, Bryan	565
Mathus, Ben	403
Matina, Joseph	430
Matinee NY	378
Matlovsky, Alisa	528
Mattern, John	528
Mattes, Hal	186
Matthes, Peter	528
Matthews, Mary Ellen	507
Maude	560
Maurer, Ingrid	556
Maurer, Michael J.	459
Maurer, Shawn	440
Maurice-Jones, Tim	440
Mauro, Richard	459
Max, Arthur	394
Maxell Corporation of America	286
Maximum Throughput, Inc.	286
Maxmen, Mimi	556
Maxtone-Graham, Jamie	440
Maxwell, Fran	403
Maxwell, Joe	440
Maxx Images, Inc.	98
May, Gary Stephen	107
May, Jim	69
May, Pamela	483
Maya, Christopher	515
Maya, Gregory	11
Maya Media Corp.	17
Mayas, Michele	107
Mayer, Christine	515, 532
Mayer, Eddy	36
Mayer, Lance	403
Mayer, Michele L.	540
Mayfield, James	403
Mayhew Breen Productions	26
Mayhew, Ina	389
Mayhew, Parris	410, 415
Maynard, Darren	528
Maysles Shorts, Inc./Maysles Films, Inc.	17
Mazet, Nicolas	536
Mazur, Alexandra	515, 532
Mazur, Bernadette	483
Mazurek, Barry	565
Mazzarella, Vinny	515
Mazzarese-Allison, Suzy	483
Mazzei, Marco	440
Mazzei, Margaret M.	383
Mazzola, Gregory A.	471
Mazzola, James R.	394, 515
Mazzola, Jeff	515
Mazzola, John J.	471
Mazzola, Matthew	515
Mazzola Jr., Ronald	471
Mazzoni Jr., John G.	471
Mazzoni, Linda	515
Mazzucca, Val	255, 257
MB Productions, Inc.	276, 278, 282
McAdams, Brit	11
McAleer, John	403
McAlister, Francis G.	420
McAllister, David A.	471
McAllister, Patrick	459, 464
McAllister, Seth	471
McAllister-Voth, Robin C.	516
McAlpine, Don	441
McArdle, Tom	69
McAuliffe, Timothy	459
McAward, Brian	430
McBrearty, Doug	420
McBride, Francis J.	459
McBride, Molly	540
McCabe, Anthony	516
McCabe, George	471
McCabe, John	410, 417
McCabe, John P.	459
McCabe, Joseph L.	471

Name	Page
McCabe, Michelle	441
McCafferty, Gary	536
McCafferty, Kevin	410, 417
McCaine, Ron	410, 414, 417
McCallion, Edna	11, 28
McCallum, Kenneth S.	471
McCallum, Marcus	11
McCally, John	441
McCann, Andrew R.	459
McCardell, Sean	459
McCarry, Charles E.	389
McCarthy, Andrew	11
McCarthy, Kevin B.	516
McCarthy, Kyle	448
McCarthy, Louise	483
McCarthy, Matthew P.	516
McCarthy, Stephen	403
McCarthy, Susannah	516
McCarthy, Tom	11
McCarthy, Virginia	525
McCartin, George	403
McClammy, Wayne	11
McClean, Brian	459
McClean, Cory	459
McClean, Harold J.	459
McClean, Kevin D.	459
McCole, David	516
McConkey, Jim	430
McConkey, Larry	413, 430
McConnell & Borow, Inc./Prop Art	366
McConnell Jr., Harold E.	516
McConville, Kevin	471
McCormack, Frank J.	459
McCormick, John D.	536
McCort, Ray	257
McCown, Chad	36
McCoy, Ann	107
McCoy, Lauretta	492
McCullagh, Brian R.	459
McCullagh, James	459
McCullough, Benjamin G.	471
McCullough, Frank	389
McDermott, Brett	459
McDermott, Kelly	561
McDermott Jr., Neil	471
McDermott, Thomas A.	516
McDevitt, John (Jack)	471
McDonagh, James P.	516
McDonald, Jeffrey T.	459
McDonald, Michael P.	459
McDonald, Michelle	556
McDonald, Ryan	502
McDonnell, John B.	516
McDonough Jr., Leslie	528
McDonough, Michael	430
McDonough, Sandy	459
McDowell, Alex	394
McElhatton, Russ	441
McElroy, Alethea	565
McElwain, John	471
McEnerney, John F.	471
McEntee, Kevin	516
McEntee, Stephen T.	420
McEntyre, Peter	413, 459
McEvoy, Jeff	69
McEwen, Gareth	69
McFadden, Michael A.	471
McFaul, Ryan	11, 28
McGann, Mark	550
McGavin, Jeanne	459
McGavin, Nicholas	459
McGavin, Robert J.	459
McGavin, William G.	459
McGee-Glover, Stephanie	483
McGee, Robin	561
McGehee, Heather (Cricket)	106
McGill, Kathleen	550
McGovern, Mark P.	459
McGowan, Patrick	441
McGowan, Patrick D.	516
McGrady, Walter	471
McGrath, Martin	441
McGrath, Mary Joan (MJ)	565
McGrath, Michael	471
McGrath, Patrick J.	471
McGrath, Ryan T.	516
McGrath, Tom	441, 459
McGreal, Colin	36
McGuigan, Kieran	441
McGuiness, Anthony	471
McGuire, Christopher TJ	441
McGuire, Daniel	536
McGuire, Gail	483
McGuire, Steven T.	420
McHenry, Christian	502
McHugh, John F.	420
McInerney, Christine	483
McIntosh, Daniel	536
McIntosh, Donald	430
McIntosh, Scott	52
McIntyre, Charles M.	536
McIntyre, David J.	471
McIntyre, John	403
McIntyre, Martin C.	423
McIntyre, Matthew J.	420
McKane, Derek	410, 414, 417, 441, 459
McKearnin, Stephen A.	420
McKelvey, Timothy	565
McKendry, Ann Durnin	516
McKenna, Charles	483
McKenna, Donna	220
McKenna, Kevin	553
McKenna, Paul	403
McKenna, Robert	410
McKenrick, Daniel	496
McKenzie, Roger	561
McKenzie, Teferra	536
McKinney, Mel	483, 492
McKinney Welding Supply Co., Inc.	318
McKiver, Thomas	492
McKnight, Kevin	441
McKnight, Sam	492
McKoy, Jennifer E.	383
McKoy, Winsome	561, 565
McLachlan, Robert	441
McLaglen, Josh	450
McLam, Taylor	52
McLaughlin, Chris	52
McLaughlin, Jack	258, 545
McLaughlin, Jan	536
McLaughlin, John A.	536
McLean, Deborah	452, 561
McLoota, Matthew	528
McMahon, David P.	420
McMahon, Greg	403
McMahon, Patrick	69
McMahon, Rodney	410
McMaster, Howard	448
McMillan Jr., James C.	471
McMillan, Karl	410, 417
McMillan, Sarah E.	516
McMillan, Timothy M.	471
McMillan-Roman, Doreen P.	383
McMullan, Tigre	459
McMurry, Gregory L.	104
McMurtrey, Debbie	69
McNabb, Barry	221
McNally, Bruce	107
McNally, David	11
McNamara, Charles A.	459
McNamara Jr., Robert J.	536
McNicholas, Keith W.	459
McNichols	352
McNutt, Stephen	441
McPeak, James A.	459
McPhee's Art Services	324
McQuoid, Simon	11
McRae, Brian	496
McRae, Donyale	492
McTigue, Colleen	565
McWilliams, Ryan	483
Meade, Joe	441
Meccariello, Joseph	410, 414
Mechanism	366
Mechanism Digital, Inc.	5, 55, 103
Media Distributors	266, 294
Media Services	222, 242
Media Services Solution Center	223
MediaMix	122, 130
Mediaracket	44
MediaVest	39
Medicine Shoppe, The	351
Medick, Aaron	410, 415
Medina Alejandro Abner	403
Medina, Anthony	394
Medina, R.N. Fran	383
Medina-Cerderia, Milagros	483
Medipix Productions, LLC	24
Meehan, Kevin V.	536
Meeker Jr., Guy	459
Meeks, Annette	483
Meere III, Charles E.	459
Meere, Thomas E.	459
Meere-Abt, Michael	459
Meere-Abt, Patricia	516
Mega Playground	88
Megatrax Production Music	80
Meheux, Phil	441

Name	Page
Mehlbrech, Alan J.	410, 415, 471
Mehling, Charles	11
Mehr-Rose, Pia	541
Mehrer Karl	425
Mehron, Inc.	348
Meienhofer, Eugene	459
Meier, Lisa	528
Meiklejohn, John	410
Meils, W. Douglas	459
Meir, Sharon	441
Meis, Rebecca J.	516
Meisenzahl, Bill	413
Melchiorre, Daniel	516
Melchiorre, Michael	420
Melendez Jr., John P.	516
Melendez, Mark A.	459
Melendez, Martha	483
Melgaard, Mimi	561
Melillo, Nicholas	11
Melina	11, 28
Melino, Bekka	394
Mellett, L. Bruce	420
Mellon, David	36
Melman, Alex	441
Melnyk, Andrew	536
Melo, Linda	483, 492
Melville, Patrick	492
Melvin, Harold	483
Melvin Jr., Eugene	516
Meminger, Hollis	403
Menard, Darius	516
Menard, Jean-Paul	516
Menard, Jenna	492
Menard, Shashanka	52
Mendelson, Andy	52
Mendelson, Matthew	459
Mendenhall, Joel	483
Mendes, Sam	11
Mendoza, Stan	448
Menendez, Carlos	389
Menke, Michelle	504
Menke, Sally	69
Mennella, Joseph E.	186
Mensching, Linda	483, 492
Menzies, Andrew	394
Menzies, Jr., Peter	441
Mercado, Hilda	441
Mercer Hotel	178
Mercer, Randy	483
Merchant Ivory Productions	27
Merci Media, Inc.	49
Mercury Lounge	249
Merdinger, Ronny	503
Meredith, Carol	483
Meridian Teterboro	150
Merims, Adam	499
Merk, Robert	464
Merkley Newmann Harty	3
Merlin Studios	44
Mermelstein, Dave	459
Merrick, John	476
Merrill, Dan	403
Merrill, Vanessa	389
Merriman, John C.	459
Merritt, James	471
Merritt, John	471
Merusi, Fred	420
Merwin-Miller, Janet	525
Merz, Larry	507
Mess Hall	83
Messina, Carla Lauren	107
Messina, Philip	394
Messina, Ramona	516
Messing, Helayne	516
Mestel, Simon	441
MetaFilm Corporation	286
Method	55, 88, 103, 289
Metivier, Timothy	403
Metro Film Cars, Inc.	322, 328, 358
Metro Weather Service	206
Metronome	249
Metropolis Studios, Inc.	130
Metropolitan Companies Inc., The	247
Metropolitan Museum of Art - Nolan Library	233
Metropolitan Pavilion	128, 190, 249
Metrovision Production Group	78, 261, 276, 282, 317
Metzger, Eric	516
Metzger, Joseph	403
Metzger, Timothy	516
Meurice Garment Care	338, 377
Mevissen, Hein	11
Mevoli, Nicholas	516
Mexicana Airlines	153
Mexico	173
Mexico AA Travel Specialist	204
Mexico-Baja California	173
Meyer, Elouise	107
Meyer, Gifford	516
Meyer Jr., Howard J.	459
Meyer, Jeffrey	516
Meyer, Jeffrey M.	476
Meyer, Tom	394
Meyerhoff, Kimberly	483
Meyerowitz, Phil	504
Meyers, Pat	556
Meyers, Robin	526
MG&G Advertising, Inc.	3
MGM Gold Communications	3
MGM Music	80
Miami Air International	150
Micallef, Eddie	528
Micallef, Jason	459
Miccio, Kathrina	483
Michael Beckman Associates, Ltd.	24
Michael, Danny	536
Michael, Jennifer	565
Michael Levine Music, Inc.	83
Michael Miller, Inc.	367, 374
Michaelanthony, Michaela	492
Michael's Classics, Inc.	358
Michaelson, Debra	448
Michalak, Cynthia	516
Michalek, David	11
Michaud, Ron	441
Michel, Michele	561
Michel, Sion	441
Michelangelo, The	178
Michelin, Gary	403
Michelin, Mike	450, 499, 528
Michelle, Janine	516, 532
Michelle's Kitchen	162
Michelson Studio	128
Michie, Drogo	394
Michigan	173
Michos, Anastas	430
Mickle, Jim	36
Microform Models, Inc.	374
Middleberg Euro	34
Middleditch, Paul	11
Midnight Media Group, Inc.	49, 276
Midtown Neon Sign Corporation	354
Midwest Express	153
Midwood Ambulance & Oxygen Service, Inc.	386
Mighty Pictures	40
Miglio, Jessica	505
Mihajlov, Sergei	459
Mik Cribben	416
Mike Lemon Casting	220, 229
Mike's Furniture, Inc.	330
Mike's Lumber Store	330
MikesGotMyBack.com	234
Miko, Joseph E.	536
Miksis, Brian	536
Mikula, Donald	492
Milano, Jody	502
Milano, Roseann	561, 565
Milcetic, John T.	459
Miler Bruce	394
Miles Associates, Inc.	24, 49
Miles, Peter	394
Milia, Michael	410
Milicevic, Milos	450
Milkis, Andy	69
Mill, New York, The	88, 104, 289
Millard Willaim	410
Millennium Hotel New York U.N. Plaza	178
Miller, Adam	403
Miller, Andrea	483
Miller, Ann	516
Miller, Bill	540
Miller Camera Support, LLC	286
Miller, Catherine	516
Miller, Charles	186, 504
Miller, Crandall	69
Miller, Eden	561
Miller, Glenn R.	459
Miller III, Harry B.	69
Miller, James	413, 441
Miller, James J.	471
Miller, James V.	471
Miller, Jamie	528
Miller, Jeffrey M.	536
Miller, Jeffrey W.	524
Miller, John C.	471
Miller, Jonathan	441
Miller, Josh	11, 28
Miller, Lisa	483
Miller, Louis	420

Company/Crew Index

Name	Page
Miller, Michael	448
Miller, Michael A.	471
Miller, Michael R.	69
Miller, Mike	11
Miller, Morgan	516
Miller, Ned	98
Miller, Nicholas	420
Miller, Nick	403
Miller, Peter J.	536
Miller, Ronald A.	420
Miller, Scott	441
Miller, Scott W.	459
Miller, Toby	459
Miller, Wayne Scott	516
Miller, William	459
Miller, William J.	471
Miller Sr., William A.	471
Miller-Arpino, Laura Lynn	516
Miller's Launch	236, 328, 549
Miller's Rental & Sales	331
Millicent, Mark	36
Millimeter Production Buyer's Guide	226
Mills, Antoine	69
Mills, Edgar	52
Mills, Francesca	561
Mills, Peter	516
Mills-Cavalluzzo, Meredith	502
Millspaugh, Paul	69
Milstein, Matthew	516
Milt, Victor/Interactive Publishing	88
Minard, Gordon	464, 496
Minard, Jon	464
Minard Lighting & Grip	306, 317
Minassian, Amie	492
Minch, Michelle	394
Mindel, Dan	441
Mindstar Productions, Inc.	222
Minerva Cleaners	338, 377
Minette, Gordon	52
Mingenbach, Louise	561
Mink, Sal	108
Mink, Symon	403
Minnerly, Barry	425
Minnesota	173
Minor Consideration, A	546
Minsky, Charles	441
Minter, Charles D.	471
Mintz, Jonathan	448
Mirabella, Angela	565
Mirage Productions Inc.	24, 39, 40, 88, 201, 289
Miranda	286
Miranda, Claudio	441
Miranda, Richard	430
Mirante, Anthony	540
Mirisch Agency, The	69, 382, 394, 430, 441, 499, 561
Mirrorlite Products	347
Mirsky Reps	26
Miskie Adele	565
Miss Jezebel's Prop House	345, 370, 374
Mississippi	173
Mississippi-Greenwood	173
Mississippi-Natchez	173
Mississippi-Tupelo	173
Mississippi-Vicksburg	173
Missouri-Kansas City	173
Miszkiel, Jasia	483
Mitchell, John A.	459
Mitchell, Monique	471
Mitchell, Richard T.	459
Mitze, Walt	4
Mixopolis, Inc.	44, 83
MJ Signs & Promotions	245, 343
Moat, Adrian	11
Mobile Messenger Service	235
Mochizuki, Yori	36
Mock, Robert M.	471
Modelbartenders.com	232
Modena, Liz	240
Moder, Danny	441
Moderne, The	178
Modisett, Tod	69
Modprop.com	346, 360, 370
Moe DiSesso Film Library	99
Moeller, Christopher	403
Moers, John	410
Moeyaert, Benoit	492
Mogg, Kirsten	565
MoHoVip, Inc.	195
Moiz	492
Mokri, Amir	441
Molecule, The	55
Mole, Laurent	492
Molina, Octavio	516
Molina, Tony	441
Molinaro, Lisa	526
Molitoris, Jo	441
Molkenthin, Jerad	459
Mollo, Cindy	69
Mollod, Sandi	26
Monacan Consulate General	165
Monaco III, Joseph	516
Monaco, Jeffrey T.	471
Monaco, Matthew	240
Monaco Sr., Roger	524
Mongelli Jr., Nicholas J.	472
Monica Randall Locations	186
Monico, Alison Nancy	528
Monroe, Montez	502
Monsey Tours	155
Monsoon Films	18, 30
Monster in my Closet LLC	323
Montalvo, Elaine	561
Montana	173
Montana Artists Agency	69, 104, 382, 394, 430, 441, 450, 493, 499, 561
Montana-Southcentral	173
Montano, Jose	394
Montauk Airport	154
Monte, Jeff	516
Montesanto, Ann	493
Montesanto, Frank	493
Montgomery, Christine A.	516
Montgomery, Jon C.	459
Montgomery, Kevin W.	472
Montgomery, Michael	472
Montgomery, Richard A.	459
Montgomery Jr., Richard C.	472
Montgomery, Timothy	472
Montiel, Cecilia	394
Monzon, Matthew	493
Mood Creations, Ltd.	18, 24, 26
Mood Designer Fabric	340
Moon, Sarah	12
Moon, Zachary	536
Moondog Edit	49
Mooney Bullock, Jennifer	483
Mooney, James	493
Moonfish Production, Ltd.	24
Moonlite Courier	235
Mooradian, George	441
Mooradian, Wendy	502
Moore, Jeffrey	410
Moore, Jennifer	565
Moore, Jonathan	403
Moore, Kevin	448
Moore P.A. Hire Inc.	126, 269, 317
Moore, Paul G.	108
Moore, Vanessa	561
Moore, William	403, 459
Moore-Theis, Pat	483, 493
Moore-Tzouris, Nedenia	536
Moosher, Christine	516
Mor, Ben	12, 28
Morabito, David	430
Morales, Carole	483
Morales, Raul	248
Morales, Ronald C.	472
Morales-Pappas, Maria	483
Moran, John T.	516
Moran, Kristine	516
Moran, Mark	430
Moran, Mike	403
Moran, Robert	420
Moran, William	472
Morand, Zeus	410, 414, 417
Morano, Reed Dawson	441
Morano, Vincent	502
Morante, Paolo	528
Mordeci, Glen	430
Morell, Gregory	516
Morello, Peter	403
Moremen, Lindsay	561
Moreno, Luis	69
Moretti, Mark	36
Morgan, Beth	561
Morgan, Clariss	483
Morgan, Dianne	483
Morgan, Donald M.	441
Morgan, Julia	528
Morgan, Mia	556
Morgans Hotel	178
Morganstein, Robert	459
Morgenstern, Vicki	483
Morin, Ricardo	55, 116
Morini, Michael M.	472
Morisot, Damien	441
Morledge, MD Louis J.	246, 386
Morley, Grace	483

Moroccan Consulate General 165
Morris, Alex 36
Morris, Colleen 565
Morris, David Evans 389
Morris, Errol 12
Morris Glasser & Son 347
Morris, Heather 483
Morris, Richard 516
Morrison, David 441
Morrison, Jon D. 459
Morrison, Julie 524
Morrison, Kathryn 561
Morrison, Marianne 483
Morrison, Phil 12, 28
Morrissey, Keith E. 516
Morristown Municipal Airport 154
Morrone, Gerard 516
Morrow, Bob 12
Morrow, Eve 483
Morse, Christine 493
Morse, Talley W. 472, 476
Morse, Thomas 536
Morsillo, Vincent 516
Mortellaro Jr., Jack Frank 516
Mortelliti, Andrew 516
Mortier, Koen 12
Mortis, Monifa 493
Morton, Chrissy 561
Morton, Perry 69
Moschini Productions 186, 201, 220
Moscoso, Amalia 493
Moser, John 69
Moser, Michael 430
Moses & Singer LLP 228
Moses, Deborah 516
Moses, Steven 441
Moshlak, David C. 536
Moshlak, Ruby 516
Moshlak-Barbalat, Molly Rain 516
Mosley, Kevin 553
Moss, Peter 441
Moss, Wayne B. 420
Mother West 83, 233
Motion Odyssey, Inc. 201, 382, 407, 413, 416, 441
Motion Picture Editors Guild (IA Local 700) 546
Motion Picture Studio Mechanics (IA Local 52) 546
Motion Picture, TV and Theatre Directory 226
Mott, John 394
Motta, Raymond 420
Motyka, Bill 389
Motz, George 430
Mougin, Claude 12
Moulton, Robert 483, 493
Mountain View Group, Ltd., The 18, 24
Movie Mobile 298
Movie Movers Transportation Equipment 158, 195, 320
Movie Services, Inc. 99
Movie Time Cars, Inc. 360
Moviecraft, Inc. 99
Moving Images 55, 57, 88, 283, 289
Moving Pictures 24, 39, 49, 88, 289
Moviola Digitial 62, 261, 266, 294
Moviola/J & R Film Company 62, 284
Mowat, Donald 483
Mowbray, Paul 472
Mowen, Bob 12
Moxie Pictures, Inc. 18
Moxness, David 441
Moya, John 403
Moyer, Donna 483
Moyer, John 430
Moyer, Steven Faulkner 441
Moyes, Dennis W. 389
Moynier, Eric 430
Mr. John, Inc. 198
MSE Media Solutions 267, 294
Muchow, Don 459
Mugavero, Melissa 528
Muhler, Michael J. 460
Muhlstock, Jeff 410, 415
Mulero, Veronica 526
Mulholland, Moyra 493
Mullen, Christie 528
Mullen, M. David 441
Mullen, Michael 460
Muller, Andy 528
Muller Jr., Fred T. 460
Muller, Gary 407
Muller, Joseph W. 460
Muller, Justin 450
Muller, Robby 441
Mullet, David 12, 28
Mullett, Peter 430
Mulligan, Mary 483
Mulligan, Zak 403
Mullins, Kevin E. 472
Multidyne 286
Munafo, Anthony G. 516
Munemi 493
Muniz, Angel 536
Muniz, Carla 483
Munkacsi, Ronald 403
Murach, Len 528
Muraoka, Alan 394
Murashige, Steven 28
Murcko, Carol A. 516
Murgas, Tina 483
Murin, David 556
Murphy, Christopher M. 553
Murphy, Cynthia 493
Murphy, Derek C. 460
Murphy, Fred 430
Murphy, James 553
Murphy, James P. 516
Murphy, John 410
Murphy, John J. 536
Murphy, Kevin 403, 460
Murphy, Maggie 528
Murphy, Michael 516, 532
Murphy, Michael S. 69
Murphy Jr., Raymond 472
Murphy, Richard 536
Murphy, Robert 472
Murphy, Sandra 483
Murphy, Scott P. 395
Murphy, Sean Patrick 240
Murphy, William R. 108
Murr, Edward 36
Murray, Brian 36
Murray, Francois 240
Murray Hill Studios, Inc. 24, 39, 58, 88, 122, 130
Murray, Malcolm C. (M.C.) 460
Murtha Agency, The 382, 395, 441
Musco Lighting 317
Muse, The 178
Museum of Modern Art Library 233
Museum of the Moving Image, The 92
Musgrove, Bryant 536
Music Bakery, The 80
Music, Roz 493
Music Video Production Association (MVPA) 547
Musky, Jane 395
Mustafa, Saade A. 414, 415, 460
Mutual Hardware 305, 306, 327, 330
Muxi, Elizabeth 565
Muzeni, Alan 516
Myer, Priska 561
Myers, Barry 12
Myers, Chris 499, 504
Myers, Grant 69
Myers, Kenneth 273, 450, 554
Myers, Margo 551
Myers, Mary 561
Myhrum, Matthew 389

N

N. Glantz & Son, Inc. 325
N.W. Production Services & RV Rental 195
N9 Productions 39, 58
NAC Production Services 360
Nadeau, John 460
Nagel, Rik/Prime Location 186
Nagle, Rick 425
Nagler, Betsy 536
Nahoum, Ken 12
Naiderman, Harold 460
Naitove + Company 26
NAK Marketing & Communications, Inc. 24
Nakanishi, Rika 395
Nakata, Ariana 395
Nallan, Daniel 472
Nallan III, William J. 472
Naparstek, Jeff 516
Napier, April 561
Napoleon Art & Productions, Inc. 49
Nardilla, Gary 410, 441
Narins, Joshua S. 430
Narvaez, Robin 484
Nash, David J. 516
Nash, Soren 403
Nasso, Julius 551
Nast, Carol 389, 517
Nastri, Arthur 537
Natale, Francine 460
Nathan, Marc 410
Nathans, Margaret 539
National 156

Company/Crew Index

National Academy of Television Arts, The . . . 547
National Aerospace Training and Research Center/ NASTAR . . . 190
National Fiber Technology, LLC. . . . 340, 348
National Flag & Display Co., Inc.. . . . 343
National Geographic Digital Motion . . . 99, 293
NationwidePictureCars.Com . . . 360
Natrona Furniture . . . 346
Nature Footage/Ocean Footage . . . 99, 293
Naud, Bob . . . 499
Navarro, Anthony . . . 517
Navarro, Guillermo . . . 441
Navesink Yachts . . . 328
Navy Arms Co. . . . 341
NBC News Archives . . . 99
NBC New York Editing Operations . . . 49
NBC New York Prosthetics Shop . . . 323
NBC New York Stages . . . 122, 134
NBC Universal Artworks . . . 88, 103
Ncyclomedia, Inc. . . . 278
Neary, Mary . . . 403
Nebraska . . . 173
Nebraska-Omaha . . . 173
NEC . . . 286
Nederlander Television & Film . . . 39
Neeb, Meegan . . . 502
Needelman, Craig . . . 410
Needelman, Craig . . . 414
Needleman, Alan . . . 540
Neese, Kelly . . . 537
Negrin, Leon . . . 403
Negrin, Michael . . . 441
Negrin, Sol . . . 430
Negron, Joel . . . 69
Neighborhood Cleaners Association International . . . 338
Nelligan, Mel . . . 526
Nelson, Arlene . . . 441
Nelson, Chris . . . 28
Nelson, Christopher S. . . . 517
Nelson, Craig . . . 430
Nelson, David . . . 448, 499
Nelson Enterprises . . . 337
Nelson, Janet . . . 395
Nelson, Jenn . . . 484
Nelson, John Killian . . . 36
Nelson, Kenneth D. . . . 420
Nelson, Peter . . . 430
Nelson Jr., Richard J. . . . 517
Nelson, Thomas . . . 537
Ne-O . . . 12
NEP Screenworks . . . 278
NEP Studios . . . 122, 134
NEP Supershooters, LP . . . 78
Nepomniaschy, Alex . . . 441
Neroda, Daniel . . . 517
Nesbit Systems, Inc. . . . 222
Nespola, Laura . . . 403
Nessen, Edward . . . 403
Neswald, Amy . . . 484
Netherlandic Consulate General . . . 165
Netherlands-Rotterdam . . . 176
NetOne, Inc. . . . 39
Nettmann Systems International . . . 261, 286
Neubig, Mary . . . 537
Neukum, Nila . . . 526
Neumann, Jeff . . . 505
Neumann, Mathias . . . 442
Neumann, Richard C. . . . 460
Neuwirth, Dana C.. . . . 517
Nevada . . . 173
Nevada-Reno-Tahoe . . . 173
Never Quit, Inc./Brian Smyj . . . 545, 549
Nevessa Production, Inc. . . . 44, 83, 269, 276, 298
Nevin, Elizabeth . . . 502
Nevins, Alexandra . . . 499
New & Unique Videos . . . 99, 293
New Amsterdam Entertainment . . . 39
New Dimension . . . 245
New Hampshire . . . 173
New Jersey . . . 173
New Jersey-Fort Lee . . . 173
New Jersey Network Media Productions . . . 39, 134
New Mexico . . . 173
New Mexico-Albuquerque . . . 173
New, Robert . . . 442
New York 411 . . . 226
New York Auto Stars . . . 360
New York Blackboard of New Jersey, Inc. . . . 374
New York-Buffalo Niagara . . . 173
New York Caterers and Party Planners . . . 232
New York City Center Studios . . . 221
New York City Q-Cards, Inc. . . . 271
New York Doll Hospital, Inc. . . . 347
New York Film Academy . . . 548
New York Film Academy Screening Room . . . 92
New York Film Flyers . . . 255, 322
New York Film & Video Guide . . . 227
New York Flowers and Plant Shed . . . 344
New York Grip Truck, Inc. . . . 306
New York Hall of Science . . . 191
New York Helmsley . . . 178
New York Hilton . . . 178
New York Jib . . . 298
New York Ladder & Scaffold Corporation . . . 126, 303, 310
New York Marriott Brooklyn . . . 178
New York Marriott Downtown . . . 178
New York Marriott East Side . . . 178
New York Marriott Marquis . . . 178
New York Movers . . . 197
New York-Nassau County . . . 173
New York Nautical . . . 328
New York Network . . . 24, 78, 88, 225, 271
New York-New York City . . . 174
New York Office . . . 18, 69, 382, 395, 403, 410, 430, 442, 493, 561
New York Palace . . . 178
NewYork-Presbyterian Emergency Medical Services . . . 386
New York Production Alliance (NYPA) . . . 547
New York Production Services . . . 201
New York Public Library - Milstein Division . . . 233
New York Public Library, the . . . 191, 234
New York Public Library for the Performing Arts . . . 234
New York-Rochester . . . 174
New York Society for Ethical Culture . . . 249
New York Speech Improvement Services . . . 208
New York State . . . 173
New York-Suffolk County . . . 174
New York Theatrical Haulers, Inc. . . . 320
New York-Upstate . . . 174
New York Videoconference Center . . . 78, 221
New York Women in Film & Television . . . 547
New Zealand . . . 176
Newark Liberty International Airport . . . 154
Newburg, Chris . . . 493
Newcomb, Robert . . . 430
Newel, LLC . . . 345
Newell, Bethany . . . 493
Newell, Evan . . . 403
Newell, Mark R.. . . . 517
Newell, William . . . 460
Newins, Edward J. . . . 472
Newman, Marc . . . 517
Newman, Spencer . . . 442
Newman, Tim . . . 410
News Broadcast Network . . . 24
Newsome, Randall . . . 531
Newsome, Rick . . . 36
Newton, Frazer . . . 517
Newton-Harding, Anne . . . 565
Newton, Tom . . . 517
Next Millennium Productions, Ltd. . . . 88, 122, 134, 290
Neziri, Merita . . . 484
Neziri, Shpresa . . . 484
Neziri, Suzana . . . 484, 493
NFL Films . . . 18, 24, 49, 74, 88, 99, 124, 134, 290
Ng, Iris Tse Min . . . 460
Ng, Philip . . . 186, 526
Ngai, William . . . 472
Ngo, Quan . . . 36
Nguyen, Ha . . . 561
NHL Hockey Archive . . . 99, 293
Nibley, Christopher . . . 442
Niccolls, Paul . . . 472
Nice Shoes . . . 88, 290
Niceberg, Andrew S. . . . 460
Nicholas, Mark . . . 420
Nicholas, Richard W. . . . 537
Nicholls, Jill . . . 395
Nichols, Dean . . . 565
Nicholson, Amy . . . 12
Nicholson, Peggy . . . 484
Nickas, Jim . . . 529
Nickason, Paul . . . 472
Nicks, Dewey . . . 12, 28
Nicksay, David . . . 499
Nielsen, Monty . . . 460
Nielson, Bridger . . . 442
Niemand, Eric . . . 561
Nierenberg, Thomas . . . 517
Niforos, James . . . 540
Niggemeyer, Jeffrey . . . 460
Nigro, Lynn Marie . . . 517
Niles, Lauren . . . 561
Nilsson, Carl . . . 442
Nilsson, Lisa K. . . . 517
Nimetz, Gregory . . . 460
Ni Rochain, Maire . . . 502
Nisa Glass Systems . . . 347

Name	Page
Nisenson, Daniel	517
Nisenson, Paul	517
Nishida, Watari	529
Nitke, Barbara	505
Nivo Productions	186, 328, 360
Nixon, Kathryn	556
Nobbs, Alexander	553
Noble, Ben	460
Noble, Chuck	496
Noble, David	472
nObrain	12
Nobu	249
Noland, Lyn	410
Noland, Tonya	493
Nolan, James (Jim)	472
Nolan, Peter	410
Nolan, Valerie	517
NOLA Studios	221
Noll, Susan	425
Non-Stop Music Library	80
Nonstop Pictures, Inc.	18
Noonan, Christopher	420
Noped, Melvin	472
Noraz, Evelyne	484
Norcostco - Eastern Costume	334, 349
Norgren, Catherine F.	556
Norm Dodge & Associates	114
Norman, Timothy	403
Normand, Michael	12
Normand, Paul D.	517
Nornang, Leda	502
Norpak Corporation	286
Norr, Carl	430
Norr, Chris	430
Norr, Maritza	403
Norris, Fred	505
Norris, Patricia	395, 561
North Carolina	174
North Carolina-Charlotte	174
North Carolina-Durham	174
North Carolina-Greensboro	174
North Carolina-Northeast	174
North Carolina-Western North Carolina	174
North Carolina-Wilmington	174
North Dakota	174
Northeastern Aviation Corporation	150
Northern Ireland	176
Northern Lights Post	49, 88, 290
Northwest Airlines	153
Northwest/KLM	153
Norton, Charles	430
Norton, David	430
Norton, Heather	403
Norton, Shelley	561
Norway	176
Norwood, John	186
Norwood Mansion	191
Notaro, Peter	448
Notick, Janna	565
Nova Disc	58
Novak, Scott H.	460
Novelty Scenic Studios	337
Novich, Adam	472
Novich, Bruce	410
Novich, Neil	472
Novick, Anna	472
Novick, Edward	537
Novo Arts, Inc.	128, 191
Novotny, Michael	395
Now Hear This	44
Nowalski, Miroslaw	420
Nowlan, Martin	460
Nowve, Lorna	240
NPI Production Services, Inc.	242
Nugent, Frank	448, 499
Nunes, Vasco	442
Nurses-In-Commercials	220, 386
Nussbaum, Joe	12
Nussbaum, Jon	472
Nussbaum, Rob	430, 460
Nutmeg Audio Post	44
Nutmeg Recording	83
Nutopia Workspace	32
Nuttgens, Giles	442
Nuzzi, Chiara	565
NY Whitehall Transportation Co., Inc.	155
NYC Fire Museum	234
NYCastings	221
Nylon Studios Inc.	83
Nyomarkay, John T.	108, 389
NYPG, Ltd.	227
NYPH Audio Visual Service	24

O

Name	Page
Oakwood Corporate Housing	178
Oare, Steve	502
Oates, Hubert J.	517
Oates, John	460
Oates Jr., John P.	517
Oates, Joseph P.	517
Oates, Kevin	517
Oates, Michael H.	472
Oates, Robert J.	517
Oates, William A.	472
Oates-Frato, Kathleen E.	517
Oates-Koenig, R.N. Elizabeth M.	383
Oates-Sparnon, Deborah A.	517
Oberle, Dan	69
Oberle, Joseph	104
Oberman, Paul	395
O'Brien, Brendan J.	537
O'Brien, Elizabeth (Beth)	460
O'Brien, Jamin	448
O'Brien, Kevin	410
O'Brien, Matthew	502
O'Brien, Melissa	403
O'Brien, Sean	472
Obscura Antiques & Oddities	374, 378
O'Callaghan, Michele	484
O'Carroll, Brian	410, 414, 417
Occhino, Murphy	529
Ochrym, Brian	410, 442
O'Connell, Karen	484
O'Connell, Kevin	460
O'Connor, Eric	403
O'Connor, Thomas M.	460
Oddball Film + Video	99, 293
Odds Costume Rental, Inc.	334
O'Dea, Sean	442
Odegaard, Brandon J.	460
Oditz, Carol	556
Odom, Gary	499
O'Donnell, Elaine	517
O'Donnell, Jimmy	410, 414
O'Donnell, Katherine	484
O'Donnell, Kory	502
O'Driscoll, Jeremiah	69
Odyssey Productions, Inc.	99
Oeser, Richard L.	517
Oetiker, Phil	430
Ogden, Richard	484
Ogden, Rita	484, 493
Ogens, Matt	12, 28
Ogilvy & Mather, Inc.	3
Ogle, Charles G.	517
Ogle Jr., Donald T.	472
OGM Music, a Division of OGM, Inc.	80
Ogu, Susan N.	517
O'Hagan, John	12
O'Hara, Shannon	565
Ohashi, Rene	442
Oheka Castle	191
Ohio Edit	49
Ohio-Cincinnati	174
Ohio-Cleveland	174
Ohio-Columbus	174
Okada, Daryn	442
Okamoto Studio	350
Oklahoma	174
Olan Montgomery Timmothy	493
O'Leary, William	460
Oliphant Studio	110
Oliva, Frank C.	517
Oliva Jr., Frank C.	517
Oliver, Ann-Marie	484
Oliver, Jono	448
Oliver, Robin Randal	450
Olivier, Charles	69
Ollen, Reginald	553
Ollendorff Fine Art	166
Olsen, Arne S.	472
Olsen Jr., Arne	472
Olsher, Jeremy	529
O'Malley, John	460
O'Malley, Neil	472
O'Malley, Ruben	403, 442
O'Malley, Thomas	529
O'Mara, Terence J.	537
Omega Media Group, Inc.	99
Omens, Caleb	529
Omni Berkshire Place	178
Omni Video Services, Ltd.	78, 276
Omnimusic	80
Omoto, Rie	493
On Location Education	541
On Point Resources, Inc.	202
On Site Energy Co., Inc.	302, 317

Company/Crew Index

On Stage Dancewear . . . 334
On Time Elite, Inc.. . . . 186, 195, 197
On Track Production Equipment . . . 300, 317
One if by Land, Two if by Sea . . . 249
O'Neal, Brendan . . . 484
O'Neil, Fintan . . . 52
O'Neill, Conor . . . 69
O'Neill, Mary-Margaret . . . 561
One Naked Egg . . . 382, 493, 507
One On One Productions . . . 221
OneSky Jets . . . 150
Onesto, Alain. . . . 410, 415
Onshore Media . . . 44, 49, 58, 88, 290
Opali, Natalie . . . 565
Open City Films . . . 27
Oppenheimer, Julie . . . 526
Opresnick, Jennifer . . . 526
Opus 1 Music Library, LLC . . . 80
Oravetz, Timothy S. . . . 517
Orbach, Yaron . . . 430
Orbit Digital . . . 88
Ordan Arietta Mindy . . . 448
Order, LLC . . . 18
O'Rear, Kathy . . . 561
Oregon . . . 174
O'Reilly, Dennis . . . 517
O'Reilly, Donald . . . 517
O'Reilly, Gavin . . . 517
Orenstein, Seth . . . 403
Orent, Stephen . . . 448
Ori, Joseph M.. . . . 460
Original License Plates/Andy Bernstein . . . 374
Origlieri, Joseph . . . 537
Origlieri, Lisa . . . 403
Orlandi, Daniel . . . 561
Orlando, Eric . . . 561
Orlando Management . . . 382, 395, 430, 442
Orofino, Vincent J.. . . . 517
O'Rourke, David . . . 52
O'Rourke, John . . . 450
Orr, James B. . . . 517
Orr, Tim . . . 442
Orsa, Jeff E. . . . 442
Orsino, Bruce P. . . . 517
Ortiz, Anthony . . . 537
Ortiz, Desiree . . . 537
Ortiz, Francisco . . . 529
Ortiz, Kenneth . . . 403
Ortiz, Nelson . . . 540
Ortolani, Stefano Maria . . . 395
Orton, George . . . 464
Orton, Richard . . . 484
Orvieto, Lawrence . . . 517
Osekoski, Paul . . . 460
O'Shea, Christopher M.. . . . 517
O'Shea III, Francis A. . . . 517
O'Shea, Michael . . . 413, 416, 430
Oshima, Jon . . . 517
Oshins, Ellen . . . 108
Oshman, Benjamin . . . 517
Oskarsdottir, Valdis . . . 69
Osmond, Polly . . . 493
Osso, Tony . . . 526
Ostrow, Robin . . . 484
Ostuni, Thomas . . . 69
Otis . . . 28
Ott, Laurent . . . 395
Ottaviano, Joanne A.A. . . . 493
Ottaviano, Susan . . . 452
Otterson Television Video, Inc. . . . 49
Ottesen, John . . . 524
Otto Kahn and James Burden, The . . . 191
Oulman, Kristine . . . 493
Outpost . . . 49, 62
Ouyoung, Juliet . . . 556
Ovasen . . . 52
Overton, C. Mark . . . 420
Owen, Lucas . . . 403
Owen, Timothy J. . . . 460
Owens, Kenneth L. . . . 420
Owgang, Cyndi . . . 540
Owings, Richard . . . 556
Ozawa, Toshiaki . . . 442, 460

P

P & S Fabrics . . . 340
P3-Production Update Magazine . . . 227
Paaswell, George . . . 551
Pac Lab . . . 74
Pacella, Mark S. . . . 36
Pachtman, Matthew . . . 556
Pacific Coast Forecasting . . . 206
Pacifici, Angelo . . . 12, 442
Pacion, Alexander . . . 389
Packaging Store . . . 166
Padgett, Daniel . . . 69
Padilla, Alfred O. . . . 460
Pados, Gyula . . . 442
Pagani, Rachel . . . 484
Pagano, Tony . . . 410, 442
Pagliaro, Robert . . . 403
Paige, Sheila . . . 526
Paikin, Daniel M. . . . 537
Painter, Barbie . . . 448
Painter, Devon . . . 556
Pak, Chong . . . 403
Pakistani Consulate General . . . 165
PAL Stage . . . 124
PAL Television East . . . 261, 276, 282, 317
Palace Digital Studios . . . 44, 55, 264
Palermo, Anthony . . . 493
Palermo, Michael . . . 69
Palma Distasi Susan . . . 403
Palmer, Briggs . . . 442
Palmer, Michael W. . . . 460
Palmieri, Gayle . . . 565
Palmieri, Genevieve . . . 529
Palmieri, Rocco . . . 460
Palminteri, Chaz . . . 12
Palumbo, Robert . . . 460
Pan American Video . . . 99
Panacciulli, Bruno F. . . . 421
Panamanian Consulate General . . . 165
Panasonic Broadcast & Television Systems Co. . . . 286
Panavision New York . . . 261, 286, 300, 305, 306, 317
Panchenko, Egor L.. . . . 537
Panchenko, Kyra . . . 484
Panczenko, Michael . . . 404
Panepinto, Stacey . . . 484
Panessa, Jeffrey . . . 472
Panetta, Lawrence . . . 537
Pangione, Daniel . . . 517
Pangione, Glen A. . . . 421
Pangione, Matthew . . . 472
Pangione, Vincent . . . 517
Pangolin Pictures, Inc. . . . 39
Pankewicz, Tim . . . 537
Pankow, Bill . . . 69
Panorama Flight Service, Inc. . . . 150, 191
Pantzer, Jerry . . . 430
Panuccio, Debi Prate . . . 517
Panuccio, Francis . . . 472
Panuccio II, Francis . . . 472
Panuccio, Jessica . . . 517
Panuccio, John . . . 472
Panzanaro, Justin . . . 472
Papadopoulos, Gus . . . 517
Papadopoulos, Marni . . . 517
Papadopoulos, Michael . . . 460
Papamichael, Phedon . . . 442
Papp, Justin . . . 517
Papp, Richard E.. . . . 517
Pappas, Andrea Denise . . . 502
Paquette, Bruce J. . . . 421
Paquette, Raymond A. . . . 472
Paquette, Robert H. . . . 472
Paquette, Ronald J. . . . 421
Paradigm . . . 382, 395, 430, 561
Paradise Catering & Mobile Kitchen . . . 162
Paragon Sports . . . 375
Paraguayan Consulate General . . . 165
Paramount, The . . . 178, 249
Paramount Courier Inc. . . . 151
Paramount Pictures - Stock Footage Library . . . 99
Paramount Production Support, Inc. . . . 306, 317
Paramount Vending . . . 347
Parekh, Andrij . . . 430
Parfitt, Tommy . . . 410
Paris, Francesca . . . 484, 493
Paris, Joseph . . . 484
Paris, Michele . . . 484
Parisian, Randy . . . 108
Park Avenue Post, Inc. . 18, 24, 44, 49, 57, 58, 88, 283, 290
Park, David . . . 430
Park, Gregory . . . 389
Park, Robbin . . . 472
Park Savoy Hotel . . . 178
Parker, Alison . . . 565
Parker, Chuck . . . 395
Parker, Gary M.. . . . 537
Parker, James . . . 448, 499
Parker, Jed . . . 69
Parker, Oneita . . . 561
Parkhurst Jr., G. Clark . . . 517
Parks, Aissatou . . . 565
Parks, Sara . . . 517
Parlay Film Productions, LLC . . . 24, 124, 128

Name	Page
Parlow, Kurt	404
Parmalee, Michael	505
Parmelee, Michael	517
Paron Fabrics West	340
Parra, Salvador	395
Parrell, Barry	442
Parrow, Neal	36
Parsons, Katrina Joy	502
Parsons, Randall	389
Parsons, Susan	502
Parsons-Meares, Ltd.	334
Partos Company	382, 395, 430, 442, 493, 561
Parts Models	229, 246
Party Line Tent Rentals	331
Party Pets, Inc.	214
Party Rental	198
Pascal, Michael	404
Pascento, Anthony J.	460
Pashayan, Richard	472
Pasicov, Stephanie	484
Passalacqua, Christopher	460
Passeri, Vincent	442
Passos, Heloisa	442
Pastecchi, David	537
Pasternak, Beth	561
Pastore, Eric	517
Pastore, Garry	517
Pastore, Micah	404
Pastorok, Morning	537
Pasztor, Beatrix Aruna	561
Patak, Chris	404
Patanjo	198
Patch, Karen	561
Patco Resources, Inc.	80, 234
Patel, Neil	389
Patelmo, Paul	404
Paterson, Owen	395
Patire, Joseph S.	421
Patnesky, Mark	404
Patricia Claire Co.	26
Patrick, Richard	448
Patsos Jr., George	472
Patsos, William	472
Patten, Marcia	565
Patterson, Jane L.	517
Patterson, Michael	12
Patterson, Miriam	499
Pattinson, Kenneth P.	472
Pattison, A. Taylor	517
Pattison, George	430, 472
Pattison, Nicky	484
Patton, Heather	565
Patton, Virginia	565
Pau, Peter	442
Paul, Anne	484, 493
Paul, Avery Elizabeth	383
Paul, Christopher	410, 414, 415, 417
Paul, Donna M.	517
Paul, George E.	460
Paul, Ronald G.	460
Paul, Steven T.	421
Paul Ziffren Sports Resource Center Library	99
Paulin, David	565
Paull, Wayne	410, 442
Paulmann, Deborah T.	484
Pavlovits, Ivan	36
Pavon, Jose	517
PAWS & Co., LLC	55, 264
Paws For Effect, Inc.	214
Payne, Jacqueline	484
Payne, Tiffany	395
Paynter, Kristen	493
PayReel	242
Pazlamatchev, Ivan	108
PCS Broadcast Services	18
Peacock, Randall	389
Peak, Tulé	395
Pearl, Daniel	442
Pearl, Eve	484
Pearl, Jeffrey	540
Pearl Paint	325
Pearlman, Jennifer	499
Pearson, Brian	421
Pearson, Christopher	442
Pearson, Jim	549
Pearson, Rob	395
Pearson, Stephen	12
Peck, Andrew	404
Peck, Ryon	36
Pecorini, Nicola	442
Pecot, Reyna	493
Pedone & Partners	3
Peebles, Brent	240
Peek, Jenny	531
Peires, Guy	430
Peitzman, Pamela	484
Pelaez, Ana	503
Pelaez, Jose	69
Peler Matthew	404
Pelikan, Jesse C.	472
Pelikan, Rudolph	421
Pellegrinelli, James	502
Pellegrini, Elizabeth	502
Pellegrino, Doug	410, 415
Pellington, Mark	12
Peloquin, Steven	460
Peltzer, Mark	517
Penczner, Marius	12, 28
Pendar-Hughes, Bob	442
Peninsula, The	178
Penn Glass Enterprises	347
Penn, Matthew	12
Pennsylvania	174
Pennsylvania Globe Gaslight Co.	350
Pennsylvania-Philadelphia	174
Pennsylvania-Pittsburgh	174
People Support Transcription & Captioning	103
Peoples, Marilyn	484
Pepe, Anthony	323
Perazzo, Evan	529
Percarpio, Thomas W.	460
Perception	49, 55, 103
Percolator Productions	24
Perdziola, Robert	108, 556
Perea, Aviva	493
Peretz, Jesse	12
Perez, Luis	442
Perez Jr., Raul	383
Performance Lighting Rentals, Inc.	306, 317
Performance Two, Inc.	545
Perkins, John	484
Perkins, Rebecca	484
Perlman, Brent	499, 529
Perlman Creative Group	245
Perlman, Donald S.	537
Perlman, Susan	517
Perno, Jill	529
Perretti, Jim	12
Perretti Productions	18
Perri, Ralph	404, 476
Perri, Rob	404
Perrin, Elizabeth	526
Perry, Sam	537
Perry, Tanaj	484
Perryman III, Dwayne B.	12
Pertalion, P. Claire	504
Peruvian Consulate General	165
Pes	12
PES Payroll	242
PESA Switching Systems	286
Pescasio, Michael	442
Pesce, James	517
Pesce, Janine	517
Petagna, Jamie Lynn	108, 517
Petagna, Ronald J.	421
Petagna Jr., Ronnie	421
Peter Kunz Co., Inc.	327, 367
Peter Pan Bus Lines	155
Peter Rosen Productions, Inc.	39
Peter Weiss Designs	367
Peter-Roberts Antiques, Inc.	345
Peters, Christine	389
Peters, Dennis	430, 460
Peterson, Barry	442
Peterson, Carl	472
Peterson, Deb	404
Peterson, John	52
Peterson, Kenneth	410, 414
Peterson, Storn	404
Peterson, Tora	518
Petersson, Mark T.	431
Petesic, Julie	484
Petraglia, Louis	472
Petraglia Jr., Louis J.	460
Petruccio, Joseph	518
Pettine, Anthony	526
Pettit, Addison	389
Pettit, Suzanne	565
Peyton, Matt	505
Pezatta, Shannon	493
Pfaffenbichler, Sebastian	442
PFS Marketwyse	24
Phase 3 Power	317
Phelan, Kate	431, 460
Phelps, Nigel	395
Phenix, Roger	537
Phil Marco Productions	18
Philadelphia Casting Co., Inc., The	220

Name	Page
Philbin, Michael T.	518
Philbin, William J.	472
Philippine Airlines	153
Phillippe, Tony	529
Phillips, Brandon	540
Phillips, David	431
Phillips, Kevin	442
Phillips, Linda	460
Phillips, Maribeth	90, 104, 499
Phillips, Mary	493
Phillips, Michael	464
Phillips, Todd	12
Phillips-Kunkel, Debra	484
Philny Effects Inc./Fireworks by Grucci Inc.	327
Philo, Tim	442
Philofilm	49
Phipps, Jacqueline	529
Phoneco, Inc.	345
Phothivongsa, Kabkeo	460
Photodisc by Getty Images	99
Photomag Sound & Image	44, 83
PhotoOp Studios	128
Photovault	99
Phox, Lance E.	460
Piana, Dario	12
Piazza, Brian C.	537
Piazza, Christopher	404
Pickering, Amy	565
Pictorvision Inc	256, 301
Picture Cars East, Inc.	360
Picture House	27
Picture Island	49, 88, 290
Picture Ray Studio	128
PicturesNow.com	99
Pienaar, André	442
Pier 59 Studios	124
Pier International Customhouse Brokerage	166
Pierce, Alan	410, 414
Pierce, Edward	389
Pierce, Kevin	395
Pierce-Roberts, Tony	442
Pierre, The	178
Pihlaja, Graydon	518
Pike, Timothy	442
Pilch, Holly Ann	502
Pilcher, Lydia	551
Pile II, Eugene N.	421
Pilgram-Noble, Helen	404
Pilhuj, George	69
Pilipski, Michael	421
Pilong, Tom	69
Pinardo, Jason	499
Pinckley, Denise	551
Pinckney, Michael	529
Pinczehelyi, Balint K.	472
Pineo, Gerard H.	518
Pinette, Jeff	404
Pinezich, Lyn	529
Pink Hippo Production Motorhomes	195
Pinkus, Jane K.	518
Pinnacle Systems, Inc.	286
Pinon, Benjamin	493
Pinson, Martha	526
Pinter, Herbert	395
Pinto, Donato	460
Pipino, Ric	493
Piranha Pictures	18, 24, 88
Piras, Sebastian	507
Pirate New York	44, 83, 220
Pirozzi, John	410
Pisarri, Ozzie	502
Pitkus, Lauri	529
Pitocchi, Susan M.	518
Pitsikoulis, Dionne	484
Pitt, Joshua	537
Pitt, Michael	448
Pitters, Amoy	493
Pitts, R. Morgan C.	518
Pivotal Post	62
Pixel Power, Inc.	286
PixelTools Corporation	286
Pizhadze, Riva	484, 493
Pizzarelli, Vera Anne	518
Pizzarello, Gerarda	108
Pizzini, Denise	395
Plachy, William J.	460
Planet, Larry	404
Plansker, Jeffery	12
Plant, Kerrie	484
Plant, Ronald R.	472
Plant, Sarah	52
Plantscapes, Inc.	344
Platarote Jr., Michael J.	518
Platarote Sr., Michael J.	518
Platt, Aaron	442
Platt, Antony	505
Platt, David	537
Platt, Kane	69
Plavsic, Bata	493
Playback Systems	59, 164, 273, 276, 278
Players Directory	227
Plaza Athénée	178
Plaza Fifty Suites Hotel, The	178
Plaza Hotel, The	178
Plexi-Craft Quality Products Corporation	346, 361
Pliskin, David W.	537
Plofker, Richard	69
Plokhooy, Dwayne	460
Plotkin, Jerry	52
Pluff III, Walter M.	518, 532
Plus 8 Digital	276, 278, 282, 284
Plymate, Rebecca	493
PMC	201
PMK, Inc.	34
PMP Studios	191
PMTV	24, 39
Pocsik, William	421
Podbielski, Robert B.	472
Point of View	24
Pokonski, Robert (Bob)	460
Polak, Alan G.	518
Polak, Raymond C.	518
Polasky, Stuart	524
Polay, Macall	505
Polcsa, Juliet	556
Poleski, Brent A.	472
Polifrone, Vincent	518
Poling, Luke	502
Polis, Matthew	52
Polito, Lin	69
Polizzi, Anthony	108, 518
Pollack, Amanda	69
Pollak, Bob	448
Pollard, James H.	472
Pollard, Thelma	484
Pollitt, Barbara A.	108
Pollock, Justin	551
Polywka, Eva	484
Pomann, Bob	52
Pomann Sound, Inc.	45, 83
Pomponio Jr., John H.	518
Ponte, Gideon	389
Ponti, Antonio	404
Ponzo, Rosemary	556, 565
Poole, Kathleen	69
Pop Films	201
Pope, Leslie A.	518
Popola, Thomas	472
Popolis, Jerry	484
Popovic, Zoran	442
Popp, Greg	12
Porporino, Mario	410, 417
Porro, Joseph	561
Portable Ice Rink Rentals	350
Portadam, Inc.	318
Portfolio	162
Portnoy, Arthur	448
Portugal	176
Portuguese Consulate General	165
Porzio, Louis J.	421
Poses, David	421
Posey, Bernadet	484
Posey-Wilkms, Bernadette	484
Posimato, John	448
Positive Impressions	245
Post Factory	62
Post Logic Studios	88, 290
Post Millennium, Inc.	49
Post Office Editorial	49, 62, 284
Post Office Media	24, 39, 88, 124, 201
Poster, Steven	442
Postman, Brian	36
PostWorks	45, 56, 57, 62, 89, 92, 283, 290, 291
Postworks, The Lab	74
Potashnik, Igor (Gary)	472
Potoskie, Thomas W.	460
Potter, Charles (Chuck)	518
Potter, Frederic	12
Potter, George	460
Potter, Howard	551
Potter, Kenneth E.	460
Potter, Mike	493
Potter-Kirshoff, Andrea	518
Potts, Sharon L.	518
Pouget, Thierry	442
Poulakakis, Tico	442
Pound, Geoffrey D.	472
Pouthier, Paul James	537

Pow! Pix, Inc. 89
Powderkeg, Inc. 55
Power, Evy 493
Power, James 518
Power, Matthew 529
PowerHouse 27. 124
PowerProduction Software 222
Powers, David. 537
Powers, Dusty. 410, 414
Powers, Lynn 529
Powers, Timothy E. 518
Powerstation 76
Powley, Elizabeth 421
Pozner, Gary 52
Poznick, Philip. 472
Prada, Francesca 4
Prange, Joaquin Diego 529
Prate, Kathi. 518
Prate, Kimberly 518
Prate, Michael J. 472
Prate Jr., Robert S. 472
Prate Sr., Robert T. 472
Prate, Thomas 473
Prate Jr., Thomas R. 473
Pratt, Ian. 473
Pratt, Jose Antonio 12
Preisner, Ariana G. 518
Preisner, Michael 518
Preiss, Jeff 12, 28
Prema Productions 201
Premier Coach, Inc. 155
Premier Executive Trailers 198
Premier Party Servers. 232
Premier Tracks 81
Premiere Locations of the Hamptons 186
Premiere Transportation 195
Prendergast, Heather 518
Presence Studios 45
Pressgrove, Craig. 404
Pressure 250
Prestemon, Steve 69
Prestige Limousine Service. 182
Prestige Trees Landscape Nursery, LLC. 344
Presto, David 484
Preston, Howard. 484
Preston, Matthew 502
Prevost, Lauretta. 404
PRG 317
Price, Charles A. 473
Price, Daria. 526
Price, David 502
Price, Douglas G. 473
Price, Ingrid. 565
Price, James. 551
Price II, Lawrence E. 460
Price, Marissa. 502
Price, Mathew 537
Price, Michael J. 460
Price, Pearleta 484
Price, Thomas Clement. 390
Pride Equipment Corporation 303, 310
Prideaux, Charles J. 476
Priestley, Andrew 404
Priestley, Thomas 431
Primalux Video 24, 39, 134, 201, 276, 282
Primas, Ronald A 386
Primavera, Christopher 473
Prime Location 231
Prime To Go 62, 284
PrimeLight Productions, Inc. 24
Primes, Robert 442
Primmer, Michael E. 537
Primrose, Robert. 537
Primus Studio 128
Prince Lumber Co., Inc. 330
Prince, Noah R. 460
Prince, Tom 499
Princeton Airport 154
Princeton Antiques Bookservice 234
Principato, Gregory. 404
Print Box, Inc. 245
Prinzi, Carl 410, 473
Prinzi, Frank 431
Prisco Jr., Michael P. 460
Prism Production Services, Inc. 24, 39, 201
Pritchett Peterson Betsy 526
Prlain, Mary. 395, 518, 532
Pro Image Studios 24, 124, 136
Pro Marine Co. 328
Pro Piano 197, 353
Probst, Christopher. 442
Procopio, Fortunato 431
Producer East Productions 24
Producers Library 99, 293

Producers Masterguide 227
Product 101. 245
Production 920, Inc. 18, 39, 201
Production Advantage, Inc. 305, 330, 340
Production Cargo 151
Production Central 57, 59, 62, 89, 125,
.... 136, 272, 276, 282, 284
Production Resource, The. 222
Production Weekly 227
Productions First Choice Inc. 258, 317
Professional Home Spa Services 234
Professional Sound Services, Inc. 269
Professional-Tapesonline 294
Projectionists (IA Local 306) 548
ProMediaSupplies.com 267, 294
Prompter Ready 272
Prop Art New York 324
Prop Central, Inc. 324, 345, 346, 367, 370
Prop Company - Kaplan &
  Associates, The. 128, 191, 345, 346, 371
Prop Specs. 339
Prop Transport, Inc. 158, 197, 320
Proper Production 201
Proper Production Locations. 186
Props for Today. 110, 345, 346, 371, 374
Props NYC 345, 346, 371, 374
Proscia, Christopher. 473
Proscia, Frank. 473
Proscia Jr., Frank 473
Proscia, Gennaro 421
Proscia, Joseph F. 473, 518
Proscia, Mark 460
Proscia Jr., Michael. 460
Proscia, Michele M. 518
Proscia, Rocco 473
Proscia, Steven M. 473
Prostowich, Peter 461
Protoactive 59
Prouse, Mark D. 108
Provenzano, Robert 518
Provost Displays 110, 114, 324, 330, 361
Provost, Larry 537
Pruger, David Jon 537
Pry, John 410
PS 260 50
PSAV Event Services 276
PSI Industries 57, 59
Public Domain. 18
Public Eye Productions 24, 39
Public, Joe 12
Public Service Truck Renting 158, 320
Publicis 3
pucciManuli. 347
Puchal, Rosanne. 484, 493
Puck Building Ballrooms 250
Puck Building Special Events 191
Puck Studios 128
Puckey, Benjamin 493
Puerto Rico 174
Pugliese, Romano C. 518
Pukowsky, Melvin 473
Pulcini, Robert. 12
Pullen, Crystal Nicole 493
Pullman, Jeff 537
Pulse Music, Inc. 83
Puma, Joan. 526
Pun, Wei K. 413, 416, 443
Puntolillo, Donna. 554
Pupo, Gualter 12
Purcell, Douglas 473
Purcell, Gregory 493
Purcigliotti, Andrea 390
Purdy, Lee. 565
Pureland Pictures, Inc. 18, 24, 201
Purificato, Philip 473
Purified Loft. 128, 191
Purman, Bob. 12
Purnell, Malcolm 404
Purple Cow Post 50
Purvines, Scott 413
Pushinsky, Jake 69
Putnam, Christine 502
Putnam Rolling Ladder 303
Pyburn Films. 18, 33
Pyramid Media 99
Pyzocha, Robert. 390

Q

Q. 493
Q Hardy 493
Q Video Services, Inc. 276, 301
Qantas 153
QTV Prompting Services. 272

Name	Page
Quackenbush, Stacy	561
Quad Cinemas	92
Quaglia, John	484, 494
Qualles, Jacqueline C.	383
Quantel, Inc.	286
Quantum Films Software	222
Quarantiello, Cheryl	504
Quarles, Aaron R.	484
Quarles, Alexander A.	518
Quarles, Sacha	484
Quellette, Dan	395
Questar, Inc.	99
Quick International Courier	151
Quik Trak Messengers	235
Quiles, Angela	503
Quiles, Christopher	473
Quinlan, Brendan	473
Quinlan, Collin P.	461
Quinlan, Gregory	461
Quinlan, James	461
Quinlan, Kate	565
Quinlan, Raymond	473, 504, 529
Quinlan, Ryan Richard	461
Quinlivan, Charles	473
Quinn, Bill	12
Quinn, Christopher	12
Quinn, Declan	431
Quinn Jr., Edwin A.	473
Quinn, Kevin M.	473
Quinn, Patrick	404
Quinn, Thomas	518
Quinones, Santiago	529
Quirk, Joseph	461
Quitoni, R.N., James A.	386
Quiyou, Lyndell	484
QuVIS	286

R

Name	Page
R & R Video	57
R/G A	55, 103
R.B.A., Inc.	166
R.J. Bennett Represents	382, 494
R.W. Commerford & Sons, Inc.	214
Raab, Jane Erica	551
Rabasse, Jean	395
Rabinowitz, Moshe S.	421
Raby, Brian J.	461
Radcliff, Anne Michele	484
Radcliffe, Charles C.	518
Radiant Artists	382, 395, 431, 443
@radical.media	18
Radio and Television Broadcast Engineers (IBEW Local 1212)	548
Radio City Music Hall	191
RadioActive Talent, Inc.	246
Radisson Lexington Hotel	178
Radka, Theresa K.K.	537
Radow, Michael	537
Rae, Mikaela	494
Raffaele, John	518
Ragazzini, Nevio	494
Rager, Donald	505
Ragozzine, Robert	404
Ragusa, Cassandra	485
Ragusa, Gail	526
Raij, Carla	529
Raimbault, Sophie	494
Raimi, Sam	12, 28
Rain Or Shine Event Services	331
Rainbow Video	57
Rainey, David G.	537
Rake, Gary	529
Rakib, Pierre	494
Rakib, Selim	485
Ramirez, Jonathan	473
Ramirez, Richard	421
Ramos, Peter	404, 411
Ramos, Philip A.	503
Rampmeyer, Mark	485
Ramscale Productions Inc.	128
Ramser, David	12
Ramsey, Brent	431
Ramsey, Greg	12
Ramsey, Gregory	431
Ramsey, Matt	69
Ramsey, Scott H.	461
Ramsey, Stephen	443, 494
Ramsey, Steven	461
Ramsey, Steven K.	473
Ramshur, Valerie Marcus	556
Rance, Floyd	404
Randall, Eliza Pelham	90, 104
Random, Ida	395
Randstad	247
Raney, Susan	518
Ranger, Nate	404
Ranieri, Paul	411
Rankin, Harry	12
Rankin, Scott	69
Rankin/Bass Productions	6, 39
Ransaw, Carol Ann	485
Ransom, Matthew	518
Ranson, Matthew	69
Raper, Kevin	390
Raphael, Audrey S.	390
Raphael, David	537
Raposa, Robert	473
Rapp, John	518
Rappaport, Ellen	4, 499, 529
Raschi, Mitje	499
Raschke-Robinson, Claudia	443
Raskin, Fred	69
Raskin, Steve	52
Rathner, Leigh	404
Ratner, Brett	12
Ratteray, Charles	36
Rattinger, Michael J.	518
Raugalis, John	461
Rausenberger, Gary	421
Raw Stock, Inc.	267
Rawlings, Kevin	485
Rawlings Jr., Richard	443
Ray Beauty Supply Co.	349
Ray Benjamin Video	50
Ray, Brenda	537
Ray, Joseph	448
Ray, Joseph J.	461
Ray, Thomas B.	461
Rayburn Music	353
Raycraft, Alysia	561
Raygun	305
Rayle-Bourne, Shannon L.	518
Raymond, Christopher	404
Raymond, Paula	518
Raynor, David	503
Razzano, Tom	504
RBY Productions, Inc.	25
Re: Search	99, 234
Rea, Ralph	473
Rea, Sabatino (Sonny)	473
Read, Edward	461, 464, 496
Ready to Eat	162
Ready to Roll Limousine Service, Inc.	182
Real Productions, Inc.	18, 25
Real Software Assistance	222
Really Fake Digital	110, 343
Reap, Thomas K.	473
Reardon, Dave	518
Rebelo, Jeffrey	485
Recar, Chuck	565
Recht, Raymond C.	390
Red Car	50
Red Thread Productions	25, 50
Reddy, Daniel	423, 461
Reddy, Raymond	421
Rede, Michele	561
Rede, Roy	395
RedHawk Communications	25
Redlin, Rosemary	494
Redlinski, Piotr	505
Reed, Adam	12
Reed, Jeremy	395
Reed, Michael	461
Reed, Peyton	12
Reed III, Roland E.	421
Reel Directory, The	227
Reel EFX, Inc.	265
Reel Life Film LLC	50
Reel Orange	99, 293
Reel People Company LLC, The	220, 229
Reels On Wheels Unlimited	152, 235
ReelsOnDemand.com	382
Rees, Carrie	404
Rees, Kim	395
Rees, Tom	186
Reese, Chauency	240
Reeve, Thomas H.	518
Reeser, Renee	36
Reeves, Schavaria	537
Refinery New York	50
Refuge	18
Regal Limousine Service	182
Regan, Kai	507
Regan, Patricia	485
Regency, The	180
reGeneration Furniture, Inc.	345, 346
Regen, Lili Abir	524

Company/Crew Index

Name	Page
Regina, Michelle	529
Regnier, Peter John	518, 524
Regnier Jr., Richard M.	518
Regnier Sr., Richard M.	518
Rehlaender, Jeffrey H.	421
Reibman, Larry	443
Reichenbach, Val	485
Reichert, Jack	411, 417
Reichman, Michael	529
Reid, James	473
Reid, Malcolm H.	421
Reider, Michael J.	518
Reidy, Charles E.	473
Reidy, Joseph	448
Reidy, Kevin C.	473
Reiff, Manfred	431
Reiker, Tami	443
Reiland, Gosta	443
Reilly, Fr. Michael P.	518
Reilly, Gail-Marie	518
Reilly, Kathleen	485
Reilly, Malicky D.	518
Reilly, Thomas A.	448, 551
Reilly-Davila, Elizabeth	485
Reilly-Lehane, Susan	485
Reisch, Michele	556
Reiser, Richard	473
Reisinger, Susan	540
Reiss, Jacqueline	494
Rejectbarn, LLC	6, 55
Relay Productions, Inc.	25
Remains	350
Rembrandt Films	6
Renaissance New York Hotel Times Square	180
Renaud, Chuck	395
Renaudin, Karen	499
Renaudin, Mark	411, 414, 417
Renaud Jr., John (Chuck)	390
Renberg, Guillaume	411
Renck, Johan	28
Renfroe, Bryant	485, 494
Reniers, Peter	431
Rennert, Christopher J.	537
Rennert Translation Group	220, 248
Rennie, David	69
Rent-A-Wreck	156
Rep Studio	45, 83
Repeta, Michael	404
Repka, Kyle	404
Repplier, Peter	448
Reshovsky, Marc	443
Resnick, Demian	529
Restivo, Giuseppe	404
Restuccia, Salvatore	461
Reticker, Meg	70
Retreat at Art Omni, The	191
Reuss, David	36
Reuter, Karen	485
Reuter, Paul	407
Reuters Television International	99, 136
Revellese-Mirante, Lisa	485
Rexer, William	431
Reyes, Betsy	485
Reynaud, Vincent	395
Reynolds, Chris	404
Reynolds, Michael	395
Reynolds, Norman	395
Reynolds, William F.	518, 532
Rey, Stella	524
Reznik, Andy	395
RGH Lighting LLC	307, 317
RGT Music Productions	83
Rhee, Judy	390
RHI Entertainment	39
Rhinofx	6, 55, 84
Rhode Island	174
Rhodes, Andy	395
Rhodes Collar/All About Dogs	214
RI, Inc./Seating Solutions	126
Rial, Kimberly	473
Ribalow, Tania	485
Ricard, John	507
Rice, Linda C.	485
Rich, Diane	110
Rich, Gary	537
Richard, Bridgland	395
Richard Kroll Research	234
Richards, Jim	461
Richards, Tony	12
Richardson, Griffin	537
Richardson, Kelly	473
Richardson, Robert	443
Richardson, Ross	443
Richardson, Tim	12
Richman, Bob	443
Richman, Geoff	70
Richman, Robert	431
Richmond, Anthony B.	443
Richmond, Tom	443
Richter, Andrea	494
Richter-Friis, Jan	443
Richter Productions, Inc.	39
Richter, Scott	70
Rick Bruck's Motorworks, Inc.	258
Rick Ulfik Productions	45, 83
Ricke, Ward	448
Ricker, Mark	390
Rider, James	411
Rieck, Lance	404
Riedel, Gay	461
Riedel, Richard	537
Riegel, Tatiana S.	70
Riemer, Ken	464
Rieser, Daniel E.	473
Riesett, Scott M.	52
Rietta, Terry	12
Rieveschl, Peter	443
Rifkin, Josh	70
Rigby, Danielle	448
Riggi, Gina	485
Riggin Design, Inc.	301
Riggins, Rose	540
Riggle, Rosalee	485
Riggs, Nancy	499
Riggs, Sarah	518
Right Eye, The	382, 395, 431, 443, 561
Riha, Neil	537
Riley, Dawn Murphy	503
Riley IV, James A.	473
Riley, Kevin	448, 499
Riley, William B.	108
Rimmel, Kurt	411, 415, 473
Rinato, Frank	404
Ringbom, Jon	108
Rinsch, Carl Erik	12, 28
Rinzler, Lisa	431
Rios, Carlos	411
Ripple, Helen	518
Risch, Timothy	404, 448
Ritacco-Sirianni, Francine	565
Ritter, Joe	448
Ritter, Kevin	565
Ritz Camera	262
Ritzinger, Heimo P.	443
Rivelli, Nicole	505
River West Scenic	114
Rivera, Al	496
Rivera Burgos Javier	505
Rivera, Lee	485
Rivera, Sonia	485
Rivers, Joseph	461
Rivers, Rob	485
Riviere, R.N., EMT Ruth V.	386
Rivo, Rebecca	551
Rizzo, Bob	221
Rizzo, Rossana	404
Rizzo, Thomas	461
RJP Creations, Inc.	343, 354
Roach Jr., George M.	476
Roach, Kevin Joseph	390, 421
Roach, Neil	443
Road Runner Camera Cars, Inc.	258
Roake, Kathryn	36, 390
Roarke, Timm	443
Robbins, Ari	416
Robbins, Carrie	390, 561
Robbins, Eric	431
Robbins Locations, Inc.	186
Robbins Media	18
Roberson, Jim	443
Roberson, Ken	221
Roberts, Kerry	240
Roberts, Leigh	52
Roberts, Roosevelt	476
Roberts, Wendy	526
Robertson, Blythe	503
Robertson, Eric J.	104
Robertson, Kat	485
Robertson, Nick	13
Robertson, Stuart	70
Robertson Taylor (North America) Inc.	230
Robespierre, Jennifer	556
Robin, Dana	551
Robinette, Jeannia	494
Robins, Larry	13
Robins, Lawrence	431
Robinson, Adam	70
Robinson, Allan S.	461

Company/Crew Index

Name	Page
Robinson, Anthony	537
Robinson, Chris	13, 70
Robinson, David	556
Robinson, Eric	404
Robinson Jr., Edward (Ted)	473
Robinson, Paul	421
Robinson, Sajata	485, 494
Robinson, Sean	421
Robinson, Steven	411, 554
Robison, Barry	395
Robotham Creative, Inc.	3
Robotham, Tom	431
Robson-Foster, Lesley	104, 431
Roccaforte, Gustave	554
Roche, David	539
Roche, John	518
Roche, Ruth	494
Rochester Two-Way Communications, Inc.	164
Rock Bottom Rentals	164
Rock-It Air Charter, Inc.	150
Rock-It Cargo	152
Rockefeller Center	191
Rocketclips, Inc.	99
Rockett, Eliot	443
Rocking Horse Cafe	162
Rocky Mountain Motion Pictures	99
Rod McBrien Productions	83
Rodgers, Aggie	561
Rodgers, Al	404
Rodgers, Helen E.	556, 565
Rodia, P. Michael (Rodi)	473
Rodney Gordon, Inc.	335
Rodriguez, Alex	70
Rodriguez, Carmen	240
Rodriguez, Deidre	561
Rodriguez, Edward	404
Rodriguez, J. Daniel	518
Rodriguez, Jesse	561
Rodriguez-Quijano, Marcos	404
Rodriguez, Ryan A.	461
Rodriguez, Ulises	503
Rodriquez, Ramon A.	240
Roe, Bill	443
Roelfs, Jan	395
Roelofs, Robert	537
Roer, Harold	518
Roer, Jason	518
Roer, Louis D.	518
Roer, Stewart B.	518
Roger Smith, The	180
Rogers, Bettie	485
Rogers, Julie	70
Rogers, Marc	464
Rogers, Molly	556
Rogers, Steve	448
Rogers, Steven J.	537
Rogers, Susan Zeeman	390
Rogers, Wendi S.	485
Rogovin, Laisann	565
Rogue Post NYC	89, 290
Rohan, Margo	561
Rohde, Evan	395
Rohn, Matthew D.	461
Rohn, Sam	186, 507
Roland, Erich	431
Roland, J. Daniel	52
Roland Music USA	83
Rollercoaster Studios, Inc.	114, 124
Rollins, Jeffrey S.	518
Rollins, Leslie E.	518
Rolston, Matthew	13
Rom, Sonja	443
Roman, Barbara	485
Roman, Serge	443
Roman, Tiel	565
Romanello, Charles J.	421
Romanello, William P.	537
Romano, Debbie A.	518
Romano, Joseph P.	537
Romano, Pete	443
Romano, Steve	404
Romeo, John	411
Romeo Scenery Studio	114
Romer, John	404
Romero, Michael	551
Romero, Pedro	395
Ronan, Brian	537
Ronn, Gary	461
Ronsvalle, Debra	526
Rooftop Edit	18, 25, 45, 50, 201
Rooftop Garden @ 620 Fifth Ave.	191
Rooftop Productions	45, 83
Rooney, Stephen	473
Rosa, Sarah E.	108
Rosado, Fernando	404
Rosario, Francisco	461
Rosati, Philip	537
Rosco Backdrops	110
Roscor	286
Rose Brand	110, 305, 330, 337, 340
Rose, Floyd T.	537
Rose, F. Michael	431
Rose, James	421
Rose, Jon	411, 417
Rose, Jonathan	390, 518
Rose, Richard C.	476
Rose, Stephen	494
Rose, Steven	448, 473
Rosen & Chadick Textiles, Inc.	340
Rosen, Chris	461
Rosen Group, The	34
Rosen, Paul	450, 529
Rosenberg, Gabrielle	395, 532
Rosenberg, Jamie	431
Rosenberg, Philip	395
Rosenbloom, Jon W.	473
Rosenblum, Daniel	537
Rosenblum, Steven	70
Rosenfeld, Hilary	556
Rosenstock, Jesse A.	519
Rosenstock, Jordan	519
Rosenstock, Scott	519
Rosenthal, Jesse D.	390
Rosenzweig, Craig	404
Rosenzweig, Steven Eric	108
Rosher, Chuck	443
Rosher, Jenna	13
Rosinsky, Gregg A.	464
Rosner, Louise	499
Ross, Amanda	485
Ross, Anne	396
Ross Eccles Cassandra	503
Ross, Ethan	531
Ross, Glenna	526
Ross, Mark	13
Ross, Thomas	529
Ross, Timothy	404
Ross, Vernon	565
Rossell, Briar	519
Rossetti, Fabrizio	70
Rossi, Antonio	404
Rossi, David	473
Rossig, Andrew	421
Rossiter, Timothy	519
Roszak, Mara	494
Roth, Amy	565
Roth, Katherine B.	556
Roth, Sonja	532
Rothenberg, Lewis	425
Rothstein, Claire	494
Rotondo, Peter	539
Rotzler, Amanda	404
Rouger, Pierre	443
Roulenko, Elena	485
Rouse, Christopher	70
Rousseau, Brenda	565
Rousselot, Philippe	443
Routt, Robert	529
Roveto Jr., Rosario	540
Rovira, Danny	421
Rovira, Paul T.	421
Rovira, Pierre	421
Rowe, Andrew	431
Rowe, Charles Sloan	526
Rowe, Stacy Lynne	526
Rowles, Michael	13
Roy, Mark A.	537
Royal Buses	195
Royal Flush Productions	83
Royal Production Services	337, 343, 349
Royal Way Limousine, Inc.	182
Royalton Hotel	180
Roybal, Jared	404
RP Rentals & Sales	303
rrrentals	335
RSA Films, Inc.	19
RTR Packaging	245
Ruark, Ann	499
Rubenstein, Sarah	240
Rubia, Jorge	13
Rubin, Edward L.	396
Rubin, Emily	540
Rubin, Shoshana	561
Rubino, Beth A.	519
Rubinstein, Mauricio	431
Rubio, Isabel	556, 562
Ruble, David	565
Rudavsky, Ondrej	13

Ruddy, Neil . . . 519
Rudelson, Aaron . . . 537
Rudis, Robert . . . 431
Rudolf, Gene . . . 396
Rudolph, David . . . 461
Rudolph, Michael R. . . . 461
Ruffler, Lisa . . . 499
Rufino, Giovanni . . . 505
Rufo, Celeste . . . 411
Ruhe, Johanna L. . . . 519
Ruhe, Martin . . . 443
Ruhlmann, Danny . . . 443
Ruidant, John . . . 494
Ruiz, Manel . . . 431
Ruiz Ziegler Monica . . . 565
Ruiz-Anchia, Juan . . . 443
Rumann, Rachel M. . . . 562
Rumes, Ilse (Boogie) . . . 461
Runnin' Shot, Inc. . . . 258
Runway, Inc. . . . 62, 284
Ruopp, Kathryn E. . . . 499, 504, 529
Ruotolo, Edward F. . . . 537
Ruschak, James . . . 240
Ruscio, Michael . . . 70
Rusnak, Paul . . . 537
Russ, Ruben F. . . . 443
Russek, Jonathan . . . 503
Russell, David . . . 505
Russell, Donald . . . 411
Russell, Mark . . . 104
Russell, Monica . . . 566
Russell, Nathaniel M. (Nat) . . . 473
Russell, Peter A. . . . 461
Russell Todd Agency . . . 382, 411, 413, 416
Russo, Barry . . . 425, 554
Russo Brothers, The . . . 13
Russo, James . . . 519
Russo, John . . . 52
Russo/Grantham Productions, Inc. . . . 83
Rustic Caterers . . . 162
Ruth, Patrick . . . 431
Rutkowski, Kelly . . . 461
Rutkowski, Richard . . . 431
Rutledge, Lisa Beth . . . 519
Rutterford, Alex . . . 13
Ruvolo, Bill . . . 13
Ryan, Alexa . . . 562
Ryan, Christopher J. . . . 461
Ryan, Darren . . . 554
Ryan, Margaret . . . 108
Ryan, Sean . . . 461
Ryan, Sharon . . . 562
Ryan Jr., Thomas T. . . . 473
Ryang, Robert . . . 70
Ryder, Sean F. . . . 519
Ryle, Mark . . . 404
Rymon, Holly . . . 503, 529
Ryzuk, Regan . . . 52

S

S.B.I. . . . 114
S.J. Golden Associates, Inc. . . . 34
S.V.E. Sales, Inc. . . . 303, 318
Saad, Nicholas . . . 473
Saad, Philip F. . . . 473
Saatchi & Saatchi Advertising . . . 3
Sabat, James J. . . . 537
Sabat Jr., James . . . 537
Sabat, Louis C. . . . 473
Sabat, Peter . . . 503
Sabat, Steven . . . 473
Saccaro, Greg . . . 411
Saccavino, Sue . . . 494
Sacchetti, Robert A. . . . 537
Saccio, Michael A. . . . 519
Saccio, Michael P. . . . 519
Saccio Jr., Philip B. . . . 519
Saccio, Philip J. . . . 519
Saccio, Roseann . . . 519
Sacco, Vittorio . . . 13
Sachs, Andrea L. . . . 461
Sadek, James . . . 421
Sadler, Lewis . . . 461
Sadler, Nic . . . 443
Saeta, Steven . . . 499
Saetta, Janet . . . 461
Safety First Divers . . . 236, 246, 549
Saffir, John . . . 529
Safhay, Amy J. . . . 344, 519
Safway Steel Products . . . 303
Saga Productions . . . 59
Sagarese, Rocco . . . 519
Sage, Jefferson . . . 396
Saia, Michael . . . 70
Saint James Studios . . . 36
Saint Laurie Merchant Tailors . . . 335, 377
Sakharov, Alik . . . 431
Saks Fifth Ave. . . . 376
Sala . . . 250
Salamanca, Robert . . . 411
Salamone, Lawrence . . . 529
Salas, Gilbert . . . 443
Salaun, Jean-Marie . . . 52
Salchow, Boris . . . 52
Saleem, Shazia . . . 485
Salerno, Anita . . . 562
Salerno, Anthony J. . . . 411
Sales, Gary . . . 448
Sales, Liz . . . 404
Salisbury Jr., David A. (Austin) . . . 554
Salk, Daniel R. . . . 554
Salle, Silvie . . . 485
Salley, Neil . . . 13
Salo, Randy M. . . . 473
Salt and Pepper Media . . . 25
Saltzman, Jared . . . 461
Saluzzi, James . . . 473
Salvatore, Kyle . . . 519
Salzburg, Diana . . . 519
Sam Flax Art and Design . . . 325
Samitz, Raymond M. . . . 421
Samperisi, Alba . . . 485, 494
Sample Clearance Limited . . . 234
Sampogna, Anne . . . 485
Sampson, Jonathan . . . 540
Samson, Michael . . . 448
Samuel, David . . . 461
Samuel, Frank . . . 13
Samul, Ryan . . . 431
Sanabria, Daniel . . . 404, 413
Sanchez, Adam J. . . . 537
Sanchez, Andres E. . . . 443
Sanchez, Emanuel L. . . . 421
Sanchez, Livio . . . 70
Sanchez, Michael F. . . . 537
Sanchez, Wilfredo . . . 485
Sandell, William . . . 396
Sanders, Chris . . . 566
Sanders, Gabriel S. . . . 537
Sanders, Ronald . . . 70
Sanders, Tom . . . 396
Sanderson, Austin K. . . . 556
Sandgren, Linus . . . 443
Sandgren, Mikael . . . 52
Sandpiper Editorial Services . . . 50
Sandra Cameron Dance Center . . . 221
Sandroni, Marc . . . 36
Sands, Robert . . . 404
Sandstrom, Joakim . . . 13
Sandtroen, Morten . . . 13
Sandu, Natalia . . . 494
Sandy, Kwmae Rubin . . . 461
Sanftner, Patricia . . . 566
Sanginiti, Leon . . . 405
Sani Lav . . . 198
Sanitate, Alessandra . . . 485
Sansone, Barbara . . . 494
Santa Barbara Location Services/
aka Location Production Coordination . . . 186
Santana, David . . . 485
Santana, Maria C. . . . 519
Santana, Paul . . . 13
Santarsiero, Drew . . . 529
Santiago, Elisa . . . 566
Santiago, Inc. . . . 19
Santiago, Roxana . . . 405
Santo, Matthew . . . 431
Santoleri, Ray . . . 485
Santora, Bud . . . 562
Santoro, Carmen S. . . . 421
Santoro, Nicoletta . . . 562
Santoro, Peter . . . 443
Santos, Anthony . . . 461
Santos, Gerard . . . 396
Santucci, Jennifer . . . 519
Sapolin, Gary . . . 507
Saraceno, Antonio . . . 13
Sarama, Michelle . . . 240
Sarao, Joseph . . . 473
Sarch, Oren . . . 70
Sargent, Christopher . . . 443
Sargo, Joseph F. . . . 519
Sariano, Daniel . . . 405
Sarjeant, Dean . . . 537
Sarluco, Michael . . . 461
Sarmiento, Ricardo . . . 411, 443
Sarnataro, Patricia . . . 556

Name	Page
Sarno, Andrew	503
Sarokin, William	537
Sarzotti, James	485, 494
SAS Scandinavian Airlines	153
Sasso, Scott William	519
Sasway, Mark	36
Saternow, Tim	390
Satin, Dave	425
Satriano, Lisa	450
Sauer, Matthew	529
Saulsbery, Jaqueline	494
Saulter, Cassandra	485
Saulter-Yacuk, Leslie	108
Saunders, Susan	240
Sava, Gerard	411, 415
Savel, Peter L.	519
Savides, Harris	431
Savini, Anthony	411
Saviola, Jesse	473
Savoy, Roy	519
Sawyer, Mary Jane	452
Sawyer, Nick	443
Saxe, Andrew	529
Sayeed, Malik	431
Sayeed, Malik Hassan	13, 28
Saye, John	461
SBP Industries	317
Scaglione, I. Nate	461
Scalettar, Peter	411
Scali, Giorgio	443
Scali, Maria	485
Scalia, Pietro	70
Scalice, Elizabeth	485
Scalice, Lizz	494
Scalzi, John D.	519
Scalzo Jr., Anthony	519
Scanlon, Bryan R.	519
Scanlon, Paul E.	519
Scanlon, Stephen E.	519
Scantlebury, Glen	70
Scarafile, Christopher	473
Scardino Jr., John	519
Scardino, Michael	537
Scarfi, Christopher E.	461
Scenic Art Studios, Inc.	110, 114
Scenic Corporation of N.Y.	114
Scerbak, Thomas J.	537
Schabel, John C.	519
Schachter, Felice	503
Schaffer, Paula	485
SchafferRogers	26
Schalk, James M.	461
Schanker, David	519
Scharer, Kathi	240
Scharf, William	70
Scharff Weisberg, Inc.	164
Scharff Weisberg Media Resource Center	25, 59
Schatz, Howard	13
Schebece, Beth	529
Scheck, William M.	519
Scheer Advertising Agency	3
Scheflow, Tibi	186, 529
Schegulla, Eva	566
Schelle, Maximillian	473
Schenck, Christopher	405, 448
Schenk, Sabine	499
Schepisi, Nick	529
Scherr, Alison	524
Schicchi, Vincent	485
Schiller, Tom	13
Schinman, Nicole	566
Schiraldi, Paul	505
Schiumo, Frank D.	473
Schleinig, Robert H.	519
Schlesinger, David	519
Schlesinger, Richard	551
Schliesser, Tobias	443
Schlitten, Elizabeth	519
Schloss, Glenn	52
Schluter Ford, Michelle	519
Schmale, Jeff	411
Schmetterling, Andrew	538
Schmidli Backdrops	110
Schmidt, Austin	443
Schmidt, Courtney	519
Schmidt, John M.	519
Schmidt, Mark	411, 485
Schmidt, Matthew	519
Schmidt, Michael J.	538
Schmidt-O'Brien, Diana	551
Schmitt, Greg	443
Schmitt, Robert W.	473
Schnall, Peter	431
Schneiberg, William V.	538
Schneider, Aaron	443
Schneider, Jeremy	411, 415
Schneider, Lauren	540
Schneider, Matthew	503
Schneider, Patrick F.	473
Schneider, Peter W.	538
Schneid, Hervé	70
Schnell, Curtis	396
Schniebolk, Beth M.	240
Schnitzer, Peggy	562
Schoenbachler, Megan	443
Schoenewald, Jennifer	461
Schofield Films	19
Schofield, John D.	499
Schofield, Stan	13
Scholastic Entertainment	6, 40
Scholl, Oliver	396
Schoneveld, Anneke	505
Schrader, Ursula Kiki	566
Schrager, Abe	443
Schreck, Donald	461
Schreiber, Klaus C.	473
Schreiner, Gary	52
Schroeder, Jeremy W.	473
Schroer, Susan	540
Schrom, Michael	431
Schrowang, Deirdre Marie	240
Schuka, Denise L.	240
Schulman, Robert	461
Schultz, Christine	566
Schumacher, Barret D.	519
Schumacher, David	539
Schurr, Karl	461
Schuster, Glenn	186
Schut, Mattias	13
Schutt, Debra	519
Schwab, Rudi	13
Schwartz, Alan	461
Schwartz, Andrew	505
Schwartz, Ari David	519
Schwartz, Ben	425
Schwartz, David	411, 414, 415, 417
Schwartz, Jeff	431
Schwartz, Jerry	532
Schwartz, John	405, 461
Schwartz, Jonathan	566
Schwartz, Marty Eli	450
Schwartz Public Relations Associates	34
Schwartz, Randy	405
Schwartzbard, Mark	405
Schwartzman, John	443
Schwarze Jr., Robert	519
Schwarz, Joshua	70
Schwarz, Kurt	473
Schweitzer, Jenny	551
Schwentner, Mark	461
Schwinn, Tom	390
Scialla, Carlo	443
Scianna, Cosimo	431
Science Faction Corp.	327
Scinto, Maryann	566
Sciretta, Joseph W.	461
Sciretta, Robert J.	461
Scoppa Jr., Edward P.	519
Scoppa Jr., Justin	519
Scoppa, Lisa	519
Scoppa, Nicole	519
Scorsese, Catherine	519
Scotland-Edinburgh	176
Scotland-Glasgow	176
Scotland-Highlands & Islands	176
Scott, Charles J.	519
Scott, Charlotte	485
Scott, Deborah	562
Scott, Jake	13, 28
Scott, Jordan	13, 28
Scott, Luke	13, 28
Scott, Michael H.	538
Scott Powers Studios, Inc.	220, 229
Scott, Ridley	13, 28
Scott, Stephen	396
Scott, Tom	26
Scott, Tony	13, 29
Scott-Gamiello, Anthony	474
Scotto, Stephen	461
Scout Source, The	186
ScreamDVD	59
Screaming Mimi's	339, 378
Screen Actors Guild (SAG)	548
Screen Gems, Ltd./Huge Productions	19
Screen International	227
ScreenLight & Grip	317
ScreenMusic International	81

Script Supervisors/Continuity &
  Allied Production Specialists Guild (IA Local 871) 548
Script Supervisors, Continuity Coordinators &
  Production Office Coordinators (Local 161) 548
Scuba/Look 83
Scudiero, Joe 13
Sculpturesque 367
Scupp, Robert J. 519
Scutakes, E. James 474
Sdanowich, Stephanie 540
Seabury Distributors 330
Seakwood, John 507
Seale, John 444
Seaman, Judy 70
Seamens Moving and Storage 197
Search, Steve 405
Sebesky, Don 52
See Factor Industry 126, 201, 269, 307, 317
See Management 382, 494, 562
See, Robert W. 474
Seehase, Chris 405
Seeley, Gary W. 474
Seeman, Lowell 234
Seeman, Phyllis 234
Seese, John S. 421
Segal, David 390
Segal, Ellen 449
Segal, Erica 499
Segschneider, Jaime 405
Sehapovic, Alija 519
Seibert, Richard 411
Seidman, Todd 390
Seig, Sam 70
Seiler, Jason M. 461
Seivard, Christopher 431
Selbert, Dara 405
Selby 13
Selden, George 461
Selective Casting By Carol Nadell 220
Selemon, Mark 519
Selesnick, Peter 444
Seliger, Mark 13, 29
Selkirk, Matthew 405
Sell, William 503
Sellers, Timothy 538
Seltzer, Gil 444
Selvadurai, David 36
Semanoff, Ben 411, 415, 444
Sember, John 538
Semmelman, Jim 540
Sena, Theo 519
Sencore 286
Seney, Korey 562
Seng, Ken 444
Senter III, John B. 461
Senties, Daniel 36
Senza Pictures 201
September Productions 19
Serafine Studios 81
Seraphic Studio, LLC 59
Seresin, Ben 444
Seresin, Michael 444
Seret Studios 186
Serge Audio 45
Serino Coyne, Inc. 3
Serio, Jennifer 485
Serio, Jorge 494
Serra, Eduardo 444
Serra, Stephen A. 519
Serraiocco, Steve 52
Serratore, Kim 485
Serrell, Bella/Ranch Dressing 396
Sesame Workshop 40
Sesler & Company 382, 431, 444
Sessoms, Maurice Lincoln 529
Set Decorators Society of America 548
Set Design Services 114
Set Shop 110, 114, 305
Sevey, Joseph 529
Sevier, Vivian 494
Sewell, Jamie 444
Sewrey, Laura 566
Seymour, Sadia 562
Seymour, Sharon 396
Shadforth, Dawn 13, 29
Shah, Byron 444
Shah, Kariemah 240
Shah, Prashant 499
Shahidi, Afshin 444
Shahi, Satish K. 461
Shainberg, Steven 13
Shamrock Communications 19
Shane, Sidney 556
Shannon, Douglas W. 461
Shannon, Laura Jean 562
Shapiro, Andrew 519
Shapiro, Kevin 494
Shapiro, Neil 444
Shapiro, Stephen 421, 524
Shapiro, Steve 52
Sharma, Vivek 70
Sharon, Shalom 494
Sharp, Colleen 70
Sharp Electronics Corporation 286
Sharpe, Wayne 52
Sharples, David 411, 415, 417
Shattered Glass 347
Shatz, Sarah 505
Shaughnessy, Moira 556
Shaw, Bob 396
Shaw, Gary 444
Shaw, Janet G. 519
Shaw, Jonathan 70
Shaw, Michael 390
Shea, Colleen 70
Shea, James S. 461
Shea, John R. 474
Shearer, Phil 396
Shearman, James 411
Sheehan, Linda 405
Sheehy, Colin 405
Shein, Elizabeth 556
Shelby, Patrick J. 474
Sheldon, Darrell 411, 417
Sheldon Prosnit Agency 382, 396, 431, 444
Shelley, Scott 413, 444
Shellito, Michael D. 519
Shelter Logic 331
Shelton, Blackford 405
Shelton, Elizabeth 556, 562
Shelton, Jas 444
Shelton, Yvette 494
Shenise, Bob 444
Shepard, Bobby 431
Shepherd, Lance A. 462
Shereese 562
Sherer, Keith 431
Sherer, Werner 485, 494
Sheridan, Dylan 519
Sheridan, James 449
Sheridan, Jim 13
Sheridan, Phillip R. 499
Sheridan, Sean 462
Sheridan, Tristan G. 411, 414, 417, 462
Sheriff-Avery, Ashunta 485
Sherman, Andrew 52
Sherman, James P. 524, 532
Sherman, Richard 396
Sherman, Roger 444, 499
Sherratt, Brian 485
Sherron, Richard 474
Sherry-Netherland 180
Sherry Rousso Associates, Inc. .. 382, 405, 431, 444
Sherwood, Matthew 519
Sherwood, Virginia 505
Shevett, Lee 474
Shevlin, Peter (Chevy) 519
Shibata, Ken 462
Shields, Laurita 556
Shiers, Linda 540
Shiffman, Nina 450, 499, 529
Shimrock, John 108
Shinn, Robert 425
Shinn, Tom 462
Shir, Howard 13
Shirt Store, Inc., The 335
Shoemaker, Jonathan 551
Shohan, Naomi 396
Sholes, Erwin 519
Shom, TK 450
Shonts, Christian 405
SHOOT Directory for Commercial Production &
  Post Production 227
Shoot First Entertainment 19
Shoot Magazine 227
Shoot New York, Inc. 201
Shooters Post & Transfer 89, 290
Shooting Star Coaches, Inc. 195
Shooting Star International 99
Shooting Stars Catering 162
Shooting Stars Int'l. 19
Shop Rite Institutional Supply, Inc. 351
Shop Studios 128, 250
Shoreham, The 180
Shore, Peggie 526
Shore, Steven 529
Short, Thomas C. 538
ShortTermProductions.Com 230

Company/Crew Index

Shotmaker Camera Cars @ Silvertrucks Lighting 258
Show Business Weekly Newspaper 227
ShowBiz Enterprises, Inc. 337
Showman Fabricators, Inc. 110, 114, 126, 337, 374
Shreve, Leslie 485, 494
Shrewsbury, Laura 566
Shrinivasan, Nithya 390
Shriver, Chris J. 390
Shropshire, Terilyn 70
Shulkind, Andrew 444
Shulman, Daniel 431
Shulman, Robert 474
Shuman, Mark 450
Shusha, Erica 411, 415
Sibert, Jonathan P. 474
Sibley, Michael 186
Sica, Joyce 485, 494
Sicangco, Eduardo 108, 556
Sicoransa, John 36
Sicurella, Kristy Prate 519
Sidel, Marc 499, 504
Sidney, Deana 396
Siebert, Andre 13
Siedlecki, Mike 70
Siega, Marcos 13
Siegel Bros. Supply Co., Inc. 303, 330
Siegel, Jonathan 449
Siegel, Rick 432
Siegel, Robert M. 462
Siegel, Ruth Ann 519
Siegel, Stephanie 566
Sierra Video Systems 286
Sigel, Maya 396
Sigel, Newton Thomas 444
Sigler, Jeffrey A. 474
Sigler, Kenneth 520
Sign Expo 343, 354
Signature Sound, Inc. 81, 234
Signorelli, James. 432
Sikelia Productions 27
Sikes, Diana 485
Silano, A. Christopher 405
Silber, Chic 524
Silber, David 421
Silberman Productions 26, 70, 382
Silecchia, Santo 474
Silicones, Inc. 361
Silk Blossom 344
Silk Gardens & Trees 344
Silkensen, Steve 70
Silva, Jorge 538
Silva, Michael 494
Silver, Gary 538
Silver, Jay 411, 417
Silver, Jeffrey 499
Silver, Pierson 405
Silver Screen Security, Ltd. 202
Silver Screen Studios 124
Silver Sound, Inc. 45
Silver-Taracido, Juli 405
Silvercup Studios 124, 136
Silvercup Studios East 124, 136
Silverman, Cara 70
Silverman, Carol A. 520
Silverman, Jeffrey 432
Silverman, Ross 396
Silverman, Steven J. 474
Silverman Stock Footage 99, 293
SilverScreen Marine 236, 246
Silverstein, Alan J. 462
Silverstein, Harlan L. 520
Silverstein, Jamie 411, 415, 444, 462
Silvertrucks Lighting 301, 307, 317
Simancas, Hector 494
Simba Productions, Inc. 25
Sime, Michael 411, 554
Simmonds, Michael. 432
Simmons, John 444
Simmons, Omar 566
Simmons Jr., Paul 566
Simms, Missy 541
Simon, Mark 520
Simon, Mili B. 494
Simon, Peter 405
Simone, Debra 486
Simonovich, Franses 503
Simons, Patricia (Avery) 520
Simpson, Craig A. 474
Simpson, Geoffrey 444
Simpson, Jerry 13, 432
Simpson, Patrick 444
Sims, Larry 494
Simunek, Charles R. 520
Simunek, William 520

Sinclair, Sharon 486
Sindeband, Markham 474
Singapore Airlines 153
Singer, Elizabeth 405
Singer, Holle 70
Singleton, Roseann 494
Singularity communications 89, 290
Singularity Corporation, The 50
Sinkler, Scott 444, 499
Sinoway, Jessica 556
Sipkin, Chad 70
Sirico, Richard A. 421
Sirota, Peggy 13
Sirugo, Bella 486
Sissel, Sandi 444
Sisti, Enzo 499
Sisul, Beatrice 70
Site4view Locations, LLC 186
Sitja, Nuria 486
Siwinski, Joseph 520
Siwinski, Todd 520
SixDay Productions, LLC 30
Size, Dennis M. 496
Skeete, Petula 486
Skelly, George 421
Skervin, Ben 494
Skiba, Marianne 486
Skidmore, John Stephen 503
Skinner, David 396
Skouras Agency, The 382, 396, 405, 411, 432, 444
Skutch, Christopher 474
Skutch, David 462
Skversky, Mark 520
Slade, David 29
SLAM! Media Group 19, 25, 40
Slate, Inc. 19, 25, 33
Slater, Amanda 449
Slater, Jane 526
Slater, Lavette 494
Slater, Linda 405
Slattery, Sharon 486
Slavin, Neal 13
Slevin, Deirdre 70
Slife, Pete 70
Slifkin, M. Eric 474
Sliwiak, Dina 486, 494
Sloan, Christopher 538
Sloan, Nina 449, 499
Sloan, Susan 383
Slosek, Kimberly 520
Sloss Law Office, P.C. 228
Slote, Ina 524, 532
Slotnick, Sara Jane 562
Slovis, Michael 432
Smart, Conrad 70
Smelin, Adam 554
Smillie Films 19
Smith, Adam 13
Smith, Alex 29
Smith, Andrew 405
Smith, Angielette 566
Smith, Angus 520
Smith Jr., Barnaby 566
Smith, Brad 432
Smith, Byron 70
Smith, Cheryl 52
Smith, Chris 13
Smith, Darrin 462
Smith, David 411, 520
Smith, Derek 405
Smith, D. Matthew 444
Smith, Dustin 474
Smith, Edward W. 421
Smith, Howard E. 70
Smith, Jeffrey 405
Smith, Jessica 566
Smith, Jim Field 13
Smith, John 70
Smith, Jonathan 411, 444
Smith, Kerrie 486
Smith, Kevin 13
Smith, Kira 538
Smith, Lee 70
Smith Limousine Service 182
Smith, Lindsey 520
Smith, Marcos 494
Smith, Martha 566
Smith, Michael 551
Smith, Natasha 240
Smith, Neil 444
Smith, Noah David 444
Smith, Norine 524
Smith, Penn 396
Smith, Rusty 396

Company/Crew Index

Name	Page
Smith, R. Vincent	520
Smith, Sheila	411
Smith, Tim M.	421
Smith, Timothy J.	474
Smith, Tomasina	486
Smith, Wayne E.	538
Smithard, Ben	444
Smolka Co.	330
Smooth-On, Inc.	345, 361
SMP Digital Graphics	343
Smuggler	19, 30
Smythe, Timothy	474
Smyth, Kevin	474
Snell & Wilcox, Inc.	286
Sniffen HD	282
Sniffen, Scott	444
Snorri, Eidur	13, 29
Snow Craft Co., Inc.	345
Snow Making by Sturm/Sturm's Special FX	327
Snyder, Adam	474
Snyder, David L.	396
Snyder, Gary A.	520
Snyder, Harriet G.	503
Snyder, Roger C.	474
Snygg, Spencer	462
Sobezynski, Yann	451
Socapa Films	261, 276, 301
Soccer Sport Supply Co.	375
Society of Camera Operators (SOC)	548
Society of Illustrators Research Library	234
Society of Motion Picture & Television Engineers (SMPTE)	548
Society of Stage Directors & Choreographers, The	548
Soddano, Michele	240
Soffian, Diane	520
Sofield, James P.	421
Sofranko, Jim	444
Soho Audio	269
SoHo Grand	180
SoHo Loft 620	128
SoHoSoleil Studio Loft Locations	128
Sol Moscot Opticians	339
Solar Film/Video Productions	45, 50, 62, 89, 284, 290
Solar Plexus, Inc.	136, 201, 276, 307, 317
Solares, Eduardo Martinez	444
Soldo, Peter	449
Solin, Laura	556
Sollett, Peter	13
Sollinger, Daniel	499
Solomon, Diana	486
Solomon, Larry	411
Solomon, Micah (Todd)	538
Solson, Joshua	462
Soltis, James	486
Soluri, Thomas	566
Somerfeld, Gretchen	526
Some's World-Wide Uniforms, Inc.	378
Something's Cooking Catering	162
Sommer, Rebecca	494
Sommers, Gary	520
Sommers, Paul	444
Somodevilla, Todd Antonio	444
Somoroff, Anne J.	520
Somoroff, Michael	13, 432
Somwaru, Sam	411, 414, 415, 417
Sonalysts' Studios	25, 55, 125, 290
Sonar	19
Sonderskov, Mark	421
Sonder, Victor	13
Sonic Safari Music	81
Sonoda, Yoshihiro	462
Sony BMG Custom Marketing Group	81
Sony Electronics Inc.	287
Sony Pictures Stock Footage	100
Soos, Christopher	444
Sopanen, Jeri	432
Sorensen, Dickson	444
Sorensen, Philip B.	462, 496
Soriano, Carmen	526
Sorice, Mark	421
Sorin, Pam	452
SOS Global Express	152
Sosbe, Kevin R.	520
Sossiadis, Karen	503
Soto, Donna	486
Soto, Nereida	486
sotuproductions@gmail.com	335
Sound City	354
Sound One Corp.	45
SoundByte Digital Audio Production, Inc.	45
Soundguild, LLC	84
SoundHound, Inc.	45
SoundImage NY	45, 84
Soundmine	84
SoundSpace	84
Soundtrack	45, 81, 84, 89, 221
Soundtrack Marketing	81
Soupios, Meredith	486
Source Stock Footage Library, Inc., The	100
SourceEcreative	222
South African Consulate General	165
South Carolina	174
South Dakota	174
South Jersey Regional Airport	154
Southard, Jonathan	451
Southern Library of Recorded Music	81
Southwell, Tom	396
Southwest	153
Southworth, Jeff	52
Souto, John M.	520
Souza, Sean	405
Sova, Peter	432
Sowd, Aaron	36
Soyk, Arthur O.	462
Sozio, Anthony V.	538
SpaceCam Systems, Inc.	256
Spacey, Kevin	13
Spagnoli, Andrew	520
Spain-Barcelona	176
Spain-Canary Islands	176
Spalla Video	100
Spalt, Johannes	396
Spangler, Suzanne	70
Spanish Consulate General	165
Spano, Mary Ann	486
Spaulding, Lucas	70
Spear, Evan	52
Special Effects Production Services, Inc.	327, 367, 374
Speciale, Joia Marie	405
Specialty Bulb Co., Inc., The	305
Specialty Business Machines	224
Specialty Signs Co., Inc.	343
Spector, Jill	494
Spectra	164
Spectra Photo/Digital	76
Spectrum	345, 350
Speeckaert, Glynn	444
Speed, Richard T.	464
Speer, Stephen	462
Spencer, Duncan M.	474
Spencer, Natalie MacGowan	494
Sperling, David	432
Sperling, Kenneth M.	474
Spherion	247
Spiegel, Michael S.	421
Spieldenner, Francis	411, 415
Spinney, Craig	540
Spinotti, Dante	444
Spinzia, Elizabeth	499
Spiotta Jr., Eugene	421
Spirit-Buffalo, Renzo	407
Spiro, Donald	505
Spisak, Neil	396
Spiteri, Michael	540
Spitz, Annie	396
Splash Studios, Inc.	45
Spodak, David	451, 499
Spontaneous	6, 19, 55
Spooner, Michele	486
Sports Cinematography Group	100, 293
Spot Welders of New York	50
Spotlight Payroll, Inc.	242
Sprance, Robin	503
Spring, Joshua W.	462
Springman, Stefan	538
Sprott, Eoin C.	520
Sprott, Patricia A.	108
Squire, Theresa	556
Squires, Eugene	432
Squires, Lee Ann	462
Squyres, Tim	70
Srubshchik, Igor	538, 554
Stable Films	25
Stabley, Anthony	396
Stacey, Terry	432
Stacker, Tim	529
Stacy Cheriff Agency	382, 432, 444
Stadler, Florian	444
Staebler, Ed	411
Stanberg, Zach	70
Staffmark	247
Stage 18	125
Stage Managers' Association	548
Stalder, W. Ernest	421
Stalker-Wilde, Julie	538

Name	Page
Staman, Pete	70
Stampfle, Debbie	405
Stamulis Jr., James A.	462
Stanciu Willingham Gabriela	566
Stanford, Daniel (Brooke)	462
Stangarone, Richard	520
Stanger, Michele	504
Stanier, John	444
Staniski, Stanley	411
Stankiewicz, Dean	421
Stankus, Marc	520
Stanley, Stuart	538
Stano, Katia	562
Stanton, Melissa	566
Stanzione, Ralph	486
Stapleton, Kenneth	449
Stapleton, Yvette	566
Star Struck Catering	162
Starace, John	70
Starace, Lia	70
Staranowicz, Michael	462
Starbuck, Anthony	538
Starch, Jonathan	449
Stardust Studios East	6, 19, 103
Starfire Swords, Ltd.	341
Stark Lighting & Generator	307, 317
Stark Naked Productions, Inc./Elsie Stark Casting	220
Stark, Tui	562
Starke, Jennifer	520
Starke, John	551
Starkey, Jeffrey M.	421
Starlite Medical Staff	386
Starr, Susan	411
Stashak, Lisa Ann	520
Stasium, Jason B.	538
Staten Island Film Locations	186
State Supply	346, 371, 374
Stauffer, Scott	538
St. Clair, Justin	494
Steacy, Brendan	444
Steadicam Operators Association	548
Stearne, William	520
Stearns, Craig	396
Steave-Dickerson, Kia	520
Steel Rose Editorial	50
Steeldeck N.Y. Inc.	126
Steele, Alexandra	529
Steele, Jon Gary	396
Steele, Kami	486
Steele, Michael	449
Stefánsson, Jón	71
Stegall, Donny	445, 462, 496
Stegerhoek, Ward	494
Steger, Jewels	562
Stegmeir, John	557
Stehman, Noelle	529
Steiger, Ueli	445
Stein, Debra	557
Stein, Jerry	538
Stein, Jonathan	421
Stein, Stuart	405
Steinberg, Joshua	474
Steinberg, Keith	474
Steinberg, Lawrence	474
Steinberg, Paul	462
Steinberg, Tony	451
Steiner, Alan R.	520
Steiner, Nancy	562
Steiner Studios	32, 92, 125, 137, 291
Steinkamp, William	71
Steinman, Laura	566
Steinman, Paul	474
Steinmetz, John	531
Steinsiek, Tate	494
Sten, James N.	520
Stenberg, Henrik	445
Stenson, Bradley	486
Stenzel, Raymond J.	421
Stenzel, William	421
Stephens, Ben	71
Stephens, Dustin	71
Stephens, Joanne	486
Stephens, Kyle R.	462
Stephenson, Edward	432
Stepper, Eric H.	520
Sterbenz, Rodney T.	520
Sterling Grant and Associates, LLC	230
Stern, David	474
Stern, Donna	71
Stern, Eric	562
Stern, Jonathan	462
Stern, Michael	29
Stern, Molly	494
Stern, Nimmers	554
Stetson, Al	474
Stettner, Franklin D.	538
Stetz, Mark	462
Steuart, James	396
Steuer, Philip	499
Steve Raskin Music	84
Stevens, Robert	445
Stevenson, Trillian	566
Stevers, Robert	462
Stewart, Carrie	520
Stewart, Dawn	529
Stewart, Eric	36
Stewart, Eve	396
Stewart, Gregory J. C.	538
Stewart, Jason	71
Stewart, Joanna	486
Stewart, Missy	396
Stewart, Shannon	423
Stewart, Todd	71
Stewart, Tony	413, 445
Stewart, Walter	462
Stidfole, James A.	520
Stief, Marshall	405
Stiegelbauer Associates	115
Stiegelbauer, David	538
Stiegelbauer, Keith P.	538
Stifanich, John R.	520
Stifel, Nell Warner	108
Still, Derrick	462
Still, Kara B.	526
Stiller, Michael	496
Stillking Films	201
Stillman, Allen	462
Stillsets	396
Stilwell, Barry	71
Stines, Steven	557
Stirling Audio Services, LLC	269
Stitch	103
Stitch Motion Graphics	265
St. John, Stephen	444
Stock, Jennifer	90, 500
Stock Options	267
Stock Shop, The/Medichrome/Anatomy Works	100
Stockdale, Muriel	557
Stockhausen, Adam	396
Stockland, Jillayne	495
Stockland Martel Films	19
Stocklin, Brian A.	462
Stocklin, Frank J	462, 464
Stocklin, Robert J.	462
Stocklin Jr., Walter	462
Stockton, David	445
Stockton, Michael Wright	106
Stoddard, Mark	411, 417
Stoddart, John	396
Stoffers, Rogier	445
Stofsky, Amy	562
Stoia, Barbara	526
Stojiljkovic, Serge	505
Stokes, John	445
Stokes, Thomas	562, 566
Stolen Car	50
Stoller, Amy	208
Stoloff, Dan	445
Stolow, Jeffery	551
Stone, Andrew	71
Stone, Debbie	495
Stone, Kris	108
Stone, Rebecca	538
Stone, Ronald C.	520
Stoner, Thomas Lee	390
Stonestreet Studios	125, 221
St. Onge, Stayc	486
Stopsky, Kenneth G.	421
StorCase Technology, Inc.	287
Storelli, Matthew D.	520
Storm, Casey	562
StormStock	100, 293
Story, Mark	13
Storyboards, Inc.	37
Storyboards Online	37
Stover, Susan Ann	551
Stowe, Abigail	566
Strader, Robert F.	474
Stradis	287
Strahan, Charles Baker	495
Strait, Robert	425
Strasburg, Ivan	445
Strassner, Miles	474
Stratosphere Multimedia	78
Stratten, Mitch	13
Strauss, Donald P.	421
Streamline Stock Footage	100
St. Regis	180

Name	Page
Strettell, Jo	495
Striano, Craig	411
Stribling, D. Barak	566
Strickland, Rebecca	449
Strickman, Eve	405
Strickman-Ripps, Inc.	220
Stricks, Michael	551
Striem, Robert	529
Striffler, Joseph G.	383
Strike Force, Inc.	317
Strippoli, Niki	566
Strober, Carol	396
Strol, Daniel	186, 529
Strong, Arthur	474
Strongboy Studios	45, 84
Stroud, Glenn	462
Stroud, Nancy	106
Strozzi, Amy	495
Strux Corporation	345
Stuart Howard Associates, Ltd.	220
Stuart Jr., Jay C.	474
Stubblefield, Joseph T.	462
Stubblefield, Wyche F.	462
Studio 57	89, 137, 282, 290
Studio 147	128
Studio Center NY	45, 84
Studio Eickholt	128, 191
Studio Instrument Rentals (S.I.R.)	353
Studio K Music Productions	45, 84
Studio Premik	84
Studio Rouge, Inc.	335, 377
Studio-On-Hudson	27
Studios At Linden Oaks	45, 125
Studley, Christopher	462
Stuhlweissenburg, Claus	411, 413, 416
Stumpf, Christina	71
Stunt Dept., Inc./Chris Barnes	236, 246, 328, 545, 549
Stunt Specialists/Peter Bucossi	545
Stuntworks	545
Sturner, Jared	474
Styles, Robert	462
Stylewar	13, 29
Suarez, Joe	451
Suarez, Patricio	432
Suarez, Santiago	13, 432
Subotic, Valdimir	445
Suffern, Richard R.T.	474
Suggs, Jeanne	14
Suggs Media Productions, Inc.	19, 25
Suhrstedt, Tim	445
Suite Spot	19, 45, 89
Sullivan, Alexander	538
Sullivan, Catherine A.	520
Sullivan County International Airport	154
Sullivan, Michael J.	474
Sullivan, Robb	71
Sullivan, Tommy	432
Sum, Anita	503
Sumerfield, Robert B.	520
Summerfield Music, Inc./ Trailer Trash Music Library	52, 81, 84
Summers, Mark	462
Summerskill, John Paul	240
Summit Aviation	150
Sumra, Jermaine	529
Sun, Michelle	405
Sun Microsystems	287
Sunara, Igor	445
Sunderlin, Diane	503
Sunset Pictures, LLC	27, 40
Supanpong, Waris	405
Super Neon Lights Co.	354
Super, Spring	495
Super-Fi	103
Superior Location Van Service, Ltd.	195
Superlative Interiors	115
Supino, Robert	462
Supply & Demand, Inc.	19
Supreme Glass Company	347
Surface Studio	110
Surgent, Christopher	529
Suriano, John	462
Surtees, Bruce	445
Susan DePhillips Illustration	37, 116
Susan Senk Public Relations	34
Suschitzky, Peter	445
Sussan Group, The	19
Sutera, Salvatore	529
Sutherland, Kate	500
Sutherland, Luke	520
Sutton, Peggy	526
Suvak, Darko	445
Suzanne Couture Modelmaking	335, 367
Swain, Jonathan B.	520
Swander, Jeffrey	486
Swanek, Eric	405
Swanson, Bergen	551
Swanson, Bruce E.	520
Swanson, Lawrence C.	520
Swanson, Russell	432
Swanson, Stephen	520
Swartz, Lindsay	503
Swass, Douglas N.	421
Swearingen, Mike	405
Sweden	176
Sweden-West Sweden	176
Swedenhjelm, Robert	476
Sweeney, Andrew	474
Sweeney, Cindy	529
Sweeney, Michael J.	462
Sweeney, Timothy	405
Sweet, Robin	551
Swenson, Chris	411
Swietlik, Dan	71
Swift, David	520
Swift, David H.	462
Swingle, Nathan	405
Swinton, Ian	421
Swiss	153
Swistak, Andrea	520
Sylvia Fay/Lee Genick & Associates Casting	229
Sylvia, James	405
Symonowicz, Peter	405
Sync Sound, Inc.	45
Sync Speed, Inc.	164, 269
Synthespian Studios	6, 19, 55, 103
Sypko, Roman A.	554
Sysko, Christine M.	520
Sysko, Steve	520
System, The	25, 59
Szabo, Christopher	462
Szani, David	405, 529
Szilagyi, Katherine	520

T

Name	Page
T-Line TV, Inc.	25
T.R.E.C.	262
Tabachnik, Jaime	405
Tablecloth Company, The	340
Taca International	153
Tackett, Michael	505
Tackley, Reginald	486
Tactical Truck	360, 378
Tadiello, Edward	108
Tadross Jr., Michael	529
Taft, Josh	14
Taglairino, Joseph	520
Tagliamonti, Amy	486
Taicher, David	411, 415, 445
Taisey, Jeff	421
Taistra, Patrick J.	474
Takagi, Keiko	495
Takagi, Orinne J. T.	538
Takaoka, Hiroo	405
Take 2 Productions	25
Taksen, Melinda	526
Talanca, Birdie	240
Talent Partners	244
Talking Wall Pictures	40
Tallerico, Elisa	486
Tallman, Seth	538
Talty, Martin	538
Tamara Backdrops	110
Tamberelli Digital	50, 164, 276, 282, 307, 317
Tamburino, Leah	486, 495
Tams, Simon T.	538
Tan, Annie	529
Tanaka, Hideyuki	14
Tandem Sound	45
Tane Digital Video	201
Tang, Randall	495
Tang, Sikay	71
Tannenbaum, Neri	551
Tanner, Elizabeth (Betsy)	421
Tanner, Jeffrey J.	520
Tanner, Mark	396
Tanzer, John C.	462
Tape Company, The	267, 294
Tape House	89
Tape Services, Inc.	267
TapeOnline.com	267, 294
TapeStockOnline.com	267, 294
Tapestry Creative Management	71, 382
Tapeworks, Inc.	46
Taranto Labs	76
Tarascio, Paul	540
Tarko, Gabor	432

Name	Page
Tarsem	29
Tartaglio, Michael J.	474
Tassone, Joseph	566
Tastefully Done Catering	162
Tatom, Susan	520
Tatro, Walter	520
Tatum, Will	504
Tavanese-Valenti, Jennifer	451
Tavani, Michael F.	474
Tavenner, Gregor	405
Tavernise, Niko	505
Tavern on the Green	250
Taxi Films, Inc.	20
Taya, Hisao	520
Taylor & Taylor Associates	230
Taylor, Adam	240
Taylor, April	529
Taylor Creative Inc.	346
Taylor, D. Hartsell	566
Taylor, Glenn M.	52
Taylor, Jonathan	445
Taylor, Josh	462
Taylor, Kimberly	486
Taylor, Lisa	520
Taylor, Lynn	495
Taylor, Michael	71
Taylor, Nate	71
Taylor, Nick	445
Taylor, Robert	462
Taylor, Rodney	445
Taylor, Sean	462
Taylor, Stev	566
Taylor-Made Productions	46, 84
Taz Studios	128
TBWA Chiat/Day, Inc.	3
TCS/Technological Cinevideo Services, Inc.	261, 276, 282
TDN Artists	71, 382, 396, 432, 445
Teague, Michelle	566
Teahan, Donald	529
TEAM	244
Team Hutchinson	545
Technicolor Creative Services - N.Y.	56, 89, 92, 290, 291
Technicolor East Coast, Inc.	74
Ted Steeg Productions, Inc.	25
Tedaldi, Claire	524
Tedeschi, David	71
Tedin, Marten	445
Teel, Julie	486
Teitelbaum, Carl	445
Teitler, William	449
Tekserve	62, 222, 224
Telephone Systems & Technologies	354
Teleprompting.com	272
Teleview	287
TellAVision	37, 104, 234, 382
Teller, Janie	541
TellurideStock.com	100
Temme, James Y.	462
Temple, Karen	452
Temple, P. David	421
TemPositions	247
Temptu	349
Ten Music	81
Tenewitz, Richard	421
Tenga, Joseph Michael	390
Tennant, David	14
Tennessee	174
Tennessee-Knoxville	174
Tennessee-Memphis	174
Tennessee-Nashville	175
Tent, Kevin	71
Teranex	287
Teran Fausto	14
Terrapin Chelsea Art Gallery	191
Terry, Daryl	486
Tessler, Jonathan	524
Testa, Bennett	540
Testa, Philip	462
Teterboro Airport	154
Texas	175
Texas-Austin	175
Texas-Dallas/Fort Worth	175
Texas-El Paso	175
Texas-Houston	175
Texas-San Antonio	175
Texas-South Padre Island	175
Thai Airways International	153
Thaler Films	40
That Cat Camera Support, LLC	301
Theater at Madison Square Garden, The	191
Theater for the New City	125
Theatrical Stage Employees (IA Local 1)	548
Theatrical Teamsters (Local 817)	548
Theatrical Wardrobe (IA Local 764)	548
thePound	50
Thewlis, Mary Rae	449
Thijisse, Leen	14
Think 3-D.Com	367
Third Eye Motion Picture Co., Inc.	27, 40
Third Millennium Films	100
Thirlaway, Simon	445
Thoen, Mia	486
Thomas, Brett	421
Thomas, Catherine	557
Thomas Cestare, Inc.	301, 307, 317
Thomas, Charity A.	390
Thomas, Deborah L.	383
Thomas, Diana	486
Thomas, James	71
Thomas, Jeff	14
Thomas, John	432
Thomas, Michael R.	486
Thomason, Nicholas Alfred	503
Thomas, Pam	14
Thomas, Randall	474
Thompson, Crystal	566
Thompson, David	411, 415
Thompson, Jason	411, 417
Thompson, Ken	405
Thompson, Kenneth	474
Thompson, Kevin	396
Thompson, Kimberly Anne	529
Thompson, Lois M.	474
Thompson, Michael A.	520
Thompson, Stephen	432
Thomson Grass Valley	287
Thomson, Walter	505, 507
Thorell, Peter David	551
Thorne, James B.	462
Thorne, Jessica	240
Thornton, Meg	566
Thornton-Jones, Nick	14
Thorpe, Adele	486
Thought Equity Motion	100, 234, 293
Thrasher, Inga	486
Threadgold, David	37
Three Great Lights	272
Thun, Nancy Lee	390
Thurber, Matthew	405
Thur, Pamela	504, 529
Tiberio III, Russell	474
Tice, Richard J.	520
Tichenor, Dylan	71
Tidemand-Johann, Kjeld	108
Tiecrafters, Inc.	335, 338, 377
Tierney, Robert Jerome	529
Tiexiera, Jennifer	71
Tillen, Jodie	396
Tillman, Greg	71
Tim Allen & Associates	100
Timan, Noah V.	538
Timberlake Studios, Inc.	335, 377
Timmer, Bart	14
Tinsley, Scott	405
Tint, Francine	562
Tirolo, David	538
Tirone, Romeo	432
Tischhauser, Peter	445
Tishcoff, Joel	462
TK Digital	20
TNT Transportation, Inc.	155
Tobi Britton's Makeup Shop	323, 349, 382
Tobin, Robert	71
Tobman, Ethan	390, 396
Tocher, Mark	52, 90, 500
Todaro, Frank	14
Todd, Demmie	507
Toelke, Arielle	495
Toga Bike Shop	191, 375
Tognacci, Matt	396
Toia, Mark	14
Toledo Jr., Hector E.	474
Toles, Alexander	520
Toll, John	445
Tollman, Annabel	562
Tolmasoff, Niclana	540
Tom C. Pickard & Co., Inc.	230
Tom Carroll Scenery, Inc.	115
Toma, Dan	532
Tomasko, Paul	62
Tomimatsu, Michi	562
TomKats, Inc.	162
Tomlinson, Anisha	71
Tomlinson, Julie	495
Tonal, Inc.	84
Toner, Victoria	503
Tong, Trevor	405
Tonkin, Bryan J.	474

Name	Page
Tonkin, Christina	520
Tonkin, Christopher	474
Tonkin, Daniel	474
Tonkin, Frankie	474
Tonkin, Kathleen	520
Tonkin, Nicholas	474
Tonnessen, B. Lynn	520
Toogood, Damien	14
Toomey, Anthony	405
Top Class Limousine	182
Top Hat Productions	20, 25, 30
Top of the Rock Weather Room	191
Torelli, Nicholas	520
Torjussen, Ceiri	52
Tormey III, PLLC John J.	228
Toro, Hernan	445
Torre, Marian	486
Torres, Angel	521
Torres, Anita	486
Torres, Jose	538
Torres, Manny	411, 415
Tortorice, Anthony	474
Tortorice Jr., Anthony J.	474
Tortoriello, Rob	71
Toser, David	557
Total Production Services	78
Toteva, Maria	108
Totino, Salvatore	445
Toto, Dominick	521
Tougas, Ginger	396
Tovoli, Luciano	445
Tower, Jon R.	462
Towne, Maryann	566
Towner, Bob	37
Townsend, Julian L.	538
Townsend, Mark	495
Townsend, Richard W.	345, 346
Towse, John	449
Towse, R. Mitchell	521
Toyama, Stacy	445
TP Rental Services, Inc.	303
Trachtman, Amy	503
Tracking Shot	258
Trackwise, Inc.	46
Traduvisual	103, 248
Trager, Robert W.	422
Trahanis, George	208
Trama, Bridget	486, 495
Trammell, Aaron	554
Trammell, Joseph E.	554
Transcript Associates, Inc.	247
Traub, Mark	540
Trautvetter, William	432
Travel Auto Bag Co., Inc.	318, 349
Traveler Productions	59
Travel Management Group/TMG	204
Travel Unlimited	204
Travisano, Ron	405
Travis, Neil	71
Traynor, James	521
TRC - Technology Resource Corporation	224
Treece, T. Ray	554
Treml, Eric	445
Trenear, John	451, 504
Trengove Studios, Inc.	367, 374
Trenner, Jeff	449
Trenton-Mercer Airport	154
Trevis, Massimiliano	445
TRF Production Music Libraries	81
TRG-RAGAMUFFIN	500
Tribeca Cinemas	92, 291
Tribeca Film Center	32
Tribeca Performing Arts Center	125, 191
Tribeca Screening Room	92, 291
Trier, Joachim	14
Trimarchi, Anthony	521
Trimarco Cuervo Rose	566
Trincere, Richard	422
Trinity Television & New Media	137
Trisolini, Matteo	507
TriStar Studios	20, 125, 137, 201
Trivigno, Kelly Ann	240
Troeger, Adam	411, 414
Trofimov, Sergey	445
Troiano, Nick	486
Troll, Wyatt	445
Troma Entertainment, Inc.	27, 100
Trombetta, Leo	71
Tropical Media, Inc.	267
Trotiner, Glen	449
Troubetzkoy Paintings, Ltd.	324
Trova, Cristian	405, 529
Trudel, Eric	503
Truesdale, Veneda	566
Truini, Adrian	462
Trujillo, Bernardo	396
Trulove, Ann	71
Trump International Hotel and Towers	180
truTV Studios	137
Tsao, Miriam Wong	566
Tseng, Derrick	462
Tsyrlin, Sasha	186, 529
Tubbs, Premik	52
Tucker, Linda	486
Tucker, Nicole	486
Tudor Hotel, The	180
Tufaro, Jim	412
Tufts, Jill	405
Tulk-Hart, Frances	562
Tulnoy Lumber & Scenic Plastics	110, 324, 330, 361
Tumblety, David	412, 462
Turek, Daniel	405
Turi, Joshua	486
Turk, Pamela Maiden	521, 532
Turken, Dana	406
Turman, Andrew	445
Turner, Alex	14
Turner Griffin Janet	566
Turner, Irapaul X.	474
Turner Jr., James A.	474
Turner, Marcus	474
Turner, Matthew H.	422
Turning Star, Inc.	110, 340
Turon Travel	204
Tuttman, David	432
Tuxen, Kasper	445
Tuzzolino, Girolamo	422
TV HEAD Productions, LLC	50
TV Pro Gear	62
TV Prompt	272
Twentyman, Lynne	526
Two Animators! LLP	6
Two Jakes	345
Tyler Camera Systems	287
Tyler, Eden	14, 29
Tyler, Elisabeth	526
Tylie Jones & Associates, Inc.	57, 73, 283
Tyroler, Sean	71
Tyson, John	449
Tzouris, William	538

U

Name	Page
U-Direct Productions	20
U.S. Coffee, Inc.	424
U.S. Color	76
U.S. Council/Carnet Help Line	166
U.S. Virgin Islands	175
Ubiqus	248
UCLA Film and Television Archive	100
Uhl, Anders	432
UK	176
UK-East Midlands	176
UK-Isle of Main	176
UK-Liverpool	176
UK-London	176
UK-South West Screen	176
UK-Yorkshire	176
Ulfik, Rick	52
Ulivella, Richard	464
Ullman, Sharon	500
Ullrich, Mattie	557
Ulrich, Eric	474
Ultrabland	46, 84, 89, 103
Ultramar Travel	204
Uncommon Trax	81
Ungar, Mike	52
Ungaro, David	445
Unger, Jonathan	521
Unger, Steffen	462
Unicorn Productions	84
Union Square Group, Ltd.	115
United Airlines Cargo	152
United Airlines/United Express	153
United Palace, The	191
United Rentals	303, 310, 317, 318
United Scenic Artists (IA Local 829)	548
United Shipping & Packaging	166
United Talent Agency	382, 432, 445
Universal Light & Sound	269
Universal Musical Instrument Co.	353
Universal Music Publishing Library/UMPL	81
Universal Studios - Stock Footage Library	100, 293
Uniworld Group, Inc.	3
Unjang, Jon Zenfeek	462
Unjang, Perry Z.	474
Unrath, Chris	422
Unterberger, Holly	526

Untitled Inc.	20
UPS	152
Urban Desire Cruises	328
Urbanik, Joseph M.	106
Urban Jr., Anthony	521
Urban Outfitters.	376
Urdaneta, Michael.	538
US Air Cargo.	152
US Air Force Motion Picture Office	100
US Airways	153
US Airways/USAirways Express	153
US Army Office of Public Affairs	100, 293
US Talent Management, Inc.	246
USA Studios	25, 50, 57, 59, 89, 290
USPS Express Mail.	152
USRental.com.	224
Utah	175
Utah Scientific.	287
Utah-Kane County.	175
Utah-Moab	175
Utah-Park City.	175
Utopia Soundstage	125
Utrecht Art & Drafting Supplies	325

V

Vaccariello, Robert A.	422
Vaccaro, Christopher.	474
Vaccaro, Craig W.	474
Vaccaro, Nicholas R.	474
Valenti, Jordan	445
Valk, Edward.	540
Vallas-Cullen, Victoria.	500
Valle Jr., Joseph A.	475
Valle Sr., Joseph A.	475
Vallee, Stephane.	445
Valli, Robert N.	475
Vallow, Kristen.	390
Valverde, Daniel	71
Van Achte Alain.	538
Van Baelen Lieven	14
Van Burger, Michael	486
Van Buskirk Jr., John.	462
Vanasco, Victoria	521
Vancata, Brad	37
Vance, Marina.	486, 495
Van De Bunt, Fred.	495
Vandergast, Thomas	432
van der Heide, Rutger.	495
Vander Linden Glenn J.	462
Van Der Ploeg Rogier.	14
Vanderpool, Nicholas	529
Vanderputten, William J.	475
Vande Water Lawrence H.	521
Van Dusen Bruce	14
Van Dyke, Brett.	445
Vane, Richard	500
van Gelder, Joost	445
Vangrofsky, Gayle Jennifer	529
Vanguard.	247
Van Heek, Bob A.	475
Vanhoutteghem, Joe	14
Van Ingen, William	462
Van Lierop Toy R.	486
Van Lieu, Walter	521
Van Patten, Steven James	540
Van, Phillip	14, 29
Van Praag, Joshua C.B.	462
Van Rossen, Mark C.	462
Van Ry Robert.	540
Van Slee, Sandrine	495
Vanson, Justin.	476
Van Starrenburg, Joost	445
Vanstone, Robert S.	422
Vant, Kristy	524
Van Wersh, Riego	445
Vapensky, Nikki.	71
Vargas, Criseida	566
Vargas, Jorge	486
Varga, Thomas G.	538
Variety, Inc.	227
Varig Brazilian Airlines.	153
Varooom Automotive Resources	360
Vasari Classic Artists' Oil Colors	325
Vassallo, Joe.	71
Vaught, Chris	412
Vazquez, Frank.	486
Veader, Anthony	486
Velasco, Danny	495
Velazquez, Sonnel	432
Velechenko, Andrew M.	422
Velez, Jason	464, 549
Velez, John.	463
Velez, Sergio.	406

Velicky, Jan	445
Velten, Billy	445
Veltri, Juliet	486
Venantini, Marleen	557
Vendetti, Christian.	529
Venditti, Jeffrey	445
Vendler, Alex.	445
Veneziano, Sandy.	396
Vennitti, Vincent	406
Venti, Joel	37
Ventura Insurance Brokerage, Inc.	230
Vera, Carlos	495
Verardi, John.	406
Verbeck, Kim.	495
Verberations! LLC	208
Vercruse, Leon H.	463
Verel, Maria.	486
Vergara, Bob.	505
Verges, Chrisann	500
Vermeer, Pieter.	432
Vermont	175
Vernola, Michael.	530
Vernon Computer Source a Division of I.T.Xchange	224
Veron, Carlos	445
Verreaux, Edward	396
Version 2 Editing.	50
Vescera, Susan.	503
Vetica, Robert.	495
Vetick, Donald M.	475
Vettel, Ann.	540
Vetter, Marilou.	406
Viano, Joseph.	475
Vicarelli, Michael.	432
Viceroy Films	25, 201
Vickers, Jamie.	396
Vickery, Lee	406
Vidbel Performing Animals	214
Video Caption Corporation	103
Video Concepts, Inc.	25, 55, 62
Video Equipment Rentals	276, 282, 284
Video Production New York.	25
Video Tape Library, Inc./VTL	100, 293
Video Village, Inc., A.	273, 554
Video Taping Service/VTS Productions	57
VideoActive Productions	25
VideoActive Productions/VoiceWorks Sound Studios	46
Videofilm Systems, Inc.	276, 282
VideoHelper, Inc.	81
VideoLink, Inc.	25
Videomaker Magazine.	227
VideoNet, Inc.	25
Videotape Products, Inc.	267, 294
Videotek	287
VidiPax LLC	57
Viera, Anthony.	539
Viesta, John	496
Vietro-Hannum, Peter	412, 415, 417, 475
Vietti, Alejo	557
Vigi, Lona	495
Vigilante, Frank.	475
Vignari, Bill	425
Vignjevich, Danielle.	486
Village Caterer & Craft Service, Inc., The	162, 424
Village Chess Shop.	347
Village Postal Center.	238
Village Video Productions	78
Villains	20, 30
Villalobos, Linda	486
Villalobos Renaldo	445
Villani, James	521
Villegas, Edward	412
Vincent, Clark	495
Vincent, John	539
Vincent, Kevin	463
Vincent, Lyle.	412, 445
Vincent, Scott	14
Vincie, Arthur.	240
Vinson, Jack	406
Vintage & Antique Musical Instruments	353
Viola, Elise G.	390
Viola, Peter.	14
Violante, Alfonso	463
Vipers, Vettes & Various Muscle Cars.	360
VIP Prompting Corporation	272
Virgin Atlantic Airways.	153
Virginia	175
Virginia-Central Virginia	175
Virtual Media.	62, 284
Viscuso, Vita	486
Visibility Public Relations, Inc.	34
Vision Earth Society	101
Visual Alchemy, LLC	273, 278, 354
Visual Matrix Corporation	287
VITAC.	103

Company/Crew Index

Name	Page
Vitagliano, Joe	412
Vitagliano, Jovan	487, 495
Vitaliano, Joan	551
Viteri, Alfredo	538
Vitucci, Jerome R.	538
Viviano, Thomas L.	521
VI[Z]rt	55
Voegeli, Andrew	412
Vogel, Joshua	521
Vogel, Julie	562
Vogel, Matthew	521
Vogt, Chris M.	521
Vogt, Mary	562
Vogt, Robert P.	521
Vogt, Tom	71
Vohr, Matt	452
Voicebank.net	225
Volpe, Eric R.	475
Volpe, Joseph	406
Volpe, Mark F.	475
Von Bartheld Peter J.	521
von Blomberg Ronald T.	344, 521, 533
von Borbely, Stefan	445
von Cannon, David	495
Von Erickson Modelmaking	367
Von Rauchhaupt Tomas	463
von Schultzendorff, Wedigo	446
von Tippelskirch Christian	504
Von Torfeld Maria	487
Voos, Christopher	412
Voudouris, Christos	446
Vozza, Anthony	551
Vranesich, Daniel	475
Vranesich, Marc F.	475
Vuolo, Robert	463

W

Name	Page
W New York	180
W New York - The Court	180
W New York - The Tuscany	180
W New York - Times Square	180
W New York - Union Square	180
Wachsler, Susan	566
Wachs, Ted	412, 414, 417, 446
Wachter, Paul	475
Wacks, Michael W.	463
Wade, Patrick D.	463
Wadsworth, Alison	487
Wager, Keith	562
Wages, William	446
Waggett, Ellen	390
Waggoner, Frederic	487
Wagner, Daniel	503
Wagner, John	463
Wagner, Robert	432
Wagreich, David	446
Wagreich, Herb	446
Wagreich, Jerry	538
Wahl, Ronald E.	240
Waititi, Taika	14
Walczak, Diana	14
Wald, Karen	526
Waldman, Harvey	449
Waldorf-Astoria	180
Walker, Anozine	487
Walker, David W.	422
Walker, Derek	412, 414
Walker, Doug	71
Walker, Ewan	495
Walker, Graham	396
Walker, James P.	422
Walker, John	406
Walker, Mariah	562
Walker, Michael	396
Walker, Mora Killeen	500
Walkieboy Inc.	164
Wall, Stacy	14, 29
Wallace III, Locke E.	538, 540
Wallach, Peter	104
Waller, Garry	446
Walling, Chris	446
Walpole, Mark	406
Walsh, Bryan	521
Walsh, Ginny	521
Walsh, James B.	476
Walsh Jr., James F.	463
Walsh, Kevin M.	521
Walsh, Kevin P.	463
Walsh, Matt	71
Walsh, Rory C.	475
Walsh Sr., James	463
Walsh, Thomas	397
Walshak, Kenneth J.	422

Name	Page
Walt Disney Co./Park Avenue Screening Room	92, 291
Walter, Kevin	406
Walter, Markus	14
Walters, Brett	406
Walters, Christopher	412
Walters, Martin	451
Walton, Dan	240
Walton Hauling & Warehouse Corporation	197, 320
Walts, Peter	463
Wan, Derek	446
Wang, Harvey	14
Warbin, Tracy	487
Ward, Ashley	495
Ward, Elizabeth Caitlin	557
Ward, Jessica	406
Ward, Kevin	446
Ward, Noreen	240
Ward, Sherman	451
Ward, Stephen	446
Wardwell, Paul T.	475
Warehouse Store Fixture Company, The	372
Warfield, Aurora	530
Warin, Vincent	446
Warnick, Craig	71
Warshaw, Jeremy	14
Warter, Fred	37
Warwick, The	180
Wasco, David	397
Washburn, James	406
Washburn, Ron	412
Washington	175
Washington-Seattle	175
Washington, Dennis	397
Waskewich, Brad	71
Wassel, John	406
Wasserman, David	475
Wasserman, Karl G. E.	538
Wassylenko, Cathy K.	108
WaterHouse, The	101
Waters, John	14
Waters, Ronald	475
Waterston, David	432
Watertown International Airport	154
Watkins, Mark	412
Watkins, Thomas F. (Tom)	521
Watkins, William T.	521
Watson, Albert	14
Watson, Brendan R.	521
Watson, Court M.	390
Watson, Lawrence	506
Watson, Leah	495
Watson, Ralph	413, 416
Watson, Robin	495
Watson, Steven	538
Watson, Thomas	487
Watt, Sharon	526
Watts, Andrew T.	463
Watts, Jon	29
Wattson, Gary	521
Wave Hill	191
Wavelength Video Services	55
WAX Music & Sound Design	84
Waxman, Jamie	240
Weapon Specialists, Ltd.	341
Weather Central, Inc.	287
Weathered, Paul R.	521
WeatherWatch Service	206
Weather Works	206
Weaver, Joel	521
Webb, Bo	412
Webb, Danielle C.	521
Webb, Ryan	463
Weber, Debra Katz	566
Weber Sones, Patricia	530
Weber, Susan	432
Weberg, Warren A.	538
Weberg, William M.	475
Webster, Dan	397
Webster Hall	250
Webster, John	530
Webster, Sara	503
Webster, Sonja	449
Wechsler, David	449
Weck, Christopher	463
Weeks, Kerry A.	521
Weeks, Loren	390
Wehr, Curtis	446
Wehrman, Laura	566
Weil, Dan	397
Weiland, Paul	14
Weinberg, Karen	487
Weiner, Howard	554
Weiner Jr., Josh	475
Weiner, Matthew	530

Name	Page
Weingarten, Mark	538
Weingartner, Mark	104, 413, 463
Weinhoff, Marla	390
Weinman, David C.	521
Weinman, Jason	521
Weinstein, Benjamin	14
Weinstein, Glen	475
Weinstein, Kim	487
Weintraub, Dara	500
Weinzimer, Rachael	521
Weisberg, Steven	530
Weisenfeld, Jody	521
Weiser, Jeff	14
Weishaar, Jeremy	406
Weisinger, Adam	530
Weisinger, Allen	487, 495
Weiss, Alexis	521
Weiss, Peter	521
Weist, Gary	390
Wekselblatt, Michael	475
Welborn, Kaleo	37
Welch, Bo	397
Welch, Sam	71
Welch, Steve	71
Welfling, Juliette	71
Welker Translation & Research	248
Well, The	50
Wellburn, Timothy	71
Weller, David J.	390
Weller, Paul T.	475
Wells, Heidi	495
Wells, Jane	530
Wells, Llewellyn	500
Wells, Reggie	495
Wells, Rosalie	566
Wellings, John A.	463
Welsch, Meredith	500
Wendell, Terry	14
Wendt, Angela	557
Wendy Goidell, Inc.	344
Wengrofsky, Brian	406
Wenk, Jonathan	506
Wenner, Gerald	432
Wenniger, Anne	521
Werblun, Steve	37
Werk, Michael	446
Werner, Andrea J.	521
Werner, Catherine	521, 533
Werner, Craig	463
Wertimer, Stephen	449
Werwa, Shelby	451, 500
Weselyj, Lubomyr M.	521
Weselyj, Oleh	475
Wessling, James	521
Wesson, Daniel H.	538
West, Alana	566
West, Derrick L.	554
West, Julian	14, 432
West, Laura	521
West Marine	328
West Side Office	32
West, Susan	463
West, Tom	521
West Virginia	175
Westchester County Airport	154
Western Costume Co.	335, 349, 378
Westervelt, Clay	446
Westfall-Tharp, Kathryn	521
Westhead, Victoria	551
Westin NY at Times Square	180
Westman, Tony	446
Weston, Jonathan	538
Weston, Thomas	413, 432
Weston, Timothy J.	475
Westprint	245
Westside Media Group	267, 294
Wetcher, Barry	506
Wexler, Haskell	446
WGBH Stock Sales	101
Whatley, Julian	446
Wheeler, Colleen	487
Wheeler, Ford	521, 533
Wheeler, Laura	530
Wheeler, Roni	449, 500
Wheels for Reels	360
Whelan, James J.	521
Whelan, Thomas J.	186, 530
Where'bouts, Inc.	186
Whetstone, Mike	397
Wheway, Robert	530
Whidden, Amanda Mary	557
Whilden, JoJo	506
Whist, Martin	397
Whitacre, Justin	406
Whitaker, James	446
Whitaker, Nicole Hirsch	446
Whitaker, Ross	14
White, Aaron	446
White, Carla	487
White Daisy	335, 378
White, Diana	521
White, Ise	562
White, Joseph	446
White Jr., Joseph	538
White, KC	413, 446
White, Kenny	52
White, Mark	390
White, Patrick E.	422
White, Peter	566
White Rain Films, Ltd.	101
White, Rheanne	495
White, Robert	463
White, Sharon	521
White, Thomas	422
White, Tsigie	566
Whitebloom, Declan	14
Whitebloom, Francis	397
Whitehall Media Productions, LLC	128
Whitehead, Cindy	562
Whitehouse, the	50
WhiteLabel product, a	20
Whitfield, Richard A.	538
Whitman, Dale	538
Whitman, Mark	412
Whitman, Tony J.	475
Whitman, Tristan	446
Whitmeyer, Joseph	487
Whitney, Charles	422
Whittaker, Karen	566
Whittall, Wendy	521
Whitten, Ben	71
Wick, Christine	521, 533
Wicker, Meghan	503
Wickstrom, Shari	37
Wickwire, Beth	562
Wideye Creative	201
Widlund, Maranda	495
Wiegand, Michael J.	521
Wiehl, Peter	446
Wiencko, Stanley	449
Wiener, Daniel	406
Wiesel, Karin	521
Wieser, George	432
Wiggins, Michael	240
Wiggins, William	521
Wiklund, Stefan	562
Wilbour Library of Egyptology	234
Wilcha, Christopher	14
Wilcox, John	52
Wilcox, Kim	557, 562
Wildchild Editorial	50
Wile, Ian B.	71
Wilk, Sean	412
Wilkens Fruit & Fir Farm	344
Wilkens, Paul	412, 413
Wilkinson, Michael	562
Will, Eric	14
Willems, Jo	446
Willer, Charlotte	495
Willett, Patricia	503
Willey, Thomas	406
William Berloni Theatrical Animals, Inc.	214
William Greaves Productions, Inc.	62
William Markle Associates	46
William M. Miller Camera Rentals	261
Williams, Anthony	495
Williams, Bill	446
Williams, Canella	503
Williams, Cheyenne	487
Williams, Christophe	71
Williams, David Gordon	422
Williams, David T.	475
Williams, Deirdre N.	566
Williams, Edward	475
Williams, James E.	521
Williams, Jennifer	397
Williams, Jerome	406
Williams, Jim	521, 533
Williams, John	500
Williams, Joseph P.	475
Williams, Jose V.	463
Williams, Kevin P.	475
Williams, Mark	446
Williams, Mickey	487
Williams, Patrece	487
Williams, Paul	422
Williams, Sher	487
Williams, Taurance	487, 495

Williams, Terry. 412
Williams, Tonero 521
Williams, Tony 14
Williams-Barnes, Cheryl 487
Willingham, Gabriela Stanciu 557
Willis, Gordon 432
Wilsher, Jarvis B. 463
Wilson, Andrea 495
Wilson, Benjamin 566
Wilson, David 397
Wilson, Edward J. 487
Wilson, Eric. 104
Wilson, Jelani 406
Wilson, Lynne 566
Wilson, Michael. 521
Wilson, Nathan 446
Wilson, Paul 412, 415
Wilson, Paul J. 475
Wilson Rivas Co., Inc., The. 424
Wilson, Robert (RJ). 521
Wilson Jr., Robert D. 521
Wilsonbuilt, Inc. 367
Wimer, Gregory. 406
Winborn, Aurelia 406
Wind Dancer Production Group. 27, 40
Windfall Productions 40
Winestine, Zack 446
Winfrey, Izear 487
Wingard, Benjamin J. 475
Wingard, Joshua 475
Wingert, Theresa. 14
Wingo, David. 52
Wings Air. 256
Wings Wildlife Production, Inc. 101, 293
Winig, Scott. 425, 446
Winkelmann, Henning. 14
Winkler, Mari Jo 551
Winkowski, Brian. 521
Winston Temps 247
Winter, Alyssa B. 533
Winter, John 500
Winter, Mark 530
Winter-Young, Robin 449, 530, 551
Winters, Bill. 432
Winters, Joan 343
Wirsing, Jeffrey 566
Wisconsin 175
Wisconsin Production Guide 227
Wise, Kenneth. 425
Wise-Tuteur, Bernadette 422
Wishengrad, Marc. 446
Wishengrad Pictures, Inc. 25
Wishingrad, Dara 397
Wish You Were Here Film & Video, Inc. 101, 293
Witherspoon, W. Randall. 566
Wits End Equipment &
  Expendables 302, 305, 317, 318, 331, 349
Wits End Production Suites. 32
WitsTrucks 305, 320
Witt, Alexander 446
Witt-Bertsche, Leslie E. 383
Wittenborn, Christie 562
Wlaysewski, Anne 562
Wlodkowski, Stan 500
WMHT Production Services 125
Wolanczyk, John. 108
Wolberg, Anthony 432
Wolcheski Jr., George A. 475
Wolcott, James 52
Wolenski, Adam 240
Wolf, Benjamin 446
Wolf, Bruce 14
Wolf, Dany 500, 551
Wolf, Jonathan David 551
Wolf, Miky 71
Wolf, Jonathan 240
Wolfe Air Aviation, Ltd. 256
Wolfe, Alan 406
Wolfe, Aleta 487
Wolff, Stephen 422
Wolin, Robert F. 390
Wolk, James F. 390
Woll, Michael. 566
Wollman Rink 191
Wollock, Daniel S. 422
Wollock-Spiegel, Susan S. 522
Wolpert, Deborah 530
Wolski, Dariusz 446
Wonder, Andrew 406
Wong, Richard H. 475
Wong, Susan 412
Wood, Andrew. 530
Wood, Bentley. 522
Wood, Mary. 52
Wood, Matthew. 71
Wood, Michael 446
Wood, Oliver 446
Wood, Richard 432
Woodburne, Roger 14
Woodfin Camp & Associates 101
Woods, Daniel 475
Woods, John J. 463
Woods, Jonathan 37
Woods, Patrick 522
Woods, Robert M. 475
Woods Jr., Robert 475
Woods, Stephen 464, 475
Woods, Thomas McGrath 475
Woodstock Airport 154
Woodward, Caroline 524
Woolard, David 557
Woolner, David 463
Woolston-Smith, Ian 412, 414, 415, 446
Wooters-Reisin, Joan 71
Word, Troy 14
Words In Process 247
Work Edit 50
Work Production Company 201
World Courier 152
World Trade Copiers 224
World Wide Audio, Inc. 46
World Yacht Dining Cruises. 250
World-Wide Business Centres. 32
Worldwide Jet 150
Worldwide Pants Incorporated 40
Worrell, Brad. 52
Worthington, Mark. 397
WPA Film Library. 101
Wray III, Clifford 566
Wright, Daniel 463
Wright, Justine 71
Wright, Michael 413
Wright, Miklos 71
Wright, Peter. 522
Wright, Phillip 432
Wright, Richard 397
Wright, Sabrina 522, 533
Wright, Steven 524, 533
Wright, Susan J. 566
Wright, Travis K. 522
Write Brothers, Inc. 222
Writers Guild of America East (WGAE) 548
WRS Motion Picture & Video Laboratory. 74
WTTW Digital Archives 101, 293
Wu, Gerald 451
Wujek, Johnny 562
Wunder, Kurt W. 422
Wurmfeld, Eden 551
www.artformedia.com 324
Wylie, Bill 37
Wylie, Michael 397
Wynkoop, Gerardus (Jerry) 463
Wyoming 175

X

X-P Shipping. 166
Xeno-Lights, Inc. 305, 307, 317
Xereas, Antonia. 557
Xytech Systems Corporation. 222
XYZ Pictures 265

Y

Yacht Owners Association. 328
Yacht Services International 328
Yacoe, Joseph 432
Yaconetti, Steve 412, 417
Yacuk, Gary W. 475
Yacuk, Richard 475
Yacuk, Thomas 383, 475
Yahaira 495
Yamaguchi, Toshiro 406
Yamashita, Nob. 37
Yamazaki, Yuki 495
Yanez, Robert 422
Yanishefsky, Sari 487
Yaple, Sean. 406
Yarbrough, Teresa M. 503
Yasaki, Yoshi 446
Yasi, Theodore 446
Yates, Toby 71
Yatsko, Kate 522
Yeandle, Dennis 506
Yeandle, Matthew 487
Yeaton, Greer 503, 530
Yedlin, Steve. 446

Yeh, William 72
Yeich, Franz J. 475
Yellow Shed Antiques 345
Yeoman, Robert 446
Yetter, Michael 463
Yezerski, Mary Kay 487
Ying, Tina 487
Yip, Derek 240
Yn Couture 335
Ynocencio, Jo 562
Yonkey, Melissa 487
Yoo, Brenda 240
Yoon, Edward 530
York Scaffold Equipment Corp. 303, 307, 310
York, Wendy 526
Yoshida, Nana N. 562
Yoshida, Ronald 538
Yostpille, Thomas G. 475
Young & Rubicam 3
Young, Dennis A. 422
Young, John 72
Young, R.N. Barbara 386
Young, William N. 422
Younts, Shane Ann 208
Your Neighborhood Office 238
Yowler, John 423
Yuen, Jerry H. 538
Yukich, Jim 14, 29
Yurich, Ernest 475
Yurich, Michael W. 475
Yusim, Anna 406
Yvette Helin Studio, LLC 323, 335, 367

Z

Zabar's 162
Zabe, Alexis 446
Zabilla, Jim 446
Zacharias, Ivan 14
Zack and J.C. 14
Zack, Denis A. 522
Zack, Kevin 522
Zadrosny, Michael 522
Zafian, Thomas 538
Zaharian, Jeni 487
Zaheer, Nausil 495
Zakarian, Louie 487, 495
Zakes, Carin 4
Zalben, Charles 551
Zambarloukos, Haris 446
Zambelli Fireworks Internationale 327
Zambrana, David F. 557
Zane, Ted 487
Zanotti, Laura 562
Zanzibar 250
Zappia, Don L. 475
Zaretsky, Lora 72
Zariwny, Travis Nicholas 397
Zarnett, Nina 475
Zecca, John 538
Zegarsky, George 422
Zeigon, Kara 522
Zeitbyte 25, 57, 89, 283
Zeleski, Thomas 475
Zero 2 Sixty. 20
Zetterberg, Robert T. 463
Zetterberg, Thomas J. 463
ZFX, Inc. 545
Zhang, Ye 538
Ziegler, Joseph 422
Zieglerova Fitzgerald, Klara 390
Zieman, John 72
Zilles, John 446
Zimmer, Stephanie 406
Zimmerman, Dan 72
Zimmerman, David 487
Zimmerman, Dean 72
Zimmerman, Eric 446
Zimmerman, Kevin 72
Zimmern, David 554
Zimmern, Peter 463, 506
Zingales, Rosalie 566
Ziska, Mikki 530
Zivkovic, Daniela 487
Zizzo, Chris 406, 463
Zizzo, Joe 432
Zócalo 250
Zolfo, Victor J. 522
Zolot, Andy 503
Zoltowski Jr., James J. 538
ZONA Design 103
Zooma Zooma Corporation 20, 30
Zophres, Mary 562
Zorrilla-de San Martin Carolina 446
Zsigmond, Vilmos 446
Zuback, Tom 506
Zuccarello, Francis 72
Zuccarini, Pete 446
Zuch, Andy 538, 554
Zuch, Bernie 538
Zuch, Steven N. 538, 554
Zucker, Carl 449
Zucker, Harriet 522, 533
Zucker, Paul 72
Zurlo, Rosemarie 487
Zviaguina, Elena 108
Zwart, Harald 14
Zydel, Brian 538
Zydel, Lenore 522
Zydel, Timothy 522

NOTES:

PICTURED:
Abandoned Hospital

LOCATION:
Staten Island, NY

PHOTOGRAPHER:
Sam Rohn

ALSAM : www.alsam.net
ASSOCIATION OF
LOCATION SCOUTS & MANAGERS

New York 411
*Qualified Listings for the
New York Production Community*
www.newyork411.com

Advertising Agencies &
Production Companies

🅐 ADVERTISER SYMBOL

Refer to the General Index for cross-referencing items in this section.

Advertising Agencies....................2
Advertising Agency Freelance Producers.....4
Animation Production Companies...........5
Commercial Directors....................7
Commercial Production Companies........15
Corporate & Video Production Companies...21
Independent Director's Reps..............26
Infomercial Production Companies.........26
Motion Picture Production Companies......27
Music Video Directors...................28
Music Video Production Companies........30
Production Offices......................31
Promo Production Companies 33
Public Relations.......................34
Storyboard Artists......................35
Television Production Companies..........38
Trailer Production Companies.............40

Advertising Agencies

A&A Group (212) 239-7360
450 Seventh Ave., Ste. 2304　FAX (212) 239-7361
New York, NY 10123　www.aa-grp.com

Advertisers Workshop (518) 523-3359
Cold Brook Plaza East　FAX (518) 523-0255
P.O. Box 645 (Near Route 86)　www.adworkshop.com
Lake Placid, NY 12946

Arnold Worldwide (212) 463-1000
110 Fifth Ave. (Near 16th St.)　FAX (212) 463-1080
New York, NY 10011　www.arnoldworldwide.com

Avrett, Free & Ginsberg, Inc. (212) 832-3800
885 Second Ave. (Near E. 47th St.)　FAX (212) 486-6518
New York, NY 10017　www.afg-adv.com

Bartle Bogle Hegarty (212) 812-6600
32 Avenue of the Americas, 19th Fl.　FAX (212) 242-4110
(Near Fifth Ave.)　www.bartleboglehegarty.com
New York, NY 10013

BBDO New York (212) 459-5000
1285 Sixth Ave. (Near W. 52nd St.)　FAX (212) 459-6645
New York, NY 10019　www.bbdo.com

Big Chair Creative Group (212) 399-3150
18 W. 21st St., PH (Near Fifth Ave.)　FAX (212) 399-3165
New York, NY 10010　www.bigchairny.com

Brouillard (212) 210-7985
466 Lexington Ave., Sixth Fl.　FAX (212) 210-8111
(Near E. 46th St.)　www.brouillard.com
New York, NY 10017

Brushfire (973) 871-1700
Two Wing Dr.　FAX (973) 871-1717
Cedar Knolls, NJ 07927　www.brushfireinc.com

Citigate Albert Frank (212) 508-3400
850 Third Ave., 11th Fl.　FAX (212) 508-3441
(Near E. 52nd St.)　www.thegateworldwide.com
New York, NY 10022

Cliff Freeman & Partners (212) 463-3200
36 W. 20th St., Fifth Fl.　FAX (212) 463-3225
(Near Houston St.)　www.clifffreeman.com
New York, NY 10011

Conill Advertising, Inc. (212) 463-2500
375 Hudson St., 11th Fl.　FAX (212) 463-2509
(Near W. Houston St.)
New York, NY 10014

Cossette Communications (212) 753-4700
415 Madison Ave., Third Fl.　FAX (212) 755-0284
(Near E. 48th St.)　www.cossette.com
New York, NY 10017

Crowley, Webb & Associates (716) 856-2932
268 Main St., Fourth Fl.　FAX (716) 856-2940
(Near Swan St.)
Buffalo, NY 14202

Dana Communications, Inc. (609) 466-9187
Two E. Broad St.　FAX (609) 466-0285
Hopewell, NJ 08525　www.danacommunications.com

Dana Communications, Inc. (212) 736-0060
350 Fifth Ave., Ste. 2620　www.danacommunications.com
New York, NY 10118

DDB Worldwide (212) 415-2000
437 Madison Ave. (Near E. 49th St.)　FAX (212) 415-3414
New York, NY 10022　www.ddb.com

Dentsu America (212) 397-3333
32 Avenue of the Americas, 16th Fl.　FAX (212) 397-3322
(Near W. 52nd St.)　www.dentsuamerica.com
New York, NY 10013

Deutsch, Inc. (212) 981-7600
111 Eighth Ave., 14th Fl.　FAX (212) 981-7525
(Near W 15th St.)
New York, NY 10011

Doremus & Company (212) 366-3000
200 Varick St., 11th Fl.　FAX (212) 366-3060
(Near Houston St.)　www.doremus.com
New York, NY 10014

EGC Group, Inc. (516) 935-4944
1175 Walt Whitman Rd.　FAX (516) 935-7017
(Near Arlington St.)　www.egcgroup.com
Melville, NY 11747

Eric Mower & Associates, Inc. (315) 466-1000
500 Plum St. (Near Evans St.)　FAX (315) 466-2000
Syracuse, NY 13204　www.mower.com

**Della Femina/
Rothschild Jeary and Partners** (212) 506-0700
902 Broadway (Near W. 20th St.)　FAX (212) 506-0751
New York, NY 10010　www.dfjp.com

Finaldi & Associates (732) 530-0174
16 Monmouth Pl.　FAX (732) 530-0174
Red Bank, NJ 07701

Foote, Cone & Belding (212) 885-3000
100 W. 33rd St. (Near Broadway)　FAX (212) 885-3988
New York, NY 10001　www.fcb.com

Furman Roth Advertising (212) 687-2300
801 Second Ave. (Near E. 43rd St.)　FAX (212) 687-0858
New York, NY 10017　www.furmanroth.com

George P. Clarke Advertising, Inc. (212) 545-7400
　FAX (212) 545-7433
　www.gpclarke.com

Gianettino & Meredith, Inc. (973) 376-2100
430 Mountain Ave., Ste. 105　FAX (973) 376-3492
Murray Hill, NJ 07974　www.gandm.net

**Gigante Vaz &
Partners Advertising, Inc.** (212) 343-0004
295 Lafayette St., Seventh Fl.　FAX (212) 343-0776
(Near E. Houston St.)　www.gigantevaz.com
New York, NY 10012

Hanft, Byrne, Raboy & Partners (212) 674-3100
205 Hudson St., Seventh Fl.　FAX (212) 228-7679
(Near Canal St.)
New York, NY 10003

J. Walter Thompson USA, Inc. (212) 210-7000
466 Lexington Ave. (Near E. 45th St.)　FAX (212) 210-7299
New York, NY 10017　www.jwt.com

Katz, Dochtermann & Epstein (212) 686-0006
129 W. 27th St., 11th Fl.　FAX (212) 686-6991
(Near Avenue of the Americas)　www.kdande.com
New York, NY 10001

Korey, Kay & Partners (212) 620-4300
130 Fifth Ave., Eighth Fl.　FAX (212) 620-7149
(Near W. 18th St.)　www.koreykay.com
New York, NY 10011

Leibler-Bronfman & Lubalin (212) 463-9292
55 Fifth Ave. (Near 12th St.)　FAX (212) 989-3102
New York, NY 10003　www.lbladvertising.com

Linett & Harrison (908) 686-0606
2500 Morris Ave.　FAX (908) 686-0623
Union, NJ 07083　www.linettandharrison.com

Lipman, Richmond, Greene (212) 684-1100
408 W. 14th St., Third Fl. FAX **(212) 929-7330**
(Near 10th Ave.)
New York, NY 10014

Lowe New York (212) 605-8000
150 E. 42nd St. www.loweworldwide.com
(Near Lexington Ave.)
New York, NY 10017

Marquardt, Roche & Partners (203) 327-0890
Five High Ridge Park FAX **(203) 353-8487**
Stamford, CT 06905 www.mrp-website.com

Merkley Newmann Harty (212) 366-3500
200 Varick St. (Near W. Houston St.) FAX **(212) 366-3637**
New York, NY 10014 www.mnh.com

MG&G Advertising, Inc. (646) 638-1447
www.mggadvertising.com

MGM Gold Communications (212) 869-7323
12 W. 31st St., Seventh Fl. FAX **(212) 869-7249**
(Near Fifth Ave.) www.mgmgoldcommunications.com
New York, NY 10001

Ogilvy & Mather, Inc. (212) 237-4000
309 W. 49th St. (Near Ninth Ave.) FAX **(310) 280-2699**
New York, NY 10019 www.ogilvy.com

Pedone & Partners (212) 627-3300
49 W. 27th St., Sixth Fl. FAX **(212) 627-3966**
(Near W. 15th St.) www.pedonepartners.com
New York, NY 10001

Publicis (212) 279-5550
Four Herald Square, 950 Sixth Ave. FAX **(212) 279-5560**
(Near W. 35th St.) www.publicis-usa.com
New York, NY 10001

Robotham Creative, Inc. (617) 817-5520
P.O. Box 539 www.robotham.com
North Scituate, MA 02060

Saatchi & Saatchi Advertising (212) 463-2000
375 Hudson St. (Near W. Houston St.) FAX **(212) 463-9855**
New York, NY 10014 www.saatchi.com

Scheer Advertising Agency (973) 762-8100
76 S. Orange Ave. FAX **(973) 762-7968**
South Orange, NJ 07079

Serino Coyne, Inc. (212) 626-2700
1515 Broadway, 36th Fl. FAX **(212) 626-2799**
(Near W. 44th St.) www.serinocoyne.com
New York, NY 10036

TBWA Chiat/Day, Inc. (212) 804-1000
488 Madison Ave., Seventh Fl. FAX **(212) 804-1200**
(Near E. 52nd St.) www.tbwachiat.com
New York, NY 10022

Uniworld Group, Inc. (212) 219-1600
100 Sixth Ave., 16th Fl. (Near Watts St.) FAX **(212) 219-6395**
New York, NY 10013 www.uniworldgroup.com

Young & Rubicam (212) 210-3000
285 Madison Ave. (Near W. 40th St.) FAX **(212) 490-9073**
New York, NY 10017 www.yandr.com

Advertising Agency Freelance Producers

Sloane Cooper	(516) 902-8700
	FAX (516) 791-9572
Andrea Davis	(917) 520-1254
Ann Faxon	(203) 438-8775
	(914) 523-0614
Kenneth Fried	(203) 323-3331
	(917) 822-8136
	FAX (203) 323-5221
Debbie Gleason	(917) 848-2553
	(718) 478-0633
Ruth Gutman	(212) 628-0106
	(917) 439-7165
	FAX (212) 628-0106
Rich Horlick	(201) 232-0495
	www.richhorlick.com
Sheran James	(949) 499-6010
	FAX (949) 499-5998
Lisa Kaplan	(917) 705-7702
	www.lisaproducer.com
Cindy Leibowitz	(212) 807-1381
	(917) 797-0080
	www.cindyleibowitz.com
Andrew Lippman	(917) 543-6500
	www.andrewlippman.tv
Walt Mitze	(917) 749-0397
	(914) 663-4499
	FAX (914) 663-4489
	www.waltmitze.com
Francesca Prada	(415) 378-8658
(Spanish & Italian)	
Ellen Rappaport	(212) 737-4992
	(917) 359-6358
Carin Zakes	(914) 325-1812
	www.carinzakes.com

Animation Production Companies

Animatus Studio (585) 232-1740
34 Winthrop St. www.animatusstudio.com
(Near Charlotte St.)
Rochester, NY 14607
Owner/Producer: Fred Armstrong
Director/Animator: Dave Puls

Animotion, Inc. (315) 471-3533
501 W. Fayette St., Ste. 141 FAX (315) 471-2730
(Near Wyoming St.) www.animotioninc.com
Syracuse, NY 13204

asterisk (212) 255-8880
20 W. 20th St., Ste. 405 www.asteriskpix.com
(Near Union Square West)
New York, NY 10011
Executive Producer: Richard O'Connor
Creative Director: Brian O'Connell

Atlantic Motion Pictures (212) 924-6170
162 W. 21st St., Fourth Fl. FAX (212) 989-8736
(Near Seventh Ave.) www.atlanticmotion.com
New York, NY 07641
President: Patrick Egan

Augenblick Studios, Inc. (718) 855-9226
20 Jay St. (Near Front St.) FAX (718) 855-9227
Brooklyn, NY 11201 www.augenblickstudios.com

Blue Sky Studios, Inc. (914) 259-6500
44 S. Broadway, 17th Fl. FAX (914) 259-6499
(Near Westchester Ave.) www.blueskystudios.com
White Plains, NY 10601
Creative Director: Chris Wedge
Animation Directors: Mark Baldo, Jan Carlee & Carlos Saldanha

Buzzco Associates, Inc. (212) 473-8800
33 Bleecker St. (Near Mott St.) FAX (212) 473-8891
New York, NY 10012
Director/Producers: Vincent Cafarelli & Candy Kugel

(917) 282-4756
Carl Paolino Studios, Inc. (917) 957-7305
Owner: Carl Paolino www.paolinostudios.com

Charged, LLC (718) 855-0216
573 Sackett St., Third Fl. FAX (718) 855-2202
(Near Third Ave.) www.charged.com
Brooklyn, NY 11217
Executive Producer: Alex Cohn
Head of Animation: Adam Pierce

Crank! It! Out!, Inc. (201) 927-0956
199 Owatonna St.
Haworth, NJ 07641
www.markmarek.org/animations/animations.html
(2D Animation, Animatics, Blue Screen Compositing, Broadcast Design, Character Animation, Character Design, Compositing, Computer Animation, Graphic Design, Green Screen Compositing, Illustrative Design, Motion Graphics, Storyboards & Visual FX)

Designomotion (917) 532-0738
67 E. 11th St., Ste. 324 www.designomotion.com
(Near Broadway)
New York, NY 10003
(2D Animation, 3D Animation, 3D Modeling, Blue/Green Screen Compositing, Broadcast Design, CGI, Compositing, Digital FX, Editorial, Graphic Design, Live Action Integration, Motion Graphics, Rotoscoping & Visual FX)
President: Joseph Silver

Digital Magic Animation, LLC (917) 576-2628
853 Broadway, Ste. 1601 www.digitalmagicanimation.com
(Near 14th St.)
New York, NY 10003
Animator: Nicole Kang

DMA Animation (212) 463-7370
89 Fifth Ave., Ste. 501 FAX (212) 463-7820
(Near E. 16th St.) www.dma-animation.com
New York, NY 10003
Creative Director: Tony Caio

Hornet, Inc. (917) 351-0520
116 W. Houston St., Fourth Fl. FAX (917) 351-0522
(Near Seventh Ave.) www.hornetinc.com
New York, NY 10012

(646) 435-9500
Humble TV (917) 593-6910
162 W. 21st St., Fourth Fl. www.humble.tv
New York, NY 10011

IBC Digital (716) 852-1724
230 Perry St., Ste. 31A FAX (716) 852-1735
Buffalo, NY 14204 www.ibcdigital.com
President/Executive Producer: Benjamin Porcari
Creative Director: Melissa Porcari
Technical Director: Trent Noble
Art Supervisor: R.C. Aradio

Ice Tea Productions (212) 557-8185
160 E. 38th St., Ste. 15B FAX (212) 687-1299
(Near Third Ave.) www.iceteaproductions.com
New York, NY 10016
Executive Producer: Rich Durkin

Integrated Studios (212) 334-4000
449 Washington St. FAX (212) 334-6969
New York, NY 10013 www.integratedstudios.com

Interface Arts (718) 788-0335
241 16th St., Ste. 2 www.interface_arts.com
(Near Sixth Ave.)
Brooklyn, NY 11215
Owner/Director: Robert Lyons
Sales Representative: Alessandra Zeka
Visual FX Supervisor: Peter Wallach
Post Production Supervisor: Jim Romaine

Inverse Media (203) 255-9620
P.O. Box 1072 www.inversemedia.com
Southport, CT 06490
(2D Paint, 3D Modeling & Compositing)

Jerard Studio, Inc. (718) 852-4128
481 Van Brunt St., Ste. 11D FAX (718) 852-2408
(Near Beard St.) www.jerardstudio.com
Brooklyn, NY 11231
President/Creative Director: John Jerard
Director/Animator/Cameraman: Chris Webb

LifeHouse Productions, LLC (860) 432-9177
P.O. Box 4007 www.lifehouseproductions.com
Manchester, CT 06045

Mechanism Digital, Inc. (646) 230-0230
514 W. 24th St., Third Fl. FAX (646) 336-8395
(Near 10th Ave.) www.mechanismdigital.com
New York, NY 10011
(2D Animation, 2D Paint, 3D Animation, 3D Modeling, Animatics, Blue Screen Compositing, Broadcast Design, CGI, Character Animation, Character Design, Compositing, Computer Animation, Digital FX, Digital Matte Painting, Digital Restoration, Editorial, Graphic Design, Green Screen Compositing, Live Action Integration, Matte Painting, Morphing, Motion Graphics, Previsualizations, Rotoscoping, Storyboards, Time-Lapse Photography, Ultimatte, Visual FX & Visual FX Supervision)
President/Visual FX Producer: Lucien J. Harriot

Rankin/Bass Productions   **(212) 582-4017**
24 W. 55th St. (Near Fifth Ave.)   www.rankinbass.com
New York, NY 10019
President: Arthur Rankin
VP Development: Peter Bakalian
Treasurer: Norman Topper

Rejectbarn, LLC   **(203) 866-1898**
23 S. Main St., Third Fl.   www.rejectbarn.com
Norwalk, CT 06854

Rembrandt Films   **(914) 763-5817**
34 Cross Pond Rd.   www.rembrandtfilms.com
(Near Ida Ln.)
Pound Ridge, NY 10576
President: Adam Snyder

Rhinofx   **(212) 986-1584**
50 E. 42nd St., 12th Fl.   FAX **(212) 986-2113**
(Near Madison Ave.)   www.rhinofx.com
New York, NY 10017
CEO/Partner: David Binstock
Executive VP/Editor/Partner: John Starace
Managing Director/Partner: Rick Wagonheim
VP/Executive Producer: Camille Geier
Sales Rep: Jay Broddock
Directors: Harry Dorrington, Arman Matin & Mark Steinberg
VP of Long Form Entertainment: Karin Levinson

Scholastic Entertainment   **(212) 389-3964**
557 Broadway (Near Prince St.)   FAX **(212) 389-3887**
New York, NY 10012   www.scholastic.com
Executive Vice President: Deborah Forte

Spontaneous   **(212) 317-0077**
575 Lexington Ave., 25th Fl.   FAX **(212) 317-1048**
(Near E. 51st St.)   www.spon.com
New York, NY 10022
Creative Director: John Leamy
Assoc. CD/Dir. of Animation: Lawrence Nimrichter
Director of Visual Effects: Andy Milkis
Head of Production: Bennett Lieber
Senior Producer: Bryce Edwards
Producers: Sarah Brown & Felili Rincon
Sales: Dana Dubay

Stardust Studios East   **(212) 334-7300**
591 Broadway, Second Fl.   FAX **(212) 334-7332**
New York, NY 10012   www.stardust.tv

Synthespian Studios   **(413) 458-0202**
96 Ballou Ln.   FAX **(413) 458-5089**
Williamstown, MA 01267   www.synthespians.net
(3D Animation, Character Animation, Computer Animation & Visual FX Supervision)
President: Diana Walczak
COO: Michael Van Himbergen
Executive Producer: Amanda Roth
Producer: Wendy Gipp
Directors: Jeff Kleiser & Diana Walczak

Two Animators! LLP   **(609) 838-1844**
3812 Quakerbridge Rd.   FAX **(609) 838-1846**
Hamilton, NJ 08619   www.twoanimators.com
(2D Animation)
Creative Director/Producer: Thomas Costantini
Animation Director/Producer: Joseph Costantini
Audio Engineer: Chris Kaplan
Writer: Gregg Boita

Commercial Directors

300ml	(212) 625-5600	www.hungryman.com
Toon Aerts	(212) 545-8500	www.publicdomainny.com
Casey Affleck	(212) 343-2020	www.rsafilms.com
Aggressive	(212) 242-7400	www.losthighwayfilms.com
Jason Alexander	(212) 685-6070	www.cfminternational.com
Monica Anderson	(212) 349-0369	www.blackwatchproductions.com
Wes Anderson	(212) 807-6901	www.moxiepictures.com
Philippe Andre	(212) 371-7711 / (212) 462-2700	www.companyfilms.net
Anouk	(212) 253-7400 / (310) 917-9191	www.celsiusfilms.com
Luis Argueta	(212) 866-5332	www.mayamediacorp.com
Robin Armstrong	(212) 481-6713	www.indartists.com
Arni and Kinski	(212) 463-7207	www.awhitelabelproduct.com
Stefan Arni	(212) 627-3600	www.hsiproductions.com
Matt Aselton	(212) 226-0661	www.epochfilms.com
Steve Ayson	(212) 545-8500	www.publicdomainny.com
Matt Badger	(212) 226-0661	www.epochfilms.com
Jorg Badura	(212) 727-1400	www.stocklandmartel.com
Geoff Barish	(310) 917-9191	www.untitled.tv
Nicholas Barker	(212) 431-3434	www.chelsea.com
Gilly Barnes	(212) 582-6050	www.mayslesfilms.com
Fabien Baron	(212) 925-8900	www.link-entertainment.com
Christopher Bean	(212) 529-3100	www.macguffin.com
Kevan Bean	(212) 529-3100	www.macguffin.com
Brian Belefant	(503) 715-2852 FAX (503) 287-5886	www.belefant.com
Brian Beletic	(212) 337-3327	www.smugglersite.com
Martin Bell	(212) 645-5800	www.cohnandco.com
Todd Bellanca	(917) 885-9513 / (310) 584-1460	www.toddbellanca.com
Sng Tong Beng	(212) 450-1616	www.cineinternational.net
Mark Benjamin	(212) 254-5285	www.benjaminproduction.com
Mark Raymon Bennett	(212) 645-5800 / (310) 917-9191	www.cohnandco.com
Peter Berg	(212) 627-3600	www.hsiproductions.com
Shari Berman	(212) 807-6901	www.moxiepictures.com
Evan Bernard	(212) 431-3434	www.chelsea.com
Ken Bernardini	(631) 351-5878	www.jalbertfilm.com
Wiebke Berndt	(212) 545-8500	www.publicdomainny.com
Brian Billow	(212) 625-5600	www.hungryman.com
Irv Blitz	(212) 627-3600	www.hsiproductions.com
Neill Blomkamp	(212) 343-2020	www.rsafilms.com
Chris Bonanno	(973) 575-5400 FAX (973) 575-6708	www.tristarstudios.com
Jan Bonny	(212) 545-8500	www.publicdomainny.com
Teddy Borsen	(212) 924-8880	www.edgefilms.us
Oliver Bradford	(212) 545-8500	www.publicdomainny.com
Mark Brinster	(818) 990-8993	www.ambitiousent.com
James Brown	(212) 337-3327	www.smugglersite.com
Gabrielle Bullard	(212) 450-1616	www.cineinternational.net
Scott Burns	(212) 627-3600	www.hsiproductions.com
Nanette Burstein	(212) 625-5600	www.hungryman.com
Paul Cade	(212) 645-5800	www.cohnandco.com
Tony Caio	(212) 463-7370 FAX (212) 463-7820	www.dma-animation.com
David Cameron	(212) 679-7199	www.theartistscompany.com

Don Cameron	(212) 463-7207	www.awhitelabelproduct.com
Paul Canney	(617) 779-8808	www.element.cc
Yves Cape	(310) 652-8778	www.lspagency.net
Rey Carlson	(212) 226-0661	www.epochfilms.com
Joe Carnahan	(212) 343-2020	www.rsafilms.com
Tony Caronia	(212) 869-8833	www.gargoylefilms.com
Nick Cassavetes	(212) 685-6070	www.cfminternational.com
Michael Cerny	(212) 794-9030	
Derek Chang	(212) 450-1616	www.cineinternational.net
Bob Chappell	(212) 387-0057	
Christian Charles	(212) 253-7400	www.celsiusfilms.com
Steve Chase	(212) 677-7500	www.gofilm.com
Peter Cherry	(212) 867-4030	www.screengemsstudios.com
John Chimples	(212) 375-0911 FAX (212) 375-0915	www.imltd.com
Spencer Chinoy	(212) 807-6901	www.moxiepictures.com
Samuel Christopher	(212) 625-5500	www.hungryman.com
Andrew Christou	(212) 807-6901	www.moxiepictures.com
Eddy Chu	(212) 242-7400	www.losthighwayfilms.com
Curtis Clark	(323) 460-4767	www.jacobandkoleagency.com
Mark Claywell	(212) 867-4030	www.screengemsstudios.com
The Coen Brothers	(212) 371-7711 (212) 462-2700	www.companyfilms.net
Donald Cohen	(914) 941-2357	www.moodcreations.com
Rob Michael Cohn	(212) 399-3150	www.bigchairny.com
Barney Cokeliss	(212) 343-2020	www.rsafilms.com
Charlie Cole	(212) 645-5800	www.cohnandco.com
Jim Collins	(212) 529-3100	www.macguffin.com
Elena Colombo	(508) 228-8073	www.september.com
Jeffrey Cooney	(212) 867-4030	www.screengemsstudios.com
Henry Corra	(212) 965-8600	www.corrafilms.com
Cosimo	(212) 905-0677	www.cosimoandcompany.com
Wayne Craig	(212) 794-9030	
Jeff Cronenweth	(310) 917-9191	www.untitled.tv
Tim Cronenweth	(310) 917-9191	www.untitled.tv
Cameron Crowe	(212) 807-6901	www.moxiepictures.com
Michael Cuesta	(212) 679-7199 (212) 625-5600	www.theartistscompany.com
Alan Cumming	(212) 941-7680	www.zoomazooma.com
John Dahl	(212) 354-8188	www.epandmedia.com
Boris Damast	(212) 794-9030	
Skip D'Amico	(212) 679-7199	www.theartistscompany.com
Lars Damoiseaux	(212) 545-8500	www.publicdomainny.com
Jonathan David	(212) 677-7500	www.gofilm.net
Marek Dawid	(212) 533-2200	
Richard DeLigter	(212) 271-0020	www.realprod.com
Henri De Maar	(212) 545-8500	www.publicdomainny.com
Christopher Desantis	(310) 917-9191	www.untitled.tv
Gerard De Thame	(212) 627-3600	www.hsiproductions.com
Tom Dey	(212) 343-2020	www.rsafilms.com
Ben Dickinson	(212) 343-2020	www.rsafilms.com
Arno Dierickx	(212) 545-8500	www.publicdomainny.com
The Directors Network 3685 Motor Ave., Ste. 220 Los Angeles, CA 90034 (Reps for Commercial Directors)	(818) 906-0006 FAX (818) 301-2224	www.thedirectorsnetwork.com
Abby Dix	(818) 906-0006	www.thedirectorsnetwork.com
Tripp Dixon	(856) 222-5675	www.nflfilms.com
David Dobkin	(212) 677-7500	www.gofilm.net
Phelim Dolan	(212) 807-7123	www.0260.com

Ben Dolphin	(212) 289-6232	www.ecreativesearch.com
Andrew Dominik	(212) 343-2020	www.rsafilms.com
Stan Dragoti	(212) 867-4030	www.screengemsstudios.com
Dan Driscoll	(508) 228-8073	www.september.com
Bruno Ducharme	(212) 450-1616	www.cineinternational.net
Laurence Dunmore	(212) 343-2020	www.rsafilms.com
Duplass Brothers	(212) 343-2020	www.rsafilms.com
Warren Du Press	(212) 253-7400	www.celsiusfilms.com
Breck Eisner	(212) 431-3434	www.chelsea.com
Sean Ellis	(212) 343-2020	www.rsafilms.com
Mona El Mansouri	(212) 462-2700	www.villains.com
Steve Eshelman	(212) 647-1300	www.crossroadsfilms.com
Lauri Faggioni	(212) 343-2020	www.rsafilms.com
Jon Fauer	(212) 643-1736, FAX (212) 643-1802	www.fauer.com
Caitlin Felton	(212) 677-7500	www.gofilm.net
Roderick Fenske	(212) 625-5600	www.hungryman.com
Alex Fernbach	(201) 963-5900	www.arf-co.tv
Tom Finerty	(212) 477-1114	www.lopespictureco.com
Kevin Fitzgerald	(212) 431-3434	www.chelsea.com
Brett Foraker	(212) 343-2020	www.rsafilms.com
David Frankham	(212) 679-7199, (212) 337-3327	www.theartistscompany.com
Larry Frey	(212) 431-3434	www.chelsea.com
Rick Friedberg	(818) 990-8993	www.ambitiousent.com
Marvin Friedman	(888) 530-3886	
Michael Frings	(212) 481-6713	www.indartists.com
Paul Fuentes	(212) 867-4030, (818) 990-8993	www.screengemsstudios.com
Beth Galthon	(201) 963-5900	www.arf-co.tv
Paul Gay	(212) 625-5600	www.hungryman.com
Nacho Gayan	(212) 337-3327	www.smugglersite.com
Michael Gersh	(718) 638-1107	
Richard Gibson	(212) 431-3434, (212) 450-1616	www.chelsea.com
Carl Ginsberg	(212) 689-7678	www.parkavenuepost.com
Robert Giraldi	(212) 966-1212	www.giraldi.com
Adam Goldstein	(212) 343-2020	www.rsafilms.com
Lionel Goldstein	(212) 545-8500	www.publicdomainny.com
Dylan Goss	(212) 645-5800	www.cohnandco.com
Fred Goss	(212) 371-7711	www.companyfilms.net
Jean-Paul Goude	(212) 463-7207	www.awhitelabelproduct.com
Martin Granger	(212) 807-6901	www.moxiepictures.com
F. Gary Gray	(212) 627-3600	www.hsiproductions.com
David Gordon Green	(212) 431-3434	www.chelsea.com
Steph Green	(212) 343-2020	www.littleminx.tv
Lauren Greenfield	(212) 431-3434	www.chelsea.com
Timothy Greenfield-Sanders	(212) 727-1400	www.stocklandmartel.com
Paula Greif	(212) 226-0661	www.epochfilms.com
Marlon Griffin	(212) 545-8500	www.publicdomainny.com
Sebastien Grousset	(212) 647-1300	www.crossroadsfilms.com
The Guard Brothers	(212) 462-2700	www.villains.com
Christopher Guest	(212) 677-7500	www.gofilm.net
H5	(212) 343-2020	www.rsafilms.com
Tim Hamilton	(212) 677-7500	www.gofilm.net
Henrik Hansen	(212) 343-2020	www.rsafilms.com
Happy	(212) 337-3327	www.smugglersite.com
Johnny Hardstaff	(212) 343-2020	www.littleminx.tv

Neil Harris	(212) 337-3327	www.smugglersite.com
Alfred Hau	(212) 450-1616	www.cineinternational.net
Michael Haussman	(212) 627-3600	www.hsiproductions.com
Haxan	(212) 431-3434	www.chelsea.com
Adrian Hayward	(212) 450-1616	www.cineinternational.net
Sonja Heiss	(212) 545-8500	www.publicdomainny.com
Norbert Heitker	(212) 545-8500	www.publicdomainny.com
Paul Henschel	(508) 228-8073	www.september.com
Jared Hess	(212) 807-6901	www.moxiepictures.com
Dennis Hitchcock	(212) 450-1616	www.cineinternational.net
Hobby	(212) 343-2020	www.rsafilms.com
Ruedi Hofmann	(212) 727-1400	www.stocklandmartel.com
James Holt	(212) 431-3434	www.chelsea.com
Bill Hudson	(212) 679-7199	www.theartistscompany.com
Steve Hudson	(212) 625-5600	www.hungryman.com
Paul Hunter	(212) 627-3600	www.hsiproductions.com
Bruce Hurwitt	(212) 647-1300	www.crossroadsfilms.com
Dominique Issermann	(212) 925-8900	www.link-entertainment.com
David Jaffe	(212) 966-1212	www.giraldi.com
Mikael Jansson	(212) 463-7207	www.awhitelabelproduct.com
Julia Jason	(212) 647-1300	www.crossroadsfilms.com
Andrews Jenkins	(212) 677-7500	www.gofilm.net
Robert Jitzmark	(212) 625-5600	www.hungryman.com
Hugh Johnson	(212) 343-2020	www.rsafilms.com
Jamie Johnson	(212) 685-6070	www.cfminternational.com
Carolyn Jones	(212) 925-8900	www.link-entertainment.com
Michael Joy	(212) 431-3434 / (212) 450-1616	www.chelsea.com
Miranda July	(212) 226-0661	www.epochfilms.com
Joseph Kahn	(212) 627-3600	www.hsiproductions.com
Miles Kahn	(718) 274-7651 / (917) 572-3182	home.earthlink.net/~phisto
Nadav Kander	(212) 727-1400	www.stocklandmartel.com
Jon Kane	(212) 888-8999	www.shootingstarsintl.com
Kaos	(212) 685-6070	www.cfminternational.com
Ian Karr	(212) 246-4634	www.ikacollective.com
Tony Kaye	(212) 655-6555	www.supplyanddemand.tv
Billy Kent	(212) 675-8287	www.firmcreative.com
Siggi Kinski	(212) 627-3600	www.hsiproductions.com
Mat Kirkby	(212) 343-2020	www.rsafilms.com
Justin Klarenbeck	(310) 917-9191	www.untitled.tv
Mark Klein	(212) 794-9030	
Jeff Kleiser	(413) 664-8176	www.synthespians.net
Rick Knief	(212) 647-1300 / (310) 917-9191	www.untitled.tv
Jesper Kouthoofd	(212) 343-2020	www.littleminx.tv
Randy Krallman	(212) 627-3600 / (212) 337-3327	www.hsiproductions.com
Johan Kramer	(212) 431-3434	www.chelsea.com
David LaChapelle	(212) 627-3600	www.hsiproductions.com
Dominic Lahiff	(212) 643-1736	www.cec-entertainment.com
Eric Laneuville	(212) 867-4030	www.screengemsstudios.com
Stan Larsen	(212) 477-1114	www.lopespictureco.com
Axel Laubscher	(212) 462-2700	www.villains.com
Robert Leacock	(917) 797-7910	
Alan Lebow	(212) 869-8833	www.gargoylefilms.com
Ian Leech	(212) 481-6713	www.indartists.com
John Leguizamo	(212) 685-6070	www.cfminternational.com

Gustavo Leme	(212) 481-6713	www.indartists.com
Matt Lenski	(212) 226-0661	www.epochfilms.com
Dan Lerner	(212) 888-8999	www.shootingstarsintl.com
Michael Lesser	(212) 691-3859	www.grandviewisland.com
David Levin	(212) 645-5800	www.cohnandco.com
Dan Levinson	(212) 807-6901	www.moxiepictures.com
Sasha Levinson	(212) 242-7400 / (212) 941-7680	www.losthighwayfilms.com
Elyse Lewin	(212) 888-8999	www.shootingstarsintl.com
Nick Lewin	(212) 647-1300	www.crossroadsfilms.com
Peter Lindbergh	(212) 463-7207	www.awhitelabelproduct.com
John Lindley	(212) 260-6545	www.perrettiproductions.com
LITTLE x	(212) 627-3600	www.hsiproductions.com
Nick Livesey	(212) 343-2020	www.rsafilms.com
Mike Long	(212) 226-0661	www.epochfilms.com
Rob Lopes	(212) 477-1114	www.lopespictureco.com
Henry Lu	(212) 807-6901	www.moxiepictures.com
Sidney Lumet	(212) 685-6070	www.cfminternational.com
Kevin MacDonald	(212) 431-3434	www.chelsea.com
Eduardo MacLean	(212) 450-1616	www.cineinternational.net
Stuart MacLeod	(212) 450-1616	www.cineinternational.net
Jeff Madoff	(212) 265-0137	www.madoffproductions.com
Kate Magee	(212) 675-8287	www.firmcreative.com
Sara Marandi	(212) 371-7711 / (212) 462-2700	www.companyfilms.net
Phil Marco	(212) 929-8082	www.philmarco.com
Andy Margetson	(212) 647-1300	www.crossroadsfilms.com
Rob Markopoulos	(856) 222-5675	www.nflfilms.com
Dick Marks	(212) 450-1616	www.cineinternational.net
Gregory Marquette	(818) 990-8993	www.ambitiousent.com
Stephen Marro	(212) 387-0057	
Bill Marshall	(212) 533-2200	
Rob Marshall	(212) 807-6901	www.moxiepictures.com
Glenn Martin	(310) 917-9191	www.untitled.tv
Renny Maslow	(212) 337-3327	www.smugglersite.com
Adam Massey	(310) 917-9191	www.untitled.tv
Gregory Maya	(212) 679-7199	www.theartistscompany.com
Brit McAdams	(212) 253-7400	www.celsiusfilms.com
Edna McCallion	(212) 226-0661	www.epochfilms.com
Marcus McCallum	(212) 647-1300	www.crossroadsfilms.com
Andrew McCarthy	(212) 685-6070	www.cfminternational.com
Tom McCarthy	(212) 647-1300	www.crossroadsfilms.com
Wayne McClammy	(212) 625-5600	www.hungryman.com
Ryan McFaul	(212) 941-7680	www.zoomazooma.com
David McNally	(212) 371-7711 / (212) 462-2700	www.companyfilms.net
Simon McQuoid	(212) 677-7500	www.gofilm.net
Charles Mehling	(212) 431-3434	www.chelsea.com
Nicholas Melillo	(818) 990-8993	www.ambitiousent.com
Melina	(212) 343-2020	www.rsafilms.com
Sam Mendes	(212) 343-2020	www.rsafilms.com
Hein Mevissen	(212) 625-5600	www.hungryman.com
David Michalek	(212) 463-7207	www.awhitelabelproduct.com
Paul Middleditch	(212) 463-7207 / (212) 627-3600	www.awhitelabelproduct.com
Josh Miller	(212) 343-2020	www.rsafilms.com
Mike Miller	(818) 990-8993	www.ambitiousent.com
Adrian Moat	(212) 343-2020	www.rsafilms.com

Sarah Moon	(212) 925-8900	www.link-entertainment.com
Ben Mor	(212) 343-2020	www.littleminx.tv
Errol Morris	(212) 807-6901	www.moxiepictures.com
Phil Morrison	(212) 226-0661	www.epochfilms.com
Bob Morrow	(212) 477-1114	www.lopespictureco.com
Koen Mortier	(212) 545-8500	www.publicdomainny.com
Claude Mougin	(212) 807-7123	www.0260.com
Bob Mowen	(212) 807-7123	www.0260.com
David Mullet	(212) 343-2020	www.littleminx.tv
Barry Myers	(212) 450-1616	www.cineinternational.net
Ken Nahoum	(212) 924-8880	www.edgefilms.us
Ne-O	(212) 337-3327	www.smugglersite.com
Amy Nicholson	(212) 625-5500	www.hungryman.com
Dewey Nicks	(212) 462-2700	www.villains.com
nObrain	(212) 463-7207	www.awhitelabelproduct.com
Michael Normand	(212) 794-9030	
Joe Nussbaum	(212) 807-6901	www.moxiepictures.com
Matt Ogens	(917) 532-0995	
John O'Hagan	(212) 343-2020	www.rsafilms.com
Angelo Pacifici	(310) 313-3762 / (818) 990-8993	www.ambitiousent.com
Chaz Palminteri	(212) 685-6070	www.cfminternational.com
Michael Patterson	(212) 242-7400	www.losthighwayfilms.com
Stephen Pearson	(212) 625-5500	www.hungryman.com
Mark Pellington	(212) 647-1300	www.crossroadsfilms.com
Marius Penczner	(212) 354-8188	www.epandmedia.com
Matthew Penn	(212) 685-6070	www.cfminternational.com
Jesse Peretz	(212) 343-2020	www.rsafilms.com
Jim Perretti	(212) 260-6545	www.perrettiproductions.com
Dwayne B. Perryman III	(917) 225-0889	www.monsoonfilmsinc.com
Pes	(212) 545-8500	www.publicdomainny.com
Todd Phillips	(212) 807-6901	www.moxiepictures.com
Dario Piana	(212) 655-6550	www.order.tv
Jeffery Plansker	(212) 655-6555	www.supplyanddemand.tv
Greg Popp	(212) 655-6555	www.supplyanddemand.tv
Frederic Potter	(212) 450-1616	www.cineinternational.net
Jose Antonio Pratt	(212) 655-6555	www.supplyanddemand.tv
Jeff Preiss	(212) 226-0661	www.epochfilms.com
Joe Public	(212) 627-3600	www.hsiproductions.com
Robert Pulcini	(212) 807-6901	www.moxiepictures.com
Gualter Pupo	(212) 625-5500	www.hungryman.com
Bob Purman	(212) 807-6901	www.moxiepictures.com
Bill Quinn	(732) 237-0525	
Christopher Quinn	(212) 431-3434	www.chelsea.com
Sam Raimi	(212) 941-7680	www.zoomazooma.com
David Ramser	(212) 679-7199	www.theartistscompany.com
Greg Ramsey	(212) 253-7400	www.celsiusfilms.com
Harry Rankin	(212) 450-1616	www.harryrankin.com
Brett Ratner	(212) 627-3600	www.hsiproductions.com
Adam Reed	(310) 917-9191	www.untitled.tv
Peyton Reed	(212) 807-6901	www.moxiepictures.com
Tony Richards	(818) 990-8993	www.ambitiousent.com
Tim Richardson	(212) 463-7207	www.awhitelabelproduct.com
Terry Rietta	(212) 462-2700	www.villains.com
Carl Erik Rinsch	(212) 343-2020	www.rsafilms.com

Nick Robertson	(212) 463-7207 www.awhitelabelproduct.com	Ridley Scott	(212) 343-2020 www.rsafilms.com
Larry Robins	(212) 477-1114 www.lopespictureco.com	Tony Scott	(212) 343-2020 www.rsafilms.com
Chris Robinson	(212) 627-3600 www.hsiproductions.com	Joe Scudiero	(212) 260-6545 www.perrettiproductions.com
Matthew Rolston	(212) 627-3600 www.hsiproductions.com	Selby	(212) 253-7400 www.celsiusfilms.com
Jenna Rosher	(212) 685-6070 www.cfminternational.com	Mark Seliger	(212) 343-2020 www.littleminx.tv
Mark Ross	(908) 233-7271	Dawn Shadforth	(212) 343-2020 www.rsafilms.com
Michael Rowles	(212) 655-6550 www.order.tv	Steven Shainberg	(508) 228-8073 www.september.com
Jorge Rubia	(212) 533-2200	Jim Sheridan	(212) 807-6901 www.moxiepictures.com
Ondrej Rudavsky	(818) 990-8993 www.ambitiousent.com	Howard Shir	(212) 941-7680 www.zoomazooma.com
The Russo Brothers	(212) 343-2020 www.rsafilms.com	Andre Siebert	(818) 990-8993 www.ambitiousent.com
Alex Rutterford	(212) 343-2020 www.rsafilms.com	Marcos Siega	(212) 625-5600 www.hungryman.com
Bill Ruvolo	(212) 689-7678 www.parkavenuepost.com	Jerry Simpson	(718) 349-9220 www.sfiproductions.com
Vittorio Sacco	(212) 645-5800 www.cohnandco.com	Peggy Sirota	(212) 627-3600 www.hsiproductions.com
Neil Salley	(508) 228-8073 www.september.com	Neal Slavin	(212) 925-8900 www.link-entertainment.com
Frank Samuel	(212) 533-2200	Adam Smith	(212) 343-2020 www.rsafilms.com
Joakim Sandstrom	(212) 679-7199 www.theartistscompany.com	Chris Smith	(212) 337-3327 www.smugglersite.com
Morten Sandtroen	(212) 675-6070 www.nonstoppictures.com	Jim Field Smith	(212) 685-6070 www.cfminternational.com
Paul Santana	(212) 655-6550 www.order.tv	Kevin Smith	(212) 807-6901 www.moxiepictures.com
Antonio Saraceno	(212) 450-1616 www.cineinternational.net	Eidur Snorri	(212) 337-3327 www.smugglersite.com
Malik Hassan Sayeed	(212) 343-2020 www.rsafilms.com	Peter Sollett	(212) 807-6901 www.moxiepictures.com
Howard Schatz	(212) 533-2200	Michael Somoroff	(212) 529-3100 www.macguffin.com
Tom Schiller	(212) 253-0333 FAX (212) 253-0330	Victor Sonder	(856) 222-5675 www.nflfilms.com
Stan Schofield	(212) 633-8700 www.schofieldfilms.com	Kevin Spacey	(212) 343-2020 www.rsafilms.com
Mattias Schut	(212) 545-8500 www.publicdomainny.com	Mark Story	(212) 647-1300 www.crossroadsfilms.com
Rudi Schwab	(617) 779-8808 www.element.cc	Mitch Stratten	(212) 625-5600 www.hungryman.com
Jake Scott	(212) 343-2020 www.rsafilms.com	Stylewar	(212) 337-3327 www.smugglersite.com
Jordan Scott	(212) 343-2020 www.rsafilms.com	Santiago Suarez	(203) 655-9500 www.ssantiagoinc.com
Luke Scott	(212) 343-2020 www.rsafilms.com		

Name	Contact
Jeanne Suggs	(212) 398-4200 www.suggsmedia.com
Josh Taft	(212) 627-3600 www.hsiproductions.com
Hideyuki Tanaka	(212) 625-5500 www.hungryman.com
David Tennant	(212) 655-6550 www.order.tv
Fausto Terán	(212) 675-8287 www.firmcreative.com
Leen Thijisse	(212) 727-1400 www.stocklandmartel.com
Jeff Thomas	(212) 371-7711 www.companyfilms.net
Pam Thomas	(212) 807-6901 www.moxiepictures.com
Nick Thornton-Jones	(212) 253-7400 www.celsiusfilms.com
Bart Timmer	(212) 545-8500 www.publicdomainny.com
Frank Todaro	(212) 807-6901 www.moxiepictures.com
Mark Toia	(212) 450-1616 www.cineinternational.net
Damien Toogood	(212) 431-3434 www.chelsea.com
Joachim Trier	(212) 343-2020 www.rsafilms.com
Alex Turner	(212) 807-7123 www.0260.com
Eden Tyler	(212) 941-7680 www.zoomazooma.com
Phillip Van	(212) 343-2020 www.littleminx.tv
Lieven Van Baelen	(212) 545-8500 www.publicdomainny.com
Rogier Van Der Ploeg	(646) 414-8444 (212) 545-8500 www.publicdomainny.com
Bruce Van Dusen	(212) 253-7400 www.celsiusfilms.com
Joe Vanhoutteghem	(212) 545-8500 www.publicdomainny.com
Scott Vincent	(212) 625-5600 www.hungryman.com
Peter Viola	(212) 472-8789
Taika Waititi	(212) 625-5600 www.hungryman.com
Diana Walczak	(413) 664-8176 www.synthespians.net
Stacy Wall	(212) 226-0661 www.epochfilms.com
Markus Walter	(212) 677-7500 www.gofilm.net
Harvey Wang	(212) 253-7400 www.celsiusfilms.com
Jeremy Warshaw	(212) 645-5800 www.cohnandco.com
John Waters	(212) 807-6901 www.moxiepictures.com
Albert Watson	(212) 675-6767 www.cyclopsnyc.com
Paul Weiland	(212) 431-3434 www.chelsea.com
Benjamin Weinstein	(212) 677-7500 www.gofilm.net
Jeff Weiser	(818) 906-0006 www.thedirectorsnetwork.com
Terry Wendell	(212) 888-8999 www.shootingstarsintl.com
Julian West	(212) 529-3100 www.macguffin.com
Ross Whitaker	(201) 963-5900 www.arf-co.tv
Declan Whitebloom	(212) 343-2020 www.rsafilms.com
Christopher Wilcha	(212) 431-3434 www.chelsea.com
Eric Will	(212) 450-1616 www.cineinternational.net
Tony Williams	(212) 450-1616 www.cineinternational.net
Theresa Wingert	(212) 529-3100 www.macguffin.com
Henning Winkelmann	(212) 529-3100 www.macguffin.com
Bruce Wolf	(212) 727-1400 www.stocklandmartel.com
Roger Woodburne	(212) 867-4030 www.screengemsstudios.com
Troy Word	(212) 675-8287 www.firmcreative.com
Jim Yukich	(212) 354-8188 www.epandmedia.com
Ivan Zacharias	(212) 337-3327 www.smugglersite.com
Zack and J.C.	(212) 242-7400 www.losthighwayfilms.com
Harald Zwart	(212) 371-7711 (212) 462-2700 www.companyfilms.net

Commercial Production Companies

4-D Creative Media (212) 599-6699
Four E. 46th St., Third Fl. (646) 483-7768
(Near Fifth Ave.) FAX (212) 499-9081
New York, NY 10017 www.4-dcreative.com
Executive Producer: Peter Cascone

903Films (212) 674-0986
515 Greenwich St., Ste. 202 FAX (212) 380-1258
New York, NY 10013 www.903films.com

AAA Acme Discount Film Works (718) 928-3812
56 Fifth Ave. (Near St. Mark's Pl.) (917) 861-4120
Brooklyn, NY 11217 www.aaaacme.com

Air Sea Land Productions, Inc. (718) 626-2646
19-69 Steinway St. (Near 20th Ave.) (888) 275-5367
Astoria, NY 11105 FAX (718) 626-1493
www.airsealand.com

Arf & Co. (201) 963-5900
710 Clinton St. (800) 929-4355
Hoboken, NJ 07030 FAX (201) 963-5757
www.arfco.tv
Executive Producer: Mark Fitzmartin
Directors: Alex Fernbach, Beth Galthon & Ross Whitaker

The Artists Company (212) 679-7199
38 W. 21st St., 12th Fl. (323) 650-4722
(Near Fifth Ave.) FAX (212) 741-1519
New York, NY 10010 www.theartistscompany.com
Executive Producers: Roberto Cecchini & Lori Lober
Vice President: Sally Antonacchio
Head of Production: Susan Burton
Directors: David Cameron, Michael Cuesta, Skip D'Amico, David Frankham, Bill Hudson, Gregory Maya, David Ramser & Joakim Sandstrom
Sales Reps: Denise Blate & Mary Eiff

Atlantic Motion Pictures (212) 924-6170
162 W. 21st St., Fourth Fl. FAX (212) 989-8736
(Near Seventh Ave.) www.atlanticmotion.com
New York, NY 10011
President/Executive Producer: Patrick Egan

Mario Battistoni (212) 888-8999
www.shootingstarsintl.com

Ben Dolphin Productions (212) 289-6232
www.ecreativesearch.com
President/Director/Cameraman: Ben Dolphin
Executive Producer: Katherine McGowan

Benjamin Productions, Inc. (212) 254-5285
60 E. Eighth St. (Near Mercer St.) FAX (212) 473-2905
New York, NY 10003 www.benjaminproduction.com
Producer: Jamie Lustberg
Director/Cameraman: Mark Benjamin

Bill Quinn Productions (732) 237-0525
P.O. Box 213
Ocean Gate, NJ 08740
Producer/Director: Bill Quinn

Black Watch Productions (212) 349-0369
49 Murray St., Ste. 1 (Near Church St.) FAX (212) 349-1335
New York, NY 10007 www.blackwatchproductions.com
Executive Producer: John Anderson
Executive Producer/Director: Monica Anderson
Production Manager: Peter Gagnon

bobsyouruncle. (212) 545-7800
638 E. Sixth St., 3rd Fl. FAX (212) 545-0398
New York, NY 10009 www.bobsyouruncle.tv

Bocce Club Pictures, LLC (212) 414-2220
104 E. 25th St., 12th Fl. FAX (212) 414-2206
(Near Park Ave.) www.bocceclubpictures.com
New York, NY 10010

Camelot Communications Group (212) 229-1150
650 Halstead Ave., Ste. 202 (914) 777-7900
Mamaroneck, NY 10543 FAX (914) 777-7904
www.camelotcommunications.tv
Executive Producer: Louis LaRose

Celsius Films (212) 253-7400
115 E. 30th St., Second Fl. FAX (212) 253-8199
(Near Park Ave. South) www.celsiusfilms.com
New York, NY 10016
Executive Producers: Robert Fisher & Stephanie Oakley
Head of Production: Holly Jenkins
Directors: Anouk, Christian Charles, Warren Du Press, Brit McAdams, Greg Ramsey, Selby, Nick Thornton-Jones, Bruce Van Dusen & Harvey Wang
East Coast Sales Reps: Carolyn Hill & Roxanne and Co.
Midwest Sales Rep: Liz Laine Reps
West Coast Sales Rep: Class Represents

Chelsea Pictures (212) 431-3434
122 Hudson St., Sixth Fl. (323) 860-8030
(Near N. Moore St.) FAX (212) 431-0199
New York, NY 10013 www.chelsea.com
Partner/Executive Producer: Allison Amon
Partner/Executive Producer/Head of Sales: Lisa Mehling
Executive Producer: Katy Greene
Head of Production: John LaChapelle
Directors: Nicholas Barker, Evan Bernard, Breck Eisner, Kevin Fitzgerald, Larry Frey, Richard Gibson, David Gordon Green, Lauren Greenfield, Haxan, James Holt, Michael Joy, Johan Kramer, Kevin MacDonald, Charles Mehling, Christopher Quinn, Damien Toogood, Paul Weiland & Christopher Wilcha
National Sales Rep: Kari Romeo
East Coast Sales Rep: Jared Shapiro
Midwest Sales Rep: Jim Robison
West Coast Sales Reps: Mark Andrews & Astrid Steel

Cine/drsa International (212) 450-1616
222 E. 44th St., Fourth Fl. (917) 865-1246
(Near Third Ave.) FAX (646) 688-2736
New York, NY 10017 www.cineinternational.net
Executive Producer: Paul Rosen
Directors: Sng Tong Beng, Gabrielle Bullard, Derek Chang, Bruno Ducharme, Richard Gibson, Alfred Hau, Adrian Hayward, Dennis Hitchcock, Michael Joy, Eduardo MacLean, Stuart MacLeod, Dick Marks, Barry Myers, Frederic Potter, Harry Rankin, Antonio Saraceno, Mark Toia, Eric Will & Tony Williams

City Lights Productions (212) 679-4400
Six E. 39th St., Third Fl. www.citylightsmedia.com
(Near Sixth Ave.)
New York, NY 10016
President/CEO: Danny Fisher
President: Jack Fisher

Cohn + Company (212) 645-5800
12 W. 23rd St., Fourth Fl. FAX (212) 645-7220
(Near Fifth Ave.) www.cohnandco.com
New York, NY 10010
President: Jack Cohn
Executive Producer: Tony Cunningham
Head of Sales: Forsberg McCarley
Directors: Martin Bell, Mark Raymon Bennett, Paul Cade, Dylan Goss & Jeremy Warshaw
Director/Cameramen: Charlie Cole, David Levin & Vittorio Sacco

Company (212) 371-7711
www.companyfilms.net
Owner/Executive Producer: Robin Benson
Executive Producer: Richard Goldstein
Head of Production: Robert Nackman
Directors: Philippe Andre, The Coen Brothers, Fred Goss, Sara Marandi, David McNally, Jeff Thomas & Harald Zwart
Head of Sales: Laura Dane

Compulsive Pictures, Inc.   **(212) 807-0050**
37 W. 20th St., Ste. 604   FAX **(212) 645-1787**
(Near Sixth Ave.)   www.compulsivepictures.com
New York, NY 10011
Executive Producers: Donald O'Connor & Jack Turney

Cornerstone Pictures   **(610) 649-3090**
47 Haverford Station Rd.   FAX **(610) 649-6206**
Haverford, PA 19041   www.cornerstonepicturesinc.com
President: Gloria Lewis
Executive Vice President: Bill German
Coordinator: Tricia Pompilio

Corra Films, Inc.   **(212) 965-8600**
Executive Producer: Alex Johnson   FAX **(212) 965-8660**
Director: Henry Corra   www.corrafilms.com

Cosimo and Company   **(212) 905-0677**
435 W. 19th St. (Near Ninth Ave.)   FAX **(973) 726-3832**
New York, NY 10011   www.cosimoandcompany.com
Director/Cameraman: Cosimo
Executive Producer: Irene Scianna

Creative Film Management
International, Inc.   **(212) 685-6070**
430 W. 14th St., Ste. 402   FAX **(212) 545-0976**
(Near Washington St.)   www.cfminternational.com
New York, NY 10014
President/Executive Producer: Lou Addesso
Executive Producer: Andrew Swee
Directors: Jason Alexander, Nick Cassavetes, Jamie Johnson, Kaos, John Leguizamo, Sidney Lumet, Andrew McCarthy, Chazz Palminteri, Matthew Penn, Jenna Rosher & Jim Field Smith

Crossroads Films   **(212) 647-1300**
136 W. 21st St., Seventh Fl.   FAX **(212) 647-9090**
(Near Sixth Ave.)   www.crossroadsfilms.com
New York, NY 10011
Executive Producer: Charlie Curran
Head of Production: Frank Dituri
Directors: Steve Eshelman, Sebastien Grousset, Bruce Hurwitt, Julia Jason, Rick Knief, Nick Lewin, Andy Margetson, Marcus McCallum, Tom McCarthy, Mark Pellington & Mark Story

cYclops productions   **(212) 675-6767**
43 Clarkson St., Second Fl.   FAX **(212) 924-3213**
(Near Greenwich St.)   www.cyclopsnyc.com
New York, NY 10014
President/Executive Producer: Michael Jurkovac
Executive Producer: Tim Mack
Head of Production: Brody McHugh
Director: Albert Watson

    (917) 544-4188
Ⓐ Directors Film Company   **31 653 865 319**
Executive Producer: Richard Coll

Edge Films/
Ken Nahoum Productions   **(212) 924-8880**
55 Van Dam St., 16th Fl.   FAX **(212) 924-0479**
(Near Hudson St.)   www.edgefilms.us
New York, NY 10013
Executive Producer: Ken Nahoum
Directors: Ken Nahoum & Teddy Borsen

Element Productions   **(617) 779-8808**
129 Braintree St.   FAX **(617) 779-8818**
Boston, MA 02134   www.element.cc
Executive Producer: Brian Smith
Head of Production: Persis Koch
Directors: Paul Canney & Rudi Schwab

epandmedia/Flashframe Films   **(212) 354-8188**
Two W. 45th St., Ste. 1200   FAX **(212) 354-8652**
(Near Fifth Ave.)   www.epandmedia.com
New York, NY 10036
President: Len Epand
Directors: John Dahl, Marius Penczner & Jim Yukich

Epoch Films, Inc.   **(212) 226-0661**
122 Hudson St., Third Fl.   FAX **(212) 226-4893**
(Near N. Moore St.)
New York, NY 10013
Executive Producers: Mindy Goldberg, Jerry Solomon & Doug Halbert
Directors: Matt Aselton, Matt Badger, Rey Carlson, Paula Greif, Miranda July, Matt Lenski, Mike Long, Edna McCallion, Phil Morrison, Jeff Preiss & Stacy Wall

    (212) 675-8287
The Firm   **(323) 663-6264**
78 Fifth Ave., Seventh Fl.   FAX **(212) 675-8251**
(Near 14th St.)   www.firmcreative.com
New York, NY 10011
Executive Producer/Partner: John Grossman
Directors: Billy Kent, Kate Magee, Fausto Terán & Troy Word
East Coast Sales Rep: Elyse Emmer
West Coast Sales Rep: Elizabeth Mang

Full Glass Films, LLC   **(212) 874-6282**
386 Park Ave. South, Ste. 303   www.fullglassfilms.com
(Near E. 27th St.)
New York, NY 10016
Partners: Stan Erdreich, Michael Parness & Elana Pianko

    (212) 869-8833
Gargoyle Films, Inc.   **(631) 724-5475**
   www.gargoylefilms.com
Executive Producer/Director: Tony Caronia
Director/Cameraman: Alan Lebow

Giraldi Productions   **(212) 966-1212**
47 Murray St. (Near W. Broadway St.)   FAX **(212) 966-6644**
New York, NY 10007   www.giraldi.com
Director: Robert Giraldi
West Coast Rep: Wil LaFayette
Midwest Rep: Robin Pickett
EP: Debbie Merlin
East Coast Rep: Kelly Salmon

    (212) 677-7500
Go Film   **(323) 860-5400**
51 E. 12th St., Seventh Fl.   FAX **(212) 677-7555**
(Near Broadway)   www.gofilm.net
New York, NY 10003
Executive Producers: Gary Rose & Jonathan Weinstein
Heads of Production: Sandy Newman & Lisa Tauscher
Production Coordinators: Emily Malito & Christiane Sabo
Directors: Ric Cantor, David Dobkin, Caitlin Felton, Christopher Guest, Tim Hamilton, Andrews Jenkins, Ras-Ish, Jakob Strom, Markus Walter & Benjamin Weinstein
East Coast Sales Reps: Amy Jones & Michael Lobikis
Midwest Sales Rep: Tracy Bernard
West Coast Sales Rep: Stephanie Stephens

Grandview Island Productions   **(212) 691-3859**
225 Varick St., Third Fl.   FAX **(212) 727-3860**
(Near W. Houston St.)   www.grandviewisland.com
New York, NY 10014
Creative Director: Carol McCann
Director/Cameraman: Michael Lesser

    (212) 260-5715
Greencard Pictures   **(212) 260-5716**
42 Bond St., Ste. 4W   FAX **(646) 216-8802**
New York, NY 10012   www.greencardpics.com

Guardian Entertainment, LTD   **(212) 727-4729**
71 Fifth Ave., Fifth Fl. (Near 15th St.)   FAX **(212) 727-4737**
New York, NY 10003   www.guardianltd.com
CEO & Executive Producer: Richard Miller
Head of Production: Hanne O'Brien

Habana Avenue   **(212) 355-8311**
954 Third Ave., Ste. 726   www.habanaavenue.com
New York, NY 10022

HSI Productions, Inc.   **(212) 627-3600**
601 W. 26th St., Ste. 1420   FAX **(212) 627-5947**
(Near 11th Ave.)   www.hsiproductions.com
New York, NY 10001
President: Stavros Merjos
Executive Producers: Maddi Carlton & Annique DeCaestecker
Directors: Stefan Arni/Siggi Kinski, Peter Berg, Irv Blitz, Scott Burns, Gerard De Thame, F. Gary Gray, Michael Haussman, Paul Hunter, Joseph Kahn, Randy Krallman, David LaChapelle, LITTLE x, Paul Middleditch, Joe Public, Brett Ratner, Chris Robinson, Matthew Rolston, Peggy Sirota & Josh Taft
Sales Representatives: Pamala Buzick & Barrie Isaacson

Humble TV   **(646) 435-9500**
     (917) 593-6910
162 W. 21st St., Fourth Fl.   www.humble.tv
New York, NY 10011

Hungry Man   **(212) 625-5600**
160 Varick St., 10th Fl.   FAX **(212) 625-5699**
(Near Canal St.)   www.hungryman.com
New York, NY 10013
Partner/Executive Producer: Kevin Byrne
Partners/Directors: Bryan Buckley & Hank Perlman
Staff Producer NY: Marisa Kaplan
Head of Sales: Stacie Gillman
Directors: 300ml, Brian Billow, Nanette Burstein, Samuel Christopher, Roderick Fenske, Paul Gay, Steve Hudson, Robert Jitzmark, Wayne McClammy, Hein Mevissen, Amy Nicholson, Stephen Pearson, Gualter Pupo, Marcos Siega, Mitch Stratten, Hideyuki Tanaka, Scott Vincent & Taika Waititi
Head of Production/Executive Producer: Cindy Becker
Casting Director: Fay Shumsey
Assistant Casting Director: Stephanie Dalle Molle

IKA Collective   **(212) 246-4634**
15 E. 32nd St., 10th Fl.   FAX **(212) 246-4635**
(Near Madison Ave.)   www.ikacollective.com
New York, NY 10016
Director: Ian Karr

Image Maintenance   **(212) 375-0911**
Three Great Jones St., Ste. 3A   FAX **(212) 375-0915**
(Near Broadway)   www.imltd.com
New York, NY 10012
Producer: Jon Doran
Director/Cameraman: John Chimples

Independent Artists, Inc.   **(212) 481-6713**
461 Park Ave. South, Ste. 300   FAX **(212) 481-8668**
(Near 31st St.)
New York, NY 10016
Executive Producer: Herb Sidel
Producer: Marc Sidel
Directors: Robin Armstrong, Michael Frings, Ian Leech & Gustavo Leme
Office Manager: Melissa Mitchell

Infinite Scenarios   **(917) 627-1057**
371 Sixth Ave., Third Fl.   www.infinitescenerios.com
Brooklyn, NY 11215

Instant Karma Films   **(917) 338-7834**
529 W. 20th St., 10th Fl.   FAX **(917) 338-7835**
New York, NY 10011   www.instantkarmafilms.tv

Jalbert Productions, Inc.   **(631) 351-5878**
President/Owner: Joe Jay Jalbert   FAX **(631) 351-5875**
Producer/Director: Ken Bernardini   www.jalbertfilm.com

KSK Studios   **(212) 481-3111**
598 Broadway, Ste. 10A   FAX **(212) 481-5404**
(Near Sixth Ave.)   www.kskstudios.com
New York, NY 10012
CEO: Manny Kivowitz
Coordinating Producer: Lauren Muir

Link Entertainment   **(212) 925-8900**
62 Greene St., Second Fl.   FAX **(212) 925-8901**
(Near Spring St.)   www.link-entertainment.com
New York, NY 10012
Executive Producer: Ann Egbert
Directors: Fabien Baron, Dominique Issermann, Carolyn Jones, Sarah Moon & Neal Slavin

     (212) 343-2020
Little Minx   **(310) 659-1577**
270 Lafayette St., Ste. 203   FAX **(212) 343-2024**
(Near Prince St.)   www.littleminx.tv
New York, NY 10012
President: Rhea Scott
Directors: Steph Green, H5, Johnny Hardstaff, Jesper Kouthoofd, Ben Mor, Josh Miller, David Mullet, Chris Nelson, Malik Sayeed, Mark Seliger, Dawn Shadforth & Phillip Van

The Lopes Picture Company, Inc.   **(212) 477-1114**
29 E. 19th St., Seventh Fl.   FAX **(212) 477-2145**
(Near Broadway)   www.lopespictureco.com
New York, NY 10003
Head of Production: Josh Levine
President: Rob Lopes
VP/Executive Producer: Rick Lopes
Directors: Tom Finerty, Stan Larsen, Rob Lopes, Bob Morrow & Larry Robins
Director/Editor: Susan Buster Thomas

Lost Highway Films   **(212) 242-7400**
30 Vandam St., Ste. 4A   FAX **(212) 242-7300**
New York, NY 10013   www.losthighwayfilms.com
Executive Producer: Marc Rosenberg
Directors: Aggressive, Eddy Chu, Sasha Levinson, Michael Patterson & Zack and J.C.
Head of Sales: Anicia Zander

MacGuffin Films, Ltd.   **(212) 529-3100**
411 Lafayette St. (Near E. Fourth St.)   FAX **(212) 529-9870**
New York, NY 10003   www.macguffin.com
President: Michael Salzer
Executive Producers: Gloria Colangelo & Sam Wool
Directors: Christopher Bean, Kevan Bean, Jim Collins, Michael Somoroff, Julian West, Theresa Wingert & Henning Winkelmann
East Coast Sales Reps: Vanessa Moseley & Maria Stenz
Midwest Sales Rep: Jay Anderson
West Coast Sales Rep: Claire Worch
Regional Sales: Sarah Lange

Madoff Productions   **(212) 265-0137**
355 W. 52nd St., Fourth Fl.   FAX **(212) 265-1925**
(Near 8th & 9th Aves)   www.madoffproductions.com
New York, NY 10019
Executive Producer: Ed Daly
Director: Jeff Madoff

Marble and Clay   **(212) 683-5380**
134 W. 26th St., Ste. 604   FAX **(212) 683-7836**
(Near Sixth Ave.)   www.marbleandclay.com
New York, NY 10001

Mark Ross Films   **(908) 233-7271**
Executive Producer/Director: Mark Ross   FAX **(908) 233-7578**

Marro & Associates/SMP   **(212) 387-0057**
242 E. 19th St. (Near Second Ave.)   FAX **(212) 387-0329**
New York, NY 10003
Executive Producer: Doug LeClaire
Directors/Cameramen: Bob Chappell & Stephen Marro

Maya Media Corp.   **(212) 866-5332**
70 La Salle St., Ste. 14-G   FAX **(212) 665-4779**
New York, NY 10027   www.mayamediacorp.com
Director: Luis Argueta

Maysles Shorts, Inc./
Maysles Films, Inc.   **(212) 582-6050**
343 Lenox Ave. (Near Broadway)   FAX **(212) 586-2057**
New York, NY 10027   www.mayslesfilms.com
Executive Producer: Lora Nelson
Directors: Gilly Barnes & Robert Leacock

Monsoon Films (917) 225-0889
2322 Seventh Ave., Ste. 1A www.monsoonfilmsinc.com
(Near Avenue B)
New York, NY 10030
Executive Producer: Mala Perna
Director/Creative Director: Dwayne B. Perryman III

Mood Creations, Ltd. (914) 941-2357
One Depot Plaza (Near Water St.) FAX (914) 941-3142
Ossining, NY 10562 www.moodcreations.com
President/Director: Donald Cohen
Producer: Scott Cohen

The Mountain View Group, Ltd. (212) 644-1561
426 State St. (Near Union St.) FAX (518) 346-0949
Schenectady, NY 12305 www.mountainviewgroup.com
Principals: Thom Gonyeau & Stephen Pruitt
Creative Director: Tom Gliserman

Moxie Pictures, Inc. (212) 807-6901
18 E. 16th St., Fourth Fl. FAX (212) 807-1456
(Near Fifth Ave.) www.moxiepictures.com
New York, NY 10003
Executive Producers: Robert Fernandez & Lizzie Schwartz
Directors: Wes Anderson, Shari Berman, Spencer Chinoy, Andrew Christou, Cameron Crowe, Martin Granger, Jared Hess, Dan Levinson, Henry Lu, Rob Marshall, Errol Morris, Joe Nussbaum, Todd Phillips, Robert Pulcini, Bob Purman, Peyton Reed, Jim Sheridan, Kevin Smith, Peter Sollett, Pam Thomas, Frank Todaro & John Waters
Sales Representative: Sarah Holbrook

New York Office (212) 545-7895
 (323) 468-2240
15 W. 26th St., Fifth Fl. FAX (212) 545-7941
(Near Broadway) www.nyoffice.net
New York, NY 10010
Directors: Daddy, Who?, Luke Forsythe, Tryan George, Mike Goode, Jeff Gorman, Herman Lederle, Peter Martinez, Gord McWatters, Keva Rosenfeld, Tim Werd, Bill Werts & Robin Willis

NFL Films (856) 222-5675
 (877) 222-3517
One NFL Plaza FAX (856) 866-4848
Mount Laurel, NJ 08054 www.nflfilms.com
Directors: Tripp Dixon, Rob Markopoulos & Victor Sonder

Nonstop Pictures, Inc. (212) 675-6070
27 W. 20th St., Ste. 700 FAX (212) 675-6071
(Near Avenue of the Americas) www.nonstoppictures.com
New York, NY 10011
Executive Producer: Doug Conte
Director/DP: Morten Sandtroen
Office Manager: Filipe Bessa

Order, LLC (212) 655-6550
145 Hudson St., Ste. 205 FAX (212) 271-8785
(Near Hubert St.) www.order.tv
New York, NY 10013
Owner/Managing Partner: Charles Salice
Co-Owner: Tim Case
Directors: Dario Piana, Michael Rowles, Paul Santana & David Tennant
West Coast Sales Rep: Connie Mellors & Co.
East Coast Sales Rep: Moustache
Midwest Sales Rep: Richard Miller Associates
Canada Sales Rep: Sparks Productions
Visual FX: Disorder

Park Avenue Post, Inc. (212) 689-7678
419 Park Ave. South, Ste. 600 FAX (212) 689-7544
(Near 29th St.) www.parkavenuepost.com
New York, NY 10016
Contact: Nigel Kettle

PCS Broadcast Services (201) 445-1711
One Robinson Ln. FAX (201) 445-8352
Ridgewood, NJ 07450 www.dwjtv.com/pcs
President: Andrew McGowan

Perretti Productions (212) 260-6545
President/Director: Jim Perretti FAX (212) 260-6561
Director: Joe Scudiero www.perrettiproductions.com
Director/Cameraman: John Lindley
Executive Coordinator: Jessica Genevieve

Phil Marco Productions (212) 929-8082
President/Director: Phil Marco FAX (212) 463-0514
Executive Producer: Patricia Phillips Marco www.philmarco.com

Piranha Pictures (212) 216-9470
347 W. 36th St., Ste. 1501 FAX (212) 216-9317
(Near Ninth Ave.) www.piranhapix.com
New York, NY 10018
Managing Director/Producer: George Moffly
Producer: Alyssa St. Vincent

Production 920, Inc. (212) 414-0606
328 Eighth Ave., Ste. 147 FAX (917) 463-3067
(Near 10th Ave.) www.production920.com
New York, NY 10001

Public Domain (646) 414-8444
32 E. 31st St., 12th Fl. FAX (212) 545-0269
(Near Madison Ave.) www.publicdomainny.com
New York, NY 10016
Executive Producer: Steven Shore
Head of Production: Megan Kelly
Directors: Toon Aerts, Steve Ayson, Wiebke Berndt, Jan Bonny, Oliver Bradford, Lars Damoiseaux, Henri De Maar, Arno Dierickx, Lionel Goldstein, Marlon Griffin, Sonja Heiss, Norbert Heitker, Koen Mortier, Pes, Mattias Schut, Bart Timmer, Lieven Van Baelen, Rogier Van Der Ploeg & Joe Vanhoutteghem

Pureland Pictures, Inc. (718) 965-0636
 FAX (718) 965-0637
 www.purelandpictures.com

Pyburn Films (212) 925-5595
1560 Broadway, 17th Fl. FAX (212) 925-7117
(Near Times Square) www.pyburn.com
New York, NY 10036
Contact: Debra Henni

@radical.media (212) 462-1500
435 Hudson St., Sixth Fl. FAX (212) 462-1600
(Near Morton St.) www.radicalmedia.com
New York, NY 10014
Chairman & CEO: Jon Kamen
Sales Representative: Maya Brewster

Real Productions, Inc. (212) 271-0020
214 Sullivan St., Second Fl. www.realprod.com
(Near Bleecker St.)
New York, NY 10012
Producer: Jim Calabrese
Director: Richard DeLigter

Refuge (212) 399-3150
18 W. 21st St., PH (Near Fifth Ave.) FAX (212) 399-3165
New York, NY 10010 www.bigchairny.com
Owner/Director: Rob Michael Cohn
Managing Partner/VP: Elise Heshler
Executive Producer: Marc Campana

Robbins Media (212) 661-7670
770 Broadway, Second Fl. FAX (212) 656-1997
New York, NY 10003 www.robbinsmedia.com

Rooftop Edit (212) 244-0744
104 W. 29th St., 12th Fl. FAX (212) 244-0690
(Near Sixth Ave.) www.rooftopedit.com
New York, NY 10001
General Manager: Anthony Forte

RSA Films, Inc. (212) 343-2020
270 Lafayette St., Ste. 203 (310) 659-1577
(Near Prince St.) FAX (212) 343-2024
New York, NY 10012 www.rsafilms.com
President: Jules Daly
VP & Executive Producer: Marjie Abrahams
Executive Producers: Phillip Fox-Mills & Tracie Norfleet
Directors: Casey Affleck, Neill Blomkamp, Joe Carnahan, Barney Cokeliss, Tom Dey, Ben Dickinson, Andrew Dominik, Laurence Dunmore, The Duplass Brothers, Lauri Faggioni, Brett Foraker, Sean Ellis, Adam Goldstein, Hobby, Henrik Hansen, Hugh Johnson, Nick Livesey, Melina, Sam Mendes, Adrian Moat, John O'Hagan, Jesse Peretz, Carl Erik Rinsch, Alex Rutterford, The Russo Brothers, Jake Scott, Jordan Scott, Luke Scott, Ridley Scott, Tony Scott, Adam Smith, Kevin Spacey, Joachim Trier & Declan Whitebloom
East Coast Sales Rep: Philip Fox-Mills & Victoria Venantini
Midwest Sales Reps.: Chris Karabas & Rob Mueller
West Coast Sales Rep: Holly Ross

Santiago, Inc. (203) 655-9500
Executive Producer: Joan Vitaliano FAX (203) 655-9558
Director: Santiago Suarez www.ssantiagoinc.com

Schofield Films (212) 633-8700
560 Broadway, Ste. 204 FAX (212) 633-9850
(Near Prince St.) www.schofieldfilms.com
New York, NY 10012
Executive Producer: Robert Berman
Director: Stan Schofield

**Screen Gems, Ltd./
Huge Productions** (212) 867-4030
222 E. 44th St., Fourth Fl. FAX (212) 450-1610
(Near Third Ave.) www.screengemsstudios.com
New York, NY 10017
Executive Producers: Eli Feldman & William Seiz
Directors: Peter Cherry, Mark Claywell, Jeffrey Cooney, Stan Dragoti, Paul Fuentes, Eric Laneuville & Roger Woodburne

September Productions (508) 228-8703
15 Madaket Rd. www.september.com
Nantucket, MA 02554
CEO & Director: Dan Driscoll
Executive Producer: Sonta Giamber
Directors: Elena Colombo, Dan Driscoll, Paul Henschel, Neil Salley & Steven Shainberg

Shamrock Communications (732) 872-9090
26 W. Highland Ave. FAX (732) 872-2586
Atlantic Highlands, NJ 07716
www.shamrockcommunications.com

Shoot First Entertainment (212) 539-3606
www.shootfirstentertainment.com

Shooting Stars Int'l. (212) 888-8999
62 W. 45th St., 10th Fl. FAX (212) 888-9161
(Near Sixth Ave.) www.shootingstarsintl.com
New York, NY 10036
President/Executive Producer: Dennis Loonan
Directors: Mario Battistoni, Jon Kane, Dan Lerner, Elyse Lewin, Chris Stifel & Terry Wendell

SLAM! Media Group (212) 924-7100
54 W. 21st St., Ste. 410 FAX (212) 229-2080
New York, NY 10010 www.slammediagroup.com

Slate, Inc. (212) 472-8789
(917) 691-3049
444 E. 82nd St., Ste. 14J (Near York Ave.)
New York, NY 10028
Director: Peter Viola

Smillie Films (212) 673-2500
54 W. 21st St., Ste. 408 FAX (646) 486-6640
New York, NY 10010

Smuggler (212) 337-3327
184 Fifth Ave., Seventh Fl. FAX (212) 337-9686
(Near E. 22nd St.) www.smugglersite.com
New York, NY 10010
Executive Producers: Brian Carmody & Patrick Milling Smith
Heads of Production: Allison Kunzman & Laura Thoel
Directors: Brian Beletic, James Brown, David Frankham, Nacho Gayan, Happy, Neil Harris, Randy Krallman, Renny Maslow, Ben Mor, Ne-O, Chris Smith, Eidur Snorri, Stylewar & Ivan Zacharias

Sonar (201) 766-5724
6600 Blvd. East, Ste. 10M www.sonarproductions.com
West New York, NJ 07093

Spontaneous (212) 317-0077
575 Lexington Ave., 25th Fl. FAX (212) 317-1048
(Near E. 51st St.) www.spon.com
New York, NY 10022
Creative Director: John Leamy
Assoc. CD/Dir. of Animation: Lawrence Nimrichter
Director of Visual Effects: Andy Milkis
Head of Production: Bennett Lieber
Senior Producer: Bryce Edwards
Producers: Sarah Brown & Felili Rincon
Sales: Dana Dubay

Stardust Studios East (212) 334-7300
591 Broadway, Second Fl. FAX (212) 334-7332
New York, NY 10012 www.stardust.tv

Stockland Martel Films (212) 727-1400
Five Union Square West FAX (212) 727-9455
(Near W. 14th St.) www.stocklandmartel.com
New York, NY 10003
Executive Producers/Partners: Maureen Martel & Bill Stockland
Directors: Jorg Badura, Timothy Greenfield-Sanders, Ruedi Hofmann, Nadav Kander, Leen Thijisse & Bruce Wolf
Head of Sales: Michelle Sack

Suggs Media Productions, Inc. (212) 398-4200
156 W. 44th St., Seventh Fl. FAX (212) 382-0922
(Near Broadway)
New York, NY 10036
Producer/Director: Jeanne Suggs

Suite Spot (212) 475-6310
126 Second Ave., Third Fl. FAX (212) 473-3748
New York, NY 10003 www.suitespotnyc.com

Supply & Demand, Inc. (212) 655-6555
145 Hudson St. FAX (212) 271-7073
New York, NY 10013 www.supplyanddemand.tv
Founder/Executive Producer: Tim Case
Co-Founder/Executive Producer: Kent Eby
Executive Producer/Managing Director: Jillian Henry
Directors: Tony Kaye, Jeffery Plansker, Greg Popp & Jose Antonio Pratt
Midwest Sales Rep: R. Miller & Associates
West Coast Sales Rep: Reber/Covington

The Sussan Group (212) 533-2200
141 Downs Ave. FAX (212) 533-0020
Stamford, CT 06902
President/Executive Producer: David L. Sussan
Directors: Marek Dawid, Bill Marshall, Jorge Rubia, Frank Samuel & Howard Schatz
Executive Producer/Head of Sales: Wayne Chrystal

Synthespian Studios (413) 458-0202
96 Ballou Ln. FAX (413) 458-5089
Williamstown, MA 01267 www.synthespians.net
President: Diana Walczak
COO: Michael Van Himbergen
Executive Producer: Amanda Roth
Producers: Wendy Gipp & Tom Leeser
Directors: Jeff Kleiser & Diana Walczak

Taxi Films, Inc. (212) 807-7120
155 Sixth Ave., 10th Fl. FAX (212) 807-7199
(Near Spring St.)
New York, NY 10013

TK Digital (347) 289-5658
167 N. Ninth St., Ste. 14 (718) 599-3020
Brooklyn, NY 11211 FAX (347) 438-3321
www.tk-digital.com

Top Hat Productions (212) 688-5490
305 Madison Ave., Ste. 449 (877) 786-7428
New York, NY 10165 FAX (800) 505-1329
www.top-hat.com

TriStar Studios (973) 575-5400
490 Route 46 East (914) 907-8766
Fairfield, NJ 07004 FAX (973) 575-6708
www.tristarstudios.com

U-Direct Productions (212) 647-9200
10 White St. (Near Broadway) FAX (212) 625-9402
New York, NY 10013 www.udirectnyc.com
President: Daniel Miller

Untitled Inc. (310) 917-9191
2241 Corinth Ave. FAX (310) 231-7612
Los Angeles, CA 90064 www.untitled.tv
Executive Producer: Jim Evans
General Manager: Larry Edwards
Head of Production: Geoff Campbell
Directors: Geoff Barish, Mark Bennett, Anouk Besson, The Cronenweths, Christopher Desantis, Justin Klarenbeck, Rick Knief, Glenn Martin, Adam Massey & Adam Reed
West Coast Sales Rep: Siobhan McCafferty
Midwest Sales Rep: Nikki Weiss
East Coast Sales Rep: Ann McKallagat

Villains (212) 462-2700
134 W. 25th St. (Near Seventh Ave.) (310) 888-8900
New York, NY 10001 FAX (212) 462-4502
www.villains.com
President: John Marshall
Directors: Mona El Mansouri, The Guard Brothers, Axel Laubscher, Dewey Nicks & Terry Rietta

a WhiteLabel product (212) 463-7207
135 W. 27th St., 10th Fl. FAX (212) 763-7228
New York, NY 10001 www.awhitelabelproduct.com
Executive Producers: Annique DeCaestecker, Oliver Hicks & Ellen Jacobson-Clarke
Directors: Arni and Kinski, Don Cameron, Jean-Paul Goude, Mikael Jansson, Peter Lindbergh, David Michalek, Paul Middleditch, nObrain, Tim Richardson & Nick Robertson

Zero 2 Sixty (212) 807-7123
121 W. 27th St. (Near Seventh Ave.) FAX (212) 807-0427
New York, NY 10001 www.0260.com
Executive Producer: Doug Robbins
Directors: Phelim Dolan, Claude Mougin, Bob Mowen & Alex Turner

Zooma Zooma Corporation (212) 941-7680
11 Mercer St., Third Fl. FAX (212) 941-8179
(Near Grand St.) www.zoomazooma.com
New York, NY 10013
President/Executive Producer: Joseph Mantegna
Producer: Henry Castillo
Directors: Todd Bellanca, Alan Cumming, Sasha Levinson, Ryan McFaul, Sam Raimi, Howard Shir & Eden Tyler
Sales Rep: Coleen McHale

Corporate & Video Production Companies

4-D Creative Media (212) 599-6699 / (646) 483-7768
Four E. 46th St., Fourth Fl. FAX (212) 499-9081
(Near Fifth Ave.) www.4-dcreative.com
New York, NY 10017

7NY (212) 962-1850
195 Chrystie St., Ste. 401C FAX (212) 962-1043
New York, NY 10002 www.7-ny.com

AAA Acme Discount Film Works (718) 928-3812
56 Fifth Ave. (Near St. Mark's Pl.) www.aaaacme.com
Brooklyn, NY 11217

ADM Productions (516) 484-6900 / (800) 236-3425
40 Seaview Blvd. www.admproductions.com
Port Washington, NY 11050

Alan Weiss Productions (212) 974-0606
355 W. 52nd St., Third Fl. FAX (212) 974-0976
(Near Ninth Ave.) www.awptv.com
New York, NY 10019
Contact: Marilou Yacoub

American Montage, Inc. (212) 334-8283
Old Chelsea Station www.americanmontage.com
P.O. Box 1042 (Near Centre Market Pl.)
New York, NY 10013
Contact: Eric Marciano

American Movie Co. (917) 414-5489 / (212) 952-1800
50 Broadway, Ste. 1206 FAX (212) 952-0152
New York, NY 10004 www.americanmovieco.com

Anderson Productions (860) 589-2776 / (800) 701-4311
34 Dell Manor Dr. FAX (860) 584-5936
Bristol, CT 06010 www.andersonprod.com
Contact: Tracy Ericson

Aurora Productions International, Inc. (631) 549-8933
1160 E. Jericho Tpke, Ste. 110 FAX (631) 549-6890
(Near Deer Park Rd.) www.auroraproductions.tv
Huntington, NY 11743
Contact: Richard Poggioli

Automatic Productions (212) 833-8000
Contacts: Laurie Heuler, Andy Kadison & Stephanie Masarsky

Aztec Video Productions (203) 775-3361
332 Federal Rd. FAX (203) 775-3394
Brookfield, CT 06804 www.aztecvideopro.com

Batwin & Robin Productions (212) 243-0229
151 W. 19th St., 10th Fl. FAX (212) 229-1616
(Near Sixth Ave.) www.batwinandrobin.com
New York, NY 10011
Contacts: Linda Batwin & Robin Silvestri

Bee Harris Productions, Inc. (914) 664-6519 / (914) 469-7695
79 Putnam St. FAX (914) 664-6422
Mount Vernon, NY 10550 www.beeharris.com
Contacts: Richie Bee & Robert Bruzio

Bill Quinn Productions (732) 237-0525 / (800) 497-0501
P.O. Box 213
Ocean Gate, NJ 08740
Contact: Bill Quinn

Black Watch Productions (212) 349-0369
49 Murray St., Ste. 1 (Near Church St.) FAX (212) 349-1335
New York, NY 10007 www.blackwatchproductions.com
Contacts: John Anderson & Monica Anderson

Bonafina Films (973) 744-8600
203 Lorraine Ave. www.bonafinafilms.com
Montclair, NJ 07043
Contact: Michael Finan

Broad Street (212) 780-5700
20 W. 22nd St. (Near W. 21st St.) FAX (212) 780-5710
New York, NY 10010 www.broadstreet.com
Contact: Walter Elzey

Burger Design/Visions Media (585) 271-5995
125 Windemere Rd. (Near Newcastle Rd.)
Rochester, NY 14610
Contact: Frederick P. Burger

CameraOne Video Production (315) 451-9790
200 Gateway Park Dr., Bldg. C www.cam1.com
(Near Henry Clay Blvd.)
Syracuse, NY 13212
Contact: John Duffy

Carolyn Wade Productions, Inc. (914) 524-9111
493 High Cliff Ln. (Near Rt. 119) FAX (914) 524-8367
Tarrytown, NY 10591
Contact: Carolyn Wade

PRIMALUX VIDEO
FULL PRODUCTION
CREWS & EQUIPMENT
STUDIO & LOCATION PACKAGES
HI-DEF, DIGITAL & BETACAM SP, DV
NTSC & PAL
35' X 30' STAGE WITH LIGHTING/GRIP EQUIPMENT
ULTIMATTE/SPECIAL EFFECTS
COMPLETE PRODUCTION AND POST PRODUCTION
ENTERTAINMENT
COMMERCIALS
CORPORATE
NEWS AND DOCUMENTARY

30 WEST 26 STREET
NEW YORK NY 10010
212/206-1402
PRIMALUX.COM

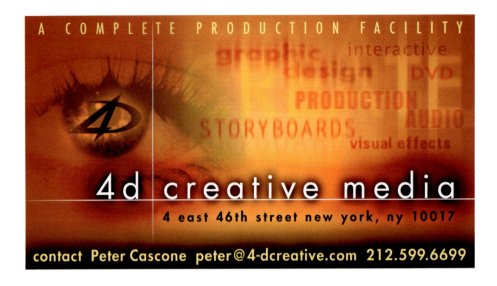

A COMPLETE PRODUCTION FACILITY

graphic · interactive
design · DVD
PRODUCTION
STORYBOARDS · AUDIO
visual effects

4d creative media
4 east 46th street new york, ny 10017

contact Peter Cascone peter@4-dcreative.com 212.599.6699

CitiCam Film & Video Services, Inc. (212) 315-2000
515 W. 57th St. (Near 10th Ave.) FAX **(212) 586-1572**
New York, NY 10019 www.citicam.net

City Lights Productions **(212) 679-4400**
Six E. 39th St., Third Fl. FAX **(212) 679-4481**
(Near Fifth Ave.) www.citylightsmedia.com
New York, NY 10016
Contacts: Danny Fisher & Jack Fisher

(585) 415-3202
Clipboard Productions **(585) 730-6064**
Contact: Carol Cieslinski

Clock Wise Productions **(212) 343-3099**
Contact: Nina Froriep FAX **(801) 843-7088**
www.clockwiseproductions.com

Collaborations In
Communications, Inc. **(973) 377-8202**
61 Riverside Dr. FAX **(973) 377-7302**
Florham Park, NJ 07932 www.collaborations.com
Contacts: Joseph V. Hupcey & Maisey Hupcey

Colossalvision **(212) 269-6333**
26 Broadway FAX **(212) 269-4334**
(Near Merchant Marines Plaza) www.colossalvision.com
New York, NY 10004
Contact: David Niles

Creative Business
Communications, Inc. **(845) 348-7670**
37 N. Broadway (Near High Ave.) FAX **(845) 348-1548**
Nyack, NY 10960 www.cbcomm.com
Contacts: Joseph Morley & Heather Winters

Creative Media Communications **(610) 789-8800**
8300 W. Chester Pike FAX **(610) 789-8807**
Upper Darby, PA 19082 www.cmcnow.com

The Creators **(914) 769-0676**
39 Washington Ave. www.creatorsmedia.com
(Near Edgewood Ave.)
Pleasantville, NY 10570
Contact: Richard DePaso

Cue & A Productions **(973) 588-3200**
21 Pine St. FAX **(973) 588-3194**
Rockaway, NJ 07866 www.cue-a.com

Custom Video Productions, Inc. **(732) 936-1001**
15 Lake Shore Dr. (Near Route 35) FAX **(732) 741-9204**
Red Bank, NJ 07701 www.cvpnj.com
Contact: Frank Farrell

Czar Productions **(860) 953-0809**
809 New Britain Ave.
Hartford, CT 06106
Contact: Gene Czarnecki

DB Production Services **(201) 302-9044**
307 Westview Ave.
Leonia, NJ 07605
Contact: Diane Berson

Dennis Powers Productions, Inc. **(212) 448-0341**
Six E. 39th St., Ste. 300 FAX **(212) 448-9602**
(Near Fifth Ave.) www.dennispowers.net
New York, NY 10016
Contact: Dennis Powers

DEVLINHAIR Productions, Inc. **(212) 941-9009**
120 Wooster St., Third Fl. FAX **(212) 941-9008**
New York, NY 10012 www.devlinhair.com

(516) 255-0100
dM works **(888) 914-6639**
246 Rockaway Ave. www.dmworks.com
(Near Hawthorne Ave.)
Valley Stream, NY 11580

DMJ Productions & Digital Media **(917) 570-5514**
369 Argyle Rd. (Near Oxford Rd.) www.dmjdigital.com
Cedarhurst, NY 11516

(212) 307-9097
DMP Productions **(917) 224-2265**
312 W. 58th St., Ste. 1 FAX **(212) 765-9723**
(Near Eighth Ave.) www.dmpproductions.tv
New York, NY 10019
Contact: Paul Dokuchitz

The Dovetail Group, Inc. **(203) 876-0800**
18 Bianca Dr. FAX **(203) 874-1335**
Milford, CT 06460

(201) 445-1711
DWJ Television **(800) 766-1711**
One Robinson Ln. FAX **(201) 445-8352**
Ridgewood, NJ 07450 www.dwjtv.com
Contacts: Anita Fethes & Daniel Johnson

Edge Films/
Ken Nahoum Productions **(212) 924-8880**
55 Van Dam St., 16th Fl. FAX **(212) 924-0479**
(Near Hudson St.) www.edgefilms.us
New York, NY 10013
Contacts: Maria Danar & Ken Nahoum

El Punto Productions (917) 204-5233
100 Manhattan Ave. Ste. 1R www.elpuntoproductions.com
Jersey City, NJ 07307

English Motion Media (212) 865-7242
243 Riverside Dr., Ste. 505 FAX (212) 961-9228
(Near 96th St.) www.e-m-m.com
New York, NY 10025
Contact: Henry English

Euro-Pacific Film & (732) 530-4451
Video Productions, Inc. (732) 581-5249
P.O. Box 7986 FAX (732) 842-6533
Shrewsbury, NJ 07702 www.euro-pacific.com
Contacts: David Calderwood & Lisa Moss

The Farm (212) 982-8500
110 E. 42nd St. (Near Park Ave.) FAX (212) 982-0056
New York, NY 10017 www.thefarm.com
Contact: John Anderson

Five Foot Five Productions, Inc. (212) 206-7706
112 W. 27th St., Ste. 510 FAX (212) 604-0626
New York, NY 10001 www.fivefootfive.com

Florentine Films/Sherman Pictures (212) 980-5966
136 E. 56th St., Ste. 4B FAX (212) 980-5944
(Near Park Ave.) www.florentinefilms.com/sherman
New York, NY 10022
Contact: Roger Sherman

FullMind, LLC. (609) 424-0115
Three Third St. FAX (609) 424-0119
Bordentown, NJ 08505 www.fullmindcreative.com

Mark Gasper (201) 656-4348
300 Observer Hwy, Fourth Fl.
Hoboken, NJ 07030
Contact: Mark Gasper

Gotham Pictures (212) 260-2626
43 E. 20th St., Ste. 7 (Near Broadway) FAX (212) 260-1200
New York, NY 10003 www.gothampictures.tv

GPI (856) 663-8092
111 Westminster Ave. FAX (856) 663-4969
Merchantville, NJ 08109 www.gugginoproductions.com
Contact: Tom Guggino

Grandview Island Productions (212) 691-3859
225 Varick St., Third Fl. FAX (212) 727-3860
(Near W. Houston St.) www.grandviewisland.com
New York, NY 10014
Contact: Michael Lesser

HBR Productions (732) 946-2737
Four E. Parkway Pl. FAX (732) 946-4043
Holmdel, NJ 07733 www.hbrproductions.com
Contact: Gladys Bensimon

Hello World Communications (212) 243-8800
118 W. 22nd St., Ste. 2A FAX (212) 691-6961
(Near Sixth Ave.) www.hwc.tv
New York, NY 10011
Contact: Ron Yoshida

hscusa.tv (718) 626-6226
19-69 Steinway St. FAX (718) 626-1493
Astoria, NY 11105 www.hscusa.tv

Infinite Scenarios (917) 627-1057
371 Sixth Ave., Third Fl. www.infinitescenerios.com
Brooklyn, NY 11215
Contacts: Brian David Cange & Thomas Halaczynsky

Instructivision, Inc. (973) 575-9992
16 Chapin Rd., Ste. 904 FAX (973) 575-9134
Pine Brook, NJ 07058 www.instructivision.com
Contacts: Rosemary Comras & Anthony Traina

Intermediapost (201) 261-3959
 (800) 811-7044
120 Route 17 North FAX (201) 261-3062
Paramus, NJ 07652 www.intermediapost.com
Contact: Michael Aiellos

 (203) 485-0392
Jack-Of-All-Trades Productions (917) 855-2041
Four Putnam Hill, Ste. 1J FAX (203) 485-0392
Greenwich, CT 06830 www.jackoftrades.biz

Jake Films, Inc. (718) 729-4688

Jalbert Productions, Inc. (631) 351-5878
230 New York Ave. (Near Leverich Pl.) FAX (631) 351-5875
Huntington, NY 11743 www.jalbertfilm.com
Contacts: Joe Jay Jalbert & Carol Randel

JHD Productions, Ltd. (631) 595-2818
62 S. Second St., Ste. E www.jhdproductionsltd.com
(Near Dunton Ave.)
Deer Park, NY 11729
Contact: Hugh Daly

Jim Houston Productions, Inc. (201) 825-7659
103 Park St. FAX (201) 825-2936
Ramsey, NJ 07446

K2imaging, Inc. (917) 952-9589
24 Tompkins Pl. (Near Court St.) www.k2imaging.com
Brooklyn, NY 11231

 (212) 480-0065
Kavanagh Productions, Inc. (800) 494-5453
32 Broadway, Ste. 1711-12 FAX (212) 480-0149
(Near Exchange Pl.) www.kavanaghproductions.com
New York, NY 10004
Contact: Bill Kavanagh

Kaye Lites, Inc. (781) 932-0005
 FAX (781) 932-0006
 www.kayelites.com

L.A. Bruell, Inc. (646) 336-5977
134 W. 26th St. (Near Seventh Ave.) FAX (646) 336-8317
New York, NY 10001 www.labruell.com
Contacts: Oshin Baroyan, Lucy Bruell & Marcel Dumont

Line By Line Productions (212) 505-0505
873 Broadway, Ste. 500 FAX (212) 505-0593
(Near W. 18th St.) www.nycproduction.com
New York, NY 10003
Contacts: Michele Bessey & Frank Garritano

Lorcott Productions, Inc. (908) 604-9098
92 Bernard Dr. FAX (908) 604-9068
Basking Ridge, NJ 07920 www.lorcott.com
Contact: Scott Levine

Lovett Productions, Inc. (212) 242-8999
17 Van Dam St., Ground Fl. FAX (212) 242-7347
New York, NY 10013 www.lovettproductions.com
Contact: Joseph Lovett

 (631) 425-5155
Make Believe TV, LLC (917) 628-6322
10 Cambridge Ave. (Near Route 110) FAX (631) 425-4622
Melville, NY 11747 www.makebelievetv.com
Contact: Mary Scott

Mark Haefeli Productions (212) 334-2164
11 Beach St., Ste. 409 FAX (646) 437-2746
New York, NY 10013 www.mhp3.com
Contacts: Joe DeAngelus & Mark Haefeli

Mark Ross Films (908) 233-7271
Contact: Mark Ross FAX (908) 233-7578

Marshad Technology Group (212) 292-8910
76 Laight St. (Near Washington St.) www.marshad.com
New York, NY 10013
Contact: Neal Marshad

Medipix Productions, LLC (609) 951-9200
Two Research Way, Third Fl. East FAX (609) 951-9201
Princeton, NJ 08540
Contact: Larry Testa

Michael Beckman Associates, Ltd. (212) 620-0933
134 W. 26th St., Ste. 901 FAX (212) 675-0291
(Near Seventh Ave.) www.beckmanmedia.com
New York, NY 10001

Miles Associates, Inc. (212) 695-1600
246 W. 38th St. (Near Seventh Ave.) FAX (212) 967-4290
New York, NY 10018 www.c4miles.tv

(973) 300-9477
Mirage Productions Inc. (888) 746-6869
111 Spring St. FAX (973) 300-9467
Newton, NJ 07860 www.mirageproductions.com

Mood Creations, Ltd. (914) 941-2357
One Depot Plaza (Near Water St.) FAX (914) 941-3142
Ossining, NY 10562 www.moodcreations.com
Contacts: Donald Cohen & Scott Cohen

Moonfish Production, Ltd. (973) 541-1112
www.moonfishproduction.com
Contacts: D. Rickards & T. Walters

Mountain View Group, Ltd. (518) 346-2034
426 State St., Ste. 300 (Near Union St.) FAX (518) 346-0949
Schenectady, NY 12305 www.mountainviewgroup.com
Contacts: Tom Gliserman, Thom Gonyeau, Melissa Gordon & Stephen Pruitt

(212) 924-7364
Moving Pictures (212) 450-7933
222 E. 44th St., Eighth Fl. (Near Spring St.) www.mpny.tv
New York, NY 10017
Contacts: Ron Honsa & Nan Penman

Murray Hill Studios, Inc. (212) 889-4200
248 E. 35th St. (Near Second Ave.) FAX (212) 889-9413
New York, NY 10016 www.murrayhillstudios.com
Contact: Jahaneen Johnsen

NAK Marketing & (917) 587-1891
Communications, Inc. (800) 847-6435
20 W. 55th St., Sixth Fl. FAX (212) 505-9399
(Near Fifth Ave.) www.nakinc.com
New York, NY 10019
Contact: Thaddeus B. Kubis

New York Network (518) 443-5333
Empire State Plaza FAX (518) 426-4198
South Concourse, Ste. 146 www.nyn.suny.edu
P.O. Box 2058 (Near State St.)
Albany, NY 12220

News Broadcast Network (212) 684-8910
451 Park Ave. South (Near 31st St.) FAX (212) 684-9650
New York, NY 10016
Contact: Laura Pair

(856) 222-5675
NFL Films (877) 222-3517
One NFL Plaza FAX (856) 866-4848
Mount Laurel, NJ 08054 www.nflfilms.com
Contact: Rick Angeli

NYPH Audio Visual Service (212) 305-1129
245 Ft. Washington Ave., Ste. 5H FAX (212) 305-1896
(Near Broadway) www.nyp.org
New York, NY 10032
Contacts: Al Pine & Jeff Szmulewicz

Park Avenue Post, Inc. (212) 689-7678
419 Park Ave. South, Ste. 600 FAX (212) 689-7544
(Near 29th St.) www.parkavenuepost.com
New York, NY 10016
Contact: Nigel Kettle

(201) 459-9044
Parlay Film Productions, LLC (973) 819-1979
930 Newark Ave., Sixth Fl. FAX (201) 459-9044
Jersey City, NJ 07306 www.parlayfilms.com

(917) 860-1845
Percolator Productions (917) 873-2271
597 Grand Ave., Ste. 1E FAX (718) 789-1874
(Near Washington Ave.) www.percolator.tv
Brooklyn, NY 11238
Contacts: Andrew Cohen & Shara Kabakow

(973) 812-8883
PFS Marketwyse (800) 737-2080
409 Minnisink Rd. FAX (973) 812-9020
Totowa, NJ 07512 www.pfsmarketwyse.com
Contact: Dennis Chominsky

Piranha Pictures (212) 216-9470
347 W. 36th St., Ste. 1501 FAX (212) 216-9317
(Near Ninth Ave.) www.piranhapix.com
New York, NY 10018
Contact: George Moffly

PMTV (610) 768-1770
681 Moore Rd., Ste. 100 FAX (610) 768-1773
King Of Prussia, PA 19406 www.pmtv.com
Contact: Brian Powers

Point of View (585) 546-4150
274 N. Goodman St. FAX (585) 546-6474
Rochester, NY 14607 www.povworks.com
Contact: Jeffrey Mead

Post Office Media (212) 302-4488
1560 Broadway, Ste. 514 FAX (212) 302-4849
New York, NY 10036 www.postofficemedia.com

Ⓐ Primalux Video (212) 206-1402
30 W. 26th St., Seventh Fl. FAX (212) 206-1826
(Near Broadway) www.primalux.com
New York, NY 10010
Contact: Judy Cashman

(718) 543-3991
PrimeLight Productions, Inc. (917) 680-5780
750 Kappock St., Ste. 805 www.primelight.net
(Near Independence Ave.)
Riverdale, NY 10463
Contact: Don Forschmidt

(203) 294-1325
Prism Production Services, Inc. (203) 996-5292
Four E. Scard Rd. FAX (203) 265-7730
Wallingford, CT 06492 www.prismpro.com
Contact: Keith Sandler

Pro Image Studios (631) 234-4310
3200 Expressway Dr. South FAX (631) 234-8256
(Near Corporate Pl.) www.proimagestudios.com
Islandia, NY 11749

Producer East Productions (631) 254-8020
10 Addison Pl. www.producereast.com
Dix Hills, NY 11746
Contacts: Harvey Birnbaum & Roz Chalman

Public Eye Productions (917) 446-8977
409 Meeker St. www.publiceyeproductions.com
South Orange, NJ 07079
Contact: Scott Sinkler

Pureland Pictures, Inc. (718) 965-0636
FAX (718) 965-0637
www.purelandpictures.com

RBY Productions, Inc. (203) 264-3666
920 Main St. North FAX (203) 264-3616
Southbury, CT 06488 www.rbyproductions.com
Contact: Evan Jones

Real Productions, Inc. (212) 271-0020
214 Sullivan St., Second Fl. www.realprod.com
(Near Bleecker St.)
New York, NY 10012
Contacts: Jim Calabrese & Richard DeLigter

Red Thread Productions (212) 367-7100
873 Broadway, Ste. 501 FAX (212) 228-6209
New York, NY 10003 www.redthreadproductions.com

RedHawk Communications (732) 440-1600
Victoria Plaza, 615 Hope Rd., Ste. 2B FAX (732) 440-1601
Eatontown, NJ 07724 www.redhawkethics.com

Relay Productions, Inc. (718) 260-9663
11 Fourth St., Second Fl. www.relayproductions.com
(Near Smith St.)
Brooklyn, NY 11231
Contacts: Richard Numeroff & Emily Quan

Rooftop Edit (212) 244-0744
104 W. 29th St., 12th Fl. FAX (212) 244-0690
(Near Sixth Ave.) www.rooftopedit.com
New York, NY 10001
Contact: Anthony Forte

Salt and Pepper Media (212) 929-2028
www.saltandpeppermedia.com

**Scharff Weisberg
Media Resource Center** (718) 610-1660
36-36 33rd St. (Near Third Ave.) FAX (718) 610-1750
Long Island City, NY 11106 www.swinyc.com

Simba Productions, Inc. (212) 216-9155
115 W. 29th St., Ste. 605 FAX (212) 216-9599
(Near Sixth Ave.) www.simbaproductions.net
New York, NY 10001
Contact: Albert Dabah

SLAM! Media Group (212) 924-7100
54 W. 21st St., Ste. 410 FAX (212) 229-2080
New York, NY 10010 www.slammediagroup.com

(212) 472-8789
Slate, Inc. (917) 691-3049
444 E. 82nd St., Ste. 14J (Near York Ave.)
New York, NY 10028
Contact: Peter Viola

Sonalysts' Studios (800) 526-8091
221 Parkway North FAX (860) 326-3748
Waterford, CT 06385 www.sonalystsmedia.com

Stable Films (212) 219-8200
86 Franklin St., Fourth Fl. FAX (212) 219-2357
(Near Church St.)
New York, NY 10013
Contact: Alex Vlack

Suggs Media Productions, Inc. (212) 398-4200
156 W. 44th St., Seventh Fl. FAX (212) 382-0922
(Near Broadway)
New York, NY 10036
Contact: Jeanne Suggs

The System (212) 957-9509
134 Parker Ave. FAX (917) 338-7596
Easton, PA 18042 www.thesystemmsp.com
Contact: Gene Perla

T-Line TV, Inc. (212) 988-3200
450 Park Ave. South, Third Fl. FAX (212) 779-4999
(Near E. 30th St.) www.t-linetv.com
New York, NY 10016
Contacts: Todd F. Ehrlich & Richard Young

Take 2 Productions (973) 508-6054
297-101 Kinderkamack Rd., Ste. 111
Oradell, NJ 07649 www.take2productions.com
Contact: George Barnes

Ted Steeg Productions, Inc. (212) 505-2088
26 W. Ninth St., Ste. 3D FAX (212) 505-2115
(Near Avenue of the Americas)
New York, NY 10011
Contact: Ted Steeg

(212) 688-5490
Top Hat Productions (877) 786-7428
305 Madison Ave., Ste. 449 FAX (800) 505-1329
New York, NY 10165 www.top-hat.com

USA Studios (212) 398-6400
29 W. 38th St. (Near Fifth Ave.) FAX (212) 398-8037
New York, NY 10018 www.usastudios.tv
Contact: Kenny Kahn

Viceroy Films (212) 725-9818
401 W. 56th St., Ste. 2M FAX (212) 725-9819
(Near Columbus Ave.) www.viceroyfilms.com
New York, NY 10019

(718) 204-1030
Video Concepts, Inc. (888) 482-4278
18-25 26th Rd. (Near 21st St.) FAX (718) 204-1017
Long Island City, NY 11102 www.videoconcepts.com
Contact: Patrick Giovanniello

Video Production New York (917) 353-2952
Two Gold St. www.videoproduction.us.com
New York, NY 10038

VideoActive Productions (212) 541-6592
1560 Broadway, Studio 610 www.videoactiveprod.com
(Near W. 57th St.)
New York, NY 10036
Contact: Steven Garrin

(800) 452-5565
VideoLink, Inc. (215) 557-8520
148 N. 17th St. FAX (215) 557-8526
Philadelphia, PA 19103 www.videolink.tv

(610) 647-3242
VideoNet, Inc. (610) 633-2862
912 St. Andrews Dr. FAX (610) 647-3774
Malvern, PA 19355 www.videonetinc.com
Contact: Ron Strobel

Wishengrad Pictures, Inc. (212) 749-7920
Contact: Marc Wishengrad www.wishpic.com

Zeitbyte (718) 666-3300
45 Main St., Ste. 1030 www.zeitbyte.com
Brooklyn, NY 11201

Independent Director's Reps

Maggie Klein & Co. (212) 447-9880
1201 Broadway, Ste. 801 FAX (212) 447-9889
(Near W. 29th St.)
New York, NY 10001

Mirsky Reps (212) 753-1312
481 Eighth Ave. (Near W. 34th St.)
New York, NY 10001

Sandi Mollod (212) 308-4880
FAX (212) 838-4338
www.sanditv.com

Naitove + Company (212) 633-6211

Patricia Claire Co. (212) 255-2252
Six W. 20th St., Ninth Fl. FAX (212) 691-9131
(Near Fifth Ave.)
New York, NY 10011

SchafferRogers (212) 229-0833
145 Avenue of the Americas FAX (212) 337-1021
Seventh Fl. (Near Dominick St.) www.schafferrogers.com
New York, NY 10013

Tom Scott (310) 230-9932
1101 Las Lomas Ave. FAX (310) 230-9932
Pacific Palisades, CA 90272

(212) 794-9030
Silberman Productions (917) 880-6747
330 E. 75th St., Ste. 33A FAX (212) 794-9232
(Near Second Ave.)
New York, NY 10021

Infomercial Production Companies

**Aurora Productions
International, Inc.** (631) 549-8933
1160 E. Jericho Tpke, Ste. 110 FAX (631) 549-6890
(Near Deer Park Rd.) www.auroraproductions.tv
Huntington, NY 11743

Concepts TV Productions, Inc. (973) 331-1500
328 W. Main St. FAX (973) 331-1550
Boonton, NJ 07005 www.conceptstv.com
Contact: Collette Liantonio

(203) 498-8818
FirstImage, LLC (800) 317-1038
Contact: Robin Desjardins FAX (203) 404-7191
www.firstimage.tv

The Lopes Picture Company, Inc. (212) 477-1114
29 E. 19th St., Seventh Fl. FAX (212) 477-2145
(Near Broadway) www.lopespictureco.com
New York, NY 10003

Mayhew Breen Productions (212) 243-0299
19 W. 21st St. (Near Fifth Ave.) FAX (212) 243-5525
New York, NY 10010 www.mayhewbreen.com
Contacts: Kirsten Malone & Marianne O'Donnell

Mood Creations, Ltd. (914) 941-2357
One Depot Plaza (Near Water St.) FAX (914) 941-3142
Ossining, NY 10562 www.moodcreations.com
Contacts: Donald Cohen & Scott Cohen

Motion Picture Production Companies

Angelika Entertainment Corporation (212) 996-8215 / (213) 840-6224
P.O. Box 4956
New York, NY 10185
FAX (213) 477-2004
www.angelikafilm.com
President: Angelika Saleh
General Manager: Barney Oldfield
Production Manager: David Maquiling
Administration: Thomas Bannister

Astoria Films (212) 330-0607
545 Eighth Ave., Ste. 401
New York, NY 10018
www.astoriafilms.com
Principal: Roy Carlo
President of Motion Pictures & Television: James IaVita
Talent & Media Relations: Tom Kelly
CFA: Errol Horowitz
Counsel: Reavis Parent

City Lights Pictures (212) 679-4400 / (646) 467-7500
Six E. 39th St., Third Fl.
(Near Fifth Ave.)
New York, NY 10016
FAX (212) 679-4481
www.citylightsmedia.com
Contacts: Danny Fisher, Jack Fisher & Marcus Lansdell

Focus Features (212) 539-4000
65 Bleecker St., Second Fl.
(Near Broadway)
New York, NY 10012
FAX (212) 539-4099
www.filminfocus.com
President: Donna Gigliotti

Forensic Films (212) 966-1110
One Worth St., Second Fl.
(Near Hudson St.)
New York, NY 10013
FAX (212) 966-1125

Fred Berner Films (212) 769-8425
500 Fifth Ave., Ste. 2700
(Near 42nd St.)
New York, NY 10110
FAX (212) 921-4249

Full Glass Films, LLC (212) 874-6282
386 Park Ave. South, Ste. 303
(Near E. 27th St.)
New York, NY 10016
www.fullglassfilms.com
Partners: Stan Erdreich, Michael Parness & Elana Pianko

Guardian Entertainment, LTD (212) 727-4729
71 Fifth Ave., Fifth Fl. (Near 15th St.) FAX (212) 727-4737
New York, NY 10003
www.guardianltd.com
Executive Producer/Producer/CEO: Richard Miller
Supervising Producer TV: Susann Brinkley
VP of Business Development/General Counsel: Clem Turner

Infinite Scenarios (917) 627-1057
371 Sixth Ave., Third Fl.
Brooklyn, NY 11215
www.infinitescenerios.com

Killer Films (212) 473-3950
380 Lafayette St., Ste. 202
(Near Great Jones St.)
New York, NY 10003
FAX (212) 473-6152
www.killerfilms.com
Producers: Pamela Koffler, Katie Roumel & Christine Vachon

Merchant Ivory Productions (212) 582-8049
250 W. 57th St., Ste. 1825
(Near Broadway)
New York, NY 10107
FAX (212) 459-9201
www.merchantivory.com
President/Director: James Ivory
Executive Producer: Richard Hawley
Director of Production: Pierre Proner

Open City Films (212) 255-0500
122 Hudson St., Fifth Fl.
(Near Spring St.)
New York, NY 10013
FAX (212) 255-0455
www.opencityfilms.com
Head of Production: Gretchen McGowan
Manager of Production & Finance: Kristina Redick
Executive Assistant: Courtney Andrialis

Picture House (212) 649-4800
597 Fifth Ave., Fourth Fl.
(Near W. 56th St.)
New York, NY 10017
FAX (212) 956-1942
www.picturehouse.com
President: Mark Ordesky

Sikelia Productions (212) 906-8800
110 W. 57th St.
(Near Avenue of the Americas)
New York, NY 10019
FAX (212) 906-8891
Director: Martin Scorsese

Studio-On-Hudson (845) 348-7674
37 N. Broadway (Near High Ave.) FAX (845) 348-1548
Nyack, NY 10960
www.studio-on-hudson.com
Executive Producers: Joseph Morley & Heather Winters

Sunset Pictures, LLC (347) 715-3858
767 Autumn Ave., Ste. 3
Brooklyn, NY 11208
FAX (347) 715-3858
www.sunsetpicturesllc.com
Director/Producer: Donovan Rodriques

Third Eye Motion Picture Co., Inc. (212) 462-1590
P.O. Box 1008
Yorktown Heights, NY 10598
FAX (212) 462-1600
Producer/Directors: Joe Berlinger & Bruce Sinofsky
Associate Producer: Mike Bonfiglio

Troma Entertainment, Inc. (212) 757-4555 / (718) 391-0110
733 Ninth Ave. (Near W. 50th St.) FAX (212) 399-9885
New York, NY 10019
www.troma.com
President: Lloyd Kaufman
Vice President: Michael Herz
Acquisitions: Jeff Shiels
Marketing Director: Josh Petraglia

Wind Dancer Production Group (212) 765-4772
200 W. 57th St., Ste. 601
(Near Seventh Ave.)
New York, NY 10019
FAX (212) 765-4785
Partners: Carmen Finestra, David McFadzean & Matt Williams

Guardian Entertainment
NY's Premier High Definition Production & Post Production Company
• All HD Formats • 24P Specialists • Featuring Sony F900's & XPRI NLE's
Cameras, Lighting, Grip, Post Production
We own the gear...we have the talent.
Got a project? Get it right the FIRST time, in less time!
SONY CINE ALTA XPRI HD NLE
71 5th Ave, 5th Fl, NY, NY 10003 • www.guardianltd.com
(212) 727-4729

Music Video Directors

Acne	(212) 343-2020	www.rsafilms.com
Jonas Åkerlund	(212) 343-2020	www.rsafilms.com
Monica Anderson	(212) 349-0369	www.blackwatchproductions.com
Matt Aselton	(212) 226-0661	www.epochfilms.com
Matt Badger	(212) 226-0661	www.epochfilms.com
Brian Beletic	(212) 337-3327	www.smugglersite.com
Todd Bellanca	(917) 885-9513 / (310) 584-1460	www.toddbellanca.com
James Brown	(212) 337-3327	www.smugglersite.com
Rey Carlson	(212) 226-0661	www.epochfilms.com
Lisa Crook	(212) 679-7199	www.theartistscompany.com
Alan Cumming	(212) 941-7680	www.zoomazooma.com
John Dahl	(212) 354-8188	www.epandmedia.com
Ben Dickinson	(212) 343-2020	www.rsafilms.com
Andrew Dosunmu	(212) 679-7199	www.theartistscompany.com
Steph Green	(212) 343-2020	www.littleminx.tv
Paula Grief	(212) 226-0661	www.epochfilms.com
The Guard Brothers	(212) 462-2700	www.villains.com
H5	(212) 343-2020	www.rsafilms.com
Happy	(212) 337-3327	www.smugglersite.com
Johnny Hardstaff	(212) 343-2020	www.littleminx.tv
Miranda July	(212) 226-0661	www.epochfilms.com
Mat Kirkby	(212) 343-2020	www.rsafilms.com
Jesper Kouthoofd	(212) 343-2020	www.littleminx.tv
Matt Lenski	(212) 226-0661	www.epochfilms.com
Sasha Levinson	(212) 941-7680	www.zoomazooma.com
Mike Long	(212) 226-0661	www.epochfilms.com
The Malloys	(212) 343-2020	www.rsafilms.com
Edna McCallion	(212) 226-0661	www.epochfilms.com
Ryan McFaul	(212) 941-7680	www.zoomazooma.com
Melina	(212) 343-2020	www.rsafilms.com
Josh Miller	(212) 343-2020	www.rsafilms.com
Ben Mor	(212) 343-2020	www.littleminx.tv
Phil Morrison	(212) 226-0661	www.epochfilms.com
David Mullet	(212) 343-2020	www.littleminx.tv
Steven Murashige	(212) 679-7199	www.theartistscompany.com
Chris Nelson	(212) 343-2020	www.rsafilms.com
Dewey Nicks	(212) 462-2700	www.villains.com
Matt Ogens	(917) 532-0995	
Otis	(212) 679-7199	www.theartistscompany.com
Marius Penczner	(212) 354-8188	www.epandmedia.com
Jeff Preiss	(212) 226-0661	www.epochfilms.com
Sam Raimi	(212) 941-7680	www.zoomazooma.com
Johan Renck	(212) 343-2020	www.rsafilms.com
Carl Erik Rinsch	(212) 343-2020	www.rsafilms.com
Malik Hassan Sayeed	(212) 343-2020	www.rsafilms.com
Jake Scott	(212) 343-2020	www.rsafilms.com
Jordan Scott	(212) 343-2020	www.rsafilms.com
Luke Scott	(212) 343-2020	www.rsafilms.com
Ridley Scott	(212) 343-2020	www.rsafilms.com

Tony Scott	(212) 343-2020 www.rsafilms.com	Stylewar	(212) 337-3327 www.smugglersite.com
Mark Seliger	(212) 343-2020 www.littleminx.tv	Tarsem	(212) 679-7199 www.theartistscompany.com
Dawn Shadforth	(212) 343-2020 www.rsafilms.com	Eden Tyler	(212) 941-7680 www.zoomazooma.com
David Slade	(212) 343-2020 www.rsafilms.com	Phillip Van	(212) 343-2020 www.littleminx.tv
Alex Smith	(212) 343-2020 www.rsafilms.com	Stacy Wall	(212) 226-0661 www.epochfilms.com
Eidur Snorri	(212) 337-3327 www.smugglersite.com	Jon Watts	(212) 337-3327 www.smugglersite.com
Michael Stern	(631) 836-3300 www.michaelstern.mabusinc.com	Jim Yukich	(212) 354-8188 www.epandmedia.com

Music Video Production Companies

7NY (212) 962-1850
195 Chrystie St., Ste. 401C   FAX (212) 962-1043
New York, NY 10002   www.7-ny.com

  (718) 928-3812
AAA Acme Discount Film Works   (917) 861-4120
56 Fifth Ave. (Near St. Mark's Pl.)   www.aaaacme.com
Brooklyn, NY 11217

  (718) 626-2646
Air Sea Land Productions, Inc.   (888) 275-5367
19-69 Steinway St. (Near 20th Ave.)   FAX (718) 626-1493
Astoria, NY 11105   www.airsealand.com

  (212) 679-7199
The Artists Company   (323) 650-4722
38 W. 21st St., 12th Fl.   FAX (212) 741-1519
(Near Fifth Ave.)   www.theartistscompany.com
New York, NY 10010
Executive Creative Director: Roberto Cecchini
Vice President: Sally Antonacchio
Directors: Lisa Crook, Andrew Dosunmu, Steven Murashige, Otis & Tarsem
Sales Rep: Laure Scott Representation

  (212) 343-2020
Black Dog Films (RSA Films)   (310) 659-1577
270 Lafayette St., Ste. 203   FAX (212) 343-2024
(Near Prince St.)   www.rsafilms.com
New York, NY 10012
Executive Producer: Kim Dellara
Directors: Acne, Jonas Åkerlund, Ben Dickinson, The Malloys, Melina, Johan Renck, Carl Erik Rinsch, Jake Scott, Jordan Scott, Luke Scott, Ridley Scott, Tony Scott, David Slade & Alex Smith
Production Coordinator: Jill Hammer

Black Watch Productions   (212) 349-0369
49 Murray St., Ste. 1 (Near Church St.)   FAX (212) 349-1335
New York, NY 10007   www.blackwatchproductions.com
Executive Producer: John Anderson
Executive Producer/Director: Monica Anderson
Production Manager: Peter Gagnon

Bocce Club Pictures, LLC   (212) 414-2220
104 E. 25th St., 12th Fl.   FAX (212) 414-2206
New York, NY 10010   www.bocceclubpictures.com

Brooklyn Films   (212) 744-2845
P.O. Box 20412   www.rkvbrooklyngroup.com
New York, NY 10021

City Lights Productions   (646) 467-7500
Six E. 39th St., Third Fl.   www.citylightsmedia.com
(Near Fifth Ave.)
New York, NY 10016
President/CEO: Danny Fisher
President: Jack Fisher

epandmedia/Flashframe Films   (212) 354-8188
Two W. 45th St., Ste. 1200   FAX (212) 354-8652
(Near Fifth Ave.)   www.epandmedia.com
New York, NY 10036
President: Len Epand
Directors: John Dahl, Marius Penczner & Jim Yukich

Epoch Films, Inc.   (212) 226-0661
122 Hudson St., Third Fl.   FAX (212) 226-4893
(Near N. Moore St.)
New York, NY 10013
Directors: Matt Aselton, Matt Badger, Rey Carlson, Paula Grief, Miranda July, Matt Lenski, Mike Long, Edna McCallion, Phil Morrison, Jeff Preiss & Stacy Wall

HSI Productions, Inc.   (212) 627-3600
601 W. 26th St., Ste. 1420   FAX (212) 627-5947
(Near 11th Ave.)   www.hsiproductions.com
New York, NY 10001

  (212) 343-2020
Little Minx   (310) 659-1577
270 Lafayette St., Ste. 203   FAX (212) 343-2024
(Near Prince St.)   www.littleminx.tv
New York, NY 10012
President: Rhea Scott
Directors: Steph Green, H5, Johnny Hardstaff, Jesper Kouthoofd, Ben Mor, Josh Miller, David Mullet, Chris Nelson, Malik Sayeed, Mark Seliger, Dawn Shadforth & Phillip Van

Mabus, Inc.   (631) 836-3300
  www.mabusinc.com

Monsoon Films   (917) 225-0889
2322 Seventh Ave., Ste. 1A   www.monsoonfilmsinc.com
(Near Avenue B)
New York, NY 10030
Executive Producer: Mala Perna
Director/Creative Director: Dwayne B. Perryman III

SixDay Productions, LLC   (917) 670-9976
One Penn Plaza, Ste. 6161   FAX (212) 290-8089
New York, NY 10119   www.sixdayproductions.com

Smuggler   (212) 337-3327
184 Fifth Ave., Seventh Fl.   FAX (212) 337-9686
(Near E. 22nd St.)   www.smugglersite.com
New York, NY 10010
Executive Producers: Brian Carmody & Patrick Milling Smith
Head of Production: Allison Kunzman
Directors: Brian Beletic, James Brown, Happy, Ben Mor, Eidur Snorri, Stylewar & Jon Watts
Sales Rep: Tommy LaBuda

  (212) 688-5490
Top Hat Productions   (877) 786-7428
305 Madison Ave., Ste. 449   FAX (800) 505-1329
New York, NY 10165   www.top-hat.com

  (212) 462-2700
Villains   (310) 888-8900
134 W. 25th St. (Near Seventh Ave.)   FAX (212) 462-4502
New York, NY 10001   www.villains.com
President: John Marshall
Directors: The Guard Brothers & Dewey Nicks
Sales Rep: Heidi Wahl

Zooma Zooma Corporation   (212) 941-7680
11 Mercer St., Third Fl. (Near Grand St.)   FAX (212) 941-8179
New York, NY 10013   www.zoomazooma.com
President/Executive Producer: Joseph Mantegna
Producer: Henry Castillo
Directors: Todd Bellanca, Alan Cumming, Sasha Levinson, Ryan McFaul, Sam Raimi & Eden Tyler
Sales Rep: Coleen McHale

Production Offices

CECO International (212) 206-8280
440 W. 15th St. (Near 10th Ave.) FAX (212) 727-2144
New York, NY 10011 www.cecostudios.com

City Stage (212) 627-3400
435 W. 19th St. (Near Ninth Ave.) FAX (212) 633-1228
New York, NY 10011 www.citystage.com

Departure Films (212) 629-9666
333 W. 39th St., Ste. 1502 FAX (212) 629-6788
New York, NY 10018 www.departure-films.com

Eastern Effects, Inc. (718) 855-1197
210 Douglass St. FAX (212) 504-9534
Brooklyn, NY 11217 www.easterneffects.com

eEmerge Production Suites (212) 404-2000
440 Ninth Ave., Eighth, 11th & 17th Fl. FAX (212) 404-3228
(Near 35th St.) www.eemerge.com
New York, NY 10001

The Film Collective (212) 334-3577
349 Broadway, Third Fl. FAX (212) 334-3565
(Near Leonard St.) www.senzapix.com
New York, NY 10013

Gigantic Pictures (212) 925-5075
59 Franklin St., Ground Fl. FAX (212) 925-5061
New York, NY 10013 www.giganticpictures.com

Greenestreet Films, Inc. (212) 609-9000
Nine Desbrosses St., Second Fl. FAX (212) 609-9099
(Near Hudson St.) www.greenestreetfilms.com
New York, NY 10013

home.work.people (212) 213-0028
636 Broadway, Ste. 1104 (310) 917-4420
New York, NY 10012 FAX (212) 677-3245
www.homeworkpeople.com

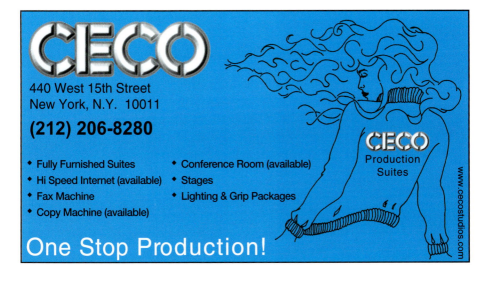

NYC PRODUCTION SPACE. REDEFINED.

eEmerge
We set the stage. You call the shots.

eEmerge is Manhattan's premiere pre and post production office space center. Fully-furnished, turn-key space, long and short-term space needs.

Visit eEmerge.com for additional information or call James Kleeman at: **212.404.3040** today.

440 9th Avenue   eEmerge.com   28 West 44th

LVR/Liman Video Rental Company (212) 594-0086 / (800) 251-4625
341 W. 38th St., Ground Fl.   FAX **(212) 594-0786**
(Near Eighth Ave.)   www.lvrusa.com
New York, NY 10018

Nutopia Workspace   (212) 400-0500
81 Franklin St.   FAX **(212) 504-8180**
New York, NY 10013   www.nutopia.us

Steiner Studios   (718) 858-1600
15 Washington Ave.   FAX **(718) 858-1690**
Brooklyn Navy Yard, NY 11205   www.steinerstudios.com

Tribeca Film Center   (212) 941-2000
375 Greenwich St. (Near Franklin St.)   FAX **(212) 941-2012**
New York, NY 10013   www.tribecafilm.com

West Side Office   (212) 904-1810
438 W. 37th St., Ste. 4G   FAX **(212) 904-1864**
New York, NY 10018   www.thewestsideoffice.com

Wits End Production Suites   (212) 242-9400 / (917) 691-3999
547 W. 49th St. (Near 10th Ave.)   FAX **(212) 242-1797**
New York, NY 10019   www.witsendnyc.com

Wits End Production Suites   (718) 361-8400
43-26 12th St. (Near 43rd Ave.)   FAX **(718) 361-8440**
Long Island City, NY 11101   www.witsendnyc.com

World-Wide Business Centres   (212) 605-0200
575 Madison Ave., Ste. 1006   FAX **(212) 605-0222**
(Near Fourth Ave.)   www.wwbcn.com
New York, NY 10022

Promo Production Companies

bobsyouruncle.   (212) 545-7800
638 E. Sixth St., Third Fl.   FAX (212) 545-0398
New York, NY 10009   www.bobsyouruncle.tv

City Lights Productions   (212) 679-4400
    (646) 467-7500
Six E. 39th St., Third Fl.   FAX (212) 679-3819
(Near Fifth Ave.)   www.citylightsmedia.com
New York, NY 10016
Contacts: Danny Fisher & Jack Fisher

The Farm   (212) 982-8500
611 Broadway, Ste. 729   FAX (707) 982-8505
(Near Park Ave.)   www.thefarm.com
New York, NY 10012
Contact: John Anderson

FDG   (646) 233-2226
Contact: Hillary E. Cutter   FAX (646) 233-2226
    www.fdg3.com

hscusa.tv   (718) 626-6226
19-69 Steinway St.   FAX (718) 626-1493
Astoria, NY 11105   www.hscusa.tv

Pyburn Films   (212) 925-5595
1560 Broadway, 17th Fl.   FAX (212) 925-7117
(Near Times Square)   www.pyburn.com
New York, NY 10036
Contact: Debra Henni

Slate, Inc.   (212) 472-8789
    (917) 691-3049
444 E. 82nd St., Ste. 14J (Near York Ave.)
New York, NY 10028
Contact: Peter Viola

Public Relations

Anna Samuel & Associates, Inc. (212) 786-0619
377 Rector Pl., Ste. 21 www.annasamuel.com
(Near West Side Hwy)
New York, NY 10280

Bender/Helper Impact (212) 689-6360
115 W. 30th St., Ste. 602 FAX **(212) 689-6601**
(Near Avenue of the Americas) www.bhimpact.com
New York, NY 10001

Dera, Roslan & Campion (212) 966-4600
584 Broadway, Ste. 1001 FAX **(212) 966-5763**
(Near Prince St.)
New York, NY 10012

Geto & Demilly, Inc. (212) 686-4551
  FAX **(212) 213-6850**
  www.getodemilly.com

The Hendra Agency Inc. (718) 622-3232
142 Sterling Pl. (Near Seventh Ave.)
Brooklyn, NY 11217

Keith Sherman & Associates (212) 764-7900
234 W. 44th St., Ste. 1004 FAX **(212) 764-0344**
New York, NY 10036 www.ksa-pr.com

LaForce & Stevens (212) 242-9353
132 W. 21st St. (Near Sixth Ave.) FAX **(212) 242-9565**
New York, NY 10011 www.laforce-stevens.com

LVM Group (212) 499-6500
60 E. 42nd St., Ste. 722 FAX **(212) 751-2862**
New York, NY 10165 www.lvmgroup.com

Middleberg Euro (212) 367-6800
110 Fifth Ave., Sixth Fl. FAX **(212) 367-7154**
New York, NY 10011 www.middleberg.com

PMK, Inc. (212) 582-1111
161 Avenue of the Americas, Ste. 10R FAX **(212) 582-6666**
(Near Spring St.)
New York, NY 10013

The Rosen Group (212) 255-8455
30 W. 26th St., Third Fl. FAX **(212) 255-8456**
(Near Sixth Ave.) www.rosengrouppr.com
New York, NY 10010

S.J. Golden Associates, Inc. (212) 683-1777
300 E. 34th St., Ste. 26C www.sjgoldenpr.com
New York, NY 10016

**Schwartz
Public Relations Associates** (212) 677-8700
444 Park Ave. South FAX **(212) 254-2507**
New York, NY 10016 www.schwartzpr.com

Susan Senk Public Relations (212) 876-5948
1755 York Ave., Ste. 33F (Near W. 16th St.)
New York, NY 10128

Visibility Public Relations, Inc. (914) 712-2610
55 Webster Ave., Ste. 406 (Near Main) FAX **(914) 712-2613**
New Rochelle, NY 10801 www.visibilitypr.com

Storyboard Artists

Above & Beyond Artists Agency (323) 464-9696
439 N. Larchmont Blvd. FAX (323) 464-5608
Los Angeles, CA 90004 www.aboveandbeyondartists.com
(Reps for Storyboard Artists)

Mike Alden (800) 289-0109
www.storyboardsinc.com

All Reel Design (914) 262-6459
www.allreel.com

Dave Arkle (800) 289-0109
www.storyboardsinc.com

Kathy Berry (212) 980-7979
www.famousframes.com

Paul Binkley (212) 980-7979
www.famousframes.com

Tim Burgard (800) 289-0109
www.storyboardsinc.com

Ray Cadd (800) 289-0109
www.storyboardsinc.com

Dan Caplan (800) 289-0109
www.storyboardsinc.com

Peter Carpenter (800) 289-0109
www.storyboardsinc.com

Ivan Cat (310) 581-4050
www.storyboardsinc.com

Kamen Chalakov (212) 980-7979
www.famousframes.com

Bernard Chang (212) 980-7979
www.famousframes.com

Jiye Choi (800) 289-0109
www.storyboardsinc.com

Chris Scalf Illustrations Inc. (248) 620-0705
www.chrisscalf.com

Jeff Coatney (212) 980-7979
www.famousframes.com

Phillipe Collot (212) 980-7979
www.famousframes.com

Elizabeth Colomba (800) 289-0109
www.storyboardsinc.com

Lorenzo Contessa (212) 663-4124
(917) 952-4485
FAX (212) 663-4124

David Cooney (718) 596-5871
(646) 221-5488

Ron Croci (212) 980-7979
www.famousframes.com

Federico D'Alessandro (800) 289-0109
www.storyboardsinc.com

Tony Daniel (800) 289-0109
www.storyboardsinc.com

Danelle Davenport (818) 590-8586
www.danelledavenport.com

John F. Davis (212) 406-2282
(917) 806-7524
FAX (212) 406-2282

Stephen DeBonrepos (212) 980-7979
www.famousframes.com

Gus DeGuzman (212) 980-7979
www.famousframes.com

Juan Diaz (212) 980-7979
www.famousframes.com

Paul Didier (212) 980-7979
www.famousframes.com

Hugo Dipietro (212) 980-7979
www.famousframes.com

Alex Echevarria (800) 289-0109
www.storyboardsinc.com

Tomoki Echigo (212) 980-7979
www.famousframes.com

Anton Evangelista (718) 881-0297
(646) 339-1842

Famous Frames, Inc. (212) 980-7979
247 E. 57th St., Second Fl. (800) 530-3375
(Near Second Ave.) FAX (212) 980-6556
New York, NY 10022 www.famousframes.com
(Reps for Storyboard Artists)

Gabriella Farkas (212) 980-7979
www.famousframes.com

Kevin Farrell (212) 980-7979
www.famousframes.comm

John Fox (310) 383-3773
www.johnfoxart.com

Frameworks Storyboards (323) 665-7736
983 Manzanita St. FAX (323) 662-4381
Los Angeles, CA 90029 www.frameworks-la.com
(Reps for Storyboard Artists)

Matt Fuller (800) 289-0109
www.storyboardsinc.com

Roger Gana (800) 289-0109
www.storyboardsinc.com

Jonathan Gesinski (212) 980-7979
www.famousframes.com

Chad Glass (800) 289-0109
www.storyboardsinc.com

Lyle Grant (800) 289-0109
www.storyboardsinc.com

Zack Grossman (800) 289-0109
www.storyboardsinc.com

Josh Hayes (800) 289-0109
www.storyboardsinc.com

Jeff Henderson (212) 980-7979
www.famousframes.com

Hillman Arts (212) 285-1995
(917) 655-0988
FAX (212) 285-8664
www.hillmanarts.com

David Hudnut	(212) 980-7979 www.famousframes.com	Mark Millicent	(212) 980-7979 www.famousframes.com
Mark Hurtado	(212) 980-7979 www.famousframes.com	Yori Mochizuki	(212) 980-7979 www.famousframes.com
Peter Ivanoff	(212) 980-7979 www.famousframes.com	Mark Moretti	(212) 980-7979 www.famousframes.com
Patrick James	(800) 289-0109 www.storyboardsinc.com	Alex Morris	(212) 980-7979 www.famousframes.com
Al Johnson	(646) 963-0498 FAX (646) 678-3836 xframes1.tripod.com	Edward Murr	(917) 721-6520 www.edmurr.com
		Brian Murray	(212) 980-7979 www.famousframes.com
Zeke Johnson	(800) 289-0109 www.storyboardsinc.com	John Killian Nelson	(212) 980-7979 www.famousframes.com
Robert Kalafut	(212) 980-7979 www.famousframes.com	Rick Newsome	(800) 289-0109 www.storyboardsinc.com
Merle Keller	(212) 980-7979 www.famousframes.com	Quan Ngo	(212) 980-7979 www.famousframes.com
Brian Koons	(800) 289-0109 www.storyboardsinc.com	Mark S. Pacella	(212) 980-7979 www.famousframes.com
Dylan Korelich	(917) 435-7329 www.dkstoryboards.com	Neal Parrow	(212) 980-7979 www.famousframes.com
Jeff Kronen	(212) 980-7979 www.famousframes.com	Ivan Pavlovits	(212) 980-7979 www.famousframes.com
George Ladas	(908) 298-3730 www.base24.com	Ryon Peck	(212) 980-7979 www.famousframes.com
David Larks	(212) 980-7979 www.famousframes.com	Brian Postman	(212) 213-6242 (917) 544-8688 FAX (212) 213-6242 www.brianpostman.com/storyboards.html
Lance Leblanc	(800) 289-0109 www.storyboardsinc.com		
Michael Lee	(212) 980-7979 www.famousframes.com	Charles Ratteray	(212) 980-7979 www.famousframes.com
Anthony Liberatore	(800) 289-0109 www.storyboardsinc.com	Renee Reeser	(212) 980-7979 www.famousframes.com
Wes Louie	(212) 980-7979 www.famousframes.com	David Reuss	(212) 980-7979 www.famousframes.com
Franck Louis-Marie	(212) 980-7979 www.famousframes.com	Kathryn Roake	(718) 788-2755
Salvatore Lucido	(212) 980-7979 www.famousframes.com	Saint James Studios 419 W. 17th St., Ste. 16-U (Near Ninth Ave.) New York, NY 10011	(212) 366-9050 (917) 921-9395 FAX (212) 366-9491 www.saintjamesstudios.com
Ernie Marjoram	(800) 289-0109 www.storyboardsinc.com		
Adolfo Martinez	(800) 289-0109 www.storyboardsinc.com	Marc Sandroni	(800) 289-0109 www.storyboardsinc.com
Steven Martinez	(212) 980-7979 www.famousframes.com	Mark Sasway	(212) 980-7979 www.famousframes.com
Eddy Mayer	(212) 980-7979 www.famousframes.com	David Selvadurai	(800) 289-0109 www.storyboardsinc.com
Chad McCown	(212) 980-7979 www.famousframes.com	Daniel Senties	(212) 980-7979 www.famousframes.com
Colin McGreal	(212) 980-7979 www.famousframes.com	John Sicoransa	(212) 674-0541 FAX (212) 674-0541 www.nonsequiturtheater.com
David Mellon	(212) 980-7979 www.famousframes.com	Aaron Sowd	(212) 980-7979 www.famousframes.com
Jim Mickle	(917) 607-5405 www.storyboardartist.net	Eric Stewart	(800) 289-0109 www.storyboardsinc.com

Storyboards, Inc.
100 Market St., Ste. E
Venice, CA 90291
(Reps for Storyboard Artists)
(310) 581-4050
(800) 289-0109
FAX (310) 581-4060
www.storyboardsinc.com

Storyboards Online
275 Madison Ave. (Near W. 48th St.)
New York, NY 10016
(212) 221-0040
(866) 419-3100
FAX (212) 751-3500
www.storyboardsonline.com

Susan DePhillips Illustration
10 Sheridan Square, Ste. 10B (Near Seventh Ave.)
New York, NY 10014
(212) 645-4857
(917) 406-9256

TellAVision
1060 20th St., Ste. 8
Santa Monica, CA 90403
(Reps for Storyboard Artists)
(310) 230-5303
FAX (310) 388-5550
www.tellavisionagency.com

David Threadgold — (212) 980-7979
www.famousframes.com

Bob Towner — (212) 980-7979
www.famousframes.com

Brad Vancata — (212) 980-7979
www.famousframes.com

Joel Venti — (800) 289-0109
www.storyboardsinc.com

Fred Warter — (212) 980-7979
www.famousframes.com

Kaleo Welborn — (212) 980-7979
www.famousframes.com

Steve Werblun — (212) 980-7979
www.famousframes.com

Shari Wickstrom — (212) 980-7979
www.famousframes.com

Jonathan Woods — (212) 890-7979
www.famousframes.com

Bill Wylie
(718) 237-8837
(917) 312-2512
FAX (718) 237-8837
www.wyliestudio.com

Nob Yamashita — (212) 980-7979
www.famousframes.com

Television Production Companies

A&E Television Networks   (212) 210-1400
235 E. 45th St. (Near Seventh Ave.)   www.aetv.com
New York, NY 10017
President/CEO: Abbe Raven

ABC Entertainment   (212) 456-7777
77 W. 66th St. (Near Columbus Ave.)   www.abc.com
New York, NY 10023

Anderson Productions   (860) 589-2776 / (800) 701-4311
34 Dell Manor Dr.   FAX (860) 584-5936
Bristol, CT 06010   www.andersonprod.com
President: Gwen Anderson
Production Manager: Tracy Ericson

Aurora Productions International, Inc.   (631) 549-8933
1160 E. Jericho Tpke, Ste. 110   FAX (631) 549-6890
(Near Deer Park Rd.)   www.auroraproductions.tv
Huntington, NY 11743

Automatic Productions   (212) 833-8000
General Manager/Sr. VP: Andy Kadison
Executive Producer: Stephanie Masarsky
Producer: Laurie Heuler

B-Train Films   (212) 645-6400
FAX (212) 645-6819
www.b-trainfilms.com

BBP, Inc.   (215) 477-4769
6100 City Ave., Ste. 1206   FAX (215) 477-9180
Philadelphia, PA 19131
President: Stanley T. Evans
Vice President: Stephen B. Ratner
Marketing Director: Victoria Mariano
Administration: Sara Bermudez

BC Video, Inc.   (212) 242-4065 / (212) 242-4117
152 W. 25th St., Second Fl.   FAX (212) 242-4190
(Near Seventh Ave.)   www.bcvideo.com
New York, NY 10001
Director/Producer: Bill Cote
Producer: John Cheshire

Boardwalk Entertainment/ Alan Wagner Productions   (212) 679-3800
210 E. 39th St. (Near Third Ave.)
New York, NY 10016
Chairman: Alan Wagner
President: Susan Wagner
VP/Creative Affairs: Elizabeth Wagner

Bradford Entertainment   (212) 308-7390
450 Park Ave., Ste. 1903   FAX (212) 935-1636
(Near E. 57th St.)   www.barbarataylorbradford.com
New York, NY 10022
President/Producer: Robert Bradford
Director: Barbara Taylor Bradford

Broadway Video   (212) 265-7600
1619 Broadway (Near W. 49th St.)   FAX (212) 713-1535
New York, NY 10019   www.broadwayvideo.com
Chairman: Lorne Michaels
CEO: Jack Sullivan
COO: Brian Offutt

CitiCam Film & Video Services, Inc.   (212) 315-2000
515 W. 57th St. (Near 10th Ave.)   FAX (212) 586-1572
New York, NY 10019   www.citicam.net

City Lights Television   (646) 519-5200
Six E. 39th St., Second Fl.   FAX (212) 679-4482
(Near Sixth Ave.)   www.citylightsmedia.com
New York, NY 10016
Contacts: Michael Krupat & Dave Noll

Comedy Central   (212) 767-8600
1775 Broadway, 10th Fl.   FAX (212) 767-8592
(Near W. 57th St.)   www.comedycentral.com
New York, NY 10019
President/CEO: Doug Herzog

Departure Films   (212) 629-9666
333 W. 39th St., Ste. 1502   FAX (212) 629-6788
New York, NY 10018   www.departure-films.com

Design TV   (212) 673-1063
Producer: John Heller

The Dovetail Group, Inc.   (203) 876-0800
18 Bianca Dr.   FAX (203) 874-1335
Milford, CT 06460
Producer/Director: Gerri Brioso
Producer/Music Director: Richard Freitas

Ellsworth Productions   (646) 698-2916
309 W. 104th St., Ste. 3C   FAX (646) 698-1613
(Near West End Ave.)
New York, NY 10025
President: Ernie Fritz

Florentine Films/Sherman Pictures   (212) 980-5966
136 E. 56th St., Ste. 4B   FAX (212) 980-5944
(Near Park Ave.)   www.florentinefilms.com/sherman
New York, NY 10022
Producer/Director: Roger Sherman

GTN Pictures, LLC   (212) 580-2554
155 W. 72nd St., Ste. 402   FAX (212) 580-1247
(Near Broadway)   www.gtnpictures.com
New York, NY 10023
President: George Nierenberg

Gullane Entertainment   (212) 463-9623
230 Park Ave. South, 13th Fl.   FAX (212) 463-9626
(Near W. 25th St.)   www.entertainment.com
New York, NY 10010

HBO Films (NY)   (212) 512-1000
1100 Avenue of the Americas   FAX (212) 512-5009
(Near W. 42nd St.)   www.hbo.com
New York, NY 10036
President: Colin Callender

The History Channel   (212) 210-1400
235 E. 45th St. (Near Second Ave.)   FAX (212) 210-9016
New York, NY 10017   www.historychannel.com
Executive Vice President: Abbe Raven

HolidayWorld Productions   (914) 698-3059
c/o Travel Marketing Media   FAX (914) 698-1952
406 Soundview Ave. (Near Harbor Heights)
Mamaroneck, NY 10543
Executive Producer: Arne Ruud

hscusa.tv   (718) 626-6226
19-69 Steinway St.   FAX (718) 626-1493
Astoria, NY 11105   www.hscusa.tv

Jalbert Productions, Inc.   (631) 351-5878
230 New York Ave. (Near Leverich Pl.)   FAX (631) 351-5875
Huntington, NY 11743   www.jalbertfilm.com
President/Owner: Joe Jay Jalbert
VP of Syndication Sales: Carol Randel

Jim Houston Productions, Inc.   (201) 825-7659
103 Park St.   FAX (201) 825-2936
Ramsey, NJ 07446
President: James Houston
VP/Production Manager: Kathleen Houston

KPI/Kralyevich Productions, Inc. (646) 356-0700
Two Rector St., 18th Fl. FAX (212) 485-8511
(Near Seventh Ave.) www.kpitv.com
New York, NY 10006
Creative Director: Vincent Kralyevich
VP of Production: Kristine Sabat

La Paloma Films (607) 433-0811
30 Chestnut St., Ste. B www.lapalomafilms.com
(Near Main St.)
Oneonta, NY 13820
Producer/Director: Joseph C. Stillman

LeFrak Productions (212) 541-9444
50 W. 57th St., Seventh Fl., Ste. 409 FAX (212) 974-8205
(Near Fifth Ave.)
New York, NY 10019
President: Francine LeFrak
Development: Sean Cassels

The Levinson/Fontana Company (212) 206-3585
185 Broome St. (Near Clinton St.) www.levinson.com
New York, NY 10002
Executive Producers: Barry Levinson & Tom Fontana

Line By Line Productions (212) 505-0505
873 Broadway, Ste. 500 FAX (212) 505-0593
(Near W. 18th St.) www.nycproduction.com
New York, NY 10003
Producers: Michele Bessey & Frank Garritano

Log In Productions (917) 864-0715
(607) 589-4709
FAX (607) 589-6151
www.logtv.com/tv
D.P., Director & Producer: Slawomir Grunberg

Lovett Productions, Inc. (212) 242-8999
17 Van Dam St., Ground Fl. FAX (212) 242-7347
New York, NY 10013 www.lovettproductions.com
President: Joseph Lovett

Marshad Technology Group (212) 292-8910
76 Laight St. (Near Washington St.) www.marshad.com
New York, NY 10013
CEO/Executive Producer: Neal Marshad
Senior Producer: Tim Cassidy

MediaVest (212) 468-4000
1675 Broadway, 14th Fl. FAX (212) 468-4050
(Near W. 52nd St.) www.bcom3group.com
New York, NY 10019
President of Programming: Jeffrey S. Grant
Manager of Programming: Nancy Florent-Beard

Mirage Productions Inc. (973) 300-9477
(888) 746-6869
111 Spring St. FAX (973) 300-9467
Newton, NJ 07860 www.mirageproductions.com

Moving Pictures (212) 924-7364
(212) 450-7933
222 E. 44th St., Eighth Fl. (Near Spring St.) www.mpny.tv
New York, NY 10017
Executive Producer: Ron Honsa

Murray Hill Studios, Inc. (212) 889-4200
248 E. 35th St. (Near Second Ave.) FAX (212) 889-9413
New York, NY 10016 www.murrayhillstudios.com

N9 Productions (212) 563-4589
245 W. 29th St., 16th Fl. www.n9productions.com
(Near Seventh Ave.)
New York, NY 10001
Director: Mark Ledzian
Executive Producer: Katie Daley

Nederlander Television & Film (212) 586-6800
1450 Broadway, 20th Fl. FAX (212) 586-5862
(Near W. 41st St.)
New York, NY 10018
Executive Producer: Gladys Nederlander

NetOne, Inc. (914) 763-3365
(800) 949-6381
12 Avery Rd. www.netonevideo.com
(Near Cross River Rd.)
Cross River, NY 10518
Contact: Rob Feiner

New Amsterdam Entertainment (212) 922-1930
1133 Avenue of the Americas, Ste. 1621 FAX (212) 922-0674
(Near E. 42nd St.) www.newamsterdamnyc.com
New York, NY 10036
CEO/Chairman: Richard P. Rubinstein
VP: Michael Messina

New Jersey Network (609) 777-5273
Media Productions (609) 777-5283
25 S. Stockton St. FAX (609) 292-6360
Trenton, NJ 08608 www.njn.net
Media Productions Manager: Fred Litwinowicz

Pangolin Pictures, Inc. (212) 245-4242
1650 Broadway, Ste. 1208 FAX (212) 245-4290
(Near W. 51st St.) www.pangolinpictures.com
New York, NY 10019

Peter Rosen Productions, Inc. (212) 535-8927
Nine E. 78th St. (Near Fifth Ave.) FAX (212) 517-5337
New York, NY 10021 www.peterrosenproductions.com
Producer/Director: Peter Rosen
Producer: Sara Lukinson
Cameraman: Joel Shapiro

PMTV (610) 768-1770
681 Moore Rd., Ste. 100 FAX (610) 768-1773
King Of Prussia, PA 19406 www.pmtv.com
President: Brian Powers

Post Office Media (212) 302-4488
1560 Broadway, Ste. 514 FAX (212) 302-4849
New York, NY 10036 www.postofficemedia.com

Primalux Video (212) 206-1402
30 W. 26th St., Seventh Fl. FAX (212) 206-1826
(Near Broadway) www.primalux.com
New York, NY 10010
President: Jeff Schwartz
Vice President: Jeff Byrd
Production Manager: Judy Cashman

(203) 294-1325
Prism Production Services, Inc. (203) 996-5292
Four E. Scard Rd. FAX (203) 265-7730
Wallingford, CT 06492 www.prismpro.com
Contact: Keith Sandler

Production 920, Inc. (212) 414-0606
328 Eighth Ave., Ste. 147 FAX (917) 463-3067
(Near 10th Ave.) www.production920.com
New York, NY 10001

Public Eye Productions (917) 446-8977
409 Meeker St. www.publiceyeproductions.com
South Orange, NJ 07079
Producer/Director: Scott Sinkler

Rankin/Bass Productions (212) 582-4017
24 W. 55th St. (Near Fifth Ave.) www.rankinbass.com
New York, NY 10019
President: Arthur Rankin
VP Development: Peter Bakalian
Treasurer: Norman Topper

RHI Entertainment (212) 977-9001
1325 Avenue of the Americas, 21st Fl. FAX (212) 977-9049
(Near W. 53rd St.) www.hallmarkent.com
New York, NY 10019

Richter Productions, Inc. (212) 947-1395
330 W. 42nd St., 24th Fl. www.richtervideos.com
(Near Ninth Ave.)
New York, NY 10036
Producer/Director/Writer: Robert Richter
Associate Producer: Amy Kessler

Scholastic Entertainment (212) 389-3964
557 Broadway (Near Prince St.) FAX **(212) 389-3887**
New York, NY 10012 **www.scholastic.com**
Executive Vice President: Deborah Forte

Sesame Workshop (212) 595-3456
One Lincoln Plaza, Fourth Fl. FAX **(212) 875-6175**
(Near Broadway) **www.sesameworkshop.org**
New York, NY 10023
President & CEO: Gary Knell

SLAM! Media Group (212) 924-7100
54 W. 21st St., Ste. 410 FAX **(212) 229-2080**
New York, NY 10010 **www.slammediagroup.com**

Talking Wall Pictures (212) 397-8686
850 Seventh Ave., Ste. 805 FAX **(212) 397-0282**
(Near W. 55th St.)
New York, NY 10019
President: John Coles
VP of Development: Jennifer Scanlon

Thaler Films (631) 851-2000
275 Marcus Blvd., Ste. M **www.thalerfilms.com**
Hauppauge, NY 11788

Third Eye Motion Picture Co., Inc. (212) 462-1590
P.O. Box 1008 FAX **(212) 462-1600**
Yorktown Heights, NY 10598
Producer/Directors: Joe Berlinger & Bruce Sinofsky
Associate Producer: Mike Bonfiglio

Wind Dancer Production Group (212) 765-4772
FAX **(212) 765-4785**
Partners: Carmen Finestra, David McFadzean & Matt Williams

Windfall Productions (201) 871-6800
120 County Rd., Ste. 100 FAX **(201) 871-1656**
Tenafly, NJ 07670
President/CEO: Ralph Molé
Sr. Producer: Jason Stewart

Worldwide Pants Incorporated (212) 975-5300
1697 Broadway (Near W. 53rd St.) FAX **(212) 975-4780**
New York, NY 10019 **www.cbs.com/lateshow**
President/CEO: Rob Burnett

Trailer Production Companies

Giaronomo Productions (212) 995-5200
665 Broadway, Ste. 1000 **www.giaronomo.com**
New York, NY 10012

Kinetic Trailers (646) 442-7790
150 W. 22nd St., Third Fl. **www.kinetictrailers.com**
New York, NY 10011

Mighty Pictures (212) 206-6557
20 W. 22nd St., Ste. 812 FAX **(212) 206-3832**
New York, NY 10010 **www.mightypics.tv**

Mirage Productions Inc. (973) 300-9477
111 Spring St. (888) 746-6869
Newton, NJ 07860 FAX **(973) 300-9467**
www.mirageproductions.com

SLAM! Media Group (212) 924-7100
54 W. 21st St., Ste. 410 FAX **(212) 229-2080**
New York, NY 10010 **www.slammediagroup.com**

Sunset Pictures, LLC (347) 715-3858
767 Autumn Ave., Ste. 3 FAX **(347) 715-3858**
Brooklyn, NY 11208 **www.sunsetpicturesllc.com**

PICTURED:
Westin Times Square

LOCATION:
Manhattan, NY

PHOTOGRAPHER:
Sam Rohn

ALSAM : www.alsam.net
ASSOCIATION OF
LOCATION SCOUTS & MANAGERS

New York 411

*Qualified Listings for the
New York Production Community*
www.newyork411.com

Post Production

HD POST

- DVCPRO HD ONLINE EDITING
- ADVANCED COLOR CORRECTION
- HD DUBBING HD FINISHING
- HDCAMSR OFFLINE EDITING
- TERANEX LAYBACKS
- FINAL CUT AVID DS NITRIS
- SYMPHONY NITRIS BLU RAY
- DIGIBETA RED WORKFLOW
- D5 CLOSED CAPTIONING
- EDITING SUITES
- 1080I
- 2K-4K 720P

5.1 AUDIO POST

- ISDN SESSIONS DOLBY E
- 5.1 & STEREO MIXING
- PROTOOLS HD DE-NOISE
- VOICEOVER ADR
- LIBRARY SOUND DESIGN
- MUSIC SCORING PHONE PATCH
- AUDIO LAYBACK
- DOLBY LM 100

SOUNDSTAGE

- GREENSCSREEN
- GRIP AND LIGHTING PACKAGE
- SOUND PACKAGE LAV BOOM
- RED CAMERA RENTAL
- CYCLORAMA KINOFLOS
- CREWS TELEPROMPTER
- DECK RENTALS GREEN ROOM

Post Production

digital arts

130 WEST 29TH STREET | 8TH FLOOR | NEW YORK NY 10001

(212) 460-9600 | www.digital-arts.net

Ⓐ ADVERTISER SYMBOL

Refer to the General Index for cross-referencing items in this section.

Audio Post Facilities 42
Commercial Editorial Houses 47
Composers & Sound Designers 51
Computer Graphics & Visual FX 53
Digital Intermediates 56
Duplication. 56
DVD Authoring & Replication 58
Editing Equipment Rentals & Sales 60
Editors 64
Film & Tape Storage 73
Film Laboratories—Motion Picture 74
Film Laboratories—Still Photography 76
Mobile Video Units,
  Satellite & Transmission Services 78
Music Libraries & Publishing 80
Music Production & Sound Design 82
Opticals 84
Post Houses 85
Post Production Supervisors 90
Screening Rooms 91
Stock Footage & Photos 93
Titling, Captioning & Broadcast Design 102
Visual FX Artists 104
Visual FX Supervisors & Producers 104

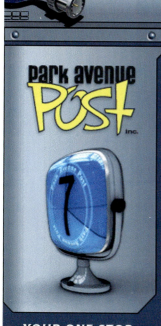

park avenue POSt inc.

- Color Correction and Finishing
- DS Nitris HD Suites
- Avid Editing HD/SD Suites
- Final Cut Pro Suites (RED Work Flow)
- Audio Recording, Sound Design
- Surround Sound Mixing
- Motion Control/Animation
- HD Up, Down & Cross Conversions
- Duplication: HD/SD Formats
- DVD Encoding and DVD Authoring
- QuickTime, WMV, Flash & MPEG Encoding
- Closed Caption and Subtitle Encoding
- Edit Suite Rentals with or w/o Editor

YOUR ONE STOP POST PRODUCTION FACILITY

Park Avenue Post, Inc. • 419 Park Avenue South
Suite 600 • New York, NY 10016
Tel: 212-689-7678 • Fax: 212-689-7544
www.parkavenuepost.com

Audio Post Facilities

91 East   **(631) 288-6363 / (631) 288-6365**
108 Mill Rd.   FAX **(631) 288-6367**
Westhampton Beach, NY 11978   **www.91east.com**
(ADR, Audio Laybacks, Audio Laybacks to High Def, Digital Sound Editing, Dubbing, ISDN, Foley, Mastering, Mixing, Music, Music Composition, Pre-Dubbing, Remote Sessions, Sound Design & Voice Over Services)

The Anx   **(212) 894-4000**
100 Avenue of the Americas   FAX **(212) 941-0439**
(Near Grand St.)
New York, NY 10013
(Dubbing, Foley, Laybacks, Mixing, Remote Sessions, Sound Editing, Synching & Transfers)

Ascent Media Management East   **(201) 767-3800**
235 Pegasus Ave.   FAX **(201) 767-4568**
Northvale, NJ 07647   **www.ascentmedia.com**
(ADR, Dubbing, Foley, Laybacks, Mixing, Music/Sound FX Library, Sound Editing & Synching and Transfers)

Audio Mixers, Inc.   **(212) 213-5335**
148 Madison Ave. (Near E. 32nd St.)   FAX **(212) 447-1340**
New York, NY 10016   **www.audiomixers.com**
(Foley, Laybacks, Mixing, Music/Sound FX Libraries, Remote Sessions, Sound Editing & Synching and Transfers)

audioEngine   **(212) 473-2700**
817 Broadway, Eighth Fl.   FAX **(212) 473-2772**
(Near E. 12th St.)   **www.audioengine.net**
New York, NY 10003
(5.1 Dolby Surround Sound Mixing, Mixing, Music/Sound FX Library & Sound Design)

Back Pocket Recording Studios   **(212) 633-1175**
37 W. 20th St., Ste. 1206   **www.russograntham.com**
(Near Sixth Ave.)
New York, NY 10011
(Mixing, Music/Sound FX Libraries, Sound Editing & Synching and Transfers)
Contact: Leonard Hospidor

Beatstreet Productions   **(212) 777-8440**
928 Broadway, Ste. 601   FAX **(212) 477-1375**
(Near E. 21st St.)   **www.beatstreetnyc.com**
New York, NY 10010
(ADR, Laybacks, Mixing, Music/Sound FX Libraries, Remote Sessions, Sound Editing & Synching and Transfers)

Bevan Sound   **(212) 768-8501**
62 W. 45th St., Tenth Fl.   FAX **(212) 768-8505**
(Near Fifth Ave.)   **www.jecomusic.com**
New York, NY 10036
(ADR, Laybacks, Mixing, Sound Editing & Synching and Transfers)
Contacts: Leigh Roberts & Gus Reyes

Big Yellow Duck   **(212) 997-1200**
62 W. 45th St., 12th Fl.   FAX **(212) 997-1293**
New York, NY 10036   **www.bigyellowduck.com**
(5.1 Surround Mixing, ADR, Foley, ISDN, Laybacks, Music Composition, Sound Design & Voice Over)
Contacts: Ralph Miccio & Matt Pedone

Bionic   **(212) 997-9100**
1375 Broadway, Seventh Fl.   FAX **(212) 997-0990**
New York, NY 10018   **www.bionic.tv**
(5.1 Surround Sound Mixing, Digital Sound Editing, Laybacks, Mixing, Music/Sound FX & Remote Sessions)

BOND Audio (212) 533-9400
665 Broadway, Ste. 1201 FAX (212) 533-9463
(Near Bond St.) www.bondedit.com
New York, NY 10012
(Digital Sound Editing, Laybacks, Mixing, Music/Sound FX Libraries & Remote Heads)

Broadway Sound (212) 333-0700
1619 Broadway, Fourth Fl. FAX (212) 333-0775
(Near W. 49th St.) www.broadwayvideo.com
New York, NY 10019
(ADR, Dolby Surround, Foley, Laybacks & Mixing)
Contacts: Ralph Kelsey & Mike Ungar

Buttons Sound, Inc. (212) 764-8650
Two W. 45th St., Ste. 603 FAX (212) 764-8672
(Near Fifth Ave.) www.buttonsny.com
New York, NY 10036
(Digital Mixing & Editing)

Buzz, Inc. (212) 302-2899
28 W. 44th St., 22nd Fl. FAX (212) 302-9844
New York, NY 10036 www.buzzny.com
(5.1 Surround, ADR, Archiving, Audio Laybacks, Audio Laybacks to High Def, Digital Editing, Dolby Surround, ISDN, Laybacks, Mastering, Mixing, Music FX Library, Sound Design, Sound Editing, Sound FX Editing, Sound FX Library, Synching, Transfers, Transmission Services & Voice Over Services)

🅐 CDM Sound Studios (212) 904-1870
  (866) 851-9788
630 Ninth Ave., Ste. 810 www.cdmstudios.com
New York, NY 10036
(ADR, Digital Editing, ISDN, Mastering, Mixing, Music Composition, Music/Sound FX, Sound Design, Sound Editing, Synching & Voice Over Services)
Contacts: Charles de Montebello, Kat Lambrix & Eric Willhelm

City Lights Post (212) 679-4400
  (646) 467-7500
Six E. 39th St., Second Fl. FAX (212) 679-4482
(Near Fifth Ave.) www.citylightsmedia.com
New York, NY 10016
Contacts: Aaron Behr, Danny Fisher & Jack Fisher

City Sound Productions (917) 232-8346
39 E. Seventh St., Ste. 2 www.citysound.com
(Near Second Ave.)
New York, NY 10003
(ADR, Laybacks, Mixing, Music/Sound FX Libraries & Sound Editing)

Creative Bubble Sound (212) 201-4201
  (212) 201-4200
79 Fifth Ave., 14th Fl. (Near 15th St.) FAX (212) 201-4210
New York, NY 10003 www.creativebubble.com
(Mixing)

Dig It Audio, Inc. (212) 206-3887
200 Varick St., Ste. 513 FAX (212) 727-3393
(Near W. Houston St.) www.digitaudio.com
New York, NY 10014
(ADR, Dolby Surround, Dubbing, Foley, Laybacks, Mixing, Music/Sound FX Library, Sound Editing & Synching and Transfers)

🅐 Digital Arts (212) 460-9000
130 W. 29th St., Eighth Fl. FAX (212) 660-3600
(Near Sixth Ave.) www.digital-arts.net
New York, NY 10001
(5.1 Surround, ADR, Audio Laybacks, Audio Laybacks to High Def, Digital Sound Editing, Dolby Surround, ISDN, Mastering, Mixing, Music Composition, Remote Sessions, Sound Design, Sound Editing & Voice Over Services)

Digital Cinema, LLC (212) 307-9612
426 W. 55th St. (Near 10th Ave.) FAX (212) 307-9045
New York, NY 10019 www.digitalcinema.com
(Digital Film Mixing Theater)
Contact: Christina Faist

Du Art Film and Video (212) 757-4580
245 W. 55th St. (Near Broadway) FAX (212) 333-7647
New York, NY 10019 www.duart.com
(Dolby Surround, Laybacks, Mixing, Sound Editing, Sound FX Libraries & Synching and Transfers)

Dubway Studios (212) 352-3070
135 W. 26th St., Ste. 202 FAX (212) 352-3072
(Near Sixth Ave.) www.dubway.com
New York, NY 11222
(ADR, Dubbing, Laybacks, Mixing, Music/Sound FX Libraries, Remote Sessions, Sound Editing & Synching and Transfers)

Everest Production Corp. (732) 560-3927
  (732) 560-3929
300 Franklin Square Dr. FAX (732) 560-0801
Somerset, NJ 08873 www.everestpro.com
(ADR, Audio Laybacks, Digital Editing, Domestic Dubbing, Dubbing, Foreign Dubbing, Laybacks, Mastering, Mixing, Synching, Transfers & Voice Over Services)
Contact: Cinar Demirci

EVTV (203) 359-8777
700 Canal St. FAX (203) 348-6000
Stamford, CT 06902 www.evtv.net
(Foley, Laybacks, Mixing, Music/Sound FX Libraries, Remote Sessions, Sound Editing & Synching and Transfers)
Contact: Michael Macari Jr.

Fred Weinberg Music and Sounds (212) 265-2536
  (561) 988-6196
161 W. 54th St., Ste. 1404 FAX (212) 265-2536
(Near Seventh Ave.) www.fredweinbergproductions.com
New York, NY 10019
(ADR, Dolby Surround, Foley, Mixing, Music/Sound FX Libraries, Remote Sessions, Scoring Stage, Sound Editing & Synching and Transfers)
Contact: Julie Blankman

Full House Productions (212) 645-2228
123 W. 18th St., Seventh Fl. FAX (212) 627-2838
(Near Sixth Ave.) www.fullhouseny.com
New York, NY 10011
(Foley, Laybacks, Mixing, Music/Sound FX Libraries, Remote Sessions, Sound Editing & Synching and Transfers)
Contact: Jeff Bush

Goldcrest Post Production (212) 243-4700
799 Washington St. (Near Horatio St.) FAX (212) 624-1701
New York, NY 10014 www.goldcrestpost.com
(ADR, Foley, Laybacks, Mixing, Sound Editing & Synching and Transfers)

Gotham Music, Inc. (908) 832-8999
  (908) 295-0680
  www.gothammusic.net
(Dolby Surround, Music/SFX Libraries, Sound Editing & Synching and Transfers)
Contact: Emanuel Kallins

Harmonic Ranch (212) 966-3141
59 Franklin St., Ste. 303 FAX (212) 431-1447
(Near Broadway) www.harmonicranch.com
New York, NY 10013
(ADR, Foley, Mixing, Music/Sound FX Libraries & Sound Editing)

HBO Studio Productions (212) 512-7800
120A E. 23rd St. (Near Park Ave.) FAX (212) 512-7788
New York, NY 10010
(Dolby Surround, Laybacks, Mixing & Music/Sound FX Libraries)

Headroom Digital Audio (212) 246-8400
11 E. 26th St., 19th Fl. FAX (212) 245-0370
(Near Fifth Ave.) www.headroomdigi.com
New York, NY 10010
(5.1 Surround, Audio Laybacks, Digital Editing, Domestic Dubbing, Dubbing, ISDN, Laybacks, Mixing, Music, Music Composition, Music FX Library, Remote Sessions, Restoration, Sound Design, Sound Editing, Sound FX Editing, Sound FX Library, Synching, Transfers & Voice Over Services)
Contacts: Claudia Gaspar, Samantha Mazza, Scott McIntosh, James Meidenbauer, Jerry Plotkin, Evan Spear & John Wilcox

Hobo Audio Company   **(212) 967-6532**
555 Eighth Ave., Fourth Fl.   FAX **(646) 607-2767**
New York, NY 10018   **www.hoboaudio.com**

HSR/NY   **(212) 687-4180**
The Graybar Bldg.   FAX **(212) 697-0536**
420 Lexington Ave., Ste. 1934   **www.hsrny.com**
(Near E. 42nd St.)
New York, NY 10170
(ADR, Dolby Surround, Foley, Laybacks, Mixing, Music/Sound FX Libraries, Remote Sessions, Sound Editing & Synching and Transfers)
Contacts: Sharon DiTullio & Sara Paterno

Ibero-American Productions, Inc.   **(212) 245-7826**
630 Ninth Ave., Ste. 700   FAX **(212) 245-1569**
(Near W. 44th St.)   **www.ibero-american.com**
New York, NY 10036
(ADR & Synching and Transfers)

Integrated Studios   **(212) 334-4000**
449 Washington St.   FAX **(212) 334-6969**
New York, NY 10013   **www.integratedstudios.com**

    (201) 261-3959
Intermediapost   **(800) 811-7044**
120 Route 17 North   FAX **(201) 261-3062**
Paramus, NJ 07652   **www.intermediapost.com**
(ADR, Foley, Laybacks, Mixing, Music/Sound FX Libraries, Sound Editing & Synching and Transfers)

iProbe Multilingual Solutions, Inc.   **(212) 489-6035**
Five W. 36th St., Ste. 402   FAX **(212) 202-4790**
(Near Fifth Ave.)   **www.iprobesolutions.com**
New York, NY 10018
(5.1 Surround, ADR, Audio Laybacks, Audio Laybacks to High Def, Digital Editing, Dolby Surround, Domestic Dubbing, Dubbing, Foley, Foreign Dubbing, ISDN, Laybacks, Mastering, Mixing, Pre-Dubbing, Remote Sessions, Restoration, Sound Design, Sound Editing, Sound FX Editing, Sound FX Library, Sound Stage, Synching, Transfers, Transmission Services & Voice Over Services)

Jonathan Helfand Music & Post   **(212) 647-9500**
44 E. 32nd St., 10th Fl.   FAX **(212) 531-6445**
(Near Park Ave. South)   **www.jhmp.com**
New York, NY 10016
(ADR, Foley, Laybacks, Mixing, Music/Sound FX Libraries, Remote Sessions, Scoring Stage, Sound Editing & Synching and Transfers)
Contact: Travis Leung

K.A.S. Music & Sound   **(718) 786-3400**
34-12 36th St. (Near 34th Ave.)   FAX **(718) 729-3007**
Astoria, NY 11106   **www.kasmusic.com**

    (212) 575-4660
Kamen Entertainment Group   **(800) 237-2448**
701 Seventh Ave., Sixth Fl.   FAX **(212) 575-4799**
(Near W. 47th St.)   **www.kamen.com**
New York, NY 10036
(Foley, Laybacks, Mixing, Music/Sound FX Libraries, Remote Sessions, Sound Editing & Synching and Transfers)
Contact: Roy Kamen

Legacy Recording Studios   **(212) 944-5770**
509 W. 38th St.   FAX **(212) 944-7258**
New York, NY 10018   **www.righttrackrecording.com**
(2-Track Mixing, 5.1 Surround Sound Mixing, Dolby Surround, Mixing, Remote Sessions, Scoring Stage & Sound Editing)

    (917) 825-5412
Loftin Productions   **(917) 399-8501**
    www.loftinpro.com
(ADR, Foley, Music/Sound FX Libraries & Sound Design and Editing)

Magno Sound & Video   **(212) 302-2505**
729 Seventh Ave. (Near W. 48th St.)   FAX **(212) 819-1282**
New York, NY 10019   **www.magnosoundandvideo.com**
(ADR, Digital Sound Editing, Dolby 5.1, Duplication, Laybacks, Mixing, Music/Sound FX Libraries & Synching and Transfers)

Manhattan Center Studios   **(212) 695-6600**
311 W. 34th St. (Near Eighth Ave.)   FAX **(212) 564-1092**
New York, NY 10001   **www.mcstudios.com**
(ADR, Audio Laybacks, Audio Restoration Services, Digital Sound Editing, Dolby Surround, Dubbing, ISDN, Foreign and Domestic Dubbing, Laybacks, Mixing, Music, Music/Sound FX Library, Restoration, Scoring/Sound Stage, Sound Editing, Sound FX Library, Synching, Transfers, Transmission Services & Voice Over Services)

Mediaracket   **(212) 961-7337**
19 W. 21st St., Ste. 1104   FAX **(212) 633-9933**
New York, NY 10010   **www.mediaracket.com**
(ADR, Foley, Laybacks, Mixing, Music/Sound FX Libraries, Sound Editing & Synching and Transfers)

Merlin Studios   **(212) 575-2744**
1560 Broadway, Ste. 1111   FAX **(212) 575-3690**
(Near W. 46th St.)
New York, NY 10036
(ADR, Foley, Mixing, Music/Sound FX Libraries, Remote Sessions & Sound Editing)

Mixopolis, Inc.   **(212) 980-5009**
Five E. 47th St., Seventh Fl.   FAX **(212) 223-4524**
(Near Fifth Ave.)   **www.mixopolis.com**
New York, NY 10017

    (845) 679-8848
Nevessa Production, Inc.   **(888) 484-8848**
One Artist Rd. (Near Route 212)   FAX **(845) 679-1208**
Saugerties, NY 12477   **www.nevessa.com**
(Dolby Surround, Mixing, Music/Sound FX Libraries, Remote Sessions, Scoring Stage, Sound Editing & Synching and Transfers)

Now Hear This   **(212) 265-1188**
250 W. 49th St., Ste. 704   **www.nhtsound.com**
(Near Broadway)
New York, NY 10019
(ADR, Digital Sound Editing, Foley, Laybacks, Mixing & Music/Sound FX Libraries)

Nutmeg Audio Post   **(212) 921-8005**
45 W. 45th St., Sixth Fl.   FAX **(212) 921-7728**
(Near Fifth Ave.)   **www.nutmegaudiopost.com**
New York, NY 10036
(ADR, Foley, Laybacks, Mixing, Music/Sound FX Libraries, Remote Sessions, Sound Editing & Synching and Transfers)

    (646) 536-3494
Onshore Media   **(310) 691-8666**
    www.onshoredigital.com
(ADR, Dolby Surround, Dubbing, Foley, Laybacks, Mixing, Music/Sound FX Library, Remote Sessions, Sound Editing & Synching and Transfers)

Palace Digital Studios   **(203) 853-1740**
29 N. Main St.   FAX **(203) 855-9608**
South Norwalk, CT 06854   **www.palacedigital.com**
(Dolby Surround, Laybacks, Mixing, Music/Sound FX Libraries, Remote Sessions, Sound Editing & Synching and Transfers)

🅐 Park Avenue Post, Inc.   **(212) 689-7678**
419 Park Ave. South, Ste. 600   FAX **(212) 689-7544**
(Near 29th St.)   **www.parkavenuepost.com**
New York, NY 10016
(Dubbing, Layback, Mixing, Music/Sound FX Libraries, Remote Sessions, Sound Editing & Synching and Transfers)

Photomag Sound & Image   **(212) 500-2700**
222 E. 44th St., 11th Fl.   FAX **(212) 682-5869**
(Near Third Ave.)   **www.postworks.com**
New York, NY 10017
(5.1 and Stereo Mixing, ADR, Foley, ISDN Remote Sessions, Laybacks, Sound Design, Transfers & Voice Over)

Pirate New York   **(212) 253-2920**
30 Irving Pl., Sixth Fl.   **www.piratenewyork.com**
(Near 15th St.)
New York, NY 10003
(Dolby Surround, Dubbing, Laybacks, Mixing, Music/Sound FX Library, Remote Sessions & Sound Editing)

Pomann Sound, Inc. (212) 869-4161
Two W. 46th St., PH FAX (212) 869-4541
New York, NY 10036 www.pomannsound.com

PostWorks (212) 894-4000
 (212) 894-4050
100 Avenue of the Americas, 10th Fl. FAX (212) 941-0439
(Near Grand St.) www.postworks.com
New York, NY 10013
(5.1 and Stereo Mixing, ADR, Foley, ISDN Remote Sessions, Laybacks, Sound Design, Sound Editing, Transfers & Voice Over)

Presence Studios (203) 221-8061
80 Wells Hill Rd., Ste. 100 www.presencestudios.com
Weston, CT 06883
(5.1 Surround, ADR, Digital Editing, Domestic Dubbing, Foley, ISDN, Laybacks, Mastering, Mixing, Mobile Facilities, Music/Sound FX Libraries, Remote Sessions, Sound Design, Sound Editing, Synching, Transfers, Transmission Services & Voice Over Services)
Contacts: Kathleen Lombard & Jon Russell

Rep Studio (607) 272-4292
110 N. Cayuga St. (Near W. State St.) FAX (607) 272-4293
Ithaca, NY 14850 www.repstudio.com
(5.1 Surround, ADR, Digital Sound Editing, Mastering, Mixing, Music Composition, Remote Sessions, Sound Design, Sound Editing, Transfers & Voice Over Services)
Contacts: Tim Reppert & Nate Richardson

Rick Ulfik Productions (212) 867-0846
211 E. 43rd St., Ste. 710 (Near Third Ave.)
New York, NY 10017
(ADR, Foley, Mixing, Music/Sound FX Libraries, Sound Editing & Synching and Transfers)
Contact: Rick Ulfik

Rooftop Edit (212) 244-0744
104 W. 29th St., 12th Fl. FAX (212) 244-0690
(Near Sixth Ave.) www.rooftopedit.com
New York, NY 10001
(Dolby Surround, Dubbing, Laybacks, Music/Sound FX Libraries, Sound Editing & Synching and Transfers)

Rooftop Productions (212) 427-5014
 www.rooftopproductions.com
(Mixing, Music/Sound FX Libraries & Sound Editing)

Serge Audio (212) 213-0808
260 Fifth Ave., Eighth Fl. www.sergeaudio.com
(Near 29th St.)
New York, NY 10001
(Audio Laybacks, Audio Laybacks to High Def, Digital Sound Editing, ISDN, Mastering, Mixing, Music Composition, Music/Sound FX Library, Remote Sessions, Sound Design, Sound Editing & Voice Over Services)

Silver Sound, Inc. (212) 757-5147
28 W. 27th St., Ste. 906 FAX (212) 757-6245
(Near Sixth Ave.) www.silversound.us
New York, NY 10001
(5.1 Surround, ADR, Audio Laybacks, Digital Editing, Dolby Surround, Foley, Mixing, Mobile Facilities, Music, Sound Design, Sound Editing, Sound FX Library & Voice Over Services)

Solar Film/Video Productions (212) 473-3040
632 Broadway, Ste. 304 FAX (212) 473-3091
(Near Houston St.) www.solarnyc.com
New York, NY 10012
(ADR, Digital Sound Editing, Foley, Laybacks, Mixing, Music/Sound FX Libraries, Sound Design, Synching and Transfers & Voice Over Services)

Sound One Corp. (212) 765-4757
1619 Broadway (Near W. 49th St.) FAX (212) 603-4363
New York, NY 10019 www.soundone.com
(ADR, Dolby Surround, Dubbing, Editing, Foley, Laybacks, Mixing, Music/Sound FX Library, Remote Sessions & Synching and Transfers)

SoundByte Digital (215) 893-3004
Audio Production, Inc. (800) 245-5395
225 S. 15th St., Ste. 2020 FAX (215) 893-9490
Philadelphia, PA 19102 www.soundbytedigital.com
(ADR, Dubbing, Foley, Laybacks, Mixing, Music/Sound FX Library, Remote Sessions, Sound Editing & Synching and Transfers)

SoundHound, Inc. (212) 575-8664
45 W. 45th St., Fourth Fl. FAX (212) 575-9412
(Near Sixth Ave.) www.soundhound.com
New York, NY 10036
(ADR, Laybacks, Mixing, Music/Sound FX Libraries, Remote Sessions, Sound Editing & Synching and Transfers)

SoundImage NY (212) 986-6445
16 W. 46th St., Eighth Fl. FAX (212) 764-0440
(Near Fifth Ave.) www.soundimageny.com
New York, NY 10036
(Laybacks, Mixing, Sound Editing & Synching and Transfers)

Soundtrack (212) 420-6010
936 Broadway, Fourth Fl. FAX (212) 777-6403
(Near W. 21st St.) www.soundtrackny.com
New York, NY 10010
Contact: Maegan Hayward

Splash Studios, Inc. (212) 271-8747
49 W. 23rd St., Sixth Fl. FAX (212) 271-8748
(Near Sixth Ave.) www.splash-studios.com
New York, NY 10010
(Dolby 5.1 Mixing, Foley and ADR Recording, ISDN, Laybacks, Mixing & Sound Editing)

Strongboy Studios (212) 203-2325
 (212) 222-1113
497 Manhattan Ave., Ste. 3 FAX (212) 222-1113
New York, NY 10027 www.strongboystudios.com

Studio Center NY (212) 986-1929
 (866) 515-2111
315 Madison Ave., 11th Fl. FAX (212) 490-9737
(Near Madison Ave.) www.studiocenter.com
New York, NY 10017
Contact: Robin Russ

Studio K Music Productions (212) 229-1642
150 W. 28th St., Ste. 902E www.parkswingorc.com
(Near Seventh Ave.)
New York, NY 10001
(Digital Sound Editing, Laybacks, Mixing & Music/Sound FX Libraries)
Contact: William Kinslow

Studios At Linden Oaks (585) 264-1780
 (585) 261-2847
170B Linden Oaks Dr. FAX (585) 264-1786
(Near Route 490) www.studiosatlindenoaks.com
Rochester, NY 14625
(ADR, Laybacks, Mixing, Music/Sound FX Libraries, Remote Sessions, Scoring Stage, Sound Editing & Synching and Transfers)

Suite Spot (212) 475-6310
126 Second Ave., Third Fl. FAX (212) 473-3748
New York, NY 10003 www.suitespotnyc.com

Sync Sound, Inc. (212) 246-5580
450 W. 56th St. (Near 10th Ave.) FAX (212) 399-6099
New York, NY 10019
(ADR, Digital Sound Editing, Dolby Surround, Foley, Laybacks, Mixing, Music/Sound FX Libraries, Remote Sessions & Synching and Transfers)
Contacts: Ken Hahn & Bill Marino

Tandem Sound (212) 255-0645
104 W. 14th St., Fourth Fl. www.tandemsound.com
(Near E. 82nd St.)
New York, NY 10011

Tapeworks, Inc. (860) 522-5997
770 Maple Ave. FAX (860) 246-2085
Hartford, CT 06114 www.tapeworksinc.com
(Digital Sound Editing, Laybacks, Mixing & Remote Sessions)
Contacts: Bill Ahearn & Doug Kupper

Taylor-Made Productions (973) 226-1461
P.O. Box 309 FAX (973) 226-1462
Caldwell, NJ 07006 www.taylormadeprod.com
(ADR, Digital Mixing, Foley, Laybacks, Music/Sound FX Libraries & Sound Editing)
Contact: Glenn M. Taylor

Trackwise, Inc. (212) 627-7700
123 W. 18th St. (Near Sixth Ave.) FAX (212) 727-3075
New York, NY 10011
(Audio Restoration Services)

Ultrabland (646) 638-2830
27 W. 24th St., Ste. 302 FAX (646) 638-2835
New York, NY 10010 www.ultrabland.com
(Audio Laybacks, Mixing, Music, Music Composition, Sound Design & Sound FX Editing)

**VideoActive Productions/
VoiceWorks Sound Studios** (212) 541-6592
1560 Broadway, Studio 610 www.videoactiveprod.com
New York, NY 10036
(ADR, Foley, Laybacks, Mixing, Music/Sound FX Libraries, Remote Sessions, Sound Editing & Synching and Transfers)
Contact: Steven Garrin

William Markle Associates (212) 246-8642
630 Ninth Ave., Ste. 417 (Near 44th St.)
New York, NY 10036
(ADR, Foley, Laybacks, Mixing, Music/Sound FX Libraries, Sound Editing & Synching and Transfers)

World Wide Audio, Inc. (646) 336-1152
41 White St., PH 5B (Near Church St.) FAX (646) 336-1153
New York, NY 10013 www.globalaudio.net

Commercial Editorial Houses

903Films (212) 674-0986
515 Greenwich St., Ste. 202   FAX (212) 380-1258
New York, NY 10013   www.903films.com

(631) 288-6363
91 East (631) 288-6365
108 Mill Rd.   FAX (631) 288-6367
Westhampton Beach, NY 11978   www.91east.com
(Compositing, Computer Graphics, Digital Offline, Digital Online, DVD Authoring, Non-Linear Offline, Non-Linear Online, Post Production Supervision & Sound Design)

American Montage, Inc. (212) 334-8283
Old Chelsea Station   www.americanmontage.com
P.O. Box 1042 (Near Centre Market Pl.)
New York, NY 10011
(Non-Linear Offline and Online)
Owner: Eric Marciano

Analog Digital International, Inc. (212) 688-5110
20 E. 49th St., Second Fl.   FAX (212) 688-5405
(Near Madison Ave.)   www.analogdigitalinc.com
New York, NY 10017
(Linear/Non-Linear Offline and Online)
President: Ayres D'Cunha

The Anx (212) 894-4000
100 Avenue of the Americas   FAX (212) 941-0439
(Near Grand St.)
New York, NY 10013

Ascent Media Management East (201) 767-3800
235 Pegasus Ave.   FAX (201) 767-4568
Northvale, NJ 07647   www.ascentmedia.com
(Computer Graphics, Linear Online, Negative Cutting, Non-Linear Offline and Online & Post-Production Supervision)

(800) 431-3801
B-Rave Studio (718) 424-5610
35-42 77th St., Ste. 31 (Near Ridge St.)
Jackson Heights, NY 11372

Beast TV (212) 206-0660
18 E. 16th St., Sixth Fl.   FAX (212) 206-0667
New York, NY 10003   www.beast.tv

Beehive, Inc. (212) 924-6060
19 W. 21st St., Ste. 1002   FAX (212) 924-1855
(Near Fifth Ave.)   www.beehive.tv
New York, NY 10010
(Non-Linear Offline and Online)
Executive Producer: Jon Vesey

Big Sky Editorial (212) 683-4004
10 E. 40th St., Ste. 1701   FAX (212) 889-6220
(Near Fifth Ave.)   www.bigskyedit.com
New York, NY 10016
(Non-Linear Offline and Online)
President: Chris Franklin
Editors: Jenn Chambers, Chris Franklin, Val Junge & Miky Wolf
Executive Producer: Cheryl Panek

Bionic (212) 997-9100
1375 Broadway, Seventh Fl.   FAX (212) 997-0990
New York, NY 10018   www.bionic.tv
(Digital Non-Linear Offline and Online & HD Editing)
Co-Owner: Steve Beal
Co-Owner/Editor: Todd Feuer
Sales/Marketing Director: Andrea Rhodes
General Manager: Ami Palombo
Producer: Meredith Collins
Audio Engineers: Andy Avitabile, Brian Beatrice & Jody Nazzaro
Editors: Todd Feuer, Dan Fisher, C. Scott Gorman & Andrew Malenda

Black Watch Editorial (212) 349-0369
49 Murray St., Ste. 1 (Near Church St.)   FAX (212) 349-1335
New York, NY 10007   www.blackwatchproductions.com
(Non-Linear Offline and Online)

Blinking Eye Media (212) 243-6243
One West St., Ste. 100   FAX (212) 242-4411
(Near Spring St.)   www.blinkingeyemedia.com
New York, NY 10004
(Non-Linear Offline and Online)

bobsyouruncle. (212) 545-7800
638 E. Sixth St., Third Fl.   FAX (212) 545-0398
New York, NY 10009   www.bobsyouruncle.tv

BOND (212) 533-9400
665 Broadway, Ste. 1201   FAX (212) 533-9463
(Near Bond St.)   www.bondedit.com
New York, NY 10012
(Graphics & Non-Linear Offline and Online)
President/Editor: Jeff Beckerman
Executive Producer: Stephanie Shayne

Broadway Video Editorial (212) 265-7600
1619 Broadway, 10th Fl.   FAX (212) 713-1535
(Near 49th St.)   www.broadwayvideo.com
New York, NY 10019
(Digital Component Online, Digital Compositing, Linear Online & Non-Linear Offline and Online)
CEO: Jack Sullivan
COO: Brian Offutt
VP of Duplication: Mark Yates
VP and Managing Director of Operations: Karen Stewart
VPs of Sound: Ralph Kelsey & Mike Ungar
Editors: Dan Bosko, Claudia D'Enjoy, Mari Keiko Gonzalez, Chris Harrison, Yossi Kimberg, Andy Milkis & Richard Plofker

Brooklyn Films (212) 744-2845
(Non-Linear Online)   www.rkvbrooklyngroup.com

Chinagraph (212) 529-1991
119 Fifth Ave., Sixth Fl. (Near 19th St.)   FAX (212) 529-1992
New York, NY 10003   www.madeinchinagraph.com
(Graphics & Non-Linear Offline)
Executive Producers: Anne Gordon & Rosemary Quigley
Editors: Eric Carlson, John Gramaglia, Thomas Ostuni, Kane Platt & Pete Slife

Chosen Pictures (646) 827-0931
(Non-Linear Offline and Online)   www.chosenpictures.com
Owner/Editor: Scott Chosed

Chromavision (212) 686-7366
49 W. 27th St., Eighth Fl.   FAX (212) 686-7310
(Near Sixth Ave.)   www.chromavision.net
New York, NY 10001
(Non-Linear Offline and Online)

City Lights Post (212) 679-4400
Six E. 39th St., Second Fl.   FAX (212) 679-4482
(Near Fifth Ave.)   www.citylightsmedia.com
New York, NY 10016
(Non-Linear Offline and Online)
President/CEO: Danny Fisher
President: Jack Fisher
VP: Aaron Behr

Consulate (212) 219-0020
536 Broadway, Ninth Fl.   FAX (212) 219-0590
(Near Spring St.)   www.consulatefilm.com
New York, NY 10012
(Non-Linear Offline and Online)
Head of Production: Charlyn Derrick
Editors: Peter Johnson, Holle Singer, Chad Sipkin & Todd Stewart
Managing Director: Lisa Binassarie

Creative Group, Inc. (212) 935-0145
1601 Broadway, 10th Fl.   FAX (212) 838-0853
(Near W. 48th St.)   www.creativegroup.tv
New York, NY 10019

Crew Cuts Film & Tape, Inc. (212) 302-2828
28 W. 44th St., 22nd Fl. FAX (212) 302-9846
(Near Fifth Ave.) www.crewcuts.com
New York, NY 10036
Executive Producer: Nancy Shames
Editors: David Cornman, Bill Cramer, Clayton Hemmert, Craig Holzer, Karen Kourtessis, Jake Jacobsen, Chris Magliozzo, Sherri Margulies, Debbie McMurtrey & Nate Taylor

Dekart Video (212) 219-9240
133 Chrystie St. (Near Broome St.) FAX (212) 966-5618
New York, NY 10002
(Linear/Non-Linear Offline and Online)

Ⓐ Digital Arts (212) 460-9600
130 W. 29th St., Eighth Fl. FAX (212) 660-3600
(Near Sixth Ave.) www.digital-arts.net
New York, NY 10001
(Digital, Digital Online, Duplication, DVD Authoring, HD Editing, Non-Linear Offline, Non-Linear Online, Post Production Supervision, Sound Design & Standards Conversions)

Diva Edit (212) 947-1395
(Non-Linear Offline and Online) www.richtervideos.com

DWJ Television (201) 445-1711
(800) 766-1711
One Robinson Ln. FAX (201) 445-8352
Ridgewood, NJ 07450 www.dwjtv.com
(Linear Online & Non-Linear Offline)
President: Daniel Johnson

Earth2mars (212) 545-8545
404 Park Ave. South, Third Fl. FAX (212) 545-7728
(Near E. 29th St.) www.earth2mars.com
New York, NY 10016
(Digital Graphics & Non-Linear Offline and Online)

Edit On Hudson (914) 524-0344
(914) 403-4411
10 Pokahoe Dr. (Near Hemlock Dr.) FAX (914) 332-1422
Sleepy Hollow, NY 10591 www.editonhudson.com
(Computer Graphics & Non-Linear Offline and Online)
President/Editor: Steve Kahn

Editors' Hideaway, Inc. (212) 661-3850
219 E. 44th St., Eighth Fl. FAX (212) 661-3609
(Near Second Ave.) www.editorshideaway.com
New York, NY 10017
(Non-Linear Offline and Online)

Everest Production Corp. (732) 560-3927
(732) 560-3929
300 Franklin Square Dr. FAX (732) 560-0801
Somerset, NJ 08873 www.everestpro.com
(Computer Animation, Computer Graphics, Duplication, DVD Authoring, HD Editing & Standards Conversions)
Contact: Cinar Demirci

Ewen Industries, Inc. (917) 771-2727
250 W. 49th St., Ste. 704 www.ewenindustries.com
New York, NY 10019
(Computer Graphics, Digital, Digital Offline and Online, HD Editing, Non-Linear Offline, Non-Linear Online & Post Production Supervision)

The Field (212) 253-2888
119 Fifth Ave., PH www.thefieldtv.com
New York, NY 10003
(Digital, Digital Offline & Editing)
Editors: Fabrizio Rossetti & Mike Siedlecki

FilmCore Editorial (212) 627-3100
149 Fifth Ave., Sixth Fl. FAX (212) 627-3101
New York, NY 10010 www.filmcore.com
(Film Editing & Non-Linear Offline)
Editors: Tiffany Burchard, Gordon Carey, Jinx Godfrey, Ruth Mamaril, Livio Sanchez & Doug Walker

GRS Systems, Inc. (212) 286-0299
216 E. 45th St. FAX (212) 286-9475
New York, NY 10017 www.grsv.com

GTV, Inc. (212) 262-6260
1697 Broadway, Ste. 404 FAX (212) 262-4709
(Near W. 53rd St.) www.gtvnyc.com
New York, NY 10019
(Analog/Digital, Compositing, Computer Animation, Computer Graphics, Digital Linear/Non-Linear Offline and Online, Duplication, DVD Authoring, Film Editing, HD Editing, Linear/Non-Linear Offline and Online, Negative Cutting, Post Production Supervision, Sound Design, Standards Conversions & Visual FX)
President/Editor: Charlie Gelber
Contact: Randi Goldman

Homestead Editorial (212) 255-4440
48 W. 25th St., Ninth Fl. FAX (212) 255-4494
(Near Sixth Ave.) www.homesteadedit.com
New York, NY 10010
(Non-Linear Offline and Online)
Executive Producer: Lance Doty
Editors: Lisa Barnable, Charly Bender, Greg Dougherty, Skip Duff, Chris Hellman, Sam Welch & John Young
Online: Paul Fernandez
Graphics: Ryoko Kurachi

Image Maintenance (212) 375-0911
Three Great Jones St., Ste. 3A FAX (212) 375-0915
(Near Broadway) www.imltd.com
New York, NY 10012
(Non-Linear Offline and Online)
Producer: Jon Doran
Editors: John Chimples & Jed Parker

Ironik Design and Post (212) 683-7225
Five Woodhaven Dr. FAX (212) 683-7225
Simsbury, CT 06070 www.ironiknyc.com
(Compositing, Computer Animation, Computer Graphics, Digital Offline, Digital Online, Duplication, HD Editing, Non-Linear Offline, Non-Linear Online & Visual FX)

Jump (212) 228-7474
625 Broadway, Seventh Fl. FAX (212) 228-6085
(Near Bleecker St.) www.nycjump.com
New York, NY 10012
(Graphics & Non-Linear Offline)
Executive Producer: Dee Tagert
Editors: David Bryen, Damien Massingham, Luis Moreno, Lin Polito, Michael Saia & Barry Stilwell

Just Add Water, Inc. (212) 838-8883
Five E. 47th St., Third Fl. FAX (212) 838-8250
(Near Fifth Ave.) www.justaddwater.tv
New York, NY 10017
(Analog, Compositing, Computer Animation and Graphics, Digital, Digital Offline and Online, Duplication, DVD Authoring, Film Editing, HD Editing, Non-Linear Offline and Online, Post Production Supervision, Sound Design & Visual FX)
Editors: Rob Cabana, Jonathan Levy, Enrico Madonna & Francis Zuccarello

KeyFrame Editing (201) 833-0425
Editor: Judy Seaman

Lost Planet Editorial, Inc. (212) 226-5678
113 Spring St., Fourth Fl. FAX (212) 431-9450
(Near Mercer St.) www.lostplanet.com
New York, NY 10012
(Non-Linear Offline)
Executive Producer: Susan Grogan
Editors: Andy Grieve & Charlie Johnston

MacKenzie Cutler (212) 979-2722
907 Broadway (Near W. 20th St.) FAX (212) 979-6909
New York, NY 10010 www.mackcut.com
(Non-Linear Offline)
Executive Producer: Melissa Miller
Editors: Gavin Cutler, Jun Diaz, Dave Koza, Ian MacKenzie, Colleen Shea & Tom Vogt

Mad River Post, Inc. (212) 375-0726
13 Crosby St., Sixth Fl. FAX (212) 375-9276
(Near Fifth Ave.) www.madriverpost.com
New York, NY 10013
(Non-Linear Offline)
President: Krystn Wagenberg
Executive Producer: Laura Relovsky
Producers: Haley Lagerfeld, Amy Lazarus & Tashana Pace
Editors: Emily Dennis, James Duffy, Stephane Dumonceau, Michael Elliot, Dick Gordon & Jason MacDonald

mad.house, inc.   **(212) 867-1515**
240 Madison Ave., 14th Fl.   FAX **(212) 697-7168**
(Near 37th St.)   **www.madhousenyc.com**
New York, NY 10016
(Graphics, Linear Online & Non-Linear Offline and Online)
Owner/Editors: Craig Warnick & Rob Tortoriello
Editors: Scott Ham, Jason Howe & Ben Whitten
Graphic Artists: Andrew Askedall & Tim Dohan
Audio Mixer/Sound Designer: John Grant
Flame Artist: Chris Davis
Business Manager: Deborah Degnan
Technology Production Manager: Laura D'Antona

Magnetic Image Video   **(212) 598-3000** / **(800) 648-8463**
149 Fifth Ave., Fourth Fl.   FAX **(212) 228-3664**
(Near 19th St.)   **www.magneticimage.com**
New York, NY 10010
(Linear/Non-Linear Offline and Online)
Owner/Editor: Harry Douglas
Editors: Vito De Candia & Totie Herman

Merci Media, Inc.   **(718) 625-1627**
50 Bridge St., Ste. 615   FAX **(718) 625-1649**
(Near Water St.)   **www.mercimedia.com**
Brooklyn, NY 11201
(Motion Graphics & Non-Linear Offline and Online)
Editors/Motion Graphic Artists: Vivek Sharma & Andrew Stone

Midnight Media Group, Inc.   **(973) 379-5959** / **(800) 392-8265**
45 E. Willow St.   FAX **(973) 379-0551**
Millburn, NJ 07041   **www.mmgi.tv**
(Non-Linear Offline and Online)
Partners: Bob Camitta, Dave Emmerling & Walter Schoenknecht
Production Manager: Bob Schaffner
Graphic Artist: Mike Fischbeck
Audio Editor: Bill McEvoy
Video Editor: Sean McManus

Miles Associates, Inc.   **(212) 695-1600**
246 W. 38th St. (Near Seventh Ave.)   FAX **(212) 967-4290**
New York, NY 10018   **www.c4miles.tv**
(Non-Linear Offline and Online)

Moondog Edit   **(212) 983-3348**
216 E. 45th St., 13th Fl.   FAX **(212) 983-3349**
(Near Third Ave.)   **www.moondogedit.com**
New York, NY 10017
(Non-Linear Offline)

Moving Pictures   **(212) 924-7364** / **(212) 450-7933**
222 E. 44th St., Eighth Fl. (Near Spring St.)   **www.mpny.tv**
New York, NY 10017
(Compositing, Computer Graphics, Graphics, HD Editing, Non-Linear Offline and Online & Post Production Supervision)
Executive Producer: Ron Honsa
Producer: Nancy Penman

Napoleon Art & Productions, Inc.   **(212) 692-9200**
420 Lexington Ave., Ste. 3020   FAX **(212) 692-0309**
(Near E. 43rd St.)   **www.napny.com**
New York, NY 10170
(Computer Graphics, Digital Offline, Digital Online & Sound Design)
President: Marty Napoleon
Editors: Matthew Gendron, Ken Kresge, Perry Morton & Matthew Ranson
Sales Reps: Jane Carter, Paul Johnson & Meredith Sorkin
Audio Engineers: Jeney Arrowood & Ron DiCesare

NBC New York Editing Operations   **(212) 664-2186**
30 Rockefeller Plaza   FAX **(212) 664-8994**
New York, NY 10112   **www.nbcuni.com/studio/newyork**
(Analog/Digital, Compositing, Computer Animation, Computer Graphics, Digital Non-Linear Offline and Online, Digital Offline and Online, Duplication, DVD Authoring, HD Editing, Linear Online, Non-Linear Offline and Online, Post Production Supervision, Sound Design & Visual FX)

NFL Films   **(856) 222-5675** / **(877) 222-3517**
One NFL Plaza   FAX **(856) 866-4848**
Mount Laurel, NJ 08054   **www.nflfilms.com/studios**
Executive Producer: Maria Patriarca
Sr. Art Director: Penny Ashman
Film Lab Manager: Mike Villanova
Colorists: Bobby Johanson & Chris Pepperman
Director of Sales: Rick Angeli
Editors: Charlie Askew, George Pilhuj, Tom Pilong & Pete Staman

Northern Lights Post   **(212) 274-1199**
135 W. 27th St., Eighth Fl.   FAX **(212) 274-1117**
(Near Sixth Ave.)   **www.nlpedit.com**
New York, NY 10001
(Computer Graphics, Non-Linear Offline and Online & Post Production Supervision)
Executive Producer: Arthur Tremeau
Producers: Damien Henderson & Jackie Vendetti
Editors: David Gioiella, Christopher Harrison, John Laskas, Mark Littman & Michael Palermo
Creative Design/Visual Effects: Christopher Harrison, Beirne Lowry & Ross Shain

Ohio Edit   **(212) 255-6446**
Seven W. 18th St., Eighth Fl.   FAX **(212) 255-5020**
(Near Fifth Ave.)   **www.ohioedit.com**
New York, NY 10011
Executive Producer: Erica Thompson
Producer: Stefanie Hirschtritt
Editors: Pete Fritz, Yuko Koseki, Antoine Mills & Frank Snider

Onshore Media   **(646) 536-3494** / **(310) 691-8666**
(Non-Linear Offline and Online)   **www.onshoredigital.com**

Otterson Television Video, Inc.   **(212) 695-7417**
251 W. 30th St. (Near Eighth Ave.)
New York, NY 10001
(Graphics & Non-Linear Offline and Online)
President: William Otterson
Operations Manager/Producer: Robert Matteo

Outpost   **(718) 599-2385**
118 N. 11th St. (Near Berry St.)   FAX **(718) 599-9747**
Brooklyn, NY 11211   **www.outpostedit.com**
(Non-Linear Offline and Online)
Contact: David Dixon

Park Avenue Post, Inc.   **(212) 689-7678**
419 Park Ave. South, Ste. 600   FAX **(212) 689-7544**
(Near 29th St.)   **www.parkavenuepost.com**
New York, NY 10016
Contact: Nigel Kettle

Perception   **(212) 563-3388**
12 W. 31st St., Sixth Fl.   FAX **(212) 563-3571**
New York, NY 10001   **www.perceptionnyc.com**
(Analog/Digital, Compositing, Computer Animation, Computer Graphics, Digital Linear/Non-Linear Offline and Online, Duplication, DVD Authoring, Film Editing, HD Editing, Linear/Non-Linear Offline and Online, Post Production Supervision & Visual FX)

Philofilm   **(212) 343-1770** / **(917) 860-9185**
401 Washington St., Ste. 2A   FAX **(212) 343-1775**
New York, NY 10013   **www.philofilm.com**

Picture Island   **(646) 638-0895**
33 Jones St., Ste. 3   FAX **(646) 202-2895**
(Near Bleecker St.)   **www.pictureisland.com**
New York, NY 10014

Post Millennium, Inc.   **(212) 319-1230**
155 Wooster St., Ste. 4E   FAX **(212) 319-1235**
(Near 47th St.)   **www.postmillennium.com**
New York, NY 10012
(Computer Graphics, Linear Online, Non-Linear Offline and Online & Post Production Supervision)

Post Office Editorial   **(212) 981-5015** / **(917) 696-6906**
311 W. 34th St., 12th Fl.   FAX **(212) 265-9114**
New York, NY 10001
(Non-Linear Offline and Online)
President/Editor: Doug Forbes
Editors: Georgina Americh & John Moser

PS 260   **(212) 447-0006**
260 Fifth Ave., PH (Near E. 29th St.)   FAX **(212) 447-0010**
New York, NY 10001   **www.ps260.com**
(Compositing, Computer Graphics, Digital Online, DVD Authoring, Film Editing, Non-Linear Offline & Non-Linear Online)
Executive Producer: Zarina Mak
Editors: Sarra Idris, Jason Kileen, JJ Lask, Maury Loeb, Robert Ryang, Dustin Stephens & John Zieman

Purple Cow Post   **(212) 206-9189**
    (516) 443-1058
688 Ave of the Americas, Ste. 306   FAX **(212) 206-8468**
(Near W. 22nd St.)   **www.purplecowpost.com**
New York, NY 10010
(Computer Graphics, Linear Online, Non-Linear Offline and Online & Post Production Supervision)
Executive Producer/Editor: Brian Kushner
Graphics: Victor Quinones & Wes Townsend
Assistant Editor: Michael Pickett

Ray Benjamin Video   **(212) 242-4820**
29 W. 15th St. (Near Fifth Ave.)   FAX **(212) 463-0584**
New York, NY 10011
(Non-Linear Offline and Online)

Red Car   **(212) 982-5555**
196 Mercer St., PH (Near Bleecker St.)   FAX **(212) 982-7179**
New York, NY 10012   **www.redcar.com**
(Non-Linear Offline)

Red Thread Productions   **(212) 367-7100**
873 Broadway, Ste. 501   FAX **(212) 228-6209**
New York, NY 10003   **www.redthreadproductions.com**

Reel Life Film LLC   **(212) 655-9268**
11 Broadway, Ste. 650   **www.rlf-nyc.com**
New York, NY 10004

Refinery New York   **(212) 391-8166**
16 W. 46th St. (Near Fifth Ave.)   FAX **(212) 391-8783**
New York, NY 10036   **www.refinerynyc.com**
(Motion Graphics, Non-Linear Offline and Online & Special Effects)

Rooftop Edit   **(212) 244-0744**
104 W. 29th St., 12th Fl.   FAX **(212) 244-0690**
(Near Sixth Ave.)   **www.rooftopedit.com**
New York, NY 10001
(Editing, Finishing & Graphics)

Sandpiper Editorial Services   **(212) 564-6643**
155 E. 34th St., Ste. 17F   FAX **(212) 564-6808**
(Near Third Ave.)
New York, NY 10016
(Non-Linear Offline)

The Singularity Corporation   **(917) 514-9057**
218 W. 40th St., Seventh Fl.   **www.singularitycorp.com**
(Near Seventh Ave.)
New York, NY 10018

Solar Film/Video Productions   **(212) 473-3040**
632 Broadway, Ste. 304   FAX **(212) 473-3091**
(Near Houston St.)   **www.solarnyc.com**
New York, NY 10012
(Avid Non-Linear Offline and Online)

Spot Welders of New York   **(212) 226-6001**
511 Canal St., Sixth Fl.   FAX **(212) 226-6006**
New York, NY 10013   **www.spotwelders.com**
(Non-Linear Offline)
CEO: David Glean
Executive Producer: Tommy Murov
Editors: Catherine Bull, Damion Clayton, Robert Duffy, Dick Gordon, Haines Hall, Michael Heldman, Pam Martin, Lucas Spaulding, Jón Stefánsson & Brad Waskewich

Steel Rose Editorial   **(212) 838-4300**
Five E. 47th St. (Near Fifth Ave.)   FAX **(212) 223-0567**
New York, NY 10017
(Non-Linear Offline and Online)

Stolen Car   **(212) 768-7600**
62 W. 45th St., Tenth Fl.   FAX **(212) 768-8505**
(Near Sixth Ave.)   **www.stolencar.net**
New York, NY 10036
(Non-Linear Offline)
Producer: Gus Reyes
Editors: Tom Donahue & Keith Krimbel

Tamberelli Digital   **(212) 244-1011**
    (877) 608-4336
516 W. 36th St., Second Fl.   FAX **(212) 947-5894**
(Near 10th Ave.)   **www.tamberelli.com**
New York, NY 10018
(Non-Linear Offline and Online)

thePound   **(212) 575-8664**
45 W. 45th St.   FAX **(212) 575-9412**
New York, NY 10036   **www.thepoundnyc.com**
(Digital Offline, Digital Online, Film Editing, HD Editing, Non-Linear Offline, Non-Linear Online, Post Production Supervision & Sound Design)

TV HEAD Productions, LLC   **(973) 588-9020**
611 Main St. (Near W. 44th St.)   FAX **(973) 588-9021**
Boonton, NJ 07005   **www.tv-head.com**
(DVD Authoring, HD Editing, Standards Conversions & Visual FX)
President: Mike Gutowitz

USA Studios   **(212) 398-6400**
29 W. 38th St. (Near Fifth Ave.)   FAX **(212) 398-8037**
New York, NY 10018   **www.usastudios.tv**
(Linear/Non-Linear Offline and Online)

Version 2 Editing   **(212) 989-1212**
601 W. 26th St., Ste. 1505   FAX **(212) 989-6640**
(Near 11th Ave.)   **www.version2.net**
New York, NY 10001
(Non-Linear Offline and Online)
Executive Producer: Linda Rafoss

The Well   **(212) 620-0220**
85 Fifth Ave. (Near E. 16th St.)   FAX **(212) 352-1881**
New York, NY 10003   **www.welledit.com**
Executive Producer: Wendy Bryant
CFO: Robert Friedman
Editors: Gary Hernandez, Eric Horowitz & Ed Kisberg
Graphic Design: Francis Oh

the Whitehouse   **(212) 568-8200**
180 Varick St., Ste. 1400   FAX **(212) 568-7882**
New York, NY 10014   **www.whitehousepost.com**
Executive Producer: Corina Dennison
Editors: Nick Allix, Heidi Black, Josh Bodnar, David Brixton, Sven Budelmann, Ian Davies, Trish Fuller, Sam Gunn, Lisa Gunning, Grant Gustafson, Steve Hamilton, Jack Hutchings, Russell Icke, Stephen Jess, Alaster Jordan, Meg Kubicka, Marc Langley, Rick Lawley, Richard Learoyd, Carlos Lowenstein, Filip Malasek, Adam Marshall, Gareth McEwen, Crandall Miller, Dan Oberle, Colby Parker, Jr., Steve Prestemon, Adam Robinson, Alex Rodriguez, John Smith, Greg Snider, Ben Stephens, Christina Stumpf, Nikki Vapensky, Matt Walsh, Christophe Williams, Matthew Wood & Kevin Zimmerman

Wildchild Editorial   **(212) 725-5333**
44 W. 28th St., 15th Fl.   FAX **(212) 725-2932**
(Near Broadway)   **www.wildchildpost.com**
New York, NY 10001
(Non-Linear Offline)

Work Edit   **(212) 719-4577**
270 W. 39th St., 11th Fl.   FAX **(212) 719-4380**
(Near Eighth Ave.)   **www.workedit.com**
New York, NY 10018
(Linear Online & Non-Linear Offline and Online)
President: Dalton Helms

Composers & Sound Designers

Joe Albano	(212) 427-5014
	www.rooftopproductions.com
Neil Argo	(323) 854-2555
	(818) 505-9600
	www.neilargo.com
Robert Arron	(212) 431-3004
Mark Barasch	(212) 986-6445
	www.soundimageny.com
David Barratt	(212) 242-0554
Robin Batteau	(212) 352-8833
	www.crushingmusic.com
John Bauers	(201) 795-3907
Christopher Benham	(917) 806-5553
	FAX (866) 809-9927
	www.12ammusic.com
Howie Beno	(212) 242-0554
Edward Bilous	(212) 447-9530
	www.smackmusic.com
Marc Black	(914) 232-5548
	www.blackmarketproductions.org
Marc Blatte	(212) 629-7400
	www.scubalook.com
Erik Blicker	(212) 673-9274
	www.gemusic.com
Gary Burke	(845) 679-8848
	www.nevessa.com
Joe Carroll	(212) 465-8540
	www.manicmoosemusic.com
Evren Celimli	(917) 202-7073
	www.evrencelimli.com
Francois Eudes Chanfrault	(310) 652-8778
	www.lspagency.net
John Crenshaw	(212) 333-0700
	www.broadwayvideo.com
Michelle DiBucci	(212) 447-9530
	www.smackmusic.com
Luisa Dunn	(818) 990-8993
	www.ambitiousent.com
Jon Ehrlich	(212) 768-8501
	www.jecomusic.com
Peter Einhorn	(845) 679-3391
	www.petereinhorn.com
Jim Farmer	(212) 349-6619
Shari Feder	(212) 633-1175
	www.russograntham.com
Lewis Flinn	(212) 254-7500
	(212) 431-3004
	www.lewisflinn.com
Gary Foote	(212) 625-2015
	www.soundguild.com
David Forman	(518) 537-6542
Joe Franco	(212) 777-8440
	www.beatstreetnyc.com
Peter Francovilla	(212) 633-1175
	www.russograntham.com
Werner Fritzsching	(212) 633-1175
	www.russograntham.com
David Gervai	(212) 677-8300
	www.compositions-inc.com
Steven Gold	(212) 677-8300
	www.compositions-inc.com
Ben Goldberg	(212) 633-1175
	www.russograntham.com
Martin Goodman	(212) 427-5014
	www.rooftopproductions.com
Ron Gozzo	(917) 805-8563
	www.rgtmusic.com
John Grant	(212) 867-1515
Marshall Grantham	(212) 633-1175
	www.russograntham.com
Grizzly Bear	(310) 652-8778
	www.lspagency.net
Steve Hansen	(212) 242-5686
	www.hi-top.com
Robb Hart	(212) 629-7400
	www.scubalook.com
Marc Healy	(212) 979-2722
	www.mackcut.com
Ryan Heiferman	(212) 997-1200
	www.bigyellowduck.com
Jonathan Helfand	(212) 647-9500
	www.jhmp.com
Chad Herndon	(212) 203-2325
	www.strongboystudios.com
Alfred Hochstrasser	(212) 989-8000
	www.musicbeast.com
Steve Jennings	(212) 625-2015
	www.soundguild.com
Bubba Kadane	(310) 652-8778
	www.lspagency.net
Matt Kadane	(310) 652-8778
	www.lspagency.net
Ralph Kelsey	(212) 333-0700
	www.broadwayvideo.com
Shane Kiester	(212) 633-1175
	www.russograntham.com
William Kinslow	(212) 229-1642
	www.parkswingorc.com
Jawanza Kobie	(302) 529-0840
Robbie Kondor	(212) 760-0077
	www.kondormusic.com
Michael Minard Lake	(845) 986-7320

Lloyd Landesman	(212) 242-0554
Clifford Lane	(212) 352-8833
	www.crushingmusic.com
Bernie Larsen	(323) 856-3000
	www.thegelleragency.com
Joey Levine	(212) 352-8833
	www.crushingmusic.com
Michael A. Levine	(212) 268-6560
	www.michaellevinemusic.com
Scott McIntosh	(212) 246-8400
	www.headroomdigi.com
Taylor McLam	(212) 352-8833
	www.crushingmusic.com
Chris McLaughlin	(212) 633-1175
	www.russograntham.com
Shashanka Menard	(718) 523-4380
	www.premik.com
Andy Mendelson	(212) 629-7400
	www.scubalook.com
Edgar Mills	(718) 523-4380
	www.premik.com
Gordon Minette	(212) 431-3004
Fintan O'Neil	(718) 746-1546
	www.northeastmusic.com
David O'Rourke	(718) 746-1546
	www.northeastmusic.com
Ovasen	(212) 989-5373
104 W. 14th St., Second Fl.	FAX (212) 989-2925
New York, NY 10011	www.ovasen.com
John Peterson	(212) 242-0554
Sarah Plant	(845) 657-8454
	(212) 663-8929
	FAX (845) 657-8454
	www.sarahplantmusic.com
Jerry Plotkin	(212) 246-8400
	www.headroomdigi.com
Matthew Polis	(212) 463-0138
	www.soundspacestudio.com
Bob Pomann	(212) 869-4161
	www.pomannsound.com
Gary Pozner	(212) 614-1891
	www.whirledmusic.com
Steve Raskin	(212) 229-1966
	www.steveraskin.com
Scott M. Riesett	(917) 825-6703
	FAX (615) 825-6702
	www.terraceproductions.com
Leigh Roberts	(212) 768-8501
	www.jecomusic.com
J. Daniel Roland	(716) 655-4903
John Russo	(212) 721-4667
	www.musicreations.net
Regan Ryzuk	(212) 625-2015
	www.soundguild.com
Jean-Marie Salaun	(212) 431-3004
	(212) 629-7400
Boris Salchow	(323) 856-3000
	www.thegelleragency.com
Mikael Sandgren	(323) 856-3000
	www.thegelleragency.com
Glenn Schloss	(212) 673-9274
	www.gemusic.com
Gary Schreiner	(212) 352-8833
	www.crushingmusic.com
Don Sebesky	(212) 352-8833
	www.crushingmusic.com
Steve Serraiocco	(718) 746-1546
	www.northeastmusic.com
Steve Shapiro	(212) 633-1175
	www.russograntham.com
Wayne Sharpe	(212) 242-0554
Andrew Sherman	(212) 431-4342
	www.fluidny.com
Cheryl Smith	(212) 777-8440
	www.beatstreetnyc.com
Jeff Southworth	(212) 352-8833
	www.crushingmusic.com
Evan Spear	(212) 246-8400
	www.headroomdigi.com
Summerfield Music, Inc./	
Trailer Trash Music Library	(818) 905-0400
	FAX (818) 905-0488
	www.summerfieldmusic.com
Glenn M. Taylor	(973) 226-1461
	www.taylormadeprod.com
Mark Tocher	(212) 340-1243
Ceiri Torjussen	(323) 856-3000
	www.thegelleragency.com
Premik Tubbs	(718) 523-4380
	www.premik.com
Rick Ulfik	(212) 867-0846
Mike Ungar	(212) 333-0700
	www.broadwayvideo.com
Kenny White	(212) 352-8833
	www.crushingmusic.com
John Wilcox	(212) 246-8400
	www.headroomdigi.com
David Wingo	(310) 652-8778
	www.lspagency.net
James Wolcott	(212) 989-9292
	www.waxnyc.com
Mary Wood	(212) 352-8833
	www.crushingmusic.com
Brad Worrell	(212) 629-7400
	www.scubalook.com

Computer Graphics & Visual FX

4-D Creative Media   (212) 599-6699
Four E. 46th St., Fourth Fl.   (646) 483-7768
(Near Fifth Ave.)   FAX (212) 499-9081
New York, NY 10017   www.4-dcreative.com
(2D/3D Animation and FX, 2D Paint, 3D Modeling, Animatics, Character Animation, Compositing, Model/Miniature Shoots, Morphing, Pre-Production Planning, Rotoscoping & Visual FX)

8 Hats High Animation & Production, Inc.   (845) 344-1888
23-27 W. Main St., Third Fl.   www.8hatshigh.com
Middletown, NY 10940
(2D/3D Animation, Animatics, Character Animation, Compositing, Digital Ink and Paint, Editorial, Graphic Design, Green Screen Compositing, Motion Capture, Motion Graphics, Photography & Storyboarding)

AccuWeather, Inc.   (814) 235-8600
385 Science Park Rd.   FAX (814) 235-8609
State College, PA 16803   www.accuweather.com
(2D/3D Animation of Weather Graphics)
Founder/CEO: Dr. Joel N. Myers
Sr. Sales Manager: Brian Kisslak

Alz Productions   (212) 594-2291
50 W. 34th St. (Near Herald Square)   FAX (212) 594-2297
New York, NY 10001   www.alz.net
(2D Paint, Animatics, Character Animation, Character Design, Graphic Design & Storyboards)
President: Albert Zee

Animated Arts   (518) 465-6448
265 Central Ave. (Near North Lake St.)   FAX (518) 465-6448
Albany, NY 12206   www.animatedarts.net
(2D/3D Animation, Animatics & Compositing)
Director: Jeffrey Radden

Animatus Studio   (585) 232-1740
34 Winthrop St.   www.animatusstudio.com
(Near Charlotte St.)
Rochester, NY 14607
(2D/3D Computer Animation, Animatics & Visual FX)
Owner/Producer: Fred Armstrong
Director/Animator: Dave Puls

Animotion, Inc.   (315) 471-3533
501 W. Fayette St., Ste. 141   FAX (315) 471-2730
(Near Wyoming St.)   www.animotioninc.com
Syracuse, NY 13204
(2D Paint, 3D Modeling, Animatics, Character Animation, Compositing & Pre-Production Planning)
Presidents: David Hicock & Larry Royer

asterisk   (212) 255-8880
20 W. 20th St., Ste. 405   www.asteriskpix.com
(Near Union Square West)
New York, NY 10011
(2D/3D Animation and FX, Character Animation, Compositing, Digital Matte Painting, Morphing, Pre-Production Planning, Rotoscoping, Ultimatte & Visual FX)

Atlantic Motion Pictures   (212) 924-6170
162 W. 21st St., Fourth Fl.   FAX (212) 989-8736
(Near Seventh Ave.)   www.atlanticmotion.com
New York, NY 10011
(2D/3D Computer Animation, Animatics, Blue/Green Screen Facilities, Digital Matte Painting & Pre-Production Planning)
President: Patrick Egan

Atomic Image Creative Media, Inc.   (212) 255-6625
311 Broadway, PH B   FAX (212) 627-8632
(Near Cornelia St.)   www.atomicimage.com
New York, NY 10007
(2D/3D Animation, Broadcast Design, CGI, Compositing, Computer Animation, Digital FX, Editorial, Graphic Design, Motion Graphics, Rotoscoping & Visual FX)

Big Film Design   (212) 627-3430
594 Broadway, Ste. 1001   FAX (212) 989-6528
New York, NY 10012   www.bigfilmdesign.com
(2D/3D Animation and FX, Compositing & Digital Matte Painting)
Creative Director/CEO: Randall Balsmeyer

Blinking Eye Media   (212) 243-6243
One West St., Ste. 100   FAX (212) 242-4411
(Near Spring St.)   www.blinkingeyemedia.com
New York, NY 10004
(2D/3D Animation and FX, 2D Paint, 3D Modeling, Animatics, Character Animation, Compositing, Digital Matte Painting, Morphing, Pre-Production Planning, Rotoscoping & Ultimatte)

Blue Sky Studios, Inc.   (914) 259-6500
44 S. Broadway, 17th Fl.   FAX (914) 259-6499
(Near Westchester Ave.)   www.blueskystudios.com
White Plains, NY 10601
(3D Animation and FX, Character Animation, Compositing & Digital Matte Painting)
CEO: Brian Keane
Senior VP/General Manager: Chuck Richardson

BOND Edit   (212) 533-9400
665 Broadway, Ste. 1201   FAX (212) 533-9463
(Near Bond St.)   www.bondedit.com
New York, NY 10012
(2D/3D Animation, Animatics, Compositing, Morphing, Pre-Production Planning, Rotoscoping & Visual FX)
President/Editor: Jeff Beckerman
Partner/Sound Designer: Joe Casalino
Executive Producer: Stephanie Shayne

Brainstorm Digital   (646) 330-5245
   (310) 230-5581
100 Water St.   FAX (646) 415-8480
Brooklyn, NY 11201   www.brainstorm-digital.com
(2D Animation, 2D Paint, 3D Animation, 3D Digitizing, 3D Modeling, Animatics, Blue/Green Screen Compositing, CGI, Compositing, Computer Animation, Digital FX, Digital Matte Painting, Digital Paint, Digital Restoration, Editorial, Image Processing, Live Action Integration, Matte Painting, Miniature Motion Control, Miniatures, Morphing, Motion Capture, Motion Control, Motion Control Photography, Motion Graphics, Photography, Pre-Production Planning, Previsualizations, Real Time Motion Control, Rotoscoping, Storyboards, Time-Lapse Photography, Ultimatte, Visual FX & Visual FX Supervision)
VFX Producer: Richard Friedlander
VFX Supervisors: Glenn Allen & Justin Ball

C-TRL Labs, Inc.   (646) 257-2210
28 Howard St., Second Fl.   www.c-trl.com
New York, NY 10013
(2D Animation, 3D Animation, 3D Modeling, Animatics, Blue Screen Compositing, Broadcast Design, Digital FX, Motion Graphics, Rotoscoping & Visual FX)

Celefex   (212) 255-3470
15 E. 32nd St., 10th Fl.   FAX (212)-246-4635
New York, NY 10016   www.celefex.com
(3D Animation and Modeling, 3D Character Animation, 3D Digital Matte Painting & Compositing)

Charlex, Inc.   (212) 719-4600
Two W. 45th St., Seventh Fl.   FAX (212) 840-2747
(Near Fifth Ave.)   www.charlex.com
New York, NY 10036
(3D Animation and FX, Compositing & Motion Graphics Design)
Contact: Anne Skopas

City Lights fx   (212) 679-4400
Six E. 39th St., Second Fl.   FAX (212) 679-4482
(Near Fifth Ave.)   www.citylightsmedia.com
New York, NY 10016
(2D/3D Computer Animation & Compositing)
President/CEO: Danny Fisher
President: Jack Fisher
VP: Aaron Behr

Creative Bubble, LLC (212) 201-4200
79 Fifth Ave., 14th Fl. (Near 15th St.) FAX **(212) 201-4210**
New York, NY 10003 **www.creativebubble.com**
(2D Paint, 2D and 3D Animation and FX, 3D Modeling, Animatics, Compositing, Digital Matte Painting, Morphing, Pre-Production Planning, Rotoscoping & Visual FX)

Curious Pictures Corporation **(212) 674-1400**
440 Lafayette St., Sixth Fl. **(212) 674-7600**
(Near E. Eighth St.) FAX **(212) 674-0081**
New York, NY 10003 **www.curiouspictures.com**
(2D/3D Character Animation, 2D/3D Digital Matte Painting, Blue/Green Screen Facilities, Cel Animation, Compositing, Digital Ink and Paint & Pre-Production Planning)

Design@Chelsea Post **(212) 727-1234**
221 W. 26th St. (Near Eighth Ave.) FAX **(212) 255-6644**
New York, NY 10001 **www.amvchelsea.com**

Designomotion **(917) 532-0738**
67 E. 11th St., Ste. 324 **www.designomotion.com**
(Near Broadway)
New York, NY 10003
(2D/3D Animation, 3D Modeling, Animatics, Blue/Green Screen Compositing, Broadcast Design, Cel Animation, CGI, Character Animation and Design, Compositing, Computer Animation, Digital FX, Digital Ink, Digital Paint, Editorial, Graphic Design, Illustrative Design, Live Action Integration, Morphing, Motion Graphics, Photography, Pre-Production Planning, Previsualization, Rotoscoping, Scanning and Recording, Stop-Motion Animation, Storyboards, Time-Lapse Photography, Ultimate, Visual FX & Visual FX Supervision)

Digital Magic Animation, LLC **(917) 576-2528**
117-14 Union Tpke, BB2 **www.digitalmagicanimation.com**
(Near 14th St.)
Kew Gardens, NY 11415
(2D/3D Animation and FX, Character Animation, Compositing, Morphing & Rotoscoping)

DMA Animation **(212) 463-7370**
89 Fifth Ave., Ste. 501 FAX **(212) 463-7820**
(Near E. 16th St.) **www.dma-animation.com**
New York, NY 10003
(2D/Paint, 3D Modeling & Character Animation)
Creative Director: Tony Caio

Du Art Film and Video **(212) 757-4580**
245 W. 55th St. (Near Broadway) FAX **(212) 333-7647**
New York, NY 10019 **www.duart.com**
(2D Animation and FX, 2D Paint, 3D Animation and FX, Compositing, Rotoscoping & Visual FX)

Ewen Industries, Inc. **(917) 771-2727**
250 W. 49th St., Ste. 704 **www.ewenindustries.com**
New York, NY 10019
(2D Animation, Animatics, Blue Screen Compositing, Broadcast Design, Character Animation, Character Design, Compositing, Computer Animation, Editorial, Graphic Design, Image Processing, Motion Graphics, Pre-Production Planning, Rotoscoping, Scanning and Recording, Storyboards, Visual FX & Visual FX Supervision)

The Field **(212) 253-2888**
119 Fifth Ave., PH **www.thefieldtv.com**
New York, NY 10003
(2D Animation, Broadcast Design & Visual FX)
Editors: Fabrizio Rossetti & Mike Siedlecki

Flickerlab **(212) 560-9228**
FAX **(212) 560-9253**
www.flickerlab.com

Fluid **(212) 431-4342**
532 Broadway, Fifth Fl. FAX **(212) 431-6525**
(Near Spring St.) **www.fluidny.com**
New York, NY 10012

Freestyle Collective **(212) 414-2200**
104 E. 25th St., 12th Fl. FAX **(212) 414-2206**
(Near Fifth Ave.) **www.freestylecollective.com**
New York, NY 10010
(2D and 3D Animation and FX & Compositing)
Creative Director: Victor Newman
Executive Producer: Elizabeth Kiehner

Fullmind, LLC **(609) 424-0115**
Three Third St. FAX **(609) 424-0119**
Bordentown, NJ 08505 **www.fullmindcreative.com**

Goldcrest Post Production/ **(212) 243-4700**
Pixel Monkeys **(212) 897-3935**
799 Washington St. FAX **(212) 243-4453**
New York, NY 10014 **www.goldcrestpost.com**

(646) 283-7767
Gotham Digital FX, Inc. **(310) 740-7326**
www.gothamdigitalfx.com
(2D Animation, 2D Paint, 3D Animation, 3D Digitizing, 3D Modeling, Animatics, Blue Screen Compositing, Broadcast Design, Cel Animation, CGI, Character Animation, Character Design, Clay Animation, Compositing, Computer Animation, Digital Film Mastering, Digital FX, Digital Ink, Digital Matte Painting, Digital Paint, Digital RestorationEditorial, Graphic Design, Green Screen Compositing, Illustrative Design, Image Processing, Live Action Integration, Matte Painting, Miniature Motion Control, Miniatures, Morphing, Motion Capture, Motion Control, Motion Control Photography, Motion Graphics, Photography, Pre-Production Planning, Previsualizations, Real Time Motion Control, Rotoscoping, Scanning and Recording, Stop-Motion Animation, Storyboards, Time-Lapse Photography, Ultimate, Visual FX & Visual FX Supervision)
Visual Effects Producer: Joseph Oberle

GTV, Inc. **(212) 262-6260**
1697 Broadway, Ste. 404 FAX **(212) 262-4709**
(Near W. 53rd St.) **www.gtvnyc.com**
New York, NY 10019
(2D Paint, 2D/3D Animation, Animatics, Blue Screen Compositing, Broadcast Design, CGI, Character Animation, Compositing, Digital Restoration, Graphic Design & Rotoscoping)

Guava **(212) 414-2222**
Eight W. 19th St., Fourth Fl. FAX **(212) 929-2669**
(Near Fifth Ave.) **www.guavanyc.com**
New York, NY 10011
(2D/3D Animation and FX, Compositing, Pre-Production Planning & Visual FX)

HBO Studio Productions **(212) 512-7800**
120A E. 23rd St. (Near Park Ave.) FAX **(212) 512-7788**
New York, NY 10010
(2D/Paint, Compositing & Pre-Production Planning)

Heirloom Biography **(914) 948-7006**
Five Augusta Pl. (Near S. Chelsea Rd.)
White Plains, NY 10603
(Compositing)
President: Peter Savigny
Director of Ops./Production Manager: Jean Palmer

Hornet, Inc. **(917) 351-0520**
116 W. Houston St., Fourth Fl. FAX **(917) 351-0522**
(Near Seventh Ave.) **www.hornetinc.com**
New York, NY 10012
(2D/3D Animation, Character Animation, Compositing, Digital Matte Painting, Morphing, Pre-Production Planning & Stop-Motion Animation)

IBC Digital **(716) 852-1724**
230 Perry St., Ste. 31A FAX **(716) 852-1735**
Buffalo, NY 14204 **www.ibcdigital.com**
(2D/3D Animation, Character Animation, Compositing & Visual FX)
President/Executive Producer: Benjamin Porcari
Creative Director: Melissa Porcari
Producer: Parrish Gust

Inverse Media **(203) 255-9620**
P.O. Box 1072 **www.inversemedia.com**
Southport, CT 06490
(2D/Paint, 3D Modeling & Compositing)

LifeHouse Productions, LLC **(860) 432-9177**
P.O. Box 4007 **www.lifehouseproductions.com**
Manchester, CT 06045
(2D Paint, 3D Animation, 3D Modeling, CGI, Computer Animation & Storyboards)
Partners: Dena L. Matthews & William R. Matthews

Mechanism Digital, Inc.   **(646) 230-0230**
514 W. 24th St., Third Fl.   FAX **(646) 336-8395**
(Near 10th Ave.)   www.mechanismdigital.com
New York, NY 10011
(2D/3D Animation, 3D Modeling, Animatics, Blue Screen Compositing, Broadcast Design, CGI, Character Animation, Character Design, Compositing, Computer Animation, Digital FX, Digital Matte Painting, Digital Paint, Digital Restoration, Editorial, Graphic Design, Green Screen Compositing, Live Action Integration, Matte Painting, Morphing, Motion Capture, Motion Graphics, Previsualizations, Rotoscoping, Storyboards, Time-Lapse Photography, Ultimate, Visual FX & Visual FX Supervision)
President/Visual FX Producers: Lucien J. Harriot

Method   **(212) 907-1200**
545 Fifth Ave., Second Fl.   FAX **(212) 907-1201**
(Near 45th St.)   www.methodstudios.com
New York, NY 10017
(2D/3D Animation and FX, Character Animation, Compositing & Digital Matte Painting)

The Molecule   **(917) 522-5690**
245 W. 55th St., Ste. 1104   FAX **(646) 349-3294**
New York, NY 10019   www.themolecule.net
(2D Animation, 2D Paint, 3D Animation, 3D Modeling, Animatics, Blue Screen Compositing, Broadcast Design, CGI, Character Animation, Character Design, Compositing, Computer Animation, Digital Film Mastering, Digital FX, Digital Matte Painting, Digital Paint, Digital Restoration, Editorial, Graphic Design, Green Screen Compositing, Image Processing, Live Action Integration, Matte Painting, Miniatures, Morphing, Motion Graphics, Pre-Production Planning, Previsualizations, Rotoscoping, Scanning and Recording, Storyboards, Ultimate, Visual FX & Visual FX Supervision)

    (212) 730-6641
Ricardo Morín   **(646) 468-3397**
(3D Modeling)   www.ricardomorin.com

Moving Images   **(212) 953-6999**
227 E. 45th St., Sixth Fl.   FAX **(212) 661-0457**
(Near Second Ave.)   www.mipost.com
New York, NY 10017
(Visual FX)
Visual Effects Director: John Miller

Palace Digital Studios   **(203) 853-1740**
29 N. Main St.   FAX **(203) 855-9608**
South Norwalk, CT 06854   www.palacedigital.com
(2D/3D Animation and FX)
VP of Operations: Maureen Connelly
President/COO: Wendy Lambert
Animators/Designers: Joe Paccia & Dan Chau

    (201) 714-9845
PAWS & Co., LLC   **(877) 448-7297**
710 Clinton St.   FAX **(201) 963-5757**
Hoboken, NJ 07030   www.pawsco.tv
(Time Manipulation Imaging System)
Technical Supervisor: Anthony Jacques
Producer: Mario Malave

Perception   **(212) 563-3388**
12 W. 31st St., Sixth Fl.   FAX **(212) 563-3571**
New York, NY 10001   www.perceptionnyc.com
(2D/3D Animation, 3D Modeling, Blue/Green Screen Compositing, Broadcast Design, CGI, Compositing, Computer Animation, Digital FX, Digital Matte Painting, Editorial, Graphic Design, Live Action Integration, Matte Painting, Motion Graphics, Previsualizations, Rotoscoping, Storyboards, Ultimate, Visual FX & Visual FX Supervision)

    (413) 528-3974
Powderkeg, Inc.   **(413) 329-5522**
    FAX **(863) 582-3974**
    www.powderkeg.com

R/G A   **(212) 946-4000**
350 W. 39th St. (Near Eighth Ave.)   FAX **(212) 946-4010**
New York, NY 10018   www.rga.com
(2D/3D Animation and FX, Compositing & Digital Matte Painting)
Chairman/CEO: Robert Greenberg
Head of Production: Steven Plumlee

Rejectbarn, LLC   **(203) 866-1898**
23 S. Main St., Third Fl.   www.rejectbarn.com
Norwalk, CT 06854

Rhinofx   **(212) 986-1584**
50 E. 42nd St., 12th Fl.   FAX **(212) 986-2113**
(Near Madison Ave.)   www.rhinofx.com
New York, NY 10017
(2D/3D Animation and FX, Character Animation, Compositing & Rotoscoping)
Chief Executive Officer/Partner: David Binstock
Executive Producer/Partner: John Starace
Managing Director/Partner: Rick Wagonheim
VP/Executive Producer: Camille Geier
Creative Director/Director: Harry Dorrington
Directors of CG: Arman Matin & Mark Steinberg
Inferno Artists: John Budion, Ronen Sharabani & Vico Sharabani
Sales Representatives: Jay Broddock
VP of Long Form Entertainment: Karin Levinson

    (800) 526-8091
Sonalysts' Studios   **(860) 326-3672**
215 Parkway North   FAX **(860) 326-3748**
Waterford, CT 06385   www.sonalystsmedia.com
(2D/Paint, 3D Modeling, Blue/Green Screen Facilities, Character Animation, Compositing & Pre-Production Planning)
Senior Vice President: Fred Litty
Vice President: Peter Walsh

Spontaneous   **(212) 317-0077**
575 Lexington Ave., 25th Fl.   FAX **(212) 317-1048**
(Near E. 51st St.)   www.spon.com
New York, NY 10022
(2D/3D Computer Animation, Compositing, Design, Live Action & Visual FX)
Creative Director: John Leamy
Assoc. CD/Dir. of Animation: Lawrence Nimrichter
Director of Visual Effects: Andy Milkis
Head of Production: Bennett Lieber
Senior Producer: Bryce Edwards
Producers: Sarah Brown & Felili Rincon
Sales: Dana Dubay

Synthespian Studios   **(413) 458-0202**
96 Ballou Ln.   FAX **(413) 458-5089**
Williamstown, MA 01267   www.synthespians.net
President: Diana Walczak
COO: Michael Van Himbergen
Executive Producer: Amanda Roth
Producer: Wendy Gipp
Directors: Jeff Kleiser & Diana Walczak

VI[Z]rt   **(212) 560-0708**
555 Eighth Ave., 10th Fl.   FAX **(212) 560-0709**
(Near W. 38th St.)   www.vizrt.com
New York, NY 10018
(Virtual Set Systems)

    (718) 204-1030
Video Concepts, Inc.   **(888) 482-4278**
18-25 26th Rd. (Near 21st St.)   FAX **(718) 204-1017**
Long Island City, NY 11102   www.videoconcepts.com
President: Patrick Giovanniello

Wavelength Video Services   **(631) 789-2949**
P.O. Box 1531   FAX **(631) 789-9366**
Lindenhurst, NY 11757
(Blue Screen & Ultimatte)
Director: Tom Guadarrama

Digital Intermediates

903Films (212) 674-0986
515 Greenwich St., Ste. 202   FAX (212) 380-0258
New York, NY 10013   www.903films.com

Deluxe New York (212) 444-5600
435 Hudson St., Ninth Fl.   www.bydeluxe.com
New York, NY 10014

Ⓐ Digital Arts (212) 460-9600
130 W. 29th St., Eighth Fl.   FAX (212) 660-3600
New York, NY 10001   www.digital-arts.net

iProbe Multilingual Solutions, Inc. (212) 489-6035
Five W. 36th St., Ste. 402   FAX (212) 202-4790
New York, NY 10018   www.iprobesolutions.com

PostWorks (212) 894-4000
(212) 894-4050
100 Avenue of the Americas   FAX (212) 941-0439
New York, NY 10013   www.postworks.com

Technicolor Creative Services - N.Y. (212) 609-9400
110 Leroy St.   FAX (212) 609-9450
New York, NY 10014   www.technicolor.com

Duplication

All Mobile Video (212) 727-1234
221 W. 26th St. (Near Seventh Ave.)   FAX (212) 255-6644
New York, NY 10001   www.allmobilevideo.com

ANS International Video (212) 673-3107
220 E. 23rd St., Second Fl.   FAX (212) 673-3816
(Near Third Ave.)   www.ansproductionsny.com
New York, NY 10010

Ascent Media Management East (201) 767-3800
235 Pegasus Ave.   FAX (201) 767-4568
Northvale, NJ 07647   www.ascentmedia.com

Broadway Video Duplication (212) 265-7600
1619 Broadway, Fourth Fl.   FAX (212) 603-0667
(Near W. 49th St.)   www.broadwayvideo.com
New York, NY 10019

Chelsea Post (212) 727-1234
221 W. 26th St. (Near Eighth Ave.)   FAX (212) 255-6644
New York, NY 10001   www.amvchelsea.com

Chromavision (212) 686-7366
49 W. 27th St., Eighth Fl.   FAX (212) 686-7310
(Near Sixth Ave.)   www.chromavision.net
New York, NY 10001

Cine Magnetics Digital & (914) 273-7500
Video Laboratories (800) 431-1102
100 Business Park Dr. (Near Route 22)   FAX (914) 273-7575
Armonk, NY 10504   www.cinemagnetics.com

City Lights Media Group (212) 679-4400
Six E. 39th St., Second Fl.   FAX (212) 679-4482
(Near Fifth Ave.)   www.citylightsmedia.com
New York, NY 10016

Deluxe New York (212) 444-5600
435 Hudson St., Ninth Fl.   www.bydeluxe.com
New York, NY 10014

Devlin Video Intl. (212) 391-1313
1501 Broadway, Ste. 408   FAX (212) 391-2744
(Near W. 43rd St.)   www.devlinvideo.com
New York, NY 10036
(All Formats & Standards Conversions)

DG FastChannel (212) 953-9300
(212) 627-2216
600 Third Ave. (Near Seventh Ave.)   FAX (212) 972-8250
New York, NY 10016   www.dgfastchannel.com

Ⓐ Digital Arts (212) 460-9600
130 W. 29th St., Eighth Fl.   FAX (212) 660-3600
(Near Sixth Ave.)   www.digital-arts.net
New York, NY 10001
(All Formats, Beta SP, D5, Digibeta, DV, DVC Pro & High Def)

(800) 446-3470
Disc Makers (212) 645-0312
16 W. 18th St.   FAX (212) 352-0573
New York, NY 10011   www.discmakers.com

(631) 752-0608
Duplication Depot, Inc. (800) 950-0608
215-B Central Ave.   FAX (631) 752-3607
(Near Engineers Ln.)   www.duplicationdepot.com
Farmingdale, NY 11735

East Coast Digital, Inc. (212) 691-4517
27 W. 20th St., Ste. 1106   www.eastcoastdigital.com
(Near Fifth Ave.)
New York, NY 10011
(All Formats, Betacam SP, Digibeta, DVCAM, HD DVC Pro, High Def, Standards Conversions & Tape Cloning)

Editors' Hideaway, Inc. (212) 661-3850
219 E. 44th St., Eighth Fl.   FAX (212) 661-3609
(Near Second Ave.)   www.editorshideaway.com
New York, NY 10017

Flow Motion Inc. (888) 818-3569
143 E. Gonzales Rd.   FAX (888) 818-3569
Oxnard, CA 93036   www.flowmotioninc.com
(CD-Audio, CD-ROM, DVD, DVD-5, DVD-9, DVD-R, Blu Ray, DVCAM & DV)

FMP Visual Communications (800) 346-5071
1010 Spring Mill Ave., Ste. 100   FAX (610) 825-4430
Conshohocken, PA 19428   www.fmpvisual.com

HAVE, Inc. (518) 828-2000
350 Power Ave. (Near Route 9G)   FAX (518) 828-2008
Hudson, NY 12534   www.haveinc.com

Hello World Communications (212) 243-8800
118 W. 22nd St., Ste. 2A   FAX (212) 691-6961
(Near Sixth Ave.)   www.hwc.tv
New York, NY 10011
(Beta SP, CD-Audio, DV, DVCAM, DVCPro, DVD, High Def, HDV, Mini HD, NTSC, Standards Conversions & VHS)

Intermediapost (201) 261-3959
120 Route 17 North (800) 811-7044
Paramus, NJ 07652 FAX (201) 261-3062
(All Formats) www.intermediapost.com

International Duplication Centre/
International Digital Centre, Inc. (212) 581-3940
216 E. 45th St., Seventh Fl. FAX (212) 581-3979
(Near Third Ave.) www.idcdigital.com
New York, NY 10017

Moving Images (212) 953-6999
227 E. 45th St., Sixth Fl. www.mipost.com
(Near Second Ave.)
New York, NY 10017

Park Avenue Post, Inc. (212) 689-7678
419 Park Ave. South, Ste. 600 FAX (212) 689-7544
(Near 29th St.) www.parkavenuepost.com
New York, NY 10016

PostWorks (212) 894-4000
  (212) 894-4050
100 Avenue of the Americas FAX (212) 941-0439
(Near Grand St.) www.postworks.com
New York, NY 10013
(Beta SP, D1, Digibeta, DVCam, DVC PRO, DVCPRO HD, DVD, HDCam, HDCam SR, HDD5, HDV, NTSC, PAL, Standards Conversions & VHS)

Production Central (212) 631-0435
873 Broadway, Ste. 205 FAX (212) 631-0436
(Near E. 18th St.) www.prodcentral.com
New York, NY 10003

PSI Industries (201) 768-8007
135 Ludlow Ave. FAX (201) 768-8314
Northvale, NJ 07647 www.psimulitimedia.com

R & R Video (212) 594-0900
505 Eighth Ave., 25th Fl. FAX (212) 594-2628
(Near W. 35th St.) www.rainbowvideo1.com
New York, NY 10018

Rainbow Video (212) 594-0545
505 Eighth Ave., 25th Fl. FAX (212) 594-2628
(Near W. 35th St.) www.rainbowvideo1.com
New York, NY 10018
(¾", ¾" SP, 1", 8mm, All Formats, All Video Formats, Beta SP, Beta SX, Betacam SP, Blu Ray, CD-Audio, CD-ROM, D2, Digibeta, Digital Betacam, DV, DVC Pro, DVCAM, DVD, DVD-5, DVD-9, DVD-R, HD Digibeta, HD DVC Pro, Hi-8mm, High Def, NTSC, Standards Conversions, Super 8, S-VHS, Tape Cloning & VHS)

Tylie Jones & Associates, Inc. (212) 972-3800
370 Lexington Ave., 10th Fl., Ste. 1007 FAX (212) 972-4419
(Near E. 41st St.) www.tylie.com
New York, NY 10017
(All Formats)

  (212) 398-6400
USA Studios (800) 872-3821
29 W. 38th St. (Near Fifth Ave.) FAX (212) 398-8037
New York, NY 10018 www.usastudios.tv

Video Taping Service/ (609) 645-1660
VTS Productions (877) 891-1002
3153 Fire Rd. FAX (609) 646-3957
Egg Harbor Township, NJ 08234
  www.videotapingservice.com
(¾", ¾" SP, 8mm, Beta SP, Betacam SP, CD-Audio, CD-ROM, DV, DVC Pro, DVCAM, DVD, DVD-R, Hi-8mm, NTSC, Standards Conversions, Super 8, S-VHS & VHS)

  (718) 482-7111
VidiPax LLC (800) 653-8434
30-00 47th Ave., Ste. 600 FAX (718) 482-1370
Long Island City, NY 11101 www.vidipax.com
(Video and Audio Tape Restoration)

Zeitbyte (718) 666-3300
45 Main St., Ste. 1030 www.zeitbyte.com
Brooklyn, NY 11201
(¾", ¾" SP, All Video Formats, Beta SP, Beta SX, Betacam SP, CD-Audio, CD-ROM, Composer Dubs, Digibeta, Digital Betacam, DV, DVC Pro, DVCAM, DVD, DVD-5, DVD-9, DVD-R, HD Digibeta, HD DVC Pro, Hi-8mm, High Def, NTSC, Standards Conversions, S-VHS & VHS)

DVD Authoring & Replication

3 Rings Media (212) 481-4499
226 Fifth Ave., Sixth Fl. FAX **(212) 213-1568**
(Near E. 27th St.) www.3ringsmedia.com
New York, NY 10001

4-D Creative Media (212) 599-6699
Four E. 46th St., Fourth Fl. (646) 483-7768
(Near Fifth Ave.) FAX **(212) 499-9081**
New York, NY 10017 www.4-dcreative.com
(Authoring Only)

A to Z Media (212) 260-0237
650 Broadway, Fourth Fl. (888) 670-0260
(Near Third St.) FAX **(212) 260-0631**
New York, NY 10012 www.atozmusic.com

Area 4 (212) 444-1171
Tribeca Film Center, 375 Greenwich St. www.area4.tv
(Near Franklin St.)
New York, NY 10013

Ascent Media Management East (201) 767-3800
235 Pegasus Ave. FAX **(201) 767-4568**
Northvale, NJ 07647 www.ascentmedia.com

Atlantic Motion Pictures (212) 924-6170
162 W. 21st St., Fourth Fl. FAX **(212) 989-8736**
New York, NY 10011 www.atlanticmotion.com

BLINK Digital (212) 661-6900
545 Fifth Ave., Second Fl. FAX **(212) 907-1233**
(Near 45th St.) www.blinkdigital.com
New York, NY 10017
(Authoring Only)

Cine Magnetics Digital & (914) 273-7500
Video Laboratories (800) 431-1102
100 Business Park Dr. (Near Route 22) FAX **(914) 273-7575**
Armonk, NY 10504 www.cinemagnetics.com

(800) 433-3472
Cinram (646) 834-1500
250 Park Ave. South, Eighth Fl. www.cinram.com
New York, NY 10003

City Lights Home Entertainment (212) 679-4400
Six E. 39th St., Third Fl. FAX **(212) 679-4481**
(Near Fifth Ave.) www.citylightsmedia.com
New York, NY 10016

Creative Bubble, LLC (212) 201-4200
79 Fifth Ave., 14th Fl. (Near 15th St.) FAX **(212) 201-4210**
New York, NY 10003 www.creativebubble.com

Devlin Video Intl. (212) 391-1313
1501 Broadway, Ste. 408 FAX **(212) 391-2744**
(Near W. 43rd St.) www.devlinvideo.com
New York, NY 10036

(800) 446-3470
Disc Makers (212) 645-0312
16 W. 18th St. FAX **(212) 352-0573**
New York, NY 10011 www.discmakers.com

dM works (516) 255-0100
246 Rockaway Ave. www.dmworks.com
(Near Hawthorne Ave.)
Valley Stream, NY 11580

Du Art Film and Video (212) 757-4580
245 W. 55th St. (Near Broadway) FAX **(212) 333-7467**
New York, NY 10019 www.duart.com
(Authoring Only)

Editors' Hideaway, Inc. (212) 661-3850
219 E. 44th St., Eighth Fl. FAX **(212) 661-3609**
(Near Second Ave.) www.editorshideaway.com
New York, NY 10017

Elrom Inc. (212) 645-5050
419 Park Ave. South, Ste. 600 FAX **(212) 689-7544**
(Near 28th St.) www.elrom.tv
New York, NY 10016

Five Foot Five Productions, Inc. (212) 206-7706
112 W. 27th St., Ste. 510 FAX **(212) 604-0626**
New York, NY 10001 www.fivefootfive.com

Flow Motion Inc. (888) 818-3569
143 E. Gonzales Rd. FAX **(888) 818-3569**
Oxnard, NY 93036 www.flowmotioninc.com

Full Circle Studios (716) 875-7740
741 Main St., The Ansonia Centre FAX **(716) 875-7162**
(Near Tupper St.) www.fullcirclestudios.com
Buffalo, NY 14203

GRS Systems, Inc. (212) 286-0299
216 E. 45th St. FAX **(212) 286-9475**
New York, NY 10017 www.grsv.com

HAVE, Inc. (518) 828-2000
350 Power Ave. (Near Route 9G) FAX **(518) 828-2008**
Hudson, NY 12534 www.haveinc.com

Hello World Communications (212) 243-8800
118 W. 22nd St., Ste. 2A FAX **(212) 691-6961**
(Near Sixth Ave.) www.hwc.tv
New York, NY 10011

(201) 261-3959
Intermediapost (800) 811-7044
120 Route 17 North FAX **(201) 261-3062**
Paramus, NJ 07652 www.intermediapost.com

International Duplication Centre/
International Digital Centre, Inc. (212) 581-3940
216 E. 45th St., Seventh Fl. FAX **(212) 581-3979**
(Near Third Ave.) www.idcdigital.com
New York, NY 10017

Masterdisk Studios (212) 541-5022
545 W. 45th St., Fifth Fl. FAX **(212) 265-5645**
New York, NY 10036 www.masterdisk.com

Murray Hill Studios, Inc. (212) 889-4200
248 E. 35th St. (Near Second Ave.) FAX **(212) 889-9413**
New York, NY 10016 www.murrayhillstudios.com

N9 Productions (212) 563-4589
245 W. 29th St., 16th Fl. www.n9productions.com
(Near Seventh Ave.)
New York, NY 10001
(Authoring Only)

Nova Disc (212) 691-8519
340 W. 11th St. (Near Washington St.) www.novadisc.net
New York, NY 10014
(Replication Only)

(646) 536-3494
Onshore Media (310) 691-8666
www.onshoredigital.com

Park Avenue Post, Inc. (212) 689-7678
419 Park Ave. South, Ste. 600 FAX **(212) 689-7544**
(Near 29th St.) www.parkavenuepost.com
New York, NY 10016

Playback Systems   **(212) 620-5530**
(Replication Only)   **(800) 540-7529**
FAX **(212) 620-5531**
www.playbackny.com

Production Central   **(212) 631-0435**
873 Broadway, Ste. 205   FAX **(212) 631-0436**
(Near E. 18th St.)   **www.prodcentral.com**
New York, NY 10003

Protoactive   **(917) 783-1654**
www.protoactive.com

PSI Industries   **(201) 768-8007**
135 Ludlow Ave.   FAX **(201) 768-8314**
Northvale, NJ 07647   **www.psimulitimedia.com**

Saga Productions   **(646) 825-9063**
75 Maiden Ln., Ste. 905   **www.sagadvd.com**
New York, NY 10038

Scharff Weisberg
Media Resource Center   **(718) 610-1660**
36-36 33rd St. (Near Third Ave.)   FAX **(718) 610-1750**
Long Island City, NY 11106   **www.swinyc.com**

ScreamDVD   **(212) 951-7171**
247 W. 35th St., Seventh Fl.   FAX **(212) 202-0915**
(Near 28th St.)   **www.screamdvd.com**
New York, NY 10001

Seraphic Studio, LLC   **(212) 561-5321**
322 W. 49th St., Ste. 2FE   FAX **(866) 369-0112**
New York, NY 10019   **www.seraphicstudio.com**

The System   **(212) 957-9509**
134 Parker Ave.   FAX **(917) 338-7596**
Easton, PA 18042   **www.thesystemmsp.com**
(Authoring Only)

Traveler Productions   **(212) 353-3289**
(Authoring Only)

USA Studios   **(212) 398-6400**
29 W. 38th St. (Near Fifth Ave.)   FAX **(212) 398-8037**
New York, NY 10018   **www.usastudios.tv**

Editing Equipment Rentals & Sales

All Mobile Video (212) 727-1234
221 W. 26th St. (Near Seventh Ave.) FAX (212) 255-6644
New York, NY 10001 www.allmobilevideo.com

American Montage, Inc. (212) 334-8283
Old Chelsea Station www.americanmontage.com
P.O. Box 1042 (Near Centre Market Pl.)
New York, NY 10011
(Non-Linear Offline and Online)

Analog Digital International, Inc. (212) 688-5110
20 E. 49th St., Second Fl. FAX (212) 688-5405
(Near Madison Ave.) www.analogdigitalinc.com
New York, NY 10017
(Linear/Non-Linear Offline and Online)

Anderson Productions (860) 589-2776
(800) 701-4311
34 Dell Manor Dr. FAX (860) 584-5936
Bristol, CT 06010 www.andersonprod.com
(Linear/Non-Linear Offline and Online)

Atlantic Motion Pictures (212) 924-6170
162 W. 21st St., Fourth Fl. FAX (212) 989-8736
New York, NY 10011 www.atlanticmotion.com

Bee Harris Productions, Inc. (914) 664-6519
(914) 469-7695
79 Putnam St. FAX (914) 664-6422
Mount Vernon, NY 10550 www.beeharris.com
(Linear Online & Non-Linear Offline and Online)

Chosen Pictures (646) 827-0931
(Non-Linear Offline and Online) www.chosenpictures.com

Departure Films (212) 629-9666
333 W. 39th St., Ste. 1502 FAX (212) 629-6788
New York, NY 10018 www.departure-films.com

Ⓐ Digital Arts (212) 460-9600
130 W. 29th St., Eighth Fl. FAX (212) 660-3600
(Near Sixth Ave.) www.digital-arts.net
New York, NY 10001
(24P Editing Systems, Avid, Digibeta, Digital Decks, Digital Non-Linear, Editing Suites, Final Cut Pro Systems, High Def, HD Decks, Non-Linear Offline & Non-Linear Online)

Diva Edit (212) 947-1395
(Non-Linear Offline and Online) www.richtervideos.com

Du Art Film and Video (212) 757-4580
245 W. 55th St. (Near Broadway) FAX (212) 333-7647
New York, NY 10019 www.duart.com
(Non-Linear Offline and Online)

Earth Video (212) 228-4254
(Non-Linear Offline and Online) www.earthvideo.net

Ⓐ East Coast Digital, Inc. (212) 691-4517
(888) 869-1013
27 W. 20th St., Ste. 1106 www.eastcoastdigital.com
(Near Fifth Ave.)
New York, NY 10011
(Analog Decks, Avid Systems, Digibeta, Digital Editing Systems, Digital Non-Linear, Final Cut Pro Systems, Hard Drive Rentals, HD Decks & Monitors)

Ⓐ Firestarter Rentals (310) 420-5146
(800) 670-7080
880 W. First St., Ste. 513 FAX (949) 363-8497
Los Angeles, CA 90012
(D5 High Def Tape Deck Rentals)

Goldcrest Post Production (212) 243-4700
799 Washington St. (Near Horatio St.) FAX (212) 624-1701
New York, NY 10014 www.goldcrestpost.com

Ⓐ Hula Post Production (212) 367-7292
20 W. 22nd St., Ste. 611 FAX (212) 367-7293
(Near Broadway) www.hulapost.com
New York, NY 10010
(24P Editing Systems, Analog, Digital and HD Decks, Avid Systems, Digibeta, Digital Editing Systems, Digital Non-Linear, Editing Suites, Final Cut Pro, Hard Drive Rentals, High Def, Linear/Non-Linear Offline and Online, Monitors, Non-Linear Hard Drive Rentals & Video Tape Monitors and Recorders)

Instructivision, Inc. (973) 575-9992
16 Chapin Rd., Ste. 904 FAX (973) 575-9134
Pine Brook, NJ 07058 www.instructivision.com
(Non-Linear Online)

Ⓐ LA Digital Post, Inc. (212) 981-8500
220 W. 42nd St., 17th Fl. FAX (212) 981-8595
New York, NY 10036 www.ladigital.com

Lovett Productions, Inc. (212) 242-8999
17 Van Dam St., Ground Fl. FAX (212) 242-7437
New York, NY 10013 www.lovettproductions.com
(Non-Linear Offline and Online)

60 Editing Equipment Rentals & Sales

LA DIGITAL POST
Toluca Lake • West Los Angeles • New York

EXPECT SOMETHING INCREDIBLE

HIGH DEFINITION & STANDARD DEFINITION
EDITING SOLUTIONS

Avid Symphony Nitris DX

Avid Media Composer Nitris DX

Avid Media Composer Adrenaline HD

Apple Final Cut Pro Studio

Digidesign Protools Audio Suite

Avid Unity Media Network

Logging • Streaming • Workflow Solutions

Peripherals • Decks • Drives

In-House Editing Suites • In-House Production Suites

On-Location System Rentals

Customized Studio Integrations

24/7 Technical Support Services

---

220 West 42nd Street
New York, New York 10036

212.981.8500
ladigital.com

LVR/Liman Video Rental Company (212) 594-0086 / (800) 251-4625
341 W. 38th St., Ground Fl. FAX (212) 594-0786
(Near Eighth Ave.) www.lvrusa.com
New York, NY 10018
(Linear Online)

Moviola Digitial (212) 247-0972
545 W. 45th St. (Near 11th Ave.) FAX (212) 265-9820
New York, NY 10036 www.moviola.com

Moviola/J & R Film Company (212) 247-0972 / (877) 668-4652
545 W. 45th St., Fourth Fl. FAX (212) 265-9820
(Near 11th Ave.) www.moviola.com
New York, NY 10036
(Non-Linear Offline)

Outpost (718) 599-2385
118 N. 11th St. (Near Berry St.) FAX (718) 599-9747
Brooklyn, NY 11211 www.outpostedit.com
(Non-Linear Offline and Online)

Pivotal Post (212) 226-5822
417 Canal St., Third Fl. www.pivotalpost.com
(Near Varick St.)
New York, NY 10013
(Film Editing & Non-Linear Offline and Online)

Post Factory (212) 627-1662
161 Avenue of the Americas, 11th Fl. FAX (212) 627-1684
(Near Spring St.) www.postfactoryny.com
New York, NY 10013
(Film Editing & Non-Linear Offline and Online)

Post Office Editorial (212) 981-5015 / (917) 696-6906
311 W. 34th St., 12th Fl. FAX (212) 265-9114
New York, NY 10001
(Non-Linear Offline and Online)

PostWorks (212) 894-4000 / (212) 894-4050
100 Avenue of the Americas FAX (212) 941-0439
(Near Grand St.) www.postworks.com
New York, NY 10013
(Non-Linear Offline and Online & Video Decks)

Prime To Go (888) 858-4180
72 Hillside Ln. www.primetogo.com
Fallsington, PA 19054
(Non-Linear Offline and Online)

Production Central (212) 631-0435
873 Broadway, Ste. 205 FAX (212) 631-0436
(Near E. 18th St.) www.prodcentral.com
New York, NY 10003

Runway, Inc. (310) 636-2000
10575 Virginia Ave. FAX (310) 636-2034
Culver City, CA 90232 www.runway.com

Solar Film/Video Productions (212) 473-3040
632 Broadway, Ste. 304 FAX (212) 473-3091
(Near Houston St.) www.solarnyc.com
New York, NY 10012
(Avid, Linear/Non-Linear Offline and Online)

Tekserve (212) 929-3645
119 W. 23rd St. (Near Sixth Ave.) FAX (212) 463-9280
New York, NY 10011 www.tekserve.com
(Linear/Non-Linear Offline and Online)

Paul Tomasko (212) 316-1920 / (845) 246-1138
1198 Glasco Tpke
Saugerties, NY 12477
(Film)

TV Pro Gear (212) 564-9933 / (818) 788-4700
540 W. 36th St., Seventh Fl. FAX (212) 564-4065
New York, NY 10018 www.tvprogear.com
(Non-Linear Offline and Online)

Video Concepts, Inc. (718) 204-1030 / (888) 482-4278
18-25 26th Rd. (Near 21st St.) FAX (718) 204-1017
Long Island City, NY 11102 www.videoconcepts.com
(Linear/Non-Linear Offline and Online)

Virtual Media (212) 490-9730
915 Broadway, 15th Fl. FAX (212) 818-0529
(Near E. 21st St.) www.virtualmediaonline.com
New York, NY 10010
(Non-Linear Offline and Online)

William Greaves Productions, Inc. (212) 265-6150
230 W. 55th St. www.williamgreaves.com
(Near Broadway)
New York, NY 10019
(Non-Linear Offline)

firestarter rentals
310.420.5146
Flame Systems Rental
Discreet Flame / Smoke HD
Day, Week, Month Rates

The Post Production Rental Company **That Never Sleeps**

Hi-Def Post Production **Rentals**

Decks – Drives – Networked Storage – AVID Editing Systems HD/SD
Final Cut Pro Systems HD/SD – Symphony Nitris DX – Media Composer Nitris DX

HULA POST
PRODUCTION
NEW YORK   LOS ANGELES

www.hulapost.com

NY ADDRESS: 20 West 22nd St., Suite 611, New York, NY 10010 · 212-367-7292
LA ADDRESS: 3747 Cahuenga Blvd. West, Studio City, CA 91604 · 818-954-0200
VENICE ADDRESS: 228 Main Street · Suite 14, Venice, CA 90291 · 310-314-3101

Editors

Doug Abel	(212) 741-9691	www.dougabel.com
Edward R. Abroms	(323) 856-3000	www.thegelleragency.com
Jonathan Alberts	(212) 545-7895	www.nyoffice.net
All Crew Agency	(818) 206-0144	www.allcrewagency.com

2920 W. Olive Ave., Ste. 201
Burbank, CA 91505
FAX (818) 206-0169
(Reps for Editors)

Michel Aller	(323) 856-3000	www.thegelleragency.com
Nick Allix	(212) 568-8200	www.whitehousepost.com
Timothy Alverson	(212) 253-6900	www.innovativeartists.com
Georgina Americh	(212) 981-5015	
Alison Amron	(212) 545-7895	www.nyoffice.net
Charlie Askew	(856) 222-5675	www.nflfilms.com
John Axelrad	(310) 395-9550	www.skouras.com
Zene Baker	(212) 253-6900	www.innovativeartists.com
Jason Ballantine	(212) 545-7895 / (310) 273-6700	www.nyoffice.net
Hernan Barangan	(212) 545-7895	www.nyoffice.net
Lisa Barnable	(212) 255-4440	www.homesteadedit.com
George Barnes	(973) 508-6054 / (305) 673-2737	
Philip Bartell	(212) 545-7895	www.nyoffice.net
Will Barton	(212) 794-9030 / (212) 545-7895	www.nyoffice.net
Jonathan Baskin	(212) 545-7895	www.nyoffice.net
Ned Bastille	(212) 253-6900	www.innovativeartists.com
Sam Bauer	(212) 997-1818	www.gershagency.com
Nicholas Beauman	(310) 395-9550	www.skouras.com
Jeff Beckerman	(212) 533-9400	
Alan Bell	(310) 395-9550	www.skouras.com
Charly Bender	(212) 255-4440	www.homesteadedit.com
Brian Berdan	(310) 395-9550	www.skouras.com
Bruce Bertrand	(973) 361-5817 / (201) 317-5388 / FAX (973) 361-2748	www.earlyfilms.net
Avril Beukes	(310) 652-8778	www.lspagency.net
Kent Beyda	(310) 273-6700	www.utaproduction.com
Heidi Black	(212) 568-8200	www.whitehousepost.com
Sue Blainey	(212) 253-6900	www.innovativeartists.com
Gena Bleier	(310) 652-8778	www.lspagency.net
Andy Blumenthal	(323) 856-3000	www.thegelleragency.com
Larry Bock	(212) 253-6900	www.innovativeartists.com
Josh Bodnar	(212) 568-8200	www.whitehousepost.com
Adam Boome	(310) 652-8778	www.lspagency.net
Charles Bornstein	(212) 253-6900	www.innovativeartists.com
Dan Bosko	(212) 265-7600	www.broadwayvideo.com
Michelle Botticelli	(212) 253-6900	www.innovativeartists.com
Scott Boyd	(323) 856-3000	www.thegelleragency.com
Maryann Brandon	(310) 273-6700	www.utaproduction.com
Geraud Brisson	(310) 652-8778	www.lspagency.net
David Brixton	(212) 568-8200	www.whitehousepost.com
Katt Brown	(212) 926-0477	www.tapestryinc.com
David Bryen	(212) 228-7474	www.nycjump.com
Jeff Buchanan	(310) 652-8778	www.lspagency.net
Sven Budelmann	(212) 568-8200	www.whitehousepost.com
Catherine Bull	(212) 226-6001	www.spotwelders.com
Tiffany Burchard	(212) 627-3100	www.filmcore.com
Edgar Burcksen	(212) 253-6900	www.innovativeartists.com

Liz Burton	(212) 271-9010	www.eenyc.com
Sheri Bylander	(212) 595-8316	
Rob Cabana	(212) 838-8883	www.justaddwater.tv
Lance Cain	(212) 545-7895	www.nyoffice.net
Malcolm Campbell	(310) 652-8778	www.lspagency.net
Jeff Canavan	(212) 253-6900	www.innovativeartists.com
Bruce Cannon	(323) 460-4767	www.jacobandkoleagency.com
Luis Carballar	(310) 652-8778	www.lspagency.net
Gordon Carey	(212) 627-3100	www.filmcore.com
John Carhart	(212) 655-9268	www.rlf-nyc.com
Eric Carlson	(212) 529-1991	www.madeinchinagraph.com
Julie Carr	(310) 652-8778	www.lspagency.net
Matthew Cassel	(310) 652-8778	www.lspagency.net
Jay Cassidy	(310) 652-8778	www.lspagency.net
Jenn Chambers	(212) 683-4004	www.bigskyedit.com
Richard Chew	(310) 395-9550	www.skouras.com
Debra Chiate	(310) 652-8778	www.lspagency.net
Jonathan Chibnall	(310) 652-8778	www.lspagency.net
John Chimples	(212) 375-0911 FAX (212) 375-0915	www.imltd.com
Shannon Chirrone	(212) 633-0822	
Scott Chosed	(646) 827-0931	www.chosenpictures.com
Pernille Bech Christensen	(310) 395-9550	www.skouras.com
Damion Clayton	(212) 226-6001	www.spotwelders.com
Cameron Clendaniel	(718) 254-8027 (617) 416-6004	www.camclendaniel.com
Anne V. Coates	(310) 273-6700	www.utaproduction.com
David Codron	(212) 253-6900	www.innovativeartists.com
Tricia Cooke	(310) 273-6700	www.utaproduction.com
David Cornman	(212) 302-2828	www.crewcuts.com
Hank Corwin	(310) 395-9550	www.skouras.com
Tom Costain	(212) 253-6900	www.innovativeartists.com
Cari Coughlin	(323) 460-4767	www.jacobandkoleagency.com
Olivier Bugge Coutte	(310) 395-9550	www.skouras.com
Bill Cramer	(212) 302-2828	www.crewcuts.com
Jacob Craycroft	(646) 734-0765	
Douglas Crise	(310) 652-8778	www.lspagency.net
Gavin Cutler	(212) 979-2722	www.mackcut.com
Vic David	(212) 962-1850 FAX (212) 962-1043	www.7-ny.com
Ian Davies	(212) 568-8200	www.whitehousepost.com
Vito De Candia	(212) 598-3000	www.magneticimage.com
Michael DeMirjian	(212) 388-1724 (215) 432-5742	www.flimflamfilm.com
Claudia D'Enjoy	(212) 265-7600	www.broadwayvideo.com
Emily Dennis	(212) 375-0726	www.madriverpost.com
Alberto De Toro	(310) 652-8778	www.lspagency.net
Nicolas De Toth	(310) 273-6700	www.utaproduction.com
Jun Diaz	(212) 979-2722	www.mackcut.com
Tom Donahue	(212) 768-7600	www.stolencar.net
Brian Donnelly	(212) 271-9010	www.eenyc.com
Dody Dorn	(310) 273-6700	www.utaproduction.com
Greg Dougherty	(212) 255-4440	www.homesteadedit.com
Harry Douglas	(212) 598-3000	www.magneticimage.com
Tom Downs	(212) 545-7895	www.nyoffice.net
Bob Ducsay	(310) 395-9550	www.skouras.com
Skip Duff	(212) 255-4440	www.homesteadedit.com
James Duffy	(212) 375-0726	www.madriverpost.com

Editors

Robert Duffy	(212) 226-6001 www.spotwelders.com	Brad Fuller	(212) 545-7895 www.nyoffice.net
Stephane Dumonceau	(212) 375-0726 www.madriverpost.com	Trish Fuller	(212) 568-8200 www.whitehousepost.com
Duwayne R. Dunham	(323) 856-3000 www.thegelleragency.com	Patrick Gallagher	(323) 460-4767 www.jacobandkoleagency.com
Andrew Eisen	(323) 856-3000 www.thegelleragency.com	Nigel Galt	(310) 652-8778 www.lspagency.net
Michael Elliot	(212) 375-0726 www.madriverpost.com	Glenn Garland	(323) 856-3000 www.thegelleragency.com
Ken Eluto	(323) 845-4144 www.montanartists.com	Christian Gazal	(310) 395-9550 www.skouras.com
George Englezos	(212) 689-7678 www.parkavenuepost.com	Charlie Gelber	(212) 262-6260 www.gtvnyc.com
Nicholas Erasmus	(212) 997-1818 www.gershagency.com	The Geller Agency 1547 Cassil Pl. Hollywood, CA 90028 (Reps for Editors)	(323) 856-3000 FAX (323) 856-3009 www.thegelleragency.com
Axuve Espinosa	(917) 621-6281		
Paul Ewen	(917) 771-2727 www.ewenindustries.com	Matthew Gendron	(212) 692-9200 www.napny.com
Julie Farol	(212) 633-0822	The Gersh Agency 41 Madison Ave., 33rd Fl. (Near E. 26th St.) New York, NY 10010 (Reps for Editors)	(212) 997-1818 (310) 274-6611 FAX (212) 997-1978 www.gershagency.com
Todd Feuer	(212) 969-9099		
Chris Figler	(323) 856-3000 www.thegelleragency.com		
Tom Finan	(310) 822-9113 www.murthaagency.com	John Gilbert	(310) 395-9550 www.skouras.com
David Finfer	(212) 997-1818 www.gershagency.com	Chris Gill	(310) 273-6700 www.unitedtalent.com
Dan Fisher	(212) 997-9100 www.bionic.tv	Megan Gill	(310) 395-9550 www.skouras.com
Sarah Flack	(310) 395-9550 www.skouras.com	David Gioiella	(212) 274-1199 (212) 794-9030 www.nlpedit.com
Peter Devaney Flanagan	(323) 856-3000 www.thegelleragency.com	Dana Glauberman	(310) 395-9550 www.skouras.com
Patrick Flynn	(917) 400-5374 homepage.mac.com/electrolex	Jinx Godfrey	(212) 627-3100 www.filmcore.com
Doug Forbes	(212) 981-5015	Mark Goldblatt	(310) 273-6700 www.utaproduction.com
Stephen Franciosa Jr.	(718) 885-3434 FAX (718) 885-3338 www.harringtontalents.com	William Goldenberg	(310) 395-9550 www.skouras.com
Jo Francis	(310) 652-8778 www.lspagency.net	Mia Goldman	(310) 273-6700 www.utaproduction.com
Richard Francis-Bruce	(310) 822-9113 www.murthaagency.com	Affonso Goncalves	(212) 545-7895 www.nyoffice.net
Chris Franklin	(212) 683-4004 www.bigskyedit.com	Conrad Gonzalez	(212) 253-6900 www.innovativeartists.com
Robert Frazen	(310) 395-9550 www.skouras.com	Mari Keiko Gonzalez	(212) 265-7600 www.broadwayvideo.com
Freakfilms, Inc./Merle Becker	(646) 325-6708 www.freakfilms.com	Timothy A. Good	(212) 253-6900 www.innovativeartists.com
Pete Fritz	(212) 255-6446 www.ohioedit.com	Dick Gordon	(212) 375-0726 (212) 226-6001 www.madriverpost.com
Lisa Fruchtman	(310) 273-6700 www.utaproduction.com		

C. Scott Gorman	(212) 997-9100 www.bionic.tv	Chris Harrison	(212) 265-7600 www.broadwayvideo.com
Yana Gorskaya	(310) 652-8778 www.lspagency.net	Christopher Harrison	(212) 274-1199 www.nlpedit.com
Susan Graef	(212) 666-6039 (347) 752-7857	James Haygood	(310) 273-6700 www.utaproduction.com
Hilmer Graham	(917) 304-2662 www.hilmeredit.com	Michael Heldman	(212) 226-6001 www.spotwelders.com
John Gramaglia	(212) 529-1991 www.madeinchinagraph.com	Chris Hellman	(212) 255-4440 www.homesteadedit.com
Schuyler Grant	(212) 633-0822	Clayton Hemmert	(212) 302-2828 www.crewcuts.com
Jacques Gravett	(212) 545-7895 www.nyoffice.net	Totie Herman	(212) 598-3000 www.magneticimage.com
Scott Gray	(212) 997-1818 www.gershagency.com	Gary Hernandez	(212) 620-0220 www.welledit.com
Bruce Green	(310) 273-6700 www.utaproduction.com	Emma E. Hickox	(310) 273-6700 www.utaproduction.com
Jerry Greenberg	(310) 273-6700 www.utaproduction.com	Paul Hirsch	(212) 253-6900 www.innovativeartists.com
Joe Gressis	(323) 856-3000 www.thegelleragency.com	Craig Holzer	(212) 302-2828 www.crewcuts.com
Andy Grieve	(212) 226-5678 www.lostplanet.com	Peter Honess	(310) 822-9113 www.murthaagency.com
Jeff Groth	(212) 545-7895 www.nyoffice.net	Eric Horowitz	(212) 620-0220 www.welledit.com
Sam Gunn	(212) 568-8200 www.whitehousepost.com	Chris Houghton	(212) 545-7895 www.nyoffice.net
Lisa Gunning	(212) 568-8200 www.whitehousepost.com	Jason Howe	(212) 867-1515 www.madhousenyc.com
Grant Gustafson	(212) 568-8200 www.whitehousepost.com	Maysie Hoy	(212) 253-6900 www.innovativeartists.com
Michael Gutowitz	(212) 271-9010 www.eenyc.com	Sean Hubbert	(323) 856-3000 www.thegelleragency.com
Andrew Hafitz	(310) 652-8778 www.lspagency.net	Amanda Hughes	(212) 271-9010 www.eenyc.com
Stephanie Hafner	(212) 752-3348 www.bluerockny.com	Jack Hutchings	(212) 568-8200 www.whitehousepost.com
Alexander Hall	(212) 545-7895 www.nyoffice.net	Russell Icke	(212) 568-8200 www.whitehousepost.com
Haines Hall	(212) 226-6001 www.spotwelders.com	Sarra Idris	(212) 447-0006 www.ps260.com
Justine Halliday	(323) 856-3000 www.thegelleragency.com	Mark Imgrund	(310) 592-8271 www.moxedit.com
Richard Halsey	(212) 253-6900 www.innovativeartists.com	Robert Ivison	(310) 652-8778 www.lspagency.net
Scott Ham	(212) 867-1515 www.madhousenyc.com	Jake Jacobsen	(212) 302-2828 www.crewcuts.com
Steve Hamilton	(212) 568-8200 www.whitehousepost.com	Stephen Jess	(212) 568-8200 www.whitehousepost.com
Kristina Hamilton-Grobler	(323) 856-3000 www.thegelleragency.com	Allyson Johnson	(310) 822-9113 www.murthaagency.com
Justine Harari	(917) 567-6316 www.justineharari.com	Peter Johnson	(212) 219-0020 www.consulatefilm.com

Charlie Johnston	(212) 226-5678 www.lostplanet.com	JJ Lask	(212) 447-0006 www.ps260.com
Alaster Jordan	(212) 568-8200 www.whitehousepost.com	John Laskas	(212) 274-1199 www.nlpedit.com
Val Junge	(212) 683-4004 www.bigskyedit.com	Rick Lawley	(212) 568-8200 www.whitehousepost.com
Steve Kahn	(914) 524-0344 www.editonhudson.com	Richard Learoyd	(212) 568-8200 www.whitehousepost.com
Robin Katz	(323) 856-3000 www.thegelleragency.com	Robert Leighton	(310) 395-9550 www.skouras.com
Myron Kerstein	(310) 273-6700 www.utaproduction.com	Martin Levenstein	(212) 545-7895 www.nyoffice.net
Jason Kileen	(212) 447-0006 www.ps260.com	Jonathan Levy	(212) 838-8883 www.justaddwater.tv
Yossi Kimberg	(212) 265-7600 www.broadwayvideo.com	Stuart Levy	(310) 395-9550 www.skouras.com
Jamie Kirkpatrick	(310) 395-9550 www.skouras.com	David Lindblom	(917) 821-0727
Ed Kisberg	(212) 620-0220 www.welledit.com	Carol Littleton	(310) 273-6700 www.utaproduction.com
Eric Kissack	(310) 652-8778 www.lspagency.net	Mark Littman	(212) 274-1199 www.nlpedit.com
Saar Klein	(310) 395-9550 www.skouras.com	Maury Loeb	(212) 447-0006 www.ps260.com
Elizabeth Kling	(310) 822-9113 www.murthaagency.com	Tony Lombardo	(310) 652-8778 www.lspagency.net
Lynzee Klingman	(310) 273-6700 www.utaproduction.com	Gregg London	(310) 395-9550 www.skouras.com
Joe Klotz	(310) 652-8778 www.lspagency.net	Melody London	(212) 545-7895 www.nyoffice.net
Michael N. Knue	(212) 253-6900 www.innovativeartists.com	Richard Lowe	(212) 545-7895 www.nyoffice.net
Yuko Koseki	(212) 255-6446 www.ohioedit.com	Carlos Lowenstein	(212) 568-8200 www.whitehousepost.com
Karen Kourtessis	(212) 302-2828 www.crewcuts.com	Aimée Lyde	(646) 228-9109 www.aimeelyde.com
Dave Koza	(212) 979-2722 www.mackcut.com	Jason MacDonald	(212) 375-0726 www.madriverpost.com
Carole Kravetz	(323) 460-4767 www.jacobandkoleagency.com	Ian MacKenzie	(212) 979-2722 www.mackcut.com
Ken Kresge	(212) 692-9200 www.napny.com	Enrico Madonna	(212) 838-8883 www.justaddwater.tv
Keith Krimbel	(212) 768-7600 www.stolencar.net	Chris Magliozzo	(212) 302-2828 www.crewcuts.com
Meg Kubicka	(212) 568-8200 www.whitehousepost.com	Filip Malasek	(212) 568-8200 www.whitehousepost.com
Edward Kulzer	(917) 359-6877 www.edkulzer.com	Andrew Malenda	(212) 997-9100 www.bionic.tv
Brian Kushner	(212) 206-9189 www.purplecowpost.com	Ruth Mamaril	(212) 627-3100 www.filmcore.com
Robert K. Lambert	(310) 273-6700 www.utaproduction.com	Sherri Margulies	(212) 302-2828 www.crewcuts.com
Marc Langley	(212) 568-8200 www.whitehousepost.com	Stephen Mark	(212) 253-6900 www.innovativeartists.com
		Adam Marshall	(212) 568-8200 www.whitehousepost.com

Pam Martin	(212) 226-6001	www.spotwelders.com
Chris Martini	(212) 643-1736	www.cec-entertainment.com
Damien Massingham	(212) 228-7474	www.nycjump.com
Jim May	(310) 395-9550	www.skouras.com
Tom McArdle	(323) 856-3000	www.thegelleragency.com
Jeff McEvoy	(212) 997-1818	www.gershagency.com
Gareth McEwen	(212) 568-8200	www.whitehousepost.com
Patrick McMahon	(323) 856-3000	www.thegelleragency.com
Debbie McMurtrey	(212) 302-2828	www.crewcuts.com
Sally Menke	(310) 273-6700	www.utaproduction.com
Andy Milkis	(212) 265-7600	www.broadwayvideo.com
Crandall Miller	(212) 568-8200	www.whitehousepost.com
Harry B. Miller III	(323) 856-3000	www.thegelleragency.com
Michael R. Miller	(310) 822-9113	www.murthaagency.com
Antoine Mills	(212) 255-6446	www.ohioedit.com
Paul Millspaugh	(212) 253-6900	www.innovativeartists.com

The Mirisch Agency
1925 Century Park East, Ste. 1070
Los Angeles, CA 90067
(Reps for Editors)
(310) 282-9940
FAX (310) 282-0702
www.mirisch.com

Tod Modisett	(323) 856-3000	www.thegelleragency.com
Cindy Mollo	(310) 652-8778	www.lspagency.net

Montana Artists Agency
7715 W. Sunset Blvd., Third Fl.
Los Angeles, CA 90046
(Reps for Editors)
(323) 845-4144
FAX (323) 845-4155
www.montanartists.com

Luis Moreno	(212) 228-7474	www.nycjump.com
Perry Morton	(212) 692-9200	www.napny.com
John Moser	(212) 981-5015	
Michael S. Murphy	(212) 253-6900	www.innovativeartists.com
Grant Myers	(212) 545-7895	www.nyoffice.net
Joel Negron	(310) 395-9550	www.skouras.com

New York Office
15 W. 26th St., Fifth Fl.
(Near Broadway)
New York, NY 10010
(Reps for Editors)
(212) 545-7895
(323) 468-2240
FAX (212) 545-7941
www.nyoffice.net

Dan Oberle	(212) 568-8200	www.whitehousepost.com
Jeremiah O'Driscoll	(310) 395-9550	www.skouras.com
Charles Olivier	(212) 545-7895	www.nyoffice.net
Conor O'Neill	(310) 395-9550	www.skouras.com
Valdis Oskarsdottir	(310) 395-9550	www.skouras.com
Thomas Ostuni	(212) 529-1991	www.madeinchinagraph.com
Daniel Padgett	(323) 856-3000	www.thegelleragency.com
Michael Palermo	(212) 274-1199	www.nlpedit.com
Bill Pankow	(310) 273-6700	www.utaproduction.com
Jed Parker	(212) 375-0911	www.imltd.com
Jose Pelaez	(917) 691-6962 / (212) 627-3072	www.josepelaez.com
George Pilhuj	(856) 222-5675	www.nflfilms.com
Tom Pilong	(856) 222-5675	www.nflfilms.com
Kane Platt	(212) 529-1991	www.madeinchinagraph.com
Richard Plofker	(212) 265-7600	www.broadwayvideo.com
Lin Polito	(212) 228-7474	www.nycjump.com
Amanda Pollack	(212) 643-1736	www.cec-entertainment.com
Kathleen Poole	(212) 271-9010	www.eenyc.com
Steve Prestemon	(212) 568-8200	www.whitehousepost.com
Jake Pushinsky	(212) 253-6900	www.innovativeartists.com
Matt Ramsey	(212) 253-6900	www.innovativeartists.com
Scott Rankin	(212) 794-9030	
Matthew Ranson	(212) 692-9200	www.napny.com
Fred Raskin	(310) 395-9550	www.skouras.com
David Rennie	(323) 856-3000	www.thegelleragency.com

Meg Reticker	(212) 545-7895	www.nyoffice.net
Geoff Richman	(310) 395-9550	www.skouras.com
Scott Richter	(323) 856-3000	www.thegelleragency.com
Tatiana S. Riegel	(212) 253-6900	www.innovativeartists.com
Josh Rifkin	(212) 545-7895	www.nyoffice.net
Stuart Robertson	(212) 633-0822	
Adam Robinson	(212) 568-8200	www.whitehousepost.com
Chris Robinson	(212) 633-0822	
Alex Rodriguez	(323) 460-4767	www.jacobandkoleagency.com
Julie Rogers	(310) 652-8778	www.lspagency.net
Steven Rosenblum	(310) 395-9550	www.skouras.com
Fabrizio Rossetti	(212) 253-2888	www.thefieldtv.com
Christopher Rouse	(212) 253-6900	www.innovativeartists.com
Michael Ruscio	(212) 253-6900	www.innovativeartists.com
Robert Ryang	(212) 447-0006	www.ps260.com
Michael Saia	(212) 228-7474	www.nycjump.com
Livio Sanchez	(212) 627-3100	www.filmcore.com
Ronald Sanders	(310) 822-9113	www.murthaagency.com
Oren Sarch	(212) 794-9030	
Pietro Scalia	(310) 395-9550	www.skouras.com
Glen Scantlebury	(310) 273-6700	www.utaproduction.com
William Scharf	(323) 460-4767	www.jacobandkoleagency.com
Hervé Schneid	(310) 273-6700	www.utaproduction.com
Joshua Schwarz	(212) 965-4632	
Judy Seaman	(201) 833-0425	
Sam Seig	(310) 652-8778	www.lspagency.net
Vivek Sharma	(718) 625-1627	www.mercimedia.com
Colleen Sharp	(310) 652-8778	www.lspagency.net
Jonathan Shaw	(323) 856-3000	www.thegelleragency.com
Colleen Shea	(212) 979-2722	www.mackcut.com
Terilyn Shropshire	(323) 460-4767	www.jacobandkoleagency.com
Mike Siedlecki	(212) 253-2888	www.thefieldtv.com

Silberman Productions (212) 794-9030 / (917) 880-6747 / FAX (212) 794-9232
330 E. 75th St., Ste. 33A
(Near Second Ave.)
New York, NY 10021
(Reps for Editors)

Steve Silkensen	(212) 545-7895	www.nyoffice.net
Cara Silverman	(212) 253-6900	www.innovativeartists.com
Holle Singer	(212) 219-0020	www.consulatefilm.com
Chad Sipkin	(212) 219-0020	www.consulatefilm.com
Beatrice Sisul	(323) 460-4767	www.jacobandkoleagency.com
Deirdre Slevin	(323) 845-4144	www.montanartists.com
Pete Slife	(212) 529-1991	www.madeinchinagraph.com
Conrad Smart	(323) 856-3000	www.thegelleragency.com
Byron Smith	(310) 395-9550	www.skouras.com
Howard E. Smith	(310) 273-6700	www.utaproduction.com
John Smith	(212) 568-8200	www.whitehousepost.com
Lee Smith	(212) 997-1818	www.gershagency.com
Frank Snider	(212) 255-6446	www.ohioedit.com
Greg Snider	(212) 568-8200	www.whitehousepost.com
Suzanne Spangler	(212) 545-7895	www.nyoffice.net
Lucas Spaulding	(212) 226-6001	www.spotwelders.com
Tim Squyres	(310) 273-6700	www.utaproduction.com
Zach Staenberg	(310) 395-9550	www.skouras.com
Pete Staman	(856) 222-5675	www.nflfilms.com
John Starace	(212) 986-1577	www.rhinoedit.tv
Lia Starace	(347) 528-2089	www.splicegirlpost.com

Jón Stefánsson	(212) 226-6001	www.spotwelders.com
William Steinkamp	(310) 652-8778	www.lspagency.net
Ben Stephens	(212) 568-8200	www.whitehousepost.com
Dustin Stephens	(212) 447-0006	www.ps260.com
Donna Stern	(212) 496-5363 / (917) 940-8973 / FAX (212) 496-5363	
Jason Stewart	(323) 856-3000	www.thegelleragency.com
Todd Stewart	(212) 219-0020	www.consulatefilm.com
Barry Stilwell	(212) 228-7474	www.nycjump.com
Andrew Stone	(718) 625-1627	www.mercimedia.com
Christina Stumpf	(212) 568-8200	www.whitehousepost.com
Robb Sullivan	(310) 395-9550	www.skouras.com
Dan Swietlik	(310) 652-8778	www.lspagency.net
Sikay Tang	(212) 633-0822	
Tapestry Creative Management 255 W. 148th St., Third Fl. New York, NY 10039 (Reps for Editors)	(212) 926-0477 / FAX (360) 926-0478	www.tapestryinc.com
Michael Taylor	(917) 743-9142 / (212) 897-6400 / FAX (212) 662-6983	www.paradigmagency.com
Nate Taylor	(212) 302-2828	www.crewcuts.com
TDN Artists 3685 Motor Ave., Ste. 220 Los Angeles, CA 90034 (Reps for Editors)	(818) 906-0006 / FAX (818) 301-2224	www.tdnartists.com
David Tedeschi	(212) 253-6900	www.innovativeartists.com
Kevin Tent	(323) 856-3000	www.thegelleragency.com
James Thomas	(310) 273-6700	www.utaproduction.com
Dylan Tichenor	(310) 273-6700	www.utaproduction.com
Jennifer Tiexiera	(212) 545-7895	www.nyoffice.net
Greg Tillman	(323) 856-3000	www.thegelleragency.com
Robert Tobin	(732) 768-5683	www.pushdesign.tv
Anisha Tomlinson	(212) 643-1736	www.cec-entertainment.com
Rob Tortoriello	(212) 867-1515	www.madhousenyc.com
Neil Travis	(310) 273-6700	www.utaproduction.com
Leo Trombetta	(310) 652-8778	www.lspagency.net
Ann Trulove	(212) 545-7895	www.nyoffice.net
Sean Tyroler	(212) 879-9800 / FAX (775) 540-4796	
Daniel Valverde	(212) 643-1736	www.cec-entertainment.com
Nikki Vapensky	(212) 568-8200	www.whitehousepost.com
Joe Vassallo	(201) 319-1023 / (646) 425-6828	
Tom Vogt	(212) 979-2722	www.mackcut.com
Doug Walker	(212) 627-3100	www.filmcore.com
Matt Walsh	(212) 568-8200	www.whitehousepost.com
Craig Warnick	(212) 867-1515	www.madhousenyc.com
Brad Waskewich	(212) 226-6001	www.spotwelders.com
Sam Welch	(212) 255-4440	www.homesteadedit.com
Steve Welch	(310) 395-9550	www.skouras.com
Juliette Welfling	(310) 652-8778	www.lspagency.net
Timothy Wellburn	(310) 652-8778	www.lspagency.net
Ben Whitten	(212) 867-1515	www.madhousenyc.com
Ian B. Wile	(212) 366-5011 / (646) 263-3296 / FAX (212) 989-5195	www.roguepost.com
Christophe Williams	(212) 568-8200	www.whitehousepost.com
Miky Wolf	(212) 683-4004	www.bigskyedit.com
Matthew Wood	(212) 568-8200	www.whitehousepost.com
Joan Wooters-Reisin	(212) 655-9268	www.rlf-nyc.com
Justine Wright	(310) 273-6700	www.unitedtalent.com
Miklos Wright	(310) 652-8778	www.lspagency.net
Toby Yates	(212) 253-6900	www.innovativeartists.com

William Yeh	(212) 253-6900 www.innovativeartists.com	Dean Zimmerman	(310) 273-6700 www.utaproduction.com
John Young	(212) 255-4440 www.homesteadedit.com	Kevin Zimmerman	(212) 568-8200 www.whitehousepost.com
Lora Zaretsky	(212) 794-9030	Francis Zuccarello	(212) 838-8883 www.justaddwater.tv
John Zieman	(212) 447-0006 www.ps260.com	Paul Zucker	(310) 652-8778 www.lspagency.net
Dan Zimmerman	(310) 273-6700 www.utaproduction.com		

Film & Tape Storage

Ascent Media Management East (201) 767-3800
235 Pegasus Ave.　　　　　　　FAX **(201) 767-4568**
Northvale, NJ 07647　　　　　**www.ascentmedia.com**

　　　　　　　　　　　　　　(201) 944-3700
Bonded Services　　　　　**(212) 956-2212**
504 Jane St.　　　　　　　　FAX **(201) 592-0727**
Fort Lee, NJ 07024　　　　　**www.bondedservices.com**

Iron Mountain Film &
Sound Archives　　　　　**(973) 812-4888**
235 Main St.　　　　　　　　FAX **(973) 812-4999**
Little Falls, NJ 07424　　　**www.ironmountain.com**

Iron Mountain Film &　　**(201) 807-1075**
Sound Archives　　　　　**(800) 899-4766**
207 Moonachie Rd.　　　　　FAX **(201) 814-0073**
Moonachie, NJ 07074　　　　**www.ironmountain.com**

　　　　　　　　　　　　　　(718) 392-4267
IWC Media Services, Inc.　**(212) 619-4447**
4401 21st St., Ste. 303　　　FAX **(718) 392-4187**
(Near 44th Ave.)　　　　　　**www.iwcmedia.com**
Long Island City, NY 11101

　　　　　　　　　　　　　　(720) 888-1000
Level 3 Communications　**(877) 253-8353**
1025 Eldorado Blvd.　　　　**www.level3.com**
Broomfield, CO 80021

Tylie Jones & Associates, Inc.　**(201) 770-1100**
801 Penhorn Ave. (Near E. 41st St.)　FAX **(201) 770-1147**
Secaucus, NJ 07094　　　　　**www.tylie.com**

Raise Your Expectations.

35mm / 16mm motion picture laboratory, HD telecine,
EFILM® digital intermediate center, 2K and 35mm screening rooms and more.

deluxe NEW YORK
435 Hudson Street 9th Floor
New York, NY 10014   212•444•5600

www.bydeluxe.com

© 2009 Deluxe Entertainment Services Group Inc. All Rights Reserved.

Film Laboratories—Motion Picture

Colorlab NYC (212) 633-8172
27 W. 20th St., Ste. 307   FAX **(212) 633-8241**
(Near Avenue of the Americas)   **www.colorlab.com**
New York, NY 10011
Contacts: Jed Ela & Nancy McLean

Deluxe New York **(212) 444-5600**
435 Hudson St., Ninth Fl.   **www.bydeluxe.com**
New York, NY 10014

Du Art Film and Video (212) 757-4580
245 W. 55th St. (Near Broadway)   FAX **(212) 333-7647**
New York, NY 10019   **www.duart.com**

Lab-Link, Inc./
Magno Sound & Video (212) 302-2505
FAX **(212) 819-1282**
www.magnosoundandvideo.com

(856) 222-5675
NFL Films (877) 222-3517
One NFL Plaza   FAX **(856) 866-4848**
Mount Laurel, NJ 08054   **www.nflfilms.com/studios**
(Color Processing)

Pac Lab (212) 505-7797
37 E. First St. (Near Second Ave.)   FAX **(212) 475-6211**
New York, NY 10003   **www.pac-lab.com**

(212) 661-2530
Postworks, The Lab (212) 894-4000
Processing, 227 E. 45th St., 17th Fl.   **www.pwny.com**
(Near Third Ave.)
New York, NY 10017
(Color Processing 16, 35, S16 and S35, Cross Processing,
HD and SD Dailies & Skip Bleach)

(212) 661-2530
Postworks, The Lab (212) 894-4000
Dailies Pickup   **www.postworks.com/theLab.asp**
100 Avenue of the Americas, 10th Fl.
(Near Grand St.)
New York, NY 10013
(Color Processing 16, 35, S16 and S35, Cross Processing,
HD and SD Dailies & Skip Bleach)

(212) 886-5200
Technicolor East Coast, Inc. (212) 609-9400
110 Leroy St. (Near Hudson St.)   FAX **(212) 609-9450**
New York, NY 10014   **www.technicolor.com**
(16mm and 35mm Color Processing, Answer Printing,
Intermediates, Print Dailies & Release Printing)

WRS Motion Picture &
Video Laboratory (412) 937-1200
213 Tech Rd.   FAX **(412) 922-1200**
Pittsburgh, PA 15205   **www.wrslabs.com**

THE WORLD OF

THE AUTHORITATIVE VOICE OF ENTERTAINMENT
BUSINESS NEWS AND INFORMATION

WWW.VARIETY.COM

Film Laboratories—Still Photography

Alkit Pro Camera   **(212) 674-1515**
                                (800) 285-1698
227 E. 45th St., Fifth Fl.   FAX **(212) 533-8044**
(Near E. 18th St.)   **www.alkit.com**
New York, NY 10017
(Black and White Processing, Color Processing, Digital Imaging, Mural Prints, One-Hour Color Processing, Quantity Duplication, Restoration & Retouching)

Baboo Color Labs, Inc.   **(212) 727-2727**
37 W. 20th St.   FAX **(212) 807-1937**
(Near Avenue of the Americas)
New York, NY 10011
(Black and White Processing, Color Processing, Digital Imaging, Mural Prints, One-Hour Black and White Processing, One-Hour Color Processing, Quantity Duplication Restoration & Retouching)

Color Edge   **(212) 633-6000**
20 W. 22nd St.   **www.coloredgecrc.com**
(Near Avenue of the Americas)
New York, NY 10010
(Black and White Processing, Color Processing, Digital Imaging, Mural Prints, One-Hour Color Processing, Quantity Duplication, Restoration & Retouching)

Duggal Color Projects, Inc.   **(212) 924-8100**
29 W. 23rd St. (Near Sixth Ave.)   FAX **(212) 242-6660**
New York, NY 10010   **www.duggal.com**
(Black and White Processing, Color Processing, Digital Imaging, Mural Prints, Quantity Duplication, Restoration & Retouching)

Duggal Underground   **(212) 941-7000**
29 W. 23rd St. (Near Fifth Ave.)   FAX **(212) 627-2293**
New York, NY 10010   **www.duggal.com**

Flatiron Color Lab   **(212) 633-9191**
108 W. 17th St. (Near Sixth Ave.)   FAX **(212) 633-9331**
New York, NY 10011   **www.flatironny.com**
(Color Processing, Digital Imaging, Mural Prints & Quantity Duplication)

Ken Horowitz
Photographic Services   **(212) 647-9939**
29 W. 15th St. (Near Fifth Ave.)   FAX **(212) 647-9941**
New York, NY 10011
(Color Processing, Digital Imaging, Mural Prints, Restoration & Retouching)

Powerstation   **(212) 924-8100**
29 W. 23rd St. (Near Broadway)   FAX **(212) 633-1266**
New York, NY 10010   **www.duggal.com**
(Black and White Processing, Color Processing, One-Hour Color Processing, Quantity Duplication & Transparencies)

Spectra Photo/Digital   **(212) 989-0626**
77 Christopher St. (Near Seventh Ave.)   FAX **(212) 366-4841**
New York, NY 10014
(Black and White Processing, Color Processing, Digital Imaging, Mural Prints, Quantity Duplication, Restoration, Retouching & Transparencies)

Taranto Labs   **(212) 691-6070**
                               www.tarantolabs.com
(Black and White Processing, Color Processing, Digital Imaging, Mural Prints, Quantity Duplication, Restoration & Retouching)

U.S. Color   **(212) 254-7200**
12 Mercer St. (Near Lafayette)   FAX **(212) 254-4073**
New York, NY 10013
(Black and White Processing, Color Processing, Digital Imaging, Mural Prints, One-Hour Color Processing, Restoration & Retouching)

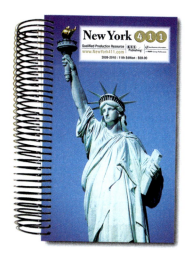
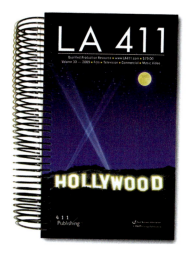

IN PRINT
411
AND ONLINE

LA411.com
NewYork411.com

Mobile Video Units, Satellite & Transmission Services

Ⓐ All Mobile Video   (212) 727-1234
221 W. 26th St. (Near Seventh Ave.)   FAX (212) 255-6644
New York, NY 10001   www.allmobilevideo.com

    (860) 589-2776
Anderson Productions   (800) 701-4311
34 Dell Manor Dr.   FAX (860) 584-5936
Bristol, CT 06010

Associated Press Television News   (212) 621-7410
450 W. 33rd St., 14th Fl.   FAX (212) 621-7419
(Near La Guardia Pl.)   www.aptn.com
New York, NY 10001

Beth Melsky Satellite Casting   (212) 505-5000
928 Broadway, Ste. 401 (Near W. 21st St.)
New York, NY 10010
(Transmission Services)

    (212) 967-6427
C&C Studios   (917) 295-6920
20 W. 37th St., Fifth Fl.   FAX (718) 504-5487
New York, NY 10018   www.candcstudios.tv

Creative Bubble, LLC   (212) 201-4200
79 Fifth Ave., 14th Fl. (Near 15th St.)   FAX (212) 201-4210
New York, NY 10003   www.creativebubble.com

DG Systems, Inc.   (212) 953-9300
600 Third Ave. (Near E. 39th St.)   FAX (212) 972-8250
New York, NY 10016   www.dgsystems.com

    (201) 445-1711
DWJ Television   (800) 766-1711
One Robinson Ln.   FAX (201) 445-8352
Ridgewood, NJ 07450   www.dwjtv.com

Envision Studios   (800) 505-0420
928 Broadway, Ste. 401   FAX (646) 415-8899
(Near W. 21st St.)
New York, NY 10010
(Transmission Services)

    (845) 426-5320
The Flight 9 Group   (888) 354-4489
212 Airport Executive Park   www.flight9.com
(Near New Clarkstown Rd.)
Nanuet, NY 10954

HBO Studio Productions   (212) 512-7800
120A E. 23rd St. (Near Park Ave.)   FAX (212) 512-7788
New York, NY 10010

Locationview   (323) 908-3388
1119 N Hudson Ave.   FAX (323) 908-3389
Hollywood, CA 90069   www.locationview.com

    (212) 594-0086
LVR/Liman Video Rental Company   (800) 251-4625
341 W. 38th St., Ground Fl.   FAX (212) 594-0786
(Near Eighth Ave.)   www.lvrusa.com
New York, NY 10018

Metrovision Production Group   (212) 989-1515
508 W. 24th St. (Near 10th Ave.)   FAX (212) 989-8278
New York, NY 10011   www.metrovision.tv

NEP Supershooters, LP   (800) 444-0054
    www.nepinc.com

New York Network   (518) 443-5333
Empire State Plaza   FAX (518) 426-4198
South Concourse, Ste. 146   www.nyn.suny.edu
P.O. Box 2058 (Near State St.)
Albany, NY 12220
(Domestic Satellite Uplink)

    (212) 840-7700
New York Videoconference Center   (888) 666-1776
39 W. 37th St., Sixth Fl.   FAX (877) 329-3465
(Near Fifth Ave.)   www.nyvideoconference.com
New York, NY 10018

    (718) 472-2944
Omni Video Services, Ltd.   (917) 562-3132
11-23 50th Ave. (Near Jackson Ave.)
Long Island City, NY 11101

    (212) 702-0700
Stratosphere Multimedia   (888) 212-0700
551 Madison Ave., Seventh Fl.   FAX (212) 702-8871
(Near E. 55th St.)   www.stratosphere-nyc.com
New York, NY 10022

    (610) 995-9750
Total Production Services   (888) 877-1178
    FAX (610) 995-9751
    www.tpsweb.com

    (631) 752-9311
Village Video Productions   (631) 753-2500
107 Alder St.   FAX (631) 845-7167
West Babylon, NY 11704   www.vvn.com

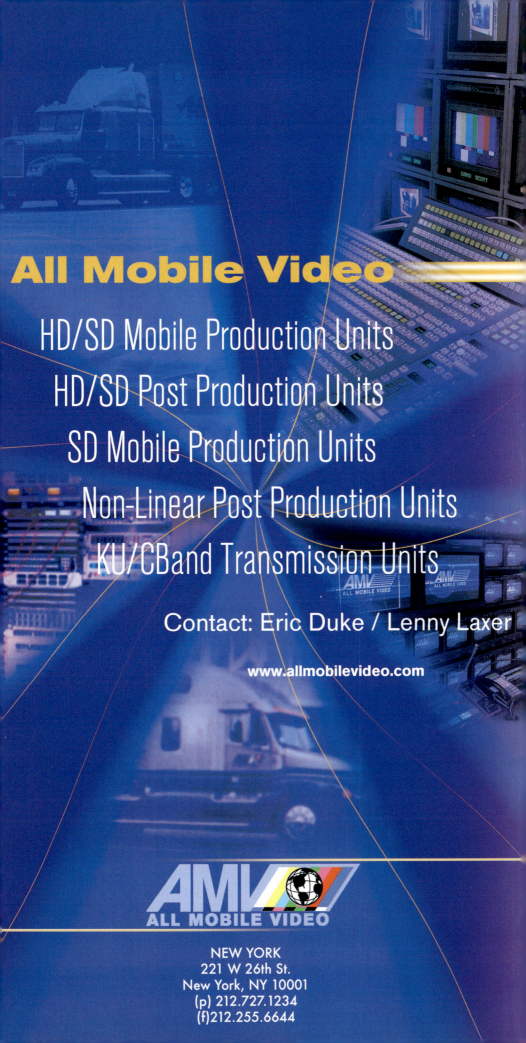

Music Libraries & Publishing

(718)music   **(718) 625-0885**
8225 Fifth Ave., Ste. 436   FAX **(718) 625-0886**
Brooklyn, NY 11209   www.718music.com
(Acoustic, Backgrounds, Contemporary, Ethnic, Music, Music Library, Licensing, Tribal & Vintage)

Amusicom   **(818) 883-8376**
22817 Ventura Blvd., Ste. 319   FAX **(818) 883-4535**
Woodland Hills, CA 91364   www.amusicom.com

Bug Music Publishing   **(323) 466-4352**
7750 Sunset Blvd.   FAX **(323) 969-0968**
Los Angeles, CA 90046   www.bugmusic.com

Cherry Lane Music Publishing   **(212) 561-3000**
Six E. 32nd St., 11th Fl.   FAX **(212) 683-2040**
(Near Fifth Ave.)   www.cherrylane.com
New York, NY 10016

Christmas and Holiday Music   **(949) 859-1615**
26642 Via Noveno   www.christmassongs.com
Mission Viejo, CA 92691
(Holiday Music)

Cinetrax   **(323) 874-9590**
8033 Sunset Blvd., Ste. 400   www.cinetrax.com
Los Angeles, CA 90046

CSS Music/Dawn Music   **(800) 468-6874**
1948 Riverside Dr.   www.cssmusic.com
Los Angeles, CA 90039
(Music & Sound FX)

EMI Music Publishing - Film Soundtrack Division   **(310) 586-2740**
2700 Colorado Ave., Ste. 100   FAX **(310) 586-2795**
Santa Monica, CA 90404   www.emimusicpub.com

Evolution Music Partners, LLC   **(323) 790-0525**
1680 N. Vine St., Ste. 500   FAX **(323) 790-0520**
Hollywood, CA 90028   www.evolutionmusicpartners.com

Extreme Production Music   **(212) 833-4900**
550 Madison Ave., Fifth Fl.   FAX **(212) 833-4977**
(Near E. 17th)   www.extrememusic.com
New York, NY 10022

FirstCom Music   **(310) 358-4915** / **(800) 858-8880**
8750 Wilshire Blvd., Second Fl.   FAX **(310) 385-4314**
Beverly Hills, CA 90211   www.firstcom.com

Gefen, Inc.   **(818) 772-9100** / **(800) 545-6900**
20600 Nordhoff St.   www.gefen.com
Chatsworth, CA 91311
(Background & Sound FX)

Groove Addicts Production Music Catalog   **(310) 572-4646** / **(800) 400-6767**
12211 W. Washington Blvd.   FAX **(310) 572-4647**
Los Angeles, CA 90066   www.grooveaddicts.com
(Acoustic & Contemporary)

Hells Kitchen Music   **(212) 397-9500**
630 Ninth Ave., Ste. 1007   FAX **(212) 581-4814**
(Near W. 44th St.)   www.hellskitchenmusic.com
New York, NY 10036

The Hollywood Edge   **(323) 603-3252** / **(800) 292-3755**
7080 Hollywood Blvd., Ste. 519   FAX **(323) 603-3298**
Los Angeles, CA 90028   www.hollywoodedge.com

Hum   **(310) 260-4949**
1547 Ninth St.   FAX **(310) 260-4944**
Santa Monica, CA 90401   www.humit.com

Jane Peterer Music Corporation   **(802) 860-7110**
29 Church St., Ste. 3   FAX **(802) 860-7112**
Burlington, VT 05401   www.jpmc.com

JRT Music   **(888) 578-6874** / **(718) 499-4635**
143 28th St. (Near Fourth Ave.)   FAX **(718) 499-0470**
Brooklyn, NY 11232   www.jrtmusic.com
(Acoustic, Backgrounds, Contemporary, Licensing, Music Library & Vintage)

Killer Tracks   **(323) 957-4455** / **(800) 454-5537**
8750 Wilshire Blvd., Ste. 220   FAX **(800) 787-2257**
Beverly Hills, CA 90211   www.killertracks.com
(Contemporary)

Leiber & Stoller Music Publishing   **(310) 273-6401**
9000 Sunset Blvd., Ste. 1107   FAX **(310) 273-1591**
Los Angeles, CA 90069
(1950s, 1960s & Vintage)

Like Dat Music   **(858) 254-6779**
P.O. Box 9476   FAX **(858) 225-0864**
Rancho Santa Fe, CA 92007   www.tjknowles.com

Los Angeles Post Music, Inc.   **(818) 501-8329**
15030 Ventura Blvd., Ste. 22-473   FAX **(818) 990-7661**
Sherman Oaks, CA 91403   www.lapostmusic.com

Manhattan Production Music   **(212) 333-5766** / **(800) 227-1954**
355 W. 52nd St., Sixth Fl.   FAX **(212) 262-0814**
(Near Ninth Ave.)   www.mpmmusic.com
New York, NY 10019

Megatrax Production Music   **(818) 255-7100** / **(888) 634-2555**
7629 Fulton Ave.   FAX **(818) 255-7199**
North Hollywood, CA 91605   www.megatrax.com

MGM Music   **(310) 449-3000**
10250 Constellation Blvd.
Los Angeles, CA 90067

The Music Bakery   **(972) 578-7863** / **(800) 229-0313**
7522 Campbell Rd., Ste. 113   FAX **(972) 424-3680**
(Near Coit)   www.musicbakery.com
Dallas, TX 75248
(Acoustic, Backgrounds, Contemporary, Ethnic, Holiday Music, Music Library & Sound FX)

Non-Stop Music Library   **(212) 242-1155**
134 W. 29th St., Ste. 906   FAX **(212) 290-7612**
(Near Avenue of the Americas)   www.nonstopmusic.com
New York, NY 10001

OGM Music, a Division of OGM, Inc.   **(323) 461-2701** / **(800) 421-4163**
6464 Sunset Blvd, Ste. 790   FAX **(323) 461-1543**
Hollywood, CA 90028   www.ogmmusic.com

Omnimusic   **(516) 883-0121** / **(800) 828-6664**
52 Main St.   FAX **(516) 883-0271**
Port Washington, NY 11050   www.omnimusic.com
(Music Library & Sound FX)

Opus 1 Music Library, LLC   **(818) 508-2040** / **(888) 757-6787**
12711 Ventura Blvd., Ste. 170   FAX **(818) 508-2044**
Studio City, CA 91604   www.opus1musiclibrary.com

Patco Resources, Inc.   **(845) 357-5300**
Nine Washington Circle   FAX **(845) 357-6427**
(Near Washington Ave.)   www.patcoresources.com
Suffern, NY 10901

Premier Tracks (760) 416-0805
1775 E. Palm Canyon Dr., Ste. H239 (866) 777-0805
Palm Springs, CA 92264   FAX **(760) 416-1855**
www.premiertracks.com

ScreenMusic International **(818) 789-2954**
18034 Ventura Blvd., Ste. 450   FAX **(818) 789-5801**
Encino, CA 91316   www.screenmusic.com
(Music Clearance, Library and Licensing)

Serafine Studios **(310) 399-9279**
P.O. Box 1798   www.frankserafine.com
Simi Valley, CA 93065

(212) 989-0011
Signature Sound, Inc. **(800) 345-6757**
71 W. 23rd St., Ste. 902   FAX **(212) 989-3576**
(Near Fifth Ave.)   www.signature-sound.com
New York, NY 10010

Sonic Safari Music **(818) 247-6219**
663 W. California Ave.   FAX **(818) 241-1333**
Glendale, CA 91203   www.sonicsafarimusic.com
(Ethnic & Tribal)

Sony BMG Custom Marketing Group **(212) 833-8000**
550 Madison Ave. (Near E. 55th St.)   FAX **(212) 833-7021**
New York, NY 10022   www.sonybmgcmg.com

Soundtrack **(212) 420-6010**
936 Broadway, Fourth Fl.   FAX **(212) 777-6403**
(Near W. 21st St.)   www.soundtrackny.com
New York, NY 10010

Soundtrack Marketing **(323) 274-3800**
1641 Riverside Dr.   FAX **(818) 500-7390**
Glendale, CA 91201   www.soundtrackmarketing.com

Southern Library of Recorded Music (760) 202-2327
39 Via San Marco   FAX **(760) 202-2327**
Rancho Mirage, CA 92270

Summerfield Music, Inc./
Trailer Trash Music Library **(818) 905-0400**
FAX **(818) 905-0488**
www.summerfieldmusic.com

Ten Music **(310) 305-3800**
312 Venice Way   FAX **(310) 305-3811**
Venice, CA 90291   www.tenmusic.tv

(201) 335 0005
TRF Production Music Libraries **(800) 899-6874**
One International Blvd, Ste. 212   FAX **(201) 335 0004**
(Near Sutin Pl.)   www.trfmusic.com
Mahwah, NJ 07495

Uncommon Trax **(312) 266-3611**
610 N. Fairbanks Court, Third Fl.   FAX **(312) 640-2860**
Chicago, IL 60611   www.uncommontrax.com
(Contemporary)

Universal Music Publishing Library/
UMPL **(310) 235-4860**
2440 Sepulveda Blvd., Ste. 100   FAX **(310) 235-4900**
West Los Angeles, CA 90064

(212) 633-7009
VideoHelper, Inc. **(877) 843-3643**
18 W. 21st St., Seventh Fl.   FAX **(866) 687-4539**
(Near Fifth Ave.)   www.videohelper.com
New York, NY 10010

Music Production & Sound Design

300 Monks (888) 211-5945
FAX (718) 228-3569
www.300monks.com

Bang Music (212) 242-2264
16 W. 18th St., Second Fl. FAX (212) 242-2430
(Near Fifth Ave.) www.bangworld.com
New York, NY 10011
Executive Producer: Lyle Greenfield
Senior Producers: Brian Jones & Sara Russo

Beatstreet Productions (212) 777-8440
928 Broadway, Ste. 601 FAX (212) 477-1375
(Near E. 21st St.) www.beatstreetnyc.com
New York, NY 10010
Composers: Joe Franco & Cheryl Smith

Big Wave Music (212) 877-9660
Executive Producer: Diane Snyder www.bigwavemusic.com

Big Yellow Duck (212) 997-1200
62 W. 45th St., 12th Fl. FAX (212) 997-1293
New York, NY 10036 www.bigyellowduck.com
Contacts: Ralph Miccio & Matt Pedone

**Bilous DiBucci Music/
Helium Vault Music Library** (212) 447-9530
FAX (212) 242-7110
www.heliumvault.com
Producers/Composers: Edward Bilous, Michelle DiBucci & Greg Kalember

Black Market Music (914) 232-5448
89 Ridge Rd. FAX (636) 720-5571
Katonah, NY 10536 www.blackmarketproductions.org
Composer: Marc Black

Broadway Sound (212) 333-0700
1619 Broadway, Fourth Fl. FAX (212) 333-0775
(Near W. 49th St.) www.broadwayvideo.com
New York, NY 10019
Composer/Sound Designers: John Crenshaw, Ralph Kelsey & Mike Ungar

Chemical Music (212) 226-7376
(917) 514-6545
www.chemicalmusic.com

Compositions (212) 677-8300
(310) 968-3685
31 Greene St., First Fl. FAX (212) 431-8778
(Near Grand St.) www.compositions-inc.com
New York, NY 10013
Composer: Steven Gold
Sound Designer: David Gervai

Creative Bubble Sound (212) 201-4201
(212) 201-4200
79 Fifth Ave., 14th Fl. (Near 15th St.) FAX (212) 201-4210
New York, NY 10003 www.creativebubble.com

Crushing Music (212) 352-8833
19 Union Square West, Eighth Fl. FAX (212) 352-8855
(Near Fifth Ave.) www.crushingmusic.com
New York, NY 10003
President/Composer: Joey Levine
Composers: Robin Batteau, Alfred Hochstrasser, Clifford Lane, Gary Schreiner, Don Sebesky, Jeff Southworth, Kenny White & Mary Wood
Composer/Contact: Taylor McLam

David Forman Music (518) 537-6542
P.O. Box 473
Germantown, NY 12526
Composer: David Forman

Ⓐ Digital Arts (212) 460-9600
130 W. 29th St., Eighth Fl. FAX (212) 660-3600
(Near Sixth Ave.) www.digital-arts.net
New York, NY 10001

Fluid (212) 431-4342
532 Broadway, Fifth Fl. FAX (212) 431-6525
(Near Spring St.) www.fluidny.com
New York, NY 10012
Managing Director: Marc Schwartz
Executive Producer: David Shapiro
Composer: Andrew Sherman

Fred Weinberg Music and Sounds (212) 265-2536
(561) 988-6196
161 W. 54th St., Ste. 1404 FAX (212) 265-2536
(Near Seventh Ave.) www.fredweinbergproductions.com
New York, NY 10019
President: Fred Weinberg
Sales Executive/Studio Manager: Julie Blankman

G & E Music (212) 673-9274
36 E. 23rd St., Ste. 7R FAX (212) 673-9140
(Near Park Ave.) www.gemusic.com
New York, NY 10010
Composers/Creative Partners: Erik Blicker & Glenn Schloss

Headroom (212) 246-8400
11 E. 26th St., 19th Fl. FAX (212) 245-0370
(Near Fifth Ave.) www.headroomdigi.com
New York, NY 10010
Producer/Composer: Jerry Plotkin
Mix Engineers/Composers/Sound Designers: Evan Spear, Scott McIntosh & John Wilcox
Studio Manager/Producer: Samantha Mazza
Production Assistant: James Meidenbauer
Client Services: Claudia Gaspar

Hells Kitchen Music (212) 397-9500
630 Ninth Ave., Ste. 1007 FAX (212) 581-4814
(Near W. 44th St.) www.hellskitchenmusic.com
New York, NY 10036

Hi-Top Productions (203) 967-2200
(212) 242-5686
One Bank St., Ste. LL2 FAX (203) 325-3308
Stamford, CT 06901 www.hi-top.com
Producer/Composer: Steve Hansen

HSR/NY (212) 687-4180
The Graybar Bldg. FAX (212) 697-0536
420 Lexington Ave., Ste. 1934 www.hsrny.com
(Near E. 42nd St.)
New York, NY 10170
Contacts: Sharon DiTullio & Sara Paterno

J.M. Salaun, Inc. (212) 431-3004
159 Mercer St. (Near Prince St.) FAX (212) 431-3026
New York, NY 10012
Composers: Robert Arron, Lewis Flinn & Gordon Minette
Composer/Sound Designer: Jean-Marie Salaun

JECO (212) 768-8501
62 W. 45th St., Tenth Fl. FAX (212) 768-8505
(Near Fifth Ave.) www.jecomusic.com
New York, NY 10036
Composer: Jon Ehrlich
Producer: Gus Reyes
Composer/Sound Designer: Leigh Roberts

Jim Farmer Music (212) 349-6619
(917) 742-9680
Composer: Jim Farmer

Jkobie Music (302) 529-0840
Owner/Composer: Jawanza Kobie FAX (302) 529-0840

John Bauers Music Productions (201) 795-3907
102 Sherman Pl. FAX (201) 795-1371
Jersey City, NJ 07307
Owner/Composer: John Bauers
Business Manager: Cathy McElroy
Creative Director: Tim Dobel
Production Manager: Donna Harris

Jonathan Helfand Music & Post (212) 647-9500
44 E. 32nd St., 10th Fl. FAX (212) 531-6445
(Near Park Ave. South) www.jhmp.com
New York, NY 10016
President/Composer: Jonathan Helfand
Engineer: Elizabeth Collins

JSM Music (212) 627-2200
59 W. 19th St. (Near Sixth Ave.) FAX (212) 645-0484
New York, NY 10011 www.jsmmusic.com
President/Owner: Joel Simon
Executive Producers: Joel Simon, Cynthia Stahl & Victoria Villalobos

Kamen Entertainment Group (212) 575-4660
(800) 237-2448
701 Seventh Ave., Sixth Fl. FAX (212) 575-4799
(Near W. 47th St.) www.kamen.com
New York, NY 10036
President: Roy Kamen

Kondor Music (818) 907-8611
Owner/Composer: Robbie Kondor FAX (818) 990-1584
www.kondormusic.com

Lewis Flinn Music (212) 254-7500
32 Union Square East, Ste. 516 www.lewisflinn.com
(Near Union Square)
New York, NY 10003
Creative Director: Lewis Flinn

MacKenzie Cutler (212) 979-2722
907 Broadway (Near W. 20th St.) FAX (212) 979-6909
New York, NY 10010 www.mackcut.com
Sound Designer: Marc Healy

Manhattan Center Studios (212) 695-6600
311 W. 34th St. (Near Eighth Ave.) FAX (212) 564-1092
New York, NY 10001 www.mcstudios.com

Manic (212) 844-2233
625 Broadway, Second Fl. FAX (212) 844-0550
(Near Bleecker St.) www.nycmanic.com
New York, NY 10012
Executive Producer: Brent Holt

Manic Moose Music (212) 465-8540
(800) 844-8644
13 W. 36th St., Eighth Fl. FAX (212) 465-8542
(Near Fifth Ave.) www.manicmoosemusic.com
New York, NY 10018
Composer: Joe Carroll

Mess Hall (917) 282-4416
P.O. Box 43115 www.messhall.com
Upper Montclair, NJ 07042
Executive Producer: Andy Messenger

Michael Levine Music, Inc. (212) 268-6560
(818) 222-2656
www.michaellevinemusic.com
Composer: Michael A. Levine

Mixopolis, Inc. (212) 980-5009
Five E. 47th St., Seventh Fl. FAX (212) 223-4524
(Near Fifth Ave.) www.mixopolis.com
New York, NY 10017

Mother West (212) 807-0405
37 W. 20th St., Ste. 1006 FAX (917) 210-2962
(Near Fifth Ave.) www.motherwest.com
New York, NY 10011
Producers: Paolo DeGregorio, Vincent Giangola, Charles Newman & Tom Rogers

Nevessa Production, Inc. (845) 679-8848
(888) 484-8848
One Artist Rd. (Near Route 212) FAX (845) 679-1208
Saugerties, NY 12477 www.nevessa.com
President/Chief Engineer: Chris Andersen
Staff Engineer: Frank Moscowitz
Composer: Gary Burke

Nutmeg Recording (212) 921-8005
45 W. 45th St., Sixth Fl. FAX (212) 921-7728
(Near Fifth Ave.) www.nutmegaudiopost.com
New York, NY 10036
President: Tony Spaneo
Operations Director: Jon Adelman
Studio Manager: Karen Johnson

Nylon Studios Inc. (646) 233-4423
39 Wooster St., Second Fl. FAX (646) 205-5220
New York, NY 10013 www.nylonstudios.com

Photomag Sound & Image (212) 500-2700
222 E. 44th St., 11th Fl. FAX (212) 682-5869
(Near Third Ave.) www.postworks.com
New York, NY 10017

Pirate New York (212) 253-2920
30 Irving Pl., Sixth Fl. www.piratenewyork.com
(Near 15th St.)
New York, NY 10003

Pomann Sound, Inc. (212) 869-4161
Two W. 46th St., PH FAX (212) 869-4541
New York, NY 10036 www.pomannsound.com
Sound Designers: Bob Pomann

Pulse Music, Inc. (212) 358-7900
817 Broadway, 11th Fl. FAX (212) 358-8686
New York, NY 10003 www.pulsemusicny.com

Rep Studio (607) 272-4292
110 N. Cayuga St. (Near W. State St.) FAX (607) 272-4293
Ithaca, NY 14850 www.repstudio.com
Head Engineer/Producer: Nate Richardson

RGT Music Productions (917) 805-8563
34-12 36th St., Ste. 1-127 FAX (718) 349-4876
(Near 20th Ave.) www.rgtmusic.com
Astoria, NY 11106
Partner/Composer: Glen Tarachow

Rick Ulfik Productions (212) 867-0846
211 E. 43rd St., Ste. 710 (Near Third Ave.)
New York, NY 10017
President/Composer: Rick Ulfik

Rod McBrien Productions (212) 595-2211
317 W. 83rd St. (Near West End Ave.) FAX (212) 721-4343
New York, NY 10024 www.rodmcbrien.com

Roland Music USA (716) 655-4903
3581 Bullis Rd. (Near Stolle Rd.)
Elma, NY 14059
President: Julianne Roland
Composer: J. Daniel Roland

Rooftop Productions (212) 427-5014
www.rooftopproductions.com
Co-Owner/Composers: Martin Goodman & Joe Albano

Royal Flush Productions (646) 456-4727
419 Grand Ave., Ste. 4 www.royalflush-productions.com
Brooklyn, NY 11238

Russo/Grantham Productions, Inc. (212) 633-1175
37 W. 20th St., Ste. 1101 FAX (212) 633-8697
(Near Sixth Ave.) www.russograntham.com
New York, NY 10011
Producer/Composer: Marshall Grantham
Composers: Shari Feder, Peter Francovilla, Werner Fritzsching, Ben Goldberg, Shane Kiester & Steve Shapiro
Composer/Sound Designer: Chris McLaughlin
Executive Producer: John Russo

Scuba/Look (212) 629-7400
19 W. 21st St., Ste. 1104 FAX (212) 629-3964
(Near Fifth Ave.) www.scubalook.com
New York, NY 10018
President: Jeanne Look
Composers: Marc Blatte, Andy Mendelson & Jean-Marie Salaun
Composer/Sound Designers: Robb Hart & Brad Worrell
Production Manager: Tom Gambale

Music Production & Sound Design

Soundguild, LLC (212) 625-2015
598 Broadway, 10th Fl. www.soundguild.com
(Near W. Houston St.)
New York, NY 10012
President: Marco Vitali
Producers/Composers: Gary Foote & Steve Jennings
Composer: Regan Ryzuk

SoundImage NY (212) 986-6445
16 W. 46th St., Eighth Fl. FAX (212) 764-0440
(Near Fifth Ave.) www.soundimageny.com
New York, NY 10036
Composer: Mark Barasch

(646) 230-7071
Soundmine (917) 215-7109
425 W. 13th St., Ste. 601 FAX (212) 656-1081
(Near Washington St.) www.soundminenyc.com
New York, NY 10014

SoundSpace (212) 463-0138
252 Seventh Ave., Ste. 4D www.soundspacestudio.com
(Near W. 24th St.)
New York, NY 10001
Sound Designer: Matthew Polis

Soundtrack (212) 420-6010
936 Broadway, Fourth Fl. FAX (212) 777-6403
(Near W. 21st St.) www.soundtrackny.com
New York, NY 10010
Executive Producer: Maegan Hayward

Steve Raskin Music (212) 229-1966
231 W. 25th St., Ste. 1A www.steveraskin.com
(Near Seventh Ave.)
New York, NY 10001
Composer: Steve Raskin

(212) 203-2325
Strongboy Studios (646) 410-2097
512 W. 151st St., Ste. 2A FAX (646) 410-2097
(Near Amsterdam Ave.) www.strongboystudios.com
New York, NY 10031
Producer/Sound Designer: Chad Herndon
Producer/Musician: Nathan Hershberger

(212) 986-1929
Studio Center NY (866) 515-2111
315 Madison Ave., 11th Fl. FAX (212) 490-9737
(Near Madison Ave.) www.studiocenter.com
New York, NY 10017
VP: Robin Russ

Studio K Music Productions (212) 229-1642
150 W. 28th St., Ste. 902E www.parkswingorc.com
(Near Seventh Ave.)
New York, NY 10001
Composer/Sound Designer: William Kinslow

Studio Premik (718) 523-4380
148-42 86th Ave. (Near 148th St.) FAX (718) 558-5774
Jamaica, NY 11435 www.premik.com
Composers: Shashanka Menard & Premik Tubbs
Engineer/Sound Designer: Edgar Mills

Summerfield Music, Inc./
Trailer Trash Music Library (818) 905-0400
FAX (818) 905-0488
www.summerfieldmusic.com

Taylor-Made Productions (973) 226-1461
P.O. Box 309 FAX (973) 226-1462
Caldwell, NJ 07006 www.taylormadeprod.com
Composer/Sound Designer: Glenn M. Taylor

Tonal, Inc. (212) 255-4369
526 W. 26th St., Ste. 417 FAX (212) 255-4729
New York, NY 10001 www.tonalsound.com

Ultrabland (646) 638-2830
27 W. 24th St., Ste. 302 FAX (646) 638-2835
New York, NY 10010 www.ultrabland.com

Unicorn Productions (845) 679-3391
31 Maurizi Ln. www.petereinhorn.com
(Near Forestwood Dr.)
Woodstock, NY 12498
President/Composer: Peter Einhorn

WAX Music & Sound Design (212) 989-9292
18 W. 21st St., 10th Fl. FAX (212) 989-5195
(Near Fifth Ave.) www.waxnyc.com
New York, NY 10010
President: Gary Sutcliffe
Head of Production/Chief Engineer: Chris Arbisi
Business Manager: Callie Janoff
Composer/Sound Designer: James Wolcott
Sales Representative: Rob Reynolds
Director of Sales & Marketing: Julia Fredahl

Opticals

Chromavision (212) 686-7366
49 W. 27th St., Eighth Fl. FAX (212) 686-7310
(Near Sixth Ave.) www.chromavision.net
New York, NY 10001

Du Art Film and Video (212) 757-4580
245 W. 55th St. (Near Broadway) FAX (212) 333-7647
New York, NY 10019 www.duart.com

HeavyLight (212) 645-8216
115 W. 27th St., 12th Fl. FAX (212) 367-8861
(Near Sixth Ave.) www.heavylightdigital.com
New York, NY 10001

Interface Arts (718) 788-0335
241 16th St., Ste. 2 www.interface_arts.com
(Near Sixth Ave.)
Brooklyn, NY 11215

Rhinofx (212) 986-1584
50 E. 42nd St., 12th Fl. FAX (212) 986-2113
(Near Madison Ave.) www.rhinofx.com
New York, NY 10017

Post Houses

903Films (212) 674-0986
515 Greenwich St., Ste. 202 FAX (212) 380-1258
New York, NY 10013 www.903films.com
(All Formats, Authoring, Avid Systems, Color Correction, Compositing, Computer Animation, Computer Graphics, Digital, Digital Colorization, Digital Editing Systems, Digital Intermediate Services, Digital Online, Duplication, DVD Design, DVD Menus, Editing, Film Editing, Final Cut Pro Systems, Finishing, Graphic Design, Graphics, HD Editing, HD Finishing, HD Online, High Def, Mastering, Motion Graphics, New Media Encoding, Non-Linear Offline and Online, Non-Linear Editing, Offline, Online, Post Supervision, Pre-Visualization, Recording, Scanning, Subtitles & Video to Still Transfers)

The Anx (212) 894-4000
100 Avenue of the Americas FAX (212) 941-0439
(Near Grand St.)
New York, NY 10013

Ascent Media Management East (201) 767-3800
235 Pegasus Ave. FAX (201) 784-2769
Northvale, NJ 07647 www.ascentmedia.com
(Color Correction, Compositing, Down/Upconversions, Film to HD/Telecine, Linear and Non-Linear Online & Titling/Character Design)

Atomic Image (212) 255-6625
311 Broadway, PH B FAX (212) 627-8632
(Near Cornelia St.) www.atomicimage.com
New York, NY 10007
(Avid and Final Cut Pro Systems, Compositing, Computer/Motion Graphics, Digital Editing Systems, Digital Online, DVD, DVD Menus and Design, Editing, Graphic Design, HD Editing, Non-Linear Offline and Online & Post Supervision)

Beyond Our Reality (212) 255-5432
Productions, Inc. (800) 583-5015
49 W. 24th St., Seventh Fl. FAX (212) 255-6866
(Near Broadway) www.beyondourreality.com
New York, NY 10010
(Color Correction, Non-Linear Offline and Online & Tape to Tape Color Correction)

The Big House Production Group (914) 944-4011
23 Spring St., Ste. 201 FAX (914) 944-8044
(Near Maple Pl.) www.bighousetv.com
Ossining, NY 10562

Bionic (212) 997-9100
1375 Broadway, Seventh Fl. FAX (212) 997-0990
New York, NY 10018 www.bionic.tv
(Avid Systems, Editing, HD Online & Non-Linear Offline and Online)

Black Watch Editorial (212) 349-0369
49 Murray St., Ste. 1 FAX (212) 349-1335
(Near Church St.) www.blackwatchproductions.com
New York, NY 10007
(Non-Linear Offline and Online)

Broadway Video (212) 265-7600
1619 Broadway (Near W. 49th St.) FAX (212) 713-1535
New York, NY 10019 www.broadwayvideo.com
(Digital Component Online, Digital Compositing, Linear Online & Non-Linear Offline and Online)

Buzz, Inc. (212) 302-2899
28 W. 44th St., 22nd Fl. FAX (212) 302-9844
New York, NY 10036 www.buzzny.com
(Color Correction, Compositing, Digital Online, Duplication, DVD Design, DVD Menus, Finishing, Graphics, HD Editing, HD Finishing, HD Online, Mastering, Motion Graphics, Negative Cutting, New Media Encoding & Non-Linear Offline and Online)

Chelsea Post (212) 727-1234
221 W. 26th St. (Near Eighth Ave.) FAX (212) 255-6644
New York, NY 10001 www.amvchelsea.com
(Computer Graphics & Linear/Non-Linear Offline and Online)

Chomet Editing (212) 696-2770
23 E. 31st St., PH North FAX (212) 696-2769
New York, NY 10016 www.chomet.com

NEXT MILLENNIUM PRODUCTIONS

POST PRODUCTION SUITES

- Avid Nitris HD
- Avid Symphony
- Avid Adrenaline HD
- Pro Tools HD w/ VO Room

31 howard st, 5a
nyc 10013

Additional Services
- Shooting Studio
- HD/SD Production
- Control Room
- Live Uplink
- Greenroom
- Crew

-Pet Friendly-

www.nmpfilms.com
917.237.1661

CitiCam Video Services, Inc.	**(212) 315-4855**
	(212) 315-2000
515 W. 57th St. (Near 10th Ave.)	FAX **(212) 586-1572**
New York, NY 10019	**www.citicam.net**

City Lights Media Group	**(212) 679-4400**
Six E. 39th St., 11th Fl.	FAX **(212) 679-3819**
(Near Fifth Ave.)	**www.citylightsmedia.com**
New York, NY 10016	
(Color Correction, Computer Graphics, HD & Non-Linear Offline and Online)	
Contact: Aaron Behr	

Colorlab NYC	**(212) 633-8172**
27 W. 20th St., Ste. 307	FAX **(212) 633-8241**
(Near Avenue of the Americas)	**www.colorlab.com**
New York, NY 10011	
(Color Correction & Film to Tape Transfers)	

Colossalvision	**(212) 269-6333**
26 Broadway	FAX **(212) 269-4334**
(Near Merchant Marines Plaza)	**www.colossalvision.com**
New York, NY 10004	
(2D/3D Graphics, HDTV, Linear and Non-Linear Online & Standards Conversion)	

Communications Plus Digital	**(212) 686-9570**
102 Madison Ave. (Near E. 29th St.)	FAX **(212) 686-8425**
New York, NY 10016	**www.cpdigital.com**
(Editing, Linear Online, Non-Linear Offline and Online & Standards Conversion)	
Contact: Bruce Cohen	

Company 3 NY	**(212) 687-4000**
535 Fifth Ave., Fifth Fl.	FAX **(212) 687-2719**
New York, NY 10017	**www.company3.com**
(Captions, Color Correction, Duplication, Film Scanning and Recording, Film to Tape Transfers, Non-Linear Online, Standards Conversion, Tape to Tape Color Correction & Telecine)	

Creative Bubble, LLC	**(212) 201-4200**
79 Fifth Ave., 14th Fl. (Near 15th St.)	FAX **(212) 201-4210**
New York, NY 10003	**www.creativebubble.com**
(Computer Graphics, Editing, Non-Linear Offline and Online & Tape to Tape Color Correction)	

Creative Group, Inc.	**(212) 935-0145**
1601 Broadway, 10th Fl.	FAX **(212) 838-0853**
(Near W. 48th St.)	**www.creativegroup.tv**
New York, NY 10019	

Deluxe New York	**(212) 444-5600**
	www.bydeluxe.com

Devlin Video Intl.	**(212) 391-1313**
1501 Broadway, Ste. 408	FAX **(212) 391-2744**
(Near W. 43rd St.)	**www.devlinvideo.com**
New York, NY 10036	
(All Formats, Authoring, Avid Systems, Captions, Color Correction, Duplication, DVD Menus, Final Cut Pro Systems, HD Editing, HD Finishing, HD Online, HD Remastering, Motion Graphics, New Media Encoding, Non-Linear Offline, Non-Linear Online, Standards Conversions & Subtitles)	

Digital Art Video, Inc.	**(718) 457-5388**
8506 60th Ave., Third Fl.	FAX **(718) 457-6499**
(Near 85th St.)	**www.digital-art.com**
Middle Village, NY 11379	
(Compositing, Computer Graphics & Linear/Non-Linear Offline and Online)	

Ⓐ **Digital Arts**	**(212) 460-9600**
130 W. 29th St., Eighth Fl.	FAX **(212) 660-3600**
(Near Sixth Ave.)	**www.digital-arts.net**
New York, NY 10001	
(Avid and Final Cut Pro Systems, Color Correction, Editing, Film to Tape Transfers, Finishing, Graphics, High Def, HD Editing, HD Finishing, HD Remastering, HD Telecine, HD Online, Post Supervision & Standards Conversions)	

	(212) 687-0111
DJM Post Production	**(212) 687-0404**
Four E. 46th St. (Near Fifth Ave.)	FAX **(212) 949-8083**
New York, NY 10017	**www.djmpost.tv**
(Avid Systems, Captions, Color Correction, Compositing, Computer Graphics, Digital Editing Systems, Duplication, Final Cut Pro Systems, Finishing, HD Editing, HD Finishing, & Linear Online)	

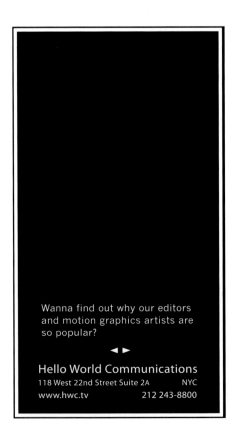

Wanna find out why our editors and motion graphics artists are so popular? ◄ ►

Hello World Communications
118 West 22nd Street Suite 2A   NYC
www.hwc.tv   212 243-8800

Du Art Film and Video (212) 757-4580
245 W. 55th St. (Near Broadway) FAX (212) 333-7647
New York, NY 10019 www.duart.com
(Color Correction, Computer Graphics, Film Scanning and Recording, Film to Tape Transfers, Non-Linear Offline and Online, Standards Conversion/Up Conversion, Subtitles & Tape to Film Transfers and Color Correction)

Dvideo Multimedia Productions (914) 251-9244
2900 Westchester Ave., Ste. 205A FAX (914) 251-9248
Purchase, NY 10577

East Coast Digital, Inc. (212) 691-4517
27 W. 20th St., Ste. 1106 www.eastcoastdigital.com
(Near Fifth Ave.)
New York, NY 10011
(Avid Systems, Computer Graphics, Digital Editing Systems, Duplication, Final Cut Pro Systems, HD Editing & Non-Linear Offline and Online)

Editors' Hideaway, Inc. (212) 661-3850
219 E. 44th St., Eighth Fl. FAX (212) 661-3609
(Near Second Ave.) www.editorshideaway.com
New York, NY 10017
(Captions, Color Correction, Computer Graphics, Duplication, Non-Linear Offline and Online, Standards Conversion & Subtitles)

Equitable Production Group (212) 314-4000
787 Seventh Ave. (Near W. 51st St.) FAX (212) 314-4001
New York, NY 10019 www.epgny.com
(Captions, Colorization & Editing)

Film-to-Tape Transfer Service (609) 924-3468

Film/Video Arts, Inc. (212) 222-1770
270 W. 96th St. www.fva.com
New York, NY 10025
(Linear/Non-Linear Offline and Online & Subtitles)

Framerunner, Inc. (212) 246-4224
555 W. 57th St., 17th Fl. FAX (212) 246-4225
(Near 11th Ave.) www.framerunner.com
New York, NY 10019
(HD Non-Linear Online)

Goldcrest Post Production (212) 243-4700
799 Washington St. (Near Horatio St.) FAX (212) 624-1701
New York, NY 10014 www.goldcrestpost.com
(Captions, Computer Graphics, Editing, Linear Online & Non-Linear Offline and Online)

GRS Systems, Inc. (212) 286-0299
216 E. 45th St. FAX (212) 286-9475
New York, NY 10017 www.grsv.com

GTV, Inc. (212) 262-6260
1697 Broadway, Ste. 404 FAX (212) 262-4709
(Near W. 53rd St.) www.gtvnyc.com
New York, NY 10019
(All Formats, Avid Systems, Color Correction, Compositing, Computer Animation, Computer/Motion Graphics, Digital Online, DVD, DVD Duplication, Editing, Final Cut Pro Systems, Finishing, Graphic Design, Graphics, HD Editing, HD Online, High Def, Non-Linear Offline and Online, Recording, Scanning, Subtitles, Tape to Tape Color Correction & Video to Still Transfers)

Guardian Entertainment, LTD (212) 727-4729
71 Fifth Ave., Fifth Fl. (Near 15th St.) FAX (212) 727-4737
New York, NY 10003 www.guardianltd.com
(Color Correction, Computer Graphics, Linear Online, Non-Linear Offline and Online, Standards Conversion, Subtitles, Tape to Film Transfers & Tape to Tape Correction)

HBO Studio Productions (212) 512-7800
120A E. 23rd St. (Near Park Ave.) FAX (212) 512-7788
New York, NY 10010
(Color Correction, Computer Graphics, Film to Tape Transfers & Linear/Non-Linear Offline and Online)

Hello World Communications (212) 243-8800
118 W. 22nd St., Ste. 2A FAX (212) 691-6961
(Near Sixth Ave.) www.hwc.tv
New York, NY 10011
(All Formats, Color Correction, Computer Graphics, Duplication, High Def, Non-Linear Offline and Online, Standards Conversion & Subtitles)
Contacts: George Stoll, Peter Walsh & Ron Yoshida

hscusa.tv (718) 626-6226
19-69 Steinway St. FAX (718) 626-1493
Astoria, NY 11105 www.hscusa.tv

Integrated Studios (212) 334-4000
449 Washington St. FAX (212) 334-6969
New York, NY 10013 www.integratedstudios.com
(Computer Animation, Computer Graphics, Final Cut Pro Systems, Graphics, HD Editing, Motion Graphics, Post Supervision, Recording, Scanning & Standards Conversions)

International Duplication Centre/
International Digital Centre, Inc. (212) 581-3940
216 E. 45th St., Seventh Fl. FAX (212) 581-3979
(Near Third Ave.) www.idcdigital.com
New York, NY 10017

(203) 322-5797
The Intervale Group, LLC (888) 233-0340
95-20 Intervale Rd. FAX (203) 329-2083
Stamford, CT 06905 www.intervalegroup.com
(Non-Linear Offline and Online)

iProbe Multilingual Solutions, Inc. (212) 489-6035
Five W. 36th St., Ste. 402 FAX (212) 202-4790
(Near Fifth Ave.) www.iprobesolutions.com
New York, NY 10018
(All Formats, Authoring, Avid Systems, Captions, Color Correction, Colorizations, Compositing, Computer Animation, Computer Graphics, Digital Colorization, Digital Editing Systems, Digital Film Mastering, Digital Intermediate Services, Digital Online, Digital Telecine, Duplication, DVD Design, DVD Menus, Edge Coding, Film Editing, Film to Tape Transfers, Final Cut Pro Systems, Finishing, Graphic Design, Graphics, HD Editing, HD Finishing, HD Remastering, HD Telecine, HD Online, Linear/Non-Linear Offline and Online, Mastering, Motion Graphics, Negative Cutting, New Media Encoding, Post Supervision, Pre-Visualization, Recording, Scanning, Standards Conversions, Subtitles, Tape to Tape Color Correction, Tape to Tape Film Simulation, Tape to Tape Transfers, Telecine, Training for Computer Graphics & Video to Still Transfers)

Ironik Design and Post (212) 683-7225
Five Woodhaven Dr. FAX (212) 683-7225
Simsbury, CT 06070 www.ironiknyc.com
(All Formats, Avid Systems, Computer Animation, Computer Graphics, Digital Editing Systems, Duplication, DVD Design, DVD Menus, Editing, Finishing, Graphic Design, Graphics, HD Editing, HD Finishing, HD Online, HD Remastering, Linear Offline, Mastering, Motion Graphics, Non-Linear Offline, Non-Linear Online, Standards Conversions & Training for Computer Graphics)
Contact: Angela Pace

LA Digital Post, Inc. (212) 981-8500
220 W. 42nd St., 17th Fl. FAX (212) 981-8595
New York, NY 10036 www.ladigital.com
(Compositing, Duplication, HD/SD Finishing, Offline, Standards Conversions & Titling)

Magno Sound & Video (212) 302-2505
729 Seventh Ave. (Near W. 48th St.) FAX (212) 819-1282
New York, NY 10019 www.magnosoundandvideo.com
(Film to Tape Transfers, Linear/Non-Linear Offline and Online & Standards Conversion)

Manhattan Center Studios (212) 695-6600
311 W. 34th St. (Near Eighth Ave.) FAX (212) 564-1092
New York, NY 10001 www.mcstudios.com
(All Formats, Avid, Color Correction, Compositing, Computer Graphics, Digital, Digital Colorization, Digital Editing Systems, Digital Film Mastering, Digital Online, Duplication, DVD, DVD Menus and Design, DVD Duplication, Editing, Finishing, Graphic Design, Graphics, High Def, HD Editing, HD Finishing, HD Remastering, HD Online, Linear/Non-Linear Offline and Online, Mastering, Post Supervision, Recording & Subtitles)

Marble and Clay (212) 683-5380
134 W. 26th St., Ste. 604 FAX (212) 683-7836
(Near Sixth Ave.) www.marbleandclay.com
New York, NY 10001
(All Formats, Authoring, Color Correction, Compositing,
Computer Animation and Graphics, Digital Editing Systems,
DVD Design and Menus, Film Editing, Final Cut Pro Systems,
Graphic Design, Graphics, HD Editing, HD Online, Mastering,
Motion Graphics, New Media Encoding, Non-Linear Offline and
Online, Post Supervision & Pre-Visualization)

Mark Haefeli Productions (212) 334-2164
11 Beach St., Ste. 409 www.mhp3.com
New York, NY 10013
(Avid Systems, Color Correction, Digital Editing Systems,
Duplication, Final Cut Pro Systems, HD Editing, HD Finishing &
Non-Linear Offline)

Mega Playground (212) 399-6342
609 Greenwich St., Eighth Fl. FAX (212) 399-6344
New York, NY 10014 www.mega-playground.com

Method (212) 907-1200
545 Fifth Ave., Second Fl. FAX (212) 907-1201
(Near 45th St.) www.methodstudios.com
New York, NY 10017
(Color Correction, Film to Tape Transfers, HDTV & Linear/Non-
Linear Offline and Online)

The Mill, New York (212) 337-3210
451 Broadway, Sixth Fl. FAX (212) 337-3259
(Near Canal St.) www.the-mill.com
New York, NY 10013
(Captions, Color Correction, Computer Graphics, Duplication,
Film Scanning and Recording, Non-Linear Online, Standards
Conversion, Tape to Tape Color Correction & Telecine)

Victor Milt/Interactive Publishing (561) 483-7734
7639 Cedarwood Circle FAX (561) 488-3016
Boca Raton, FL 33434 www.interpubco.com
(Non-Linear Offline and Online & Standards Conversion)
Contact: Kim Milt

(973) 300-9477
Mirage Productions Inc. (888) 746-6869
111 Spring St. FAX (973) 300-9467
Newton, NJ 07860 www.mirageproductions.com

Moving Images (212) 953-6999
227 E. 45th St., Sixth Fl. FAX (212) 661-0457
(Near Second Ave.) www.mipost.com
New York, NY 10017
(Color Correction, Film to Tape Transfers, Linear/Non-Linear
Offline and Online, Standards Conversion & Subtitles)

(212) 924-7364
Moving Pictures (212) 450-7933
222 E. 44th St., Eighth Fl. (Near Spring St.) www.mpny.tv
New York, NY 10017
(Compositing, Graphics & Non-Linear Offline and Online)

Murray Hill Studios, Inc. (212) 889-4200
248 E. 35th St. (Near Second Ave.) FAX (212) 889-9413
New York, NY 10016 www.murrayhillstudios.com

NBC Universal Artworks (212) 664-5972
30 Rockefeller Plaza, Ste. 1622W www.nbcartworks.com
New York, NY 10012
(Computer Graphics, Graphic Design, Graphics, Motion
Graphics & New Media Encoding)

New York Network (518) 443-5333
Empire State Plaza FAX (518) 426-4198
South Concourse, Ste. 146 www.nyn.suny.edu
P.O. Box 2058 (Near State St.)
Albany, NY 12220
(Captions, Color Corrections, Computer Graphics, Duplication,
Non-Linear Offline and Online, Subtitles & Tape to Tape
Color Correction)

Ⓐ Next Millennium Productions, Ltd. (917) 237-1661
31 Howard St., Ste. 5A FAX (917) 237-1663
New York, NY 10013 www.nmpfilms.com
(All Formats, Avid Systems, Color Correction, Compositing,
Digital Editing Systems, Digital Online, Finishing, HD Editing,
HD Online, Non-Linear Offline and Online,
Post Supervision & Recording)

(856) 222-5675
NFL Films (877) 222-3517
One NFL Plaza FAX (856) 866-4848
Mount Laurel, NJ 08054 www.nflfilms.com
(Digital Component Online, Film to Tape Transfers, HDTV,
Linear/Non-Linear Offline and Online & Standards Conversion)

Nice Shoes (212) 683-1704
352 Park Ave. South, 16th Fl. FAX (212) 683-9233
(Near E. 25th St.) www.niceshoes.com
New York, NY 10010
(Color Correction, Colorization, Film to Tape Transfers, High Def,
Non-Linear, Standards Conversions & Tape to Tape Transfers)
Contact: Kristen Kupjian

Northern Lights Post (212) 274-1199
135 W. 27th St., Eighth Fl. FAX (212) 274-1117
(Near Sixth Ave.) www.nlpedit.com
New York, NY 10001
(Color Correction, Compositing, Computer Graphics, Down/
Upconversions, File Transfers, Linear and Non-Linear Online &
Titling/Character Generation)

(646) 536-3494
Onshore Media (310) 691-8666
www.onshoredigital.com
(Color Correction, Computer Graphics, Digital Film Scanning
and Recording, HDTV, Non-Linear Offline and Online &
Standards Conversion)

(646) 731-3100
Orbit Digital (212) 894-4000
1619 Broadway, Seventh Fl. FAX (646) 731-3198
New York, NY 10019 www.pwny.com

Park Avenue Post, Inc. (212) 689-7678
419 Park Ave. South, Ste. 600 FAX (212) 689-7544
(Near 29th St.) www.parkavenuepost.com
New York, NY 10016
(Color Correction, Colorization, Compositing, Computer
Graphics, Editing, Linear Online, Non-Linear Offline and Online,
Standards Conversion & Subtitles)

Picture Island (646) 638-0895
33 Jones St., Ste. 3 FAX (646) 202-2895
(Near Bleecker St.) www.pictureisland.com
New York, NY 10014

Piranha Pictures (212) 216-9470
347 W. 36th St., Ste. 1501 FAX (212) 216-9317
(Near Ninth Ave.) www.piranhapix.com
New York, NY 10018
(2D/3D Animation, Computer Graphics, Editing, HD, Non-
Linear Offline and Online, Digital Component Online, Digital
Compositing, Music Supervision, Sound Mixing & Titling and
Character Generation)

Post Logic Studios (212) 520-3150
435 Hudson St., Seventh Fl. FAX (212) 520-3155
(Near Morton) www.postlogic.com
New York, NY 10014
(Color Correction, Film to Tape Transfers, High Def &
Standards Conversion)

Post Office Media (212) 302-4488
1560 Broadway, Ste. 514 FAX (212) 302-4849
New York, NY 10036 www.postofficemedia.com

PostWorks   **(212) 894-4000**
100 Avenue of the Americas   **(212) 894-4050**
(Near Grand St.)   FAX **(212) 941-0439**
New York, NY 10013   **www.postworks.com**
(Avid Systems, Computer Graphics, Digital Intermediate Services, Duplication, Film Scanning and Recording, Film to Tape Transfers, Final Cut Pro Systems, HD Editing, HD Online, Linear Online, Non-Linear Offline and Online, Quality Control, Standards Conversion, Subtitles, Tape to Film Transfers, Tape to Tape Color Correction & Telecine)

Pow! Pix, Inc.   **(212) 531-6444**
44 E. 32nd St. (Near Park Ave.)   FAX **(212) 531-6447**
New York, NY 10016   **www.powpix.com**
(Avid Systems, HD Editing, HD Finishing, Mobile Facility, New Media Encoding, Non-Linear Offline & Non-Linear Online)

Production Central   **(212) 631-0435**
873 Broadway, Ste. 205   FAX **(212) 631-0436**
(Near E. 18th St.)   **www.prodcentral.com**
New York, NY 10003

    (212) 366-5011
Rogue Post NYC   **(917) 817-1673**
18 W. 21st St., Sixth Fl.   **www.roguepost.com**
(Near Fifth Ave.)
New York, NY 10010
(All Formats, Color Correction, Digital Film Mastering, DVD, DVD Menus and Design, DVD Duplication, Editing, Film Editing, Final Cut Pro Systems, Finishing, Graphic Design, Graphics, High Def, HD Editing, HD Finishing, HD Remastering, HD Online, Non-Linear Offline and Online, Post Supervision & Video to Still Transfers)

Shooters Post & Transfer   **(215) 861-0100**
The Curtis Center, Ste. 1050   FAX **(215) 861-0098**
Independence Square West   **www.shootersinc.com**
Philadelphia, PA 19106
(All Formats, Avid Systems, Compositing, Computer Animation, Computer Graphics, Digital Film Mastering, Digital Intermediate Services, Film Restoration, Film Scanning, Film to Tape Transfers, Final Cut Pro Systems, Graphic Design, Graphics, HD Editing, HD Finishing, HD Online, HD Telecine, Motion Graphics, Non-Linear Offline, Non-Linear Online, Pre-Visualization, Scanning & Tape to Tape Color Correction)

Singularity communications   **(212) 481-3558**
40 W. 27th St., Second Fl.   **www.singularitycorp.com**
(Near Sixth Ave.)
New York, NY 10001
(Editing, Film Editing & Non-Linear Offline and Online)

Solar Film/Video Productions   **(212) 473-3040**
632 Broadway, Ste. 304   FAX **(212) 473-3091**
(Near Houston St.)   **www.solarnyc.com**
New York, NY 10012
(Avid, Computer Graphics, Linear/Non-Linear Offline and Online & Standards Conversion)

Soundtrack   **(212) 420-6010**
936 Broadway, Fourth Fl.   FAX **(212) 777-6403**
(Near W. 21st St.)   **www.soundtrackny.com**
New York, NY 10010
Contact: Maegan Hayward

Studio 57   **(631) 650-0057**
140 Hoffman Ln. (Near Space Court)   FAX **(631) 650-0010**
Islandia, NY 11749   **www.studio57online.com**
(Color Correction, Computer Graphics, Duplication, Non-Linear Offline and Online & Tape to Tape Color Correction)

Suite Spot   **(212) 475-6310**
126 Second Ave., Third Fl.   FAX **(212) 473-3748**
New York, NY 10003   **www.suitespotnyc.com**

Tape House   **(212) 894-4000**
100 Avenue of the Americas   FAX **(212) 941-0439**
(Near Grand St.)   **www.tapehouse.com**
New York, NY 10013

Technicolor Creative Services - N.Y.   **(212) 609-9400**
110 Leroy St. (Near Hudson St.)   FAX **(212) 609-9450**
New York, NY 10014   **www.technicolor.com**
(Digital Intermediates Services, Film Scanning and Recording & Film to Tape Transfers)
Contact: Steve Coffey

Ultrabland   **(646) 638-2830**
27 W. 24th St., Ste. 302   FAX **(646) 638-2835**
New York, NY 10010   **www.ultrabland.com**
(All Formats, Computer Graphics, Final Cut Pro Systems, Finishing, Graphic Design, HD Editing, HD Finishing, HD Online & Motion Graphics)

USA Studios   **(212) 398-6400**
29 W. 38th St. (Near Fifth Ave.)   FAX **(212) 398-8037**
New York, NY 10018   **www.usastudios.tv**
(Captions, Color Correction, Colorization, Editing, Film to Tape Transfers, Standards Conversion & Subtitles)

Zeitbyte   **(718) 666-3300**
45 Main St., Ste. 1030   **www.zeitbyte.com**
Brooklyn, NY 11201
(All Formats, Authoring, Avid Systems, Captions, Color Correction, Colorizations, Compositing, Computer Animation, Computer Graphics, Digital Colorization, Digital Editing Systems, Digital Intermediate Services, Digital Online, Duplication, DVD Design, DVD Menus, Film Editing, Final Cut Pro Systems, Finishing, Graphic Design, Graphics, HD Editing, HD Finishing, HD Online, HD Remastering, HD Telecine, Linear Offline, Linear Online, Mastering, Mobile Facility, Motion Graphics, New Media Encoding, Non-Linear Offline, Non-Linear Online, Post Supervision, Pre-Visualization, Recording, Scanning, Standards Conversions, Subtitles, Tape to Tape Color Correction, Tape to Tape Film & Video to Still Transfers)

Post Production Supervisors

Molly Bradford (917) 449-6793

Rosanna Herrick (917) 287-6575
www.townandcountrycreative.com

Maribeth Phillips (212) 691-1390
(917) 826-3399
FAX (212) 691-1390

Eliza Pelham Randall (310) 962-9463
(323) 525-1225
www.queenofspades.com

Jennifer Stock (516) 569-7759
www.jenstock.com

Mark Tocher (212) 340-1243

Screening Rooms

57 Screening Room   **(212) 765-0990**
140 W. 57th St.   FAX **(212) 957-6020**
New York, NY 10019   www.57screeningroom.com

DGA Theater   **(212) 581-0370**
(16mm, 35mm, Dolby SR and SRD & SDDS)   www.dga.org

Ⓐ Frederick P. Rose Hall
Home of Jazz at Lincoln Center   **(212) 258-9535**
Broadway at 60th St.   FAX **(212) 258-9906**
New York, NY 10019   www.jalc.org/venues

Goldcrest Post Production   **(212) 243-4700**
799 Washington St.   FAX **(212) 624-1701**
(Near Horatio St.)   www.goldcrestpost.com
New York, NY 10014
(35mm, Dolby SRD, Dolby SDDS & Video Facilities)

Helen Mills Theater   **(212) 243-6200**
135 W. 26th St., Ste. 11A   FAX **(212) 243-1325**
New York, NY 10001   www.helenmills.com
(Beta, Digibeta, Digital Projection, Dolby, DVD, High Def, Mini DV, Satellite Teleconferencing, VHS & Video Projection)

The Kitchen   **(212) 255-5793**
512 W. 19th St. (Near 10th Ave.)   www.thekitchen.org
New York, NY 10011
(Video)

Magno Sound & Video   **(212) 302-2505**
729 Seventh Ave. (Near W. 48th St.)   FAX **(212) 764-1679**
New York, NY 10019   www.magnosoundandvideo.com
(16mm, 35mm, Dolby SRD, DTS Surround, HD & Video)

Mark Forman Productions Corp. (212) 633-9960
300 W. 23rd St., Ste. 14A/B   FAX **(212) 807-0121**
(Near Eighth Ave.)   **www.screeningroom.com**
New York, NY 10011
(HDTV)

The Museum of the Moving Image **(718) 784-4520**
3601 35th Ave. (Near 36th St.)   FAX **(718) 784-4681**
Long Island City, NY 11106   **www.movingimage.us**
(16mm, 35mm, 70mm & Video)

New York Film Academy
Screening Room   **(212) 674-4300**
100 E. 17th St.   FAX **(212) 477-1414**
(Near Union Square East)   **www.nyfa.com**
New York, NY 10003
(16mm, 35mm, Dolby SRD & Video)

                             (212) 894-4000
PostWorks   **(212) 894-4050**
100 Avenue of the Americas   FAX **(212) 941-0439**
(Near Grand St.)   **www.postworks.com**
New York, NY 10013
(2K Digital Projection & 35mm, HD/2K Color Correction for DI and 5.1)

Quad Cinemas   **(212) 255-2243**
34 W. 13th St. (Near Sixth Ave.)   FAX **(212) 255-2247**
New York, NY 10011   **www.quadcinema.com**
(16mm & 35mm)

Steiner Studios   **(718) 858-1600**
15 Washington Ave.   FAX **(718) 858-1690**
Brooklyn Navy Yard, NY 11205   **www.steinerstudios.com**

Technicolor Creative Services - N.Y. **(212) 609-9400**
110 Leroy St. (Near Hudson St.)   FAX **(212) 609-9450**
New York, NY 10014   **www.technicolor.com**
(35mm, Digital Projection & Dolby)

Tribeca Cinemas   **(212) 941-2001**
54 Varick St. (Near Laight St.)   FAX **(212) 965-4651**
New York, NY 10013   **www.tribecacinemas.com**
(16mm, 35mm, 5.1, Beta, Digibeta, Digital Projection, Dolby, Dolby SR, DV CAM, DVD, Film, HDCAM, High Def, Mini DV, VHS & Video Projection)

Ⓐ Tribeca Screening Room   **(212) 941-2000**
375 Greenwich St. (Near Franklin St.)   FAX **(212) 941-2012**
New York, NY 10013   **www.tribecafilm.com**
(16mm, 35mm, THX & Video)

Walt Disney Co./
Park Avenue Screening Room   **(212) 735-5348**
500 Park Ave.   **www.buenavistapost.com**
(Near E. 59th St.)
New York, NY 10022
(35mm, Dolby SRD & Video Facilities)

private screenings

company meetings

dailies screenings

TRIBECA SCREENINGROOM
375 GREENWICH STREET | NY NY 10013 | 212.941.2000

Stock Footage & Photos

ABCNews VideoSource (212) 456-5421 / (800) 789-1250
125 West End Ave. (Near W. 65th St.) FAX (212) 456-5428
New York, NY 10023   www.abcnewsvsource.com
Footage: ABC News From 1963–Present

**(A) Action Footage/
Warren Miller Entertainment** (303) 253-6300 / (800) 729-3456
5720 Flatiron Pkwy   www.warrenmiller.com
Boulder, CO 80301
Footage: Comedy, Extreme/Adventure Sports, Scenics, Time-Lapse & Vintage

Action Sports/Scott Dittrich Films (212) 681-6565 / (310) 459-2526
www.sdfilms.com
Footage: Aerials, Animals, Cities, Clouds, Natural Disasters, People, Pollution, Scenics, Sports, Sunsets, Time-Lapse & Waves

Adventure Pictures (415) 431-1122
350 Alabama St., Ste. 1   FAX (415) 431-1128
San Francisco, CA 94110   www.adpix.com
Footage: Adventure, Sports, Time-Lapse & Travel

**Air Power Video &
Film Stock Library** (516) 869-3082
Nine Rose Hill Dr.   FAX (516) 869-3085
(Near Gracewood Dr.)   www.airpowerstock.com
Manhasset, NY 11030
Footage: Commercial Aviation & Military

Air Sea Land Productions, Inc. (718) 626-2646 / (888) 275-5367
19-69 Steinway St. (Near 20th Ave.)   FAX (718) 626-1493
Astoria, NY 11105   www.airsealand.com
Footage: Aerials, Animals, Cityscapes, Landscapes, Mountains, Nature, Scenics, Seasons, Trains & Underwater

Al Giddings Images, Inc. (406) 333-4300
75 Bridger Hollow Rd.   FAX (406) 333-4308
Pray, MT 59065   www.algiddings.com
Footage and Photos: Aquatic Subjects, Natural History & Oceans

Alan Benoit Photography (480) 967-2241 / (602) 526-1800
1101 E. Mesquite St.   FAX (480) 926-8888
Gilbert, AZ 85296
Photos: All Subjects

All-Stock (310) 317-9996 / (800) 323-0079
P.O. Box 1705   www.all-stock.com
Pacific Palisades, CA 90272
Footage: All Subjects

AM Stock-Cameo Film Library (818) 762-7865
10513 Burbank Blvd.   FAX (818) 762-6480
(Near Cahuenga Blvd.)   www.amstockcameo.com
North Hollywood, CA 91601
Footage: 35mm and HD: Airports, Architecture, Cities, Hotels, Houses, Landscapes, Motels, Office Buildings, Planes, Police Stations, Restaurants, Schools & Vehicles

Ambient Images (310) 312-6640 / (800) 627-8057
11600 Rochester Ave., Ste. 11   FAX (310) 312-5590
Los Angeles, CA 90025   www.ambientimages.com
Photos: California and New York Aerials, Cityscapes & Landscapes

**America by Air
Stock Footage Library** (800) 488-6359
154 Euclid Blvd.   FAX (413) 235-1462
Lantana, FL 33462   www.americabyair.com
Footage: 35mm and High Def: Aerials, Contemporary, Ground & International Establishing Shots

American Playback Images (818) 954-9870
27748 Caraway Ln., Ste. 1   FAX (818) 955-5112
Santa Clarita, CA 91350   www.americanplayback.com
Footage: Americana, Cartoons, Commercials, Historical, Movie Clips, News & Playback

American Stock Photography (213) 386-4600 / (800) 786-6300
4203 Locust St.   FAX (213) 365-7171
Philadelphia, PA 19104   www.americanstockphotos.com
Photos: Contemporary & Historical

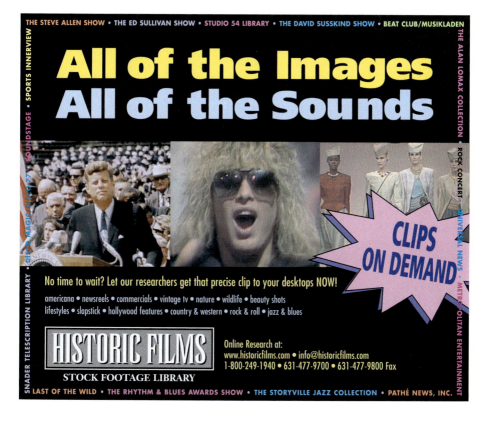

Anchor Archives   (213) 369-6903
Footage: 1950's Americana, Celebrities, Nautical,
Travelogue & Vintage

      (518) 392-5500
Animals Animals/Earth Scenes   (800) 392-5503
17 Railroad Ave. (Near Thomas St.)   FAX (518) 392-5550
Chatham, NY 12037   www.animalsanimals.com
Photos: Animals & Earth Scenes

Animation Entertainment   (858) 793-1900
3830 Valley Center Dr., Ste. 705-833   FAX (858) 793-1942
San Diego, CA 92130   www.animationtrip.com/licensing
Footage and Photos: Computer Animation and Illustrations,
High-Tech Imagery & Special FX

      (888) 250-2739
Apex Stock   (323) 443-2580
6725 W. Sunset Blvd., Ste. 490   FAX (323) 443-2579
Hollywood, CA 90028   www.apexstock.com

ARC Science Simulations   (800) 759-1642
P.O. Box 1955   www.arcscience.com
Loveland, CO 80539
Footage: High Resolution 2D and 3D Earth-From-Space
Animation
Photos: Earth Textures, Earth-From-Space & High Resolution
Cloud Layers

Archer-Telecine
Stock Footage Libraries   (818) 889-8246
P.O. Box 8426
Universal City, CA 91618
Footage: 1957–Present Worldwide Skylines/Traffic, Jets,
Resorts, Scenics & Time-Lapse Clouds

      (646) 613-4600
Archive Films by Getty Images   (800) 462-4379
One Hudson Square   www.gettyimages.com
75 Varick St. Fifth Fl. (Near Grand St.)
New York, NY 10013
Footage: Americana, Business/Industry, Cartoons, Celebrities,
Destinations, Educational, Events, Film Genres, Home Movies,
Lifestyle, News, Newsreels, Political, Sports & Travel

      (541) 863-4429
Artbeats   (800) 444-9392
1405 N. Myrtle Rd.   FAX (541) 863-4547
Myrtle Creek, OR 97457   www.artbeats.com

Battlegrounds   (502) 339-7934
9801 Somerford Rd.   FAX (502) 339-7934
Louisville, KY 40242   www.battlegroundsvideo.com
Footage: Generic & Military

action footage

WARREN MILLER entertainment

EYE CATCHING FOOTAGE
59 Years Filming Around the World.

Extreme / Action Adventure Sports • Bloopers
Scenics • Time Lapse • Vintage
16mm / 35mm / HD

STOCK FOOTAGE SALES
wmefootage.com
303.253.6300
stockfootage@warrenmiller.com

BBC Motion Gallery, Los Angeles   (818) 299-9712   (800) 966-5424
4144 Lankershim Blvd., Ste. 200   FAX **(818) 299-9763**
North Hollywood, CA 91602   www.bbcmotiongallery.com
Footage: Arts, Bloopers, Communications, Current Events, Destinations, Entertainment, Historical, Leisure, Lifestyles, Medicine, Music, Natural History, News, Politics, Reality, Science, Stock, Technology, Travel and Locations, Universal Newsreels & Wildlife

BBC Motion Gallery, New York   **(212) 705-9399**
747 Third Ave. (Near E. 46th St.)   FAX **(212) 705-9342**
New York, NY 10017   www.bbcmotiongallery.com
Footage: Arts, Bloopers, Communications, Current Events, Destinations, Entertainment, Historical, Leisure, Lifestyles, Medicine, Music, Natural History, News, Politics, Reality, Science, Stock, Technology, Travel and Locations, Universal Newsreels & Wildlife

BBC Motion Gallery, Toronto   **(416) 362-3223**
130 Spadina Ave., Ste. 401   FAX **(416) 362-3553**
Toronto, ON M5V 2L4 Canada   www.bbcmotiongallery.com
Footage: Arts, Bloopers, Communications, Current Events, Destinations, Entertainment, Historical, Leisure, Lifestyles, Medicine, Music, Natural History, News, Politics, Reality, Science, Stock, Technology, Travel and Locations, Universal Newsreels & Wildlife

Best Shot   **(813) 877-2118**
4301 W. Cayuga St.   FAX **(813) 874-3655**
Tampa, FL 33614   www.bestshotfootage.com
Footage: All Subjects

Bill Bachmann Studios   **(407) 333-9988**
www.billbachmann.com
Photos: Abstracts, Beaches, Business, Caribbean, Medical, Minorities & World Travel

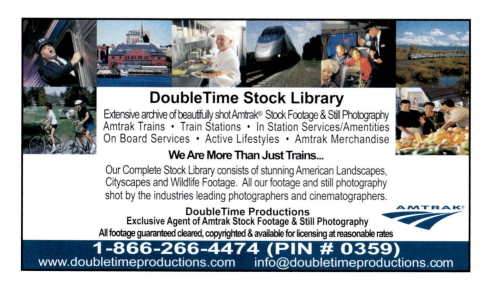

Stock Footage & Photos

BlackLight Films   (323) 436-7070
3371 Cahuenga Blvd. West   (323) 436-2229
Hollywood, CA 90068   FAX (323) 436-2230
www.blacklightfilms.com
Footage: Aerials, Agriculture, Americana, Animals, Architecture, Cityscapes, Clouds, Contemporary, Cultures, Deserts, Driving Shots, Flowers, Historical Landmarks, International People and Scenery, Landscapes, Lifestyles, Mountains, Nature, Oceans, Rivers, Rural, Scenics, Seasons, Skies, Storms, Suns and Moons, Time-Lapse, Trains, Transportation, Travel & Wildlife

Blackstone Stock Footage   (615) 731-5310
509 Upsall Dr.   FAX (615) 731-5232
Antioch, TN 37013   www.blackstonestockfootage.com
Footage: All Subjects

Blue Fier Photography/Blue Fier   (818) 344-5527
   (866) 225-8334
7450 Beckford Ave.   FAX (818) 344-5556
Reseda, CA 91335   www.bluefier.com
Photos: Clouds, Deserts, Forests, Mountains, Panoramics, Roads, Scenics, Skies, Skylines, Sunsets & Water

Blue Sky Stock Footage/
Bill Mitchell   (310) 305-8384
   (877) 992-5477
   FAX (310) 305-8985
www.blueskyfootage.com
Footage: 35mm, Super16mm and HD Real-Time and Time-Lapse: Aerials, Aerospace, Agriculture, Airplanes, Americana, Animals, Architecture, Cityscapes, Clouds, Deserts, Driving Shots, Eclipses, Experimental, Flowers, Forests, Highways, Historical Landmarks, International People and Scenery, Landscapes, Lightning, Motion Control, Mountains, Nature, Oceans, Rivers, Rural, Seasons, Skies, Space, Sports, Stars/Comets/Planets, Storms, Suns and Moons, Traffic, Trains, Transportation & Underwater

Boeing Image Licensing   (206) 662-1551
P.O. Box 3707, M/C 14-84   FAX (206) 655-1320
Seattle, WA 98124   www.boeingimages.com
Footage: Aerials, Aerospace, Airplanes, Archival, Cityscapes, Computer Graphics, Contemporary, Deserts, Experimental, Historical Landmarks, Landscapes, Mountains, Oceans, Skies, Space, Suns and Moons, Technology, Transportation & Travel

The Bridgeman Art Library   (212) 828-1238
65 E. 93rd St. (Near Madison Ave.)   FAX (212) 828-1255
New York, NY 10128   www.bridgemanart.com
Photos: Fine Art & History

Budget Films, Inc.   (323) 660-0187
   (323) 660-0800
4427 Santa Monica Blvd.   FAX (323) 660-5571
Los Angeles, CA 90029   www.budgetfilms.com
Footage: Beauty, Current Events, Technology & Vintage

Dennis Burkhart/Encounter Video   (503) 285-8974
   (800) 677-7607
14825 NW Ash St.   FAX (503) 285-3726
Portland, OR 97231   www.encountervideo.com
Footage: California Coast, Cook Islands, Easter Island, Egypt, Himalayas, Kenya, National Parks, Oregon Coast, Pacific Northwest, Paris, Time-Lapse & Wildlife

Camera One   (206) 523-3456
8523 15th Ave. NE   FAX (206) 523-3668
Seattle, WA 98115
Footage: Aerials, Archeology, Caribbean, Cities, Clouds, Eclipses, Europe, Landscapes, Lightning, Moons, National Parks, Nature, Northwest, Outdoor Sports, Scenics, Southwest, Storms, Sunrises and Sunsets, Time-Lapse, Underwater, Whitewater & Wildlife

The Canadian Press Images   (416) 507-2195
   (416) 364-0321
36 King St. East, Fourth Fl.   www.cp.org
Toronto, ON M5C 2L9 Canada
Photos: Canadian News

Caribbean Images   (212) 875-1507
   (917) 859-1115
159 W. 80th St., Ste. 1C   FAX (212) 875-1507
(Near Amsterdam)   www.wrenvideo.com
New York, NY 10024
Footage: Aerials, Scenics, Sports, Underwater & Wildlife

Carl Barth Images   (805) 969-2346
   (805) 637-0881
P.O. Box 5325   FAX (805) 969-5057
Santa Barbara, CA 93150
Footage: Aerials, Contemporary Establishing Shots, Moving Car Backgrounds, Scenics, Skylines & Vintage Archival 1960s

CBS News Archives/
BBC Motion Gallery   (212) 705-9399
747 Third Ave.   www.bbcmotiongallery.com
(Near 46th St.)
New York, NY 10017
Footage: CBS News 1954–Present

CelebrityFootage   (310) 360-9600
320 S. Almont Dr.   FAX (310) 360-9696
Beverly Hills, CA 90211   www.celebrityfootage.com
Footage: Award Ceremonies, Celebrities, Entertainment, Events, High Def, Hollywood, Movie Premieres, People, Red Carpet Arrivals & Stars

Chertok Associates Inc. -
Jazz On Film   (845) 461-7986
18 Old Schoolhouse Rd. (Near Congers Rd.)
New City, NY 10956
Footage: 1930s–1960s Vintage Jazz, African-American Lifestyle, Early Television, Music, Musicians, Nightclubs, Pop Culture, Street Scenes & Tap Dance

Chicagoland News Footage   (312) 455-1212
1613 W. Huron St.
Chicago, IL 60622
Footage: Chicagoland Rescues, Crimes, Fires, Gangs, Medical Emergencies & Natural Disasters

Clay Lacy Aviation, Inc.   (818) 989-2900
   (800) 423-2904
7435 Valjean Ave.   FAX (818) 909-9537
Van Nuys, CA 91406   www.claylacy.com
Footage: Aerials

The Clip Joint for Film   (818) 842-2525
833-B N. Hollywood Way   FAX (818) 842-2644
Burbank, CA 91505
Footage: All Subjects

CNN ImageSource   (404) 827-3326
One CNN Center   FAX (404) 827-1840
North Tower, Fourth Fl.   www.cnnimagesource.com
Atlanta, GA 30303
Footage and Photos: 1980–Present Current Events

Collegiate Images   (954) 343-8000
   (818) 625-1606
   FAX (954) 343-8001
www.collegiateimages.com

The Communications Group, Inc.   (919) 828-4086
   (888) 479-3456
P.O. Box 50157   FAX (919) 832-7797
Raleigh, NC 27650   www.cgfilm.com
Footage: Aerials, Boston, High Def, North Carolina Cities, Farms and Landscapes & The Big Dig

Compro Productions, Inc.   (770) 918-8163
2055 Boar Tusk Rd. NE   www.compro-atl.com
Conyers, GA 30012
Footage: Asian and European Cities, Landscapes and People

Corbis   (800) 260-0444
   (212) 777-6200
902 Broadway, Third Fl.   FAX (212) 533-4034
(Near E. 20th St.)   www.corbis.com
New York, NY 10010
Photos: All Subjects

Corbis   (800) 260-0444
   (323) 602-5700
3455 S. La Cienega Blvd.   FAX (323) 602-5701
Los Angeles, CA 90016   www.corbis.com
Photos: All Subjects

Corbis Motion   (212) 375-7622
   (866) 473-5264
902 Broadway (Near E. 20th St.)   FAX (212) 375-7700
New York, NY 10010   www.corbismotion.com
Footage: All Subjects

Corbis Stock Market (800) 999-0800
902 Broadway, Fourth Fl. FAX (800) 283-0808
(Near 25th Ave.) www.corbis.com
New York, NY 10010
Photos: All Subjects

Creative Arts Television (860) 868-1771
P.O. Box 739 FAX (860) 868-9999
Kent, CT 06757
Footage: Performing and Visual Arts Documentaries

Creative Production Group (818) 508-3308
12711 Ventura Blvd., Ste. 160 (818) 508-3311
Studio City, CA 91604 FAX (818) 508-2022
www.creativeproductiongroup.com
Footage: Military & Newsreels

CTV Archives Sales (416) 384-7389
Nine Channel Nine Court (800) 628-7780
Toronto, ON M1S 4B5 Canada FAX (416) 384-7384
www.ctv.ca
Footage: Classic News, Documentary and Sports

Culver Pictures (718) 752-9393
51-02 21st St., Ste. 4B FAX (718) 752-9394
(Near Sixth Ave.) www.culverpictures.com
Long Island City, NY 11101
Photos: All Subjects Up Until 1950

Custom Medical Stock Photo, Inc. (773) 267-3100
3660 W. Irving Park Rd. (800) 373-2677
Chicago, IL 60618 FAX (773) 267-6071
www.cmsp.com
Footage and Photos: Medical & Science

David Scharf Photography (323) 666-8657
2100 Loma Vista Pl. FAX (323) 666-0449
Los Angeles, CA 90039 www.scharfphoto.com
Film/Video Footage and Photos: Scanning Electron Microscopy

dick clark productions
Media Archives (310) 786-8971
9200 Sunset Blvd. www.dickclarkproductions.com
West Hollywood, CA 90069
Footage: 1950s–1990s Pop/Rock Music Performances

Documentary (617) 926-0491
Educational Resources (800) 569-6621
101 Morse St. FAX (617) 926-9519
Watertown, MA 02472 www.der.org
Footage: Anthropology, Cultures & People Around the World

Ⓐ Doubletime Productions (516) 869-1170
162 Pond View Dr. (866) 226-4474
Port Washington, NY 11050 FAX (516) 869-1171
www.doubletimeproductions.com
Footage and Photos: AMTRAK Official Licensing, Animals, Beaches and Sunsets, Chicago, Cityscapes, Deserts, Florida, Landscapes, Lifestyles, Mountains, New York Panoramic and Rural Scenes, North American Wildlife, Northwest, Rocky Mountain Scenery, Scenics, Southwest, Traffic, Trains, Transportation & Travel

DV/HDcuts (310) 497-5636
FAX (505) 438-0924
www.dvcuts.com
Footage: Airplanes, Americana, Cityscapes, Clouds, Deserts, Driving Shots, Experimental, Highways, Historical Landmarks, International People and Scenery, Landscapes, Lightning, Mountains, Nature, Oceans, Rivers, Seasons, Stars/Comets/Planets, Storms, Suns and Moon, Time-Lapse, Traffic, Trains, Transportation & Underwater

eFootage, Inc. (626) 395-9593
87 N. Raymond Ave., Ste. 850 (818) 481-6922
Pasadena, CA 91103 FAX (626) 792-5394
www.efootage.com
Footage: All Subjects

Film & Video Stock Shots, Inc. (818) 760-2098
10442 Burbank Blvd. (888) 436-6824
North Hollywood, CA 91601 FAX (818) 760-3294
www.stockshots.com
Footage: Aerials, Archival, Cartoons, Current Images, Extreme Sports, Landscapes, Lifestyles, Manufacturing, Medical, Microscopy, Nature, Science, Slapstick, Space, Sports, Time-Lapse, Underwater, Wildlife & Worldwide Locations

FILM Archives, Inc. (212) 696-2616
35 W. 35th St., Ste. 504 (Near 30th St.) (212) 696-0417
New York, NY 10001 FAX (212) 696-0021
www.filmarchivesonline.com
Footage: 1896–Present

Film Bank, Inc./Corbis Motion (866) 473-5264
902 Broadway (212) 375-7622
New York, NY 10010 www.corbismotion.com
Footage: Aerials, Animals, Animation, Archival and Contemporary Sports, Medical, Nature, News, People, Science, Special FX, Technology, Time-Lapse, Underwater & Worldwide Locations

Finley-Holiday Film Corporation (562) 945-3325
12607 E. Philadelphia St. (800) 345-6707
Whittier, CA 90601 FAX (562) 693-4756
www.finley-holiday.com
Footage and Photos: Aerospace, American History, Landmarks, National Parks, Outer Space, Scenics & Wildlife

Fish Films Footage World (818) 905-1071
4548 Van Noord Ave. (800) 442-0550
Studio City, CA 91604 FAX (818) 905-0301
www.footageworld.com
Footage: Aerials, Americana, Archival, Cartoons, Cities, Classic TV, Commericals, Contemporary, Culture, Educational, Extreme Sports, Graphics, High Def, Historical, Landmarks, Lifestyles, Nature, Newsreels, Oddities, Scenics, Time-Lapse, Travel, Underwater & Wildlife

FoodPix (323) 257-4400
99 Pasadena Ave. FAX (323) 257-3122
South Pasadena, CA 91030 www.foodpix.com
Photos: Food

Footage Hollywood (818) 760-1500
10520 Magnolia Blvd. FAX (818) 760-1532
North Hollywood, CA 91601 www.footagehollywood.com
Footage: Celebrity Newsreel, Interviews & Vintage–Present Film Trailers

The Footage Store (818) 556-6080
2121 Scott Rd., Ste. 201 FAX (818) 556-6080
Burbank, CA 91504 www.footagestore.com
Footage: All Subjects

FootageFinder (775) 323-0965
940 Matley Ln., Ste. 1 (Near Mill St.) (800) 852-2330
Reno, NV 89502 FAX (775) 323-1055
www.footagefinder.com
Footage: Fighter Jets, Ghost Towns, Las Vegas and Reno Nevada, Outdoor Activities, Steam Locomotives, Western States & WWII Aircraft

Framepool Inc. (646) 982-5120
32 Avenue of the Americas, 25th Fl. (800) 331-1314
New York, NY 10013 FAX (866) 928-6637
www.framepool.com
Footage: Aerials, Aerospace, Agriculture, Animals, Cityscapes, Clouds, Commercials, Contemporary, Cultures, Deserts, Flowers, International People and Scenery, Landscapes, Lightning, Lifestyles, Mountains, Nature, Scenics, Seasons, Space, Stars/Comets/Planets, Storms, Time-Lapse, Traffic, Transportation, Wildlife & Underwater

Framepool Inc. (310) 402-4626
10905 Ohio Ave., Ste. 116 (800) 331-1314
Los Angeles, CA 90024 FAX (866) 928-6637
www.framepool.com
Footage: Aerials, Aerospace, Agriculture, Animals, Cityscapes, Clouds, Commercials, Contemporary, Cultures, Deserts, Flowers, International People and Scenery, Landscapes, Lightning, Lifestyles, Mountains, Nature, Scenics, Seasons, Space, Stars/Comets/Planets, Storms, Time-Lapse, Traffic, Transportation, Underwater & Wildlife

Freewheelin' Films Stock Footage (970) 925-2640 / (888) 740-0360
44895 Hwy 82   FAX (970) 925-9369
Aspen, CO 81611   www.fwf.com
Footage: Aerials, Cityscapes, Motor Sports, Scenics, Sports & Travelogues

Getty Images (646) 613-4600 / (800) 462-4379
One Hudson Square   www.gettyimages.com
75 Varick St., Fifth Fl. (Near Grand St.)
New York, NY 10013
Photos: All Subjects, Illustration & Film

Ⓐ Global ImageWorks, LLC (201) 384-7715
65 Beacon St.   FAX (201) 501-8971
Haworth, NJ 07641   www.globalimageworks.com
Footage: 9/11, Aerials, Cityscapes, Contemporary, Destinations, Entertainment, Extreme Weather, Global Conflict, Global Warming, Historic, Interviews, Katrina, Lifestyles, Music, Nature, Politics, Pop Culture, Rap, Rock n Roll, Science, Technology, Terrorism, Time Lapse, Underwater & Wildlife

Global Vision Images (514) 879-0020
2600 William Tremblay St., Ste. 150   FAX (514) 879-0047
Montreal, QC H1Y 3J2 Canada   www.visionglobale.ca
Footage: Architecture, Computer Graphics, Countries, Events, Industry, Landscapes, Natural Phenomena, Nature, People, Sports, Transportation & Wildlife

Greg Hensley Productions (970) 984-3158
200 South E. St., Ste. 113   www.greghensley.com
New Castle, CO 81647
Footage: 35mm, High Def, Time-Lapse & Wildlife

HBO Archives (877) 426-1121
1100 Sixth Ave. (Near 42nd St.)   FAX (212) 512-5225
New York, NY 10036   www.hboarchives.com
Footage: Entertainment News Collection, Contemporary Stock From HBO Films, High Def, Iconic Sports, Newsreels & Royalty-Free Wildlife Footage

Ⓐ Historic Films (631) 477-9700 / (800) 249-1940
211 Third St. (Near Front St.)   FAX (631) 477-9800
Greenport, NY 11944   www.historicfilms.com
Footage: All Subjects, Hollywood, Musical Performances & Newsreels

The Hollywood Film Registry (310) 456-8184
5473 Santa Monica Blvd., Ste. 408   FAX (323) 957-2159
Los Angeles, CA 90029
Footage: Current Events & Historical

Hollywood Licensing, LLC (310) 442-5685
12233 W. Olympic Blvd., Ste. 170   FAX (310) 442-5683
Los Angeles, CA 90064   www.hollywoodlicensing.com
Footage: All Subjects, America's Funniest Home Videos & Red Bull Extreme Sports

Hot Shots/Corbis Motion (212) 375-7622 / (866) 473-5264
902 Broadway (Near 20th St.)   FAX (212) 375-7700
New York, NY 10010   www.corbismotion.com
Footage: Aerials, Archival, Contemporary, Cultures, Landmarks, Lifestyles, Nature, Newsreels, Scenics, Time-Lapse & Worldwide Locations

Image Bank Films and Archive Films by Getty Images (646) 613-4600 / (800) 462-4379
One Hudson Square   www.gettyimages.com
75 Varick St., Fifth Fl. (Near Fifth Ave.)
New York, NY 10013
Footage: Archival & Contemporary

Inter Video (818) 843-3624
    www.intervideo24.com
Footage: Aviation, Computer Graphics, Medical, News, Space, Sports, Travel & Weather

International Travel Films (323) 461-9994
224 N. Rossmore Ave.   FAX (323) 461-9996
Los Angeles, CA 90004
Footage: People, Ships, Trains & Worldwide Locations

ITN Source (212) 385-2077
116 John St., Ste. 701   FAX (646) 792-4668
New York, NY 10038   www.itnsource.com
Footage: News

Jalbert Productions, Inc. (631) 351-5878
230 New York Ave. (Near Leverich Pl.)   FAX (631) 351-5875
Huntington, NY 11743   www.jalbertfilm.com
Footage: Extreme and Outdoor Sports & Sports Celebrities

Joan Kramer & Associates, Inc. (310) 446-1866 / (212) 567-5545
10490 Wilshire Blvd., Ste. 1701   FAX (310) 446-1856
(Near Warner)   home.earthink.net/~ekeeeek
Los Angeles, CA 90024
Photos: Corporate, Glamour, Industrial, Leisure, People, Scenics, Underwater & World Travel

John E. Allen, Inc. (201) 391-3299
P.O. Box 452   FAX (201) 391-6335
Newfoundland, PA 18445
Footage: Archival

John Sandy Productions, Inc. (303) 721-6121 / (877) 418-7101
P.O. Box 5104   FAX (303) 721-0466
Englewood, CO 80155   www.jsptv.com
Footage: Extreme and Outdoor Sports, Mountain Biking & Skiing

KeywestFilms.com (305) 451-2227
P.O. Box 1476   FAX (305) 852-2821
Key Largo, FL 33037   www.keywestfilms.com
Footage: South Pacific & Tropical

The Library of Moving Images (323) 469-7499
6671 Sunset Blvd., Ste. 1581   FAX (323) 469-7559
Hollywood, CA 90028   www.libraryofmovingimages.com
Footage: 1890s–1990s Historical Hollywood & 20th Century Images and Events

LifeStockPhotos.com (951) 609-8020
    www.lifestockphotos.com

Linear Cycle Productions (818) 347-9880
P.O. Box 2608   FAX (818) 347-9880
North Hills, CA 91393   www.linearcycleproductions.com
Footage: People & Vintage–1990

Louis Wolfson II Florida Moving Image Archive (305) 375-1505
101 W. Flagler St.   FAX (305) 375-4436
Miami, FL 33130   www.fmia.org
Footage: Caribbean, Cuba, Florida, Miami & Space Program

MacGillivray Freeman Films (949) 494-1055
P.O. Box 205   FAX (949) 494-2079
Laguna Beach, CA 92652   www.macfreefilms.com
Footage: Aerials, Aesthetic Sports, Clouds, Exotic/Tropical Locations, Nature, Oceans, Scenics & Underwater

March of Time Newsreels and Documentaries (212) 512-7171 / (212) 512-5664
1100 Sixth Ave.   FAX (212) 512-7040
New York, NY 10036   www.themarchoftime.net

Masterfile (416) 929-3000 / (800) 387-9010
Three Concorde Gate, Fourth Fl.   FAX (416) 929-2104
Toronto, ON M3C 3N7 Canada   www.masterfile.com
Photos: All Subjects

Maxx Images, Inc. (604) 985-2560
711 W. 15th St.   FAX (604) 985-2890
N.Vancouver, BC V7M 1T2 Canada   www.maxximages.com
Footage: Aerials, British Columbia, Killer Whales, Mountains, Oceans, Underwater & Wildlife

Ned Miller (847) 816-9020 / (847) 975-9020
P.O. Box 7160   www.nedmiller.com
Libertyville, IL 60048
Footage: Chicago

Moe DiSesso Film Library (661) 255-7969
24233 Old Rd. FAX (661) 255-8179
Santa Clarita, CA 91321 www.animalactors4hire.com
Footage: Animals

Movie Services, Inc. (954) 321-8883
3780 SW 30th Ave. FAX (954) 321-8703
Fort Lauderdale, FL 33312
Footage: All Subjects

Moviecraft, Inc. (708) 460-9082
P.O. Box 438 www.moviecraft.com
Orland Park, IL 60462
Footage: Americana, Archival, Cartoons, Industrial, Newsreels & Pre-1965 Television

National Geographic Digital Motion (202) 857-5868 / (877) 730-2022
FAX (202) 429-5755
www.ngdigitalmotion.com
Footage: Aerials, Archeology, Arts, Cultures, Entertainment, History, Landscapes, Locations/Destinations, People, Scenery, Science, Sports, Technology, Underwater, Wildlife & World News

Nature Footage/Ocean Footage (831) 375-2313
300 Foam St. FAX (831) 621-9559
Monterey, CA 93940 www.naturefootage.com

Ⓐ NBC News Archives (212) 664-3797 / (818) 840-4249
30 Rockefeller Plaza, Ste. 327W FAX (212) 703-8558
(Near E. 49th St.) www.nbcnewsarchives.com
New York, NY 10112
Footage: NBC News: 1940s–Present

New & Unique Videos (619) 644-3000 / (800) 365-8433
7323 Rondel Court FAX (619) 644-3001
San Diego, CA 92119 www.newuniquevideos.com
Footage: Aerials, Animals, Archival Film, Beaches and Sunsets, Bloopers, Cities, Contemporary, Corporate/Industrial, Current Events, International, Lifestyles, Medical, Military, People, Scenics, Sports, Travel and Locations, Technological, Underwater & Wildlife

NFL Films (856) 222-5675 / (877) 222-3517
One NFL Plaza FAX (856) 866-4848
Mount Laurel, NJ 08054 www.nflfilms.com
Footage: NFL

NHL Hockey Archive (201) 750-5860 / (201) 750-5800
Footage: NHL Hockey 1920s–Present FAX (201) 750-5850

Oddball Film + Video (415) 558-8112
275 Capp St. FAX (415) 558-8116
San Francisco, CA 94110
Footage: Archival, Contemporary, High Def & Offbeat

Odyssey Productions, Inc. (503) 223-3480
2800 NW Thurman St. FAX (503) 223-3493
Portland, OR 97210 www.odysseypro.com
Footage: All Subjects

Omega Media Group, Inc. (770) 449-8870
3100 Medlock Bridge Rd., Ste. 100 FAX (770) 449-5463
Norcross, GA 30071 www.omegamediagroup.com
Footage: All Subjects

Pan American Video (707) 822-3800 / (800) 726-2634
Footage: Archive 1900–1970s FAX (707) 822-0800
www.panamvideo.com

Paramount Pictures - Stock Footage Library (818) 432-4025
5555 Melrose Ave.
Hollywood, CA 90038
www.thoughtequity.com/paramountpictures
Footage: 1920s–Present Paramount Features & Television

Paul Ziffren Sports Resource Center Library (323) 730-4646
2141 W. Adams Blvd. FAX (323) 730-0546
Los Angeles, CA 90018 www.aafla.org
Photos: Sports

Photodisc by Getty Images (646) 613-4600 / (800) 462-4379
One Hudson Square www.gettyimages.com
75 Varick St., Fifth Fl. (Near Grand St.)
New York, NY 10013
Footage: Royalty-Free, All Subjects

Photovault (415) 552-9682
1045 17th St. www.photovault.com
San Francisco, CA 94107
Footage: All Subjects

PicturesNow.com (415) 435-1076
Photos: Historic Art and Illustration FAX (415) 435-5027
www.picturesnow.com

Producers Library (818) 752-9097 / (800) 944-2135
10832 Chandler Blvd. FAX (818) 752-9196
North Hollywood, CA 91601 www.producerslibrary.com
Footage: 1950s Americana, Hollywood History & Outtakes

Pyramid Media (310) 398-6149 / (800) 421-2304
P.O. Box 1048 FAX (310) 398-7869
Santa Monica, CA 90406 www.pyramidmedia.com
Footage: Animals, Geography, Health, Nature, Safety, Science & Sports

Questar, Inc. (312) 266-9400 / (800) 544-8422
FAX (312) 266-9523
www.questar1.com
Footage: Cities, Cultures, Foreign Locations, Landscapes, People & Wildlife

Re: Search (646) 365-1300
432 Park Ave. South, Ste. 1009 FAX (646) 365-1304
(Near 29th St.) www.researchandrights.com
New York, NY 10016
Footage and Photos: All Subjects

Reel Orange (949) 548-4524
316 La Jolla Dr. (Near Cliff Drive) www.reelorange.com
Newport Beach, CA 92663
Footage: Aerials, Environmental & Grand Canyon

Reuters Television International (646) 223-6600 / (818) 953-4105
Three Times Square, Fourth Fl. FAX (646) 223-6615
(Near Broadway) www.reuters.com
New York, NY 10036
Footage: 1896–Present News Archive

Rocketclips, Inc. (562) 438-6300
Footage: Lifestyles & People www.rocketclips.com

Rocky Mountain Motion Pictures (323) 461-9900
937 N. Citrus Ave. FAX (323) 461-0100
Los Angeles, CA 90038 www.rmmp.com
Footage: All Subjects

Shooting Star International (323) 469-2020
1441 N. McCadden Pl. FAX (323) 464-0880
Los Angeles, CA 90028 www.shootingstaragency.com
Photos: Celebrities, Entertainment, Geography, Glamour, Historical, Human Interest, Movie Stills & News

Silverman Stock Footage (917) 470-9104
210 Douglass St. www.silvermanstockfootage.com
Brooklyn, NY 11217
Footage: Aerials, Airplanes, Americana, Animals, Architecture, Archival, Cityscapes, Clouds, Contemporary, Cultures, Deserts, Extreme Sports, Flowers, International People, Landscapes, Lifestyles, Nature, Oceans, Scenics, Space, Storms, Suns and Moons, Time-Lapse, Traffic & Underwater

Sony Pictures Stock Footage (310) 244-3704 / (866) 275-6919
10202 W. Washington Blvd., Turner 4314
Culver City, CA 90232
www.sonypicturesstockfootage.com
Footage: Action, Aerials, Aerospace, Airplanes, Americana, Animals, Architecture, Cityscapes, Clouds, Contemporary, Cultures, Deserts, Driving Shots, Explosions, Fires, Forests, Futuristic, Highways, Historical Landmarks, International People and Scenery, Landscapes, Lightning, Mountains, Nature, Oceans, Pyrotechnics, Rivers, Rural, Scenic, Seasons, Skies, Space, Stars/Comets/Planets, Storms, Suns and Moons, Traffic, Trains, Transportation, Travel, Underwater & Wildlife

The Source
Stock Footage Library, Inc. (520) 298-4810
140 S. Camino Seco, Ste. 308   FAX (520) 290-8831
Tucson, AZ 85710   www.sourcefootage.com
Footage: Aerials, Business, Destinations, Sports, Technology & Time-Lapse

Spalla Video (212) 765-4646 / (914) 476-4880
99 Buena Vista Ave., First Fl.
Yonkers, NY 10701
Footage: Celebrities & Events

Sports Cinematography Group (212) 744-5333 / (310) 785-9100
73 Market St.   FAX (310) 564-7500
Venice, CA 90291
www.sportscinematographygroup.com
Footage: All Sports Subjects, Extreme Sports, Lifestyles, Motor Racing, Nature & Wildlife

The Stock Shop/ (212) 453-3426
Medichrome/Anatomy Works (800) 233-1975
116 E. 27th St., Fifth Fl.   FAX (212) 447-9732
(Near Lexington Ave.)
New York, NY 10016
Photos: Medical & Medical Illustrations

StormStock (817) 276-9500
P.O. Box 122020   FAX (817) 795-1132
Arlington, TX 76012   www.stormstock.com
Footage: 16mm, 35mm, Blizzards, Beaches, Caribbean, Clouds, Disasters, Environmental, Fires, Flash Floods, Hail, High Def, High Resolution, Hurricane Katrina, Hurricanes, Landscapes, Lightning, Microbursts, Natural Disasters, Natural History, Nature, Oceans, Radar, Science, Seasons, Skies, Storm Clouds, Storms, Sunrises, Sunsets, Time-Lapse, Tornadoes, Traffic & Waves

Streamline Stock Footage (212) 925-2547 / (323) 660-5868
594 Broadway, Ste. 900   FAX (212) 334-7696
(Near W. Houston St.)   www.streamlinefilms.com
New York, NY 10012
Footage: Contemporary & Vintage

TellurideStock.com (970) 728-6503 / (970) 729-0122
P.O. Box 1215
Telluride, CO 81435
Footage: Action Sports, Avalanche, Forest Fires, International Travel, Scenics & Sports POV

Third Millennium Films (212) 675-8500
89 Fifth Ave., Ste. 1002   FAX (212) 675-6042
(Near W. 14th St.)   www.thirdmillenniumfilms.net
New York, NY 10003
Footage: Archival, Animals, Lifestyles, New York City Aerials, Time-Lapse, Vintage & World Locations

Thought Equity Motion (646) 495-6123 / (866) 815-6599
770 Broadway, Ste. 236   FAX (646) 495-6042
New York, NY 10003   www.thoughtequity.com
Footage: 16mm, 35mm, Abstracts, Adventure Sports, Aerials, Agriculture, Air Force, Airplanes, Airports, Americana, Animals, Anthropology, Archeology, Architecture, Archival, Arts, Aviation, Award Ceremonies, Bald Eagles, Beaches, Blizzards, Bloopers, Business, Caribbean, Celebrities, Ceremonies, Cityscapes, Clearance, Clouds, College Sports, Comedy, Commercials, Communications, Computer Graphics, Contemporary, Conventions, Crimes, Crowds, Cultures, Current Events, Deserts, Disasters, Driving Shots, Eclipses, Educational, Entertainment, Environmental, Events, Experimental, Explosions, Extreme Sports, Film, Feature Films, Fires, Flash Floods, Flowers, Forests, Gangs, Geography, Grand Canyon, Hail, HBO, High Def, High Resolution, High-Speed, Highways, Historical, Historical Landmarks, Hollywood, Home Movies, Hurricanes, Icons, Industry, International, Jets, Killer Whales, Landmarks, Landscapes, Leisure, Lifestyles, Lightning, Medical Emergencies, Medicine, Military, Minorities, Moons, Motion Control, Motor Racing, Mountains, Music, National Geographic, National Parks, Natural Disasters, Natural History, Nature, Nautical, NBC News, NCAA, Neighborhoods, News, North American Wildlife, Oceans, Outdoor Sports, Outtakes, People, Photos, Planets, Police, Political, Pollution, Pop Culture, Radar, Research, Rights and Clearances, Rivers, Rocky Mountains, Royalty-Free, Rural, Sailing, Scenics, Science, Seasons, Skies, Sony, Space, Space Program, Sports, Stars, Storm Clouds, Storms, Stunts, Sunrises, Suns, Sunsets, Technology, Television, Time-Lapse, Tornadoes, Traffic, Trains, Transportation, Travel, Underwater, Vintage, Waves, Whitewater, Wildlife, World War I, World War II & Yacht Racing

Tim Allen & Associates (850) 763-5795
1118 Jenks Ave.   FAX (850) 785-3508
Panama City, FL 32401   www.timallenphotography.com
Photos: All Subjects

Troma Entertainment, Inc. (212) 757-4555 / (718) 391-0110
733 Ninth Ave. (Near W. 50th St.)   FAX (212) 399-9885
New York, NY 10019   www.troma.com
Footage: Feature Films

UCLA Film and Television Archive (323) 466-8559
1015 N. Cahuenga Blvd.   FAX (323) 461-6317
Los Angeles, CA 90038
Footage: 1900s–1980s Newsreels

Universal Studios -
Stock Footage Library (818) 777-1695
100 Universal Plaza   FAX (818) 866-0763
Bldg. 2313A, Lower Level
Universal City, CA 91608
Footage: All Subjects   www.universalstudios.com/studio

US Air Force Motion Picture Office (310) 235-7511
10880 Wilshire Blvd., Ste. 1240   FAX (310) 235-7500
Los Angeles, CA 90024
Footage: Air Force

US Army Office of Public Affairs (310) 235-7621 / (310) 235-7622
10880 Wilshire Blvd., Ste. 1250   FAX (310) 235-6075
Los Angeles, CA 90024
www.defenselink.mil/faq/pis/PC12FILM.html
Footage: U.S. Army

Video Tape Library, Inc./VTL (323) 656-4330
1509 N. Crescent Heights Blvd., Ste. 2   FAX (323) 656-8746
Los Angeles, CA 90046   www.videotapelibrary.com
Footage: Aerials, Americana, Animals, Archival, Bloopers, Cities, Cultures, Extreme and Recreational Sports, HD Footage, Historical, Landmarks, Landscapes, Lifestyles, News, People, Professionals, Technological, Time-Lapse, Travel Locations & Underwater

Vision Earth Society (305) 945-6789
1825 N. E. 149th St. FAX (305) 945-0300
Miami, FL 33181 www.visionearth.org
Footage and Photos: Underwater

The WaterHouse (800) 451-3737
Mile Marker 102.5 FAX (305) 451-5147
Key Largo, FL 33037 www.stephenfrinkcollection.com
Photos: Underwater

WGBH Stock Sales (617) 300-3901
One Guest St. FAX (617) 300-1056
Boston, MA 02135 www.wgbhstocksales.org
Footage: Aerials, Americana, Cultures, Deserts, Eclipses, Fires, International People and Scenery, Landscapes, Nature, Rivers, Rural, Scenics, Technology, Trains, Underwater & Wildlife

(206) 682-5417
White Rain Films, Ltd. (800) 816-5244
2009 Dexter Ave. North FAX (206) 682-3038
Seattle, WA 98109 www.whiterainfilms.com
Footage: Aerials, Icons, International People and Scenery, Time-Lapse & Wildlife

Wings Wildlife Production, Inc. (949) 830-7845
Two McLaren, Ste. A FAX (949) 830-5116
Irvine, CA 92618 www.wildlifelibrary.com
Footage: 35mm African and North American Wildlife

Wish You Were Here
Film & Video, Inc. (818) 371-9649
www.wywhstock.com
Footage: Film, High Def & Video: Aerials, Cities, Cultures, Destinations, Events, Landmarks, People, Scenics, Time-Lapse & Wildlife

Woodfin Camp & Associates (718) 624-4620
115 St. Felix St. (Near Eighth Ave.)
Brooklyn, NY 11217 www.woodfincamp.com
Photos: Artists, Occupations, People Around the World, Places, Politicians & Writers

(800) 777-2223
WPA Film Library (708) 460-0555
16101 S. 108th Ave. FAX (708) 460-0187
Orland Park, IL 60467 www.wpafilmlibrary.com
Footage: 1895-21st Century, Americana, Classic Commercials and Industrial Films, High Def, Historic, Music, Politics & UFO Collection

WTTW Digital Archives (773) 509-5412
5400 N. St. Louis Ave. FAX (773) 509-5307
Chicago, IL 60625 www.wttwdigitalarchives.com
Footage: Aerials, Airplanes, Americana, Architecture, Archival, Cityscapes, Contemporary, Cultures, Deserts, Flowers, Historical Landmarks, International People and Scenery, Landscapes, Lifestyles, Mountains, Nature, Oddities, Rural, Scenics, Seasons, Sports, Trains & Transportation

Titling, Captioning & Broadcast Design

asterisk   (212) 255-8880
20 W. 20th St., Ste. 405   www.asteriskpix.com
(Near Union Square West)
New York, NY 10011
(Feature Film Titles, Logos, Station ID Packages, TV Network/Cable ID's and Packages & TV Show Titles and Opens)

Atlantic Motion Pictures   (212) 924-6170
162 W. 21st St., Fourth Fl.   FAX (212) 989-8736
New York, NY 10011   www.atlanticmotion.com

Beehive, Inc.   (212) 924-6060
19 W. 21st St., Ste. 1002   FAX (212) 924-1855
(Near Fifth Ave.)   www.beehive.tv
New York, NY 10010
(Commercials, Logos, Promos, TV Network/Cable ID's and Packages & TV Show Opens)

Ben Hillman & Company, Inc.   (917) 887-4365 / (413) 229-3448
115 W. 30th St., Ste. 1206   www.benhillman.com
(Near Sixth Ave.)
New York, NY 10001

Big Film Design   (212) 627-3430
594 Broadway, Ste. 1001   FAX (212) 989-6528
New York, NY 10012   www.bigfilmdesign.com
(Feature Film Titles)

Blinking Eye Media   (212) 243-6243
One West St., Ste. 100   FAX (212) 242-4411
(Near Spring St.)   www.blinkingeyemedia.com
New York, NY 10004
(Feature Film Titles, Logos, Station ID Packages, TV Network/Cable ID's and Packages & TV Show Titles and Opens)

BOND   (212) 533-9400
665 Broadway, Ste. 1201   FAX (212) 533-9463
(Near Bond St.)   www.bondedit.com
New York, NY 10012
(Commercials, Feature Film Titles, Logos, Music Videos, Promos, Subtitles, Trailers, TV Network/Cable IDs and Packages & TV Show Opens and Titles)

CaptionMax   (212) 462-0060
159 W. 25th St., 10th Fl.   FAX (212) 462-0061
(Near Seventh Ave.)   www.captionmax.com
New York, NY 10001
(Audio Description, Closed Captioning & Multi-Language DVD Subtitling)

Chromavision   (212) 686-7366
49 W. 27th St., Eighth Fl.   FAX (212) 686-7310
(Near Sixth Ave.)   www.chromavision.net
New York, NY 10001
(Commercials, Feature Film Titles, Logos, Music Videos, Promos, Station ID Packages & TV Show Titles)

Creative Bubble, LLC   (212) 201-4200
79 Fifth Ave., 14th Fl. (Near 15th St.)   FAX (212) 201-4210
New York, NY 10003   www.creativebubble.com
(Commercials, Logos, Music Videos, Promos, Station ID Packages, TV Network/Cable ID's and Packages, TV Show Opens & Trailers)

Design@Chelsea Post   (212) 727-1234
221 W. 26th St. (Near Eighth Ave.)   FAX (212) 255-6644
New York, NY 10001   www.amvchelsea.com

Designomotion   (917) 532-0738
67 E. 11th St., Ste. 324   www.designomotion.com
(Near Broadway)
New York, NY 10003
(Animated Logos, Cable ID's, Cable Packages, ID's, Logos, Opens, Station ID Packages, Titles, TV Show, Visual Description & TV Network ID's and Packages)

Ⓐ Digital Arts   (212) 460-9600
130 W. 29th St., Eighth Fl.   FAX (212) 660-3600
New York, NY 10001   www.digital-arts.net
(Closed Captioning)

DMA Animation   (212) 463-7370
89 Fifth Ave., Ste. 501   FAX (212) 463-7820
(Near E. 16th St.)   www.dma-animation.com
New York, NY 10003
(Feature Film Titles, Logos & TV Show Opens)

Du Art Film and Video   (212) 757-4580
245 W. 55th St. (Near Broadway)   FAX (212) 333-7647
New York, NY 10019   www.duart.com
(Feature Film Titles, Logos, Subtitles & TV Show Titles and Opens)

Elrom Inc.   (212) 645-5050
419 Park Ave. South   FAX (212) 689-7544
New York, NY 10016   www.elrom.tv

EyeballNYC   (212) 431-5234
187 Lafayette St., Second Fl.   FAX (212) 431-6793
(Near Broome St.)   www.eyeballnyc.com
New York, NY 10013
(Commercials, Promos, TV Network/Cable ID's and Packages & TV Show Opens)

FDG   (646) 233-2226
   FAX (646) 233-2226
   www.fdg3.com
(Audio Description, AVI Subtitles, Closed Captioning, Domestic, DVD Subtitles, Feature Film, Foreign, Real Time Captioning, Subtitles & Video Subtitles)

Freestyle Collective   (212) 414-2200
104 E. 25th St., 12th Fl.   FAX (212) 414-2206
(Near Fifth Ave.)   www.freestylecollective.com
New York, NY 10010
(Feature Film Titles, Logos, Station ID Packages, TV Network/Cable ID's and Packages & TV Show Titles and Opens)

GTV, Inc.   (212) 262-6260
1697 Broadway, Ste. 404   FAX (212) 262-4709
(Near W. 53rd St.)   www.gtvnyc.com
New York, NY 10019
(Commercials, Logos, Music Videos, Promos, Station ID Packages, Trailers & TV Network/Cable ID's and Packages)

Hornet, Inc.   (917) 351-0520
116 W. Houston St., Fourth Fl.   FAX (917) 351-0522
(Near Seventh Ave.)   www.hornetinc.com
New York, NY 10012
(Commercials, Feature Film Titles, Logos, Music Videos, Promos, Station ID Packages, TV Network/Cable ID's and Packages & TV Show Titles/Opens)

hscusa.tv   (718) 626-6226
19-69 Steinway St.   FAX (718) 626-1493
Astoria, NY 11105   www.hscusa.tv

Interface Arts   (718) 788-0335
241 16th St., Ste. 2   www.interface_arts.com
(Near Sixth Ave.)
Brooklyn, NY 11215
(Feature Film Titles, Logos, Station ID Packages, Trailers & TV Show Titles and Opens)

InterNation, Inc.   (212) 619-5545 / (800) 222-8799
299 Broadway, Ste. 1400   FAX (212) 619-5887
(Near Duane St.)   www.internation.com
New York, NY 10007
(Foreign Language Graphics & Subtitles)

iProbe Multilingual Solutions, Inc. (212) 489-6035
Five W. 36th St., Ste. 402 FAX **(212) 202-4790**
(Near Fifth Ave.) **www.iprobesolutions.com**
New York, NY 10018
(Animated Logos, Audio Description, AVI Subtitles, Cable ID's, Cable Packages, Closed Captioning, Domestic, DVD Subtitles, Feature Film, Foreign, ID's, Logos, Opens, Real Time Captioning, Station ID Packages, Subtitles, Titles, TV Show, Visual Description, Video Subtitles, TV Network ID's & TV Network Packages)

LVT Laser Subtitling (212) 343-1910
609 Greenwich, Ste. 4B FAX **(212) 965-1338**
New York, NY 10014 **www.lvt.usa.com**
(Laser Subtitles)

Mechanism Digital, Inc. (646) 230-0230
514 W. 24th St., Third Fl. FAX **(646) 336-8395**
(Near 10th Ave.) **www.mechanismdigital.com**
New York, NY 10011
(Animated Logos, Cable ID's, Cable Packages, Feature Film, ID's, Logos, Opens, Promos, Station ID Packages, Titles, TV Network ID's, TV Network Packages & TV Show)

Method (212) 907-1200
545 Fifth Ave., Second Fl. FAX **(212) 907-1201**
(Near 45th St.) **www.methodstudios.com**
New York, NY 10017
(Commercials & Feature Film Titles)

NBC Universal ArtWorks (212) 664-5972
30 Rockefeller Plaza, Ste. 1622W FAX **(212) 664-2377**
New York, NY 10112 **www.nbcartworks.com**

**People Support
Transcription & Captioning** (877) 914-5999
221 W. 26th St. **www.peoplesupport.com**
New York, NY 10001

Perception (212) 563-3388
12 W. 31st St., Sixth Fl. FAX **(212) 563-3571**
New York, NY 10001 **www.perceptionnyc.com**
(Captions, Feature Film, Foreign and Domestic, ID's, Logos, Opens, Packages, Station ID Packages, Subtitles, Titles, TV Network/Cable TV Show & Visual Description)

R/G A (212) 946-4000
350 W. 39th St. (Near Eighth Ave.) FAX **(212) 946-4010**
New York, NY 10018 **www.rga.com**
(Commercials, Feature Film Titles, Logos, Promos & TV Show Opens)

Stardust Studios East (212) 334-7300
591 Broadway, Second Fl. FAX **(212) 334-7332**
New York, NY 10012 **www.stardust.tv**

Stitch (212) 584-9700
16 W. 46th St., 11th Fl. FAX **(212) 391-8783**
(Near Fifth Ave.) **www.stitch.net**
New York, NY 10036

Super-Fi (212) 924-6536
45 Main St., Ste. 521 (Near Front St.) **www.superfi.tv**
Brooklyn, NY 11201

Synthespian Studios (413) 458-0202
96 Ballou Ln. FAX **(413) 458-5089**
Williamstown, MA 01267 **www.synthespians.net**
(Commercials, Feature Film Titles, Logos, Music Videos, Station ID Packages & TV Show Titles and Opens)

Traduvisual (646) 546-5350
FAX **(646) 895-7599**
www.traduvisual.com
(Animated Logos, Audio Description, AVI Subtitles, Closed Captioning, Domestic, DVD Subtitles, Feature Film, Foreign, Logos, Real Time Captioning, Subtitles, Titles, TV Show, Visual Description & Video Subtitles)

Ultrabland (646) 638-2830
27 W. 24th St., Ste. 302 FAX **(646) 638-2835**
New York, NY 10010 **www.ultrabland.com**
(Animated Logos, Cable ID's, Logos, Opens, TV Show & TV Network ID's and Packages)

 (800) 705-1203
Video Caption Corporation (800) 705-1204
6030 Route 82, Ste. 203 **www.vicaps.com**
Stanfordville, NY 12581
(AVI Subtitles, Closed Captioning, Domestic, DVD Subtitles, Feature Film, Foreign, NLE Direct, Subtitles, Titles, TV Network Packages, TV Show & Video Subtitles)

VITAC (724) 514-4000
101 Hillpointe Dr. FAX **(724) 514-4111**
Canonsburg, PA 15317 **www.vitac.com**

ZONA Design (212) 244-2900
350 Fifth Ave., Ste. 321 FAX **(212) 244-3101**
(Near W. 34th St.) **www.zonadesign.com**
New York, NY 10118
(Feature Film Titles, Logos, Station ID Packages, TV Network/Cable ID's and Packages & TV Show Titles and Opens)

Visual FX Artists

Bruce Bertrand (2D & 3D)
(973) 361-5817
(201) 317-5388
FAX (973) 361-2748
www.earlyfilms.net

John Cirabisi
(212) 255-6625
FAX (212) 627-8632
www.atomicimage.com

Designomotion
67 E. 11th St., Ste. 324
(Near Broadway)
New York, NY 10003
(917) 532-0738
www.designomotion.com

Keegan Martin
(818) 990-8993
www.ambitiousent.com

The Mill, New York
451 Broadway, Sixth Fl.
(Near Canal St.)
New York, NY 10013
(212) 337-3210
FAX (212) 337-3259
www.the-mill.com

Joseph Oberle (2D, 3D & Digital Matte Painting)
(646) 283-7767
(310) 740-7326
www.josephoberle.com

TellAVision
1060 20th St., Ste. 8
Santa Monica, CA 90403
(Reps for 3D Artists)
(310) 230-5303
FAX (310) 388-5550
www.tellavisionagency.com

Visual FX Supervisors & Producers

Eric Alba
(310) 947-8502
(310) 628-1249
FAX (815) 717-9846
www.ericalba.org/work
(Visual FX Designer, Consultant, Producer & Supervisor)

Glenn Allen
(646) 330-5245
www.brainstorm-digital.com

Justin Ball
(646) 330-5245
www.brainstorm-digital.com

Luke Ditommaso
(917) 522-5690
FAX (646) 349-3294
www.themolecule.net

Michael Fink
(310) 200-8418
FAX (310) 459-7525
www.utaproduction.com

Richard Friedlander
(646) 330-5245
www.brainstorm-digital.com

Lucien J. Harriot
(917) 806-5484
www.supevisorvfx.com

Chris Healer
(917) 522-5690
FAX (646) 349-3294
www.themolecule.net

David Isyomin
(212) 987-2265
(Visual FX Supervisor)

Ed Manning
(917) 532-5241
(212) 844-2233
(Visual FX Supervisor)

Gregory L. McMurry
(310) 273-6700
www.utaproduction.com

Montana Artists Agency
7715 W. Sunset Blvd., Third Fl.
Los Angeles, CA 90046
(Reps for Visual FX Supervisors)
(323) 845-4144
FAX (323) 845-4155
www.montanartists.com

Joseph Oberle
(646) 283-7767
(310) 740-7326
www.gothamdigitalfx.com
(2D, 3D, Visual FX Consultant, Visual FX Producer & Visual FX Supervisor)

Maribeth Phillips (Visual FX Producer)
(212) 691-1390
(917) 826-3399
FAX (212) 691-1390

Eliza Pelham Randall
(310) 962-9463
(323) 525-1225
FAX (866) 244-7117
www.queenofspades.com
(2D, 3D, Consultant, Producer, Visual FX Consultant & Visual FX Supervisor)

Eric J. Robertson
(917) 509-4696
FAX (866) 262-7768
(2D, 3D, Visual FX Producer & Visual FX Supervisor)

Lesley Robson-Foster (Visual FX Supervisor)
(917) 621-7202
(310) 633-3435
www.robsonfoster.com

Mark Russell
(310) 273-6700
www.unitedtalent.com

Peter Wallach
(718) 788-0335
(917) 653-3195
www.interface_arts.com

Mark Weingartner (Visual FX Supervisor)
(818) 702-1777
(818) 970-6833
FAX (818) 702-1779

Eric Wilson
(413) 528-9772
(413) 329-5522
FAX (413) 528-3974
www.eric.powderkeg.com

PICTURED: Grand Army Plaza
LOCATION: Brooklyn, NY
PHOTOGRAPHER: Sam Rohn
ALSAM : www.alsam.net
ASSOCIATION OF LOCATION SCOUTS & MANAGERS

New York 411
Qualified Listings for the New York Production Community
www.newyork411.com

Sets & Stages

One Stop Production!

International Corporation

440 West 15th Street
New York, N.Y. 10011
www.cecostudios.com

(212) 206 - 8280

- Sound Stages with Hard Cycs
- MOS Stage
- Working Kitchen
- Production Suites
- Lighting & Grip
- Location Packages

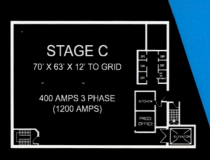

STAGE C
70' X 63' X 12' TO GRID
400 AMPS 3 PHASE
(1200 AMPS)

STAGE B
63' X 60' X 15' TO GRID
600 AMPS 3 PHASE
(1800 AMPS)

STAGE A
64' X 64' X 15' TO GRID
600 AMPS 3 PHASE
(1800 AMPS)

Stages • Locations
Production Suites

fax (212) 727 - 2144 • lighting fax (212) 675 - 6812

Sets & Stages

Ⓐ ADVERTISER SYMBOL

**Refer to the General Index for
cross-referencing items in this section.**

Backings & Scenic Artists (Local 52 NY) ... 106
Backings & Scenic Artists (Local 829 NY) .. 107
Backings & Scenic Artists 109
Set Design, Construction & Rentals 111
Set Sketchers 116
Stages............................. 117
Stages—Portable 126
Still Photography Studios & Lofts 127
TV Studios.......................... 130
Stage Chart......................... 138

Backings & Scenic Artists (Local 52 NY)

Greta Alexander	(215) 923-4248	Alicia M. Jacobson	(215) 243-1312 (215) 439-0743
Margaret Boritz	(215) 546-6251 (215) 425-5743	Heather (Cricket) McGehee	(215) 923-6044 (609) 494-2081
Jennifer M. Desnouee	(215) 423-0794	Michael Wright Stockton	(215) 592-7691
Anne Donovan	(215) 232-3782	Nancy Stroud	(215) 829-0493 (215) 829-9419
Frank P. Dukes	(215) 465-7579 (856) 371-5659	Joseph M. Urbanik	(215) 443-8818

Backings & Scenic Artists (Local 829 NY)

Peter Allburn (Backdrops)	(201) 725-7748
Roxanne T. Amico	(610) 776-7860
Rand F. Angelicola	(212) 727-7704
Artistic F/X, Inc./Don Geyra P.O. Box 248 New Rochelle, NY 10802	(914) 632-6667 FAX (914) 632-6667 www.artisticfx.net
Jane Asch	(732) 469-2835
Stuart E. Auld	(917) 676-9164
J. Lourdes Aviles	(786) 371-7491 (914) 423-2055
Campbell Baird	(212) 633-1953 (908) 387-1994
Nikolai Bartossik	(212) 396-3474 www.absolutearts.com/portfolios/n/nikart
Richard Block	(412) 241-0782
Susan A. Blume	(201) 488-6490
Avery Brandon	(212) 316-0858
Stephen Caldwell	(914) 231-9286 (917) 952-4545
Daniel Ciampa	(631) 838-3650
Mary C. Citarella	(212) 989-2812 (917) 558-4515
Tamar Cohn	(718) 783-1130 (718) 812-2347
Cathy Jo Colby-Grauer	(203) 431-6198
Jennifer Cole	(215) 407-5858
Hallie A. Coletta	(845) 634-0273
Sarah Conly	(212) 865-3294
Lorenzo Contessa	(212) 663-4124 (917) 952-4485 FAX (212) 663-4124
Jeffrey Czaja	(201) 939-8635 (201) 747-2224
James F. Donahue	(718) 783-3004
Arthur Dworin	(212) 962-3193
Cindy Anita Fain	(212) 501-9090 (917) 796-4641
Harry Feiner	(212) 362-4584 FAX (212) 362-0587 www.harryfeinertheatredesign.com
Kate Fenton	(347) 407-3876
Mark Fitzgibbons	(718) 237-0787
Amber Fleming-Shon	(917) 566-6051
Gail Fuller	(212) 929-4621
Julia Garrison	(718) 938-1594
Emily Gaunt	(201) 865-6045
Stephen Geiger	(845) 358-7630 (914) 629-8056
Karyn Gerred	(215) 592-7308
Jim Gilmartin	(212) 427-0742
Lane Glisson	(718) 788-0910
Steven P. Glisson	(718) 788-0910
Peter G. Hackman	(212) 923-6436 FAX (212) 923-6436
Matthew C. Hansel	(917) 952-5874
Tim Hawkins	(516) 428-4189 (845) 292-6942
Christopher Hebel	(646) 489-9800
Warren Jorgenson	(914) 882-7676
Janet Lee Kalas	(212) 927-4062
J. Fry Karins	(732) 988-7251
Christopher Kay	(917) 701-5654
Phillip Kennedy	(845) 753-8118 (914) 450-6626
Suzanne Kent	(718) 788-0283
Renee Kildow	(718) 383-0180
Maxine Willi Klein	(212) 222-4161
Vladimir Lagransky	(973) 956-0105
Richard Laurenzi	(718) 783-7487
Pamela Lenau	(212) 362-7093
Elizabeth Lieberman	(203) 353-9193
Lisa Lorms	(973) 744-0291 (973) 744-0291
Amy Lyons	(646) 229-1190
Peter S. Mania	(201) 935-9456
Gary Stephen May	(860) 868-1047
Michele Mayas	(646) 729-4512
Ann McCoy	(646) 249-5937
Bruce McNally	(718) 624-4884
Carla Lauren Messina	(212) 243-4461 (631) 725-5111
Elouise Meyer	(516) 333-1758 (516) 728-3964

Sal Mink	(845) 754-8460
Paul G. Moore	(845) 794-6017
William R. Murphy	(914) 332-8185 (914) 262-6334
John T. Nyomarkay	(201) 963-6629
Ellen Oshins	(212) 929-3203
Randy Parisian	(215) 968-3865 (215) 370-6142
Ivan Pazlamatchev	(845) 510-4165 (845) 642-2560
Robert Perdziola	(212) 366-1815
Jamie Lynn Petagna	(732) 566-7226 (917) 613-9796
Gerarda Pizzarello	(732) 828-8997
Anthony Polizzi	(917) 992-4208
Barbara A. Pollitt	(845) 354-4005
Mark D. Prouse	(845) 526-0965 (845) 803-2065
William B. Riley	(914) 617-8864
Jon Ringbom	(914) 528-3906 FAX (914) 528-3462
Sarah E. Rosa	(917) 692-6574
Steven Eric Rosenzweig	(518) 329-3975 (917) 733-8598
Margaret Ryan	(845) 628-7367 (914) 714-3166
Leslie Saulter-Yacuk	(845) 424-3697 (845) 406-8999
John Shimrock	(718) 788-4441
Eduardo Sicangco	(212) 989-3408 FAX (212) 929-2825
Patricia A. Sprott	(607) 746-6188 (917) 991-5443
Nell Warner Stifel	(215) 387-6096
Kris Stone	(917) 519-1011 (212) 228-4963
Edward Tadiello	(201) 790-3162 (201) 963-1983 FAX (201) 963-1983
Kjeld Tidemand-Johann	(845) 304-9666 (845) 358-6308
Maria Toteva	(646) 312-9504
Cathy K. Wassylenko	(718) 622-4508 (917) 733-2140
John Wolanczyk	(631) 757-2336 (917) 593-8900
Elena Zviaguina	(347) 251-3081 (646) 287-4669

Backings & Scenic Artists

Andrew Tedesco Studios, Inc. (212) 924-8438
www.andrewtedesco.com
(Airbrushing, Custom Backings, Decorative Painting, Faux Finishes, Murals, Patinas, Scenic Painting & Trompe L'Oeil)

Elise Bennett (212) 877-7565
(Scenic Artist) (917) 447-6511

Pamela Berkeley (413) 229-0005
(Scenic Artist) FAX (413) 229-0005

Betsy Davis Backdrops (212) 645-4197
601 W. 26th St., Ste. 308 FAX (212) 645-4197
(Near 11th Ave.) www.betsydavisbackdrops.com
New York, NY 10001

Susan Blume (201) 488-6490
www.whimsicaldesignsllc.com

Michael Boak (612) 722-5854
(Scenic Artist) (917) 868-0759

Avery Brandon (212) 316-0858
(Scenic Artist) (646) 239-3800
FAX (212) 362-4854

Ziska Childs (970) 963-3651
(Scenic Artist) (970) 948-0650
FAX (970) 963-3652
www.ziskachilds.com

Bill Clarke (212) 222-5915
(Scenic Designer) (646) 342-8690
FAX (212) 222-5915

Cobalt Studios (845) 583-7025
P.O. Box 79, 134 Royce Rd. FAX (845) 583-7025
(Near Route 17B) www.cobaltstudios.net
White Lake, NY 12786
(Backdrops, Murals, Painted Backings & Scrims)

Hallie Coletta (845) 429-1999
(845) 634-0273
www.colettadesign.com

Cyc-O-Builders/Re-Cyc Co. (212) 308-3106
Eight E. 48th St., Ste. 5A (Near Madison Ave.)
New York, NY 10017
(Custom Cycloramas)

Dazian Fabrics (201) 549-1000
124 Enterprise Ave. South (877) 232-9426
Secaucus, NJ 07094 FAX (201) 549-1055
(Custom Backings) www.dazian.com

Evolving Image (917) 680-7075
335 E. 13th St., Ste. 3 (917) 676-5959
(Near First Ave.) www.evolvingimage.com
New York, NY 10003
(Custom Backings, Faux Finishes, Murals, Scenic Painting & Trompe L'Oeil)

Fierce Release Designs Corp. (718) 946-3283
3861 Oceanview Ave. (646) 279-7454
Brooklyn, NY 11224 www.fiercerelease.com
(Airbrushing, Custom Backings, Faux Finishes, Murals, Scenic Painting & Trompe L'Oeil)

Oliphant Backdrops

Over 1500 backdrops in stock for rent
WE SHIP EVERYWHERE

www.ostudio.com
20 West 20th Street
New York, NY 10011
212-741-1233

Dianne Rossetti Finn	(212) 799-2355
(Scenic Artist)	FAX (212) 799-2355

	(718) 788-0910
Steven Glisson	(917) 445-8257
(Scenic Artist)	FAX (718) 788-0910

Jerard Studio, Inc.	(718) 852-4128
481 Van Brunt St., Ste. 11D	FAX (718) 852-2408
(Near Beard St.)	www.jerardstudio.com
Brooklyn, NY 11231	
(Custom Backings, Faux Finishes, Murals, Scenic Painting & Trompe L'Oeil)	

Janet Kalas	(212) 927-4062
(Scenic Artist)	FAX (212) 781-5231

Kraus & Sons, Inc.	(212) 620-0408
158 W. 27th St. (Near Sixth Ave.)	FAX (212) 924-4081
New York, NY 10001	www.krausbanners.com
(Custom Backings & Scrims)	

Sandro La Ferla	(212) 620-0693
(Custom and Rental Backdrops)	

	(845) 628-7367
Maggie Leigh	(914) 714-3166
(Scenic Artist)	FAX (845) 628-7367

Ⓐ **Oliphant Studio**	(212) 741-1233
	FAX (212) 366-6772
	www.ostudio.com
(Airbrushing, Backdrops, Backings, Custom, Decorative Painting, Faux Finishes, Murals, Muslin, Paint, Painted Backdrops, Patinas, Rentals, Scenic Artist & Trompe L'Oeil)	

Props for Today	(212) 244-9600
330 W. 34th St. (Near Eighth Ave.)	FAX (212) 244-1053
New York, NY 10001	www.propsfortoday.com
(Surfaces)	

	(800) 555-3772
Provost Displays	(610) 279-3970
	FAX (610) 279-3968
	www.provostdisplays.com

Really Fake Digital	(800) 761-6995
	FAX (323) 227-9033
	www.reallyfake.com
(Backdrops, Backings, Custom, Digital Imaging, Murals, Photo Backings & Printed Scrims and Fabrics)	

	(718) 420-1420
Diane Rich	(917) 734-7713
(Scenic Artist)	FAX (718) 420-1420

	(203) 708-8900
Rosco Backdrops	(800) 767-2669
52 Harbor View Ave.	FAX (203) 708-8919
Stamford, CT 06902	www.roscodigital.com
(Custom and Rental Backdrops)	

Rose Brand	(800) 223-1624
Four Emerson Ln. (Near W. 15th St.)	www.rosebrand.com
Secaucus, NJ 07094	
(Custom Backings, Muslin, Scrims & Surfaces)	

Scenic Art Studios, Inc.	(845) 534-5300
Two Mill St. (Near Route 32)	FAX (845) 534-5394
Cornwall, NY 12518	www.scenicartstudios.com
(Custom Backdrops, Faux Finishes, Murals, Scenic Painting & Trompe L'Oeil)	

	(212) 352-1384
Schmidli Backdrops	(800) 724-0171
601 W. 26th St., Ste. 1235	FAX (212) 807-7262
(Near 11th Ave.)	www.schmidli.com
New York, NY 10001	
(Custom and Rental Backdrops)	

	(212) 255-3500
Set Shop	(800) 422-7381
36 W. 20th St. (Near Sixth Ave.)	FAX (212) 229-9600
New York, NY 10011	www.setshop.com
(Custom and Rental Backdrops, Faux Finishes, Murals, Scenic Painting, Surfaces & Trompe L'Oeil)	

Showman Fabricators, Inc.	(718) 935-9899
47-22 Pearson Pl. (Near Davis Court)	FAX (718) 855-9823
Long Island, NY 11101	www.showfab.com

Surface Studio	(212) 244-6107
242 W. 30th St., 12th Fl.	FAX (212) 244-8522
(Near Seventh Ave.)	www.surfacestudio.com
New York, NY 10001	
(Hard Background Surfaces & Rentals)	

Tamara Backdrops	(773) 596-5588
	www.backdrops.com
(Custom and Rental Backings, Murals & Trompe L'Oeil)	

	(212) 740-9550
Tulnoy Lumber & Scenic Plastics	(800) 899-5833
1620 Webster Ave. (Near 173rd St.)	FAX (718) 299-8920
Bronx, NY 10457	www.tulnoylumber.com
(Faux Finishes)	

	(718) 254-0534
Turning Star, Inc.	(877) 849-3182
229 Bond St. (Near Ninth St.)	FAX (718) 254-0538
Brooklyn, NY 11217	www.turningstar.com
(Flameproofing)	

Set Design, Construction & Rentals

Acadia Scenic (201) 653-8889
130 Bay St. FAX (201) 653-4717
Jersey City, NJ 07302

Acme Stimuli Design & Production (845) 688-5107
2640 Route 214 (212) 465-1071
Lanesville, NY 12450 www.acmestimuli.com
(Custom Fabrication, Foam Sculpting, Set Construction,
Turnkey Art & Welding)

Aero Mock-Ups, Inc. (888) 662-5877
34 Burges Pl. www.aeromockups.com
Wayne, NJ 07470
(Airplane Interiors)

All Access Staging & Productions (973) 579-0067
One N. Park Dr. FAX (973) 579-0068
Newton, NJ 07860 www.allaccessinc.com
(Custom Fabrication, Grading & Ramps)

🅐 **The Art Department, LLC** (732) 431-0601
17 Bannard St., Ste. 12 FAX (732) 431-0604
Freehold, NJ 07728 www.the-art-dept.tv
(Custom Fabrication, Foam Sculpting, High-Tech Sets,
Landscapes, Ramps, Recycled Sets & Set Construction)

🅐 **Artificial Reality** (718) 707-9797
11-36 49th Ave. (Near 21st St.) (917) 992-4251
Long Island City, NY 11101 FAX (718) 707-3363
www.artificialrealityny.com

Artists@Work, Inc. (215) 203-8100
1100 Shackamaxon St. FAX (215) 203-8108
Philadelphia, PA 19125 www.artistsatwork.com

Bednark Studio (212) 365-8611
315 Third Ave. www.bednarkstudio.com
Brooklyn, NY 11215
(Custom Fabrication, Flat Rentals, Landscapes, Recycled Sets,
Set Construction, Steel Fabrication & Turnkey Art)

Canal Street Studio (212) 274-0060
472 Greenwich St. (Near Canal St.)
New York, NY 10013

Capital Scenic, Inc. (845) 429-4800
P.O. Box 382, (914) 490-2000
55 W. Railroad Ave., Ste. 3C FAX (845) 429-2138
Garnerville, NY 10923 www.capitalscenic.com

**CBS Television Design &
Set Construction** (212) 975-7612
524 W. 57th St. (Near 10th Ave.) FAX (212) 975-7530
New York, NY 10019 www.cbsscenic.com

Center Line Studios, Inc. (845) 534-7143
P.O. Box 510, Two Mill St. FAX (845) 534-4560
(Near Route 9W) www.centerlinestudios.com
Cornwall, NY 12518

STIEGELBAUER
ASSOCIATES INC

- CONSTRUCTION
- GRAPHICS
- VAC-U-FORM
- SIGNAGE
- CNC MACHINING
- STORAGE

The Scenery Solution!!

BUILDING 20 BROOKLYN NAVY YARD BROOKLYN N.Y. 11205
TEL: 718 624-0835 FAX: 718 624-0844 E MAIL STIEGASSOC@AOL.COM

Composition Workshop	(718) 855-1211
45 Summit St.	(718) 852-6698
Brooklyn, NY 11231	FAX (718) 855-5200
	www.compositionworkshop.com

Constructive Display, Inc.	(718) 237-3131
499 Van Brunt St., Ste. 5A	FAX (718) 237-4182
(Near Beard St.)	www.constructivedisplay.com
Brooklyn, NY 11231	

Creative Engineering	(718) 937-5292
5-50 54th Ave. (Near Second St.)	FAX (718) 937-1271
Long Island City, NY 11101	
	www.creativeengineeringinc.com

Custom Creations	(201) 223-5125
142 32nd St.	FAX (201) 255-0404
Union City, NJ 07087	www.custom-creations.com

Daddy-O Productions, Inc.	(718) 625-2135
	(917) 494-8474
63 Flushing Ave., Unit 119	FAX (718) 625-8579
Bldg. 280, Ste. 821 Brooklyn Navy Yard	www.daddy-o.com
(Near Cumberland St.)	
Brooklyn, NY 11205	

Damage Studios/	(917) 293-3884
Andrea Purcigliotti	(917) 293-3884
130 Seigel St., Fourth Fl. Left	FAX (917) 293-3884
(Near Humboldt St.)	www.damagestudiosnyc.com
Brooklyn, NY 11206	

Erector Sets, Inc.	(215) 289-1505
4324 Tackawanna St.	www.erectorsetsinc.com
Philadelphia, PA 19124	

Ⓐ **Flat Washer**	(917) 805-5935
	FAX (718) 383-3532
	www.flat-washer.com

Global Scenic Studios, Ltd.	(203) 334-2130
46 Brookfield Ave.	FAX (203) 333-3077
Bridgeport, CT 06610	www.globalservicesscenic.com

Ⓐ **Gotham Scenic, LLC**	(212) 741-3499
Pier 40, Second Fl. South	FAX (212) 633-6120
New York, NY 10014	www.gothamscenic.com

Jerard Studio, Inc.	(718) 852-4128
481 Van Brunt St., Ste. 11D	FAX (718) 852-2408
(Near Beard St.)	www.jerardstudio.com
Brooklyn, NY 11231	

John Creech Design & Production	(718) 237-1144
129 Van Brunt St.	FAX (718) 237-4133
Brooklyn, NY 11231	www.webuildeverything.com

KLAD	(973) 744-6352
	(201) 280-3841
56 Woodlawn Ave.	www.klad.com
Clifton, NJ 07013	

Ⓐ **Konduit Inc.**	(718) 433-1383
5-21 46th Rd.	FAX (718) 433-1714
Long Island City, NY 11101	www.konduitsetmakers.com

Largent Studios, Ltd.	(718) 254-9220
	(917) 687-5150
499 Van Brunt St., Ste. 9A	FAX (718) 254-9610
(Near Reed St.)	www.largentstudios.com
Brooklyn, NY 11231	

Architectural & Scenic Design Elements for Advertising & Entertainment

For 20 years, we've been building the most recognizable and intricate sets in the industry. From sketches to final production, we work with our clients giving the most dependable, innovative and cost-effective service in the industry.

Specializing In:

Set Design | Art Direction | Computer Renderings
Graphic Design | Set Construction & Painting | Custom Props
Model Making | Steel & Aluminum Fabrication | Platforms
Flats, Jacks, Windows & Doors | Vacuuforming

For Your Convenience:

22' Ceilings | Design Space | First Floor Access
Storage Space | Wi-Fi Access | Workshop Space

Montauk, NY Lighthouse

ESPN SET DESIGN

Yohji Yamamoto retail

artificialrealityny.com
718.707.9797   f 718.707.3363
11-36 49th Avenue
Long Island City, NY 11101

©2008 Artificial Reality

The Light House, Inc.	(800) 721-6191
	(908) 253-0011
	FAX (908) 253-3633
	www.lighthouselights.com
(Custom Fabrication, High-Tech Sets, Landscapes, Ramps, Recycled Sets, Set Construction & Steel Fabrication)	

Norm Dodge & Associates	(212) 289-1092
	www.normdodge.com

	(800) 555-3772
Ⓐ **Provost Displays**	(610) 279-3970
501 W. Washington St., Ste. 3	FAX (610) 279-3968
Norristown, PA 19401	www.provostdisplays.com

River West Scenic	(201) 432-0180
430 Communipaw Ave.	FAX (201) 432-9111
Jersey City, NJ 07304	

Rollercoaster Studios, Inc.	(973) 428-6009
A-1 Merry Ln. (Near River Rd.)	FAX (973) 428-6029
East Hanover, NJ 07936	www.rollercoasterstudios.com

Romeo Scenery Studio	(845) 940-5990
P.O. Box 1319	FAX (866) 302-4201
Hopewell Junction, NY 12533	www.scenerystudio.com

S.B.I.	(212) 629-3523
320 W. 37th St. (Near Eighth Ave.)	FAX (212) 629-3524
New York, NY 10018	www.sbiwood.com

Scenic Art Studios, Inc.	(845) 534-5300
Two Mill St. (Near Route 32)	FAX (845) 534-5394
Cornwall, NY 12518	www.scenicartstudios.com

Ⓐ **Scenic Corporation of N.Y.**	(718) 237-5333
63 Flushing Ave., Bldg. 292, Ste. 102	FAX (718) 522-0328
(Near Cumberland)	www.scenicorp.com
Brooklyn, NY 11205	

	(718) 380-6379
Set Design Services	(917) 584-0238
161-06 Jewel Ave., Ste. 3G	FAX (718) 380-6379
(Near 161st St.)	
Flushing, NY 11365	

	(212) 255-3500
Set Shop	(800) 422-7381
36 W. 20th St. (Near Sixth Ave.)	FAX (212) 229-9600
New York, NY 10011	www.setshop.com

Showman Fabricators, Inc.	(718) 935-9899
47-22 Pearson Pl. (Near Davis Court)	FAX (718) 855-9823
Long Island, NY 11101	www.showfab.com

Ⓐ Stiegelbauer Associates (718) 624-0835 Brooklyn Navy Yard, Bldg. 20 FAX **(718) 624-0844** Brooklyn, NY 11205	**Tom Carroll Scenery, Inc.** (201) 432-9047 25 Pollock Ave. FAX **(201) 434-1146** Jersey City, NJ 07305 www.tomcarrollscenery.com
Superlative Interiors (718) 786-2689 209 E. 76th St., Ste. 2A FAX **(718) 786-3109** (Near 36th Ave.) New York, NY 10021	**Union Square Group, Ltd.** (212) 979-7588 853 Broadway, Ste. 1601 FAX **(212) 979-8355** (Near E. 14th St.) www.usg-events.com New York, NY 10003

Set Design, Construction & Rentals

Set Sketchers

Above & Beyond Artists Agency (323) 464-9696
439 N. Larchmont Blvd.   FAX (323) 464-5608
Los Angeles, CA 90004 www.aboveandbeyondartists.com
(Reps for Set Sketchers)

Art Dept./Brian Kelly   (917) 288-8694
543 Kosciusko St.   www.brooklynartdept.com
(Near Stuyvesant St.)
Brooklyn, NY 11221

                                    (970) 963-3651
Ziska Childs   (970) 948-0650
(Sketch Artist)   FAX (970) 963-3652
                                www.ziskachilds.com

                                    (718) 596-5871
David Cooney   (646) 221-5488

                                    (212) 406-2282
John F. Davis   (917) 806-7524
                                FAX (212) 406-2282

                                    (212) 730-6641
Ricardo Morín   (646) 319-8666
510 W. 55th St., Ste. 309   www.ricardomorin.com
(Near 10th Ave.)
New York, NY 10019

                                    (212) 645-4857
Susan DePhillips Illustration   (917) 406-9256
10 Sheridan Square, Ste. 10B (Near Seventh Ave.)
New York, NY 10014

SILVERCUP STUDIOS

MAIN LOT
42-22 22ND STREET
LONG ISLAND CITY, NY 11101
718-906-2000 ~ FAX: 718-906-2585

STAGE	SIZE	GRID	CYC
1	78' X 157'	18'	
2	70' X 117'	18'	Y
3	49' X 117'	18'	Y
4	70' X 114'	18'	Y
5	64' X 42'	35'	Y
6	53' X 40'	18'	Y
7	57' X 40'	18'	Y
8	62' X 36'	20'	Y
9	84' X 75'	18'	Y
10	53' X 118'	18'	Y
A	88' x 156'	20'	
B	70' X 290'	20'	
X	120' X 140'	22'	

EAST LOT
34-02 STARR AVENUE
LONG ISLAND CITY, NY 11101
718-906-3000 ~ FAX: 718-906-3042

STAGE	SIZE	GRID	CYC
C	173' X 90'	28'	Y
D	210' X 80'	28'	
E	210' X 80'	28'	
F	210' X 80'	28'	
G	210' X 72'	28'	Y
H	188' X 50'	28'	Y

ALSO ON SITE:
SILVERTRUCKS LIGHTING
LOCATION LIGHTING & GRIP EQUIPMENT
WWW.SILVERTRUCKSLIGHTING.COM

SILVERCUP@SILVERCUPSTUDIOS.COM ~ WWW.SILVERCUPSTUDIOS.COM

CITY STAGE

New York's Favorite Full-Service Production Facility

3 STATE-OF-THE-ART SOUND STAGES

Stage 1- 46x56x16
Stage 3- 47x52x13
Stage 5- 47x52x13 (with CYC)

All equipped with:
- Sound-proof client rooms • Production offices • Dressing rooms
- Lighting and grip • Expendables • Video • Full catering

"We also do Entertainment related Events and Parties, short and long term office rentals."

See our 2 page spread!

Call Brian Coles- 212 627-3400
435 W. 19th St. NY 10011
Take a Virtual Tour @ www.citystage.com

Stages

The 1896 (718) 451-6531
592 Johnson Ave. FAX (718) 381-2893
Brooklyn, NY 11237 www.the1896.com

Abingdon Theatre Arts Complex (212) 868-2055
312 W. 36th St., First Fl. FAX (212) 868-2056
(Near Eighth Ave.) www.abingdontheatre.org
New York, NY 10018
Contact: Stephen Squibb

(917) 414-5489
American Movie Co. (212) 952-1800
50 Broadway, Ste. 1206 FAX (212) 952-0152
New York, NY 10004 www.americanmovieco.com

(212) 531-5300
Apollo Theater Foundation (212) 531-5312
253 W. 125th St. (Near Eighth Ave.) FAX (212) 749-2743
New York, NY 10027 www.apollotheater.com
Contact: James Moody

(646) 432-5000
Bravo Studios (800) 441-4876
40 W. 27th St., Second Fl. FAX (646) 432-5013
(Near Sixth Ave.) www.newyorksoundstage.com
New York, NY 10001
Contacts: Tim Donovan & Ryan Eugene Kelley

(718) 349-9146
Broadway Stages (718) 786-5428
203 Meserole Ave. (Near Jewel St.) FAX (718) 349-9148
Brooklyn, NY 11222 www.broadway-stages.com
Contact: Dawn Dianda

(718) 456-7570
Brooklyn Fire Proof (718) 675-9334
120 Ingraham St. FAX (718) 456-7394
Brooklyn, NY 11237 www.brooklynfireproof.com

C&C Studios (212) 967-6427
(917) 295-6920
20 W. 37th St., Fifth Fl. FAX (718) 504-5487
New York, NY 10018 www.candcstudios.tv

Ⓐ CECO International (212) 206-8280
440 W. 15th St. (Near 10th Ave.) FAX (212) 727-2144
New York, NY 10011 www.cecostudios.com
Contact: Jody Baran

Chelsea Broadcast Services, Inc. (212) 727-1234
221 W. 26th St. (Near Seventh Ave.) FAX (212) 255-6644
New York, NY 10001 www.allmobilevideo.com
Contact: Eric Duke

(212) 268-0028
Ⓐ Cine Magic Stages (917) 805-2177
210 Elizabeth St., Basement FAX (212) 268-0363
New York, NY 10012 www.cinemagicstages.com

Cinema World Studios (718) 389-9800
220 Dupont St. FAX (718) 389-9897
(Near McGuinness Blvd.) www.cinemaworldstudios.com
Brooklyn, NY 11222
Contact: Mark Oppenheimer

Ⓐ City Stage (212) 627-3400
435 W. 19th St. (Near Ninth Ave.) FAX (212) 633-1228
New York, NY 10011 www.citystage.com
Contact: Brian Coles

Connecticut Film Center Norwalk (203) 348-2500
345 Ely Ave. FAX (203) 348-5200
Norwalk, CT 06854 www.ctfilmcenter.com

Context Studios (718) 384-8300
One N. 12th St., Second Fl., Box B7 www.contextnyc.com
(Near Kent Ave.)
Brooklyn, NY 11211
Contact: Ed Montgomery

CITY

3 STATE OF-THE-ART SOUND STAGES

All stages equipped with:
Luxurious sound proof elevated client rooms
Production offices with high speed internet access
Closed circuit televisions
Dressing rooms with make-up stations
Kitchen/prep areas

FACILITY:

- Lighting, grip and dolly equipment
- Expendables
- Express passenger elevator
- Silent air conditioning
- Fax and copy
- 3pin electrical system
- Flexible rates and start time
- 2 Wall Cyc
- Stage manager provided at no additional cost
- Additional dressing rooms available
- Located in the heart of Chelsea

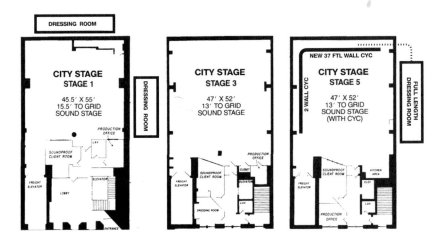

Contact: Brian Coles - Director of Operations

435 WEST 19TH STREET, NEW YORK, NY 10011

S T A G E

"We've shot all of VH1's Midnight Minutes at City Stage. The folks there have been great. The atmosphere is low-key and relaxed, but completely professional. When we go to City Stage, it dosen't feel like work."

Bill Flanagan, VP/Editorial Director, VH1

"Citystage is our home. We have been shooting weekly our Original work there for years. Brian and his crew understand the meaning of customer service."

Alyson Perlongo, Producer, Origional Media

"For Fifteen years City Stage has been my first choice. it's a great space."

Donna Watts, MTV Networks

"Their facility is high end and well maintained. A perfect choice with all the celeb talent we shoot regularly for our promo's. They run a highly professional crew and outfit."

Damien Vena, Line Producer, HBO Creative Services

Take a Virtual Tour @ www.citystage.com

212 627-3400 FAX 212 633-1228

Dakota Studio	(212) 691-2197
78 Fifth Ave., Eighth Fl.	FAX (212) 691-2239
(Near W. 14th St.)	www.dakotastudio.com
New York, NY 10011	
Contact: Matthew Sess	

Digital Arts	(212) 460-9600
130 W. 29th St., Eighth Fl.	www.digital-arts.net
New York, NY 10001	

	(917) 492-1757
Digital Laundry	(914) 414-2185
173 E. 120th St.	www.digitallaundry.net
New York, NY 10035	
Contacts: George Rivera, Robert "Bruce" Martin & Robin Rivera	

East Hampton Studios	(631) 537-0313
P.O. Box 583	FAX (631) 702-2159
Wainscott, NY 11975	
www.theneweasthamptonstudios.com	

	(718) 492-7400
East of Hollywood NY	(718) 439-3930
Two 52nd St.	www.eastofhollywoodny.com
Brooklyn, NY 11232	

Ⓐ Globus Studios	(212) 243-1008
44 W. 24th St. (Near Sixth Ave.)	www.globus.cc
New York, NY 10010	
Contact: Ron Globus	

Gramercy Broadcast Center	(212) 614-4088
230 Park Avenue South (Near 19th St.)	FAX (212) 614-4198
New York, NY 10003	www.gramercybroadcast.com
Contact: Tony Minecola	

	(212) 512-7800
HBO Studio Productions	(212) 512-7912
120A E. 23rd St. (Near Park Ave.)	FAX (212) 512-7788
New York, NY 10010	

Hill Studio & Scenic	(856) 423-8910
35 W. Broad St.	FAX (856) 224-0224
Paulsboro, NJ 08066	
Contact: John Burzichelli	

	(212) 463-0061
Horvath & Associates Studios, Ltd.	(212) 989-7570
335 W. 12th St. (Near Greenwich St.)	FAX (212) 989-7570
New York, NY 10012	www.horvathstudios.com
Contact: Simon Hooper	

STAGE 1	· 16,320 SF 120' × 136'	9,000 AMPS 35' TO GRID
STAGE 2	· 16,320 SF 120' × 136'	9,000 AMPS 35' TO GRID
STAGE 3	· 27,200 SF 200' × 136'	12,000 AMPS 45' TO GRID
STAGE 4	· 16,320 SF 120' × 136'	9,000 AMPS 45' TO GRID
STAGE 5	· 21,760 SF 160' × 136'	12,000 AMPS 45' TO GRID
BUILDING 7	· 5,000 SF 100' × 50'	
BUILDING 8	· 10,000 SF 100' × 100'	
BUILDING 9	· 10,000 SF 100' × 100'	

- Five State-of-the-Art Sound Stages Totaling 100,000 sf
- Full Service Facility for Start-to-Finish Production
- 25,000 sf of Mill Shop Space
- 185,000 sf of Other Support Space: Production Offices, Dressing Rooms, Green Rooms, Hair and Makeup, Wardrobe, Commissary, etc.
- State-of-the-Art 100 seat HD Screening Room
- Silent HVAC
- 28' × 20' Elephant Doors Interconnecting Stages
- 24 Hour Security
- 15 Acre Private Enclave
- On Site Parking

STAGE 1   **2-WALL CYCLORAMA**
100'L × 60'W × 28'H

STEINER
STUDIOS

15 Washington Avenue
Brooklyn Navy Yard
New York 11205

(718) 858-1600
www.steinerstudios.com

FEATURE FILMS   TELEVISION   PHOTOGRAPHY   COMMERCIALS

Illusion Studio (516) 294-1038
P.O. Box 21   FAX (516) 747-4139
Mineola, NY 11501
Contact: Joe Matina

Industria Super Studio (212) 366-1114
775 Washington St. (Near W. 12th St.)   FAX (212) 691-3934
New York, NY 10014   www.industrianyc.com
Contact: Paige Hanson

Integrated Studios (212) 334-4000
449 Washington St.   FAX (212) 334-6969
New York, NY 10013   www.integratedstudios.com

(212) 967-1029
Jewel Street Studios   (917) 751-0358
94 Jewel St., Ground Fl.   FAX (718) 554-7494
Brooklyn, NY 11222   www.jewelstreetstudios.com

Kaufman Astoria Studios (718) 392-5600
34-12 36th St. (Near 34th Ave.)   FAX (718) 706-7733
Astoria, NY 11106   www.kaufmanastoria.com
Contact: Peter Romano

(917) 533-6022
Ⓐ **LIC Film Studios**   (718) 606-2560
10-43 47th Ave., Ste. 1   www.filmstudiorenting.com
Long Island City, NY 11101

The Light House, Inc. (800) 721-6191
221 Evans Way, Ste. C   FAX (908) 253-3633
Branchburg, NJ 08876   www.lighthouselights.com

Ⓐ **MediaMix** (201) 262-3700
Four Pearl Court   FAX (201) 262-3798
Allendale, NJ 07401   www.mediamixstudios.com
Contact: Joe Vargas

Murray Hill Studios, Inc. (212) 889-4200
248 E. 35th St. (Near Second Ave.)   FAX (212) 889-9413
New York, NY 10016   www.murrayhillstudios.com

NBC New York Stages (212) 664-2013
30 Rockefeller Plaza   FAX (212) 664-5056
(Near W. 49th St.)   www.nbcny.filmmakersdestination.com
New York, NY 10112
Contact: Mary Gallagher

NEP Studios (212) 401-4971
FAX (212) 679-7964
www.nepinc.com

Next Millennium Productions, Ltd. (917) 237-1661
31 Howard St., Ste. 5A   FAX (917) 237-1663
New York, NY 10013   www.nmpfilms.com

Studio Suite 15 at Pal T.V.

PENTHOUSE STUDIO • LIGHTING AND GRIP
COURTEOUS SERVICE • REASONABLE RATES
CONVENIENT MIDTOWN LOCATION

#1# 212-741-9111
Fax # 212-741-7772

#236 W. 27th St., 15th Fl., New York, NY 10001
www.StudioSuite15.com

Full-Service Sound Stages, Television Studios, and Post Production Facilities

Studio A

Kitchen Set

Studio B/Talk Show Set

Green Screen Cove

Conference Room Set

Control Room

Edit 1

Edit 2

Audio Booth w/ Pro Tools

Studio A
- 58' x 55' x 16' to grid
- 152 - 2.4K dimmers
- 50 - 6K dimmers
- ETC Express 48/96 console
- 3-wall hard cyc
- Drive-in access
- Ultimatte cove

Studio B
- 35' x 35' x 16' to grid
- 50 - 2.4K dimmers
- ETC Express 24/48 console
- 3-wall hard cyc
- Drive-in access
- Ultimatte cove

- 800 amps 3-phase per studio
- Complete lighting and grip packages
- Kitchen and news/talk show sets
- Make-up, green room & production offices

- Full control room with live web streaming
- Final Cut HD/Pro Tools with VO booth
- Extremely quiet with plenty of free parking
- Convenient to mass transit

Feature films, broadcast television, TV commercials, corporate or music videos, whatever you produce, MediaMix can help you shoot it, edit it, and deliver it – on time and on budget. And, yes, we're in the zone. Just 20 miles and 30 minutes from Rockefeller Center.

MediaMix knows that your clients are asking you to do more for less. We can help either by offering you the best pricing available on individual facilities or by partnering with you to provide one package price for everything that you would usually outsource.

Location production • Studio production • Teleprompting • Jimmy Jib
Avid & Final Cut editing • After Effects • DVD authoring • CD-ROM authoring
CD and DVD replication

MediaMix does it all. Call us when planning your next project to see what we can do for you.

MediaMix
www.MediaMixStudios.com
4 Pearl Court, Allendale, New Jersey 07401
(888) 5-MediaMix   (888-563-3426)

Call us and we will beat the best price you can find for comparable facilities by at least 10%

Crew and out-of-pocket expenses excluded.
One coupon per client. Expires August 31, 2010.

NFL Films One NFL Plaza Mount Laurel, NJ 08054 Contact: Rick Angeli	**(856) 222-5675** **(877) 222-3517** FAX **(856) 866-4848** **www.nflfilms.com**

Ⓐ **PAL Stage** 236 W. 27th St., 15th Fl. PH New York, NY 10001	**(212) 741-9111** **(212) 333-5359** FAX **(212) 741-7772** **www.paleast.com**

Parlay Film Productions, LLC   **(201) 459-9044**
    (973) 819-1979
930 Newark Ave., Sixth Fl.   FAX **(201) 459-9044**
(Near Newark Ave.)   **www.parlayfilms.com/studio**
Jersey City, NJ 07306
Contacts: Sam Nalband, John Welsh III & Cameron Zonfrilli

Pier 59 Studios   **(212) 691-5959**
Chelsea Piers, #59, Second Fl.   FAX **(212) 691-9022**
New York, NY 10011   **www.pier59studios.com**
Contact: Ana Schechter

Post Office Media   **(212) 302-4488**
1560 Broadway, Ste. 514   FAX **(212) 302-4849**
New York, NY 10036   **www.postofficemedia.com**

PowerHouse 27   **(585) 730-6064**
    (585) 415-3202
27 Saint Bridget's Dr.   FAX **(585) 730-6065**
(Near St. Paul St.)   **www.powerhouse27.com**
Rochester, NY 14605
Contact: Carol Cieslinski

Pro Image Studios   **(631) 234-4310**
3200 Expressway Dr. South   FAX **(631) 234-8256**
(Near Corporate Pl.)   **www.proimagestudios.com**
Islandia, NY 11749
Contact: Harry Oates

Ⓐ **Production Central** 873 Broadway, Ste. 205 (Near E. 18th St.) New York, NY 10003	**(212) 631-0435** FAX **(212) 631-0436** **www.prodcentral.com**

Rollercoaster Studios, Inc.   **(973) 428-6009**
A-1 Merry Ln. (Near River Rd.)   FAX **(973) 428-6029**
East Hanover, NJ 07936   **www.rollercoasterstudios.com**
Contact: Scott Schauder

Silver Screen Studios   **(212) 336-6300**
W. 23rd St. & The Hudson River   FAX **(212) 336-6808**
New York, NY 10011   **www.chelseapiers.com**
Contact: Paul Rindone

Ⓐ **Silvercup Studios** 42-22 22nd St. (Near Queens Plaza South) Long Island City, NY 11101 Contact: Lisa Sanchez	**(718) 906-2000** FAX **(718) 906-2585** **www.silvercupstudios.com**

Ⓐ **Silvercup Studios East** 34-02 Starr Ave. (Near Van Dam St.) Long Island City, NY 11101 Contact: Lisa Sanchez	**(718) 906-3000** FAX **(718) 906-2146** **www.silvercupstudios.com**

LIC FILM STUDIOS
10-43 47th Avenue, Suite One
Long Island City, New York 11101
(718) 606-2560
www.filmstudiorenting.com

Gary Fisher Dawson   (917) 533-6022

Eliminating your barriers...
Illuminating your business...

An affordable alternative venue for the professional and student filmmaker.

Sonalysts' Studios — (800) 526-8091
215 Parkway North — (860) 326-3672
Waterford, CT 06385 — FAX (860) 326-3748
Contact: Fred Litty — www.sonalystsmedia.com

Stage 18 — (203) 852-8185
18 Leonard St. — FAX (203) 838-3126
Norwalk, CT 06850 — www.vfstv.com
Contact: Dale Cihi

Ⓐ Steiner Studios — (718) 858-1600
15 Washington Ave. — FAX (718) 858-1690
Brooklyn Navy Yard, NY 11205 — www.steinerstudios.com

Stonestreet Studios — (212) 229-0020
48 W. 21st St., Eighth Fl. — FAX (800) 701-9530
(Near Sixth Ave.) — www.stonestreetstudios.com
New York, NY 10010
Contact: Joanna Shattuck

Studios At Linden Oaks — (585) 264-1780
170B Linden Oaks Dr. — (585) 261-2847
(Near Route 490) — FAX (585) 264-1786
Rochester, NY 14625 — www.studiosatlindenoaks.com
Contact: David Lippa

Theater for the New City — (212) 254-1109
155 First Ave. (Near 10th St.) — FAX (212) 979-6570
New York, NY 10003 — www.theaterforthenewcity.net
Contact: Crystal Field

Tribeca Performing Arts Center — (212) 220-1459
199 Chambers St., Ste. S 110C — FAX (212) 732-2482
(Near West St.) — www.tribecapac.org
New York, NY 10007

TriStar Studios — (973) 575-5400 / (914) 907-8766
490 Route 46 East — FAX (973) 575-6708
Fairfield, NJ 07004 — www.tristarstudios.com

Utopia Soundstage — (845) 679-7600
293 Tinker St. — www.utopiasoundstage.com
Woodstock, NY 12498

WMHT Production Services — (518) 880-3400
Four Global View — FAX (518) 880-3409
Troy, NY 12180 — www.wmht.org
Contact: David Wennberg

STEELDECK®

STAGING SYSTEMS

- Car Ramps
- Drum Risers
- Seating Tiers
- Raked Stages
- Camera Risers
- Catwalks/Runways
- Lighting Towers
- Press Platforms

- Strong
- Simple
- Durable
- Versatile
- Economical
- Sales
- Rentals
- Installations

877-60-STAGE steeldeckny.com

Stages—Portable

Ⓐ All Access Staging & Productions (973) 579-0067
One N. Park Dr. FAX **(973) 579-0068**
Newton, NJ 07860 www.allaccessinc.com
(Disabled Persons' Lifts and Ramps, Platforms, Ramps, Risers, Rolling Risers & Step Units)

Bernhard-Link Theatrical LLC **(201) 727-9440**
 FAX **(201) 727-9455**
 www.bltprod.com
(Flats, Platforms, Portable Stages & Step Units)

Circuit Lighting, Inc. **(732) 968-9533**
299 Route 22 East FAX **(732) 968-9231**
Green Brook, NJ 08812 www.circuitlighting.com

Main Attractions **(732) 225-3500**
 FAX **(732) 225-2110**
 www.mainattractions.com

 (718) 389-8727
Moore P.A. Hire Inc. **(917) 747-5372**
21 Box St. (Near Manhattan Ave.) www.moorepahire.com
Brooklyn, NY 11222
(Platforms, Portable Stages, Risers & Rolling Risers)

New York Ladder & **(800) 229-3352**
Scaffold Corporation **(914) 423-2960**
122 Woodworth Ave. FAX **(914) 476-4140**
Yonkers, NY 10702 www.newyorkladder.com
(Scaffolding & Risers)

RI, Inc./Seating Solutions **(631) 845-0449**
60 Austin Blvd. (Near Old Willets Path) FAX **(631) 845-0470**
Commack, NY 11725 www.sitonthis.com
(Bleachers, Portable Stages & Risers)

See Factor Industry **(718) 784-4200**
37-11 30th St. (Near 37th Ave.) FAX **(718) 784-0617**
Long Island City, NY 11101 www.seefactor.com

Showman Fabricators, Inc. **(718) 935-9899**
47-22 Pearson Pl. (Near Davis Court) FAX **(718) 855-9823**
Long Island, NY 11101 www.showfab.com

 (718) 599-3700
Ⓐ Steeldeck N.Y. Inc. **(877) 607-8243**
143-145 Banker St. FAX **(718) 599-3800**
(Near Norman Ave.) www.steeldeckny.com
Brooklyn, NY 11222
(Platforms, Portable Stages & Risers)

JEWEL STREET STUDIOS
THE EASIEST, MOST PRIVATE ACCESS OF ANY STUDIO IN NEW YORK.

- 3200sf (49×68)
- 17' ceilings
- 27' Wide Cyc with Flying Ceiling
- Ground Floor
- Drive-in Access
- In the Greenpoint Stage Area
- Private Parking
- Floor Drains for water FX
- Expendables, grip, electric
- Stylish Lounge, Green Room
- The Best Staff

212.967.1029
94 Jewel Street
Brooklyn NY 11222
INFO@JEWELSTREETSTUDIOS.COM

WWW.JEWELSTREETSTUDIOS.COM

Still Photography Studios & Lofts

2StopsBrighter (212) 868-5555
(212) 868-5556
231 W. 29th St., Ste. 1007 www.2stopsbrighter.com
New York, NY 10001

The Altman Building (212) 741-3400
135 W. 18th St. (Near Seventh Ave.) FAX **(212) 741-3424**
New York, NY 10011 www.altmanbldg.com

American Movie Co. (917) 414-5489
(212) 952-1800
50 Broadway, Ste. 1206 FAX **(212) 952-0152**
New York, NY 10010 www.americanmovieco.com

Atelier 34 Studio (212) 532-7727
34 W. 28th St., Sixth Fl. FAX **(212) 481-8549**
New York, NY 10001 www.atelier34studio.com

Atlantic Motion Pictures (212) 924-6170
162 W. 21st St., Fourth Fl. FAX **(212) 989-8736**
New York, NY 10011 www.atlanticmotion.com

B-hive Stages (212) 925-3778
38 Greene St., Fifth Fl. FAX **(212) 925-3799**
New York, NY 10013 www.bhivestages.com

Bathhouse Studios (212) 388-1111
540 E. 11th St. (Near Avenue B) FAX **(212) 388-1713**
New York, NY 10009 www.bathhousestudios.com
Contacts: Sarah Garrity & David Gipson

(718) 349-9146
Broadway Stages (718) 786-5428
203 Meserole Ave. (Near Jewel St.) FAX **(718) 349-9148**
Brooklyn, NY 11222 www.broadway-stages.com
Contact: Dawn Dianda

Brooklyn Studios (718) 392-1007
211 Meserole Ave. FAX **(718) 392-1008**
Brooklyn, NY 11222 www.brooklynstudios.net

Camart Studio (212) 691-8840
Contact: John Carriglio FAX **(212) 691-8841**
www.camart.com

Capsule Studio (212) 777-8027
873 Broadway, Ste. 204 www.capsulestudio.com
(Near E. 18th St.)
New York, NY 10003

Composition Workshop (718) 855-1211
(718) 852-6698
45 Summit St. FAX **(718) 855-5200**
Brooklyn, NY 11231 www.compositionworkshop.com

Crosseyed Studio (212) 929-7550
162 Charles St., Second Fl. FAX **(212) 929-4215**
(Near Washington St.)
New York, NY 10014
Contact: Abby Gennet

The Culinary Loft LLC (212) 431-7425
515 Broadway, Ste. 5A FAX **(212) 431-7816**
(Near Broome St.)
New York, NY 10012
Contact: Corinne Colen

Dakota Studio (212) 691-2197
78 Fifth Ave., Eighth Fl. FAX **(212) 691-2239**
(Near W. 14th St.) www.dakotastudio.com
New York, NY 10011

Digital Arts (212) 460-9600
130 W. 29th St., Eighth Fl. www.digital-arts.net
New York, NY 10001

Divine Studio (212) 387-9655
21 E. Fourth St., Ste. 605 FAX **(212) 387-7944**
(Near Lafayette St.) www.divinestudios.com
New York, NY 10003

Eagles Nest Studio (212) 736-6221
259 W. 30th St., 13th Fl. FAX **(212) 736-0084**
(Near Eighth Ave.) www.eaglesnestnyc.com
New York, NY 10001

Ex Eggs, Inc. (212) 234-7110
www.exeggs.com

Gary's Loft, Inc. (917) 837-2420
28 W. 36th St., PH FAX **(212) 656-1940**
New York, NY 10018 www.garysloft.com
Contact: Gary Handel

(212) 564-4084
🅐 Go Studios (917) 584-5900
245 W. 29th St., Seventh Fl. FAX **(212) 868-3057**
New York, NY 10001 www.go-studios.com

Still Photography Studios & Lofts 127

Home Studios, Inc. (212) 475-4663
873 Broadway, Ste. 301 (973) 865-4577
(Near 18th St.) FAX (212) 475-2446
New York, NY 10003 www.homestudiosinc.com

Ⓐ Jewel Street Studios (212) 967-1029
94 Jewel St., Ground Fl. (917) 751-0358
Brooklyn, NY 11222 FAX (718) 554-7494
www.jewelstreetstudios.com

Metropolitan Pavilion (212) 463-0071
125 W. 18th St. (Near Seventh Ave.) (212) 463-0200
New York, NY 10011 FAX (212) 463-0946
www.metropolitanevents.com

Michelson Studio (212) 633-1111
163 Bank St. (Near Washington St.) FAX (212) 633-2833
New York, NY 10014 www.michelsonstudio.com

Novo Arts, Inc. (212) 674-3093
57 E. 11th St., 10th Fl. FAX (212) 979-5381
(Near Broadway) www.novoarts.com
New York, NY 10003

Parlay Film Productions, LLC (201) 459-9044
930 Newark Ave., Sixth Fl. (973) 819-1979
(Near Newark Ave.) FAX (201) 459-9044
Jersey City, NJ 07306 www.parlayfilms.com/studio
Contacts: Sam Nalband, John Welsh III & Cameron Zonfrilli

PhotoOp Studios (631) 537-0033
P.O. Box 1107, One Tradesmans Path (917) 293-3884
Bridgehampton, NY 11932 FAX (631) 537-0033
www.photoopstudios.com

Picture Ray Studio (212) 929-6370
245 W. 18th St., Ground Fl. FAX (212) 243-2998
(Near Seventh Ave.) www.pictureraystudio.com
New York, NY 10011

Primus Studio (212) 966-3803
64 Wooster St., Ste. 3E FAX (212) 966-3803
(Near Broome St.) www.primusnyc.com
New York, NY 10012

**The Prop Company -
Kaplan & Associates** (212) 691-7767
111 W. 19th St., Eighth Fl. FAX (212) 727-3055
(Near Sixth Ave.)
New York, NY 10011

Puck Studios (212) 274-8900
295 Lafayette St., Ste. 705 FAX (212) 226-6835
(Near Houston St.)
New York, NY 10012

Purified Loft (718) 522-2354
135 Plymouth St., Loft 204 FAX (718) 522-2354
Brooklyn, NY 11201 www.purifiedloft.com

Ramscale Productions Inc. (212) 206-6580
55 Bethune St., PH 13th Fl. FAX (212) 206-6683
(Near Washington St.) www.ramscale.com
New York, NY 10014

Shop Studios (212) 245-6154
442 W. 49th St. (Near Ninth Ave.) (212) 582-1650
New York, NY 10019 FAX (212) 582-3112
www.shopstudios.com
Contacts: Jacques Rosas & Eric Steding

SoHo Loft 620 (212) 260-4300
620 Broadway, Ste. 2R FAX (212) 260-0403
(Near E. Houston St.) www.soholoft620.com
New York, NY 10012
Contact: Nancy Ney

SoHoSoleil Studio Loft Locations (212) 431-8824
136 Grand St., Loft 5WF (917) 449-8353
(Near Crosby St.) FAX (212) 925-1086
New York, NY 10013 www.sohosoleil.com

Studio 147 (212) 620-7883
147 W. 15th St. (Near Seventh Ave.) (212) 620-7877
New York, NY 10011 FAX (212) 620-7903
www.studio147.net

Studio Eickholt (646) 613-9610
93 St. Marks Pl., Third Fl. FAX (646) 613-9610
New York, NY 10013 studioeickholt.tripod.com

Taz Studios (212) 254-0669
873 Broadway, Ste. 605 (201) 939-0370
(Near E. 18th St.) www.tazstudio.com
New York, NY 10003
Contact: William Neumann

Whitehall Media Productions, LLC (908) 232-2182
102 Elm St., PH (Near Broad St.) FAX (908) 232-1995
Westfield, NJ 07090 www.whitehallstudio.com
Contact: Nadine Raphael

GoStudios

245 west 29th st nyc
www.go-studios.com
212 564 4084

Make a scene at Murray Hill's newest studio.

Our ready-to-shoot studios and one-of-a-kind control room are now available for rent!

- 2 Studios
- 2 In-House Sets (entertainment and news)
- Audio Post-Production Room
- Avid Edit Bays

- Available after 3 PM Monday–Friday and all day Saturday and Sunday
- SD only
- Ideal for Corporate and Industrial Shoots
- Satellite Media Tours

truTV STUDIOS

For more information, please contact Rob Pumo at 212.973.3209 or Robert.Pumo@turner.com or Margie Whitfield at 212.973.2811 or Margie.Whitfield@turner.com. Or see the article on our state-of-the-art control room at www.trutvstudios.com.

TV Studios

Bravo Studios (646) 432-5000 / (800) 441-4876
40 W. 27th St., Second Fl.   FAX (646) 432-5013
(Near Sixth Ave.)   www.bravofilm.com
New York, NY 10001
Contacts: Tim Donovan & Ryan Eugene Kelley

Brooklyn College Television Center   (718) 951-5585
2900 Bedford Ave. (Near Campus Rd.)   www.bctvr.org
Brooklyn, NY 11210
Contact: George Casturani

Brooklyn Studios   (718) 392-1007
211 Meserole Ave.   FAX (718) 392-1008
Brooklyn, NY 11222   www.brooklynstudios.net

Ⓐ **C&C Studios**   (212) 967-6427 / (917) 295-6920
20 W. 37th St., Fifth Fl.   FAX (718) 504-5487
New York, NY 10018   www.candcstudios.tv

Ⓐ **Chelsea Broadcast Services, Inc.**   (212) 727-1234
221 W. 26th St. (Near Seventh Ave.)   FAX (212) 255-6644
New York, NY 10001   www.allmobilevideo.com
Contact: Eric Duke

Context Studios   (718) 384-8300
One N. 12th St., Second Fl., Box B7   www.contextnyc.com
(Near Kent Ave.)
Brooklyn, NY 11211
Contact: Ed Montgomery

Kaufman Astoria Studios   (718) 392-5600
34-12 36th St. (Near 34th Ave.)   FAX (718) 706-7733
Astoria, NY 11106   www.kaufmanastoria.com

Magno Sound & Video   (212) 302-2505
729 Seventh Ave.   FAX (212) 819-1282
(Near W. 48th St.)   www.magnosound.com
New York, NY 10019

Ⓐ **Manhattan Center Studios**   (212) 695-6600
311 W. 34th St. (Near Eighth Ave.)   FAX (212) 564-1092
New York, NY 10001   www.mcstudios.com
Contact: Daphne Walter

MediaMix   (201) 262-3700
Four Pearl Court   FAX (201) 262-3798
Allendale, NJ 07401   www.mediamixstudios.com
Contact: Joe Vargas

Ⓐ **Metropolis Studios, Inc.**   (212) 722-5500
1443 Park Ave. (Near 106th St.)   FAX (212) 722-7341
New York, NY 10029   www.metropolis-studios.com
Contact: Gray Winslow

Murray Hill Studios, Inc.   (212) 889-4200
248 E. 35th St. (Near Second Ave.)   FAX (212) 889-9413
New York, NY 10016   www.murrayhillstudios.com

Chelsea Television Studios
AMV / Unitel

Multi-Camera Sound Stages

Large Audience Facilities

Satellite and Fiber for Live Transmission

Chelsea Television Studios
Studio A - 98' x 89' x 19'
Studio B - 80' x 65' x 19'
Studio C - 52' x 42' x 14.5'
Studio D - 27' x 17' x 12'

AMV / Unitel
Studio 53 - 104' x 47' x 19'
Studio 57A - 101' x 47' x 19'

Contact: Eric Duke / Paula Pevzner

www.allmobilevideo.com

AMV — ALL MOBILE VIDEO

CHELSEA TELEVISION STUDIOS
221 W 26th St.
New York, NY 10001
(p) 212.727.1234
(f) 212.255.6644

AMV / UNITEL
515 W. 57th St.
New York, NY 10019
(p) 212.265.3600
(f) 212.581.8368

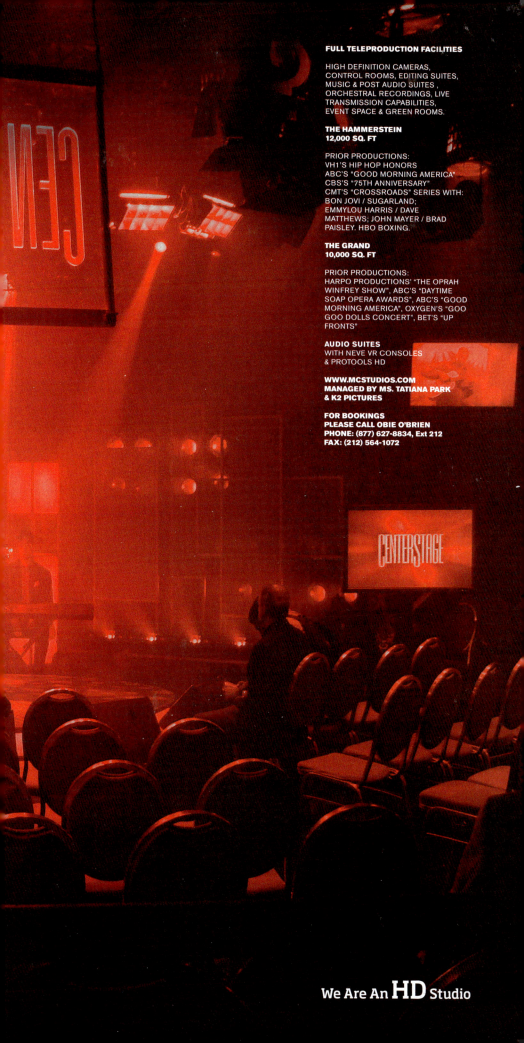

FULL TELEPRODUCTION FACILITIES

HIGH DEFINITION CAMERAS, CONTROL ROOMS, EDITING SUITES, MUSIC & POST AUDIO SUITES , ORCHESTRAL RECORDINGS, LIVE TRANSMISSION CAPABILITIES, EVENT SPACE & GREEN ROOMS.

THE HAMMERSTEIN
12,000 SQ. FT

PRIOR PRODUCTIONS:
VH1'S HIP HOP HONORS
ABC'S "GOOD MORNING AMERICA"
CBS'S "75TH ANNIVERSARY"
CMT'S "CROSSROADS" SERIES WITH:
BON JOVI / SUGARLAND;
EMMYLOU HARRIS / DAVE MATTHEWS; JOHN MAYER / BRAD PAISLEY. HBO BOXING.

THE GRAND
10,000 SQ. FT

PRIOR PRODUCTIONS:
HARPO PRODUCTIONS' "THE OPRAH WINFREY SHOW", ABC'S "DAYTIME SOAP OPERA AWARDS", ABC'S "GOOD MORNING AMERICA", OXYGEN'S "GOO GOO DOLLS CONCERT", BET'S "UP FRONTS"

AUDIO SUITES
WITH NEVE VR CONSOLES & PROTOOLS HD

WWW.MCSTUDIOS.COM
MANAGED BY MS. TATIANA PARK & K2 PICTURES

FOR BOOKINGS
PLEASE CALL OBIE O'BRIEN
PHONE: (877) 627-8834, Ext 212
FAX: (212) 564-1072

We Are An **HD** Studio

NBC New York Stages (212) 664-2013
30 Rockefeller Plaza   FAX (212) 664-5056
(Near W. 49th St.) www.nbcny.filmmakersdestination.com
New York, NY 10112
Contact: Mary Gallagher

NEP Studios (212) 401-4971
FAX (212) 679-7964
www.nepinc.com

New Jersey Network (609) 777-5273
Media Productions (609) 777-5283
25 S. Stockton St.   FAX (609) 292-6360
Trenton, NJ 08608   www.njn.net
Contact: Fred Litwinowicz

Ⓐ Next Millennium Productions, Ltd. (917) 237-1661
31 Howard St., Ste. 5A   FAX (917) 237-1663
New York, NY 10013   www.nmpfilms.com

(856) 222-5675
NFL Films (877) 222-3517
One NFL Plaza   FAX (856) 866-4848
Mount Laurel, NJ 08054   www.nflfilms.com
Contact: Rick Angeli

Primalux Video (212) 206-1402
30 W. 26th St, Seventh Fl.   FAX (212) 206-1826
(Near Sixth Ave.)   www.primalux.com
New York, NY 10010
Contact: Judy Cashman

REUTERS/CHIP EAST

NEWSWORTHY
IN THE HEART OF TIMES SQUARE

Breaking news meets a state-of-the-art studio at Thomson Reuters Headquarters. Call today, and make sure your next production grabs headlines.

For information, call +1 646 223 6620 or email TVRSSNY@reuters.com.

© Thomson Reuters 2009. All rights reserved.

Pro Image Studios (631) 234-4310	**Silvercup Studios** (718) 906-2000
3200 Expressway Dr. South FAX (631) 234-8256	42-22 22nd St. FAX (718) 906-2585
(Near Corporate Pl.) www.proimagestudios.com	(Near Queens Plaza South) www.silvercupstudios.com
Islandia, NY 11749	Long Island City, NY 11101
Contact: Harry Oates	Contact: Lisa Sanchez
Production Central (212) 631-0435	**Silvercup Studios East** (718) 906-3000
873 Broadway, Ste. 205 FAX (212) 631-0436	34-02 Starr Ave. (Near Van Dam St.) FAX (718) 906-2146
(Near E. 18th St.) www.prodcentral.com	Long Island City, NY 11101 www.silvercupstudios.com
New York, NY 10003	Contact: Lisa Sanchez
Ⓐ Reuters Television International (646) 223-6620	(201) 836-5427
Three Times Square, Fourth Fl. FAX (646) 223-6629	**Solar Plexus, Inc.** (201) 281-5973
(Near Broadway) www.reuters.com	135 Oakdene Ave. FAX (201) 836-5427
New York, NY 10036	Teaneck, NJ 07666 www.solarplexusprods.com

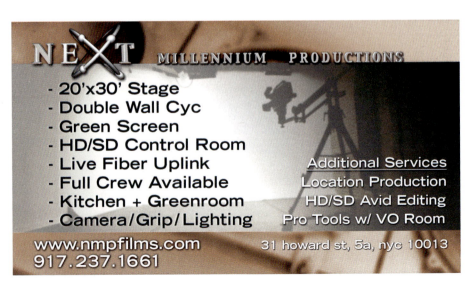

NEXT MILLENNIUM PRODUCTIONS

- 20'x30' Stage
- Double Wall Cyc
- Green Screen
- HD/SD Control Room
- Live Fiber Uplink
- Full Crew Available
- Kitchen + Greenroom
- Camera/Grip/Lighting

Additional Services
Location Production
HD/SD Avid Editing
Pro Tools w/ VO Room

www.nmpfilms.com
917.237.1661

31 howard st, 5a, nyc 10013

Location. Location. Location.

Only Manhattan offers you unbeatable access to the kind of talent and equipment a demanding project like yours requires. Metropolis Studios has everything you need to make world-class television in the heart of New York City: all-digital equipment, multiple HD formats, generous production and office space, plus easy access to public transport and three international airports.

We're everything you need, right where you need it.

- 7,000 sq. ft. column-free stage; fully-equipped, audience-rated
- All-digital component equipment
- 3:4 and 16:9 aspect ratios
- All-digital AES audio
- Solid State Logic Aysis Air++
- ETC Expression 3 lighting console
- Comprehensive lighting package
- Component/composite VTRs
- HD conversion available
- 10,000 sq. ft. office & support space
- Upper Manhattan location
- Free on-site indoor parking

Metropolis Studios
1443 Park Avenue, New York, NY 10029
212-722-5500 fax 212-722-7341
www.metropolis-studios.com

Steiner Studios (718) 858-1600
15 Washington Ave.   FAX (718) 858-1690
Brooklyn Navy Yard, NY 11205   www.steinerstudios.com

(631) 650-0057
Studio 57 (631) 766-0777
140 Hoffman Ln. (Near Space Court)   FAX (631) 650-0010
Islandia, NY 11749   www.studio57online.com

Trinity Television & New Media   (212) 602-0767
74 Trinity Pl., Fourth Fl.   FAX (212) 602-0770
(Near Rector St.)   www.trinitytvandnewmedia.com
New York, NY 10006
Contact: William Jarrett

TriStar Studios   (973) 575-6971
490 Route 46 East   FAX (973) 575-6708
Fairfield, NJ 07004   www.tristarstudios.com

(212) 973-2811
 **truTV Studios**   (212) 973-3209
600 Third Ave., 19th Fl. (Near 39th St.)   FAX (212) 973-8925
New York, NY 10016   www.trutvstudios.com

TV Studios

Stage Chart: 30,400—6,250 Sq. Ft.

STAGE NAME	PHONE	STAGE NUMBER	LENGTH	WIDTH	HEIGHT	AREA SQUARE FEET	SOUND STAGE	INSERT	POWER/AMPS	CYCLORAMAS
Connecticut Film Center--Norwalk	203-348-2500	1	160	190	24	30400	●		4000AC	
Steiner Studios	718-858-1600	3	135	200	45	27000	●	●	12000A	
Kaufman Astoria Studios	718-392-5600	E	217	120	40	26040	●		12000AC	
Steiner Studios	718-858-1600	5	135	160	45	22000	●	●	12000A	
East Hampton Studios	631-537-6300	1	166	110	56	18260	●		2000AC	
Silvercup Studios	718-906-2000	B	290	70	20	18000	●		2400AC	
Silvercup Studios	718-906-2000	X	140	120	22	16800	●		2800AC	
Silvercup Studios East	718-906-3000	D	210	80	28	16800	●		2400AC	
Silvercup Studios East	718-906-3000	E	210	80	28	16800	●		3600AC	
Silvercup Studios East	718-906-3000	F	210	80	28	16800	●		3600AC	
Steiner Studios	718-858-1600	1	135	120	35	16200	●	●	9000A	2 Wall
Steiner Studios	718-858-1600	2	135	120	35	16200	●	●	9000A	
Steiner Studios	718-858-1600	4	135	120	45	16200	●	●	9000A	
Silvercup Studios East	718-906-3000	C	173	90	28	15500	●		3600AC	2 Wall Hard
Silvercup Studios East	718-906-3000	G	210	72	28	15120	●		3600AC	2 Wall Hard
Sonalysts Studios	800-526-8091	15	150	100	40	15000	●		4800AC	
Silver Screen Studios	212-336-6300	D	120	120	22	14400	●		1200AC	
Silvercup Studios	718-906-2000	1	157	78	18	12300	●		2400AC	
Kaufman Astoria Studios	718-392-5600	G	134	90	31	12060	●		6000AC	
Kaufman Astoria Studios	718-392-5600	H	134	90	31	12060	●		6000AC	
Silvercup Studios	718-906-2000	A	156	87	20	11000	●		1200AC	
Cinema World Studios	718-389-9800	B	50	200	38	10000	●		6000AC	
NBC New York Studios	212-664-2013	8H	131	76	24	10000	●			●
Steiner Studios	718-858-1600	8	100	100	28	10000		●	200A	
Steiner Studios	718-858-1600	9	100	100	28	10000		●	200A	
Silvercup Studios East	718-906-3000	H	188	50	28	9400	●		3600AC	2 Wall Hard
Broadway Stages	718-786-5428	B	144	62	30	8928	●		3000AC	2 Wall Hard
Chelsea Television Stages	212-727-1234	A	98	89	19	8722	●		1800AC	
Studio 57	631-650-0057	57	130	65	16	8450	●		2000AC	1 Wall Hard
Silvercup Studios	718-906-2000	2	117	70	18	8400	●		2400AC	2 Wall Hard
Broadway Stages	718-786-5428	D	160	50	24	8000	●		1200AC	
Kaufman Astoria Studios	718-392-5600	J	180	80	21	8000	●		9000AC	
Silvercup Studios	718-906-2000	4	118	65	18	7700	●		2400AC	2 Wall Hard
Cinema World Studios	718-389-9800	1	120	63	20	7560	●		6000AC	2 Wall Hard w/Cov
NEP Studio	212-401-4971	52	75	100	17	7500			6100AC	
Brooklyn Fire Proof	718-456-7570	A	99	73	16.5	7227	●		1200AC	35'
Sonalysts Studios	800-752-1946	7	100	70	35	7000	●		1800AC	2 Wall Hard
Silver Screen Studios	212-336-6300	E	115	60	22	6900	●		600AC	
Silver Screen Studios	212-336-6300	F	115	60	22	6900	●		1000AC	
Silvercup Studios	718-906-2000	10	118	53	18	6500	●		1200AC	2 Wall Hard
Metropolis Studios, Inc.	212-722-5500	1	85	75	30	6375	●		21000AC/DC	
Silvercup Studios	718-906-2000	9	84	75	18	6250	●		2400AC	2 Wall Hard

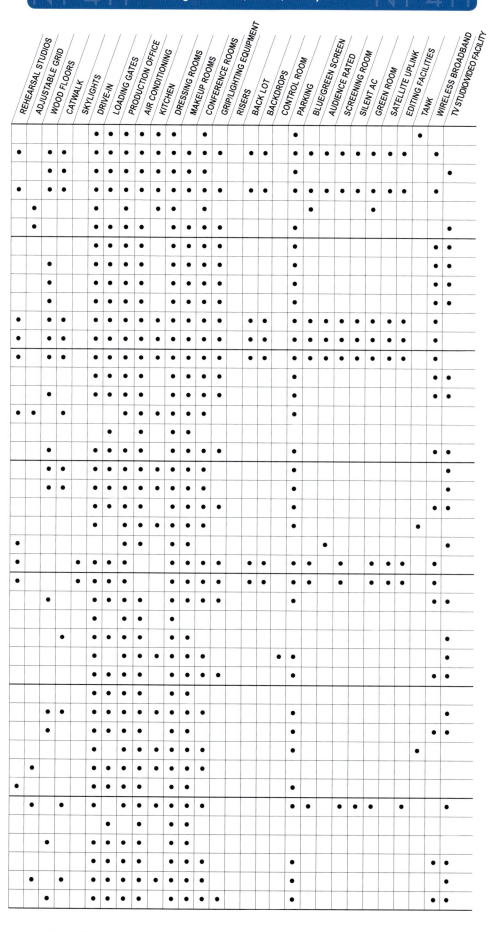

Stage Chart: 30,400—6,250 Sq. Ft.

Stage Chart: 6,000—3,000 Sq. Ft.

STAGE NAME	PHONE	STAGE NUMBER	LENGTH	WIDTH	HEIGHT	AREA SQUARE FEET	SOUND STAGE	INSERT	POWER/AMPS	CYCLORAMAS
Hill Studio & Scenic	856-423-8910	1	100	60	25	6000			7200AC	2 Wall Hard
Illusion Studio	516-294-1038	1	100	60	20	6000			600AC	2 Wall Hard
NEP Studio	212-401-4971	5th Ave	100	60	20	6000			1500AC	
Pier 59 Studios	212-691-5959	C	80	72	35	5760	●		1800AC	
Silvercup Studios	718-906-2000	3	117	49	18	5700	●		2400AC	2 Wall Hard
Broadway Stages	718-786-5428	C	98	23	30	5500	●		1200AC	
NBC New York Studios	212-664-2013	6B	126	50	16	5480	●			●
NBC New York Studios	212-664-2013	6A	109	45	17	5425	●			●
Horvath & Associates Studios Ltd.	212-463-0061	2	72	75	17	5400	●		1500AC	2 Wall Hard
New Jersey Network Media Prods.	609-777-5273	D	81	65	26	5265	●		160AC	1 Wall Soft
Chelsea Television Stages	212-727-1234	B	80	65	19	5200	●		1200AC	
Boylan Studios	212-924-7550	A	84	60	14	5000			200AC	
Broadway Stages	718-786-5428	1	100	50	23	5000			1200AC	
Sonalysts Studios	800-526-8091	5	100	50	35	5000	●		1200AC	2 Wall Hard
Steiner Studios	718-858-1600	7	100	50	24	5000		●	200A	
NEP Studio	212-401-4971	Penn A	72	68	18	4896			5800AC	
NEP Studio	212-401-4971	Penn B	72	68	18	4896			5800AC	
NBC New York Studios	212-664-2013	8G	96	50	17	4875	●			●
NFL Films	856-222-5675		60	80	24	4800	●	●		2 Wall Hard
Pier 59 Studios	212-691-5959	10	66	70	15	4620			400AC	2 Wall Hard
CECO International	212-206-8280	C	70	63	12	4410			1200AC	
NBC New York Studios	212-664-2013	3K	68	64	13	4170	●			●
CECO International	212-206-8280	A	64	64	15	4096	●		1800AC	2 Wall Hard
Boylan Studios	212-924-7550	B	66	60	14	4000			200AC	
Kaufman Astoria Studios	718-392-5600	F	75	54	21	4000	●		3000AC	
NEP Studio	212-401-4971	54	65	60	20	4000			5400AC	1 Wall Hard
CECO International	212-206-8280	B	63	60	15	3780	●		1800AC	2 Wall Hard
The Light House, Inc.	800-721-6191	B	75	50	18	3750	●		1200AC	2 Wall Hard
NBC New York Studios	212-664-2013	3B	78	48	17	3744	●			●
Pro Image Studios	631-234-4310	A	72	52	14	3744	●	●	4800AC	1 Wall Hard
Tristar Studios	973-565-5400		71	52	17	3692	●	●	500 AC	
Rollercoaster Studios, Inc.	973-428-6009	B	60	60	12	3600	●		1200AC	2 Wall Hard
WMHT Production Services	518-880-3400	A	60	60	16	3600			900AC	Hard Corner, Pro C
Industria Super Studio	212-366-1114	6	58	50	11	3555			400AC	3 Wall Hard
NEP Studio	212-401-4971	47	72	47	13.5	3384			2400AC	2 Wall Hard
NBC New York Studios	212-664-2013	3C	77	47	15	3310	●		1600AC	●
Pier 59 Studios	212-691-5959	7	65	50	16	3250			600AC	
Cine Magic Stages	212-268-0028		67	47	15	3200	●		1800AC	2 Wall Hard
Stage 18	800-568-1064	1	60	53	18	3180	●		1800	3 Wall Hard
Pier 59 Studios	212-691-5959	1	70	45	16	3150			600AC	3 Wall Hard
Industria Super Studio	212-366-1114	5	66	42	14	3009			250AC	
Camart Studio	212-691-8840	1	60	50	12	3000			200AC	

REHEARSAL STUDIOS	ADJUSTABLE GRID	WOOD FLOORS	CATWALK	SKYLIGHTS	DRIVE-IN	LOADING GATES	PRODUCTION OFFICE	AIR CONDITIONING	KITCHEN	DRESSING ROOMS	MAKEUP ROOMS	CONFERENCE ROOMS	GRIP/LIGHTING EQUIPMENT	RISERS	BACK LOT	BACKDROPS	CONTROL ROOM	PARKING	BLUE/GREEN SCREEN	AUDIENCE RATED	SCREENING ROOM	SILENT AC	GREEN ROOM	SATELLITE UPLINK	EDITING FACILITIES	TANK	WIRELESS BROADBAND	TV STUDIO/VIDEO FACILITY
			•		•	•	•	•	•	•	•							•										
					•			•	•	•	•																	
	•					•	•	•	•	•	•	•																
		•																										
					•	•	•	•		•	•	•						•									•	•
		•					•	•		•	•																	
•							•	•		•	•									•								•
																				•								
					•	•	•	•	•	•	•	•						•										
	•					•		•	•	•	•	•		•				•	•	•			•	•				•
					•	•	•	•		•	•																	•
•				•	•	•		•		•	•	•						•										
•		•				•	•	•																				
	•		•		•		•	•	•	•	•	•						•	•		•	•	•			•		•
•				•	•	•	•			•	•	•	•		•	•		•	•		•		•	•	•		•	
	•					•	•	•		•	•	•																
	•					•	•	•		•	•	•																
•							•	•		•	•									•								•
					•		•			•	•																	•
					•	•		•																				
		•			•	•			•	•	•	•																
•							•	•		•	•																	•
		•			•	•	•	•	•	•	•	•																
•				•	•	•		•		•	•	•						•										
		•	•		•			•	•	•	•	•						•										•
	•				•	•	•	•	•	•	•	•																
		•			•	•	•	•	•	•	•	•																
					•	•	•	•	•	•	•	•						•										
•							•	•		•	•									•								•
					•		•	•	•	•	•	•	•	•		•	•	•	•				•	•	•		•	•
					•	•	•	•	•	•	•	•						•	•									
						•	•	•	•	•	•	•						•										
					•			•		•		•																
	•				•	•		•		•	•	•																
•							•	•		•	•													•				•
								•																				
						•	•	•		•	•	•	•						•								•	
			•		•	•	•	•	•	•	•	•	•		•	•	•	•	•		•	•	•		•	•	•	•
					•				•																			
				•				•		•		•																
		•						•	•	•	•																	

Stage Chart: 2,800—1,320 Sq. Ft.

STAGE NAME	PHONE	STAGE NUMBER	LENGTH	WIDTH	HEIGHT	AREA SQUARE FEET	SOUND STAGE	INSERT	POWER/AMPS	CYCLORAMAS
Theater for the New City	212-254-1109	1	70	40	23	2800				
Pier 59 Studios	212-691-5959	2	60	45	16	2700			600AC	3 Wall Hard
Pier 59 Studios	212-691-5959	4	60	45	16	2700			600AC	2 Wall Hard
Pier 59 Studios	212-691-5959	5	60	45	16	2700			600AC	1 Wall Hard
Pier 59 Studios	212-691-5959	6	60	45	18	2700			600AC	
Pier 59 Studios	212-691-5959	9	45	60	15	2700			200AC	1 Wall Hard
Silvercup Studios	718-906-2000	5	64	42	36	2700	●		2400AC	1 Wall Hard
Theater for the New City	212-254-1109	2	60	45	18	2700				
Theater for the New City	212-254-1109	4	60	45	18	2700				
NEP Studio	212-401-4971	33	57	47	13.5	2647			900AC	2 Wall Hard
City Stage	212-627-3400	1	55	45	15	2475	●		1200AC	
City Stage	212-627-3400	3	52	47	13	2444	●		900AC	
City Stage	212-627-3400	5	52	47	13	2444	●		900AC	1 Wall Hard
Brooklyn College Television Center	718-951-5585	B	60	40	14	2400				2 Wall Hard Curved
Pro Image Studios	631-234-4310	B	60	40	14	2400	●		2000AC	
Rollercoaster Studios, Inc.	973-428-6009	A	60	40	18	2400	●		1200AC	3 Wall Hard
Tristar Studios	973-565-5400		60	40	17	2400				
WMHT Production Services	518-880-3400	B	60	40	16	2400			900AC	3 Wall Soft
Silvercup Studios	718-906-2000	7	57	40	18	2300	●		1800AC	2 Wall Hard
Studios at Linden Oaks	585-264-1780	1	65	35	16	2275	●	●	1400AC	2 Wall Hard
HBO Studio Productions, Inc.	212-512-7800	A	47	48	16	2256	●		200AC	3 Wall Hard
Silvercup Studios	718-906-2000	8	62	36	20	2200	●		1200AC	2 Wall Hard
Context Studios	718-384-8300	1	44	48	15	2112		●	450AC	1 Wall Hard
Silvercup Studios	718-906-2000	6	53	40	18	2100	●		1800AC	2 Wall Hard
Industria Super Studio	212-366-1114	3	47	45	14	2092			150AC	2 Wall Hard
New Jersey Network Media Prods.	609-777-5273	A	45	45	17	2025	●		400AC	1 Wall Soft
Production Central	212-631-0435	1	35	45	14	2000	●	●	600AC	
Media Mix	201-262-3700	1	48	40	17	1920	●	●	800AC	3 Wall Hard
Tribeca Performing Arts Center	212-220-1459	2	30	39.5	18.5	1891	●		60AC	1 Wall Soft
Apollo Theater Foundation	212-531-5300		45	40	19	1800	●		600AC	2 Wall Hard
Manhattan Center Studios	212-695-6600	2	60	30	15	1800			250AC	
Industria Super Studio	212-366-1114	9	44	40	14	1760			150AC	3 Wall Cove Hard
Industria Super Studio	212-366-1114	1	46	38	11	1748			100AC	3 Wall Hard w/Cove
Globus Studio	212-243-1008	A	50	32	15	1600	●	●	1200AC	3 Wall Hard
Chelsea Television Stages	212-727-1234	C	42	38	14	1596		●	600AC	
Industria Super Studio	212-366-1114	4	52	25	14	1552			100AC	
Industria Super Studio	212-366-1114	2	47	25	11	1500			100AC	3 Wall Hard
Pier 59 Studios	212-691-5959	3	50	30	16	1500			600AC	Half Egg Hard
Tribeca Performing Arts Center	212-220-1459	1	30	46	19	1380	●		200AC	1 Wall Hard Curved
Dakota Studio	212-691-2197	1	55	25	12	1375	●		300AC	2 Wall Hard
Industria Super Studio	212-366-1114	8	40	34	14	1360			100AC	3 Wall Cove Hard
Boylan Studios	212-924-7550	C	66	20	14	1320			200AC	

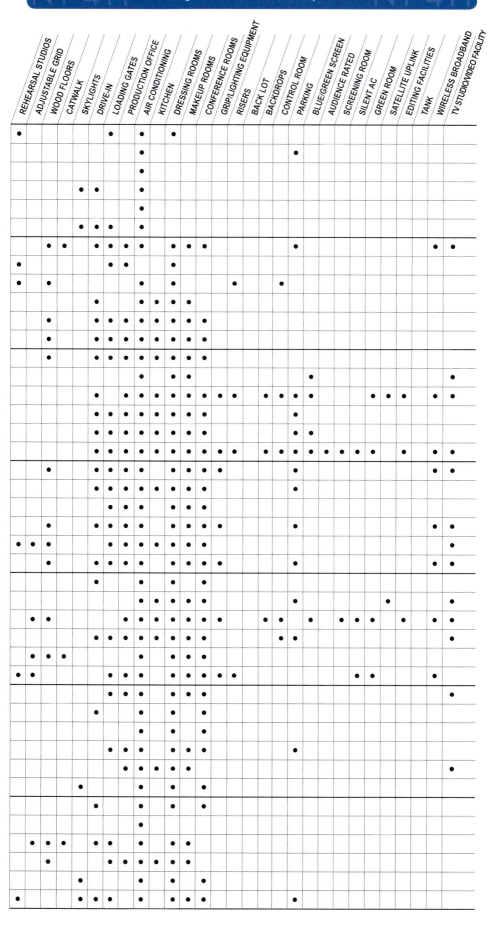

Stage Chart: 2,800—1,320 Sq. Ft.

Stage Chart: 1,200—156 Sq. Ft.

STAGE NAME	PHONE	STAGE NUMBER	LENGTH	WIDTH	HEIGHT	AREA SQUARE FEET	SOUND STAGE	INSERT	POWER/AMPS	CYCLORAMAS
NEP Studio	212-401-4971	37	38	31	11	1200			900AC	2 Wall Hard
Rollercoaster Studios, Inc.	973-428-6009	D	30	40	18	1200	●		1200AC	
Apollo Theater Foundation	212-531-5300	Main	37	29	28	1073			800AC	2 Wall Hard
Trinity Television and New Media	212-602-0794	Main	24	42	11	1008	●	●	1000Ac	3 Wall Soft
Primalux Video	212-206-1402	1	37	26	11	962	●		300AC	1 Wall Soft
Bravo Stages	212-679-9779	1	32	30	14	960	●		600AC	1 Wall Hard
Brooklyn Fire Proof	718-456-7570	B	40	24	16.5	960	●		800AC	
Murray Hill Studios, Inc.	212-889-4200	A	23	40	14	920				2 Wall Hard
Reuters Television	646-223-6620	1	30	30	15	900	●			1 Wall Hard
Rollercoaster Studios, Inc.	973-428-6009	C	30	30	12	900			1200AC	1 Wall Hard
Magno Sound & Video	212-302-2505	3A	37	24	11	888	●			
Production Central	212-631-0435	2	25	35	16	875	●	●	300AC	
TruTV Studios	212-973-2811	B	35	24	8.6	840		●	100AC	
Gramercy Broadcast Center	212-614-4088	3	38	19	12	722	●		400AC	3 Wall Soft
Context Studios	718-384-8300	2	24	30	13	720	●	●	300AC	
Sonalysts Studios	800-526-8091	4	28	24	12	672		●	100AC	
Industria Super Studio	212-366-1114	7	33	19	14	627			100AC	3 Wall Curved Hard
Brooklyn Fire Proof	718-456-7570	C	25	25	16.5	625	●		800AC	
Theater for the New City	212-254-1109	3	30	20	11	600				
Sonalysts Studios	800-526-8091	3	30	19	12	570		●	100AC	
Stonestreet Studios	212-229-0020	B	30	17	11	510	●		300AC	
Stonestreet Studios	212-229-0020	A	30	16	11	480	●		440AC	
Globus Studio	212-243-1008	B	25	16	15	400	●		500AC	2 Wall Hard
Abingdon Theatre Company	212-868-2055	Havoc	17	20	14	340			1400AC	
Murray Hill Studios, Inc.	212-889-4200	B	23	33	8	322				
Chelsea Television Stages	212-727-1234	D	20	16	14	320		●	600AC	2 Wall Hard
Magno Sound & Video	212-302-2505	3B	24	12	11	288	●			
Gramercy Broadcast Center	212-614-4088	4	17	15	16	255	●		400AC	3 Wall Soft
Abingdon Theatre Company	212-868-2055	Strelsin	15	13	12	156			400AC	

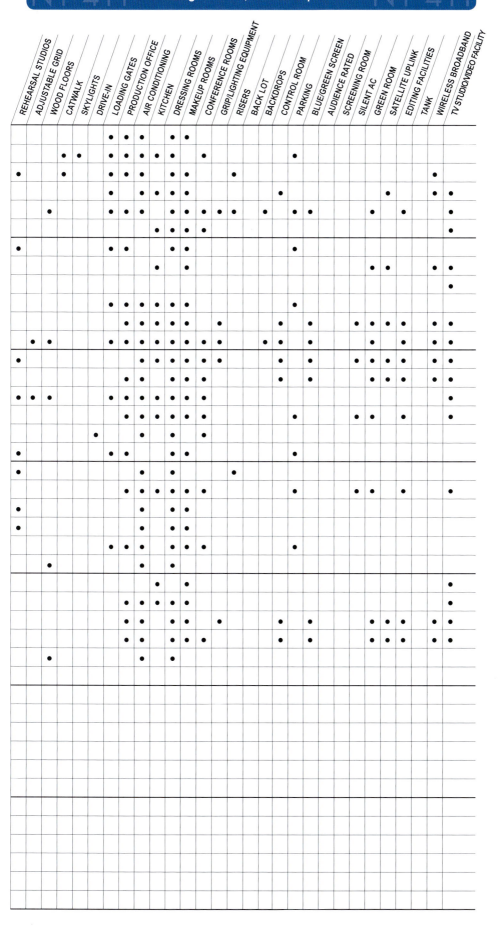

Stage Chart: 1,200—156 Sq. Ft.

NOTES:

Don't put success on hold because you missed an A-List call.
Let BuyerZone answer your needs.

Join the millions who have already saved time and money on purchases like **Phone Systems, Copiers** and more by taking advantage of BuyerZone's FREE, no obligation services including:

- Price quotes from multiple suppliers
- Purchasing advice: Buyer's guides, pricing articles, tips and more
- Supplier ratings/comparisons

It's fast, it's free and you're in control.

REQUEST FREE QUOTES NOW!
Call (866) 623-5564 or visit BuyerZoneBusiness.com

NOTES:

Location Services & Equipment

PICTURED:
Penthouse Apartment
LOCATION:
Brooklyn, NY
PHOTOGRAPHER:
Sam Rohn
ALSAM : www.alsam.net
ASSOCIATION OF
LOCATION SCOUTS & MANAGERS

New York 411
*Qualified Listings for the
New York Production Community*
www.newyork411.com

YOUR NEXT STAY IN NYC IS ON US

An exclusive portfolio of residences & homes in the most prestigious addresses in North America available for

Scouting & Production

Book one of our private homes and get a free week stay at the

Jumeirah Essex House

- Essex House, NYC
- Westhampton, NY
- Greenwich, CT
- New Rochelle, NY
- Eastchester, NY

TO BOOK CALL 888-522-1099 OR EMAIL
LB@LAURENBERGERCOLLECTION.COM
WWW.LAURENBERGERCOLLECTION.COM

Location Services & Equipment

Ⓐ ADVERTISER SYMBOL

Refer to the General Index for
cross-referencing items in this section.

Air Charters	150
Air Freight & Couriers	151
Airlines	153
Airports	154
Bus Charters	155
Car Rentals	156
Cargo & Passenger Vans	157
Caterers	159
Communications Equipment	163
Counsulates General	165
Crating & Packing	166
Customs Brokers & Carnets	166
Film Commissions—North America	167
Film Commissions—International	176
Hotels & Short-Term Housing	177
Limousine & Car Services	181
Location Libraries, Management & Scouts	183
Locations	187
Motorhomes & Portable Dressing Rooms	192
Moving, Storage & Transportation	196
Parking Services	198
Portable Restrooms	198
Production Services—North America	200
Production Services—International	201
Security & Bodyguards	202
Travel Agencies	204
Water Trucks	205
Weather	206

HAMPTONS LOCATIONS®
PRIME LOCATIONS • SCOUTING • PRODUCTION

HAMPTONS • NORTH FORK • FLORIDA • POCONOS

NANCY GRIGOR
TEL: 631-267-1001 • FAX: 631-267-2462
TOLL FREE: 888-711-1001
P.O. BOX 372 • AMAGANSETT, NY 111930

www.hamptonslocations.com

Air Charters

Air Royale International
230 Park Ave., 10th Fl.
New York, NY 10169
(212) 983-6800
(800) 776-9253
FAX (212) 983-6861
www.airroyale.com

Atlantic Aviation Services
233 Industrial Ave.
Teterboro, NJ 07608
(201) 288-1740
FAX (201) 288-1753
www.atlanticaviation.com

Blue Star Jets
One Dag Hammarskjold Plaza
885 Second Ave., 16th Fl.
New York, NY 10017
(212) 446-9037
(866) 538-8463
FAX (212) 446-9061
www.bluestarjets.com

East Hampton Airlines
90 Industrial Rd. (Near Main St.)
Wainscott, NY 11975
(631) 537-3737
(800) 359-8654
FAX (631) 537-3755

Eastway Aviation
Long Island MacArthur Airport
101 Hering Dr.
Ronkonkoma, NY 11779
(631) 737-9911
(800) 927-0209
FAX (631) 737-4926
www.eastwayav.com

Executive Fliteways, Inc.
One Clark Dr. (Near S. Second St.)
Ronkonkoma, NY 11779
(631) 588-5454
(800) 533-3363
FAX (631) 588-5527
www.fly-efi.com

Helicopter Flight Services
(212) 355-0801
(888) 933-5969
www.heliny.com

Jet Aviation Business Jets
112 Charles A. Lindbergh Dr.
Teterboro, NJ 07608
(201) 288-8400
(800) 736-8538
FAX (201) 462-4136
www.jetaviation.com

Jet Productions
7240 Hayvenhurst Ave., Ste. 148
Van Nuys, CA 91406
(818) 781-4742
(877) 895-1790
FAX (818) 781-4743
www.jetproductions.net

Jets.com
75 Rockefeller Plaza, Ste. 1816
New York, NY 10019
(800) 370-7719
www.jets.com

Meridian Teterboro
485 Industrial Ave.
Teterboro, NJ 07608
(201) 288-5040
(800) 882-2333
FAX (201) 288-1229
www.meridianteb.com

Miami Air International
5000 NW 36th St., Ste. 307
Miami, FL 33122
(305) 876-3600
(305) 876-3670
FAX (305) 871-4222
www.miamiair.com

Northeastern Aviation Corporation
8200 Republic Airport
(Near Broad Hollow Rd.)
Farmingdale, NY 11735
(631) 756-4600
(800) 234-0046
FAX (631) 756-0698
www.northeasternaviation.com

OneSky Jets
P.O. Box 217
Manchester, NH 03105
(603) 663-1017
(866) 663-7591
FAX (603) 218-6238
www.onesky.com

Panorama Flight Service, Inc.
67 Tower Rd.
Westchester County Airport
(Near Purchase St.)
White Plains, NY 10604
(914) 328-9800
(914) 424-0951
FAX (914) 328-1055
www.panoramaflightservice.com

Rock-It Air Charter, Inc.
LA International Airport
6201 W. Imperial Hwy
Los Angeles, CA 90045
(310) 568-3781
FAX (310) 568-3785
www.rockitair.com

Summit Aviation
7144 Republic Airport
(Near Broad Hollow Rd.)
East Farmingdale, NY 11735
(631) 756-2545
(800) 255-4625
FAX (631) 756-0809
www.summitjet.com

Worldwide Jet
14555 N. Scottsdale Rd., Ste. 280
Scottsdale, AZ 85254
(856) 825-4540
www.worldwidejet.com

...WHEN IT'S HOT !!!!!

BLUEBIRD EXPRESS OFFERS EXPEDITED SOLUTIONS FOR...

- FILM DAILIES FOR LOCAL OR LOCATION SHOOTS
- SAME DAY RUSHES, NEXT FLIGHT OUT, OVERNIGHT (DOMESTIC OR INTERNATIONAL)
- CENSOR BOARD APPROVAL PRINTS
- DO NOT XRAY ACCCEPTANCE WITH AIRLINES
- WHEN YOU ARE WORKING LATE & THE SHIPPING DEPARTMENT IS CLOSED
- SECURITY ISSUES (PIRATING)- CODE NAMES – SPLIT SHIPMENTS
- REPLACEMENT REELS
- CAMERA / LIGHTING EQUIPMENT/ PROPS
- PROCESSING PAPERWORK (COMMERCAIL INVOICES / CARNETS)
- FILM FESTIVAL COORDINATION
- WHEN A DEADLINE IS APPROACHING ...IT'S CRUNCH TIME

BLUEBIRD EXPRESS DELIVERS...

✓ PERSONAL, IMMEDIATE, RESPONSE ...NO RECORDED MESSAGE
✓ FLEXIBILITY... AIR OR GROUND - PICKUP AND DELIVER ANYWHERE
✓ AVAILABILITY 24 / 7/ 365
✓ AUTOMATIC CONFIRMATION OF SHIPMENT STATUS
✓ ONLINE TRACK/TRACE, ORDER ENTRY, CUSTOM SHIPMENT MANAGEMENT REPORTS
✓ IMMEDIATE INVOICING FOR INTERNAL CUSTOMER BILL BACKS

"YOU'LL CALL BECAUSE YOU KNOW WE CAN DELIVER"

JFK: 516 255-0800 - YYZ: 905 672-2922 – LAX: 310 645-0300 - LHR: 011 44 208 848-0800

E-mail: customerservice@bluebird-courier.com

Air Freight & Couriers

A to Z Couriers (212) 253-6500
106 Ridge St. (Near Delancey St.) FAX (212) 253-6565
New York, NY 10002 www.atozcouriers.com

(718) 349-7343
Advanced Express, Inc. (888) 744-7322
240 W. 37th St., Seventh Fl. FAX (212)-594-3566
(Near Vernon Blvd.) www.advancedexpress.com
New York, NY 10018

American Airlines Cargo (800) 227-4622
JFK Airport, Cargo Bldg. 123 www.aa.com/cargo
(Near JFK Expy)
Jamaica, NY 11430

(718) 458-3666
Axis Global Systems (800) 568-4901
46-35 54th Rd. (Near 46th St.) FAX (718) 458-5122
Maspeth, NY 11378 www.axisg.com

Behind the Scenes (818) 344-9287
FAX (818) 344-9284
www.btsfreight.com

(908) 965-0900
Bellair Express (800) 444-7049
FAX (908) 965-0246
www.bellair.com

🅐 Bluebird Express Courier, LLC (516) 255-0800
145 Hook Creek Blvd., Bldg. C5C FAX (516) 255-9364
Valley Stream, NY 11581 www.bluebird-courier.com

Broadway Bound (718) 482-8384
3705 Greenpoint Ave. www.broadwaybound-rba.com
(Near Broome St.)
Long Island City, NY 11101

Delta Cargo (800) 352-2746
JFK Airport, Cargo Bldg. 67 www.delta.com/airlogistics
(Near JFK Expwy)
Jamaica, NY 11430

Delta Dash (800) 352-2746

DHL (800) 225-5345
www.dhl.com

(323) 779-6900
Distribution by Air, Inc./DBA (800) 553-1449
2701 El Segundo Blvd. FAX (323) 779-6958
Hawthorne, CA 90250 www.dbaco.com

Federal Express (800) 238-5355
www.fedex.com

(800) 762-3787
FedEx Custom Critical (800) 255-2421
www.customcritical.fedex.com

Future Express (800) 863-2928
P.O. Box 447 FAX (732) 821-7584
Milltown, NJ 08850 www.futureexpress.com

(718) 392-6686
Graf Air Freight (800) 238-6686
1046 47th Ave. (Near Vernon Blvd.)
Long Island City, NY 11101

Paramount Courier Inc. (212) 684-3311
14 E. 39th St. FAX (212) 684-3075
New York, NY 10016 www.paramountcourier.com

(214) 821-4400
Production Cargo (212) 679-5670
FAX (214) 821-4404
www.productioncargo.com

(800) 488-4400
Quick International Courier (718) 995-3616
www.quickintl.com

Reels On Wheels Unlimited (914) 576-6300
(877) 576-6300
P.O. Box 100 FAX **(914) 633-6932**
New Rochelle, NY 10804 **www.reelsonwheels.com**

Rock-It Cargo **(516) 825-7356**
600 Bayview Ave. **www.rockitcargo.com**
(Near S. Conduit)
Inwood, NY 11096

SOS Global Express **(800) 628-6363**
www.sosglobal.com

United Airlines Cargo **(800) 722-5243**
1325 Avenue of the Americas FAX **(718) 632-1809**
(Near 53rd St.) **www.ualcargo.com**
New York, NY 10019

UPS **(212) 608-8871**
(866) 696-3656
130 Church St. (Near Chubb Ave.) **www.ups.com**
New York, NY 10007

US Air Cargo **(888) 300-0099**
JFK Airport, Cargo Area C, Bldg. 84 FAX **(718) 656-2163**
(Near JFK Expwy)
Jamaica, NY 11430

USPS Express Mail **(800) 275-8777**
www.usps.com

World Courier **(516) 354-2600**
(800) 221-6600

Airlines

Aero California	(800) 237-6225	
Aerolineas Argentinas	(800) 333-0276	www.aeroargentinas.com
Aeromexico	(800) 237-6639 / (617) 868-3397 / FAX (617) 868-3397	www.aeromexico.com
Air Canada	(888) 247-2262 / (888) 422-7533	www.aircanada.ca
Air France	(800) 237-2747	www.airfrance.com
Air Jamaica	(800) 523-5585	www.airjamaica.com
Air New Zealand	(800) 262-1234 / (866) 629-4919	www.airnz.com
Alaska Airlines	(800) 426-0333	www.alaskaair.com
Alitalia	(800) 223-5730	www.alitaliausa.com
American Airlines	(800) 433-7300	www.aa.com
ANA All Nippon Airways	(800) 235-9262	www.anaskyweb.com
Asiana Airlines	(800) 227-4262	www.flyasiana.com
Avianca	(800) 284-2622	www.avianca.com
British Airways	(800) 247-9297	www.britishairways.com
Cathay Pacific	(800) 233-2742	www.cathaypacific.com
China Airlines	(800) 227-5118	www.china-airlines.com
Continental Airlines	(800) 525-0280	www.continental.com
Delta Airlines	(800) 241-4141	www.delta.com
Egypt Air	(800) 334-6787	www.egyptair.com
El Al Israel Airlines	(800) 223-6700	www.elal.com
Finnair	(800) 950-5000	www.finnair.com
Garuda-Indonesia	(800) 342-7832	www.garuda-indonesia.com
Grupo Taca	(800) 327-9832 / (800) 225-2272	www.taca.com
Hawaiian Airlines	(800) 367-5320	www.hawaiianair.com
Iberia Airlines	(800) 772-4642	www.iberia.com
Japan Airlines	(800) 525-3663	www.jal.com
jetBlue	(800) 538-2583	www.jetblue.com
Korean Air	(213) 484-1900 / (800) 438-5000	www.koreanair.com
LanChile Airlines	(310) 416-9061 / (866) 435-9526	
LOT Polish Airlines	(212) 789-0970	www.lot.com
LTU	(866) 266-5588 / FAX (407) 831-2470	www.ltu-airways.com
Malaysia Airlines	(800) 552-9264	www.malaysiaairlines.com.my
Martinair-Holland	(800) 627-8462	www.martinairusa.com
Mexicana Airlines	(800) 531-7921	www.mexicana.com
Midwest Express	(800) 452-2022	www.midwestexpress.com
Northwest Airlines	(800) 225-2525 / (800) 447-4747	
Northwest/KLM	(800) 692-6955	www.klm.com
Philippine Airlines	(800) 435-9725	www.philippineair.com
Qantas	(800) 227-4500	www.qantas.com.au
SAS Scandinavian Airlines	(800) 221-2350	www.scandinavian.net
Singapore Airlines	(800) 742-3333	www.singaporeair.com/americas
Southwest	(800) 435-9792	www.iflyswa.com
Swiss	(877) 359-7947	www.swiss.com
Taca International	(800) 400-8222	www.taca.com
Thai Airways International	(800) 426-5204	www.thaiair.com
United Airlines/United Express	(800) 241-6522	www.united.com
US Airways	(800) 428-4322	www.usairways.com
USAirways/USAirways Express	(800) 428-4322	www.usairways.com
Varig Brazilian Airlines	(800) 468-2744	www.varigbrasil.com
Virgin Atlantic Airways	(800) 862-8621 / (800) 821-5438	www.virgin-atlantic.com

Airports

Adirondack Regional Airport (518) 891-4600
96 Airport Rd. FAX (518) 891-0870
Saranac Lake, NY 12983

Air Pegasus Heliport (212) 563-4442
335 12th Ave. (Near W. 30th St.) FAX (212) 563-0526
New York, NY 10001

Albany International Airport (518) 242-2200
737 Albany Shaker Rd. FAX (518) 242-2641
(Near Wolf Rd.) www.albanyairport.com
Albany, NY 12211

Atlantic City International Airport (609) 645-7895
Egg Harbor Township, NJ 08234 FAX (609) 641-4348
www.acairport.com

Binghamton Regional Airport (607) 763-4471
2534 Airport Rd., Box 16 FAX (607) 763-4475
(Near Route 17) www.binghamtonairport.com
Johnson City, NY 13790

(860) 292-2000
Bradley International Airport (888) 624-1533
Schoephoester Rd. www.bradleyairport.com
Windsor Locks, CT 06096

(716) 630-6000
Buffalo-Niagara International Airport (877) 359-2642
4200 Genesee St. (Near Holtz Dr.) FAX (716) 630-6070
Buffalo, NY 14225 www.buffaloairport.com

Camden County Airport (856) 767-1233
817 Watsontown-New Freedom Rd. FAX (856) 768-1659
Berlin, NJ 08009 www.camdencountyairportinc.com

Central Jersey Regional Airport (908) 526-2822
1034 Millstone River Rd. FAX (908) 526-7308
Hillsborough, NJ 08844 www.centraljerseyairport.com

Chautauqua County Airport (716) 484-0204
3163 Airport Dr. (Near Route 120) FAX (716) 487-1322
Jamestown, NY 14701

(212) 248-7240
Downtown Manhattan Heliport (212) 435-6353
Pier 6, Cuentes Slip, East River FAX (212) 363-6792
(Near FDR Dr.) www.panynj.gov
New York, NY 10004

Finger Lakes Regional Airport (315) 568-0110
2727 Martin Rd. (Near Thorpe Rd.) FAX (315) 568-4397
Seneca Falls, NY 13148

**John F. Kennedy
International Airport** (718) 244-4444
Van Wyck Expwy (Near Nassau Expwy) www.panynj.gov
Jamaica, NY 11430

LaGuardia Airport (718) 533-3400
Port Authority Administrative Offices www.panynj.gov
Hangar Seven (Near Grand Central Pkwy East)
Flushing, NY 11371

Massena International Airport (315) 769-7605
90 Aviation Rd. (Near N. Racquette River Rd.)
Massena, NY 13662

Montauk Airport (631) 668-3738
E. Lake Dr. FAX (631) 668-2615
Montauk, NY 11954

Morristown Municipal Airport (973) 538-3366
Eight Airport Rd. FAX (973) 538-6947
Morristown, NJ 07960 www.mmuair.com

Newark Liberty International Airport (973) 961-6154
Building One FAX (973) 981-4215
Newark, NJ 07114 www.panynj.gov

Princeton Airport (609) 921-3100
41 Airpark Rd. (Near 206 Fwy) FAX (609) 921-1291
Princeton, NJ 08540 www.princetonairport.com

South Jersey Regional Airport (609) 267-3131
68 Stacy Haines Rd. FAX (609) 267-0836
Lumberton, NJ 08048

Sullivan County International Airport (845) 583-6600
County Rd. 183A FAX (845) 583-5080
(Near County Rd. 183) www.scgnet.us
White Lake, NY 12786

Teterboro Airport (201) 288-1775
399 Industrial Ave. FAX (201) 288-6512
Teterboro, NJ 07608 www.teb.com

(609) 882-1600
Trenton-Mercer Airport (609) 882-1601
Airport Administrative Office FAX (609) 771-0732
1100 Terminal Circle Dr., Ste. 301
West Trenton, NJ 08628
www.mercercounty.org/airport/index.htm

Watertown International Airport (315) 639-3809
22529 Airport Dr. FAX (315) 639-6247
(Near Foster Park Rd.)
Dexter, NY 13634

Westchester County Airport (914) 995-4860
240 Airport Rd., Ste. 202 FAX (914) 995-4268
(Near Rye Lake Ave.) www.westchestergov.com/airport
White Plains, NY 10604

Woodstock Airport (860) 928-4652
Route 169, P.O. Box 95 FAX (860) 928-4652
South Woodstock, CT 06267

Bus Charters

AA Executive (516) 792-1735
Town Car & Limousine (800) 716-2799
333 Hempstead Ave., Ste. 209 FAX (516) 256-0092
(Near Catalpa Dr.) www.exectownlimo.com
Malverne, NY 11565

Academy Bus Tours (201) 420-7000
111 Paterson Ave. FAX (201) 420-8087
Hoboken, NJ 07030 www.academybus.com

American Ground Transportation (212) 979-0500
237 First Ave. (Near E. 14th St.) www.1888nyclimo.com
New York, NY 10003

Atlantic Express (718) 442-9100
Transportation Group (800) 336-3886
Seven North St. FAX (718) 442-5104
(Near Richmond Terrace) www.atlanticexpress.com
Staten Island, NY 10302

Bestway Coach Express (718) 222-0717
183 Seventh St. (Near Second Ave.) FAX (718) 222-0729
Brooklyn, NY 11215 www.bestwaycoach.com

Campus Coach Lines (212) 682-1050
545 Fifth Ave., Ste. 609 (Near 45th St.) FAX (212) 687-1010
New York, NY 10017

De Camp Bus Lines (973) 783-7500
101 Greenwood Ave. FAX (973) 746-6648
Montclair, NJ 07042 www.decamp.com

Golden Touch Transportation, Inc. (718) 886-5204
109-15 14th Ave. (Near 110th St.) FAX (718) 661-4341
College Point, NY 11356
www.goldentouchtransportation.com

Ⓐ **H & B Super Express, Inc.** (718) 966-8186
Three Stafford Ave. FAX (718) 317-2491
(Near Grantwood Ave.) www.hbsuperexpress.com
Staten Island, NY 10312

  (718) 251-0910
L.A. Express Charter Service (917) 681-2377
2123 Mill Ave. (Near Avenue M) FAX (516) 781-5777
Brooklyn, NY 11234 www.laebuses.com

  (718) 623-9000
Monsey Tours (800) 232-8687
870 Dean St. (Near Classon Ave.) FAX (718) 623-1850
Brooklyn, NY 11238 www.monseybus.com

NY Whitehall (718) 361-8547
Transportation Co., Inc. (866) 361-8547
46-25 54th Ave. (Near Second St.) FAX (718) 392-9139
Masteth, NY 11378

Peter Pan Bus Lines (800) 343-9999
P.O. Box 1776 www.peterpanbus.com
Springfield, MA 01102

Premier Coach, Inc. (212) 599-3600
1150 Longwood Ave. www.premiercoachny.com
(Near Spofford Ave.)
Bronx, NY 10474

  (718) 984-2812
TNT Transportation, Inc. (800) 868-8411
10 Manley St. (Near Arthur Kill Rd.) FAX (718) 984-2907
Staten Island, NY 10309 www.tnttransportation.com

H & B *Super Express Inc.*
Luxury Limo Bus
VIP Party Coach & Mini Bus
In Business over 20 years
Office: 888-305-4400
Cell: 917-299-2524
All major credit cards accepted.
www.hbsuperexpress.com
E-mail: h-b@si.rr.com
24 / 7 Service

Car Rentals

A A Amcar   (212) 222-8500
315 W. 96th St. (Near West End Ave.)   www.aamcar.com
New York, NY 10025

Alamo   (800) 462-5266
www.alamo.com

All State Auto Rental   (212) 736-1188
629 W. 50th St. (Near 11th Ave.)
New York, NY 10019

    (908) 851-9495
All-Most New Rentals/Vans-to-Go   (800) 570-8267
43 Progress St.   FAX (908) 851-0546
Union, NJ 07083   www.almostnewrentals.com

Avis   (800) 352-7900
www.avis.com

    (718) 426-7039
Barn Truck Rental   (718) 426-7042
FAX (718) 898-4573
www.barntruckrental.com

    (212) 661-5906
Budget/Sears   (800) 527-0700
FAX (972) 404-7867
www.budget.com

Dollar Rent A Car   (800) 800-4000
www.dollar.com

Enterprise   (800) 736-8222
www.enterprise.com

Hertz   (800) 654-3131
www.hertz.com

National   (800) 227-7368
www.nationalcar.com

    (800) 961-0998
Rent-A-Wreck   (914) 961-5100
333 Tuckahoe Rd.   www.rentawreck.com
(Near Van Dam St.)
Yonkers, NY 10710

C.C. RENTAL

cars • cargo vans • 15 passenger vans • minivans • suv's
14ft or 20ft cubetrucks (with lifts or ramps)
daily, weekly, monthly rentals

www.ccrentalnyc.com
430 West 37th St., New York, NY 10018 (between 9th and 10th)
212 • 239 • 3333

Cargo & Passenger Vans

All-Most New Rentals/Vans-to-Go (908) 851-9595 / (800) 570-8267
43 Progress St. FAX (908) 851-0546
Union, NJ 07083 www.almostnewrentals.com

Angel Aerial Corporation (212) 460-8899 / (800) 503-9240
185 Broome St. (Near Clinton St.) FAX (212) 460-8244
New York, NY 10002

Ⓐ **Barn Truck Rental** (718) 426-7039 / (718) 426-7042
(Passenger Vans) FAX (718) 898-4573
www.barntruckrental.com

Budget Truck Rental (212) 465-1911
510 W. 35th St. (Near 10th Ave.) FAX (212) 594-1238
New York, NY 10001 www.budgettruck.com
(Cargo Vans)

Budget Truck Rental (212) 397-2893
415 W. 45th St. (Near Ninth Ave.) FAX (212) 674-2497
New York, NY 10036 www.budgettruck.com
(Cargo Vans)

Budget Truck Rental (212) 533-0155
307 E. 11th St. (Near First Ave.) FAX (212) 674-2497
New York, NY 10003 www.budgettruck.com
(Cargo Vans)

BARN RENTALS
Trucks • Vans • Flatbeds • Pickups
15-Passenger Vans • Cars
57-05 Broadway, Woodside, New York 11377
Minutes from Manhattan, near Kaufman & Silvercup Studios
(718) 426-7039
WWW.BARNTRUCKRENTAL.COM

Budget Truck Rental   **(212) 987-3642**
220 E. 117th St. (Near Third Ave.)   FAX **(212) 987-4403**
New York, NY 10035   www.budgettruck.com
(Cargo Vans)

Cars on Location   **(203) 732-4745**
  (800) 736-9178
768 Derby Ave.   FAX **(203) 732-4193**
Seymour, CT 06483   www.carsonlocation.com
(Passenger Vans)

Chelsea Motor Rental   **(212) 564-9555**
549 W. 26th St. (Near 11th Ave.)   FAX **(212) 564-0677**
New York, NY 10001

Ⓐ **Courier Car Rental**   **(212) 239-3333**
430 W. 37th St. (Near W. 40th St.)   FAX **(973) 882-9887**
New York, NY 10018   www.ccrentalnyc.com
(Passenger Vans)

Edge Auto & Truck Rental   **(212) 947-3343**
333 10th Ave.   FAX **(212) 947-3364**
New York, NY 10001   www.edgeautorental.com

Hertz Truck & Van   **(888) 999-5500**
41-85 Doremus Ave.   www.hertztrucks.com
Newark, NJ 07105

Movie Movers   **(276) 650-3378**
Transportation Equipment   **(818) 252-7722**
400 Movie Movers East   www.moviemovers.com
Axton, VA 24054
(Crew Cabs)

  (212) 957-4004
Prop Transport, Inc.   **(212) 594-2521**
630 Ninth Ave., Ste. 309   FAX **(212) 957-6569**
New York, NY 10036   www.proptransport.com
(Passenger Vans)

Public Service Truck Renting   **(718) 786-4000**
25-61 49th Ave. (Near 27th St.)   FAX **(718) 392-8227**
Long Island City, NY 11101   www.pstruck.com
(Cargo Vans)

Star Struck Catering
CHEF JONATHAN FORGASH

CHEFS FOR FILM AND FASHION

STAGE ★ LOCATION ★ EVENTS

FULL SERVICE MOBILE KITCHEN

WWW.STARSTRUCKCATERING.COM
917.626.8960 ★ 718.956.0725

Caterers

An Affair to Remember (201) 666-9605
(201) 599-2499
23 Emerson Plaza East FAX (201) 666-9734
Emerson, NJ 07630 www.affairtoremember.8m.com

Andrews Catering (631) 424-2700
(631) 750-1400
FAX (631) 424-2097
www.andrewscatering.com

ASAP Caterers/FoodThoughts (877) 228-3737
25 Grove St.
Hackensack, NJ 07601
(Mobile Kitchen Facility)

Atlantic Coast Catering (856) 778-9728

Balducci's (212) 653-8320
155A W. 66th St. www.balduccis.com
(Near Columbus Ave.)
New York, NY 10023

Bellizzi's Broadway Catering (212) 629-4818
(917) 923-3639

Bimmy's Caterers (718) 361-3144
47-00 33rd St., Second Fl. FAX (718) 361-6662
(Near 47th Ave.)
Long Island City, NY 11101

David Dreishpoon's Gourmet
516.868.0801 CELL 917.682.2020
WWW.DAVIDSCRAFTSERVICES.COM

FLEET OF WALK ON HOT TRUCKS
THE ONLY CATERER IN TOWN TO SERVE HOT BREAKFAST, HOT LUNCH AND HOT CRAFT

CREDITS
CURRENT: THE NAMESAKE • FIND ME GUILTY • NYC MARATHON • CHAPPELLE SHOW • HEARTBURN
SOMEONE TO WATCH OVER ME • INTERNAL AFFAIRS • THE FRESHMAN GREENCARD • MALCOLM X • ERASER
BIG DADDY • THE ROYAL TANNENBAUMS • A BEAUTIFUL MIND • MR. DEEDS • ANGER MANAGEMENT
HE ETERNAL SUNSHINE OF THE SPOTLESS MIND • TAXI • SECRET WINDOW • LAW AND ORDER 2ND – 14TH SEASONS
NYPD BLUE (ALL NY LOCATION SHOOTS) • OZ 1ST – 6TH SEASONS • THIRD WATCH 1ST – 4TH SEASON • ED • HITCH
FEAR FACTOR (NY) • GUESS WHO • FUR • LITTLE CHILDREN • THE BEDFORD DIARIES • THE BLACK DONNELLYS
THE DEVIL WEARS PRADA • 2005 NYC MARATHON • EL CANTANTE ANAMORPH • PURPLE VIOLETS • EMPTY CITY
HE TINA FEY PILOT • EXTREME MAKEOVER HOME EDITION • NEW AMSTERDAM • DON'T MESS WITH THE ZOHAN
ACCIDENTAL HUSBAND • DEATH IN LOVE • THE WRESTLER • DAMAGES • THE PRIVATE LIVES OF PIPPA LEE

1000's of events covered
Over 20 years of experience

Specializing in...

- **Feature Films**
- **Commercials**
- **Outdoor Musical Events**
- **Concerts**
- **Crew Meals**
- **Wrap Parties**
- **Drop Off Service**
- **Craft Services**

We have a fleet of fully equipped mobile kitchens!!

OFFICE: (973) 754-9502
FAX: (973) 754-9503
EMAIL: kevin@kevoocatering.com

www.kevoocatering.com

Cabbages and Kings — (203) 226-0531
34 Franklin St. (Near Saugatuck)   FAX (203) 222-8564
Westport, CT 06880

Call Cuisine Caterers — (212) 752-7070
1032 First Ave. (Near E. 56th St.)   FAX (212) 832-3848
New York, NY 10022

Camelot Catering — (732) 257-4373
19 Summerhill Rd.   FAX (732) 251-5420
Spotswood, NJ 08884   www.cambridgeinn.com

Carl Michaels Catering — (917) 488-9208
www.carlmichaelscatering.com

Carl Posey Catering — (908) 719-3334
2475 Lamington Rd.   FAX (908) 719-3044
Bedminster, NJ 07921   www.grillmasternj.net

Champignon — (212) 366-4410
200 Seventh Ave. (Near W. 21st St.)   FAX (212) 929-6002
New York, NY 10011   www.champignoncatering.com

(631) 351-6030
Ⓐ **Corinne's Concepts In Catering** — (800) 919-9261
845 E. Jericho Tpke (Near Totten Ave.)   FAX (631) 351-1587
Huntington Station, NY 11746
www.interactivegourmet.com

Ⓐ **David Dreishpoon's Gourmet** — (917) 682-2020
126 Commonwealth Ave.   www.davidscraftservices.com
(Near Washington St.)
Merrick, NY 11566

Ⓐ **Directors' Catering** — (718) 386-7475
284 Meserole St. (Near Bushwick Ave.)   FAX (718) 386-7846
Brooklyn, NY 11206   www.directorscatering.com

Taste the Gourmet Difference™

Breakfast • Lunch • Dinner • Craft Service

Feature Films - Commercials - TV - Concerts - Music Videos

Serving the entertainment industry for over 28 years

Fully Equipped Mobile Kitchen Fleet

1.800.919.9261
www.corinnescatering.com

THE DIRECTORS' catering

serving new york's film, commercial & entertainment industries for over 40 years.

Breakfast ★ Lunch & Dinner
Coffee Service ★ Mobile Kitchens ★ Craft Service

Professional Staff To Service You,
When You Want It, Where You Want It, We'll Be There.

phone: 718-386-7475 or 212-431-4995   mobile: 516-510-3480
www.directorscatering.com

A Dream Cuisine Fine Catering, LLC (718) 389-3638 / (718) 757-9984
1073 Manhattan Ave., Ground Fl. FAX (718) 389-1341
(Near Eagle St.) www.dreamcuisinenyc.com
Brooklyn, NY 11222

Executive Charm (212) 321-1822
46B Saratoga Blvd. (Near Austin Blvd.) FAX (516) 889-4123
Island Park, NY 11558 www.cateredevent.com

The Galaxy Global Eatery (212) 777-3631
15 Irving Pl. (Near E. 15th St.) FAX (212) 777-3224
New York, NY 10003 www.galaxyglobaleatery.com

Giorgio's of Gramercy Park (212) 477-0007
27 E. 21st St. (Near Broadway) FAX (212) 228-3354
New York, NY 10010

Gourmet To U, LLC (732) 367-1997 / (908) 216-1575
FAX (732) 367-1954

Great American Catering (212) 480-2015
47 West St. (Near Rector) www.gacatering.com
New York, NY 10006

Henry's International Cuisine (201) 686-7540
307 Hollywood Ave. FAX (908) 352-2007
Hillside, NJ 07205
(24-Hour Service & Mobile Kitchen Facilities)

Hudson Valley Locations, Inc. (914) 643-6976
431 Buena Vista Rd. www.hudsonvalleylocations.com
(Near Second St.)
New City, NY 10956

Dream Cuisine Fine Catering, LLC
Production Catering • Location

1073 Manhattan Avenue • Brooklyn, NY
T: 718.389.3638 F: 718.389.1341 M: 718.757.9984

Lamb & Jaffy • An American Bistro
Dinner: Wed - Sun • Garden • Brunch

Ⓐ Kevoo Catering	(973) 754-9502
52 Rockland Ave.	(201) 314-6828
West Paterson, NJ 07424	FAX (973) 754-9503
(Mobile Kitchen Facilities)	www.kevoocatering.com

La Bonne Cusine Catering — (212) 531-3477
478 Central Park West, Ste. 314 — www.lbccatering.com
(Near 107th St.)
New York, NY 10025

La Cuisine — (203) 488-7100
750 E. Main St. — FAX (203) 488-7144
Branford, CT 06405

LaNoce's Fine Food For Film, LLC — (860) 355-5441 / (860) 234-4445
Four Grandview Ln.
New Milford, CT 06776

Lorraine's Food Factory — (585) 442-6574 / (800) 582-2837
777 Culver Rd. (Near Main St.)
Rochester, NY 14609 — www.lorrainesfoodfactory.com

Manganaro's Hero-Boy — (212) 947-7485
492 Ninth Ave. (Near W. 37th St.)
New York, NY 10018

Marion's A Go-Go — (212) 995-1776 / (212) 475-4354
354 Bowery (Near E. Fourth St.) — FAX (212) 979-2492
New York, NY 10012

Michelle's Kitchen — (212) 996-0012
1614 Third Ave. (Near E. 61st St.) — FAX (212) 996-0087
New York, NY 10128 — www.michelleskitchen.com

Paradise Catering & Mobile Kitchen — (646) 932-3496
311 E. 45th St. (Near Second Ave.)
New York, NY 10017

Portfolio — (212) 691-3845
Four W. 19th St. (Near Fifth Ave.) — FAX (212) 691-4307
New York, NY 10011 — www.portfoliorestaurant.com

Ready to Eat — (212) 229-1013
525 Hudson (Near W. 10th St.) — FAX (212) 229-1373
New York, NY 10014 — www.readytoeat.net

Rocking Horse Cafe — (212) 463-9511
182 Eighth Ave. (Near W. 19th Ave.) — FAX (212) 243-3245
New York, NY 10011 — www.rockinghorsecafe.com

Rustic Caterers — (201) 816-0176
Four W. Palasides Ave. — FAX (201) 816-3547
Englewood, NJ 07631 — www.rusticcaterers.net

Ⓐ Shooting Stars Catering	(609) 859-3696
	(609) 352-6308
	FAX (609) 859-4333

Something's Cooking Catering — (212) 691-0002
22-10 39th Ave. — FAX (718) 391-0001
Long Island City, NY 11101

Ⓐ Star Struck Catering	(917) 626-8960
	(718) 956-0725
	FAX (718) 228-5592
	www.starstruckcatering.com

Tastefully Done Catering — (201) 553-9090
820 10th Ave. (Near W. 54th St.) — FAX (201) 553-9099
New York, NY 10019 — www.tastefullydone.com

TomKats, Inc. — (615) 256-9596 / (800) 670-2248
641 Fogg St. — FAX (615) 256-5055
Nashville, TN 37203 — www.tomkats.com
(24-Hour Service & Mobile Kitchen Facilities)

The Village Caterer & Craft Service, Inc. — (212) 529-2207 / (646) 321-3535
122 MacDougal St., Ste. 20 — FAX (212) 529-2207
(Near Carmine St.) — www.villagecaterer.com
New York, NY 10012

Zabar's — (212) 787-2000
2245 Broadway (Near W. 80th St.) — FAX (212) 580-4477
New York, NY 10024 — www.zabars.com

Shooting Stars Catering — We Have Served The Film Industry Since 1988 With Great Food, Friendly Staff, and New Mobile Kitchens. Serving the Film Industry Fine Food on Location. 609-859-3696. OFFICE 609.859.3696 CELL: 609.352.6308 FAX: 609.859.4333. We also rent catering trucks.

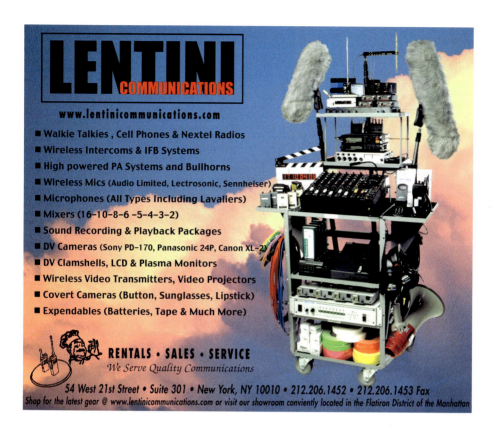

Communications Equipment

AAA Communications (212) 459-2475 / (800) 925-5437 210 Fairfield Rd. FAX **(973) 808-8588** Fairfield, NJ 07004 www.aaacomm.com (Cellular Phones, Pagers & Walkie Talkies)	**All Star Radios** (212) 505-7666 / (917) 957-1252 379 Park Ave. South, Fourth Fl. FAX **(212) 505-7667** New York, NY 10016 www.allstarradios.com

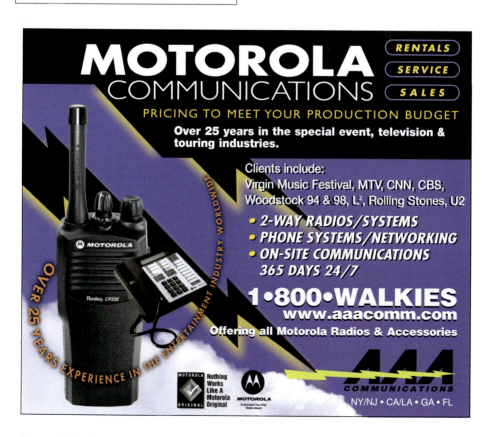

Communications Equipment 163

AllCell Rentals	(215) 985-2355
	(800) 724-2355
(Cellular Phones, Pagers & Radios)	FAX (215) 985-0223
	www.allcellrentals.com

Apache Rental Group	(818) 842-9944
3910 W. Magnolia Blvd.	FAX (818) 842-9269
Burbank, CA 91505	www.apacherentalgroup.com
(Cellular Phones, Repeaters & Walkie Talkies)	

	(212) 543-2089
BearCom	(888) 841-3600
	www.bearcom.com

	(914) 345-9292
CP Communications, Inc.	(800) 762-4254
200 Clearbrook Rd.	FAX (914) 345-9222
Elmsford, NY 10523	www.cpcomms.com
(Base Stations, Intercom Systems, Walkie Talkies & Wireless Mics)	

	(800) 996-1810
Event Radio Rentals, Inc.	(212) 444-8083
	FAX (646) 862-8934
	www.eventradiorentals.com
(2-Ways, Aircards, Bullhorns, Cellular Phones, Pagers & Nextels)	

	(888) 679-6111
Exchange Communications	(505) 501-1029
233 N. Guadalupe, Ste. 290	FAX (888) 694-8111
Santa Fe, NM 87501	www.exchangecom.net
(Office Phone Systems & Temporary Land Lines)	

Gotham Sound and	(212) 629-9430
Communications, Inc.	(866) 468-4268
330 W. 38th St., Ground Fl., Ste. 105	FAX (212) 629-9436
(Near Eighth Ave.)	www.gothamsound.com
New York, NY 10018	

Ⓐ **Hello World Communications** (212) 243-8800
118 W. 22nd St., Ste. 2A FAX (212) 691-6961
(Near Sixth Ave.) www.hwc.tv
New York, NY 10011
(2-Ways, Bullhorns, Cellular Phones, Helicopter Headsets, Internet Connectivity, Junxion Boxes, Radios, Rentals, Repeaters, Walkie Talkies, Wireless Internet, Wireless Mics & Wireless Routers)

Keep in Touch	(212) 921-1911
Communications, Inc.	(800) 250-2320
251 W. 39th St., Seventh Fl.	FAX (212) 333-5900
New York, NY 10018	
(Walkie Talkies)	

Ⓐ **Lentini Communications** (212) 206-1452
54 W. 21st St., Ste. 301 FAX (212) 206-1453
(Near Fifth Ave.)
New York, NY 10010 www.lentinicommunications.com
(Cell Phones, Walkie Talkies, Wireless IFB/Intercoms & Wireless Internet Junction Boxes)

	(212) 620-5530
Playback Systems	(800) 540-7529
242 W. 30th St., Ste. 500	FAX (212) 620-5531
(Near Seventh Ave.)	www.playbackny.com
New York, NY 10001	
(Bullhorns, Cellular Phones & Walkie Talkies)	

Rochester Two-Way	(585) 987-1340
Communications, Inc.	(585) 652-6656
(Walkie Talkies)	FAX (585) 652-6656

	(646) 660-4221
Rock Bottom Rentals	(877) 809-4502
	www.rockbottomrentals.com
(Base Stations, Bullhorns, Cellular Phone/Fax Equipment, Nextels, Pagers, Repeaters, Satellite Phones & Walkie Talkies)	

	(212) 582-2345
Scharff Weisberg, Inc.	(718) 610-1660
36-36 33rd St. (Near 36th Ave.)	FAX (212) 757-6367
Long Island City, NY 11106	www.scharffweisberg.com
(Cellular Phones & Walkie Talkies)	

Spectra	(212) 744-2255
172 E. 75th St. (Near Third Ave.)	FAX (212) 628-7069
New York, NY 10021	www.spectra-ny.com
(Satellite Phones)	

Sync Speed, Inc. (610) 659-1033
10 E. Manoa Rd. www.syncspeedinc.com
Havertown, PA 19083
(2-Ways, Base Stations, Bullhorns, Helicopter Headsets, Installation, Intercom Systems, Internet Connectivity, Mobile Services, Radios, Rentals, Repeaters, Walkie Talkies, Wired/Wireless Intercom Systems, Wireless Internet & Wireless Mics)

	(212) 244-1011
Tamberelli Digital	(877) 608-4336
516 W. 36th St., Second Fl.	FAX (212) 947-5894
(Near 10th Ave.)	www.tamberelli.com
New York, NY 10018	
(Nextels & Walkie Talkies)	

Walkieboy Inc.	(212) 691-2662
250 W. 49th St., Ste. 805	FAX (212) 691-2663
New York, NY 10019	

We offer the gear we choose to use

audio - video - lighting
projectors - cell phones
wireless routers
walkie talkies

◄ ►

Hello World Communications
118 West 22nd Street Suite 2A   NYC
www.hwc.tv   212 243-8800

Consulates General

Australian Consulate General (212) 351-6500
150 E. 42nd St., 34th Fl. FAX (212) 351-6501
(Near Lexington Ave.) www.australianyc.org
New York, NY 10017

Austrian Consulate General (212) 737-6400
31 E. 69th St. (Near Madison Ave.) FAX (212) 585-1992
New York, NY 10021 www.austria-ny.org

Belgian Consulate General (212) 586-5110
1065 Avenue of the Americas, 22nd Fl. FAX (212) 582-9657
(Near W. 54th St.) www.diplobel.us
New York, NY 10018

Brazilian Consulate General (212) 827-0976
1185 Avenue of the Americas, 21st Fl. FAX (212) 827-0225
(Near W. 46th St.) www.brazilny.org
New York, NY 10036

British Consulate General (212) 745-0200
845 Third Ave. (Near E. 51st St.) FAX (212) 754-3062
New York, NY 10022 www.britainusa.com

Colombian Consulate General (212) 370-0004
10 E. 46th St. (Near Madison Ave.) FAX (212) 972-1725
New York, NY 10017

French Consulate General (212) 606-3600
934 Fifth Ave. (Near E. 74th St.)
New York, NY 10021

German Consulate General (212) 610-9700
871 United Nations Plaza FAX (212) 610-9702
(Near E. 49th St.) www.germany.info/consular
New York, NY 10017

Greek Consulate General (212) 988-5500
69 E. 79th St. (Near Park Ave.) FAX (212) 734-8492
New York, NY 10075

Haitian Consulate General (212) 697-9767
271 Madison Ave. (Near E. 39th St.) FAX (212) 681-6991
New York, NY 10016 www.haitianconsulate-nyc.org

Icelandic Consulate General (212) 593-2700
(646) 282-9360
800 Third Ave., 36th Fl. FAX (212) 593-6269
(Near E. 49th St.)
New York, NY 10022

Indonesian Consulate General (212) 879-0600
Five E. 68th St. (Near Madison Ave.) FAX (212) 570-6206
New York, NY 10065 www.indonesianewyork.org

Irish Consulate General (212) 319-2555
345 Park Ave., 17th Fl. FAX (212) 980-9475
(Near E. 51st St.)
New York, NY 10154

Israeli Consulate General (212) 499-5000
800 Second Ave. (Near E. 43rd St.) www.israelfm.org
New York, NY 10017

Jamaican Consulate General (212) 935-9000
767 Third Ave., Second Fl. FAX (212) 935-7507
(Near E. 48th St.) www.congenjamaica-ny.com
New York, NY 10017

Japanese Consulate General (212) 371-8222
299 Park Ave. (Near E. 48th St.) FAX (212) 371-1294
New York, NY 10171 www.cgj.org

Korean Consulate General (646) 674-6000
(212) 692-9120
335 E. 45th St. www.koreanconsulate.org
(Near Second Ave.)
New York, NY 10017

Lebanese Consulate General (212) 744-7905
Nine E. 76th St. (Near Fifth Ave.) FAX (212) 794-1510
New York, NY 10021

Lithuanian Consulate General (212) 354-7840
420 Fifth Ave., Third Fl. FAX (212) 354-7911
(Near E. 38th St.) www.ltconsny.org
New York, NY 10018

Monacan Consulate General (212) 286-0500
565 Fifth Ave., 23rd Fl. FAX (212) 286-1574
(Near E. 46th St.) www.monaco-consulate.com
New York, NY 10017

Moroccan Consulate General (212) 758-2625
10 E. 40th St., 24th Fl. FAX (212) 779-7441
(Near Fifth Ave.) www.moroccanconsulate.com
New York, NY 10016

Netherlandic Consulate General (212) 246-1429
One Rockefeller Plaza, 11th Fl. FAX (212) 586-7222
(Near Fifth Ave.) www.cgny.org
New York, NY 10020

Pakistani Consulate General (212) 879-5800
12 E. 65th St. (Near Madison Ave.) FAX (212) 517-6987
New York, NY 10021 www.pakistanconsulateny.org

Panamanian Consulate General (212) 840-2450
1212 Sixth Ave., Sixth Fl. FAX (212) 840-2469
(Near W. 47th St.)
New York, NY 10036

Paraguayan Consulate General (310) 417-9500
(212) 682 9441
6033 West Century Blvd., Ste. 985 FAX (310) 417-9520
(Near Third Ave.) www.paraguayconsulatela.com
Los Angeles, CA 90045

Peruvian Consulate General (646) 735-3828
(646) 735-3864

Portuguese Consulate General (212) 221-3165
590 Fifth Ave. www.portugal.com
New York, NY 10036

South African Consulate General (212) 213-4880
333 E. 38th St., Ninth Fl. (Near First Ave.)
New York, NY 10016

Spanish Consulate General (212) 355-4080
150 E. 58th St. (Near Lexington Ave.) FAX (212) 644-3751
New York, NY 10155

Crating & Packing

Ollendorff Fine Art **(888) 668-3872**
www.ollendorff.com

Packaging Store **(718) 706-8900**
37-11 35th Ave. (Near 37th St.) FAX **(718) 706-9295**
Long Island City, NY 11101 www.packnyc.com

United Shipping & Packaging **(212) 475-2214**
200 E. 10th St. (Near Second Ave.) www.uspny.com
New York, NY 10003

(718) 276-1522
(800) 767-1530
X-P Shipping
155-06 S. Conduit Ave. FAX **(718) 341-5233**
(Near 166th St.)
Jamaica, NY 11434

Customs Brokers & Carnets

All In One Customhouse Brokers **(908) 820-9443**
331 Second St.
Elizabeth, NJ 07206

Frank Spadaro
Customhouse Brokers **(212) 226-3316**
156-15 146 Ave. (Near 157th St.) FAX **(718) 949-1309**
Jamaica, NY 11434

Jet Air Service, Inc. **(718) 656-7430**
230-59 International Airport Center Blvd. FAX **(718) 244-0942**
Jamaica, NY 11431 www.jetairservice.com

Pier International
Customhouse Brokerage **(212) 425-3909**
61 Broadway, Ste. 1115 FAX **(212) 968-0552**
(Near Exchange Pl.) www.pierintl.com
New York, NY 10006

R.B.A., Inc. **(718) 482-8384**
3705 Greenpoint Ave. www.finearttransport.com
(Near Fifth Ave.)
Long Island City, NY 11101

U.S. Council/Carnet Help Line **(800) 282-2900**
FAX **(847) 381-3857**
www.atacarnet.com

Film Commissions—North America

Alabama (334) 242-4195
Alabama Film Office, 401 Adams Ave. FAX **(334) 242-2077**
Montgomery, AL 36104   **www.alabamafilm.org**
Contact: Courtney Murphy

Alabama-Mobile (251) 438-7100
Mobile Film Office   FAX **(251) 438-7104**
164 Saint Emanuel St.   **www.mobilefilmoffice.com**
Mobile, AL 36602
Contact: Eva Golson

Alaska (907) 269-8491
Alaska Film Office   **www.alaskafilm.org**
550 W. Seventh Ave., 17th Fl.
Anchorage, AK 99501
Contact: Shelly James

(602) 771-1193
Arizona (800) 523-6695
Arizona Film Office   FAX **(602) 771-1211**
1700 W. Washington St., Ste. 220
Phoenix, AZ 85007   **www.azcommerce.com/film**

Arizona-Cochise County (520) 432-9215
Cochise County Film Office   **www.explorecochise.com**
1415 Melody Ln., Bldg. G
Bisbee, AZ 85603

(928) 634-7593
Arizona-Cottonwood (928) 649-0509
Cottonwood Film Office   FAX **(928) 634-7594**
1010 S. Main St.   **www.cottonwoodchamberaz.org**
Cottonwood, AZ 86326

(928) 425-4495
Arizona-Globe (800) 804-5623
The Globe-Miami Regional Film Office   FAX **(928) 425-3410**
1360 N. Broad St.   **www.globemiamichamber.com**
Globe, AZ 85501

Arizona-Page-Lake Powell (928) 645-2741
Page-Lake Powell Film Office   FAX **(928) 645-3181**
P.O. Box 727   **www.pagelakepowellchamber.org**
Page, AZ 86040

Arizona-Phoenix (602) 262-4850
Phoenix Film Office   FAX **(602) 534-2295**
200 W. Washington St., 19th Fl.   **www.filmphoenix.com**
Phoenix, AZ 85003

(928) 777-1204
Arizona-Prescott (866) 878-2489
Prescott Film Office, P.O. Box 2059
Prescott, AZ 86302
www.cityofprescott.net/business/film/

(928) 204-1123
Arizona-Sedona (928) 254-9115
Sedona Film Office, P.O. Box 478   FAX **(928) 204-1064**
Sedona, AZ 86339   **www.sedonafilmoffice.com**
Contact: Judy Schultz

(520) 770-2151
Arizona-Tucson (877) 311-2489
Tucson Film Office   FAX **(520) 884-7804**
100 S. Church Ave.   **www.filmtucson.com**
Tucson, AZ 85701

(928) 684-5479
Arizona-Wickenburg (928) 684-0977
Wickenburg Film Office   FAX **(928) 684-5470**
216 N. Frontier St.   **www.wickenburgchamber.com**
Wickenburg, AZ 85390

Arizona-Yuma (928) 314-9247
Yuma Film Commission, P.O. Box 172   FAX **(928) 314-2280**
Yuma, AZ 85364   **www.filmyuma.com**
Contacts: Jeff Byrd & Bonny Rhodes

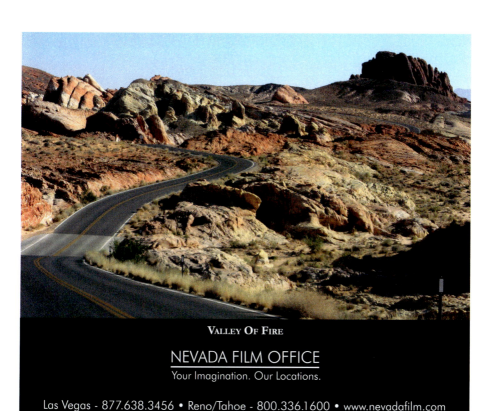

VALLEY OF FIRE

NEVADA FILM OFFICE
Your Imagination. Our Locations.

Las Vegas - 877.638.3456 • Reno/Tahoe - 800.336.1600 • www.nevadafilm.com

Arkansas (501) 682-7676
Arkansas Film Office (501) 682-7326
One State Capitol Mall, Fourth Fl. FAX (501) 682-3456
Little Rock, AR 72201 www.arkansasedc.com
Contact: Joe Glass

**Association of
Film Commissioners International** (307) 637-4422
109 E. 17th St., Ste. 18 FAX (413) 375-2903
Cheyenne, WY 82001 www.afci.org

Bahamas (242) 356-5216
Bahamas Film Commission FAX (242) 356-5904
P.O. Box N-3701 www.bahamasfilm.com
Nassau Bahamas
Contact: Angela Archer

British Virgin Islands (284) 494-4119
British Virgin Islands Film Commission FAX (284) 494-8138
P.O. Box 134 www.bvitourism.com/film/
Road Town, Tortola, Virgin Islands (British)

California (323) 860-2960
 (800) 858-4749
California Film Commission FAX (323) 860-2972
7080 Hollywood Blvd., Ste. 900 www.film.ca.gov
Los Angeles, CA 90028
Contact: Amy Lemisch

Canada-Alberta (780) 422-8584
Alberta Film Commission FAX (780) 422-8582
Fifth Fl., Commerce Pl., 10155-102 St. www.albertafilm.ca
Edmonton, AB T5J 4L6 Canada
Contact: Dan Chugg

Canada-Argenteuil Laurentians (450) 562-2446
Argenteuil-Laurentians Film Commission FAX (450) 562-1911
430 Grace St. www.filmlaurentides.ca
Lachute, QC J8H 1M6 Canada

Canada-British Columbia (604) 660-2732
BC Film Commission FAX (604) 660-4790
201-865 Hornby St. www.bcfilmcommission.com
Vancouver, BC V6Z 2G3 Canada

Canada-Calgary (403) 221-7868
Calgary Film Commission FAX (403) 221-7828
731 First St. SE www.calgaryeconomicdevelopment.com
Calgary, AB T2G 2G9 Canada
Contact: Beth Thompson

Canada-Columbia Shuswap (250) 832-8194
Columbia Shuswap Film Commission FAX (250) 832-3375
P.O. Box 978 www.csrd.bc.ca
Salmon Arm, BC V1E 4P1 Canada

 (780) 917-7627
Canada-Edmonton (800) 463-4667
Edmonton Film Commission FAX (780) 425-5283
Fifth Fl., World Trade Center, 9990 Jasper Ave.
Edmonton, AB T5J 1P7 Canada
Contact: Patti Tucker www.filminedmonton.com

Canada-Manitoba (204) 947-2040
Manitoba Film & Sound FAX (204) 956-5261
410-93 Lombard Ave. www.mbfilmsound.ca
Winnipeg, MB R3B 3B1 Canada
Contact: Carole Vivier

Canada-Montreal (514) 872-2883
Montreal Film & TV Commission FAX (514) 872-3409
303 Notre Dame St. East, Sixth Fl. www.montrealfilm.com
Montreal, QC H2Y 3Y8 Canada

 (250) 386-3976
Canada-Nanaimo (888) 537-3456
Greater Victoria Film Commission FAX (250) 386-3967
P.O. Box 34, 794 Fort St. www.filmvictoria.com
Victoria, BC V8W 1H2 Canada
Contact: Beverley Dondale

OUR PEOPLE. OUR LOCATIONS.
AND NOW OUR INCENTIVE.
Are why producers choose San Antonio.

Drew Mayer-Oakes
Film Marketing Manager
210.207.6730
Drew@FilmSanAntonio.com
FilmSanAntonio.com

© 2008 GREATER MIAMI CONVENTION & VISITORS BUREAU

in the spotlight…

MIAMI™
MIAMIBOUTIQUEHOTELS.COM

Canada-New Brunswick (506) 869-6868
New Brunswick Film, P.O. Box 5001   FAX **(506) 869-6840**
Moncton, NB E1C 8R3 Canada   **www.nbfilm.com**
Contact: Roger Cyr

Canada-Newfoundland (709) 738-3456
Newfoundland & Labrador Film   FAX **(709) 739-1680**
12 King's Bridge Rd.   **www.nlfdc.ca**
St. John's, NF A1C 3K3 Canada
Contact: Chris Bonnell

Canada-Northwest Territories (867) 920-8793
NWT Film Commission   FAX **(867) 873-0101**
P.O. Box 1320
Yellowknife, NT X1A 2L9 Canada
www.iti.gov.nt.ca/artscrafts/filmcommission.shtml
Contact: Carla Wallis

Canada-Nova Scotia (902) 424-7177
Nova Scotia Film Development Corp.   FAX **(902) 424-0617**
1724 Granville St., Second Fl.   **www.film.ns.ca**
Halifax, NS B3J 1X5 Canada
Contact: Ann MacKenzie

Canada-Nunavut Territory (867) 975-6000
Nunavut Film Commission   FAX **(867) 975-5981**
P.O. Box 1000, Stn. 1120   **www.gov.nu.ca**
Iqaluit, NU XOA OHO Canada
Contact: Ed McKenna

Canada-Okanagan (250) 717-0087
Okanagan Film Commission   FAX **(250) 868-0512**
1450 KLO Rd.   **www.okanaganfilm.com**
Kelowna, BC V1W 3Z4 Canada

Canada-Ontario (416) 314-6858
Ontario Media Development   FAX **(416) 314-6876**
175 Bloor St. East, South Tower, Ste. 501   **www.omdc.on.ca**
Toronto, ON M4W 3R8 Canada
Contact: Donna Zuchlinski

(902) 368-6300
Canada-Prince Edward Island (800) 563-3734
PEI Film Commission, P.O. Box 340   FAX **(902) 368-6301**
Charlottetown, PE C1A 7K7 Canada   **www.techpei.com**
Contact: Scot MacDonald

Canada-Quebec City (418) 641-6766
Quebec City Film & TV Commission   FAX **(418) 691-5777**
43 Buade St., Third Fl., Ste. 310   **www.filmquebec.com**
Quebec G1R 4A2 Canada
Contacts: Lorraine Boily, Geneviève Doré & Karine Latulippe

Canada-Saskatchewan (306) 798-9800
Sask Film, 1831 College Ave.   FAX **(306) 798-7768**
Regina, SK S4P 3V5 Canada   **www.saskfilm.com**
Contact: Susanne Bell

Canada-Thompson-Nicola (250) 377-8673
Thompson-Nicola Film Commission   FAX **(250) 372-5048**
300-465 Victoria St.   **www.tnrd.bc.ca**
Kamloops, BC V2C 2A9 Canada

Canada-Toronto (416) 338-3456
Toronto Film & TV Office   FAX **(416) 392-0675**
City Hall, Rotunda North 100 Queen St. West
Toronto, ON M5H 2N2 Canada   **www.toronto.ca/tfto**
Contact: Rhonda Silverstone

Canada-Yukon (867) 667-5400
Yukon Film & Sound Commission   FAX **(867) 393-7040**
P.O. Box 2703   **www.reelyukon.com**
Whitehorse, YT Y1A 2C6 Canada
Contact: Margarita Ramon

(303) 592-4065
Colorado (800) 726-8887
Colorado Film Commission   FAX **(303) 722.1158**
241 S. Cherokee St., Ste. E   **www.coloradofilm.org**
Denver, CO 80223
Contact: Kevin Shand

(303) 938-2066
Colorado-Boulder (303) 442-2911
Boulder Film Commission   FAX **(303) 938-2098**
2440 Pearl St.   **www.bouldercoloradousa.com**
Boulder, CO 80302

(303) 567-4660
Colorado-Clear Creek County (800) 882-5278
Chamber & Tourism Bureau   FAX **(303) 567-0967**
of Clear Creek County   **www.clearcreekcounty.org**
2060 Miner St., P.O. Box 100
Idaho Springs, CO 80452

(719) 635-7506
Colorado-Colorado Springs (800) 888-4748
Colorado Springs   FAX **(719) 635-4968**
Convention & Visitors Bureau
515 S. Cascade Ave.
Colorado Springs, CO 80903
www.filmcoloradosprings.com

Colorado-Fremont/Custer County (719) 275-2331
Fremont/Custer County Film Office   FAX **(719) 275-2332**
403 Royal Gorge Blvd.
Canon City, CO 81212

Colorado-Southwest (970) 247-0312
www.swcolotravel.org

Colorado-Telluride (310) 994-9753
Telluride Film Commission   FAX **(970) 728-4720**
P.O. Box 182   **www.filmtelluride.com**
Telluride, CO 81435

Connecticut (860) 256-2800
CT Commission on Culture and Tourism   FAX **(860) 256-2763**
One Constitution Plaza   **www.ctfilm.com**
Hartford, CT 06103
Contacts: Mark Dixon & Ellen Woolf

(302) 739-4271
Delaware (866) 284-7483
Delaware Tourism Office   FAX **(302) 739-5749**
99 Kings Hwy   **www.visitdelaware.com**
Dover, DE 19901
Contact: Nikki Boone

District of Columbia (202) 727-6608
DC Film & TV   FAX **(202) 727-3246**
441 Fourth St., NW Ste. 760N   **www.film.dc.gov**
Washington, DC 20001
Contact: Crystal Palmer

(809) 694-2291
Dominican Republic (809) 330-2234
Serie23 Film Commission   FAX **(305) 946-8531**
Ayuntamiento Serie23   **www.drfilm.org**
San Pedro de Macoris 21000 Dominican Republic

(877) 352-3456
Florida (818) 508-7772
Governor's Office of   FAX **(850) 410-4770**
Film & Entertainment   **www.filminflorida.com**
The Capitol, Ste. 2001
Tallahassee, FL 32399
Contact: Paul Sirmons

Florida-Cape Canaveral (877) 572-3224
Space Coast Film Commission   FAX **(321) 433-4476**
430 Brevard Ave., Ste. 150   **www.space-coast.com**
Cocoa Village, FL 32922

(863) 534-2506
Florida-Central Florida (800) 828-7655
Central Florida Motion Picture/TV   FAX **(863) 534-0886**
600 N. Broadway, Ste. 300   **www.filmcentralflorida.com**
Bartow, FL 33830

Florida-Collier County (239) 659-3456
Collier County Film Commission   FAX **(239) 213-3053**
755 Eighth Ave. South   **www.shootinparadise.com**
Naples, FL 34102

New York State's best kept location secret...

BUFFALO NIAGARA

We're easy on your pocket

- Lucrative New York State **TAX INCENTIVE (30%)**
- Inexpensive lodging, catering and hospitality services
- **FREE** permits, police and municipal locations
- Experienced and affordable crew base

We've got what you want

- Varied urban settings with architecture from every era
- Easy road closures and neighborhood control
- Available subway (above and below ground)
- Abandoned steel mills and industrial sites
- Coastline, canal and TWO Great Lakes
- Assorted rural settings (just minutes away from downtown Buffalo)
- **SNOW**... guaranteed

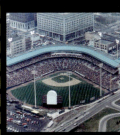

Check out Buffalo Niagara... We'll roll out the red carpet for you!

BUFFALO NIAGARA FILM COMMISSION

Tim Clark
Film Commissioner
clark@buffalocvb.org
office: (716) 852-0511 ext. 227
mobile: (716) 432-0350
www.filmbuffaloniagara.org

Florida-Emerald Coast (800) 322-3319
Emerald Coast TDC Film Commission FAX (850) 651-7149
P.O. Box 609 www.destin-fwb.com/film
Fort Walton Beach, FL 32549

Florida-Fort Lauderdale (954) 627-0128
(800) 741-1420
The Broward Alliance Film Commission FAX (954) 524-3167
110 E. Broward Blvd., Ste. 1990 www.filmbroward.com
Fort Lauderdale, FL 33301

Florida-Jacksonville (904) 630-1622
Jacksonville Film & TV Office FAX (904) 630-2919
One W. Adams St., Ste. 200 www.filmjax.com
Jacksonville, FL 32202

Florida-Key West (305) 293-1800
(800) 345-6539
Florida Keys & Key West FAX (305) 296-0788
Film Commission www.filmkeys.com
1201 White St., Ste. 102
Key West, FL 33040

Florida-Miami Beach (305) 673-7070
Miami Beach Film Commission FAX (305) 673-7063
1700 Convention Center Dr. www.filmiamibeach.com
Miami Beach, FL 33139

Florida-Miami-Dade (305) 375-3288
Miami-Dade Mayor's Office FAX (305) 375-3266
of Film & Entertainment www.filmiami.org
111 NW First St., Ste. 2540
Miami, FL 33128

Florida-Orlando (407) 422-7159
Metro Orlando Film & FAX (407) 841-9069
Entertainment Commission www.filmorlando.com
301 E. Pine St., Ste. 900
Orlando, FL 32801

Florida-Palm Beach County (561) 233-1000
(800) 745-3456
Palm Beach County Film & FAX (561) 233-3113
Television Commission www.pbfilm.com
1555 Palm Beach Lakes Blvd., Ste. 900
West Palm Beach, FL 33401

Florida-Tampa Bay (813) 342-4058
(800) 826-8358
Tampa Bay Film Commission FAX (813) 223-0083
401 E. Jackson St., Ste. 2100 www.filmtampabay.com
Tampa, FL 33602
Contact: Lindsey Norris

Georgia (404) 962-4052
Georgia Film, Video & Music Office FAX (404) 962-4053
75 Fifth St., Ste. 1200 www.georgia.org
Atlanta, GA 30308
Contact: Bill Thompson

Georgia-Savannah (912) 651-3696
(912) 651-2360
Savannah Film Commission FAX (912) 651-0982
P.O. Box 1027 www.savannahfilm.org
Savannah, GA 31402

Hawaii (808) 586-2570
Hawaii Film Office, P.O. Box 2359 FAX (808) 586-2572
Honolulu, HI 96804 www.hawaiifilmoffice.com
Contact: Donne Dawson

Hawaii-Big Island (808) 327-3663
(808) 981-8395
Big Island Film Office FAX (808) 981-2096
25 Aupuni St., Ste. 109 www.filmbigisland.com
Hilo, HI 96720

Hawaii-Honolulu (808) 527-6108
Honolulu Film Office FAX (808) 527-6102
530 S. King St., Ste. 306 www.filmhonolulu.com
Honolulu, HI 96813

Hawaii-Kauai (808) 241-6386
Kauai Film Commission FAX (808) 241-6399
4444 Rice St., Ste. 200 www.filmkauai.com
Lihue, HI 96766
Contact: Art Umezu

Hawaii-Maui (808) 270-7415
(808) 270-7710
Maui County Film Office FAX (808) 270-7995
One Main Plaza 2200 www.filmmaui.com
Main St., Ste. 305
Wailuku, HI 96793
Contact: Benita Brazier

Idaho (208) 334-2470
(800) 942-8338
Idaho Film Office FAX (208) 334-2631
700 W. State St., Box 83720 www.filmidaho.com
Boise, ID 83720
Contacts: Kat Haase & Peg Owens

Illinois (312) 814-3600
Illinois Film Office FAX (312) 814-8874
100 W. Randolph St., Third Fl. www.filmillinois.state.il.us
Chicago, IL 60601
Contact: Betsy Steinberg

Illinois-Chicago (312) 744-6415
Chicago Film Office FAX (312) 744-1378
121 N. LaSalle St., Ste. 806 www.chicagofilmoffice.us
Chicago, IL 60602

Indiana (317) 234-2087
Film Indiana FAX (317) 232-4146
One N. Capitol Ave., Ste. 700 www.filmindiana.com
Indianapolis, IN 46204
Contact: Erin Newell

Iowa-Cedar Rapids (319) 398-5009
(800) 735-5557
Cedar Rapids Convention & FAX (319) 398-5089
Visitors Bureau, 119 First Ave. SE www.cedar-rapids.com
Cedar Rapids, IA 52406

Iowa-Des Moines (515) 242-4726
Iowa Film Office, 200 E. Grand Ave. FAX (515) 242-4809
Des Moines, IA 50309 www.traveliowa.com/film/
Contact: Tom Wheeler

Jamaica-Kingston (876) 978-7755
(876) 978-5122
Jamaica Film Commission FAX (876) 978-0140
18 Trafalgar Rd. www.filmjamaica.com
Kingston 10 Jamaica
Contact: Del Crooks

Kansas (785) 296-4927
Kansas Film Commission FAX (785) 296-3490
1000 SW Jackson St., Ste. 100 www.filmkansas.com
Topeka, KS 66612

Kansas-Wichita (316) 660-6308
(800) 288-9424
Greater Wichita Convention & FAX (316) 265-0162
Visitors Bureau/Wichita Film Commission
100 S. Main, Ste. 100 www.visitwichita.com
Wichita, KS 67202

Kentucky (502) 564-3456
(800) 345-6591
Kentucky Film Office FAX (502) 564-7588
500 Mero St. 2200 Capital Plaza Tower
Frankfort, KY 40601 www.kyfilmoffice.com

Louisiana (225) 342-5403
Entertainment Industry, P.O. Box 94185 www.lafilm.org
Baton Rouge, LA 70804
Contacts: Alex Schott & Chris Stelly

Louisiana-New Orleans (504) 658-0912
FAX (504) 658-0934
www.cityofno.com/portal.aspx

Maine (207) 624-7631
Maine Film Office　FAX (207) 624-7631
59 State House Station　www.filminmaine.com
Augusta, ME 04333　FAX (207) 287-8070
Contact: Lea Girardin

Maryland (410) 767-6340
Maryland Film Office　(800) 333-6632
401 E. Pratt St., 14th Fl.　FAX (410) 333-0044
Baltimore, MD 21202　www.marylandfilm.org
Contact: Jack Gerbes

Maryland-Baltimore (410) 887-3334
Baltimore County Film Commission　FAX (410) 887-5781
400 Washington Ave.
Baltimore, MD 21204

Massachusetts-Boston (617) 635-3911
　(617) 635-4455
City of Boston Film Bureau　FAX (617) 635-4428
City Hall, Ste. 802　www.cityofboston.gov/arts
Boston, MA 02201

Mexico (52 55) 5448 5383
　(52 55) 5448 5322
National Film Commission - Mexico　FAX (52 55) 5448 5381
Av. Division Del Norte 2462 Quinto Piso
Col. Portales, C.P. 03300 Mexico
www.comefilm.gob.mx/english/inicio.html
Contact: Jorge Santoyo

Mexico-Baja California (664) 634-6330
State Film Commission　FAX (664) 634-7157
P.O. Box 2448　www.bajafilm.com
Chula Vista, CA 91912

Michigan (800) 477-3456
　(517) 373-0638
Michigan Film Office　FAX (517) 241-2930
702 W. Kalamazoo　www.michigan.gov/filmoffice
P.O. Box 30739
Lansing, MI 48909
Contact: Janet Lockwood

Minnesota (651) 645-3600
Minnesota Film & TV Board　FAX (651) 645-7373
2446 University Ave. West, Ste. 100　www.mnfilmandtv.org
Saint Paul, MN 55114
Contact: Lucinda Winter

Mississippi (601) 359-3297
　(601) 359-3422
Mississippi Film Office　FAX (601) 359-5048
P.O. Box 849　www.visitmississippi.org/film
Jackson, MS 39205

Mississippi-Greenwood (662) 453-9197
　(800) 748-9064
Greenwood Film Office　FAX (662) 453-5526
P.O. Drawer 739　www.gcvb.com
Greenwood, MS 38935

Mississippi-Natchez (601) 446-6345
　(800) 647-6724
Natchez Film Commission　FAX (601) 442-0814
640 S. Canal St., Box C　www.visitnatchez.org
Natchez, MS 39120

Mississippi-Tupelo (662) 841-6521
　(800) 533-0611
Tupelo Film Commission　FAX (662) 841-6558
P.O. Box 47　www.tupelo.net
Tupelo, MS 38802

Mississippi-Vicksburg (800) 221-3536
Vicksburg Convention &　FAX (601) 636-9475
Visitors Bureau, P.O. Box 110　www.visitvicksburg.com
Vicksburg, MS 39181

Missouri-Kansas City (816) 691-3833
　(800) 767-7700
Film Commission of Greater Kansas City　FAX (816) 691-3880
1100 Main St., Ste. 2200　www.kcfilm.com
Kansas City, MO 64105

Montana (406) 841-2876
　(800) 553-4563
Montana Film Office　FAX (406) 841-2877
301 S. Park Ave.　www.montanafilm.com
Helena, MT 59620
Contacts: John Ansotegui & Sten Iversen

Montana-Southcentral (406) 222-0438
Montana Film Center, P.O. Box 253
Livingston, MT 59047

Nebraska (402) 471-3746
　(800) 228-4307
Nebraska Film Office　FAX (402) 471-3778
P.O. Box 94666　www.filmnebraska.org
Lincoln, NE 68509

Nebraska-Omaha (402) 444-7737
Omaha Film Office　FAX (402) 444-4511
1001 Farnam St., Ste. 200　www.visitomaha.com
Omaha, NE 68102

Ⓐ Nevada (702) 486-2711
　(877) 638-3456
Nevada Film Office Las Vegas　FAX (702) 486-2712
555 E. Washington Ave., Ste. 5400　www.nevadafilm.com
Las Vegas, NV 89101
Contact: Charles Geocaris

Nevada-Reno-Tahoe (775) 687-1814
　(800) 336-1600
Nevada Film Office Reno/Tahoe　FAX (775) 687-4497
108 E. Proctor　www.nevadafilm.com
Carson City, NV 89701

New Hampshire (603) 271-2220
New Hampshire Film & TV Office　FAX (603) 271-3163
20 Park St.　www.nh.gov/film
Concord, NH 03301
Contact: Matthew Newton

New Jersey (973) 648-6279
New Jersey Motion Picture Commission　FAX (973) 648-7350
153 Halsey St., P.O. Box 47023　www.njfilm.org
Newark, NJ 07101
Contact: Joseph Friedman

New Jersey-Fort Lee (201) 592-3663
　(201) 693-2763
Fort Lee Film Commission　FAX (201) 585-7222
309 Main St.　www.fortleefilm.org
Fort Lee, NJ 07024

New Mexico (505) 476-5600
　(800) 545-9871
New Mexico Film Office　FAX (505) 476-5601
418 Montezuma Ave.　www.nmfilm.com
Santa Fe, NM 87501
Contact: Lisa Stroot

New Mexico-Albuquerque (505) 768-3283
Albuquerque Film Office　FAX (505) 768-3280
P.O. Box 1293　www.filmabq.com
Albuquerque, NM 87103

Ⓐ New York State (212) 803-2330
Governor's Office for　FAX (212) 803-2339
Motion Picture & Television Development
633 Third Ave., 33rd Fl.
New York, NY 10017　www.nylovesfilm.com/index.asp
Contact: Pat Swinney Kaufman

Ⓐ New York-Buffalo Niagara (716) 852-0511
　(888) 228-3369
Buffalo Niagara Film Commission　FAX (716) 852-0131
617 Main St., Ste. 200　www.filmbuffaloniagara.org
Buffalo, NY 14203

New York-Nassau County (516) 571-3168
Nassau County Film Office　FAX (516) 571-6195
One West St., Ste 326A　www.longislandfilm.com
Mineola, NY 11501

Ⓐ New York-New York City   **(212) 489-6710**
NYC Mayor's Office of Film,   FAX **(212) 307-6237**
Theatre & Broadcasting   **www.nyc.gov/film**
1697 Broadway
New York, NY 10019

New York-Rochester   **(585) 279-8308**
Rochester/Finger Lakes Film Office   FAX **(585) 232-4822**
45 East Ave., Ste. 400   **www.filmrochester.org**
Rochester, NY 14604

New York-Suffolk County   **(631) 853-4800**
Suffolk County Film Office   FAX **(631) 853-4888**
H. Lee Dennison Bldg., Second Fl.
100 Veterans Hwy
Hauppauge, NY 11788
www.suffolkcountyfilmcommission.com

     (518) 584-3255
New York-Upstate   **(800) 526-8970**
Capital-Saratoga Film Commission   FAX **(518) 587-0318**
28 Clinton St.   **www.capital-saratogafilm.com**
Saratoga Springs, NY 12866

     (919) 733-9900
North Carolina   **(866) 468-2273**
North Carolina Film Office   FAX **(919) 715-0151**
301 N. Wilmington St.   **www.ncfilm.com**
Raleigh, NC 27699
Contact: Aaron Syrett

North Carolina-Charlotte   **(704) 347-8942**
Charlotte Regional Film Office   FAX **(704) 347-8981**
1001 Morehead Square Dr., Ste. 200   **www.charlotteusa.com**
Charlotte, NC 28203

North Carolina-Durham   **(919) 680-8313**
Durham Film Office, 101 E. Morgan St.   FAX **(919) 683-8353**
Durham, NC 27701   **www.durham-nc.com**

North Carolina-Greensboro   **(336) 393-0001**
Piedmont Triad Film Commission   FAX **(336) 668-3749**
7025 Albert Pick Rd., Ste. 303   **www.piedmontfilm.com**
Greensboro, NC 27409

     (252) 482-4333
North Carolina-Northeast   **(888) 872-8562**
Northeast Partnership Film Office   FAX **(252) 482-3366**
119 W. Water St.   **www.ncnortheast.com**
Edenton, NC 27932

**North Carolina-
Western North Carolina**   **(828) 687-7234**
Western North Carolina Film Commission   FAX **(828) 687-7552**
134 Wright Brothers Way   **www.wncfilm.net**
Fletcher, NC 28732
Contact: Mary Trimarco

North Carolina-Wilmington   **(910) 343-3456**
Wilmington Regional   FAX **(910) 343-3457**
Film Commission, Inc.   **www.wilmingtonfilm.com**
1223 N. 23rd St.
Wilmington, NC 28405

     (701) 328-2509
North Dakota   **(800) 435-5663**
North Dakota Film Commission   FAX **(701) 328-4878**
1600 E. Century Ave., Ste. 2   **www.ndtourism.com**
Bismarck, ND 58502

Ohio-Cincinnati   **(513) 784-1744**
Cincinnati & Northern Kentucky   FAX **(513) 768-8963**
Film Commission   **www.film-cincinnati.org**
602 Main St., Ste. 712
Cincinnati, OH 45202

Ohio-Cleveland   **(216) 623-3910**
Greater Cleveland Film Commission   FAX **(216) 623-0876**
1301 E. Ninth St., Ste. 120   **www.clevelandfilm.com**
Cleveland, OH 44113

Ohio-Columbus   **(614) 264-2324**
Greater Columbus Film Commission
P.O. Box 12735   **www.filmcolumbus.com**
Columbus, OH 43212

     (405) 230-8440
Oklahoma   **(800) 766-3456**
Oklahoma Film & Music Office   FAX **(405) 230-8640**
120 N. Robinson, Sixth Fl.   **www.oklahomafilm.org**
Oklahoma City, OK 73102
Contact: Jill Simpson

Oregon   **(503) 229-5832**
Oregon Film & Video Office   FAX **(503) 229-6869**
121 SW Salmon St., Ste. 1205   **www.oregonfilm.org**
Portland, OR 97204

Pennsylvania   **(717) 783-3456**
Pennsylvania Film Office   FAX **(717) 787-0687**
Commonwealth Keystone Bldg.   **www.filminpa.com**
400 North St., Fourth Fl.
Harrisburg, PA 17120
Contact: Janie Shecter

Pennsylvania-Philadelphia   **(215) 686-2668**
Greater Philadelphia Film Office   FAX **(215) 686-3659**
100 S. Broad St., Ste. 600   **www.film.org**
Philadelphia, PA 19110

     (412) 261-2744
Pennsylvania-Pittsburgh   **(888) 744-3456**
Pittsburgh Film Office   FAX **(412) 471-7317**
130 Seventh St., Ste. 202   **www.pghfilm.org**
Pittsburgh, PA 15222

Puerto Rico   **(787) 758-4747**
Puerto Rico Film Commission   FAX **(787) 756-5706**
355 F.D. Roosevelt Ave.   **www.puertoricofilm.com**
Ste. 106 P.O. Box 362350
Hato Rey 00918 Puerto Rico
Contact: Laura Velez

     (401) 222-3456
Rhode Island   **(401) 222-6666**
Rhode Island Film & TV Office   FAX **(401) 222-3018**
One Capitol Hill, Third Fl.   **www.film.ri.gov**
Providence, RI 02908
Contact: Steven Feinberg

South Carolina   **(803) 737-0490**
South Carolina Film Commission   FAX **(803) 737-3104**
1201 Main St., Ste. 1600   **www.filmsc.com**
Columbia, SC 29201
Contact: Jeff Monks

     (605) 773-3301
South Dakota   **(800) 952-3625**
South Dakota Film Office   FAX **(605) 773-3256**
711 E. Wells Ave.   **www.filmsd.com**
Pierre, SD 57501
Contact: Lesa Jarding

     (615) 741-3456
Tennessee   **(877) 818-3456**
Tennessee Film, Entertainment and   FAX **(615) 741-5554**
Music Commission   **www.film.tennessee.gov**
312 Eighth Ave. North, Ninth Fl.
Nashville, TN 37243

     (865) 246-2629
Tennessee-Knoxville   **(865) 637-4550**
East Tennessee Television &   FAX **(865) 523-2071**
Film Commission   **www.ettfc.com**
17 Market Square, Ste. 201 (Near Market St.)
Knoxville, TN 37902
Contact: Thomas Duncan

Tennessee-Memphis   **(901) 527-8300**
Memphis & Shelby County   FAX **(901) 527-8326**
Film Commission
516 Tennessee St., Ste. 215
Memphis, TN 38103

Tennessee-Nashville (615) 880-1827 / (615) 862-4700
Mayor's Office of Film FAX (615) 862-6025
222 Second Ave. North, Ste. 418 www.filmnashville.com
Nashville, TN 37201

Texas (512) 463-9200
Texas Film Commission FAX (512) 463-4114
P.O. Box 13246 www.texasfilmcommission.com
Austin, TX 78711
Contact: Bob Hudgins

Texas-Austin (512) 583-7229 / (512) 583-7230
Austin Film Commission FAX (512) 583-7281
301 Congress Ave., Ste. 200 www.austintexas.org
Austin, TX 78701

Texas-Dallas/Fort Worth (214) 571-1050
Dallas Film Commission FAX (214) 665-2907
325 N. St. Paul St., Ste. 700
Dallas, TX 75201 www.dallasfilmcommission.com

Texas-El Paso (915) 534-0698 / (800) 351-6024
El Paso Film Commission FAX (915) 532-2963
One Civic Center Plaza www.visitelpaso.com
El Paso, TX 79901

Texas-Houston (713) 227-1407 / (713) 437-5251
Houston Film Commission FAX (713) 223-3816
901 Bagby, Ste. 100 www.filmhouston.texaswebhost.com
Houston, TX 77002

Ⓐ Texas-San Antonio (210) 207-6730 / (800) 447-3372
San Antonio Film Commission FAX (210) 207-6843
203 S. St. Mary's St. Second Fl. www.filmsanantonio.com
San Antonio, TX 78205

Texas-South Padre Island (956) 761-3005 / (800) 657-2373
South Padre Island Film Commission www.sopadre.com
7355 Padre Blvd.
Port Isabel, TX 78597

U.S. Virgin Islands (340) 775-1444 / (340) 774-8784
U.S. Virgin Island Film Promotion Office FAX (340) 774-4390
P.O. Box 6400
St. Thomas 00804, Virgin Islands
Contact: Caroline Simon

Utah (801) 538-8740 / (800) 453-8824
Utah Film Commission FAX (801) 538-1397
Council Hall/Capitol Hill www.film.utah.gov
300 N. State St.
Salt Lake City, UT 84114
Contact: Marshall Moore

Utah-Kane County (435) 644-5033 / (800) 733-5263
Kane County Film Commission FAX (435) 644-5923
78 South 100 East www.kaneutah.com
Kanab, UT 84741

Utah-Moab (435) 259-1346
Moab to Monument Valley FAX (435) 259-2574
Film Commission, P.O. Box 640 www.filmmoab.com
Moab, UT 84532

Utah-Park City (435) 649-6100 / (800) 453-1360
Park City Film Commission FAX (435) 649-4132
1910 Prospector Ave., Ste. 103 www.parkcityfilm.com
Park City, UT 84060

Vermont (802) 828-3618
Vermont Film Commission FAX (802) 828-0607
10 Baldwin St. Drawer 33 www.vermontfilm.com
(Near Bailey Ave.)
Montpelier, VT 05633
Contact: Joseph Bookchin

Virginia (804) 545-5530 / (800) 854-6233
Virginia Film Office FAX (804) 545-5531
901 E. Byrd St., West Tower, 19th Fl. www.film.virginia.org
Richmond, VA 23219

Virginia-Central Virginia (804) 216-2772
Central Virginia Film Office FAX (804) 862-1200
One New Millennium Dr. www.cvfo.org
Petersburg, VA 23805

Washington (206) 264-0667
Washington State Film Office FAX (206) 382-4343
1218 Third Ave., Ste. 1515 www.washingtonfilmworks.org
Seattle, WA 98101

Washington-Seattle (206) 684-5030 / (206) 684-0903
Seattle Film & Music Office FAX (206) 684-0379
700 Fifth Ave., Ste. 5752 www.seattle.gov/filmandmusic
P.O. Box 94708
Seattle, WA 98124

West Virginia (866) 698-3456 / (304) 550-1871
West Virginia Film Office FAX (304) 558-1662
90 MacCorkle Ave. SW www.wvfilm.com
S. Charleston, WV 25303
Contact: Pamela Haynes

Wisconsin (414) 287-6235
Wisconsin Film Office www.filmwisconsin.net
648 N. Plankinton Ave., Ste. 425
Milwaukee, WI 53203
Contact: Melissa Musante

Wyoming (307) 777-3400 / (800) 458-6657
Wyoming Film Office FAX (307) 777-2877
I-25 at College Dr. www.filmwyoming.com
Cheyenne, WY 82002
Contacts: Michell Howard & Colin Stricklin

Film Commissions—International

Australia-Melbourne
61 3 9660 3240
61 3 9660 3200
FAX 61 3 9660 3201
www.film.vic.gov.au
Melbourne Film Office/Film Victoria
Level 7, 189 Flinders Ln.
Melbourne, Victoria 3000 Australia

Australia-New South Wales
61 2 9264 6400
FAX 61 2 9264 4388
www.fto.nsw.gov.au
Level 13, 227 Elizabeth St.
Sydney, NSW 2000 Australia

Australia-Queensland
61 7 3224 4114
61 7 3224 5838
FAX 61 7 3224 6717
www.pftc.com.au
Pacific Film and Television Commission
Level 15, 111 George St., Brisbane
Queensland, Queensland 4000 Australia
Contact: Jess Conoplia

Austria
43 1 58858 0
FAX 43 1 586 8659
www.location-austria.at
Opernring 3/2
1010 Vienna Austria

Austria-Cine Tirol
43 512 5320 182
FAX 43 512 5320 140
www.cinetirol.com
Cine Tirol Film Commission
Tirol Werbung Maria-Theresien-Strasse 55
Innsbruck A-6010 Austria

Brazil-Amazon
92 633 2850
FAX 92 233 9973
www.amazonasfilm.com.br
Av. Sete de Setembro 1546
Manaus-AM, Amazonas 69005-141 Brazil

France
33 1 53 83 98 98
FAX 33 1 53 83 98 99
www.filmfrance.net
33, rue des Jeûneurs, 75 002
Paris, France

Germany-Bavaria
089 544602 16
FAX 089 544602 23
www.film-commission-bayern.de
Sonnenstrasse 21
Munich, Bavaria 80331 Germany

Germany-Berlin
0331 743 87 30
FAX 0331 743 87 99
www.bbfc.de
Berlin Brandenburg Film Commission
August-Bebel-Strasse 26-53, 14482 Postdam-Babelsberg
Germany

Ireland
353 91 561 398
FAX 353 91 561 405
www.irishfilmboard.ie
Location Services, Rockford House
St. Augustine St.
Galway, Ireland

Italy-Campania
39 81 509 1533
39 338 696 9028
FAX 39 81 509 8470
www.campaniafilmcommission.org
Via Lago Patria 200
Giugliano in Campania 80014 Italy

Netherlands-Rotterdam
31 10 436 0747
FAX 31 10 436 0553
www.rff.rotterdam.nl
Llooydstraat 9F
Rotterdam 3015 EA Netherlands

New Zealand
64 4 385 0766
FAX 64 4 384 5840
www.filmnz.com
23 Frederick St.
Wellington 6011 New Zealand

Northern Ireland
44 28 9023 2444
FAX 44 28 9023 9918
www.niftc.co.uk
21 Alfred St.
Belfast BT2 8ED Ireland

Norway
47 55 56 4343
FAX 47 90 88 7385
www.norwegianfilm.com
Georgernes Verft 12
Bergen N-5011 Norway

Portugal
351 213 230 800
FAX 351 213 343 1952
www.icam.pt
Rua S. Pedro de Alcantara, 45-1
Lisboa 1269-138 Portugal

Scotland-Edinburgh
44 131 622 7337
FAX 44 131 622 7338
www.edinfilm.com
63 George St.
Edinburgh EH2 2JG United Kingdom

Scotland-Glasgow
0845 300 7300
www.scottishscreen.com
Scottish Screen
Second Fl. 249 W. George St.
Glasgow G2 4QE United Kingdom

Scotland-Highlands & Islands
44 1463 710221
FAX 44 1463 710848
www.scotfilm.org
Inverness Castle
Inverness, IV2 3EG United Kingdom

Spain-Barcelona
34 93 454 8066
FAX 34 93 323 8048
www.barcelonafilm.com
Barcelona Plató Film Commission
C/ Mallorca, 209, Principal-1
Barcelona 08036 Spain
Contact: Júlia Goytisolo

Spain-Canary Islands
34 922 321 331
FAX 34 922 237 876
www.tenerifefilm.com
Tenerife Film, C/Áurea Diaz Flores
s/n., 38005 Santa Cruz de Tenerife
Islas Canarias Spain

Sweden
46 8 665 11 00
46 8 665 12 55
FAX 46 8 666 37 48
www.swedenfilmcommission.com
P.O. Box 27183
Stockholm S-10252 Sweden

Sweden-West Sweden
46 520 49 09 07
FAX 46 520 49 09 01
www.swedenfilmcommission.com
Film I Vast, Box 134
Trollhattan 461 23 Sweden

UK
44 20 7861 7861
FAX 44 20 7861 7862
www.ukfilmcouncil.org.uk
UK Film Council
10 Little Portland St.
London WIW 7JG United Kingdom

UK-East Midlands
44 115 910 5564
44 115 934 9090
FAX 44 115 950 0988
www.em-media.org.uk
35-37 St. Mary's Gate
Nottingham NG1 1PU United Kingdom

UK-Isle of Main
44 1624 687173
FAX 44 1624 687171
www.gov.im/dti/iomfilm
First Fl., Hamilton House, Peel Rd.
Douglas IMI 5EP United Kingdom

UK-Liverpool
44 151 708 2967
FAX 44 151 708 2984
www.liverpool.gov.uk
233 The Tea Factory, 82 Wood St.
Liverpool L1 4DQ United Kingdom

UK-London
44 207 613 7676
FAX 44 207 613 7677
www.filmlondon.org.uk
Film London, The Tea Building
56 Shoreditch High St., Ste. 6.10
London E1 6JJ United Kingdom

UK-South West Screen
44 117 952 9977
FAX 44 117 952 9988
www.swscreen.co.uk
St. Bartholomews Court
Lewins Mead
Bristol BS1 5BT United Kingdom

UK-Yorkshire
44 (0) 113 294 4410
FAX 44 (0) 113 294 4989
www.screenyorkshire.co.uk
Studio 22, 46 The Calls
Leeds LS2 7EY United Kingdom

Hotels & Short-Term Housing

60 Thompson (212) 204-6491
60 Thompson St. (Near Broome St.) (877) 431-0400
New York, NY 10012 FAX (212) 204-5005
www.thompsonhotels.com

Accredited Accommodations Inc. (212) 695-3404
(Short-Term Housing) (800) 277-0413
FAX (212) 695-4655
www.furnapts.com

Acocella Group (212) 991-5750
27 W. 24th St., Ste. 704 FAX (212) 367-0976
New York, NY 10010 www.tagrelo.com

The Algonquin (212) 840-6800
59 W. 44th St. (Near Sixth Ave.) (888) 304-2047
New York, NY 10036 FAX (212) 944-1419
www.algonquinhotel.com

Ameritania Hotel (212) 247-5000
230 W. 54th St. (Near Broadway) FAX (212) 247-3313
New York, NY 10019 www.nychotels.com

Amsterdam Court Hotel (212) 459-1000
226 W. 50th St. (Near Broadway) FAX (212) 265-5070
New York, NY 10019 www.nychotels.com

Avalon Hotel (212) 299-7000
(Short-Term Housing) (888) 442-8256
FAX (212) 299-7001
www.avalonhotelnyc.com

Bed & Breakfast (212) 645-8134
Network of New York (800) 900-8134
130 Barrow St., Ste. 508 www.bedandbreakfastnetny.com
(Near Washington St.)
New York, NY 10014

Bedford Hotel (212) 697-4800
(Short-Term Housing) (800) 221-6881
FAX (212) 697-1093
www.bedfordhotel.com

Beekman Tower (212) 355-7300
Three Mitchell Pl. (Near E. 49th St.) (866) 298-4606
New York, NY 10017 FAX (212) 753-9366
www.thebeekmanhotel.com

The Benjamin (212) 715-2500
125 E. 50th St. (Near Lexington Ave.) (212) 320-8002
New York, NY 10022 FAX (212) 715-2525
www.thebenjamin.com

The Bentley (212) 644-6000
500 E. 62nd St. (Near York Ave.) FAX (212) 207-4800
New York, NY 10021 www.nychotels.com

BridgeStreet (212) 594-7744
Corporate Housing Worldwide (866) 594-7744
FAX (212) 594-8987
www.bridgestreet.com

Bryant Park Hotel (212) 869-0100
40 W. 40th St. (Near Sixth Ave.) (877) 640-9300
New York, NY 10018 FAX (212) 869-4446
www.bryantparkhotel.com

The Carlton on Madison Avenue (212) 532-4100
88 Madison Ave. FAX (212) 231-6911
New York, NY 10016 www.carltonhotelny.com

The Carlyle (212) 744-1600
35 E. 76th St. (Near Madison Ave.) (800) 227-5737
New York, NY 10021 FAX (212) 717-4682
www.thecarlyle.com

Casablanca Hotel (212) 869-1212
147 W. 43rd St. (Near Broadway) (888) 922-7225
New York, NY 10036 FAX (212) 391-7585
www.casablancahotel.com

Chambers (212) 974-5656
15 W. 56th St. (Near Fifth Ave.) FAX (212) 974-5657
New York, NY 10019 www.chambershotel.com

Chelsea Inn (212) 645-8989
46 W. 17th St. (Near Sixth Ave.) (800) 640-6469
New York, NY 10011 FAX (212) 645-1903
www.chelseainn.com

Churchill Corporate Services (212) 686-0444
245 W. 17th St. (800) 658-7366
New York, NY 10011 www.furnishedhousing.com
(Short-Term Housing)

Churchill Residence Suites (973) 636-9400
15 Park Row www.churchillsuitesdowntown.com
(Near Ann St.)
New York, NY 10038

Citi Furnished (212) 689-4900
250 Park Ave. South www.citifurnished.com
New York, NY 10003
(Short-Term Housing)

Eastgate Tower Suite Hotel (212) 687-8000
222 E. 39th St. FAX (212) 490-2634
New York, NY 10016 www.affinia.com
(Short-Term Housing)

The Fitzpatrick Manhattan (212) 355-0100
687 Lexington Ave. (Near E. 57th St.) (800) 367-7701
New York, NY 10022 FAX (212) 308-5166
www.fitzpatrickhotels.com

Ⓐ Flatotel (212) 887-9400
135 W. 52nd St. FAX (212) 887-9893
New York, NY 10019

The Four Seasons (212) 758-5700
57 E. 57th St. (Near Park Ave.) (800) 332-3442
New York, NY 10022 FAX (212) 758-5517
www.fourseasons.com

Glenwood NYC (212) 535-0500
(Short-Term Housing) (877) 535-0500
www.glenwoodnyc.com

Gramercy Park Hotel (212) 920-3300
Two Lexington Ave. FAX (212) 201-2170
New York, NY 10010 www.gramercyparkhotel.com

Grand Hyatt (212) 883-1234
Park Ave. at Grand Central Station (800) 233-1234
(Near Park Ave.) FAX (212) 697-3772
New York, NY 10017 www.newyork.hyatt.com

Hotel Beacon (212) 787-1100
2130 Broadway (Near W. 75th St.) (800) 572-4969
New York, NY 10023 FAX (212) 724-0839
www.beaconhotel.com

Hotel Elysée (212) 753-1066
60 E. 54th St. (Near Madison Ave.) (800) 535-9733
New York, NY 10022 FAX (212) 980-9278
www.elyseehotel.com

Hotel Metro (212) 947-2500
45 W. 35th St. (Near Sixth Ave.) FAX (212) 279-1310
New York, NY 10001 www.hotelmetronyc.com

Hotel Wales (212) 876-6000
1295 Madison Ave. (Near E. 92nd St.) FAX (212) 860-7000
New York, NY 10128 www.waleshotel.com

Hudson Hotel (212) 554-6000
356 W. 58th St. (Near Ninth Ave.) (800) 697-1791
New York, NY 10019 FAX (212) 554-6001
www.hudsonhotel.com

Inn At Irving Place (212) 533-4600
56 Irving Pl. (Near E. 17th St.) FAX **(212) 533-4611**
New York, NY 10003 www.innatirving.com

(800) 782-8021
InterContinental Barclay (212) 755-5900
111 E. 48th St. FAX **(212) 644-0079**
New York, NY 10017 www.new-york.interconti.com

(212) 247-0300
Juhmeirah Essex House (888) 645-5697
160 Central Park South FAX **(212) 315-1839**
(Near Seventh Ave.) www.essexhouse.com
New York, NY 10019

The Kitano (212) 885-7000
66 Park Ave. (Near E. 38th St.) FAX **(212) 885-7100**
New York, NY 10016 www.kitano.com

(917) 306-5600
A Lauren Berger Collection (917) 388-2512
www.laurenbergercollection.com

(212) 245-5000
Le Parker Meridien (212) 748-7420
118 W. 57th St. (Near Sixth Ave.) FAX **(212) 307-1776**
New York, NY 10019 www.parkermeridien.com

(212) 838-1400
The Lowell (800) 221-4444
28 E. 63rd St. (Near Madison Ave.) FAX **(212) 319-4230**
New York, NY 10021 www.lhw.com

(212) 944-6050
The Mansfield (800) 255-5167
12 W. 44th St. (Near Fifth Ave.) FAX **(212) 764-4477**
New York, NY 10036 www.mansfieldhotel.com

The Marcel (212) 696-3800
201 E. 24th St. (Near Third Ave.) FAX **(212) 696-0077**
New York, NY 10011 www.nychotels.com

(212) 744-4300
The Mark (800) 843-6275
25 E. 77th St. (Near Madison Ave.) FAX **(212) 744-2749**
New York, NY 10021 www.mandarinoriental.com

(212) 417-3100
The Marmara - Manhattan (800) 621-9029
301 E. 94th St. (Near Second Ave.) FAX **(212) 427-3042**
New York, NY 10128 www.marmara-manhattan.com
(Extended Stay Housing)

(212) 953-5707
Marriott ExecuStay (800) 877-2800
FAX **(212) 953-5755**
www.execustay.com

Mercer Hotel (212) 965-3800
147 Mercer St. (Near Prince St.) FAX **(212) 965-3838**
New York, NY 10012 www.mercerhotel.com

(212) 765-0505
The Michelangelo (800) 237-0990
152 W. 51st St. (Near Seventh Ave.) FAX **(212) 541-6604**
New York, NY 10019 www.michelangelohotel.com

Millennium Hotel
New York U.N. Plaza (212) 758-1234
One United Nations Plaza FAX **(212) 702-5051**
(Near First Ave.) www.millennium-hotels.com
New York, NY 10017

The Moderne (212) 397-6767
243 W. 55th St. (Near Broadway) FAX **(212) 397-8787**
New York, NY 10019 www.nychotels.com

(212) 686-0300
Morgans Hotel (800) 334-3408
237 Madison Ave. (Near E. 37th St.) FAX **(212) 779-8352**
New York, NY 10016 www.morganshotel.com

(212) 485-2400
The Muse (877) 692-6873
130 W. 46th St. (Near Sixth Ave.) FAX **(212) 485-2900**
New York, NY 10036 www.themusehotel.com

New York Helmsley (212) 490-8900
212 E. 42nd St. (Near Second Ave.) FAX **(212) 405-4299**
New York, NY 10017 www.helmsleyhotels.com

(212) 586-7000
New York Hilton (800) 445-8667
1335 Avenue of the Americas FAX **(212) 315-1374**
(Near W. 53rd St.) www.hilton.com
New York, NY 10019

(718) 246-7000
New York Marriott Brooklyn (800) 236-2427
333 Adams St. (Near Willoughby St.) FAX **(718) 246-0563**
Brooklyn, NY 11201 www.marriott.com

(212) 385-4900
New York Marriott Downtown (800) 228-9290
85 West St. (Near Spring St.) FAX **(212) 227-8136**
New York, NY 10006 www.marriott.com

(212) 755-4000
New York Marriott East Side (800) 236-2427
525 Lexington Ave. (Near E. 49th St.) FAX **(212) 751-3440**
New York, NY 10017 www.marriott.com

(212) 398-1900
New York Marriott Marquis (800) 228-9290
1535 Broadway (Near W. 45th St.) FAX **(212) 704-8930**
New York, NY 10036 www.marriott.com

(212) 888-7000
New York Palace (800) 697-2522
455 Madison Ave. (Near E. 50th St.) FAX **(212) 303-6000**
New York, NY 10022 www.newyorkpalace.com

Oakwood Corporate Housing (888) 745-3429
(Extended Stay Housing) www.oakwood.com/production

(212) 753-5800
Omni Berkshire Place (800) 843-6664
21 E. 52nd St. (Near Madison Ave.) FAX **(212) 754-5018**
New York, NY 10022 www.omnihotels.com

(212) 764-5500
The Paramount (800) 225-7474
235 W. 46th St. (Near Eighth Ave.) FAX **(212) 554-6511**
New York, NY 10036

Park Savoy Hotel (212) 245-5755
(Short-Term Housing) FAX **(212) 765-0668**
www.parksavoyhotel.com

(212) 247-2200
The Peninsula (800) 262-9467
700 Fifth Ave. (Near W. 55th St.) FAX **(212) 903-3949**
New York, NY 10019 www.peninsula.com

(212) 838-8000
The Pierre (800) 332-3442
Two E. 61st St. (Near Fifth Ave.) FAX **(212) 758-1615**
New York, NY 10021 www.fourseasons.com/pierre

(212) 734-9100
Plaza Athénée (800) 447-8800
37 E. 64th St. (Near Madison Ave.) FAX **(212) 772-0958**
New York, NY 10021 www.plaza-athenee.com

(212) 751-5710
The Plaza Fifty Suites Hotel (800) 637-8483
155 E. 50th St. (Near Third Ave.) FAX **(212) 753-1468**
New York, NY 10022 www.mesuite.com

The Plaza Hotel (800) 257-7544
Fifth Ave. at Central Park South
New York, NY 10019 www.fairmont.com/theplaza

(212) 755-4400
Radisson Lexington Hotel (800) 448-4471
(Short-Term Housing) FAX **(212) 308-0194**
www.lexingtonhotelnyc.com

Here's the plot. Flatotel gives you the artsy feel of a boutique hotel and the comfort of the largest guestrooms in the city. Plus, our Midtown location means you're just minutes from everything — major attractions, soundstages and television networks. Our Moda restaurant serves excellent Italian cuisine and our outdoor lounge is famous for its happy hour. Choose Flatotel the next time you're in the city and work and play in style.

FLATOTEL
INTIMATE • TAILORED • COSMOPOLITAN

A New York City Hotel

135 West 52nd Street
Reservations at 212.887.9400 ~ 1.800.FLATOTEL
www.flatotel.com

The Regency
540 Park Ave. (Near E. 61st St.)
New York, NY 10021
(212) 759-4100
(800) 235-6397
FAX (212) 826-5674
www.loewshotels.com

Renaissance New York Hotel Times Square
714 Seventh Ave. (Near W. 48th St.)
New York, NY 10036
(212) 765-7676
(800) 236-2427
FAX (212) 765-1962
www.nycrenaissance.com

The Roger Smith
501 Lexington Ave. (Near E. 47th St.)
New York, NY 10017
(212) 755-1400
(800) 445-0277
FAX (212) 319-9130
www.rogersmith.com

Royalton Hotel
44 W. 44th St. (Near Sixth Ave.)
New York, NY 10036
(212) 869-4400
(800) 635-9013
FAX (212) 869-8965
www.royalton.com

Sherry-Netherland
781 Fifth Ave. (Near E. 59th St.)
New York, NY 10022
(212) 355-2800
FAX (212) 319-4306
www.sherrynetherland.com

The Shoreham
33 W. 55th St. (Near Fifth Ave.)
New York, NY 10019
(212) 247-6700
(800) 553-3347
FAX (212) 765-9741
www.shorehamhotel.com

SoHo Grand
310 W. Broadway (Near Canal St.)
New York, NY 10013
(212) 965-3000
(800) 965-3000
FAX (212) 965-3200
www.sohogrand.com

St. Regis
Two E. 55th St. (Near Fifth Ave.)
New York, NY 10022
(212) 753-4500
(800) 759-7550
FAX (212) 787-3447
www.starwood.com

Trump International Hotel and Towers
One Central Park West
(Near W. 59th St.)
New York, NY 10023
(212) 299-1000
(888) 448-7867
FAX (212) 299-1150
www.trumpintl.com

The Tudor Hotel
304 E. 42nd St. (Near Second Ave.)
New York, NY 10017
(212) 986-8800
(800) 879-8836
FAX (212) 986-1758
www.tudorhotelny.com

W New York
541 Lexington Ave. (Near E. 49th St.)
New York, NY 10022
(212) 755-1200
(877) 946-8357
FAX (212) 319-8344
www.whotels.com

W New York - The Court
130 E. 39th St. (Near Lexington Ave.)
New York, NY 10016
(212) 685-1100
(877) 946-8357
FAX (212) 889-0287
www.whotels.com

W New York - The Tuscany
120 E. 39th St. (Near Lexington Ave.)
New York, NY 10016
(212) 686-1600
(877) 946-8357
FAX (212) 779-7822
www.whotels.com

W New York - Times Square
1567 Broadway (Near W. 47th St.)
New York, NY 10036
(212) 930-7400
(877) 946-8357
FAX (212) 930-7500
www.whotels.com

W New York - Union Square
201 Park Ave. South (Near E. 17th St.)
New York, NY 10003
(212) 253-9119
(877) 946-8357
FAX (212) 253-9229
www.whotels.com

Waldorf-Astoria
301 Park Ave. (Near E. 49th St.)
New York, NY 10022
(212) 355-3000
(800) 925-3673
FAX (212) 872-7272
www.waldorf.com

The Warwick
65 W. 54th St. (Near Sixth Ave.)
New York, NY 10019
(212) 247-2700
FAX (212) 247-2725
www.warwickhotels.com

Westin NY at Times Square
270 W. 43rd St.
New York, NY 10036
(866) 837-4183
(212) 201-2700
FAX (212) 201-2701
www.westinny.com

Limousine & Car Services

Ⓐ AA Executive Town Car & Limousine (516) 792-1735 / (800) 716-2799
333 Hempstead Ave., Ste. 209 FAX (516) 256-0092
(Near Catalpa Dr.) www.exectownlimo.com
Malverne, NY 11565

American Classic Limousines (212) 979-0500 / (888) 692-5466
237 First Ave. (Near E. 14th St.) www.1888nyclimo.com
New York, NY 10003

American Ground Transportation (212) 979-0500
237 First Ave. (Near E. 14th St.) www.1888nyclimo.com
New York, NY 10003

Attitude New York, Inc. (212) 397-0004
P.O. Box 223 www.attitudenewyork.com
Planetarium Station
New York, NY 10024

Bens Luxury Car & Limousine Service, Inc. (718) 433-2776 / (888) 446-5466
50-19 49th St. (Near 11th St.) FAX (718) 706-8968
Queens, NY 11377 www.benslimo.com

Bermuda Limousine International (212) 647-8400 / (800) 223-1383
537 W. 20th St. (Near West Side Hwy) FAX (212) 633-2685
New York, NY 10011 www.bermudalimo.com

Big Apple Car, Inc. (718) 236-7788

BLS Limo (800) 843-5752
18-20 Steinway St. (Near Berrian Blvd.) FAX (718) 274-2408
Astoria, NY 11105 www.blslimo.com

Carizma Limo (516) 825-3664 / (800) 247-9385
P.O. Box 160 FAX (516) 825-7306
Valley Stream, NY 11582 www.carizmatransportation.com

EXECUTIVE TOWN CAR & LIMO
Professional On Time Service
Serving New York's Television, Movie and Production Industry for over 15 years!
All new Lincoln's, Mercedes and SUVs
1-800-716-2799
exectown@aol.com
www.exectownlimo.com

intaBORO
Two-Way Radio Car
Safe • Reliable • Courteous • Professional
Luxury Town Cars • 24/7
Thirty-eight years serving New York's TV, Movie & Production Industry
Call now to set up your Voucher Account
718-845-1705
J. David Krauser x3024   Steve Strum x3027

Carmel	(212) 666-6666 (800) 922-7635
Crown Limousine 42-37 Crescent St. (Near 42nd Rd.) Long Island City, NY 11101	(212) 246-2626 (800) 692-7696 FAX (718) 943-0391 www.1800mycrown.com
Dial 7 4323 35th St. (Near 43rd Ave.) Queens, NY 11101	(212) 777-7777 (800) 777-8888 www.dial7.com
Dial Car 2106 Avenue X Brooklyn, NY 11235	(718) 743-8383
Diva Limousine, Ltd. 22 Butler St. Elizabeth, NJ 07206	(800) 427-3482 FAX (908) 248-0250 www.divalimo.com
Garden State Limo 58 First St. Hackensack, NJ 07601	(800) 300-3356 (800) 481-8626 www.gardenstatelimo.us
Highbridge Car Service	(212) 927-4600
ⓐ Intaboro 88-19 101 Ave. Jamaica, NY 11416	(718) 845-1705 FAX (718) 845-1709
The Limo Tour 1636 Third Ave., Ste. 420 (Near 92nd St.) New York, NY 10128	(212) 423-0101 FAX (212) 423-0404 www.limotours.com
LimoRes.net 134 W. 37th St. New York, NY 10018	(646) 898-2322 (877) 546-6186 FAX (212) 967-9812
ⓐ Mansfield's Executive Transportation 603 W. 148th St. New York, NY 10031	(212) 281-0017 (646) 286-3868 FAX (212) 926-9789
Prestige Limousine Service 85 Goodway Dr. (Near Winton) Rochester, NY 14623	(585) 272-9760 FAX (585) 424-5419 www.prestigelimo-of-wny.com
Ready to Roll Limousine Service, Inc. 1850 Amsterdam Ave. New York, NY 10031	(212) 714-1900 (800) 666-7689 FAX (212) 694-0010 www.rtrlimo.com
Regal Limousine Service 26 Bogert St. Closter, NJ 07624	(800) 383-7028 www.regallimousineservice.com
Royal Way Limousine, Inc. 300 E. 54th St. (Near Second Ave.) New York, NY 10022	(212) 593-3291 (866) 253-3705 www.royalwaylimo.com
Smith Limousine Service 636 W. 47th St. (Near 11th Ave.) New York, NY 10036	(212) 247-0711 FAX (212) 586-6353
Top Class Limousine 24 Ashburton Ave. (Near N. Broadway) Yonkers, NY 10701	(914) 423-5466 (800) 427-5450 FAX (914) 423-2277 www.topclasslimo.com

Debbie Regan LOCATIONS
tel: 212.591.1313
tel: 516.626.1928

NYC, NY, NJ, & CT
- Mansions
- Lofts
- Apartments
- Offices
- Schools
- Equestrian
- Suburban
- Beach Houses
& More!

www.debbiereganlocations.com

Location Libraries, Management & Scouts

AKA Locations (212) 620-4777
511 Sixth Ave., Ste. 167   FAX (212) 620-4888
(Near W. 13th St.)   www.akalocations.com
New York, NY 10011

(561) 483-0477
Ⓐ **All-Star Locations** (561) 445-7300
6921 Giralda Circle   FAX (561) 483-5477
Boca Raton, FL 33433   www.all-starlocations.com
(South Florida: Architectural Properties, Bar and Restaurant Locations, Castles, Coastal and Marine Locations, Estates, Houses, International Locations, Office Buildings, Retail Spaces & Warehouses)

Allencrest Associates (732) 747-5162
                             (917) 757-7493
41 Eastport Court   FAX (732) 747-5162
Red Bank, NJ 07701   www.allencrestlocations.com

Ⓐ **ALSAM/Association of Location Scouts and Managers**   www.alsam.net

David Appelson (212) 866-6287
                  (917) 841-4470
                  www.alsam.net

atomic torpedo.com (917) 716-9738
                       www.atomictorpedo.com

WWW.LOCATIONCONTROL.COM

Michael J. Battin
235 West 22nd Street, Suite #3-R
New York, NY 10011 USA

(OFC) 212.627.2467
(FAX) 212.691.5581
(CELL) 917.287.7211
EMAIL: MJBATTIN@LOCATIONCONTROL.COM

MANAGEMENT SCOUTING PERMITS PARKING SECURITY
COMMERCIALS • FEATURES • CONCERTS • EVENTS

Producers, it's the rush hour, make your next stop . . .

THE LOCATION STATION

Mark D. McKennon
Scout • Manager

Film • TV • Commercial • Still

Worked with producers, directors, DPs, photographers and agencies who have called the shots for shows, films, video and ads created for CBS, PBS, TNT, NBC, NTV (Japan), MBC (Korea), Miramax, Fox 2000, Lions Gate Films, Intel, Hewlett Packard, Hyundai, Honda, Volvo, Time Warner Cable, independent features, etc.

718.768.5539 (Phone/Fax) / 917.744.8730
scoutmanmark@gmail.com / www.scoutman.com

Reliable, versatile location support, New York metro and beyond . . .

Jimmy Ayoub
(212) 598-4467
(917) 847-6514
FAX (212) 598-4378
www.jimmyayoub.com

Jane Barrer
(917) 509-4674
(646) 290-7130

Bear Locations
P.O. Box 803
New York, NY 10009
(917) 449-4523
FAX (212) 202-5247
www.bearlocations.com
(Architectural Properties, Bar and Restaurant Locations, Castles, Churches, Coastal and Marine Locations, Estates, Houses, Mountain Locations, Office Buildings, Retail Spaces, Stages & Warehouses)

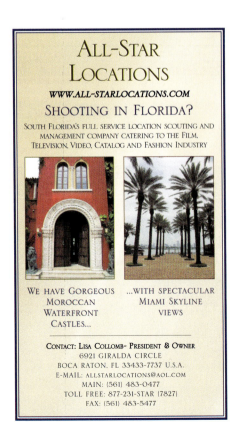

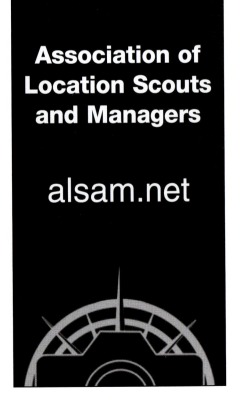

Location Libraries, Management & Scouts

Carl Bellavia
(201) 200-0960
(201) 294-9435
www.carlbellavia.com

Betty Rankin Locations Unlimited (201) 567-2809
FAX (215) 947-2950
www.bettyrankin.com

Mitchell Brozinsky
(917) 922-2248
(845) 708-2377
www.locationguy.net

Chasing Locations
(917) 673-3444
(212) 566-8480
50 Murray St., Ste. 415 www.chasinglocations.com
(Near Church St.)
New York, NY 10007

Robert Chemtob
(212) 222-4081
(917) 886-3398
www.alsam.net

Jeri Cohen
(917) 940-7195
www.alsam.net

Jay Cullnan
(917) 749-8169
(Architectural Properties, Bar and Restaurant Locations,
Churches, Coastal and Marine Locations, Houses, Mountain
Locations, New York City Five Boroughs and Surrounding Area,
Office Buildings, Retail Spaces, Stages & Warehouses)

Dan Snyder Locations
(212) 925-8203
(917) 523-4168
FAX (270) 714-7275
www.dansnyderlocations.com

🅐 Debbie Regan Locations, Ltd.
(212) 591-1313
(516) 626-1928
FAX (516) 626-2337
www.debbiereganlocations.com

Monty Diamond
(212) 477-1562
(917) 553-9834
www.alsam.net

Featured In Films/Patti Brashears (631) 424-8047
FAX (631) 549-3175
www.featuredinfilms.com

John Fedynich
(973) 338-7746
(973) 464-2904

David Fitzgerald
(973) 744-4577
(973) 865-4577
www.alsam.net

Mitch Ganem
(917) 447-4719
(212) 568-0311
www.alsam.net

Peter Garruba
(914) 841-1789
(845) 358-2006
www.alsam.net

Theo Gerike
(484) 682-9010

Deren Getz
(212) 387-9001
(917) 741-9836
www.getzlocations.com

🅐 Hamptons Locations
(631) 267-1001
P.O. Box 372 FAX (631) 267-2462
Amagansett, NY 11930 www.hamptonslocations.com

Gary Handel
(718) 858-4702
FAX (718) 852-7715
www.garysloft.com

Gahan Haskins
(646) 567-9060
(917) 770-3223
www.riverboys.com

R. Richard Hobbs
(917) 747-0856
(973) 472-7646
FAX (212) 202-5280
nyc.locationscout.us

Home Planet Productions
(845) 358-2006
(914) 841-1789
FAX (845) 348-6310

Larry Horodner
(917) 721-8074
(201) 653-0878

Chip Hourihan
(718) 928-3812
(917) 861-4120

Hudson Valley Locations, Inc. (914) 643-6976
431 Buena Vista Rd. www.hudsonvalleylocations.com
(Near Second St.)
New City, NY 10956

John Hutchinson
(212) 777-2538
(917) 705-2529
FAX (212) 473-8268
www.hutchinsonlocations.com
(Architectural Properties, Bar and Restaurant Locations,
Castles, Coastal and Marine Locations, Deserts, Estates,
International Locations, Mountain Locations & Warehouses)

J.Q. Locations (917) 582-4504
(Location Management & Scout)

Jenny Landey Productions, Inc. (631) 324-5770
247 Kings Point Rd. FAX (631) 329-6234
(Near Head Rock Rd.) www.jennylandeyproductions.com
East Hampton, NY 11937

Josh Karan
(212) 923-1680
(917) 923-2584
www.alsam.net

Ernie Karpeles
(914) 833-0343
(917) 750-4542
www.alsam.net

Steven Knee
(212) 734-0605
(917) 439-5588
www.locationny.com

Isabelle Kostic
(212) 684-8500
(917) 592-2191
c/o Site4View www.site4view.com
799 Broadway, Ste. 608
New York, NY 10003

Michael Kriaris
(917) 882-0062
(718) 464-7294
www.alsam.net

🅐 Location Control, Inc./Coneheads
(212) 627-2467
(917) 287-7211
235 W. 22nd St., Ste. 3R FAX (212) 691-5581
(Near Seventh Ave.) www.locationcontrol.com
New York, NY 10011

🅐 The Location Station/
(718) 768-5539
Mark McKennon
(917) 744-8730
FAX (718) 554-1532
www.scoutman.com

Locations Extrordinaire, Inc.
(631) 226-1767
(561) 487-5050
FAX (561) 487-5828
www.locationse.com
(Architectural Properties, Bar and Restaurant Locations,
Castles, Coastal and Marine Locations, Estates, Historic
Properties, Houses, Office Buildings & Stages)

Location Libraries, Management & Scouts

Long Island Locations/Lee Davis	(631) 267-6240	**Robbins Locations, Inc.**	(212) 633-6440

12 Handy Ln., P.O. Box 1106
Amagansett, NY 11930

FAX (212) 727-0665
www.robbinslocations.com

Charles Lum   (917) 319-2525 / (212) 242-5543

Sam Rohn   (718) 230-3651 / (917) 771-3651
www.nylocations.com

Jeff MacLean   (212) 741-3240 / (781) 863-1555
www.ennisinc.com

Santa Barbara Location Services/aka Location Production Coordination   (805) 969-5555
1805 E. Cabrillo Blvd., Ste. B   FAX (805) 969-9595
Santa Barbara, CA 93108   www.santabarbara-locations.com
(Ojai, San Luis Obispo, Santa Barbara, Santa Ynez Valley & Ventura)
Contact: Ronnie Haran Mellen

John Maher   (914) 232-9608 / (917) 750-0392 / FAX (914) 232-9608
www.alsam.net

Hal Mattes   (718) 745-8010 / (917) 771-0549
www.alsam.net

Tibi Scheflow   (917) 822-2489
www.alsam.net

Glenn Schuster   (917) 282-7360
www.glennschuster.com

Joseph E. Mennella   (718) 253-0140 / (917) 449-7507
www.alsam.net

The Scout Source   (973) 746-2552
104 Gates Ave.
Montclair, NJ 07042

Charles Miller   (203) 595-0392 / (917) 991-0001 / FAX (203) 595-0397
www.alsam.net

Seret Studios   (212) 372-7170
73 West St.   FAX (212) 972-7940
Brooklyn, NY 11222   www.seretstudios.com
(Architectural Properties, Bar and Restaurant Locations, Historic Properties, Houses, Office Buildings, Retail Spaces & Warehouses)

Monica Randall Locations   (516) 921-7438
Box 75   www.monicarandall.com
Oyster Bay, NY 11771

Michael Sibley   (917) 846-7977
www.alsam.net

Moschini Productions   (212) 620-3961
54 Barrow St., Ste. 2B   FAX (212) 208-0975
New York, NY 10014   www.moschini.com

Site4view Locations, LLC   (212) 614-8500
799 Broadway, Ste. 608   FAX (212) 614-8586
(Near E. 11th St.)   www.site4view.com
New York, NY 10003

Rik Nagel/Prime Location   (917) 449-2929
www.primelocationnyc.com

Staten Island Film Locations   (718) 477-1530 / (718) 473-2969
www.statenislandfilmlocations.vpweb.com
(Architectural Properties, Bar and Restaurant Locations, Churches, Coastal and Marine Locations, Estates, Houses, International Locations, Office Buildings, Retail Spaces, Stages & Warehouses)

Philip Ng   (646) 515-6531 / (718) 332-6455

Nivo Productions   (516) 922-5853 / (305) 215-8519
167 Cove Rd.   FAX (516) 922-5854
Oyster Bay, NY 11771   www.nivoproductions.com

Daniel Strol   (845) 424-3247 / (914) 673-4666
www.alsam.net

John Norwood   (212) 473-7195 / (917) 509-4500
www.alsam.net

Sasha Tsyrlin   (973) 783-1190 / (973) 960-2131 / FAX (973) 783-4909
www.alsam.net

On Time Elite, Inc.   (800) 779-6642 / (201) 653-5565
50-58 Marshall St.   FAX (201) 653-5957
Hoboken, NJ 07030   www.ontimeelite.com
Contact: Candace Orth

Thomas J. Whelan   (914) 479-0040 / (646) 279-4670

Where'bouts, Inc.   (718) 222-4940 / (917) 405-5717
www.wherebouts.com
(Architectural Properties, Bar and Restaurant, Castles, Churches, Coastal and Marine Locations, Deserts, Estates, Houses, International Locations, Licensed Broker, Mountain Locations, Office Buildings, Retail Spaces, Stages & Warehouses)

Premiere Locations of the Hamptons   (631) 537-1669 / (917) 690-1075
P.O. Box 803   FAX (631) 907-4236
East Hampton, NY 11937   www.premierelocations.com
(The Hamptons, North Fork of Long Island & Bellport)

Proper Production Locations   (212) 255-2839 / (917) 554-2280
213 W. 21st St., Ste. 2A   FAX (212) 255-6185
(Near Seventh Ave.)   www.properproduction.com
New York, NY 10011
Contacts: Michele Howell & Christine Miele

Tom Rees   (973) 761-4404 / (201) 407-0097
www.tjreeslocations.com

Come play in our house!

Frederick P. Rose Hall is perfect for dance, theater, opera, benefits, conferences, product launches and corporate events.

Centrally located in Columbus Circle, our two versatile theaters, soaring atrium, full-service catering and intimate jazz club ensure a spectacular event.

Rose Theater
1200+ seats and one of the world's most acoustically versatile concert venues.

The Allen Room
425+ seats with the Manhattan skyline as its backdrop.

For more information:
212-258-9980
booking@jalc.org
www.jalc.org/booking

jazz at lincoln center
Frederick P. Rose Hall, Home of Jazz at Lincoln Center
Broadway at 60th Street

Locations

101 River Views (212) 431-2262
101 Sixth Ave. (646) 342-0448
New York, NY 10013 FAX (212) 431-4712
www.101riverviews.com

Ⓐ 1887 Townhouse (212) 877-5400
59 W. 85th St. www.1887townhouse.com
New York, NY 10024
(Houses)
Contact: Dan Starer

The 1896 (718) 451-6531
592 Johnson Ave. FAX (718) 381-2893
Brooklyn, NY 11237 www.the1896.com

20 Greene Gallery (212) 334-3347
20 Greene St. www.20greene.com
New York, NY 10013

620 Loft & Garden (212) 588-8634
620 Fifth Ave. FAX (212) 479-8634
New York, NY 10020 www.topoftherocknyc.com/events

Alger House (212) 627-8838
45 Downing St. (Near Bedford St.) FAX (212) 645-7799
New York, NY 10014 www.algerhouse.com
Contact: Sam Milliken

The Altman Building (212) 741-3400
135 W. 18th St. (Near Seventh Ave.) FAX (212) 741-3424
New York, NY 10011 www.altmanbldg.com

Amtrak (215) 349-2735
30th St. Station, Fifth Fl. FAX (215) 349-1872
Philadelphia, PA 19104 www.amtrak.com
Contact: Rick Remington

Art & Industry/Doctor Proper, Ltd. (212) 477-0116
FAX (212) 477-1420
www.aid20c.com

**Association of the Bar
of the City of New York** (212) 382-6637
42 W. 44th St. (Near Sixth Ave.) FAX (212) 869-2145
New York, NY 10036 www.abcny.org
Contact: Nicholas Marricco

The Beacon Theatre (212) 465-6106
2124 Broadway (Near 74th St.) FAX (212) 465-6568
New York, NY 10023 www.thegarden.com/specialevents

Boeing (314) 232-3002
P.O. Box 3707, M/C 14/84 FAX (206) 655-1320
Seattle, WA 98124 www.boeingimages.com
Contact: Kevin Kelly

Broad Street Ballroom (646) 624-2524
41 Broad St. FAX (646) 624-2526
(Near Beaver Street and Exchange Place)
New York, NY 10004
www.broadstreetballroom.com
(Colleges/Schools & Historic Properties)

Brooklyn Museum of Art (718) 501-6202
200 Eastern Pkwy FAX (718) 501-6145
Rights & Reproductions www.brooklynmuseum.org
(Near Washington Ave.)
Brooklyn, NY 11238

Brooklyn Studios (718) 392-1007
211 Meserole Ave. FAX (718) 392-1008
Brooklyn, NY 11222 www.brooklynstudios.net

Ⓐ Chelsea Piers (212) 336-6777
23rd St. & The Hudson River FAX (212) 336-6725
(Near 23rd St.)
New York, NY 10011 www.chelseapiers.com/onlocation
Contacts: Lauren McCourt, Sherwin Johnson & Jenna Weinerman

Church Street Boxing Gym (212) 571-1333
25 Park Pl. (Near Church St.) FAX (212) 571-3777
New York, NY 10007 www.nyboxinggym.com

Crosseyed Studio	**(212) 929-7550**
162 Charles St., Second Fl.	FAX **(212) 929-4215**
(Near Washington St.)	
New York, NY 10014	
Contact: Abby Gennet	

The Culinary Loft LLC	**(212) 431-7425**
515 Broadway, Ste. 5A	FAX **(212) 431-7816**
(Near Spring St. & Broome St.)	**www.culinaryloft.com**
New York, NY 10012	
Contact: Corinne Colen	

The Cutting Room	**(212) 691-1900**
19 W. 24th St. (Near Broadway)	FAX **(212) 691-0104**
New York, NY 10010	

Dakota Studio	**(212) 691-2197**
78 Fifth Ave., Eighth Fl.	FAX **(212) 691-2239**
(Near W. 14th St.)	**www.dakotastudio.com**
New York, NY 10011	

Deep Hollow Ranch	**(631) 668-3901**
Ranch Rd./Montauk Hwy, Box 835	FAX **(631) 668-3902**
Montauk, NY 11954	**www.deephollowranch.com**

Dieu Donné	**(212) 226-0573**
315 W. 36th St., Ground Fl., Ste. 101	FAX **(212) 226-6088**
(Near Eighth Ave.)	**www.dieudonne.org**
New York, NY 10018	

Divine Studio	**(212) 387-9655**
21 E. Fourth St., Ste. 605	FAX **(212) 387-7944**
(Near Lafayette St.)	**www.divinestudios.com**
New York, NY 10003	

Douglas House, Inc.	**(845) 359-1477**
275 Kings Hwy (Near Princes Gate)	FAX **(845) 359-2945**
Orangeburg, NY 10962	**www.thedouglashouse.com**
Contacts: Heather Douglas & Marjorie Douglas	

East Point-Waterfront Peninsula Estate	**(631) 549-0356**
167 E. Shore Rd.	**www.eastpointlocation.com**
(Near Harbor Hill Dr.)	
Huntington, NY 11743	

A **Frederick P. Rose Hall**	
Home of Jazz at Lincoln Center	**(212) 258-9535**
Broadway at 60th St.	FAX **(212) 258-9906**
New York, NY 10019	**www.jalc.org/venues**

Gary's Loft, Inc.	**(917) 837-2420**
28 W. 36th St., PH	FAX **(212) 656-1940**
New York, NY 10018	**www.garysloft.com**

Glass House New York	**(646) 303-8006**
103 Hog Hill Rd.	**www.glasshouseny.com**
Yorktown Heights, NY 10514	

Gleason's Gym, Inc.	**(718) 797-2872**
77 Front St., Second Fl.	**www.gleasonsgym.net**
(Near Main St.)	
Brooklyn, NY 11201	

Gotham Bike Shop	**(212) 732-2453**
112 W. Broadway (Near Reade St.)	FAX **(212) 732-2247**
New York, NY 10013	**www.gothambikes.com**
Contact: Dave Nazaroff	

	(718) 383-5941
Greenpoint Reformed Church	**(917) 446-2109**
136 Milton St.	**www.greenpointchurch.org**
Brooklyn, NY 11222	

	(212) 372-7170
Greenpoint Terminal	**(917) 755-6411**
73 West St.	FAX **(212) 972-7940**
Brooklyn, NY 11222	**www.seretstudios.com**

Harlem Brownstone Location	**(212) 690-1007**
	FAX **(212) 690-1026**
	www.harlembrownstonelocation.com

THE LOG CABIN LOCATION

Looking for a log cabin on a lake for your next shoot?

We have it. An elegant cabin on 84 private acres ready for your next production:

✧ Cabin on private 6.5 acre lake ✧
Stables, barns, wood fencing ✧ Trails,
woods, fields ✧ Wooden dock, boats ✧
Stone fireplace ✧ Hardwood flooring

Check out the photo's on our website:
www.TheLogCabinLocation.com

Contact: Anita Raisch
Office: (908) 362-5415
Location: (908) 362-6036

Easy access off Rt 80 in Blairstown, NJ

Shoot On Location

Film
- Law & Order (series)
- Are You Smarter Than A 5th Grader? (series)
- Head & Shoulders Shampoo (TV spot)
- The Girl in the Park (feature)
- On the Hook (feature)
- Missing Person (feature)

Photo
- Babies 'R' Us
- Type A Inc.
- Cutting Edge Magazine
- Service Magazine
- Macy's West
- More Magazine
- Hermon Miller
- Vogue Knitting Magazine

Contact:
Anne Houlihan
Sales Manager/Special Events
212.216.2006
ahoulihan@javitscenter.com

THE JAVITS CENTER
Marketplace for the World®

Javits Convention Center
655 West 34th Street
New York, NY 10001
www.javitscenter.com

Helen Mills Theater 135 W. 26th St., Ste. 11A New York, NY 10001	(212) 243-6200 FAX (212) 243-1325 www.helenmills.com
Home Studios, Inc. 873 Broadway, Ste. 301 (Near 18th St.) New York, NY 10003	(212) 475-4663 (973) 865-4577 FAX (212) 475-2446 www.homestudiosinc.com
Hudson Theatre At **Millenium Broadway** 145 W. 44th St. (Near Broadway) New York, NY 10036	(212) 768-4400 FAX (212) 789-7698
Ⓐ **Jacob K. Javits Convention Center** 655 W. 34th St. (Near 11th Ave.) New York, NY 10001	(212) 216-2000 FAX (212) 216-2588 www.javitscenter.com
JFK Terminal 4	(718) 751-3710 FAX (718) 751-3719 www.jfkiat.com
Ⓐ **Lightbox-NY LLC** 841 Barretto St., Box 14 Bronx, NY 10474	(718) 759-6419 FAX (718) 732-2144 www.lightbox-ny.com
Location 05 568 Broadway, Ste. 805 New York, NY 10012	(212) 219-2144 (917) 991-8405 FAX (212) 219-3863 www.location05.com
Ⓐ **The Log Cabin Location** 24 Sunset Lake Rd. Blairstown, NJ 07825	(908) 362-5415 (908) 362-6036 FAX (908) 908-7972 www.thelogcabinlocation.com
Madison Square Garden Four Penn Plaza New York, NY 10001	(212) 465-6106 FAX (212) 465-6568 www.thegarden.com/specialevents
Ⓐ **Manhattan Penthouse** 80 Fifth Ave., 17th Fl. (Near 14th St.) New York, NY 10011 Contact: Sam Milliken	(212) 727-8437 FAX (212) 645-7799 www.manhattanpenthouse.com
Metropolitan Pavilion 125 W. 18th St. (Near Seventh Ave.) New York, NY 10011	(212) 463-0071 (212) 463-0200 FAX (212) 463-0946 www.metropolitanevents.com
Ⓐ **National Aerospace Training and** **Research Center/NASTAR** 125 James Way Southampton, PA 18966	(215) 355-9100 (866) 482-0933 FAX (267) 989-1251 www.nastarcenter.com

---

MANHATTAN TOWNHOUSE

13 spacious rooms, great light, beautiful architectural details, gourmet kitchen, 9 fireplaces, fully furnished, all props free, sunny garden on West 85ᵀᴴ St.

Dan Starer (212) 877-5400

www.1887townhouse.com

---

2 Great Shoot Sites

Manhattan Penthouse
Entire top 17th Floor with huge arched windows, high ceilings, Fifth Avenue at 14th Street, easy access, great light, best 360 degree views in Manhattan

Alger Mansion
Huge furnished carriage home in Village, many interesting decorative features, high ceilings, freight elevator, quiet

Sam Milliken: 212-627-8838
Photos: mansionscatering.com

New York Hall of Science (718) 699-0005
47-01 111th St. (Near 48th Ave.) FAX (718) 699-1341
Queens, NY 11368 www.nyscience.org

The New York Public Library (212) 930-0830
476 Fifth Ave. (Near 42nd St.) (212) 930-0730
New York, NY 10018 FAX (212) 642-0100
www.nypl.org

Norwood Mansion (781) 924-1310
241 W. 14th St. (Near Seventh Ave.) FAX (212) 989-6442
New York, NY 10011
Contact: Raf Borello

Novo Arts, Inc. (212) 674-3093
57 E. 11th St., 10th Fl. FAX (212) 979-5381
(Near Broadway) www.novoarts.com
New York, NY 10003

Oheka Castle (631) 692-2707
135 W. Gate Dr. (Near W. Jericho Tpke) FAX (631) 692-7712
Cold Spring Hills, NY 11743 www.oheka.com

**The Otto Kahn and
James Burden Mansions** (212) 722-4745
1-7 E. 91st. St. FAX (212) 996-1784
New York, NY 10128

Panorama Flight Service, Inc. (914) 328-9800
67 Tower Rd. (914) 424-0951
Westchester County Airport FAX (914) 328-1055
White Plains, NY 10604
www.panoramaflightservice.com

PMP Studios (212) 967-9909
320 W. 37th St. (212) 563-2047
New York, NY 10018 FAX (212) 967-9919
www.320studiosnyc.com

**The Prop Company -
Kaplan & Associates** (212) 691-7767
111 W. 19th St., Eighth Fl. FAX (212) 727-3055
(Near Sixth Ave.)
New York, NY 10011

Puck Building Special Events (212) 257-6085
295 Lafayette St., Ste. 705 FAX (212) 343-1201
(Near Houston St.)
New York, NY 10012
Contact: Jaimie Marks

Purified Loft (718) 522-2354
135 Plymouth St., Loft 204 FAX (718) 522-2354
Brooklyn, NY 11201 www.purifiedloft.com

Radio City Music Hall (212) 465-6106
1260 Sixth Ave. (Near W. 50th St.) FAX (212) 465-6568
New York, NY 10020 www.thegarden.com/specialevents
Contact: Jennifer Bretschneider

The Retreat at Art Omni (212) 249-7406
P.O. Box 368 www.retreatartomi.com
Ghent, NY 12075

Rockefeller Center (212) 588-8634
45 Rockefeller Plaza, 12th Fl. FAX (212) 479-8634
New York, NY 10111 www.rockefellercenter.com

Rooftop Garden @ 620 Fifth Ave. (212) 698-2000
620 Fifth Ave. FAX (212) 332-6550
New York, NY 10111 www.topoftherocknyc.com

Studio Eickholt (646) 613-9610
93 St. Marks Pl., Third Fl. FAX (646) 613-9610
New York, NY 10013 www.eickholtgallery.com

Terrapin Chelsea Art Gallery (212) 645-3041
121 W. 15th St. (Near Sixth Ave.) FAX (212) 367-7281
New York, NY 10011 www.terrapinindustries.com

**The Theater at
Madison Square Garden** (212) 465-6106
Four Penn Plaza FAX (212) 465-6568
New York, NY 10001 www.thegarden.com/specialevents

Toga Bike Shop (212) 799-9625
110 West End Ave. (Near 64th St.) FAX (212) 799-2834
New York, NY 10023 www.togabikes.com
Contact: Dave Nazaroff

Ⓐ Top of the Rock Weather Room (212) 698-2000
30 Rockefeller Center FAX (212) 332-6550
New York, NY 10112 www.topoftherocknyc.com

Tribeca Performing Arts Center (212) 220-1459
199 Chambers St., Ste. S 110C FAX (212) 732-2482
(Near West St.) www.tribecapac.org
New York, NY 10007
Contact: Amy Coombs

The United Palace (212) 568-6700
4140 Broadway (Near 175th St.) (212) 568-6701
New York, NY 10033 FAX (212) 568-4488

Wave Hill (718) 549-3200
675 W. 252nd St. FAX (718) 884-8952
(Near Sycamore Ave.) www.wavehill.org
Bronx, NY 10471
Contact: Susie Brown

Wollman Rink (212) 439-6900
830 Fifth Ave. FAX (212) 628-8322
New York, NY 10065 www.wollmanskatingrink.com

ON TIME Elite

for the rest of the story visit our website
www.ontimeelite.com

- A dozen plus floor plans to choose from!
- Serving the industry for 20 years
- Five Star VIP Accommodations
- Production/mobile office, makeup, wardrobe
- Multi User - High Speed Broadband Internet!
- All buses have brand new interiors
- Non-Union & Union drivers
- Buses equipped with Plasma TV, Navigation system, iPod Connectivity and Direct TV

Call 1.800.779.6642
Available 24 hours

A Picture is worth a thousand words

NY 411 — Motorhomes & Portable Dressing Rooms

A. van Hoek Ltd.	(917) 701-5367
71 Montrose Ave.	(718) 599-4388
Brooklyn, NY 11206	www.retrofuturistic.com
(Airstream Trailers, Honeywagons, Mobile Offices & Star Trailers)	
BBL Mobile, Inc.	(800) 848-4140
8004 NW 154 St., Ste. 379	FAX (805) 241-8793
Miami Lakes, FL 33016	www.bblmobile.com
ⓐ **Big Shot, Inc.**	(212) 244-7468
367 Lighthouse Ave.	FAX (718) 967-0176
(Near Lamont Ave.)	www.bigshotsinc.com
Staten Island, NY 10306	
Cars on Location	(203) 732-4745
768 Derby Ave.	(800) 736-9178
Seymour, CT 06483	FAX (203) 732-4193
	www.carsonlocation.com
ⓐ **Cassone Leasing, Inc.**	(631) 585-7800
1950 Lakeland Ave.	(800) 640-8844
Ronkonkoma, NY 11779	FAX (631) 585-7895
	www.cassone.com
CitiVans	(212) 354-8267
Class Act Location Service	(203) 735-9326
	(866) 735-9326
	FAX (203) 732-4193
	www.classactservices.com
Don's Location Vans	(800) 698-7544
	(631) 698-7770
	FAX (631) 698-7748
	www.donslocationvans.com

The Finest Location Vehicles for Your Upcoming Production or Fashion Shoot!

QUALITY SERVICE AT ECONOMY RATES!

Call today: (718) 657-9609

* Wireless internet
royalbuses@aol.com

* Union / non-union drivers
www.royalbuses.com

Royal Buses
Luxury Vehicles 1-800 336-3666

Shooting Star COACHES

A Leader in the Industry!

24 HR Telephone: **718.643.0649**

Upgrading & Adding Brand New "Cutting Edge" Vehicles to our Fleet Every Year
Brand New 2008 Busses • Sizes Ranging From 33ft. to 42ft.
Union and Non Union Drivers
EVERY VEHICLE A "POP OUT" • **ALL VEHICLES FULLY FUNCTIONAL WITH POP OUTS OPEN OR CLOSED!**
Wide & Super Wide Expanding Single / Full Wall / Double/ Triple or Quadruple "Pop Out's" on <u>ALL</u> Vehicles!
VIP & Celebrity Coaches • DVD VCR & TRACKING DIRECT TV
All Leather Sofas & Wood Laminate and Ceramic Tile Floors
The Industries NEWEST, Most Spacious & Comfortable Vehicles
Extra Large Make-Up Stations • Removable Make-Up Tables
Huge Production & Work Surfaces
Front & Rear / Left & Right Side and Rear Entrances
Rear Garage Models with "Hydraulic Lift Gate"
Up To 45' of Wardrobe Racks • Steamers • Tables • Beach Carts
Rolling Racks • Torpedo Heaters• Portable Putt Putt Gennies
Directors Chairs • Pop -Up Tents • Digital Fax • etc...
2 Banger Hair / Make-Up / Mobile Restroom (Honeywagon)

*MULTI USER HIGH SPEED BROADBAND
SECURE WIRELESS INTERNET (WI-FI)
AVAILABLE ON <u>ALL</u> OF OUR VEHICLES!
DIGITAL CELLULAR FAX AVAILABLE ON REQUEST
*VISIT OUR NEW WEB SITE FOR MUCH MORE
INFORMATION AND VEHICLE SPECIFICATIONS
OF THE REST OF OUR VEHICLES

*Custom Graphics & Full Vinyl Wrap Specialists

More Expanding "Pop-Out" Coaches than ANYONE in the Industry! Choice of <u>11</u> "Slide Out" Floorplans
Introducing our Exclusive Full Wall Slide & the Industries 1st Full Rear Opening "Garage" Coach !

SILVERSTAR "Mobile Hotel Suite"
Specialty Vehicle • 42 ft Diesel Coach
Ultra Wide Expander • 4 Pop Outs
VIP STAR Talent / Hair / Make-up Wardrobe

DIPLOMAT 1 & 2
2 Identical Luxury Expanding Diesel Coaches
for VIP Talent / Hair / Make-Up / Wardrobe

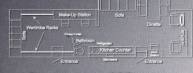

STARCOACH 1 & 2
2 Identical Expanding Coaches Ideal for
Production / Hair / Make-up / Wardrobe / Talent

EUROLINER
Super Wide Expanding Rear Wardrobe Garage
Production / Hair / Make-up Wardrobe / Talent

*Please check our website for more Floorplans and Information

Shooting Star Coaches
WWW.SHOOTINGSTARCOACHES.COM

image created for Superior "the crown series" by chris van oosterhout

Superior location vans
ph# 718 782 2494 www.superiorlocationvans.com
union and non-union jobs welcome

Driftwood RV Center/Atlantic City	(609) 641-1630
	(888) 350-4678
6623 Black Horse Pike	FAX (609) 646-7574
Egg Harbor Township, NJ 08234	

E.S., Inc.   (800) 736-8888
P.O. Box 670476
Flushing, NY 11367

Forbes Brothers
Production Vehicles   (516) 428-8124
P.O. Box 266   www.forbesproduction.com
Montauk, NY 11954
(Makeup Trailers, Motorhomes, Production Trailers, Shower Trailers, Star Trailers & Wardrobe Trailers)

Haddad's   (412) 655-8822
221 Curry Hollow Rd.   FAX (412) 655-9320
Pittsburgh, PA 15236

Motorhomes & Portable Dressing Rooms

BIG SHOT INC

Has been serving the commercial photo industry in New York City since 1996. Our custom motor coaches are designed to provide maximum comfort and functionality for both client and crew.

Call Frankie

367 Lighthouse Ave. • Staten Island, NY 10306 • Phone (212) BIG-SHOT (244-7468)
Fax (718) 979-0176 • web: www.bigshotsinc.com • Email: bigshotsinc@aol.com

BIG SHOT INC ON LOCATION

JLS Wheels (212) 566-2806
109 Luquer St., Ste. 3A FAX (212) 343-9816
Brooklyn, NY 11231 www.jlswheels.com

Kelner's Rentals, Inc. (610) 399-6879
1151 Fielding Dr. FAX (610) 399-8537
West Chester, PA 19382

Lightnin' Rentals (770) 963-1234
2555 University Pkwy FAX (770) 338-4151
Lawrenceville, GA 30043 www.lightnin.net

Location City, Inc. (800) 562-2489

MAPS/ (212) 290-2914
Mobile Arts Production Services (888) 843-7880
FAX (212) 290-2683
www.mapsproduction.com

MoHoVip, Inc. (917) 716-1814
54 W. 85th St., Ste. BR FAX (917) 720-9821
New York, NY 10024 www.mohovip.com
(Motorhomes)

Movie Movers (276) 650-3378
Transportation Equipment (818) 252-7722
400 Movie Movers East www.moviemovers.com
Axton, VA 24054

N.W. Production Services & (800) 260-6646
RV Rental (949) 212-9735
FAX (949) 361-2836
www.nwproduction.com

(800) 779-6642
On Time Elite, Inc. (201) 653-5565
50-58 Marshall St. FAX (201) 653-5957
Hoboken, NJ 07030 www.ontimeelite.com
Contact: Candace Orth

(848) 203-2818
Pink Hippo Production Motorhomes (917) 680-5908
www.pinkhippomotorhomes.com

Premiere Transportation (888) 771-0588
FAX (615) 261-2108
www.myluxurybus.net
(Makeup Trailers, Mobile Offices, Mobile Screening Rooms, Motorhomes & Star Trailers)

(718) 657-9609
Royal Buses (800) 336-3666
108-20 180th St. (Near 94th Ave.) FAX (718) 206-3862
Jamaica, NY 11433 www.royalbuses.com
(Honeywagons, Mobile Offices, Motorhomes, Production Trailers, Star Trailers & Wardrobe Trailers)

(718) 643-0649
Shooting Star Coaches, Inc. (888) 643-0649
99 Joralemon St., Ste. 2A FAX (973) 581-1485
(Near Brooklyn Queens Expwy) www.shootingstar.com
Brooklyn, NY 11201

Superior Location Van Service, Ltd. (718) 782-2494
83 Wythe Ave. FAX (718) 599-7370
Brooklyn, NY 11211 www.superiorlocationvans.com

PINK HIPPO
production motorhomes

NEW 2008 PRODUCTION MOTOR HOME

40 FOOT DIESEL SINGLE SLIDE OUT
DOUBLE DOOR ENTRANCE
FULLY EQUIPPED 20 FT WARDROBE AREA
REAR LOADING LIFT
6.5 FOOT HAIR/MAKEUP STATION
TABLES, CHAIRS, COOLERS AND TENT
INDOOR/OUTDOOR SURROUND SOUND SYSTEM
GPS NAVIGATION SYSTEM

CONTACT JIMMY AT 848.203.2818
NEW YORK & MIAMI
WWW.PINKHIPPOMOTORHOMES.COM

Moving, Storage & Transportation

Advantage Movers (212) 400-8679
217 E. 86th St. www.advantagemovers.net
(Near Third Ave.)
New York, NY 10028

Anthony Augliera Inc. (203) 937-9080
34 Hamilton St. FAX **(203) 937-0140**
West Haven, CT 06516 www.augliera.com

(212) 594-1300
Dependable Transport & Messenger **(212) 465-2300**
240 W. 37th St., Eighth Fl. FAX **(212) 594-4375**
(Near Seventh Ave.) www.dependablemessenger.com
New York, NY 10018

Divine Moving and Storage (212) 244-4011
317 W. 35th St. **(866) 688-7666**
New York, NY 10001 www.divinemoving.com

(212) 988-9292
Flat Rate Movers **(800) 486-3528**
466 Broome St., Fifth Fl. FAX **(212) 269-2769**
(Near Greene St.) www.flatrate.com
New York, NY 10013

Integrity Movers (212) 625-9090
(718) 556-5999
www.integritymoversinc.com

Manor Moving and Storage (212) 531-1500
(866) 626-6748
219 W. 100th St. (Near Broadway) FAX (212) 531-2500
New York, NY 10025 www.manormoving.com

Mario's Express Service, Inc. (732) 346-6666
45 Fernwood Ave. www.mariosexpress.com
Edison, NJ 08837

New York Movers (800) 956-6966
(718) 782-0555
45 S. First St. (Near Wythe Ave.) FAX (718) 384-2247
Brooklyn, NY 11211 www.newyorkmovers.com

On Time Elite, Inc. (800) 779-6642
(201) 653-5565
50-58 Marshall St. FAX (201) 653-5957
Hoboken, NJ 07030 www.ontimeelite.com
Contact: Linda Safir

Pro Piano (212) 206-8794
(800) 367-0777
85 Jane St. (Near Washington Ave.) FAX (212) 633-1207
New York, NY 10014 www.propiano.com

Prop Transport, Inc. (212) 957-4004
(212) 594-2521
630 Ninth Ave., Ste. 309 FAX (212) 957-6569
New York, NY 10036 www.proptransport.com

Seamens Moving and Storage (212) 997-1117
(800) 440-0342
43-20 Van Dam St. www.seamensmoving.com
(Near Varick St.)
New York, NY 10018

**Walton Hauling &
Warehouse Corporation** (212) 246-8685
609 W. 46th St. (Near 11th Ave.) FAX (212) 586-4628
New York, NY 10036

Parking Services

Location Control, Inc./Coneheads (212) 627-2467
235 W. 22nd St., Ste. 3R (917) 287-7211
(Near Seventh Ave.) FAX (212) 691-5581
New York, NY 10011 www.locationcontrol.com

Portable Restrooms

Aparo's Little John (631) 968-9107
  (800) 479-9818

🅐 **Call-A-Head Corporation** (718) 634-2085
304 Cross Bay Blvd. (800) 634-2085
(Near Shad Creek Rd.) FAX (800) 634-8127
Broad Channel, NY 11693

Elite Coaches (800) 631-9366
3168 Bordentown Ave. (732) 721-3443
Old Bridge, NJ 08857 FAX (732) 721-7068
  www.elitecoaches.com

Emil Norsic & Son, Inc. (631) 283-0604
1625 County Road 39 FAX (631) 287-1232
Southampton, NY 11968 www.norsic.com

Kohler Rental (410) 969-9100
7767 Old Telegraph Rd., Ste. 6 (866) 732-8734
Severn, MD 21144 FAX (410) 969-7276
  www.kohlereventservices.com

🅐 **Mr. John, Inc.** (800) 628-8955
200 Smith St. FAX (732) 417-0367
Keasbey, NJ 08832 www.mrjohn.com

Party Rental (718) 927-1255
713 Snediker Ave. (Near Linden Blvd.) FAX (718) 927-0082
Brooklyn, NY 11207 www.partyrentalslimited.com

Patanjo (631) 475-0978
19 Stiriz Rd. (Near Beaver Dam Rd.) (800) 852-5111
Brookhaven, NY 11719

Premier Executive Trailers (845) 883-9538
70 Coy Rd. (866) 883-9538
Clintondale, NY 12515 FAX (845) 883-5573
  www.premier-exec.com

Sani Lav (631) 981-7433
2164 Pond Rd. (Near S. First St.) (800) 244-7264
Ronkonkoma, NY 11779 FAX (631) 981-7423

CALLAHEAD®
Service People Trust

304 Crossbay Blvd. • Broad Channel, New York 11693
Tel: **(800) 634-2085** • Fax: **(800) 634-8127**
W W W . C A L L A H E A D . C O M

We're One Of New York State's Largest Portable Sanitation Companies Currently Servicing Over 4,000 Locations!

Servicing New York City's 5 Boroughs, Westchester, Nassau and Suffolk Counties

The ToileTree
The Aerohead
V.I.P. Toilet
Special Event Toilet

SANITATION EQUIPMENT OF EVERY DESCRIPTION
Outdoor Units • Highrise Units • Handicap Units
Trailer Units • Job-Site Units • Portable Sinks
Guard Sheds • Storage Sheds • Porcelain Systems
Holding Tanks • Hand Cleaning Systems • VIP Toilets
Comfort Stations • Fuel Oil Delivery

The Comfort Station

SAME DAY DELIVERY
All units delivered in brand new condition.
Rent it by Day, Week or Month
Rentals • Sales • Service
Ask about our service guarantees.
Serviced daily to weekly
and everything in between.

The Newport 1100 Series
The Newport 1600 Series (Also available in 2500 Series)

SERVING NEW YORK FOR 33 YEARS!

The Restroom Station

MISSION STATEMENT
'To Develop and Evolve a Human Necessity'
– Charles W. Howard, PRESIDENT & C.E.O.

Fuel Oil Delivery • Portasheds • Comfort Stations • VIP Toilets • Guard Sheds • Holding Tanks • Handicap Toilets

Production Services—North America

7NY (212) 962-1850
195 Chrystie St., Ste. 401C FAX (212) 962-1043
New York, NY 10002 www.7-ny.com

903Films (212) 674-0986
515 Greenwich St., Ste. 202 FAX (212) 380-1258
New York, NY 10013 www.903films.com

a.k.a. films (212) 473-2228
51 E. 12th St., Sixth Fl. FAX (212) 473-6068
(Near Broadway) www.akafilms.com
New York, NY 10003
Contact: Kerrie King

AAA Acme Discount Film Works (718) 928-3812
56 Fifth Ave. (Near St. Mark's Pl.) www.aaaacme.com
Brooklyn, NY 11217

(516) 484-6900
ADM Productions (800) 236-3425
40 Seaview Blvd. www.admproductions.com
Port Washington, NY 11050

(718) 626-2646
Air Sea Land Productions, Inc. (888) 275-5367
19-69 Steinway St. (Near 20th Ave.) FAX (718) 626-1493
Astoria, NY 11105 www.airsealand.com

(917) 414-5489
American Movie Co. (212) 952-1800
50 Broadway, Ste. 1206 FAX (212) 952-0152
New York, NY 10004 www.americanmovieco.com

(212) 625-9327
Atlantic Television, Inc. (917) 568-7218
524 Broadway, Fourth Fl. FAX (212) 625-9346
(Near Spring) www.atlantictv.com
New York, NY 10012
Contact: Howard Krupa

Beyond Our Reality (212) 255-5432
Productions, Inc. (800) 583-5015
49 W. 24th St., Seventh Fl. FAX (212) 255-6866
(Near Broadway) www.beyondourreality.com
New York, NY 10010

Black Watch Productions (212) 349-0369
49 Murray St., Ste. 1 (Near Church St.) FAX (212) 349-1335
New York, NY 10007 www.blackwatchproductions.com
Contacts: John Anderson & Monica Anderson

Bocce Club Pictures, LLC (212) 414-2220
104 E. 25th St., 12th Fl. FAX (212) 414-2206
New York, NY 10010 www.bocceclubpictures.com

Bollywood Hollywood Production, Inc. (732) 762-4277
2088 Route 130 North FAX (732) 777-0227
Monmouth Junction, NJ 08852
www.bollywoodhollywood.com

Brooklyn Independent Studios (718) 432-1025
65 Roebling St., Ste. 202 FAX (718) 432-7353
Brooklyn, NY 11211 www.brooklynindie.com

(914) 591-5888
Christopher Films (917) 208-1698
One Bridge St.
Irvington, NY 10533
Contact: James Parker

Cinergy Pictures, Inc. (212) 533-1023
Contacts: Petra Hoebel & Per Melita FAX (646) 219-0233

CitiCam Film & Video Services, Inc. (212) 315-2000
515 W. 57th St. (Near 10th Ave.) FAX (212) 586-1572
New York, NY 10019 www.citicam.net

City Lights Productions (646) 467-7500
Six E. 39th St., Third Fl. www.citylightsmedia.com
(Near Fifth Ave.)
New York, NY 10016

(917) 544-4188
Directors Film Company 31 653 865 319
Contact: Richard Coll

Clock Wise Productions (212) 343-3099
Contact: Nina Froriep FAX (801) 843-7088
www.clockwiseproductions.com

(718) 636-0990
E. Paul DiMartino Jr. (917) 689-5997
FAX (718) 360-9229
www.milkywaymedia.net

Echelon Productions, Inc. (212) 769-4429
243 W. 70th St., Fifth Fl. FAX (212) 769-4453
(Near Amsterdam Ave.) www.echelonusa.com
New York, NY 10023
Contact: Daniel Hank

Full Glass Films, LLC (212) 874-6282
386 Park Ave. South, Ste. 303 www.fullglassfilms.com
(Near E. 27th St.)
New York, NY 10016

Greenestreet Films, Inc. (212) 609-9000
Nine Desbrosses St., Second Fl. FAX (212) 609-9099
(Near Hudson St.) www.greenestreetfilms.com
New York, NY 10013
Contact: Rich Glassey

Guardian Entertainment, LTD (212) 727-4729
71 Fifth Ave., Fifth Fl. (Near 15th St.) FAX (212) 727-4737
New York, NY 10003 www.guardianltd.com
Contact: H. Anderson

Harrington Talents (718) 885-3434
213 Fordham St. FAX (718) 885-3338
Bronx, NY 10464 www.harringtontalents.com

Licata International Productions (212) 645-5050
531 W. 19th St. FAX (212) 645-2780
New York, NY 10011 www.kenlicata.com
Contact: Ken Licata

Mobile Video Productions, Inc.
636 Avenue of the Americas
Suite 3D
New York, NY 10011
Phone #: 212-924-9616
Fax #: 212-924-9604
E-Mail: mvp@dmc1.net

ALL FORMATS - FILM/HD/VIDEO
CREWS*EQUIPMENT*SERVICES

New York's Premier Production & Post Production Services

★ NYC's friendliest & most experienced production crews
★ Single or multi-camera Productions
★ All formats, from Mini-DV & Beta SP to HD, RED One & 35MM
★ HD edit suite and post production

7NY 212-962-1850
www.7-ny.com
195 Chrystie Street, Suite 401-C New York, NY 10002

Line By Line Productions (212) 505-0505
873 Broadway, Ste. 500 FAX **(212) 505-0593**
(Near W. 18th St.) **www.nycproduction.com**
New York, NY 10003
Contacts: Michele Bessey & Frank Garritano

(516) 767-1393
Locksley Productions (516) 270-4444
Three Derby Rd. **homepage.mac.com/locksleyproductions**
(Near Port Washington Blvd.)
Port Washington, NY 11050
Contact: Keith Browne

MAPS/ (212) 290-2914
Mobile Arts Production Services (888) 843-7880
FAX **(212) 290-2683**
www.mapsproduction.com

Maslow Media Group (202) 965-1100
2233 Wisconsin Ave. NW, Ste. 400 FAX **(202) 965-6171**
Washington, DC 20007 **www.maslowmedia.com**

(973) 300-9477
Mirage Productions Inc. (888) 746-6869
111 Spring St. FAX **(973) 300-9467**
Newton, NJ 07860 **www.mirageproductions.com**

Moschini Productions (212) 620-3961
54 Barrow St., Ste. 2B FAX **(212) 208-0975**
New York, NY 10014 **www.moschini.com**

Motion Odyssey, Inc. (917) 597-0037
www.motionodyssey.com

New York Production Services (212) 675-8287
78 Fifth Ave., Seventh Fl. FAX **(212) 675-8251**
(Near W. 14th St.) **www.newyorkproductionservices.com**
New York, NY 10011
Contact: John Grossman

PMC (212) 541-4620
1650 Broadway, Ste. 1103 FAX **(212) 333-5767**
(Near Eighth Ave.) **www.pmcglobal.com**
New York, NY 10019
Contact: George Braun

Post Office Media (212) 302-4488
1560 Broadway, Ste. 514 FAX **(212) 302-4849**
New York, NY 10036 **www.postofficemedia.com**

Prema Productions (212) 352-0082
110 Horatio St., Ste. 105 FAX **(212) 352-0082**
(Near Washington St.) **www.premaproductions.com**
New York, NY 10014
Contact: Mario Chioldi

Primalux Video (212) 206-1402
30 W. 26th St., Seventh Fl. FAX **(212) 206-1826**
(Near Broadway) **www.primalux.com**
New York, NY 10010

(203) 294-1425
Prism Production Services, Inc. (203) 996-5292
Four E. Scard Rd. FAX **(203) 265-7730**
Wallingford, CT 06492 **www.prismpro.com**
Contact: Keith Sandler

Production 920, Inc. (212) 414-0606
328 Eighth Ave., Ste. 147 FAX **(917) 463-3067**
(Near 10th Ave.) **www.production920.com**
New York, NY 10001

(212) 255-2839
Proper Production (917) 554-2280
213 W. 21st St., Ste. 3A FAX **(212) 255-6185**
(Near Seventh Ave.) **www.properproduction.com**
New York, NY 10011
Contacts: Michele Howell & Christine Miele

Pureland Pictures, Inc. (718) 965-0636
FAX **(718) 965-0637**
www.purelandpictures.com

Rooftop Edit (212) 244-0744
104 W. 29th St., 12th Fl. FAX **(212) 244-0690**
(Near Sixth Ave.) **www.rooftopedit.com**
New York, NY 10001
Contact: Anthony Forte

See Factor Industry (718) 784-4200
37-11 30th St. (Near 37th Ave.) FAX **(718) 784-0617**
Long Island City, NY 11101 **www.seefactor.com**
Contacts: Bobby Flecker & Mark Friedman

Senza Pictures (212) 334-3577
349 Broadway, Third Fl. FAX **(212) 334-3565**
(Near Leonard St.) **www.senzapix.com**
New York, NY 10013

(212) 243-1351
Shoot New York, Inc./hornet (917) 991-7899
P.O. Box 1321, Old Chelsea Station FAX **(212) 243-1184**
New York, NY 10113 **www.shootnewyork.com**
Contacts: Jennifer D. Frantz & Anthony J. Vozza

(201) 836-5427
Solar Plexus, Inc. (201) 281-5973
135 Oakdene Ave. FAX **(201) 836-5427**
Teaneck, NJ 07666 **www.solarplexusprods.com**

Tane Digital Video (212) 279-3150
555 Eighth Ave., Ste. 1203 **www.tanedv.com**
New York, NY 10018

TriStar Studios (973) 575-6971
490 Route 46 East FAX **(973) 575-6708**
Fairfield, NJ 07004 **www.tristarstudios.com**

Viceroy Films (212) 725-9818
401 W. 56th St., Ste. 2M FAX **(212) 725-9819**
(Near Columbus Ave.) **www.viceroyfilms.com**
New York, NY 10019

Wideye Creative (917) 324-5299
375 South End Ave., Ste. 17T FAX **(212) 321-9670**
New York, NY 10280 **www.wideyecreative.com**

Work Production Company (212) 535-5551
511 Sixth Ave., No. 167 (Near 13th St.) FAX **(212) 535-5588**
New York, NY 10011 **www.workproductions.com**
President: Wendy Gordon

Production Services—International

(800) 245-6639
Cine South de Mexico (011) 52 55 5684 0869
FAX **(011) 52 55 5679 7097**
Contact: Mark Pittman **www.filmmexico.com**

(212) 450-1616
Cine/drsa International (917) 865-1246
222 E. 44th St., Fourth Fl. FAX **(646) 688-2736**
(Near Third Ave.) **www.cineinternational.net**
New York, NY 10017
Contact: Paul Rosen

(917) 544-4188
Directors Film Company 31 653 865 319
Contact: Richard Coll

Euro-Pacific Film & (732) 530-4451
Video Productions, Inc. (732) 581-5249
P.O. Box 7986 FAX **(732) 842-6533**
Shrewsbury, NJ 07702 **www.euro-pacific.com**
Contacts: David Calderwood & Lisa Moss

(323) 939-9639
Global Production Network (310) 570-0065
FAX **(323) 417-1599**
www.globalproductionnetwork.com

Licata International Productions (212) 645-5050
531 W. 19th St. FAX **(212) 645-2780**
New York, NY 10011 **www.kenlicata.com**

+ 6 012 333 0681
Pop Films (917) 392-7337
www.popfilms-asia.com

Stillking Films (310) 466-9161
3530 Greenwood Ave. **www.stillking.com**
Los Angeles, CA 90066
(Bulgaria, Chile, Czech Republic, London, South Africa & Spain)
Contact: Doug Lewis

Security & Bodyguards

21st Century Security, Inc. (516) 377-5646 / (800) 649-4827
710 Sunrise Hwy, Stes. 1 & 2   FAX (516) 377-5651
(Near Jerome Ave.) www.21stcenturysecurity.com
Baldwin, NY 11510

Axel Protection Systems, Inc. (347) 386-5545 / (718) 206-4800
90-24 161st St. (Near Jamaica Ave.)   FAX (718) 206-2977
Jamaica, NY 11432   www.axelpro.net

Bulldog Service (718) 474-7194
P.O. Box 940818   FAX (718) 474-7194
Far Rockaway, NY 11694

Cambridge Security Services Corp. (212) 889-2111 / (800) 536-9984
419 Park Ave. South, Ste. 300   FAX (212) 889-5131
New York, NY 10016
www.cambridgesecurityservices.com

CK Security Group, Inc. (718) 227-5547 / (917) 803-1103
FAX (718) 227-5547
www.cksecuritygroup.com

Ⓐ **EPIC Security Corp.** (212) 580-3434 / (800) 548-3434
The EPIC Building, 2067 Broadway   www.epicsecurity.com
(Near W. 72nd St.)
New York, NY 10023

FJC Security Services (516) 328-6000
275 Jericho Tpke (Near S. Fourth St.)   FAX (516) 328-5373
Floral Park, NY 11001   www.fjcsecurity.com

Global Security Services (212) 260-7444 / (800) 883-8614
www.globsec.com
(Armed Guards, Bodyguards, Location Bodyguards, Location Security, Off-Duty Officers, Studio Security & Unarmed Guards)

Gold Shield Executive Services (718) 815-4844 / (212) 619-4844
900 South Ave.   www.goldshieldexecutive.com
(Near Glen St.)
Staten Island, NY 10314

International Protective Service Agency (212) 947-1681
481 Eighth Ave., Ste. 1570   FAX (212) 594-0889
New York, NY 10001   www.ipsasecurity.com

John Shields Security (212) 682-6094
60 E. 42nd St. (Near Madison Ave.)   FAX (212) 297-0841
New York, NY 10165

Knight Security (212) 609-3400
www.knightsecurityny.com

Lifestyle Resources (212) 947-9792
23 W. 36th St., Ste. 4B   FAX (212) 736-9115
(Near Fifth Ave.)   www.sterlinglifestyle.com
New York, NY 10018

Ⓐ **On Point Resources, Inc.** (917) 609-9798 / (914) 760-8860
P.O. Box 193   FAX (914) 668-8577
Fleetwood, NY 10552   www.onpointrinc.com

Silver Screen Security, Ltd. (718) 746-7130 / (212) 415-9125
P.O. Box 605026   FAX (718) 746-7129
Bayside, NY 11360   www.silverss.com

EPIC SECURITY CORP — SPECIAL SERVICES

When you're ready to demand more from your security service!℠

POLICE & BLAZER STYLE UNIFORMS

24 HR EPIC COMMAND & DISPATCH CENTER

PRODUCTION INDUSTRY SPECIALISTS

(212) 580-3434

THE EPIC BUILDING • 2067 BROADWAY • NYC 10023

New York's Top Security Service for 30+ Years.
Serving All 5 Boroughs & The NY/NJ Metro Area.

- ARMED & UNARMED SECURITY OFFICERS
- TRAINED BY NY PRIVATE POLICE ACADEMY®
- STUDIO & LOCATION SECURITY
- TEMPORARY & SPECIAL EVENTS SECURITY
- **INTELIFAX** INVESTIGATION SERVICES®/EMPLOYEE SCREENING
- TOP SECURITY AT UNBEATABLE RATES℠

LICENSED BY NYS DEPT OF STATE/NJ DIV OF STATE POLICE

FIDELITY BONDED • FULLY INSURED • $20 MILLION CGL

Mark J. Lerner, PhD President & CEO
Criminologist

Steven F. Goldman, Exec. VP
Licensed Private Detective

Selwyn Falk, CPP Vice Pres.
CPP — Certified Protection Professional
BOARD CERTIFIED IN SECURITY MANAGEMENT

NYS/NJ APPROVED TRAINING

EST. 1978 — PRIVATE POLICE ACADEMY®
30+ YEARS

**OUTSIDE MANHATTAN
CALL TOLL FREE: 1-800-548-3434**

QUARTER CENTURY CLUB — ASIS INTERNATIONAL

Because the times demand it®

SECURITY GUARDS

©MMIX

EPIC SECURITY CORP.®

INTELIFAX is a US Registered Service Mark of EPIC Security Corp.

Travel Agencies

Air-Tech (212) 219-7000
P.O. Box 472 www.airtech.com
Mastic Beach, NY 11951

Arilang Travel (212) 563-3350
(800) 223-6225
350 Fifth Ave., Ste. 2206 FAX (212) 239-0989
(Near E. 34th St.)
New York, NY 10118

Astor Travel, Inc. (212) 302-4692
119 W. 40th St., 14th Fl. (Near Broadway)
New York, NY 10018

Cloud Tours (718) 721-3808
(800) 223-7880
31-09 Newtown Ave., Third Fl. FAX (718) 721-4019
(Near 52nd St.) www.cloudtours.com
Long Island City, NY 11102

Entertainment Travel, Inc. (212) 840-7800
(Near Exchange Pl.) www.entertainmenttvl.com

Frenchway Travel, Inc. (212) 243-3500
(800) 243-3575
11 W. 25th St., Eighth Fl. FAX (212) 243-3535
(Near Broadway) www.frenchwaytravel.com
New York, NY 10010

International Travel Exchange (212) 808-5368
(800) 727-7830
211 E. 43rd St., Ste. 604 FAX (212) 808-0491
(Near Third Ave.) www.americatravelclub.com
New York, NY 10017

Kennedy Travel (212) 840-8659
130 W. 42nd St., Ste. 401 FAX (212) 730-2269
(Near Avenue of the Americas) www.kennedytravel.com
New York, NY 10036

The Kima Travel Group (718) 729-8200
(800) 848-5462
44-02 11th St., Ste. 606 FAX (718) 729-5952
(Near 44th Ave.)
Long Island City, NY 11101

Linden Travel Bureau, Inc. (212) 404-6300
909 Third Ave. FAX (212) 421-2790
New York, NY 10022 www.lindentravel.com

Lois Lane Travel (212) 243-5277
(212) 243-7601
230 Fifth Ave., Ste. 604 FAX (212) 243-8213
(Near 22nd St.)
New York, NY 10001

Mexico AA Travel Specialist (212) 421-5110
59 E. 54th St., Ste. 52 FAX (212) 753-9237
(Near Madison Ave.)
New York, NY 10022

Travel Management Group/TMG (323) 256-8750
6176 Outlook Ave. FAX (323) 993-0456
Los Angeles, CA 90042 www.tmg.la

Travel Unlimited (212) 431-0303
(800) 249-5917
87 Walker St., Ste. 5A FAX (646) 613-1078
(Near Lafayette St.) www.bestfareintown.com
New York, NY 10013

Turon Travel (212) 925-5453
(800) 952-7646
Two Wooster St., Ground Fl. FAX (212) 219-1865
(Near Canal St.) www.turontravel.com
New York, NY 10013

Ultramar Travel (888) 856-2929
14 E. 47th St. (Near Fifth Ave.) FAX (212) 856-0129
New York, NY 10017 www.ultramartravel.com

Water Trucks

Angel Aerial Corporation	(212) 460-8899
185 Broome St. (Near Clinton St.)	(800) 503-9240
New York, NY 10002	FAX (212) 460-8244
	www.angelaerial.com

Ⓐ Aqua-Effects	(800) 451-2436
P.O. Box 2083	FAX (732) 730-2126
Lakewood, NJ 08701	www.allchemical.com

Ⓐ Auto Props	(973) 470-9354
Eight Lexington Ave.	FAX (973) 815-1497
Wallington, NJ 07057	www.autoprops-waterworks.com

Blakley Equipment	(914) 664-5500
	(800) 662-5857
491 E. Third St. (Near Columbus Ave.)	FAX (914) 664-5815
Mount Vernon, NY 10553	www.blakleytree.com

Hill Studio & Scenic	(856) 423-8910
35 W. Broad St.	FAX (856) 224-0224
Paulsboro, NJ 08066	

Autoprops-Waterworks.com

Cars For All Your Film Needs

Motion Picture, Music Videos,
Print Ads, Still Photography,
Special Events, Parades, Store Fronts

973-470-9354

Weather

AccuWeather, Inc. (814) 235-8600
385 Science Park Rd. FAX (814) 235-8609
State College, PA 16803 www.accuweather.com

CompuWeather (800) 825-4445
FAX (800) 825-4441
www.compuweather.com

Metro Weather Service (800) 488-7866
FAX (516) 568-8853
www.metroweather.com

Pacific Coast Forecasting (818) 787-1287
(877) 359-4723
7530 Hayvenhurst Ave. FAX (818) 787-3187
Van Nuys, CA 91406 www.pcforecasting.com

Weather Works (800) 427-3456
(908) 850-8660
FAX (908) 850-8664
www.weatherworksinc.com
(24-Hour Live Meteorologists, Hurricane Surveillance, Live Forecasts & Nationwide and Worldwide Weather)

WeatherWatch Service (863) 709-1221
FAX (863) 709-1221
www.weatherwatchservice.com
(24-Hour Live Meteorologists, Hurricane Surveillance, Live Forecasts, Nationwide Weather, Recorded Forecasts & Worldwide Weather)

PICTURED:
Old Bank

LOCATION:
Manhattan, NY

PHOTOGRAPHER:
Sam Rohn

ALSAM : www.alsam.net
ASSOCIATION OF
LOCATION SCOUTS & MANAGERS

New York 411

*Qualified Listings for the
New York Production Community*
www.newyork411.com

Production Support

Production Support

Get Fast Results!

Printing and **Mailing Services** *all* under one roof.

FULL COLOR PRINTING SERVICES
Post cards • Brochures • Posters • Invitations
Ad journals • Press kit pocket folders • Programs
Business cards • Letterhead • Envelopes
Remittance envelopes • Note pads
Membership cards • Newsletters

Quark, Adobe and Microsoft files accepted

MAILING SERVICES
Presorting of mail: standard, non-profit and first class
CASS certification, NCOA updating of lists
Combining and Deduping of multiple lists
Envelope inserting • Addressing
Wafer sealing of self mailers
Application of postage stamps
Permit mailing including bar coding
Laser letter personalization

GET A QUICK PRICE QUOTE at
tim@westprintny.com

Personalized service from *real* people, not a website form.

WESTPRINT NY
212 989-2948 in NYC
201 553-9701 in NJ
tim@westprintny.com

AUTHORIZED Print Service Provider
Adobe

Ⓐ ADVERTISER SYMBOL

Refer to the General Index for cross-referencing items in this section.

Acting/Dialect Coaches..................208
Animals & Trainers......................209
Casting Directors.......................215
Casting Facilities......................221
Choreographers..........................221
Computer Consultants & Software.........222
Computers, Office Equipment & Supplies..223
Digital Casting & Video Conferencing....225
Directories & Trade Publications........226
Entertainment Attorneys.................228
Extras Casting Agencies.................229
Hand & Leg Models.......................229
Insurance Brokers & Guarantors..........230
Janitorial & Strike Services............231
Large Scale Event Planning..............232
Libraries, Research & Clearance.........233
Massage Therapists......................234
Messenger Services......................235
Nautical Film Services & Coordination...236
Notaries................................238
Payroll & Production Accountants
  (Local 161 NY)........................239
Payroll & Production Accountants........241
Promotional Products....................245
Talent & Modeling Agencies..............246
Technical Advisors......................246
Transcription & Secretarial Services....247
Translation & Interpretation Services...248
Wrap Party Locations....................249

Animal Actors Inc.
(908) 537-7800

Steve McAuliff
mcauliff@eclipse.net
www.animalactorsinc.com

—— Recent Credits Include ——

Sherlock Holmes   Sorcerer's Apprentice   Last Night
Pelham 1 2 3   Taking The Ninth   Taking Woodstock
When In Rome   Surrogates   Lymelife
Law & Order   Gossip Girl   Damages

Acting/Dialect Coaches

Susan Cameron	(917) 841-5776
(Dialect/Speech Coaching)	www.susancameron.net

New York Speech (212) 242-8435
Improvement Services (800) 773-2593
253 W. 16th St., Ste. 1B www.nyspeech.com
New York, NY 10011
(Dialect/Speech Coaching)

Amy Stoller	(917) 319-7448
(Dialect/Speech Coaching)	www.stollersystem.com

George Trahanis	(718) 624-7329
	(917) 981-8253

Verberations! LLC	(917) 696-3633
	(800) 205-8029
(Dialect/Speech Coaching)	FAX (212) 271-3280
	www.verberations.com/dialects

Shane Ann Younts	(212) 877-2567
	www.shaneannyounts.com

SPEECH INSTRUCTION

NEW YORK SPEECH IMPROVEMENT SERVICES, PC
253 W 16th St NYC 10011

SPEECH AND VOICE IMPROVEMENT

Regional and Foreign Accent Elimination
All Stage Dialects for All Acting Roles

Consultant to the Major Acting Schools and Agents
NYS Lic. Speech Therapists • 30th Anniversary

212-242-8435 • 1-800-SPEAKWELL

Sam Chwat, MS, CCC - SP, Director
E-mail: samspeech@aol.com

Current and past clients include:
Robert DeNiro, Julia Roberts, Patrick Stewart,
Tony Danza, Leonardo DiCaprio, Kathleen Turner,
Richard Gere, Olympia Dukakis, Willem Dafoe,
Kate Hudson, Andie MacDowell, Heath Ledger,
Shia LaBeouf, Vincent Donofrio, Jon Bon Jovi,
Gregory Hines, Shakira, Petra Nemcova,
Jude Law, Marcia Gay Harden & Stars of Major TV,
Film & Broadway productions.
Available for on-set assignments.

www.samspeech.com

Movies — Partial Listing
Harry Potter I-VII
Dr. Dolittle I & II
101 & 102 Dalmatians
Evan Almighty
Marley & Me
Beverly Hills Chihuahua
Hotel for Dogs
Eight Below
The Shaggy Dog
Lassie Come Home
Charlie & The Chocolate Factory
The Crow I-III
Ace Ventura I & II
Hidalgo

TV — Partial Listing
Frasier
Monk
CSI / CSI Miami / CSI NY
Ghost Whisperer
Malcolm in the Middle
Two and A Half Men
The Sopranos

Birds & Animals Unlimited

East Coast 866.226.9215 • West Coast 877.542.1355 • London 01923685146
www.birdsandanimals.com

Animals & Trainers

76 Carriage Company (215) 923-8516 / (215) 389-8687
1119 N. Bodine St. FAX (215) 923-7776
Philadelphia, PA 19123 www.phillytour.com
(Horses)

Ⓐ **All Creatures Great & Small** (914) 232-3623 / (914) 682-8870
Three Little Ln. (Near Route 127) FAX (914) 232-3621
White Plains, NY 10605 www.animalagent.com
(Domestic & Exotic)

Ⓐ **All Star Animals** (516) 569-5014 / (516) 984-4664
187 Lakeview Dr. (Near Hereford Rd.) FAX (516) 569-5178
Hewlett, NY 11557 www.allstaranimals.com
(Birds, Cats, Dogs, Elephants, Exotics & Farm Animals)

Ⓐ **All-Tame Animals, Inc.** (212) 873-5000
440 West End Ave. FAX (212) 799-3568
New York, NY 10024 www.alltameanimals.com
(Birds, Cats, Dogs, Exotics, Farm Animals & Horses)

Ⓐ **American Humane Association** (818) 501-0123 / (800) 677-3420
FAX (818) 501-8725
www.americanhumane.org/film

Ⓐ **Animal Actors, Inc.** (908) 537-7800 / (908) 966-4580
Four American Way FAX (908) 537-7801
Glen Gardner, NJ 08826 www.animalactorsinc.com
(Birds, Cats, Dogs, Exotics, Farm Animals & Horses)

Animal Works (212) 501-6972
138 Highmount Ave. (Near Grand Ave.) FAX (845) 353-0357
Nyack, NY 10960
(Domestics & Exotics)

Ⓐ **Animals for Advertising, Inc.** (212) 245-2590
310 W. 55th St., Ste. 6H www.animalsforadvertising.com
(Near Eighth Ave.)
New York, NY 10019
(Birds, Cats, Dogs, Exotics & Farm Animals)

Aquavisions (516) 546-5944 / (516) 229-8265
(Exotic Fish) www.aquavisions.net

Barbara's Animal People (484) 363-1887
P.O. Box 1405 www.barbarasanimalpeople.com
Pottstown, PA 19464
(Domestics, Exotics & Farm Animals)

Benay's Bird & Animal Source, Inc. (818) 881-0053
4776 Nomad Dr. FAX (818) 888-5548
Woodland Hills, CA 91364 www.benaysanimals.com
(Birds, Cats, Coati, Dogs, Exotics, Farm Animals, Horses, Monkeys, Raccoons, Reptiles, Rodents, Sea Lions, Skunks, Squirrels & Wildlife)

Ⓐ **Birds & Animals Unlimited East** (866) 226-9215
www.birdsandanimals.com
(Birds, Cats, Dogs, Exotics, Farm Animals, Horses, Insects, Livestock, Primates, Reptiles, Small Animals & Snakes)

Bow Wow Productions (760) 948-9430 / (800) 926-9969
FAX (760) 948-9434
www.bowwowproductions.com
(Birds, Cats, Dogs, Exotics & Farm Animals)

Brian McMillan's Hollywood Animals (323) 665-9500 / (323) 481-4806
4103 Holly Knoll Dr. FAX (323) 665-9200
Los Angeles, CA 90027 www.hollywoodanimals.com
(Bears, Hyenas, Leopards, Lions, Panthers, Tigers & White Lion)

www.AllTameAnimals.com

Domestic, Exotic & Farm Animals
For Television, Theatre, Fashion, Parties, Film & Advertising.

clients: As the World Turns, One Life to Live, Late Show with David Letterman, Law & Order, AmEx, MC, Ralph Lauren, Abercrombie, ABT, The GAP, Barneys New York, Vogue, Neiman Marcus, Saks, Juicy Couture, Target...

Exclusive supplier of Animals
for the Metropolitan Opera

212-873-5000

NANCY NOVOGRAD

AllTameAnimals@aol.com

440 West End Ave., New York, NY 10024

Brockett's Film Fauna, Inc.   (805) 379-3141
437 W. Carlisle Rd.   FAX (805) 379-4585
Thousand Oaks, CA 91361   www.brockettsfilmfauna.com
(Alligators, Birds, Crocodiles, Frogs, Insects, Lizards, Small Animals, Snakes & Spiders)

**Chateau Theatrical Animals &
Chateau Stable**   (212) 246-0520
608 W. 48th St. (Near 11th St.)   FAX (718) 828-4636
New York, NY 10036   www.chateaustables.net
(Horses & Horse-Drawn Carriages)

All Star Animals
★ ★ ★ ★ ★
516-569-5014
www.allstaranimals.com

Locations Available
Fully Insured

★ ★ ★ FEATURE FILMS ★ ★ ★

The Extra Man	After. Life	The Private Lives of Pippa Lee
The Good Heart	Achchamundu! Achchamundu!	Paper Man
The Imperialists Are Still Alive	Shadowboxer	Stephanie Daley
Multiple Sarcasms	Birds of America	Marconi Bros.
Buddy Gilbert Comes Alive	Dedication	Return To Sleepaway Camp
No Reservations	Watching The Detectives	If I Didn't Care
Tenderness	Wonderwall	★ TV /COMMERCIALS ★
Pleasure of Your Company	Twisted Fortune	Maybelline Giant Eagle
How to Lose Friends and Alienate People	Life in Flight	Bayer Aspirin Advair
	Strangers With Candy	Ford Target
The Toe Tactic	Diminished Capacity	Avon Purina

BAMBI BROOK   BARBARA AUSTIN

ANIMAL AGENCY INC.

Fully Insured

PRINT · FILM · TV · BROADWAY · COORDINATORS · STUNTS

CALL: (212)575-9396
EMAIL: dawnanimalagency@aol.com

- The Largest Animal Rental Service in the East
- We Own Over 500 Domestic & Exotic Animals
- Country and Farm Locations Available
- Home of "Nipper & Chipper" RCA Commercials)
- Over 300 Film & TV Credits Recently Including:

The Lovely Bones
Pink Panther 2
Sex and the City
(The Movie & TV Series)
The Baster Salt
Push
The Wackness
Pretty Bird
Cupid
30 Rock
Rescue Me
Damages
The View
Ugly Betty
Animal Planet
Law and Order –
   CI & SVU
As the World Turns
Sopranos
Late Night with Conan O'Brian
Late Show with David Letterman
MTV

In business since 1960, we have successfully used animals in commercials, print, TV, film, video, and theater including Radio City Music Christmas Spectacular (29 Years) and NYC Opera (35 Seasons)

Many Props: Wagon and Horse-Drawn Carriages

ANIMALS FOR ADVERTISING

Over thirty years of print, tv, and film experience

A chicken to wear sneakers???
Easy, when you know how. And do I know how!!!

☆ Cigar-smoking basset & poodle
 (Carpet-Fresh, David Letterman)

☆ Flying pigeons, doves too
 (Walt Disney)

☆ Sleeping & driving cats
 ("Toonces," Saturday Night Live)

☆ Acrobatic elephants
 (Anne Klein)

☆ Cooperative cows
 (Reeses, Land O'Lakes, Hardee's)

☆ Chickens wearing sneakers
 (American Red Cross)

and lots more
for tv, movies, and Broadway

Conan, Spin City, Happiness, Trick,
Project Runway, Disco Nights, Zoolander, The Debtors.

Need an animal, reptile, or bird for your next shoot? Call me.

LINDA HANRAHAN
310 WEST 55TH STREET, NEW YORK, NY 10019

(212) 245-2590

animals4advertising@nyc.rr.com   www.animalsforadvertising.com

---

Ⓐ Dawn Animal Agency, Inc.   (212) 575-9396
413 W. 47th St.   www.dawnanimalagency.com
(Near Ninth Ave.)
New York, NY 10036
(Domestics & Exotics)

Dawn Wolfe's   (856) 524-4006
Pawsitively Famous Animal Actors   (877) 280-5117
   FAX (877) 280-5117
www.pawsitivelyfamousanimalactors.com

No Animals Were Harmed®

No production budgets were hurt either.
We're FREE for SAG domestic productions!

Get American Humane on your set to protect
your animal actors, your production and
your reputation. It's the smart thing to do.
It's the right thing to do.

We've been part of the entertainment industry
since 1940. Make sure *No Animals Were Harmed*
on *your* set!

Call us at (818) 501-0123 or go online:
www.americanhumane.org/film

AMERICAN HUMANE
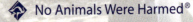
No Animals Were Harmed®

All Creatures Great & Small

New York's Leading *Professional* Animal Agency

www.AnimalAgent.com

- Exotic & Domestic Animals of all kinds
- Professional on-set Trainers & Handlers
- Accurate Bids & Fast Turnaround
- 50+ years of Reliable Performance
- On-staff Zoologist

CLIENTS INCLUDE:

AFLAC, Vogue, Disney, Electrolux, Maybelline, Animal Planet, Discovery, National Geo, MTV, ESPN, D&G, GQ, DKNY, Tiffany, Vera Wang, Nike, GAP, AmEx, Mastercard, Verizon, A&H, Cole Haan, Barneys, Nordstrom, Tribeca Film Festival, Cottonelle, Glamour, Maxim, Vanity Fair, Staples, Target, Budweiser, VH1, PBS, Pepsi, Coach, Page 6, HP, Macys, Rolling Stone, Aeropostale, Iams, Meow Mix, Pedigree, Westminster Dog Show

Ruth Manecke, Zoologist
Cathryn Long, Animal Specialist

(914) 232-3623
(914) 682-8870

Cat@AnimalAgent.com

Deep Hollow Ranch (631) 668-3901
Ranch Rd./Montauk Hwy, Box 835 FAX (631) 668-3902
Montauk, NY 11954 www.deephollowranch.com
(Horses)

Dusty Promotions, LLC (866) 552-2262
(Horses) www.dustypromotions.com

Exotics Unlimited (718) 720-4677
16 Sunset Ave. FAX (718) 390-0280
Staten Island, NY 10314
(Birds, Insects, Monkeys & Reptiles)

A Horse Drawn Affair (518) 329-5249
258 Crest Ln. www.ahorsedrawnaffair.com
(Near E. Ancram Rd.)
Ancramdale, NY 12503

(516) 766-1100
Party Pets, Inc. (516) 857-4387
P.O. Box 439 www.partypets.com
Baldwin, NY 11510

Paws For Effect, Inc. (877) 729-7439
www.pawsforeffect.net
(Birds, Cats, Dogs, Exotics & Livestock)

(860) 491-3421
R.W. Commerford & Sons, Inc. (860) 491-4201
48 Torrington Rd., P.O. Box 188 FAX (860) 491-9428
Goshen, CT 06756 www.commerfordzoo.com
(Camels, Elephants, Goats, Horses, Ponies & Sheep)

(860) 213-0260
Rhodes Collar/All About Dogs (860) 536-7190
11 Allen St. www.rhodescollar.com
Mystic, CT 06355

Vidbel Performing Animals (518) 734-4137
Box 149 Siam Rd.
Windham, NY 12496
(Dogs, Exotic Birds & Ponies)

William Berloni (860) 345-8734
Theatrical Animals, Inc. (860) 478-3935
181 Little City Rd. FAX (860) 345-3184
Higganum, CT 06441 www.theatricalanimals.com
(Birds, Cats, Dogs, Farm Animals & Reptiles)

Film ■ **Television** ■ **Theatre**
Commercials ■ **Voice Overs**
Also Spanish Consultants & Translation Services

Stark Naked Productions
Come find your "dream" cast

Elsie C. Stark
Casting Director

39 West 19th Street, 12th Floor
New York, NY 10011
Tel: 212.366.1903 Fax: 212.366.0495
www.starknakedproductions.com

"Your DreamCasters"

Casting Directors

Amerifilm Casting, Inc. (212) 253-2528
www.amerifilmcasting.com

Amhalise Casting (212) 539-3691
111 E. 14th St., Ste. 251   FAX (718) 222-2744
New York, NY 10003   www.amhalisecasting.com
(Babies, Celebrities, Children, Commercials, Film,
Real People & Spanish Language Casting)

Ⓐ Amy Gossels Casting (212) 472-6981
(212) 717-4277
1471 Third Ave.
New York, NY 10028
(Babies, Celebrities, Children, Circus/Variety Acts,
Commercials, Film, Podcasting, Real People, Reality,
TV & Webisodes)
Contacts: Amy Gossels & Eliza Khan

Anetka Enterprises (212) 929-2339
247 W. 38th St., Seventh Fl.   FAX (212) 989-9105
New York, NY 10018   www.crcasting.com

Ⓐ Baby Wranglers Casting, Inc. (212) 568-1200
689 Fort Washington Ave., Ste. 1AA (Near W. 190th St.)
New York, NY 10040
(Babies & Children)

**Bambini Casting & Wrangling/
Michele Avantario** (914) 646-5839
(Babies & Children)
Contact: Michele Avantario

Barbara McNamara Casting, LLC (212) 645-6051
249 W. 34th St., Ste. 500   FAX (212) 645-6044
New York, NY 10001   www.barbmcasting.com

AMY GOSSELS CASTING
UNION NON-UNION & REAL

commercials   film   television   print   videos
1471 THIRD AVE. NEW YORK CITY 10028   212 472 6981

Beth Melsky Casting (212) 505-5000
928 Broadway, Ste. 300 (Near 21st St.)
New York, NY 10010

(212) 289-3208
Boland/Eggmann Casting (917) 449-3982
230 E. 87th St., Ste. 3D (Near Third Ave.)
New York, NY 10128
Contacts: Mary Clay Boland & Katharina Eggmann

Carol Hanzel Casting (212) 242-6113
48 W. 21st St., Seventh Fl. FAX (212) 242-6208
(Near Fifth Ave.)
New York, NY 10010

(646) 336-6146
Casting Solutions (212) 875-7573
P.O. Box 20164 FAX (515) 474-5291
New York, NY 10011 www.castingsolutions.tv
(Commercials, Film, Foreign Language Casting, Real People, Reality, TV, Voice Casting & Webisodes)
Contact: Liz Ortiz-Mackes

Chantiles Vigneault Casting, Inc. (212) 924-2278
39 W. 19th St., 12th Fl. FAX (212) 924-2484
(Near Fifth Ave.) www.cvcasting.com
New York, NY 10011
Contacts: Sharon Chantiles & Jeffrey Vigneault

Chloe Productions, Inc. (212) 523-0460
250 W. 54th St., Ste. 705 FAX (212) 523-0042
(Near Eighth Ave.) www.chloepro.com
New York, NY 10019
(Celebrities)

Jodi Collins (212) 643-1736
www.cec-entertainment.com

Danny Goldman & Associates (323) 463-1600
1006 N. Cole Ave. FAX (323) 463-3139
Hollywood, CA 90038   www.dannygoldmancasting.com
(Babies, Children, Commercials, Industrials, Real People & Voice Casting)
Contacts: Mariko Ballentine, Chris Devane, Danny Goldman, Alan Kaminsky & Josh Rappaport

donald case casting

COMMERCIALS • TELEVISION • THEATRE • FILM

386 PARK AVE SOUTH SUITE 809
NEW YORK, NY 10016

(212)889-6555
FAX: (212)889-4074

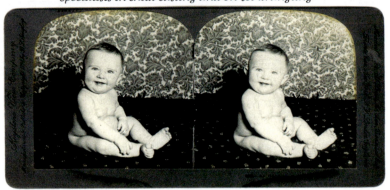

Baby Wranglers Casting, Inc.
Specialists in child casting and on-set wrangling

Tel/Fax: 212.568.1200 689 Ft. Washington Ave., #1AA NY, NY 10040
Dr. John V. Hicks, Kathleen Mazzie, Claudia Schneider

Ⓐ Donald Case Casting (212) 889-6555
386 Park Ave. South, Ste. 809 FAX **(212) 889-4074**
(Near E. 27th St.) www.donaldcasecasting.com
New York, NY 10016

Donna DeSeta Casting (212) 274-9696
525 Broadway, Third Fl. FAX **(212) 274-9795**
(Near Spring St.) www.donnadesetacasting.com
New York, NY 10012

Donna Grossman Casting (212) 598-2344
12 W. 27th St., 10 North, Aqua Studios (Near Broadway)
New York, NY 10001 www.donnagrossmancasting.com
(Babies, Children, Commercials, Real People, Reality,
TV & Webisodes)
Contacts: Paul Bernstein & Lisa Feiner

Doreen Frumkin Casting (212) 595-2781
FAX **(212) 595-6422**

Everything Events & (973) 338-6995
Entertainment, LLC (323) 230-5527
41 Watchung Plaza, Ste. 236 FAX **(973) 200-4291**
Montclair, NJ 07042 www.eeande.com
(Celebrities, Circus/Variety Acts, Commercials, Film, Real
People, Reality & TV)

(860) 672-3205
Extreme Skills Productions **(860) 480-4164**
149 Popple Swamp Rd. FAX **(860) 672-4938**
Cornwall Bridge, CT 06754
(Circus & Variety)

Godlove & Company, Inc. (212) 627-7300
151 W. 25th St., 11th Fl. FAX **(212) 627-3977**
(Near Seventh Ave.) www.godlovecasting.com
New York, NY 10001
(Commercials, TV & Webisodes)
Contacts: Linda Godlove & Ken Lupano

Grant Wilfley Casting (212) 685-3537
123 W. 18th St., Eighth Fl. FAX **(212) 684-7039**
New York, NY 10011

The Great Voice Co. (201) 541-8595
110 Charlotte Pl. FAX **(201) 541-8608**
Englewood Cliffs, NJ 07632 www.greatvoice.com
(Voice Casting)

Harriet Bass Casting (212) 598-9032
648 Broadway, Ste. 912 FAX **(212) 420-8424**
(Near Bleecker St.)
New York, NY 10012

SCOTT POWERS STUDIOS, INC
CASTING

*CREATIVE SOLUTIONS
TO YOUR
MOST CHALLENGING CASTINGS*

135 W. 29TH ST., STE. 404, NEW YORK, NY 10001 USA TEL 212.242.4700 FAX 212.242.4768
CASTING@SCOTTPOWERS.COM HTTP://SCOTTPOWERS.COM/CASTING.HTML

CENTRAL CASTING
★ EST. 1925 ★

Offering a full range of background services for every type of production from offices in Los Angeles and New York. Central Casting meets all of your needs with:

- Background Talent for Feature Films, Television, Commercials, and Print Media

- SAG, AFTRA, and Non-Union Background Actors

- Dedicated Casting Directors

- Service Available 24/7

- State-of-the-Art Computer Imaging

- Largest Background Database in the Country

- In-House Payroll Services

NEW YORK
Phone: 646.205.8244
Fax: 212.947.4859

LOS ANGELES
Phone: 818.562.2700
Fax: 818.562.2786

www.centralcasting.org

Herman & Lipson Casting, Inc. (212) 807-7706
Film Center Bldg. FAX (212) 989-7734
630 Ninth Ave., Ste. 1410 (Near W. 44th St.)
New York, NY 10036

Hidden Talents Casting (212) 734-7560
Three New York Ave. FAX (914) 949-5616
White Plains, NY 10606 www.hiddentalents.com
(Real People)

The Hollywood-Madison Group (310) 956-1098
11684 Ventura Blvd., Ste. 258
Studio City, CA 91604 www.hollywood-madison.com
(Celebrities)

House Production & Casting (212) 929-0200
450 W. 15th St., Ste. 202 FAX (212) 929-5350
New York, NY 10011 www.houseprod.com
(Children, Commercials, Foreign Language Casting, Real People, TV, Voice Casting & Webisodes)

HSR/NY (212) 687-4180
The Graybar Bldg. FAX (212) 697-0536
420 Lexington Ave., Ste. 1934 www.hsrny.com
(Near E. 42nd St.)
New York, NY 10170
(Voice Casting)
Contacts: Sharon DiTullio & Sara Paterno

Impossible Casting (212) 255-3029
122 W. 26th St., Sixth Fl. FAX (212) 255-3132
(Near Sixth Ave.) www.impossiblecasting.com
New York, NY 10001

(212) 619-5545
InterNation, Inc. (800) 222-8799
299 Broadway, Ste. 1400 FAX (212) 619-5887
(Near Duane St.) www.internation.com
New York, NY 10007
(Foreign Language Casting and Voice-Overs)

iProbe Multilingual Solutions, Inc. (212) 489-6035
Five W. 36th St., Ste. 402 FAX (212) 202-4790
(Near Fifth Ave.) www.iprobesolutions.com
New York, NY 10018
(Foreign Language Voice Overs and Voice Casting)

**Judy Henderson &
Associates Casting** (212) 877-0225
330 W. 89th St. (Near West End Ave.)
New York, NY 10024

Judy Keller Casting, Inc. (212) 463-7676
247 W. 38th St., Seventh Fl. FAX (212) 807-8698
New York, NY 10018 www.judykellercasting.com

Kathy Wickline Casting (215) 739-9952
1080 N. Delaware Ave. FAX (215) 634-6454
Philadelphia, PA 19125 www.wicklinecasting.com
Contacts: Karen Brager & Kathy Wickline

(212) 459-9293
Kelli Lerner Casting (310) 492-5987
330 W. 56th St., Ste. 25E www.kellilernercasting.com
(Near Eighth Ave.)
New York, NY 10019

(646) 781-9182
❶ Ken Lazer Casting (646) 523-4429
FAX (646) 514-7995
www.kenlazercasting.com
(Babies, Children, Circus/Variety Acts, Commercials, Film, Foreign Language Casting, Real People, Reality, TV, Voice Casting & Webisodes)

❶ Kipperman Casting, Inc. (212) 736-3663
12 W. 37th St., Third Fl. FAX (212) 736-5660
(Near Fifth Ave.) www.kipperman.com
New York, NY 10018

Liz Lewis Casting Partners (212) 645-1500
151 W. 19th St., Third Fl. FAX (212) 645-2483
(Near Sixth Ave.) www.lizlewis.com
New York, NY 10011

Donna McKenna (212) 643-1736
www.cec-entertainment.com

Mike Lemon Casting (215) 627-8927
413 N. Seventh St., Ste. 602 FAX (215) 627-8923
Philadelphia, PA 19123 www.mikelemoncasting.com

Moschini Productions (212) 620-3961
54 Barrow St., Ste. 2B FAX (212) 208-0975
New York, NY 10014 www.moschini.com
(Children, Circus/Variety Acts, Commercials, Film, Podcasting, Real People, Reality, TV & Webisodes)

Nurses-In-Commercials (212) 712-6462
(Nurses & Health Professionals) FAX (718) 585-3872

The Philadelphia Casting Co., Inc. (215) 592-7575
800 N. Second St., Ste. 179 www.philacast.com
Philadelphia, PA
Contacts: Sam Gish & Susan Gish

Pirate New York (212) 253-2920
30 Irving Pl., Sixth Fl. www.piratenewyork.com
(Near 15th St.)
New York, NY 10003
(Voice Casting)

(214) 890-0660
The Reel People Company LLC (212) 564-4141
(Real People) FAX (214) 890-7830
Contact: Kristi Comuzzi www.reelpeoplecompany.com

Rennert Translation Group (212) 867-8700
216 E. 45th St., 17th Fl. FAX (212) 867-7666
(Near Third Ave.) www.rennert.com
New York, NY 10017
(Foreign Language Voice-Overs)

❶ Scott Powers Studios, Inc. (212) 242-4700
135 W. 29th St., Ste. 404 FAX (212) 242-4768
(Near Sixth Ave.)
New York, NY 10001
Contacts: James Loughlin & Scott Powers

Selective Casting By Carol Nadell (212) 757-1510
FAX (212) 246-5365
www.selectivecasting.com
(Industrials, Interactive, Foreign Language, Film & Theater)

**❶ Stark Naked Productions, Inc./
Elsie Stark Casting** (212) 366-1903
39 W. 19th St., 12th Fl. FAX (212) 366-0495
(Near Sixth Ave.) www.starknakedproductions.com
New York, NY 10011
(Babies, Celebrities, Children, Commercials, Film, Foreign Language Casting, Podcasting, Real People, TV, Voice Casting & Webisodes)
Contacts: Elizabeth Gans, CB Maltese & Elsie Stark

Strickman-Ripps, Inc. (212) 966-3211
66 W. Broadway, Ste. 602 FAX (212) 966-4740
(Near Murray St.) www.strickman-ripps.com
New York, NY 10007
(Non-Union, Real People & SAG)
Contacts: Mary Anne Driscoll, Lori Fink, Rebecca Hewitt, Stacy Horowitz, Jennifer Kitchin & Jill Strickman-Ripps

Stuart Howard Associates, Ltd. (212) 414-1544
207 W. 25th St., Sixth Fl. (Near Seventh Ave.)
New York, NY 10001
Contacts: Stuart Howard, Howard Meltzer & Amy Schecter

Casting Facilities

Abingdon Theatre Arts Complex (212) 868-2055
312 W. 36th St., First Fl. FAX (212) 868-2056
(Near Eighth Ave.) www.abingdontheatre.org
New York, NY 10018
Contact: Stephen Squibb

Acting Management, Inc. (212) 989-8709
247 W. 38th St., Seventh Fl. FAX (212) 807-8698
(Near Eighth Ave.)
New York, NY 10018

Cap 21 Studios (212) 807-0202
18 W. 18th St., Sixth Fl. FAX (212) 807-0166
(Near Fifth Ave.) www.cap21.org
New York, NY 10011

Center Stage/NY (212) 929-2228
48 W. 21st. St., Fourth Fl. FAX (212) 929-2722
(Near Sixth Ave.) www.centerstageny.com
New York, NY 10010

City Stage (212) 627-3400
435 W. 19th St. (Near Ninth Ave.) FAX (212) 633-1228
New York, NY 10011 www.citystage.com

Context Studios (718) 384-8300
One N. 12th St., Second Fl., Box B7 www.contextnyc.com
(Near Kent Ave.)
Brooklyn, NY 11211

Divine Studio (212) 387-9655
21 E. Fourth St., Ste. 605 FAX (212) 387-7944
(Near Lafayette St.) www.divinestudios.com
New York, NY 10003

New York City Center Studios (212) 247-0430
130 W. 56th St. (Near Seventh Ave.) FAX (212) 246-9778
New York, NY 10019 www.nycitycenter.org

(212) 840-7700
New York Videoconference Center (888) 666-1776
39 W. 37th St., Sixth Fl. FAX (877) 329-3465
(Near Fifth Ave.) www.nyvideoconference.com
New York, NY 10018

NOLA Studios (212) 582-1417
250 W. 54th St. (Near Broadway) FAX (212) 582-8728
New York, NY 10019

NYCastings (212) 219-3339
243 W. 30th St., Third Fl. www.nycastings.com/studio
New York, NY 10001

One On One Productions (212) 691-6000
34 W. 27th St., 11th Fl. FAX (212) 633-1492
(Near Sixth Ave.) www.oneononenyc.com
New York, NY 10001

Sandra Cameron Dance Center (212) 431-1825
199 Lafayette St. (Near Broome St.) FAX (212) 219-7003
New York, NY 10012 www.sandracameron.com

Soundtrack (212) 420-6010
936 Broadway, Fourth Fl. FAX (212) 777-6403
(Near W. 21st St.) www.soundtrackny.com
New York, NY 10010

Stonestreet Studios (212) 229-0020
48 W. 21st St., Eighth Fl. FAX (800) 701-9530
(Near Sixth Ave.) www.stonestreetstudios.com
New York, NY 10010
Contact: Joanna Shattuck

Choreographers

(917) 553-5363
John Carrafa (323) 954-7730
www.johncarrafa.com

Clear Talent Group/CTG (212) 840-4100
325 W. 38th St., Ste. 1203 FAX (212) 967-4567
(Near Eighth Ave.) www.cleartalentgroup.com
New York, NY 10018
(Reps for Choreographers)

Kate Gyllenhaal (917) 796-7838

Christopher Harrison (212) 279-0790
FAX (212) 279-3119
www.anti-gravity.com

(212) 994-9500
Melanie LaPatin (917) 696-7340
FAX (212) 994-9501
www.dancetimessquare.com

Felice Lesser (212) 594-3388
www.fldt.org

(212) 496-0413
Barry McNabb (917) 375-5971
www.barrymcnabb.com

Bob Rizzo (212) 496-6802
FAX (212) 724-3449
www.bobrizzo.com

Ken Roberson (212) 445-0160
FAX (212) 246-7138

Computer Consultants & Software

Applied Information Management, Inc. (516) 773-3294
70 Polo Rd. (Near Chelsea Pl.) FAX (516) 482-8574
Great Neck, NY 11023 www.aim-harpoon.com
(Residuals, Rights Licensing, and Royalty/Participation Accounting Software)

Cine-Com Payroll (310) 306-0165
748 Washington Blvd. FAX (310) 306-2550
Marina del Rey, CA 90292 www.cine-com.net
(Payroll and Production Accounting Software)

Datafaction, Inc. (323) 291-5700
5100 W. Goldleaf Circle, Ste. 250 FAX (323) 291-3111
Los Angeles, CA 90056 www.df.com
(Production Accounting Software)

DriveSavers Data Recovery (800) 440-1904
(Data Recovery) www.drivesavers.com

Entertainment Partners/Vista Production Accounting Software (646) 473-9000
875 Sixth Ave., 15th Fl. FAX (212) 947-4787
(Near W. 31st St.) www.entertainmentpartners.com
New York, NY 10001
(Bidding, Budgeting and Production Accounting Software)

Entertainment Publishers (310) 440-5800
(800) 820-7601
FAX (310) 440-5812
www.entertainmentpublisher.com
(Contract Software)

Final Draft, Inc. (800) 231-4055
(818) 995-8995
FAX (818) 995-4422
www.finaldraft.com
(Screenwriting Software)

Ⓐ Media Services (212) 366-9390
(866) 414-9615
30 W. 22nd St., Fifth Fl. FAX (212) 366-9398
(Near Sixth Ave.) www.media-services.com
New York, NY 10010
(Accounting, AICP/AICE Actualizing/Bidding, Budgeting, Scheduling and Screenwriting Software)

Mindstar Productions, Inc. (703) 404-1100
8300 Boone Blvd., Ste. 500 FAX (703) 404-5549
Vienna, VA 22182 www.mindstarprods.com
(Breakdown, Budgeting, Scheduling and Shot Logging Software)

Nesbit Systems, Inc. (609) 397-7720
243 N. Union St. www.nesbit.com
Fourth Fl., NJ 08540

PowerProduction Software (408) 559-0800
(800) 457-0383
www.powerproduction.com
(AICP Bidding and Actualizing, Costume Management and Storyboarding Software)

The Production Resource (818) 637-4896
(888) 345-1920
www.powerbid.com
(Commercial Bidding and Actualizing Software)

Quantum Films Software (323) 938-4912
P.O. Box 480255 www.quantumfilms.net
Los Angeles, CA 90048
(Entertainment Industry Software Workflow, Requirements Analysis & System Design)

Real Software Assistance (617) 679-0000
139 Main St. FAX (617) 679-0640
Cambridge, MA 02142 www.realsoftwaresystems.com
(Production Accounting Software)

SourceEcreative (800) 525-0230
(561) 392-9701
FAX (800) 437-9919
www.sourceecreative.com
(Television Commercial Information Database)

Tekserve (212) 929-3645
119 W. 23rd St. FAX (212) 463-9280
New York, NY 10011 www.tekserve.com

Write Brothers, Inc. (818) 843-6557
348 E. Olive Ave., Ste. H FAX (818) 843-8364
Burbank, CA 91502 www.screenplay.com
(Script Formatting Software)

Xytech Systems Corporation (845) 744-5679
(818) 303-7800
38 Basel Rd. www.xytechsystems.com
Pine Bush, NY 12566
(Facility Management Software)

www.showbizsoftware.com
(800) 5-Showbiz

Computers, Office Equipment & Supplies

ABC Office Essentials Co., Inc.   (212) 532-7771
284 Madison Ave. (Near E. 40th St.)   FAX **(212) 532-7773**
New York, NY 10017   www.abc-office-essentials.com
(Coffee Service and Kitchen Equipment)

**Alpha Business
Machine Corporation**   (212) 643-5555
151 W. 30th St. (Near Seventh Ave.)   FAX **(212) 564-4851**
New York, NY 10001
(Copiers, Fax Machines, Printers & Typewriters)

Ⓐ American Copy Machines   (212) 244-2727
141 W. 28th St. (Near Sixth Ave.)   FAX **(212) 244-2739**
New York, NY 10001   www.americancopymachines.com
(Copiers & Fax Machines)

Business Equipment Rentals   (212) 582-2020
250 W. 49th St. (Near Broadway)   FAX **(212) 582-0751**
New York, NY 10019   www.bizrentalny.com
(Computers, Copiers, Fax Machines, Printers & Shredders)

   (585) 427-2222
Business Methods, Inc.   (800) 724-2480
150 Metro Park (Near E. Henrietta Rd.) FAX **(585) 427-0887**
Rochester, NY 14623   www.businessmethods.net
(Computers, Copiers, Fax Machines, Overhead Projectors & Printers)

   (212) 398-6500
Candle Business Systems, Inc.   (800) 578-2679
1501 Broadway, Ste. 503   FAX **(212) 398-6539**
(Near W. 44th St.)   www.candlebusiness.com
New York, NY 10036
(Computers, Copiers & Fax Machines)

Computer Rent   (212) 767-0400
(Computers, Fax Machines & Printers)   FAX **(212) 619-6844**
www.computerpropsnyc.com

Egads Computer Corporation   (212) 557-4656
211 E. 43rd St., Ste. 1002   FAX **(212) 557-5780**
(Near Third Ave.)   www.egadscomputer.com
New York, NY 10017
(Computer, Macintosh, Plasma Displays & Printers)

   (888) 679-6111
Exchange Communications   (505) 501-1029
233 N. Guadalupe, Ste. 290   FAX **(888) 694-8111**
Santa Fe, NM 87501   www.exchangecom.net
(Copiers, Fax Machines & Phone Systems)

Gramercy Office Equipment   (212) 674-7700
175 Fifth Ave. (Near 23rd St.)   FAX **(212) 674-7598**
New York, NY 10010
(Typewriters)

LDI Color Toolbox   (212) 375-6133
1500 Broadway, 10th Fl.   FAX **(212) 375-6134**
(Near W. 43rd St.)   www.ldicolortoolbox.com
New York, NY 10036
(Computers, Copiers, Fax Machines & Typewriters)

Lentini Communications   (212) 206-1452
54 W. 21st St., Ste. 301   FAX **(212) 206-1453**
(Near Fifth Ave.)   www.lentinicommunications.com
New York, NY 10010
(Wireless Internet Junction Boxes)

Lincoln Business Machines   (212) 769-0606
111 W. 68th St. (Near Columbus Ave.) FAX **(212) 787-4246**
New York, NY 10023   www.golbm.com
(Computers, Fax Machines, Printers & Typewriters)

   (212) 366-9390
Media Services Solution Center   (866) 414-9615
30 W. 22nd St., Fifth Fl.   FAX **(212) 366-9398**
(Near Sixth Ave.)   www.media-services.com
New York, NY 10010
(Computers)

Rental Headquarters

Daily / Weekly / Monthly

"New York's #1 source for productionn support and props"

- B/W & Color Copiers
- Computers
- Notebooks
- B/W & Color Printers
- 2 HOURS DELIVERY
- PROMPT SERVICE

- Fax Machines
- Monitors, Plasma
- Safes
- Much, much more...
- RENT WITH OPTION TO OWN
- RELIABLE EQUIPMENT

FREE
✓ Delivery
✓ Set up
✓ Pick up

"WE WILL WORK WITH YOU TO MEET YOUR PRODUCTION BUDGET"

American Copy Machines
Open 24/7   Est. 1977   **(212)244-2727**
141 West 28th St., NY
www.americancopymachines.com

Specialty Business Machines   **(212) 587-9600**
253 W. 35th St., Ste. 12A   FAX **(212) 587-9617**
New York, NY 10001   **www.specialtybusiness.com**
(Computers, Copiers, Fax Machines, Printers & Typewriters)

Tekserve   **(212) 929-3645**
119 W. 23rd St.   FAX **(212) 463-9280**
New York, NY 10011   **www.tekserve.com/rentals**
(Desktop Computers, Laptops, Macintosh, Monitors & Projectors)

TRC -   **(609) 720-1885**
Technology Resource Corporation   **(888) 601-0200**
29 Emmons Dr., Ste. E10   FAX **(609) 720-1701**
Princeton, NJ 08540   **www.trcrent.com**
(Computers, Macintosh & Printers)

USRental.com   **(800) 877-3682**
18 N. Water St.   **www.usrental.com**
Greenwich, CT 06830
(Computers, Macintosh & Printers)

Vernon Computer Source   **(203) 969-0060**
a Division of I.T.Xchange   **(800) 347-7333**
77 Selleck St.   FAX **(203) 969-0050**
Stamford, CT 06902   **www.vernoncomputersource.com**
(Computer Projectors, Computers, Macintosh & Printers)

World Trade Copiers   **(212) 267-4378**
150 Fulton St. (Near Broadway)   FAX **(212) 267-3376**
New York, NY 10038   **www.worldtradecopiers.com**
(Copiers, Fax Machines & Printers)

Digital Casting & Video Conferencing

Beth Melsky Satellite Casting (212) 505-5000
928 Broadway, Ste. 401 (Near W. 21st St.)
New York, NY 10010

Envision Studios (800) 505-0420
928 Broadway, Ste. 401 FAX **(646) 415-8899**
(Near W. 21st St.)
New York, NY 10010

House Production & Casting (212) 929-0200
450 W. 15th St., Ste. 202 FAX **(212) 929-5350**
New York, NY 10011 www.houseprod.com

New York Network (518) 443-5333
Empire State Plaza FAX **(518) 426-4198**
South Concourse, Ste. 146 www.nyn.suny.edu
P.O. Box 2058 (Near State St.)
Albany, NY 12220

(877) 294-9910
Voicebank.net (661) 294-9912
P.O. Box 803095 FAX **(661) 294-9764**
Valencia, CA 91380 www.voicebank.net

Directories & Trade Publications

Advertising Age (212) 210-0281
711 Third Ave. (Near E. 44th St.) FAX (212) 210-0200
New York, NY 10017 www.adage.com

Adweek (646) 654-5500
770 Broadway, Seventh Fl. FAX (646) 654-5365
(Near E. Ninth St.) www.adweek.com
New York, NY 10003

 (800) 562-2706
Adweek Directories (818) 487-4550
770 Broadway, Seventh Fl. www.adweek.com/directories
(Near Ninth St.)
New York, NY 10003
(Advertising, Marketing & Media)

The Alternative Pick (212) 675-4176
1123 Broadway, Ste. 7A FAX (212) 675-4403
(Near W. 26th St.) www.altpick.com
New York, NY 10010
(Design, Illustration and Photography for Print, Television and Web)

 (323) 969-4333
American Cinematographer (800) 448-0145
P.O. Box 2230 FAX (323) 876-4973
Hollywood, CA 90078 www.theasc.com/magazine

Back Stage (800) 562-2706
770 Broadway, Fourth Fl. FAX (646) 654-5744
(Near W. Eighth St.) www.backstage.com
New York, NY 10003

Baseline, Inc. (310) 393-9999
520 Broadway, Ste. 230 www.pkbaseline.com
Santa Monica, CA 90401
(Film Industry Online Information Service)

Billboard (646) 654-5500
770 Broadway (Near E. Ninth St.) FAX (646) 654-5518
New York, NY 10003 www.billboard.com

 (212) 979-6700
The Black Book (800) 841-1246
740 Broadway, Second Fl. FAX (212) 673-4321
New York, NY 10003 www.blackbook.com
(Illustration & Photography)

Breakdown Services, Ltd. (212) 869-2003
850 Seventh Ave., Ste. 600 FAX (212) 869-2004
(Near 55th St.) www.breakdownservices.com
New York, NY 10019
(Information Service for Actors and Talent Agents)

 (212) 210-0100
Creativity (212)-210-0793
711 Third Ave., Third Fl. FAX (212) 210-0497
(Near E. 45th St.)
New York, NY 10017

 (310) 289-2000
DGA Directory of Members (310) 289-2082
7920 Sunset Blvd. FAX (310) 289-5384
Los Angeles, CA 90046 www.dga.org

DGA Quarterly (310) 289-5333
7920 Sunset Blvd. www.dga.org
Los Angeles, CA 90046

Digital Content Producer (818) 236-3667
 www.digitalcontentproducer.com

DM News (646) 638-6120
 www.dmnews.com

DV Magazine (212) 378-0467
(Digital Video and Media) www.dv.com

Emmy (ATAS Magazine) (818) 754-2800
5220 Lankershim Blvd. FAX (818) 761-2827
North Hollywood, CA 91601 www.emmys.tv

 (310) 440-5800
Entertainment Publishers (800) 820-7601
(Guild and Union Contracts) FAX (310) 440-5812
 www.entertainmentpublisher.com

Film & Video Magazine (212) 621-4900
110 William St., 11th Fl. (Near Dey St.) FAX (212) 621-4800
New York, NY 10038 www.filmandvideomagazine.com

Film, TV & Music Directory (561) 279-4685
c/o Peter Glenn Publications FAX (561) 279-4672
235 SE Fifth Ave., Ste. R www.pgdirect.com
Delray Beach, FL 33483

Filmmaker Magazine (212) 563-0211
104 W. 27th St., 12th Fl. FAX (212) 563-1933
New York, NY 10001 www.filmmakermagazine.com

The Hollywood Reporter (646) 654-5630
770 Broadway (Near E. Ninth St.) FAX (646) 654-5637
New York, NY 10003 www.hollywoodreporter.com

The Hollywood Reporter Blu-Book (323) 525-2184
5055 Wilshire Blvd., Sixth Fl. FAX (323) 525-2091
Los Angeles, CA 90036 www.hollywoodreporter.com
(Commercial, Film and Television Production)

**Independent Film and
Video Monthly** (212) 807-1400
P.O. Box 391620 (Near Spring St.) FAX (212) 463-8519
Cambridge, MA 02139 www.aivf.org

**International
Cinematographer's Guild Magazine** (323) 876-0160
7755 Sunset Blvd. FAX (323) 878-1180
Los Angeles, CA 90046 www.cameraguild.com

Kemps Film, TV & Video Handbook (912) 232-5939
 FAX (912) 232-6434
 www.kftv.com
(International Film, Television and Video Production)

The Knowledge (011) 44 173 237 7047
CMP Information Ltd. FAX (011) 44 173 237 7440
Sovereign House Sovereign Way
Tonbridge
Kent TN9 1RW United Kingdom
 www.theknowledgeonline.com
(Commercial, Film, and TV Production for Great Britain)

LA 411 (800) 545-2411
5900 Wilshire Blvd., 29th Fl. www.la411.com
Los Angeles, CA 90036
(Commercial, Film, Music Video, Television and Video
Production for Southern California)

Millimeter Production Buyer's Guide (866) 627-2467
249 W. 17th St., 13th Fl. www.millimeter.com
(Near Seventh Ave.)
New York, NY 10001

**Motion Picture,
TV and Theatre Directory** (212) 245-0969
P.O. Box 276 FAX (212) 245-0974
Tarrytown, NY 10591 www.mpe.net

 (800) 545-2411
New York 411 (646) 746-6891
360 Park Ave. South, 14th Fl. FAX (646) 746-6894
(Near E. 26th St.) www.newyork411.com
New York, NY 10010
(Commercial, Film, Music Video, Television and Video
Production for NY, NJ and CT)

New York Film & Video Guide (732) 572-9193
(800) 572-9190
FAX (732) 572-9194
www.nyfilmguide.com
(Commercial and Feature Film Production)

NYPG, Ltd. (212) 243-0404
Empire State Building FAX (212) 243-9779
350 Fifth Ave., Ste. 4016 (Near 34th St.) www.nypg.com
New York, NY 10118
(Commercial Production)

P3-Production Update Magazine (818) 785-6362
7021 Hayvenhurst Ave., Ste. 205 FAX (818) 785-8092
Van Nuys, CA 91406 www.p3update.com

Players Directory (310) 247-3058
2210 W. Olive Ave. FAX (310) 601-4445
Burbank, CA 91506 www.playersdirectory.com
(Casting)

(212) 777-4002
Producers Masterguide (212) 995-5555
60 E. 8th St., 34th Fl. (Near Broadway) FAX (212) 777-4101
New York, NY 10003 www.producers.masterguide.com
(Commercial, Film, Television and Video Production & Guild
and Union Contracts)

Production Weekly (415) 223-3994
www.productionweekly.com

The Reel Directory (415) 531-9760
P.O. Box 1910 www.reeldirectory.com
Boyes Hot Springs, CA 95416
(Film and Television Production for Northern California)

Screen International (718) 596-0200
60 Pineapple St., Ste. 6A FAX (718) 596-0032
(Near Hicks St.) www.screendaily.com
Brooklyn, NY 11201

**SHOOT Directory for Commercial
Production & Post Production** (203) 227-1699
21 Charles St., Ste. 203 FAX (203) 227-2787
(Near W. Eighth St.) www.shootonline.com
Westport, CT 06880

Shoot Magazine (203) 227-1699
21 Charles St., Ste. 203 FAX (203) 227-2787
Westport, CT 06880 www.shootonline.com

Show Business Weekly Newspaper (212) 986-4100
211 E. 43rd St., Ste. 310 FAX (212) 972-5107
(Near Third Ave.) www.showbusinessweekly.com
New York, NY 10017

Variety, Inc. (646) 746-7001
360 Park Ave. South (Near E. 26th St.) FAX (646) 746-6977
New York, NY 10010 www.variety.com

(530) 891-8410
Videomaker Magazine (800) 284-3226
P.O. Box 4591 FAX (530) 891-8443
Chico, CA 95927 www.videomaker.com

Wisconsin Production Guide (414) 852-8855
www.badgerguide.com

Entertainment Attorneys

Baker Botts, LLP (212) 408-2500
30 Rockefeller Plaza (Near 49th St.) FAX **(212) 408-2501**
New York, NY 10112 www.bakerbotts.com

Steven C. Beer (212) 801-9294
200 Park Ave. (Near 29th St.) FAX **(212) 801-6400**
New York, NY 10066 www.stevenbeer.com

Boylan, Brown, Code,
Vigdor & Wilson (585) 232-5300
2400 Chase Square FAX **(585) 238-9055**
Rochester, NY 14604 www.boylanbrown.com

Cowan, DeBaets,
Abrahams & Sheppard (212) 974-7474
41 Madison Ave., 34th Fl. FAX **(212) 974-8474**
(Near 26th St.) www.cdas.com
New York, NY 10010

Dunnington, Bartholow & Miller LLP (212) 682-8811
1359 Broadway, Sixth Fl. FAX **(212) 661-7769**
New York, NY 10018 www.dunnington.com

Frankfurt, Kurnit, Klein & Selz (212) 980-0120
488 Madison Ave., Tenth Fl. FAX **(212) 593-9175**
(Near 51st St.) www.fkks.com
New York, NY 10022

Franklin, Weinrib,
Rudell & Vassallo, P.C. (212) 935-5500
488 Madison Ave., 18th Fl. FAX **(212) 308-0642**
(Near 51st St.) www.fwrv.com
New York, NY 10022

Furgang & Adwar, LLP (212) 725-1818
1325 Avenue of the Americas, 28th Fl. FAX **(212) 941-9711**
New York, NY 10020 www.furgang.com

Jacobson & Colfin, P.C. (212) 691-5630
60 Madison Ave., Ste. 1026 FAX **(212) 645-5038**
New York, NY 10010 www.thefirm.com

Law Offices of Mark Litwak (310) 859-9595
433 N. Camden Dr., Ste. 1010 FAX **(310) 859-0806**
Beverly Hills, CA 90210 www.marklitwak.com

Law Offices of Rosalind Lichter (212) 941-4075
375 Greenwich St., Ste. 712 FAX **(212) 941-4076**
(Near N. Moore St.) www.rlichterlaw.com
New York, NY 10013

Loeb & Loeb, LLP (212) 407-4000
345 Park Ave. (Near 51st St.) FAX **(212) 407-4990**
New York, NY 10154 www.loeb.com

Moses & Singer LLP (212) 554-7848
405 Lexington Ave. (Near E. 42nd St.) FAX **(212) 554-7700**
New York, NY 10174 www.mosessinger.com

Sloss Law Office, P.C. (212) 627-9898
555 W. 25th St., Fourth Fl. FAX **(212) 627-9498**
(Near 10th Ave.) www.slosslaw.com
New York, NY 10001

(212) 410-4142
John J. Tormey III, PLLC (845) 735-9691
217 E. 86th St., PMB 221 FAX **(212) 410-2380**
(Near Second Ave.) www.tormey.org
New York, NY 10028

Extras Casting Agencies

Audience Associates/Big Crowds (818) 985-8811
3940 Laurel Canyon Blvd., Ste. 1152 www.bigcrowds.com
Studio City, CA 91604
(Large Crowds: 100–20,000 & TV Audiences)

Background, Inc. (212) 609-1103
601 W. 26th St., Ste. M224 FAX (212) 366-1101
(Near 11th Avenue) www.bgroundinc.com
New York, NY 10001
(Small and Large Crowds & Union and Non-Union)
Contact: Kerry Ann O'Sullivan

Barbara McNamara Casting, LLC (212) 645-6051
249 W. 34th St., Ste. 500 FAX (212) 645-6044
New York, NY 10001 www.barbmcasting.com

Bill Dance Casting (818) 754-6634
4605 Lankershim Blvd., Ste. 401 FAX (818) 754-6643
North Hollywood, CA 91602 www.billdancecasting.com

Central Casting (646) 205-8244
875 Sixth Ave., 24th Fl. FAX (212) 947-4859
(Near Seventh Ave.) www.centralcasting.org
New York, NY 10011

Extra Connection (212) 472-6981
1471 Third Ave. (Near E. 79th St.) (212) 717-4277
New York, NY 10028

Extra Talent Agency (212) 807-8172
1133 Broadway, Ste. 1201 FAX (212) 807-8174
New York, NY 10010 www.extratalentagency.com

Grant Wilfley Casting (212) 685-3537
123 W. 18th St., Eighth Fl. FAX (212) 684-7039
New York, NY 10011

Mike Lemon Casting (215) 627-8927
413 N. Seventh St., Ste. 602 FAX (215) 627-8923
Philadelphia, PA 19123 www.mikelemoncasting.com

The Reel People Company (212) 564-4141
(214) 890-0660
www.reelpeoplecompany.com

Scott Powers Studios, Inc. (212) 242-4700
135 W. 29th St., Ste. 404 FAX (212) 242-4768
(Near Sixth Ave.) www.scottpowers.com/casting.html
New York, NY 10001

Sylvia Fay/
Lee Genick & Associates Casting (212) 889-2626
71 Park Ave. (Near E. 38th St.)
New York, NY 10016
Contact: Lee Genick

Hand & Leg Models

Ashly Covington (804) 307-9946
(Hand Model) www.handmodelusa.com

Elaine Gordon Management (212) 936-1001
(516) 623-7736
2942 Harbor Rd. (Near Lindermere Dr.) FAX (516) 623-8863
Merrick, NY 11566
(Reps for Body Parts Models)

Ford Models, Inc. (212) 219-6500
111 Fifth Ave., Ninth Fl. FAX (212) 219-6550
New York, NY 10003 www.fordmodels.com
(Reps for Body Parts Models)

Jimmy Furino (212) 758-1188
(212) 563-3234
(Foot & Hand Model)

Bernard Maisner (212) 477-6776
(On-Camera Writing and Calligraphy) FAX (732) 899-9859
www.bernardmaisner.com

Parts Models (212) 744-6123
7529 FDR Station FAX (212) 396-3014
New York, NY 10150 www.partsmodels.com
(Reps for Body Parts Models)

Insurance Brokers & Guarantors

Arts & Entertainment
Insurance Brokerage (781) 639-2723
259 Humphrey St., P.O. Box 1048 FAX (781) 639-2844
Marblehead, MA 01945 www.videoinsurance.com

(212) 406-4499
C & S Int'l Insurance Brokers Inc. (800) 257-0883
19 Fulton St., Ste. 308A FAX (212) 406-7584
(Near Water St.) www.csins.com
New York, NY 10038

(212) 5934200
Casswood Insurance Agency, Ltd. (800) 972-2242
379 Broadway (Near W. 14th St.) FAX (866) 558-7841
Saratoga Springs, NY 12866 www.casswood.com

(516) 394-7553
CBS Coverage Group, Inc. (516) 938-9000
111 Express St. FAX (516) 938-7511
Plainview, NY 11803 www.cbsinsurance.com

(212) 603-0231
D.R. Reiff & Associates (800) 827-7363
320 W. 57th St. (Near Eighth Ave.) FAX (212) 247-0739
New York, NY 10019 www.reiffinsurance.com

(212) 867-3550
Dewitt Stern Group (212) 297-1444
420 Lexington Ave., Ste. 2700 FAX (212) 573-4026
(Near E. 43rd St.) www.dewittstern.com
New York, NY 10170

(212) 683-2433
Film Emporium (800) 371-2555
274 Madison Ave., Ste. 404 FAX (212) 683-2740
(Near E. 40th St.) www.filmemporium.com
New York, NY 10016

HSBC Bank, USA N.A. (212) 525-1234
452 Fifth Ave., 15th Fl. FAX (212) 525-6784
(Near 40th St.) www.us.hsbc.com/film
New York, NY 10018

Robertson Taylor
(North America) Inc. (212) 279-4519
330 Seventh Ave., Ninth Fl. FAX (212) 279-4536
New York, NY 10001 www.robertson-taylor.com

ShortTermProductions.Com (310) 207-5432
12300 Wilshire Blvd., Ste. 400 FAX (310) 207-8526
Los Angeles, CA 90025 www.shorttermproductions.com

Sterling Grant and Associates, LLC (877) 954-7200
2200 E. Camelback, Ste. 222 FAX (602) 954-9624
Phoenix, AZ 85016 www.sterling-grant.com

Taylor & Taylor Associates (212) 490-8511
90 Park Ave., Third Fl. FAX (212) 490-7236
(Near E. 39th St.) www.taylorinsurance.com
New York, NY 10016

Tom C. Pickard & Co., Inc. (800) 726-3701
820 Pacific Coast Hwy FAX (800) 318-9840
Hermosa Beach, CA 90254 www.tcpinsurance.com

(212) 702-3300
Ⓐ **Ventura Insurance Brokerage, Inc.** (800) 795-8075
475 Park Ave. South, 17th Fl. FAX (212) 702-3333
(Near E. 48th St.) www.venturainsurance.com
New York, NY 10016

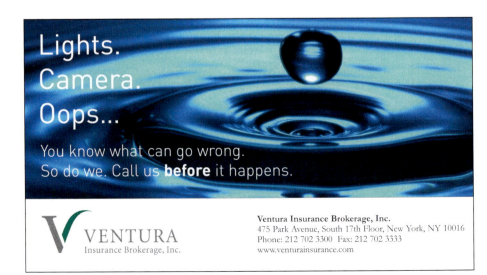

Lights.
Camera.
Oops...
You know what can go wrong.
So do we. Call us **before** it happens.

VENTURA
Insurance Brokerage, Inc.

Ventura Insurance Brokerage, Inc.
475 Park Avenue, South 17th Floor, New York, NY 10016
Phone: 212 702 3300 Fax: 212 702 3333
www.venturainsurance.com

Janitorial & Strike Services

Ⓐ Chelrae Carting LLC (347) 862-3977
841 Barretto St., Box 14 FAX **(917) 591-2868**
Bronx, NY 10474

Ko Karting (917) 405-0683
332 Bleecker St., Ste. 38H
New York, NY 10014

Prime Location (917) 449-2929
533 E. Fifth St., Ste. 22 www.primelocationnyc.com
New York, NY 10009

Large Scale Event Planning

B. Rodwin & Co.   **(212) 255-0355**
359 Bleecker St. (Near W. 10th St.)   FAX **(212) 255-9605**
New York, NY 10014   **www.brodwinco.com**
(Event Planning)

Barkley Kalpak Associates   **(212) 947-1502**
315 W. 39th St., Studio 607   **www.bka.net**
(Near Eighth Ave.)
New York, NY 10018
(Event Planning)

Cal James Entertainment, Inc.   **(212) 967-9791**
484 W. 43rd St., Ste. 36H   FAX **(212) 967-9791**
(Near 10th Ave.)   **www.caljames.com**
New York, NY 10036
(Entertainment)

Castle & Pierpont   **(212) 244-8668**
353 W. 39th St. (Near Eighth Ave.)   FAX **(212) 244-8662**
New York, NY 10018   **www.castlepierpont.com**
(Event Planning & Party Supplies)

Charles Banfield Productions   **(310) 975-9401**
(Event Planning)   FAX **(212) 851-1182**
   www.charlesbanfield.com

Danis & Danis   **(212) 779-8790**
45 Sutton Pl., Ste. 20C   FAX **(212) 684-4964**
(Near E. 59th St.)   **www.danis-danis.com**
New York, NY 10016
(Event Planning)

Empire Entertainment, Inc.   **(212) 343-1645**
560 Broadway, Ste. 202   FAX **(212) 343-1646**
(Near Prince St.)   **www.empireentertainment.com**
New York, NY 10012
(Event Planning)

Eric Silvey Entertainment   **(212) 486-9517**
225 E. 27th St.   **www.ericsilveyentertainment.com**
(Near Third Ave.)
New York, NY 10022
(Event Planning)

Event Designs New York   **(646) 422-0054**
207 E. 84th St., Ste. 201   FAX **(646) 422-0056**
(Near Third Ave.)   **www.edny.com**
New York, NY 10028
(Corporate Event Planning)

Everything Events &   **(973) 338-6995**
Entertainment, LLC   **(323) 230-5527**
41 Watchung Plaza, Ste. 236   FAX **(973) 200-4291**
Montclair, NJ 07042   **www.eeande.com**
(Caterers, Corporate Event Planning, Entertainment, Event
Show Production, Event Staffing, Party Supplies & Rentals)

   (203) 485-0392
Jack-Of-All-Trades Productions   **(917) 855-2041**
Four Putnam Hill, Ste. 1J   FAX **(203) 485-0392**
Greenwich, CT 06830   **www.jackoftrades.biz**
(Corporate Event Planning, Entertainment & Event
Show Production)

Modelbartenders.com   **(212) 499-0886**
145 W. 28th St., Ste. 10SW   FAX **(212) 499-0884**
(Near Avenue of the Americas)   **www.modelbartenders.com**
New York, NY 10001
(Event Staffing)

New York Caterers and
Party Planners   **(212) 396-9351**
421 E. 65th St. (Near York Ave.)   FAX **(212) 396-9352**
New York, NY 10021   **www.ny-caterers.com**
(Caterers & Event Planning)

Premier Party Servers   **(212) 499-0886**
145 W. 28th St., Ste. 10 SW
(Near Avenue of the Americas)
New York, NY 10001   **www.premierpartyservers.com**
(Event Planning)

Libraries, Research & Clearance

American Folk Art Museum Research Library (212) 265-1040
45 W. 53rd St. (Near Fifth Ave.) FAX (212) 265-2350
New York, NY 10019 www.folkartmuseum.org

American Heritage Magazine Picture Library (212) 206-5107
90 Fifth Ave. (Near 15th St.) FAX (212) 367-3151
New York, NY 10011 www.americanheritage.com
(Picture Library)

American Museum of Natural History Library (212) 769-5400
Central Park West at 79th St. FAX (212) 769-5009
New York, NY 10024 library.amnh.org

American Society of Composers, Authors & Publishers (ASCAP) (212) 621-6000
One Lincoln Plaza (Near 63rd St.) www.ascap.com
New York, NY 10023
(Music Clearance and Licensing)

Anthology Film Archives (212) 505-5181
32 Second Ave. www.anthologyfilmarchives.org
(Near Second St.)
New York, NY 10003

Archival Film Research (212) 989-2025
 (917) 207-6818
799 Greenwich St., Loft Six South FAX (212) 989-4607
New York, NY 10014 www.archivalfilmresearch.com

Brooklyn Museum of Art (718) 501-6307
 (718) 501-6511
200 Eastern Pkwy FAX (718) 501-6125
(Near Washington Ave.)
Brooklyn, NY 11238

BZ/Rights & Permissions, Inc. (212) 924-3000
2350 Broadway, Ste. 224 FAX (212) 924-2525
(Near Avenue of the Americas) www.bzrights.com
New York, NY 10024

Ⓐ Clearance Domain LLC (800) 562-1231
 (310) 898-1233
 FAX (888) 562-5120
 www.clearancedomain.com

Collegiate Images (954) 343-8000
 (818) 625-1606
(Stock Footage Research) FAX (954) 343-8001
 www.collegiateimages.com

Diamond Time, Ltd. (212) 274-1006
630 Ninth Ave., Ste. 1012 FAX (212) 274-1938
(Near 44th St.) www.diamondtime.net
New York, NY 10036
(Copyright Clearance and Research)

Eastern Script Service, Inc. (508) 478-4252
 (613) 542-3999
53 Pine Island Rd. FAX (508) 478-3715
Milford, MA 01757 www.easternscript.com
(Script Clearance and Research)

Elizabeth Bardsley & Associates, Inc. (818) 563-4008
3727 W. Magnolia Blvd., Ste. 450 FAX (818) 823-1938
Burbank, CA 91510 www.elizabethbardsley.com
(Research Services & Script Annotations)

Film Art LA (323) 461-4900
 FAX (323) 461-4959
 www.filmartla.com
(Art and Photography Copyright Clearance and Research)

Frick Art Reference Library (212) 288-8700
10 E. 71st St. (Near Fifth Ave.) FAX (212) 879-2091
New York, NY 10021 www.frick.org

Global ImageWorks, LLC (201) 384-7715
65 Beacon St. FAX (201) 501-8971
Haworth, NJ 07641 www.globalimageworks.com
(Clearances, Film Copyright Research, Footage Clearance, Footage Research, Music Clearances, Music Research, Photography Clearances, Photography Research, Research & Stock Footage Clearances)

Joan Pearce Research Associates (323) 655-5464
8111 Beverly Blvd., Ste. 308 FAX (323) 655-4770
Los Angeles, CA 90048 home.earthlink.net/~jpra/
(Errors and Omissions & Research)

Metropolitan Museum of Art - Nolan Library (212) 570-3788
1000 Fifth Ave. (Near 80th St.) www.metmuseum.org
New York, NY 10028

Mother West (212) 807-0405
37 W. 20th St., Ste. 1006 FAX (917) 210-2962
(Near Fifth Ave.) www.motherwest.com
New York, NY 10011
(Music Clearance)

Museum of Modern Art Library (212) 708-9433
 (212) 708-9400
11 W. 53rd St. (Near Fifth Ave.) FAX (212) 333-1122
New York, NY 10019 www.moma.org
(By Appointment Only)

New York Public Library - Milstein Division (212) 930-0828
Humanities & Social Sciences Library
Fifth Ave. and 42nd St., Rm. 121
New York, NY 10018
www.nypl.org/research/chss/lhg/genea.html

New York Public Library for the Performing Arts (212) 870-1630
40 Lincoln Center Plaza (Near Columbus Ave.)
New York, NY 10023
www.nypl.org/research/lpa/lpa.html

The New York Public Library (212) 930-0830
476 Fifth Ave. (Near 42nd St.) (212) 930-0730
New York, NY 10018 FAX (212) 642-0100
www.nypl.org

NYC Fire Museum (212) 691-1303
278 Spring St. (Near Holland Tunnel) FAX (212) 924-0430
New York, NY 10013 www.nycfiremuseum.org

Patco Resources, Inc. (845) 357-5300
Nine Washington Circle FAX (845) 357-6427
(Near Washington Ave.) www.patcoresources.com
Suffern, NY 10901
(Music Clearance)

Princeton Antiques Bookservice (609) 344-1943
2917 Atlantic Ave. (800) 253-6863
Atlantic City, NJ 08401 FAX (609) 344-1944
www.princetonantiques.com
(Rare Book Search Service)

Re: Search (646) 365-1300
432 Park Ave. South, Ste. 1009 FAX (646) 365-1304
(Near 29th St.) www.researchandrights.com
New York, NY 10016
(Rights Clearance, Stock Footage Research & Visual Licensing)

Richard Kroll Research (845) 353-5258
202 Birchwood Ave. (917) 697-0371
Upper Nyack, NY 10960 FAX (845) 353-5258

Sample Clearance Limited (212) 707-8804
162 W. 56th St., Ste. 306 FAX (212) 707-8952
(Near Seventh Ave.)
New York, NY 10019
(Clearance and Licensing of Music Samples)

Signature Sound, Inc. (212) 989-0011
71 W. 23rd St., Ste. 902 (800) 345-6757
(Near Fifth Ave.) FAX (212) 989-3576
New York, NY 10010 www.signature-sound.com
(Music Clearance and Licensing)

Society of Illustrators Research Library (212) 838-2560
128 E. 63rd St. (Near Lexington Ave.) FAX (212) 838-2561
New York, NY 10021 www.societyillustrators.org
(By Appointment Only)

TellAVision (310) 230-5303
1060 20th St., Ste. 8 FAX (310) 388-5550
Santa Monica, CA 90403 www.tellavisionagency.com
(Reps for Footage & Visual Research/Treatment Design Companies)

Thought Equity Motion (646) 495-6123
770 Broadway, Ste. 236 (866) 815-6599
New York, NY 10003 FAX (646) 495-6042
www.thoughtequity.com

Wilbour Library of Egyptology (718) 638-5000
200 Eastern Pkwy FAX (718) 638-3731
(Near Washington Ave.) www.brooklynart.org
Brooklyn, NY 11238

Massage Therapists

Susanna Green (917) 363-6353

🅐 **Heidi's Fabulous Fatigue Fighters Worldwide** (212) 996-0640
(917) 301-2022
www.fabulousfatiguefighters.com

MikesGotMyBack.com (917) 455-0559
www.mikesgotmyback.com

Professional Home Spa Services (848) 459-0012
25 First Ave. www.prohomespa.com
New York, NY 10003

Lowell Seeman (718) 891-3732
FAX (718) 843-2818

Phyllis Seeman (718) 843-0029

Messenger Services

A to Z Couriers (212) 253-6500
106 Ridge St. (Near Delancey St.) FAX (212) 253-6565
New York, NY 10002 www.atozcouriers.com

Bombay Couriers (212) 398-0780
59 W. 37th St. www.iccworld.com
(Near Avenue of the Americas)
New York, NY 10018

Breakaway Courier Systems (212) 947-4455
335 W. 35th St., 10th Fl. (212) 947-7777
(Near Eighth Ave.) FAX (212) 947-3335
New York, NY 10001 www.breakawaycourier.com

Choice Courier (212) 370-1999
 FAX (212) 370-0440
 www.choicecourier.com

City Expeditor, Inc. (212) 353-2042
125 E. 23rd St. (Near Lexington Ave.) FAX (212) 228-8320
New York, NY 10010 www.cityexpeditor.com

 (212) 594-1300
Dependable Transport & Messenger (212) 465-2300
240 W. 37th St., Eighth Fl. FAX (212) 594-4475
(Near Seventh Ave.) www.dependablemessenger.com
New York, NY 10018

Dynamex (212) 564-2222
302 Fifth Ave., Fourth Fl. FAX (212) 868-5910
(Near 31st St.) www.dynamex.com
New York, NY 10001

Mobile Messenger Service (212) 247-7400
443 W. 54th St. (Near Ninth Ave.) FAX (212) 315-3083
New York, NY 10019 www.mobilemessengerservice.com

Moonlite Courier (212) 473-2246
125 E. 23rd St. (Near Park Ave.) FAX (212) 529-1625
New York, NY 10010 www.moonlitecourier.com

Quik Trak Messengers (212) 463-7070
267 W. 17th St., Third Fl. FAX (212) 463-8318
(Near Eighth Ave.) www.quik-trak.com
New York, NY 10011

 (914) 576-6300
Reels On Wheels Unlimited (877) 576-6300
P.O. Box 100 FAX (914) 633-6932
New Rochelle, NY 10804 www.reelsonwheels.com

Nautical Film Services & Coordination

**Captain Mike's Diving/
Michael Carew**
530 City Island Ave.
City Island, NY 10464
(718) 885-1588
(347) 865-4230
FAX (718) 885-2543
www.captainmikesdiving.com

Cinema Rentals, Inc.
25876 The Old Road, Ste. 174
Stevenson Ranch, CA 91381
(661) 222-7342
(877) 877-9605
FAX (661) 253-3643
www.cinemarineteam.com

Ⓐ Miller's Launch
Pier 7 1/2
Staten Island, NY 10301
(Marine Coordination)
(718) 727-7303
FAX (718) 448-6326
www.millerslaunch.com

Safety First Divers
(516) 486-5733

SilverScreen Marine
127 E. 10th St., No. 7/8
New York, NY 10003
(212) 505-0694
(917) 797-2884
www.silverscreenmarine.com

Stunt Dept., Inc./Chris Barnes
221 Dogwood Ln.
Manhasset, NY 11030
(516) 236-9644
FAX (516) 869-0843
www.stuntdept.com

MILLER'S LAUNCH
PIER 7 1/2, STATEN ISLAND, NY

Miller's Launch's fleet includes vessels ranging from 10 feet to 150 feet. Each of these vessels is specially equipped for doing a vast amount of different jobs for our customers:

- **Crew Boats**
- **Camera Platform Vessels**
- **Prop Boats**
- **Tug Boats & Barges**
- **Utility & Work Boats**

Depending on your needs, Miller's Launch can fully customize your vessel to contain any of the specialized equipment you may need. All of our vessels are equipped with sophisticated navigation and communication tools.

Professional crews onboard and shore side in New York and New Jersey guarantee that your vessel is expertly maintained and ably navigated.

Call Miller's Launch anytime 24 hours a day at **(718) 727-7303** to learn more about the specialized vessels and "can do" attitude that will make your expedition a success.

CONTACT:
sven@millerslaunch.com

www.millerslaunch.com

Notaries

Village Postal Center (212) 505-0303
532 La Guardia Pl. (Near Bleecker St.) FAX **(212) 979-7462**
New York, NY 10012

Your Neighborhood Office (212) 989-8303
332 Bleecker St. (Near W. 10th St.) FAX **(212) 691-8661**
New York, NY 10014   www.neighborhoodoffice.com

Payroll & Production Accountants (Local 161 NY)

Tara Noel Andrus	(917) 442-2865
Diana Marie Ascher	(917) 523-8104
Theodore Au	(917) 523-8432
Joshua Bell	(917) 288-2366
Eric Robert Bellamy	(718) 720-7143 / (917) 520-5293
Kevin A. Black	(347) 512-8163
Anna Bosco	(973) 479-1587
Stephen M. Boyle	(914) 831-7036 / (914) 980-7085
Janice Brabaw	(646) 246-4957
Scott Franklin Brant (Assistant Production Accountant)	(203) 587-1158
Craig Brown (Assistant Production Accountant)	(412) 716-4185
Lauren Brundage	(718) 204-9825 / (646) 322-0718
Nicole Bukowski (Assistant Production Accountant)	(917) 838-8070
Brian Cantaldi	(917) 670-8851
Salvatore Carino	(516) 459-0823
Gina Castellano (Assistant Production Accountant)	(718) 288-4269
Amy S. Comstock	(212) 399-1008 / (646) 251-7748
Janette Cosby	(518) 695-9482 / (518) 669-1360
Jen Cox (Production Accountant)	(917) 334-7242
John Craigmile	(212) 533-6424 / (917) 375-0264
Scotch James Crisostomo	(206) 218-5151
Joshua Dease (Assistant Production Accountant)	(803) 528-3604
Katherine De Jesus (Assistant Production Accountant)	(917) 698-1959
Monica Delgado (Assistant Production Accountant)	(516) 561-2966
Joan DeVilla	(516) 897-6028 / (917) 903-1758
David Farr (Assistant Production Accountant)	(203) 417-6573
John Finn	(607) 832-4400 / (917) 572-7992
Maryann Fondulas	(201) 526-4265
Jennifer Freed	(973) 744-3574 / (973) 495-8725
Rosa Garces	(917) 453-3789
Rebecca Garland	(203) 606-7977
Rachel A. Gibson	(212) 690-9169 / (917) 793-0620
Rebecca Glew (Assistant Production Accountant)	(347) 602-6865
Niko Dee Godfrey (Assistant Production Accountant)	(917) 861-5222
Robert Gori (Assistant Production Accountant)	(914) 620-0191
Mollie Vera Grace (Assistant Production Accountant)	(401) 212-7983
Steve Guilbaud	(718) 224-4494
Eli Gurevich	(917) 669-3825
Vanuel Deshawn Hamilton	(917) 691-1634
Marlus C. Harding	(718) 858-3519
James Hinton	(646) 682-9533 / (310) 482-1180
Sean Hogan	(718) 389-4509 / (917) 587-1384
Morgan Howard	(917) 775-5235 / (212) 206-1070
Elizabeth Huizinga	(718) 607-6237
Peter Hutchinson (Production Accountant)	(212) 206-1099 / (917) 385-3008
Keith Linwood Jacobs (Assistant Production Accountant)	(917) 621-7430
Anne K. Johnson (Production Accountant)	(212) 267-3748 / (917) 207-8673
Meera Joshi	(310) 975-4613
Kenneth M. Kroll	(201) 939-5898
Dan Kukkonen	(626) 644-5197
Sara Lane (Production Accountant)	(917) 202-4921
Adam Leach (Assistant Production Accountant)	(610) 566-4407 / (610) 453-2736
Tatyana Lehman	(212) 541-7678 / (917) 705-1671
Stephen Lippross	(310) 435-3766
Joseph Lombardi	(845) 429-6579 / (845) 642-2783
Pietro Lorino Jr.	(973) 763-3346
Jennifer Lovin	(917) 306-6179
Richard Mancuso	(212) 787-7750

Keira Marcus	(347) 227-8799 / (646) 382-7571
Maria A. Marini	(914) 613-8355 / (914) 263-4340
Gregory Martin	(917) 848-5179
Elaine Martinelli (Assistant Production Accountant)	(516) 294-1405 / (516) 790-3021
Liz Modena	(917) 353-2063
Matthew Monaco (Assistant Production Accountant)	(203) 858-9069
Sean Patrick Murphy	(508) 528-1101 / (508) 498-0812
Francois Murray	(718) 694-0494 / (646) 296-1134
Lorna Nowve	(212) 595-4589
Brent Peebles (Production Accountant)	(917) 664-5298
Chauency Reese (Production Accountant)	(347) 693-0505
Kerry Roberts	(917) 362-3199
Carmen Rodriguez	(646) 533-1026
Ramon A. Rodriquez	(718) 404-8070
Sarah Rubenstein	(718) 791-0499
James Ruschak	(718) 788-4727
Michelle Sarama	(914) 723-9050
Susan Saunders	(718) 793-2513
Kathi Scharer	(212) 979-6961 / (917) 613-7442
Beth M. Schniebolk	(212) 633-6872
Deirdre Marie Schrowang	(212) 861-8487 / (917) 841-7316
Denise L. Schuka	(914) 528-9587 / (914) 582-2306
Kariemah Shah	(914) 237-4129 / (646) 321-0527
Natasha Smith	(347) 581-8304
Michele Soddano	(845) 294-6262 / (845) 551-8888
John Paul Summerskill	(646) 957-1640
Birdie Talanca	(910) 392-1516 / (910) 264-8333
Adam Taylor	(718) 928-9431 / (917) 748-8846
Jessica Thorne	(607) 437-1956
Kelly Ann Trivigno	(917) 445-1351
Arthur Vincie	(917) 968-8138
Ronald E. Wahl	(212) 369-9059 / (917) 680-6044
Dan Walton	(646) 234-2089
Noreen Ward	(914) 954-9604
Jamie Waxman	(631) 243-6448 / (631) 484-0069
Michael Wiggins (Production Accountant)	(917) 593-0559
Adam Wolenski (Assistant Production Accountant)	(201) 978-6867
Jonathan Wolf	(212) 721-8696 / (917) 495-1620
Derek Yip (Production Accountant)	(917) 887-8259
Brenda Yoo	(646) 678-2720

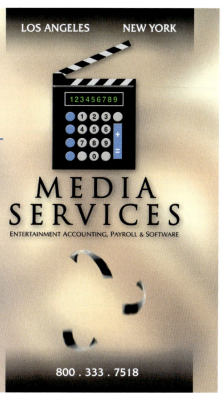

Payroll & Production Accountants

ABS Payroll &
Production Accounting Services (212) 675-4600
1115 Broadway, Ste. 1200   www.abspayroll.net
New York, NY 10010
(Payroll, Post Production Accounting & Production Accountants)

(209) 296-4087
American Residuals & Talent, Inc. (603) 367-9955
26 Gregs Way   FAX (603) 367-9941
Tamworth, NH 03886   www.artpayroll.com
(Celebrity Contracts & SAG/AFTRA Commercial
Signatory Services)

Broadcast Business Consultants (212) 687-3525
246 N. Franklin Tpke   www.broadcastbusiness.com
(Near W. 31st St.)
Ramsey, NJ 07446

CAPS Universal (212) 925-1415
588 Broadway, Ste. 803   FAX (212) 925-1502
New York, NY 10012   www.capsuniversalpayroll.com
(Celebrity Contracts, Payroll, Production Software, SAG/AFTRA
Commercial Signatory Services & Union Compliance Signatory)

Cast & Crew Entertainment Services (212) 594-5686
450 Seventh Ave., Ste. 1703   FAX (212) 594-5762
(Near W. 32nd St.)   www.castandcrew.com
New York, NY 10123

Chloe Productions, Inc. (212) 523-0460
250 W. 54th St., Ste. 705   FAX (212) 523-0042
(Near Eighth Ave.)   www.chloepro.com
New York, NY 10019
(Celebrity Contracts & Payroll)

(508) 481-2212
CrewStar, Inc. (888) 746-6871
One Boston Rd.   FAX (508) 481-7785
Southborough, MA 01772   www.crewstar.com

(914) 837-6279
EMS, Inc. (818) 386-0905
445 Gramatan Ave., Ste. E-A2   FAX (818) 386-9341
Mount Vernon, NY 10552   www.emspayroll.com
(Payroll, Production Accountant, Production Software, SAG/AFTRA
Commercial Signatory Services & Union Compliance Signatory)

Entertainment Partners (646) 473-9000
875 Sixth Ave. (Near 31st St.)   FAX (212) 947-4707
New York, NY 10001   www.entertainmentpartners.com

IndiePay, Inc. (212) 206-1724
333 Hudson St., Ste. 201   FAX (212) 206-1070
New York, NY 10013   www.indiepayroll.com

The Jacobson Group (310) 444-5255
11835 W. Olympic Blvd., Ste. 500   FAX (310) 444-5256
Los Angeles, CA 90064   www.jacobsongrp.com

JFA, Inc. (212) 206-1099
511 W. 25th St., Ninth Fl.   FAX (212) 206-1070
New York, NY 10001   www.jfafilm.com

Maslow Media Group (202) 965-1100
2233 Wisconsin Ave. NW, Ste. 400   FAX (202) 965-6171
Washington, DC 20007   www.maslowmedia.com

Ⓐ Media Services 30 W. 22nd St., Fifth Fl. (Near Sixth Ave.) New York, NY 10010	(212) 366-9390 (866) 414-9615 FAX (212) 366-9398 www.media-services.com
Ⓐ NPI Production Services, Inc. 2550 Hollywood Way Fourth Fl., Ste. 430 (Near Buena Vista) Burbank, CA 91505 (Payroll)	(866) 296-2267 (818) 566-7878 FAX (818) 566-7879 www.npiproductionservices.com
PayReel	(800) 352-7397 (303) 526-4900 FAX (303) 526-4901 www.payreel.com
Ⓐ PES Payroll 260 W. 36th St., Eighth Fl. New York, NY 10018	(212) 695-6622 FAX (212) 695-6615 www.pespayroll.com
Spotlight Payroll, Inc. 494 Eighth Ave., Ste. 1000 (Near W. 35th St.) New York, NY 10001	(212) 868-3820 FAX (212) 868-3821 www.spotlight.net

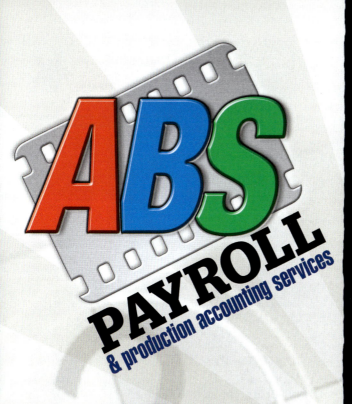

ABS
PAYROLL
& production accounting services

Commercials

Documentaries

Films

Industrials

Internet (New Media)

Live Performances

Music Videos

Print Media

"The Independent Filmmaker's Choice"

Serving the Entertainment Industry since 1985

Shorts

Special Events

Staff Payrolls

Television

Training

Theatre

Union/non-union talent and crew payroll

Production and post-production accounting

Corporate Accounting and bookkeeping

Workers Compensation Insurance

**NEW YORK
(212) 675-4600**

**LOS ANGELES
(818) 848-9200**

abspayroll.net

Prompt, Accurate, &
★ Customized Services ★
COAST to COAST

ARTpayroll.com

TV & Radio Commercials
Film
TV
Industrial
Music Video
Interactive Media
Live Theatre
Crew

SAG
AFTRA
AFM
ACTRA
IATSE
Actor's Equity

Union or Non-Union Budgeting & Processing
Production & Signatory Services
Business Affairs
Celebrity & Talent Negotiations
Traffic & Network Clearance
Employer of Record
Workers Compensation Insurance

A·R·T
★ Complete Support from start to finish ★

Headquarters (603) 367-9955 • Northern California (209) 296-4087 • Southern California (805) 526-9119 • Boston/Traffic (617) 921-5893

Talent Partners	(212) 727-1800	TEAM	(212) 871-6200
	www.talentpartners.com	250 W. 54th St., Ste. 705	FAX (212) 523-0041
		New York, NY 10019	www.teamservices.net
		(Payroll)	

PRODUCTION ACCOUNTING

Our services include:
A full-time accounting staff
On location our in-house staff
Complete production accounting services
Post Production accounting services
Hardware
24/7 hardware support
IT Department in our Los Angeles office
MediaWin accounting software and 24/7 support

www.media-services.com
310-440-9630

Promotional Products

Addiss Pat Enterprises, Inc. (703) 448-9770
(Embroidery & Silkscreening) (877) 448-9770
FAX (703) 448-9771
www.addissent.com

Alpha Engraving Co. (212) 247-5266
254 W. 51st St. (Near Eighth Ave.) FAX (212) 247-2014
New York, NY 10019 www.alphaengraving.com

Athletic Style Custom Merchants (212) 838-2564
118 E. 59th St. (Near Park Ave.) FAX (212) 888-9184
New York, NY 10022 www.athleticstyle.com
(Embroidery, Laser Printing & Silkscreening)

Bonnie Ott Promotions, Inc. (212) 338-0333
305 E. 40th St. (Near Second Ave.) FAX (212) 338-0330
New York, NY 10016 www.bonnieott.com
(Embroidery & Silkscreening)

(845) 429-4800
Capital Scenic, Inc. (914) 490-2000
P.O. Box 382 FAX (845) 429-2138
55 W. Railroad Ave., Ste. 3C www.capitalscenic.com
Garnerville, NY 10923

Captiv 8 Hats (212) 473-2440
57 E. 11th St., Fifth Fl. FAX (212) 473-2739
New York, NY 10003 www.captiv8promos.com
(Embroidery & Silkscreening)

Casablanca Promotions, Inc. (212) 338-9000
303 Fifth Ave., Ste. 1502 FAX (212) 338-0355
(Near Fifth Ave.) www.casablancapromotions.com
New York, NY 10016
(Embroidery & Silkscreening)

The Corporate Image Unlimited (212) 949-6699
125 Maiden Ln., Third Fl. FAX (212) 949-0629
(Near Water St.) www.corporatepromos.com
New York, NY 10038
(Embroidery & Silkscreening)

Economy Novelty & Printing (212) 481-3022
407 Park Ave. South, Ste. 26A FAX (212) 481-4514
(Near E. 28th St.) www.thinkideas.com
New York, NY 10016
(Embroidery & Silkscreening)

Empire Promotional Products (212) 268-9910
231 W. 29th St., Ste. 205 www.empirepromos.com
New York, NY 10001
(Apparel, Bags, Embossing, Embroidery, Hats, Laser Printing, Merchandising, Packaging, Silkscreening & T-Shirts)

(212) 691-7056
Free Advertising, Inc. (800) 637-3323
2201 Plaza Dr. FAX (732) 634-2230
Woodbridge, NJ 07095
(Embroidery & Silkscreening)

(914) 376-5301
Greek 101.com (888) 473-3550
646 Saw Mill River Rd. FAX (914) 476-4333
(Near Clement St.) www.greek101.com
Yonkers, NY 10710
(Fraternity and Sorority Items)

In Record Time, Inc. (212) 262-4414
575 Eighth Ave., Ste. 1900 (800) 575-4414
(Near 38th St.) FAX (212) 262-4512
New York, NY 10018 www.inrecordtime.com
(Embossing, Embroidery & Silkscreening)

Industrial Contacts, Inc. (516) 408-1400
265 Post Ave., Ste. 130 FAX (212) 689-3952
(Near Lexington Ave.) www.indcontacts.com
Westbury, NY 11590
(Embroidery & Silkscreening)

MJ Signs & Promotions (201) 594-9800
123 Patterson St. FAX (201) 594-9436
Hillsdale, NJ 07642

(212) 768-9434
N.G. Slater Corporation (800) 848-4621
42 W. 38th St. (Near Fifth Ave.) FAX (212) 869-7368
New York, NY 10018 www.ngslater.com
(Embroidery & Silkscreening)

New Dimension (212) 964-0400
99 Nassau St. (Near Beekman)
New York, NY 10038 www.newdimensioninc.com
(Embossing, Embroidery & Silkscreening)

Perlman Creative Group (201) 445-6188
668 Wyckoff Ave. FAX (201) 445-6288
Wyckoff, NJ 07481 www.perlmancreative.com
(Graphic Design)

Positive Impressions (800) 895-5505
150 Clearbrook Rd. www.positiveimpressions.com
(Near Executive Blvd.)
Elmsford, NY 10523
(Embroidery & Silkscreening)

Print Box, Inc. (212) 741-1381
350 Fifth Ave., Ste. 2619 FAX (212) 463-9071
(Near 34th St.) www.promobrands.com
New York, NY 10118
(Embroidery & Silkscreening)

Product 101 (212) 691-5888
20 W. 22nd St., Ste. 1609 FAX (212) 691-9139
(Near Fifth Ave.) www.product101.com
New York, NY 10010

RTR Packaging (212) 620-0163
27 W. 20th St., Ste. 603 FAX (212) 620-0018
(Near Fifth Ave.) www.bagvertising.com
New York, NY 10011
(Specialty Bags and Packaging)

(212) 989-2948
Westprint (201) 553-9701
2417 Central Ave. FAX (212) 989-3805
Union City, NJ 07087

Talent & Modeling Agencies

Bongarbiz (914) 734-1177
426 Smith St. (Near Requa St.) FAX (914) 734-8035
Peekskill, NY 10566 www.bongarbiz.com
(Circus, Specialty & Variety Acts)

Bryan Bantry (212) 935-0200
FAX (212) 935-2698
www.bryanbantry.com

Classic Model & Talent, Inc. (212) 532-7800
381 Park Ave. South, Ste. 1216 FAX (212) 684-0299
(Near E. 27th St.) www.classicagency.com
New York, NY 10016

Clear Talent Group/CTG (212) 840-4100
325 W. 38th St., Ste. 1203 FAX (212) 967-4567
(Near Eighth Ave.) www.cleartalentgroup.com
New York, NY 10018
(Athletes, Children, Choreographers, Commercial Talent, Models & Talent)

Cleri Model Management (732) 650-9730
(212) 721-6900
145 Talmadge Rd., Ste. 11 FAX (732) 650-9230
Edison, NJ 08817 www.clerimodels.com

Dorothy Palmer Talent Agency, Inc. (212) 765-4280
235 W. 56th St., Ste. 24-K
(Near Broadway)
New York, NY 10019
www.dorothypalmertalentagencyinc.com

The Endeavor Agency (212) 625-2500
152 W. 57th St., 25th Fl.
New York, NY 10019

Everything Events & Entertainment, LLC (973) 338-6995
(323) 230-5527
41 Watchung Plaza, Ste. 236 FAX (973) 200-4291
Montclair, NJ 07042 www.eeande.com
(Athletes, Choreographers, Commercial Talent, Models & Talent)

Ford Models, Inc. (212) 219-6500
111 Fifth Ave., Ninth Fl. FAX (212) 219-6550
New York, NY 10003 www.fordmodels.com

Gonzalez Model and Talent Agency (212) 982-5626
112 E. 23rd St., PH www.gonzalezmodels.com
(Near Park Ave. South)
New York, NY 10010

Grassy Hill (212) 539-3161
(Talent Management)

Ikon New York, Inc. (212) 691-2363
260 W. 39th St., 18th Fl. FAX (212) 691-3622
(Near Seventh Ave.) www.ikonmodels.com
New York, NY 10018

Parts Models (212) 744-6123
7529 FDR Station FAX (212) 396-3014
New York, NY 10150 www.partsmodels.com
(Body Parts Models)

RadioActive Talent, Inc. (212) 315-1919
www.radiotv.com

US Talent Management, Inc. (585) 244-0592
235 Alexander St. FAX (585) 244-4324
(Near Anderson Ave.) www.ustalent.com
Rochester, NY 14607

Technical Advisors

Aerial Focus/Tom Sanders (805) 455-3142
www.aerialfocus.com
(BASE Jumping, Hang Gliding, Skydiving & Ultralight Aircraft)

AzRa Historical Resources/USHist (530) 877-4173
(818) 516-9559
13763 Granad Dr. www.ushist.com
Magalia, CA 95954
(Historical Re-Enactments)

Call the Cops (888) 548-0911
(Homicide, Police Dialogue, Procedure, SWAT, Tactics & Vice Patrol)

Caravan West Productions (661) 268-8300
35660 Jayhawker Rd. www.caravanwest.com
Agua Dulce, CA 91390
(Firearms Instructor: Westerns: 1860–1910)

Cinema Rentals, Inc. (661) 222-7342
(877) 877-9605
25876 The Old Rd., Ste. 174 FAX (661) 253-3643
Stevenson Ranch, CA 91381 www.cinemarentals.com
(Marine and Underwater Safety)
Contact: Jim Pearson

**Cinematicstunts.com/
John-Eric Schuman** (877) 447-8868
www.cinematicstunts.com
(Firearms)

Cop Call Consulting, Inc. (917) 833-6189
(877) 926-7225
P.O. Box 2307033 FAX (845) 623-2021
New York, NY 10023 www.copcallny.com
(Crime Scene, Homicide, Police Dialogue, Procedure, SWAT & Tactics)

**David Zema, Inc./
Voice of Success Programs** (212) 675-4978
1123 Broadway, Ste. 1012 (Near 25th St.) www.davidzema.com
New York, NY 10010
(Speech & Voice)

Gleason's Gym, Inc. (718) 797-2872
77 Front St., Second Fl. www.gleasonsgym.net
(Near Main St.)
Brooklyn, NY 11201

Melanie LaPatin (212) 994-9500
(917) 696-7340
156 W. 44th St., Third Fl. FAX (212) 994-9501
(Near Broadway) www.dancetimessquare.com
New York, NY 10036
(Ballroom, Partner and Social Dance, Body Language & Dance Sport and Conceptualization)

Robert H. Leviton, MD, MPH, FACEP (718) 920-9135
(914) 715-8102
(Medical) FAX (718) 920-9106

Martial Arts, Inc. (917) 623-0853

Louis J. Morledge, MD (212) 583-2830
150 E. 58th St., 18th Fl. FAX (212) 583-0444
New York, NY 10155
(Medical)

Safety First Divers (516) 486-5733
(Marine Coordination & Water Safety)

SilverScreen Marine (212) 505-0694
(917) 797-2884
127 E. 10th St., No. 7/8 www.silverscreenmarine.com
(Near Third Ave.)
New York, NY 10003
(Marine Consulting and Coordination, Script Analysis, Underwater Services, Underwater Film and Video & Water Safety)

Stunt Dept., Inc./Chris Barnes (516) 236-9644
(Marine Coordination & Water Safety) FAX (516) 869-0843
www.stuntdept.com

Transcription & Secretarial Services

A Plus Recording & Transcribing (212) 813-6700
167 W. 21st St. FAX (212) 813-6715
(Near Seventh Ave.) www.aplusnyc.com
New York, NY 10011
(Transcription & Word Processing)

Accomplished Office Service (212) 227-7440
(800) 221-7242
22 Courtland St., Ste. 802 FAX (212) 227-7524
(Near Broadway) www.ubiqus.com
New York, NY 10007

Adecco (212) 391-7000
551 Fifth Ave., Ste. 910 FAX (212) 391-7956
(Near 42nd St.) www.adeccousa.com
New York, NY 10010

ANP Transcriptions (877) 797-7047
(845) 369-8624
75 Montebello Rd., Ste. 201 FAX (845) 369-7234
Suffern, NY 10901 www.anptranscriptions.com
(Foreign Language Transcription, Scripts, Transcription & Word Processing)

Avid Productions Transcription Services (703) 932-0978
8639 Victoria Rd. www.avidproductions.com
Springfield, VA 22151
(Scripts, Temporary Personnel, Transcription & Word Processing)

Daily Transcripts, Inc. (718) 775-3191
(888) 291-0447
165 Lexington Ave., Third Fl. www.dailytranscription.com
New York, NY 10016

Elliott Film Transcription Service (212) 752-2504
210 E. 63rd St., Ste. 10C FAX (212) 752-2504
(Near Third Ave.)
New York, NY 10065

Elrom Inc. (212) 645-5050
419 Park Ave. South FAX (212) 689-7544
New York, NY 10016 www.elrom.tv

iProbe Multilingual Solutions, Inc. (212) 489-6035
Five W. 36th St., Ste. 402 FAX (212) 202-4790
(Near Fifth Ave.) www.iprobesolutions.com
New York, NY 10018
(Foreign Language Transcription, Scripts, Transcription & Word Processing)

The Metropolitan Companies Inc. (212) 983-6060
110 E. 42nd St., Ste. 802 FAX (212) 983-7406
(Near Park Ave.) www.metstaff.com
New York, NY 10017

Randstad (212) 687-8605
489 Fifth Ave., Fifth Fl. FAX (212) 697-4225
(Near E. 41st St.)
New York, NY 10017

Spherion (212) 983-8800
420 Lexington Ave. (Near 43rd St.) FAX (212) 983-8797
New York, NY 10170 www.spherion.com

Staffmark (212) 271-3900
10 E. 40th St., 20th Fl. FAX (212) 271-3988
(Near E. 42nd St.) www.staffmark.com
New York, NY 10016

TemPositions (212) 490-7400
420 Lexington Ave., Ste. 2100 FAX (212) 867-1759
(Near E. 43rd St.) www.tempositions.com
New York, NY 10170

Transcript Associates, Inc. (212) 757-7113
(800) 452-6855
250 49th St., Ste. 600 FAX (212) 586-6774
(Near Broadway)
New York, NY 10019

Vanguard (212) 682-6400
633 Third Ave., 12th Fl. FAX (212) 682-7416
(Near E. 41st St.) www.temporarypersonnel.com
New York, NY 10017

Winston Temps (212) 687-7890
(212) 557-5000
122 E. 42nd St. (Near Lexington Ave.) FAX (212) 682-1056
New York, NY 10168 www.winstonresources.com

Words In Process (201) 445-9302
335 E. Glen Ave. FAX (201) 445-2762
Ridgewood, NJ 07450

You need transcripts.
On time. On budget. With the right words and proper punctuation.

Here's your solution.

- **Save money and budget easily** with our guaranteed prices.
- **Slash costs** with free dubbing from Beta, DV, ¾", VHS, or DAT.
- **Get special discounts** by pre-scheduling your shoots.
- **Make your job easier** with our *high-quality, time coded transcripts*.
- **Save time** with our convenient townhouse location in the heart of Chelsea.

Call us today and be a hero.

A Plus Recording & Transcribing
167 W 21 St @ 7th Ave New York City
(212) 813-6700 www.aplusnyc.com

Translation & Interpretation Services

1-800-Translate (212) 355-4455
865 United Nations Plaza (800) 872-6752
(Near E. 48th St.) FAX (888) 872-6752
New York, NY 10017 www.1-800-translate.com

ABC WordExpress (800) 570-0700
Worldwide Language Services (310) 260-7700
FAX (800) 570-5950
www.wordexpress.net

ANP Transcriptions (877) 797-7047
75 Montebello Rd., Ste. 201 (845) 369-8624
Suffern, NY 10901 FAX (845) 369-7234
(Localization & Transcription) www.anptranscriptions.com

Elrom Inc. (212) 645-5050
419 Park Ave. South FAX (212) 689-7544
New York, NY 10016 www.elrom.tv

Ⓐ InterNation, Inc. (212) 619-5545
299 Broadway, Ste. 1400 (800) 222-8799
(Near Duane St.) FAX (212) 619-5887
New York, NY 10007 www.internation.com

iProbe Multilingual Solutions, Inc. (212) 489-6035
Five W. 36th St., Ste. 402 FAX (212) 202-4790
(Near Fifth Ave.) www.iprobesolutions.com
New York, NY 10018
(6912 Languages and Transcription including Arabic, Cantonese, Chinese, Danish, Dutch, Finnish, French, French Canadian, German, Greek, Hebrew, Hindi, Italian, Japanese, Korean, Mandarin, Norwegian, Polish, Portuguese, Russian, Spanish, Swedish, Turkish, Urdu, Vietnamese & Localization)

Magnum Group, Inc. (215) 413-1614
610 S. Second St. (800) 320-1662
Philadelphia, PA 19147 FAX (215) 413-1615
www.magnumgroupinc.com

Raul Morales (718) 881-4802
976 McLean Ave., Ste. 211 (917) 509-7201
Yonkers, NY 10704 www.especial.com
(Spanish)

Ⓐ Rennert Translation Group (212) 867-8700
216 E. 45th St., 17th Fl. FAX (212) 867-7666
(Near Third Ave.) www.rennert.com
New York, NY 10017
(Over 100 Languages)

Traduvisual (646) 546-5350
(English, French, Italian & Spanish) FAX (646) 895-7599
www.traduvisual.com

Ubiqus (212) 227-7440
22 Cortland St., Ste. 802 (800) 221-7242
New York, NY 10007 FAX (212) 227-7524
(Transcription) www.ubiqus.com

Welker Translation & Research (212) 787-3556
186 Riverside Dr. (Near W. 91st St.) FAX (212) 875-9549
New York, NY 10024
(Portuguese & Spanish)

Wrap Party Locations

320 Studios NYC   (212) 967-9909 / (212) 563-2047
320 W. 37th St., 14th Fl.   www.320studiosnyc.com
New York, NY 10018

Asia Society   (212) 288-6400
725 Park Ave.   www.asiasociety.org
(Near E. 70th St.)
New York, NY 10021

Association of the Bar of the City of New York   (212) 382-6637
42 W. 44th St. (Near Sixth Ave.)   FAX (212) 869-2145
New York, NY 10036   www.abcny.org
Contact: Nicholas Marrico

Bateaux New York   (212) 352-1366
(Charter Cruises)   www.bateauxnewyork.com
Contact: Steven Brumble

The Bowery Ballroom   (212) 533-2111
Six Delancey St.   www.boweryballroom.com
(Near Bowery)
New York, NY 10002
Contact: John Moore

Broad Street Ballroom   (646) 624-2524
41 Broad St.   FAX (646) 624-2526
(Near Beaver St.)
New York, NY 10004   www.broadstreetballroom.com

Broadway Stages   (718) 349-9146 / (718) 786-5428
203 Meserole Ave.   FAX (718) 349-9148
(Near Jewel St.)   www.broadway-stages.com
Brooklyn, NY 11222

Cathedral Church of St. John the Divine   (212) 316-7490
1047 Amsterdam Ave.   www.stjohndivine.org
(Near W. 112th St.)
New York, NY 10025
Contact: Mary Lyons

Ⓐ Chelsea Piers   (212) 336-6800
23rd St. & The Hudson River   FAX (212) 336-6725
(Near 23rd St.)   www.chelseapiers.com
New York, NY 10011

The China Club   (212) 398-3800
268 W. 47th St. (Near Broadway)   FAX (212) 302-6217
New York, NY 10036   www.chinaclubnyc.com
Contact: Timmy Gleason

City Hall   (212) 964-4118
131 Duane St. (Near Church St.)   FAX (212) 577-6287
New York, NY 10013
Contact: Heidi Vanderwal

City Stage   (212) 627-3400
435 W. 19th St. (Near Ninth Ave.)   FAX (212) 633-1228
New York, NY 10011   www.citystage.com

Clubfone, Inc.   (212) 580-5538
178 Columbus Ave., Ste. 23-1146   FAX (212) 580-5538
(Near W. 68th St.)   www.clubfone.com
New York, NY 10023
(Party Planners/Site Locators)

Copacabana   (212) 239-2672
560 W. 34th St. (Near 11th Ave.)   www.copacabanany.com
New York, NY 10001
Contact: Peter Dorn

The Culinary Loft LLC   (212) 431-7425
515 Broadway, Ste. 5A   FAX (212) 431-7816
(Near Broome St.)   www.culinaryloft.com
New York, NY 10012
Contact: Corinne Colen

Diva   (212) 941-9024
341 W. Broadway (Near Grant)
New York, NY 10013

Element   (212) 254-2200
225 E. Houston St.   FAX (212) 254-2219
New York, NY 10002   www.elementny.com

Fabbri Mansion (House of the Redeemer)   (212) 289-0399
Seven E. 95th St. (Near Fifth Ave.)   FAX (212) 410-7899
New York, NY 10128   www.houseoftheredeemer.org
Contact: Judy Counts

Heartland Brewery   (646) 572-2337
93 South St.   www.heartlandbrewery.com
(Near Fulton St.)
New York, NY 10038
Contact: Jamie Kirk

Le Cirque 2000   (212) 644-0202
One Beacon Court, 151 E. 58th St.   FAX (212) 644-0388
(Near Lexington Ave.)   www.lecirque.com
New York, NY 10022
Contact: Camille Dulac

Le Parker Meridien   (212) 245-5000 / (212) 748-7420
118 W. 57th St. (Near Sixth Ave.)   FAX (212) 708-7407
New York, NY 10019   www.parkermeridien.com
Contact: Patrick Fortemps

Lightbox-NY LLC   (718) 759-6419
841 Barretto St., Box 14   FAX (718) 732-2144
Bronx, NY 10474   www.lightbox-ny.com

Manhattan Center Studios - Ballrooms   (877) 627-8834
311 W. 34th St. (Near Eighth Ave.)   FAX (212) 564-1092
New York, NY 10001   www.mcstudios.com
Contacts: Sara Rosenberg & Lisa Schamis

Mercury Lounge   (212) 260-4700
217 E. Houston St.   www.mercuryloungenyc.com
(Near Avenue A)
New York, NY 10002
Contact: John Moore

Metronome   (212) 505-7400
915 Broadway (Near W. 21st St.)   FAX (212) 505-5529
New York, NY 10010   www.metronomenyc.com

Metropolitan Pavilion   (212) 463-0071 / (212) 463-0200
125 W. 18th St. (Near Seventh Ave.)   FAX (212) 463-0946
New York, NY 10011   www.metropolitanevents.com

New York Society for Ethical Culture   (212) 874-5210
Two W. 64th St. (Near Broadway)   FAX (212) 595-7258
New York, NY 10023   www.nysec.org
Contact: Paula Sheldon

Nobu   (212) 219-0500
105 Hudson St. (Near Franklin St.)   FAX (212) 219-1441
New York, NY 10013   www.noburestaurants.com
Contact: Ann Yamamoto

One if by Land, Two if by Sea   (212) 255-8649
17 Barrow St.   www.oneifbyland.com
(Near Seventh Ave. South)
New York, NY 10014
Contact: Brian Semple

The Paramount   (212) 764-5500 / (800) 225-7474
235 W. 46th St. (Near Eighth Ave.)   FAX (212) 554-6511
New York, NY 10036
Contact: Andrea Amico

Pressure   **(212) 352-1161**
110 University Pl., Fifth Fl.   www.pressurenyc.com
(Near E. 13th St.)
New York, NY 10003

Puck Building Ballrooms   **(212) 274-8900**
295 Lafayette St., Ste. 705   **(212) 427-2818**
(Near Houston St.)   www.puckbuilding.com
New York, NY 10012

Sala   **(212) 979-6606**
344 Bowery (Near Great Jones St.)   FAX **(212) 979-5392**
New York, NY 10012   www.salanyc.com

Shop Studios   **(212) 245-6154**
442 W. 49th St. (Near Ninth Ave.)   **(212) 582-1650**
New York, NY 10019   FAX **(212) 582-3112**
  www.shopstudios.com

Tavern on the Green   **(212) 873-3200**
Central Park West   www.tavernonthegreen.com
(Near W. 67th St.)
New York, NY 10023
Contact: Arthur Tarzy

Webster Hall   **(212) 353-1600**
125 E. 11th St. (Near Fourth Ave.)   www.websterhall.com
New York, NY 10003
Contact: Tim Bauman

World Yacht Dining Cruises   **(212) 630-8800**
Pier 81, W. 41st St. (Near 12th Ave.)   **(800) 498-4276**
New York, NY 10036   FAX **(212) 630-8899**
Contact: Jo-Anne Falco   www.worldyacht.com

Zanzibar   **(212) 957-9197**
645 Ninth Ave. (Near W. 45th St.)   FAX **(212) 957-6946**
New York, NY 10036   www.zanzibarnyc.com
Contact: Arnie Papa

Zócalo   **(212) 717-7772**
172 E. 82nd St.   www.zocalonyc.com
(Near Lexington Ave.)
New York, NY 10028
Contact: Robert Shapiro

Camera & Sound Equipment

PICTURED:
Red Hook Warehouse

LOCATION:
Brooklyn, NY

PHOTOGRAPHER:
Sam Rohn

ALSAM : www.alsam.net
ASSOCIATION OF
LOCATION SCOUTS & MANAGERS

New York 411
*Qualified Listings for the
New York Production Community*
www.newyork411.com

CAMERA COPTERS

CALIFORNIA - FLORIDA - NEW YORK - USA

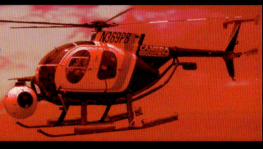

The ONE-STOP SOURCE for aerial production services...

WESCAM · **CINEFLEX HD** · GYRON Systems International, LTD · IMAX · TYLER

- Helicopters & Airplanes
- Camera Mounts & Systems
- Aerial Coordination & Stunts
- Film, Video, & Print Photography
- Location Scouting & Pre-Production
- FAA Approved Motion Picture Safety Manual

Paul Barth - SAG Pilot
Aerial Coordinator

We have the following systems IN-HOUSE (you pay no shipping charges !)

The Pictorvision (formerly WESCAM) 35mm film system.

Tyler Middle Mount II. Film & Video cameras up to 60 lbs.

CINEFLEX HD - new gyrostabilized Sony F950 Cinealta. HDCAM & HDSR. Beautiful downconverts to Digibeta, DVCPro, etc...

Recent credits: "Madison", "The Amazing Race", "Joan of Arcadia", "CSI: Miami" "Three Wishes", "The Simple Life", "The Help", "Reno 911 - The Movie", "Gumball 3000 The Movie", running footage for Kawasaki Jet-Skis and Volvo...

Our "BIG RIG" brings a complete aerial production unit to your location, including helicopter, camera systems, crew, jet fuel, and more. Call for details.

email: info@cameracopters.com
or call us toll-free at: **888-463-7953**

www.cameracopters.com

Camera & Sound Equipment

Ⓐ ADVERTISER SYMBOL

Refer to the General Index for
cross-referencing items in this section.

Aerial Equipment 252
Aerial—Fixed Wing & Helicopter Pilots 257
Camera Cars & Tracking Vehicles 258
Camera Rentals—Motion Picture 259
Camera Rentals—Still Photography 262
Motion Control 263
Raw Stock 266
Sound Equipment Rentals & Sales 268
Teleprompting & Cue Card Services 270
Video Assist Services 273
Video Cameras & Equipment 274
Video Display, Playback & Projection 277

CINEMA COPTERS

Contact Us:

Toll Free: 1-888-NYC-HELI

Office: 1-908-474-9700

Fax: 1-908-474-0488

Email: Cinema@LibertyHelicopters.com

- Professional Aerial Film & Video
- HD / SD / 35 mm   -   16:9 / 4:3
- Gyro Stabalized Platforms
- Experienced SAG Pilot's
- Over 10 Camera & Story Ships
- Location Scouting & Pre-Production
- Aerial & Ground Coordination
- Over 20 Years of Experience

SPACECAM   FLIR SYSTEMS   WESCAM   CINEFLEX HD

www.LibertyHelicopters.com

Aerial Equipment

Aerial Focus/Tom Sanders (805) 455-3142
Aircraft: Ultralights   www.aerialfocus.com
Cameras: Helmet
Equipment: BASE Jumping Equipment, Hang Gliders, Parachutes & Skydiving Equipment

Aerialexposures.com, LLC (800) 786-4153
W. 30th St. (Near 12th Ave.)   www.aerialexposures.com
New York, NY 10001
Camera Mounts: Gyro-Stabilized Helicopter Mounts

Aerialexposures.com, LLC

Professional Helicopter Aerial Video   NY-NJ-CT-PA

HD / SD / PAL   1080i / 720P   24P/30P/60P/60i   16:9 or 4:3

We provide the new Panasonic HDX-900, an ultra smooth gyro-stabilized camera mount and a professional aerial cinematographer.

Thirteen affordable helicopters to choose from!
Twinstars, Astars, Schweizer 300C & Robinson R44

Contact: Arnie Itzkowitz - (800) 786-4153   (973) 838-4153
e-mail: arnieitz@optonline.net - www.aerialexposures.com

Member PAPA - Professional Aerial Photographers Association

Al Cerullo
HOVER-VIEWS UNLIMITED

(516) 496-2946 DIRECT
(516) 496-8029 FAX
(516) 315-8063 MOBILE

All Gyrostabilized Camera Systems Available
Authorized Tyler Camera Systems Dealer

35 YEARS EXPERIENCE

Film Credits: The Taking of Pelham 123, Ironman 2, Salt, The Sorcerer's Apprentice, Angels and Demons, Knowing, State of Play, Fighting, The Bourne Ultimatum, 21, Marley & Me, Pride and Glory, Stop-Loss, The Incredible Hulk, The Nanny Diaries, Spiderman 1, 2, & 3, I Am Legend, Superman 1, 2 & Returns, Jumper, Be Kind Rewind, Ladder 49, Conspiracy Theory, The Brave One, Working Girl, and many more- *check the website for a complete listing.*

TV Credits: CSI: NY, Law and Order, House, Past Life, The Wire, Kings, Royal Pains, Heroes, Ugly Betty, Dirty Sexy Money- *check the website for a complete listing.*

Aerial Film Pilot / Aerial Coordinator
F.A.A. Certified
Member SAG/AFTRA
Member Motion Picture Pilot Association
Wyvern Approved

2009 SOC Lifetime Achievement Award Recipient

www.hoverviews.com   hoverviews@aol.com

Air Metro Helicopters, Inc.   (845) 429-1200
                                   (212) 883-0999
22 Gagen Rd. (Near Route 9-W)   FAX (845) 429-1200
West Haverstraw, NY 10993   www.airmetro.net
Camera Mounts: Fixed Wing & Helicopter

AIRCAM Aerial Video and Photography   (800) 943-4420
                                           (516) 393-1914
One Media Crossways   FAX (516) 364-4592
(Near Crossways Park Dr.)   www.nyaircam.com
Woodbury, NY 11797
Aircraft: Helicopters
Cameras: Gyro-Stabilized Camera Systems

Ⓐ Airpower Aviation Resources, Inc.   (805) 402-0052
336 West End Ave., Ste. 3B   www.airpower-aviation.com
New York, NY 10023
Aircraft: Civilian and Military Fixed Wing Aircraft & Helicopters
Services: Aerial Coordination, Aerial Production & Pilots

Ⓐ Atlantic Cine Equipment, Inc.   (212) 944-0003
                                       (410) 243-4181
210 W. 29th St.   FAX (443) 524-0210
Baltimore, MD 21211   www.aceeast.com
Aerial Equipment: Gyro-Stabilized 5-Axis Camera Systems & Stab-C/Gyron-FS
Camera Mounts: Nose Mounts & Side Mounts
Camera Mounts/Systems: Gyron Super-G
Cameras: Gyro-Stabilized Camera Systems
Equipment: Air to Ground Radios & Fuel Trucks
Services: Aerial Coordination and Production, Consultation, Ground Production, Ground Safety Consultation, Ground Safety Personnel and Pilots, Helicopter Refueling, Pilots, Second Unit Directors & Stabilized Shooting Coordination

CHASE SCENE IN: TRANSFORMERS

Helinet Aviation is a highly experienced full-service aviation aerial film company. We provide camera and picture ships, both rotor and fixed wing, as well as film and HD aerial camera systems. Our film pilots and aerial coordinators have years of experience with commercials, documentaries and feature films. We are easy to work with, whether you utilize our resources or those of our network of worldwide vendors. Call John Burton at Helinet to discuss how to get the best aerial services for your budget.

FOR INFO: 1.866.HELINET (435-4638)
HELINET.COM

Automobile Film Club of America, Inc.	(718) 447-2255 (718) 447-0438
10 Cross St. (Near Bay St.) Staten Island, NY 10304	FAX (718) 447-2289 www.autofilmclub.com
Aircraft: Fixed-Wing Aircraft & Helicopters	
Ⓐ **Camera Copters, Inc.**	(888) 463-7953 (305) 793-7033
Aircraft: Helicopters	www.cameracopters.com
Ⓐ **Helinet Aviation Services**	(201) 727-1558
111 Charles A. Lindbergh Dr. Teterboro, NJ 07608	FAX (201) 727-0121 www.helinet.com
Aircraft: Helicopters Camera Mounts: Fixed Wing & Gyro-Stabilized	
HeloAir, Inc.	(804) 226-3400 (888) 359-4356 www.heloair.com

Hover-Views Unlimited, Inc./	(516) 496-2946
Al Cerullo	(516) 315-8063
P.O. Box 1164	FAX (516) 496-8029
Syosset, NY 11791	www.hoverviews.com
Aircraft: Helicopters	
Camera Mounts: Fixed Wing	

	(818) 781-4742
Jet Productions	(877) 895-1790
7240 Hayvenhurst Ave., Ste. 148	FAX (818) 781-4743
Van Nuys, CA 91406	www.jetproductions.net
Aircraft: Fixed-Wing Aircraft	

	(818) 902-0800
Kevin LaRosa	(818) 422-3777
Services: Helicopter Pilot	FAX (818) 902-1168
	www.jetcopters.com

Liberty Helicopters	(908) 474-9700
	www.libertyhelicopters.com

	(201) 440-5050
Val Mazzucca	(917) 952-9200
Services: Helicopter Pilot	www.tlicharters.com

	(212) 736-0883
New York Film Flyers	(845) 255-1087
529 W. 42nd St. (Near 10th St.)	FAX (845) 255-0798
New York, NY 10036	www.nyfilmflyers.com
Aircraft: Fixed Wing Aircraft & Helicopters	
Camera Mounts: Fixed Wing	

Aerial Experts

EAST COAST BASED GYRO-STABILIZED FILM SYSTEMS

ace

atlantic cine equipment
New York • Baltimore / Washington DC
www.aceeast.com
212.944.0003
Moving Cameras Since 1986

Pictorvision Inc — (818) 785-9282 / (800) 876-5583 / FAX (818) 785-9787
7701 Haskell Ave., Ste. B
Van Nuys, CA 91406
www.pictorvision.com
Camera Mounts/Systems: Wescam
Camera Mounts: Fixed Wing, Gyro-Stabilized & XR Stabilized Remote Head

SpaceCam Systems, Inc — (818) 889-6060 / FAX (818) 889-6062
31111 Via Colinas, Ste. 201
Westlake Village, CA 91362
www.spacecam.com
Camera Mounts: Gyro-Stabilized

Wings Air — (212) 845-9822 / (877) 292-7554 / FAX (212) 845-9822
136 Tower Rd., Hangar M
White Plains, NY 10604
www.wingsair.net
Aerial Equipment: Stab-C/Gyron
Aircraft: Helicopters
Camera Mounts: Belly Mounts, Gyro-Stabilized Mounts, Helicopter Mounts, Nose Mounts, Side Mounts, Tyler Camera Mounts, Wescam Mounts & XR Stabilized Remote Head
Camera Mounts/Systems: Gyron, Spacecam, Tyler & Wescam
Equipment: Air to Ground Radios, Aircraft Intercom Systems, Night Sun Searchlights, Overwater Safety Equipment & Safety Equipment
Services: Aerial Coordination, Aerial Production, Consultation & Pilots

Wolfe Air Aviation, Ltd. — (866) 487-4643 / FAX (626) 584-4099
39 E. Walnut St.
Pasadena, CA 91103
www.wolfeair.com
Aircraft: Fixed Wing Aircraft & Helicopters

AERIAL
CINEMATOGRAPHY

BRIAN HELLER
401 · 751 · 1381

REPRESENTED BY
TURLEY CINEMATOGRAPHERS
212 · 924 · 8505

Aerial—Fixed Wing & Helicopter Pilots

Whit Baldwin (804) 226-3400
(Helicopter Pilot) (888) 359-4356
www.heloair.com

Kevin LaRosa (818) 902-0800
(818) 422-3777
FAX (818) 902-1168
www.jetcopters.com

Val Mazzucca (201) 440-5050
(917) 952-9200
www.tlicharters.com

Ray McCort (212) 714-6037
(Helicopter Pilot) FAX (212) 202-7356

CAMERA CARS - PROCESS TRAILERS - TOW DOLLIES - CRANES - CAR RIGS

T. 212 425-4840 C. 646 529-2585
actioncameracars@gmail.com www.actioncameracars.com

ALSO AVAILABLE: HOOD MOUNT - HOSTESS TRAY - SUCTION CUP KIT

Camera Cars & Tracking Vehicles

Action ATV (917) 696-4486
(ATV Camera Car) www.actionatv.com

Ⓐ Action Camera Cars, Inc. (212) 425-4840
(646) 529-2585
www.actioncameracars.com
(Air Ride Camera Cars, Car Rigs, Cranes, Process Trailers & Tow Dollies)

Camera Cars Unlimited, Inc. (818) 889-9903
5331 Derry Ave., Ste. A FAX (818) 889-4970
Agoura Hills, CA 91301 www.cameracarsunlimited.com
(Camera Car Cranes, Off-Road and Standard Camera Cars, Process Trailers & Tow Dollies)

Mark Forman Productions Corp. (212) 633-9960
300 W. 23rd St., Ste. 14A/B FAX (212) 807-0121
(Near Eighth Ave.) www.screeningroom.com
New York, NY 10011
(Camera Bicycles)

Jack McLaughlin (914) 329-6253
(ATV Camera Car) www.jmstunts.com

(718) 834-5660
Productions First Choice Inc. (212) 882-1666
FAX (718) 834-8348
(2 and 3-Axle Insert Cars, Air-Ride Process Trailers, Camera Car Cranes, Crane Ready Camera Cars, Process Trailers/Trucks, Technocranes & Tow Dollies)

(914) 668-4711
Rick Bruck's Motorworks, Inc. (800) 375-5755
22 S. Terrace Ave. FAX (914) 668-2411
(Near Mt. Vernon Ave.)
Mount Vernon, NY 10550

Road Runner Camera Cars, Inc. (914) 777-7400
420 Center Ave. (Near Waverly Ave.) FAX (860) 354-5073
Mamaroneck, NY 10543 www.cameracars.net
(Camera Car with Generator, Process Trailers & Tow Dollies)

(917) 613-0091
(407) 240-9127
Runnin' Shot, Inc.
(Camera Cars & Process Trailers) FAX (407) 856-8491
www.runninshot.com

**Shotmaker Camera Cars @
Silvertrucks Lighting** (718) 906-3045
Silvercup Studios/East FAX (718) 906-3075
34-02 Starr Ave. www.silvercupstudios.com/trucks.htm
(Near Van Dam St.)
Long Island City, NY 11101
(Camera Cars & Process Trailers)

Tracking Shot (718) 786-5428
203 Meserole Ave. (Near Diamond St.) FAX (718) 349-9148
Brooklyn, NY 11222
(Camera Cars, Process Trailers & Tow Dollies)

PAL east TELEVISION

- Over 15 years of experience!
- SONY AND PANASONIC HD Camera Packages
- Specializing in PAL Broadcast Equipment Rentals
- PAL Camera Packages:
  - PAL DIGITAL BETACAM
  - PAL DVCAM CAMCORDERS
  - DIGITAL BETA, BETA SP & DVCAM VTR's
- Audio Equipment
- Lighting and Grip Rentals
- PAL/NTSC and DVD Tape Transfers

PH. 212.741.9111
FAX. 212.741.7772

236 WEST 27TH STREET,
15TH FLOOR,
NEW YORK, NEW YORK
10001

WWW.PALEAST.COM
INFO@PALEAST.COM

Camera Rentals—Motion Picture

Abel Cine Tech, Inc. (888) 223-1599 / (212) 462-0100
609 Greenwich St., Fifth Fl. FAX (212) 462-0179
(Near Leroy St.) www.abelcine.com
New York, NY 10014
16mm: Aaton Prod Super 16mm Xterà, & A-Minima
Heads: Cartoni, O'Connor & Sachtler
High Def: PhantomHD, Phantom65, VariCam, HPX2000, HPX3000, HVX200, Sony F900R, Sony EX1, PS Technik & MovieTube Adaptors
Lenses: Angenieux, Animorphic, Canon, Century, Cooke S4s, Elite, Fujinon, Leicas, Super Speeds, Elephoto, Ultra Primes & Variable HDV: JVC & Sony
Accessories: CamTram System, Digital Micro Force Zoom Control, Filters, Heads, Jibs, MovieTube Lens Adapter, Remote Heads, Underwater Housings & Visual FX Camera Systems
Other: Multi-Camera Systems

Arri CSC (212) 757-0906
619 W. 54th St. (Near 11th Ave.) FAX (212) 713-0075
New York, NY 10019 www.cameraservice.com
16mm: All Arri
35mm: All Arri
65mm: All Arri

Atlantic Cine Equipment, Inc. (212) 944-0003 / (410) 243-4181
210 W. 29th St. FAX (443) 524-0210
Baltimore, MD 21211 www.aceeast.com
Accessories: CamRemote, Gyro-Stabilized 5 Axis Heads, Gyron FS, Kenworthy-Nettmann Snorkel, MicroPlus, MiniMote, Mini-C, MocroMote, Remote and Robotic Systems and Accessories, Stab-C & Super-G

Boston Camera Rental Co. (617) 277-2200
1686 Commonwealth Ave. FAX (617) 277-6800
Brighton, MA 02135 www.bostoncamera.com
16mm: Arri SR2 & Arri SR3
35mm: Arri 353, Arri 435, Arri 535B & Moviecam Compact

BVR, Ltd. (212) 541-5390 / (800) 797-4287
355 W. 52nd St. FAX (212) 541-5751
New York, NY 10019 www.bvr.com

Camera Obscura, Ltd. (212) 533-3713 / (917) 854-9590
Four Rivington St. (Near Bowery) FAX (212) 533-0621
New York, NY 10002 www.camerascura.com
35mm: Arri 435ES & 535B
Accessories: Filters, Heads & Lenses

Cine Magic Stages (212) 268-0028 / (917) 805-2177
210 Elizabeth St. (Near Prince St.) FAX (212) 268-0363
New York, NY 10012 www.cinemagicstages.com
16mm: Photo-Sonics Action Master
35mm: Photo-Sonics 4ER and 4BR & Photo-Sonics 4ML
Lenses: Borescope Cinewand T56, Century/Clairmont/Zeiss Swing and Shift & Revolution Modular Lens System

Cinema Rentals, Inc. (661) 222-7342 / (877) 877-9605
25876 The Old Rd., Ste. 174 FAX (661) 253-3643
Stevenson Ranch, CA 91381 www.cinemarentals.com
35mm: Stunt, Crash and Underwater Cameras
Video: Digital Underwater Video & Lipstick Camera

Cinema-Vision (212) 620-8191
210 11th Ave., Ste. 403 (Near 25th St.) FAX (212) 620-8198
New York, NY 10001 www.motionpicturerentals.com
16mm: Aaton, Arri SR2, Bolex Cameras and Lenses, Photo-Sonics Actionmaster Regular/Super-16 & SR3 Regular/Super-16mm
35mm: Aaton, Arri 435 Xtreme, Arri 535B, Moviecam Photo-Sonics ER & Photo-Sonics C (2500fps)
Lenses: Angenieux HR, Angenieux Optimo, Arri Shift and Tilt, Cooke S4, Innovision Probe 2, Revolution Modular Lens Systems & Zeiss Primes
Accessories: Expendables, Filters, Heads & TripodsOther: Repairs & Sales

RENTAL - SALES - SERVICE
35mm - Super35 - 16mm - Super16 - Super-8 - HD - Red 4K

ARRI Master Primes
Cooke S4
ARRI Ultra Primes
Zeiss Super Speeds
Zeiss 2.1 Primes
Zeiss Variable Primes
ARRI Marcos
Nikkor
Angenieux Optimo Series Zooms
Cooke Zooms
Innovision Probe II, II+, HD
Revolution Lens System
ARRI/Clairmont Shift and Tilt
Red One Zooms

Arricam LT
ARRI 535B
Moviecam Compact & SL
ARRI 435 Xtreme
ARRI 235
ARRI 35-III 3rd Gen.
ARRI 416 Plus
Aaton XTR Prod
Red One
Panasonic Varicam 3700
Sony F900R
P+S Technik

PHOTO-SONICS
East-Coast Representative
High-Speed Cameras
35mm 4ER Pin-Registered
35mm 4C - to 2500 FPS
16mm Actionmaster 3000

Vintage and Prop Packages Available

210 11th Ave (25th St), New York, NY 10001   ph (212)620-8191   fax (212)620-8196
www.motionpicturerentals.com

CPT Rental, Inc.   **(718) 424-1600**
36-01A 48th Ave. (Near 36th St.)   FAX **(718) 457-4778**
Long Island City, NY 11101   www.cptrental.com
16mm: Aaton XTR, Arri Bl, S, SR2, SR3 & Photosonics Actionmaster
35mm: All Arri, High Speed Cameras, Mitchell, Moviecam Compact, SL & Photosonics 4ER and 4C
High Def: Camera Packages & PS Technik Adaptors
Lenses: HD Scope, Optimo Zoom, Periscope & T-Rex
Video: Panasonic & Sony

Du-All Camera Corp.   **(212) 643-1042**
                         (212) 643-1319
231 W. 29th St., Ste. 210   FAX **(212) 643-9335**
(Near Seventh Ave.)   www.duallcamera.com
New York, NY 10001
Accessories: Expendables, Filters, GlideCam, Heads, Jib Arms, Lenses, P&S Technik Mini and Pro 35 Adapters & Tripods
Super 8mm: Bauer, Beaulieu 4008 ZM-2,
Canon 1014 XL-S & Nizo
16mm & Super 16mm: Aaton LTR-7 and LTR-54, Bolex Rex 5 and SBM & Ikonoscop A-Cam
16mm Arri: S/B, SR, SR2 & SR3
35mm: Eyemo
35mm Arri: 2C, 3, BL1, BL3, BL4 & Moviecam
Other: Sales & Repairs

FTC/Orlando   **(407) 422-8246**
                (800) 683-1156
35mm: Arri 2C, Steadicam & Ultracam   FAX **(407) 843-0738**
                  www.ftcorlando.com

Hand Held Films, Inc.   **(212) 502-0900**
66 White St., Ground Fl.   FAX **(212) 502-0906**
(Near Broadway)   www.handheldfilms.com
New York, NY 10013
16mm: Aaton, Arri, Bolex, SR2, SR3 & Super 16
35mm: Compact
Heads: Lambda, O'Connor, Sachtler & Weaver-Steadman
High Def: 24P, 720P, Panasonic, PS Technik Adaptors, Sony & Ultra Primes
Lenses: Angenieux, Animorphic, Arri Ultra, Close-Focus, Cooke, Elite, Hawk, Innovision Probe, Macro, Optimo Zoom, Revolution, Slant-Focus, Superspeeds, Swing/Tilts, Telephoto & Zeiss
Super 8mm: Beaulieu
Accessories: Color Video Doors/Taps, Digital Micro Force Zoom Control, Filters, Hardware/Wireless Remote Control & Jibs

Hit & Run Productions   **(718) 809-9057**
                     (718) 782-8381
65 Roebling St., Ste. 202   FAX **(718) 782-8388**
Brooklyn, NY 11211   www.hitandrunproductions.com
16mm: Arri, SR & Super16
Heads: Sachtler
Lenses: Zeiss

joe's production & grille, inc.   **(917) 733-5915**
                     (800) 688-4212
                  www.joesgrille.com
16mm: Super 16mm Bolex RX5 & Panasonic HVX200
Lenses: Angenieux, Anamorphic, Century & Zeiss
High Def: 1080I, 24P, 720P & Panasonic
Video: Digital & Panasonic

Location Camera, Ltd. (215) 576-5600
300 Pennsylvania Ave. (215) 513-0243
Oreland, PA 19075 FAX (215) 576-6022
High Def: Panasonic Varicam HD www.locationcamera.com

Mammoth Production Packages (585) 381-2470
3800 Monroe Ave. FAX (585) 381-2462
(Near Woodland Rd.) www.mammothpro.com
Pittsford, NY 14534
16mm Arri: SR2 & SR3
35mm Arri: 35-3, 435 Advance & 535B

Metrovision Production Group (212) 989-1515
508 W. 24th St. (Near 10th Ave.) FAX (212) 989-8278
New York, NY 10011 www.metrovision.tv
16mm: Aaton XTRprod
35mm: Aaton 35-111

Moviola Digitial (212) 247-0972
545 W. 45th St. (Near 11th Ave.) (800) 327-3724
New York, NY 10036 FAX (212) 265-9820
www.moviola.com

Nettmann Systems International (818) 623-1661
www.camerasystems.com/agents.htm
Accessories: Gyron FS/Stab-C, Kenworthy Nettman Snorkel, Mini-C, Nettmann Cam-Remote and Mini-Mote, Stab-C Compact, Super-G & Vectorvision

Ⓐ PAL Television East (212) 741-9111
236 W. 27th St., 10th Fl. FAX (212) 741-7772
New York, NY 10001 www.paleast.com

Panavision New York (212) 606-0700
150 Varick St., Second Fl. FAX (212) 244-4457
(Near 10th Ave.) www.panavision.com
New York, NY 10013
35mm: Aaton, Arri & Panavision
65mm: Panavision
Lenses: Frazier Lens System

Socapa Films (800) 718-2787
375 Greenwich St., Tribeca Film Center www.socapa.org
(Near N. Moore St.)
New York, NY 10013
Accessories: Glidecam V-16

TCS/Technological Cinevideo Services, Inc. (212) 247-6517
341 W. 38th St., Fourth Fl. FAX (212) 489-4886
(Near Ninth Ave.) www.tcsfilm.com
New York, NY 10018
16mm: Aaton, Arri, Arri 416, Bolex, C-Motion, Canon, Moviecam, SR2, SR3 & Super16
35mm: Arricam LT & Compact
Heads: Arri, Bogen, Cartoni, Lambda, O'Connor, Ronford, Sachtler, Weaver-Steadman & Wireless
High Def: 1080i, 24P, 720P, Cooke, Mini DVs, Multi-Camera Systems, Panasonic, Phantom HD, PS Technik Adaptors, Red One, Sony F35 & Ultra Primes
Lenses: Angenieux, Animorphic, Arri Ultra, Century, Close-Focus, Cooke, Digiprimes, Lo-Angle Prism, Master Primes, Optimo Zoom, Telephoto, Variable, Zeiss & Zooms
Video: Digital, Panasonic & Sony
Accessories: Color Video Doors/Taps, Digital Lens Control, Digital Micro Force Zoom Control, Filters, Jibs, Hardware/Wireless Remote Control, Heads, Light Meter Housings, Sliders, Steadicam Systems & Video Tap/Assist Packages

William M. Miller Camera Rentals (914) 779-1203
48 Lawrence Park Crescent (917) 406-0474
(Near Midland Ave.) FAX (914) 779-1203
Bronxville, NY 10708 www.williammmiller.net
16mm: Arri SR3
Lenses: Zeiss
Accessories: Filters, Heads & Lenses

Camera Rentals—Still Photography

Adorama Rentals — (212) 627-8487
42 W. 18th St. (Near Sixth Ave.) — FAX **(212) 929-9013**
New York, NY 10011 — www.adoramarentals.com

Calumet Photographic Pro Center — (212) 989-8500 / (800) 225-8638
22 W. 22nd St. — FAX **(212) 627-9088**
New York, NY 10010 — www.calumetphoto.com

Cress Photo — (973) 694-1280
P.O. Box 4262 — FAX **(973) 694-6965**
Wayne, NJ 07474 — www.flashbulbs.com

CSI Rentals — (212) 243-7368
133 W. 19th St., Ground Fl. — FAX **(212) 243-2102**
New York, NY 10011 — www.csirentals.com

Foto Care, Ltd. — (212) 741-2990
136 W. 21st St. (Near Sixth Ave.) — FAX **(212) 741-3217**
New York, NY 10011 — www.fotocare.com

K&M Camera — (212) 532-1106 / (800) 343-9826
385 Broadway (Near First Ave.) — FAX **(212) 532-4403**
New York, NY 10013 — www.kmcamera.com

The Lens & Repro Equipment Corporation — (212) 675-1900
33 W. 17th St., Fifth Fl. — FAX **(212) 989-5018**
(Near Sixth Ave.) — www.lensandrepro.com
New York, NY 10011

Ritz Camera — (212) 877-8760
2400 Broadway (Near W. 88th St.) — FAX **(212) 877-7423**
New York, NY 10024 — www.ritzcamera.com

T.R.E.C. — (212) 727-1941 / (800) 622-1941
127 W. 24th St. (Near Seventh Ave.) — FAX **(212) 727-2008**
New York, NY 10011 — www.trecrental.com

Motion Control

Atlantic Motion Pictures	(212) 924-6170	🅐 **Richard Coppola/Motion Control**	(718) 428-3636
162 W. 21st St., Fourth Fl.	FAX (212) 989-8736		(917) 864-8307
(Near Seventh Ave.)	www.atlanticmotion.com		FAX (718) 428-8291
New York, NY 10011		www.motioncontrol.coppola.com	
	(212) 268-0028	🅐 **Gear + Rose Motion Control**	(914) 421-5019
🅐 **Cine Magic Stages**	(917) 805-2177		www.gearandrose.com
210 Elizabeth St., Basement	FAX (212) 268-0363	(Zebra Real-Time Portable System and Accessories)	
New York, NY 10012	www.cinemagicstages.com		

Ⓐ Gizmo Special Effects	(973) 884-2911
220 Reynolds Ave.	www.gizmosfx.com
Parsippany, NJ 07054	

Palace Digital Studios	(203) 853-1740
29 N. Main St.	FAX (203) 855-9608
South Norwalk, CT 06854	www.palacedigital.com

	(201) 714-9845
Ⓐ PAWS & Co., LLC	(877) 448-7297
710 Clinton St.	FAX (201) 963-5757
Hoboken, NJ 07030	www.pawsco.tv

Reel EFX, Inc.
5539 Riverton Ave.
North Hollywood, CA 91601
(Multiple Computer Controlled Still Camera System)
(818) 762-1710
(213) 308-7289
FAX (818) 762-1734
www.reelefx.com

Stitch Motion Graphics
16 W. 46th St., 11th Fl.
(Near Fifth Ave.)
New York, NY 10036
(212) 584-9700
(212) 391-8783
FAX (212) 391-8783
www.stitch.net

XYZ Pictures
555 W. 57th St., Ste. 1710
(Near 11th Ave.)
New York, NY 10019
(HD and SD Animation)
(212) 246-4224
(917) 363-4722
FAX (212) 246-4225
www.xyzpictures.com

Raw Stock

Ametron Audio Video
1546 N. Argyle Ave.
Hollywood, CA 90028
(323) 466-4321
(323) 464-1144
FAX (323) 871-0127
www.ametron.com

B&H Photo Video Pro Audio
420 Ninth Ave. (Near W. 34th St.)
New York, NY 10001
(Video Only)
(212) 444-5085
(212) 239-7760
FAX (212) 239-7766
www.bhphotovideo.com

Broadcast Store
9420 Lurline Ave., Ste. C
Chatsworth, CA 91311
(Tape Only)
(818) 998-9100
FAX (818) 998-9106
www.broadcaststore.com

Carpel Video
429 E. Patrick St.
Frederick, MD 21701
(Video Only)
(800) 238-4300
FAX (301) 694-9510
www.carpelvideo.com

Colorlab NYC
27 W. 20th St., Ste. 307
(Near Avenue of the Americas)
New York, NY 10011
(212) 633-8172
FAX (212) 633-8241
www.colorlab.com

Edgewise Media Services, Inc.
630 Ninth Ave. (Near 44th St.)
New York, NY 10036
(212) 977-9330
(800) 444-9330
www.edgewise-media.com

Ⓐ Empress Media, Inc.
306 W. 38th St., Ninth Fl.
(Near Eighth Ave.)
New York, NY 10018
(212) 643-4898
(888) 683-6773
FAX (212) 643-4894
www.empressintel.com

EVS/Express Video Supply, Inc.
(818) 552-4590
(800) 238-8480
FAX (818) 552-4591
www.evsonline.com

Film Emporium
274 Madison Ave., Ste. 404
(Near E. 40th St.)
New York, NY 10016
(212) 683-2433
(800) 371-2555
FAX (212) 683-2740
www.filmemporium.com

Film Source LA
(818) 484-3236
(866) 537-1114
FAX (818) 688-0101
www.filmsourcela.com

Fujifilm USA, Inc.
Motion Picture Divison
(888) 424-3854
FAX (323) 465-8279
www.fujifilmusa.com

Global Media Resources, Inc.
(818) 508-6760
(805) 967-1879
FAX (818) 508-6710
www.globalmediaresource.com

Kodak
360 W. 31st St., Second Fl.
(Near Ninth Ave.)
New York, NY 10001
(Film Only)
(212) 631-3400
FAX (212) 631-2662
www.kodak.com

Lentini Communications
54 W. 21st St., Ste. 301
(Near Fifth Ave.)
New York, NY 10010
(212) 206-1452
FAX (212) 206-1453
www.lentinicommunications.com

Media Distributors
645 W. 27th St. (Near 12th Ave.)
New York, NY 10001
(212) 375-1800
(877) 827-7862
FAX (212) 564-5540
www.mediadistributors.com

Moviola Digitial
545 W. 45th St. (Near 11th Ave.)
New York, NY 10036
(Video Only)
(212) 581-7111
(800) 327-3724
FAX (212) 265-9820
www.moviola.com

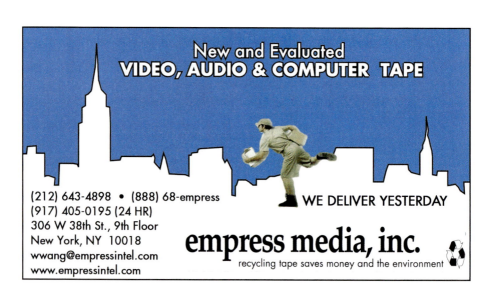

MSE Media Solutions (323) 721-1656
6013 Scott Way (800) 626-1955
Los Angeles, CA 90040 FAX (323) 721-1506
www.msemedia.com

ProMediaSupplies.com (336) 664-1004
6812 Renwick Court FAX (336) 605-3212
Greensboro, NC 27410 www.promediasupplies.com
(New Video Stock)

Raw Stock, Inc. (212) 255-0445
  (888) 729-7862
1133 Broadway, Seventh Fl., Ste. 712 FAX (212) 463-9420
(Near W. 26th St.) www.raw-stock.com
New York, NY 10010
(Film Only)

Stock Options (416) 504-4956
  (877) 799-5400
787 King St. W. FAX (416) 504-3015
Toronto, ON M5V 1N6 Canada www.stockoptionscorp.com
(Film Only)

The Tape Company (800) 851-3113
  (212) 769-2291
Folcroft West Business Park FAX (818) 566-8989
Darby Commons, Fairfax Ste. 5
Folcroft, PA 19032 www.thetapecompany.com

Tape Services, Inc. (800) 370-8273
  (917) 797-2499
FAX (603) 425-2220
www.tapeservices.com

TapeOnline.com (877) 893-8273
  (615) 263-1838
FAX (615) 263-1411
www.tapeonline.com

TapeStockOnline.com (888) 322-8273
  (310) 352-4230
FAX (310) 352-4233
www.tapestockonline.com

Tropical Media, Inc. (818) 955-8818
  (800) 650-1616
FAX (818) 955-8838
www.tropicalmedia.com

Videotape Products, Inc. (818) 566-9898
  (800) 422-2444
2721 W. Magnolia Blvd. FAX (818) 566-8989
Burbank, CA 91505 www.myvtp.com

Westside Media Group (310) 979-3500
12233 W. Olympic Blvd., Ste. 152
Los Angeles, CA 90064 www.westsidemediagroup.com

LENTINI COMMUNICATIONS

www.lentinicommunications.com

- DAT, DVD & Hardrive TC Recorders
- Wireless Mics (Audio Limited, Lectrosonic, Sennheiser)
- Microphones (All Types Including Lavaliers)
- Mixers (16-10-8-6 -5-4-3-2)
- Wireless Intercom & IFB Systems
- Sound Recording & Playback Packages
- DV Cameras (Sony PD-170, Panasonic 24P, Canon XL-2)
- DV Clamshells, LCD & Plasma Monitors
- Wireless Video Transmitters, Video Projectors
- Covert Cameras (Button, Sunglasses, Lipstick)
- Walkie Talkies & Cell Phones & Nextel Radios,
- Expendables (Batteries, Tape & Much More)

RENTALS • SALES • SERVICE
We Serve Quality Communications

54 West 21st Street • Suite 301 • New York, NY 10010 • 212.206.1452 • 212.206.1453 Fax
Shop for the latest gear @ www.lentinicommunications.com or visit our showroom conviently located in the Flatiron District of the Manhattan

Sound Equipment Rentals & Sales

Big Mo Pro, Inc. (973) 439-1656
323 New Road, Ste. 3 FAX (973) 439-1670
Parsippany, NJ 07054 www.bigmopro.com
(Analog, DAT Recording Tape, Expendables, Microphones, Players, Playback Systems, Preamps, Speakers, Specialty Microphones, Theatrical Sound Systems, Vintage Gear & Wireless Systems)

C&C Studios (212) 967-6425
 (917) 295-6920
20 W. 37th St., Fifth Fl. FAX (718) 504-5487
New York, NY 10018 www.candcstudios.tv

Channelbass (917) 548-5630
 (917) 406-5594
141 Devoe St., Ste. 2 FAX (718) 486-5819
(Near Manhattan Ave.) www.channelbass.net
Brooklyn, NY 11211

Dreamhire, LLC (212) 691-5544
 (800) 234-7536
36-36 33rd St., Ste. 102 FAX (212) 563-5525
(Near 36th Ave.) www.dreamhire.com
Long Island City, NY 11106
(Analog, Audio Props, DAT Recording, Digital Audio Workstations, Microphones, Preamps, Speakers, Microphones, Vintage Gear & Wireless Systems)

Forte' Sound (213) 304-1605
 www.fortesound.com

Gotham Sound and (212) 629-9430
Communications, Inc. (866) 468-4268
330 W. 38th St., Ground Fl., Ste. 105   FAX (212) 629-9436
(Near Eighth Ave.) www.gothamsound.com
New York, NY 10018

GRS Systems, Inc. (212) 286-0299
216 E. 45th St. FAX (212) 286-9475
New York, NY 10017 www.grsv.com

Hello World Communications (212) 243-8800
118 W. 22nd St., Ste. 2A FAX (212) 691-6961
(Near Sixth Ave.) www.hwc.tv
New York, NY 10011
(DAT Recording Tape, Digital Audio Workstations, Digital Multi-Track Portable Recorders, Microphones, Speakers & Wireless Systems)

Ins & Outs, Inc. (845) 256-0899
 (914) 388-4920
60 Jansen Rd. (Near Sarafian Rd.)   FAX (845) 256-1484
New Paltz, NY 12561 www.insandoutssound.com

Ⓐ **Lentini Communications** (212) 206-1452
54 W. 21st St., Ste. 301 FAX (212) 206-1453
(Near Fifth Ave.) www.lentinicommunications.com
New York, NY 10010

LVR/Liman Video Rental Company (212) 594-0086
 (800) 251-4625
341 W. 38th St., Ground Fl. FAX (212) 594-0786
(Near Eighth Ave.) www.lvrusa.com
New York, NY 10018

Mammoth Production Packages (585) 381-2470
3800 Monroe Ave. FAX (585) 381-2462
(Near Woodland Rd.) www.mammothpro.com
Pittsford, NY 14534

Moore P.A. Hire Inc.	(718) 389-8727 (917) 747-5372
21 Box St. (Near Manhattan Ave.) www.moorepahire.com Brooklyn, NY 11222 (Analog, Audio Props, Microphones, Playback Systems, Players, Preamps, Speakers, Theatrical Sound Systems, Underwater Speakers & Wireless Systems)	

Nevessa Production, Inc.	(845) 679-8848 (888) 484-8848
One Artist Rd. (Near Route 212) Saugerties, NY 12477	FAX (845) 679-1208 www.nevessa.com

❶ **Professional Sound Services, Inc.**	(212) 586-1033 (800) 883-1033
311 W. 43rd St., Ste. 1100 (Near Eighth Ave.) New York, NY 10036	FAX (212) 586-0970 www.pro-sound.com

See Factor Industry	(718) 784-4200
37-11 30th St. Long Island City, NY 11101	FAX (718) 784-0617 www.seefactor.com
(Analog, Microphones, Playback Systems, Preamps, Speakers, Specialty Microphones, Theatrical Sound Systems, Vintage Gear & Wireless Systems)	

Soho Audio	(212) 226-2429 (917) 902-2219
376 Broome St., Fourth Fl. (Near Mott St.) New York, NY 10013	FAX (212) 966-7650 www.sohoaudio.com

Stirling Audio Services, LLC	(732) 417-1001 (800) 652-8346
180 Northfield Ave. Edison, NJ 08837	FAX (732) 417-1010 www.stirlingaudioservices.com
(Microphones, Preamps, Speakers, Specialty Microphones, Theatrical Sound Systems, Vintage Gear & Wireless Systems)	

Sync Speed, Inc.	(610) 659-1033
10 E. Manoa Rd. Havertown, PA 19083	www.syncspeedinc.com
(Analog, Audio Props, DAT Recording Tape, Digital Multi-Track Portable Recorders, Expendables, Microphones, Playback Systems, Players, Preamps, Speakers, Specialty Microphones, Theatrical Sound Systems & Wireless Systems)	

Universal Light & Sound	(917) 743-3676
280 Madison Ave., Ste. 912 New York, NY 10016	www.ulsnyc.com

The Worldwide Leader In Prompting Services & Rentals

Highly skilled and experienced operators and technicians

The widest range of prompting hardware and software, including entirely wireless solutions

Equipment rental without an operator available

TV SHOWS . FEATURE FILMS . LIVE EVENTS . CONFERENCES . CONCERTS . AWARDS
POLITICAL CAMPAIGNS . CORPORATE VIDEOS . COMMERCIALS

QTV Prompting Services
306 5th Floor Avenue, 3rd Floor, New York, NY 10001
Tel +1 212 929 7755   Fax +1 212 929 2105
Email events@qtv.com

QTV
www.qtv.com

Teleprompting & Cue Card Services

A-Prompt (845) 359-4137 FAX (413) 638-7765 www.teleprompter.com	Available Teleprompting (973) 508-6054 www.availableteleprompting.com

TV Prompt — TELEPROMPTING SERVICES

**TV Specials
Video/Film
Public Speaking**

15", 12" & 6" Flat-Panels
Free Standing
Presidential
Large Screen Displays
DC Packages

EXPERIENCE & SERVICE
Contact: Duncan Chinnock
646.485.4355
48 West 21st Street, 7th Floor
New York, NY 10010

www.tvprompt.com

A-Prompt

Teleprompting Video, Film, Television, Award shows, Public speaking, Concerts, or any type of teleprompting need. State-of-the-art equipment and very experienced operators New York or Worldwide.

845-359-4137
www.teleprompter.com

Bleecker Prompting, Inc. 320 W. 76th St., Ste. 7G (Near West End Ave.) New York, NY 10023	(212) 579-2327 (718) 755-4211

Flashcards/Liz Forsyth 319 W. 18th St., Ste. 3G New York, NY 10011	(212) 691-4381 (917) 716-4767 www.cuecards.com

Foxtrot Production Services 20 Clifford Pl. East Norwich, NY 11732	(516) 628-8759 (516) 428-3063

ⓐ HPC Productions 155 Ridge St., Ste. 1A (Near Houston St.) New York, NY 10002	(212) 475-1649 (646) 418-3766 FAX (212) 475-1649 www.hpc-productions.com

ⓐ Intelliprompt Inc.	(212) 765-0555 www.intelliprompt.com

ⓐ Jerry Berg Computer Prompting 373 Necconset Hwy, Ste. 302 Hauppauge, NY 11788	(631) 366-2715 FAX (631) 366-4852

New York City Q-Cards, Inc. Three Deal Ln. Livingston, NJ 07039	(973) 533-1242 (917) 204-4454 FAX (973) 533-1242 www.nycqcards.com

New York Network (518) 443-5333
Empire State Plaza FAX (518) 426-4198
South Concourse, Ste. 146 www.nyn.suny.edu
P.O. Box 2058 (Near State St.)
Albany, NY 12220

Teleprompting & Cue Card Services

Excellence in Prompting for over 40 years

Our commitment to service is unmatched in the industry.

Our desire to make every production the best it can be and our pride in our work makes us second to none.

Call James O'Brien or Chris O'Brien at VIP.
Telephone #: (212) 247-7786
Facsimile #: (212) 247-7786
James' Cell: (917) 295-2199
Chris' Cell: (917) 295-2122
E-Mail VIP for Information

www.vipprompting.com

JERRY BERG
COMPUTER PROMPTING SERVICE
DIV. Jered Enterprises Inc

373 Nesconset Highway #302
Hauppauge, NY 11788

Tel: 631-366-2715
Fax: 631-366-4852

Email: bergprompting@aol.com
www.jerrybergprompting.com

Production Central — (212) 631-0435
873 Broadway, Ste. 205 — FAX (212) 631-0436
(Near E. 18th St.) — www.prodcentral.com
New York, NY 10003

Prompter Ready — (973) 746-8860 / (201) 220-1773
Nine Wellesley Rd. — FAX (973) 746-8866
Upper Montclair, NJ 07043

Ⓐ QTV Prompting Services — (212) 929-7755
306 Fifth Ave., Third Fl. — FAX (212) 929-2105
(Near Fifth Ave.) — www.qtv.com
New York, NY 10001

Ⓐ Teleprompting.com — (888) 488-0100
www.teleprompting.com

Three Great Lights — (973) 727-6532
FAX (973) 352-6112
www.threegreatlights.com

Ⓐ TV Prompt — (646) 485-4355 / (917) 991-8239
www.tvprompt.com

Ⓐ VIP Prompting Corporation — (212) 247-7786
FAX (845) 359-6277
www.vipprompting.com

Intelliprompt
(212) 765-0555

630 9th Avenue,
Ste 907, NYC NY 10036

Computerized Teleprompter
System with single and multiple LCD camera mounts (6" Hand Held), dual 15" podium LCD's, 15" LCD interview monitors.
Operator and equipment packages to suit your requirements.
Intelliprompt Software.

Prompt@Intelliprompt.com
www.intelliprompt.com

HPC PRODUCTIONS

TELEPROMPTING FOR COMMERCIALS, PROMOS, CORPORATE AND POLITICAL EVENTS

- Experienced and courteous operators
- Battery power available
- All LCD, flat screen equipment
- Speech and camera – mounted prompters (all sizes for film and video)
- affordable rates

SERVICE MANAGER • PAUL CRESS
155 Ridge St. Suite #1A
New York, NY. 10002
212 475 1649 • 646 418 3766
email: hpcinnyc@yahoo.com
www.hpc-productions.com

Video Assist Services

Adam Smelin Enterprises (914) 420-4022
110 N. Chatsworth Ave. FAX **(914) 833-2012**
(Near Glenn Rd.)
Larchmont, NY 10538

Austin Salisbury Productions (212) 777-2121
20 E. Ninth St., Ste. 22A **(917) 991-4966**
(Near University Pl.) FAX **(212) 777-2121**
New York, NY 10003

Rhys Carpenter (212) 781-1375
 (917) 597-1546
FAX **(208) 246-4793**

Gregory Edwards (718) 398-0515

Feature Video Systems, Inc./
Joel Holland (914) 271-6528
P.O. Box 45 www.featurevideo.com
Croton-On-Hudson, NY 10520

IGS Video Services, LLC (917) 776-5434

Peter Kremer (203) 975-7999

Kenneth Myers (866) 322-6039
 (203) 912-4505
FAX **(203) 322-6039**

Playback Systems (212) 620-5530
242 W. 30th St., Ste. 500 **(800) 540-7529**
(Near Seventh Ave.) FAX **(212) 620-5531**
New York, NY 10001 www.playbackny.com

A Video Village, Inc. (484) 322-0640
 (888) 223-5115
www.videovillage.com

Visual Alchemy, LLC (973) 332-6425
10 Village Park Rd. **(973) 239-3964**
Cedar Grove, NJ 07044 FAX **(973) 239-3965**
www.visualalchemy.tv

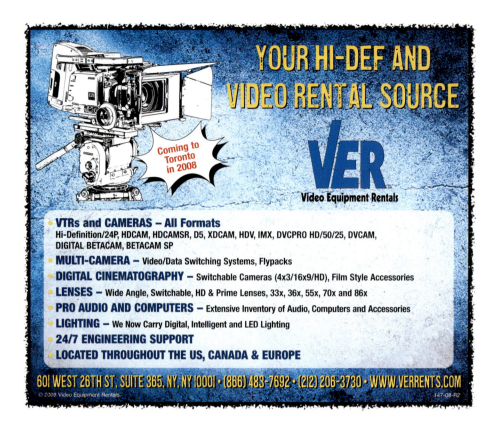

Video Cameras & Equipment

Abel Cine Tech, Inc. (212) 462-0100 / (888) 223-1599
609 Greenwich St., Fifth Fl. FAX (212) 462-0199
(Near Leroy St.) www.abelcine.com
New York, NY 10014
(24P, Digital, HDV, High Def, Mini DV, Monitors, Phantom HD High Speed Camera, Projectors, Recorders, Specialty Cameras & Underwater Housings)

All Mobile Video (212) 727-1234
221 W. 26th St. (Near Seventh Ave.) FAX (212) 255-6644
New York, NY 10001 www.allmobilevideo.com
(3/4", Betacam SP, Digital Betacam & VHS)

Atlantic Television, Inc. (212) 625-9327 / (917) 568-7218
524 Broadway, Fourth Fl. www.atlantictv.com
(Near Spring)
New York, NY 10012
(24P, Analog Systems, Betacam, Blue/Green Screen Facilities, Broadcast Systems, Camera Carts, Digiprimes, Digital, HDV, High Def, Lipstick Cameras, Magliner, Mini DV, Monitors, Multi-Camera Systems, Sound Equipment, Specialty Cameras, Steadicam Systems & Underwater Housings)

Bexel (212) 246-5051 / (800) 225-6185
625 W. 55th St. (Near 11th Ave.) FAX (212) 246-6373
New York, NY 10019 www.bexel.com
(3/4", Betacam, Digital Betacam, DVC Pro, Hi-8 & VHS)

Big Foot Productions, Inc. (718) 729-1900
37-09 36th Ave. (Near 37th St.) FAX (718) 729-8638
Long Island City, NY 11101 www.bigfootnyc.com
(Betacam SP, Digital Betacam & DVCam)

Boston Camera Rental Co. (617) 277-2200
1686 Commonwealth Ave. FAX (617) 277-6800
Brighton, MA 02135 www.bostoncamera.com
(DVCam, HD Cameras & Mini DV)

BVR, Ltd. (212) 541-5390
(800) 797-4287
355 W. 52nd St. (Near Ninth Ave.) FAX (212) 541-5751
New York, NY 10019 www.bvr.com
(Betacam SP, Digital Betacam, DVCam, HD, Hi-8 & Mini DV)

Cinema Rentals, Inc. (661) 222-7342
(877) 877-9605
25876 The Old Rd., Ste. 174 FAX (661) 253-3643
Stevenson Ranch, CA 91381 www.cinemarentals.com
(Digital and Hi-8 Underwater Video & Lipstick Camera)

CitiCam Video Services, Inc. (212) 315-4855
(212) 315-2000
515 W. 57th St. (Near 10th Ave.) FAX (212) 586-1572
New York, NY 10019 www.citicam.net

Clark Media (610) 694-9800
(Beta SP & DV) FAX (610) 694-9700
www.hidef.tv

dv Depot (212) 333-5100
251 W. 39th St., Seventh Fl. FAX (212) 333-5900
(Near Seventh Ave.) www.dvdepot.com
New York, NY 10018
(24P, HDV, High Def, Lipstick Cameras, Mini DV, Monitors, Multi-Camera Systems & Sound Equipment)

E.C. Professional Video (212) 333-5570
(212) 586-6156
253 W. 51st St. FAX (212) 262-0888
New York, NY 10019

Gear For Hire HD (212) 688-5490
(877) 786-7428
305 Madison Ave., Ste. 449 FAX (800) 505-1329
New York, NY 10165 www.gearforhireny.com

GRS Systems, Inc. (212) 286-0299
216 E. 45th St. FAX (212) 286-9475
New York, NY 10017 www.grsv.com

Hand Held Films, Inc. (212) 502-0900
66 White St., Ground Fl. FAX (212) 502-0906
(Near Broadway) www.handheldfilms.com
New York, NY 10013
(24P, Broadcast Systems, Digiprimes, Digital, HDV, High Def, Magliner, Mini DV, Underwater Housings Video Assist Systems & Wireless Monitoring)

HB Group, Inc. (203) 234-8107
(800) 331-1804
60 Dodge Ave. FAX (203) 239-4882
North Haven, CT 06473 www.hbgroupinc.com
(Betacam SP, Digital Betacam & DVCam)

Hello World Communications (212) 243-8800
118 W. 22nd St., Ste. 2A FAX (212) 691-6961
(Near Sixth Ave.) www.hwc.tv
New York, NY 10011
(Digital, HDV, High Def & Lenses)

Instructivision, Inc. (973) 575-9992
16 Chapin Rd., Ste. 904 FAX (973) 575-9134
Pine Brook, NJ 07058 www.instructivision.com
(Video Camera Systems)

K.P. Pro Video, Inc. (800) 670-6555
(718) 441-8263
FAX (718) 4410777
www.kpprovideo.com

Keslow Television, Inc. (KTV) (212) 239-1500
444 W. 36th St. (Near 10th Ave.) FAX (212) 239-1212
New York, NY 10018 www.keslow.com
(Broadcast Video Equipment)

We offer the audio, video & lighting gear you have been fantasizing about. And when you visit, we'll happily introduce you to our video - DVD production, editing & motion graphics services.

◄►

Hello World Communications
118 West 22nd Street Suite 2A   NYC
www.hwc.tv   212 243-8800

Video Cameras & Equipment

Lentini Communications (212) 206-1452
54 W. 21st St., Ste. 301 FAX (212) 206-1453
(Near Fifth Ave.) www.lentinicommunications.com
New York, NY 10010

  (212) 594-0086
LVR/Liman Video Rental Company (800) 251-4625
341 W. 38th St., Ground Fl. FAX (212) 594-0786
(Near Eighth Ave.) www.lvrusa.com
New York, NY 10018
(Betacam SP, Digital Betacam, DV, DVC Pro, DVCam & Mini DV)

Manhattan Place Entertainment (212) 682-2000
310 E. 44th St. (Near Second Ave.) FAX (212) 682-2058
New York, NY 10017 www.manhattanplace.tv
(Betacam SP)

MB Productions, Inc. (973) 439-0044
Four Edison Pl. FAX (973) 439-9844
Fairfield, NJ 07004 www.mbvideo.com
(Camera Packages, Monitors & Video Projection)

Metrovision Production Group (212) 989-1515
508 W. 24th St. (Near 10th Ave.) FAX (212) 989-8278
New York, NY 10011 www.metrovision.tv
(Betacam SP & Digital Camcorders)

  (973) 379-5959
Midnight Media Group, Inc. (800) 392-8265
45 E. Willow St. FAX (973) 379-0551
Millburn, NJ 07041 www.mmgi.tv
(24P, Betacam SP, DVCAM, DVCPro, HDV &
Multi-Camera Systems)

  (845) 679-8848
Nevessa Production, Inc. (888) 484-8848
One Artist Rd. (Near Route 212) FAX (845) 679-1208
Saugerties, NY 12477 www.nevessa.com
(DVCam)

Omni Video Services, Ltd. (718) 472-2944
11-23 50th Ave. (Near Jackson Ave.) FAX (718) 472-5944
Long Island City, NY 11101
(Betacam SP & Digital Betacam)

PAL Television East (212) 741-9111
236 W. 27th St., 10th Fl. FAX (212) 741-7772
New York, NY 10001 www.paleast.com

  (212) 620-5530
Playback Systems (800) 540-7529
242 W. 30th St., Ste. 500 FAX (212) 620-5531
(Near Seventh Ave.) www.playbackny.com
New York, NY 10001

  (212) 947-9797
Plus 8 Digital (818) 333-1000
540 W. 35th St. (Near 10th Ave.) FAX (212) 244-4457
New York, NY 10001 www.plus8digital.com
(Sony F900 and F950 & Viper)

❶ Primalux Video (212) 206-1402
30 W. 26th St., Seventh Fl. FAX (212) 206-1826
(Near Broadway) www.primalux.com
New York, NY 10010
(24P, Betacam, Blue Screen Facilities, Digital, Flatscreens,
Green Screen Facilities, HDV, High Def, Mini DV, Monitors &
Sound Equipment)

Production Central (212) 631-0435
873 Broadway, Ste. 205 FAX (212) 631-0436
(Near E. 18th St.) www.prodcentral.com
New York, NY 10003
(¾", 24P, Analog Systems, Betacam, Blue/Green Screen
Facilities, Broadcast Systems, Camera Carts, Digiprimes, Digital,
Flatscreens, Flypacks, HDV, Hi-8, High Def, Magliner, Mini DV,
Monitors, Multi-Camera Systems, Playback Systems, Portable
AVID Systems, Projectors, Recorders, Sound Equipment,
Ultimatte, Video Assist Systems & Wireless Monitoring)

  (212) 279-9640
PSAV Event Services (888) 882-4228
534 W. 35th St. (Near 10th Ave.) FAX (212) 279-8690
New York, NY 10001 www.psav.com
(Audiovisual Equipment & Video Cameras and Display)

  (201) 930-9855
Q Video Services, Inc. (800) 921-3478
P.O. Box 383 FAX (201) 930-9850
Park Ridge, NJ 07656 www.qvideo.tv
(Steadicams)

Socapa Films (800) 718-2787
375 Greenwich St., Tribeca Film Center www.socapa.org
(Near N. Moore St.)
New York, NY 10013
(DV Cameras and Accessories)

  (201) 836-5427
Solar Plexus, Inc. (201) 281-5973
135 Oakdene Ave. FAX (201) 836-5427
Teaneck, NJ 07666 www.solarplexusprods.com
(Century Optics Wide Angle Lenses, Fuji 9X 14X Zoom,
Ikegami HL DV7 WS, Manfrotto Remote Zoom Control,
Panasonic DVX 100A & Sachtler Video 18 Head)

  (212) 244-1011
Tamberelli Digital (877) 608-4336
516 W. 36th St., Second Fl. FAX (212) 947-5894
(Near 10th Ave.) www.tamberelli.com
New York, NY 10018
(24P HD, Audio and Wireless Mics, Betacam SP, Digital
Betacam, DVCam & Mini DV Cameras and Recorders)

**TCS/Technological
Cinevideo Services, Inc.** (212) 247-6517
341 W. 38th St., Fourth Fl. FAX (212) 489-4886
(Near Ninth Ave.) www.tcsfilm.com
New York, NY 10018

  (212) 206-3730
❶ Video Equipment Rentals (866) 483-7692
601 W. 26th St., Ste. 365 www.verrents.com
(Near 11th Ave.)
New York, NY 10001
(24P, Broadcast Systems, Flatscreens, Flypacks, HDV, High
Def, Multi-Camera Systems, Projectors, Sound Equipment &
Specialty Cameras)

Videofilm Systems, Inc. (203) 866-7319
18 Leonard St. FAX (203) 838-3126
Norwalk, CT 06850 www.vfstv.com
(Component Betacam, Digital Betacam, DVCam, DVC Pro &
Sony High Definition)

VISUAL ALCHEMY, LLC
video & computer services for film production

see our new catalog at
www.visualalchemy.tv

➤ Specialists in 24 frame film to video synchronization

➤ Video & computer prop rentals
(see our online catalog at www.visualalchemy.tv)

➤ Custom computer graphics & animation design

➤ Digital Video Assist

➤ Complete video production services

➤ Video Walls & Video Projection

➤ Episodic TV:
"Law & Order" "30 Rock"
"Law & Order: SVU" "Cashmere Mafia"
"Law & Order: Criminal Intent"

➤ Feature Films:
"Syriana" "The Invasion"
"21" "Jumper"
"Zach & Miri" "PS I Love You"
"The Departed" "Gone Baby Gone"

➤ Commercial Clients:
Maysles Films Backyard Prods.
Believe Media Crossroads Films
Pen & Inc. Anonymous Content
Headquaters Public Domain

973-332-6425

Michael Sime
info@visualalchemy.tv

Video Display, Playback & Projection

Computer Rent (212) 767-0400
225 Broadway www.computerpropsnyc.com
(Near Barkley)
New York, NY 10007

Fresh Air Flicks (877) 215-5500
FAX (877) 215-5500
www.freshairflicks.com
(Front Screen Projections, High-Output Large Screen Video Projection, Inflatable Movie Screens, LED Screens, Mobile LED Screens, Outdoor Movie Systems, Rear Screen Projections, Video Projection & Video Walls)

GRS Systems, Inc. (212) 286-0299
216 E. 45th St. FAX (212) 286-9475
New York, NY 10017 www.grsv.com

HB Group, Inc. (203) 234-8107
(800) 331-1804
60 Dodge Ave. FAX (203) 239-4882
North Haven, CT 06473 www.hbgroupinc.com

Hello World Communications (212) 243-8800
118 W. 22nd St., Ste. 2A FAX (212) 691-6961
(Near Sixth Ave.) www.hwc.tv
New York, NY 10011
(Front and Rear Screen Projections & Video Projection)

Ⓐ K2imaging, Inc. (917) 952-9589
24 Tompkins Pl. (Near Court St.) www.k2imaging.com
Brooklyn, NY 11231
(High-Output Large Screen Video Projection & Video Projection)

MB Productions, Inc.	(973) 439-0044
Four Edison Pl.	FAX (973) 439-9844
Fairfield, NJ 07004	www.mbvideo.com
(Flatscreens, Front and Rear Screen Projections, High-Output Front/Rear Large Screen Video Projection, LED Screens, Mobile LED Screens, Projection, Video Playback & Video Walls)	

Ⓐ **Ncyclomedia, Inc.**	(212) 242-3177
160 Bleecker St., Ste. 6HE	FAX (212) 242-8438
New York, NY 10012	www.ncyclomedia.com

NEP Screenworks	(800) 868-2898
	www.screenworksnep.com

Playback Systems	(212) 620-5530
	(800) 540-7529
242 W. 30th St., Ste. 500	FAX (212) 620-5531
(Near Seventh Ave.)	
New York, NY 10001	

Plus 8 Digital	(212) 947-9797
	(818) 333-1000
540 W. 35th St. (Near 10th Ave.)	FAX (212) 244-4457
New York, NY 10001	www.plus8digital.com

Ⓐ **Visual Alchemy, LLC**	(973) 332-6425
	(973) 239-3964
10 Village Park Rd.	FAX (973) 239-3965
Cedar Grove, NJ 07044	www.visualalchemy.tv

Video Display, Playback & Projection

PICTURED:
Granite Plaza Midtown

LOCATION:
Manhattan, NY

PHOTOGRAPHER:
Mitch Ganem

ALSAM : www.alsam.net
ASSOCIATION OF
LOCATION SCOUTS & MANAGERS

New York 411
*Qualified Listings for the
New York Production Community*
www.newyork411.com

zeitbyte
digital media

Zeitbyte specializes in delivering your High Definition video to the Internet and beyond.

We offer a wide spectrum of HD services:

- HD Webcasting
- Custom HD Web Video Players
- HD Camera Crews
- HD Editing & Color Correction
- Volume & Custom Encoding
- Blu-Ray Authoring & Duplication
- Content Management Systems

Zeitbyte is a one-stop shop offering a full range of services for High Definition and Standard Definition video.

Contact us today @ 718-666-3300.

Zeitbyte, LLC
45 Main St., Suite #1030
Brooklyn, N.Y. 11201
http://www.zeitbyte.com
718-666-3300

High Def

ⓐ ADVERTISER SYMBOL

Refer to the General Index for
cross-referencing items in this section.

HD Cameras & Equipment 280
HD Duplication 283
HD Editing Equipment. 284
HD Equipment Manufacturers. 285
HD Post Houses 288
HD Screening Rooms 291
HD Stock Footage. 292
HD Tape Stock 294

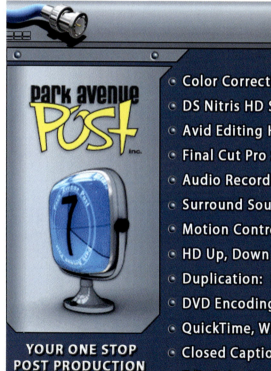

park avenue Post Inc.

- Color Correction and Finishing
- DS Nitris HD Suites
- Avid Editing HD/SD Suites
- Final Cut Pro Suites (RED Work Flow)
- Audio Recording, Sound Design
- Surround Sound Mixing
- Motion Control/Animation
- HD Up, Down & Cross Conversions
- Duplication: HD/SD Formats
- DVD Encoding and DVD Authoring
- QuickTime, WMV, Flash & MPEG Encoding
- Closed Caption and Subtitle Encoding
- Edit Suite Rentals with or w/o Editor

YOUR ONE STOP POST PRODUCTION FACILITY

Park Avenue Post, Inc. • 419 Park Avenue South
Suite 600 • New York, NY 10016
Tel: 212-689-7678 • Fax: 212-689-7544
www.parkavenuepost.com

HD Cameras & Equipment

24fps Productions, Inc. (646) 638-0659
144 W. 27th St., 12th Fl. FAX (212) 206-6986
New York, NY 10001 www.24fpsproductions.com

Abel Cine Tech, Inc. (888) 223-1599
(212) 462-0100
609 Greenwich St., Fifth Fl. FAX (212) 462-0199
(Near Leroy St.) www.abelcine.com
New York, NY 10014
(1080i, 24P, 720P, Accessories, D-5, Decks, HD-CAM, HDSR, HDV, Monitors, Panasonic, Phantom HD High-Speed Camera, Projectors, PS Technik Adaptors, SDX 900, Sony & VTR Systems)

Air Sea Land Productions, Inc. (718) 626-2646
(888) 275-5367
19-69 Steinway St. (Near 20th Ave.) FAX (718) 626-1493
Astoria, NY 11105 www.airsealand.com
(1080i, 24P, 720P, Editing Facilities, HD-CAM, HDV, Monitors, Panasonic & Sony)

Ⓐ All Mobile Video (212) 727-1234
221 W. 26th St. (Near Seventh Ave.) FAX (212) 255-6644
New York, NY 10001 www.allmobilevideo.com
(Mobile Trucks)

Atlantic Cine Equipment, Inc. (212) 944-0003
(410) 243-4181
210 W. 29th St. FAX (443) 524-0210
Baltimore, MD 21211 www.aceeast.com
(1080i, 24P, 720P, Accessories, Multi-Camera Systems & Panasonic)

Atlantic Television, Inc. (212) 625-9327
(917) 568-7218
524 Broadway, Fourth Fl. www.atlantictv.com
(Near Spring)
New York, NY 10012
(1080i, 24P, 720P, Accessories, Blue/Green Screen Facilities, Cooke S4s, Decks, DVC-Pro, Editing Facilities, HD-CAM, HDSR, HDV, Monitors, Multi-Camera Concert Packages, Multi-Camera Systems, Panasonic, SDX 900, Sony, Ultra Prims, VTR Systems, Wireless Monitoring & Zeiss Digiprimes)

B&H Photo Video Pro Audio (212) 444-5085
(212) 239-7760
420 Ninth Ave. (Near W. 34th St.) FAX (212) 239-7766
New York, NY 10001 www.bhphotovideo.com

Bexel (212) 246-5051
(800) 225-6185
625 W. 55th St. (Near 11th Ave.) FAX (212) 246-6373
New York, NY 10019 www.bexel.com

Beyond Our Reality (212) 255-5432
Productions, Inc. (800) 583-5015
49 W. 24th St., Seventh Fl. FAX (212) 255-6866
(Near Broadway) www.beyondourreality.com
New York, NY 10010

Big Foot Productions, Inc. (718) 729-1900
37-09 36th Ave. (Near 37th St.) FAX (718) 729-8638
Long Island City, NY 11101 www.bigfootnyc.com

Boston Camera Rental Co. (617) 277-2200
1686 Commonwealth Ave. FAX (617) 277-6800
Brighton, MA 02135 www.bostoncamera.com

BVR, Ltd. (212) 541-5390
(800) 797-4287
355 W. 52nd St. (Near Ninth Ave.) FAX (212) 541-5751
New York, NY 10019 www.bvr.com

Cablecam International, Inc. (818) 349-4955
(818) 601-6333
21303 Itasca St. FAX (818) 349-3879
Chatsworth, CA 91311 www.cablecam.com

Cinema-Vision (212) 620-8191
210 11th Ave., Ste. 403 (Near 25th St.) FAX (212) 620-8198
New York, NY 10001 www.motionpicturerentals.com

Clark Media (610) 694-9800
FAX (610) 694-9700
www.hidef.tv

HD RENTALS & EDITING

Cameras & VTR's
HDCAM-SR
HD-D5
DVCPRO 50/DVCPRO HD
XDCAM HD
HDV

Editing & Project Mastering
Avid Symphony Nitris HD
Final Cut Pro HD

Alchemist Platinum - Motion Compensated
HD Up/Down/Cross Conversion

HD Screening

GRS SYSTEMS
216E 45th St. New York, NY 10017
Tel 212-286-0299 Fax 212-286-9475
www.grsv.com

Colossalvision (212) 269-6333
26 Broadway FAX (212) 269-4334
(Near Merchant Marines Plaza) www.colossalvision.com
New York, NY 10004

crewHD.com (973) 508-6054
www.crewhd.com

Digital Arts (212) 460-9600
130 W. 29th St., Eighth Fl. FAX (212) 660-3600
(Near Sixth Ave.) www.digital-arts.net
New York, NY 10001
(1080i, 24P, 720P, D-5, Decks, DVC-Pro, Editing Facilities, Green Screen Facilities, HD-CAM, HDSR, Panasonic & Sony)

Gear For Hire HD (212) 688-5490
(877) 786-7428
305 Madison Ave., Ste. 449 FAX (800) 505-1329
New York, NY 10165 www.gearforhireny.com

GRS Systems, Inc. (212) 286-0299
216 E. 45th St. FAX (212) 286-9475
New York, NY 10017 www.grsv.com

Hand Held Films, Inc. (212) 502-0900
66 White St., Ground Fl. FAX (212) 502-0906
(Near Broadway) www.handheldfilms.com
New York, NY 10013
(1080i, 720P, Accessories, Cooke S4s, DVC-Pro, HD-CAM, HDSR, HDV, Monitors, Multi-Camera Systems, Panasonic, PS Technik Adaptors, SDX 900, Sony, Ultra Primes, Wireless Monitoring & Zeiss Digiprimes)

HB Group, Inc. (203) 234-8107
(800) 331-1804
60 Dodge Ave. FAX (203) 239-4882
North Haven, CT 06473 www.hbgroupinc.com

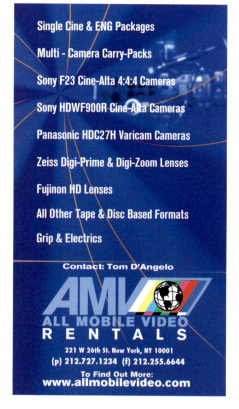

Ⓐ Hello World Communications   **(212) 243-8800**
118 W. 22nd St., Ste. 2A   FAX **(212) 691-6961**
(Near Sixth Ave.)   **www.hwc.tv**
New York, NY 10011
(1080i, 24P, 720P, Decks, DVC-Pro, Editing Facilities, Green Screen Facilities, HDV, Monitors, Multi-Camera Systems, Panasonic, Projectors, Sony & VTR Systems)

Ⓐ K.P. Pro Video, Inc.   **(800) 670-6555**
   (718) 441-8263
87-07 Jamaica Ave.   FAX **(718) 4410777**
Woodhaven, NY 11421   **www.kpprovideo.com**

K2imaging, Inc.   **(917) 952-9589**
24 Tompkins Pl. (Near Court St.)   FAX **(917) 591-6981**
Brooklyn, NY 11231   **www.k2imaging.com**

Keslow Television, Inc. (KTV)   **(212) 239-1500**
444 W. 36th St. (Near 10th Ave.)   FAX **(212) 239-1212**
New York, NY 10018   **www.keslow.com**

LVR/Liman Video Rental Company   **(212) 594-0086**
   (800) 251-4625
341 W. 38th St., Ground Fl.   FAX **(212) 594-0786**
(Near Eighth Ave.)   **www.lvrusa.com**
New York, NY 10018

MB Productions, Inc.   **(973) 439-0044**
Four Edison Pl.   FAX **(973) 439-9844**
Fairfield, NJ 07004   **www.mbvideo.com**

Metrovision Production Group   **(212) 989-1515**
508 W. 24th St. (Near 10th Ave.)   FAX **(212) 989-8278**
New York, NY 10011   **www.metrovision.tv**

PAL Television East   **(212) 741-9111**
236 W. 27th St., 10th Fl.   FAX **(212) 741-7772**
New York, NY 10001   **www.paleast.com**

Plus 8 Digital   **(212) 947-9797**
   (818) 333-1000
540 W. 35th St. (Near 10th Ave.)   FAX **(212) 244-4457**
New York, NY 10011   **www.plus8digital.com**

Primalux Video   **(212) 206-1402**
30 W. 26th St., Seventh Fl.   FAX **(212) 206-1826**
(Near Broadway)   **www.primalux.com**
New York, NY 10010
(1080i, 24P, 720P, Accessories, Blue Screen Facilities, Editing Facilities, Green Screen Facilities, HD-CAM, HDV, Monitors, Panasonic & Sony)

Production Central   **(212) 631-0435**
873 Broadway, Ste. 205   FAX **(212) 631-0436**
(Near E. 18th St.)   **www.prodcentral.com**
New York, NY 10003
(1080i, 24P, 720P, Accessories, Blue/Green Screen Facilities, Converters, Decks, DVC-Pro, Editing Facilities, HD-CAM, HDV, Monitors, Multi-Camera Concert Packages, Multi-Camera Systems, Panasonic, Portable Ultimatte & Projectors)

Sniffen HD   **(212) 354-7741**
   (203) 264-2028
533 Bagley Rd.   **www.sniffen.com**
Southbury, CT 06488

Studio 57   **(631) 650-0057**
   (631) 766-0777
140 Hoffman Ln. (Near Space Court)   FAX **(631) 650-0010**
Islandia, NY 11749   **www.studio57online.com**

Tamberelli Digital   **(212) 244-1011**
   (877) 608-4336
516 W. 36th St., Second Fl.   FAX **(212) 947-5894**
(Near 10th Ave.)   **www.tamberelli.com**
New York, NY 10018

TCS/Technological Cinevideo Services, Inc.   **(212) 247-6517**
341 W. 38th St., Fourth Fl.   FAX **(212) 489-4886**
(Near Ninth Ave.)   **www.tcsfilm.com**
New York, NY 10018
(1080i, 24P, 2K Cameras, 4K Cameras, 720P, Accessories, Converters, Cooke S4s, Decks, DVC-Pro, HD-CAM, HDSR, HDV, Monitors, Multi-Camera Concert Packages, Multi-Camera Systems, Panasonic, PS Technik Adaptors, Red One, SDX 900, Sony, Sync Generators, Ultra Primes, VTR Systems, Wireless Monitoring & Zeiss Digiprimes)

Video Equipment Rentals   **(212) 206-3730**
   (866) 483-7692
601 W. 26th St., Ste. 365   **www.verrents.com**
(Near 11th Ave.)
New York, NY 10001

Videofilm Systems, Inc.   **(203) 866-7319**
18 Leonard St.   FAX **(203) 838-3126**
Norwalk, CT 06850   **www.vfstv.com**

HD Duplication

24fps Productions, Inc. (646) 638-0659
FAX (212) 206-6986
www.24fpsproductions.com

All Mobile Video (212) 727-1234
221 W. 26th St. FAX (212) 255-6644
New York, NY 10001 www.allmobilevideo.com

Ascent Media Management East (201) 767-3800
235 Pegasus Ave. FAX (201) 784-2769
(Near Livingston St.) www.ascentmedia.com
Northvale, NJ 07647

Chelsea Post (212) 727-1234
221 W. 26th St. (Near Eighth Ave.) FAX (212) 255-6644
New York, NY 10001 www.amvchelsea.com

Chromavision (212) 686-7366
49 W. 27th St., Eighth Fl. FAX (212) 686-7310
(Near Sixth Ave.) www.chromavision.net
New York, NY 10001

Devlin Video International (212) 391-1313
1501 Broadway, Ste. 408 FAX (212) 391-2744
(Near W. 43rd St.) www.devlinvideo.com
New York, NY 10036

DG FastChannel (212) 953-9300
600 Third Ave. (Near Seventh Ave.) (212) 627-2216
New York, NY 10016 FAX (212) 972-8250
www.dgfastchannel.com

Digital Arts (212) 460-9600
130 W. 29th St., Eighth Fl. FAX (212) 660-3600
(Near Sixth Ave.) www.digital-arts.net
New York, NY 10001

Elrom Inc. (212) 645-5050
419 Park Ave. South FAX (212) 689-7544
New York, NY 10016 www.elrom.tv

GRS Systems, Inc. (212) 286-0299
216 E. 45th St. FAX (212) 286-9475
New York, NY 10017 www.grsv.com

Hello World Communications (212) 243-8800
118 W. 22nd St., Ste. 2A FAX (212) 691-6961
(Near Sixth Ave.) www.hwc.tv
New York, NY 10011

International Duplication Centre/
International Digital Centre, Inc. (212) 581-3940
216 E. 45th St., Seventh Fl. FAX (212) 581-3979
(Near Third Ave.) www.idcdigital.com
New York, NY 10017

Moving Images (212) 953-6999
227 E. 45th St., Sixth Fl. www.mipost.com
(Near Second Ave.)
New York, NY 10017

Ⓐ Park Avenue Post, Inc. (212) 689-7678
419 Park Ave. South, Ste. 600 FAX (212) 689-7544
(Near 29th St.) www.parkavenuepost.com
New York, NY 10016

(212) 894-4000
PostWorks (212) 894-4050
100 Avenue of the Americas FAX (212) 941-0439
(Near Grand St.) www.postworks.com
New York, NY 10013

Tylie Jones & Associates, Inc. (212) 972-3800
370 Lexington Ave., 10th Fl., Ste. 1007 FAX (212) 972-4419
(Near E. 41st St.) www.tylie.com
New York, NY 10017

Ⓐ Zeitbyte (718) 666-3300
45 Main St., Ste. 1030 www.zeitbyte.com
Brooklyn, NY 11201

HD Editing Equipment

Air Sea Land Productions, Inc. (718) 626-2646
19-69 Steinway St. (Near 20th Ave.) (888) 275-5367
Astoria, NY 11105 FAX (718) 626-1493
www.airsealand.com

All Mobile Video (212) 727-1234
221 W. 26th St. FAX (212) 255-6644
New York, NY 10001 www.allmobilevideo.com

Digital Arts (212) 460-9600
130 W. 29th St., Eighth Fl. FAX (212) 660-3600
(Near Sixth Ave.) www.digital-arts.net
New York, NY 10001

Du Art Film and Video (212) 757-4580
245 W. 55th St. (Near Broadway) FAX (212) 333-7647
New York, NY 10019 www.duart.com

Firestarter Rentals (310) 420-5146
880 W. First St., Ste. 513 (800) 670-7080
Los Angeles, CA 90012 FAX (949) 363-8497

Goldcrest Post Production (212) 243-4700
799 Washington St. (Near Horatio St.) FAX (212) 624-1701
New York, NY 10014 www.goldcrestpost.com

GRS Systems, Inc. (212) 286-0299
216 E. 45th St. FAX (212) 286-9475
New York, NY 10017 www.grsv.com

LA Digital Post, Inc. (212) 981-8500
220 W. 42nd St., 17th Fl. FAX (212) 981-8595
New York, NY 10036 www.ladigital.com

LVR/Liman Video Rental Company (212) 594-0086
341 W. 38th St., Ground Fl. (800) 251-4625
(Near Eighth Ave.) FAX (212) 594-0786
New York, NY 10018 www.lvrusa.com

Moviola/J & R Film Company (212) 247-0972
545 W. 45th St., Fourth Fl. (877) 668-4652
(Near 11th Ave.) FAX (212) 265-9820
New York, NY 10036 www.moviola.com

Plus 8 Digital (212) 947-9797
540 W. 35th St. (Near 10th Ave.) (818) 333-1000
New York, NY 10001 FAX (212) 244-4457
www.plus8digital.com

Post Office Editorial (212) 981-5015
311 W. 34th St., 12th Fl. (917) 696-6906
New York, NY 10001 FAX (212) 981-5015

Prime To Go (888) 858-4180
72 Hillside Ln. www.primetogo.com
Fallsington, PA 19054

Production Central (212) 631-0435
873 Broadway, Ste. 205 FAX (212) 631-0436
(Near E. 18th St.) www.prodcentral.com
New York, NY 10003

Runway, Inc. (310) 636-2000
10575 Virginia Ave. FAX (310) 636-2034
Culver City, CA 90232 www.runway.com

Solar Film/Video Productions (212) 473-3040
632 Broadway, Ste. 304 FAX (212) 473-3091
(Near Houston St.) www.solarnyc.com
New York, NY 10012

Video Equipment Rentals (212) 206-3730
601 W. 26th St., Ste. 365 (866) 483-7692
(Near 11th Ave.) www.verrents.com
New York, NY 10001

Virtual Media (212) 490-9730
915 Broadway, 15th Fl. FAX (212) 818-0529
(Near E. 21st St.) www.virtualmediaonline.com
New York, NY 10010

HD Equipment Manufacturers

Acrodyne Industries (Ai) — (888) 881-4447
10706 Beaver Dam Rd.
Cockeysville, MD 21030
www.acrodyne.com
(Transmitters)

AJA Video — (530) 274-2048 / (800) 251-4224
443 Crown Point Circle, Ste. C
Grass Valley, CA 95945
FAX (530) 274-9442
www.aja.com
(Interface Tools & Video Converters)

Amphibico — (514) 333-8666
459 Deslauriers
Montreal, QC H4N 1W2 Canada
FAX (514) 333-1339
www.amphibico.com
(Underwater Camera Housings and Accessories)

Angenieux — 33 477 90 78 00
42570 Saint-Héand
France
FAX 33 477 90 78 03
www.angenieux.com
(Lenses)

Astro Systems, Inc. — (626) 336-7001 / (877) 882-7876
418 Cloverleaf Dr., Ste. C
Baldwin, CA 91706
FAX (626) 336-7005
www.astro-systems.com
(Video Monitors and Processing Tools)

Autodesk — (514) 393-1616 / (800) 869-3504
FAX (514) 393-0110
www.autodesk.com
(Video Editing and FX Systems)

Avid Technology, Inc. — (978) 640-6789 / (800) 949-2843
One Park West
Tewksbury, MA 01876
FAX (978) 640-1366
www.avid.com
(Video Editing and FX Systems)

Band Pro Film & Digital, Inc. — (818) 841-9655
3403 W. Pacific Ave.
Burbank, CA 91505
FAX (818) 841-7649
www.bandpro.com
(Camera Accessories, Cameras, Lenses & Prime Lenses)

Barco, Inc. — (916) 859-2500 / (888) 414-7226
11101-A Trade Center Dr.
Rancho Cordova, CA 95670
FAX (916) 859-2515
www.barco.com
(Video Processing Tools)

Blackmagic Design — 61 3 9682 4770
11 Gateway Court
Port Melbourne, Victoria 3207 Australia
FAX 61 3 9682 4790
(Video Cards)
www.blackmagic-design.com

BOXX Technologies, Inc. — (512) 835-0400 / (877) 877-2699
10435 Burnet Rd., Ste. 120
Austin, TX 78758
FAX (512) 835-0434
www.boxxtech.com
(Video Editing and FX Systems)

Canon — (800) 321-4388
One Canon Plaza
Lake Success, NY 11042
www.canonhdec.com
(Lenses)

CELCO — (909) 481-4648
8660 Red Oak Ave.
Rancho Cucamonga, CA 91730
FAX (909) 481-6899
www.celco.com
(Film Recorders)

Chyron Corporation — (631) 845-2000
Five Hub Dr.
Melville, NY 11747
FAX (631) 845-3895
www.chyron.com
(Video Graphics Systems)

Cobalt Digital, Inc. — (217) 344-1243 / (800) 669-1691
2406 E. University Ave.
Urbana, IL 61802
FAX (217) 344-1245
www.cobaltdigital.com
(Video Conversion Tools)

da Vinci Systems, Inc. — (954) 688-5600
4397 NW 124 Ave.
Coral Springs, FL 33065
FAX (954) 575-5936
www.davsys.com
(Color Image Enhancement and Restoration Tools)

Digital Projection, Inc. — (770) 420-1350
55 Chastain Rd., Ste. 115
Kennesaw, GA 30144
FAX (770) 420-1360
www.digitalprojection.com
(DLP-Based Projection Systems)

Digital Vision, Inc. — (818) 769-8111
4605 Lankershim Blvd., Ste. 700
North Hollywood, CA 91602
FAX (818) 769-1888
www.digitalvision.se
(Video Processing Tools)

Doggicam, Inc. — (818) 845-8470
1500 W. Verdugo Ave.
Burbank, CA 91506
FAX (818) 845-8477
www.doggicam.com
(Remote Heads)

Dolby Laboratories, Inc. — (415) 645-5000
100 Potrero St.
San Francisco, CA 94103
FAX (415) 645-4000
www.dolby.com
(Audio Processing Systems)

Doremi Labs, Inc. — (818) 562-1101
1020 Chestnut St.
Burbank, CA 91506
FAX (818) 562-1109
www.doremilabs.com
(Disk Recorders & Video Servers)

Draper, Inc. — (800) 238-7999
411 S. Pearl St.
Spiceland, IN 47385
FAX (765) 987-7142
www.draperinc.com
(Front and Rear Projection Screens)

DSC Laboratories — (905) 673-3211
3565 Nashua Dr.
Mississauga, ON L4V 1R1 Canada
FAX (905) 673-0929
www.dsclabs.com
(Camera Test Systems)

DVS Digital Video, Inc. — (818) 846-3600
300 E. Magnolia Blvd., Ste. 102
Burbank, CA 91502
FAX (818) 846-3648
www.dvsus.com
(Video Processing Tools)

Electrosonic — (888) 343-3602
(Display and Projection Systems)
www.electrosonic.com

Evertz — (905) 335-3700 / (877) 995-3700
5288 John Lucas Dr.
Burlington, ON L7L 5Z9 Canada
FAX (905) 335-3573
www.evertz.com
(Video Processing Tools)

eyeon Software, Inc. — (416) 686-8411
2181 Queen St. East, Ste. 201
Toronto, ON M4E 1E5 Canada
FAX (416) 698-9315
www.eyeonline.com
(Video Compositing and FX Systems)

Faraday Technology, Ltd. — 44 (0) 1782 661501
Croft Rd. Industrial Estate
Newcastle-Under-Lyme
Staffordshire ST5 0QZ United Kingdom
FAX 44 (0) 1782 630101
www.faradaytech.co.uk
(Delay Lines & Filters)

FOR-A Corporation of America — (714) 894-3311
11125 Knott Ave., Ste. A
Cypress, CA 90630
FAX (714) 894-5399
www.for-a.com
(Video Processing Tools)

Fujinon, Inc. — (973) 633-5600
10 High Point Dr.
Wayne, NJ 07470
FAX (973) 633-5216
www.fujinon.com
(Lenses)

Gyron Systems International, A Division of Wolfe Air Aviation, Ltd. — (866) 487-4643
39 E. Walnut St.
Pasadena, CA 91103
FAX (626) 584-4099
www.gyron.com
(Aerial Equipment)

Iconix (800) 783-1080
418 Chapala St. www.iconixvideo.com
Santa Barbara, CA 93101
(D-Cinema Camera, HDTV Broadcast & Ice Cube and Lipstick Cameras)

Ikegami Electronics (USA), Inc. (201) 368-9171
37 Brook Ave. FAX (201) 569-1626
Maywood, NJ 07607 www.ikegami.com

IMAGICA Corp. of America (310) 277-1790
1840 Century Park East, Ste. 750 FAX (310) 277-1791
Los Angeles, CA 90067 www.imagica-la.com
(Projection Systems)

JVC Professional Products (973) 317-5000
1700 Valley Rd. FAX (973) 317-5030
Wayne, NJ 07470 www.jvc.com/pro
(HD Pro-Camcorders and Systems)

Key Digital Systems (914) 667-9700
521 E. Third St. FAX (914) 668-8666
Mount Vernon, NY 10553 www.keydigital.com
(Video Processing Tools)

 (913) 492-4666
Keywest Technology (800) 331-2019
14563 W. 96th Terrace FAX (913) 322-1864
Lenexa, KS 66215 www.keywesttechnology.com
(Video Processing Tools)

Leader Instruments Corporation (800) 645-5104
6484 Commerce Dr. FAX (714) 527-7490
Cypress, CA 90630 www.leaderusa.com
(Video Monitors and Accessories)

 (800) 372-2447
LSI (866) 574-5741
1621 Barber Ln. www.lsi.com
Milpitas, CA 95035
(Communications Semiconductors)

Maxell Corporation of America (201) 794-5900
22-08 Route 208 FAX (201) 796-8790
Fair Lawn, NJ 07410 www.maxell.com
(Tape Stock)

 (514) 925-3350
Maximum Throughput, Inc. (888) 684-1011
1751 Richardson St., Ste. 5-204 FAX (514) 925-3378
Montreal, QC H3K 1G6 Canada www.max-t.com
(Network-Attached Storage Devices)

MetaFilm Corporation (310) 335-9340
P.O. Box 12555 FAX (310) 410-1143
Marina del Rey, CA 90230 www.metafilmcorp.com
(Recorders & Scanners)

Miller Camera Support, LLC (973) 857-8300
218 Little Falls Rd. FAX (973) 857-8188
Cedar Grove, NJ 07009 www.millertripods.com

Miranda (514) 333-1772
3499 Douglas-B.-Floreani FAX (514) 333-9828
Montreal, QC H4S 2C6 Canada www.miranda.com
(Video Processing Tools)

 (516) 671-7278
Multidyne (800) 488-8378
191 Forest Ave. FAX (516) 671-3362
Locust Valley, NY 11560 www.multidyne.com
(Fiber Optic Transport Products)

NEC (800) 338-9549
395 N. Service Rd., Ste. 407 www.necus.com
Melville, NY 11747
(Display Systems/Monitors)

Nettmann Systems International (818) 623-1661
(Aerial Equipment & Remote Heads) FAX (818) 623-1671
  www.camerasystems.com

Norpak Corporation (613) 592-4164
10 Hearst Way FAX (613) 592-6560
Kanata, ON K2L 2P4 Canada www.norpak.ca
(TV Data Broadcasting Tools)

Panasonic Broadcast & (201) 348-7000
Television Systems Co. (323) 436-3500
One Panasonic Way www.panasonic.com/broadcast
Secaucus, NJ 07094
(Camera Systems & Processing/Storage Tools)

Panasonic Broadcast & (323) 436-3500
Television Systems Co. (323) 436-3615
3330 Cahuenga Blvd. West
Los Angeles, CA 90068 www.panasonic.com/broadcast

Panavision New York (212) 606-0700
150 Varick St., Second Fl. FAX (212) 244-4457
(Near 10th Ave.) www.panavision.com
New York, NY 10013
(Camera Lenses and Systems)

PESA Switching Systems (256) 726-9200
103 Quality Circle, Ste. 210 FAX (256) 726-9271
Huntsville, AL 35806 www.pesa.com
(Routing Switcher Systems)

Pinnacle Systems, Inc. (650) 526-1600
280 N. Bernardo Ave. FAX (650) 526-1601
Mountain View, CA 94043 www.pinnaclesys.com
(Video Editing and FX Systems)

Pixel Power, Inc. (954) 943-2026
1000 W. McNab Rd. FAX (954) 943-2035
Pompano Beach, FL 33069 www.pixelpower.com
(Video Graphics Systems)

PixelTools Corporation (408) 374-5327
10721 Wunderlich Dr. FAX (408) 374-8074
Cupertino, CA 95014 www.pixeltools.com
(Software Encoding and Repair Utilities)

Quantel, Inc. 44 (0) 1635 48 222
Turnpike Rd. FAX 44 (0) 1635 815 815
Newbury, Berkshire RG14 2NX United Kingdom
(Video Editing and FX Systems) www.quantel.com

 (785) 272-3656
QuVIS (800) 554-8116
2921 Wanamaker Dr., Ste. 107 FAX (785) 272-3657
Topeka, KS 66614 www.quvis.com
(Video Processing Tools and Storage)

 (847) 299-8080
Roscor (800) 843-3679
1061 Feehanville Dr. FAX (847) 299-4206
Mount Prospect, IL 60056 www.roscor.com
(Broadcast Facility Systems Design and Integration)

 (605) 339-0100
Sencore (800) 736-2673
3200 Sencore Dr. www.sencore.com
Sioux Falls, SD 57107
(Broadcast Facility Systems & Video Servers)

 (201) 529-8200
Sharp Electronics Corporation (866) 484-7825
Professional Display Division FAX (201) 529-9636
Sharp Plaza, Mail Stop One www.sharpusa.com
Mahwah, NJ 07495
(Display and Projection Tools, Projection Systems & Video Monitors)

Sierra Video Systems (530) 478-1000
P.O. Box 2462 FAX (530) 478-1105
Grass Valley, CA 95945 www.sierravideo.com
(Modular Terminal Equipment & Routing Switchers)

Snell & Wilcox, Inc. (818) 556-2616
3519 Pacific Ave. FAX (818) 556-2626
Burbank, CA 91505 www.snellwilcox.com
(Video Processing Tools)

Sony Electronics Inc.　　　(866) 766-9272
　　　　　　pro.sony.com/bbsc/ssr/home.do

StorCase Technology, Inc.　　(714) 438-1850
　　　　　　　　　　　　　　　(800) 435-0642
17600 Newhope St.　　　FAX (714) 438-1847
Fountain Valley, CA 92708　www.storcase.com
(Data Storage Enclosures)

Stradis　　　　　　　　　(404) 320-0110
1800 Century Blvd. NE, Ste. 1225　FAX (404) 320-3132
Atlanta, GA 30345　　　　www.stradis.com
(MPEG-2 Video Decoders)

Sun Microsystems　　　(650) 960-1300
　　　　　　　　　　　　　　(800) 555-9786
4150 Network Circle　　　www.sun.com
Santa Clara, CA 95054
(Video Servers and Systems)

Teleview　　　　　　　82 70 7018 8900
401 Sehwa Blvd. 355-1, Yatap-dong, Bundang-gu
Seongnam-Si, Kyunggi 463-070 Korea
(Receivers)　　　　　　　www.teleview.co.kr

Teranex　　　　　　　(407) 858-6000
12600 Challenger Pkwy, Ste. 100　FAX (407) 858-6048
Orlando, FL 32826　　　www.teranex.com
(Converters, Noise Reducers & Post Processors)

Thomson Grass Valley　(818) 729-7700
　　　　　　　　　　　　　　(800) 547-8949
2255 N. Ontario St., Ste. 150　FAX (818) 729-7777
Burbank, CA 91504　www.thomsongrassvalley.com
(Cameras & Video Processing Tools)

Tyler Camera Systems　(818) 989-4420
　　　　　　　　　　　　　　(800) 390-6070
14218 Aetna St.　　　FAX (818) 989-0423
Van Nuys, CA 91401　www.tylermount.com
(Gyro-Stabilized Helicopter Camera Mounts)

Utah Scientific　　　　(801) 575-8801
4750 Wiley Post Way, Ste. 150　FAX (801) 537-3099
Salt Lake City, UT 84116　www.utsci.com
(Switchers)

Videotek　　　　　　　(800) 231-9673
(Video Processing Tools)　www.videotek.com

Visual Matrix Corporation　(818) 843-4831
P.O. Box 11028　　　FAX (818) 843-6544
Burbank, CA 91504　www.visual-matrix.com
(Converters)

Weather Central, Inc.　(608) 274-5789
401 Charmany Dr., Ste. 200　FAX (608) 278-2746
Madison, WI 53719　www.weathercentral.tv
(Weather Graphics Systems)

HD Equipment Manufacturers

HD Post Houses

903Films   **(212) 674-0986**
515 Greenwich St., Ste. 202   FAX **(212) 380-1258**
New York, NY 10013   **www.903films.com**

Air Sea Land Productions, Inc.   **(718) 626-2646**
   (888) 275-5367
19-69 Steinway St. (Near 20th Ave.)   FAX **(718) 626-1493**
Astoria, NY 11105   **www.airsealand.com**
(Captions, Color Correction, Computer Graphics, Non-Linear Offline and Online & Subtitles)

Area 4   **(212) 444-1171**
Tribeca Film Center   **www.area4.tv**
375 Greenwich St.
New York, NY 10013
(Captions, Compositing, Computer Graphics, Duplication, File Transfers & Non-Linear Offline and Online)

Ascent Media Management East   **(201) 767-3800**
235 Pegasus Ave.   FAX **(201) 784-2769**
(Near Livingston St.)   **www.ascentmedia.com**
Northvale, NJ 07647
(Color Correction, Compositing, Down/Upconversions, Film to HD/Telecine, Linear and Non-Linear Online & Titling/Character Generation)

Atomic Image   **(212) 255-6625**
311 Broadway, PH B   FAX **(212) 627-8632**
(Near Cornelia St.)   **www.atomicimage.com**
New York, NY 10007
(Compositing, Color Correction, Computer Graphics, Non-Linear Online & Titling/Character Generation)

Beyond Our Reality   **(212) 255-5432**
Productions, Inc.   **(800) 583-5015**
49 W. 24th St., Seventh Fl.   FAX **(212) 255-6866**
(Near Broadway)   **www.beyondourreality.com**
New York, NY 10010
(Color Correction, Non-Linear Offline and Online & Tape to Tape Color Correction)

Bionic   **(212) 997-9100**
1375 Broadway, Seventh Fl.   FAX **(212) 997-0990**
New York, NY 10018   **www.bionic.tv**
(Online)

Buzz, Inc.   **(212) 302-2899**
28 W. 44th St., 22nd Fl.   FAX **(212) 302-9844**
New York, NY 10036   **www.buzzny.com**
(Color Correction, Compositing, Computer Graphics, Downconversions, Duplication, File Transfers, Non-Linear Online, Titling/Character Generation & Upconversions)

Charlex, Inc.   **(212) 719-4600**
Two W. 45th St., Seventh Fl.   FAX **(212) 840-2747**
(Near Fifth Ave.)   **www.charlex.com**
New York, NY 10036
(Compositing, Computer Graphics & Non-Linear Online)

Chelsea Post   **(212) 727-1234**
221 W. 26th St. (Near Eighth Ave.)   FAX **(212) 255-6644**
New York, NY 10001   **www.amvchelsea.com**
(Color Correction, Compositing, Down/Upconversions, File Transfers, Linear and Non-Linear Online & Titling/Character Generation)

City Lights Post   **(212) 679-4400**
Six E. 39th St., Second Fl.   FAX **(212) 679-4482**
(Near Fifth Ave.)   **www.citylightsmedia.com**
New York, NY 10016
(Color Correction, Computer Graphics & Non-Linear Offline and Online)
Contacts: Aaron Behr, Danny Fisher & Jack Fisher

Colossalvision   **(212) 269-6333**
26 Broadway   FAX **(212) 269-4334**
(Near Merchant Marines Plaza)   **www.colossalvision.com**
New York, NY 10004
(Color Correction, Compositing, Computer Graphics, Down/Upconversions, File Transfers, Film to HD/Telecine and Datacine, HD to Film Transfers, Linear and Non-Linear Online & Titling/Character Generation)

Company 3 NY   **(212) 687-4000**
535 Fifth Ave., Fifth Fl.   FAX **(212) 687-2719**
New York, NY 10017   **www.company3.com**
(Color Correction, Compositing, Down/Upconversions, File Transfers, Film to HD/Telecine and Datacine & Linear and Non-Linear Online)

Creative Bubble, LLC   **(212) 201-4200**
79 Fifth Ave., 14th Fl. (Near 15th St.)   FAX **(212) 201-4210**
New York, NY 10003   **www.creativebubble.com**
(Computer Graphics, Non-Linear Offline and Online & Tape to Tape Color Correction)

Creative Group, Inc.   **(212) 935-0145**
1601 Broadway, 10th Fl.   FAX **(212) 838-0853**
(Near W. 48th St.)   **www.creativegroup.tv**
New York, NY 10019
(Color Correction, Compositing, Computer Graphics, Down/Upconversions, File Transfers, Linear and Non-Linear Online & Titling/Character Generation)

Deluxe New York   **(212) 444-5600**
435 Hudson St., Ninth Fl.   **www.bydeluxe.com**
New York, NY 10014

Designomotion   **(917) 532-0738**
67 E. 11th St., Ste. 324   **www.designomotion.com**
(Near Broadway)
New York, NY 10003

Devlin Video Intl.   **(212) 391-1313**
1501 Broadway, Ste. 408   FAX **(212) 391-2744**
(Near W. 43rd St.)   **www.devlinvideo.com**
New York, NY 10036
(Captions, Color Correction, Downconversions, Duplication, Motion Graphics, Non-Linear Offline, Non-Linear Online, Standards Conversions, Subtitles & Upconversions)

Digital Arts   **(212) 460-9600**
130 W. 29th St., Eighth Fl.   FAX **(212) 660-3600**
(Near Sixth Ave.)   **www.digital-arts.net**
New York, NY 10001
(Captions, Color Correction, Compositing, Computer Graphics, Down/Upconversions, Duplication, File Transfers, Non-Linear Online & Titling/Character Generation)

    (212) 687-0111
DJM Post Production   **(212) 687-0404**
Four E. 46th St. (Near Fifth Ave.)   FAX **(212) 949-8083**
New York, NY 10017   **www.djmpost.com**
(Captions, Color Correction & Linear/Non-Linear Offline and Online)

Du Art Film and Video   **(212) 757-4580**
245 W. 55th St. (Near Broadway)   FAX **(212) 333-7647**
New York, NY 10019   **www.duart.com**
(Color Correction, Compositing, Computer Graphics, Down/Upconversions, File Transfers, Film to HD/Telecine and Datacine, HD to Film Transfers, Non-Linear Online & Titling/Character Generation)

Film/Video Arts, Inc.   **(212) 222-1770**
270 W. 96th St.   **www.fva.com**
New York, NY 10025
(Linear/Non-Linear Offline and Online & Subtitles)

Framerunner, Inc.   **(212) 246-4224**
555 W. 57th St., 17th Fl.   FAX **(212) 246-4225**
(Near 11th Ave.)   **www.framerunner.com**
New York, NY 10019
(Color Correction, Computer Graphics, Non-Linear Offline and Online, Standards Conversions & Subtitles)

Goldcrest Post Production   **(212) 243-4700**
799 Washington St. (Near Horatio St.)   FAX **(212) 624-1701**
New York, NY 10014   **www.goldcrestpost.com**
(Compositing & Computer Graphics)

GRS Systems, Inc.   **(212) 286-0299**
216 E. 45th St.   FAX **(212) 286-9475**
New York, NY 10017   **www.grsv.com**

GTV, Inc.   **(212) 262-6260**
1697 Broadway, Ste. 404   FAX **(212) 262-4709**
(Near W. 53rd St.)   **www.gtvnyc.com**
New York, NY 10019
(Color Correction, Compositing, Computer Graphics, Down/Upconversions, Non-Linear Online & Titling/Character Generation)

Guardian Entertainment, LTD   **(212) 727-4729**
71 Fifth Ave., Fifth Fl. (Near 15th St.)   FAX **(212) 727-4737**
New York, NY 10003   **www.guardianltd.com**
(Color Correction, Compositing, Linear Online, Non-Linear Offline and Online, Standards Conversion, Subtitles, Tape to Film Transfers & Tape to Tape Correction)

HBO Studio Productions   **(212) 512-7800**
120A E. 23rd St. (Near Park Ave.)   FAX **(212) 512-7788**
New York, NY 10010
(Color Correction, Compositing, Down/Upconversions, File Transfers, Film to HD/Telecine and Datacine & Non-Linear Online)

Hello World Communications   **(212) 243-8800**
118 W. 22nd St., Ste. 2A   FAX **(212) 691-6961**
(Near Sixth Ave.)   **www.hwc.tv**
New York, NY 10011
(Color Correction, Compositing, Computer Graphics, Duplication, Linear/Non-Linear Offline and Online, Standards Conversion & Subtitles)
Contacts: Peter Walsh & Ron Yoshida

International Duplication Centre/
International Digital Centre, Inc.   **(212) 581-3940**
216 E. 45th St., Seventh Fl.   FAX **(212) 581-3979**
(Near Third Ave.)   **www.idcdigital.com**
New York, NY 10017

LA Digital Post, Inc.   **(212) 981-8500**
220 W. 42nd St., 17th Fl.   FAX **(212) 981-8595**
New York, NY 10036   **www.ladigital.com**
(Compositing, Duplication, HD/SD Finishing, Offline, Standards Conversions & Titling)

Magno Sound & Video   **(212) 302-2505**
729 Seventh Ave. (Near W. 48th St.)   FAX **(212) 819-1282**
New York, NY 10019   **www.magnosoundandvideo.com**
(Down/Upconversions, File Transfers & Non-Linear Online)

Method   **(212) 907-1200**
545 Fifth Ave., Second Fl.   FAX **(212) 907-1201**
(Near 45th St.)   **www.methodstudios.com**
New York, NY 10017
(Color Correction, Compositing, Computer Graphics, Down/Upconversions, File Transfers, Non-Linear Online & Titling/Character Generation)

The Mill, New York   **(212) 337-3210**
451 Broadway, Sixth Fl.   FAX **(212) 337-3259**
(Near Canal St.)   **www.the-mill.com**
New York, NY 10013
(Captions, Color Correction, Computer Graphics, Duplication, Film Scanning and Recording, Non-Linear Online, Standards Conversion, Tape to Tape Color Correction & Telecine)

    (973) 300-9477
Mirage Productions Inc.   **(888) 746-6869**
111 Spring St.   FAX **(973) 300-9467**
Newton, NJ 07860   **www.mirageproductions.com**
(Film to HD/Telecine & HD to Film Transfers)

Moving Images   **(212) 953-6999**
227 E. 45th St., Sixth Fl.   **www.mipost.com**
(Near Second Ave.)
New York, NY 10017
(Color Correction, Compositing, Computer Graphics, Down/Upconversions, File Transfers, Film to HD/Datacine, Film to HD/Telecine, Non-Linear Online & Titling/Character Generation)

    (212) 924-7364
Moving Pictures   **(212) 450-7933**
222 E. 44th St., Eighth Fl.   **www.mpny.tv**
New York, NY 10017

Next Millennium Productions, Ltd. (917) 237-1661
31 Howard St., Ste. 5A FAX **(917) 237-1663**
New York, NY 10013 **www.nmpfilms.com**
(Color Correction, Compositing, Downconversions & Non-Linear Offline and Online)

NFL Films (856) 222-5675
  (877) 222-3517
One NFL Plaza FAX **(856) 866-4848**
Mount Laurel, NJ 08054 **www.nflfilms.com**
(Digital Component Online, Film to Tape Transfers, Linear/Non-Linear Offline and Online & Standards Conversion)

Nice Shoes (212) 683-1704
352 Park Ave. South, 16th Fl. FAX **(212) 683-9233**
(Near E. 25th St.) **www.niceshoes.com**
New York, NY 10010
(Color Correction, Compositing, Computer Graphics, Down/Upconversions, File Transfers, Film to HD/Telecine and Datacine, HD to Film Transfers, Non-Linear Online & Titling/Character Generation)

Northern Lights Post (212) 274-1199
135 W. 27th St., Eighth Fl. FAX **(212) 274-1117**
(Near Sixth Ave.) **www.nlpedit.com**
New York, NY 10001
(Color Correction, Compositing, Computer Graphics, Down/Upconversions, File Transfers, Linear and Non-Linear Online & Titling/Character Generation)

Onshore Media (646) 536-3494
  (310) 691-8666
  www.onshoredigital.com
(Color Correction, Down/Upconversions, File Transfers, Linear and Non-Linear Online & Titling/Character Generation)

Park Avenue Post, Inc. (212) 689-7678
419 Park Ave. South, Ste. 600 FAX **(212) 689-7544**
(Near 29th St.) **www.parkavenuepost.com**
New York, NY 10016
(Color Correction, Compositing, Downconversions, File Transfers & Linear and Non-Linear Online)

Picture Island (646) 638-0895
33 Jones St., Ste. 3 FAX **(646) 202-2895**
(Near Bleecker St.) **www.pictureisland.com**
New York, NY 10014

Post Logic Studios (212) 520-3150
435 Hudson St., Seventh Fl. FAX **(212) 520-3155**
(Near Morton) **www.postlogic.com**
New York, NY 10014
(Color Correction, Down/Upconversions & HD to Film Transfers)

PostWorks (212) 894-4000
  (212) 894-4050
100 Avenue of the Americas FAX **(212) 941-0439**
(Near Grand St.) **www.postworks.com**
New York, NY 10013
(Color Correction, Compositing, Computer Graphics, Digital Intermediate Services, Down/Upconversions, File Transfers, Film to HD/Telecine and Datacine, HD to Film Transfers, Linear and Non-Linear Online, Quality Control & Titling/Character Generation)

Rogue Post NYC (212) 366-5011
  (917) 817-1673
18 W. 21st St., Tenth Fl. **www.roguepost.com**
New York, NY 10010
(Color Correction, Down/Upconversions, File Transfers & Linear/Non-Linear Online)

Shooters Post & Transfer (215) 861-0100
The Curtis Center, Ste. 1050 FAX **(215) 861-0099**
Independence Square West **www.shootersinc.com**
Philadelphia, PA 19106
(Color Correction, Compositing, Computer Graphics, Downconversions, File Transfers, Film to HD/Datacine, Non-Linear Online, Tape to Tape Correction, Titling/Character Generation & Upconversions)

Singularity communications (212) 481-3558
40 W. 27th St., Second Fl. **www.singularitycorp.com**
(Near Sixth Ave.)
New York, NY 10001
(Non-Linear Online)

Solar Film/Video Productions (212) 473-3040
632 Broadway, Ste. 304 FAX **(212) 473-3091**
(Near Houston St.) **www.solarnyc.com**
New York, NY 10012
(Color Correction, Compositing, Computer Graphics, Down/Upconversions, File Transfers, Linear and Non-Linear Online & Titling/Character Generation)

Sonalysts' Studios (800) 526-8091
215 Parkway North FAX **(860) 326-3748**
Waterford, CT 06385 **www.sonalystsmedia.com**
Contact: Fred Litty

Studio 57 (631) 650-0057
  (631) 766-0777
140 Hoffman Ln. (Near Space Court) FAX **(631) 650-0010**
Islandia, NY 11749 **www.studio57online.com**
(Color Correction, Compositing, Downconversions, Non-Linear Online & Titling/Character Generation)

Technicolor Creative Services - N.Y. (212) 609-9400
110 Leroy St. (Near Hudson St.) FAX **(212) 609-9450**
New York, NY 10014 **www.technicolor.com**
(Color Correction, Compositing, Down/Upconversions, File Transfers, Film to HD/Telecine and Datacine, HD to Film Transfers (Film Out), Non-Linear Online & Titling/Character Generation)

USA Studios (212) 398-6400
  (800) 872-3821
29 W. 38th St. (Near Fifth Ave.) FAX **(212) 398-4145**
New York, NY 10018 **www.usastudios.tv**

HD Screening Rooms

Goldcrest Post Production (212) 243-4700
799 Washington St. (Near Horatio St.) FAX **(212) 624-1701**
New York, NY 10014 **www.goldcrestpost.com**

Magno Sound & Video (212) 302-2505
729 Seventh Ave. (Near W. 48th St.) FAX **(212) 819-1282**
New York, NY 10019 **www.magnosoundandvideo.com**

Mark Forman Productions Corp. (212) 633-9960
300 W. 23rd St., Ste. 14A/B FAX **(212) 807-0121**
(Near Eighth Ave.) **www.screeningroom.com**
New York, NY 10011

(212) 894-4000
PostWorks (212) 894-4050
100 Avenue of the Americas FAX **(212) 941-0439**
(Near Grand St.) **www.postworks.com**
New York, NY 10013

Steiner Studios (718) 858-1600
15 Washington Ave. FAX **(718) 858-1690**
Brooklyn Navy Yard, NY 11205 **www.steinerstudios.com**

Technicolor Creative Services - N.Y. (212) 609-9400
110 Leroy St. (Near Hudson St.) FAX **(212) 609-9450**
New York, NY 10014 **www.technicolor.com**

Tribeca Cinemas (212) 941-2001
54 Varick St. (Near Beach St.) FAX **(212) 941-2012**
New York, NY 10013 **www.tribecacinemas.com**

Tribeca Screening Room (212) 941-2000
375 Greenwich St. (Near Franklin St.) FAX **(212) 941-2012**
New York, NY 10013 **www.tribecafilm.com**

Walt Disney Co./
Park Avenue Screening Room (212) 735-5348
500 Park Ave. **www.buenavistapost.com**
(Near E. 59th St.)
New York, NY 10022

HD Stock Footage

Action Footage/   (303) 253-6300
Warren Miller Entertainment   (800) 729-3456
5720 Flatiron Pkwy   www.wmefootage.com
Boulder, CO 80301
(Extreme/Adventure Sports)

     (310) 459-2526
Action Sports/Scott Dittrich Films   (212) 681-6565
P.O. Box 301   FAX (310) 456-1743
Malibu, CA 90265   www.sdfilms.com
(Animals, Nature, People & Sports)

     (718) 626-2646
Air Sea Land Productions, Inc.   (888) 275-5367
19-69 Steinway St. (Near 20th Ave.)   FAX (718) 626-1493
Astoria, NY 11105   www.airsealand.com
(Aerials, Animals, Cityscapes, Landscapes, Mountains, Nature, Scenics, Seasons, Trains & Underwater)

     (310) 317-9996
All-Stock   (800) 323-0079
P.O. Box 1705   www.all-stock.com
Pacific Palisades, CA 90272
(Animals, Nature, People & Sports)

America by Air   (386) 663-4567
Stock Footage Library   (800) 488-6359
154 Euclid Blvd.   FAX (413) 235-1462
Lantana, FL 33462   www.hdfootage.com
(Aerials, Contemporary & International)

Animation Entertainment   (858) 793-1900
3830 Valley Center Dr., Ste. 705-833   FAX (858) 793-1942
San Diego, CA 92130   www.animationtrip.com/licensing
(Computer Animation)

     (541) 863-4429
Artbeats   (800) 444-9392
1405 N. Myrtle Rd.   FAX (541) 863-4547
Myrtle Creek, OR 97457   www.artbeats.com
(Aerials, Backgrounds, Effects, Establishments, Lifestyles, Nature & Reference)

     (818) 299-9712
BBC Motion Gallery, Los Angeles   (800) 966-5424
4144 Lankershim Blvd., Ste. 200   FAX (818) 299-9763
North Hollywood, CA 91602   www.bbcmotiongallery.com

BBC Motion Gallery, New York   (212) 705-9399
747 Third Ave. (Near E. 46th St.)   FAX (212) 705-9342
New York, NY 10017   www.bbcmotiongallery.com

BBC Motion Gallery, Toronto   (416) 362-3223
130 Spadina Ave., Ste. 401   FAX (416) 362-3553
Toronto, ON M5V 2L4 Canada
     www.bbcmotiongallery.com

     (323) 436-7070
BlackLight Films   (323) 436-2229
3371 Cahuenga Blvd. West   FAX (323) 436-2230
Hollywood, CA 90068   www.blacklightfilms.com

Blue Sky Stock Footage/   (310) 305-8384
Bill Mitchell   (877) 992-5477
(All Subjects)   FAX (310) 305-8985
     www.blueskyfootage.com

     (323) 660-0187
Budget Films, Inc.   (323) 660-0800
4427 Santa Monica Blvd.   FAX (323) 660-5571
Los Angeles, CA 90029   www.budgetfilms.com
(Beauty, Clouds, Deserts, Fireworks, Moons, National Parks, Nature & Sunsets)

Camera One   (206) 523-3456
8523 15th Ave. NE   FAX (206) 523-3668
Seattle, WA 98115   www.cameraone.us
(Aerials, Archeology, Caribbean, Cities, Clouds, Eclipses, Europe, Landscapes, Lightning, Moons, National Parks, Nature, Northwest, Outdoor Sports, Scenics, Southwest, Storms, Sunrises and Sunsets, Time-Lapse (Natural and Traffic/Urban), Underwater, Whitewater & Wildlife)

CelebrityFootage   (310) 360-9600
320 S. Almont Dr.   FAX (310) 360-9696
Beverly Hills, CA 90211   www.celebrityfootage.com
(Celebrities, Entertainment, Events, Hollywood, Movie Premieres & People)

Collegiate Images   (954) 343-8000
(College Sports)   FAX (954) 343-8001
     www.collegiateimages.com

     (919) 828-4086
The Communications Group, Inc.   (888) 479-3456
P.O. Box 50157   FAX (919) 832-7797
Raleigh, NC 27650   www.cgfilm.com
(Aerials, Boston, North Carolina Cities, Farms and Landscapes & The Big Dig)

     (212) 375-7622
Corbis Motion   (866) 473-5264
902 Broadway (Near E. 20th St.)   FAX (212) 375-7700
New York, NY 10010   www.corbismotion.com
(Scenics, Sports & Wildlife)

DV/HDcuts   (310) 497-5636
     FAX (505) 438-0924
     www.dvcuts.com
(Airplanes, Americana, Cityscapes, Clouds, Deserts, Driving Shots, Experimental, Highways, Historical Landmarks, International People and Scenery, Landscapes, Lightning, Mountains, Nature, Oceans, Rivers, Seasons, Stars/Comets/Planets, Storms, Suns and Moon, Time-Lapse, Traffic, Trains, Transportation & Underwater)

     (818) 905-1071
Fish Films Footage World   (800) 442-0550
4548 Van Noord Ave.   FAX (818) 905-0301
Studio City, CA 91604   www.footageworld.com
(All Categories, Aerials, Alaska, Animals, Cities, Nature, Time-Lapse, Weather & Wildlife)

The Footage Store   (818) 556-6080
2121 Scott Rd., Ste. 201   FAX (818) 556-6080
Burbank, CA 91504   www.footagestore.com
(Beauty, Nature, Scenics, Time Lapse & Wildlife)

     (310) 402-4626
Framepool Inc.   (800) 331-1314
10905 Ohio Ave., Ste. 116   FAX (866) 928-6637
Los Angeles, CA 90024   www.framepool.com
(Aerials, Agriculture, Animals, Architecture, Cityscapes, Clouds, Contemporary, Cultures, Deserts, Flowers, Forests, International People and Scenery, Landscapes, Lightning, Lifestyles, Mountains, Nature, Rivers, Skies, Space, Sports, Suns and Moons, Technology, Time-Lapse & Wildlife)

     (646) 982-5120
Framepool Inc.   (800) 331-1314
32 Avenue of the Americas, 25th Fl.   FAX (866) 928-6637
New York, NY 10013   www.framepool.com
(Aerials, Agriculture, Animals, Architecture, Cityscapes, Clouds, Contemporary, Cultures, Deserts, Flowers, Forests, International People and Scenery, Landscapes, Lightning, Lifestyles, Mountains, Nature, Rivers, Skies, Space, Sports, Suns and Moons, Technology, Time-Lapse & Wildlife)

Getty Images   (800) 462-4379
One Hudson Square   www.gettyimages.com
75 Varick St., Fifth Fl. (Near Grand St.)
New York, NY 10013
(All Subjects)

Global ImageWorks, LLC   (201) 384-7715
65 Beacon St.   FAX (201) 501-8971
Haworth, NJ 07641   www.globalimageworks.com
(All Subjects)

Greg Hensley Productions   (970) 984-3158
200 South E. St., Ste. 113   www.greghensley.com
New Castle, CO 81647
(Avalanches, Cities, Clouds, Comets, Eclipses, Fireworks, Flowers, Lightning, Moons, Mountain Sports, Oceans, People, Plants, Rivers, Seasons, Storms, Sunrises, Sunsets, Trees, US Parks & Wildlife)

The Hollywood Film Registry   (310) 456-8184
5473 Santa Monica Blvd., Ste. 408   FAX (323) 957-2159
Los Angeles, CA 90029
(All Subjects)

    (805) 965-9848
Home Planet Productions   (818) 422-4144
    FAX (805) 965-2329
    www.homeplanetproductions.com

Howard Hall Productions   (858) 259-8989
2171 La Amatista Rd.   FAX (858) 792-1467
Del Mar, CA 92014   www.howardhall.com
(Aerials, Animals, Clouds, Landscapes, Mountains, Nature, Oceans, Skies, Suns and Moons, Time-Lapse, Underwater & Wildlife)

Image Bank Films and   (646) 613-4600
Archive Films by Getty Images   (800) 462-4379
One Hudson Square   FAX (646) 613-4501
75 Varick St., Fifth Fl.   www.gettyimages.com
(Near Fifth Ave.)
New York, NY 10013
(Business, Destinations, Nature, People, Space, Sports & Wildlife)

Inter Video   (818) 843-3624
    www.intervideo24.com
(Aviation, Computer Graphics, Medical, News, Space, Sports, Travel & Weather)

    (202) 857-5868
National Geographic Digital Motion   (877) 730-2022
    FAX (202) 429-5755
    www.ngdigitalmotion.com
(Archeology, Architecture, Ceremonies, Cities, Landmarks, Natural Disasters, Natural History, People, Wildlife & World Scenes)

Nature Footage/Ocean Footage   (831) 375-2413
300 Foam St.   FAX (831) 621-9559
Monterey, CA 93940   www.naturefootage.com

    (619) 644-3000
New & Unique Videos   (800) 365-8433
7323 Rondel Court   FAX (619) 644-3001
San Diego, CA 92119   www.newuniquevideos.com
(Aerials, Animals, Archival Film, Beaches and Sunsets, Bloopers, Cities, Contemporary, Corporate/Industrial, Current Events, International, Lifestyles, Medical, Military, People, Scenics, Sports, Travel and Locations, Technological, Underwater & Wildlife)

    (201) 750-5860
NHL Hockey Archive   (201) 750-5800
(NHL Hockey 1920s–Present)   FAX (201) 750-5850

    (415) 558-8112
Oddball Film + Video   (415) 558-8122
275 Capp St.   FAX (415) 558-8116
San Francisco, CA 94110   www.oddballfilm.com
(Americana, International, Nature, Timelapse & Wildlife)

    (818) 752-9097
Producers Library   (800) 944-2135
10832 Chandler Blvd.   FAX (818) 752-9196
North Hollywood, CA 91601   www.producerslibrary.com
(Cities)

Reel Orange   (949) 548-4524
316 La Jolla Dr.   www.reelorange.com
Newport Beach, CA 92663
(Aerials, Environmental & Grand Canyon)

Silverman Stock Footage   (917) 470-9104
210 Douglass St.   www.silvermanstockfootage.com
Brooklyn, NY 11217
(Aerials, Airplanes, Americana, Animals, Architecture, Archival, Cityscapes, Clouds, Contemporary, Cultures, Deserts, Extreme Sports, Flowers, International People, Landscapes, Lifestyles, Nature, Oceans, Scenics, Space, Storms, Suns and Moons, Time-Lapse, Traffic & Underwater)

    (310) 785-9100
Sports Cinematography Group   (212) 744-5333
73 Market St.   FAX (310) 564-7500
Venice, CA 90291   www.sportscinematographygroup.com
(All Sports Subjects: Extreme Sports, Mountain Sports, Stadium Sports & Water Sports)

StormStock   (817) 276-9500
P.O. Box 122020   FAX (817) 795-1132
Arlington, TX 76012   www.stormstock.com
(Blizzards, Beaches, Caribbean, Clouds, Disasters, Environmental, Fires, Flash Floods, Hail, Hurricane Katrina, Hurricanes, Landscapes, Lightning, Microbursts, Natural Disasters, Natural History, Nature, Oceans, Radar, Science, Seasons, Skies, Storm Clouds, Storms, Sunrises, Sunsets, Time-Lapse, Tornadoes, Traffic & Waves)

    (646) 495-6123
Thought Equity Motion   (866) 815-6599
770 Broadway, Ste. 236   FAX (646) 495-6046
New York, NY 10003   www.thoughtequity.com

Universal Studios -
Stock Footage Library   (818) 777-1695
100 Universal Plaza   FAX (818) 866-0763
Bldg. 2313A, Lower Level
Universal City, CA 91608
(Selected Subjects)   www.universalstudios.com/studio

    (310) 235-7621
US Army Office of Public Affairs   (310) 235-7622
10880 Wilshire Blvd., Ste. 1250   FAX (310) 235-6075
Los Angeles, CA 90024
(US Army)   www.defenselink.mil/faq/pis/PC12FILM.html

Video Tape Library, Inc./VTL   (323) 656-4330
1509 N. Crescent Heights Blvd., Ste. 2   FAX (323) 656-8746
Los Angeles, CA 90046   www.videotapelibrary.com
(Aerials, Americana, Animals, Archival, Bloopers, Cities, Cultures, Extreme and Recreational Sports, Historical, Landmarks, Landscapes, Lifestyles, News, People, Professionals, Time-Lapse, Travel Locations & Underwater)

Wings Wildlife Production, Inc.   (949) 830-7845
Two McLaren, Ste. A   FAX (949) 830-5116
Irvine, CA 92618   www.wildlifelibrary.com
(African and North American Wildlife)

Wish You Were Here
Film & Video, Inc.   (818) 371-9649
    www.wywhstock.com
(Aerials, Destinations, Landmarks, Scenics, Time-Lapse & Wildlife)

WTTW Digital Archives   (773) 509-5412
5400 N. St. Louis Ave.   FAX (773) 509-5307
Chicago, IL 60625   www.wttwdigitalarchives.com
(Cityscapes, Flowers, Music Performance/Concerts, National Parks, Rural, Scenics, Trains, Tsunami Disaster and Relief, U.S. Landmarks & U.S. Troops/Iraq)

HD Tape Stock

Ametron Audio Video
1546 N. Argyle Ave.
Hollywood, CA 90028
(323) 466-4321
(323) 464-1144
FAX (323) 871-0127
www.ametron.com

B&H Photo Video Pro Audio
420 Ninth Ave. (Near W. 34th St.)
New York, NY 10001
(212) 444-5085
(212) 239-7760
FAX (212) 239-7766
www.bhphotovideo.com

Broadcast Store
9420 Lurline Ave., Ste. C
Chatsworth, CA 91311
(818) 998-9100
FAX (818) 998-9106
www.broadcaststore.com

Carpel Video
429 E. Patrick St.
Frederick, MD 21701
(800) 238-4300
FAX (301) 694-9510
www.carpelvideo.com

Edgewise Media Services, Inc.
1215 N. Highland Ave.
Hollywood, CA 90038
(323) 769-0900
(800) 824-3130
FAX (323) 466-6815
www.edgewise-media.com

Edgewise Media Services, Inc.
917 E. Katella Ave.
Anaheim, CA 92805
(714) 919-2020
(800) 444-9330
FAX (714) 919-2010
www.edgewise-media.com

Edgewise Media Services, Inc.
630 Ninth Ave. (Near 44th St.)
New York, NY 10036
(212) 977-9330
(800) 444-9330
FAX (212) 977-9644
www.edgewise-media.com

Empress Media, Inc.
306 W. 38th St., Ninth Fl.
(Near Eighth Ave.)
New York, NY 10018
(212) 643-4898
(888) 683-6773
FAX (212) 643-4894
www.empressintel.com

EVS/Express Video Supply, Inc.
(818) 552-4590
(800) 238-8480
FAX (818) 552-4591
www.evsonline.com

Film Emporium
Sunset Gower Studios
1438 N. Gower St., Bldg. 35, Box 72
Hollywood, CA 90028
(323) 464-5144
(866) 611-3456
FAX (323) 464-7348
www.filmemporium.com

Film Emporium
274 Madison Ave., Ste. 404
(Near E. 40th St.)
New York, NY 10016
(212) 683-2433
(800) 371-2555
FAX (212) 683-2740
www.filmemporium.com

Film Source LA
(818) 484-3236
FAX (818) 688-0101
www.filmsourcela.com

Fujifilm USA, Inc.
Motion Picture Divison
(888) 424-3854
FAX (323) 465-8279
www.fujifilmusa.com

Global Media Resources, Inc.
(818) 508-6760
(805) 967-1879
FAX (818) 508-6710
www.globalmediaresource.com

Media Distributors
645 W. 27th St. (Near 12th Ave.)
New York, NY 10001
(212) 375-1800
(877) 827-7862
FAX (212) 564-5540
www.mediadistributors.com

Moviola Digitial
545 W. 45th St. (Near 11th Ave.)
New York, NY 10036
(212) 581-7111
(800) 327-3724
FAX (212) 265-9820
www.moviola.com

MSE Media Solutions
6013 Scott Way
Los Angeles, CA 90040
(323) 721-1656
(800) 626-1955
FAX (323) 721-1506
www.msemedia.com

Professional-Tapesonline
P.O. Box 927
Hightstown, NJ 08520
(888) 359-8273
(609) 443-4779
FAX (609) 443-3395
www.professional-tapesonline.com

ProMediaSupplies.com
6812 Renwick Court
Greensboro, NC 27410
(336) 664-1004
FAX (336) 605-3212
www.promediasupplies.com

The Tape Company
(800) 851-3113
www.thetapecompany.com

TapeOnline.com
(877) 893-8273
(615) 263-1838
FAX (615) 263-1411
www.tapeonline.com

TapeStockOnline.com
(888) 322-8273
(310) 352-4230
FAX (310) 352-4233
www.tapestockonline.com

Videotape Products, Inc.
2721 W. Magnolia Blvd.
Burbank, CA 91505
(818) 566-9898
(800) 422-2444
FAX (818) 566-8989
www.myvtp.com

Westside Media Group
12233 W. Olympic Blvd., Ste. 152
Los Angeles, CA 90064
(310) 979-3500
www.westsidemediagroup.com

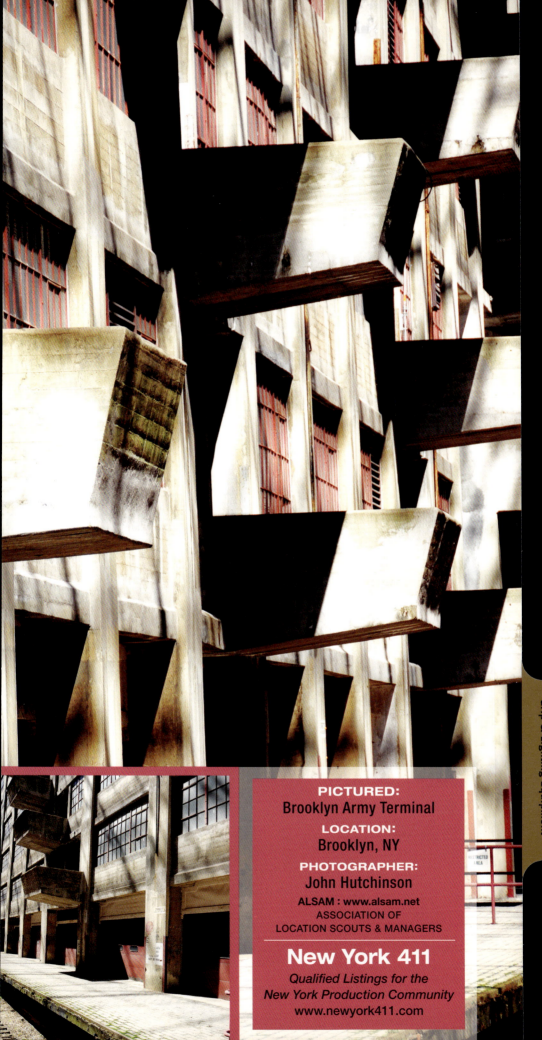

PICTURED:
Brooklyn Army Terminal

LOCATION:
Brooklyn, NY

PHOTOGRAPHER:
John Hutchinson

ALSAM : www.alsam.net
ASSOCIATION OF
LOCATION SCOUTS & MANAGERS

New York 411

*Qualified Listings for the
New York Production Community*
www.newyork411.com

Grip & Lighting Equipment

GENERATORS
CAMERA CARS
LIGHTING & GRIP
EQUIPMENT TRUCKS

Full Line of Tungsten & HMI Lighting

Specialty Lighting Including:

Aurasofts
Super Troopers
Square Wave/Flicker Free HMI's
Kino Flotm Flicker Free Fluorescents
Xenotech BriteLitetm Xenon Arc Lites
Camera Cars & Cranes

Grip & Lighting Equipment

LOCATED AT:
Silvercup Studios East
34-02 STARR AVENUE, LONG ISLAND CITY, NY 11101
718-906-3000 FAX: 718-906-3042

Ⓐ ADVERTISER SYMBOL

Refer to the General Index for
cross-referencing items in this section.

Booms, Cranes & Camera Support........ 296
Climate Control Systems................ 302
Construction & Yard Equipment Rentals.... 303
Grip & Lighting Expendables............. 304
Grip Equipment 306
Hoisting & Lift Equipment/Cherry Pickers... 308
Lighting Equipment & Generators......... 311
Production Equipment & Accessories...... 318
Trucks & Vans........................ 319

Kits
AND EXPENDABLES

WE'VE MOVED

43-77 9th Street
Long Island City, NY 11101

ph: 212•947•0700
718•482•1824

fax: 212•563•2310
718•482•1853

kitsandexpendables.com

NEW YORK   NEW JERSEY   BALTIMORE

FEATURE SYSTEMS INC.
FILM EQUIPMENT RENTAL

ph 212•736•0447
201•531•2299
fax 212•465•1987
201•531•2290

**We've Moved!
223 Veterans Blvd
Carlstadt, NJ 07072**

featuresystems.com

Kitstrucks
EXPENDABLES ON LOCATION

a full service expendables shop
parked on your job

ph 201•531•9700
cell 917•921•4751
fax 201•531•9701

155 Anderson Avenue,
Moonachie, NJ 07074

kitstrucks.com

Booms, Cranes & Camera Support

ACS/Aerial Camera Support (917) 470-9092
(203) 380-9942
www.jibrentals.com
Cranes: Jimmy Jib, Mini-Jib & Triangle
Dollies: Chapman Super PeeWee & Custom Sled
Accessories: Lightweight Aluminum and Steel Dolly Track & Remote Heads

Action Camera Cars, Inc. (212) 425-4840
(646) 529-2585
www.actioncameracars.com
Cranes: Matthews MC-88 with Remote Stabilized Head and Mark III Ride-on & Techno 15' and 30'
Accessories: Car Rigs, Hostess Tray, Hood Mounts & Suction Cup Mount Kit

Agnello Films (201) 741-4367
Booms: Trovato Camjib
Cranes: Tulip

Arri CSC (212) 757-0905
619 W. 54th St. (Near 11th Ave.) FAX (212) 713-0075
New York, NY 10019 www.cameraservice.com
Cranes: Giraffe, Phoenix & Jimmy Jib
Dollies: Chapman, Fisher & Panther
Accessories: Remote Heads

ASL Productions, Inc. (718) 626-2646
(888) 275-5367
19-69 Steinway St. (Near 19th St.) FAX (718) 626-1493
Astoria, NY 11105 www.airsealand.com
Accessories: Dutch Heads & Remote Heads
Arms: Jimmy Jib

Ⓐ **Atlantic Cine Equipment, Inc.** (212) 944-0003
(410) 243-4181
210 W. 29th St. FAX (443) 524-0210
Baltimore, MD 21211 www.aceeast.com
Arms: MC88 3 Section
Cranes: SuperTechno 50, SuperTechno 30 & Techno 15
Dollies: Fisher 10 Tracking Rail Runner, Rig Runner and Track Runner
Accessories: Remote Heads & Stabilized Systems

Ⓐ **Black Dog Jib Productions, Inc.** (718) 974-4770
211-10 73rd Ave., Ste. 2A FAX (800) 883-1537
(Near Broadway) www.blackdogjib.com
New York, NY 11364
Cranes: Jimmy Jib III & Jimmy Jib Triangles
Dollies: All-Terrain Wheels & Stanton Dolly Track
Accessories: 3-Axis Remote Dutch Heads, 35mm & 16mm Film Kits

BUDCO Enterprises, Inc. (631) 434-6500
145 Plant Ave. FAX (631) 434-7555
Hauppauge, NY 11788 www.budco.us

BVR, Ltd. (212) 541-5390
(800) 797-4287
355 W. 52nd St. (Near Ninth Ave.) FAX (212) 541-5751
New York, NY 10019 www.bvr.com
Booms: Mini 7 Jib
Dollies: Chapman Super Pee Wee III & Startrack Doorway Dolly
Accessories: Heads, Pedestals, Tracks & Tripods

Cablecam International, Inc. (818) 349-4955
(818) 601-6333
21303 Itasca St. FAX (818) 349-3879
Chatsworth, CA 91311 www.cablecam.com
Accessories: Cable-Suspended Camera Tracking Systems & Mounts

CableTrak Systems, Inc. (845) 626-4218
(917) 670-9766
115 Ridgeview Rd. FAX (845) 626-5607
Kerhonkson, NY 12446
Cranes: Cablecam Device & Extended Jimmy Jib

Camera Moves (570) 828-8882
P.O. Box 309 FAX (570) 828-7787
Dingmans Ferry, PA 18328 www.cameramoves.com
Cranes: Jimmy Jibs

Eastern Effects, Inc. (718) 855-1197
210 Douglass St. FAX (212) 504-9534
Brooklyn, NY 11217 www.easterneffects.com
Accessories: Car Mounts, Car Rigs & Dolly Tracks
Dollies: Fisher 10 and 11 & Matthews Doorway

atlantic cine equipment
New York • Baltimore / Washington DC
www.aceeast.com

ACE SuperTechno 30 with the ACE/Nettmann Stab-C captures stunt scene on "I Am Legend"

ACE nose mount with the ACE/Nettmann Super-G shooting aerials

New* For 2008

* **AF-200-2 Helicopter Nose Mount:** East coast based nose mount for gyro-stabilized film and video "Ball" systems working on A-Star & Twin Star helicopters
* **Nettmann Stab-C Compact:** 80lb, 5 axis gyro-stabilized remote head, camera car and helicopter ready
* **TrackRunner Mini:** World's smallest professional track system with built-in cable management
* **SuperTower 6**: Stand-alone or track-mounted telescopic tower with 4' to 7' rise

technocranes • gyro-stabilized remote heads
high-speed tracking systems • telescopic towers
remote heads • specialized HD robotic systems
gyro-stabilized helicopter mounts

feature films / television / commercials

212.944.0003

Moving Cameras Since 1986

FastLights (800) 437-5494
FAX (617) 314-9676
www.fastlights.com
Arms: Fisher Jib 21, Jimmy Jib, Porta-Jib, Triangle Jimmy, Trovato & Trovato Jr. Jib Arms
Cranes: Jib Arms, Portable Jimmy Jib & Triangle Jimmy Jib
Dollies: Doorway, Fisher 10, Fisher 11, PeeWee & Super PeeWee II
Accessories: Body Mounts, Dolly Tracks, Glidecam Stabilization System, Matthews Steel Track, Pan/Tilt Heads, Remote Camera Systems, Steadicam Systems, Track Wheel Sets & Wide Angle Lenses

Ⓐ Feature Systems (212) 736-0447
(201) 531-2299
223 Veterans Blvd. (Near 10th Ave.)   FAX (212) 465-1987
Carlstadt, NJ 07072   www.featuresystems.com
Dollies: Fisher & Light Weight Track

Goblin Lighting Services, Inc. (718) 447-7157
(917) 439-8906
730 Richmond Terrace   FAX (718) 720-5200
(Near Lafayette Ave.)   www.goblininc.com
Staten Island, NY 10301
Dollies: Chapman & Fisher

Hertz Equipment Rental Corporation (888) 777-2700
(212) 255-4208
www.hertzequip.com

High Output, Inc. (781) 364-1800
(800) 787-4747
FAX (781) 364-1900
www.highoutput.com
Arms: Fisher, Miller Pro, Porta Jib, Straight Shooter & Super Maxi
Cranes: Enlouva, Phoenix, Piccolo & Tulip
Dollies: Chapman, Elemack, Fisher, Western & Wheelchair

Ⓐ Ichabod Crane, Inc. (845) 258-1786
(914) 536-8370
34 Little York Rd.   FAX (845) 258-1816
Warwick, NY 10990

Ⓐ Majestic Light (212) 477-1147
(800) 310-4783
111 E. 14th St., Ste. 131   FAX (212) 529-9547
(Near Fourth Ave.)   www.majesticlight.us
New York, NY 10003
Cranes: Pegasus Super Technocrane
Accessories: Weaver Steadman Remotes

Mammoth Production Packages (585) 381-2470
3800 Monroe Ave.   FAX (585) 381-2462
(Near Woodland Rd.)   www.mammothpro.com
Pittsford, NY 14534
Cranes: Jimmy Jib, Piccolo & Tulip
Dollies: Fisher 10 and 11

Movie Mobile (718) 482-8200
11-38 49th Ave. (Near 21st St.)   FAX (718) 482-9865
Long Island City, NY 11101
Cranes: Chapman
Dollies: Chapman

Nevessa Production, Inc. (845) 679-8848
(888) 484-8848
One Artist Rd. (Near Route 212)   FAX (845) 679-1208
Saugerties, NY 12477   www.nevessa.com
Booms: Jimmy Jib III

Ⓐ New York Jib (888) 488-0100
Arms: 24' Jimmy Jib & 24' Triangle Jimmy   www.nyjib.com
Cranes: 24' Jib Arms
Accessories: 2 Axis Remote Heads & Pan/Tilt Heads

NEW YORK Jib
Howard Heitner
Jimmy Jib Camera Crane
Owner / Operator
▶ Television   ▶ Live Events
▶ Entertainment   ▶ Films
▶ Sports   ▶ Concerts
▶ Commercials   ▶ Music Videos
▶ Infomercials   ▶ Corporate
Providing dynamic camera moves to the Tri-state Area!
CALL **888-488-0100**
www.nyjib.com

On Track Production Equipment   **(203) 209-2462**
1803 Huntington Tpke   FAX **(203) 380-1224**
Trumbull, CT 06611
Cranes: Super Technocrane
Dollies: Car Rigs & Peewee III

Panavision New York   **(212) 606-0700**
30-40 48th Ave. (Near 10th Ave.)   FAX **(212) 244-4694**
Long Island City, NY 11101   www.panavision.com
Cranes: Straight Shoot'R & Techno
Dollies: Chapman, Fisher, Hybrid & PeeWee

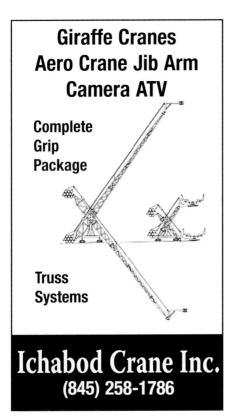

Pictorvision Inc
7701 Haskell Ave., Ste. B
Van Nuys, CA 91406
(818) 785-9282
(800) 876-5583
FAX (818) 785-9787
www.pictorvision.com
Accessories: Camera Mounts, Gyro-Stabilized Camera Mounts, Wescam Aerial Systems & XR Stabilized Remote Heads

Q Video Services, Inc.
P.O. Box 383
Park Ridge, NJ 07656
(201) 930-9855
(800) 921-3478
FAX (201) 930-9850
www.qvideo.tv
Jimmy Jibs: 6'–30' & Bartek Wireless Focus

Ⓐ **Riggin Design, Inc.**
Cranes: Telescopic
(845) 679-4215
www.technojib.com

Ⓐ **Silvertrucks Lighting**
Silvercup Studios/East
34-02 Starr Ave. (Near Van Dam St.)
Long Island City, NY 11101
(718) 906-3045
FAX (718) 906-3042
www.silvercupstudios.com/trucks.htm
Cranes: Enlouva & Pegasus
Dollies: Fisher

Socapa Films
375 Greenwich St., Tribeca Film Center
(Near N. Moore St.)
New York, NY 10013
(800) 718-2787
www.socapa.org
Arms: Media Logic 8'

Ⓐ **That Cat Camera Support, LLC**
60 Butternut Ln.
Stratford, CT 06614
(917) 842-6555
(203) 377-8997
FAX (203) 377-8997

Thomas Cestare, Inc.
188 Herricks Rd. (Near Garfield Ave.)
Mineola, NY 11501
(516) 742-5550
FAX (516) 742-5551
www.thomascestareinc.com
Cranes: Piccolo
Dollies: Elemack & Phantom

MOBILE AIR CONDITIONING
"Our Business Is Keeping You Cool"

ANY LOCATION
Studios Remote Sets Buildings Schools
Holding areas Warehouses Tents Spot Cooling

A.G.E. SERVICES
53 Hanse Avenue • Freeport, NY 11520
Tel (516) 546-5903
Fax (516) 546-0198
www.setcoolers.com
visit or website for 24/7 contact info

Climate Control Systems

Ⓐ A.G.E. Services, Inc. - Mobile Air Conditioning (516) 546-5903
53 Hanse Ave. (Near St. Mary's Pl.) FAX (516) 546-0198
Freeport, NY 11520 www.ageservices.com
(Air Conditioning Units & Heaters)

AAA Event Services (888) 580-7368 / (973) 808-6290
(Air Conditioning Units & Heaters) FAX (973) 808-8588
www.aaaeventservices.com

Aggreko Event Services (908) 474-1322 / (877) 603-6021
3351-4 Tremley Point Rd. FAX (908) 474-1323
Linden, NJ 07036
www.aggreko.com/equipserv/event-services.asp
(Air Conditioning Units & Heaters)

Air Conditioner Rental and Leasing (412) 381-9700 / (800) 581-4844
1001 Freyburg St. FAX (412) 381-9701
Pittsburgh, PA 15203 www.acrental.com
(Air Conditioning, Fans & Heaters)

Foley Power Systems (732) 885-3040 / (732) 885-5555
855 Centennial Ave. FAX (732) 885-5291
Piscataway, NJ 08855 www.foleyinc.com
(Air Conditioning Units & Heaters)

Kits and Expendables (212) 947-0700 / (718) 482-1824
43-77 Ninth St. (Near 10th Ave.) FAX (212) 563-2310
Long Island City, NY 10018
www.kitsandexpendables.com
(Air Conditioning Units & Heaters)

Kitstrucks (201) 531-9700 / (917) 921-4751
155 Anderson Ave. FAX (201) 531-9701
Moonachie, NJ 07074 www.kitstrucks.com
(Mobile Service: Air Conditioning Units & Heaters)

Kohler Rental (410) 969-9100 / (866) 732-8734
7767 Old Telegraph Rd., Ste. 6 FAX (410) 969-7276
Severn, MD 21144 www.kohlereventservices.com

Main Attractions (732) 225-3500
FAX (732) 225-2110
www.mainattractions.com

On Site Energy Co., Inc. (212) 331-0600 / (800) 736-8251
40 Charlotte Ave. FAX (516) 937-1516
(Near W. Old Country Rd.) www.onsite-energy.com
Hicksville, NY 11802
(Air Conditioning Units & Heaters)

Wits End Equipment & Expendables (212) 242-9400 / (917) 691-3999
547 W. 49th St. (Near 10th Ave.) FAX (212) 242-1797
New York, NY 10019 www.witsendnyc.com
(Air Conditioning Units & Heaters)

Wits End Equipment & Expendables (718) 361-8400
43-26 12th St. (Near 43rd Ave.) FAX (718) 361-8440
Long Island City, NY 11101 www.witsendnyc.com
(Air Conditioning Units & Heaters)

Construction & Yard Equipment Rentals

Angel Aerial Corporation (212) 460-8899 / (800) 503-9240
185 Broome St. (Near Clinton St.) FAX (212) 460-8244
New York, NY 10002

Boston Road Equipment Rentals, Inc. (718) 654-8710
3211 Boston Rd. (Near La Conia Ave.) FAX (718) 515-5821
Bronx, NY 10469

Chief Equipment, Inc. (516) 868-1400 / (516) 354-4048
319 W. Sunrise Hwy
Freeport, NY 11520

Greenpoint Tool Rentals Corporation (718) 782-7887
310 Nassau Ave. (Near Apollo St.) FAX (718) 782-9338
Brooklyn, NY 11222 www.gtrentals.com

Hertz Equipment Rental Corporation (973) 589-7540 / (800) 559-2216
41-85 Doremus Ave. FAX (973) 589-8453
Newark, NJ 07105 www.hertzequip.com

Hinkel Equipment Rental (215) 416-0568 / (800) 689-9365
2410 High Rd. FAX (215) 938-0609
Huntingdon Valley, PA 19006 www.hinkrent.com

Homefront Hardware (212) 545-1447
202 E. 29th St. (Near Third Ave.) FAX (212) 545-0092
New York, NY 10016 www.hfront.com

Kohler Rental (410) 969-9100 / (866) 732-8734
7767 Old Telegraph Rd., Ste. 2 FAX (410) 969-7226
Severn, MD 21144 www.kohlereventservices.com
(Tents)

Lapietra Machinery & Equipment, Inc. (718) 439-0900 / (800) 942-9950
5320 Third Ave. (Near 54th St.) FAX (718) 439-0094
Brooklyn, NY 11220 www.a1tool.com

❹ New York Ladder & Scaffold Corporation (800) 229-3352 / (914) 423-2960
122 Woodworth Ave. FAX (914) 476-4140
Yonkers, NY 10702 www.newyorkladder.com
(Scaffolding)

Pride Equipment Corporation (631) 224-5000 / (800) 564-7743
150 Nassau Ave. (Near Moffit Blvd.) FAX (631) 224-4830
Islip, NY 11751 www.prideequipment.com

Putnam Rolling Ladder (212) 226-5147
32 Howard St. (Near Lafayette St.) FAX (212) 941-1836
New York, NY 10013 www.putnamrollingladder.com

RP Rentals & Sales (718) 456-7397
1855 Stanhope St. FAX (718) 456-6900
(Near Onderdonk Ave.) www.rprentals.com
Ridgewood, NY 11385

S.V.E. Sales, Inc. (704) 398-0007 / (800) 762-8267
(Portable Roadway Systems) FAX (704) 398-0540
www.mudtraks.com

Safway Steel Products (718) 321-3914 / (800) 640-8778
31-31 123rd St. (Near 31st Ave.) FAX (718) 321-8106
Flushing, NY 11354 www.safway.com

Siegel Bros. Supply Co., Inc. (718) 387-0300 / (800) 872-8872
880 Meeker Ave. (Near Varick Ave.) FAX (718) 387-1874
Brooklyn, NY 11222

TP Rental Services, Inc. (212) 713-1999
417 W. 50th St. (Near Ninth Ave.) FAX (212) 713-1752
New York, NY 10019 www.tprental.com

United Rentals (718) 762-6969
28-44 College Pt. Blvd. FAX (718) 762-6610
(Near 138th St.) www.unitedrentals.com
Flushing, NY 11354

❹ York Scaffold Equipment Corp. (718) 784-6666
37-20 12th St. (Near 37th Ave.) FAX (718) 482-9016
Long Island City, NY 11101 www.yorkscaffold.com

NewYork Ladder & Scaffolding Corp.

- *Installation*
- *Rental*
- *Sales*

1.800.229.3352

YORK SCAFFOLD EQUIPMENT CORP.

- Frame & Systems Scaffold
- Rolling Towers
- Suspended Systems

Sales & Rentals
718-784-6666
37-20 Twelfth Street, LIC, NY 11101
www.yorkscaffold.com

BARBIZON LIGHTING COMPANY

Lights, Camera, Action!
The show can't go on without Barbizon.

GEL & DIFFUSION
Correction, Diffusion, Color Effects
Available in Sheets, Rolls & Acrylic Panels

LAMPS
Pars, MSR, CSR, HMI/HID, HPL, Fluorescent, LCD
Projection & Specialty Bulbs

LIGHTING EQUIPMENT
Tungsten/HMI Location Kits, State of the Art LED,
Fluorescent, Moving Lights and On-Camera Lighting

PRODUCTION SUPPLIES
Slates, View Finders, Gaffer's Glass, Light Meters, Camera Filters,
Setwear Gloves & Pouches, Leatherman, Tools, Flashlights
Sound Blankets, Tents / Shelters

RIGGING & ROPE
Clamps, Safety Cables, Spanset, Shackles, Pipe, Fittings,
Chain, Sash Cord, Trickline, Hemp, Grip Chain

CABLE, WIRING, CONNECTORS & DISTRO
Zip Cord, Quick-Ons, SJ/SJO/SJT, THHN,
Cable Assemblies, Stage Pin, Twist Lock,
Portable Distribution and Control Systems

EXPENDABLES
Paper Lanterns, Foam Core, B-Board, China Markers,
Show Cards, Seamless Paper, Batteries, Dust Off,
Camera & Gaffer's Tape, Eye Cushions, Paint

GRIP
Stands, Mounting Equipment, Apple Boxes, Hardware,
Flags, Scrims, Overheads, Sandbags/Shotbags

CASES & CARTS
Pelican, Porta Brace, Kata, Hand Trucks, Hampers, Crates

CLOTH
Commando, Duvetyne, Bobbinette/Cinenet, Muslin,
Keying Cloth, Backgrounds

Barbizon is the LARGEST SUPPLIER of Location Lighting and Production Supplies!
456 West 55th Street (Between 9th & 10th) New York, NY 10019
In NYC Call 212-586-1620
OPEN MONDAY - FRIDAY 8AM - 5:30PM   SATURDAYS 9AM - 1PM

Atlanta Boston Charlotte Chicago Dallas Denver Miami New York Orlando Phoenix Washington, D.C. London Sydney

WWW.BARBIZON.COM   866-502-2724

Grip & Lighting Expendables

Arri CSC (212) 757-0906
619 W. 54th St. (Near 11th Ave.) FAX (212) 713-0075
New York, NY 10019 www.cameraservice.com

B&H Photo Video Pro Audio (212) 444-5085 / (212) 239-7760
420 Ninth Ave. (Near W. 34th St.) FAX (212) 239-7766
New York, NY 10001 www.bhphotovideo.com

▲ Barbizon (212) 586-1620
456 W. 55th St. (Near 10th Ave.) FAX (212) 247-8818
New York, NY 10019 www.barbizon.com

▲ Bulbtronics (631) 249-2272 / (800) 654-8542
720 Ninth Ave. (Near W. 49th St.) FAX (631) 249-6066
New York, NY 10019 www.bulbtronics.com

▲ Bulbtronics (631) 249-2272 / (800) 227-2852
45 Banfi Plaza (Near Carolyn Blvd.) FAX (631) 249-7742
Farmingdale, NY 11735 www.bulbtronics.com

CECO International (212) 206-8280
440 W. 15th St. (Near 10th Ave.) FAX (212) 727-2144
New York, NY 10011 www.cecostudios.com

Cress Photo (973) 694-1280
P.O. Box 4262 FAX (973) 694-6965
Wayne, NJ 07474 www.flashbulbs.com
(Flash Bulbs, Flash Guns & Flashpans)

Eastern Effects, Inc. (718) 855-1197
210 Douglass St. FAX (212) 504-9534
Brooklyn, NY 11217 www.easterneffects.com
(Bulbs & Camera, Lighting and Production Expendables)

Expendables Plus, Inc. (718) 609-6464 / (917) 964-6464
91 Moultrie St. (Near Calyer St.) FAX (718) 609-6119
Brooklyn, NY 11222

FastLights (800) 437-5494
FAX (617) 314-9676
www.fastlights.com
(Bulbs and Lighting Expendables, Camera Expendables,
Layout Boards & Production Expendables)

Feature Systems (212) 736-0447 / (201) 531-2299
223 Veterans Blvd. (Near 10th Ave.) FAX (212) 465-1987
Carlstadt, NJ 07072 www.featuresystems.com

Goblin Lighting Services, Inc. (718) 447-7157 / (917) 439-8906
730 Richmond Terrace FAX (718) 720-5200
(Near Lafayette Ave.) www.goblininc.com
Staten Island, NY 10301

High Output, Inc. (781) 364-1800 / (800) 787-4747
FAX (781) 364-1900
www.highoutput.com

Hotlights, Inc. (212) 645-5295 / (800) 362-5295
133 W. 19th St. (Near Seventh Ave.) FAX (212) 989-6918
New York, NY 10011 www.hotlights.com

Kaye Lites, Inc. (781) 932-0005
34-B Holton St. FAX (781) 932-0006
Woburn, MA 01801 www.kayelites.com

Kits and Expendables (212) 947-0700 / (718) 782-1824
43-77 Ninth Ave. (Near 10th Ave.) FAX (212) 563-2310
Long Island City, NY 11101 www.kitsandexpendables.com
(Production Expendables)

Kitstrucks (201) 531-9700 / (917) 921-4751
155 Anderson Ave. FAX (201) 531-9701
Moonachie, NJ 07074 www.kitstrucks.com
(Mobile Services)

Lentini Communications	(212) 206-1452
54 W. 21st St., Ste. 301	FAX (212) 206-1453
(Near Fifth Ave.)	www.lentinicommunications.com
New York, NY 10010	
Liberty Electrical Supply Co., Inc.	(718) 342-5790
326 Rockaway Ave.	FAX (718) 498-1455
(Near New York Ave.)	www.libertyelectrical.com
Brooklyn, NY 11212	
The Light House, Inc.	(800) 721-6191
	FAX (908) 253-3633
	www.lighthouselights.com
	(215) 576-5600
Location Lighting, Ltd.	(215) 353-0543
300 Pennsylvania Ave.	FAX (215) 576-6022
Oreland, PA 19075	www.locationlighting.com
Mutual Hardware	(718) 361-2480
3627 Vernon Blvd. (Near 36th Ave.)	FAX (718) 786-9591
Long Island City, NY 11106	www.mutualhardware.com
Panavision New York	(212) 606-0700
30-40 48th Ave. (Near 10th Ave.)	FAX (212) 244-4694
Long Island City, NY 11101	www.panavision.com
	(802) 651-6915
Production Advantage, Inc.	(800) 424-9991
P.O. Box 1700	FAX (802) 651-6914
Willston, VT 05449	www.productionadvantageonline.com

Raygun	(212) 337-1935
435 W. 19th St. (Near Ninth Ave.)	FAX (212) 337-1936
New York, NY 10011	www.raygunco.com
Rose Brand	(800) 223-1624
Four Emerson Ln. (Near W. 15th St.)	www.rosebrand.com
Secaucus, NJ 07094	
	(212) 255-3500
Set Shop	(800) 422-7381
36 W. 20th St. (Near Sixth Ave.)	FAX (212) 229-9600
New York, NY 10011	www.setshop.com
	(631) 589-3393
The Specialty Bulb Co., Inc.	(800) 331-2852
80 Orville Dr., P.O. Box 231	FAX (631) 563-3089
(Near Veteran's Hwy)	www.bulbspecialists.com
Bohemia, NY 11716	
Wits End Equipment & Expendables	(718) 361-8400
43-26 12th St. (Near 43rd Ave.)	FAX (718) 361-8440
Long Island City, NY 11101	www.witsendnyc.com
(Mobile Services)	
	(212) 242-9400
WitsTrucks	(917) 691-3999
547 W. 49th St. (Near 10th Ave.)	FAX (212) 242-1797
New York, NY 10019	www.witsendnyc.com
(Mobile Services)	
Xeno Lights, Inc.	(212) 941-9494
One Worth St. (Near Hudson Street)	FAX (212) 941-9495
New York, NY 10013	www.xenolights.com

Grip & Lighting Expendables

Grip Equipment

Altman Rentals, Inc.
57 Alexander St.
(Near Ashburton Ave.)
Yonkers, NY 10701
(212) 569-7777
(914) 476-7987
FAX (914) 476-1204
www.altmanrentals.com

Arri CSC
619 W. 54th St. (Near 11th Ave.)
New York, NY 10019
(212) 757-0906
FAX (212) 713-0075
www.cameraservice.com

CECO International
440 W. 15th St. (Near 10th Ave.)
New York, NY 10011
(212) 206-8280
FAX (212) 727-2144
www.cecostudios.com

Cine 60
(347) 527-1175
(917) 239-8119
www.cine60newyork.com

The Cooper Film Company, Inc.
(201) 358-1016
(201) 704-3266

East Coast Lighting, Inc.
48 Eagle St. (Near Franklin St.)
Brooklyn, NY 11222
(718) 383-8100
FAX (718) 383-8122
www.eclny.net

Eastern Effects, Inc.
210 Douglass St.
Brooklyn, NY 11217
(718) 855-1197
FAX (212) 504-9534
www.easterneffects.com
(10-Ton Grip and Lighting Truck, Electric, Grip and Rigging Hardware Supplies, Rigging, Scaffolding & Trucks)

Eclipse
515 W. 47th St.
New York, NY 10036
(917) 497-9128

Elefant Films
(888) 435-3326
FAX (212) 757-5141
www.elefantfilms.com

FastLights
(800) 437-5494
FAX (617) 314-9676
www.fastlights.com
(Chain Hoists/Truss Systems, Couplers, Cranes, Electric Equipment, Grip Supplies, Grip Truck, Hydraulic Cranes, Man Baskets, Offset Jibs, Rigging, Scaffolding, Scissorlifts, Swivel Clamps, Truck Cranes & Trucks)

Feature Systems
223 Veterans Blvd. (Near 10th Ave.)
Carlstadt, NJ 07072
(212) 736-0447
(201) 531-2299
FAX (212) 465-1987
www.featuresystems.com

Fort Gates Films Unlimited
Eight Eagle Point Dr.
Great Neck, NY 11024
(516) 236-3666
www.fortgatesfilms.com
(Lighting, Lighting Equipment, Grip & Six Ton Grip and Lighting Truck)

GDR Equipment Co.
755 W. Nyack Rd.
(Near Western Hwy)
West Nyack, NY 10994
(212) 956-6447
(845) 348-3972
FAX (845) 348-1580
www.gdrequipment.com

Goblin Lighting Services, Inc.
730 Richmond Terrace
(Near Lafayette Ave.)
Staten Island, NY 10301
(718) 447-7157
(917) 439-8906
FAX (718) 720-5200
www.goblininc.com

Hand Held Films, Inc.
66 White St., Ground Fl.
New York, NY 10013
(212) 502-0900
FAX (212) 502-0906
www.handheldfilms.com

High Output, Inc.
(781) 364-1800
(800) 787-4747
FAX (781) 364-1900
www.highoutput.com

Hotlights, Inc.
133 W. 19th St. (Near Seventh Ave.)
New York, NY 10011
(212) 645-5295
(800) 362-5295
FAX (212) 989-6918
www.hotlights.com

Ichabod Crane, Inc.
34 Little York Rd.
Warwick, NY 10990
(845) 258-1786
(914) 536-8370
FAX (845) 258-1816

K/A/S Lighting
36-45 37th St. (Near 36th Ave.)
Astoria, NY 11101
(718) 786-7990
FAX (718) 786-5083
www.kaslighting.com

Kaye Lites, Inc.
(781) 932-0005
FAX (781) 932-0006
www.kayelites.com

KJ Films, LLC
15 Ridgebury Rd.
East Haddam, CT 06423
(860) 995-5106
(860) 873-2419
www.kjfilms.com

Liberty Lighting Limited
(212) 580-7237
www.libertylightinglimited.com

Light Foot Grip & Lighting
37-09 36th Ave.
Long Island City, NY 11101
(718) 729-1900
FAX (718) 729-8638
www.lightfootnyc.com

The Light House, Inc.
(800) 721-6191
FAX (908) 253-3633
www.lighthouselights.com

Location Lighting, Ltd.
300 Pennsylvania Ave.
Oreland, PA 19075
(215) 576-5600
(215) 353-0543
FAX (215) 576-6022
www.locationlighting.com

Luna Lighting
203 Meserole Ave.
(Near McGuinness Blvd.)
Brooklyn, NY 11222
(718) 349-9146
(718) 786-5428
FAX (718) 349-9148

Mammoth Production Packages
3800 Monroe Ave.
(Near Woodland Rd.)
Pittsford, NY 14534
(585) 381-2470
FAX (585) 381-2462
www.mammothpro.com

Minard Lighting & Grip
283 Hope Valley Rd.
Amston, CT 06231
(860) 228-9069
(860) 682-2728
FAX (860) 228-8209

Mutual Hardware
3627 Vernon Blvd. (Near 36th Ave.)
Long Island City, NY 11106
(718) 361-2480
FAX (718) 786-9591
www.mutualhardware.com

New York Grip Truck, Inc.
246 Franklin St.
Bloomfield, NJ 07003
(973) 464-6147

Panavision New York
30-40 48th Ave. (Near 10th Ave.)
Long Island City, NY 11101
(212) 606-0700
FAX (212) 244-4694
www.panavision.com

Paramount Production Support, Inc. (718) 729-6525
32-69 Gale Ave. (Near 32nd Pl.)
Long Island City, NY 11101
FAX (718) 729-6315
www.paramount.com

Performance Lighting Rentals, Inc.
P.O. Box 264
Ingomar, PA 15127
(412) 781-5655
(866) 882-9466
FAX (412) 781-5705
www.perflight.com

RGH Lighting LLC (212) 647-1114
236 W. 30th St. (Near Seventh Ave.) (212) 947-4744
New York, NY 10001 FAX (212) 647-1451
www.rghlighting.com

See Factor Industry (718) 784-4200
37-11 30th St. (Near 37th Ave.) FAX (718) 784-0617
Long Island City, NY 11101 www.seefactor.com

Ⓐ Silvertrucks Lighting (718) 906-3045
Silvercup Studios/East FAX (718) 906-3042
34-02 Starr Ave. www.silvercupstudios.com/trucks.htm
(Near Van Dam St.)
Long Island City, NY 11101

Solar Plexus, Inc. (201) 836-5427
135 Oakdene Ave. (201) 281-5973
Teaneck, NJ 07666 FAX (201) 836-5427
www.solarplexusprods.com

Stark Lighting & Generator (347) 538-6501
27 Huguenot St. (888) 454-4487
New Paltz, NY 12561 FAX (845) 255-4280
www.starklighting.com

Tamberelli Digital (212) 244-1011
516 W. 36th St., Second Fl. (877) 608-4336
(Near 10th Ave.) FAX (212) 947-5894
New York, NY 10018 www.tamberelli.com

Thomas Cestare, Inc. (516) 742-5550
188 Herricks Rd. (Near Garfield Ave.) FAX (516) 742-5551
Mineola, NY 11501 www.thomascestareinc.com

Xeno-Lights, Inc. (212) 941-9494
One Worth St. (Near Hudson St.) FAX (212) 941-9495
New York, NY 10013 www.xenolights.com

York Scaffold Equipment Corp. (718) 784-6666
37-20 12th St. (Near 37th Ave.) FAX (718) 482-9016
Long Island City, NY 11101 www.yorkscaffold.com

ABLE EQUIPMENT RENTAL: WE UNDERSTAND YOUR PRODUCTION NEEDS

GENERATOR: ULTRA SILENT · CRYSTAL SYNC · PARALLELING

Aerial Work Platforms · Forklifts, Rough Terrain & Straight Mast
Air Tools And Compressors · Welders & Generators · Portable Air Conditioners
Portable Fume Free Heaters · Temporary Distribution

1.800.518.1321 · 631.841.3333
ABLEEQUIPMENT.COM · INFO@ABLEEQUIPMENT.COM
COPIAGUE, NY · EDISON, NJ · ROCK TAVERN, NY

Hoisting & Lift Equipment/Cherry Pickers

ABC Rental Center (516) 437-7667
2016 Hillside Ave. FAX (516) 437-7672
(Near New Hyde Park Rd.)
New Hyde Park, NY 11040
(Forklifts & Personnel Lifts)

Ⓐ Able Equipment Rental, Inc. (631) 841-3333
21 Dixon Ave. (Near Galvani St.) (866) 468-2666
Copiague, NY 11726 FAX (631) 841-3066
www.gotboom.com

INIFINITI HANDLING SYSTEMS

We provide Daily, Weekly, and Monthly rentals of Scissor Lifts & Boom Lifts as well as Forklifts, gas and electric up to 20,000 lb. capacities. Electric Pallet Jacks up to 6,000 lb. capacities. We also rent Motrec Electric Tow Tractors. We provide 24 hour service from two locations covering Albany to Long Island. We also sell New and Used equipment and provide parts and service.

New York

Garden City, LI
603 Chestnut Street
Garden City, NY 11530
Tel: **(516) 280-7589**
Fax: (516) 280-7595

Upstate, NY
420 Highland Ave. Ext.
Middletown, NY 10940
Tel: **(845) 343-0641**
Fax: (845) 342-3627

www.ihslift.com

Adams Rents (718) 341-1234
243-29 Merrick Blvd. (Near 244th St.)
Rosedale, NY 11422
(Forklifts, Man Baskets & Scissorlifts)

Ahern Rentals, Inc. (856) 429-2280
(609) 309-1035
1905 Route 206 FAX (609) 859-2041
Southampton, NJ 08088 www.ahernrentals.com
(Booms, Camera Baskets, Forklifts, Jibs, Lightbars, Man Baskets, Scaffolding & Scissorlifts)

Angel Aerial Corporation (212) 460-8899
(800) 503-9240
185 Broome St. (Near Clinton St.) FAX (212) 460-8244
New York, NY 10002 www.angelaerial.com

Blakley Equipment (914) 664-5500
(800) 662-5857
491 E. Third St. (Near Columbus Ave.) FAX (914) 664-5815
Mount Vernon, NY 10553 www.blakleytree.com
(Man Baskets, Personnel Lifts, Scissorlifts & Truck Mounted Booms)

BUDCO Enterprises, Inc. (631) 434-6500
145 Plant Ave. FAX (631) 434-7555
Hauppauge, NY 11788 www.budco.us

Hertz Equipment Rental Corporation (973) 589-7540
(800) 559-2216
FAX (973) 589-8453
www.hertzequip.com

NewYork Ladder & Scaffolding Corp.

- *Installation*
- *Rental*
- *Sales*

1.800.229.3352

YORK SCAFFOLD EQUIPMENT CORP.

YORK

- Frame & Systems Scaffold
- Rolling Towers
- Suspended Systems

Sales & Rentals
718-784-6666
37-20 Twelfth Street, LIC, NY 11101
www.yorkscaffold.com

Hinkel Equipment Rental (215) 416-0568
(800) 689-9365
2410 High Rd. FAX (215) 938-0609
Huntingdon Valley, PA 19006 www.hinkrent.com
(Condor Man Baskets, Forklifts, Personnel Lifts, Scissorlifts & Truck Mounted Booms)

Independent Aerial Equip. (908) 527-1211
765 York St. FAX (908) 527-1271
Elizabeth, NJ 07201 www.independentaerials.com

Ⓐ Infiniti Handling Systems (516) 280-7589
(Booms, Forklifts & Scissorlifts) FAX (516) 280-7595

Ⓐ New York Ladder & (800) 229-3352
Scaffold Corporation (914) 423-2960
122 Woodworth Ave. FAX (914) 476-4140
Yonkers, NY 10702 www.newyorkladder.com
(Scaffolding)

Pride Equipment Corporation (631) 224-5000
(800) 564-7743
150 Nassau Ave. (Near Moffit Blvd.) FAX (631) 224-4830
Islip, NY 11751 www.prideequipment.com
(Booms, Forklifts, Manlifts & Scissorlifts)

United Rentals (718) 456-8546
(800) 543-5438
104 Gardner Ave. (Near Randolph St.) FAX (718) 366-2213
Brooklyn, NY 11237 www.unitedrentals.com
(Booms, Forklifts & Scissorlifts)

United Rentals (203) 259-8387
(800) 972-9415
185 Thorpe St. FAX (203) 255-7531
Fairfield, CT 06824 www.unitedrentals.com

United Rentals (845) 561-2599
(800) 679-2981
5311 Route 9W (Near N. Hill Ln.) FAX (845) 561-2035
Newburgh, NY 12550 www.unitedrentals.com

United Rentals (631) 244-2541
(866) 694-9845
262 McCormick Dr. (Near Union Ave.) FAX (631) 244-2726
Bohemia, NY 11716 www.unitedrentals.com
(Booms, Forklifts, Manlifts & Scissorlifts)

United Rentals (718) 762-6969
28-44 College Pt. Blvd. FAX (718) 762-6610
(Near 138th St.) www.unitedrentals.com
Flushing, NY 11354
(Booms, Forklifts, Manlifts & Scissorlifts)

Ⓐ York Scaffold Equipment Corp. (718) 784-6666
37-20 12th St. (Near 37th Ave.) FAX (718) 482-9016
Long Island City, NY 11101 www.yorkscaffold.com
(Scaffolding)

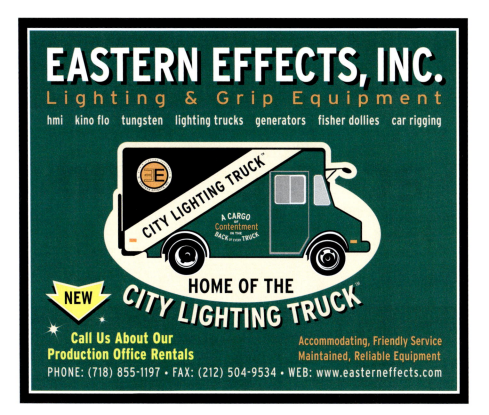

Lighting Equipment & Generators

AAA Event Services (888) 580-7368
(Generators) (973) 808-6290
FAX (973) 808-8588
www.aaaeventservices.com

ABC Rental Center (516) 437-7667
2016 Hillside Ave. FAX (516) 437-7672
(Near New Hyde Park Rd.)
New Hyde Park, NY 11040
(Generators)

Able Equipment Rental, Inc. (631) 840-6666
21 Dixon Ave. (Near Galvani St.) FAX (631) 841-3066
Copiague, NY 11726 www.gotboom.com

Ⓐ Aggreko Event Services (908) 474-1322
 (877) 603-6021
3351-4 Tremley Point Rd. FAX (908) 474-1323
Linden, NJ 07036
www.aggreko.com/equipserv/event-services.asp
(Generators)

Air Conditioner Rental and Leasing (412) 381-9700
 (800) 581-4844
1001 Freyburg St. FAX (412) 381-9701
Pittsburgh, PA 15203 www.acrental.com
(Generators)

All Terrain Power Co., Inc. (718) 852-4922
 (516) 607-6649
FAX (718) 267-0002
www.allterrainpower.com
(Generators)

Altman Rentals, Inc. (212) 569-7777
 (914) 476-7987
57 Alexander St. FAX (914) 476-1204
(Near Ashburton Ave.) www.altmanrentals.com
Yonkers, NY 10701

Angel Aerial Corporation (212) 460-8899
 (800) 503-9240
185 Broome St. (Near Clinton St.) FAX (212) 460-8244
New York, NY 10002 www.angelaerial.com

Annapolis Mobile Power Services, Inc. (410) 758-0450
111 Poplar School Rd. FAX (410) 758-1914
Centreville, MD 21617 www.annapolismobilepower.com
(Generators)

Arri CSC (212) 757-0906
619 W. 54th St. (Near 11th Ave.) FAX (212) 713-0075
New York, NY 10019 www.cameraservice.com

Available Light (718) 707-9670
 (917) 871-0358
29-20 37th Ave. (Near 30th St.) FAX (718) 707-9693
Long Island City, NY 11101 www.alny.net

Barbizon (212) 586-1620
456 W. 55th St. (Near 10th Ave.) FAX (212) 247-8818
New York, NY 10019 www.barbizon.com

BarnDoor Lighting Outfitters (203) 773-1335
 (888) 276-3667
2155 State St. FAX (203) 773-9474
Hamden, CT 06517 www.barndoorlighting.com
(Chimeras, Dedo Lighting, Generators, HMIs & Kino Fluorescent Lighting)

Bogen Imaging, Inc. (201) 818-9500
565 E. Crescent Ave. FAX (201) 818-9177
Ramsey, NJ 07446 www.bogenimaging.us
(Sales Only)

Bulbtronics (631) 249-2272
 (800) 227-2852
45 Banfi Plaza (Near Carolyn Blvd.) FAX (631) 249-7742
Farmingdale, NY 11735 www.bulbtronics.com
(Bulbs & Lamps)

Let Us Quote Your Next Project

For feature films, commercials, still photography, television, video, independent film projects, industrials, student films and special events.

Ask for details about free delivery and pickup.

Lighting and Grip Packages

1, 3 & 5 Ton Grip, Electric, Tungsten and HMI Packages, Maintenance, Repair, Upgrades Including HMI and Flicker Free Ballast Repair

- Fisher 10 & 11 Dollies
- Filmair Track
- Arri Flicker Free HMI's
- Mole-Richardson Quartz
- Arri & Lowel Lighting Kits
- Matthews Grip Equipment
- Kino Flo Fluorescents
- K5600 Jokers & Bug Lights
- Dedo Light Kits
- Chimeras
- Honda Crystal Generators
- Hand Held Generators
- Fog & Wind Machines
- Torpedo Heaters
- Portable Jib Arms

EAST COAST LIGHTING, INCORPORATED

48 Eagle Street, Brooklyn, NY 11222
(718) 383-8100   FAX (718) 383-8122   PAGER (888) 961-5107
Visit us at www.eclny.net or e-mail eastcoastlighting@eclny.net

---

Bulbtronics — (631) 249-2272 / (800) 654-8542
720 Ninth Ave. (Near W. 49th St.)   FAX (631) 249-6066
New York, NY 10019   www.bulbtronics.com
(Bulbs & Lamps)

Ⓐ CECO International — (212) 206-8280
440 W. 15th St. (Near 10th Ave.)   FAX (212) 727-2144
New York, NY 10011   www.cecostudios.com

Cine 60 — (347) 527-1175 / (917) 239-8119
www.cine60newyork.com

Circuit Lighting, Inc. — (732) 968-9533
299 Route 22 East   FAX (732) 968-9231
Green Brook, NJ 08812   www.circuitlighting.com

CSI Rentals — (212) 243-7368
133 W. 19th St., Ground Fl.   FAX (212) 243-2102
New York, NY 10011   www.csirentals.com

One Stop Production!

CECO International Corporation

440 West 15th Street
New York, N.Y. 10011
www.cecostudios.com

(212) 206 - 8280

- Stages
- Locations
- Production Suites

fax
(212) 727 - 2144

lighting fax
(212) 675 - 6812

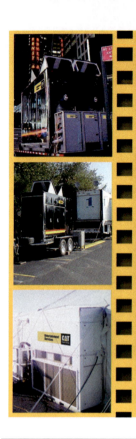

Movie Silent Generators, A/C, Heat with Red Light Operation

- 24 hours a day/7 days a week
- Cables, ramps, transformers and distribution
- Qualified site technicians
- Creative solutions
- Competitive prices

LOS ANGELES 866.762.5228	**NEW YORK** 877.456.7854	**DALLAS** 888.908.4228
ORLANDO 877.228.2852	**TAMPA** 866.769.3761	**NEW ENGLAND** 888.296.4492

Entertainment Services CAT Rental Power

es-cat.com

East Coast Lighting, Inc. (718) 383-8100
48 Eagle St. (Near Franklin St.) FAX (718) 383-8122
Brooklyn, NY 11222 www.eclny.net

Eastern Effects, Inc. (718) 855-1197
210 Douglass St. FAX (212) 504-9534
Brooklyn, NY 11217 www.easterneffects.com
(24-Hour Service, Blue/Green Screen, Dedo Lighting, Desisti, Fluorescent Lighting, Generators, HMI, Lighting Equipment, Small Generators & Xenon Lighting)

Eclipse (917) 497-9128
515 W. 47th St.
New York, NY 10036

Entertainment Services (877) 456-7854
10 Lafayette Pl.
Kenilworth, NJ 07033
(Generators)

---

rghlighting.com   (212) 244 . 8300   236 W 30 ST NY, NY   theflug.com

scheimpflüg

DIGITAL	LIGHTING	ELECTRONICS	PRODUCTION
Digital Capture	HMI	Generators	Fog Machines
DSLR/Medium Format	Tungsten	Inverters	Gels & Diffusion
Archiving	Studio Strobe	Distro-Boxes	Effects Fans
Fine Art Prints	Kino	Cable & Wire	Table & Chairs
Travel-Ready Techs	Light Banks	Expert Technicians	Wardrobe Gear

Check out our selection of **Generator and Grip Trucks** online

NEW YORK & THE WORLD

When You Need Flawless Execution, You Need Aggreko Event Services.

For 20 years, we have provided temporary power and climate control solutions to the television and film industries. Your local event team proudly supplies the expertise and specialized equipment needed, wherever your project takes you.

- **The Ultimate in Quiet Power:** 500- to 7600 amp Generators
- **Portable Air Conditioning:** Studio/Sound Stage Systems, 1- to 200 tons
- **Cam-Lok Distribution**
- **Special Effects:** Breath Effect, Ice & Fog
- **UL-Listed Electrical Distribution**

888.245.6381
www.aggreko.com

Projects include:
King Kong ■ Evan Almighty ■ Ocean's Thirteen

aggreko

Farm Boy Films (212) 475-6166
126 Second Ave., Third Fl. FAX (212) 475-6166
(Near E. Seventh St.)
New York, NY 10003
members.aol.com/farmbfilms/homepage.html
(Kino Flo & Tungsten)

FastLights (800) 437-5494
FAX (617) 314-9676
www.fastlights.com
(24-Hour Service, Blacklight, Blue/Green Screen, Dedo Lighting, Fluorescent Lighting, Generators, Giant Tungsten/HMI Lighting Balloons, HMI, Light Towers, Lighting Equipment, Lithium Ion Battery Belts, Small Generators, Soft Box Lighting, Theatrical Lighting & Xenon Lighting)

Feature Systems (212) 736-0447
(201) 531-2299
223 Veterans Blvd. (Near 10th Ave.) FAX (212) 465-1987
Carlstadt, NJ 07072 www.featuresystems.com

Fisher Light (800) 888-0187
(Fisher Lights and Balloons) www.fisherlight.com

(732) 885-3040
Foley Power Systems (732) 885-5555
855 Centennial Ave. FAX (732) 885-5291
Piscataway, NJ 08855 www.foleyinc.com
(Generators)

Fort Gates Films Unlimited (516) 236-3666
Eight Eagle Point Dr. www.fortgatesfilms.com
Great Neck, NY 11024

Lighting Equipment & Generators

Goblin Lighting Services, Inc. (718) 447-7157
730 Richmond Terrace (917) 439-8906
(Near Lafayette Ave.) FAX (718) 720-5200
Staten Island, NY 10301 www.goblininc.com

GripAndElectric.com (917) 476-9967
FAX (718) 247-6023
www.gripandelectric.com
(24-Hour Service, Blue/Green Screen, Bulbs, Chimeras, Fluorescent Lighting, HMIs, Light Towers, Line Frequency Meters, Small Generators & Soft Box Lighting)

Hand Held Films, Inc. (212) 502-0900
66 White St., Ground Fl. FAX (212) 502-0906
New York, NY 10013 www.handheldfilms.com
(Blacklight, Chimeras, Dedo Lighting, Fluorescent Lighting, Generators, Green Screen & HMIs)

Hello World Communications (212) 243-8800
118 W. 22nd St., Ste. 2A FAX (212) 691-6961
(Near Sixth Ave.) www.hwc.tv
New York, NY 10011
(24-Hour Service, Chimeras & Fluorescent Lighting)

Hertz Equipment Rental Corporation (888) 777-2700
(212) 255-4208
www.hertzequip.com

High Output, Inc. (781) 364-1800
(800) 787-4747
FAX (781) 364-1900
www.highoutput.com

Hit & Run Productions (718) 809-9057
65 Roebling St., Ste. 202 (718) 782-8381
Brooklyn, NY 11211 FAX (718) 782-8388
www.hitandrunproductions.com
(Chimeras, Fluorescent Lighting & HMIs)

Hotlights, Inc. (212) 645-5295
133 W. 19th St. (Near Seventh Ave.) (800) 362-5295
New York, NY 10011 FAX (212) 989-6918
www.hotlights.com

Illumination Dynamics (704) 679-9400
(866) 544-4483
FAX (704) 679-9420
www.illuminationdynamics.com

Jupiter Ltg. Co, Inc. (212) 633-9890
236 W. 27th St., 15th Fl. FAX (212) 741-7772
New York, NY 10001

K/A/S Lighting (718) 786-7990
36-45 37th St. (Near 36th Ave.) FAX (718) 786-5083
Astoria, NY 11101 www.kaslighting.com

Kaye Lites, Inc. (781) 932-0005
FAX (781) 932-0006
www.kayelites.com

KJ Films, LLC (860) 995-5106
15 Ridgebury Rd. (860) 873-2419
East Haddam, CT 06423 www.kjfilms.com

KL Lighting (718) 292-1257
2680 Park Ave. (Near E. 141st St.) FAX (718) 742-2461
Bronx, NY 10451 www.klprods.com

Kohler Rental (410) 969-9100
7767 Old Telegraph Rd., Ste. 6 (866) 732-8734
Severn, MD 21144 FAX (410) 969-7276
www.kohlereventservices.com
(Generators)

Liberty Lighting Limited (212) 580-7237
www.libertylightinglimited.com

Light Foot Grip & Lighting (718) 729-1900
37-09 36th Ave. FAX (718) 729-8638
Long Island City, NY 11101 www.lightfootnyc.com

The Light House, Inc. (800) 721-6191
FAX (908) 253-3633
www.lighthouselights.com

Location Lighting, Ltd. (215) 576-5600
300 Pennsylvania Ave. FAX (215) 576-6022
Oreland, PA 19075 www.locationlighting.com

Location Power Source, Ltd. (800) 932-5235
20 Beachwood Ave. (516) 330-7044
(Near Port Washington Blvd.) FAX (516) 883-2676
Port Washington, NY 11050
(Generators)

Luna Lighting (718) 349-9146
203 Meserole Ave. (718) 786-5428
(Near McGuinness Blvd.) FAX (718) 349-9148
Brooklyn, NY 11222

LVR/Liman Video Rental Company (212) 594-0086
341 W. 38th St., Ground Fl. (800) 251-4625
(Near Eighth Ave.) FAX (212) 594-0786
New York, NY 10018 www.lvrusa.com
(Generators & Video Lighting)

Mammoth Production Packages (585) 381-2470
3800 Monroe Ave. FAX (585) 381-2462
(Near Woodland Rd.) www.mammothpro.com
Pittsford, NY 14534

**ONE MAN. ONE TRUCK.
THREE TONS OF OPTIONS.**
JOHNFRISBIE@GRIPANDELECTRIC.COM
917-476-9967

Metrovision Production Group (212) 989-1515
508 W. 24th St. (Near 10th Ave.) FAX **(212) 989-8278**
New York, NY 10011 www.metrovision.tv

(860) 228-9069
Minard Lighting & Grip (860) 682-2728
283 Hope Valley Rd. FAX **(860) 228-8209**
Amston, CT 06231

(718) 389-8727
Moore P.A. Hire Inc. (917) 747-5372
21 Box St. (Near Manhattan Ave.) www.moorepahire.com
Brooklyn, NY 11222
(Lighting Balloons, Small Generators & Theatrical Lighting)

(641) 673-0411
Musco Lighting (800) 825-6020
FAX **(888) 397-8736**
www.musco.com

(212) 331-0600
On Site Energy Co., Inc. (800) 736-8251
40 Charlotte Ave. FAX **(516) 937-1516**
(Near W. Old Country Rd.) www.onsite-energy.com
Hicksville, NY 11802
(Generators)

On Track Production Equipment (203) 209-2462
1803 Huntington Tpke FAX **(203) 380-1224**
Trumbull, CT 06611

PAL Television East (212) 741-9111
236 W. 27th St., 10th Fl. FAX **(212) 741-7772**
New York, NY 10001 www.paleast.com

Panavision New York (212) 606-0700
30-40 48th Ave. (Near 10th Ave.) FAX **(212) 244-4694**
Long Island City, NY 11101 www.panavision.com

Paramount Production Support, Inc. (718) 729-6525
32-69 Gale Ave. (Near 32nd Pl.) FAX **(718) 729-6315**
Long Island City, NY 11101 www.paramount.com

(412) 781-5655
Performance Lighting Rentals, Inc. (866) 882-9466
P.O. Box 264 FAX **(412) 781-5705**
Ingomar, PA 15127 www.perflight.com

Phase 3 Power (718) 643-0649
99 Joralemon St., Ste. 2A FAX **(718) 643-1821**
(Near Brooklyn Queens Expwy)
Brooklyn, NY 11201

PRG (845) 567-5700
539 Temple Hill Rd. FAX **(845) 567-5800**
New Windsor, NY 12575 www.prg.com
(Lighting Balloons & Theatrical Lighting)

(718) 834-5660
Productions First Choice Inc. (212) 882-1666
(Generators) FAX **(718) 834-8448**

Ⓐ RGH Lighting LLC (212) 647-1114
236 W. 30th St. (Near Ninth Ave.) FAX **(212) 647-1451**
New York, NY 10001 www.rghlighting.com
(Chimeras, Dedo Lighting, Electrical Safety Equipment,
Generators, HMIs, Lithium Ion Battery Belts, Small Generators,
Soft Box Lighting, Strobe Lighting & Tube Balloons)

(908) 412-8630
SBP Industries (800) 458-4231
1301 New Market Ave. FAX **(908) 412-8635**
South Plainfield, NJ 07080 www.sbp4juice.com
(24-Hour Service, Generators,
Small Generators & Transformers)

ScreenLight & Grip (781) 326-5088
502 Sprague St. FAX **(781) 326-4751**
Dedham, MA 02026 www.screenlightandgrip.com

See Factor Industry (718) 784-4200
37-11 30th St. (Near 37th Ave.) FAX **(718) 784-0617**
Long Island City, NY 11101 www.seefactor.com
(Bulbs, Electrical Safety Equipment, Generators, HMIs, Light
Towers, Small Generators, Strobe Lighting,
Theatrical Lighting & Transformers)

Ⓐ Silvertrucks Lighting (718) 906-3045
Silvercup Studios/East FAX **(718) 906-3042**
34-02 Starr Ave. (Near Van Dam St.)
Long Island City, NY 11101
www.silvercupstudios.com/trucks.htm

(201) 836-5427
Solar Plexus, Inc. (201) 281-5973
135 Oakdene Ave. FAX **(201) 836-5427**
Teaneck, NJ 07666 www.solarplexusprods.com

(347) 538-6501
Stark Lighting & Generator (888) 454-4487
27 Huguenot St. FAX **(845) 255-4280**
New Paltz, NY 12561 www.starklighting.com
(Lighting Truck & Van Generator)

(212) 925-1738
Strike Force, Inc. (201) 218-7164
24 Park Ave. FAX **(212) 925-3705**
Glen Rock, NJ 07452 www.strikeforcegenerators.com
(Generators)

(212) 244-1011
Tamberelli Digital (877) 608-4336
516 W. 36th St., Second Fl. FAX **(212) 947-5894**
(Near 10th Ave.) www.tamberelli.com
New York, NY 10018

Thomas Cestare, Inc. (516) 742-5550
188 Herricks Rd. (Near Garfield Ave.) FAX **(516) 742-5551**
Mineola, NY 11501 www.thomascestareinc.com

United Rentals (718) 762-6969
28-44 College Pt. Blvd. FAX **(718) 762-6610**
(Near 138th St.) www.unitedrentals.com
Flushing, NY 11354
(Generators)

(212) 242-9400
Wits End Equipment & Expendables (917) 691-3999
547 W. 49th St. (Near 10th Ave.) FAX **(212) 242-1797**
New York, NY 10019 www.witsendnyc.com
(Generators)

Wits End Equipment & Expendables (718) 361-8400
43-26 12th St. (Near 43rd St.) FAX **(718) 361-8440**
Long Island City, NY 11101 www.witsendnyc.com
(Generators)

Xeno-Lights, Inc. (212) 941-9494
One Worth St. (Near Hudson St.) FAX **(212) 941-9495**
New York, NY 10013 www.xenolights.com

Production Equipment & Accessories

AAA Event Services (888) 580-7368
(973) 808-6290
FAX (973) 808-8588
www.aaaeventservices.com
(Barricades, Chairs, Coolers, Tables & Tents)

Barbizon (212) 586-1620
456 W. 55th St. (Near 10th Ave.) FAX (212) 247-8818
New York, NY 10019 www.barbizon.com

Calzone Case Company (203) 367-5766
(800) 243-5152
225 Black Rock Ave. FAX (203) 336-4406
Bridgeport, CT 06605 www.calzonecase.com
(Equipment Cases)

Expendables Plus, Inc. (718) 609-6464
(917) 964-6464
91 Moultrie St. (Near Calyer St.) FAX (718) 609-6119
Brooklyn, NY 11222
(Chairs, Coffee Urns, Coolers & Tables)

Gerriets International (609) 758-9121
(609) 902-7092
130 Winterwood Ave. FAX (609) 758-9596
Ewing, NJ 08638 www.gi-info.com
(Fiber Optic Drops, Projection Screens & Scrims)

High Output, Inc. (781) 364-1800
(800) 787-4747
FAX (781) 364-1900
www.highoutput.com

Kits and Expendables (212) 947-0700
(718) 482-1824
43-77 Ninth St. FAX (212) 563-2310
(Near 10th Ave.) www.kitsandexpendables.com
Long Island City, NY 11101
(Canopies, Chairs, Coolers, Heaters, Tables & Tents)

Kitstrucks (201) 531-9700
(917) 921-4751
155 Anderson Ave. FAX (201) 531-9701
Moonachie, NJ 07074 www.kitstrucks.com
(Mobile Services: Canopies, Chairs, Coolers, Heaters, Tables & Tents)

Lentini Communications (212) 206-1452
54 W. 21st St., Ste. 301 FAX (212) 206-1453
(Near Fifth Ave.) www.lentinicommunications.com
New York, NY 10010
(Equipment Cases and Carts)

Main Attractions (732) 225-3500
85 Newfield Ave. FAX (732) 225-2110
Edison, NJ 08837 www.mainattractions.com

(212) 246-4390
McKinney Welding Supply Co., Inc. (212) 246-4305
535 W. 52nd St. (Near 10th Ave.) FAX (212) 582-3105
New York, NY 10019 www.mckinneynyc.com
(Helium & Industrial Gases)

Portadam, Inc. (856) 740-0606
(800) 346-4793
3082 S. Black Horse Pike FAX (856) 740-0614
Williamstown, NJ 08094 www.portadam.com
(Water Diversion and Structures)

S.V.E. Sales, Inc. (704) 398-0007
(800) 762-8267
(Portable Roadway Systems) FAX (704) 398-0540
www.mudtraks.com

Travel Auto Bag Co., Inc. (212) 840-0025
(800) 840-0095
264 W. 40th St., 11th Fl. FAX (212) 302-8267
(Near Eighth Ave.) www.travelautobag.com
New York, NY 10018
(Wardrobe Handling and Storage Equipment)

United Rentals (718) 762-6969
28-44 College Pt. Blvd. FAX (718) 762-6610
(Near 138th St.) www.unitedrentals.com
Flushing, NY 11354
(Traffic Safety Equipment)

(212) 242-9400
Wits End Equipment & Expendables (917) 691-3999
547 W. 49th St. (Near 10th Ave.) FAX (212) 242-1797
New York, NY 10019 www.witsendnyc.com
(Mobile Services: Chairs, Coolers, Tables & Tents)

Wits End Equipment & Expendables (718) 361-8400
43-26 12th St. (Near 43rd Ave.) FAX (718) 361-8440
Long Island City, NY 11101 www.witsendnyc.com
(Mobile Services: Chairs, Coolers, Tables & Tents)

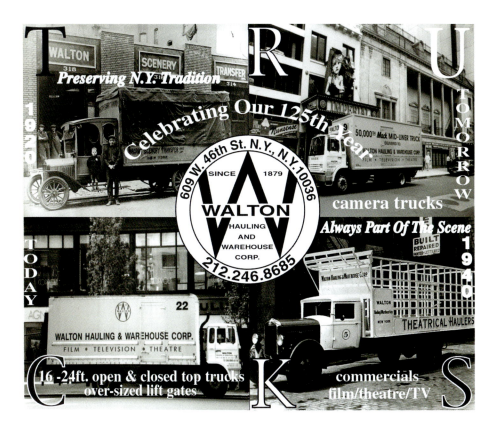

Trucks & Vans

Angel Aerial Corporation (212) 460-8899 / (800) 503-9240
185 Broome St. (Near Clinton St.) FAX (212) 460-8244
New York, NY 10002
www.angelaerial.com

Barn Truck Rental (718) 426-7039 / (718) 426-7042
(Passenger Vans, Pickups & Vans) FAX (718) 898-4573
www.barntruckrental.com

Budd Enterprises, Ltd. (212) 421-8846
P.O. Box 2254 Grand Central Station FAX (212) 319-5897
New York, NY 10163

Budget Truck Rental (212) 465-1911
510 W. 35th St. (Near 10th Ave.) FAX (212) 594-1238
New York, NY 10001 www.budgettruck.com
(High Cubes & Straight Trucks)

Budget Truck Rental (212) 397-2893
415 W. 45th St. (Near Ninth Ave.) FAX (212) 674-2497
New York, NY 10036 www.budgettruck.com
(High Cubes & Straight Trucks)

Budget Truck Rental (212) 533-0155
307 E. 11th St. (Near First Ave.) FAX (212) 674-2497
New York, NY 10003 www.budgettruck.com
(High Cubes & Straight Trucks)

Budget Truck Rental (212) 987-3642
220 E. 117th St. (Near Third Ave.) FAX (212) 987-4403
New York, NY 10035 www.budgettruck.com
(High Cubes & Straight Trucks)

Cars on Location (203) 732-4745 / (800) 736-9178
768 Derby Ave. FAX (203) 732-4193
Seymour, CT 06483 www.carsonlocation.com
(Flatbeds)

ANTHONY AUGLIERA INCORPORATED

Theatrical Transfer

Hauling Broadway Since Vaudeville

203-937-9080
203-937-0140 (Fax)

34 Hamilton Street
West Haven, CT 06516

www.augliera.com

Chelsea Motor Rental (212) 564-9555
549 W. 26th St. (Near 11th Ave.)   FAX (212) 564-0677
New York, NY 10001
(Trucks & Vans)

Courier Car Rental (212) 239-3333
430 W. 37th St. (Near W. 40th St.)   FAX (973) 882-9887
New York, NY 10018   www.ccrentalnyc.com
(High Cubes, Pickups & Vans)

(212) 594-1300
Dependable Transport & Messenger (212) 465-2300
240 W. 37th St., Eighth Fl.   FAX (212) 594-4375
(Near Seventh Ave.)   www.dependablemessenger.com
New York, NY 10018

Eastern Effects, Inc. (718) 855-1197
210 Douglass St.   FAX (212) 504-9534
Brooklyn, NY 11217   www.easterneffects.com
(Camera and Lighting Trucks & Vans)

Elefant Films (888) 435-3326
FAX (212) 757-5141
www.elefantfilms.com

(212) 736-0447
Feature Systems (201) 531-2299
223 Veterans Blvd. (Near 10th Ave.)   FAX (212) 465-1987
Carlstadt, NJ 10018   www.featuresystems.com

(888) 777-2700
Hertz Equipment Rental Corporation (888) 999-5500
www.hertzequip.com

Movie Movers (276) 650-3378
Transportation Equipment (818) 252-7722
400 Movie Movers East   www.moviemovers.com
Axton, VA 24054
(Flatbeds, Pickups, Stake Beds & Top Kicks)

New York Theatrical Haulers, Inc. (718) 875-4400
262 Van Brunt St. (Near Delavin St.)   FAX (718) 832-0660
Brooklyn, NY 11231
(18', 22' and 24' Trucks)

(212) 957-4004
Prop Transport, Inc. (212) 594-2521
630 Ninth Ave., Ste. 309   FAX (212) 957-6569
New York, NY 10036   www.proptransport.com
(Liftgate Trucks & Vans)

Public Service Truck Renting (718) 786-4000
25-61 49th Ave. (Near 27th St.)   FAX (718) 392-8227
Long Island City, NY 11101   www.pstruck.com
(Flatbeds, High Cubes, Tractors & Vans)

Ⓐ **Walton Hauling &**
Warehouse Corporation (212) 246-8685
609 W. 46th St. (Near 11th Ave.)   FAX (212) 586-4628
New York, NY 10036

WitsTrucks (718) 361-8400
43-26 12th St.   FAX (718) 361-8440
Long Island City, NY 11101   www.witsendnyc.com
(12', 14' and 15' Trucks)

(212) 242-9400
WitsTrucks (917) 691-3999
547 W. 49th St. (Near 10th Ave.)   FAX (212) 242-1797
New York, NY 10019   www.witsendnyc.com
(12', 14' and 15' Trucks)

PICTURED:
Port Authority Grain Terminal

LOCATION:
Brooklyn, NY

PHOTOGRAPHER:
John Hutchinson

ALSAM : www.alsam.net
ASSOCIATION OF
LOCATION SCOUTS & MANAGERS

New York 411
*Qualified Listings for the
New York Production Community*
www.newyork411.com

Your set the way it was envisioned.

Classic. Modern. Traditional.
Props. Residential Furnishings. Office Furnishings.
Production Offices. Green Rooms.
Accessories. Cleared Art.

arenson prop center

396 Tenth Avenue
New York, NY 10001
212.564.8383
www.aof.com/props

Props & Wardrobe

Ⓐ ADVERTISER SYMBOL

Refer to the General Index for cross-referencing items in this section.

Aerial Picture Vehicles................... 322
Animatronics, Puppets & Makeup FX...... 323
Architectural Elements 324
Art Fabrication, Licensing & Rentals....... 324
Arts & Crafts Supplies................... 325
Atmospheric/Lighting
   Special FX & Pyrotechnics............. 326
Boats & Nautical Props.................. 328
Building/Surface Materials & Hardware 329
Canopies & Tents 331
Car Prep, Rigging & Prototypes 332
Color-Correct Props 333
Costume Makers & Rentals 334
Draperies & Window Treatments 336
Dry Cleaners.......................... 338
Eyewear & Jewelry 339
Fabrics............................... 340
Firearms & Weapons................... 341
Flags, Graphics & Signage 342
Flowers, Greens & Plants 344
Foam................................ 345
Furnishings—Antique & Vintage 345
Furnishings—Contemporary 346
Games, Toys & Amusements 347
Glass................................ 347
Hair, Makeup & Wardrobe Supplies 348
Ice 350
Lamps & Lighting Fixtures............... 350
Medical & Scientific Props............... 351
Memorabilia & Collectibles 352
Metals & Foils 352
Musical Instrument Rentals.............. 353
Neon 354
Photo, Video & Electronic Props.......... 354
Picture Vehicles....................... 355
Plastics, Plexiglas & Fiberglass 361
Product Placement 362
Prop Fabrication & Mechanical FX........ 363
Prop Houses......................... 368
Restaurant & Kitchen Equipment 372
Specialty Props....................... 373
Sporting Goods....................... 375
Studio Services....................... 376
Tailoring & Alterations 377
Uniforms & Surplus.................... 378
Vintage Clothing & Accessories 378

Aerial Picture Vehicles

Airpower Aviation Resources, Inc. (805) 402-0052
336 West End Ave., Ste. 3B www.airpower-aviation.com
New York, NY 10023

Automobile Film Club of America, Inc.
(718) 447-2255
(718) 447-0438
10 Cross St. FAX (718) 447-2289
Staten Island, NY 10304 www.autofilmclub.com

Helinet Aviation Services (201) 727-1558
111 Charles A. Lindbergh Dr. FAX (201) 727-0121
Teterboro, NJ 07608 www.helinet.com

Jet Productions
(818) 781-4742
(877) 895-1790
7240 Hayvenhurst Ave., Ste. 148 FAX (818) 781-4743
Van Nuys, CA 91406 www.jetproductions.net

Metro Film Cars, Inc.
(973) 450-1692
(973) 699-7707
114 Brighton Ave. FAX (973) 751-8320
Belleville, NJ 07109

New York Film Flyers
(212) 736-0883
(845) 255-1087
529 W. 42nd St. FAX (845) 255-0798
New York, NY 10036 www.nyfilmflyers.com

Animatronics, Puppets & Makeup FX

Norman Bryn (203) 869-5065 / (917) 218-9441
(Makeup FX)
www.makeup-artist.com

Carl Paolino Studios, Inc. (917) 282-4756 / (917) 957-7305
www.paolinostudios.com
(Animatronics, Puppets & Makeup FX)

Castelli Models & Effects (973) 680-1485
17 Herman St.   FAX (973) 680-1486
Glen Ridge, NJ 07028   www.castellimodels.com
(Puppets)

Custom Creations (201) 223-5125
142 32nd St.   FAX (201) 255-0444
Union City, NJ 07087   www.custom-creations.com
(Animatronics & Puppets)

Design to Deceive/Joshua Turi (201) 522-0680
www.designtodeceive.com
(Animatronics, Articulated Dummies, Body Suits, Cadavers, Castings, Characters, Creatures, Foam Sculpting, Hand Puppets, Life-Like Replicas, Makeup FX, Masks, Mechanical Puppets, Models, Molds, Oversized Props, Prosthetics, Puppets, Radio-Controlled Puppets, Sculpting, Special FX Props, Statues & Vacuum-Forming)

Suzanne DeSimone (845) 883-6317 / (914) 456-0229
(Makeup FX)   FAX (845) 883-9672

Ellen Rixford Studio (212) 865-5686
308 W. 97th St., Ste. 71   www.ellenrixford.com
(Near West End Ave.)
New York, NY 10025
(Body Suits & Conventional and Mechanical Puppets)

Flexitoon (212) 877-2757
46 W. 73rd St., Ste. 3A   FAX (212) 799-1987
(Near Central Park West)   www.flexitoon.com
New York, NY 10023
(Puppets)

Carl Fullerton (201) 767-7690
(Makeup FX)

The Gemini Co., Inc. (718) 858-7222
63 Flushing Ave., Ste. 157   www.thegeminicompany.com
Bldg. 131, Ste. 3J
Brooklyn, NY 11205

General Mayhem (516) 767-2793 / (917) 951-7039
61 Haven Ave.   FAX (516) 767-2793
Port Washington, NY 11050   www.gmayhem.com
(Life-Like Replicas, Makeup FX & Prosthetics)

Ⓐ Geppetto Studios, Inc. (718) 398-9792
201 46th St., Second Fl.   www.geppettostudios.com
Brooklyn, NY 11220

Giordano FX (973) 615-7263
518 Central Ave., Ste. 2L
Carlstadt, NJ 07072
www.myspace.com/scareproductions
(Animatronics, Articulated Dummies, Body Suits, Cadavers, Castings, Characters, Computer Enhanced Puppetry, Creatures, Foam Sculpting, Hand Puppets, Life-Like Replicas, Makeup FX, Marionettes, Masks, Mechanical Puppets, Miniatures, Models, Molds, Oversized Props, Prosthetics, Puppets, Radio-Controlled Puppets, Remote-Controlled FX, Robotics, Sculpting, Special FX Props, Statues, Vacuum-Forming & Welding)

Jerard Studio, Inc. (718) 852-4128
481 Van Brunt St., Ste. 11D   FAX (718) 852-2408
(Near Beard St.)   www.jerardstudio.com
Brooklyn, NY 11231
(Animatronics, Costume Mechanics, Masks & Puppets)

Craig Lyman (212) 580-0584 / (646) 732-4243
(Makeup FX)   FAX (212) 580-0596

Monster in my Closet LLC (973) 676-0777 / (973) 479-3555
364 Glenwood Ave.   www.monsterinmycloset.com
(Near Dodd St.)
East Orange, NJ 07017
(Animatronics, Articulated Dummies, Body Suits, Cadavers, Castings, Characters, Creatures, Foam Sculpting, Hand Puppets, Life-Like Replicas, Makeup FX, Masks, Mechanical Puppets, Molds, Oversized Props, Prosthetics, Puppets, Radio-Controlled Puppets, Remote-Controlled FX, Sculpting, Special FX Props & Statues)

NBC New York Prosthetics Shop (212) 664-4093
30 Rockefeller Plaza   FAX (212) 664-5056
New York, NY 10112
www.nbcny.filmmakersdestination.com
(Animatronic Animals, Articulated Urethane Dummies, Body Suits, Body Parts, Cadavers, Castings, Character Body Suits, Characters, Creature Suits, Creatures, Custom Animal FX, Foam Sculpting, Full Body Suits, Hand Puppets, Life-Like Replicas, Makeup FX and Prosthetics, Mannequins, Masks, Mechanical Puppets, Miniatures, Models, Molds, Oversized Props, Prosthetics, Puppeteered FX, Puppet Fabrication, Radio-Controlled Puppets, Remote-Controlled Articulation, Remote-Controlled FX, Remote-Controlled Props, Sculpting, Sculpture, Slip Rubber Masks, Special FX Props, Statues, Ultra-Realistic Rental Babies & Vacuum Forming)

Anthony Pepe (718) 777-1649
(Makeup FX)   www.demonicpumpkins.com

Tobi Britton's Makeup Shop (646) 382-8819 / (212) 807-0447
131 W. 21st St. (Near Seventh Ave.)   FAX (212) 727-0975
New York, NY 10011   www.themakeupshop.com
(Makeup FX)

Yvette Helin Studio, LLC (718) 389-8797 / (917) 617-5935
1205 Manhattan Ave., Ste. 1-3-6   FAX (718) 559-6924
(Near Franklin St.)   www.yvettehelinstudio.com
Brooklyn, NY 11222
(Puppets)

Geppetto
Costumes, Puppets, Props & INSTALLATION ARTS
For Film, Stage, Television, Display, and Special Events
718-398-9792
www.geppettostudios.com
Since 1982

Architectural Elements

Architectural Antiques Exchange (215) 922-3669
715 N. Second St. FAX (215) 922-3680
Philadelphia, PA 19123 www.architecturalantiques.com
(Architectural Salvage)

Prop Central, Inc. (718) 786-2689
209 E. 76th St., Ste. 2A FAX (718) 786-3109
(Near 36th Ave.)
New York, NY 10021

Provost Displays (800) 555-3772
(610) 279-3970
FAX (610) 279-3968
www.provostdisplays.com

Tulnoy Lumber & Scenic Plastics (212) 740-9550
(800) 899-5833
1620 Webster Ave. (Near 173rd St.) FAX (718) 299-8920
Bronx, NY 10457 www.tulnoylumber.com

Art Fabrication, Licensing & Rentals

Andrew Kolb & Son, Ltd. (718) 292-1486
728 E. 136th St. (Near 28th St.) FAX (718) 402-6360
Bronx, NY 10454 www.andrewkolbart.com
(Art Rentals & Custom Art)

Arrangements, Inc. Marine Division (914) 238-1300
P.O. Box 126 FAX (914) 238-9776
Mount Kisco, NY 10549
(Marine Art & Ship Models)

Art & Industry/Doctor Proper, Ltd. (212) 477-0116
50 Great Jones St. (Near Lafayette St.) FAX (212) 477-1420
New York, NY 10012 www.aid20c.com
(1930s–1970s Furniture and Art)

ART: ASAP (212) 956-0805
(800) 821-4717
415 W. 50th St. FAX (212) 956-0796
New York, NY 10019 www.artasap.com

Art for Film, LLC (917) 856-5432
(646) 251-4734
110 Clifton Pl., Ste. 4D www.artforfilmnyc.com
(Near Classon)
Brooklyn, NY 11238

Available Art (917) 279-4686
(Art Rentals) www.availableart.com

Chris Bobin (646) 742-0630
347 Fifth Ave., Ste. 1102 www.chrisbobin.com
New York, NY 10016
(Fabrication)

Film Art LA (323) 461-4900
FAX (323) 461-4959
www.filmartla.com

Framing For Movies (800) 705-8801
676 Broadway www.framingformovies.com
Bayonne, NJ 07002
(Framing)

Peter G. Hackman (212) 923-6436
(Fine Art Reproductions & Sculpture) FAX (212) 923-6436

June Bateman Fine Art (212) 925-7951
(917) 806-8200
1133 Broadway, Ste. 519 FAX (212) 925-7951
New York, NY 10010 www.junebateman.com

McPhee's Art Services (818) 749-7097
10944 Peony Pl. NW FAX (818) 567-2999
Silverdale, WA 98383 www.clearedartservices.com
(Cleared Artwork Sales, Custom Digital Fabrication, Family Photos & Posters)

Prop Art New York (917) 804-4543
www.modernartforrent.com
(Modern Paintings and Photographs)

Troubetzkoy Paintings, Ltd. (212) 688-6544
(800) 335-3735
306 E. 61st St., Third Fl. FAX (212) 688-2627
(Near Second Ave.) www.troubetzkoypaintings.com
New York, NY 10021
(Custom Paintings)

(212) 431-0607
www.artformedia.com (212) 219-1464
84 Walker St. (Near Broadway) FAX (212) 219-0183
New York, NY 10013 www.artformedia.com

Arts & Crafts Supplies

7th Avenue Stationers   (212) 695-4900
210 W. 35th St.   FAX **(212) 643-0480**
(Near Seventh Ave.) **www.seventhavenuecollectors.com**
New York, NY 10001

A.I. Friedman, Inc.   **(212) 243-9000**
   (800) 736-5676
44 W. 18th St. (Near Sixth Ave.)   FAX **(212) 929-7320**
New York, NY 10011

Arthur Brown & Brother Co., Inc.   **(212) 575-5555**
Two W. 45th St. (Near Fifth Ave.)   FAX **(212) 575-5825**
New York, NY 10036   **www.artbrown.com**

Charrette   **(800) 367-3729**
   FAX **(800) 626-7889**
   www.charrette.com

The Compleat Sculptor   **(212) 243-6074**
   (800) 972-8578
90 Vandam St.   FAX **(212) 243-6374**
New York, NY 10013   **www.sculpt.com**

David Davis   **(800) 965-6554**
499 Van Brunt St., Ste. 6A   **www.daviddavisart.com**
Brooklyn, NY 11231

Dualoy Leather   **(212) 736-3360**
45 W. 34th St., Ste. 811   FAX **(212) 594-8327**
(Near Sixth Ave.)   **www.dualoy.com**
New York, NY 10001
(Leathers)

Guerra Paint & Pigment   **(212) 529-0628**
510 E. 13th St. (Near Avenue A)   FAX **(212) 529-0787**
New York, NY 10009   **www.guerrapaint.com**

Lee's Art Shop, Inc.   **(212) 247-0110**
220 W. 57th St. (Near Broadway)   **www.leesartshop.com**
New York, NY 10019

N. Glantz & Son, Inc.   **(718) 439-7707**
218 57th St. (Near Second Ave.)   FAX **(718) 492-5463**
Brooklyn, NY 11220   **www.nglantz.com**

Pearl Paint   **(212) 431-7932**
308 Canal St. (Near Broadway)   FAX **(212) 274-8290**
New York, NY 10013   **www.pearlpaint.com**

Pearl Paint   **(201) 447-0300**
776 Route 17 North   FAX **(201) 447-4102**
Paramus, NJ 07652   **www.pearlpaint.com**

Pearl Paint   **(516) 542-7700**
2000 Hempstead Tpke (Near Front St.)   FAX **(516) 542-7683**
East Meadow, NY 11554   **www.pearlpaint.com**

Sam Flax Art and Design   **(212) 813-6666**
900 Third Ave. (Near E. 54th St.)   FAX **(212) 813-6660**
New York, NY 10022   **www.samflaxny.com**

Sam Flax Art and Design   **(212) 620-3000**
12 W. 20th St. (Near Fifth Ave.)   FAX **(212) 620-3060**
New York, NY 10011   **www.samflaxny.com**

Utrecht Art & Drafting Supplies   **(800) 223-9132**
111 Fourth Ave. (Near E. 12th St.)   FAX **(212) 420-9632**
New York, NY 10003   **www.utrecht.com**

Vasari Classic Artists' Oil Colors   **(800) 932-9375**
323 W. 39th St., Sixth Fl.   FAX **(212) 947-6974**
(Near Eighth Ave.)   **www.shopvasaricolors.com**
New York, NY 10018
(Oil Paints)

Atmospheric/Lighting Special FX & Pyrotechnics

Acme Special Effects	(212) 874-7700
	(917) 549-1896
202 W. 88th St.	www.acmespecialeffects.com
(Near Amsterdam Ave.)	
New York, NY 10024	

Arri CSC	(212) 757-0906
619 W. 54th St. (Near 11th Ave.)	FAX (212) 713-0075
New York, NY 10019	www.cameraservice.com
(Fog and Wind Machines)	

BERGFX	(917) 974-7501
	www.bergfx.com

Mark Bero	(718) 383-6170
(Pyrotechnics)	

	(212) 874-7700
Fred Buchholz	(917) 549-1896
(Pyrotechnics)	www.acmespecialeffects.com

Cress Photo	(973) 694-1280
P.O. Box 4262	FAX (973) 694-6965
Wayne, NJ 07474	www.flashbulbs.com
(Special FX Flashbulbs and Flashguns)	

Dancing Waters	(407) 574-6275
1410 SE Tenth St.	FAX (239) 772-5817
Cape Coral, FL 33990	www.dancingwaters.com
(Theatrical Show Fountains)	

	(800) 437-3939
Ⓐ Drew Jiritano Special Effects	(201) 863-4475
	FAX (201) 863-0351
(Atmospheric FX, Pyrotechnics & Special FX)	www.djfx.com

EFEX Rentals, Inc.	(718) 505-9465
58-05 52nd Ave. (Near 58th St.)	FAX (718) 505-9631
Woodside, NY 11377	
(Atmospheric FX, Pyrotechnics & Weather FX)	

	(310) 312-9772
Future Lighting	(310) 346-1649
(Projection of Clouds, Fire and Snow)	www.futurelighting.net

	(203) 527-9602
FX	(860) 324-0025
165 Union City Rd.	FAX (203) 527-9604
Prospect, CT 06712	
(Pyrotechnics)	

GZ Entertainment & Stunts (201) 675-1118
15 Storig Ave. www.gzfxandstunts.com
Closter, NJ 07624
(Atmospheric FX, Blacklights, Confetti Special FX and Cannon Systems, Fog FX/Machines, Mechanical FX, Projections, Pyrotechnics, Rain FX/Machines, Smoke FX/Machines, Snow FX/Machines, Weather FX/Machines & Wind FX/Machines)

Hill Studio & Scenic (856) 423-8910
35 W. Broad St. FAX (856) 224-0224
Paulsboro, NJ 08066
(Atmospheric FX)

 (212) 645-5295
Hotlights, Inc. (800) 362-5295
133 W. 19th St. (Near Seventh Ave.) FAX (212) 989-6918
New York, NY 10011 www.hotlights.com
(Fog Machines & Wind Machines)

Ⓐ J & M Effects (718) 875-0140
524 Sackett St. (Near Nevins St.) FAX (718) 596-8329
Brooklyn, NY 11217 www.jmfx.net
(Atmospheric FX, Pyrotechnics & Weather FX)

 (914) 403-0483
K-F/X, Inc. (914) 937-9345
49 Townsend St. FAX (914) 937-7274
Port Chester, NY 10573

 (212) 721-9769
Lasers by Technological Artisans (888) 353-1320
Five North View Court www.taiserver.com
Pleasantville, NY 10570
(Laser FX)

Mutual Hardware (718) 361-2480
3627 Vernon Blvd. (Near 36th Ave.) FAX (718) 786-9591
Long Island City, NY 11106 www.mutualhardware.com
(Fog Machines)

Peter Kunz Co., Inc. (845) 687-0400
55 Creek Rd. (Near Tow Path) FAX (845) 687-0579
High Falls, NY 12440 www.peterkunzeffects.com
(Atmospheric FX & Pyrotechnics)

Philny Effects Inc./ (631) 286-0088
Fireworks by Grucci Inc. (800) 227-0088
One Grucci Ln. (Near Horse Block Rd.) FAX (631) 286-9036
Brookhaven, NY 11719 www.grucci.com

Science Faction Corp. (212) 586-1911
149 E. 73rd St.
New York, NY 10021
(Laser FX)

Snow Making by Sturm/
Sturm's Special FX (262) 245-6594
P.O. Box 691 www.snowmaker.com
Lake Geneva, WI 53147
(Pyrotechnics, Snow Machines & Weather FX)

Special Effects
Production Services, Inc. (201) 405-0101
186 Paul Court FAX (201) 405-0632
Hillsdale, NJ 07642
(Laser, Lightning and Plasma FX)

 (800) 245-0397
Zambelli Fireworks Internationale (800) 860-0955
P.O. Box 1463 FAX (724) 658-8318
New Castle, PA 16101 www.zambellifireworks.com

Atmospheric/Lighting Special FX & Pyrotechnics

Boats & Nautical Props

All Seasons Marine Corp. (718) 253-5434
5300 Kings Plaza (Near Avenue U)   FAX **(718) 763-0090**
Brooklyn, NY 11234
(Camera and Support Boats)

Automobile Film Club (718) 447-2255
of America, Inc. (718) 447-0438
10 Cross St. (Near Bay St.)   FAX **(718) 447-2289**
Staten Island, NY 10304   www.autofilmclub.com
(Picture Boats)

CineMarine Team - (661) 222-7342
Cinema Rentals, Inc. (877) 877-9605
25876 The Old Road, Ste. 174   FAX **(661) 253-3643**
Stevenson Ranch, CA 91381   www.cinemarineteam.com
(Camera and Picture Boats & Marine Coordination)

Circle Line Cruises (212) 630-8147
Pier 83, W. 42nd St. (Near 12th Ave.)   FAX **(212) 631-0569**
New York, NY 10036   www.circleline.com
(Sightseeing Boat Charters)

Defender Industries, Inc. (800) 628-8225
42 Great Neck Rd.   FAX **(800) 654-1616**
Waterford, CT 06385   www.defender.com
(Marine Equipment)

Executive Yacht Management, Inc. (310) 306-2555
644 Venice Blvd.   FAX **(310) 306-1147**
Marina del rey, CA 90291   www.yacht-management.com
(Camera/Picture Boats, Charters, Marine Props, Nautical Equipment/Supplies, Powerboats, Sailboats & Yachts)

Kosnac Equipment Rental, Inc. (718) 876-5447
1435 Richmond Terrace   FAX **(718) 876-5448**
(Near Broadway)
Staten Island, NY 10310
(Camera, Picture and Support Boats)

(917) 691-5688
Lots of Yachts/Lots of Spots (800) 773-2812
(Sailing Vessels & Yachts)   FAX **(212) 677-5212**
www.lotsofyachts.com

(973) 450-1692
Metro Film Cars, Inc. (973) 699-7707
114 Brighton Ave.   FAX **(973) 751-8320**
Belleville, NJ 07109

Miller's Launch (718) 727-7303
Pier 7 1/2   FAX **(718) 448-6326**
Staten Island, NY 10301   www.millerslaunch.com
(Barges, Camera/Picture Boats, Canoes, Charters, Charts, Inflatables, Jet Skis, Kayaks, KiteBoards, Maps, Marine Props, Nautical Equipment/Supplies, Nautical Props, Powerboats, Sailboats, Support Boats, Surfboards, Tugboats & Yachts)

(732) 671-9358
Navesink Yachts (954) 462-4583
113 Marvin Rd.   www.navesinkyachts.com
Middletown, NJ 07748
(Canoes, Charters, Charts, Inflatables, Jet Skis, Kayaks, KiteBoards, Maps, Marine Props, Nautical Equipment/Supplies, Nautical Props, Powerboats, Sailboats, Support Boats, Surfboards, Tugboats & Yachts)

New York Nautical (212) 962-4522
158 Duane St. (Near Thomas St.)   FAX **(212) 406-8420**
New York, NY 10013   www.newyorknautical.com
(Charts, Maps & Nautical Instruments)

(516) 922-5853
Nivo Productions (305) 215-8519
167 Cove Rd.   FAX **(516) 922-5854**
Oyster Bay, NY 11771   www.nivoproductions.com
(Runabouts, Speedboats, Vintage Powerboats, Sailboats & Yachts)

Pro Marine Co. (718) 885-3420
P.O. Box 58   FAX **(718) 885-2120**
Bronx, NY 10464
(Camera, Picture and Support Boats)

Stunt Dept., Inc./Chris Barnes (516) 236-9644
FAX **(516) 869-0843**
www.stuntdept.com
(Camera Boats, Marine Coordination & Water Safety)

Urban Desire Cruises (800) 922-4813
210 E. 73rd St.   www.urbandesirecruises.com
(Near Third Ave.)
New York, NY 10021
(Camera and Picture Boats)

West Marine (212) 594-6065
12 W. 37th St. (Near Fifth Ave.)   FAX **(212) 594-0721**
New York, NY 10018   www.westmarine.com
(Powerboat and Sailboat Equipment)

Yacht Owners Association (212) 736-1010
1123 Broadway, Ste. 317   FAX **(212) 594-3297**
(Near Seventh Ave.)   www.yachtsny.com
New York, NY 10010
(Referral for Yacht Charters)

(732) 752-1463
Yacht Services International (718) 885-3294
P.O. Box 703   www.yachtservicesintl.com
Green Brook, NJ 08812
(Barges, Camera/Picture Boats, Charters, Inflatables, Jet Skis, Kayaks, Marine Props, Nautical Equipment/Supplies, Nautical Props, Powerboats, Sailboats, Support Boats, Surfboards, Tugboats & Yachts)

Le Noble Lumber Co., Inc.

The Leading Provider of Scenic & Construction Materials for the Motion Picture & TV Industries Since 1965

Tel: 212.246.0150
Fax: 212.262.7105
www.LeNobleLumber.com

(212) 246-0150

38-20 Review Avenue
Long Island City, NY 11101
Tel: 718.784.5230
Fax: 718.784.1422

Quality Material Delivered When You Need It.

Building/Surface Materials & Hardware

Acme Marble Co., Inc. (718) 965-3560 / (718) 788-0527
160 17th St. (Near Fourth Ave.) FAX (718) 788-0528
Brooklyn, NY 11215
(Granite, Marble & Onyx)

Architectural Antiques Exchange (215) 922-3669
715 N. Second St. FAX (215) 922-3680
Philadelphia, PA 19123 www.architecturalantiques.com
(Antique Bars, Columns, Fixtures, Mantels and Signs)

Blue Bell Lumber & Moulding Co., Inc. (212) 923-0200
501 E. 164th St. FAX (212) 923-3695
(Near Washington Ave.)
Bronx, NY 10456

Blue Bell Lumber & Moulding Co., Inc. (212) 923-0200
4309 Broadway (Near W. 177th St.) FAX (212) 923-3695
New York, NY 10033

Dazian Fabrics (201) 549-1000 / (877) 232-9426
124 Enterprise Ave. South FAX (201) 549-1055
Secaucus, NJ 07094 www.dazian.com
(Flameproofing Supplies & Theatrical Paints)

Epstein's Paint Center (212) 265-3960
822 10th Ave. (Near W. 55th St.) FAX (212) 765-8841
New York, NY 10019 www.epsteinspaint.com
(Carpet, Flooring, Paint, Wallpaper & Window Treatments)

Fabulous Wallcoverings (973) 673-2220
470 Prospect Ave., Ste. 105 FAX (973) 736-3017
West Orange, NJ 07052 www.fabulouswallcoverings.com
(Contemporary & Vintage)

I. Weiss and Sons, Inc. (718) 706-8139 / (888) 325-7192
2-07 Borden Ave. (Near Second St.) FAX (718) 482-9410
Long Island City, NY 11101 www.iweiss.com
(Curtain Track & Theatrical Hardware)

Kitstrucks (201) 531-9700 / (917) 921-4751
155 Anderson Ave. FAX (201) 531-9701
Moonachie, NJ 07074 www.kitstrucks.com
(Mobile Service)

Ⓐ LeNoble Lumber Co., Inc. (212) 246-0150
38-20 Review Ave. FAX (212) 262-7105
Long Island City, NY 11101 www.lenoblelumber.com
(Custom, Flooring, Formica, Hardware, Lumber, Plywood, Windows, Wood Moulding & Wood Veneers)

"Quality & Service Fit for a Prince"
Since 1923

Kolbe Windows
Custom Doors:
Wood, Metal & Access
Moulding
Flooring
Formica
Paint
Hardware
Caulking
Scaffolds
Ladders
Janitorial
Safety Gear

Fine Lumber
Plywood
Drywall
QuietRock
Insulation
Masonry
Plumbing
Roofing
Electrical
Blades & Saws
Power Tools
Keys Cut

Pick-Ups & Same Day Delivery
Large Stock & Competitive Pricing
90 Ft. Boom Service Available

404 West 15th St. New York NY
Phone: (212) 777-1150 Fax: (646) 638-3900
www.PrinceLumber.com

Liberty Electrical Supply Co., Inc. (718) 342-5790
326 Rockaway Ave. FAX **(718) 498-1455**
(Near New York Ave.) **www.libertyelectrical.com**
Brooklyn, NY 11212

Main Attractions (732) 225-3500
85 Newfield Ave. FAX **(732) 225-2110**
Edison, NJ 08837 **www.mainattractions.com**

(212) 875-9403
Mike's Furniture, Inc. **(212) 595-8884**
520 Amsterdam Ave. FAX **(212) 875-8949**
(Near W. 85th St.) **www.mikeslumber.com**
New York, NY 10024
(Stained and Unfinished Furniture)

(212) 595-8884
Mike's Lumber Store **(212) 875-9403**
254 W. 88th St. (Near Broadway) FAX **(212) 874-6921**
New York, NY 10024 **www.mikeslumber.com**
(Hardware & Lumber)

Mutual Hardware (718) 361-2480
3627 Vernon Blvd. (Near 36th Ave.) FAX **(718) 786-9591**
Long Island City, NY 11106 **www.mutualhardware.com**
(Scenic Supplies & Theatrical Hardware)

Ⓐ Prince Lumber Co., Inc. **(212) 777-1150**
404 W. 15th St. (Near Ninth Ave.) FAX **(646) 638-3900**
New York, NY 10011 **www.princelumber.com**
(Flooring, Formica, Hardware, Lumber, Masonry, Paints/
Painting Equipment, Plywood, Windows, Wood Moulding &
Wood Veneers)

(802) 651-6915
Production Advantage, Inc. **(800) 424-9991**
P.O. Box 1700 FAX **(802) 651-6914**
Willston, VT 05449 **www.productionadvantageonline.com**
(Scenic Supplies & Theatrical Hardware)

(800) 555-3772
Provost Displays **(610) 279-3970**
FAX **(610) 279-3968**
www.provostdisplays.com

Rose Brand (800) 223-1624
Four Emerson Ln. (Near W. 15th St.) **www.rosebrand.com**
Secaucus, NJ 07094
(Theatrical Hardware, Paint and Supplies)

Seabury Distributors (973) 335-8266
16 Hillcrest Rd. FAX **(973) 335-8218**
Towaco, NJ 07082
(Fiberboard Forms, Laminates & Plywood)

(718) 387-0300
Siegel Bros. Supply Co., Inc. **(800) 872-8872**
880 Meeker Ave. (Near Varick Ave.) FAX **(718) 387-1874**
Brooklyn, NY 11222

Smolka Co. (212) 686-2300
231 E. 33rd St. (Near Second Ave.) FAX **(212) 686-2308**
New York, NY 10016 **www.smolka.com**
(Bathroom Accessories and Fixtures)

(212) 740-9550
Tulnoy Lumber & Scenic Plastics **(800) 899-5833**
1620 Webster Ave. (Near 173rd St.) FAX **(718) 299-8920**
Bronx, NY 10457 **www.tulnoylumber.com**

Canopies & Tents

AAA Event Services (888) 580-7368 / (973) 808-6290 / FAX (973) 808-8588
(Tents)
www.aaaeventservices.com

Ace Party Rental (718) 445-2600 / (516) 352-4220 / FAX (718) 445-4501
171-27 Station Rd. (Near 172nd St.)
Flushing, NY 11358
www.acepartyrental.com

All Affairs (718) 234-4300 / (212) 675-5530 / FAX (718) 234-6400
2255 59th St. (Near Bay Pkwy)
Brooklyn, NY 11230
www.allaffairs.com

All Occasions/PartyBuster.com (718) 789-9200 / (888) 531-1800 / FAX (718) 789-9222
1111 Rogers Ave.
(Near Clarendon Rd.)
Brooklyn, NY 11226
www.partybuster.com

Camping Station (877) 664-8444 / (718) 418-2622 / FAX (718) 497-2168
1628 Jefferson Ave.
(Near Wyckoff Ave.)
Flushing, NY 11385
www.campingstation.net

Frank's Sport Shop (718) 299-9628 / FAX (718) 583-1652
430 E. Tremont Ave. (Near Park Ave.)
Bronx, NY 10457
www.frankssports.com

Kits and Expendables (212) 947-0700 / (718) 482-1824 / FAX (718) 563-2310
43-77 Ninth St. (Near 10th Ave.)
Long Island City, NY 11101
www.kitsandexpendables.com

Kitstrucks (201) 531-9700 / (917) 921-4751 / FAX (201) 531-9701
155 Anderson Ave.
Moonachie, NJ 07074
www.kitstrucks.com

Kohler Rental (410) 969-9100 / (866) 732-8734 / FAX (410) 969-7276
7767 Old Telegraph Rd., Ste. 6
Severn, MD 21144
www.kohlereventservices.com
(Tents)

Main Attractions (732) 225-3500 / FAX (732) 225-2110
85 Newfield Ave.
Edison, NJ 08837
www.mainattractions.com

Miller's Rental & Sales (732) 985-3050 / FAX (732) 985-4415
764 US Highway 1 (Near Melville Rd.)
Edison, NJ 08817
www.millersrentals.com

Party Line Tent Rentals (914) 592-1200 / (914) 592-2016 / FAX (914) 592-1635
11 Vreeland Ave. (Near Route 9A)
Elmsford, NY 10523
www.partylinerentals.com

Rain Or Shine Event Services (518) 587-8755 / (800) 647-6054
184 Lake Ave. (Near East Ave.)
Saratoga Springs, NY 12866
www.tentrent.com

Shelter Logic (800) 932-9344 / FAX (860) 274-9302
150 Calendar Rd.
(Near Buckingham St.)
Watertown, CT 06795
www.shelterlogic.com

Wits End Equipment & Expendables (212) 242-9400 / (917) 691-3999 / FAX (212) 242-1797
547 W. 49th St. (Near 10th Ave.)
New York, NY 10019
www.witsendnyc.com
(Tents)

Car Prep, Rigging & Prototypes

Automobile Film Club of America, Inc. (718) 447-2255
10 Cross St. (Near Bay St.) (718) 447-0438
Staten Island, NY 10304 FAX (718) 447-2289
www.autofilmclub.com

Cars on Location (800) 736-9178
768 Derby Ave. (203) 732-4745
Seymour, CT 06483 FAX (203) 732-4193
www.carsonlocation.com

EFEX Rentals, Inc. (718) 505-9465
58-05 52nd Ave. (Near 58th St.) FAX (718) 505-9631
Woodside, NY 11377

Giordano FX (973) 615-7263
518 Central Ave., Ste. 2L
Carlstadt, NJ 07072
www.myspace.com/scareproductions
(Car Manipulation, Car Mounts & Lifts)

Color-Correct Props

Colour Correction People, Inc. (212) 947-2882
222 W. 37th St., Eighth Fl. FAX (212) 947-4848
(Near Seventh Ave.) www.colourcorrection.com
New York, NY 10018

Comp 24 (212) 627-4000
(800) 848-7716
127 W. 30th St., Fourth Fl. FAX (212) 627-4287
(Near Seventh Ave.) www.comp24.com
New York, NY 10001

🅐 **Graphics for Industry, Inc.** (212) 889-6202
307 W. 36th St., 10th Fl. FAX (212) 545-1276
(Near Eighth Ave.) www.gfiusa.net
New York, NY 10001

It's In The Works, Inc. (212) 502-6511
127 W. 30th St., Fourth Fl. www.itsintheworks.net
(Near E. 27th St.)
New York, NY 10001

Looking for Color Correct Packaging for TV or Print
Call
Graphics for Industry, Inc.
Serving the Industry Since 1946

307 West 36th Street, New York, NY 10018
212-889-6202
email:mpahmer@gfiusa.net

Costume Makers & Rentals

Adele Recklies Co. (718) 768-9036
420 Fourth Ave., Ste. 1 FAX (718) 768-9036
(Near Eighth St.) www.beadcrachetsnakes.com
Brooklyn, NY 11215
(Crocheting & Knitting)

Aegean Imports (650) 593-8300
4600 El Camino Rd., Ste. 215 FAX (650) 559-0243
Los Altos, CA 94022
(Greek Fisherman's Caps)

Barclay Church Supply (718) 863-0474
3348 Campbell Dr. (Near Agar Pl.)
Bronx, NY 10465
(Religious Garments)

Ben Kahn Furs (212) 279-0633
424 Fifth Ave., First Fl. (Near 39th St.) FAX (212) 827-5004
New York, NY 10018
(Fur Coats)

Chris Bobin (646) 742-0630
(Costume Construction) www.chrisbobin.com

(212) 957-7000
Bra*Tenders (888) 438-2272
630 Ninth Ave., Ste. 601 FAX (212) 957-7010
New York, NY 10036 www.bratenders.com
(Specialty/Vintage Look Undergarments and Hosiery)

(610) 279-3970
Character Translations, Inc. (800) 555-3774
(Character Costume Construction) FAX (610) 279-3968
www.charactertranslations.com

(518) 374-7442
The Costumer, Inc. (518) 374-7459
1020-1030 Barrett St. (Near Union St.) FAX (518) 374-0087
Schenectady, NY 12305 www.thecostumer.com
(Costume Rentals, Construction and Design)

Creative Costume Company (212) 564-5552
242 W. 36th St., Eighth Fl. FAX (212) 564-5613
(Near Seventh Ave.) www.creativecostume.com
New York, NY 10018
(Character and Period Costume Rentals & Costume Design)

Early Halloween (212) 691-2933
130 W. 25th St., 11th Fl. FAX (212) 243-1499
(Near Sixth Ave.) www.earlyhalloween.com
New York, NY 10001
(Vintage Costume Rentals; By Appointment Only)

(718) 273-7139
Every Thing Goes (718) 720-5378
140 Bay St. (Near Victory Blvd.) www.etgstores.com
Staten Island, NY 10301

Francine Tint Costume Design/
Soft Sculpture (212) 475-3366

(718) 823-9792
Frank Bee Stores (718) 823-3033
3435 E. Tremont Ave. FAX (718) 824-2979
(Near Bruckner Blvd.) www.costumeman.com
Bronx, NY 10465
(Costume Rentals)

Frankie Steinz Costume (212) 925-1373
24 Harrison St. www.frankiesteinz.com
(Near Greenwich St.)
New York, NY 10013

Geppetto Studios, Inc. (718) 398-9792
201 46th St., Second Fl. www.geppettostudios.com
Brooklyn, NY 11220

Giordano FX (973) 615-7263
518 Central Ave., Ste. 2L
Carlstadt, NJ 07072
www.myspace.com/scareproductions
(Animal/Character Costumes, Armor, Construction, Custom, Design, Embroidery, Full Costume Construction and Design, Futuristic Costuming, Leathers, Mascots, Masks, Police, Military, Period, Rentals, Screenprinting, Spacesuits, Special FX Costumes, Uniforms, Vintage, Western Wear & Wigs)

(914) 376-5301
Greek 101.com (888) 473-3550
646 Saw Mill River Rd. FAX (914) 476-4333
(Near Clement St.) www.greek101.com
Yonkers, NY 10710
(Fraternity and Sorority Items)

Hat/Cap Exchange (302) 478-9338
P.O. Box 250 FAX (866) 270-7668
Ouray, CO 81427 www.hatcapexchange.com

Helen Uffner Vintage Clothing, LLC (718) 937-0220
30-10 41st Ave., Third Fl. FAX (718) 937-0227
(Near Northern Blvd.) www.uffnervintage.com
Long Island City, NY 11101
(1860s–1970s Costume Rentals)

(212) 695-6888
J. Levine Books & Judaica (800) 553-9474
Five W. 30th St. (Near Fifth Ave.) FAX (212) 643-1044
New York, NY 10001 www.levinejudaica.com
(Jewish Religious Garments)

Justin Justin (718) 721-9022
11-27 31st Dr., Ste. 4 www.justinjustin.com
(Near Vernon Blvd.)
Long Island City, NY 11106
(Custom Menswear)

(212) 803-1600
LaCrasia Gloves (917) 912-4174
1181 Broadway, Eighth Fl. FAX (212) 686-5250
(Near 28th St.) www.wegloveyou.com
New York, NY 10001
(Custom and Rental Gloves)

(212) 226-4182
Celeste Livingston (646) 456-0013
(Costume Construction)

Mask Arts Co./ (212) 243-4039
Stanley Allan Sherman (917) 836-6764
203 W. 14th St., Ste. 5F www.maskarts.com
(Near Seventh Ave.)
New York, NY 10011
(Custom Leather Work & Masks)

(973) 575-3503
Norcostco - Eastern Costume (800) 220-6940
333A Route 46 West FAX (973) 575-2563
Fairfield, NJ 07004 www.norcostco.com
(Theatrical Costume Rentals)

Odds Costume Rental, Inc. (212) 268-6227
231 W. 29th St., Third Fl. FAX (212) 629-3032
(Near Seventh Ave.)
New York, NY 10001
(1900–Present Costume Rentals)

(212) 725-1174
On Stage Dancewear (866) 725-1174
197 Madison Ave. (Near E. 35th St.) FAX (212) 725-4524
New York, NY 10016 www.onstagedancewear.com
(Dancewear & Dance Shoes)

Parsons-Meares, Ltd. (212) 242-3378
519 Eighth Ave., 11th Fl. FAX (212) 741-1869
New York, NY 10018
(Costume Construction)

Rodney Gordon, Inc.   **(212) 594-6658**
519 Eighth Ave., 11th Fl.   FAX **(212) 594-6693**
(Near W. 36th St.)
New York, NY 10018
(Hat and Mask Construction)

rrrentals   **(212) 242-6120**
245 W. 29th St., 11th Fl.   FAX **(212) 242-6127**
New York, NY 10001   **www.rrrentalsny.com**
(Beading, Contemporary, Design, Evening Gowns, Gloves, Hats, Knitwear, Leathers, Masks, Rentals, Shoes/Boots, Undergarments & Wedding Gowns)

Saint Laurie Merchant Tailors   **(212) 643-1916**
22 W. 32nd St., Fifth Fl.   FAX **(212) 695-4709**
(Near Fifth Ave.)   **www.saintlaurie.com**
New York, NY 10001
(Costume Construction and Design)

The Shirt Store, Inc.   **(212) 557-8040**
51 E. 44th St. (Near Fifth Ave.)   FAX **(212) 557-1628**
New York, NY 10017   **www.shirtstore.com**
(Custom Shirtmaking)

SOTU Productions   **(718) 963-1034**
102 N. Eighth St., Fourth Fl.   **www.sotuproductions.com**
Brooklyn, NY 11211
(1900s–Contemporary, Animals, Armor, Beading, Construction, Custom, Dancewear, Design, Embroidery, Ethnic Apparel, Evening Gowns, Flight Gear, Full Costume Construction and Design, Furs, Futuristic Costuming, Gloves, Hats, Knitwear, Leathers, Mascots, Masks, Masquerade Costuming, Police, Military, Period–Present, Religious Garments, Rentals, Screenprinting, Shoes/Boots, Spacesuits, Special FX Costumes, Undergarments, Uniforms, Vintage, Wedding Gowns, Western Wear & Wigs)

Studio Rouge, Inc.   **(212) 989-8363**
152 W. 25th St., Seventh Fl.   FAX **(212) 989-5575**
(Near Seventh Ave.)   **www.studiorouge.com**
New York, NY 10001
(Contemporary, Dancewear, Evening Gowns, Full Costume Construction, Knitwear, Leathers & Period–Present)

Suzanne Couture Modelmaking   **(212) 714-9310**
227 W. 29th St. (Near Seventh Ave.)   FAX **(212) 714-0759**
New York, NY 10001
    www.suzannecouturemodelmaking.com
(Animal/Character Costumes, Construction, Custom, Design, Full Costume Construction, Furs, Futuristic Costuming, Leathers, Mascots, Masks, Religious Garments, Spacesuits, Special FX Costumes & Western Wear)

Tiecrafters, Inc.   **(212) 629-5800**
252 W. 29th St. (Near Eighth Ave.)   FAX **(212) 629-0115**
New York, NY 10001   **www.tiecrafters.com**
(Custom Ties and Neckwear)

Timberlake Studios, Inc.   **(212) 967-4736**
322 Seventh Ave., Ste. 2F   FAX **(212) 967-4737**
(Near W. 28th St.)   **www.timberlakestudios.com**
New York, NY 10001
(Costume Construction and Design)

    (818) 508-2111
Western Costume Co.   **(888) 293-7837**
11041 Vanowen St.   FAX **(818) 508-2153**
North Hollywood, CA 91605   **www.westerncostume.com**
(Costume Construction and Rentals)

White Daisy   **(716) 397-2234**
P.O. Box 170   **www.whitedaisyshop.com**
Jamestown, NY 14702
(Tie-Dyed Clothing)

Yn Couture   **(917) 863-9492**
    www.yncouture.net
(All Eras, Construction and Design, Contemporary, Custom, Full Costume Construction & Leather Costumes)

    (718) 389-8797
Yvette Helin Studio, LLC   **(917) 617-5935**
1205 Manhattan Ave., Ste. 1-3-6   FAX **(718) 559-6924**
(Near Franklin St.)   **www.yvettehelinstudio.com**
Brooklyn, NY 11222
(Costume Construction and Design)

Draperies & Window Treatments

Allstate Glass Corp. (212) 226-2517
85 Kenmare St. (Near Mulberry St.)   FAX (212) 966-7904
New York, NY 10012
(Blinds & Shades)

Circle Visual, Inc. (212) 719-5153
225 W. 37th St., 16th Fl.   FAX (212) 704-0918
(Near Seventh Ave.)   www.circlevisual.com
New York, NY 10018
(Custom)

(201) 549-1000
Dazian Rentals   (877) 232-9426
124 Enterprise Ave. South   FAX (201) 549-1055
Secaucus, NJ 07094   www.dazian.com

(201) 770-9950
Ⓐ **Drape Kings**   (888) 372-7363
3200 Liberty Ave., Ste. 2C   FAX (201) 770-9956
North Bergen, NJ 07047   www.drapekings.com
(Theatrical Draperies)

Eldridge Textile Co. (732) 544-4500
22 Meridian Rd.   www.eldridgetextile.com
(Near Madison Ave.)
Eatontown, NJ 07724
(Window Treatments)

Epstein's Paint Center (212) 265-3960
822 10th Ave. (Near W. 55th St.)   FAX (212) 765-8841
New York, NY 10019   www.epsteinspaint.com
(Blinds, Shades & Shutters)

(609) 758-9121
Gerriets International   (609) 902-7092
130 Winterwood Ave.   FAX (609) 758-9596
Ewing, NJ 08638   www.gi-info.com
(Theatrical Draperies)

(718) 706-8139
I. Weiss and Sons, Inc.   (888) 325-7192
2-07 Borden Ave. (Near Second St.)   FAX (718) 482-9410
Long Island City, NY 11101   www.iweiss.com
(Fiber Optic Curtains & Theatrical Draperies and Rigging)

(201) 222-1677
Ⓐ **Joseph C. Hansen Company, Inc.**   (212) 248-8055
629 Grove St., Lot 26   FAX (201) 222-1699
Jersey City, NJ 07310   www.jchansen.com
(Custom Curtains and Draperies)

Justin Justin (718) 721-9022
11-27 31st Dr., Ste. 4   www.justinjustin.com
(Near Vernon Blvd.)
Long Island City, NY 11106
(Curtains)

Nelson Enterprises (908) 479-6902
1014 Route 173 East FAX (908) 479-6903
Bloomsbury, NJ 08804 www.nelson-enterprises.com
(Theatrical Draperies)

Novelty Scenic Studios (516) 671-5940
40 Sea Cliff Ave. (Near Glen Keith Rd.) FAX (516) 674-2213
Glen Cove, NY 11542
(Theatrical Draperies and Rigging)

Rose Brand (800) 223-1624
Four Emerson Ln. (Near W. 15th St.) www.rosebrand.com
Secaucus, NJ 07094
(Theatrical Draperies and Rigging)

Royal Production Services (212) 781-1440
(Pipe & Drape)

ShowBiz Enterprises, Inc. (212) 989-5005
 (800) 746-9249
FAX (800) 989-6006
www.showbizenterprises.com

Showman Fabricators, Inc. (718) 935-9899
47-22 Pearson Pl. (Near Davis Court) FAX (718) 855-9823
Long Island, NY 11101 www.showfab.com
(Theatrical Draperies)

pipe & drape
heights 6"-50 feet
film & television tricks
30 + colors and styles
carpet, rope & stanchions
traveler & quick track, Kabuki
complete packages or a la carte

RENTALS | SALES | SERVICES | 24/7 | FABRICATION | NATIONWIDE
+1-201-770-9950 www.drapekings.com 888-DRAPE-ME

Draperies & Window Treatments

Dry Cleaners

Aphrodite French Cleaners (718) 782-8668
35 Division Pl. (Near Morgan Ave.)
Brooklyn, NY 11222

Aphrodite French Cleaners (212) 579-1160
322 Columbus Ave. (Near W. 75th St.)
New York, NY 10023

Aphrodite French Cleaners (212) 755-7305
1187 Second Ave. (Near E. 62nd St.)
New York, NY 10021

Aphrodite French Cleaners (212) 475-4869
30 University Pl. (Near E. Ninth St.)
New York, NY 10003

Cambridge Cleaners (212) 986-4420
719 Second Ave. (Near E. 39th St.)
New York, NY 10016

Chris French Cleaners (212) 475-5444
57 Fourth Ave. (Near E. Ninth St.) FAX **(212) 253-1784**
New York, NY 10003

Clevergreen Cleaners (781) 306-9705
109 Charles St. (617) 710-0999
Boston, MA 02114 FAX **(781) 306-9708**
(Rush Service Available) www.clevergreencleaners.com

Ernest Winzer Theatrical & (718) 294-2400
Leather Cleaner (877) 946-9371
1828 Cedar Ave., P.O. Box 294 FAX **(718) 294-2729**
(Near 179th) www.winzercleaners.com
Bronx, NY 10453

Fancy Cleaners (212) 982-2007
254 Third Ave. (Near E. 21st St.) www.fancycleaners.com
New York, NY 10010
(Same Day Service Available)

Fancy R&S Leather Cleaners (212) 481-1112
242 E. 14th St. (Near Third Ave.)
New York, NY 10003

Fashion Award Cleaners (212) 289-5623
2205 Broadway (Near E. 94th St.)
New York, NY 10024

Flat Rate Cleaners (646) 825-3857
www.flatratecleaners.com

Hallak Cleaners (212) 832-0750
(888) 343-2111
1232 Second Ave. (Near E. 65th St.) FAX **(201) 343-0223**
New York, NY 10021 www.hallakcleaners.com

Lincoln Terrace Cleaners (212) 874-9146
149 Amsterdam Ave. FAX **(212) 874-3066**
(Near W. 66th St.)
New York, NY 10023

Meurice Garment Care (212) 475-2778
(800) 240-3377
31 University Pl. (Near E. Eighth St.) FAX **(516) 627-2943**
New York, NY 10003 www.meuricegarmentcare.com

Meurice Garment Care (212) 759-9057
(800) 240-3377
245 E. 57th St. (Near Second Ave.) FAX **(516) 627-2943**
New York, NY 10022 www.meuricegarmentcare.com

Meurice Garment Care (516) 627-6060
(800) 240-3377
20 Park Ave. (Near Plamdome Rd.) FAX **(516) 627-2943**
Manhasset, NY 11030 www.meuricegarmentcare.com

> **Ⓐ Minerva Cleaners** (718) 729-4566
> (917) 687-3211
> 29-09 Broadway FAX **(718) 729-4344**
> Astoria, NY 11106

Neighborhood Cleaners
Association International (212) 967-3002
252 W. 29th St., Seventh Fl. FAX **(212) 967-2240**
(Near Eighth Ave.)
New York, NY 10001

Tiecrafters, Inc. (212) 629-5800
252 W. 29th St. (Near Eighth Ave.) FAX **(212) 629-0115**
New York, NY 10001 www.tiecrafters.com
(Tie and Scarf Cleaning)

MINERVA CLEANERS
Est. 1969
FILM • THEATRE • TV

Quality dry cleaning • Shirts hand finished
All types of laundry • 24-hr. service • Overnight service
Same day cleaning & laundry

Pick-up & Delivery available 24 hrs.
7 days a week!

718-729-4566

Emergency service available
Fax: 718-729-4344 • 24-hr Cell 917-687-3211
Incorporated in the states of NJ and CT

Eyewear & Jewelry

Every Thing Goes   (718) 273-7139 / (718) 720-5378
140 Bay St. (Near Victory Blvd.)   www.etgstores.com
Staten Island, NY 10301

The Eye Shop   (212) 673-9450
50 W. Eighth St. (Near Sixth Ave.)
New York, NY 10011
(Eyeglasses & Sunglasses)

The Family Jewels   (212) 633-6020
130 W. 23rd St., Ground Fl.   www.familyjewelsnyc.com
(Near Seventh Ave.)
New York, NY 10011
(Vintage Jewelry and Accessories)

Fanelli Antique Timepieces   (212) 517-2300
790 Madison Ave., Ste. 202 (Near E. 67th St.)
New York, NY 10065
(Antique Watches)

Helen Uffner Vintage Clothing LLC   (718) 937-0220
30-10 41st Ave., Third Fl.   FAX (718) 937-0227
(Near Northern Blvd.)   www.uffnervintage.com
Long Island City, NY 11101
(Vintage Accessories, Eyeglasses, Jewelry and Watches)

Prop Specs   (323) 935-7776
(Antique–Present Eyeglasses)   FAX (323) 935-7778
www.propspecs.com

Screaming Mimi's   (212) 677-6464
382 Lafayette St. (Near E. Fourth St.)   FAX (212) 677-6523
New York, NY 10003   www.screamingmimis.com
(Jewelry & Accessories)

Sol Moscot Opticians   (866) 667-2687
118 Orchard St. (Near Delancey St.)   www.moscots.com
New York, NY 10002
(Eyeglasses & Sunglasses)

Fabrics

Be Seated, Inc. (212) 924-8444
66 Greenwich Ave. (Near Seventh Ave.) www.tabwa.com
New York, NY 10011
(Hand-Woven Textiles)

Circle Visual, Inc. (212) 719-5153
225 W. 37th St., 16th Fl. FAX (212) 704-0918
(Near Seventh Ave.) www.circlevisual.com
New York, NY 10018
(Draperies, Pillows, Trimming & Window Treatments)

Ⓐ Dazian Fabrics (201) 549-1000
124 Enterprise Ave. South (877) 232-9426
Secaucus, NJ 07094 FAX (201) 549-1055
(Theatrical Fabrics) www.dazian.com

Decorators Walk/Schumacher (212) 415-3900
979 Third Ave., Ste. 611 (Near E. 59th St.)
New York, NY 10022

Dye-Namix, Inc. (212) 941-6642
151 Grand St., Second Fl. FAX (212) 941-7407
(Near Broadway) www.dyenamix.com
New York, NY 10013
(Dyeing, Painting & Silkscreening)

Eldridge Textile Co. (732) 544-4500
22 Meridian Rd. www.eldridgetextile.com
(Near Madison Ave.)
Eatontown, NJ 07724
(Linens)

The Family Jewels (212) 633-6020
130 W. 23rd St., Ground Fl. www.familyjewelsnyc.com
(Near Seventh Ave.)
New York, NY 10011
(Vintage Textiles)

Gerriets International (609) 758-9121
130 Winterwood Ave. (609) 902-7092
Ewing, NJ 08638 FAX (609) 758-9596
www.gi-info.com
(Drops, Scrims, Textiles & Theatrical Fabrics)

Hamburger Woolen Co., Inc. (516) 352-7400
23 Denton Ave., P.O. Box 796 (800) 221-3464
(Near Bellmont Ave.) FAX (516) 352-7704
New Hyde Park, NY 11040 www.hwcny.com

Helen Uffner Vintage Clothing LLC (718) 937-0220
30-10 41st Ave., Third Fl. FAX (718) 937-0227
(Near Northern Blvd.) www.uffnervintage.com
Long Island City, NY 11101

I. Weiss and Sons, Inc. (718) 706-8139
2-07 Borden Ave. (Near Second St.) (888) 325-7192
Long Island City, NY 11101 FAX (718) 482-9410
www.iweiss.com
(Flameproofing, Theatrical Fabrics & Trimmings)

Marvco Corporation (516) 621-0654
P.O. Box 1302 FAX (561) 621-0654
Roslyn Heights, NY 11577
(Linens)

Mood Designer Fabric (212) 730-5003
225 W. 37th St., Third Fl. FAX (212) 221-1932
(Near Eighth Ave.) www.moodfabrics.com
New York, NY 10018

National Fiber Technology, LLC (978) 686-2964
300 Canal St. FAX (978) 686-1497
Lawrence, MA 01840 www.nftech.com
(Fur and Hair Fabrics)

P & S Fabrics (212) 226-1534
360 Broadway (Near Franklin St.) (212) 226-1572
New York, NY 10013 FAX (212) 343-1838

Paron Fabrics West (212) 768-3266
206 W. 40th St. (Near Seventh Ave.) FAX (212) 768-3260
New York, NY 10018 www.paronfabrics.com

Production Advantage, Inc. (800) 424-9991
P.O. Box 1700 (802) 651-6915
Willston, VT 05449 FAX (802) 651-6914
www.productionadvantageonline.com
(Theatrical Fabrics)

Rose Brand (800) 223-1624
Four Emerson Ln. (Near W. 33rd) www.rosebrand.com
Secaucus, NJ 07094
(Theatrical Fabrics)

Rosen & Chadick Textiles, Inc. (212) 869-0142
561 Seventh Ave., Second Fl. FAX (212) 730-5865
(Near 40th St.) www.rosenandchadickfabrics.com
New York, NY 10018

The Tablecloth Company (973) 942-1555
514 Totowa Ave. (800) 227-5251
Paterson, NJ 07522 FAX (800) 377-3720
(Table Linens) www.tablecloth.com

Turning Star, Inc. (718) 254-0534
229 Bond St. (Near Ninth St.) (877) 849-3182
Brooklyn, NY 11217 FAX (718) 254-0538
(Flameproofing) www.turningstar.com

DAZIAN FABRICS

SALES
FR Velvet
Velour
Metallic
Sheers
Scrim
Muslin
Masking
Blackout
Cyclorama
Keying
Stretch
Lighting +
Projection Fabrics.
Custom Sewing +
Printing Services

RENTALS
Theatrical,
Austrian Puff +
Event Draperies.
Star Drop, Bead +
Fiber Optic Curtains.
Scrims, Backdrops +
Projection Surfaces.

East Rental 877.232.9426
877.532.9426

West Rental 877.432.9426
877.277.9426

www.dazian.com

Firearms & Weapons

Centre Firearms Co., Inc. (212) 244-4040
10 W. 37th St., Seventh Fl. FAX (212) 947-1233
(Near Fifth Ave.) www.centrefirearms.com
New York, NY 10018

Cinematicstunts.com/
John-Eric Schuman (877) 447-8868
41 Kalina Dr. www.cinematicstunts.com
Saugerties, NY 12477

(718) 809-9057
Hit & Run Productions (718) 782-8381
65 Roebling St., Ste. 202 FAX (718) 782-8388
Brooklyn, NY 11211 www.hitandrunproductions.com
(Guns & Period Firearms)

I.M.A./International
Military Antiques, Inc. (908) 903-1200
1000 Valley Rd. FAX (908) 903-0106
Gillette, NJ 07933 www.ima-usa.com
(Period Guns, Military Material and Swords)

J & M Effects (718) 875-0140
524 Sackett St. (Near Nevins St.) FAX (718) 596-8329
Brooklyn, NY 11217 www.jmfx.net
(Edged Weapons & Firearms)

Navy Arms Co. (304) 262-9870
219 Lawn St. FAX (304) 262-1658
Martinsburg, WV 25401 www.navyarms.com
(Period Guns)

Starfire Swords, Ltd. (607) 589-7244
74 Railroad Ave. (Near Sabin Rd.) FAX (607) 589-6630
Spencer, NY 14883 www.starfireswords.com
(Axes, Daggers & Swords)

Ⓐ Weapon Specialists, Ltd. (212) 941-7696
33 Greene St., Ste. 1 West FAX (212) 941-7654
(Near Grand St.) www.weaponspecialists.com
New York, NY 10013
(Armor, Edged Weapons, Explosives & Guns)

National Flag & Display

MANUFACTURERS OF BANNERS AND FLAGS SINCE 1935

Custom Banners
- Press Backdrops
- Building Wraps
- Wall Murals
- Fabric Architecture
- Theatrical Flats

Flags & Accessories
- U.S., State & Foreign Flags
- Hand Held Flags
- Patriotic Fans & Bunting
- Hardware & Accessories
- *Purchase or Rental*

22 W. 21st Street
New York, NY 10010
T. 212-462-4000
F. 212-462-2624
sales@nationalflag.com

www.nationalflag.com

Flags, Graphics & Signage

AAA American Flag Decorating Co., Inc. (212) 279-3524 / (212) 279-4644
36 W. 37th St., Ninth Fl. FAX (212) 695-8392
(Near Sixth Ave.)
New York, NY 10018

Ace Banner Flag & Graphics (212) 620-9111
107 W. 27th St. (Near Sixth Ave.) FAX (212) 463-9128
New York, NY 10001 www.acebanner.com
(Banners, Digital Prints, Displays, Flags, Graphics & Posters)

All Suffolk Flag Rental Company (631) 589-2295 / (800) 734-4144
812 Sayville Ave. (Near 13th St.) FAX (631) 589-8141
Bohemia, NY 11716

Arista Flag Corporation (845) 246-7700
157 W. Saugerties Rd. FAX (845) 246-7786
(Near Bandcamp Rd.) www.aristaflag.com
Saugerties, NY 12477
(Banners & Flags)

Art Flag Co., Inc. (212) 334-1890 / (877) 278-3524
Eight Jay St. (Near Hudson St.) FAX (212) 941-9631
New York, NY 10013 www.artflag.com
(Banners & Flags)

Baumwell Graphics, Inc. (704) 814-4550 / (888) 266-7245
8923 Providence Estates Ct. www.chromatype.com
Charlotte, NC 28270
(Custom Magazines and Newspapers, Graphic Design, Graphic Props, Giclee Printing, Labels, Large Format Printing, Laser Engraving & Typesetting)

Bernard Maisner, Master Calligrapher (212) 477-6776
www.bernardmaisner.com
(Period Calligraphy and Documents)

Big Apple Visual Group (212) 629-3650 / (877) 244-2775
247 W. 35th St. (Near Eighth Ave.) FAX (212) 629-4954
New York, NY 10001 www.bigapplegroup.com

Carl Waltzer Digital Service (212) 674-7848 / (212) 475-8748
873 Broadway, Ste. 412 FAX (212) 475-9359
(Near 18th St.) www.waltzer.com
New York, NY 10003
(Graphic Design)

Circle Visual, Inc. (212) 719-5153
225 W. 37th St., 16th Fl. FAX (212) 704-0918
(Near Seventh Ave.) www.circlevisual.com
New York, NY 10018
(Custom Banners, Displays & Silkscreening)

Color Reflections, Inc. (215) 627-4686
400 Green St. FAX (215) 627-9030
Philadelphia, PA 19123 www.color-reflections.com

Comp 24 (212) 627-4000 / (800) 848-7716
127 W. 30th St., Fourth Fl. FAX (212) 627-4287
(Near Seventh Ave.) www.comp24.com
New York, NY 10001

Custom Creations (201) 223-5125
142 32nd St. FAX (201) 255-0444
Union City, NJ 07087 www.custom-creations.com

A date with sunrise design... (917) 568-6027
(Graphic Design) (212) 987-7419

Dazian Fabrics (201) 549-1000
124 Enterprise Ave. South (877) 232-9426
Secaucus, NJ 07094 FAX (201) 549-1055
(Custom Banners & Displays) www.dazian.com

Dweller By The Stream Bindery (845) 657-8700
768 Bostock Rd. FAX (845) 657-8700
(Near Upper Boiceville)
Boiceville, NY 12412
(Custom Hand Book Binding & Graphic Design)

Eclectic • Encore Props, Inc. (212) 645-8880
620 W. 26th St., Fourth Fl. FAX (212) 243-6508
(Near 11th Ave.) www.eclecticprops.com
New York, NY 10001

Kraus & Sons, Inc. (212) 620-0408
158 W. 27th St. (Near Sixth Ave.) FAX (212) 924-4081
New York, NY 10001 www.krausbanners.com

Let There Be Neon, Inc. (212) 226-4883
38 White St. (Near Church St.) FAX (212) 431-6731
New York, NY 10013 www.lettherebeneon.com
(Custom Signs)

Manhattan Neon Sign Corporation (212) 714-0430
514 W. 36th St. (Near 10th Ave.) FAX (212) 947-3906
New York, NY 10018 www.manhattanneon.com
(Illuminated and Non-Illuminated Signage)

MJ Signs & Promotions (201) 594-9800
123 Patterson St. FAX (201) 594-9436
Hillsdale, NJ 07642

Ⓐ National Flag & Display Co., Inc. (212) 462-4000
22 W. 21st St. (Near Fifth Ave.) FAX (212) 462-2624
New York, NY 10010 www.nationalflag.com
(Banners & Flags)

Really Fake Digital (800) 761-6995
FAX (323) 227-9033
www.reallyfake.com
(Custom, Digital Imaging, Graphics & Signage)

RJP Creations, Inc. (973) 786-6993
290 Decker Pond Rd., Bldg. B2 FAX (973) 786-6997
Andover, NJ 07821 www.rjpcreations.com
(Signage)

Royal Production Services (212) 781-1440
(Flag Rentals)

Sign Expo (212) 925-8585
102 Franklin St., Fourth Fl. FAX (212) 925-5628
New York, NY 10013 www.signexpo.com

SMP Digital Graphics (212) 691-6766
135 W. 20th St. (Near Sixth Ave.) FAX (212) 989-6386
New York, NY 10011

(212) 243-8521
Specialty Signs Co., Inc. (800) 394-3433
54 W. 21st St., Ste. 201 FAX (212) 243-6457
(Near Sixth Ave.) www.specialtysigns.com
New York, NY 10010

Joan Winters (212) 475-6605
(Graphics)

Flags, Graphics & Signage

Flowers, Greens & Plants

Lawrence Amanuel
(Greensman)
(914) 522-9297
(845) 928-3849
FAX (845) 928-3850

American Foliage & Design Group, Inc.
122 W. 22nd St. (Near Sixth Ave.)
New York, NY 10011
(212) 741-5555
FAX (212) 741-9499
www.americanfoliagedesign.com
(Artificial and Live Flowers and Plants)

James M. Breen
(Greensman)
(610) 742-4442
(610) 358-4416

Castle & Pierpont
353 W. 39th St. (Near Eighth Ave.)
New York, NY 10018
(212) 244-8668
FAX (212) 244-8662
www.castlepierpont.com

Charles Lubin Company, Inc.
145 Saw Mill River Rd., Third Fl.
(Near Lake Ave.)
Yonkers, NY 10701
(914) 968-5700
FAX (914) 968-5723
www.lubinflowers.com
(Artificial Flowers and Plants)

Chelsea Garden Center
580 11th Ave. (Near 38th St.)
New York, NY 10036
(212) 727-7100
(877) 846-0565
FAX (212) 414-8750
www.chelseagardencenter.com
(Flowers, Plants, Shrubs & Trees)

New York Flowers and Plant Shed
209 W. 96th St.
(Near Amsterdam Ave.)
New York, NY 10025
(212) 662-4400
(800) 753-9595
FAX (212) 663-0589
www.plantshed.com
(Flowers, Plants & Trees)

Plantscapes, Inc.
113 Division Ave. (Near Park Ave.)
Blue Point, NY 11715
(631) 473-7300
FAX (631) 363-0759

Prestige Trees Landscape Nursery, LLC
92 Millhurst Rd.
Englishtown, NJ 07726
(732) 446-7888
www.prestigetrees.com
(Landscape Construction & Large Trees)

Amy J. Safhay
(Greensman)
(914) 736-7344
FAX (914) 450-8889

Silk Blossom
100 Randolph Rd.
Somerset, NJ 08873
(732) 271-8080
FAX (732) 271-8092
(Artificial Flowers, Plants and Trees)

Silk Gardens & Trees
113 W. 28th St.
(Near Avenue of the Americas)
New York, NY 10001
(212) 629-0600
FAX (212) 629-0612
(Artificial Flowers, Plants and Trees)

Ronald T. von Blomberg
(Greensman)
(631) 283-8447
(631) 926-2013

Wendy Goidell, Inc.
140 Riverside Dr., Ste. 15J (Near W. 87th St.)
New York, NY 10024
(212) 362-6168
(917) 787-8189
(Flowers & Plants)

Wilkens Fruit & Fir Farm
1335 White Hill Rd.
(Near Mohansic Ave.)
Yorktown Heights, NY 10598
(Fir and Spruce Trees)
(914) 245-5111
FAX (914) 245-4099
www.wilkensfarm.com

Foam

Industrial Plastics (212) 226-2010
P.O. Box 210   FAX (212) 226-2015
West Orange, NJ 07052   www.industrialplasticsnyc.com

Smooth-On, Inc. (800) 762-0744
2000 Saint John St.   FAX (610) 252-6200
Easton, PA 18042   www.smooth-on.com

Snow Craft Co., Inc. (516) 739-1399
200 Fulton Ave. (Near Thorens St.)   FAX (516) 739-1637
Garden City Park, NY 11040

Strux Corporation (516) 768-3969
P.O. Box 536   FAX (631) 422-5740
Lindenhurst, NY 11757   www.strux.com

Furnishings—Antique & Vintage

Anything But Costumes (908) 788-1727
111 Mine St.   FAX (609) 397-3970
Flemington, NJ 08822   www.anythingbutcostumes.com
(Set Dressing & Vintage Furniture)

Art & Industry/Doctor Proper, Ltd. (212) 477-0116
50 Great Jones St. (Near Lafayette St.)   FAX (212) 477-1420
New York, NY 10012   www.aid20c.com
(1930s–1970s Furniture and Art)

Baxter & Liebchen (718) 797-0630
33 Jay St.   www.baxterliebchen.com
Brooklyn, NY 11201

Braswell Galleries (203) 327-5101
733 Canal St.   (203) 515-2424
Stamford, CT 06902   FAX (203) 359-3827
www.braswellgalleries.com

Bridge Furniture & Props (718) 916-9706
126 Lombardy St., Second Fl.   FAX (718) 663-7130
(Near Porter)   www.bridgeprops.com
Brooklyn, NY 11222

Decorators Walk/Schumacher (212) 415-3900
979 Third Ave., Ste. 611 (Near E. 59th St.)
New York, NY 10022

Eclectic • Encore Props, Inc. (212) 645-8880
620 W. 26th St., Fourth Fl.   FAX (212) 243-6508
(Near 11th Ave.)   www.eclecticprops.com
New York, NY 10001
(Antique–Present)

Evergreen Antiques (212) 744-5664
1249 Third Ave. (Near E. 72nd St.)   FAX (212) 744-5666
New York, NY 10021   www.evergreenantiques.com

Every Thing Goes (718) 273-0568
17 Brook St. (Near Victory Blvd.)   (718) 720-5378
Staten Island, NY 10301   FAX (718) 448-6842
www.etgstores.com

Every Thing Goes (718) 273-0568
123 Victory Blvd. (Near Brook St.)   (718) 720-5378
Staten Island, NY 10301   FAX (718) 448-6842
www.etgstores.com
(Vintage–Contemporary)

Fanelli Antique Timepieces (212) 517-2300
790 Madison Ave., Ste. 202 (Near E. 67th St.)
New York, NY 10065
(Antique Clocks and Watches)

Jacques Carcanagues, Inc. (212) 925-8110
21 Greene St. (Near Grand St.)   FAX (212) 925-8112
New York, NY 10013   www.jacquescarcanagues.com
(Asian Antiques)

Lost City Arts (212) 375-0500
18 Cooper Square (Near E. Sixth St.)   FAX (212) 375-9422
New York, NY 10003   www.lostcityarts.com
(20th Century Design)

Miss Jezebel's Prop House (516) 656-9653
FAX (352) 726-8403

Newel, LLC (212) 758-1970
425 E. 53rd St. (Near Sutton Pl.)   FAX (212) 371-0166
New York, NY 10022   www.newel.com
(Antiques)

Peter-Roberts Antiques, Inc. (212) 477-9690
84 Wooster St.   FAX (212) 477-9692
New York, NY 10012   www.peter-roberts.com
(American Arts and Crafts)

Phoneco, Inc. (608) 582-4124
19813 E. Mill Rd., P.O. Box 70   FAX (608) 582-4593
Galesville, WI 54630   www.phonecoinc.com
(Vintage Telephones)

Prop Central, Inc. (718) 786-2689
209 E. 76th St., Ste. 2A   FAX (718) 786-3109
(Near 36th Ave.)
New York, NY 10021

**The Prop Company -
Kaplan & Associates** (212) 691-7767
111 W. 19th St., Eighth Fl.   FAX (212) 727-3055
(Near Sixth Ave.)
New York, NY 10011

Props for Today (212) 244-9600
330 W. 34th St. (Near Eighth Ave.)   FAX (212) 244-1053
New York, NY 10001   www.propsfortoday.com
(Antique–Present)

Props NYC (212) 352-0101
509 W. 34th St., Second Fl.   (212) 741-7160
(Near 10th Ave.)   FAX (212) 741-8552
New York, NY 10001   www.propsnyc.com

reGeneration Furniture, Inc. (212) 741-2102
38 Renwick St. (Near Canal St.)   FAX (212) 741-2342
New York, NY 10013   www.regenerationfurniture.com
(1950s–1970s)

Spectrum (800) 668-3899
510 Squankum Yellow Brook Rd.   FAX (253) 322-0212
Farmingdale, NJ 07727   www.greatchandliers.com
(Reproductions)

Richard W. Townsend (914) 232-5867
www.richardmakesfurniture.com

Two Jakes (718) 782-7780
320 Wythe Ave. (Near Grand St.)   FAX (718) 782-7259
Brooklyn, NY 11211   www.twojakes.com
(20th Century Office Furniture)

Yellow Shed Antiques (845) 628-0362
571 Route Six, P.O. Box 706 (Near Cherry Ln.)
Mahopac, NY 10541
(Antique Furniture, Clocks and Accessories)

Furnishings—Contemporary

Adirondack Rents
30-40 48th Ave.
Long Island City, NY 11101
(718) 204-4500
(212) 682-6484
FAX (800) 477-1330
www.adirondackrents.com

Ⓐ Arenson Prop Center
396 10th Ave. (Near W. 33rd St.)
New York, NY 10001
(Home and Office Furniture and Accessories)
(212) 564-8383
FAX (212) 947-4856
www.aof.com

Braswell Galleries
733 Canal St.
Stamford, CT 06902
(203) 327-5101
(203) 515-2424
FAX (203) 359-3827
www.braswellgalleries.com

Bridge Furniture & Props
126 Lombardy St., Second Fl.
Brooklyn, NY 11222
(Accessories, Acrylic, Lighting, Office, Prop House, Reproductions, Rugs & Upholstery)
(718) 916-9706
FAX (718) 663-7130
www.bridgeprops.com

Eclectic • Encore Props, Inc.
620 W. 26th St., Fourth Fl.
(Near 11th Ave.)
New York, NY 10001
(212) 645-8880
FAX (212) 243-6508
www.eclecticprops.com

Evolving Image
335 E. 13th St., Ste. 3
(Near First Ave.)
New York, NY 10003
(Custom Painted Furniture)
(917) 680-7075
(917) 676-5959
www.evolvingimage.com

FormDecor, Inc.
24 Commerce Rd., Ste. L
Fairfield, NJ 07004
(Accessories, Acrylic, Custom, Eclectic, Garden and Patio, Glassware, Hand Props, Lighting, Office, Prop House, Reproductions, Rugs & Upholstery)
(714) 367-9272
www.formdecor.com

Greenroom
270 Lafayette St., Ste. 204
New York, NY 10012
(Garden and Patio, Prop House, Rugs & Upholstery)
(212) 625-1818
FAX (212) 219-9994
www.yourgreenroom.com

Lale For Home
308 W. 93rd St., Ste. 6
(Near West End Ave.)
New York, NY 10025
(Accessories)
(212) 280-4937
FAX (212) 941-7692
www.laleforhome.com

Lamu Industries
2926 Route 32 (Near Hommelville Rd.)
Saugerties, NY 12477
(Mahogany Tables)
(518) 678-2244
www.lamu.com

Lost City Arts
18 Cooper Square (Near E. Sixth St.)
New York, NY 10003
(212) 375-0500
FAX (212) 375-9342
www.lostcityarts.com

Modprop.com
1044 Madison Ave., Ste. 3R
(Near 79th St.)
New York, NY 10021
(212) 628-7582
www.modprop.com

Natrona Furniture
32 W. 20th St.
New York, NY 10011
(212) 404-7649
(212) 929-7600
FAX (212) 255-7641
www.natrona.com

Plexi-Craft
Quality Products Corporation
514 W. 24th St. (Near 10th Ave.)
New York, NY 10011
(Lucite and Plexiglas Furniture and Accessories)
(212) 924-3244
FAX (212) 924-3508
www.plexi-craft.com

Prop Central, Inc.
209 E. 76th St., Ste. 2A
(Near 36th Ave.)
New York, NY 10021
(718) 786-2689
FAX (718) 786-3109

The Prop Company -
Kaplan & Associates
111 W. 19th St., Eighth Fl.
(Near Sixth Ave.)
New York, NY 10011
(212) 691-7767
FAX (212) 727-3055

Props for Today
330 W. 34th St. (Near Eighth Ave.)
New York, NY 10001
(212) 244-9600
FAX (212) 244-1053
www.propsfortoday.com

Props NYC
509 W. 34th St., Second Fl.
(Near 10th Ave.)
New York, NY 10001
(212) 352-0101
(212) 741-7160
FAX (212) 741-8552
www.propsnyc.com

reGeneration Furniture, Inc.
38 Renwick St. (Near Canal St.)
New York, NY 10013
(212) 741-2102
FAX (212) 741-2342
www.regenerationfurniture.com

State Supply
1361 Amsterdam Ave.
(Near W. 126th St.)
New York, NY 10027
(212) 663-2300
FAX (212) 663-3802
www.statesupplyprops.com

Taylor Creative Inc.
150 W. 28th St., Ste. 1001
New York, NY 10001
(646) 336-6808
(888) 245-4044
FAX (646) 336-6810
www.taylorcreativeinc.com

Richard W. Townsend
(Custom)
(914) 232-5867
www.richardmakesfurniture.com

Games, Toys & Amusements

Chess Forum (212) 475-2369
219 Thompson St. (Near Bleecker St.) (917) 673-7792
New York, NY 10012 FAX (212) 475-3905
www.chessforum.com

Compleat Strategist (212) 685-3880
11 E. 33rd St. (Near Fifth Ave.) (212) 685-3881
New York, NY 10016 FAX (212) 685-2123
www.thecompleatstrategist.com
(Adventure, Dice, Fantasy, Hobby, Poker and Wargame Supplies)

Jan's Hobby Shop (212) 861-5075
1435 Lexington Ave. (Near E. 94th St.) (212) 987-4765
New York, NY 10128
(Models)

M. Gordon Novelty, Inc. (212) 254-8616
52 W. 29th St. (Near Broadway)
New York, NY 10001
(Magic Supplies & Novelties)

Manhattan Dollhouse Shop (201) 446-6518
767 Fifth Ave. www.manhattandollhouse.com
(Near 58th St.)
New York, NY 10153
(Dollhouses, Dolls & Miniatures)

New York Doll Hospital, Inc. (212) 838-7527
787 Lexington Ave. (Near E. 61st.)
New York, NY 10021

Paramount Vending (212) 935-9577
500 W. 43rd (Near 10th Ave.) FAX (212) 563-9843
New York, NY 10036
(Contemporary and Vintage Arcade Games, Casino Equipment, Jukeboxes, Pinball and Vending Machines)

pucciManuli (917) 945-2644
(484) 466-2067
FAX (484) 466-2437
www.puccimanuli.com
(Antiques, Dolls/Miniatures, Games, Model Cars and Trains & Novelties)

Village Chess Shop (212) 475-9580
230 Thompson St. (Near W. Third St.) FAX (212) 475-9192
New York, NY 10012 www.chess-shop.com

Glass

Allstate Glass Corp. (212) 226-2517
85 Kenmare St. (Near Mulberry St.) FAX (212) 966-7904
New York, NY 10012 www.allstateglasscorp.com

Braswell Galleries (203) 327-5101
733 Canal St. (203) 515-2424
Stamford, CT 06902 FAX (203) 359-3827
www.braswellgalleries.com

Capitol Glass & Sash Co., Inc. (212) 243-4528
401 Washington St. (Near Laight St.) FAX (212) 924-4216
New York, NY 10013

EFEX Rentals, Inc. (718) 505-9465
58-05 52nd Ave. (Near 58th St.) FAX (718) 505-9631
Woodside, NY 11377
(Breakaway)

Glass Restorations (212) 517-3287
1597 York Ave. (Near 84th St.) FAX (212) 517-3287
New York, NY 10028
(Fabrication & Restoration)

J & M Effects (718) 875-0140
524 Sackett St. (Near Nevins St.) FAX (718) 596-8329
Brooklyn, NY 11217 www.jmfx.net
(Breakaway)

Knickerbocker Plate Glass Company (212) 247-8500
439 W. 54th St. (Near Ninth Ave.) FAX (212) 489-1449
New York, NY 10019 www.knickerbockerplateglass.com

Mirrorlite Products (914) 930-8906
12A White St. FAX (914) 930-8907
Buchanan, NY 10511 www.rearprojection.com
(Mirrors)

Morris Glasser & Son (212) 831-8750
305 Third Ave. FAX (212) 369-2526
Brooklyn, NY 11215

Nisa Glass Systems (212) 265-0882
667 10th Ave. (Near W. 47th St.) FAX (212) 445-0727
New York, NY 10036

Penn Glass Enterprises (718) 346-0900
8406 Liberty Ave. (Near 84th Ave.) FAX (718) 641-5967
Ozone Park, NY 11417

Shattered Glass (718) 372-8202
122 Bay 40th St. (Near Benson Ave.) FAX (718) 372-8419
Brooklyn, NY 11214
(Custom Glass and Mirrors)

Supreme Glass Company (212) 247-3967
31-17 38th Ave. (Near Northern Blvd.) FAX (718) 729-3875
Long Island City, NY 11101

Hair, Makeup & Wardrobe Supplies

ADM Tronics Unlimited, Inc. (201) 767-6040
224-S Pegasus Ave. FAX (201) 784-0260
Northvale, NJ 07647 www.admtronics.com
(Makeup Adhesives)

Alcone NYC (212) 757-3734
 (800) 466-7446
322 W. 49th St. (Near Eighth Ave.) FAX (718) 729-8296
New York, NY 10011 www.alconeco.com
(Professional Makeup)

A Beauty Props (516) 223-4030
 (516) 250-8952
162 E. Merrick Rd. FAX (516) 223-0348
Freeport, NY 11520 www.barberprops.com

Bra*Tenders (212) 957-7000
 (888) 438-2272
630 Ninth Ave., Ste. 601 FAX (212) 957-7010
New York, NY 10036 www.bratenders.com
(Wardrobe and Lingerie Cleaning, Handling and Storage Supplies)

De Meo Brothers, Inc. (973) 778-8100
Two Brighton Ave. (Near Sixth Ave.) FAX (973) 778-8126
Passaic, NJ 07055
(Wigs & Wigmaking Supplies)

Kits and Expendables (212) 947-0700
 (718) 482-1824
43-77 Ninth St. (Near 10th Ave.) FAX (212) 563-2310
Long Island City, NY 11101 www.kitsandexpendables.com
(Garment Racks, Hampers, Irons, Mirrors & Steamers)

Kitstrucks (201) 531-9700
 (917) 921-4751
155 Anderson Ave. FAX (201) 531-9701
Moonachie, NJ 07074 www.kitstrucks.com
(Mobile Service: Garment Racks, Hampers, Irons, Mirrors & Steamers)

Lacey Costume Wigs (212) 695-1996
 (800) 562-9911
318 W. 39th St., 10th Fl. FAX (212) 695-3860
(Near Eighth Ave.)
New York, NY 10018
(Hair Goods & Wigs)

Manhattan Wardrobe Supply (212) 268-9993
 (888) 401-7400
245 W. 29th St., Eighth Fl. FAX (212) 268-1210
(Near Eighth Ave.) www.wardrobesupplies.com
New York, NY 10001
(Hair and Makeup Supplies & Wardrobe Cleaning, Handling and Storage Supplies)

Mehron, Inc. (845) 426-1700
 (800) 332-9955
100 Red Schoolhouse Rd. FAX (845) 426-1515
(Near Ram Ridge Rd.) www.mehron.com
Chestnut Ridge, NY 10977
(Makeup)

National Fiber Technology, LLC (978) 686-2964
300 Canal St. FAX (978) 686-1497
Lawrence, MA 01840 www.nftech.com
(Hair and Fur Fabrics)

WARDROBE SUPPLIES

www.travelautobag.com

FREE CATALOG

- GARMENT BAGS: CANVAS-NYLON
- CLEAR WARDROBE BAGS: ZIPPERED
- ROLLING WARDROBE CASES
- PRO GARMENT STEAMERS
- GARMENT HANGERS: ALL TYPES
- CHROME WIRE, PLASTIC, WOOD
- COLLAPSIBLE ROLLING RACKS

SINCE 1933

TRAVEL AutoBag
264 W 40TH ST • NYC 10018
TEL: 212-840-0025
E-MAIL: info@travelautobag.com

Norcostco - Eastern Costume	(973) 575-3503
333A Route 46 West	(800) 220-6940
Fairfield, NJ 07004	FAX (973) 575-2563
	www.norcostco.com

Ray Beauty Supply Co.	(212) 757-0175
721 Eighth Ave. (Near 46th St.)	(800) 253-0993
New York, NY 10036	FAX (212) 459-8918
(Hair Supplies)	www.raybeauty.com

Ⓐ **Royal Production Services** (212) 781-1440
(Directors Chairs, Makeup and Wardrobe Mirrors & Portable Wardrobe Racks)

Temptu	(212) 675-4000
26 W. 17th St., Ste. 503	FAX (212) 675-4075
New York, NY 10011	www.temptu.com
(Makeup Supplies, Skin Care Products & Theatrical Makeup)	

	(646) 382-8819
Tobi Britton's Makeup Shop	(212) 807-0447
131 W. 21st St. (Near Seventh Ave.)	FAX (212) 727-0975
New York, NY 10011	www.themakeupshop.com

	(212) 840-0025
Ⓐ **Travel Auto Bag Co., Inc.**	(800) 840-0095
264 W. 40th St., 11th Fl.	FAX (212) 302-8267
(Near Eighth Ave.)	www.travelautobag.com
New York, NY 10018	
(Cases, Hangers, Steamers, Rolling Racks & Wardrobe Handling and Storage Equipment)	

	(818) 508-2111
Western Costume Co.	(888) 293-7837
11041 Vanowen St.	FAX (818) 508-2153
North Hollywood, CA 91605	www.westerncostume.com
(Wardrobe Supplies)	

	(212) 242-9400
Wits End Equipment & Expendables	(917) 691-3999
547 W. 49th St. (Near 10th Ave.)	FAX (212) 242-1797
New York, NY 10019	www.witsendnyc.com
(Garment Racks, Hampers, Irons, Mirrors & Steamers)	

Wits End Equipment & Expendables	(718) 361-8400
43-26 12th St. (Near 43rd Ave.)	FAX (718) 361-8440
Long Island City, NY 11101	www.witsendnyc.com
(Garment Racks, Hampers, Irons, Mirrors & Steamers)	

Hair, Makeup & Wardrobe Supplies

Ice

AA Armato & Son   (212) 737-1742
239 E. 88th St., Ste. 1 (Near Third Ave.)
New York, NY 10128
(Cube and Dry Ice)

Arctic Glacier   (908) 241-4833
205 W. Westfield Ave.   FAX **(908) 241-6316**
Roosevelt Park, NJ 07204
(Block, Cube and Dry Ice & Ice Sculpture)

Diamond Ice   (212) 355-3734
556 River Ave. (Near E. 150th St.)   FAX **(718) 292-0781**
Bronx, NY 10451
(Block, Cube and Dry Ice)

Fear No Ice   (631) 242-9380
697 Acorn St., Ste. D   FAX **(631) 274-3173**
(Near Deer Park Ave.)   www.fearnoice.com
Deer Park, NY 11729
(Sculpture)

Okamoto Studio   (212) 842-0630
35-03 31st St. (Near 10th St.)   FAX **(212) 842-0633**
Long Island City, NY 11106   www.okamotostudionyc.com
(Ice Sculptures)

Portable Ice Rink Rentals   (516) 676-5242
16 La Marcus Ave.   FAX **(516) 676-5242**
(Near Glen Cove Ave.)
Glen Cove, NY 11542
(Portable Ice Rinks)

Lamps & Lighting Fixtures

Braswell Galleries   (203) 327-5101 / (203) 515-2424
733 Canal St.   FAX **(203) 359-3827**
Stamford, CT 06902   www.braswellgalleries.com

Bridge Furniture & Props   (718) 916-9706
126 Lombardy St., Second Fl.   FAX **(718) 663-7130**
(Near Porter)   www.bridgeprops.com
Brooklyn, NY 11222

Broome Lampshades, Inc.   (212) 431-9666
325 Broome St. (Near Bowery)   FAX **(212) 431-9866**
New York, NY 10002   www.lampshadesny.com

Ⓐ **City Knickerbocker, Inc.**   (212) 586-3939 / (212) 586-3940
665 11th Ave., Second Fl.   FAX **(212) 262-2889**
New York, NY 10019   www.cityknickerbocker.com

Just Shades, Inc.   (212) 966-2757
21 Spring St., Ground Fl.   FAX **(212) 334-6129**
(Near Elizabeth St.)   www.justshadesny.com
New York, NY 10012
(Lampshades)

Lighting by Gregory, Inc.   (212) 226-1276 / (800) 796-1965
158 Bowery (Near Broome St.)   FAX **(212) 226-2705**
New York, NY 10012   www.lightingbygregory.com
(Ceiling Fans, Lamps & Track Lighting)

Lost City Arts   (212) 375-0500
18 Cooper Square (Near E. Sixth St.)   FAX **(212) 375-9342**
New York, NY 10003   www.lostcityarts.com
(20th Century Vintage)

Pennsylvania Globe Gaslight Co.   (203) 484-7749 / (203) 214-8761
300 Shaw Rd.   FAX **(203) 484-7758**
North Branford, CT 06471   www.pennglobe.com
(Vintage Gaslight Replicas)

Remains   (212) 675-8051
130 W. 28th St. (Near Sixth Ave.)   FAX **(212) 675-8052**
New York, NY 10001   www.remains.com
(Antique Lighting Fixtures)

Spectrum   (800) 668-3899
510 Squankum Yellow Brook Rd.   FAX **(253) 322-0212**
Farmingdale, NJ 07727   www.greatchandliers.com
(Reproduction Chandeliers)

City Knickerbocker Lighting
Founded in 1906
Commercial and Retail
Repairs, Sales and Rentals
Convenient Access for Pickup/Delivery
CELEBRATING OUR 100TH YEAR!
Great New Location...
665 11th Ave. (at 48th St.)
NYC, NY 10019
212-586-3939
www.cityknickerbocker.com

Medical & Scientific Props

Aimes, Inc. (718) 993-4400
2417 Third Ave. (Near 134th St.) FAX (718) 993-4260
Bronx, NY 10451 www.aimesmed.com

Ⓐ American Resource (212) 279-7767
Medical Equipment (877) 633-6673

Anything But Costumes (908) 788-1727
111 Mine St. FAX (609) 397-3970
Flemington, NJ 08822 www.anythingbutcostumes.com

Cinema World Studios (718) 389-9800
220 Dupont St. FAX (718) 389-9897
(Near McGuinness Blvd.) www.cinemaworldstudios.com
Brooklyn, NY 11222

Marburger Surgical (718) 822-6820
1646 Eastchester Rd. FAX (718) 822-6824
Bronx, NY 10461
(Lab & Medical)

The Medicine Shoppe (212) 255-9111
306 Eighth Ave. (Near W. 25th St.) FAX (212) 242-2587
New York, NY 10001

(800) 698-5007
Shop Rite Institutional Supply, Inc. (914) 490-5687
253 E. 204th St., Ste. 201 FAX (718) 563-5369
(Near E. Mosholu Pkwy South)
New York, NY 10458

877.MED.ONSET
American Resource
MEDICAL PROPS

"The most up-to-date medical rental facility east of the L.A. river". (*Set Décor Magazine*)

Massive, state-of-the-art.
Most knowledgeable in the USA.

Memorabilia & Collectibles

Argosy Book Stores, Inc. (212) 753-4455
116 E. 59th St. (Near Lexington Ave.) FAX **(212) 593-4784**
New York, NY 10022 **www.argosybooks.com**
(Ephemera & Vintage Photos, Posters and Prints)

Gaslight Advertising Archives, Inc. **(631) 462-4444**
17 Bernard Ln. (Near Commack Rd.) FAX **(631) 462-7394**
Commack, NY 11725 **www.gaslightarchives.com**
(Ephemera, Magazines, Photos, Posters & Prints)

Jerry Ohlinger's
Movie Material Store, Inc. **(212) 989-0869**
253 W. 35th St. (Near Eighth Ave.) FAX **(212) 989-1660**
New York, NY 10001 **www.moviematerials.com**
(Movie Memorabilia and Posters)

Metals & Foils

(800) 638-2522
Admiral Metals **(800) 423-6472**
1046 University Ave. (Near Culver Rd.) FAX **(585) 244-4730**
Rochester, NY 14607 **www.admiralmetals.com**
(Aluminum, Brass, Copper & Stainless Steel)

Alufoil Products **(631) 231-4141**
135 Oser Ave. (Near Marcus Blvd.) FAX **(631) 231-1435**
Hauppauge, NY 11788 **www.alufoil.com**
(Plain and Colored Boards, Foils and Foil Paper)

Grand Brass Lamp Parts **(212) 226-2567**
51 Railroad Ave. FAX **(212) 226-2573**
West Haven, CT 06516 **www.grandbrass.com**
(Brass)

(718) 291-8060
Hadco Metal Trading Co., LLC **(800) 221-0344**
104-20 Merrick Blvd. FAX **(718) 291-8388**
(Near Liberty Ave.) **www.hadco-metal.com**
Jamaica, NY 11433

(732) 846-8333
McNichols **(800) 237-3820**
FAX **(732) 846-5555**
www.mcnichols.com
(Expanded and Perforated Metal, Grating, Tread Grip & Wire Cloth)

Musical Instrument Rentals

Beethoven Pianos
232 W. 58th St. (Near Broadway)
New York, NY 10019
(212) 765-7300
(800) 241-0001
FAX (212) 765-6544
www.beethovenpianos.com

Braswell Galleries
733 Canal St.
Stamford, CT 06902
(203) 327-5101
(203) 515-2424
FAX (203) 359-3827
www.braswellgalleries.com

Drum Rentals/Vintage Drums
1133 Broadway, Seventh Fl. (Near W. 26th St.)
New York, NY 10010
(212) 255-0445

Pro Piano
85 Jane St. (Near Washington Ave.)
New York, NY 10014
(Amplifiers, Drums, Pianos & Synthesizers)
(212) 206-8794
(800) 367-0777
FAX (212) 633-1207
www.propiano.com

Rayburn Music
44 W. 62nd St. (Near Broadway)
New York, NY 10023
(Bagpipes, Guitars & Orchestral)
(212) 541-6236
FAX (212) 541-6630
www.rayburnmusicny.com

Ⓐ Studio Instrument Rentals (S.I.R.)
475 10th Ave., Second Fl.
(Near 36th St.)
New York, NY 10018
(212) 627-4900
FAX (212) 627-7079
www.sirny.com

Universal Musical Instrument Co.
732 Broadway (Near Waverly Pl.)
New York, NY 10003
(Band, Guitars & Orchestral)
(212) 254-6917
FAX (516) 593-2397

Vintage & Antique Musical Instruments
P.O. Box 434
Bronx, NY 10471
(718) 548-6008
(914) 523-2228
FAX (718) 548-6008
www.allmusicalinstruments.net

Neon

Artkraft Strauss Sign Corporation (212) 265-5155
1776 Broadway, Ste. 1810   FAX (212) 265-5262
(Near W. 57th St.)   www.artkraft.com
New York, NY 10019

Let There Be Neon, Inc. (212) 226-4883
38 White St. (Near Church St.)   FAX (212) 431-6731
New York, NY 10013   www.lettherebeneon.com

Lite Brite Neon (718) 855-6082
232 Third St., Ste. C1B   FAX (718) 855-6083
Brooklyn, NY 11215   www.litebriteneon.com

Manhattan Neon Sign Corporation (212) 714-0430
514 W. 36th St. (Near 10th Ave.)   FAX (212) 947-3906
New York, NY 10018   www.manhattanneon.com

Midtown Neon Sign Corporation (212) 736-3838
10-40 45th. St. (Near 10th Ave.)   FAX (212) 629-0455
Long Island City, NY 11101

RJP Creations, Inc. (973) 786-6993
290 Decker Pond Rd., Bldg. B2   FAX (973) 786-6997
Andover, NJ 07821   www.rjpcreations.com

Sign Expo (212) 925-8585
102 Franklin St., Fourth Fl.   FAX (212) 925-5628
New York, NY 10013   www.signexpo.com

Super Neon Lights Co. (718) 236-5667
7813 16th Ave. (Near 78th St.)   FAX (718) 236-6101
Brooklyn, NY 11214

Photo, Video & Electronic Props

Computer Rent (212) 767-0400
225 Broadway   www.computerpropsnyc.com
(Near Barkley)
New York, NY 10007
(Computer and Video Props)

Cress Photo (973) 694-1280
P.O. Box 4262   FAX (973) 694-6985
Wayne, NJ 07474   www.flashbulbs.com
(Vintage Still Cameras and Flash Equipment)

Harry Poster Vintage TVs (201) 794-9606
1310 Second St.   www.harryposter.com
Fair Lawn, NJ 07410
(Vintage Televisions)

**The Lens & Repro
Equipment Corporation** (212) 675-1900
33 W. 17th St., Fifth Fl.   FAX (212) 989-5018
(Near Sixth Ave.)
New York, NY 10011
www.lensandrepro.com/PROPS/index.html
(Vintage Motion Picture and Still Cameras)

(212) 575-0210
Sound City (212) 575-1060
58 W. 45th St. (Near Sixth Ave.)   FAX (212) 221-7907
New York, NY 10036   www.soundcityny.com
(Electronics, Stereos & Video Equipment)

Telephone Systems & Technologies (631) 286-0344

(973) 332-6425
Visual Alchemy, LLC (973) 239-3964
10 Village Park Rd.   FAX (973) 239-3965
Cedar Grove, NJ 07044   www.visualalchemy.tv

Picture Vehicles

1 A Allstar Picture Cars (310) 463-4489 / (818) 609-0777
17757 Victory Blvd. (Near Balcom Ave) FAX (818) 609-0666
Reseda, CA 91335   www.allstarpicturecars.com
(Antique to Contemporary Buses, Cars, Convertibles, Emergency Vehicles, Limousines, Motorcycles, Trucks & Vehicle Transportation)

76 Carriage Company (215) 923-8516 / (215) 389-8687
1119 N. Bodine St.   FAX (215) 923-7776
Philadelphia, PA 19123   www.phillytour.com
(Carriages & Wagons)

A. van Hoek Ltd. (917) 701-5367 / (718) 599-4388
71 Montrose Ave.   www.retrofuturistic.com
Brooklyn, NY 11206
(Airstream Trailers, Antique, Buses, Classic, Exotics, Futuristic, Limousines, Luxury, RVs, Sleighs, Trailers, Vehicle Transportation & Vintage)

AA Executive Town Car & Limousine (516) 792-1735 / (800) 716-2799
333 Hempstead Ave., Ste. 209   FAX (516) 256-0092
(Near Catalpa Dr.)   www.exectownlimo.com
Malverne, NY 11565
(Limousines)

Ⓐ Auto Props (973) 470-9434
Eight Lexington Ave.   FAX (973) 815-1497
Wallington, NJ 07057   www.autoprops-waterworks.com

Automobile Film Club of America, Inc. (718) 447-2255 / (718) 447-0438
10 Cross St. (Near Bay St.)   FAX (718) 447-2289
Staten Island, NY 10304   www.autofilmclub.com
(Vintage–Contemporary Cars, Emergency Vehicles, Military Vehicles, Motorcycles, Police Cars, Trucks and Taxicabs)

Cars for Films (973) 484-9755 / (973) 818-6973
166-174 Mt. Pleasant Ave.   FAX (973) 484-9757
Newark, NJ 07104   www.carsforfilms.net
(Classic–Contemporary Cars, Custom/Exotics, Military Vehicles, Motorcycles, Police Cars, Trucks & Vintage Cars)

Ⓐ Cars on Location (203) 732-4745 / (800) 736-9178
768 Derby Ave.   FAX (203) 732-4193
Seymour, CT 06483   www.carsonlocation.com
(Classic–Contemporary Cars, Custom/Exotics, Military Vehicles, Motorcycles, Police Cars, Race Cars, Stunt Cars & Trucks)

Classic Cars (845) 786-2942
Four Katavolos   FAX (845) 786-2942
Tomkins Cove, NY 10986

Ⓐ Cooper Film Cars (212) 929-3909
137 Perry St. (Near Greenwich St.)   FAX (212) 633-6952
New York, NY 10014   www.cooperclassiccars.com
(Contemporary & Vintage)

Ⓐ Creative Film Cars (212) 864-4060
167 Madison Ave., Ste. 604   FAX (212) 696-4060
New York, NY 10016   www.creativefilmcars.com
(Ambulances, Antiques, Buses, Classics, Contemporary, Exotics, Fire Trucks, Hearses, Military Vehicles, Motorcycles, Motorhomes, Police Vehicles, Scooters, Taxis, Tractors & Trucks)

Filmcars and Vintage Checker Taxicabs (718) 748-6707 / (917) 748-4010
359 97th St. (Near Fourth Ave.)   FAX (718) 745-8371
Brooklyn, NY 11209   www.filmcars.com
(1910–1970 Vintage Cars & Checker Taxicabs)

METRO FILM CARS INC.

Movies ★ Music Videos ★ Still Shoots ★ Commercials
Music and Sound Tracking for Movies & TV . . . .Call for info

Helicopters & Jet Planes · Trucks, etc. · Boats · Ambulances · Military Vehicles · Subway Car
Race Car · Taxis · Dragsters · Luxury & Sports Cars · Volkswagen & Aston Martin Cars
Police & Detective Cars · NYPD Tow Truck · NYC DOT Tow Truck · Large Heavy Crane
Tractor Trailers · Stunt Drivers · School Buses · City Buses · Convertibles · Sheriff Police Cars
Black & White · Non Descript Police · Dump Trucks · Buses · Low Riders
**Antique & Modern Airplanes · Old Airstream Trailers · 1980s Winnebago
FBI Police Surveilance Van**

Credits: Borat: The Movie, Sex and the City, All My Children, Halloween 8, Saturday Night Live, Cosby, Nissan, Maxim Magazine, Allure Magazine, Essence Magazine, Nike, Wendy's, Burlington Coat Factory, Lexus, Honda, Aston Martin, Samsonite Luggage Commercial

Car Prep + NEW CAR CARRIER (Enclosed type) with a special Tow Vehicle
Office: (973) 450-1692   Fax: (973) 751-8320   metro4film@aol.com

---

Giordano FX (973) 615-7263
518 Central Ave., Ste. 2L
Carlstadt, NJ 07072
www.myspace.com/scareproproductions
(Ambulances, Antique, Classic, Contemporary, Convertibles, Cutaways, Damaged, Domestics, Emergency Vehicles, European, Exotics, Fishing Boats, Hearses, High Performance, Hot Rods, Jeeps, Limousines, Lowriders, Luxury, Motorboats, Motorcycles, Muscle Cars, Police Vehicles, Rescue Vehicles, Semi Trucks, Sports Cars, Taxis, Tractor Trailers, Trailers, Trucks, Vehicle Transportation & Vintage)

A Horse Drawn Affair (518) 329-5249
258 Crest Ln. (Near E. Ancram Rd.) FAX (518) 329-5250
Ancramdale, NY 12503
www.ahorsedrawnaffair.com
(Carriages, Sleighs & Wagons)

Hunter Ambulance, Inc. (718) 372-0700
(Ambulances) FAX (516) 371-0871
www.hunterambulance.com

❹ Lost Soul Picture Cars (973) 979-1503
Three Melissa Dr. (201) 982-5255
North Haledon, NJ 07508 www.lostsoulent.com

Manhattan Motorcars (212) 594-6200
270 11th Ave. (Near W. 27th St.) (888) 765-5769
New York, NY 10001 FAX (212) 594-4430
(Exotics) www.manhattanmotorcars.com

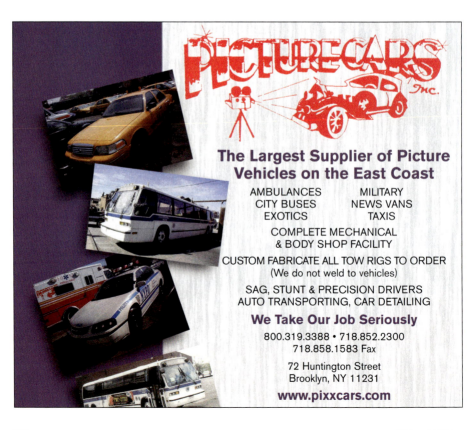

Cooper Film Cars

Serving the Industry Since 1978

Insured and NYS Licensed Dealer
Online Database with 1,000s of Options
Unparalled Knowledge, Experience, and Support
Quick Results and NO Excuses

212-929-3909

info@cooperclassiccars.com   www.cooperclassiccars.com

Prime West Village/Meat Packing District Location

Rent Our Unique Drive-In Gallery/Studio for
Photo Shoots or Private Events!

Located Directly Across from our Classic Car Gallery
132 Perry Street Between Greenwich St. and Washington St. in the West Village

Exclusive Packages Available For Cars with Studio Space

Lost Soul Entertainment
Picture Cars

Supplier of modern and vintage automobiles
Police Cars, Taxi Cabs, Ambulances, Fire Trucks, Classic Cars, Non Descript Vehicles

We Offer:
- Flat Bed Service • Custom Paint • Custom Decals • Drivers Available
- Matching Cars • Clear Glass • Stunt Rigging • Fuel Cells

"Any Vehicle, Any Location, Your Vision Is Our Dedication"

Matt: (973) 979-1503   Bryan: (201) 982-5255

www.lostsoulent.com

Motorhomes & Portable Dressing Rooms

 Plush Luxury Coaches &
Picture Car Towing Service

Al Breen: (201) 376-6921

Ⓐ Metro Film Cars, Inc. (973) 450-1692
114 Brighton Ave. (973) 699-7707
Belleville, NJ 07109 FAX (973) 751-8320
(Airstream Trailers, Antiques, Buses, Contemporary,
Helicopters, Military Vehicles, Motorcycles, Police Cars, Tanks,
Taxis & Tractor Trailers)

Michael's Classics, Inc. (607) 588-7002
37336 Route 23 (Near State Hwy 30) FAX (607) 588-9707
Grand Gorge, NY 12434
(Damaged, Military Vehicles, Motorcycles, Tanks, Troop
Carriers, UniMogs & Vehicle Transportation)

MOVIE TIME CARS INC.

Complete Line of Picture Cars

www.movietimecars.com

1-877 CARS 4 FILM

movietimecars@me.com

Tel: 201.964.0177
Fax: 201.964.0179

759-63 Riverside Ave.
Lyndhurst, NJ 07071

VEHICLES FOR ALL YOUR PRODUCTION NEEDS

We Offer a Wide Selection of
EXOTIC, ANTIQUE, CLASSIC CARS
POLICE, DETECTIVE
STUNT CARS • MILITARY &
EMERGENCY VEHICLES
AIRPLANES,
SAILBOATS,
ROW BOATS,
POWER BOATS

Specialty Services Available

(973) 667-3711

WheelsForReels@aol.com

Autoprops-Waterworks.com
Cars For All Your Film Needs

Motion Picture, Music Videos,
Print Ads, Still Photography,
Special Events, Parades, Store Fronts

973-470-9354

CARS ON LOCATION

When You Need Cars For Stars

(800) 736-9178

(203) 732-4745 • Fax (203) 732-4193

Email: info@carsonlocation.com

www.carsonlocation.com

ANY VEHICLE • ANY PERIOD • ANY WHERE • TRANSPORTATION
CUSTOM PAINTING • CAR COORDINATOR • OTHER RELATED PROPS

Modprop.com   (212) 628-7582
1044 Madison Ave., Ste. 3R   www.modprop.com
(Near 79th St.)
New York, NY 10021
(Vintage Bicycles, Cars and Motorbikes)

Ⓐ Movie Time Cars, Inc.   (201) 964-0177
759-763 Riverside Ave.   (201) 964-0178
Lyndhurst, NJ 07071   FAX (201) 964-0179
www.movietimecars.com

NAC Production Services   (516) 766-0000
3844 Hampton Rd. (Near Daly Blvd.)   (800) 834-8733
Oceanside, NY 11572   FAX (516) 678-0000
www.picturecars.net

NationwidePictureCars.Com   (310) 659-1711
FAX (310) 652-2841
www.nationwidepicturecars.com
(Classic–Contemporary Cars, Motorcycles and Trucks)

New York Auto Stars   (203) 395-5292
    (305) 785-4929
(Ambulances, ATVs, Cabin Cruisers, Camera Cars, Cigarette Boats, Classic, Convertibles, Damaged, Emergency Vehicles, European, Futuristic, Hearses, Horse and Buggy, HumVees, Limousines, Lowriders, Luxury, Military Vehicles, Motorcycles, Muscle Cars, Police Vehicles, RVs, Scooters, Sleighs, Sports Cars, Storage, Tanks, Taxis, Vehicle Coordination, Vehicle Transportation & Vintage)

Nivo Productions   (516) 922-5853
    (305) 215-8519
167 Cove Rd.   FAX (516) 922-5854
Oyster Bay, NY 11771   www.nivoproductions.com
(Camera Cars, Convertibles, Custom, Exotics, Limousines, Luxury Sedans, Military Vehicles, Motorcycles, Muscle Cars, Police Vehicles, RVs, Sports Cars & Trucks)

Ⓐ Picture Cars East, Inc.   (718) 852-2300
    (800) 319-3388
72 Huntington St. (Near Henry St.)   FAX (718) 858-1583
Brooklyn, NY 11231   www.pixxcars.com

Tactical Truck   (540) 341-7140
P.O. Box 984   FAX (540) 341-7146
Marshall, VA 20116   www.tacticaltruck.com
(Military Vehicles)

Varooom Automotive Resources   (917) 887-4608
107 Suffolk St., Ste. 409
New York, NY 10002
(Vintage–Contemporary Cars, Muscle Cars, Motorcycles and Scooters)

Vipers, Vettes &   (516) 377-3943
Various Muscle Cars   (516) 729-1805
www.vipersvettes.com
(Classic–Contemporary, Exotics, High Performance and Muscle Cars)

Ⓐ Wheels for Reels   (973) 667-3711
(Airplanes, Buses, Cars & Trucks)

Plastics, Plexiglas & Fiberglass

Castelli Models & Effects (973) 680-1485
17 Herman St. FAX (973) 680-1486
Glen Ridge, NJ 07028 www.castellimodels.com
(Vacuum-Forming)

IASCO-TESCO (952) 920-7393
(888) 919-0899
FAX (952) 920-2947
www.iasco-tesco.com
(Mold-Making Materials, Plastics, Resins & Vacuum-Forming Materials)

Just Plastics (212) 569-8500
250 Dyckman St., Second Fl. FAX (212) 569-6970
(Near Seaman Ave.) www.justplastics.com
New York, NY 10034
(Acrylic)

Plexi-Craft
Quality Products Corporation (212) 924-3244
514 W. 24th St. (Near 10th Ave.) FAX (212) 924-3508
New York, NY 10011 www.plexi-craft.com
(Acrylic and Plexiglas Fabrication)

Ⓐ Provost Displays (800) 555-3772
(610) 279-3970
(Vacuum-Forming) FAX (610) 279-3968
www.provostdisplays.com

Silicones, Inc. (336) 886-5018
(800) 533-8709
FAX (336) 886-7122
www.silicones-inc.com

Smooth-On, Inc. (800) 762-0744
2000 Saint John St. (610) 252-5800
Easton, PA 18042 FAX (610) 252-6200
www.smooth-on.com
(Liquid Plastics and Rubber)

Tulnoy Lumber & Scenic Plastics (718) 901-1700
(800) 899-5833
1620 Webster Ave. (Near E. 173rd St.) FAX (718) 299-8920
Bronx, NY 10457 www.tulnoylumber.com
(Vacuum-Forming)

Product Placement

AIM Productions, Inc.   (718) 729-9288
37-11 35th Ave., Ste. 3B   FAX (718) 786-0137
(Near 37th St.)
Astoria, NY 11101

Clearance Domain LLC   (800) 562-1231
    (310) 898-1233
    FAX (888) 562-5120
    www.clearancedomain.com

Impact Product Placement   (718) 271-5271
    (718) 813-7383
62-54 97th Pl., Ste. 14C (Near 63rd Dr.)
Rego Park, NY 11374

Prop Fabrication & Mechanical FX

Art Dept. (917) 288-8694
(Prop Fabrication) www.brooklynartdept.com

Artificial Reality (718) 707-9797
(917) 992-4251
11-36 49th Ave. (Near 21st St.) FAX (718) 707-3363
Long Island City, NY 11201 www.artificialrealityny.com

Bandolier, Inc. (718) 643-1399
20 Jay St., Ste. 1006 FAX (718) 643-6929
(Near Plymouth St.) www.bandolierinc.com
Brooklyn, NY 11201

Chris Bobin (646) 742-0630
347 Fifth Ave., Ste. 1102 www.chrisbobin.com
New York, NY 10016
(Embroidery, Fabric Props, Fabrications & Prototyping)

Brooklyn Model Works, Inc. (718) 834-1944
60 Washington Ave. FAX (718) 596-8934
(Near Flushing Ave.) www.brooklynmodelworks.com
Brooklyn, NY 11205
(Action Props, Artificial Foods, Breakaways, Custom, Electronics, Foam Sculpting, FX Props, Gadgetry, Mechanical FX, Miniatures, Models, Oversized Props, Product Pours, Prop Fabrication, Prototyping, Radio-Controlled, Remote-Controlled, Rigging, Rubber Props, Sculpted Props, Skeleton Replication, Toy Fabrication, Vacuum-Forming & Welding)

Capital Scenic, Inc. (845) 429-4800
(914) 490-2000
P.O. Box 382 FAX (845) 429-2138
55 W. Railroad Ave., Ste. 3C www.capitalscenic.com
Garnerville, NY 10923

Carl Paolino Studios, Inc. (917) 282-4756
(917) 957-7305
www.paolinostudios.com
(Breakaways, Custom Props, Mechanical FX, Miniatures, Models, Over-Sized Props & Rigging)

Castelli Models & Effects (973) 680-1485
17 Herman St. FAX (973) 680-1486
Glen Ridge, NJ 07028 www.castellimodels.com
(Artificial Food, Miniatures, Over-Sized Props & Rigging)

Cimmelli, Inc. (845) 735-2090
16 Walter St. (Near Railroad Ave.) FAX (845) 735-1643
Pearl River, NY 10965
(Mechanical FX & Models)

Clockwork Apple, Inc. (718) 858-3192
63 Flushing Ave. FAX (718) 858-0359
Bldg. 280, Ste. 268, Third Fl. www.clockwork-apple.com
Brooklyn Navy Yard
Brooklyn, NY 11205
(Models)

SUZANNE COUTURE MODELMAKING

212 . 714 . 9310 TEL
212 . 836 . 9898 CEL

227 WEST 29 STREET
NEW YORK, NY 10001

PROPS   FOR PRINT
SETS   TELEVISION
COSTUMES   DISPLAY
AWARDS   TRADE SHOWS
                SPECIAL EVENTS

suzannecouturemodelmaking.com

PT CRUISER HANDBAG
CHRYSLER

SIX FOOT CORRECTION FLUID
FED EX / KINKO

CBS EARLY SHOW COW
NYC COW PARADE

OVERSIZE BOTTLE
COCA COLA

Constructive Display, Inc. (718) 237-3131
499 Van Brunt St., Ste. 5A FAX (718) 237-4182
(Near Beard St.) www.constructivedisplay.com
Brooklyn, NY 11231
(Action Props, Artificial Foods, Custom, Foam Sculpting, FX Props, Mechanical FX, Miniatures, Models, Oversized Props, Prop Fabrication, Prototyping, Rubber Props, Sculpted Props, Toy Fabrication & Welding)

Creative Engineering (718) 937-5292
5-50 54th Ave. (Near Second St.) FAX (718) 937-1271
Long Island City, NY 11101
www.creativeengineeringinc.com
(Miniatures, Models & Over-Sized Props)

Custom Creations (201) 223-5125
142 32nd St. FAX (201) 255-0444
Union City, NJ 07087 www.custom-creations.com
(Foam Sculpture & Mechanical FX)

EFEX Rentals, Inc. (718) 505-9465
58-05 52nd Ave. (Near 58th St.) FAX (718) 505-9631
Woodside, NY 11377
(Breakaways, Rigging & Turntables)

Ellen Rixford Studio (212) 865-5686
308 W. 97th St., Ste. 71 www.ellenrixford.com
(Near West End Ave.)
New York, NY 10025
(Models & Sculpture)

Ⓐ The Gemini Co., Inc. (718) 858-7222
63 Flushing Ave., Ste. 157 www.thegeminicompany.com
Brooklyn, NY 11205

Geppetto Studios, Inc. (718) 398-9792
201 46th St., Second Fl. www.geppettostudios.com
Brooklyn, NY 11220

Ⓐ Giordano FX (973) 615-7263
518 Central Ave., Ste. 2L
Carlstadt, NJ 07072
www.myspace.com/scareproductions
(Action Props, Artificial Foods, Breakaways, Custom, Electronics, Extreme Sports, Flying, Foam Sculpting, FX Props, Gadgetry, Hydraulics, Mechanical FX, Miniatures, Models, Motion Control Systems, Oversized, Product Pours, Prop Fabrication, Prototyping, Radio-Controlled, Remote-Controlled, Rigging, Robotics, Rubber Props, Sculpted Props, Skeleton Replication, Toy Fabrication, Vacuum-Forming, Waterjet Cutting, Weapon Fabrication & Welding)

Global Antiques &
Fine Reproductions (212) 533-8500
67 E. 11th St. (Near E. 11th St.) FAX (212) 995-2832
New York, NY 10003
(Custom Reproduction Furniture)

GZ Entertainment & Stunts (201) 675-1118
15 Storig Ave. www.gzfxandstunts.com
Closter, NJ 07624
(Action Props, Breakaways, Ceramics, Computer-Controlled, Custom, Electronics, Extreme Sports, Flying, Foam Sculpting, FX Props, Gadgetry, Hydraulics, Marine Equipment, Mechanical FX, Miniatures, Models, Motion Control Systems, Prop Fabrication, Prototyping, Radio-Controlled, Remote-Controlled, Rigging, Robotics, Rubber Props, Sculpted Props, Skeleton Replication, Turntables, Vacuum-Forming, Weapon Fabrication & Welding)

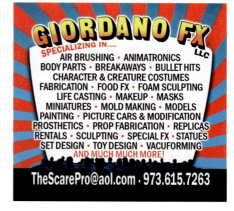

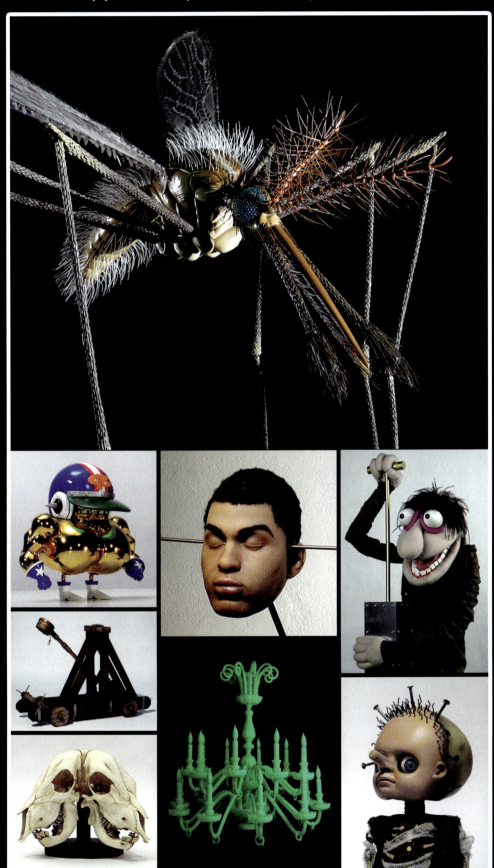

Ⓐ Hero Props (646) 734-2198
18 Bridge St., Ste. 1A FAX **(718) 222-3021**
Brooklyn, NY 11201 **www.heropropsnyc.com**

I. Weiss and Sons, Inc. (718) 706-8139
 (888) 325-7192
2-07 Borden Ave. (Near Second St.) FAX **(718) 482-9410**
Long Island City, NY 11101 **www.iweiss.com**
(Rigging)

I.C.B.A., Inc./Bargsten (201) 420-8680
50 Dey St., Ste. 4404 FAX **(201) 792-5776**
Jersey City, NJ 07306
(Models & Rigging)

J & M Effects (718) 875-0140
524 Sackett St. (Near Nevins St.) FAX **(718) 596-8329**
Brooklyn, NY 11217 **www.jmfx.net**
(Action Props, Breakaways & Radio-Controlled Props)

Jan's Hobby Shop (212) 861-5075
 (212) 987-4765
1435 Lexington Ave. (Near E. 94th St.)
New York, NY 10128
(Models)

Jeffrey Meyer Turntables (212) 777-1465
 (917) 836-7009
873 Broadway (Near 18th St.) **www.jmturntables.com**
New York, NY 10003
(Turntables)

Jerard Studio, Inc. (718) 852-4128
481 Van Brunt St., Ste. 11D FAX **(718) 852-2408**
(Near Beard St.) **www.jerardstudio.com**
Brooklyn, NY 11231
(Action Props, Models & Sculpture)

John Creech Design & Production (718) 237-1144
129 Van Brunt St. FAX **(718) 237-4133**
Brooklyn, NY 11231 **www.webuildeverything.com**

K-F/X, Inc. (914) 403-0483
 (914) 937-9345
49 Townsend St. FAX **(914) 937-7274**
Port Chester, NY 10573

Largent Studios, Ltd. (718) 254-9220
499 Van Brunt St., Ste. 9A FAX **(718) 254-9610**
(Near Reed St.) **www.largentstudios.com**
Brooklyn, NY 11231
(Action Props, Flying, Foreground Miniatures, FX Props, Gadgetry, Motion Control Rigs, Oversized Props, Prop Fabrication, Prototyping, Rigging, Sculpted Props, Turntables & Welding)

Manhattan Model Shop (212) 473-6312
40 Great Jones St. (Near Lafayette St.) FAX **(212) 979-9841**
New York, NY 10012 **www.manhattanmodelshop.com**
(Action Props, Custom, Foam Sculpting, Mechanical FX, Miniatures, Models, Oversized Props, Prop Fabrication, Prototyping, Sculpted Props & Toy Fabrication)

McConnell & Borow, Inc./Prop Art (718) 230-9400
239 Saint Marks Ave. FAX **(718) 230-9402**
(Near Vanderbilt Ave.) **www.propartnyc.com**
Brooklyn, NY 11238
(Miniatures & Models)

Mechanism (718) 788-7865
122 18th St., Second Fl. **www.mechanism.tv**
Brooklyn, NY 11215
(Action Props, Custom, Foam Sculpting, FX Props, Gadgetry, Mechanical FX, Models, Prop Fabrication, Prototyping, Sculpted Props & Toy Fabrication)

Michael Miller, Inc. (914) 793-1999
(Artificial Food & Models) www.michaelmillerinc.com

Peter Kunz Co., Inc. (845) 687-0400
55 Creek Rd. (Near Tow Path) FAX (845) 687-0579
High Falls, NY 12440 www.peterkunzeffects.com
(Miniatures, Over-Sized Props & Rigging)

Peter Weiss Designs (845) 878-4391
(914) 645-1118
FAX (845) 878-4391
(Miniatures, Models, Over-Sized Props & Rigging)

Prop Central, Inc. (718) 786-2689
209 E. 76th St., Ste. 2A FAX (718) 786-3109
(Near 36th Ave.)
New York, NY 10021
(Prop Fabrication)

Sculpturesque (201) 573-9150
Seven Etheridge Pl. (201) 458-3590
Park Ridge, NJ 07656 FAX (201) 307-8889
www.sculpturesqueart.com

Special Effects Production Services, Inc. (201) 405-0101
186 Paul Court FAX (201) 405-0632
Hillsdale, NJ 07642
(Glassblowing, High-Tech Props & Laser and Plasma Devices)

(A) Suzanne Couture Modelmaking (212) 714-9310
227 W. 29th St. (Near Seventh Ave.) FAX (212) 714-0759
New York, NY 10001
www.suzannecouturemodelmaking.com
(Action Props, Artificial Foods, Breakaways, Custom, Foam Sculpting, FX Props, Gadgetry, Mechanical FX, Miniatures, Models, Oversized Props, Product Pours, Prop Fabrication, Prototyping, Rigging, Rubber Props, Sculpted Props, Skeleton Replication, Toy Fabrication, Vacuum-Forming, Weapon Fabrication & Welding)

Think 3-D.Com (646) 873-0050
180 Cross Hwy (203) 682-6405
Westport, CT 06880 FAX (203) 682-6405
www.think3-d.com
(3D Design, Action Props, Artificial Foods, Mechanical FX, Miniatures, Models, Over-Sized Props, Rigging, Sculpted Props & Vacuum-Forming)

Trengove Studios, Inc. (212) 268-0020
60 W. 22nd St., Ste. 2 (800) 366-2857
(Near Seventh Ave.) FAX (212) 268-0030
New York, NY 10010 www.trengovestudios.com
(Artificial Food & FX Props)

Von Erickson Modelmaking (347) 239-6976
206 Classon Ave. www.vonerickson.com
Brooklyn, NY 11205
(Custom, Foam Sculpting, Miniatures, Models, Oversized Props, Prop Fabrication, Prototyping, Sculpted Props, Toy Fabrication & Vacuum-Forming)

Wilsonbuilt, Inc. (917) 776-5414
63 Flushing Ave., Ste. 197 www.wilsonbuilt.com
(Near Reed St.)
Brooklyn, NY 11205
(Custom Props & Mechanical FX)

Yvette Helin Studio, LLC (718) 389-8797
1205 Manhattan Ave., Ste. 1-3-6 (917) 617-5935
(Near Franklin St.) FAX (718) 559-6924
Brooklyn, NY 11222 www.yvettehelinstudio.com
(Foam Sculpture)

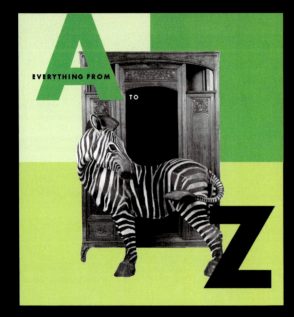

Prop Houses

Anything But Costumes (908) 788-1727
111 Mine St. FAX (609) 397-3970
Flemington, NJ 08822   www.anythingbutcostumes.com

Art & Industry/Doctor Proper, Ltd. (212) 477-0116
50 Great Jones St. (Near Lafayette St.) FAX (212) 477-1420
New York, NY 10012   www.aid20c.com

The Art Department, LLC (732) 431-0601
17 Bannard St., Ste. 12 FAX (732) 431-0604
Freehold, NJ 07728   www.the-art-dept.tv

Ⓐ Bridge Furniture & Props (718) 916-9706
126 Lombardy St., Second Fl. FAX (718) 663-7130
Brooklyn, NY 11222   www.bridgeprops.com

BRIDGE FURNITURE & PROPS

126 Lombardy Street 2nd Floor Brooklyn, NY 11222 Tel: 718.916.9706

BRIDGE PROPS .COM

THINK OF US AS THE GENIE THAT GRANTS EVERY WISH

 **STATE SUPPLY**

1361 Amsterdam Avenue
New York, NY 10027

212.663.2300
fax 212.663.3802

www.statesupplyprops.com

Ⓐ Eclectic • Encore Props, Inc.   (212) 645-8880
620 W. 26th St., Fourth Fl.   FAX (212) 243-6508
(Near 11th Ave.)   www.eclecticprops.com
New York, NY 10001

Miss Jezebel's Prop House   (516) 656-9653
    FAX (352) 726-8403

Ⓐ Modprop.com   (212) 628-7582
1044 Madison Ave., Ste. 3R   www.modprop.com
(Near 79th St.)
New York, NY 10021

Prop Central, Inc.   (718) 786-2689
209 E. 76th St., Ste. 2A   FAX (718) 786-3109
(Near 36th Ave.)
New York, NY 10021

The Prop Company -	
Kaplan & Associates	**(212) 691-7767**
111 W. 19th St., Eighth Fl.	FAX **(212) 727-3055**
(Near Sixth Ave.)	
New York, NY 10011	

🅐 Props for Today	**(212) 244-9600**
330 W. 34th St. (Near Eighth Ave.)	FAX **(212) 244-1053**
New York, NY 10001	www.propsfortoday.com

	(212) 352-0101
🅐 Props NYC	**(212) 741-7160**
509 W. 34th St., Second Fl.	FAX **(212) 741-8552**
(Near 10th Ave.)	www.propsnyc.com
New York, NY 10001	

🅐 State Supply	**(212) 663-2300**
1361 Amsterdam Ave.	FAX **(212) 663-3802**
(Near W. 126th St.)	www.statesupplyprops.com
New York, NY 10027	

Prop Houses

Restaurant & Kitchen Equipment

Anything But Costumes   (908) 788-1727
111 Mine St.   FAX (609) 397-3970
Flemington, NJ 08822   www.anythingbutcostumes.com

Artamus Restaurant Equipment   (800) 734-1880
1201 Astoria Blvd. (Near 12th St.)   FAX (718) 274-2876
Long Island City, NY 11102

    (212) 925-3786
Bari Restaurant Equipment   (212) 925-3845
240 Bowery (Near Prince St.)   FAX (212) 941-7054
New York, NY 10012   www.bariequipment.com

Carole Stupell, Ltd.   (212) 260-3100
29 E. 22nd St. (Near Park Ave.)   FAX (212) 260-3101
New York, NY 10010   www.carolestupell.com
(Fine China and Porcelain, Glassware & Silverware)

    (212) 473-7670
CSI/William Steinberg   (718) 657-5177
266 Bowery (Near Houston St.)   FAX (212) 226-5425
New York, NY 10012   www.globeslicersusa.com
(Vintage–Present Cash Registers, Grinders, Scales and Slicing Machines)

**Daroma
Restaurant Equipment Corp.**   (212) 260-2463
231 Bowery (Near Prince St.)   FAX (212) 979-1335
New York, NY 10002
(Commercial Kitchen and Restaurant Equipment)

    (718) 777-8600
Ⓐ Manhattan Propane   (631) 492-2048
(Propane)   FAX (631) 492-2051
   www.manhattanpropane.com

**The Warehouse Store
Fixture Company**   (203) 575-0111
84 Progress Ln.   FAX (203) 575-9140
Waterbury, CT 06705

We Delivered Propane to:
Manhattan
Brooklyn • Queens

Servicing to the entertainment industry around New York City

Call us at **631-492-2048**
For 24 hour delivery available

manhattanpropane.com
sales@manhattanpropane.com

Specialty Props

Aero Mock-Ups, Inc. (888) 662-5877
34 Burges Pl. www.aeromockups.com
Wayne, NJ 07470
(Airplane Interiors)

American Taximeters & Communications, Inc. (718) 937-4600 / (800) 882-0280
21-46 44th Dr. (Near 23rd St.) FAX (718) 937-4805
Long Island City, NY 11101 www.at-c.com
(Taxi Meters and Accessories)

Aquarium Design (845) 352-1640
80 Red School House Rd., Ste. 217 FAX (845) 352-1506
(Near Garden State Pkwy) www.aquariumdesign.com
Spring Valley, NY 10977

Aquavisions (516) 546-5944 / (516) 729-1805
www.aquavisions.net
(Aquariums and Accessories)

Arrangements, Inc. Marine Division (914) 238-1300
P.O. Box 126 FAX (914) 238-9776
Mount Kisco, NY 10549
(Marine Art & Ship Models)

Barclay Church Supply (718) 863-0474
3348 Campbell Dr.
Bronx, NY 10465
(Church Goods & Religious Articles)

Be Seated, Inc. (212) 924-8444
66 Greenwich Ave. www.tabwa.com
New York, NY 10011
(Baskets & Pottery)

Beauty Props (516) 223-4030
200 E. Sunrise Hwy FAX (516) 223-0348
Freeport, NY 11520 www.barberprops.com
(Vintage Barber Shop & Beauty Equipment)

Carole Stupell, Ltd. (212) 260-3100
29 E. 22nd St. (Near Park Ave.) FAX (212) 260-3101
New York, NY 10010 www.carolestupell.com
(China, Decorative Items, Gifts & Silverware)

(212) 794-3858
Choices: The Recovery Bookstore (866) 245-4818
220 E. 78th St. (Near Third Ave.) www.choices-nyc.com
New York, NY 10021
(Self-Help and Recovery Posters and Gifts)

Computer Rent (212) 767-0400
225 Broadway www.computerpropsnyc.com
(Near Barkley)
New York, NY 10007
(Computers)

Constructive Display, Inc. (718) 237-3131
499 Van Brunt St., Ste. 5A FAX (718) 237-4182
(Near Beard St.) www.constructivedisplay.com
Brooklyn, NY 11231

Creative Engineering (718) 937-5292
5-50 54th Ave. (Near Second St.) FAX (718) 937-1271
Long Island City, NY 11101
(Science Fiction Props) www.creativeengineeringinc.com

Eclectic • Encore Props, Inc. (212) 645-8880
620 W. 26th St., Fourth Fl. FAX (212) 243-6508
(Near 11th Ave.) www.eclecticprops.com
New York, NY 10001
(Full-Service Prop House)

The Gemini Co., Inc. (718) 858-7222
63 Flushing Ave., Ste. 157 www.thegeminicompany.com
Brooklyn, NY 11205

Giordano FX (973) 615-7263
518 Central Ave., Ste. 2L
Carlstadt, NJ 07072
www.myspace.com/scareproductions

(914) 376-5301
Greek 101.com (888) 473-3550
646 Saw Mill River Rd. FAX (914) 476-4333
(Near Clement St.) www.greek101.com
Yonkers, NY 10710
(Fraternity and Sorority Items)

(201) 666-6604
Holy Land Art Company, Inc. (800) 334-3621
12 Sullivan St. FAX (201) 666-6069
Westwood, NJ 07675 www.holylandartcompany.com
(Church Goods & Religious Articles)

(212) 695-6888
J. Levine Books & Judaica (800) 553-9474
Five W. 30th St. FAX (212) 643-1044
New York, NY 10001 www.levinejudaica.com
(Jewish Religious Articles)

When You Want The Best.
AERO MOCK-UPS — Better than the real thing
www.aeromockups.com

- Fully functional 20' narrow-body airline interior
- 20' of coach or 1st class cabins
- Color-corrected cabin lighting
- Fastened seatbelt / no smoking signs
- Overhead luggage bins
- Window shades
- Oxygen mask drop
- Free set dressing

For Information Call:
(888) 662-5877
Email: info@aeromockups.com

The Lawbook Exchange, Ltd. (732) 382-1800
(800) 422-6686
33 Terminal Ave. www.lawbookexchange.com
Clark, NJ 07066

Lost and Found Props (646) 230-7747
601 W. 26th St., Ste. 414 FAX (646) 230-7749
New York, NY 10001 www.lostandfoundprops.com
(Antiques, Chairs, Fabrics, Home Decor, Organics, Surfaces, Tables, Tabletop Items & Vintage)

Michael Miller, Inc. (914) 793-1999
(Artificial Chocolate, Food and Ice) FAX (914) 793-2120
www.michaelmillerinc.com

(508) 485-9333
Microform Models, Inc. (877) 489-3011
158 Winter St. www.microformmodels.com
Marlborough, MA 01752
(Scaled Model Cars, Fences, Figures, Furniture, Light Posts, Planes, Shrubs, Trees and Trucks)

Miss Jezebel's Prop House (516) 656-9653
(Full-Service Prop House) FAX (352) 726-8403

New York Blackboard (973) 926-1600
of New Jersey, Inc. (800) 652-6273
83 Route 22 West FAX (973) 926-3440
Hillside, NJ 07205 www.nyblackboard.com
(Chalkboards, Corkboards, Directories, Easels & Menu Boards)

(212) 505-9251
Obscura Antiques & Oddities (917) 592-0736
280 E. 10th St. www.obscuraantiques.com
New York, NY 10009
(Taxidermy)

Original License Plates/ (718) 279-1890
Andy Bernstein (917) 494-6551
www.platehut.com
(Contemporary and Vintage License Plates)

Props for Today (212) 244-9600
330 W. 34th St. (Near Eighth Ave.) FAX (212) 244-1053
New York, NY 10001 www.propsfortoday.com
(Full-Service Prop House)

(212) 352-0101
Props NYC (212) 741-7160
509 W. 34th St., Second Fl. FAX (212) 741-8552
(Near 10th Ave.) www.propsnyc.com
New York, NY 10001
(Full-Service Prop House)

Showman Fabricators, Inc. (718) 935-9899
47-22 Pearson Pl. (Near Davis Court) FAX (718) 855-9823
Long Island, NY 11101 www.showfab.com
(Airplane Interiors)

Special Effects
Production Services, Inc. (201) 405-0101
186 Paul Court FAX (201) 405-0632
Hillsdale, NJ 07642
(Science Fiction FX and Props)

State Supply (212) 663-2300
1361 Amsterdam Ave. FAX (212) 663-3802
(Near W. 126th St.) www.statesupplyprops.com
New York, NY 10027
(Full-Service Prop House)

(212) 268-0020
Trengove Studios, Inc. (800) 366-2857
60 W. 22nd St., Ste. 2 FAX (212) 268-0030
(Near Seventh Ave.) www.trengovestudios.com
New York, NY 10010
(Artificial Food, Ice Cubes, Pours and Splashes)

Sporting Goods

Blatt Billiards Supply Corp. (212) 674-8855
809 Broadway (Near W. 11th St.) (800) 252-8855
New York, NY 10003 FAX **(212) 598-4514**
www.blattbilliards.com

Capitol Fishing Tackle (212) 929-6132
132 W. 36th St. (Near Seventh Ave.) FAX **(212) 929-0039**
New York, NY 10018 www.capitolfishing.com

Captain Mike's Diving/ (718) 885-1588
Michael Carew (347) 865-4230
530 City Island Ave. FAX **(718) 885-2543**
City Island, NY 10464 www.captainmikesdiving.com
(Scuba Gear)

Church Street Boxing Gym (212) 571-1333
25 Park Pl. (Near Church St.) FAX **(212) 571-3777**
New York, NY 10007 www.nyboxinggym.com
(Boxing Equipment & Portable Boxing and Wrestling Rings)

Cougar (914) 693-8877
917 Sawmill River Rd. FAX **(914) 693-9453**
(Near Ashford Ave.)
Ardsley, NY 10502
(Archery and Scuba Diving Equipment)

(212) 966-8730
Eastern Mountain Sports (888) 463-6367
591 Broadway (Near Houston St.) www.ems.com
New York, NY 10012
(Camping and Climbing Equipment)

Eclectic • Encore Props, Inc. (212) 645-8880
620 W. 26th St., Fourth Fl. FAX **(212) 243-6508**
(Near 11th Ave.) www.eclecticprops.com
New York, NY 10001

Everlast Sporting Goods Mfg. (212) 239-0990
183 Madison Ave., Ste. 1701 (Near W. 36th St.)
New York, NY 10016
(Boxing Equipment & Exercise Gear)

Gerry Cosby & Co., Inc. (212) 563-6464
11 Penn Plaza (Near Seventh Ave.) FAX **(212) 967-0876**
New York, NY 10001 www.cosbysports.com

Gleason's Gym, Inc. (718) 797-2872
77 Front St., Second Fl. www.gleasonsgym.net
(Near Main St.)
Brooklyn, NY 11201

(212) 688-4222
Gym Source (888) 496-7687
40 E. 52nd St. (Near Madison Ave.) FAX **(212) 750-2886**
New York, NY 10022 www.gymsource.com
(Exercise and Gym Equipment)

Paragon Sports (212) 255-8036
867 Broadway (Near 18th St.) FAX **(212) 929-1831**
New York, NY 10003 www.paragonsports.com

(212) 427-6050
Soccer Sport Supply Co. (800) 223-1010
1745 First Ave. www.homeofsoccer.com
(Near E. 90th St.)
New York, NY 10128

Toga Bike Shop (212) 799-9625
110 West End Ave. (Near 64th St.) FAX **(212) 799-2834**
New York, NY 10023 www.togabikes.com

Studio Services

Bergdorf Goodman (212) 872-8772
754 Fifth Ave. (Near W. 57th St.) FAX (212) 872-8721
New York, NY 10019
Contact: Elizabeth Gregg

Bloomingdale's (212) 705-3673
1000 Third Ave. (Near E. 60th St.) FAX (212) 705-3939
New York, NY 10022
Contacts: Barbara D'Orsaneo & Cary Stiber

Bra*Tenders (212) 957-7000
(888) 438-2272
630 Ninth Ave., Ste. 601 FAX (212) 957-7010
New York, NY 10036 www.bratenders.com
Contact: Alan Kaplan

Giorgio Armani (212) 366-9720
114 Fifth Ave. (Near 17th St.) www.giorgioarmani.com
New York, NY 10011

Saks Fifth Ave. (877) 551-7257
611 Fifth Ave., Fifth Fl. FAX (601) 968-5281
(Near E. 50th St.) www.saksfifthavenue.com
New York, NY 10022
Contact: Connie Buck

Urban Outfitters (212) 375-1277
162 Second Ave. www.urbanoutfitters.com
(Near E. 10th St.)
New York, NY 10003
Contact: Melissa Blanar

Urban Outfitters (212) 475-0009
628 Broadway (Near W. Houston St.) FAX (212) 539-1994
New York, NY 10012 www.urbanoutfitters.com
Contact: Suzanne Keamnock

Tailoring & Alterations

Ernest Winzer (718) 294-2400
Theatrical & Leather Cleaner (877) 946-9371
1828 Cedar Ave., P.O. Box 294 FAX **(718) 294-2729**
(Near 179th) www.winzercleaners.com
Bronx, NY 10453

Justin Justin **(718) 721-9022**
11-27 31st Dr., Ste. 4 www.justinjustin.com
(Near Vernon Blvd.)
Long Island City, NY 11106
(Men's Tailoring)

(212) 226-4182
Celeste Livingston **(646) 456-0013**

(212) 475-2778
Meurice Garment Care **(800) 240-3377**
31 University Pl. (Near E. Eighth St.) FAX **(516) 627-2943**
New York, NY 10003 www.meuricegarmentcare.com

(212) 759-9057
Meurice Garment Care **(800) 240-3377**
245 E. 57th St. (Near Second Ave.) FAX **(516) 627-2943**
New York, NY 10022 www.meuricegarmentcare.com

(516) 627-6060
Meurice Garment Care **(800) 240-3377**
20 Park Ave. (Near Plamdome Rd.) FAX **(516) 627-2943**
Manhasset, NY 11030 www.meuricegarmentcare.com

(718) 729-4566
Minerva Cleaners **(917) 687-3211**
29-09 Broadway FAX **(718) 729-4344**
Astoria, NY 11106

Saint Laurie Merchant Tailors **(212) 643-1916**
22 W. 32nd St., Fifth Fl. FAX **(212) 695-4709**
(Near Fifth Ave.) www.saintlaurie.com
New York, NY 10001

Studio Rouge, Inc. **(212) 989-8363**
152 W. 25th St., Seventh Fl. FAX **(212) 989-5575**
(Near Seventh Ave.)
New York, NY 10001

Tiecrafters, Inc. **(212) 629-5800**
252 W. 29th St. (Near Eighth Ave.) FAX **(212) 629-0115**
New York, NY 10001 www.tiecrafters.com
(Tie Alterations)

Timberlake Studios, Inc. **(212) 967-4736**
322 Seventh Ave., Ste. 2F FAX **(212) 967-4737**
(Near W. 28th St.) www.timberlakestudios.com
New York, NY 10001

Uniforms & Surplus

City Intercoms, Inc. (201) 750-1176 / (800) 248-9468
P.O. Box 565 FAX (201) 750-1339
New York, NY 10002
(Police Badges and Uniform Accessories)

I.M.A./International Military Antiques, Inc. (908) 903-1200
1000 Valley Rd. FAX (908) 903-0106
Gillette, NJ 07933 www.ima-usa.com
(Period Military Material)

Some's World-Wide Uniforms, Inc. (201) 843-1199 / (800) 631-7077
314 Main St. FAX (201) 843-3014
Hackensack, NJ 07601 www.somes.com
(Fire, Military & Police)

Tactical Truck (540) 341-7140
P.O. Box 984 FAX (540) 341-7146
Marshall, VA 20116 www.tacticaltruck.com
(Military Equipment and Tents)

Western Costume Co. (818) 508-2111 / (888) 293-7837
11041 Vanowen St. FAX (818) 508-2153
North Hollywood, CA 91605 www.westerncostume.com

Vintage Clothing & Accessories

Bra*Tenders (212) 957-7000 / (888) 438-2272
630 Ninth Ave., Ste. 601 FAX (212) 957-7010
New York, NY 10036 www.bratenders.com
(Vintage Look Undergarments and Hosiery)

Early Halloween (212) 691-2933
130 W. 25th St., 11th Fl. FAX (212) 243-1499
(Near Sixth Ave.) www.earlyhalloween.com
New York, NY 10001
(By Appointment Only)

Every Thing Goes (718) 273-7139 / (718) 720-5378
140 Bay St. (Near Victory Blvd.) www.etgstores.com
Staten Island, NY 10301

The Family Jewels (212) 633-6020
130 W. 23rd St., Ground Fl. www.familyjewelsnyc.com
(Near Seventh Ave.)
New York, NY 10011
(Antique, Designer, Hats, Lace, Purses, Rentals,
Undergarments, Used, Vintage, Victorian & Western)

Helen Uffner Vintage Clothing LLC (718) 937-0220
30-10 41st Ave., Third Fl. FAX (718) 937-0227
(Near Northern Blvd.) www.uffnervintage.com
Long Island City, NY 11101
(1860s–1970's Original & Accessories)

LaCrasia Gloves (212) 803-1600 / (917) 912-4174
1181 Broadway, Eighth Fl. FAX (212) 686-5250
(Near 28th St.) www.wegloveyou.com
New York, NY 10001

Matinee NY (917) 837-3645 / (212) 996-7080
(Vintage) www.vintagecoolclothes.com

Obscura Antiques & Oddities (212) 505-9251 / (917) 592-0736
280 E. 10th St. www.obscuraantiques.com
New York, NY 10009

Screaming Mimi's (212) 677-6464
382 Lafayette St. (Near E. Fourth St.) FAX (212) 677-6523
New York, NY 10003 www.screamingmimis.com
(1940s–1980s Never Worn and Used Sales and Rentals)

White Daisy (716) 397-2234
P.O. Box 170 www.whitedaisyshop.com
Jamestown, NY 14702
(Tie-Dyed Clothing)

NEW YORK
WE ARE ALL IN THIS TOGETHER

Association of Location Scouts and Managers

alsam.net

🅐 ADVERTISER SYMBOL

Refer to the General Index for cross-referencing items in this section.

Agents, Reps & Job Referral Services 380
Ambulance/Paramedics & Nurses
  (Local 52 NY) 383
Ambulance/Paramedics & Nurses. 384
Art Directors/Production Designers
  (Local 829 NY) 388
Art Directors/Production Designers 391
Camera Assistants (Local 600 NY) 398
Camera Assistants 407
Camera Operators (Local 600 NY) 408
Camera Operators...................... 413
Camera Operators—Aerial (Local 600 NY). . 414
Camera Operators—Steadicam
  (Local 600 NY) 415
Camera Operators—Steadicam 416
Camera Operators—Underwater
  (Local 600 NY) 417
Carpenters/Shop Craft (Local 52 NY) 418
Craft Service (Local 52 NY) 423
Craft Service 424
Digital Imaging Technicians (Local 600 NY) . 425
Digital Imaging Technicians.............. 425
Directors of Photography (Local 600 NY) ... 426
Directors of Photography................ 433
First Assistant Directors (DGA NY) 447
First Assistant Directors................. 450
Food Stylists & Home Economists 452
Gaffers & Electricians (Local 52 NY)....... 453
Gaffers & Electricians 464
Grips (Local 52 NY) 465
Grips 476
Hair & Makeup Artists (Local 798 NY) 477
Hair & Makeup Artists 488
Lighting Directors 496
Producers 497
Production Coordinators (Local 161 NY) ... 501
Production Coordinators 503
Production Managers 504
Production Stills Photographers (Local 600). . 505
Production Stills Photographers.......... 507
Props Department (Local 52 NY) 508
Props Department 523
Script Supervisors (Local 161 NY) 525
Script Supervisors..................... 526
Second Assistant Directors (DGA NY) 527
Second Assistant Directors 531
Set Decorators 532

Sound Mixers (Local 52 NY) 534
Sound Mixers 539
Stage Managers (DGA NY) 540
Studio Teachers/Welfare Workers......... 541
Stunt Coordinators & Performance Drivers. . 542
Trade Associations/Unions 546
Training Centers 548
Underwater Technicians 549
Unit Production Managers (DGA NY) 550
VTR Operators (Local 52 NY)............ 552
VTR Operators 554
Wardrobe Stylists/Costume Designers
  (Local 829 NY)...................... 555
Wardrobe Stylists/Costume Designers 558
Wardrobe Supervisors (Local 764 NY) 563
NY Union Commercial Work Rules........ 567
IATSE (AFL-CIO) Guidelines............. 571
IATSE Commercial
  Production Agreements—Jurisdictions 573
IATSE Commercial Production Agreement
  Work Rules & Conditions 574
P&W Rules—IATSE Commercial
  Production Agreement................. 575
Minimum Wage Rates
  Within LA County..................... 576
Minimum Wage Rates
  Outside LA County 578
Northeast Corridor Agreement
  Locals 600, 161 & 798 580
Local 600—International Photographers
  Working Rules & Conditions 581
Local 161—Script Supervisors
  Working Rules & Conditions 582
Local 789—Hair & Makeup
  Working Rules & Conditions 583
Local 52—Studio Mechanics
  Minimum Daily Rates 584
Local 52—Studio Mechanics
  Working Rules & Conditions 585
Local 829—Scenic Artists
  Minimum Wage Rates.................. 586
Local 829—Scenic Artists
  Working Rules & Conditions 587
Directors Guild of America
  Minimum Daily Salaries................ 589
Directors Guild of America Work Rules..... 590
Screen Actors Guild Guidelines 592

Agents, Reps & Job Referral Services

Aartist Loft (212) 274-0961
580 Broadway, Ste. 606 FAX (212) 274-0962
(Near W. Houston) www.aartistloft.com
New York, NY 10012
(Reps for Makeup Artists and Wardrobe Stylists)

Above & Beyond Artists Agency (323) 464-9696
439 N. Larchmont Blvd. FAX (323) 464-5608
Los Angeles, CA 90004 www.aboveandbeyondartists.com
(Reps for Art Directors/Production Designers, Set Sketchers
and Storyboard Artists)

All Crew Agency (818) 206-0144
2920 W. Olive Ave., Ste. 201 FAX (818) 206-0169
Burbank, CA 91505 www.allcrewagency.com
(Reps for Assistant Directors, Directors of Photography, Production
Designers, Editors, Hair and Makeup Artists, Script Supervisors,
Storyboard Artists and Wardrobe Stylists/Costume Designers)

Ambitious Entertainment (818) 990-8993
15120 Hartsook St., Ste. 1 www.ambitiousent.com
Sherman Oaks, CA 91403
(Reps for Art Directors/Production Designers, Commercial
Directors and Directors of Photography)

Art Department (212) 925-4222
48 Greene St., Fourth Fl. FAX (212) 925-4422
(Near Broome St.) www.art-dept.com
New York, NY 10013
(Reps for Hair Stylists, Makeup Artists and Wardrobe Stylists)

Artists by Timothy Priano (212) 929-7771
131 Varick St., Ste. 905 FAX (212) 929-7760
New York, NY 10013 www.artistsbytimothypriano.com
(Reps for Hair and Makeup Artists, Set Decorators and
Wardrobe Stylists)

ArtMix Photography (718) 596-2400
(310) 473-0770
297 Bond St. FAX (718) 596-2401
Brooklyn, NY 11231 www.artmixphotography.com
(Reps for Still Photographers)

Atlantic Television, Inc. (212) 625-9327
(917) 568-7218
524 Broadway, Fourth Fl. FAX (212) 625-9346
(Near Spring) www.atlantictv.com
New York, NY 10012
(Reps for Directors of Photography and Camera Operators)

Bryan Bantry (212) 935-0200
(Reps for Hair and Makeup Artists) FAX (212) 935-2698
www.bryanbantry.com

Clear Talent Group/CTG (212) 840-4100
325 W. 38th St., Ste. 1203 FAX (212) 967-4567
(Near Eighth Ave.) www.cleartalentgroup.com
New York, NY 10018

Creative Entertainment Connections (212) 643-1736
260 W. 35th St., Ste. 603 FAX (212) 643-1802
New York, NY 10001 www.cec-entertainment.com
(Reps for Art Directors/Production Designers, Camera
Operators, Casting Directors, Costume Designers, Directors of
Photography, Editors, Hair and Makeup Artists, Line Producers,
Location Managers & UPMs)

Crew 1 TV, Inc. (212) 665-8277
224 W. 35th St., Ste. 610 FAX (212) 594-5874
(Near 7th and 8th Avenues) www.crew1tv.com
New York, NY 10001
(TV Crew Referral)

Crew Connection (800) 352-7397
(303) 526-4900
FAX (303) 526-4901
www.crewconnection.com
(Nationwide and International Crew Booking)

crewHD.com (973) 508-6054
www.crewhd.com

CrewStar, Inc. (508) 481-2212
(888) 746-6871
One Boston Rd. FAX (508) 481-7785
Southborough, MA 01772 www.crewstar.com
(Crew Referral)

Dattner Dispoto & Associates (310) 474-4585
10635 Santa Monica Blvd., Ste. 165 FAX (310) 474-6411
Los Angeles, CA 90025 www.ddatalent.com
(Reps for Directors of Photography)

Dawn to Dusk Agency (212) 431-8631
(323) 850-6783
www.dawn2duskagency.com
(Reps for Hair and Makeup Artists and Wardrobe Stylists)

Dion Peronneau Agency   (323) 299-4043
FAX (323) 299-4269
www.dionperonneau.com
(Reps for Hair and Makeup Artists and Wardrobe Stylists)

Ⓐ The Directors Network   (818) 906-0006
3685 Motor Ave., Ste. 220   FAX (818) 301-2224
Los Angeles, CA 90034   www.thedirectorsnetwork.com
(Reps for Commercial Directors)

The Endeavor Agency   (212) 625-2500
152 W. 57th St., 25th Fl.
New York, NY 10019

   (212) 741-3240
Ennis, Inc.   (781) 863-1555
(Reps for Hair and Makeup Artists)   FAX (781) 863-1554
www.ennisinc.com

   (646) 453-1585
Exclusive Artists Management   (646) 453-1583
596 Broadway, Ste. 601   www.eamgmt.com
New York, NY 10012
(Reps for Hair and Makeup Artists & Wardrobe Stylists)

   (212) 980-7979
Famous Frames, Inc.   (800) 530-3375
247 E. 57th St., Second Fl.   FAX (212) 980-6556
(Near Second Ave.)   www.famousframes.com
New York, NY 10022
(Reps for Storyboard Artists)

Frameworks Storyboards   (323) 665-7736
983 Manzanita St.   FAX (323) 662-4381
Los Angeles, CA 90029   www.frameworks-la.com
(Reps for Storyboard Artists)

The Geller Agency   (323) 856-3000
1547 Cassil Pl.   FAX (323) 856-3009
Hollywood, CA 90028   www.thegelleragency.com
(Reps for Costume Designers, Directors of Photography, Editors, First Assistant Directors, Production Designers and Stunt Coordinators)

   (212) 997-1818
The Gersh Agency   (310) 274-6611
41 Madison Ave., 33rd Fl.   FAX (212) 997-1978
(Near E. 26th St.)   www.gershagency.com
New York, NY 10010
(Reps for Art Directors/Production Designers, Directors of Photography, Editors and Wardrobe Stylists/Costume Designers)

Halley Resources   (212) 206-0901
231 W. 29th St., Ste. 701   FAX (212) 206-0904
(Near Seventh Ave.)   www.halleyresources.com
New York, NY 10001
(Reps for Food Stylists, Hair and Makeup Artists, Prop Stylists and Wardrobe Stylists/Costume Designers)

   (212) 213-0028
home.work.people   (310) 917-4420
636 Broadway, Ste. 1106   FAX (212) 677-3245
New York, NY 10012   www.homeworkpeople.com
(Referral for Broadcast Designers and Producers, Creative Management/Executives and Crew)

Illusions Management   (212) 242-7050
129 W. 27th St., PH (Near Sixth Ave.)   FAX (212) 206-6228
New York, NY 10001   www.clickmodel.com/illusions.php
(Reps for Hair and Makeup Artists and Wardrobe Stylists)

Ⓐ Innovative Artists   (212) 253-6900
235 Park Ave. South, Seventh Fl.
New York, NY 10003   www.innovativeartists.com
(Reps for Art Directors/Production Designers, Directors of Photography and Wardrobe Stylists/Costume Designers)

International
Creative Management - ICM   (212) 556-5600
825 Eighth Ave.   www.icmtalent.com
New York, NY 10019

The Jacob & Kole Agency   (323) 460-4767
6715 Hollywood Blvd., Ste. 216   FAX (323) 460-4804
Los Angeles, CA 90028   www.jacobandkoleagency.com
(Reps for Directors of Photography and Production Designers)

   (646) 275-0280
Luna Llena Management, Inc.   (917) 864-6412
168 Second Ave., Ste. 254   www.llmgmt.com
New York, NY 10003
(Reps for Hair and Makeup Artists)

The Mack Agency   (818) 753-6300
5726 Woodman Ave., Ste. 4   FAX (818) 753-6311
Van Nuys, CA 91401   www.themackagency.net
(Reps for Art Directors/Production Designers and Directors of Photography)

Magnet NY   (212) 352-3223
270 Lafayette St., Ste. 901   FAX (212) 941-7441
New York, NY 10012   www.themagnetagency.com
(Reps for Art Directors, Hair and Makeup Artists and Wardrobe Stylists)

INNOVATIVE ARTISTS

DIRECTORS OF PHOTOGRAPHY
PRODUCTION DESIGNERS
STYLISTS / COSTUME DESIGNERS

Commercials & Music Videos   Features & Television
JEFF MAHONEY   DEBBIE HAEUSLER
ROBBYN FOXX   HEATHER GRIFFITH
    CRAIG MIZRAHI

1617 Broadway   Tel: 310.656.5153
Santa Monica, CA 90404   Fax: 310.656.5156

Mark Edward, Inc. (212) 279-1999
325 W. 38th St., Ste. 1011 www.markedwardinc.com
(Near Eighth Ave.)
New York, NY 10018
(Reps for Hair and Makeup Artists)

The Mirisch Agency (310) 282-9940
1925 Century Park East, Ste. 1070 FAX (310) 282-0702
Los Angeles, CA 90067 www.mirisch.com
(Reps for Costume Designers, Directors of Photography, Editors, Producers and Production Designers)

Montana Artists Agency (323) 845-4144
7715 W. Sunset Blvd., Third Fl. FAX (323) 845-4155
Los Angeles, CA 90046 www.montanartists.com
(Reps for Directors of Photography, Editors, First Assistant Directors, Hair and Makeup Artists, Producers, Production Designers, Visual FX Supervisors and Wardrobe Stylists/Costume Designers)

Motion Odyssey, Inc. (917) 597-0037
www.motionodyssey.com
(Reps for Camera Assistants, Directors of Photography and Steadicam Operators)

The Murtha Agency (310) 822-9113
4240 Promenade Way, Ste. 232 FAX (310) 822-6662
Marina Del Rey, CA 90292 www.murthaagency.com
(Reps for Directors of Photography and Production Designers)

(212) 545-7895
New York Office (323) 468-2240
15 W. 26th St., Fifth Fl. FAX (212) 545-7941
(Near Broadway) www.nyoffice.net
New York, NY 10010
(Reps for Camera Assistants, Camera Operators, Costume Designers, Directors of Photography, Editors, Hair and Makeup Artists and Production Designers)

One Naked Egg (212) 925-1111
675 Hudson St., Ste. 4N FAX (212) 929-6552
(Near 13th St.) www.onenakedegg.com
New York, NY 10014
(Reps for Hair and Makeup Artists and Production Still Photographers)

Orlando Management (818) 781-9233
15134 Martha St. www.orlandomanagement.com
Sherman Oaks, CA 91411
(Reps for Directors of Photography and Production Designers)

Paradigm (212) 897-6400
360 Park Ave. South, 16th Fl. FAX (212) 764-8941
(Near Seventh Ave.) www.paradigmagency.com
New York, NY 10010
(Reps for Costume Designers, Directors of Photography, Line Producers and Production Designers)

Partos Company (310) 458-7800
227 Broadway, Ste. 204 FAX (310) 587-2250
Santa Monica, CA 90401 www.partos.com
(Reps for Directors of Photography, Hair and Makeup Artists, Production Designers and Wardrobe Stylists)

R.J. Bennett Represents (212) 673-5509
530 E. 20th St., Ste. 2B www.rjbennettrepresents.com
(Near First Ave.)
New York, NY 10009
(Reps for Hair and Makeup Artists)

Radiant Artists (323) 463-0022
6715 Hollywood Blvd., Ste. 220 FAX (323) 375-0231
Los Angeles, CA 90028 www.radiantartists.com
(Reps for Costume Designers, Directors of Photography and Production Designers)

(818) 953-4930
ReelsOnDemand.com (866) 667-3357
84 E. Santa Anita Ave. FAX (818) 688-3991
Burbank, CA 91502 www.reelsondemand.com
(Online Demo Reels and Portfolios)

The Right Eye (212) 924-8505
41 Union Square West, Ste. 1004 FAX (212) 924-8544
(Near W. 16th St.) www.therighteye.com
New York, NY 10003
(Reps for Directors of Photography, Production Designers and Wardrobe Stylists/Costume Designers)

Russell Todd Agency (818) 985-1130
5238 Goodland Ave. FAX (818) 985-1134
Valley Village, CA 91607 www.russelltoddagency.com
(Reps for Camera Operators)

See Management (212) 255-2500
307 Seventh Ave., Ste. 1607 FAX (212) 255-2020
New York, NY 10001 www.seemanagement.com
(Reps for Hair and Makeup Artists and Wardrobe Stylists)

(310) 966-4005
Sesler & Company (416) 504-1223
11840 Jefferson Blvd. FAX (323) 988-0930
Los Angeles, CA 90230 www.seslercompany.com
(Reps for Directors of Photography)

Sheldon Prosnit Agency (310) 652-8778
800 S. Robertson Blvd., Ste. 6 FAX (310) 652-8772
Los Angeles, CA 90035 www.lspagency.net
(Reps for Directors of Photography and Production Designers)

(212) 564-7892
Sherry Rousso Associates, Inc. (212) 564-7893
One River Pl., Ste. 1828 FAX (212) 564-7849
(Near 12th Ave.) www.sradp.com
New York, NY 10036
(Reps for Camera Assistants and Directors of Photography)

(212) 794-9030
Silberman Productions (917) 880-6747
330 E. 75th St., Ste. 33A FAX (212) 794-9232
(Near Second Ave.)
New York, NY 10021
(Reps for Commercial Directors and Editors)

The Skouras Agency (310) 395-9550
1149 Third St., Third Fl. FAX (310) 395-4295
Santa Monica, CA 90403 www.skouras.com
(Reps for Camera Assistants, Camera Operators, Directors of Photography and Production Designers)

Stacy Cheriff Agency (310) 314-2606
10923 Ayres Ave. www.stacycheriffagency.com
Los Angeles, CA 90064
(Reps for Directors of Photography)

Tapestry Creative Management (212) 926-0477
255 W. 148th St., Third Fl. FAX (360) 926-0478
New York, NY 10039 www.tapestryinc.com
(Reps for Editors)

Ⓐ TDN Artists (818) 906-0006
3685 Motor Ave., Ste. 220 FAX (818) 301-2224
Los Angeles, CA 90034 www.tdnartists.com
(Reps for Directors of Photography, Editors & Production Designers)

TellAVision (310) 230-5303
1060 20th St., Ste. 8 FAX (310) 388-5550
Santa Monica, CA 90403 www.tellavisionagency.com
(Reps for 3D FX Artists, Storyboard Artists & Visual Research/Treatment Design)

(646) 382-8819
Tobi Britton's Makeup Shop (212) 807-0447
131 W. 21st St. (Near Seventh Ave.) FAX (212) 727-0975
New York, NY 10011 www.themakeupshop.com
(Referral for Makeup Artists)

United Talent Agency (310) 273-6700
9560 Wilshire Blvd., Ste. 500 FAX (310) 247-1111
Beverly Hills, CA 90212 www.unitedtalent.com
(Reps for Directors of Photography)

Ambulance/Paramedics & Nurses (Local 52 NY)

John Antonacchio	(718) 543-6760 / (917) 641-3002
Maria Baan	(646) 354-3399
Maureen Beitler, R.N.	(212) 787-9193 / (917) 370-5625
Bruce Bell, EMT-P (Paramedic)	(646) 594-8325 / (845) 353-6806
Mary Frances Berkelbach	(609) 368-3559
Debra Birnbaum, R.N.	(954) 464-9498
Deborah Blake	(212) 491-4142 / (917) 226-2664
Jacqueline Brandwein	(718) 956-3248
Robert S. Broder	(212) 593-9706 / (917) 783-0785
Joseph Brunner	(516) 315-1553 / (516) 546-3233
Lisa L. Caracciola	(516) 971-3591
Chester Coleman	(718) 252-5506 / (917) 451-0915
C.K. Collins, EMT-P (Paramedic)	(631) 864-9445 / (631) 445-1958 / FAX (631) 864-9445
ⓐ Leslie Collins, R.N. (Baby Wrangler)	(516) 624-4944 / (516) 428-6447 / FAX (516) 624-8026
Kathy Cossu	(718) 605-7507 / (917) 669-6729 / FAX (718) 608-0515
Kristy Victoria Davenport	(212) 978-3840 / (866) 721-8896 / FAX (866) 306-0963
Ilysa R. Del Giudice	(516) 221-1960 / (516) 973-0173
Denise M. Depalma	(609) 263-5447
Victoria Dilks	(215) 860-2260 / (215) 962-4839
William Duncklee	(718) 843-8906 / (917) 697-7342
Marjorie Gayle Edwards	(718) 585-8529 / (212) 724-2800
Jonathan Ellis	(845) 216-0371
Kathy Fellegara, R.N.	(914) 961-0674 / (914) 523-3185
Rich Fellegara (Paramedic)	(914) 961-0674 / (917) 692-3134
Daniel Frommer	(516) 480-8881
Carolyn A. Gershenson, R.N.	(516) 466-5316 / (516) 527-2343 / FAX (516) 466-7088
Peter M. Gershenson, M.D. (EMT)	(516) 466-5316 / (516) 641-3977 / FAX (516) 466-7088
Patricia A. Jones-Malewich	(212) 684-3205 / (917) 533-7884
Kathleen M. Kelly, R.N.	(215) 698-1651 / (267) 968-1724 / FAX (215) 698-3175
Adam Levy	(516) 779-0077 / (516) 621-6965
Marie Loughran, R.N.	(917) 647-6381
Loretta Marsh	(908) 303-8238 / (800) 225-0256
Margaret M. Mazzei	(215) 579-1409 / (267) 408-2610
Jennifer E. McKoy	(201) 441-4603
Doreen P. McMillan-Roman	(631) 767-5583
Fran Medina, R.N.	(845) 986-9268 / (845) 258-8199
Elizabeth M. Oates-Koenig, R.N.	(845) 496-5085 / (845) 234-0495
Avery Elizabeth Paul	(203) 605-6809
Raul Perez Jr.	(917) 204-1543
Jacqueline C. Qualles	(845) 341-0054 / (845) 342-5484
Susan Sloan	(212) 713-5540
Joseph G. Striffler	(631) 252-7235
Deborah L. Thomas	(212) 406-7106 / (212) 312-5228
Leslie E. Witt-Bertsche	(516) 248-7882 / (516) 987-9221
Thomas Yacuk	(845) 424-4531

SET NURSE • BABYWRANGLER • TUTOR

Leslie Collins R.N.B.S. BA Elm. Ed.
Commercials • Series • Film • Music Videos
(516) 624-4944   (516) 428-6447 Cell

- Standby Ambulance Service (ALS & BLS)
- Movie, TV and Video Shoots
- We provide Paramedics, EMT's, and Nurses
- Prop Vehicles
- Sporting Events for professional teams, school games, or kids classes
- Concerts of all Kinds

We service the NY Metropolitan area and all of Long Island

Whatever your particular needs may be, our family can provide exactly the services that you need.

Please Call 718-372-0700, ask for Wayne

Web: http://www.HunterAmbulance.com

Email: info@hunterambulance.com

Ambulance/Paramedics & Nurses

Jacque Ambadjes (516) 414-2940
(Paramedic) (516) 319-6582

Ambu-Care (877) 633-4569
(EMTs & Paramedics) www.ambu-care.com

Amphibious Medics (646) 736-7487

Assured Protection, LLC (212) 518-7516
1420 York Ave., Ste. 3B FAX (646) 607-4323
New York, NY 10021 www.assuredprotection.com

On-Site Medical Services
Call: (718) 645-1000

MIDWOOD
AMBULANCE SERVICE

Providing: Paramedics and Emergency Medical Technicians
Advanced Life Support & Basic Life Support Ambulances
24 HOURS A DAY

On Camera Service Also Available

Serving New York City for over 50 years

Emergency Medical Services
212-472-2222
Superb care when every second counts

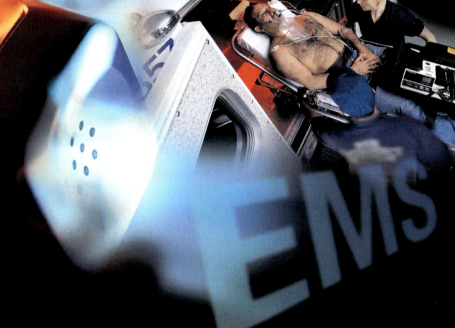

The Unforeseen Event...
Protect Yourself; Protect Your Staff

Contact NewYork-Presbyterian Emergency Medical Services:
- Pre-hospital critical care services for the production industry
- State-of-the-art ambulances and biomedical equipment
- Expertly qualified Physicians, Paramedics, EMT's, RN's
- On-site First-Aid, Basic Life Support, Advanced Life Support
- Charters for on-camera needs, entertainment and sports events

Scheduling & rates, EMS Administration: **212-746-0885**
Emergency Assistance 24 hours a day: **212-472-2222**

NewYork-Presbyterian
EMERGENCY MEDICAL SERVICES

The University Hospital of Columbia and Cornell
525 East 68th Street, NY, NY 10065

Bambini Casting & Wrangling/
Michele Avantario (914) 646-5839
(Baby Wrangler)

Bolte Medical
Urgent Care Center NYC (212) 588-9314
141 E. 55th St., Ste. 8-H www.boltemedical.com
New York, NY 10022

(718) 920-9135
Cine-Med (914) 715-8102
FAX (718) 920-9106
(Ambulances, EMTs, Medics, Nurses, Technical Advisors & Travel Medicine)

Cinema World Medical Division (718) 389-9800
220 Dupont St. FAX (718) 389-9897
(Near McGuinness Blvd.) www.cinemaworldstudios.com
Brooklyn, NY 11222
(Baby Wranglers & Nurses)

Lisa Davis (917) 806-8572

Ⓐ **Hunter Ambulance, Inc.** (718) 372-0700
FAX (516) 371-0871
www.hunterambulance.com
(Ambulances, EMTs, Medics, Nurses, Rescue Technicians, Safety Consultants & Technical Advisors)

Kathy's Medical Production (718) 605-7507
Company, Inc./Kathy Cossu, R.N. (917) 669-6729
(Ambulances, Baby Wranglers & Nurses) FAX (718) 608-0515

Ⓐ **Midwood Ambulance &**
Oxygen Service, Inc. (718) 645-1000
FAX (718) 375-9661
www.midwoodambulance.com

Ⓐ **Louis J. Morledge, MD** (212) 583-2830
150 E. 58th St., 18th Fl. FAX (212) 583-0444
(Near Lexington Avenue)
New York, NY 10155
(CAST Exams, EMTs, Lifeguards, Nurses, Paramedics, Safety Consultants & Travel Medicine)

Ⓐ **NewYork-Presbyterian** (212) 472-2222
Emergency Medical Services (212) 746-0885
525 E. 68th St., Ste. M-101 FAX (212) 746-5476
New York, NY 10065 www.nyp.org

Nurses-In-Commercials (212) 712-6462
FAX (718) 585-3872

Ⓐ **Ronald A. Primas, M.D.,** (212) 737-1212
FACP, FACPM, CTH (212) 737-2333
FAX (212) 517-3814
www.doctortothestars.com
(Cast Exams, EMTs, Medics, Nurses, Safety Consultants, Technical Advisors & Travel Medicine)

(718) 648-8707
James A. Quitoni, R.N. (718) 951-2901

Ruth V. Riviere, R.N., EMT (917) 699-8478
FAX (718) 796-9396

(718) 634-3194
Starlite Medical Staff (917) 756-6479
221 Beach 80th St., Ste. 5J FAX (718) 634-4727
(Near Rockaway Beach Blvd.) www.starlitemedicalstaff.com
Rockaway Beach, NY 11693

Barbara Young, R.N. (215) 464-3255

MORLEDGE MEDICAL

PREMIER Services 24/7/365
CAST exams • Hotel & House Calls by Appointment
Travel Medicine • Yellow Fever vaccination center
212-229-9000
LOUIS J. MORLEDGE, MD
150 East 58th Street, 18th Fl., New York, NY 10022 (East of Lexington Ave.)
www.morledgemedical.com
On-location Visits | Team of Board-certified Physicians and Specialists
LOS ANGELES/VANCOUVER

www.DoctortheStars.com

212-737-1212

24/7 Discrete, Confidential Production Shoot (Set) Calls & House/Hotel Calls

24/7 Travel Medicine Consultations and Vaccinations (NYS Approved Yellow Fever Vaccination Site) by Appointment

24/7 Specialty Referrals: including Dental, Psychiatric, OB/GYN, ENT, Acupuncture, Chiropractic, and more!

24/7 Cast Exams by Appointment

24/7 Urgent Care Center By Appointment

Technical Consultations

Board Certified Physicians with Major Teaching Hospital Affiliations. VIP Service

Dr. Primas is a contributing consultant to Natural Geographic Traveler, Self, Health, Manhattan Living and Forbes magazines as a travel medicine expert. He has been featured in The New York Times, The Wall Street Journal, The International Herald Tribune, New York Resident, CNN, The Discovery Channel, ABC News, CBS, CBS World News, NY1 and Fox News on traveler's health related issues.

Dr. Primas has also had guest appearances on Making the Band I, II & IV, Making the Cut, Band in a Bubble, Kimora: Life in the Fab Lane, the Food Network Channel, Discovery Health: Travel Emergencies, Discovery Health: Nightmare in New York.

DOCTOR TO THE STARS™

Ronald A. Primas, MD, FACP, FACPM, CTH

Art Directors/Production Designers (Local 829 NY)

Name	Contact
Irfan Akdag	(201) 750-9404 / (917) 854-7100 / FAX (201) 750-9405
Sonia M. Alio	(718) 857-5382
Peter Allburn	(201) 725-7748
Kevin Allen	(973) 744-6352 / (201) 280-3841 / FAX (973) 744-7193 / www.klad.com
Michael S. Anania	(973) 673-0668
Cameron Anderson	(513) 218-2398
Loy Arcenas	(212) 387-0345
Jonathan Arkin	(646) 207-6930 / (973) 763-6631
Simona M. Auerbach	(212) 579-4398 / (917) 806-5498
Michael Auszura	(203) 292-3799 / (917) 847-0867
Campbell Baird	(212) 633-1953 / (908) 387-1994
Russell Barnes	(917) 676-9996 / (212) 500-5600
Teri Bella	(917) 512-4975 / (917) 701-0191
Elise Bennett	(917) 447-6511
Roshelle Berliner	(310) 652-8778 / www.lspagency.net
Andrew Bernard	(212) 545-7895 / www.nyoffice.net
Kevin Bird	(310) 458-7800 / www.partos.com
Beowulf Boritt	(212) 317-0602
Cassandra Boyd	(917) 686-2447
Jenny Burton	(201) 750-9404 / (917) 539-3910 / FAX (201) 750-9405 / www.jacobandkoleagency.com
Richard W. Butler	(914) 827-2662 / (914) 473-5173
Rick Butler	(323) 845-4144 / (914) 473-5173 / www.montanartists.com
Stephen Caldwell	(914) 231-9286 / (917) 952-4545
Luke Cantarella	(949) 878-3727 / (646) 263-4989
Teresa M. Carriker-Thayer	(845) 266-3218
Stephanie Carroll	(212) 529-9029 / FAX (212) 529-9029
Stephen Carter	(212) 545-7895 / (718) 832-3279 / www.nyoffice.net
Len X. Clayton	(718) 488-8433 / (917) 554-6885
Edward Coco	(917) 749-5382
Lester Cohen	(323) 460-4767 / (845) 687-4503 / www.jacobandkoleagency.com
Benjamin Conable	(917) 449-0415
Jeremy Conway	(310) 395-9550 / www.skouras.com
Patrice Andrew Davidson	(212) 286-5019
Dan Davis	(323) 460-4767 / www.jacobandkoleagency.com
John F. Davis	(212) 406-2282 / (917) 806-7524
Matteo De Cosmo	(718) 302-9010 / (917) 757-1511
Jennifer E. Dehghan	(201) 787-9691 / homepage.mac.com/jdehghan
Paul De Pass	(212) 362-2648
Norm Dodge	(212) 289-1092 / www.normdodge.com
David Doernberg	(310) 273-6700 / www.utaproduction.com
Diann E. Duthie	(212) 496-1416
Martin D. Fahrer	(718) 721-5928
Sorangel Fersobe	(201) 332-3361 / (917) 476-4941
M. Alison Ford	(914) 772-3905 / (914) 762-8014
Armond Francone	(718) 852-9823 / (917) 488-5400
Lisa Frantz	(917) 834-4335
Chad K. Frazier	(917) 306-0070
Mary Frederickson	(212) 459-0192 / (917) 570-4257 / www.maryfrederickson.com
Christopher H. Freeman	(518) 828-3459 / (212) 286-0075
Mark Friedberg	(310) 822-9113 / www.murthaagency.com
Timothy Galvin	(215) 635-1227
Regina Garcia	(718) 846-3104 / (917) 617-7115
Terry Gipson (Production Designer)	(845) 876-8995 / www.gipsondesigngroup.com

Steven Glazman	(212) 645-2492 / (646) 388-2347	Kai Lee	(212) 897-3944 / (917) 771-7370 / FAX (212) 624-1727 / www.worldsaway.tv
Anne Goelz	(914) 953-3981	Wing Lee	(718) 596-0334
Dina Goldman	(310) 395-9550 / www.skouras.com	Edmund (Ted) Lefevre Jr.	(973) 744-6331 / (917) 816-7350
Sandra Goldmark	(212) 942-8001	Sharon Lomofsky	(212) 997-1818 / www.gershagency.com
Jess Gonchor	(310) 822-9113 / www.murthaagency.com	Nicholas Lundy	(212) 253-6900 / www.innovativeartists.com
John Hobbie	(609) 567-0342 / (214) 507-1849	Thomas Lynch	(206) 302-7000
Troy Hourie	(718) 832-3438 / (917) 482-1966	Kenneth Raymond Macleod	(201) 653-6889 / (201) 218-0413
Andrew Jackness	(917) 969-1125 / (310) 282-9940 / www.andrewjackness.com	Tina Marie Manfredi	(718) 622-3680
Malchus Janocko	(718) 956-4065 / (917) 304-4201	John Marsala	(917) 916-6579
Rachel Short Janocko	(718) 852-1597 / (917) 449-4025	Ina Mayhew	(845) 679-4664 / (646) 279-5099
Deborah Jensen	(718) 398-7981 / (917) 674-5984	Charles E. McCarry	(860) 982-9116 / (845) 358-0671
Tory Jones	(212) 673-3788 / (917) 847-3614	Frank McCullough	(212) 647-8718 / (646) 825-1580
Susan Kaufman	(212) 254-3236 / FAX (212) 254-3236	Carlos Menendez	(310) 474-4585 / www.dattnerdispoto.com
Paul D. Kelly	(212) 663-3713 / (917) 882-6731	Vanessa Merrill	(845) 405-1080
Jeannette Kim	(914) 393-7790	David Evans Morris	(718) 782-3077 / (917) 617-2097
Raymond Klausen	(212) 769-3112	Bill Motyka	(201) 579-7983 / (973) 222-9477
Betsy Klompus	(718) 499-2562 / (917) 439-6242	Dennis W. Moyes	(201) 933-5156
Ray Kluga	(212) 253-6900 / www.innovativeartists.com	Matthew Myhrum	(917) 362-2678
Marion S. Kolsby	(212) 691-3387	Carol Nast	(212) 242-7942
David Korins	(212) 545-7895 / www.nyoffice.net	John Nyomarkay	(310) 652-8778 / (201) 963-6629 / www.lspagency.net
Ryan Kravetz	(646) 351-9424	Alexander Pacion	(917) 319-4774 / (310) 288-8000
Georges N. Krivobok	(718) 522-5944 / (917) 375-1473	Gregory Park	(914) 909-3855
Sarah Lambert	(845) 856-6958	Randall Parsons	(212) 491-7081 / (917) 334-3995
Kevin Largent	(718) 254-9220 / (917) 687-5150 / FAX (718) 254-9610 / www.largentstudios.com	Neil Patel	(212) 255-6958 / (212) 337-9522
Suttirat Larlarb	(323) 845-4144 / www.montanartists.com	Randall Peacock	(212) 352-3223 / www.magnetny.com
Richard Lassalle	(212) 997-1818 / www.gershagency.com	Christine Peters	(917) 523-2632
		Addison Pettit	(718) 858-7989
Julian LaVerdiere	(310) 395-9550 / (212) 244-2334 / FAX (212) 244-2334 / www.julianlaverdiere.com	Edward Pierce	(201) 837-7828
		Gideon Ponte	(212) 352-3223 / www.themagnetagency.com

Clement Price-Thomas	(310) 395-9550
	www.skouras.com
Andrea Purcigliotti	(917) 293-3884
	FAX (917) 293-3885
	www.damagestudiosnyc.com
Robert Pyzocha	(718) 384-8653
	(347) 351-3886
Kevin Raper	(212) 228-0984
Audrey S. Raphael	(718) 262-9047
Raymond C. Recht	(212) 663-6458
John (Chuck) Renaud Jr.	(718) 782-9294
	(323) 468-2240
Judy Rhee (Production Designer)	(212) 634-8157
Mark Ricker	(310) 395-9950
	www.skouras.com
Kevin Joseph Roach	(917) 609-2572
Kathryn Roake	(718) 788-2755
Carrie Robbins	(212) 564-8625
Susan Zeeman Rogers	(978) 902-8816
Jonathan Rose	(212) 279-0871
	(917) 224-9763
	jonathanrose.weebly.com
Jesse D. Rosenthal	(856) 802-9220
	(609) 304-3800
Tim Saternow	(860) 983-6468
Tom Schwinn	(212) 877-1886
David Segal	(212) 924-0375
Todd Seidman	(718) 290-4931
	www.seidmandesign.com
Michael Shaw	(917) 691-6756
	(845) 727-7667
	www.mshawdesign.com
Nithya Shrinivasan	(323) 459-3698
Chris J. Shriver	(212) 219-9638
Thomas Lee Stoner	(845) 358-2039
Joseph Michael Tenga	(718) 545-6036
Charity A. Thomas	(718) 399-2983
	(917) 622-4311
Nancy Lee Thun	(201) 656-2844
Ethan Tobman	(917) 952-0520
	(212) 997-1818
	www.gershagency.com
Kristen Vallow	(310) 458-7800
	www.partos.com
Elise G. Viola	(845) 691-5914
	(845) 417-5299
Ellen. Waggett	(718) 701-5018
	(917) 974-9708
Court M. Watson	(917) 405-6345
Loren Weeks	(323) 845-4144
	www.montanartists.com
Marla Weinhoff	(310) 474-4585
	www.marlaweinhoffstudio.com
Gary Weist	(203) 222-0946
David J. Weller	(718) 855-5843
	(212) 979-7761
Ford Wheeler	(212) 736-0181
	(917) 334-5604
Mark White	(310) 652-8778
	www.lspagency.net
Robert F. Wolin	(718) 672-8699
James F. Wolk	(212) 986-9354
Klara Zieglerova Fitzgerald	(917) 940-2235

Art Directors/Production Designers

Fanae Aaron	(323) 463-0022	www.radiantartists.com
Above & Beyond Artists Agency	(323) 464-9696	
439 N. Larchmont Blvd.	FAX (323) 464-5608	
Los Angeles, CA 90004	www.aboveandbeyondartists.com	
(Reps for Art Directors/Production Designers)		
Heidi Adams	(818) 753-6300	www.themackagency.net
Maher Ahmad	(310) 273-6700	www.utaproduction.com
Floyd Albee	(310) 395-9550	www.skouras.com
Ambitious Entertainment	(818) 990-8993	www.ambitiousent.com
15120 Hartsook St., Ste. 1		
Sherman Oaks, CA 91403		
(Reps for Art Directors/Production Designers)		
Nathan Amondson	(818) 753-6300	www.themackagency.net
Amy Ancona	(212) 997-1818	www.gershagency.com
Atli Arason	(818) 753-6300	www.themackagency.net
Steve Arnold	(310) 395-9550	www.skouras.com
Michelle Ashley	(323) 449-1538	
(Set Decorator)	FAX (323) 851-2249	
Paul Avery	(212) 545-7895	www.nyoffice.net
Phillip Barker	(310) 474-4585	www.dattnerdispoto.com
Guy Barnes	(310) 822-9113	www.murthaagency.com
Benoit Barouh	(323) 460-4767	www.jacobandkoleagency.com
K.K. Barrett	(310) 273-6700	www.utaproduction.com
Poppy Bartlett	(212) 352-3223	www.themagnetagency.com
June Bateman	(212) 925-7951 / (917) 806-8200	
	FAX (212) 925-7951	www.junebateman.com
Amelia Battaglio	(917) 405-8758 / (718) 522-2845	www.detaglia.com
Eric Beauchamp	(323) 251-5113 / (310) 656-0400	www.ericbeauchamp.com
Judy Becker	(310) 273-6700	www.utaproduction.com
Michael Bednark	(212) 352-3223	www.themagnetagency.com
Susan Beeson-de Havenon	(843) 577-3233 / (917) 922-3490	FAX (843) 577-3416
Max Bellhouse	(212) 352-3223	www.magnetny.com
Cat Belluschi	(917) 363-0082	
Joseph Bennett	(310) 273-6700	www.utaproduction.com
Laurence Bennett	(212) 253-6900	www.innovativeartists.com
Richard Berg	(212) 253-6900	www.innovativeartists.com
Julie Berghoff	(212) 997-1818	www.gershagency.com
Max Biscoe	(212) 253-6900	www.innovativeartists.com
Dan Bishop	(310) 395-9550	www.skouras.com
Jim Bissell	(310) 395-9550	www.skouras.com
Michael Boak	(612) 722-5854 / (917) 868-0759	
Gavin Bocquet	(310) 395-9550	www.skouras.com
Frank Bollinger	(323) 856-3000	www.thegelleragency.com
Michael Bolton	(310) 395-9550	www.skouras.com
David Bomba	(310) 395-9550	www.skouras.com
John Lord Booth	(310) 395-9550	www.skouras.com
Billy Bostock	(310) 458-7800	www.partos.com
Merideth Boswell	(310) 822-9113	www.murthaagency.com
Brian Branstetter	(310) 395-9550	www.skouras.com
Charles Breen	(212) 997-1818	www.gershagency.com
Michael Broaddus	(323) 463-0022	www.radiantartists.com
Tom Brown	(310) 474-4585	www.dattnerdispoto.com
Martina Buckley	(212) 253-6900	www.innovativeartists.com
Kim Buddee	(310) 652-8778	www.lspagency.net
Elizabeth Burhop/ ART department TV, Inc.	(917) 495-4305 / (323) 646-0426	www.artdept.tv
Don Burt	(310) 395-9550	www.skouras.com
Linda Burton	(212) 545-7895	www.nyoffice.net

Damien Byrne	(212) 545-7895 www.nyoffice.net	David Weller Design 505 Court St., Ste. 7P Brooklyn, NY 11231	(212) 979-7761 www.wellerdesign.com
Eugenio Caballero	(310) 652-8778 www.lspagency.net	Jennifer A. Davis	(310) 395-9550 www.skouras.com
Ellen Caldwell	(917) 817-1875	John F. Davis	(212) 406-2282 (917) 806-7524 FAX (212) 406-2282
Allan Cameron	(310) 395-9550 www.skouras.com		
Franco Carbone	(212) 997-1818 www.gershagency.com	Jamie Dean	(212) 352-3223 www.themagnetagency.com
Charisse Cardenas	(310) 822-9113 www.murthaagency.com	Jennifer Deghan	(212) 924-8505 www.therighteye.com
Jean-Philippe Carp	(212) 545-7895 www.nyoffice.net	Jackson DeGovia	(310) 395-9550 www.skouras.com
Shawn Carroll	(212) 924-8505 www.therighteye.com	Linda DeScenna	(310) 395-9550 www.skouras.com
Stefania Cella	(212) 253-6900 www.innovativeartists.com	Cece de Stefano	(212) 253-6900 www.innovativeartists.com
Scott Chambliss	(212) 253-6900 www.innovativeartists.com	Debbie De Villa	(323) 845-4144 www.montanartists.com
David Chapman	(212) 253-6900 www.innovativeartists.com	Chris Dileo	(818) 753-6300 www.themackagency.net
Scott Chestnut	(310) 395-9550 www.skouras.com	Leslie Dilley	(212) 997-1818 www.gershagency.com
John Chichester	(323) 460-4767 www.jacobandkoleagency.com	Marco Belli DiMaccio	(212) 625-2500 (213) 880-1209 www.marcodimaccio.com
James Chinlund	(212) 352-3223 www.magnetny.com	Eric Dixon	(917) 930-0945
Barry Chusid	(310) 273-6700 www.utaproduction.com	Maria Djurkovic	(310) 273-6700 www.utaproduction.com
Mike Conte	(917) 774-0984	Simon Dobbin	(310) 652-8778 www.lspagency.net
Claudio Contreras	(310) 395-9550 www.skouras.com	John Doliner	(818) 781-9233 www.orlandomanagement.com
Michael Corenblith	(310) 395-9550 www.skouras.com	Daniel Dorrance	(212) 253-6900 www.innovativeartists.com
Tony Cowley	(212) 253-6900 www.innovativeartists.com	Thomas Drotar	(818) 990-8993 www.ambitiousent.com
Stuart Craig	(310) 395-9550 www.skouras.com	Tom Duffield	(310) 273-6700 www.unitedtalent.com
Ivo Cristante	(323) 460-4767 www.jacobandkoleagency.com	Philip Duffin	(818) 753-6300 www.themackagency.net
Paul Cross	(310) 474-4585 www.dattnerdispoto.com	Matt Duncan (Production Designer, Prop Master, Set Buyer & Set Decorator)	(917) 804-8177 www.mattduncandesign.com
Nathan Crowley	(310) 395-9550 www.skouras.com		
Howard Cummings	(310) 273-6700 www.utaproduction.com	Guy Hendrix Dyas (Production Designer)	(323) 276-0807 www.guyhendrixdyas.com
Bruce Curtis	(212) 997-1818 www.gershagency.com	Chad Dzlewior	(212) 352-3223 www.magnetny.com
Charlie Daboub	(323) 460-4767 www.jacobandkoleagency.com	Debra Echard	(323) 463-0022 www.radiantartists.com
Philip Dagort	(323) 460-4767 www.jacobandkoleagency.com	Jason Edmonds	(310) 458-7800 www.partos.com
		William A. Elliott	(310) 822-9113 www.murthaagency.com

Deborah Evans	(310) 395-9550 www.skouras.com	Michael Grasley	(310) 652-8778 www.lspagency.net
David Faithfull	(323) 463-0022 www.radiantartists.com	Sarah Greenwood	(310) 395-9550 www.skouras.com
Chris Farmer	(818) 753-6300 www.themackagency.net	Arv Grewal	(310) 395-9550 www.skouras.com
Mark Fisichella	(310) 652-8778 www.lspagency.net	Joaquin Grey	(323) 460-4767 www.jacobandkoleagency.com
David Fitzpatrick	(310) 652-8778 www.lspagency.net	Clay Griffith	(212) 253-6900 www.innovativeartists.com
Jan Peter Flack	(310) 458-7800 www.partos.com	David Gropman	(310) 395-9550 www.skouras.com
Jack Flanagan	(212) 352-3223 www.magnetny.com	Bruno Hadjadj	(212) 545-7895 www.nyoffice.net
Molly Flanegin	(818) 753-6300 www.themackagency.net	Jeff Hall	(818) 990-8993 www.ambitiousent.com
Ricky Floyd	(212) 352-3223 www.themagnetagency.com	Peter J. Hampton	(310) 822-9113 www.murthaagency.com
Tom Foden	(310) 395-9550 www.skouras.com	Caroline Hanania	(310) 395-9550 www.skouras.com
Roger Ford	(310) 395-9550 www.skouras.com	Richard C. Hankins	(212) 253-6900 www.innovativeartists.com
Damon Fortier	(212) 253-6900 www.innovativeartists.com	John Hansen	(917) 855-1188 (323) 449-1538 FAX (323) 851-2249
Robert Fox	(310) 652-8778 www.lspagency.net	Sean Hargreaves	(310) 395-9550 www.skouras.com
Robbie Freed	(310) 474-4585 www.dattnerdispoto.com	Stan Harris	(646) 246-3722 www.devedog.com
Larry Fulton	(310) 273-6700 www.utaproduction.com	Tom Hartman	(310) 458-7800 www.partos.com
Alex Fymat	(212) 545-7895 www.nyoffice.net	Ron Hellman	(212) 352-3223 www.magnetny.com
Tracey Gallacher	(310) 395-9550 www.skouras.com	Jeremy Hindle	(310) 273-6700 www.utaproduction.com
The Geller Agency 1547 Cassil Pl. Hollywood, CA 90028 (Reps for Production Designers)	(323) 856-3000 FAX (323) 856-3009 www.thegelleragency.com	Richard Holland	(310) 273-6700 www.unitedtalent.com
		Paul Holt	(323) 845-4144 www.montanartists.com
Leslie Genser	(201) 481-3831	Jan Houllevigue	(212) 545-7895 www.nyoffice.net
The Gersh Agency 41 Madison Ave., 33rd Fl. (Near E. 26th St.) New York, NY 10010 (Reps for Art Directors/Production Designers)	(212) 997-1818 (310) 274-6611 FAX (212) 997-1978 www.gershagency.com	Angela Howard	(212) 545-7895 www.nyoffice.net
		Denise Hudson	(310) 652-8778 www.lspagency.net
Chris Giammalvo	(917) 969-8443 (212) 545-7895 www.chrisg.tv	Clark Hunter	(212) 253-6900 www.innovativeartists.com
		Mark Hutman	(212) 997-1818 www.gershagency.com
Darren Gilford	(818) 753-6300 www.themackagency.net	Innovative Artists 235 Park Ave. South, Seventh Fl. New York, NY 10003 (Reps for Art Directors/Production Designers)	(212) 253-6900 www.innovativeartists.com
Aaron Goffman (Prop Master)	(800) 655-3305 (323) 997-7999 www.goffman.tv		
Chris Goodmanson (Set Decorator)	(562) 900-8265 web.mac.com/brotchuby		
George Goodridge	(212) 643-1736 www.cec-entertainment.com	Gemma Jackson	(310) 395-9550 www.skouras.com

Regan Jackson (310) 652-8778
www.lspagency.net

The Jacob & Kole Agency (323) 460-4767
6715 Hollywood Blvd., Ste. 216 FAX (323) 460-4804
Los Angeles, CA 90028 www.jacobandkoleagency.com
(Reps for Production Designers)

Chris Jones (212) 545-7895
www.nyoffice.net

Steven Jones-Evans (212) 997-1818
www.gershagency.com

Francois Jordaan (310) 458-7800
www.partos.com

Chester Kaczenski (310) 652-8778
www.lspagency.net

Kevin Kavanaugh (310) 395-9550
www.skouras.com

Michael Keeling (310) 458-7800
www.partos.com

Morgan Kennedy (310) 474-4585
www.dattnerdispoto.com

Steve Kimmel (310) 652-8778
FAX (323) 669-0343
www.lspagency.net

Paul Kirby (310) 395-9550
www.skouras.com

Doug Kraner (212) 253-6900
www.innovativeartists.com

Michael Krantz (323) 460-4767
www.jacobandkole.com

Francois-Renaud Labarthe (310) 652-8778
www.lspagency.net

Neil Lamont (310) 652-8778
www.lspagency.net

Peter Lamont (310) 652-8778
www.lspagency.net

Steve Lawrence (310) 395-9550
www.skouras.com

David Lazan (212) 253-6900
www.innovativeartists.com

Charles Lee (310) 652-8778
www.lspagency.net

George Liddle (310) 822-9113
www.murthaagency.com

Stephen Lineweaver (212) 253-6900
www.innovativeartists.com

Barbara Ling (310) 395-9550
www.skouras.com

Cory Lorenzen (212) 997-1818
www.gershagency.com

Hugo Luczyc-Wyhowski (310) 395-9550
www.skouras.com

Patrick Lumb (310) 273-6700
www.unitedtalent.com

The Mack Agency (818) 753-6300
5726 Woodman Ave., Ste. 4 FAX (818) 753-6311
Van Nuys, CA 91401
(Reps for Art Directors/Production Designers)

Magnet NY (212) 352-3223
270 Lafayette St., Ste. 901 FAX (212) 941-7441
New York, NY 10012 www.themagnetagency.com
(Reps for Art Directors)

Grant Major (310) 273-6700
www.utaproduction.com

Aran Mann (212) 997-1818
www.gershagency.com

Cathy Marshall (973) 625-7472
(201) 317-8108
FAX (973) 627-3703
(Art Director, Production Designer, Prop Master,
Set Decorator & Set Dresser)

Paul Martin (310) 652-8778
www.lspagency.net

Jacqui Masson (213) 483-4400
(213) 220-3530
FAX (213) 483-4400
www.nyoffice.net

Arthur Max (310) 822-9113
www.murthaagency.com

James R. Mazzola (718) 945-7494
(917) 882-3484

Alex McDowell (818) 753-6300
www.themackagency.net

Anthony Medina (212) 253-6900
www.innovativeartists.com

Bekka Melino (212) 545-7895
www.nyoffice.net

Andrew Menzies (212) 253-6900
www.innovativeartists.com

Philip Messina (310) 395-9550
www.skouras.com

Tom Meyer (310) 273-6700
www.unitedtalent.com

Drogo Michie (212) 352-3223
www.themagnetagency.com

Bruce Miller (310) 652-8778
www.lspagency.net

Peter Miles (212) 255-2500
www.seemanagement.com

Michelle Minch (212) 997-1818
www.gershagency.com

The Mirisch Agency (310) 282-9940
1925 Century Park East, Ste. 1070 FAX (310) 282-0702
Los Angeles, CA 90067 www.mirisch.com
(Reps for Production Designers)

Montana Artists Agency (323) 845-4144
7715 W. Sunset Blvd., Third Fl. FAX (323) 845-4155
Los Angeles, CA 90046 www.montanartists.com
(Reps for Production Designers)

Jose Montano (310) 395-9550
www.skouras.com

Cecilia Montiel (323) 460-4767
www.jacobandkoleagency.com

John Mott (323) 856-3000
www.thegelleragency.com

Alan Muraoka (310) 652-8778
www.lspagency.net

Scott P. Murphy	(323) 845-4144	Kevin Pierce	(212) 924-8505
	www.montanartists.com		www.therighteye.com

The Murtha Agency (310) 822-9113
4240 Promenade Way, Ste. 232   FAX (310) 822-6662
Marina Del Rey, CA 90292   www.murthaagency.com
(Reps for Production Designers)

		Herbert Pinter	(310) 822-9113
			www.murthaagency.com
		Denise Pizzini	(323) 856-3000
			www.thegelleragency.com
Jane Musky	(310) 395-9550		
	www.skouras.com	Mary Prlain	(917) 412-1392
		(Set Decorator)	www.maryprlain.com
Rika Nakanishi	(818) 753-6300		
	www.themackagency.net	Dan Quellette	(323) 460-4767
			www.jacobandkoleagency.com
Ariana Nakata	(310) 458-7800		
	www.partos.com	Jean Rabasse	(323) 460-4767
			www.jacobandkoleagency.com
Janet Nelson	(310) 395-9550		
	www.skouras.com	Radiant Artists	(323) 463-0022

6715 Hollywood Blvd., Ste. 220   FAX (323) 375-0231
Los Angeles, CA 90028   www.radiantartists.com
(Reps for Production Designers)

New York Office (212) 545-7895 / (323) 468-2240
15 W. 26th St., Fifth Fl.   FAX (212) 545-7941
(Near Broadway)   www.nyoffice.net
New York, NY 10010
(Reps for Production Designers)

		Ida Random	(310) 395-9550
			www.skouras.com
Jill Nicholls	(212) 352-3223	Roy Rede	(818) 508-9222
	www.magnetny.com		
		Jeremy Reed	(310) 273-6700
Patricia Norris	(310) 822-9113		www.unitedtalent.com
	www.murthaagency.com	Kim Rees	(213) 482-1987 / (323) 463-0022
			www.radiantartists.com
Michael Novotny	(310) 652-8778		
	www.lspagency.net	Chuck Renaud	(917) 204-6034 / (212) 545-7895
			www.chuckrenaud.com
Paul Oberman	(310) 652-8778		
	www.lspagency.net	Vincent Reynaud	(310) 652-8778
			www.lspagency.net

Orlando Management (818) 781-9233
15134 Martha St.   www.orlandomanagement.com
Sherman Oaks, CA 91411
(Reps for Production Designers)

		Michael Reynolds	(212) 352-3223
			www.magnetny.com
Stefano Maria Ortolani	(310) 822-9113	Norman Reynolds	(310) 395-9550
	www.murthaagency.com		www.skouras.com
Laurent Ott	(310) 652-8778	Andy Reznik	(310) 458-7800
	www.lspagency.net		www.partos.com

Paradigm (212) 897-6400
360 Park Ave. South, 16th Fl.   FAX (212) 764-8941
(Near Seventh Ave.)   www.paradigmagency.com
New York, NY 10010
(Reps for Production Designers)

		Andy Rhodes	(310) 395-9550
			www.skouras.com
		Bridgland Richard	(212) 997-1818
			www.gershagency.com
Chuck Parker	(212) 253-6900		
	www.innovativeartists.com	The Right Eye	(212) 924-8505

41 Union Square West, Ste. 1004   FAX (212) 924-8544
(Near W. 16th St.)   www.therighteye.com
New York, NY 10003
(Reps for Production Designers)

Salvador Parra	(310) 652-8778		
	www.lspagency.net		

Partos Company (310) 458-7800
227 Broadway, Ste. 204   FAX (310) 587-2250
Santa Monica, CA 90401   www.partos.com
(Reps for Production Designers)

		Barry Robison	(310) 273-6700
			www.utaproduction.com
Owen Paterson	(310) 273-6700	Jan Roelfs	(310) 395-9550
	www.unitedtalent.com		www.skouras.com
Tiffany Payne	(818) 753-6300	Evan Rohde	(310) 652-8778
	www.themackagency.net		www.lspagency.net
Tulé Peak	(310) 652-8778	Pedro Romero	(212) 253-6900
	www.lspagency.net		www.innovativeartists.com
Rob Pearson	(212) 253-6900	Gabrielle Rosenberg	(212) 229-2729 / (917) 863-0547
	www.innovativeartists.com		www.changeinc.com
Nigel Phelps	(310) 273-6700	Philip Rosenberg	(212) 997-1818
	www.utaproduction.com		www.gershagency.com

Art Directors/Production Designers

Anne Ross	(310) 395-9550 www.skouras.com	Johannes Spalt	(323) 463-0022 www.radiantartists.com
Edward L. Rubin	(212) 253-6900 www.innovativeartists.com	Neil Spisak	(310) 395-9550 www.skouras.com
Gene Rudolf	(520) 722-3423 (877) 773-3598 FAX (520) 722-3423	Annie Spitz	(310) 652-8778 www.lspagency.net
Jefferson Sage	(310) 395-9550 www.skouras.com	Anthony Stabley	(323) 440-1455 www.supergrandefilms.com
William Sandell	(212) 997-1818 www.gershagency.com	Craig Stearns	(212) 253-6900 www.innovativeartists.com
Tom Sanders	(310) 273-6700 www.utaproduction.com	Jon Gary Steele	(310) 273-6700 www.utaproduction.com
Gerard Santos	(212) 352-3223 www.magnetny.com	James Steuart	(310) 474-4585 www.dattnerdispoto.com
Curtis Schnell	(310) 652-8778 www.lspagency.net	Eve Stewart	(310) 474-4585 www.dattnerdispoto.com
Oliver Scholl	(212) 997-1818 www.gershagency.com	Missy Stewart	(310) 273-6700 www.utaproduction.com
Stephen Scott	(310) 652-8778 www.lspagency.net	Stillsets	(212) 352-3223 www.themagnetagency.com
Bella Serrell/Ranch Dressing	(323) 463-0022 www.radiantartists.com	Adam Stockhausen	(310) 822-9113 www.murthaagency.com
Sharon Seymour	(310) 395-9550 www.skouras.com	John Stoddart	(310) 395-9550 www.skouras.com
Bob Shaw	(310) 822-9113 www.murthaagency.com	Carol Strober	(310) 652-8778 www.lspagency.net
Phil Shearer	(818) 990-8993 www.ambitiousent.com	Mark Tanner	(310) 474-4585 www.dattnerdispoto.com
Sheldon Prosnit Agency 800 S. Robertson Blvd., Ste. 6 Los Angeles, CA 90035 (Reps for Production Designers)	(310) 652-8778 FAX (310) 652-8772 www.lspagency.net	TDN Artists 3685 Motor Ave., Ste. 220 Los Angeles, CA 90034 (Reps for Production Designers)	(818) 906-0006 FAX (818) 301-2224 www.tdnartists.com
Richard Sherman	(212) 997-1818 www.gershagency.com	Kevin Thompson	(310) 273-6700 www.utaproduction.com
Naomi Shohan	(310) 822-9113 www.murthaagency.com	Jodie Tillen	(212) 253-6900 www.innovativeartists.com
Deana Sidney	(212) 924-8505 www.therighteye.com	Ethan Tobman	(212) 997-1818 www.gershagency.com
Maya Sigel	(323) 460-4767 www.jacobandkoleagency.com	Matt Tognacci	(818) 990-8993 www.ambitiousent.com
Ross Silverman	(323) 683-5263	Ginger Tougas	(323) 460-4767 www.jacobandkoleagency.com
David Skinner	(323) 460-4767 www.jacobandkoleagency.com	Bernardo Trujillo	(310) 652-8778 www.lspagency.net
The Skouras Agency 1149 Third St., Third Fl. Santa Monica, CA 90403 (Reps for Production Designers)	(310) 395-9550 FAX (310) 395-4295 www.skouras.com	Sandy Veneziano	(310) 822-9113 www.murthaagency.com
Penn Smith	(818) 753-6300 www.themackagency.net	Edward Verreaux	(310) 273-6700 www.utaproduction.com
Rusty Smith	(212) 997-1818 www.gershagency.com	Jamie Vickers	(310) 505-2445 (310) 458-7800 www.partos.com
David L. Snyder	(212) 253-6900 www.innovativeartists.com	Graham Walker	(212) 253-6900 www.innovativeartists.com
Tom Southwell	(323) 460-4767 www.jacobandkoleagency.com	Michael Walker	(310) 458-7800 www.partos.com

Thomas Walsh	(212) 253-6900	Francis Whitebloom	(310) 458-7800
	www.innovativeartists.com		www.partos.com
David Wasco	(310) 273-6700	Jennifer Williams	(310) 652-8778
	www.utaproduction.com		www.lspagency.net
Dennis Washington	(310) 822-9113	David Wilson	(212) 545-7895
	www.murthaagency.com		www.nyoffice.net
Dan Webster	(310) 652-8778	Dara Wishingrad	(212) 924-8505
	www.lspagency.net		www.therighteye.com
Dan Weil	(310) 273-6700	Mark Worthington	(323) 460-4767
	www.utaproduction.com		www.jacobandkoleagency.com
Bo Welch	(310) 273-6700	Richard Wright	(310) 652-8778
	www.unitedtalent.com		www.lspagency.net
Mike Whetstone	(310) 652-8778	Michael Wylie	(212) 253-6900
	www.lspagency.net		www.innovativeartists.com
Martin Whist	(310) 273-6700	Travis Nicholas Zariwny	(212) 643-1736
	www.unitedtalent.com		www.cec-entertainment.com

Camera Assistants (Local 600 NY)

Olga Abramson	(215) 828-9926
Amy Albano	(917) 913-9452
Ernie Albritton	(718) 562-9011
Blake Alcantara	(914) 261-7289
Ramsey Alkaysi	(973) 214-9801 (973) 338-0473
Aleksandr Allen (Film Loader & Second AC)	(641) 821-9512
Stuart Allen (First AC)	(212) 242-6310 (917) 518-1337
Sebastian Almeida (First AC)	(917) 520-7924
Beth Anderson	(978) 821-4132
Alexander Andres (Second AC)	(724) 774-5128 (724) 312-0914
Rebecca Arndt	(617) 645-4810
Wayne Arnold (First AC)	(410) 960-7851
Eli Aronoff (First AC)	(917) 324-5695
Ian Axilrod (Second AC)	(310) 463-9887
Jeffrey Baker (First AC)	(610) 635-0906 (610) 909-0610
Matthew Balzarini (Second AC)	(732) 673-6670
David Baron (First AC)	(845) 352-9182 (845) 323-7303 FAX (845) 426-4667 us.imdb.com/name/nm0056219/
Monica Barrios-Smith (Second AC)	(704) 889-2386 (704) 737-5711
Robert Becchio (First AC)	(914) 643-2476 (508) 693-7532
Jonathan Beck	(917) 376-2569
James Belletier (First AC)	(201) 776-7298 (201) 866-6067
Angela Bellisio (Second AC)	(917) 579-6953
Jason Bellitto	(910) 520-8416
Braden Belmonte	(917) 952-9049
Hilary Benas	(804) 690-4007
Robert Benedetti	(732) 617-1613
Nicola Benizzi	(917) 496-3737 (212) 254-2073
Richard Berger (First AC)	(212) 749-3362
Charles Beyer (First AC)	(732) 530-2874 (917) 767-3165
Joshua Blakeslee (First AC)	(401) 737-6183
Troy Blischok (First AC, High Def, Remote Heads, Steadicam & Underwater)	(910) 228-8280 www.troyblischok.com
Ben Bloodwell	(917) 880-5993 (718) 816-8009
Patrick Borowiak (First AC)	(910) 233-4000 (910) 395-2320
Ethan Borsuk	(203) 464-2752
Frank Bourassa	(516) 428-5912 (631) 722-8333
Ian Bracone	(845) 236-4097 (917) 301-5610
Tom Bracone (First AC)	(845) 236-4097 (917) 301-5687 FAX (845) 236-1062 www.tombracone.com
Ralph Brandofino (First AC)	(908) 688-6317 (908) 400-6019
Barbara Bravo	(201) 410-6750 (201) 418-8698
Steven Briante	(917) 589-6279
Jason Brignola	(927) 992-0700
John Broughton (First AC)	(212) 665-5090
Lauren Brown	(551) 427-2914
Deborah Brozina (First AC)	(212) 979-8030 FAX (212) 979-9645
Adriana Brunetto-Lipman	(917) 612-5866
Cima Bue (First AC)	(845) 482-2023 (845) 701-0983
Robert Bullard (First AC)	(401) 447-0291 (401) 247-9050
Janice Burgess (Second AC)	(978) 356-1826 (978) 771-6705
Matthew Burke	(917) 690-2149
Michael Burke	(802) 223-7851 (347) 324-7140
Graham Burt	(203) 858-7689
Jamie Bussant	(516) 250-4276 (631) 957-5844

Kate Butler (215) 242-0871
(First AC, French & German) (215) 284-4310

Kenneth Butts (201) 251-9397
(First AC)

George Byers (914) 337-2133
(First AC) (914) 263-7151

Travis Cadalzo (718) 683-1104
(Second AC)

Maria Calvaruso (718) 418-4512
(First AC)

Michael Cambria (718) 984-2696
(First AC) (917) 750-8094

James Candreva (516) 768-2708
(First AC) www.jimcandreva.com

Nick Candreva (631) 741-2652

Don Canfield (914) 526-4896
(First AC) www.gearandrose.com

Jeffrey Canfield (845) 641-1554

Christian Carmody (718) 369-9519
(First AC) (917) 769-7245

Ian Carmody (646) 262-4179
(Second AC)

Thomas Carroll (914) 584-5956
(914) 271-8734

Anne Carson (347) 365-0973
(Film Loader)

Daniel Casey (412) 327-4720
(Second AC)

Matthew Caulk (410) 923-6288
(410) 274-7015

Deborah Cavanaugh (212) 786-3410
(917) 250-5069

Christopher Cenatiempo (212) 534-3024
(Second AC) (203) 767-1163

Drew Cerria (973) 764-4714
(First AC)

LeRoy Chen (646) 456-4690
(First AC)

Nina Chien (212) 941-8278
(First AC) (310) 990-0196

Sung Rae Cho (646) 318-6229
(First AC)

Joseph Christofori (617) 645-7622
(First AC) (413) 733-7688
www.joechristo.com

Justeen Cicio (908) 591-4141

Thomas Cioccio (718) 486-9836
(First AC) (917) 518-6309

Nathan Clapp (202) 625-2004
(First AC) (202) 262-3434

Harry Clark (203) 834-9874
(First AC) (203) 981-0921

John Clemens (201) 681-0608
(First AC) (908) 832-8965

Phil Cohen (917) 903-1176
(First AC) (914) 813-2712

Paul Colangelo (917) 576-7124
(First AC) (212) 879-7829

Alisa Colley (718) 794-9122
(917) 693-0183

Keith Conod (201) 791-4084
(201) 264-2206

Daniel Cook (215) 699-8005
(First AC)

Alan Corder (704) 532-4273
(704) 609-0745

Kathleen Corgan (212) 262-3174
(First AC) (917) 617-0454

Donald Cornett (212) 219-9610
(First AC) (917) 373-7301

Michelle Coughlan (917) 882-4205

Tim Coughlan (617) 787-0436
(617) 968-4803

John Coughlin (917) 499-7569

W Cronin (216) 932-3548
(First AC) (216) 288-6969

Rene Crout (917) 940-1976
(First AC)

Rick Crumrine (724) 775-2756
(First AC)

Michael Csatlos (201) 741-5113
(First AC, High Def, Motion Control, Remote Heads, Second Unit, Special FX, Steadicam & Underwater)

Michael Cunningham (212) 353-9153

Benjamin Dailey (917) 535-7545

James Daly (802) 318-5368

Nicholas Deeg (917) 721-0941
(212) 691-6925

Anthony Defonzo (917) 842-9362
(718) 239-2885

Anthony Defrancesco (267) 259-0190

Julian Delacruz (212) 316-6675
(Second AC) (917) 992-5354

Christopher Del Sordo (973) 953-0693

Vincent DeMaio (718) 921-2806

Nick Demas (718) 812-3091

Camera Assistants (Local 600 NY)

Marque DeWinter	(800) 379-0442
Alfonso Diaz	(212) 691-4659
Mike DiFeo	(908) 247-0967
Angelo DiGiacomo (First AC)	(631) 979-1739 / (631) 379-7997 / FAX (631) 499-3201
Robert DiGiacomo (First AC)	(516) 480-1907 / (516) 433-2192
Sean Donnelly	(914) 384-2918
Melissa Donovan (First AC)	(917) 723-6364
Steven Doty	(562) 810-4564
Patrick Doyle	(516) 640-2080 / (516) 801-1928
Shane Duckworth (Second AC)	(505) 660-3406
Gregory Dunaj (Chyron Operator)	(609) 397-4059
Russell Dunn (Chyron Operator)	(203) 226-7111
Colin Duran	(843) 452-2339
Jeff Dutemple (First AC)	(917) 513-8327
Philip Dutton (First AC)	(860) 868-9733 / (917) 972-4912
Autumn Eakin Second AC	(314) 398-2846
Jay Eckardt (First AC)	(917) 334-8394
Edwin Effrein (First AC)	(973) 985-9120 / (973) 853-6565
Steven Eliopoulos (First AC)	(617) 480-2856
Peter Elliot (First AC)	(845) 365-0173 / (914) 907-8605
Sam Elliot	(917) 402-3738
Arthur Ellis (First AC)	(347) 244-0071
Osa Elmfors (First AC)	(212) 226-5872
Kris Enos (Second AC)	(212) 260-3202 / (917) 544-9597
Jonathan Ercole (First AC)	(917) 509-0244 / (914) 288-9033
Wilfredo Estrada-Carrasquillo (First AC)	(787) 287-1018
William Evans (Second AC)	(646) 246-6957
Deborah Fastuca	(212) 600-4378 / (412) 996-3723
Jay Feather (First AC)	(917) 273-1136 / (718) 852-5744
Rick Fee (First AC)	(781) 749-2947
Danny Feighery	(917) 376-7857
Gavin Fernandez	(718) 494-0831 / (917) 340-9222
Stanley Fernandez (First AC)	(718) 605-5671 / (917) 579-1625
Gregory Finkel	(917) 992-3449
Jamieson Fitzpatrick (Second AC)	(617) 510-9313 / (781) 944-4964
David Flanigan (First AC)	(917) 541-3002
Matthew Flannery (First AC)	(917) 282-2163
John Floresca	(917) 541-0987
William Floyd (First AC)	(201) 709-6512 / (973) 759-7263
Charles Foerschner	(516) 994-6734
Doug Foote (First AC)	(718) 832-1470 / (917) 225-7908
Megan Forste (First AC)	(310) 993-2817
Jon Fortunato (First AC)	(914) 727-0192
Pyare Fortunato (First AC)	(917) 554-5116 / (718) 384-7991
Richard Fredette (Second AC)	(802) 654-9295
Rob Fritche	(914) 489-8538
Joshua Friz	(603) 991-4751
Jonathan Furmanski (First AC)	(718) 599-9512 / (646) 431-2806
Daniel Galiardi (First AC)	(516) 594-0544
Mara Galus (Second AC)	(646) 269-2990
Carlos Garcia	(787) 752-0369 / (787) 473-5033
Michael Garofalo (First AC)	(516) 455-9017 / (631) 470-4892
Fernando Gayesky	(212) 254-8919 / (646) 236-0665
Paul Gibilisco (Second AC)	(914) 406-0682

Spencer Gillis	(718) 644-1640
Rick Gioia (First AC)	(914) 213-0199
John (Woody) Glaser (First AC)	(973) 962-6642 / (201) 310-0999 / FAX (973) 962-6221
Christopher Gleaton	(347) 203-0060 / (718) 862-9060
James Goldsmith	(516) 931-7162 / (917) 602-7426
Chuck Gomez (First AC)	(347) 834-2835
Gabriel Goodenough (First AC)	(410) 963-3071 / (410) 243-6999
Bradley Grant	(773) 209-2964
Michael Grantland	(917) 407-9577
William Gray	(410) 458-8342 / (410) 737-8008
Katie Greaves	(845) 336-5123 / (845) 853-5546
Thomas Greco	(215) 513-0243 / (215) 872-0635 / FAX (215) 513-0247 / www.locationcamera.com (Aerial, First AC, High Def, Remote Heads & Steadicam)
Christopher Green (First AC)	(212) 666-5899 / (917) 923-7912
Ronald Green (First AC)	(410) 233-7691
Lisa Guevara (First AC)	(917) 538-0349
Lauren Haber (First AC)	(607) 227-0437
Craig Haft	(516) 528-2473
Nicholas Hahn	(347) 365-1296 / (347) 512-8510
James Hair (First AC)	(718) 522-5853 / (646) 734-6775
Cai Hall	(860) 488-0287
Andrew Hamilton (Film Loader)	(313) 443-4067
John Hamilton (Second AC)	(301) 585-1073 / (202) 270-2081
Barbara Hanania (First AC)	(781) 259-0828
William Hand (Second AC)	(843) 224-8076
Zsolt Haraszti (High Def & Second AC)	(843) 813-4567
Douglas Hart (First AC)	(718) 937-7250
Herb Harton (First AC)	(910) 791-3643 / (910) 620-1629
Kevin Haverty (First AC)	(347) 463-7021
Anthony Hechanova	(718) 297-3244 / (917) 566-2438
Elizabeth Hedges (Second AC)	(917) 862-4732
Becki Heller	(802) 578-2585
Michelle Hemion (Second AC)	(704) 488-9674
Sarah Hendrick	(516) 317-2223
John Heneghan	(212) 228-1246 / (917) 817-4963
Erin Henning	(562) 212-0200
Daniel Hersey (First AC)	(212) 228-6133 / (917) 923-4662
Liz Heslep	(617) 308-4572
Marc Hillygus	(917) 400-1873
Marc Hirschfeld (First AC)	(212) 757-4453
Jack Hirschorn (First AC)	(718) 643-0760
Wesley Hodges (Second AC)	(646) 872-6563
Christian Hollyer (Second AC)	(508) 845-9760 / (508) 642-9945
Ira Holzman (First AC)	(516) 269-5411
Jon Hopkins	(631) 667-5361 / (516) 662-1614
Ralph Hotchkiss (First AC)	(212) 864-2977
Laura Hudock	(917) 502-1324
Amanda Hudson	(917) 400-0898 / (347) 365-7356
Kenneth Hudson (First AC)	(910) 762-8797
Larry Huston (First AC)	(212) 777-7541 / (646) 206-0896 / FAX (212) 533-5958
Fabio Iadeluca	(201) 410-3951
Sebastian Iervolino	(917) 981-1999 / (212) 477-1303
Michael Indursky (Film Loader, First AC, High Def, Second AC & Second Unit)	(631) 466-4107
Scott Inge (First AC)	(804) 402-0314 / (804) 752-0195
Milly Itzhak	(917) 549-0627

Will Iversen	(301) 455-7149
Susan Jacob	(203) 494-1350 / (203) 393-3832 / www.susanjacob.com
(First AC, High Def, Second AC, Second Unit, Special FX & Steadicam)	
Mary Anne Janke (First AC)	(781) 367-3362
E.W. Jew (First AC)	(212) 947-6517
Adam Johnson	(646) 234-4868
Christophe Johnson	(917) 940-0972
Alexander Jones	(617) 504-1713 / (207) 967-5084
Dan Jones (First AC)	(843) 364-4082
Quenell Jones	(718) 801-0778
Glenn Kaplan (First AC)	(805) 480-0414 / (310) 245-4833
Kevin Kasarda	(212) 865-1413 / (917) 887-6412
Lee Kazista (First AC)	(201) 725-8288
Dan Keck	(212) 496-9062 / (917) 687-4065
Stan Keitt (First AC)	(917) 414-1456
Patrick Kelly (First AC)	(978) 561-1230 / (617) 840-7048
Meg Kettell (Second AC)	(646) 489-3566
Kevin Kilcher	(585) 748-6619 / (212) 652-5694
Mark Killian	(617) 529-3444
Aaron Kirby	(510) 301-8328
James Klayer	(212) 673-2309 / (917) 916-7216
Rachael Kliman	(203) 687-8180
Rob Koch (First AC)	(914) 263-5381
Scott Koenigsberg	(516) 805-0781
Jennifer Koestler (Second AC)	(718) 693-1775 / (917) 670-4419
Doug Kofsky	(646) 226-3232
Dianne Koronkiewicz (First AC)	(917) 709-2919
Denny Kortze (Second AC)	(917) 232-0452
Stephen Kozlowski	(212) 203-9205
Michael Krebs (First AC)	(410) 828-5708 / (410) 371-7209
Dave Kudrowitz	(617) 875-4513
Suad Kutlug	(917) 309-3394
Thomas Lairson (Second AC)	(310) 749-9337 / (406) 932-6410
April Lanci-Leseur	(323) 428-3395
(Aerial, Film Loader, High Def, Motion Control, Remote Heads, Second AC, Second Unit & Special FX)	
Jose Lara	(914) 557-9665
Spencer Laroche	(917) 518-7973 / (718) 513-0716
Kate Larose	(504) 669-2036
Mary Latvis (First AC)	(718) 784-1907
Robert Lau (First AC)	(917) 833-9311 / (718) 375-2078
Ahnna Lee (Film Loader)	(513) 673-4145
Damon LeMay	(617) 877-9153
Michael Leonard (First AC)	(856) 728-7637 / (609) 220-4505
Sammy Leonard	(646) 240-1630 / (718) 872-7211
Jordan Levie	(847) 363-9978
Charlie Lew (First AC)	(617) 731-5294
Shawn Lewallen (First AC)	(910) 251-8314
Franziska Lewis	(646) 339-8624
Alexis Li (Second AC)	(213) 400-4141
Todd Liebler (First AC)	(718) 222-9277 FAX (718) 222-3906
Gus Limberis	(516) 298-6824
Scott Lipkowitz	(516) 458-2045
Deborah Lipman (First AC)	(917) 239-8632
Hamilton Longyear	(941) 400-3043
Nathan Lopez	(805) 453-0366
Frank Love	(704) 806-3729
Zoraida Luna Luna	(939) 717-5298
John MacDonald (First AC)	(203) 938-4770 / (917) 576-9752
James Madrid	(917) 331-4705

Scott Maguire	(917) 648-5492	William Moore	(212) 362-5912
(First AC)	www.scottmaguire.com		(917) 656-4354
Peter Mallamo	(704) 566-4921	Mike Moran	(631) 375-5747
	(704) 618-0202	Peter Morello	(973) 509-7464
Mitch Malpica	(570) 828-6766		(973) 865-4673
Joe Mancusi	(203) 561-0830		FAX (973) 509-1645
Robert Mancuso	(516) 581-1468	John Moya	(917) 826-6597
(First AC)	(516) 887-5822		(212) 396-3320
Derek Manganelli	(917) 660-6969	Zak Mulligan	(917) 991-1412
Gareth Manwaring	(315) 247-6267	Ronald Munkacsi	(910) 548-4553
Marc Marinelli	(914) 462-6677	(First AC)	
Alexander Martin	(646) 709-7985	Kevin Murphy	(732) 528-9374
Kevin Martinek	(973) 224-4682		(732) 233-7924
Nicole Martinez	(336) 408-6536	Soren Nash	(201) 766-2765
(Second AC)			(413) 519-2955
Ben Mathus	(330) 414-4457	Mary Neary	(347) 612-4312
Fran Maxwell	(914) 779-1330		(516) 835-5108
(Chyron Operator)		Leon Negrin	(212) 249-7796
Lance Mayer	(212) 517-7628		(917) 252-3702
(Second AC)	(646) 342-5396		FAX (212) 570-0148
James Mayfield	(215) 235-1722	Laura Nespola	(347) 678-8048
John McAleer	(201) 370-2107	Edward Nessen	(646) 336-1506
(First AC)		(First AC)	(917) 975-6259
Stephen McCarthy	(617) 469-5214	New York Office	(212) 545-7895
(First AC)		15 W. 26th St., Fifth Fl.	(323) 468-2240
George McCartin	(215) 704-0327	(Near Broadway)	FAX (212) 545-7941
John McIntyre	(910) 799-3910	New York, NY 10010	www.nyoffice.net
(Second AC)	(910) 297-7264	(Reps for Camera Assistants)	
Paul McKenna	(631) 988-0763	Evan Newell	(917) 843-8697
Greg McMahon	(718) 715-2662	Timothy Norman	(212) 988-3393
Abner Medina Alejandro	(787) 732-4891	Maritza Norr	(646) 236-2915
	(787) 605-4574	Heather Norton	(718) 488-9219
Hollis Meminger	(917) 656-2024	(First AC)	(917) 365-2119
Dan Merrill	(917) 838-3613	Melissa O'Brien	(917) 763-6215
Timothy Metivier	(800) 650-4193	Eric O'Connor	(917) 400-9357
(First AC)	(917) 975-5475	Ruben O'Malley	(718) 986-4858
Joseph Metzger	(541) 619-6742	(Second AC)	www.rubenomalley.com
Gary Michelin	(201) 385-7663	Seth Orenstein	(917) 376-7650
Adam Miller	(646) 326-4103	Lisa Origlieri	(201) 738-2622
Nick Miller	(323) 401-5848	(Second AC)	(973) 228-0365
Symon Mink	(917) 569-5252	Kenneth Ortiz	(718) 267-6319
(First)	www.symonmink.com		(646) 270-0169
Christopher Moeller	(646) 245-5229	Lucas Owen	(718) 781-9309
Jonathan Moore	(443) 621-3213		(718) 836-5846
		Robert Pagliaro	(718) 549-4887
		(First AC)	(917) 743-1429
		Chong Pak	(609) 865-8257
		Susan Palma Distasi	(973) 981-9281
		(Chyron Operator)	

Michael Panczenko	(410) 992-1695 / (443) 538-5804
Kurt Parlow (First AC)	(410) 963-6626
Michael Pascal (First AC)	(718) 438-1980 / (347) 405-3805
Micah Pastore	(347) 407-4131
Chris Patak (First AC)	(917) 363-9099
Paul Patelmo (Video)	(914) 699-1116 / (914) 393-5439 / FAX (914) 699-1116
Mark Patnesky (Second AC)	(724) 344-9504
Andrew Peck	(330) 990-3872
Matthew Pebler (Second AC)	(480) 363-8035
Ralph Perri (Remote Heads)	(203) 667-0550
Rob Perri	(323) 533-6915
Deb Peterson	(323) 708-5203
Storn Peterson (First AC)	(718) 340-8270 / (917) 686-7127
Christopher Piazza	(315) 882-2226
Helen Pilgram-Noble	(646) 321-3435
Jeff Pinette	(860) 368-9342
Larry Planet (First AC)	(516) 244-1470
Antonio Ponti (First AC)	(718) 237-9745 / (917) 806-3407
Craig Pressgrove (First AC)	(917) 783-1747
Lauretta Prevost	(703) 346-8102
Andrew Priestley (First AC)	(212) 439-0755 / (917) 715-2629
Gregory Principato (First AC & Steadicam)	(908) 317-4730 / (908) 656-7613
Malcolm Purnell	(917) 821-8975 / (718) 638-6185
Patrick Quinn (First AC)	(917) 558-1224 / www.patrickquinn.org
Robert Ragozzine (First AC)	(212) 924-5837 / (917) 971-5078
Peter Ramos	(516) 520-4669 / (516) 650-4817
Floyd Rance (First AC)	(718) 789-3567 / www.mvaaff.com
Nate Ranger (First AC)	(917) 957-5354 / (212) 513-1393
Leigh Rathner (First AC)	(518) 669-8520
Christopher Raymond	(212) 686-2395 / (917) 533-7613
Carrie Rees	(917) 757-0738
Michael Repeta	(910) 233-0109 / (910) 392-2530
Kyle Repka (Film Loader & Second AC)	(267) 312-5602
Giuseppe Restivo	(718) 545-2724 / (718) 813-8463
Chris Reynolds (First AC)	(646) 515-0908
Lance Rieck (First AC)	(718) 636-0205 / (917) 767-1903
Frank Rinato (First AC)	(908) 508-1909
Timothy Risch (First AC)	(276) 475-3943 / (310) 429-3866
Rossana Rizzo	(917) 648-0900
Eric Robinson	(646) 295-9068
Al Rodgers (First AC)	(516) 318-8936 / (631) 647-5650
Edward Rodriguez (First AC)	(718) 828-4125 / (917) 541-9589
Marcos Rodriguez-Quijano	(787) 763-8710 / (787) 644-0867
Steve Romano (First AC)	(914) 844-4243 / (914) 777-0355
John Romer	(917) 734-9145 / (914) 962-2233
Fernando Rosado	(787) 810-4481
Craig Rosenzweig (First AC)	(516) 467-4238 / (917) 294-4012 / www.craigrosenzweig.com
Timothy Ross	(718) 687-8917
Antonio Rossi (First AC)	(917) 407-7538 / (212) 580-7561
Amanda Rotzler	(412) 596-0154
Jared Roybal	(917) 566-2571
Mark Ryle	(646) 259-1895
Liz Sales	(646) 250-2680
Daniel Sanabria	(914) 633-9869 / FAX (914) 633-0337
Robert Sands (First AC)	(212) 580-0549 / (917) 204-8551

Leon Sanginiti (First AC)	(215) 882-1651 (856) 740-0889	Jeffrey Smith	(646) 346-0559
Roxana Santiago	(787) 363-8224	Sean Souza	(212) 924-9787 (917) 653-8627
Daniel Sariano (Second AC)	(718) 643-6467 (646) 957-6551	Joia Marie Speciale	(917) 696-2586 www.joiaspeciale.com
Christopher Schenck (First AC)	(828) 290-8713 (310) 503-9110 www.chrisschenck.com	Debbie Stampfle (Second AC)	(917) 538-4012
John Schwartz (First AC)	(212) 799-7875 (917) 826-8863	Stuart Stein (First AC)	(703) 276-8428 (703) 623-7531
Randy Schwartz	(646) 361-7704	Marshall Stief	(516) 659-2894
Mark Schwartzbard	(917) 453-7784 www.markschwartzbard.com	Eve Strickman	(917) 566-9058
Steve Search (First AC)	(203) 438-1614 (917) 282-0508	Michelle Sun (First AC)	(213) 268-3236
Chris Seehase	(917) 509-4771	Waris Supanpong	(347) 489-0317
Jaime Segschneider	(914) 720-2578	Eric Swanek (First AC)	(908) 447-9975
Dara Selbert	(646) 483-8571 (212) 472-7657	Mike Swearingen	(917) 783-8764
Matthew Selkirk	(585) 545-0265	Timothy Sweeney	(617) 823-3252
Linda Sheehan (First AC)	(732) 830-2792	Nathan Swingle	(914) 213-8027
Colin Sheehy (Second AC)	(714) 318-6286 (412) 404-2374	James Sylvia	(508) 954-9070
Blackford Shelton (First AC)	(443) 253-9828 (410) 602-8088	Peter Symonowicz	(732) 292-1956 (732) 616-2270
Sherry Rousso Associates, Inc. One River Pl., Ste. 1828 (Near 12th Ave.) New York, NY 10036 (Reps for Camera Assistants)	(212) 564-7892 FAX (212) 564-7849 www.sradp.com	David Szani (Second AC)	(201) 372-1172
		Jaime Tabachnik (Second AC)	(917) 207-7685 www.jaimetabachnik.com
		Hiroo Takaoka (First AC)	(917) 406-4376
Christian Shonts	(704) 560-0876 (704) 568-7720	Gregor Tavenner	(917) 860-9368
A. Christopher Silano (First AC)	(718) 575-1050	Ken Thompson (Second AC)	(203) 561-0055
Pierson Silver (Second AC)	(718) 797-4244 (917) 279-9023	Matthew Thurber (First AC)	(781) 461-0759
Juli Silver-Taracido	(787) 724-1687	Scott Tinsley	(212) 620-4701 (917) 561-6419
Peter Simon	(917) 715-7473	Trevor Tong (Second AC)	(917) 373-0995
Elizabeth Singer	(347) 886-8696	Anthony Toomey	(212) 987-6990 (917) 673-6990
The Skouras Agency 1149 Third St., Third Fl. Santa Monica, CA 90403 (Reps for Camera Assistants)	(310) 395-9550 FAX (310) 395-4295 www.skouras.com	Ron Travisano (First AC)	(973) 783-5474 (917) 797-7449
		Cristian Trova (First AC)	(347) 262-6779 (413) 499-5759
Linda Slater (Second AC)	(646) 456-4420	Jill Tufts (First AC)	(617) 298-9899 (617) 308-0858
Andrew Smith	(845) 380-7883		
Derek Smith (First AC)	(910) 343-0007 (910) 262-4230	Daniel Turek (First AC)	(910) 452-0100 (910) 233-0690

Dana Turken	(917) 776-3935	Brian Wengrofsky (First AC)	(917) 568-2124
Sergio Velez (First AC)	(718) 908-8732 (718) 463-1427	Justin Whitacre	(631) 678-7665
		Daniel Wiener	(215) 514-7639
Vincent Vennitti (First AC)	(917) 847-9807 (718) 225-5353	Thomas Willey (Second AC)	(207) 244-5540 (207) 266-0088
John Verardi (First AC)	(910) 262-2640 (910) 270-0369	Jerome Williams (First AC)	(917) 209-4621 (718) 714-5705
Marilou Vetter (First AC)	(718) 788-7859 (917) 833-0964	Jelani Wilson	(212) 862-3599 (917) 557-0860
Lee Vickery (First AC)	(718) 852-2950 (917) 449-0504	Gregory Wimer (First AC)	(802) 223-0394 (802) 578-6827
Jack Vinson	(914) 473-3047	Aurelia Winborn (First AC)	(917) 603-7893
Joseph Volpe (First AC)	(201) 842-0193 (201) 315-7354	Alan Wolfe (First AC)	(718) 852-5444 (917) 324-2214
John Walker	(804) 339-7262	Andrew Wonder	(516) 946-1079 www.andrewwonder.com
Mark Walpole (First AC)	(703) 549-3468 (202) 258-9915	Toshiro Yamaguchi	(718) 781-8215
Kevin Walter	(201) 637-0435	Sean Yaple	(910) 763-0775 (910) 352-7804
Brett Walters (First AC)	(917) 806-2195	Anna Yusim (First AC)	(917) 523-8854 (718) 638-1514
Jessica Ward (Second AC)	(310) 343-3038	Stephanie Zimmer	(917) 207-2274
James Washburn	(570) 686-7694	Chris Zizzo	(631) 757-3710 (917) 355-0229 FAX (631) 757-3758 www.freewebs.com/busyboy
John Wassel	(570) 636-1726 (570) 401-0253		
Jeremy Weishaar (First AC)	(917) 863-7885		

Camera Assistants

Jeff Adorno	(914) 576-0547 (646) 391-8908	**Mai Iskander**	(646) 515-5995 (310) 458-7800 www.partos.com

Jeff Adorno (914) 576-0547 / (646) 391-8908

Tet Akay (212) 420-1563 / (917) 826-0444
(First) www.translucentfilmstudios.com

Kristoffer Brearton (917) 981-9943
www.krisb.com

Benjamin Centoducati (718) 815-3471

Andrea Dorman (732) 728-9288 / (917) 545-2538
(First) FAX (732) 728-9296

Ari Goldstein (718) 796-7053 / (646) 256-9575

Samuel Henriques (718) 499-4586 / (917) 544-4379
www.samhenriques.com

John Hunter (212) 564-7892
www.sradp.com

Mai Iskander (646) 515-5995 / (310) 458-7800
www.partos.com

Stan Keitt (917) 414-1456
(First AC)

Samuel Levy (310) 474-4585
www.dattnerdispoto.com

Alex MacDonald (310) 963-3267
(Aerial & Motion Control)

Motion Odyssey, Inc. (917) 597-0037
(Reps for Camera Assistants) www.motionodyssey.com

Gary Muller (818) 515-7271

Paul Reuter (347) 204-7481
www.paulreuter.com

Renzo Spirit-Buffalo (212) 875-9349
www.spiritbuffalo.com

Camera Operators (Local 600 NY)

Henry Adebonojo	(718) 949-2222 / (818) 206-0144
Bill Akerlund	(212) 505-0434
Brett Albright	(646) 270-9001 / (347) 715-7293
S. Dana Altomare	(917) 225-1225
Alex Applefeld	(410) 342-3462
Todd Armitage	(917) 601-9892
Miguel Armstrong	(212) 288-4467 / (917) 589-6485
Jim Arnold	(704) 904-1574 / (704) 663-5853
Michael Audick	(703) 204-1492
James Ball	(703) 608-1293 / (703) 922-9502
Bruce Balton	(570) 296-2733 / (917) 952-8570 / www.brucebalton.com
Robert Balton	(570) 828-8882
Axel Baumann	(718) 852-5481
Wylda Bayron	(646) 460-0263
Charles Bedi	(201) 390-0441 / (973) 478-6307
Bob Bellairs	(516) 735-6944
Michael Berg	(845) 548-0352
Win Bernfeld	(914) 232-0001
George Bianchini (Steadicam)	(917) 744-7614 / (212) 545-7895 / www.steadi-g.com
Manuel Billeter	(718) 243-1781 / (917) 586-0707
Maceo Bishop (Steadicam)	(917) 776-4976 / (818) 985-1130 / www.russelltoddagency.com
Bob Bogen (Action Sports & High Def)	(917) 881-2752
Dennis Boni	(301) 365-3007 / (202) 255-1691
Ira Brenner	(212) 724-4676 / (917) 864-2100
Gerard Brigante (Aerial, High Def, Motion Control, Remote Heads, Second Unit & Underwater)	(609) 506-8029
Robert Brillant	(973) 300-0263 / (917) 509-2500
Mark Britt	(516) 220-0318
Michael Buck	(848) 459-8653
John Burdick	(412) 231-2311
Terrence Burke	(917) 887-2283 / (201) 363-0373
Jeffrey Byrd	(212) 233-5851
Steven C. Calitri	(617) 501-3814
Jerry Cancel	(914) 843-8373
Michael Caracciolo	(201) 660-8430
Oliver Cary	(917) 209-6214
Jose Castro	(917) 226-2841
Cliff Charles	(917) 709-6653 / www.cliffcharles.com
John Chimples	(917) 886-9872
Dominick Ciardiello	(917) 763-0462
Daniel Cirella	(631) 645-1663 / (212) 799-9088
Trevor Cohen	(516) 729-2552
Joseph Collins	(212) 679-5512 / (917) 617-1247
Raymond Collins	(201) 248-3857 / www.therighteye.com
Edgar Colon	(787) 647-8969 / (787) 780-4429
R. B. Conover	(203) 943-5427 / (203) 877-8075
Stephen Consentino (High Def & Steadicam)	(914) 837-0120 / FAX (212) 214-0648
Stephen Coombs	(973) 476-4499 / (973) 729-7930
John Correira (High Def, Steadicam & Underwater)	(401) 316-9980 / (508) 336-3124
Lawrence Cullen	(973) 890-8666 / (973) 714-0761
Niels Dachler (Aerial)	(718) 415-3337
Joseph D'Alessandro	(910) 392-0387 / (910) 352-7607
Joe De Bonis	(201) 966-9110
Jon Delgado	(646) 382-5511 / (212) 260-5781
Robert Del Russo	(973) 812-8434 / (973) 534-2747
John DeMato	(718) 431-3542 / (718) 729-7343
Daniel DeNitto	(845) 246-1709
Kerwin DeVonish	(347) 739-1611
Matthew Doll	(910) 540-4747 / (910) 792-5584

Brian Dowley	(617) 510-2320 (617) 661-3041 www.briandowley.com		William Hays	(646) 207-2648 (212) 229-1730
Steve Drellich	(718) 781-3660		Samuel Henriques	(718) 499-4586 (917) 544-4379 www.samhenriques.com
Predrag Dubravcic (Aerial, High Def, Remote Heads, Special FX & Underwater)	(845) 704-7054 www.predrag.net		Jonathan Herron	(718) 499-1763 (917) 748-1866 www.reelsondemand.com/jonherron
Kevin Egan	(732) 922-8555 (732) 567-8413		Yahel Herzog	(917) 991-8723
David E. Elkins (Second Unit)	(336) 768-8958 (336) 770-1335 www.davidelkins.com		Charles Hill	(703) 317-1354
			Jeffrey Hodges	(212) 243-2024
Ted Erne	(917) 705-3681		Jay Hufford	(347) 742-3966
Jerome Fauci	(310) 540-3221 (818) 985-1130		Charles Huntley	(212) 579-8593 (917) 561-3627
James Fideler (High Def)	(347) 702-2312		Mai Iskander	(646) 515-5995 (310) 458-7800 www.partos.com
Max Fischer	(804) 261-5723 (804) 675-2635		Anthony Jacques	(718) 638-0002 (718) 208-9776
Eric Fisher	(781) 254-3423		Alec Jarnagin	(917) 804-6606 www.floatingcamera.com
Teddy Flandreau	(917) 865-9164 (203) 797-8489		Jeff Kantor	(845) 246-1433
Joe Gabriel	(917) 749-2934		John Keating	(847) 363-9978
David Garcia-Vlasits	(646) 345-3835		Eric Kendra	(908) 887-4126
Nick Gardner	(410) 327-0670 (202) 270-7324		David Kimelman (Steadicam)	(954) 347-0243 (561) 392-1055 www.davidkimelman.tv
Matt Garite	(516) 221-8753			
John Geisler	(917) 863-8600		David Knight	(310) 928-1525 (818) 985-1130 www.russelltoddagency.com
Don Glenn	(917) 445-2241			
Frank Godwin	(910) 381-4433 (910) 232-4028		Jay Kulick	(203) 329-2226 (917) 647-0277
Afton Grant	(781) 883-4235		Rod Lamborn	(212) 545-7895 (646) 418-1137 www.nyoffice.net
Randy Greer	(410) 383-8779 (410) 404-3836		Calen Lang	(917) 209-8676 (802) 763-8654
Carlos Guerra	(917) 533-7225 (718) 789-0486		Barbara Langdon	(201) 395-9939 (973) 390-0827
Mark Gunning	(617) 293-3761 (617) 327-1342		Thomas Lappin	(718) 788-3469 (310) 463-3177
Manuel Gutierrez	(973) 713-4893		Michael Latino	(413) 329-8721 (413) 229-3265
Chip Hackler	(910) 790-9724			
Amy Hall	(917) 568-8726 (646) 707-0484		Chris LaVasseur	(718) 748-9671 (917) 513-0578
Christopher Hall	(212) 862-4097 (347) 247-8558		Greg Lederway	(631) 804-0389
Leslie Hankey	(212) 496-0273		Rachael Levine (Remote Heads & Second Unit)	(917) 575-5907 www.rachaellevine.com
Shaun Harkins	(917) 670-9677		Steven Liebowitz (High Def)	(212) 262-5453 www.videodimensions.net
Jason Harvey	(917) 913-1757			
Helene Haviland	(410) 429-5122		Ludovic Littee	(917) 855-7019 (212) 759-5863
Chris Hayes	(917) 626-9050			

Dennis A. Livesey	(212) 876-6657 (917) 699-4680 FAX (212) 876-6849 www.dennisalivesey.com	Gary Nardilla	(212) 315-4855 FAX (212) 586-1572 www.citicam.net
John Lizzio (High Def, Second Unit & Steadicam)	(917) 887-1424 (201) 313-9680	Marc Nathan	(973) 429-1070
		Craig Needelman	(215) 880-7039
Bob Long	(973) 670-1784	New York Office 15 W. 26th St., Fifth Fl. (Near Broadway) New York, NY 10010 (Reps for Camera Operators)	(212) 545-7895 (323) 468-2240 FAX (212) 545-7941 www.nyoffice.net
Victor Longtin	(718) 544-4176 (917) 751-9352		
Michael Loscalzo	(516) 428-4930		
Charles Marcus	(917) 593-8722 (718) 368-4184	Tim Newman	(201) 420-6619 (917) 607-5385
Albino Marsetti	(917) 609-7441	Peter Nolan	(212) 242-1152
Greg Martin	(212) 249-4328 (917) 209-8802	Lyn Noland	(212) 799-2942
		Bruce Novich	(914) 582-4394
Philip Martinez	(917) 309-3605	Kevin O'Brien	(973) 539-6461
Parris Mayhew	(917) 673-3950 (212) 924-8505 www.therighteye.com	Brian O'Carroll (High Def)	(917) 674-3016 (212) 979-6887 FAX (212) 979-6887 www.nydp.tv
John McCabe	(203) 321-1095 (917) 968-9457	Brian Ochrym	(973) 300-9477 (888) 746-6869 FAX (973) 300-9467 www.mirageproductions.com
Kevin McCafferty	(212) 924-9616		
Ron McCaine	(203) 524-0219		
Derek McKane	(310) 395-9550 (631) 754-3550 www.skouras.com	Jimmy O'Donnell	(203) 256-5798
		Alain Onesto	(631) 266-2263
Robert McKenna	(917) 553-1099	Tony Pagano	(914) 645-2748 (914) 533-2890 FAX (914) 533-6406
Rodney McMahon	(347) 730-6515 (347) 806-8256		
Karl McMillan	(312) 301-9000	Tommy Parfitt	(917) 416-7582 (718) 759-0117
Joseph Meccariello	(610) 942-4593 (215) 870-2507	Christopher Paul	(212) 545-7895 (914) 698-2626 www.nyoffice.net
Aaron Medick (Steadicam)	(917) 714-3686 (212) 643-1736 FAX (718) 278-0298 www.steadycine.com	Wayne Paull	(203) 227-9020 (203) 247-2414
		Doug Pellegrino	(973) 383-7550
Alan J. Mehlbrech	(917) 753-1146 www.alanmehlbrech.com	Kenneth Peterson	(919) 933-9493 (919) 624-8362
John Meiklejohn	(212) 666-1453	Alan Pierce (Action Sports, Aerial, High Def, Motion Control, Remote Heads, Second Unit, Special FX & Underwater)	(203) 464-1773 (860) 683-8446 www.piercepictures.com
Michael Milia	(917) 669-8141		
William Millard	(203) 655-9369		
John Moers	(201) 893-9029 011 420 602 266 597	John Pirozzi	(212) 529-5535 (323) 333-5476
Jeffrey Moore	(910) 262-7397 (910) 392-7674	Mario Porporino	(917) 439-9165 FAX (973) 226-6061
Zeus Morand	(718) 625-4970 (917) 364-8920	Dusty Powers	(910) 520-5240 (910) 270-4422
Jeff Muhlstock	(201) 251-1511	Carl Prinzi	(212) 924-7678 (917) 612-8436
John Murphy	(203) 966-3088 (203) 722-8027	John Pry	(917) 282-0977 (718) 728-4051

Peter Ramos	(516) 520-4669 (516) 650-4817	David Sharples (Action Sports, High Def & Second Unit)	(732) 233-6490
Paul Ranieri	(845) 634-0684	James Shearman	(631) 645-5690
Jack Reichert	(732) 212-0790	Darrell Sheldon	(910) 233-7866 (910) 686-9594
Mark Renaudin	(914) 310-8981 (914) 332-7054	Tristan G. Sheridan	(718) 274-5473 (917) 673-5132
Guillaume Renberg (Motion Control & Remote Heads)	(917) 796-2773 (212) 865-3249 www.remotehead.net	Erica Shusha	(847) 477-9314
James Rider	(917) 763-5620	Jay Silver	(718) 809-9655 (718) 383-1325 www.jaysilverdp.com
Kurt Rimmel	(914) 924-2254		
Carlos Rios	(914) 522-0937 (914) 637-0169	Jamie Silverstein	(718) 369-9891 (917) 796-4217
Steven Robinson	(917) 348-4998 (212) 567-7611 FAX (212) 567-0941	Michael Sime	(973) 332-6425 (973) 239-3964 FAX (973) 239-3965 www.visualalchemy.tv
John Romeo	(917) 743-8268 (212) 727-1161 www.johnromeo.net	The Skouras Agency 1149 Third St., Third Fl. Santa Monica, CA 90403 (Reps for Camera Operators)	(310) 395-9550 FAX (310) 395-4295 www.skouras.com
Jon Rose	(914) 714-4042 (914) 949-6945	David Smith	(609) 397-1030
Celeste Rufo (High Def)	(201) 739-2912 (201) 346-0499	Jonathan Smith (High Def & Second Unit)	(646) 552-5747
Russell Todd Agency 5238 Goodland Ave. Valley Village, CA 91607 (Reps for Camera Operators & Steadicam Operators)	(818) 985-1130 FAX (818) 985-1134 www.russelltoddagency.com	Sheila Smith	(703) 527-4870 (703) 447-4060
		Larry Solomon (High Def)	(516) 678-3693
Donald Russell (Aerial, High Def, Motion Control, Remote Heads, Second Unit & Special FX)	(718) 696-8040	Sam Somwaru	(201) 310-5633 (917) 822-0823 www.soundandmotion.net
Greg Saccaro	(516) 796-6961	Francis Spieldenner	(201) 384-8154 (917) 604-4130
Robert Salamanca	(718) 803-3328	Ed Staebler	(516) 480-4475
Anthony J. Salerno (Action Sports & Second Unit)	(917) 439-9163 FAX (908) 668-4804 www.crewsnvideo.com	Stanley Staniski	(202) 265-3510
Ricardo Sarmiento	(917) 539-7467 FAX (212) 995-8582 www.sarmientofilms.com	Susan Starr	(212) 677-5809
		Mark Stoddard	(703) 534-8935
Gerard Sava	(914) 478-6322 (914) 468-4800	Craig Striano	(212) 679-3020 (917) 447-7160
Anthony Savini	(631) 665-8605 (516) 443-8164	Claus Stuhlweissenburg (Steadicam)	(917) 797-3014 www.steadiclaus.com
Peter Scalettar	(646) 221-7678	Chris Swenson	(917) 689-1530 (914) 524-0019
Jeff Schmale	(443) 865-0278	David Taicher	(610) 644-5191
Mark Schmidt	(917) 440-4581		
Jeremy Schneider	(407) 922-4585	David Thompson	(818) 985-1130 (443) 255-3325
David Schwartz (Aerial, High Def, Second Unit, Steadicam & Underwater)	(856) 216-0694 (856) 261-2314 FAX (856) 216-0695	Jason Thompson	(646) 753-2402 (917) 687-6966
		Manny Torres (Action Sports, High Def, Remote Heads, Second Unit & Steadicam)	(917) 770-1903
Richard Seibert	(516) 423-9089		
Ben Semanoff (Steadicam)	(212) 688-5490 (877) 786-7428 FAX (800) 505-1329 www.bensemanoff.com	Adam Troeger	(718) 974-4770

Jim Tufaro	(973) 460-9579	Christopher Walters	(347) 623-7508 (347) 623-7508
David Tumblety	(718) 230-1207 (917) 864-0838	Ron Washburn	(631) 225-7937 (631) 807-7014
Chris Vaught	(973) 616-6401	Mark Watkins	(914) 238-7196
Peter Vietro-Hannum	(917) 324-5175	Bo Webb	(910) 762-7843 (910) 297-1211
Edward Villegas	(718) 387-7863		
Lyle Vincent	(917) 664-9367 www.murthaagency.com	Mark Whitman	(973) 226-2177 (347) 219-2899
		Sean Wilk	(212) 581-9548
Joe Vitagliano	(508) 650-1801 (617) 306-2246	Paul Wilkens	(203) 470-1924
		Terry Williams	(410) 653-5038
Andrew Voegeli	(646) 361-3806 (212) 567-3109	Paul Wilson	(646) 234-2623 (718) 388-5997
Christopher Voos	(631) 375-3435	Susan Wong	(917) 846-9809
Ted Wachs	(917) 865-1255 (212) 371-6269 www.oraclecreative.com	Ian Woolston-Smith (High Def, Second Unit & Steadicam)	(203) 470-3885 www.iancam.com
Derek Walker	(718) 852-3494 (917) 676-2086	Steve Yaconetti	(516) 671-7433

Camera Operators

Atlantic Television, Inc. (212) 625-9327
524 Broadway, Fourth Fl. (917) 568-7218
(Near Spring) FAX (212) 625-9346
New York, NY 10012 www.atlantictv.com
(Reps for Camera Operators)

George Barnes (973) 508-6054
(305) 673-2737

Jeb Bergh (516) 429-6376

Danny Buonsanto (917) 723-5156
(310) 947-9971
www.metropolitanpictures.net

Paul Burns (917) 533-7294
(800) 706-7977
(Steadicam) FAX (973) 762-4287

Don Canfield (914) 526-4896
(Motion Control) www.gearandrose.com

Justin Crabill (917) 912-6521

Michael Crain (917) 597-0037
(Steadicam)

Mik Cribben (800) 235-2713
(917) 513-3795
(Steadicam) FAX (212) 620-0084
www.mikcribben.com

Vic David (212) 962-1850
FAX (212) 962-1043
www.7-ny.com

Dan Davis (908) 713-0365
(908) 246-6485
(Steadicam) FAX (908) 713-0508
www.blast.net/davis

Bill DeHuff (860) 583-9303
(860) 212-8005
FAX (860) 584-0669
www.sonlightprods.com

Richard Eliano (917) 930-3736

David E. Elkins (336) 768-8958
(336) 770-1335
(Second Unit) www.davidelkins.com

Richard S. Freedman (212) 253-1885
(917) 716-5799

Chris Hayes (917) 626-9050

Sandy Hays (818) 985-1130
(Steadicam) www.russelltoddagency.com

Jeffrey Hirschorn (212) 979-8437
(212) 260-4211
(Steadicam)

Dave Isern (917) 913-2989
(323) 868-2492
(Steadicam) www.daveisern.com

Adam Keith (201) 930-9855
(800) 921-3478
(Steadicam) FAX (201) 930-9850
www.qvideo.tv

Ronald Kienhuis (917) 359-3917
(516) 829-0470
FAX (516) 829-2666

Gabor Kover (201) 461-4511
(201) 741-2777
(Aerial, High Def, Remote Heads & Second Unit)

Bruce MacCallum (212) 935-1612
(917) 825-7210

Paul Magee (610) 623-4250
(Steadicam) FAX (610) 623-4250

Scott Maguire (917) 648-5492
www.scottmaguire.com

Larry McConkey (609) 397-4702
(310) 557-9906
FAX (609) 397-4938

Peter McEntyre (631) 789-0878
(201) 650-4947
(Video)

Bill Meisenzahl (917) 658-6238
www.gotoguynyc.com

James Miller (212) 772-0800
(Video)

Motion Odyssey, Inc. (917) 597-0037
(Reps for Steadicam Operators) www.motionodyssey.com

Michael O'Shea (610) 246-1218
(Steadicam)

Wei K. Pun (917) 215-4028
(310) 314-2606
www.weidp.com
(Action Sports, Aerial, Film, High Def, Second Unit & Special FX)

Scott Purvines (347) 683-6463
www.actlab.utexas.edu/~scottp/portfolio

Russell Todd Agency (818) 985-1130
5238 Goodland Ave. FAX (818) 985-1134
Valley Village, CA 91607 www.russelltoddagency.com
(Reps for Camera Operators & Steadicam Operators)

Daniel Sanabria (914) 633-9869
FAX (914) 633-0337

Scott Shelley (917) 318-6797

Tony Stewart (866) 725-7714
(609) 462-7361
FAX (609) 883-5919
www.stewartfilms.com

Claus Stuhlweissenburg (917) 797-3014
(Steadicam) www.steadiclaus.com

Ralph Watson (310) 822-9113
(Steadicam) www.murthaagency.com

Mark Weingartner (818) 702-1777
(818) 970-6833
FAX (818) 702-1779

Thomas Weston (201) 664-0404
(201) 674-3314

KC White (908) 400-6793
(Aerial, High Def & Second Unit) FAX (908) 647-9480
www.kcwhite.net

Paul Wilkens (203) 748-4333

Michael Wright (562) 493-5265
(562) 243-6453
(Steadicam)

Camera Operators—Aerial (Local 600 NY)

Dennis Boni	(301) 365-3007 / (202) 255-1691
Ira Brenner	(212) 724-4676 / (917) 864-2100
Gerard Brigante	(609) 506-8029
John Burdick	(412) 231-2311
John Chimples	(917) 886-9872
Niels Dachler	(718) 415-3337
Joe De Bonis	(201) 966-9110
Brian Dowley	(617) 510-2320 / (617) 661-3041 / www.briandowley.com
Predrag Dubravcic	(845) 704-7054 / www.predrag.net
Ted Erne	(917) 705-3681
Max Fischer	(804) 261-5723 / (804) 675-2635
John Geisler	(917) 863-8600
Randy Greer	(410) 383-8779
Leslie Hankey	(212) 496-0273
Shaun Harkins	(917) 670-9677
Jeff Kantor	(845) 246-1433
David Knight	(310) 928-1525 / (818) 985-1130 / www.russelltoddagency.com
Chris LaVasseur	(718) 748-9671 / (917) 513-0578
Bob Long	(973) 670-1784
Ron McCaine	(203) 524-0219
Derek McKane	(310) 395-9550 / (631) 754-3550 / www.skouras.com
Joseph Meccariello	(610) 942-4593 / (215) 870-2507
Zeus Morand	(718) 625-4970 / (917) 364-8920
Saade A. Mustafa	(917) 375-0074 / (718) 968-7657
Craig Needelman	(215) 880-7039
Brian O'Carroll	(917) 674-3016 / (212) 979-6887
Jimmy O'Donnell	(203) 256-5798
Christopher Paul	(212) 545-7895 / (914) 698-2626 / www.nyoffice.com
Kenneth Peterson	(919) 933-9493 / (919) 624-8362
Alan Pierce	(203) 464-1773 / (860) 683-8446
Dusty Powers	(910) 520-5240 / (910) 270-4422
Mark Renaudin	(914) 332-7054 / (914) 310-8981
David Schwartz	(856) 216-0694 / (856) 261-2314
Tristan G. Sheridan	(718) 274-5473 / (917) 673-5132
Sam Somwaru	(201) 310-5633 / (917) 822-0823 / www.soundandmotion.net
Adam Troeger	(718) 974-4770
Ted Wachs	(917) 865-1255 / (212) 371-6269 / www.oraclecreative.com
Derek Walker	(917) 676-2086 / (718) 852-3494
Ian Woolston-Smith	(203) 470-3885 / www.iancam.com

Camera Operators—Steadicam (Local 600 NY)

George Bianchini	(917) 744-7614
	(212) 545-7895
	www.steadi-g.com
Maceo Bishop	(917) 776-4976
	(818) 985-1130
Gerard Brigante	(609) 506-8029
Michael Caracciolo	(201) 660-8430
Raymond Collins	(201) 248-3857
	www.therighteye.com
Stephen Consentino	(914) 837-0120
	FAX (212) 214-0648
Niels Dachler	(718) 415-3337
Joe De Bonis	(201) 966-9110
Don Glenn	**(917) 445-2241**
Afton Grant	(781) 883-4235
Carlos Guerra	(917) 533-7225
	(718) 789-0486
William Hays	(646) 207-2648
	(212) 229-1730
Jonathan Herron	(718) 499-1763
	(917) 748-1866
	www.reelsondemand.com/jonherron
Alec Jarnagin	(917) 804-6606
Eric Kendra	(908) 887-4126
David Kimelman	(954) 347-0243
	(561) 392-1055
	www.davidkimelman.tv
Greg Lederway	(631) 804-0389
John Lizzio	(917) 887-1424
	(201) 313-9680
Bob Long	(973) 670-1784
Philip Martinez	(917) 309-3605
Parris Mayhew	(917) 673-3950
	(212) 924-8505
	www.therighteye.com
Aaron Medick	(917) 714-3686
	(212) 643-1736
	FAX (718) 278-0298
	www.steadycine.com
Alan J. Mehlbrech	(917) 753-1146
	www.alanmehlbrech.com
Jeff Muhlstock	(201) 251-1511
Saade A. Mustafa	(917) 375-0074
Alain Onesto	(631) 266-2263
Christopher Paul	(212) 545-7895
	(914) 698-2626
	www.nyoffice.net
Doug Pellegrino	(973) 383-7550
Kurt Rimmel	(914) 924-2254
Gerard Sava	(914) 478-6322
	(917) 468-4800
Jeremy Schneider	(407) 922-4585
David Schwartz	(856) 216-0694
	(856) 261-2314
	FAX (856) 216-0695
Ben Semanoff	(212) 688-5490
	(877) 786-7428
	FAX (800) 505-1329
	www.bensemanoff.com
David Sharples	(732) 233-6490
Erica Shusha	(847) 477-9314
Jamie Silverstein	(718) 369-9891
	(917) 796-4217
Sam Somwaru	(201) 310-5633
	(917) 822-0823
	www.soundandmotion.net
Francis Spieldenner	(201) 384-8154
	(917) 604-4130
David Taicher	(610) 644-5191
David Thompson	(818) 985-1130
	(443) 255-3325
Manny Torres	(917) 770-1903
Peter Vietro-Hannum	(917) 324-5175
Paul Wilson	(646) 234-2623
	(718) 388-5997
Ian Woolston-Smith	203-470-3885

Camera Operators—Steadicam

Erik Anderson	(212) 924-8505
	www.therighteye.com
Paul Burns	(917) 533-7294
Michael Crain	(917) 597-0037
Dan Davis	(908) 713-0365
	(908) 246-6485
	FAX (908) 713-0508
	www.blast.net/davis
Sandy Hays	(818) 968-1130
	www.russelltoddagency.com
Jeffrey Hirschorn	(212) 979-8437
	FAX (212) 260-4211
Dave Isern	(917) 913-2989
	(323) 868-2492
	www.daveisern.com
Adam Keith	(201) 930-9855
	(800) 921-3478
	FAX (201) 930-9850
	www.qvideo.tv
Paul Magee	(610) 623-4250
	FAX (610) 623-4250
Mik Cribben	(800) 235-2713
	(917) 513-3795
	FAX (212) 620-0084
	www.mikcribben.com
Motion Odyssey	(917) 597-0037
(Reps for Steadicam Operators)	www.motionodyssey.com
Michael O'Shea	(610) 246-1218
Wei K. Pun	(917) 215-4028
	(310) 314-2606
	www.weidp.com
Ari Robbins	(212) 643-1736
	www.cec-entertainment.com
Russell Todd Agency	(818) 985-1130
(Reps for Steadicam Operators)	FAX (818) 985-1134
	www.russelltoddagency.com
Claus Stuhlweissenburg	(917) 797-3014
	www.steadiclaus.com
Ralph Watson	(310) 822-9113
	www.murthaagency.com

Camera Operators—Underwater (Local 600 NY)

Michael Berg	(845) 548-0352
Jeb Bergh	(516) 429-6376
Ira Brenner	(212) 724-4676 / (917) 864-2100
Gerard Brigante	(609) 506-8029
Mark Britt	(516) 220-0318
John Chimples	(917) 886-9872
Tim Cothren	(202) 680-3350
Joe De Bonis	(201) 966-9110
Predrag Dubravcic	(845) 704-7054
Don Glenn	(917) 445-2241
Amy Hall	(917) 568-8726
Leslie Hankey	(212) 496-0273
Shaun Harkins	(917) 670-9677
Jason Harvey	(917) 913-1757
Jonathan Herron	(718) 499-1763 / (917) 748-1866 www.reelsondemand.com/jonherron
Rod Lamborn	(212) 545-7895 / (646) 418-1137 www.nyoffice.net
Calen Lang	(917) 209-8676
John Lizzio	(917) 887-1424 / (201) 313-9680
Michael Loscalzo	(516) 428-4930
John McCabe	(203) 321-1095 / (917) 968-9457
Kevin McCafferty	(212) 924-9616
Ron McCaine	(203) 524-0219
Derek McKane	(631) 754-3550 / (310) 395-9550
Karl McMillan	(312) 301-9000
Zeus Morand	(718) 625-4970 / (917) 364-8920
Brian O'Carroll	(917) 674-3016 / (212) 979-6887 FAX (212) 979-6887 www.nydp.tv
Christopher Paul	(212) 545-7895 / (646) 418-1137 www.nyoffice.net
Mario Porporino	(917) 439-9165 FAX (973) 226-6061
Jack Reichert	(732) 212-0790
Mark Renaudin	(914) 310-8981
Jon Rose	(914) 714-4042 / (914) 949-6945
David Schwartz	(856) 216-0694 / (856) 261-2314 FAX (856) 216-0695
David Sharples	(732) 233-6490
Darrell Sheldon	(910) 233-7866 / (910) 686-9594
Tristan G. Sheridan	(718) 274-5473 / (917) 673-5132
Jay Silver	(718) 809-9655 / (718) 383-1325 www.jaysilverdp.com
Sam Somwaru	(201) 310-5633 / (917) 822-0823 www.soundandmotion.net
Mark Stoddard	(703) 534-8935
Jason Thompson	(646) 753-2402 / (917) 687-6966
Peter Vietro-Hannum	(917) 324-5175
Ted Wachs	(917) 865-1255 / (212) 371-6269 www.oraclecreative.com
Steve Yaconetti	(516) 671-7433

Carpenters/Shop Craft (Local 52 NY)

Vincent Accardi	(631) 327-6341
Michael Acevedo	(845) 742-3034
Kenneth J. Albanese	(845) 735-3294
Nicholas Albanese	(845) 323-7833 / (845) 735-3294
Joseph Anthony Alfieri	(631) 289-6963
Joseph S. Alfieri	(631) 289-6963
Derrick J. Alford	(212) 247-8283 / (718) 596-4513
James C. Allen	(917) 494-1730
Jose Amor	(917) 692-4596
Scott G. Anderson	(215) 468-5271 / (267) 250-9648
Francisco Andraca	(646) 345-8154
Robert J. Antalocy	(845) 325-4524
Henry Antonacchio	(718) 863-0684 / (917) 707-9191
Juan Enrique V. Aviles	(201) 224-0536 / (201) 966-9428
Bill Ballou	(805) 559-4291
Yosef Barbalat	(917) 414-2389
Brian A. Becker	(973) 340-1751 / (973) 418-6993
Richard Bennett	(973) 485-3358 / (973) 903-1557
Robert Bennett	(516) 316-5346
Martin Bernstein	(718) 768-0886
Henry T. Biernacki	(518) 767-2286
Joseph A. Bisogna	(973) 366-8436
Walter E. Blake	(860) 514-0784
Peter Blechman	(516) 944-8437 / (516) 319-2382
Douglas A. Bleier	(914) 242-0239 / (914) 376-9667
Frank A. Boccia	(718) 816-7688 / (347) 752-0132
Gary E. Boesch	(732) 270-2667 / (732) 814-7333
Douglas M. Bowen	(718) 596-7414 / (917) 514-7365
Thomas F. Bowen	(215) 745-5594 / (215) 306-4724
Daniel Brandes	(570) 424-2301 / (570) 242-5213
Thomas Brennan	(908) 277-2344
Paul Brush	(732) 341-1359 / (732) 666-2045
Kenneth Brzozowski	(518) 494-5367
Timothy H. Buchman	(201) 848-9491
David H. Buck	(860) 535-1287
Charles Buli	(201) 398-6759
Peter Bundrick	(914) 693-8859
Ryan Bundrick	(914) 760-1666 / (914) 693-2015
Michelle Burnworth	(267) 671-0119 / (215) 888-8682
James Cappello	(845) 634-6401 / (914) 329-0052
Bill Capucilli	(914) 478-1899 / (914) 426-4359
James P. Cariot	(914) 534-8054
James Carlino	(917) 523-5793
Joe Caruso	(845) 294-0560 / (917) 299-4803
Charles Cecil	(516) 766-4209 / (516) 975-1627
John J. Ciccimarro	(203) 470-1512
Charles Cirigliano	(508) 257-4682
Laurence Clark	(212) 254-8614 / (917) 406-4809
Rodney Clark	(212) 534-1215
Keith Cleary	(215) 862-2774 / (215) 862-9020
John Coda	(718) 597-4379 / (914) 661-9142
Isaac J. Cohen	(917) 207-8643
Tobias S. Core	(917) 294-7094
Thomas Costabile	(914) 273-5753
Jack Coyle	(617) 513-9191
Gregory Criscuolo	(212) 227-0062 / (917) 749-0529
Larry B. Cronk	(201) 293-3031
Michael S. Cucciarre	(201) 794-1061
Peter Culen	(914) 631-8385
Michael P. Curry Jr.	(917) 752-3155 / (917) 887-6189
Michael Curry Sr.	(212) 734-0455
Michael Cycan	(516) 582-8310 / (516) 353-1083

Richard A. Daddi	(860) 599-1431
Michael Davidson	(215) 668-0683
Matthew J. De Nicola	(631) 207-2884
Alex Devlin	(718) 545-3391
Frank R. Di Dio	(718) 966-6749
Daniel P. Dietrich	(917) 647-3061
Robert Di Grigoli	(732) 477-9281 (732) 740-7581
Robert Dillon	(516) 459-0195
Paul George Divone	(212) 477-3676 (917) 335-3514
Scott R. Dixon	(914) 709-1514
Charles D. Doherty	(856) 985-6200 (856) 222-5821
James T. Doherty	(856) 232-1247 (215) 984-3311
George Donohue	(732) 768-3483 (732) 706-0704
Richard Bryan Douglas	(516) 665-7578
Tomm Doyle	(212) 489-1305
Joseph J. Drobka	(860) 528-5184
Peter T. Duhaime	(203) 732-8803
George D. Dummitt	(212) 532-4692
Henry Duys	(718) 510-3827
Charles (Chip) Eccles	(412) 828-9664 (412) 596-9664
Michael A. Esposito	(910) 793-6069
Bernard A. Farbrother	(914) 443-8182 (212) 456-5714
John B. Farrell	(201) 943-1651 (201) 951-3756
Wes Faulkenberry Jr.	(516) 546-0531 (516) 902-0141
Edward Ferraro	(516) 889-3578 (917) 867-4098
David Flaiz	(631) 261-0539 (516) 721-4726
Eric Friedewald	(917) 414-3783 (646) 414-1876
Charles Furey	(732) 281-0949
Gerard J. Furey	(732) 929-3369
John S. Gallagher	(484) 764-7763
Fred J. Gallo	(212) 327-4038
Marcial Garlitos	(718) 389-2143 (917) 520-6853
Daniel P. Geary	(973) 812-1465 (973) 207-5645
Hubert Gee	(212) 877-3143 (646) 753-1052
William J. Geiger	(516) 223-2940 (718) 433-3921
John E. Geisz	(814) 235-0868
Ezra K. Gertsen	(212) 567-5434 (631) 804-8291
Glenn H. Gertsen	(914) 225-2201 (914) 321-5408
Jesse H. Gertsen	(845) 225-2201 (914) 438-3293
K. Scott Gertsen	(203) 323-9172
Ryan M. Gertsen	(914) 469-2921
Gregg Gilmartin	(516) 826-5249
James P. Gilroy Jr.	(610) 459-8936 (215) 401-6887
John J. Gilroy	(610) 449-0290
Michael Goldstein	(518) 623-9440
Gregory W. Goodwin	(516) 978-8583
Glenn E. Gordon	(203) 982-3304
Timothy P. Gorman	(718) 438-7901
Jon E. Graf	(215) 551-4416 (215) 829-1787
John H. Grammer	(914) 457-1735
Robert (Crow) Grant	(845) 782-7914 (914) 753-2302
Roger Gray	(845) 565-3274 (845) 534-7143
Glen A. Gregory	(516) 536-1480
Thomas J. Gregory	(516) 889-8975 (516) 987-7832
William R. Gregory	(347) 489-6109
Sam Greto	(914) 937-1629 (914) 973-0414
Gary Grill	(973) 746-7589 (973) 809-4313
John Grimolizzi	(845) 986-8421 (917) 389-0036
Gregory V. Hagler	(203) 366-6330
Kenneth Hammer	(732) 270-9626
Daniel Hanessian	(914) 593-0447 (914) 251-6854
Gabe Harris	(212) 222-8161 (917) 862-2597
Richard Hartman	(215) 576-0914

Linda Lee Harvey	(917) 701-3341
Brent Haywood	(718) 218-9239 (917) 838-4131
Michael Herlihy	(631) 549-3249
Paul Hewitt	(215) 424-6416
David Hill	(607) 437-4733
Gavin Holmes	(917) 771-9546
Harold Horn	(718) 338-7398 (917) 491-4461
Mark Horstmann	(914) 986-3559
John C. Jackson	(212) 873-0005 (212) 274-0060
Christopher D. Janks	(917) 709-9180
Daniel J. Janssen	(518) 668-9015
Edward J. Johnson	(215) 545-7216
John R. Johnston	(413) 229-5919
Gerard J. Jordan	(718) 357-7505 (917) 896-0146
Michael Kall	(718) 343-7798 (917) 225-3932
Joseph P. Kamfor Jr.	(845) 356-0759 (845) 729-8070
Richard S. Kamin	(516) 791-1875 (516) 884-6515
Michael T. Kearns	(914) 803-1343 (203) 913-1321
Colin T. Keech	(215) 922-0198
Robert Keller	(212) 677-5763 (917) 969-7266
Todd. Kelsey	(518) 696-2328
Martin Kirchoff	(718) 349-2951
George Kouzoujian Jr.	(212) 989-1502
Gordon Krause	(212) 989-2739
Bernard J. Kuhn Jr.	(203) 877-1935
Don Kushner	(888) 761-8324
Roger P. Lang	(631) 580-1759
Steven E. Lawler	(973) 571-0099 (973) 650-7716
Hoang Anh Le	(856) 482-6889 (609) 458-6183
Bret Lehne	(646) 299-1783 (718) 972-4960
William Lehne	(718) 972-4960 (917) 586-0490
Mark E. Leining	(732) 821-4429
Paul Lodes	(215) 338-6265
Richard B. Lohrer Jr.	(917) 882-9774
Frank Love	(570) 296-5315 (914) 391-8516
Ulf Loven	(212) 979-1561
Peter Lukeris	(203) 426-9201
Dennis Madigan	(267) 235-9443
Brian R. Mahon	(631) 661-4195
James Maiello	(212) 614-0626 (718) 499-4185
Paul Maiello	(215) 232-6467
Tim Main	(718) 387-3279
Christopher G. Markunas	(215) 281-5927 (215) 327-6310
Peter Matejczyk	(732) 264-6412
Francis G. McAlister	(212) 203-5365 (212) 475-7495
Doug McBrearty	(609) 859-1177
Stephen T. McEntee	(215) 732-3316
Steven T. McGuire	(203) 867-7533
John F. McHugh	(914) 762-8014 (914) 772-3557
Matthew J. McIntyre	(215) 333-3104
Stephen A. McKearnin	(201) 343-0886
David P. McMahon	(215) 355-2189 (267) 981-8202
Michael Melchiorre	(201) 664-5796
L. Bruce Mellett	(718) 383-0820 (917) 673-9094
Fred Merusi	(973) 293-3292 (973) 293-8095
Louis Miller	(973) 761-8321 (718) 755-6745
Nicholas Miller	(212) 663-0037
Ronald A. Miller	(718) 783-5507
Robert Moran	(516) 457-7243
Wayne B. Moss	(973) 948-2805
Raymond Motta	(646) 207-9952
Kenneth D. Nelson	(212) 262-9820 (212) 262-9280
Mark Nicholas	(516) 867-4201
Christopher Noonan	(603) 835-2984
Miroslaw Nowalski	(800) 973-5718
C. Mark Overton	(914) 376-2992
Kenneth L. Owens	(203) 671-5074

Bruno F. Panacciulli	(631) 581-4924 / (516) 383-1123
Glen A. Pangione	(201) 784-9421 / (917) 871-7171
Bruce J. Paquette	(914) 478-3631
Ronald J. Paquette	(914) 478-7013
Joseph S. Patire	(973) 835-7949 / (201) 723-9680
Steven T. Paul	(609) 822-0668 / (800) 556-0593
Brian Pearson	(646) 637-2340 / (718) 224-4130
Rudolph Pelikan	(516) 739-0705 / (516) 739-0706
Ronald J. Petagna	(732) 441-2755 / (908) 313-9760
Ronnie Petagna Jr.	(732) 441-2755 / (732) 580-1380
Eugene N. Pile II	(814) 445-2214
Michael Pilipski	(914) 754-8323
William Pocsik	(908) 238-7089
Louis J. Porzio	(732) 416-9358
David Poses	(718) 596-9610
Elizabeth Powley	(267) 312-3908
Gennaro Proscia	(718) 829-6621
Moshe S. Rabinowitz	(516) 379-1948 / (516) 375-4140
Richard Ramirez	(718) 596-2326 / (646) 221-0064
Gary Rausenberger	(845) 564-4425 / (845) 742-0497
Raymond Reddy	(631) 979-8127 / (516) 724-0159
Roland E. Reed III	(215) 232-0257 / (267) 252-9325
Jeffrey H. Rehlaender	(631) 757-4803
Malcolm H. Reid	(718) 398-2797 / (646) 734-8949
Kevin Roach	(917) 609-2572
Paul Robinson	(917) 603-6136
Sean Robinson	(212) 543-4294 / (917) 640-9536
Charles J. Romanello	(973) 779-6683
James Rose	(212) 228-1309
Andrew Rossig	(845) 987-6893
Danny Rovira	(631) 423-8938 / (917) 992-4251
Paul T. Rovira	(631) 846-9449
Pierre Rovira	(631) 893-2982 / (917) 233-0506
James Sadek	(718) 398-4507 / (917) 439-0311
Raymond M. Samitz	(718) 649-5332
Emanuel L. Sanchez	(646) 285-8340
Carmen S. Santoro	(856) 478-4012
John S. Seese	(267) 257-8786
Stephen Shapiro	(917) 693-4696 / FAX (718) 434-4653
David Silber	(516) 759-7405
Richard A. Sirico	(718) 998-6536 / (718) 496-6362
George Skelly	(407) 421-4226
Edward W. Smith	(518) 623-4427
Tim M. Smith	(646) 526-7783
James P. Sofield	(609) 768-4151 / (609) 738-9360
Mark Sonderskov	(917) 805-5935 / FAX (718) 383-3532
Mark Sorice	(516) 365-7806
Michael S. Spiegel	(908) 276-5432
Eugene Spiotta Jr.	(631) 730-8243 / (516) 330-7595
W. Ernest Stalder	(212) 254-9859
Dean Stankiewicz	(215) 339-5133 / (215) 250-3318
Jeffrey M. Starkey	(203) 375-2478
Jonathan Stein	(516) 378-4545 / (516) 220-9500
Raymond J. Stenzel	(631) 475-6488
William Stenzel	(631) 739-3176 / (631) 475-6488
Kenneth G. Stopsky	(201) 439-0367 / (201) 725-6916
Donald P. Strauss	(845) 783-1681 / (845) 325-2861
Douglas N. Swass	(516) 375-0629
Ian Swinton (Construction Coordinator)	(860) 342-1001 / FAX (860) 342-1036
Jeff Taisey	(516) 395-2499 / (516) 244-4499
Elizabeth (Betsy) Tanner	(917) 826-3281
P. David Temple	(212) 924-7870
Richard Tenewitz	(845) 496-0771 / (914) 522-6485
Brett Thomas	(201) 890-1498

Robert W. Trager	(215) 639-4496 / (215) 509-0295
Richard Trincere	(631) 324-5985 / (917) 842-6197
Matthew H. Turner	(267) 254-8850
Girolamo Tuzzolino	(718) 232-6105 / (646) 261-7035
Chris Unrath	(215) 922-3086
Robert A. Vaccariello	(516) 739-8277 / (516) 291-0131
Robert S. Vanstone	(215) 634-0340 / (215) 719-2828
Andrew M. Velechenko	(973) 662-0011
David W. Walker	(973) 697-8489 / (800) 678-9442
James P. Walker	(631) 828-9906
Kenneth J. Walshak	(631) 376-1209 / (917) 696-2246
Patrick E. White	(215) 262-9479
Thomas White	(201) 337-2049 / (201) 752-3766
Charles Whitney	(732) 262-8629
David Gordon Williams	(856) 795-3534 / (856) 220-8455
Paul Williams	(215) 739-3955 / (267) 278-0778
Bernadette Wise-Tuteur	(914) 739-7518
Stephen Wolff	(215) 740-3517
Daniel S. Wollock	(718) 636-9490
Kurt W. Wunder	(215) 551-4789
Robert Yanez	(212) 924-3272
Dennis A. Young	(203) 501-3534
William N. Young	(215) 949-9332 / (215) 509-8541
George Zegarsky	(914) 941-6421
Joseph Ziegler	(914) 588-8121

Craft Service (Local 52 NY)

Michael C. Barnes	(856) 981-1695	Cindy Keen	(856) 374-2832 (856) 237-9185
Patricia A. Barnes	(856) 889-2909	Claudia Litwack	(215) 339-5133 (215) 668-2591
Angeline Cleary	(267) 614-1570 (215) 862-2774	Martin C. McIntyre	(856) 358-1011 (856) 275-5267
Jeff J. Davis	(609) 886-9691 (609) 827-6783	Daniel Reddy	(856) 563-4130
Lena Drobot	(856) 303-9004 (609) 332-8804	Shannon Stewart	(215) 438-1557 (267) 254-2453
Jeanene K. Fiedler	(856) 232-9205 (609) 706-9692	John Yowler	(856) 427-7841 (609) 560-0974
William Hamilton Jr.	(215) 492-0201 (215) 812-7994		

Craft Service

As You Like It Craft Service   **(201) 240-8128**
(24-Hour Service, Breakfasts, Catering For Non-Union/Crowd Extras, Coffee Service, Juices, Lunch & Smoothies)

Cabbages and Kings   **(203) 226-0531**
34 Franklin St. (Near Saugatuck)   FAX **(203) 222-8564**
Westport, CT 06880

   (845) 216-5211
D's Craft Service   **(203) 743-4395**
67A Sheridan St., Ste. 6
Danbury, CT 06810

David Dreishpoon's Gourmet   **(917) 682-2020**
126 Commonwealth Ave.   **www.davidcraftservices.com**
(Near Washington St.)
Merrick, NY 11566

E.S., Inc.   **(800) 736-8888**
P.O. Box 670476
Flushing, NY 11367

East Side Bagels   **(212) 794-1655**
1496 First Ave. (Near E. 78th St.)   FAX **(212) 794-2529**
New York, NY 10021

EatCatering by Danielle Wilson   **(201) 736-2511**
FAX **(201) 455-2579**
www.eatcateringnyc.com

   (973) 754-9502
Kevoo Catering   **(201) 314-6828**
52 Rockland Ave.   FAX **(973) 754-9503**
West Paterson, NJ 07424   **www.kevoocatering.com**

   (860) 355-5441
LaNoce's Fine Food For Film, LLC   **(860) 234-4445**
Four Grandview Ln.
New Milford, CT 06776

U.S. Coffee, Inc.   **(516) 733-7600**
51 Alpha Plaza (Near W. John St.)   FAX **(516) 433-7870**
Hicksville, NY 11801   **www.firstcoffee.com**

The Village Caterer &   **(212) 529-2207**
Craft Service, Inc.   **(646) 321-3535**
122 MacDougal St., Ste. 20   FAX **(212) 529-2207**
(Near Carmine St.)   **www.villagecaterer.com**
New York, NY 10012

   (917) 548-3407
The Wilson Rivas Co., Inc.   **(718) 296-1840**
7442 Atlantic Ave.
Ozone Park, NY 11416

Digital Imaging Technicians (Local 600 NY)

J. Eric Camp	(703) 869-9484
Jeffrey Cirbes	(845) 494-7556 / (845) 477-3721
Robert Daraio	(914) 774-2646
Othmar Dickbauer	(212) 228-7473 / (917) 319-0301 / www.tornadopixels.com
Jeff Flohr	(978) 846-3601
Thomas Gilmour	(212) 627-4520 / (917) 328-6956
Thomas Guadarrama	(516) 458-9806 / (631) 842-0831
Ryan Heide	(917) 604-5851
J.M. Hurley	(973) 204-7000
Gary Isaacs	(917) 209-4884
Nicholas Kay	(973) 460-0230
Sam Kretchmar	(847) 951-8423
Abby Levine	(917) 859-4342
John Mania	(201) 652-7162
Barry Minnerly	(203) 952-6369 / (203) 857-4529
Rick Nagle	(917) 923-6001
Susan Noll	(631) 423-4575
Lewis Rothenberg	(201) 615-2202 / (201) 939-0422 / FAX (201) 939-0423 / www.tnsproductions.com
Barry Russo	(201) 871-9697
Dave Satin	(917) 951-3536
Ben Schwartz	(646) 326-7702 / www.imdb.com/name/nm2366642
Robert Shinn	(973) 809-1665
Robert Strait	(732) 306-6217 / (732) 636-4760
Bill Vignari	(917) 273-9719
Scott Winig	(917) 856-0211 / (336) 777-1057
Kenneth Wise	(718) 981-7096

Digital Imaging Technicians

Scott Billups (Film)	(818) 990-8993 / www.ambitiousent.com
Mariusz Cichon	(347) 365-0556
Jeff Kantor	(917) 825-5380
Karl Mehrer	(917) 952-9589 / FAX (917) 591-6981 / www.k2imaging.com

Directors of Photography (Local 600 NY)

Peter Abraham — (917) 453-1219

Phil Abraham — (310) 395-9550 / (212) 260-7943 / FAX (310) 395-4295
(Film & High Def)

Peter Agliata — (718) 625-7923

Martin Ahlgren — (646) 327-8813
(Film & High Def)

Martin Albert — (917) 913-9630
www.mbalbert.com
(Film & High Def)

Maryse Alberti — (917) 572-8397
www.dattnerdispoto.com
(Film & High Def)

All Crew Agency — (818) 206-0144
2920 W. Olive Ave., Ste. 201 — FAX (818) 206-0169
Burbank, CA 91505 — www.allcrewagency.com
(Reps for Directors of Photography)

Joe Arcidiacono — (917) 686-5091 / (212) 420-8845

Dominic Azoto — (917) 885-4998

Joaquin Baca-Asay — (310) 314-2606 / (917) 701-5753
www.stacycheriffagency.com

John Bailey — (310) 273-6700 / (212) 496-7042
www.utaproduction.com
(Film & High Def)

Florian Ballhaus — (323) 377-2242 / (310) 314-2606
www.florianstadler.com

Randall Balsmeyer — (212) 627-3430
FAX (212) 989-6528
www.bigfilmdesign.com
(Film, High Def, Second Unit & Special FX)

Larry Banks — (718) 264-2602
(Film & High Def)

Robert Barocci — (917) 545-0807
www.robertbarocci.com
(Film & High Def)

Michael F. Barrow — (212) 227-1156 / (917) 685-8139
(Film & High Def)

Peter Barrow — (917) 297-2056 / (845) 758-5714
www.peterbarrow.com
(Action Sports, Film, High Def & Remote Heads)

Michael Barry — (914) 241-2265 / (914) 649-3299
(Film & High Def)

Chris Bean — (212) 529-3100 / (203) 854-5067 / FAX (212) 529-9870
www.macguffin.com
(Film & High Def)

Kevan Bean — (212) 529-3100

Regis Becker — (410) 326-2329 / (410) 353-1857

Adam Beckman — (323) 460-4767
www.jacobandkoleagency.com
(Film & High Def)

Mark Benjamin — (212) 254-5285 / (917) 763-6370
(Film & High Def)

Carlos Bermudez — (617) 306-0976 / (781) 862-3979

Bernard Berner — (914) 329-4695
(Film & High Def)

David Bernkopf — (917) 842-8841
www.davidb-vfx.com
(Film, High Def & Special FX)

Nixon Binney — (845) 883-6956
(Film & High Def)

Peter Blanck — (914) 723-0564 / (413) 229-8951

Marc Blandori — (212) 533-3713 / (917) 854-9590
(Film & High Def)

Kip Bogdahn — (917) 742-2668 / (310) 314-2606
www.stacycheriffagency.com

Oliver Bokelberg — (212) 997-1818
www.gershagency.com

Stephen Bower — (203) 438-4487
FAX (203) 438-4549
www.stephenbower.com
(Film, Remote Heads, Second Unit & Underwater)

Mathew Brady — (212) 982-1010

Steve Brill — (212) 685-4940
FAX (212) 685-4927
www.ldg.com

Raymond Brislin — (571) 435-5144 / (910) 793-3029
(Film & High Def)

James Brown — (212) 505-0138
(Film & High Def)

John Budde — (212) 533-3138 / (646) 298-4611
(Film & High Def)

Bobby Bukowski — (310) 474-4585 / (505) 638-5326
www.dattnerdispoto.com
(Film & High Def)

Bill Burke — (267) 992-4548

Paolo Caimi — (212) 564-7892
www.sradp.com
(Film)

James Callanan — (718) 768-1085 / (917) 434-1910
(Film & High Def)

Murdoch Campbell — (301) 320-2996

Patrick Capone — (201) 944-2957 / (201) 739-9685

Michael Carmine — (718) 224-3355
FAX (718) 224-3355
www.mikecarmine.com
(Action Sports, Film, High Def, Second Unit & Special FX)

Dan Carp — (718) 981-3501 / (917) 833-2647
(Film & High Def)

David C. Castillo — (201) 795-1912
(Film & High Def)

Vanja Cernjul (Film & High Def)	(917) 446-2755	Andrew Dintenfass	(818) 753-6300 (212) 288-3530 www.themackagency.net
Giselle Chamma	(212) 366-9455 (917) 853-5764 www.gisellechamma.com	Richard Dobbs	(203) 373-0400
		Ben Dolphin	(212) 289-6232
Robert Chappell (Film & High Def)	(860) 677-7632 (323) 667-2565	Peter Donahue (Film & High Def)	(212) 346-7623 (310) 474-4585 www.dattnerdispoto.com
Allan Charles	(410) 986-1400	Dicran (Deke) Donelian (Film & High Def)	(212) 387-7955 (310) 395-9550 FAX (212) 217-2711 www.dekedonelian.com
Mihai Chebac (Film & High Def)	(617) 558-0688 (617) 964-9544		
Richard Chisolm	(410) 467-2997	Jack Donnelly (Film & High Def)	(914) 764-0917 FAX (914) 764-0951 www.jacobandkoleagency.com
Matthew Clark	(845) 735-5126 (917) 860-6209	Patrick Donnelly	(917) 371-4314
Charlie Cole	(213) 876-4040	Robert Draper	(818) 807-9381 (207) 236-6059
William Coleman	(212) 534-0142	Stuart Dryburgh	(917) 783-9117
Jeffrey Confer	(267) 968-5245		
Douglas Cooper (Film & High Def)	(646) 334-0985 (212) 477-8978	David M. Dunlap	(845) 677-8644 (845) 235-4562
		Robert Elliot (Film & High Def)	(212) 874-5509
Simon Coull	(310) 860-3741 www.simoncoull.com	Frederick Elmes	(914) 923-0337
Stefan Czapsky (Film & High Def)	(310) 474-4585 (607) 369-5504 www.dattnerdispoto.com	Gene Engels (Film)	(973) 875-8599 (201) 953-2283
David Dart	(609) 760-3599	Geoffrey Erb	(631) 728-3399 (526) 639-9390
Dattner Dispoto & Associates 10635 Santa Monica Blvd., Ste. 165 Los Angeles, CA 90025 (Reps for Directors of Photography)	(310) 474-4585 FAX (310) 474-6411 www.ddatalent.com	Evan Estern (Film & High Def)	(860) 824-4546
Don Davis (Film & High Def)	(631) 653-8030	Boyd Estus (Aerial, Film & High Def)	(617) 515-2090 (617) 876-7268
Scott Davis	(978) 363-5524 (978) 979-0475	Brant Fagan	(603) 826-3445 (203) 858-3998
Austin de Besche	(617) 510-0219 (781) 646-6004	Brian Fass	(212) 534-7594 (917) 532-6338 FAX (212) 534-7594 www.brianfass.com
Frank DeMarco (Film & High Def)	(917) 653-7010 (212) 929-5266		
Jim Denny (Film & High Def)	(212) 228-6944 (917) 913-5921	Jon Fauer (Film & High Def)	(212) 643-1736 (212) 570-2920 FAX (212) 643-1802 www.fauer.com
Joe DeSalvo (Film & High Def)	(818) 753-6300 (212) 732-1853 www.themackagency.net	Jim Fealy (Film)	(212) 228-0215 (310) 474-4585 www.dattnerdispoto.com
Jean de Segonzac	(212) 533-6362	Gerald Feil	(917) 414-8050 (917) 836-5000
Alan Deutsch (Film & High Def)	(212) 337-1017 (917) 226-6747	Alexander Fernbach (Film & High Def)	(201) 963-5900
Craig DiBona (Film & High Def)	(212) 535-9232 (323) 856-3000 www.thegelleragency.com	Peter Fernberger (Film & High Def)	(917) 701-9421
Richard DiGregorio	(617) 826-9607	Kenneth Ferris	(917) 288-1969 (570) 828-2736
Phil Dillon (Film & High Def)	(866) 625-7050 (404) 307-4904 www.tdnartists.com	Russell Fine (Film & High Def)	(310) 474-4585 (212) 620-4320 www.dattnerdispoto.com

Neil Fleitell	(301) 530-8958	James Gucciardo	(917) 518-6266
(Film & High Def)		(Film & High Def)	www.jimgucciardo.com

Neil Fleitell (301) 530-8958
(Film & High Def)

Stefan Forbes (917) 450-3847
(Film & High Def) www.freaktheframe.com

Herbert O. Forsberg (201) 652-6661
(Film) www.hforsberg.com

Joey Forsyte (310) 714-1702

Ron Fortunato (917) 776-9082

John Foster (718) 369-0404
(917) 407-0125
(Film & High Def)

Sergei Franklin (212) 228-4254
(646) 247-7871
www.sergeifranklin.com

Jonathan Freeman (212) 997-1818
(212) 579-8064
www.gershagency.com

Robert Gantz (203) 227-3260
(310) 474-4585
(Film & High Def) www.dattnerdispoto.com

John Gates (508) 655-1180
(Film & High Def)

Luke Geissbühler (917) 880-7118
(212) 634-8157
(Film & High Def) www.homepage.mac.com/lgdp

The Geller Agency (323) 856-3000
1547 Cassil Pl. FAX (323) 856-3009
Hollywood, CA 90028 www.thegelleragency.com
(Reps for Directors of Photography)

Dejan Georgevich (323) 856-6278
(212) 877-5561
(Film & High Def)

The Gersh Agency (212) 997-1818
41 Madison Ave., 33rd Fl. FAX (212) 997-1978
(Near E. 26th St.) www.gershagency.com
New York, NY 10010
(Reps for Directors of Photography)

Dan Gillham (212) 545-7895
(917) 224-6966
(Film & High Def) www.nyoffice.net

Michael Givens (843) 521-0558
(843) 252-1860
(Film & High Def) www.michaelgivens.com

Fritz Goforth (704) 362-3018
(704) 619-3093

Joseph Goldman (212) 777-0785
(646) 872-9194
(Film & High Def)

Patricia Govoni (323) 468-2240
(212) 989-0569

Arthur Green (845) 353-5428

Michael Green (201) 825-9248
(201) 788-3782
(Film & High Def)

Gary Grieg (202) 333-0778
(Film & High Def)

David Griffiths (212) 925-1530
(646) 269-0427
(Film & High Def) FAX (212) 925-1530
www.therighteye.com

James Gucciardo (917) 518-6266
(Film & High Def) www.jimgucciardo.com

Craig Haagensen (310) 463-5161
(973) 853-6853
(Film & High Def)

Rob Hahn (203) 222-8080

Robert Haley (908) 531-6305

Robert Hanna (646) 241-4849

Wolfgang Held (212) 545-7895
(212) 620-0029
(Film & High Def) www.nyoffice.net

Brian Heller (401) 751-1381
(Film & High Def)

Alec Hirschfeld (631) 329-9048
(631) 375-0840
FAX (631) 610-8272

Jeffrey Hirschorn (212) 979-8437
(212) 260-4211
(Film & High Def)

Petr Hlinomaz (212) 580-9867
(917) 355-6587
(Film & High Def)

Nicholas Hoffman (917) 843-3624
(Film, High Def & Remote Heads)

Adam Holender (212) 755-0325

Jerome Holway (610) 524-5979
(610) 659-7305
(Film & High Def) www.jerryholway.com

Tom Houghton (212) 690-1007
(323) 821-3351
(Film & High Def) FAX (212) 690-1026
www.tomhoughton.com

Timothy Housel (908) 237-1550
(908) 391-4630

Brian Rigney Hubbard (212) 997-1818
(917) 224-7213
(Film & High Def) www.vermillionsyndicate.com

John Hunter (212) 564-7892
(201) 693-6192
www.sradp.com

Mott Hupfel (310) 474-4585
(917) 698-1711
(Film & High Def) www.dattnerdispoto.com

Tom Hurwitz (212) 928-4466
(Film & High Def) FAX (212) 927-7302
www.tomhurwitz.com

Michael Huss (212) 688-5981
(917) 754-3123
(Film & High Def) FAX (212) 206-1538

Innovative Artists (212) 253-6900
235 Park Ave. South, Seventh Fl.
New York, NY 10003 www.innovativeartists.com
(Reps for Directors of Photography)

Thomas Inskeep (410) 727-0648
(410) 598-9753

David Insley (301) 509-9340
(Film & High Def)

Robert Ipcar (718) 499-9064
(Film & High Def)

Tim Ives (917) 685-5946 / (718) 875-1519
(Film & High Def) www.timives.com

The Jacob & Kole Agency (323) 460-4767
6715 Hollywood Blvd., Ste. 216 FAX (323) 460-4804
Los Angeles, CA 90028 www.jacobandkoleagency.com
(Reps for Directors of Photography)

Jamie Jacobson (970) 270-4639
(Film & High Def)

Anthony Jannelli (908) 273-9266
(Film & High Def)

Lukasz Jogalla (718) 369-1858 / (917) 770-3204
(Film & High Def)

Kevin Jones (323) 460-4767 / (917) 539-6970
(Film & High Def) www.jacobandkoleagency.com

Edward Joyce (781) 209-0980

Learan Kahanov (917) 680-4272
(Film & High Def) FAX (215) 647-4272
www.lkdp.com

Chaim Kantor (212) 647-7300
FAX (212) 647-7318
www.cameraguild.com

Thomas Kaufman (301) 891-3009

Stephen Kazmierski (323) 845-4144 / (212) 431-8239
www.montanartists.com

Ken Keller (212) 300-7094

Greg Kelly (301) 977-8922
(Film & High Def)

Glenn Kershaw (203) 451-3462 / (818) 509-5976

Kyle Kibbe (310) 474-4585 / (212) 242-2271
(Film) www.dattnerdispoto.com

David Kimelman (954) 347-0243 / (561) 392-1055
www.davidkimelman.tv

Adam Kimmel (212) 228-7523 / (323) 460-4767
(Film & High Def) FAX (212) 228-7523
www.jacobandkole.com

William Klayer (212) 539-1158 / (646) 287-2046

David Knox (914) 478-4416
(Film & High Def)

Gabor Kover (201) 461-4511 / (201) 741-2777
(Aerial, Film, High Def, Remote Heads & Second Unit)

Peter Kowalski (818) 384-3378
www.peterkowalski.com

Thomas Krueger (917) 363-4567

Ellen Kuras (310) 860-3741 / (917) 270-3708
(Film & High Def) www.utaproduction.com

Spencer Lasky (203) 858-9533

Ashley Lazarus (212) 724-7462 / (212) 877-1012
FAX (212) 724-9498

Robert Leacock (917) 797-7910
(Film & High Def)

Alan Lebow (718) 829-5663 / (917) 499-8298
(Film & High Def) www.alpdigital.com

Robert Lechterman (914) 582-9454
www.robertlechterman.com
(Film, High Def & Remote Heads)

Donald Lenzer (631) 267-6571
(Film & High Def)

Michael Lesser (212) 691-3859
(Film & High Def)

Samuel Levy (310) 474-4585 / (646) 263-0543
(Film) FAX (310) 474-6411
www.dattnerdispoto.com

Darren Lew (917) 690-7192 / (718) 596-6556
(Film & High Def)

Charles Libin (323) 460-4767 / (917) 747-3797
(Film & High Def) www.luminaria.net/reels/reelindex.html

Andy Lilien (646) 652-9985

Jeanne Lipsey (310) 395-9550 / (917) 699-0499
www.skouras.com

P. J. Lopez (787) 403-6936 / (787) 721-5247
(Film, High Def & Remote Heads)

Tom Lucak (631) 765-6559
(Film & High Def)

Bruce MacCallum (212) 935-1612
(Film & High Def)

The Mack Agency (818) 753-6300
5726 Woodman Ave., Ste. 4 FAX (818) 753-6311
Van Nuys, CA 91401 www.themackagency.net
(Reps for Directors of Photography)

Paul Magee (610) 623-4250
(Film & High Def) FAX (610) 623-4250

Constantine Makris (631) 477-5076 / (516) 742-6330

Jan Maliszewski (781) 861-6141 / (617) 212-2515
(Film & High Def)

Rick Malkames (914) 723-5558 / (914) 924-5558
(Film & High Def)

Tom Mangravite (212) 242-2475
(Film)

Teodoro Maniaci (212) 997-1818 / (718) 783-8295
www.gershagency.com

Phil Marco (212) 929-8082
FAX (212) 463-0514
www.philmarco.com

Barry Markowitz (917) 364-4392
(Film & High Def) www.jacobandkoleagency.com

Horacio Marquinez	(917) 885-8403
Edward Marritz	(917) 880-7839 (212) 222-9352
Igor Martinovic (Film & High Def)	(917) 304-6545
Michael Marzovilla (Film)	(212) 608-1822 (917) 402-8088
Peter Masterson	(603) 383-9586 (978) 505-0965
Joseph Matina (Film & High Def)	(516) 294-1038
Brian McAward	(860) 350-9445 (203) 241-5087
Jim McConkey (Film & High Def)	(914) 645-5953 (609) 397-6688
Larry McConkey	(609) 397-4702 (310) 557-9906 FAX (609) 397-4938
Michael McDonough	(310) 652-8778 (917) 957-2740 www.lspagency.net
Donald McIntosh (Film & High Def)	(781) 862-5534
Anastas Michos	(917) 923-8479 (212) 280-3129
Richard Miranda	(301) 469-8420
The Mirisch Agency 1925 Century Park East, Ste. 1070 Los Angeles, CA 90067 (Reps for Directors of Photography)	(310) 282-9940 FAX (310) 282-0702 www.mirisch.com
Montana Artists Agency 7715 W. Sunset Blvd., Third Fl. Los Angeles, CA 90046 (Reps for Directors of Photography)	(323) 845-4144 FAX (323) 845-4155 www.montanartists.com
David Morabito	(914) 232-3633 (917) 952-9500
Mark Moran	(603) 898-4911
Glen Mordeci (Film & High Def)	(917) 822-7932 www.sradp.com
Michael Moser (Action Sports & High Def)	(202) 293-1780 www.mosermedia.com
George Motz (Film & High Def)	(323) 460-4767 (718) 768-0019 FAX (212) 627-3844 www.jacobandkoleagency.com
John Moyer	(412) 741-2693 (412) 585-3613
Eric Moynier	(917) 318-9145 (818) 206-0144
Peter Mullett (Film)	(410) 804-2896
Fred Murphy	(212) 997-1818 (212) 608-3215 www.gershagency.com
Joshua S. Narins (Aerial, Second Unit & Underwater)	(917) 861-3060
Sol Negrin (Film & High Def)	(516) 287-3288 (631) 543-5032
Craig Nelson (Film & High Def)	(212) 535-4015
Peter Nelson (Film & High Def)	(845) 626-4502 (212) 505-7641
New York Office 15 W. 26th St., Fifth Fl. (Near Broadway) New York, NY 10010 (Reps for Directors of Photography)	(212) 545-7895 (323) 468-2240 FAX (212) 545-7941 www.nyoffice.net
Robert Newcomb (Film)	(704) 362-0552
Carl Norr	(917) 771-4125
Chris Norr (Film & High Def)	(323) 845-4144 (917) 407-8649 FAX (323) 845-4155 www.montanartists.com
Charles Norton	(617) 968-2136 (617) 876-2953
David Norton (Film & High Def)	(845) 657-2404 (310) 907-0703 www.skouras.com
Rob Nussbaum (Film & High Def)	(973) 865-0326 (973) 492-8056
Phil Oetiker (Film)	(718) 832-5854 (917) 279-6561
Yaron Orbach	(917) 443-0100
Orlando Management 15134 Martha St. Sherman Oaks, CA 91411 (Reps for Directors of Photography)	(818) 781-9233 www.orlandomanagement.com
Michael O'Shea (Film & High Def)	(610) 246-1218
Jerry Pantzer (Film & High Def)	(212) 222-7072 (917) 549-5787 FAX (212) 865-7272
Paradigm 360 Park Ave. South, 16th Fl. (Near Seventh Ave.) New York, NY 10010 (Reps for Directors of Photography)	(212) 897-6400 FAX (212) 764-8941 www.paradigmagency.com
Andrij Parekh (Film & High Def)	(310) 395-9550 (646) 644-1444 www.andrijparekh.com
David Park	(917) 439-9007 (212) 254-2746
Partos Company 227 Broadway, Ste. 204 Santa Monica, CA 90401 (Reps for Directors of Photography)	(310) 458-7800 FAX (310) 587-2250 www.partos.com
George Pattison (Film & High Def)	(631) 261-9115 (516) 527-9915
Guy Peires (Film & High Def)	(323) 791-3989
Dennis Peters	(917) 468-1564

Mark T. Petersson (Film & High Def)	(917) 992-0813 (518) 392-7860	Andrew Rowe (High Def)	(207) 837-9155 (207) 785-4380
Kate Phelan	(718) 789-2765 (917) 744-3327	Mauricio Rubinstein	(917) 747-8216 (212) 799-2790 www.jacobandkoleagency.com
David Phillips (Film & High Def)	(212) 643-2859 (310) 474-4585 www.dattnerdispoto.com	Robert Rudis (Film & High Def)	(914) 686-7289
Thomas Priestley (Film)	(910) 256-9066 (910) 297-3882	Manel Ruiz	(212) 966-3997 (917) 679-0022 www.dattnerdispoto.com
Frank Prinzi	(917) 842-9399 (917) 441-7524	Patrick Ruth (Film & High Def)	(617) 298-9899 (617) 308-0701
Fortunato Procopio (Film & High Def)	(917) 209-3427 www.fortunatoprocopio.com	Richard Rutkowski (Film & High Def)	(212) 732-9331 (917) 406-6657 www.360d.com/rr
Declan Quinn (Film & High Def)	(323) 460-4767 (845) 534-8148 www.jacobandkoleagency.com	Alik Sakharov (Film & High Def)	(201) 662-7072
Radiant Artists 6715 Hollywood Blvd., Ste. 220 Los Angeles, CA 90028 (Reps for Directors of Photography)	(323) 463-0022 FAX (323) 375-0231 www.radiantartists.com	Ryan Samul (Film & High Def)	(212) 997-1818 (917) 776-0847 www.ryansamul.com
Brent Ramsey (Film & High Def)	(303) 898-3894 (203) 461-9652	Matthew Santo	(646) 245-7617 (212) 472-7746
Gregory Ramsey	(212) 254-8929	Harris Savides (Film & High Def)	(310) 395-9550 (917) 991-7576 FAX (310) 395-4295
Manfred Reiff	(212) 786-4397 www.manfredreiff.com	Malik Sayeed	(917) 319-6555 (310) 474-4585 www.dattnerdispoto.com
Peter Reniers (Film & High Def)	(917) 861-6283	Peter Schnall	(917) 689-6039
William Rexer (Film & High Def)	(310) 395-9550 (212) 431-0362	Michael Schrom (Film)	(212) 239-3939
Robert Richman	(973) 509-7375	Jeff Schwartz (Film & High Def)	(718) 225-2583 (212) 206-1402 FAX (212) 206-1826 www.primalux.com
The Right Eye 41 Union Square West, Ste. 1004 (Near W. 16th St.) New York, NY 10003 (Reps for Directors of Photography)	(212) 924-8505 FAX (212) 924-8544 www.therighteye.com	Cosimo Scianna (Film & High Def)	(973) 726-3215
Lisa Rinzler	(212) 997-1818 (212) 431-0994 www.gershagency.com	Christopher Seivard	(717) 432-5865 (917) 952-4716
Eric Robbins	(646) 529-2508	Sesler & Company 11840 Jefferson Blvd. Culver City, CA 90230 (Reps for Directors of Photography)	(310) 966-4005 (416) 504-1223 FAX (323) 988-0930 www.seslercompany.com
Lawrence Robins (Film & High Def)	(802) 649-8988 (802) 233-2839 www.larryrobins.com	Sheldon Prosnit Agency 800 S. Robertson Blvd., Ste. 6 Los Angeles, CA 90035 (Reps for Directors of Photography)	(310) 652-8778 FAX (310) 652-8772 www.lspagency.net
Tom Robotham (Film & High Def)	(617) 817-5520 www.robotham.com		
Lesley Robson-Foster	(917) 621-7202 (310) 633-3435 www.robsonfoster.com	Bobby Shepard	(914) 557-5365 (914) 699-5342
Erich Roland	(703) 352-7855	Keith Sherer (Film, High Def, Second Unit & Special FX)	(843) 216-4813 (843) 327-0090
F. Michael Rose	(917) 231-6978		
Jamie Rosenberg www.sradp.com/?a=p&gid=75 (Action Sports, Aerial, Film, High Def, Remote Heads & Special FX)	(212) 741-0876 (212) 564-7892	Sherry Rousso Associates, Inc. One River Pl., Ste. 1828 (Near 12th Ave.) New York, NY 10036 (Reps for Directors of Photography)	(212) 564-7892 (212) 564-7893 FAX (212) 564-7849 www.sradp.com
		Daniel Shulman	(917) 533-5768

Rick Siegel (Film & High Def)	(917) 602-4499 / FAX (212) 202-3995 / www.rickspix.net
James Signorelli	(917) 817-3433
Jeffrey Silverman (Film & High Def)	(802) 368-2591
Michael Simmonds	(212) 673-2518 / (917) 848-2306
Jerry Simpson (Film & High Def)	(718) 349-9220
The Skouras Agency / 1149 Third St., Third Fl. / Santa Monica, CA 90403 / (Reps for Directors of Photography)	(310) 395-9550 / FAX (310) 395-4295 / www.skouras.com
Michael Slovis (Film & High Def)	(973) 746-5015 / (973) 632-3934 / www.thegelleragency.com
Brad Smith	(609) 234-0466 / (610) 845-0520
Michael Somoroff (Film & High Def)	(212) 529-3100
Jeri Sopanen	(212) 799-0679
Peter Sova (Film & High Def)	(212) 253-6900 / (607) 538-9355 / www.innovativeartists.com
David Sperling (Film & High Def)	(732) 530-7504 / www.onsetsoftware.com
Eugene Squires (Film & High Def)	(413) 369-4171
Terry Stacey (Film & High Def)	(310) 273-6700 / (917) 886-8784 / www.utaproduction.com
Stacy Cheriff Agency / 10923 Ayres Ave. / Los Angeles, CA 90064 / (Reps for Directors of Photography)	(310) 314-2606 / www.stacycheriffagency.com
Edward Stephenson (Film & High Def)	(516) 456-0461
Patricio Suarez (Film & High Def)	(212) 564-7892 / (914) 447-0226 / www.sradp.com
Santiago Suarez	(203) 536-2533 / (203) 661-5148
Tommy Sullivan (Film)	(910) 540-3695 / (910) 371-1180
Russell Swanson	(310) 248-2000 / (203) 470-9720 / www.russellswanson.net
Gabor Tarko (Film & High Def)	(917) 273-9611 / www.gabortarko.com
TDN Artists / 3685 Motor Ave., Ste. 220 / Los Angeles, CA 90034 / (Reps for Directors of Photography)	(818) 906-0006 / FAX (818) 301-2224 / www.tdnartists.com
John Thomas	(212) 253-6900 / (973) 783-7360 / www.innovativeartists.com
Stephen Thompson (Film & High Def)	(910) 512-0566 / (910) 845-2758
Romeo Tirone (Film & High Def)	(323) 460-4767 / (917) 385-9550 / www.jacobandkoleagency.com
William Trautvetter (Film & High Def)	(401) 847-4797 / (401) 935-4973
David Tuttman (Film & High Def)	(914) 584-7642 / (914) 923-0856
Anders Uhl	(631) 796-4841
United Talent Agency / 9560 Wilshire Blvd., Ste. 500 / Beverly Hills, CA 90212 / (Reps for Directors of Photography)	(310) 273-6700 / FAX (310) 247-1111 / www.unitedtalent.com
Thomas Vandergast	(610) 356-3404
Sonnel Velazquez	(787) 502-8846 / (310) 990-4325 / www.sonnelvelazquez.com
Pieter Vermeer (Film & High Def)	(818) 753-6300 / (917) 679-7328 / www.themackagency.net
Michael Vicarelli	(201) 679-1018
Robert Wagner (Film & High Def)	(212) 206-0003 / FAX (212) 206-0003 / www.robertwagnerfilms.com
David Waterston (Film & High Def)	(310) 474-4585 / www.dattnerdispoto.com
Susan Weber (Film & High Def)	(570) 223-8381
Gerald Wenner	(203) 410-3112 / (203) 773-0212
Julian West	(212) 807-8532
Thomas Weston (Film & High Def)	(201) 664-0404 / (201) 674-3314
George Wieser	(212) 564-7892 / (917) 912-2573 / www.sradp.com
Gordon Willis	(508) 540-8186
Bill Winters (Film & High Def)	(914) 672-2494 / www.billwinters.net
Anthony Wolberg (Film & High Def)	(310) 395-9550 / (718) 643-0017 / www.skouras.com
Richard Wood	(718) 981-0641
Phillip Wright	(757) 435-7646 / (757) 627-9996
Joseph Yacoe (Film & High Def)	(818) 753-6300 / (631) 680-6100 / www.themackagency.net
Joe Zizzo (Film & High Def)	(310) 395-9550 / (917) 952-8672 / www.skouras.com

Directors of Photography

Nasar Abich	(310) 652-8778
	www.lspagency.net
	(212) 545-7895
Damian Acevedo	(323) 468-2240
(Film & High Def)	www.nyoffice.net
	(310) 274-6611
Tom Ackerman	(212) 997-1818
	www.gershagency.com
Lance Acord	(310) 474-4585
	www.dattnerdispoto.com
Tom Agnello	(201) 741-4367
(Film)	
Brian Agnew	(310) 652-8778
	www.lspagency.net
Magni Agustsson	(310) 652-8778
	www.lspagency.net
Bill Ahrens	(212) 564-7892
	www.sradp.com
Maxime Alexandre	(310) 273-6700
	www.utaproduction.com
All Crew Agency	(818) 206-0144
2920 W. Olive Ave., Ste. 201	FAX (818) 206-0169
Burbank, CA 91505	www.allcrewagency.com
(Reps for Directors of Photography)	
Gonzalo Amat	(212) 897-6400
	www.paradigmagency.com
Ambitious Entertainment	(818) 990-8993
15120 Hartsook St., Ste. 1	www.ambitiousent.com
Sherman Oaks, CA 91403	
(Reps for Directors of Photography)	
Mitch Amundsen	(212) 997-1818
	www.gershagency.com
Tarin Anderson	(310) 652-8778
	www.lspagency.net
Gregory Andracke	(917) 414-4520
(Film, High Def & Second Unit)	
Daniel Aranyo	(310) 652-8778
	www.lspagency.net
Daniel Ardilley	(310) 652-8778
(Film & High Def)	www.lspagency.net
Sergio Arguello	(310) 314-2606
	www.stacycheriffagency.com

David A. Armstrong	(212) 253-6900
	www.innovativeartists.com
Randy Arnold	(310) 652-8778
	www.lspagency.net
John Aronson	(310) 822-9113
	www.murthaagency.com
Yorgos Arvanitis	(310) 652-8778
	www.lspagency.net
Howard Atherton	(310) 822-9113
	www.murthaagency.com
	(212) 625-9327
Atlantic Television, Inc.	(917) 568-7218
524 Broadway, Fourth Fl.	FAX (212) 625-9346
(Near Spring)	www.atlantictv.com
New York, NY 10012	
(Reps for Directors of Photography)	
Bernard Auroux	(310) 717-1428
(Film & High Def)	
Rebecca Baehler	(323) 460-4767
	www.jacobandkoleagency.com
Christopher Baffa	(310) 474-4585
	www.dattnerdispoto.com
Ian Baker	(310) 395-9550
	www.skouras.com
Tony Balderrama	(310) 314-2606
	www.stacycheriffagency.com
Alex Barber	(310) 474-4585
	www.dattnerdispoto.com
Mia Barker	(917) 494-6495
(Film & High Def)	www.skouras.com
Jeff Barklage	(866) 625-7050
(Film & High Def)	www.tdnartists.com
	(973) 508-6054
George Barnes	(305) 673-2737
John Barr	(310) 822-9113
	www.murthaagency.com
Michael Barrett	(310) 273-6700
	www.unitedtalent.com
John S. Bartley	(310) 822-9113
	www.murthaagency.com

SASAHARA

MARK SASAHARA
Director of Photography

Phantom HD Technician

(718) 440-1013

msasaharaphoto@mindspring.com

www.msasahara.com

Bojan Bazelli	(310) 474-4585 www.dattnerdispoto.com	John Boyd	(818) 990-8993 www.ambitiousent.com
Rhet Bear	(212) 253-6900 www.innovativeartists.com	Russell Boyd	(310) 822-9113 www.murthaagency.com
Christophe Beaucarne	(323) 460-4767 www.jacobandkoleagency.com	Geoff Boyle	(310) 474-4585 www.dattnerdispoto.com
Keith Behrle (Film & High Def)	(973) 464-1079 FAX (973) 228-6301	Tom Bracone (Film & High Def)	(845) 236-4097 (917) 301-5687 FAX (845) 236-1062 www.tombracone.com
Jonathan Belinski (Film & High Def)	(917) 882-0126 www.jonathanbelinski.com	Mike Braden (Film & High Def)	(585) 473-5303 (585) 615-6481 www.mikaren.com
Bruce Benedict	(212) 924-8505 (949) 837-5311 FAX (212) 924-8544 homepage.mac.com/cinebruce	Caroline Brandes	(212) 924-8505 www.therighteye.com
Peter Benison	(818) 206-0144 www.allcrewagency.com	Ira Brenner (Film & High Def)	(212) 724-4676 (917) 864-2100
Jeremy Benning	(310) 966-4005 www.seslercompany.com	Steve Brill	(212) 685-4940 FAX (212) 685-4927 www.ldg.com
Michael Berg	(845) 548-0352	Robert Brinkmann	(310) 822-9113 www.murthaagency.com
Andreas Berger	(310) 458-7800 www.partos.com	Mark Brinster (Film & High Def)	(818) 990-8993 www.ambitiousent.com
Michael D. Bernard (Film & High Def)	(310) 474-4585 (213) 353-9900 www.dattnerdispoto.com	Bryan Brousseau	(718) 626-6226 FAX (718) 626-1493 www.hscusa.tv
Lana Bernberg	(323) 845-4144 www.montanartists.com	Jeffrey T. Brown	(212) 643-1736 www.cec-entertainment.com
Paul Berner (Film & High Def)	(914) 282-1878 FAX (914) 967-8422	Nicolaj Bruel (Film & High Def)	(212) 253-6900 www.innovativeartists.com
Barry Berona	(818) 753-6300 www.themackagency.net	Eigil Bryld	(310) 395-9550 www.skouras.com
Alain Betrancourt (Film & High Def)	(310) 395-9550 www.skouras.com	Alexander Buono	(310) 474-4585 www.dattnerdispoto.com
John Beymer	(310) 306-8682 (917) 744-8706	Don Burgess	(212) 997-1818 www.gershagency.com
Adam Biddle	(818) 753-6300 www.themackagency.net	David Burr	(310) 822-9113 www.murthaagency.com
Christopher Bierlein (Film & High Def)	(917) 783-1062 (212) 260-1215 www.chrisbierlein.com	Stephen H. Burum	(310) 822-9113 www.murthaagency.com
Ivan Bird	(310) 474-4585 www.dattnerdispoto.com	Bill Butler (Film & High Def)	(212) 253-6900 www.innovativeartists.com
Stephen Blackman	(323) 463-0022 www.radiantartists.com	Patrick Cady	(212) 997-1818 www.gershagency.com
Jarin Blaschke	(212) 924-8505 www.therighteye.com	Greg Califano (Film)	(732) 208-6450 (732) 974-2012
Nigel Bluck	(310) 395-9550 www.skouras.com	Thomas Callaway	(323) 856-3000 www.thegelleragency.com
John Bonanno (Film)	(212) 932-1549	Paul Cameron (Film & High Def)	(310) 463-4640 www.dattnerdispoto.com
Norman Bonney	(212) 564-7892 www.sradp.com	Valentina Caniglia (Film & High Def)	(646) 387-3376 www.valentinacaniglia.net
Eli Born	(212) 897-6400 www.paradigmagency.com	James Carman (Film & High Def)	(917) 208-8806 FAX (212) 533-8806 www.timetravelerarts.com
Harlan Bosmajian	(646) 325-7921		
Chase Bowman	(212) 643-1736 www.cec-entertainment.com		

Russell Carpenter	(310) 474-4585 www.dattnerdispoto.com	Ericson Core	(212) 997-1818 www.gershagency.com
Andrew Carranza	(212) 924-8505 www.therighteye.com	Ivan Corona	(818) 753-6300 www.themackagency.net
Joe Caruso (Film & High Def)	(772) 234-3031	Adrian Correia	(212) 643-1736 www.cec-entertainment.com
Lula Carvalho	(212) 997-1818 www.gershagency.com	Mick Coulter	(310) 395-9550 www.skouras.com
Pedro Castro (Film & High Def)	(310) 652-8778 www.pedrocastro.net	Brandon Cox	(212) 253-6900 www.innovativeartists.com
Matthew Caton	(212) 924-8505 www.therighteye.com	Tom Cox	(212) 564-7892 www.sradp.com
Sarah Cawley	(212) 897-6400 www.paradigmagency.com	Nelson Cragg	(323) 856-3000 www.thegelleragency.com
Doug Chamberlain	(310) 458-7800 www.partos.com	Michael Crain	(917) 597-0037
Michael Chapman (High Def)	(310) 273-6700 www.utaproduction.com	Crew Connection (Referral for Directors of Photography)	(800) 352-7397 (303) 526-4900 FAX (303) 526-4901 www.crewconnection.com
Cliff Charles (Film & High Def)	(917) 709-6653 www.cliffcharles.com	Jeff Cronenweth	(310) 474-4585 www.dattnerdispoto.com
Chuy Chavez	(212) 997-1818 www.gershagency.com	Richard Crudo	(212) 643-1736 www.cec-entertainment.com
Claudio Chea	(212) 253-6900 www.innovativeartists.com	Jeffrey Cunningham	(212) 643-1736 www.cec-entertainment.com
Enrique Chediak (Film & High Def)	(310) 273-6700 www.unitedtalent.com	Joseph D'Alessandro (Film)	(910) 392-0387 (910) 352-7607
Christopher Chomyn	(323) 856-3000 www.thegelleragency.com	Paul Daley	(310) 314-2606 www.stacycheriffagency.com
James Chressanthis	(310) 652-8778 www.lspagency.net	Shane Daly	(310) 474-4585 www.dattnerdispoto.com
Chunghoon Chung	(310) 474-4585 www.dattnerdispoto.com	Michael Dana (Film)	(914) 263-7651 (207) 935-3079 www.nex10.com
Andrew Cifelli (Film & High Def)	(609) 298-2175 (609) 744-9675	Lee Daniel	(212) 997-1818 www.gershagency.com
David Claessen (Film & High Def)	(212) 897-6400 www.paradigmagency.com	Greg Daniels	(818) 753-6300 www.themackagency.net
Curtis Clark (Film & High Def)	(323) 460-4767 www.jacobandkoleagency.com	David Darby (Film & High Def)	(909) 626-7785 (212) 564-7892 FAX (909) 625-6925 www.daviddarby.com
Manuel Alberto Claro	(310) 652-8778 www.lspagency.net	Dattner Dispoto & Associates 10635 Santa Monica Blvd., Ste. 165 Los Angeles, CA 90025 (Reps for Directors of Photography)	(310) 474-4585 FAX (310) 474-6411 www.ddatalent.com
Jonathan Cliff	(310) 458-7800 www.partos.com		
Patrice Lucien Cochet	(212) 997-1818 www.gershagency.com	Didier Daubeach	(212) 564-7892 www.sradp.com
Joseph Colangelo	(818) 753-6300 www.themackagency.net	Allen Daviau	(310) 395-9550 www.skouras.com
Peter L. Collister	(212) 997-1818 www.gershagency.com	Elliot Davis	(310) 395-9550 www.skouras.com
Pierrot Colonna	(212) 564-7892 www.sradp.com	Benoit Debie	(310) 652-8778 www.lspagency.net
Joseph Consentino (Film & High Def)	(203) 241-5261 (203) 438-4460	Anghel Decca	(310) 273-6700 www.unitedtalent.com
Carolyn Constantine	(212) 924-8505 www.therighteye.com		

Directors of Photography

Bruno Delbonnel	(310) 273-6700 www.unitedtalent.com	Mark Eberle (Aerial)	(818) 906-0006 www.tdnartists.com
Ricardo Della Rosa	(310) 652-8778 www.lspagency.net	Eric Edwards (Film)	(212) 253-6900 www.innovativeartists.com
Antoine Denisov	(212) 924-8505 www.therighteye.com	David Eggby	(310) 822-9113 www.murthaagency.com
Darcy Dennett (High Def)	(917) 549-7787	Ron Egozi (Film, High Def & Remote Heads)	(917) 690-0573 www.ronegozi.com
Caleb Deschanel	(212) 997-1818 www.gershagency.com	Mark Ellensohn (Film & High Def)	(310) 503-0133 FAX (818) 502-1707
Ketil Dietrichson (Film & High Def)	(310) 652-8778 www.lspagency.net	Marc Laliberté Else (Film & High Def)	(310) 474-4585 www.dattnerdispoto.com
Joe di Gennaro (Film & High Def)	(818) 761-2377 (818) 749-4957 homepage.mac.com/joe.digennaro/	Robert Elswit	(310) 273-6700 www.unitedtalent.com
Patrick Michael Dolan (Film)	(310) 480-0507	Ross Emery	(310) 474-4585 www.dattnerdispoto.com
Lawrence Dolkart (Film & High Def)	(323) 463-0022 www.radiantartists.com	Kevin Emmons	(818) 906-0006 www.tdnartists.com
Mark Dombrow (Film & High Def)	(610) 291-3069	Eric Engler	(818) 753-6300 www.themackagency.net
Steve Drellich (Film & High Def)	(718) 781-3660	Everything Events & Entertainment, LLC 41 Watchung Plaza, Ste. 236 Montclair, NJ 07042 (Referral for Directors of Photography)	(973) 338-6995 (323) 230-5527 FAX (973) 200-4291 www.eeande.com
Dave Drez	(310) 314-2606 www.stacycheriffagency.com	Jallo Faber	(310) 273-6700 www.unitedtalent.com
David Dubois	(310) 652-8778 www.lspagency.net	Luca Fantini	(212) 564-7892 www.sradp.com
Predrag Dubravcic (Aerial, Film, High Def, Remote Heads, Special FX & Underwater)	(845) 704-7054 (323) 460-4767 www.predrag.net	Steven Fierberg (Film & High Def)	(323) 896-1777 (310) 246-3180 www.fierberg.com
Michael Duff (Film & High Def)	(914) 478-3871 (212) 924-8505 FAX (914) 478-2131	Steven Finestone (Film & High Def)	(310) 838-5698 (310) 713-9994 FAX (310) 558-4711
Mike Duff	(212) 924-8505 www.therighteye.com	Bruce L. Finn (Film & High Def)	(310) 317-1557 (323) 845-4144 FAX (310) 317-1558 www.montanartists.com
Simon Duggan	(310) 474-4585 www.dattnerdispoto.com	Dick Fisher (Film & High Def)	(520) 907-1900 (877) 489-8866 www.dickfisher.net
Ray Dumas (Film & High Def)	(310) 966-4005 www.seslercompany.com	Michael Fitzmaurice (Film)	(310) 458-7800 www.partos.com
Andrew Dunn	(310) 395-9550 www.skouras.com	Mo Flam (Film & High Def)	(551) 358-1449
Giles Dunning (Film & High Def)	(212) 253-6900 (310) 656-0400 www.innovativeartists.com	Tim Fleming	(212) 997-1818 www.gershagency.com
Marcos Durian	(818) 753-6300 www.themackagency.net	John C. Flinn	(212) 253-6900 www.innovativeartists.com
Patrick Duroux	(323) 460-4767 www.jacobandkoleagency.com	Larry Fong	(323) 460-4767 www.jacobandkoleagency.com
Marcelo Durst	(310) 458-7800 www.partos.com	Stephane Fontaine	(323) 460-4767 www.jacobandkoleagency.com
John Ealer (Film)	(212) 545-7895 www.nyoffice.net	Anthony Forma (High Def)	(914) 673-2170
Timothy Eaton (Film & High Def)	(866) 535-1972		

Mark Forman (High Def)	(212) 633-9960 (212) 633-8482 FAX (212) 807-0121 www.screeningroom.com
Crille Forsberg (Film & High Def)	(310) 273-6700 www.utaproduction.com
Ian Forsyth	(323) 460-4767 www.jacobandkoleagency.com
Eric Foster (Film & High Def)	(310) 652-8778 www.lspagency.net
Steve Fraasa (Film & High Def)	(323) 937-0677 (323) 365-0536 FAX (323) 937-0677 www.stevenfraasa.com
Robert Fraisse	(310) 474-4585 www.dattnerdispoto.com
Michael Franks (Film & High Def)	(212) 529-5126 (310) 839-8828 www.mfranks.com
Greig Fraser	(310) 273-6700 www.utaproduction.com
Patrick Fraser	(818) 753-6300 www.themackagency.net
Walt Fraser	(212) 253-6900 www.innovativeartists.com
David J. Frederick	(310) 261-3541 (310) 474-6299 www.soc.org
Christopher Freilich (Film & High Def)	(609) 439-2845 www.virtuosofilms.com
Jim Frohna	(310) 314-2606 www.stacycheriffagency.com
Tak Fujimoto	(310) 395-9550 www.skouras.com
Guy Furner	(212) 924-8505 www.therighteye.com
Vincent Galindez (Film)	(917) 771-0355
Scott Galinsky (Film & High Def)	(310) 395-9550 www.skouras.com
Joe Gallagher	(323) 856-3000 www.thegelleragency.com
Christopher Gallo	(818) 753-6300 www.themackagency.net
Omer Ganai	(310) 273-6700 www.unitedtalent.com
James Gardner (Film & High Def)	(310) 966-4005 www.seslercompany.com
Mark Garrett	(310) 474-4585 www.dattnerdispoto.com
Eric Gautier	(310) 652-8778 www.lspagency.net
David Geddes	(212) 253-6900 www.innovativeartists.com
Adam Geiger (Aerial, High Def & Underwater)	(774) 563-0068 (508) 645-2899 www.sealightpictures.com
The Geller Agency 1547 Cassil Pl. Hollywood, CA 90028 (Reps for Directors of Photography)	(323) 856-3000 FAX (323) 856-3009 www.thegelleragency.com
Darren Genet	(212) 253-6900 www.innovativeartists.com
The Gersh Agency 41 Madison Ave., 33rd Fl. (Near E. 26th St.) New York, NY 10010 (Reps for Directors of Photography)	(212) 997-1818 (310) 274-6611 FAX (212) 997-1978 www.gershagency.com
Helge Gerull	(310) 395-9550 www.skouras.com
Xavi Gimenez	(310) 652-8778 www.lspagency.net
Michael Giovingo (Film & High Def)	(212) 319-6555 (203) 421-3355 FAX (203) 421-3355
Steven Gladstone (Film & High Def)	(917) 886-5858 (718) 625-0556 FAX (718) 625-4921 www.gladstonefilms.com
Stephen Goldblatt	(310) 395-9550 www.skouras.com
Paul Goldsmith	(310) 474-4585 www.dattnerdispoto.com
Dana Gonzales	(310) 652-8778 www.lspagency.net
Magdalena Gorka	(818) 753-6300 www.themackagency.net
Stuart Graham	(323) 460-4767 www.jacobandkoleagency.com
Milton Grana-Mena (Film & High Def)	(787) 791-2878 (787) 431-1433
Joe Grasso (Film & High Def)	(212) 253-6900 www.innovativeartists.com
Kevin Graves	(323) 856-3000 www.thegelleragency.com
Jack Green	(212) 997-1818 www.gershagency.com
Jesse Green	(310) 395-9550 www.skouras.com
Adam Greenberg	(212) 997-1818 www.gershagency.com
Robbie Greenberg (Film)	(310) 458-7800 www.partos.com
David Gribble	(310) 652-8778 www.lspagency.net
Phil Gries (Film & High Def)	(516) 656-3456 (516) 317-8957 FAX (516) 656-5677 www.atvaudio.com
Xavier Perez Grobet	(310) 474-4585 www.dattnerdispoto.com
Charlie Gruet	(212) 564-7892 www.sradp.com

Directors of Photography

Slawomir Grunberg (High Def)	(917) 864-0715 (607) 589-4709 FAX (607) 589-6151 www.logtv.com/tv	Richard Henkels (Film & High Def)	(310) 273-6700 www.unitedtalent.com
Alexander Gruszynski	(212) 897-6400 www.paradigmagency.com	David Hennings	(212) 253-6900 www.innovativeartists.com
Ottar Gudnason	(310) 474-4585 www.dattnerdispoto.com	Scott Henriksen	(323) 460-4767 www.jacobandkoleagency.com
Eric Guichard	(323) 460-4767 www.jacobandkoleagency.com	Jonathan Herron	(718) 499-1763 (917) 748-1866 www.reelsondemand.com/jonherron
Sanji F. Gupta	(818) 906-0006 www.tdnartists.com	Ron Hersey	(323) 856-3000 www.thegelleragency.com
Eric J. Haase (Film & High Def)	(212) 253-6900 www.innovativeartists.com	Joshua Hess	(310) 395-9550 www.skouras.com
Ari Haberberg (Film & High Def)	(212) 533-2789 (917) 776-0015	Julien Hirsch	(310) 652-8778 www.lspagency.net
Grosvenor Miles Hafela (Film & High Def)	(617) 875-1737 (508) 833-4398 www.lightgatemedia.com	Julian Hohndorf	(310) 314-2606 www.stacycheriffagency.com
		Hank Holton	(609) 737-2659
Karl Hahn	(323) 460-4767 www.jacobandkoleagency.com	Nathan Hope	(310) 822-9113 www.murthaagency.com
Conrad Hall	(310) 395-9550 www.skouras.com	Doug Hostetter	(818) 753-6300 www.themackagency.net
Dennis S. Hall	(212) 253-6900 www.innovativeartists.com	John Houtman	(310) 966-4005 www.seslercompany.com
Geoffrey Hall	(310) 474-4585 www.dattnerdispoto.com	Angus Hudson	(310) 474-4585 www.dattnerdispoto.com
Amir Hamed	(212) 564-7892 www.sradp.com	Tim Hudson	(212) 545-7895 www.nyoffice.net
Peter Hannan	(310) 474-4585 www.dattnerdispoto.com	Paula Huidobro	(212) 997-1818 www.gershagency.com
Massimo Hanozet (Film & High Def)	(212) 564-7892 www.sradp.com	Rob Humphreys	(310) 458-7800 www.partos.com
Warren Hansen	(323) 460-4767 www.jacobandkoleagency.com	Jim Hunter	(818) 906-0006 www.tdnartists.com
Anthony Hardwick (Film & High Def)	(310) 463-9894 (212) 897-6400 www.paradigmagency.com	John Hunter (Film & High Def)	(212) 564-7892 www.sradp.com
Rob Hardy	(310) 474-4585 www.dattnerdispoto.com	Shane Hurlbut	(212) 997-1818 www.gershagency.com
Peter Hartmann (Film & High Def)	(310) 966-4005 www.seslercompany.com	Slawomir Idziak	(310) 395-9550 www.skouras.com
Jason Harvey	(818) 753-6300 (917) 913-1757 www.themackagency.net	Jakob Ihre	(310) 395-9550 www.skouras.com
Kim Mitchell Haun (Film & High Def)	(818) 501-4898 (818) 968-5111 FAX (818) 788-5633	Innovative Artists 235 Park Ave. South, Seventh Fl. New York, NY 10003 (Reps for Directors of Photography)	(212) 253-6900 www.innovativeartists.com
David Hausen (Film & High Def)	(212) 967-4080 (917) 312-3123 FAX (212) 941-3866 www.surreel.com	John Inwood (Film & High Def)	(917) 690-4313
		Judy Irola	(323) 856-3000 www.thegelleragency.com
Simon Hawken	(323) 463-0022 www.radiantartists.com	Matthew Irving	(212) 253-6900 www.innovativeartists.com
David Hellman	(310) 395-9550 www.skouras.com	Toby Irwin	(310) 273-6700 www.unitedtalent.com

Levie Isaacks (212) 253-6900
www.innovativeartists.com

Dave Isern (917) 913-2989
(323) 868-2492
(Film & High Def) www.daveisern.com

Mai Iskander (646) 515-5995
(310) 458-7800
(Film & High Def) www.partos.com

The Jacob & Kole Agency (323) 460-4767
6715 Hollywood Blvd., Ste. 216 FAX (323) 460-4804
Los Angeles, CA 90028 www.jacobandkoleagency.com
(Reps for Directors of Photography)

Frederik Jacobi (212) 545-7895
www.nyoffice.net

Igo Jadue-Lillo (323) 460-4767
www.jacobandkoleagency.com

Peter James (310) 395-9550
www.skouras.com

Alec Jarnagin (917) 804-6606
www.floatingcamera.com

Jendra Jarnagin (212) 643-1736
(718) 871-6683
FAX (309) 405-0526
www.floatingcamera.com

Johnny E. Jensen (212) 253-6900
www.innovativeartists.com

David Johnson (212) 997-1818
www.gershagency.com

Hugh Johnson (310) 822-9113
www.murthaagency.com

Shelly Johnson (323) 460-4767
www.jacobandkoleagency.com

Imre Juhasz (323) 788-4132
(212) 545-7895
(Film & High Def) www.imrejuhasz.net

Kristian Kachikis (310) 474-4585
www.dattnerdispoto.com

Emmanuel Kadosh (310) 474-4585
www.dattnerdispoto.com

Lance Kaplan (917) 318-3582
www.lancekaplan.com

Daniel Karp (818) 990-8993
(Film & High Def) www.ambitiousent.com

Glen Keenan (310) 966-4005
www.seslercompany.com

Steve Keith-Roach (310) 273-6700
www.unitedtalent.com

Gavin Kelly (323) 856-3000
www.thegelleragency.com

Ken Kelsch (818) 781-9233
(Film & High Def) www.orlandomanagement.com

Francis Kenny (212) 997-1818
www.gershagency.com

Scott Kevan (212) 997-1818
www.gershagency.com

Jan Kiesser (212) 253-6900
(Film & High Def) www.innovativeartists.com

Shawn Kim (310) 652-8778
www.lspagency.net

Jeffrey Kimball (818) 753-6300
www.themackagency.net

Jim Kimura (818) 906-0006
www.tdnartists.com

Sean Kirby (310) 652-8778
www.lspagency.net

Alar Kivilo (310) 273-6700
www.unitedtalent.com

Peter Klein (212) 564-7892
www.sradp.com

Thomas Kloss (310) 652-8778
(Film & High Def) www.lspagency.net

James Kniest (310) 966-4005
www.seslercompany.com

Douglas Koch (310) 966-4005
www.seslercompany.com

Matthias Koenigswieser (310) 652-8778
www.lspagency.net

Lajos Koltai (310) 395-9550
www.skouras.com

Peter Konczal (646) 765-5300
(732) 463-1568
(Film & High Def) FAX (732) 463-1568

Petra Korner (212) 253-6900
www.innovativeartists.com

Thomas Krueger (323) 460-4767
(Film & High Def) www.jacobandkoleagency.com

Howard Krupa (212) 625-9327
(917) 647-9750
(Film) www.atlantictv.com

Alwin Kuchler (212) 997-1818
www.gershagency.com

Jules Labarthe (917) 370-8622

Flavio Labiano (310) 474-4585
www.dattnerdispoto.com

Ed Lachman (310) 273-6700
(Film) www.utaproduction.com

Kjell Lagerroos (310) 474-4585
www.dattnerdispoto.com

Alex Lamarque (212) 253-6900
www.innovativeartists.com

Rod Lamborn (212) 545-7895
(Film & High Def) www.nyoffice.net

John Landi (732) 236-1296
(732) 238-0562
(High Def)

Stöps Langensteiner (310) 652-8778
www.lspagency.net

Christophe Lanzenberg (310) 273-6700
(Film & High Def) www.unitedtalent.com

David Lanzenberg (310) 395-9550
www.skouras.com

Andre Lascaris (212) 253-6900
www.innovativeartists.com

Directors of Photography

Chris Lavasseur	(212) 643-1736	Julio Macat	(310) 652-8778
	www.cec-entertainment.com		www.lspagency.net

Jim LeBlanc   (619) 563-0173 / (619) 778-4433
(Film & High Def)

Matthew MacCarthy   (212) 643-1736
www.cec-entertainment.com

Jason Lehel   (212) 253-6900
www.innovativeartists.com

The Mack Agency   (818) 753-6300
5726 Woodman Ave., Ste. 4   FAX (818) 753-6311
Van Nuys, CA 91401   www.themackagency.net
(Reps for Directors of Photography)

Denis Lenoir   (310) 652-8778
www.lspagency.net

Peter Mackay   (212) 564-7892
www.sradp.com

John R. Leonetti   (212) 997-1818
(Film & High Def)   www.gershagency.com

Dylan Macleod   (310) 966-4005
www.seslercompany.com

Yorick Le Saux   (310) 652-8778
www.lspagency.net

Glen MacPherson   (310) 822-9113
www.murthaagency.com

Andrew Lesnie   (310) 273-6700
www.unitedtalent.com

Eric Maddison   (310) 474-4585
www.dattnerdispoto.com

Philippe Le Sourd   (310) 395-9550
www.skouras.com

Chris Magee   (818) 906-0006
www.tdnartists.com

Chuck Levey   (917) 992-2026
(Film & High Def)

Scott Maguire   (917) 648-5492
www.scottmaguire.com

Robert Levi   (917) 334-9610 / (212) 777-6933
(Film & High Def)   FAX (212) 253-0330

Denis Maloney   (212) 253-6900
www.innovativeartists.com

Jordan Levy   (310) 314-2606
(Film & High Def)   www.jordanlevy.com

Chris Manley   (310) 652-8778
www.lspagency.net

Peter Levy   (310) 822-9113
www.murthaagency.com

David Mansfield   (212) 875-1507 / (917) 859-1115
(Aerial, High Def & Underwater)   FAX (917) 875-1507
www.wrenvideo.com

Rain Li   (212) 253-6900
www.innovativeartists.com

Rich Marino   (978) 807-9197
(High Def)   www.richmarino.com

Matthew Libatique   (310) 273-6700
www.unitedtalent.com

Stephen Marro   (212) 387-0057

Jong Lin   (310) 652-8778
www.lspagency.net

Adam Marsden   (310) 966-4005
www.seslercompany.com

Karl Walter Lindenlaub   (310) 395-9550
www.skouras.com

Nicola Marsh   (212) 253-6900
www.innovativeartists.com

Joe Livolsi   (631) 327-3516
www.crabmeadowfilms.com

Pascal Marti   (212) 545-7895
(Film)   www.nyoffice.net

Walt Lloyd   (818) 753-6300
www.themackagency.net

Alejandro Martinez   (310) 652-8778
www.lspagency.net

Mateo Londono   (310) 474-4585
(Film)   www.dattnerdispoto.com

Thomas Marvel   (310) 474-4585
www.dattnerdispoto.com

Gordon Lonsdale   (212) 253-6900
www.innovativeartists.com

Bryan Maslin   (585) 820-6099
(Film & High Def)   www.maslindigital.tv

Rick Lopez   (212) 545-7895
www.nyoffice.net

Steve Mason   (310) 822-9113
www.murthaagency.com

Vic Losick   (212) 580-1266
(Film & High Def)   FAX (212) 580-3444
www.viclosick.com

Shawn Maurer   (212) 253-6900
(Film & High Def)   www.innovativeartists.com

Patrick Loungway   (818) 519-1190

Tim Maurice-Jones   (310) 273-6700
www.unitedtalent.com

Emmanuel Lubezki   (323) 460-4767
www.jacobandkoleagency.com

Jamie Maxtone-Graham   (323) 856-3000
www.thegelleragency.com

Franz Lustig   (323) 460-4767
www.jacobandkoleagency.com

Joe Maxwell   (818) 753-6300
(Film & High Def)   www.themackagency.net

John Lynch   (310) 395-9550
www.skouras.com

Marco Mazzei   (818) 753-6300
www.themackagency.net

Chris Mably   (310) 458-7800
www.partos.com

Don McAlpine	(212) 997-1818	Claudio Miranda	(310) 474-4585
	www.gershagency.com		www.dattnerdispoto.com

Michelle McCabe — (917) 443-5361
www.michellemccabe.com

The Mirisch Agency — (310) 282-9940
1925 Century Park East, Ste. 1070   FAX (310) 282-0702
Los Angeles, CA 90067   www.mirisch.com
(Reps for Directors of Photography)

John McCally — (203) 222-8003
(Film & High Def)

Danny Moder — (212) 253-6900
www.innovativeartists.com

Russ McElhatton — (323) 856-3000
www.thegelleragency.com

Amir Mokri — (818) 753-6300
www.themackagency.net

Patrick McGowan — (310) 314-2606
www.stacycheriffagency.com

Tony Molina — (310) 474-4585
www.dattnerdispoto.com

Martin McGrath — (323) 460-4767
www.jacobandkoleagency.com

Jo Molitoris — (310) 474-4585
www.dattnerdispoto.com

Tom McGrath — (310) 474-4585
www.dattnerdispoto.com

Montana Artists Agency — (323) 845-4144
7715 W. Sunset Blvd., Third Fl.   FAX (323) 845-4155
Los Angeles, CA 90046   www.montanartists.com
(Reps for Directors of Photography)

Kieran McGuigan — (310) 273-6700
www.utaproduction.com

Christopher TJ McGuire — (310) 652-8778
www.lspagency.net

George Mooradian — (818) 753-6300
www.themackagency.net

Derek McKane — (310) 395-9550
(Film & High Def)   www.skouras.com

Reed Dawson Morano — (631) 834-7126
(Aerial, Film & High Def)   www.reedmorano.com

Kevin McKnight — (212) 564-7892
www.sradp.com

Donald M. Morgan — (323) 856-3000
www.thegelleragency.com

Robert McLachlan — (310) 273-6700
www.unitedtalent.com

Damien Morisot — (212) 545-7895
(Film)   www.nyoffice.net

Stephen McNutt — (212) 253-6900
www.innovativeartists.com

David Morrison — (323) 463-0022
(Film & High Def)   www.radiantartists.com

Joe Meade — (718) 966-1774
(Film & High Def)

Steven Moses — (323) 460-4767 / (323) 463-0022
www.jacobandkoleagency.com

Phil Meheux — (310) 395-9550
www.skouras.com

Peter Moss — (818) 906-0006
www.tdnartists.com

Sharon Meir — (212) 997-1818
www.gershagency.com

Motion Odyssey, Inc. — (917) 597-0037
www.motionodyssey.com
(Reps for Directors of Photography)

Alex Melman — (212) 997-1818
www.gershagency.com

David Moxness — (310) 474-4585
www.dattnerdispoto.com

Peter Menzies, Jr. — (310) 395-9550
www.skouras.com

Steven Faulkner Moyer — (917) 806-6814
(Film, High Def, Second Unit, Special FX & Underwater)

Hilda Mercado — (323) 460-4767
www.jacobandkoleagency.com

M. David Mullen — (212) 545-7895
(Film & High Def)   www.nyoffice.net

Simon Mestel — (310) 966-4005
(Film & High Def)   www.seslercompany.com

Robby Muller — (310) 822-9113
www.murthaagency.com

Ron Michaud — (860) 523-8948 / (203) 982-6420
(Film & High Def)

The Murtha Agency — (310) 822-9113
4240 Promenade Way, Ste. 232   FAX (310) 822-6662
Marina Del Rey, CA 90292   www.murthaagency.com
(Reps for Directors of Photography)

Sion Michel — (212) 564-7892
www.sradp.com

Gary Nardilla — (212) 315-4855
(Film & High Def)   FAX (212) 586-1572
www.citicam.net

James Miller — (212) 772-0800

Jonathan Miller — (917) 865-7106
FAX (347) 402-8545
www.millerfilms.com

Guillermo Navarro — (310) 458-7800
(Film)   www.partos.com

Scott Miller — (310) 652-8778
www.lspagency.net

Michael Negrin — (212) 253-6900
www.innovativeartists.com

Dan Mindel — (310) 395-9550
www.skouras.com

Arlene Nelson — (818) 753-6300
www.themackagency.net

Charles Minsky — (212) 253-6900
www.innovativeartists.com

Alex Nepomniaschy — (212) 253-6900
www.innovativeartists.com

Mathias Neumann	(310) 474-4585 www.dattnerdispoto.com	Barry Parrell	(310) 966-4005
Robert New	(212) 253-6900 www.innovativeartists.com	Partos Company 227 Broadway, Ste. 204 Santa Monica, CA 90401 (Reps for Directors of Photography)	(310) 458-7800 FAX (310) 587-2250 www.partos.com
New York Office 15 W. 26th St., Fifth Fl. (Near Broadway) New York, NY 10010 (Reps for Directors of Photography)	(212) 545-7895 (323) 468-2240 FAX (212) 545-7941 www.nyoffice.net	Vincent Passeri	(818) 753-6300 www.themackagency.net
		Heloisa Passos	(310) 395-9550 www.skouras.com
Spencer Newman (Film & High Def)	(310) 458-7800 (310) 358-7619 www.partos.com	Peter Pau	(212) 997-1818 www.gershagency.com
Christopher Nibley (Film & High Def)	(818) 509-0613 www.nibley.com	Wayne Paull (Film & High Def)	(203) 227-9020 (203) 247-2414
Bridger Nielson	(323) 460-4767 www.jacobandkoleagency.com	Daniel Pearl	(818) 753-6300 www.themackagency.net
Carl Nilsson	(310) 474-4585 www.dattnerdispoto.com	Christopher Pearson	(310) 652-8778 www.lspagency.net
Vasco Nunes (Film)	(212) 545-7895 www.nyoffice.net	Nicola Pecorini	(310) 395-9550 www.skouras.com
Giles Nuttgens	(310) 474-4585 www.dattnerdispoto.com	Bob Pendar-Hughes	(323) 463-0022 www.radiantartists.com
Brian Ochrym (Film & High Def)	(973) 300-9477 (888) 746-6869 FAX (973) 300-9467 www.mirageproductions.com	Luis Perez	(310) 474-4585 www.dattnerdispoto.com
		Michael Pescasio	(212) 897-6400 www.paradigmagency.com
Sean O'Dea	(310) 474-4585 www.dattnerdispoto.com	Barry Peterson	(310) 273-6700 www.utaproduction.com
Rene Ohashi (Film & High Def)	(310) 966-4005 www.seslercompany.com	Sebastian Pfaffenbichler	(310) 395-9550 www.skouras.com
Daryn Okada	(310) 822-9113 www.murthaagency.com	Kevin Phillips	(212) 897-6400 www.paradigmagency.com
Ruben O'Malley (Film)	(718) 986-4858 www.rubenomalley.com	Tim Philo (Film & High Def)	(718) 499-0596 (718) 344-0319
Orlando Management 15134 Martha St. Sherman Oaks, CA 91411 (Reps for Directors of Photography)	(818) 781-9233 www.orlandomanagement.com	André Pienaar (Film & High Def)	(310) 458-7800 www.partos.com
Tim Orr (Film & High Def)	(646) 642-9089 www.utaproduction.com	Tony Pierce-Roberts	(310) 395-9550 www.skouras.com
Jeff E. Orsa	(323) 460-4767 www.jacobandkoleagency.com	Timothy Pike	(310) 395-9550 www.skouras.com
Toshiaki Ozawa (Film & High Def)	(908) 281-4057 (310) 474-4585 FAX (310) 474-6411 www.dattnerdispoto.com	Aaron Platt	(212) 545-7895 www.nyoffice.net
		Zoran Popovic	(212) 253-6900 www.innovativeartists.com
Angelo Pacifici (Film & High Def)	(310) 313-3762 (818) 990-8993 www.ambitiousent.com	Steven Poster	(213) 819-0000 (310) 205-5812 www.gershagency.com
Gyula Pados	(310) 395-9550 www.skouras.com	Thierry Pouget	(212) 545-7895 www.nyoffice.net
Tony Pagano (Film & High Def)	(914) 645-2748 (914) 533-2890 FAX (914) 533-6406	Tico Poulakakis	(310) 458-7800 www.partos.com
Briggs Palmer	(818) 591-2972 FAX (818) 591-2972 www.briggspalmer.com	Robert Primes	(212) 253-6900 www.innovativeartists.com
Phedon Papamichael (Film & High Def)	(212) 253-6900 www.innovativeartists.com	Christopher Probst	(310) 652-8778 www.lspagency.net

Wei K. Pun   (917) 215-4028 / (310) 314-2606
www.weidp.com
(Action Sports, Aerial, Film, High Def, Remote Heads, Second Unit, Special FX & Steadicam)

Radiant Artists   (323) 463-0022
6715 Hollywood Blvd., Ste. 220   FAX (323) 375-0231
Los Angeles, CA 90028   www.radiantartists.com
(Reps for Directors of Photography)

Stephen Ramsey   (310) 429-2541 / (323) 650-4974
(Film & High Def)

Claudia Raschke-Robinson   (917) 349-2112 / (212) 941-4075
(Film & High Def)   FAX (212) 941-4076
www.claudiaraschke.com

Richard Rawlings Jr.   (310) 822-9113
www.murthaagency.com

Larry Reibman   (310) 251-2956
(Film & High Def)

Tami Reiker   (310) 474-4585
www.dattnerdispoto.com

Gosta Reiland   (310) 395-9550
www.skouras.com

Marc Reshovsky   (818) 753-6300
www.themackagency.net

Robert Richardson   (310) 395-9550
www.skouras.com

Ross Richardson   (310) 395-9550
(Film & High Def)   www.skouras.com

Bob Richman   (323) 460-4767
(Film & High Def)   www.jacobandkoleagency.com

Anthony B. Richmond   (310) 273-6700
www.unitedtalent.com

Tom Richmond   (310) 273-6700
www.unitedtalent.com

Jan Richter-Friis   (310) 474-4585
(Film)   www.dattnerdispoto.com

Peter Rieveschl   (917) 656-7667
(Film & High Def)   FAX (212) 202-4016

The Right Eye   (212) 924-8505
41 Union Square West, Ste. 1004   FAX (212) 924-8544
(Near W. 16th St.)   www.therighteye.com
New York, NY 10003
(Reps for Directors of Photography)

Heimo P. Ritzinger   (818) 906-0006
www.tdnartists.com

Neil Roach   (323) 460-4767
www.jacobandkoleagency.com

Timm Roarke   (323) 460-4767
www.jacobandkoleagency.com

Jim Roberson   (323) 856-3000
www.thegelleragency.com

Eliot Rockett   (323) 856-3000
www.thegelleragency.com

Bill Roe   (310) 822-9113
www.murthaagency.com

Sonja Rom   (310) 474-4585
www.dattnerdispoto.com

Serge Roman   (212) 564-7892
www.sradp.com

Pete Romano   (310) 822-9113
(Underwater)   www.murthaagency.com

Chuck Rosher   (310) 788-0684 / (212) 371-6269
www.oraclecreative.com

Pierre Rouger   (310) 474-4585
www.dattnerdispoto.com

Philippe Rousselot   (212) 997-1818
www.gershagency.com

Martin Ruhe   (310) 474-4585
www.dattnerdispoto.com

Danny Ruhlmann   (310) 474-4585
www.dattnerdispoto.com

Juan Ruiz-Anchia   (212) 997-1818
www.gershagency.com

Ruben F. Russ   (323) 460-4767
www.jacobandkoleagency.com

Nic Sadler   (323) 460-4767
www.jacobandkoleagency.com

Gilbert Salas   (310) 314-2606
www.stacycheriffagency.com

Andres E. Sanchez   (310) 314-2606
www.stacycheriffagency.com

Linus Sandgren   (310) 395-9550
www.skouras.com

Peter Santoro   (818) 326-8548 / (818) 769-7688
(Film & High Def)   FAX (818) 985-8131

Christopher Sargent   (310) 395-9550
www.skouras.com

Ricardo Sarmiento   (917) 539-7467
(Film & High Def)   FAX (212) 995-8582
www.sarmientofilms.com

Nick Sawyer   (310) 474-4585
www.dattnerdispoto.com

Giorgio Scali   (818) 753-6300
www.themackagency.net

Tobias Schliesser   (310) 395-9550
www.skouras.com

Austin Schmidt   (212) 643-1736
www.cec-entertainment.com

Greg Schmitt   (323) 463-0022
www.radiantartists.com

Aaron Schneider   (212) 253-6900
www.innovativeartists.com

Megan Schoenbachler   (212) 545-7895
(Film)   www.nyoffice.net

Abe Schrager   (718) 263-0010 / (347) 806-1101
FAX (718) 577-9966

John Schwartzman   (310) 822-9113
www.murthaagency.com

Carlo Scialla   (212) 564-7892
(Film, High Def, Second Unit & Special FX)   www.sradp.com

John Seale	(310) 822-9113 www.murthaagency.com	John Simmons	(818) 753-6300 www.themackagency.net
Peter Selesnick (Film & High Def)	(323) 460-4767 www.jacobandkoleagency.com	Geoffrey Simpson	(310) 822-9113 www.murthaagency.com
Gil Seltzer (Film, High Def, Remote Heads, Second Unit & Special FX)	(917) 309-4848 www.gilseltzerdp.com	Patrick Simpson	(818) 753-6300 www.themackagency.net
		Scott Sinkler (High Def)	(917) 446-8977 www.publiceyeproductions.com
Ben Semanoff	(212) 688-5490 (877) 786-7428 FAX (800) 505-1329 www.bensemanoff.com	Sandi Sissel	(212) 997-1818 www.gershagency.com
Ken Seng (Film)	(718) 755-7100	The Skouras Agency 1149 Third St., Third Fl. Santa Monica, CA 90403 (Reps for Directors of Photography)	(310) 395-9550 FAX (310) 395-4295 www.skouras.com
Ben Seresin	(310) 395-9550 www.skouras.com	D. Matthew Smith	(323) 460-4767 www.jacobandkoleagency.com
Michael Seresin	(310) 395-9550 www.skouras.com	Jonathan Smith (Film & High Def)	(646) 552-5747
Eduardo Serra	(310) 273-6700 www.unitedtalent.com	Neil Smith	(516) 671-8435 (516) 458-7518 FAX (516) 671-2853
Sesler & Company 11840 Jefferson Blvd. Los Angeles, CA 90230 (Reps for Directors of Photography)	(310) 966-4005 (416) 504-1223 FAX (323) 988-0930 www.seslercompany.com	Noah David Smith (Film & High Def)	(917) 882-9127 www.noahdavidsmith.com
Jamie Sewell	(323) 460-4767 www.jacobandkoleagency.com	Ben Smithard	(310) 474-4585 www.dattnerdispoto.com
Byron Shah	(212) 997-1818 www.gershagency.com	Scott Sniffen (Film & High Def)	(212) 354-7741 (203) 982-5142 www.sniffen.com
Afshin Shahidi	(818) 753-6300 www.themackagency.net	Jim Sofranko (Film)	(845) 657-2099 (212) 545-7895 FAX (845) 657-5876 www.nyoffice.net
Neil Shapiro	(310) 395-9550 www.skouras.com		
Gary Shaw (Film)	(212) 564-7892 www.sradp.com	Eduardo Martinez Solares	(310) 652-8778 www.lspagency.net
Sheldon Prosnit Agency 800 S. Robertson Blvd., Ste. 6 Los Angeles, CA 90035 (Reps for Directors of Photography)	(310) 652-8778 FAX (310) 652-8772 www.lspagency.net	Paul Sommers	(212) 997-1818 www.gershagency.com
		Todd Antonio Somodevilla (Film & High Def)	(323) 463-0022 www.radiantartists.com
Scott Shelley (High Def)	(917) 318-6797	Christopher Soos (Film & High Def)	(323) 460-4767 www.jacobandkoleagency.com
Jas Shelton	(310) 652-8778 www.lspagency.net	Dickson Sorensen (Film & High Def)	(215) 598-8177 www.sorensenfilm.com
Bob Shenise (High Def)	(800) 476-3702 (518) 489-1037 www.sheniseproductions.com	Glynn Speeckaert	(310) 474-4585 www.dattnerdispoto.com
Roger Sherman (Film & High Def)	(212) 980-5966 FAX (212) 980-5944 www.florentinefilms.com/sherman	Dante Spinotti	(310) 822-9113 www.murthaagency.com
		Stephen St. John	(310) 474-4585 www.dattnerdispoto.com
Sherry Rousso Associates, Inc. One River Pl., Ste. 1828 (Near 12th Ave.) New York, NY 10036 (Reps for Directors of Photography)	(212) 564-7892 (212) 564-7893 FAX (212) 564-7849 www.sradp.com	Stacy Cheriff Agency 10923 Ayres Ave. Los Angeles, CA 90064 (Reps for Directors of Photography)	(310) 314-2606 www.stacycheriffagency.com
Andrew Shulkind	(212) 897-6400 www.paradigmagency.com	Florian Stadler (Film & High Def)	(323) 377-2242 (310) 314-2606 www.florianstadler.com
Newton Thomas Sigel	(310) 474-4585 www.dattnerdispoto.com	John Stanier	(310) 395-9550 www.skouras.com
Jamie Silverstein	(718) 369-9891 (917) 796-4217	Brendan Steacy	(310) 966-4005 www.seslercompany.com

Donny Stegall (High Def)	(732) 742-8222 (732) 448-1895	**Hernan Toro** (Film & High Def)	(917) 412-4777 www.hernantoro.com
Ueli Steiger (Film)	(310) 458-7800 www.partos.com	**Salvatore Totino**	(310) 395-9550 www.skouras.com
Henrik Stenberg	(310) 474-4585 www.dattnerdispoto.com	**Luciano Tovoli**	(323) 460-4767 www.jacobandkoleagency.com
Robert Stevens	(310) 652-8778 www.lspagency.net	**Stacy Toyama**	(212) 564-7892 www.sradp.com
Tony Stewart (Film & High Def)	(866) 725-7714 (609) 462-7361 FAX (609) 883-5919 www.stewartfilms.com	**Eric Treml**	(310) 474-4585 www.dattnerdispoto.com
		Massimiliano Trevis	(310) 474-4585 www.dattnerdispoto.com
David Stockton	(310) 474-4585 www.dattnerdispoto.com	**Sergey Trofimov**	(310) 474-4585 www.dattnerdispoto.com
Rogier Stoffers	(323) 460-4767 www.jacobandkoleagency.com	**Wyatt Troll**	(310) 474-4585 www.dattnerdispoto.com
John Stokes	(310) 822-9113 www.murthaagency.com	**Andrew Turman**	(310) 395-9550 www.skouras.com
Dan Stoloff (Film & High Def)	(212) 897-6400 www.paradigmagency.com	**Kasper Tuxen**	(310) 652-8778 www.lspagency.net
Ivan Strasburg	(310) 652-8778 www.lspagency.net	**David Ungaro**	(310) 652-8778 www.lspagency.net
Valdimir Subotic	(212) 545-7895 www.nyoffice.net	**United Talent Agency** 9560 Wilshire Blvd., Ste. 500 Beverly Hills, CA 90212 (Reps for Directors of Photography)	(310) 273-6700 FAX (310) 247-1111 www.unitedtalent.com
Tim Suhrstedt	(212) 253-6900 www.innovativeartists.com		
Igor Sunara (Film & High Def)	(212) 439-1569	**Jordan Valenti** (Film & High Def)	(310) 652-8778 www.lspagency.net
Bruce Surtees	(212) 997-1818 www.gershagency.com	**Stephane Vallee**	(323) 460-4767 www.jacobandkoleagency.com
Peter Suschitzky	(310) 395-9550 www.skouras.com	**Brett Van Dyke**	(310) 966-4005 www.seslercompany.com
Darko Suvak (Film & High Def)	(310) 273-6700 www.unitedtalent.com	**Joost van Gelder**	(310) 273-6700 www.unitedtalent.com
David Taicher (Film & High Def)	(610) 640-0303 (610) 633-3000 FAX (610) 640-0304	**Joost Van Starrenburg** (Film & High Def)	(323) 460-4767 www.jacobandkoleagency.com
		Riego Van Wersh	(323) 460-4767 www.jacobandkoleagency.com
Jonathan Taylor	(310) 652-8778 www.lspagency.net	**Jan Velicky**	(310) 273-6700 www.unitedtalent.com
Nick Taylor	(323) 460-4767 www.jacobandkoleagency.com	**Billy Velten**	(818) 906-0006 www.tdnartists.com
Rodney Taylor	(310) 474-4585 www.dattnerdispoto.com	**Jeffrey Venditti** (Film & High Def)	(310) 656-0400 (310) 663-7677 www.innovativeartists.com
TDN Artists (Reps for Directors of Photography)	(818) 906-0006 FAX (818) 301-2224 www.tdnartists.com		
Marten Tedin	(323) 460-4767 www.jacobandkoleagency.com	**Alex Vendler** (Film & High Def)	(212) 545-7895 www.nyoffice.net
Carl Teitelbaum (Film)	(212) 431-3860	**Carlos Veron**	(310) 395-9550 www.skouras.com
Simon Thirlaway	(310) 652-8778 www.lspagency.net	**Reynaldo Villalobos**	(212) 253-6900 www.innovativeartists.com
Peter Tischhauser	(310) 314-2606 FAX (310) 815-1202 www.stacycheriffagency.com	**Lyle Vincent**	(310) 822-9113 www.murthaagency.com
John Toll	(310) 822-9113 www.murthaagency.com	**Stefan von Borbely**	(310) 395-9550 www.skouras.com

Wedigo von Schultzendorff	(310) 395-9550	www.skouras.com
Christos Voudouris (Film)	(212) 545-7895	www.nyoffice.net
Ted Wachs	(917) 865-1255	
William Wages	(212) 253-6900	www.innovativeartists.com
David Wagreich (Film & High Def)	(310) 652-8778	www.lspagency.net
Herb Wagreich (Film & High Def)	(914) 941-6812	
Garry Waller (Film & High Def)	(805) 217-7141 / (310) 822-9113	www.murthaagency.com
Chris Walling	(323) 856-3000	www.thegelleragency.com
Derek Wan (High Def)	(213) 626-2633 / (323) 788-3883 / FAX (213) 626-2629	www.allinone-usa.com
Kevin Ward (Film & High Def)	(818) 701-7676	www.shoottothrill.net
Stephen Ward	(212) 675-2556	
Vincent Warin	(310) 395-9550	www.skouras.com
Curtis Wehr	(212) 253-6900	www.innovativeartists.com
Michael Werk	(212) 564-7892	www.sradp.com
Clay Westervelt (Film & High Def)	(818) 990-8993	www.ambitiousent.com
Tony Westman	(212) 253-6900	www.innovativeartists.com
Haskell Wexler	(310) 395-9550	www.skouras.com
Julian Whatley	(310) 474-4585	www.dattnerdispoto.com
James Whitaker	(310) 395-9550	www.skouras.com
Nicole Hirsch Whitaker	(323) 463-0022	www.radiantartists.com
Aaron White	(212) 897-6400	www.paradigmagency.com
Joseph White	(323) 856-3000	www.thegelleragency.com
KC White (Aerial, Film & High Def)	(908) 647-9480 / (908) 400-6793 / FAX (908) 647-9480	www.kcwhite.net
Tristan Whitman	(818) 906-0006	www.tdnartists.com
Peter Wiehl (Film & High Def)	(917) 626-5872 / FAX (203) 261-7755	
Jo Willems	(310) 474-4585	www.dattnerdispoto.com
Bill Williams (Film & High Def)	(203) 894-9174	
Mark Williams	(310) 474-4585	www.dattnerdispoto.com
Nathan Wilson (Film & High Def)	(212) 545-7895	www.nyoffice.net
Zack Winestine (Film)	(212) 633-2040	
Scott Winig	(310) 458-7800	www.partos.com
Marc Wishengrad	(212) 749-7920	www.wishpic.com
Alexander Witt	(310) 822-9113	www.murthaagency.com
Benjamin Wolf (Film & High Def)	(347) 451-9945	
Dariusz Wolski	(310) 395-9550	www.skouras.com
Michael Wood	(310) 395-9550	www.skouras.com
Oliver Wood	(310) 822-9113	www.murthaagency.com
Ian Woolston-Smith (Aerial, Film, High Def, Remote Heads, Second Unit, Special FX & Steadicam)	(203) 470-3885	www.iancam.com
Yoshi Yasaki	(310) 458-7800	www.partos.com
Theodore Yasi	(732) 625-3074 / (201) 647-4722 / FAX (732) 625-3075	
Steve Yedlin (Film & High Def)	(212) 253-6900	www.innovativeartists.com
Robert Yeoman	(310) 822-9113	www.murthaagency.com
Alexis Zabe	(310) 652-8778	www.lspagency.net
Jim Zabilla	(212) 564-7892	www.sradp.com
Haris Zambarloukos	(310) 273-6700	www.utaproduction.com
John Zilles	(310) 474-4585	www.dattnerdispoto.com
Eric Zimmerman	(818) 753-6300	www.themackagency.net
Carolina Zorrilla-de San Martin (Film)	(212) 564-7892	www.sradp.com
Vilmos Zsigmond	(818) 753-6300	www.themackagency.net
Pete Zuccarini	(212) 997-1818	www.gershagency.com

First Assistant Directors (DGA NY)

Brad Abrams	(917) 568-3190
Robert Albertell	(917) 757-6902
Jose Alvarez	(973) 731-1016 / (917) 838-6422
Margaret Ambrosoni	(212) 410-3566
Marlene Arvan	(212) 807-8834
David Backus	(718) 636-9142 / (917) 453-3143
Jan Ballhaus	(818) 985-8161
Peter Barbera	(212) 475-2885 / (646) 382-4946
Alan Berger	(516) 679-5128
Jeffrey Bernstein	(917) 658-7866
Michael Billig	(914) 837-5803
Timothy Bird	(718) 840-0257
Julie A. Bloom	(718) 789-5320 / (917) 579-1790
Arle Bordas (English & Spanish)	(917) 453-1537
Vebe Borge	(212) 737-3558 / (914) 490-8976
Ian Brister	(212) 255-1351
Kenneth Brown	(203) 520-7164
Douglas Bruce	(520) 284-2082
Pierre Cailliarec	(973) 233-0535
Alfred Califano	(732) 295-4377
Matthew Vose Campbell	(917) 860-0461
Michael Cavagrotti	(201) 785-0101 / (201) 674-7388 / FAX (201) 785-0202
Bonnie Champion	(704) 321-9405 / (704) 576-2582
Mariela Comitini	(973) 931-8668
David Cox	(212) 334-1910 / (917) 449-4503
William Danial Curren	(860) 354-2350
Neil Daly	(646) 642-6250
Patricia Danziger	(203) 222-7217 / (203) 247-6546 / FAX (203) 222-7137
Daniel Deitchman	(201) 362-4737 / (646) 688-4424 / FAX (212) 428-6711 / www.dandeitchman.com
John Devlin	(212) 647-0555 / (917) 532-7226
Timothy Donohue	(845) 516-0008
Pat Dorfman	(718) 729-4688
David Dreyfuss	(718) 601-9760
Nancy Early	(914) 453-8751
Laurie Eichengreen	(212) 724-5953
Carol Eilenberg	(347) 246-6195
Stephen Elliot Jr.	(212) 864-4547
Peter Epstein	(914) 769-6310 / (914) 419-7222
Adam Escott	(718) 230-3612
George Fares	(917) 544-1839 / (917) 388-3951
Tom Fatone	(646) 325-8550
Stuart Feldman	(973) 226-8589
Joseph Donato Ferone	(718) 359-3436 / (917) 270-8080 / FAX (718) 359-4165
John Ficalora	(914) 591-5238 / FAX (914) 591-9603
Robert Fisher	(914) 381-6128
Bettiann Fishman	(212) 243-1413 / (917) 587-7804
Adam K. Free	(914) 764-4329 / FAX (914) 764-4894
Amy Friedman-Norton	(845) 657-2404
The Geller Agency 1547 Cassil Pl. Hollywood, CA 90028 (Reps for First Assistant Directors)	(323) 856-3000 / FAX (323) 856-3009 / www.thegelleragency.com
Steve Gilbert	(212) 799-0798
Jeffry S. Gitter	(212) 255-5299 / (917) 304-7505
Peter Giuliano	(417) 683-6014 / (310) 273-6700 / www.utaproduction.com
Stephen Andrew Glanzrock	(212) 255-8733 / FAX (320) 205-8733
James Edward Golden	(212) 924-3333
Joanne Golden	(212) 665-8445
Bruce H. Greenfield	(212) 665-6462
Don Greenholz	(212) 580-1072
Laurie Gross	(212) 734-9129
Louis J. Guerra	(516) 628-2529 / (917) 703-2022
Neil Hallenborg	(609) 914-0311 / (609) 351-1952 / FAX (609) 914-0233

Timothy Hayes	(631) 329-5840
Eric Henriquez	(610) 351-2220 / (917) 374-2048
William Hevessy	(813) 886-2137 / (813) 220-8010
Samuel Hoffman	(212) 529-1707
Dylan Hopkins	(845) 348-0340 / (914) 441-5461
Stephen Howard	(212) 567-8760 / (914) 633-9569
Michael Ingber	(845) 878-4130
Peter Jackson	(516) 944-3975
Robert B. Jackson	(203) 858-0326
David Johnson	(203) 438-2780
Miles Johnstone	(917) 439-6469
Marcie Kammel	(212) 807-1320
Johnna Kleban	(908) 647-1755
Jon W. Knoop	(718) 274-6131
Mark Kovacs	(973) 762-6630 / (973) 632-5556 / FAX (973) 762-6904
Dana Kuznetzkoff	(323) 462-6447
Paul Laurens	(310) 401-5058
Jeffrey Lazar	(212) 533-0010 / FAX (212) 533-0010
Lark Levine	(860) 927-4631
Richard Levine	(212) 533-0010
Gaetano Lisi	(212) 876-1328
Marco Londoner	(917) 797-6166
John Lowe	(212) 604-4862 / (917) 826-6344 / homepage.mac.com/lowelife
Donald Lumpkin	(212) 243-0939 / (917) 282-3784 / FAX (212) 633-0315
Vince Maggio	(718) 825-3212
Sheila Mahoney	(516) 324-6430
A. Domonic Mandy	(310) 994-5593
Ann Mann	(212) 799-7666
Kyle McCarthy	(212) 595-6074
Howard McMaster	(212) 316-1178 / (917) 572-7484 / FAX (212) 316-2131
Stan Mendoza	(973) 783-4661
Debra Michaelson	(201) 816-1973 / (818) 831-6977
Michael Miller	(516) 721-2660
Jonathan Mintz	(646) 342-7050
Kevin Moore	(917) 647-0870
David Nelson	(914) 381-3054 / (914) 282-5693
Peter Notaro	(516) 379-0030
Frank Nugent	(914) 591-2773 / (914) 582-1565 / FAX (914) 591-3252
Jamin O'Brien	(212) 431-3090
Jono Oliver	(914) 405-9025 / (800) 921-4665
Mindy Ordan Arietta	(201) 358-8173
Stephen Orent	(631) 544-6320
Barbie Painter	(917) 681-0867
James Parker	(914) 591-5888 / (917) 208-1698
Richard Patrick	(914) 764-1234
Michael Pitt	(646) 391-7288
Bob Pollak	(203) 247-3777 / (203) 761-1310 / FAX (203) 761-8797
Arthur Portnoy	(914) 664-0123
John Posimato	(212) 683-4483 / (212) 681-0682
Joseph Ray	(201) 567-0544 / (212) 840-1234
Joseph Reidy	(646) 314-9422 / (917) 705-9282
Thomas A. Reilly	(914) 241-8455
Peter Repplier	(917) 816-6341
Ward Ricke	(212) 873-9866
Danielle Rigby	(860) 455-0660
Kevin Riley	(201) 403-3183 / (201) 750-1703 / FAX (201) 750-1922 / www.rileysight.com
Timothy Risch	(310) 429-3866 / (276) 475-3943
Joe Ritter	(718) 852-7980 / (646) 957-1230
Steve Rogers	(818) 398-7450
Steven Rose	(212) 496-2713
Gary Sales	(305) 527-3919
Michael Samson	(847) 864-7733
Christopher Schenck	(828) 290-8713 / (310) 503-9110 / homepage.mac.com/chris_schenck/

Ellen Segal	(631) 241-4741	Jeff Trenner	(845) 265-4120 (914) 325-1435 FAX (845) 265-7689
James Sheridan	(347) 546-0906	Glen Trotiner	(212) 727-7665 (310) 236-4013 FAX (212) 727-7379 www.glentrotiner.com
Jonathan Siegel	(212) 722-1888 (917) 902-4402 www.linkedin.com/in/jonathansiegel		
Amanda Slater	(646) 228-5759	John Tyson	(212) 252-2005 (917) 678-4205
Nina Sloan	(973) 744-0210 (201) 259-7818 FAX (973) 744-6621	Harvey Waldman	(212) 877-7706 (212) 595-4595
Peter Soldo	(917) 902-4226	Sonja Webster	(201) 266-4148
Kenneth Stapleton	(201) 612-9113 FAX (201) 612-1125	David Wechsler	(917) 696-7466 (212) 769-3444
Jonathan Starch	(646) 221-9042	Stephen Wertimer	(212) 795-6784 (310) 281-5545
Michael Steele	(718) 789-5320 (917) 734-7961	Roni Wheeler	(917) 974-1397 (908) 810-1468 FAX (908) 810-1467 www.fultonstreetfilms.com
Rebecca Strickland	(212) 477-7779 (917) 767-4219		
William Teitler	(212) 749-9182 (917) 609-6910	Stanley Wiencko	(347) 787-1432
		Robin Winter-Young	(917) 698-2507
Mary Rae Thewlis	(347) 743-0198	Carl Zucker	(914) 674-9150
John Towse	(516) 628-2409		

First Assistant Directors

Tony Adler	(323) 856-3000	www.thegelleragency.com
Vincent Agostino	(310) 930-6570	
Benita Allen	(310) 652-8778	www.lspagency.net
Fernando Altschul	(323) 856-3000	www.thegelleragency.com
Todd Amateau	(310) 652-8778	www.lspagency.net
David Appelson	(212) 866-6287 / (917) 841-4470	FAX (917) 591-2868
Jane Barrer	(917) 509-4674 / (646) 290-7130	
Eric Berkal	(917) 656-7417	
Craig Borden	(323) 856-3000	www.thegelleragency.com
Jack Briggs	(212) 995-2781	
Ira Brooks	(845) 368-1820 / (917) 861-6084	FAX (845) 368-1840
Gary Buonanno	(203) 637-3935	
Chris Carroll	(212) 643-1736	www.cec-entertainment.com
Audrey S. Cohen	(305) 385-2204 / (310) 208-6776	FAX (310) 208-6776
Margaret M. Denk	(917) 602-8540	
Phil Dupont	(323) 856-3000	www.thegelleragency.com
Kate Eisemann	(917) 873-2256	FAX (203) 259-0124
Sergio Ercolessi	(310) 652-8778	www.lspagency.net
Paul Etheredge	(323) 856-3000	www.thegelleragency.com
Luc Etienne	(310) 273-6700	www.utaproduction.com
Richard Fox	(323) 856-3000	www.thegelleragency.com
Brad Garfield	(914) 834-2666 / (914) 522-9202	FAX (914) 833-3685 www.northridgeproductions.com
Walter Gasparovic	(310) 273-6700	www.unitedtalent.com
The Geller Agency 1547 Cassil Pl. Hollywood, CA 90028 (Reps for First Assistant Directors)	(323) 856-3000	FAX (323) 856-3009 www.thegelleragency.com
James Grasso	(310) 455-7169	
Alex Hapsas	(845) 365-3066	
J. Michael Haynie	(310) 652-8778	www.lspagency.net
Chip Hourihan	(718) 928-3812 / (917) 861-4120	
Robert B. Jackson	(203) 858-0326	
Michael Jordan	(845) 236-3566	
Adam Kagan	(917) 559-3639	www.kaganfamily.com/adam
Erwin Kramer	(212) 567-5545 / (888) 446-1866	FAX (310) 446-1856 home.earthlink.net/~ekeeeek
Mark Krumper	(407) 353-2099	
Steven Levy	(212) 355-8311 / (310) 499-4804	FAX (310) 496-3110 www.stevenjlevy.com
Jules Lichtman	(310) 652-8778	www.lspagency.net
Gary Marcus	(310) 273-6700	www.utaproduction.com
Josh McLaglen	(310) 273-6700	www.unitedtalent.com
Mike Michelin	(201) 694-0988	FAX (201) 939-6847
Milos Milicevic	(310) 273-6700	www.utaproduction.com
Montana Artists Agency 7715 W. Sunset Blvd., Third Fl. Los Angeles, CA 90046 (Reps for First Assistant Directors)	(323) 845-4144	FAX (323) 845-4155 www.montanartists.com
Justin Muller	(323) 856-3000	www.thegelleragency.com
Kenneth Myers	(866) 322-6039 / (203) 912-4505	FAX (203) 322-6039
Robin Randal Oliver	(323) 856-3000	www.thegelleragency.com
John O'Rourke	(323) 856-3000	www.thegelleragency.com
Paul Rosen	(917) 749-0272	
Lisa Satriano	(310) 273-6700	www.utaproduction.com
Marty Eli Schwartz	(310) 273-6700	www.unitedtalent.com
Nina Shiffman	(718) 858-7858	
TK Shom	(310) 652-8778	www.lspagency.net
Mark Shuman	(917) 554-5858 / (718) 349-7889	

Yann Sobezynski	(917) 698-7831 (718) 310-1200 www.coldcutsproductions.com	John Trenear	(212) 962-6121 (917) 536-3481 FAX (212) 962-6121
Jonathan Southard	(323) 856-3000 www.thegelleragency.com	Martin Walters	(310) 273-6700 www.unitedtalent.com
David Spodak	(561) 272-8721	Sherman Ward	(610) 804-5048 www.picsnwords.com
Tony Steinberg	(323) 856-3000 www.thegelleragency.com	Shelby Werwa	(212) 929-4456
Joe Suarez	(212) 643-1736 www.cec-entertainment.com	Gerald Wu	(407) 697-7654
Jennifer Tavanese-Valenti	(917) 747-0578		

Food Stylists & Home Economists

Nir Adar (212) 206-0901
www.halleyresources.com

Dyne Benner (212) 688-7571
www.foodforads.com

Jacqueline Buckner (212) 737-5746
(303) 204-4001
(Food Stylist) www.thebestfoodstylist.com

dantasticfood (215) 794-0527
(267) 261-7369
FAX (215) 794-7871
www.dantasticfood.com

Michelle Francisco (718) 683-7003
www.thatfoodstylistchick.com

Ed Gabriels (212) 206-0901
www.halleyresources.com

Travis Grandon (212) 741-3240
www.ennisinc.com

Victoria Granof (212) 925-4222
www.art-dept.com

Sarah Greenberg (212) 873-1764
(917) 364-6199
FAX (212) 873-1764
www.sarahfood-stylist.com

Halley Resources (212) 206-0901
231 W. 29th St., Ste. 701 FAX (212) 206-0904
(Near Seventh Ave.) www.halleyresources.com
New York, NY 10001
(Food Stylists)

Janet Hanson (201) 750-7952
(Food Stylist)

Marilinda Hodgdon (212) 735-6583
FAX (212) 735-6982
www.marilinda.com

Suzette Kaminski (212) 279-1999
www.markedwardinc.com

Barbara Listenik (718) 946-3283
FAX (718) 946-3084
www.fiercerelease.com

Ellen Lucas (917) 363-4255
www.ellenlucas.com

Deborah McLean (212) 206-0901
www.halleyresources.com

Susan Ottaviano (212) 206-0901
www.halleyresources.com

Mary Jane Sawyer (212) 741-3240
(781) 863-1555
www.ennisinc.com

Pam Sorin (212) 741-3240
www.ennisinc.com

Karen Temple (212) 924-7870
www.foodstylist.com

Matt Vohr (212) 206-0901
www.halleyresources.com

Gaffers & Electricians (Local 52 NY)

Lowell B. Achziger	(609) 397-5585 (609) 397-3970
Greg Addison	(917) 836-1858 (718) 928-3311
William Almeida	(201) 991-8012 (917) 283-6780
Daniel Amadie	(215) 588-8030
Brian C. Aman	(845) 225-5611
Tricia Anastasia (Electrician)	(609) 652-9523
David T. Anderson	(212) 420-6043
Thomas M. Anderson	(718) 788-4694
Michael Arisohn	(518) 312-3456
Zachary Arkin	(516) 897-7438
Richard E. Asbury	(610) 642-0220 (610) 348-9917
Michael Audino	(724) 654-7320
Rafael August	(917) 673-0095
Donald (Lee) Ayrton	(860) 588-6932
Joseph M. Baccari	(718) 379-0731
Steven N. Baker	(718) 815-1398 (917) 337-9784
Tamu-ra Bakr	(347) 256-3510
Christian Baldi	(516) 433-3886 (516) 884-9222
Joseph W. Baliski	(856) 931-3936 (609) 209-5417
David G. Baney	(603) 305-3631
Joseph J. Banks Jr.	(516) 326-9126 (212) 385-0567
Raphael (Andre) Banks	(516) 872-2459 (800) 864-5363
Clayton Barrow	(443) 370-2747
Michael F. Barrow	(212) 227-1156
Robert A. Baumgartner	(323) 646-7060
Richard W. Baxter	(914) 248-8316
Grady J. Bayersdorfer	(201) 836-0507 (201) 927-5977
Kelly Beaton	(718) 497-4994 (917) 363-2484
Gustavo Bechini	(212) 608-0602 (917) 749-0874
Joseph Beck	(516) 221-1657
Richard Beck	(718) 499-9689
John J. Begley	(718) 886-7573 (917) 992-1371
J. R. Beket	(203) 874-0791
James J. BeKiaris (Gaffer)	(718) 229-3834 (646) 734-0729
George Bell III	(609) 296-9539
Samuel Bender	(845) 225-7482 (914) 391-8708
Michael Berg	(845) 548-0352
Timothy Berg	(732) 679-6395 (917) 885-0853
John Berry (Electrician)	(845) 658-8835 (914) 388-0537
Christopher J. Beste	(302) 654-8975
Michael Bicknell	(212) 260-5460
J.B. Billeci (Electrician)	(917) 929-7655
Sarah E. Black	(212) 260-7154
Peter J. Blahut	(631) 716-0748
Robert G. Blair	(914) 941-2699
Tom Blancato	(212) 645-9480 (917) 226-0769
Pamela Blum	(914) 754-7487 (914) 769-8040
Joseph J. Bolesta (Electrician)	(718) 447-7157 FAX (718) 720-5200 www.goblininc.com
Joseph P. Bonacorda	(516) 223-2607 (516) 305-3357
Eric A. Boncher	(718) 891-4434 (646) 279-6655
Hugo Bonilla	(646) 621-5020
James W. Boorman	(310) 713-0129
Christopher Bower	(201) 795-9888
Peter Boynton	(203) 530-9968
Nicole Brait	(646) 236-8316
Salvatore R. Branca	(908) 850-5445 (973) 229-5801
David W. Brandon	(610) 292-8417 (610) 304-5565
Michael W. Brennan	(215) 943-1055 (908) 735-0692
Lynn Breschel (Electrician)	(845) 258-1786 FAX (845) 258-1816
Kelly J. Britt	(908) 317-0599 (908) 419-3504

Thomas Brouard	(914) 561-4950
John Budde	(212) 533-3138 / (646) 298-4611
Jorge P. Burgos	(718) 402-6351 / (917) 773-4165
Glynis J. Burke (Gaffer)	(201) 385-8344
Michael F. Burke	(212) 781-8499 / (201) 385-8344
William Burke	(212) 675-7803 / (917) 782-8471
James (Jamie) Burnett	(860) 330-2476
Peter C. Caldwell (Gaffer)	(203) 840-0104 / (203) 858-0376
Robert Caldwell	(215) 533-2137 / (215) 743-2783
Steven C. Calitri	(718) 429-6431
William J. Callahan	(718) 921-4813 / (917) 972-3284
David Cambria	(917) 225-9999 / (401) 438-3525 / FAX (917) 591-3225
Casey Campbell	(917) 628-1040
Daniel B. Canton	(203) 761-1271
John Cardoni	(212) 420-8507 / (917) 304-4316
Dominique Caron	(215) 687-0175
Rhys Carpenter	(212) 781-1375 / (917) 597-1546 / FAX (208) 246-4793
Guy M. Caso	(201) 785-3889
Ann D. Cavanaugh	(201) 784-3287
David Wade Cecil	(267) 977-3841 / (267) 977-3841
Christopher Cellary	(201) 825-3763
Duane Chan-Shue	(917) 207-2081
Samuel Chase	(718) 852-9615 / (917) 771-3279
Justin T. Cheatham	(718) 693-5266 / (718) 490-3180
David G. Chedd	(212) 614-0058
Tony (Ty) Chennault	(646) 342-9044
John Cheshire Jr.	(917) 748-7888 / (212) 737-5624
Molly Cheshire	(610) 347-2483
Radium L. Cheung	(718) 633-3644 / (917) 539-1529
Neil Christie	(516) 931-3736
Angelo P. Cicero	(888) 899-7658
Richard J. Citrone	(401) 789-3889
Peter J. Clare	(201) 930-1280 / (201) 788-8615
Andrew Clarke (Gaffer)	(212) 533-3142
John (Jack) Coffen	(631) 661-3938 / (516) 659-4595
Edward A. Cohen	(212) 228-6043 / (888) 727-5935
Fred Cohen (Gaffer)	(212) 982-9728
Ian D. Cohen	(646) 408-8405 / (718) 609-9942
Richard Cohn (Gaffer)	(718) 499-6223
Peter Thomas Colavito	(718) 266-1810 / (917) 673-1195
Steven J. Comesky	(516) 756-3638 / (516) 319-6618
Andrew Conner	(610) 518-5343 / (610) 804-5557
Kelly Conners	(732) 918-1355 / (732) 221-6200
Tracy Conners	(732) 787-2198
Luis Contreras	(908) 303-0078 / (908) 876-3683
John Coots	(973) 698-4193
Anthony Corapi	(423) 515-5963
Anthony J. Cortosi	(215) 925-1640 / (215) 319-6037
Howard Cournoyer	(973) 868-4073
Patrick Cousins	(718) 686-0177
Thomas P. Coyne	(718) 729-9395
Matthew Craig	(917) 992-9384
Andrea Cronin-Souza	(212) 924-9787 / (917) 553-8578
Patrick C. Crooks	(917) 597-0389
Ralph F.S. Crowley	(212) 222-8455 / (917) 312-5057
Nick Cupkovic	(212) 410-0536 / (917) 384-0170
Gavin Curran	(212) 874-3319 / (917) 864-7565
Paul Daley	(212) 337-8890 / (917) 445-9545
Douglas A. Dalisera (Gaffer)	(845) 365-2663
Steve Danieli	(973) 571-1088 / (973) 205-1970
Jeffrey A. Danielson	(212) 348-9873

John Dardis	(323) 663-4282
Philip Darrell	(860) 535-2118
Glenn Davis	(609) 652-9331 / (609) 442-9888
Andrew J. Day (Gaffer)	(973) 744-7110 / (917) 757-1163
Christopher De Blau	(201) 447-4631 / (551) 804-7108
Jerry W. DeBlau (Gaffer)	(201) 791-2906 / (201) 965-1650 / FAX (201) 703-9137
John W. De Blau III	(201) 796-6377
Michael J. Delaney Jr.	(732) 530-9272
Kane C. Delaney	(310) 746-7020
Maggie Delaney	(843) 367-1476
Michael J. Delaney (Electrician)	(732) 530-9272
Vincent P. Delaney	(213) 463-4858
Jon M. Delgado	(212) 260-5781
Moira Demos	(646) 638-3503 / (917) 837-4462
Jim Denny	(212) 228-6944 / (917) 913-5921
Tony Denoi	(302) 322-6540 / (610) 696-1848
Anthony De Rosa	(914) 265-5260 / (914) 265-5560
Michael A. De Rosa	(914) 265-2147
Thomas F. Devine	(215) 482-4291 / (215) 778-4881
Keith J. Devlin	(718) 638-4039 / (718) 724-9398
Philip J. Devonshire (Electrician)	(908) 665-9882
James F. Dillinger Jr.	(516) 379-8011
Chris Dixon	(917) 482-6963
Kenneth R. Dodd	(201) 796-2793 / (201) 665-2050
Christopher E. Dolan	(201) 666-7984 / (201) 741-9026
Dede P. Dolan	(845) 642-8904
James A. (Peaches) Dolan	(201) 934-9116 / (201) 913-4881
James P. Dolan	(201) 768-0164 / (201) 390-3396
Richard N. Dolan	(201) 594-1975 / (973) 449-7275
Ronald P. Dolan	(603) 883-2770
Thomas W. Dolan	(201) 505-4775
Mitchell Donian (Gaffer)	(212) 807-1504
Christian G. Drechsler	(917) 817-0158
Jesse C. Dublanica	(646) 824-5426
John G. Duncan Jr.	(610) 544-9253
Don Earl	(609) 625-5410
Steven D. Edick	(860) 839-4175
Leighton S. Edmondson	(646) 734-0048 / (718) 418-5323
Mark Egyud (Electrician)	(917) 697-0885
Daniel R. Ehrenbard	(973) 744-6080
Micah Eisenmann	(646) 361-4841 / (718) 701-0459
David Elwell	(212) 722-1898 / (646) 345-3685
Eugene W. Engels	(973) 875-8599
Jay M. Engels	(973) 600-0447
Russell W. Engels	(973) 875-9779
Ryan Engels	(973) 875-8599 / (973) 768-8943
Wade S. Engels	(973) 875-8599 / (973) 875-0550
Jeffrey A. Eplett	(718) 302-5687 / (917) 309-1964
Christian L. Epps	(678) 525-6105
Gerald Evans	(607) 844-8383
John Faherty	(201) 222-3475 / (201) 417-2869
Robert A. Falcone	(917) 715-0633
Andrew Falk	(917) 816-5358
James Fallon	(716) 480-0883
Michael Fanelli	(914) 833-0620
Peter Fanelli	(914) 834 5220
William Farber (Gaffer)	(516) 364-8835 / (516) 510-5564
Gregory Farrell	(631) 447-0095 / (631) 523-8718
Robert J. Fedeli	(203) 924-9632
Ronald M. Fedeli	(203) 255-6326
Sean P. Fedigan	(845) 298-6068 / (914) 589-1671
Daniel W. Feith	(860) 489-1419
James J. Ferris	(646) 645-4223
Raffaello Ferrucci (Gaffer)	(212) 645-7715 / (917) 468-3936 / FAX (917) 940-9555

Mark John Fiedler	(856) 863-8517 (856) 318-1405	Michael J. Gallart (Gaffer)	(973) 279-1970 (973) 493-4324
William Fiedler	(856) 232-9205 (856) 337-3764	Jim E. Galvin	(201) 303-9669
Charles A. Fields	(914) 736-6083 (914) 972-4047	Robert Gambardella	(908) 653-0661 (908) 377-7453
Kenneth P. Finlay (Gaffer)	(201) 342-9440 (201) 739-6863 FAX (201) 342-9440	Julie A. Gant	(303) 554-0248
Joseph Edward Fittipaldi	(304) 257-8383	Arthur C. Gardner	(201) 948-0010 (917) 982-7135
Kevin G. Fitzpatrick	(516) 933-8775 (516) 680-5513	Steven Garner	(212) 725-4915 (917) 226-2180
Kevin G. Fitzpatrick Jr.	(516) 933-8775 (516) 369-9426	Arthur N. Giegerich	(914) 496-2559
Morris Flam	(845) 687-4507	Shaun C. Gilbert	(203) 414-9785
John L. Flanagan	(516) 932-8816 (516) 241-7626	John Gilgar Jr.	(646) 286-1368
David Flowers	(203) 501-0413	Paul S. Gilly	(718) 227-2884
Richard Fogel	(201) 933-0883 (201) 923-3761	Anthony D. Girolami	(631) 661-1633 (631) 661-8636
Patrick B. Fontana	(516) 795-4812 (516) 857-3934	Peter R. Girolami	(845) 359-3562 (917) 226-6669
Edward Foody	(201) 568-4583	Richard J. Girolami	(201) 951-2838
Casey J. Ford	(516) 376-2028	Richard J. Girolami Jr.	(201) 491-6569
Matthew Ford	(646) 321-8360	Louis Gisone	(917) 710-6327
Richard J. Ford	(718) 876-6783	Lisa Marie Gleeson	(917) 543-8942
Thomas M. Ford	(646) 431-6296	Joseph Goldman (Electrician)	(212) 777-0785 (646) 872-9194
Jay Fortune	(631) 462-5939 (516) 457-3798	Damian Gonzales	(973) 594-0410 (201) 803-7414
Raymond Fortune	(718) 631-0896	Robert F. Gonzalez	(201) 599-2168
Avra Fox-Lerner	(347) 439-1629	Justin Gravatt	(917) 304-7172
Michael Fradianni www.michaelfradianni.remaxbenchmark.com (Electrician & Gaffer)	(845) 742-0456 (845) 238-2024	Michael N. Green	(718) 388-3453 (917) 584-9708
Reba Frankel	(646) 772-0328	Steven Greenberg	(212) 888-6582 (917) 523-6599
David Franzoni	(732) 409-0166	Shawn Greene	(617) 256-0871
Henry Thomas Franzoni	(949) 716-4338	Scott Gregoire	(718) 832-6035 (917) 328-8476
Jon-David Freedman	(850) 784-3522	James Gregory	(203) 731-1157
Walter Fricke	(973) 429-2427	Jamison Grella	(917) 822-4186
Samuel G. Friedman	(212) 614-9008 (917) 539-3827	Andrew Greve	(646) 283-2875
Christopher H. Frumkes	(212) 769-0873 (917) 575-9466	David Grill	(201) 818-0434 (201) 825-0391
James W. Fryer	(518) 273-0538	Joseph L. Grimaldi	(845) 721-4400
Daryl D. Furr	(718) 782-4551 (917) 641-6541	Charles Grubbs	(609) 448-3977 (609) 240-2068
Jamie Gallagher	(203) 562-5383	Robert Gurgo (Gaffer)	(732) 892-5910 (732) 267-5198
		David Gurney	(716) 390-3222

Jerome Hall	(718) 320-5052 / (917) 875-1223
Ned Hallick	(718) 788-0110
Thomas B. Hamilton II	(917) 747-7784
Christopher M. Hammond	(201) 224-4160 / (201) 681-4437
Andrew Hansen	(917) 450-4133
David Lee Harges	(917) 861-8727
James J. Harker	(917) 453-8914
George W. Harrington	(732) 817-1955 / (888) 884-3669
Shane Harrington	(732) 817-1955 / (732) 977-3224
Sheila Harrington-Hughes	(609) 927-2348
David L. Harrison	(610) 586-1697 / (215) 960-2683
Michael Haskell	(610) 495-9697
Edward (Ted) Hayash	(888) 346-9757
Christopher Hayes	(516) 872-6548 / (516) 521-6940
Timothy D. Healy	(201) 217-1719
Susan Heller	(212) 627-4078 / (917) 523-0573
Michael Sean Hennessy	(609) 232-2481 / (215) 306-4726
Xavier Henselmann	(212) 533-8060 / (917) 482-6847
Matthew Higham	(914) 777-7685 / (917) 225-8616
Gary D. Hildebrand	(732) 530-2945 / (917) 647-4524
Jeremy K. Hill	(516) 872-3573
George Hines	(718) 416-0062 / (917) 755-2693
William Hines	(732) 758-9899 / (732) 996-4558
Petr Hlinomaz (Gaffer)	(212) 580-9867 / (917) 355-6587
John S. Hockenberry Jr.	(610) 622-5863
Andrew Holliday (Electrician)	(718) 935-1929 / (917) 650-7389
Ira Holzman	(516) 269-5411
Mary M. Hoole	(610) 892-3810 / (215) 585-5109
Charles Houston	(718) 622-4575 / (917) 348-7459
Matt Howard	(845) 424-4465 / (914) 282-3172
Daniel Howie	(718) 622-7872 / (917) 824-2076
Michael Hunold	(212) 795-0784
Richard Illy	(203) 261-3008 / (203) 279-0571 / FAX (203) 261-3008
Matthew Ishibashi	(609) 448-2411
Abigail Iverson	(312) 608-8364
F. Lee Iwanski	(718) 424-8918 / (646) 208-8261
Michael A. Jackson	(646) 286-3435
Frank Jacoby Sr. (Electrician)	(609) 646-2649
Bernard James	(908) 464-8406 / (908) 812-6661
Kevin Janicelli (Gaffer)	(845) 528-0761
Roberto Jimenez	(718) 434-2240 / (917) 490-3530
Jeremy C. Johnson	(914) 753-5806
Rolf Johnson	(631) 271-8857
Beverly Jones	(201) 281-3216 / (917) 762-8455
Learan Kahanov	(917) 680-4272 / www.lkdp.com
Mark Kahn	(212) 595-1570 / (917) 579-6938
Keith Kalohelani	(212) 724-4742 / (917) 533-3407
Jenny Kane (Electrician)	(212) 228-3847
Josh Karan	(212) 923-1680
Daniel F. Karlok	(201) 783-7059
Philip Kathrens	(571) 277-6698
Renee K. Kayon	(310) 374-1761
Jonathan P. Kealey	(718) 786-1829 / (800) 372-3281
Jeffery W. Keaton	(917) 345-9827
Robert Keene	(203) 838-6057
Edward T. Kelly	(631) 242-7934
James Kelly	(631) 242-7934 / (631) 383-1672
John J. Kelly Jr.	(631) 669-7598 / (516) 309-0069
Philip J. Kenny	(860) 680-3009
Scott Kincaid	(917) 710-6916 / (718) 726-2059
David L. Kissinger Li	(215) 943-1579 / (267) 218-0539

William Klayer (Gaffer)	(212) 539-1158 / (646) 287-2046
Jeremy Knaster	(212) 662-8204 / (917) 975-3475
Peter Koola	(845) 687-9332 / (917) 586-7256
Russ Korker Sr.	(732) 219-0531
Daniel Kubicek	(646) 541-0798
John W. Kuegel	(718) 852-5084 / (718) 852-4922
Nina Kuhn	(917) 868-2857
Amy Kupferberg (Electrician)	(212) 249-4886
Charles Lalino	(516) 822-0969 / (516) 987-5456
Jeffrey Lalino	(516) 933-3785 / (516) 822-0969
Stephen J. Lalino	(516) 796-5729
Alan Lampel (Electrician)	(212) 927-1666 / (917) 922-1104
Jason A. Lanci	(718) 319-8352 / (917) 284-3947
David Landau	(201) 377-8894
John Landi	(732) 236-1296 / (732) 238-0562
Thomas J. Landi	(718) 980-6677 / (516) 410-8576
Jean Pierre Laplanche	(908) 665-9297 / (908) 317-3694
Eric A. Leigh	(845) 680-0257 / (914) 715-6105
Jonathon Leigh	(917) 273-2198 / (516) 938-0545
Kurt Lennig	(718) 398-8977 / (917) 833-0106
Joseph Leo	(201) 267-2024
Michael Leo	(201) 814-1214 / (201) 895-3429
Michael Lesser	(212) 691-3859
David LeVine	(347) 538-6501 / (888) 454-4487
Daniel H. Levy	(201) 794-9280 / (201) 926-0198
Todd Lichtenstein (Electrician)	(973) 731-0333 / (973) 768-5954
Craig Ligget (Gaffer)	(610) 565-4973 / (610) 304-5552
Robert C. Linke	(203) 825-2347
Christopher Liscinsky	(845) 268-4986 / (914) 263-3846
Steve Litecky	(505) 231-0282 / (575) 773-4918
Jim Litten	(212) 580-1965 / (917) 653-1603
Kerry A. Lombard	(203) 268-9925
Chris Lombardozzi (Electrician)	(718) 853-5590 / (718) 219-1551
William P. Louthe	(609) 889-3660 / (609) 972-9271
Edward F. Love Jr.	(509) 967-5240
Andrew Lowe	(718) 361-1712
Jonathan Lumley (Gaffer)	(212) 242-0736 / (917) 658-7750 / FAX (212) 675-1584
Jonathan Luton	(718) 499-4726 / (917) 334-1668
Eugene Lynch	(845) 325-5930
William Lynch	(908) 925-7306
Robert T. Mabin	(610) 644-1965 / (610) 517-4341
John D. Mabry	(518) 696-4381
Lorne J. Macdougall	(845) 353-8331 / (800) 491-3702
William MacGhee (Electrician)	(917) 862-7087
Thomas Madden Jr.	(908) 566-4823
Allan E. Mader	(201) 943-2850
James Mah	(845) 528-6483 / (917) 273-2978
John Maher (Electrician)	(914) 633-8472 / (914) 413-3541
Paul E. Mallick	(212) 721-0456 / (212) 300-5654
Dennis Malone	(631) 661-6764 / (516) 522-9729
James Malone (Rigging Gaffer)	(631) 669-0369 / (516) 521-4970
James J. Manzione	(516) 365-4580 / (516) 581-8290
Sean Manzione	(516) 365-4580
Roger Marbury	(718) 832-1664
Michael Maronna	(347) 728-5545 / (718) 389-5009
Jeanette Martorano	(516) 729-8035
Salvatore (Sal) Martorano Jr.	(516) 378-5815 / (516) 235-4015

Frida Marzouk	(347) 393-8836
Michael Marzovilla	(212) 608-1822 / (917) 402-8088
Peter Marzulli	(718) 499-9280 / (917) 806-2783
Michael J. Maurer	(718) 278-5055 / (917) 584-7339
Richard Mauro	(201) 836-5427
Patrick McAllister	(410) 758-1912
Timothy McAuliffe	(516) 799-8015 / (516) 650-8263
Francis J. McBride	(718) 769-0654 / (917) 808-4253
John P. McCabe	(917) 968-9457
Andrew R. McCann	(212) 923-7800
Sean McCardell	(718) 783-4756 / (917) 204-6167
Brian McClean	(917) 599-6659 / (718) 474-5211
Cory McClean	(718) 529-3428 / (646) 624-1653
Harold J. McClean	(718) 322-8025 / (917) 481-1644
Kevin D. McClean	(718) 474-5211
Frank J. McCormack	(201) 244-8697 / (917) 656-2228
Brian R. McCullagh	(631) 589-5175 / (347) 563-8125
James McCullagh	(718) 423-5528 / (917) 406-5528
Brett McDermott	(845) 371-2919 / (845) 300-3579
Jeffrey T. McDonald	(602) 684-5147
Michael P. McDonald	(516) 676-8861
Sandy McDonough	(800) 721-6191 / FAX (908) 253-3633 / www.lighthouselights.com
Peter McEntyre	(631) 789-0878 / (201) 650-4947
Jeanne McGavin	(201) 666-5067
Nicholas McGavin	(201) 358-1172 / (201) 294-1685
Robert J. McGavin	(201) 358-1172
William G. McGavin	(201) 666-5947
Mark P. McGovern	(908) 850-0847
Tom McGrath	(310) 740-0103 / (212) 929-0144 / www.bigdipperfilms.com
Derek McKane	(310) 395-9550 / www.skouras.com
Tigre McMullan	(845) 265-1074 / (914) 456-3192
Charles A. McNamara	(323) 839-5949
Keith W. McNicholas	(917) 209-8266
James A. McPeak	(610) 328-5769
Guy Meeker Jr. (Electrician)	(212) 722-3349
Charles E. Meere III	(516) 867-6581 / (914) 420-5088
Thomas E. Meere	(718) 428-8944
Michael Meere-Abt	(718) 648-9549 / (347) 322-6696
Eugene Meienhofer	(646) 541-0798
W. Douglas Meils	(212) 280-4549 / (917) 608-8173
Mark A. Melendez	(516) 676-5242 / (516) 316-6702
Matthew Mendelson	(516) 449-9714
Dave Mermelstein	(609) 581-5594
John C. Merriman	(973) 743-4437 / (917) 553-4437 / FAX (973) 748-7889
Howard J. Meyer Jr.	(602) 951-0582
Jason Micallef	(718) 351-6109 / (718) 809-7490
Sergei Mihajlov	(917) 923-8254
John T. Milcetic	(914) 736-3221 / (917) 407-0786
Glenn R. Miller	(845) 679-4226
Scott W. Miller	(212) 420-9333 / (917) 749-0355
Toby Miller	(330) 464-1149
William Miller	(914) 635-2659
John A. Mitchell	(973) 223-1021
Richard T. Mitchell (Electrician)	(215) 884-6444 / (215) 290-8498
Jerad Molkenthin	(908) 689-5776 / (484) 994-8463
Jon C. Montgomery	(212) 673-9759
Richard A. Montgomery (Electrician)	(914) 963-3011
William Moore (Gaffer)	(212) 362-5912 / (917) 656-4354
Robert Morganstein	(609) 348-1975
Jon D. Morrison	(412) 551-5327 / (412) 257-0594
Don Muchow	(718) 596-8134

Michael J. Muhler	(609) 324-3838 / (609) 954-6694
Michael Mullen	(516) 724-1393
Fred T. Muller Jr. (Electrician)	(631) 884-6814
Joseph W. Muller	(631) 472-4544
Derek C. Murphy	(718) 275-5162 / (917) 297-7677
Kevin Murphy	(212) 488-7136 / (917) 882-9414
Malcolm C. (M.C.) Murray	(800) 558-4878
Saade A. Mustafa	(917) 375-0074 / (718) 968-7657
John Nadeau	(718) 797-1656 / (646) 523-2211
Harold Naiderman	(212) 564-1522
Francine Natale	(609) 903-9222
Richard C. Neumann	(516) 457-7710
William Newell	(917) 566-8159
Iris Tse Min Ng	(917) 251-5698
Andrew S. Niceberg	(516) 921-8283 / (516) 721-1525
Monty Nielsen	(347) 853-5756
Jeffrey Niggemeyer	(310) 339-8188
Gregory Nimetz	(609) 484-4642 / (732) 269-2663
Ben Noble	(917) 279-6700
Scott H. Novak	(973) 746-8997 / (973) 610-5850
Martin Nowlan	(718) 789-2765 / (917) 771-5355
Rob Nussbaum	(973) 865-0326 / (973) 492-8056
John Oates (Electrician)	(917) 748-9051
Elizabeth (Beth) O'Brien	(718) 490-7878
Kevin O'Connell	(201) 533-9588
Thomas M. O'Connor	(718) 930-8194
Brandon J. Odegaard	(860) 582-1901 / FAX (860) 582-1901
William O'Leary (Gaffer)	(917) 327-5886
John O'Malley	(917) 353-1512
Joseph M. Ori	(212) 595-0406 / (917) 697-3648
Paul Osekoski	(845) 831-0122 / (914) 830-1965
Timothy J. Owen	(718) 728-8902 / (917) 554-7183
Toshiaki Ozawa (Gaffer)	(908) 281-4057 / (310) 474-4585 / FAX (310) 474-6411
Alfred O. Padilla	(718) 703-3551 / (917) 922-7624
Michael W. Palmer	(310) 489-6453
Rocco Palmieri	(718) 648-9738 / (917) 620-4852
Robert Palumbo	(718) 622-2492 / (718) 791-6270
Michael Papadopoulos	(212) 447-6348
Anthony J. Pascento	(516) 678-4409
Christopher Passalacqua	(212) 888-0789 / (917) 838-1141
George E. Paul	(718) 626-6093
Ronald G. Paul (Gaffer)	(914) 739-3869 / (917) 348-6271
Steven Peloquin	(201) 963-4602
Thomas W. Percarpio	(845) 651-4581
Dennis Peters	(917) 468-1564
Louis J. Petraglia Jr.	(347) 219-0076
Kate Phelan	(718) 789-2765 / (917) 744-3327
Linda Phillips	(516) 378-4359 / (516) 680-4050
Kabkeo Phothivongsa (Electrician)	(917) 685-9727
Lance E. Phox	(732) 728-9288 / (917) 860-8793 / FAX (732) 728-9296
Donato Pinto	(718) 984-6083
William J. Plachy	(914) 358-0386 / (914) 353-3966
Dwayne Plokhooy	(201) 702-8419
Robert (Bob) Pokonski	(732) 723-1199 / (917) 313-7656
Thomas W. Potoskie	(917) 374-1016
George Potter	(201) 670-8685 / (551) 486-1769
Kenneth E. Potter	(201) 670-8685 / (201) 248-0230
Lawrence E. Price II	(856) 547-2797
Michael J. Price (Electrician)	(516) 375-5231
Noah R. Prince	(718) 832-7043 / (646) 258-1943
Michael P. Prisco Jr.	(973) 452-6566
Mark Proscia	(862) 668-2700
Michael Proscia Jr.	(732) 673-1943

Peter Prostowich	(718) 626-3108 / (917) 871-0358
Collin P. Quinlan	(201) 792-3135 / (631) 277-4474
Gregory Quinlan	(631) 422-1728
James Quinlan	(201) 792-3135 / (516) 819-4060
Ryan Richard Quinlan	(631) 289-7455
Joseph Quirk	(212) 533-0015 / (917) 854-5928
Brian J. Raby	(215) 850-2199
Scott H. Ramsey	(914) 238-4953
Steven Ramsey	(718) 693-6626 / (917) 679-8162
John Raugalis	(845) 473-0633 / (914) 474-4432
Joseph J. Ray	(212) 956-1478
Thomas B. Ray	(917) 913-1336
Edward Read	(516) 735-3467 / (917) 513-4333 / www.readbroslighting.com
Daniel Reddy	(609) 397-5585
Michael Reed	(917) 673-8521
Salvatore Restuccia	(917) 841-3752
Jim Richards	(212) 222-0315 / (646) 734-5899
Gay Riedel	(201) 262-5467
Joseph Rivers	(914) 213-4480 / (845) 635-8004
Thomas Rizzo	(516) 641-9928 / (516) 223-3132
Allan S. Robinson	(973) 515-0809 / (347) 645-8121
Ryan A. Rodriguez	(718) 267-1115 / (917) 696-5365
Matthew D. Rohn	(212) 724-2725 / (917) 762-0327
Gary Ronn	(212) 864-6953 / (917) 334-9012
Francisco Rosario	(347) 776-0699 / (718) 738-3890
Chris Rosen	(212) 673-5522
David Rudolph	(212) 828-1669 / (617) 312-3893
Michael R. Rudolph	(845) 259-3026 / (917) 940-2337
Ilse (Boogie) Rumes	(718) 218-8083 / (917) 349-4903
Peter A. Russell	(631) 724-6045 / (917) 887-2107
Kelly Rutkowski (Electrician)	(212) 598-0281 / (646) 734-4882
Christopher J. Ryan	(917) 793-3040 / (917) 749-8625
Sean Ryan	(570) 814-5779
Andrea L. Sachs	(718) 383-7460 / (917) 254-1512
Lewis Sadler	(917) 254-1512
Janet Saetta	(718) 434-2240
Jared Saltzman	(973) 779-8101 / (973) 318-4815
David Samuel	(212) 420-0806
Kwmae Rubin Sandy	(917) 586-9886 / (212) 289-8103
Anthony Santos	(917) 353-3143
Michael Sarluco	(516) 603-6221 / (516) 883-0405
John Saye	(845) 928-2684 / (347) 739-2410
I. Nate Scaglione	(215) 468-6555
Christopher E. Scarfi	(212) 677-2785 / (917) 576-6825
James M. Schalk	(212) 573-5570 / (631) 289-4924
Jennifer Schoenewald	(215) 334-5258 / (215) 419-2966
Donald Schreck	(212) 580-8893 / (917) 685-5524
Robert Schulman	(908) 679-0722
Karl Schurr (Electrician)	(609) 652-9523
Alan Schwartz	(888) 681-8975
John Schwartz	(201) 792-0227 / (917) 566-2569
Mark Schwentner	(914) 964-8587 / (917) 318-1031
Joseph W. Sciretta	(516) 825-1641 / (516) 729-4680
Robert J. Sciretta	(212) 545-0954
Stephen Scotto	(914) 776-5613
Jason M. Seiler	(718) 321-0429 / (917) 925-6958
George Selden	(917) 592-1718
John B. Senter III	(212) 677-5711
Satish K. Shahi	(646) 486-4075 / (917) 870-4040
Douglas W. Shannon	(212) 315-2756
James S. Shea	(203) 384-9447

Lance A. Shepherd	(845) 634-8809 (917) 880-8164
Sean Sheridan	(718) 499-3042 (646) 263-8676
Tristan G. Sheridan	(718) 274-5473 (917) 673-5132
Ken Shibata	(212) 686-0775 (917) 714-8538
Tom Shinn	(512) 636-3934
Robert M. Siegel	(914) 693-5783
Alan J. Silverstein	(610) 494-7762 (302) 373-5190
Jamie Silverstein (Gaffer)	(718) 369-9891 (917) 796-4217
David Skutch	(973) 744-2737 (973) 715-2793
Darrin Smith	(203) 981-4631
Spencer Snygg	(610) 782-0572 (646) 209-6726
Joshua Solson	(917) 805-4448
Yoshihiro Sonoda	(646) 234-0230
Philip B. Sorensen	(212) 595-9835 (917) 887-3432
Arthur O. Soyk	(914) 359-9275 (914) 329-4078
Stephen Speer	(212) 873-9788
Joshua W. Spring	(301) 229-9612
Lee Ann Squires	(914) 469-3581
James A. Stamulis Jr.	(516) 233-2025 (917) 887-8882
Daniel (Brooke) Stanford	(718) 834-5312 (917) 776-7123
Michael Staranowicz	(215) 482-5795 (215) 669-9507
Donny Stegall	(732) 742-8222 (732) 448-1895
Paul Steinberg (Electrician)	(718) 438-0535
Kyle R. Stephens	(732) 951-1334 (973) 534-6724
Jonathan Stern	(646) 283-4550
Mark Stetz	(917) 502-9936
Robert Stevers	(212) 254-8789
Walter Stewart	(818) 907-0685
Derrick Still	(212) 283-0007 (917) 699-7568 FAX (718) 617-8488
Allen Stillman	(212) 608-6328
Brian A. Stocklin	(347) 231-8519
Frank J Stocklin	(301) 490-3544
Robert J. Stocklin	(917) 922-4467
Walter Stocklin Jr.	(516) 798-4268
Glenn Stroud	(845) 638-2517
Joseph T. Stubblefield	(718) 499-5840
Wyche F. Stubblefield	(718) 499-5840
Christopher Studley	(212) 228-4963 (415) 260-6030
Robert Styles	(845) 471-3236 (845) 464-2023
Mark Summers	(212) 529-2826 (917) 826-9114
Robert Supino	(212) 864-4139
John Suriano (Electrician)	(347) 221-2092
Michael J. Sweeney	(609) 786-1498
David H. Swift	(954) 898-4414
Christopher Szabo	(201) 634-9333 (201) 745-5157
John C. Tanzer	(323) 770-6111
Josh Taylor	(512) 565-1528
Robert Taylor	(718) 459-6813
Sean Taylor	(407) 748-4243
James Y. Temme	(646) 345-3062
Philip Testa (Gaffer)	(212) 627-1723 (917) 686-3027 FAX (212) 627-7081
James B. Thorne	(212) 473-5168 (917) 572-8653
Joel Tishcoff	(917) 757-1356 (718) 399-6665
Jon R. Tower	(310) 573-9295
Adrian Truini	(212) 924-5747 (917) 991-5567
Derrick Tseng	(718) 797-3245
David Tumblety	(718) 230-1207 (917) 864-0838
Steffen Unger	(917) 570-5571
Jon Zenfeek Unjang	(206) 579-5917
John Van Buskirk Jr.	(201) 296-0574 (201) 832-0490
Glenn J. Vander Linden	(845) 353-1939
William Van Ingen	(401) 596-3021
Joshua C.B. Van Praag	(347) 351-8537
Mark C. Van Rossen	(732) 335-3744

John Velez	(908) 804-3010 (914) 736-0420	Mark Weingartner (Gaffer)	(818) 702-1777 (818) 970-6833 FAX (818) 702-1779
Leon H. Vercruse	(914) 736-0420 (914) 537-6405	John A. Wellings	(607) 753-6222
Kevin Vincent	(347) 210-2834	Craig Werner (Electrician)	(908) 281-6057
Alfonso Violante	(973) 773-0051	Susan West	(609) 484-9740 (609) 432-1732
Tomas Von Rauchhaupt	(718) 383-9134 (917) 627-5252	Robert White	(917) 399-1953 (212) 260-0689
Robert Vuolo	(917) 620-8594	Jose V. Williams	(973) 374-4322
Michael W. Wacks	(201) 945-7573 (201) 446-3909	Jarvis B. Wilsher	(888) 280-0994
Patrick D. Wade	(917) 497-7816	John J. Woods	(718) 383-7031 (917) 414-6046
John Wagner	(718) 939-1028	David Woolner	(518) 312-3456
James F. Walsh Jr.	(201) 440-3227 (201) 647-6323	Daniel Wright	(201) 871-0289 (917) 617-4536
James Walsh Sr. (Gaffer)	(201) 967-9893 (201) 638-5488 FAX (201) 967-9893	Gerardus (Jerry) Wynkoop	(631) 789-5189 (631) 553-5576
Kevin P. Walsh	(973) 764-3044 (973) 476-0763	Michael Yetter	(917) 613-0685 (718) 574-0811
Peter Walts	(917) 750-2165	Robert T. Zetterberg	(516) 735-5812 (516) 389-0912
Andrew T. Watts	(718) 274-7895	Thomas J. Zetterberg	(631) 588-0243 (516) 548-2959
Ryan Webb	(917) 213-9611	Peter Zimmern	(646) 729-6868
Christopher Weck	(917) 450-8902 (212) 995-8730	Chris Zizzo (Gaffer)	(631) 757-3710 (917) 355-0229 FAX (631) 757-3758

www.freewebs.com/busyboy

Gaffers & Electricians (Local 52 NY)

Gaffers & Electricians

Frederick C. Anderson (856) 768-8477
(Electrician)

Stephen C. Barrow (803) 649-0017
(Gaffer) (917) 226-8562

Andy Futo (954) 577-0550
(Gaffer) (954) 439-4437
FAX (954) 577-0870

Marisa Gara (716) 284-4613
(Electrician)

Nicola Guarneri (347) 729-6896
www.nicolaguarneri.com

Ted Hayash (818) 653-5786
(Gaffer) (818) 893-0092
www.tedhayash.com

Alan Hostetter (212) 475-6166
(917) 328-1179
FAX (212) 473-3748
members.aol.com/farmbfilms/homepage.html

David E. Houlle (314) 647-0665
(Gaffer) (888) 661-1965
FAX (314) 647-0665
www.sspsinc.com

Stephen Kaye (617) 538-8212
(781) 932-0005
FAX (781) 932-0006
www.kayelites.com

Patrick McAllister (410) 758-1912
(Electrician) (410) 758-0450
FAX (410) 758-1914
www.annapolismobilepower.com

Robert Merk (203) 924-7281
(Electrician)

Gordon Minard (910) 814-1804
(910) 890-3428

Jon Minard (860) 228-9069
(860) 682-2728
FAX (860) 228-8209

George Orton (518) 584-9182
(518) 330-8274

Michael Phillips (518) 587-8870
(Electrician)

Edward Read (516) 735-3467
(917) 513-4333
www.readbroslighting.com

Ken Riemer (585) 787-2040
(585) 766-9420
FAX (585) 787-2040
www.kenriemer.com

Marc Rogers (203) 637-4068
(Gaffer)

Gregg A. Rosinsky (203) 253-4539

Richard T. Speed (314) 645-3205
(Gaffer)

Frank J. Stocklin (301) 490-3544
(Electrician) (301) 286-6339

Richard Ulivella (201) 294-6042
www.u3studios.com

Jason Velez (917) 497-9128

Stephen Woods (732) 673-5717
(Electrician)

Grips (Local 52 NY)

Manuel Abad III	(716) 435-3446
Joseph F. Abbatecola	(516) 443-0078
Robert A. Agredo	(718) 884-5097 / (917) 572-4110
Martin Albert	(917) 913-9630 / www.mbalbert.com
Peter Alexeev	(917) 509-1032
Michael Alfieri	(845) 369-6505 / (845) 406-7699
Bob Andres (Key)	(973) 464-6147 / FAX (718) 599-2077
David Araki	(212) 334-1108 / (917) 495-4498
Douglas H. Armstrong	(212) 832-3389
Tony Arnaud	(212) 334-7875 / (917) 660-1175
William S. Arnot	(917) 417-4701 / (415) 455-9556
Vincent Arteca	(718) 843-7790 / (917) 519-7531
Bruce A. Atwater	(631) 736-5401 / (516) 680-5363
Donald Aurnhammer	(201) 467-9226
Stephen A. Baker	(631) 744-8846 / (631) 929-3131
Edward R. Baklarz	(732) 335-8987
Joseph R. Baklarz	(732) 787-2170
Richard Baklarz	(732) 787-7446
Robert Baklarz	(732) 495-2937
Bruce Balton	(570) 296-2733 / (917) 952-8570 / www.brucebalton.com
Cesar S. Baptista	(917) 405-0983
Gene Baratta	(732) 239-1376
James Baratta	(732) 239-8098
James P. Barnes	(856) 468-3471 / (856) 623-1060
Michael Barnes	(856) 728-7275 / (215) 557-9982
Gerald A. Barrett Jr.	(732) 237-7113 / (732) 760-1187
Alison C. Barton	(212) 828-1669 / (617) 797-0583
Wesley S. Battle	(914) 712-7525 / (914) 837-4835
Robert G. Bauer	(610) 274-0291
Rodney Bauer	(516) 354-4248
Daniel Beaman	(201) 513-3758
Christopher Beattie	(610) 721-1250
Ruark Behan	(973) 235-0378 / (917) 836-3771
Christopher P. Belanger	(401) 596-5099
Joseph Belschner	(407) 529-6474
Peter A. Betulia	(212) 262-3174 / (917) 518-4286
Michael J. Betzag	(718) 326-2766 / (917) 886-2033
Donald M. Bialer	(212) 988-6408 / (917) 653-3460
Adam Bianchi	(212) 388-1861
Vincent J. Biscaino	(718) 858-6621 / (646) 523-1635
Ray Blackburn	(212) 751-4043 / (917) 648-4969
Matt Blades	(718) 488-9219 / (917) 804-4274
Alan Blagg	(917) 825-5216
Steven A. Blaho	(914) 788-6863
Laurent Blanchette	(845) 228-1739 / FAX (845) 228-1334
Marina Blanchette	(845) 380-0349
Arthur Blum	(323) 449-3759
John T. Bobick	(631) 499-6472 / (631) 255-7782
Garrett Boehling	(914) 923-1948 / (917) 670-9369
John Boesch	(201) 325-9363 / (201) 681-3134
James C. Bokor Jr.	(201) 797-3288
Keith Robert Bokor	(973) 823-9449
Thomas J. Boles III	(201) 947-0619 / (201) 376-3949
John H. Bolz	(516) 659-5007 / (516) 742-8409 / FAX (516) 742-7214
James Boniece	(914) 738-8564 / (914) 260-7312
Robert Bortner	(570) 559-7823 / (917) 572-0085
Rolf H. Bortner	(212) 737-0542 / (917) 389-9116
David Bowers	(917) 674-3342
Paul Boyd	(617) 427-0894
Rik Brady	(516) 448-3801

Sheridan R. Braxton	(610) 352-6524 / (610) 804-5551
John Breen	(215) 545-5225
Michael Brennan	(845) 692-4358 / (914) 975-0219
Kevin Bright	(917) 847-6113
Earle Brokenshire	(646) 246-3536
David M. Bromberg	(212) 724-7396
Bernard X. Brongniart	(917) 749-8727
Sydney Brook	(212) 926-3421 / (917) 941-8091
Jim L. Brown	(203) 459-4645
Richard Bruck	(914) 282-9033
Rick Bruck	(914) 668-4711 / (800) 375-5755 / FAX (914) 668-2411
John Brush	(732) 573-0209
Michael Buck	(732) 500-2956
Charles E. Buckland IV	(860) 667-9746
Peter Bulavinetz	(646) 498-4280 / (718) 279-0241
Keith Bunting Jr.	(718) 852-4699 / (800) 304-2182
James P. Burke	(518) 632-5697
Kenneth J. Burke	(315) 497-2879
Terrence C. Burke	(201) 363-0373 / (917) 887-2283
Terrence Laron Burke	(718) 379-5194 / (917) 596-2407
F. Joseph Burrell	(845) 399-5779 / (718) 353-0474
Sam Burrell	(917) 597-9205 / (718) 353-0474
Michael P. Byrne	(609) 924-7446 / (917) 942-1337
Gregory Cahill	(718) 789-0294 / (917) 886-0936
Kevin Cahill	(917) 776-0706 / (212) 228-0515
Keith Califano	(201) 610-0510 / (201) 303-0587
Kevin Califano	(732) 995-6451
Ryan J. Callahan	(215) 508-0452 / (215) 704-1671
Tony Campenni	(888) 853-5408
James F. Campolo	(845) 639-6073
Paul Candrilli	(201) 261-3812
Greg Canicio	(631) 697-0161
Michael Cappa	(516) 541-6839 / (516) 398-1632
Mitchell Carner	(716) 891-4783
David M. Carr	(917) 299-3901
Joel F. Carucci	(516) 570-0457 / (516) 353-0577
James A. Casey	(610) 626-4317 / (610) 501-0260
Charles Casillo	(718) 835-5789
Joseph Casillo	(718) 835-5789 / (917) 657-1045
Dan Cassidy	(917) 373-6829 / (619) 445-0958
Michael C. Cassidy	(801) 731-4209
Sean Cassidy	(516) 797-7467
William Cassidy	(631) 289-2109 / (516) 982-4611 / FAX (631) 654-4875
Eric Castaldo	(845) 561-4194 / (914) 299-5971
Francis L. Catalano	(212) 879-0246 / (917) 815-0378
Mark Catania	(856) 256-2075 / (800) 413-4085
Donald J. Cerrone	(212) 861-2703
Michael J. Cerullo	(201) 939-2321 / (973) 202-2477
Kai Wai Cheng	(516) 395-7020 / (516) 826-3344
Frederick Chesterman	(845) 216-4917 / (845) 359-2302
Andrew Cheung	(212) 877-9852
Archangelo V. Ciotti	(914) 725-4959 / (917) 956-1730
Marcel Ciurea	(917) 415-5422 / (718) 278-4817
Phil Clark	(718) 237-2145
Thomas Clark	(845) 228-1862 / (914) 953-5685
William R. Claxton	(718) 786-5884 / (917) 733-4691 / FAX (718) 786-5970
Dominick Cocuzzo	(718) 746-5606 / (718) 746-4414
Pat A. Cocuzzo	(718) 746-5606 / (347) 992-1842
Charles J. Colon	(718) 429-6782
Luis Colon	(516) 749-3961
Addison P. Cook	(718) 398-2947 / (917) 678-4737
R. Caswell Cooke	(201) 218-9287

James G. Cooper	(201) 358-1016 (201) 704-3266
John E. Corbett	(845) 477-2071 (845) 721-2113
Jason Cortazzo	(484) 431-8320 (610) 490-1720
Howard A. Cosgrove	(310) 737-9360
Damian F. Costa	(818) 402-9371
Daniel R. Cournoyer	(212) 722-7607
Anthony Cox	(718) 384-3238
Divine T. Cox	(914) 654-8082 (917) 632-5000
John Cuneo Jr.	(856) 939-2938
David A. Dabrowski	(302) 983-8979
Jeremiah Jay Dalton	(917) 685-7606
Joseph Damiano	(914) 941-5107 (914) 584-4801
Benjamin A. D'andrea	(914) 310-8385
Timothy A. Davies	(201) 656-2810 (201) 725-5955
Aaron Dawley	(718) 782-5370 (917) 869-0619
James F. Delahanty	(845) 987-8179 (845) 987-9043
Edward De Meglio	(484) 461-3889
Francis R. Demers	(203) 421-0143
Daniel J. De Nitto	(845) 246-1709
Eugene C. De Pasquale III	(631) 668-4108 (917) 824-6594
John J. De Siena	(516) 295-1399
James N. De Wolf	(201) 845-4634 (201) 914-0187
Frank R. Di Dio	(718) 966-6749
Pedro Diez	(646) 479-2138 (212) 254-6582
Gabriel D. Di Rienzo	(212) 956-6447 (845) 348-3972 www.gdrequipment.com
Stephen Disador	(845) 279-7459
John (Douglas) Dolan	(201) 315-3016
John P. Dolan	(973) 427-3009 (201) 315-3016 FAX (973) 427-5161
John J. Donaghy	(856) 468-6510 (856) 901-9597
Christopher Donohue	(718) 470-0365
Damien Donohue	(718) 470-0365 (917) 697-1101
John (JD) Donohue	(631) 321-1682 (516) 702-9292
Joseph G. Donohue Jr.	(718) 423-0170
Joseph G. Donohue III	(718) 229-0212 (646) 498-5684
Peter G. Donohue	(845) 735-8074 (917) 474-9074
S. Patrick Donovan	(718) 388-2928 (800) 362-7243
Sean M. Donovan	(513) 531-6107
Joe Doughan	(201) 891-5781 (201) 264-7934
Kevin Dougherty	(732) 787-4617
Daniel Dour	(914) 561-2551
Richard Dowgin	(845) 258-2879 (917) 742-5860
Gregory M. Dressel	(631) 767-5811
Charles E. Duer	(856) 933-2644
John G. Duncan Sr.	(610) 544-9253 (610) 742-1406
John W. Duvall	(914) 715-7773
Scott Eberle	(917) 513-8889
Terry R. Eckert	(702) 460-1999
James Edmiston	(718) 597-6065 (646) 522-6714
Edward J. Egan III	(201) 666-7143
Kevin M. Egan	(201) 265-5340
William T. Egan	(201) 265-4096 (201) 265-5340
Michael Eichner	(973) 770-1918
Christopher Elassad	(646) 533-4200 (718) 680-4583
George Elias	(718) 261-1950 (646) 642-6644
Dayson Engels	(973) 948-3716 (973) 277-9295
Glen K. Engels	(570) 828-2213
Kenneth Engels	(516) 759-6984 (917) 494-4912
Johnny Erbes-Chan	(917) 531-4883
Michael J. Fabiano	(203) 938-3320
Michael Farese III	(585) 392-1888
John Farina	(914) 693-3912 (914) 450-5225
Thomas Farmer	(212) 925-2244 (914) 666-7070
Matthew Farrell	(201) 403-5074
Richard Fedeli	(203) 500-4785
George C. Feldbauer	(908) 789-8919 FAX (908) 789-8919

Robert Feldmann	(917) 502-4389
Timothy J. Ferraer	(973) 769-4457
Edwin M. Figueroa	(212) 567-9100 / (917) 556-9433
Daniel M. Finn	(607) 746-9677
James M. Finnerty	(305) 258-1052
John Finnerty	(516) 221-8431 / (516) 826-8979
John M. Finnerty	(516) 579-8646
Joseph A. Finnerty	(516) 221-5887
Gerard J. Fiore	(516) 679-2963 / (516) 369-1492
Robert J. Fiore	(516) 520-0838
Glenn Fishel	(212) 289-2685 / (917) 744-7358
Andrew Fishman	(212) 717-2872 / (917) 690-5831
Brian J. Fitzsimons	(732) 747-2526 / (201) 320-3686
Glenn Fjotland	(212) 304-8234 / (917) 648-1200
Joseph Fleming	(516) 739-0706 / (516) 410-9086
Kevin W. Flynn	(201) 568-0466 / (646) 734-5894
Timothy J. Flynn	(973) 625-4151 / (973) 592-2184
Steven C. Fornes	(908) 692-7354
David Fortino	(215) 389-1347 / (215) 465-4222
Joseph Fortunato	(917) 750-1586
Ralph Fratianni	(718) 767-8834 / (917) 618-0503
Steven Fratianni	(718) 939-9209
Kenneth J. Fundus	(516) 798-3583 / FAX (516) 798-3583
Anthony Fungrai	(212) 691-4516 / (917) 859-8031
Jordan Gable	(215) 465-6958 / (267) 977-7634
John Gabriele	(212) 799-1234
Jason Galante	(718) 252-8837
Richard Galante Jr.	(718) 253-1913 / (347) 306-2358
Daniel Galdo	(973) 249-9660
Randall Gallagher	(212) 942-0422 / (917) 843-0213
Steven Gallo	(646) 342-2226 / (212) 869-7700
John J. Galuppo Jr.	(718) 667-1421 / (347) 675-9216
Dennis Gamiello Jr.	(914) 494-3580
Anthony F. Gamiello	(631) 324-1534 / (914) 557-4260
Christopher Gamiello	(914) 328-7592 / (914) 906-9704
Dennis Gamiello	(631) 324-1534 / (914) 391-6721
Robert E. Ganz	(201) 489-6413 / (917) 836-8594
John Gardenier	(201) 943-1936 / (201) 638-3940
Julia M. Gardner-Patsos	(516) 872-3469
George B. Gartland	(516) 641-4207
James B. Gartland	(516) 319-3916
James V. Gartland	(845) 623-1196 / (914) 392-8275
Justin T. Garvey	(860) 743-4048
William F. Garvey	(203) 562-6265
John Gatland	(631) 664-8498
Eric Gearity	(718) 932-1255 / (917) 881-2490
Kim Giglia	(718) 238-3456 / (917) 288-9333
Billy Gilleran	(818) 324-2553
Charles Gilleran	(213) 369-3099
Kevin Casey Gilligan	(732) 842-3257 / (612) 281-9512
Stephen Girouard	(347) 683-3310
Charles Goodman	(212) 304-9381 / (917) 359-8097
Paul V. Goroff	(203) 209-2462
Bradley J. Goss	(516) 541-0026 / (516) 581-4686
Kirk Goss	(631) 941-3881
James M. Grady	(732) 264-9417 / (732) 241-0264
Anthony D. Graf	(267) 258-7625
Jonathan Graham	(516) 536-8742 / (516) 805-1960
Christopher F. Graneto	(347) 683-3498
George E. Grant	(917) 691-4429
Francis C. Grasso	(856) 962-0306
Mark Grasso	(856) 784-3562
Jeremy S. Grites	(718) 383-9843 / (917) 865-5767

James P. Gruebel	(718) 843-1732 (917) 483-3157	John House	(718) 596-4699
Ian Grunke	(914) 552-0997 (914) 939-7564	Victor W. Huey	(212) 732-4587 (347) 693-9686
Paul Grunke	(603) 748-2685	Michael Hughes	(860) 340-5496
Matthew L. Guarriello	(718) 984-8877 (646) 302-6833	John Hulbert	(914) 628-2420
Vincent J. Guarriello	(718) 667-0139 (917) 205-5071	Anthony J. Itri	(718) 967-8871 (347) 723-1460
Melissa Guimaraes	(917) 453-0093	Frank Itri	(718) 980-1862 (718) 689-0694
Richard J. Guinness Jr.	(516) 795-5601 (516) 541-4527	Anthony R. Iulo	(201) 784-8874
		Robert (Bob) Izzo	(917) 539-9277
Kevin Hackenberg	(215) 859-0607 (215) 769-7310	Edward R. Jabara	(718) 836-2203
Nicholas Haines-Stiles	(212) 920-1038	Gary P. Jackiewicz	(917) 715-9778
Adam M. Hall	(917) 405-0931	Robert A. Jackson	(914) 423-9289
H. Jay Halligan	(732) 859-3037	Rory A. Jackson	(914) 968-3653
John J. Halligan	(732) 345-8110	James P. Jacob	(718) 726-6531 (917) 759-1815
Paul J. Halligan	(732) 872-8008 (732) 245-6715	Frank Jacoby Jr.	(609) 407-7191
Thomas E. Halligan Jr.	(215) 529-5423 (732) 222-4788	Jeffrey C. Jirgal	(845) 623-5583 (845) 685-7671
Matthew L. Hanlon	(215) 836-9995 (267) 250-7169	Thomas Jirgal	(845) 735-4266 (845) 461-3959
Eugene P. Hannafey	(732) 747-9005 FAX (732) 530-5949	Jasper Lee Johnson III	(732) 968-9574 (732) 558-5306
Robert Harlow	(347) 701-3601	Thomas L. Johnson Jr.	(917) 650-1130
William Harrer Jr.	(484) 251-1710	Patrick G. Johnson	(646) 331-1555 (718) 227-7736
James Harris	(914) 362-8113		
Douglas Hart	(718) 937-7250	Salvatore J. Johnson	(718) 227-7736 (347) 728-0166
Richard J. Hebrank	(845) 878-6574 (914) 475-0213	Thomas Johnson	(718) 227-7736 (646) 331-2555
James Heerdegen	(347) 228-7009	Edward Jones Jr.	(973) 676-9871 (973) 592-8382
Zachary Henderson	(646) 785-6154		
Christopher L. Hensel	(267) 242-0344	William P. Jones	(215) 462-4430 (215) 266-0498
Christopher Hernandez	(914) 621-7850	Bruce R. Jordan	(718) 225-0611 (718) 344-4588
Pedro Hernandez	(570) 643-2790 (570) 977-1057	Steven A. Jordan	(609) 484-0661
John James Herron	(570) 686-3873 (570) 807-3319	Brandon Kamin	(516) 791-1875 (516) 232-1417
Neire Hester	(212) 369-8161 (347) 386-1483	Michael J. Kammerer	(201) 430-4253 (201) 344-6537
Thomas J. Hill	(201) 814-0084	Michael J. Kammerer Jr.	(732) 571-2302 (732) 996-7823
Brent P. Hirn	(914) 353-3724 (914) 261-6600	Peter Kantor	(917) 373-9344
Thomas J. Hocking	(845) 878-3830 (914) 391-8065	Keith F. Kastner	(516) 731-6646 (516) 314-5109
Dana S. Hook	(732) 530-5195 (732) 687-2765	John Keating	(718) 278-0015 (917) 945-6542

Casey Kehoe	(323) 668-2713
Harold Reid Kelly	(732) 829-1657 (732) 829-7469
Joseph W. Kelly	(516) 485-9527
Timothy J. Kelly	(212) 327-3101 (917) 673-0779
Richard Kelusak	(609) 457-6010
Thomas Kempf	(347) 558-5044
Kenneth G. Keneally	(212) 997-2272
Daniel P. Kennedy	(516) 623-8332 (516) 553-5984
John D. (Jack) Kennedy	(646) 423-7787
John T. Kennedy Jr.	(516) 763-2935 (516) 793-2985
Patrick J. Kennedy	(631) 378-3894
Thomas G. Kennedy	(516) 255-9377
Timothy Keogh	(917) 864-4017
Richard C. Kerekes	(800) 796-7363
Edward T. Kerwick Jr.	(631) 543-4937 (917) 808-4740
Thomas E. Kerwick Jr.	(631) 471-7748 (631) 445-3810
Kevin Kerwick	(631) 807-9006
Thomas Kerwick	(631) 471-7748 (516) 662-7655
William V. Kerwick	(631) 360-1217 (516) 650-2279
Richard J. Khorigan	(718) 353-8843 (207) 938-4232
Dmitry Kibrik	(718) 975-0394 (917) 734-8805
Chris C. Kilduff	(718) 849-1953 (347) 563-3342
Roger Kimpton	(212) 580-5103 (917) 364-2211
Daniel D. Kirsch	(845) 651-1153 (914) 830-0977
Michael Kirsch	(347) 645-7663
Graham Klatt	(848) 459-2521 (732) 961-0378
Anthony Klein	(718) 352-4107
Mark A. Klein	(646) 533-7863 (718) 352-6771
Todd S. Klein	(212) 665-6039 (917) 403-7025
Edward J. Knott III	(772) 293-1011
Morton Korn	(845) 358-5975 (914) 217-5671
Ronald P. Koval	(518) 587-9160
Edward Koza III	(908) 337-2494
John M. Krause	(718) 599-7899 (917) 721-8740
Christopher Kubicek	(215) 275-4273
Thomas Kudlek	(516) 763-2787 (516) 850-1101
Robert Kummert	(973) 663-0082
Zbigniew Kuros	(718) 499-5851 (718) 614-1167
Carl J. Landi	(352) 551-4995
Sal J. Lanza	(845) 878-9829 (917) 953-2414
Vincent M. Lanza	(718) 863-0373 (917) 855-6024
Edward Larkin	(718) 428-0726 (917) 668-4380
Edward M. Larkin Jr.	(214) 929-3279
Daniel Larro	(609) 390-1883
David John La Rue	(508) 544-5190
Charles (Buddy) Lawn	(215) 236-9420
Francis (Bosko) Leach	(212) 673-5512 (917) 613-9421
Joseph Leggiere	(201) 337-8024 (201) 651-8880
Edward R. (Ted) Lehane	(718) 832-6834 (917) 673-7548
Christopher Leonard	(516) 826-6489 (516) 805-1485
James M. Leonard	(914) 476-9339
Randy Levine	(732) 716-0917
William Ley	(973) 586-7756
Robert J. Liccio Jr.	(856) 232-9401
Mitchell Lillian	(845) 258-1786 (914) 536-8370 FAX (845) 258-1816
Jeffrey M. Lo Maglio	(917) 309-7722
Roberto J. Lopez	(917) 662-2083
Paul Loret	(973) 344-6223 (201) 517-6215
David William Lowe	(610) 747-0494 (215) 905-3847
Brendan Lowry	(631) 544-9195 (631) 433-2669
David F. Lowry	(631) 462-6657 (631) 499-4988
David F. Lowry III	(631) 462-6657
Edward W. Lowry	(631) 421-6010 (516) 297-2430

Gerard J. Lowry	(631) 425-7773 (646) 294-1081
Kevin Lowry	(646) 523-4649
Martin Lowry	(631) 544-9195 (631) 433-2705
Patrick J. Lowry	(631) 549-7280 (631) 484-4221
Shaun Lowry	(631) 544-9195 (631) 433-2670
Thomas E. Lowry	(904) 225-5122
William Lowry Jr.	(718) 599-3084 (917) 880-8739
Matthew J. Luberda	(631) 680-8947
Neil Luberda	(631) 821-5480 (516) 339-6503
Peter Lunarola	(718) 227-5506 (718) 835-2689
Matthew Lynch	(914) 562-4504 (718) 589-7600
Stephen Lynch	(718) 383-0048 (917) 912-4410
Todd Mac Nicholl	(845) 856-3826
Constantine Gus Magalios	(631) 957-7385
Dan Mahoney	(917) 544-1794
Brendon Malone	(631) 669-0369
Sean Malone	(816) 304-2448
Christopher G. Manos	(215) 462-7833 (215) 290-1023
John Marcotte	(646) 996-5598
Robert Markus	(212) 254-5046 (917) 686-4307
Charles Marroquin	(845) 987-8058 (646) 734-9124
Rick L. Marroquin	(212) 749-3230 (917) 699-4018
Keith Marshall	(914) 469-7948 (800) 366-2377
Edgar Martin	(718) 852-4699
Greg Martin	(212) 249-4328 (917) 209-8802
Gary Martone	(718) 423-9232
Chris N. Marzulli	(914) 772-5199
Thomas Marzulli	(212) 627-5592 (646) 641-2137
Louis M. Massa	(917) 972-0417
Gregory A. Mazzola	(718) 351-3455
John J. Mazzola	(718) 946-2429 (917) 295-7559
Ronald Mazzola Jr.	(917) 453-3427
John G. Mazzoni Jr.	(609) 586-5365
David A. McAllister	(732) 684-6115 (917) 560-4105
Seth McAllister	(718) 246-5090 (917) 449-8763
George McCabe	(718) 318-6234 (347) 782-3574
Joseph L. McCabe	(718) 634-7572
Kenneth S. McCallum	(610) 924-9684 (215) 480-2655
Kevin McConville	(570) 698-7381 (570) 470-5902
Benjamin G. McCullough	(516) 488-3122
Neil McDermott Jr.	(631) 385-4689
John (Jack) McDevitt	(914) 987-7796 (914) 408-1355
John McElwain	(973) 713-0219
John F. McEnerney	(718) 963-3532 (917) 674-1147
Michael A. McFadden	(203) 645-6909
Walter McGrady	(917) 592-9729
Michael McGrath	(212) 928-1326 FAX (212) 928-1328
Patrick J. McGrath	(732) 571-9583 (732) 996-2371
Anthony McGuiness	(516) 561-3952 (516) 638-9080
David J. McIntyre	(215) 425-6571 (215) 407-3306
James C. McMillan Jr.	(631) 277-9442 (516) 645-2922
Timothy M. McMillan	(949) 933-4092
Alan J. Mehlbrech	(215) 339-5250 (215) 719-2929
James Merritt	(914) 679-2639
John Merritt	(845) 781-5035
James J. Miller	(516) 860-4337 (516) 632-5123
James V. Miller	(516) 799-9793 (516) 250-1620
John C. Miller	(609) 476-2027
Michael A. Miller	(201) 573-8659
William A. Miller Sr.	(631) 734-4162
William J. Miller	(914) 690-2887
Charles D. Minter	(302) 981-0595 (610) 869-9292
Monique Mitchell	(201) 864-8023 (917) 620-2326
Robert M. Mock	(610) 466-0640
Jeffrey T. Monaco	(845) 623-1615 (845) 494-9965

Nicholas J. Mongelli Jr.	(718) 331-7566 / (646) 529-2029
Kevin W. Montgomery	(631) 928-9187 / (516) 480-4200
Michael Montgomery	(845) 621-1792 / (917) 560-8658
Richard C. Montgomery Jr.	(914) 963-3011
Timothy Montgomery	(631) 654-0547 / (516) 426-9561
Ronald S. Morales	(347) 416-6087
William Moran	(212) 787-1180
Michael M. Morini	(917) 589-2010
Talley W. Morse	(718) 279-0299
Paul Mowbray	(609) 625-0430
Kevin E. Mullins	(973) 208-9178 / (973) 479-5081
Raymond Murphy Jr.	(201) 263-0064 / (201) 263-0065
Robert Murphy	(718) 468-0437 / (917) 362-3424
Daniel Nallan	(631) 544-0727 / (516) 769-1244
William J. Nallan III	(516) 679-8529
Edward J. Newins	(888) 814-7857 / (917) 679-7022
William Ngai	(914) 359-8911
Paul Niccolls	(917) 579-5631 / (201) 459-6062
Paul Nickason	(973) 783-9580 / (646) 325-4199
David Noble	(410) 336-4901
James (Jim) Nolan	(718) 218-8448 / (917) 207-4352
Melvin Noped	(917) 838-0913
Adam Novich	(914) 584-1838
Neil Novich	(914) 674-9126 / (914) 815-0859
Anna Novick	(212) 665-2127 / (734) 717-0840
Jon Nussbaum	(973) 838-8869 / (973) 886-5547
Michael H. Oates	(201) 886-1547 / (201) 886-2343
William A. Oates	(201) 945-8162 / (917) 247-8132
Sean O'Brien	(732) 775-0467
Donald T. Ogle Jr.	(609) 435-2657
Arne Olsen Jr.	(973) 919-4777
Arne S. Olsen	(718) 815-7397
Neil O'Malley	(516) 449-7906
Jeffrey Panessa	(917) 705-5161
Matthew Pangione	(201) 784-9421 / (973) 563-8697
Francis Panuccio	(718) 631-2641 / (917) 966-3271
Francis Panuccio II	(718) 631-2641 / (646) 262-5213
John Panuccio	(516) 735-6065 / (516) 205-0626
Justin Panzanaro	(732) 968-9434 / (908) 930-4978
Raymond A. Paquette	(914) 747-1788
Robert H. Paquette	(914) 423-3567 / (914) 450-8916
Robbin Park	(847) 331-4909
Richard Pashayan	(203) 952-3409
George Patsos Jr.	(631) 367-1959 / (516) 242-3831
William Patsos (Key)	(516) 561-7943
Kenneth P. Pattinson	(610) 532-2149
George Pattison	(631) 261-9115 / (516) 527-9915
Jesse C. Pelikan	(516) 739-0705 / (516) 315-8411
Carl Peterson	(201) 385-6881
Louis Petraglia	(718) 380-3249 / (646) 208-5768
William J. Philbin	(860) 527-4613
Balint K. Pinczehelyi	(646) 894-5275
Ronald R. Plant	(516) 541-3306 / (917) 693-1238
Robert B. Podbielski	(516) 997-2342 / (917) 744-6087
Brent A. Poleski	(646) 533-9727
James H. Pollard	(201) 797-7250 / (551) 206-7676
Thomas Popola	(845) 657-6802
Igor (Gary) Potashnik	(718) 854-7955 / (917) 776-5162
Geoffrey D. Pound	(914) 827-3155 / (914) 329-5464
Philip Poznick	(631) 266-6957 / (631) 258-4755
Michael J. Prate	(631) 266-6957 / (631) 258-4755
Robert S. Prate Jr.	(631) 368-7679 / (631) 877-1806
Robert T. Prate Sr.	(631) 368-7679 / (631) 871-0389

Thomas Prate	(631) 266-6956 / (631) 266-6957
Thomas R. Prate Jr.	(631) 266-6957
Ian Pratt	(347) 439-4954 / (718) 633-8005
Charles A. Price	(516) 965-9566 / (516) 797-4374
Douglas G. Price	(917) 754-7184
Christopher Primavera	(201) 943-8578 / (201) 501-2534
Carl Prinzi	(212) 924-7678 / (917) 824-6211
Christopher Proscia	(845) 774-8420 / (845) 304-0971
Frank Proscia	(914) 371-4297
Frank Proscia Jr.	(845) 354-6314 / (845) 642-6684
Joseph F. Proscia	(845) 504-5501 / (845) 598-8082
Rocco Proscia	(718) 792-7018 / (646) 739-2940
Steven M. Proscia	(914) 368-3918
Melvin Pukowsky	(718) 491-4960 / (917) 309-7491
Douglas Purcell	(201) 322-6814 / (201) 760-9050
Philip Purificato	(718) 738-5986 / (646) 321-1835
Christopher Quiles	(917) 312-5177
Brendan Quinlan	(631) 750-3178 / (631) 445-8359
Raymond Quinlan	(631) 513-3327 / (631) 289-7355
Charles Quinlivan	(212) 206-8161
Edwin A. Quinn Jr.	(845) 504-5464
Kevin M. Quinn	(201) 236-3899
Jonathan Ramirez	(516) 739-0705 / (516) 650-9393
Steven K. Ramsey	(718) 834-0830 / FAX (718) 834-0830
Robert Raposa	(845) 783-6901 / (917) 248-4804
Ralph Rea	(516) 825-1483
Sabatino (Sonny) Rea	(516) 825-1483 / (516) 395-4982
Thomas K. Reap	(267) 246-6378
James Reid	(631) 737-5672
Charles E. Reidy	(212) 979-8710
Kevin C. Reidy	(201) 221-6648
Richard Reiser	(845) 687-7515 / (914) 413-3572
Kimberly Rial	(215) 462-4430 / (267) 226-7577
Kelly Richardson (Dolly Grip, Jib Operator & Key Grip)	(203) 380-9942 / www.dollyrental.com
Daniel E. Rieser	(610) 668-9683 / (215) 401-6666
James A. Riley IV	(845) 878-9266 / (845) 590-9736
Kurt Rimmel	(914) 924-2254
Edward (Ted) Robinson Jr.	(718) 854-2128 / (917) 670-4313
P. Michael (Rodi) Rodia	(718) 858-2423 / (917) 771-6424
Stephen Rooney	(917) 693-3326
Steven Rose	(212) 249-2219 / (646) 319-5167
Jon W. Rosenbloom	(917) 974-3216
David Rossi	(212) 595-1244 / (917) 664-4202
Nathaniel M. (Nat) Russell	(718) 431-2296 / (917) 743-5999
Thomas T. Ryan Jr.	(914) 969-0159 / (914) 497-5933
Nicholas Saad	(203) 767-8640
Philip F. Saad	(917) 842-6555
Louis C. Sabat	(631) 754-4907 / (631) 664-1500
Steven Sabat	(631) 754-4907 / (631) 463-1257
Randy M. Salo	(917) 349-0565
James Saluzzi	(631) 265-1698
Joseph Sarao	(609) 892-9876 / (718) 419-6889
Jesse Saviola	(646) 772-8650
Christopher Scarafile	(718) 622-7395 / (917) 586-5657
Maximillian Schelle	(973) 726-0420
Frank D. Schiumo	(732) 671-0711 / (917) 380-5446
Robert W. Schmitt	(718) 631-3859 / (646) 236-1650
Patrick F. Schneider	(845) 657-8398
Klaus C. Schreiber	(212) 982-9813 / (917) 696-7737
Jeremy W. Schroeder	(718) 768-8612 / (888) 855-0732
Kurt Schwarz	(718) 599-6872 / (917) 604-6397

Grips (Local 52 NY)

Anthony Scott-Gamiello	(718) 539-1353 / (347) 392-0564
E. James Scutakes	(516) 922-0983 / (516) 680-2950
Robert W. See	(856) 429-7111 / (856) 795-6741
Gary W. Seeley	(201) 805-3921
John R. Shea	(631) 543-4124
Patrick J. Shelby	(917) 853-0856
Richard Sherron	(718) 845-8279 / (718) 207-0746
Lee Shevett	(212) 982-1820 / (917) 886-9228
Robert Shulman	(718) 625-3586 / (845) 800-8979 / FAX (718) 625-3586
Jonathan P. Sibert	(856) 853-7655 / (609) 805-2028
Jeffrey A. Sigler	(201) 383-8325
Santo Silecchia	(201) 348-3290
Steven J. Silverman	(212) 947-2255
Craig A. Simpson	(215) 389-2883 / (877) 523-0092
Markham Sindeband	(718) 782-8071 / (917) 364-4004
Christopher Skutch	(973) 233-9389 / (973) 632-3637
M. Eric Slifkin	(718) 583-7053 / (212) 722-9084
Dustin Smith	(212) 724-4075
Timothy J. Smith	(631) 261-1129 / (516) 651-4838
Kevin Smyth	(917) 863-8804
Timothy Smythe	(212) 308-2772
Adam Snyder	(718) 625-0130 / (917) 827-4097
Roger C. Snyder	(518) 842-0628
Duncan M. Spencer	(215) 468-8608
Kenneth M. Sperling	(800) 474-7361 / (914) 419-9462
Joshua Steinberg	(917) 942-3632
Keith Steinberg	(646) 739-0083
Lawrence Steinberg	(718) 591-9868
Paul Steinman	(718) 243-2800 / (917) 224-7555
David Stern	(917) 701-7803
Al Stetson	(845) 621-1730 / (914) 645-8790
Robert F. Strader	(516) 458-3452
Miles Strassner	(732) 613-9277
Arthur Strong	(631) 220-4624 / (631) 673-7967
Jay C. Stuart Jr.	(703) 837-9266 / (917) 780-2199
Jared Sturner	(914) 777-7400 / (914) 774-9156 / www.cameracars.net
Richard R.T. Suffern	(917) 805-5055 / (917) 649-5178
Michael J. Sullivan	(718) 398-6569 / (415) 793-1974
Andrew Sweeney	(718) 832-2809 / (917) 586-5277
Patrick J. Taistra	(201) 931-1202 / (201) 362-7184
Michael J. Tartaglio	(609) 653-1271 / (800) 918-7581
Michael F. Tavani	(860) 974-1577
Randall Thomas	(203) 835-6457
Kenneth Thompson	(718) 822-6691 / (718) 312-9569
Lois M. Thompson	(718) 723-1099
Russell Tiberio III	(203) 981-4487
Hector E. Toledo Jr.	(732) 940-9077 / (732) 688-8576
Bryan J. Tonkin	(718) 305-3431 / (917) 939-3130
Christopher Tonkin	(718) 274-2629
Daniel Tonkin	(718) 274-2629
Frankie Tonkin	(718) 746-3573 / (917) 439-7499
Nicholas Tonkin	(718) 746-3573 / (917) 295-1133
Anthony Tortorice	(484) 840-0785 / (215) 901-0263
Anthony J. Tortorice Jr.	(215) 271-8920
Irapaul X. Turner	(718) 529-5875 / (646) 373-3297
James A. Turner Jr.	(718) 448-7526
Marcus Turner	(718) 636-8469
Eric Ulrich	(917) 650-8667
Perry Z. Unjang	(917) 653-6879
Christopher Vaccaro	(201) 321-3437
Craig W. Vaccaro	(973) 632-0874
Nicholas R. Vaccaro	(973) 633-0342 / (973) 393-1956

Joseph A. Valle Jr.	(631) 418-5513
Joseph A. Valle Sr.	(860) 354-4447
Robert N. Valli	(925) 631-9271
Bob A. Van Heek	(302) 654-5169
William J. Vanderputten	(212) 691-4387 (917) 418-8918
Donald M. Vetick	(609) 895-1010 (609) 658-9300
Joseph Viano	(631) 462-9116 (917) 758-2582
Peter Vietro-Hannum	(917) 324-5175
Frank Vigilante	(917) 513-3043
Eric R. Volpe	(201) 714-9376
Mark F. Volpe	(323) 222-4929
Daniel Vranesich	(973) 779-6042
Marc F. Vranesich	(973) 423-4759 (201) 980-3259
Paul Wachter	(914) 948-2610 (914) 671-9255
Rory C. Walsh	(516) 797-6656 (516) 655-8958
Paul T. Wardwell	(718) 648-1113 (718) 757-1209
David Wasserman	(917) 312-5907
Ronald Waters	(212) 987-9552 (917) 763-3744
William M. Weberg	(914) 478-5228 (917) 301-5180
Josh Weiner Jr.	(800) 347-2574
Glen Weinstein	(845) 265-3170 (914) 629-4829
Michael Wekselblatt	(914) 654-1354
Paul T. Weller	(212) 239-4171
Oleh Weselyj	(860) 320-4654
Timothy J. Weston	(215) 230-3402 (215) 824-8284
Tony J. Whitman	(310) 395-8706
David T. Williams	(860) 360-2862
Edward Williams	(212) 780-1710 (845) 439-3506
Joseph P. Williams	(845) 227-8306
Kevin P. Williams	(718) 601-0849
Paul J. Wilson	(732) 872-1678 (732) 687-7889
Benjamin J. Wingard	(732) 951-2412 (609) 828-0505
Joshua Wingard	(215) 741-0888 FAX (215) 752-4086
George A. Wolcheski Jr.	(203) 468-7593
Richard H. Wong	(626) 307-8872
Daniel Woods	(570) 588-9705 (201) 491-1191
Robert M. Woods	(845) 298-1899 (845) 797-1175
Robert Woods Jr.	(917) 664-8217
Stephen Woods	(732) 673-5717
Thomas McGrath Woods	(203) 355-1817 (203) 274-2774
Gary W. Yacuk	(516) 232-3828
Richard Yacuk	(516) 681-0959 (516) 244-1758
Thomas Yacuk	(845) 424-4531
Franz J. Yeich	(973) 571-1912 (973) 220-5692
Thomas G. Yostpille	(516) 287-4457 (516) 897-7997
Ernest Yurich	(718) 323-6114 (917) 747-2427
Michael W. Yurich	(718) 323-6114 (917) 502-9264
Don L. Zappia	(914) 963-8497 (914) 562-3513
Nina Zarnett	(212) 206-0178 (917) 450-8716
Thomas Zeleski	(631) 567-0399

Grips

Martin W. Brennan	(860) 283-0877
James W. Finnerty Jr.	(516) 767-7010 (917) 916-0370
Richard A. Galante Sr.	(718) 252-8837 (516) 546-0722
Edward R. Geller	(302) 764-1646 (302) 562-9498
Jay Geller	(302) 652-1883 (302) 743-2144
Charles Gill	(716) 634-5529 FAX (716) 634-5529
Howard Krupa	(212) 625-9327 FAX (212) 625-9346 www.atlantictv.com
John Merrick	(704) 347-5846 (704) 904-2816
Jeffrey M. Meyer	(315) 436-4723 FAX (315) 425-9068 www.geocities.com/collectorpimp07
Talley W. Morse	(718) 279-0299 (954) 328-7528 FAX (718) 279-0299
Ralph Perri (Key)	(203) 667-0550
Charles J. Prideaux	(917) 513-7476 (720) 565-1191 www.paladinentertainment.com
George M. Roach Jr.	(215) 533-9164
Roosevelt Roberts	(718) 816-6739
Richard C. Rose	(802) 372-8829 (914) 522-9652
Robert Swedenhjelm	(585) 394-4037 FAX (585) 394-4037
Justin Vanson	(917) 887-3963
James B. Walsh	(818) 802-8707

Hair & Makeup Artists (Local 798 NY)

Mary Aaron (212) 627-4304
(Makeup)

Brian Abbott (917) 972-7408
(Makeup)

Patrick Alemi (845) 893-9911
(Hair)

Marleen Alter (617) 510-8792
(Makeup)

Monserra Alvarez (212) 923-7996
(Hair)

Belinda Anderson (347) 731-3926
(Hair)

Bert Anderson (718) 704-7206
(Hair)

Matiki A. Anoff (718) 622-5365
(Makeup)

Janet Arena (917) 439-7022
(Makeup Artist)

Lazaro Arencibia (646) 265-9940
(Hair)

Willie (Cody) Armstrong (646) 387-6353
(Hair)

Pamela Arnone (212) 333-2633
(Makeup)

Jill Astmann (212) 979-0845
(Makeup)

Angelina Avallone (203) 232-8424
(Makeup)

Brian Badie (347) 645-4464
Hair

Robert Baker (212) 740-4915
(Makeup)

Vivian Baker (888) 857-2730
(Makeup)

Linda Balletto (203) 284-8863
(Makeup)

Caryn Bardunias (631) 872-9819
(Makeup)

Carole Barone (212) 586-1953
(Makeup) FAX (212) 586-1953

Stephanie Barr (917) 885-6502
(Makeup)

Donna Battersby-Green (718) 263-4303
(Hair)

Guy Bayo (646) 468-5737
(Hair)

Adrienne Bearden (610) 918-2759
(Makeup)

Michelle Beck (607) 326-3441
(Makeup)

Deborah Bell (973) 224-2866
(Makeup)

Patty Bell (412) 298-3936
(Makeup)

Charlene Belmond (917) 453-6133
(Hair)

Juanita Bennett (215) 776-1532
(Makeup)

Kevin Bennett (917) 658-4204
(Makeup)

Barry Berger (917) 868-4435
(Makeup)

Simone Berritto (347) 723-9251
(Makeup)

Sonya Bertolozzi (917) 734-6174
(Makeup)

Kate Best (917) 295-9546
(Makeup)

Annette Bianco (917) 387-2651
(Hair)

Teresa Bianco (201) 615-9796
(Makeup)

Wayne Bilotti (212) 787-8611
(Hair)

Chris Bingham (212) 242-1903
(Makeup)

Katherine Biscoe (323) 839-0550
(Makeup)

Stephen Bishop (917) 685-1966
(Hair)

Jean Block (212) 967-9470
(Hair) (917) 843-4781
FAX (212) 268-7177
www.hairtheatrix.com

Margot Boccia (917) 880-9191
(Makeup)

Cyndie Boehm (347) 715-0357
(Makeup)

Laura Bonanni-Castorino (917) 837-0061
(Hair) (732) 970-3103
FAX (732) 970-3103

Karen Borgo (718) 921-0796
(Makeup)

Rebecca Borman (347) 256-4321
(Makeup)

Lorraine Boushell (917) 613-2627
Makeup

Kimberly Braisin (917) 370-1193
(Makeup)

Darianne Bramberg (516) 510-7261
(Makeup)

Veronica Brayman (917) 848-1675
(Hair)

Christina Brice (917) 783-6051
(Makeup)

Justen Brosnan (Makeup)	(917) 270-9204
David Brown (Hair)	(212) 807-0846
Dale Brownell (Hair)	(607) 847-8156
Tanya Bruhwiler (Makeup)	(917) 294-4267
Erin Daye Bruinsma-Gort (Makeup)	(516) 623-6969
Michelle Bruno (Makeup)	(212) 569-2669
Susan Bruzenas (Hair)	(917) 509-2669
Nicole Bryl (Makeup)	(212) 553-5695
Norman Bryn (Makeup)	(203) 869-5065
Francesco Buccellato (Makeup)	(917) 887-8809
Milton Buras (Hair)	(212) 706-0381
Nathan Busch (Hair)	(917) 952-3173
Laurie Cacioli (Hair)	(212) 866-1110
Ljiljana Cado (Makeup)	(215) 905-3843
John Caglione Jr. (Makeup)	(516) 617-1989
Chris Calabrese (Hair)	(973) 715-7319
Colleen Callaghan (Hair)	(201) 232-3646
Kymbra Callaghan (Makeup)	(201) 394-0458
Victor Callegari (Makeup)	(212) 769-1311
Joseph Campayno (Makeup)	(212) 529-0977
Carol Campbell (Hair)	(862) 216-0203
Lynn Campbell (Makeup)	(917) 407-3711
Christine Cantrell (Hair)	(516) 437-2836
Candace Carell (Makeup)	(917) 602-8106
Jean Carney (Makeup)	(617) 254-3456
Joyce Carollo (Hair)	(516) 781-2579
Vincenza Carovillano (Makeup)	(718) 863-9376
Ruth Gayle Carsch (Hair)	(347) 526-4118
Craig Carter (Hair)	(917) 385-0224
Roderick Carter (Makeup)	(412) 260-4109
Lori Cartwright (Hair)	(914) 962-2639
Elaine Casillo-Baez (Hair)	(201) 441-7185
Janet Cassidy (Makeup)	(212) 496-8564
Alexis Caydem (Hair)	(212) 243-4314
Benedett Celada (Makeup)	(212) 353-8308
Valentin Celada (Makeup)	(212) 677-5515
Michelle Champagne (Hair)	(201) 641-5994
Kay Chandy (Makeup)	(917) 257-6190
Rose Chatterton (Hair)	(917) 282-7270
Limor Chernichaw (Makeup)	(201) 261-7353
Larry Cherry (Hair)	(516) 378-9718
Judy Chin (Makeup)	(917) 750-1662
Michelle Chinnery (Makeup)	(917) 885-0788
Robert Chiu (Hair)	(917) 848-4856
Jane Choi (Makeup)	(917) 450-5122 www.janechoimakeup.com
Leslie Christin (Makeup)	(800) 314-0262
Brandon Claflin (Makeup)	(917) 494-4454
Luann Claps (Makeup)	(917) 623-0953
Sandra Claravall (Makeup)	(917) 415-1189
Chris Clark (Hair)	(917) 703-7535
Toni Coburn (Hair)	(212) 242-9423
Joanne Cocuzza-Offenhartz (Hair)	(914) 833-3835
Elizabeth Cohen (Makeup)	(718) 636-5599
Joseph Cola (Makeup)	(732) 207-5233

Mary Cook (Hair)	(212) 348-0069 / (917) 287-0909
Sharon Cordice (Makeup)	(724) 417-6636
Martial Corneville (Hair)	(212) 234-4755
Susan Corrado (Hair)	(917) 553-6969
Monica Costea (Hair)	(917) 640-9033
Pauline Coutroulis (Makeup)	(201) 401-0556
Joseph Cranzano (Makeup)	(215) 822-8204
Anita Crawford (Hair)	(917) 574-1888
Ana Crespo (Makeup)	(917) 767-6280
Joseph Cuervo (Makeup)	(917) 597-0539
Melissa Cullen (Makeup)	(848) 250-7026
Aleksandra Cummins (Hair)	(917) 478-7560
Daisy Curbean (Hair)	(347) 248-8453
Christine Curich (Hair)	(917) 301-1940
John Curtin (Hair)	(917) 327-7117
Alan Cutler (Makeup Artist)	(917) 301-6235
Michelle Cutler (Makeup)	(917) 359-0452
Lillian Cvecich (Hair)	(718) 357-4918
Mary A. D'Angelo-Hedrick (Hair)	(888) 260-7341
Diane D'Agostino (Hair)	(973) 768-9149
Crista Davi-Coppers (Makeup)	(201) 446-6233
Lisa Davis-Godley (Makeup)	(917) 806-8572
April Dawson (Makeup)	(914) 949-9762
Robin Day (Hair)	(917) 856-8256 / (718) 432-5665
Richard Dean (Makeup)	(212) 741-0202
Angelina De Angelis (Hair)	(917) 312-5428
Sherry Deberson (Hair)	(412) 885-1594
Phyllis Della (Hair)	(212) 223-2336
Melanie Demitri (Makeup Artist)	(888) 919-7163
Victor De Nicola (Hair)	(718) 886-2907
Thomas L. Denier Jr. (Makeup)	(631) 741-8982
Margina Dennis (Makeup)	(212) 608-7747
Suzanne DeSimone (Makeup)	(914) 456-0229
Felice Diamond (Makeup)	(516) 695-7987
Michael di Cesare (Hair)	(917) 642-7781
Karen Dickenson (Hair)	(917) 453-6494
John Digioia (Hair)	(646) 331-6699
Joanne Dimirco (Hair)	(212) 975-2460
Jane Di Persio (Makeup)	(917) 362-8657
Andrea Divincenzo-River (Hair)	(917) 304-0280
Diane Dixon (Hair)	(610) 247-5188
Christine Domaniecki (Makeup)	(973) 223-4529 / (973) 759-4977 / FAX (973) 844-9044 / www.make-upartistsatlarge.com
Naomi Donne (Makeup)	(212) 674-9776
Paula Dorf (Makeup)	(212) 724-8464
Jorjee Douglass (Makeup)	(917) 723-9637
Katherine Doumbia (Makeup)	(917) 894-5760
Katherine Drazen-Difulvio (Hair)	(212) 316-9896
Marjorie Durand (Makeup)	(917) 817-6697
Davion Edwards (Hair)	(917) 734-0665
Dennis Eger (Makeup)	(631) 252-3761
Paulette Elkind (Makeup)	(212) 315-3088 / (917) 673-8390
Mitchell Ely (Makeup)	(917) 535-6787
Jack Engel (Makeup)	(914) 318-6238

Sunday Englis (Makeup)	(516) 747-6829
Gary English (Hair)	(917) 306-2304
Richard Esposito (Hair)	(718) 518-9478
Eldo Ray Estes (Makeup)	(917) 817-0704
Wendy Evans (Hair)	(914) 882-8559
Andrea Fairweather (Makeup) www.fairweatherfaces.com	(917) 304-0749
Robert Fama (Hair)	(347) 604-3389
Scott Farley (Hair)	(917) 359-4134
Joseph Farulla (Makeup)	(201) 290-6558
Adele Fass (Makeup)	(646) 734-5275
Cynthia Faye (Makeup) www.angelfaceinc.com	(908) 654-1381
Anna Febres (Hair)	(718) 567-3763
Fern Feller (Makeup)	(917) 842-0469
Christine Fennell (Hair)	(516) 639-9632
H. Roxanne Ferguson (Hair)	(323) 216-5959
Enrico Ferrante (Hair)	(917) 496-6025
Jay Ferrara (Hair)	(718) 884-9380
Paul Ferraro (Hair)	(201) 317-1324
Donna Fischetto (Hair)	(516) 431-3249
Janet Flora (Makeup)	(917) 748-6896
Jeong Fonkalsrud (Makeup)	(973) 744-1022
Amrita-Diane Ford (Makeup)	(917) 846-9641
C. Romani Ford (Makeup)	(212) 662-4681
Kristen Foster (Hair)	(646) 642-8475
Kristi Fuhrmann (Makeup)	(917) 990-3409
Carl Fullerton (Makeup)	(201) 767-7690
Joanne Gair (Makeup)	(646) 432-9293
Angela Gallagher (Makeup)	(201) 214-1245
Helen M. Gallagher (Makeup)	(646) 335-2685
Fabian Garcia (Hair)	(917) 971-1343
Cindy Gardner (Colorist, Hair, Makeup & Wigs)	(818) 599-2723
Rachel Geary (Makeup)	(412) 292-1809
Paul Gebbia (Makeup)	(973) 812-2388
Alenalsa George (Makeup)	(718) 712-2166
Kay Georgiou (Hair)	(646) 705-3447
Lana Gersman (Makeup)	(212) 691-4234
Gregg Giannillo (Hair)	(917) 225-7074
Anita Gibson (Makeup)	(917) 355-4441
Doreen Gillis (Makeup)	(212) 288-1860
Hildie Ginsberg (Makeup)	(917) 532-6690
Susan Ginsberg (Makeup)	(516) 484-8055
Valerie Gladstone (Hair)	(718) 768-6119
Lorraine Godfrey (Hair)	(347) 513-7749
Thom Gonzales (Hair)	(973) 325-1697
Patricia Grande (Hair)	(917) 656-7794
Gloria Grant (Makeup)	(917) 697-1718
Bobby Grayson (Hair)	(917) 757-5357
Daniel Green Jr. (Makeup)	(917) 544-9736
Meredith Greene (Makeup)	(570) 476-8010
Wanda Gregory (Hair)	(201) 921-4261
Nicole Grieco (Makeup)	(917) 374-2266
Linda Grimes (Makeup)	(212) 477-3901 / (917) 854-3999
Anthony Gueli (Hair)	(347) 610-5109
Nzingha Gumb (Makeup)	(646) 228-7846

Robin Gurin (908) 832-9421
(Makeup)

Mitchell Hale (917) 572-8080
(Hair)

John Hall Jr. (215) 345-6847
(Makeup)

Stanley Hall (973) 902-6651
(Hair)

Souraya Hamdi (212) 729-8440
(Makeup) www.sourayahamdi.com

Maya Hardinge (917) 854-6212
(Makeup)

Lisa Harrell (631) 484-9025
(Hair)

Mary Jeanete Harrington (917) 593-0068
(Hair)

Dierdre Harris (718) 578-9691
(Hair)

Christopher Harrison (718) 921-7264
(Makeup) (917) 586-0077

Dallas Hartnett (201) 424-0968
(Hair)

Jason Hayes (917) 733-6033
(Hair)

Sherry Heart (646) 295-7032
(Hair)

Dianne Heller (610) 888-3679
(Makeup)

Jean Henry (917) 699-6247
(Hair)

Darwin Hensley (800) 916-0754
(Makeup)

Erin Hicks (917) 562-6393
(Hair)

Lori Hicks (718) 768-2922
(Makeup)

Gudrun Holt (201) 394-2394
(Hair)

Steven Horak (201) 585-2254
(Makeup)

Tisa Howard (917) 743-8523
(Makeup)

Sharon Ilson-Burke (917) 921-9612
(Makeup)

Lindsay Irish Desarno (610) 357-2455
(Makeup)

Keira Iritano (917) 928-0837
(Hair)

Demian Isla (646) 486-1032
(Hair)

Jennifer Ivey (770) 246-9633
(Makeup)

Ann Marie Izner-Preston (717) 227-3512
(Hair)

John James (646) 262-2223
(Hair)

J. Jared Janas (201) 349-4444
www.backstageartistry.com
(Body Painting, Colorist, Grooming, Hair, Makeup, Special FX Makeup & Wigs)

Tracy Jansen (201) 914-9322
(Makeup)

Angela Johnson (914) 419-6519
(Makeup)

D Michell Johnson (718) 486-5395
(Hair)

Florence Johnson (212) 288-3491
(Makeup)

Jennifer Johnson (212) 795-0840
(Hair)

Lisa Johnson (212) 662-8316
(Hair)

Robert Johnson (215) 564-1323
(Makeup)

David Johnstone (212) 505-1751
(Hair)

Herita Jones (800) 707-1915
(Makeup)

Jeanne Josefczyk (724) 448-7332
(Makeup)

Daedra Kaehler (917) 656-0633
(Makeup)

Mary Kahler (917) 608-8838
(Makeup)

Robin Kaiser (917) 783-5287
(Makeup)

Persefon Karakosta (646) 337-4215
(Makeup)

Keira Karlin (908) 654-8255
(Makeup)

Theodora Katsoulogiannakis (646) 207-4444
(Hair)

Bilgi Kaya (973) 568-6751
(Makeup)

Sandye Kaye (347) 681-7743
(Makeup)

Sanna Kayeriley (917) 318-6382
(Makeup)

Michelle Kearns (323) 788-4775
(Makeup) www.smak.com

Cassandra Keating (646) 591-3432
(Makeup)

Stephen Kelley (201) 280-9791
(Makeup)

Barbara Kelly (646) 286-0476
(Makeup)

Paula Kelly (212) 304-0838
(781) 964-9000
(Body Painting, Hair, Makeup, Special FX Makeup & Wigs)

Renee Kelly (718) 457-7980
(Hair)

Hair & Makeup Artists (Local 798 NY)

Robert Kelly (212) 819-0030
(Makeup)

Shanah-Ann Kendall (917) 445-7381
(Hair)

Rachel Kick (412) 576-1238
(Makeup)

Steven Kirkham (212) 929-2556
(Hair)

Lori Klein (212) 996-9390
(Makeup)

Sarit Klein (917) 412-4701
(Makeup)

Todd Kleitsch (917) 414-1920
(Makeup)

Jeffrey Knaggs (646) 675-9981
(Hair)

Frances Kolar (718) 344-1678
(Makeup)

Donald Kozma (845) 590-6479
(Makeup)

Tamah Krinsky (917) 592-3234
(Makeup) www.seemanagement.com

Michael Kriston (917) 940-8381
(Hair)

Anna Krommydas (917) 689-9511
(Hair)

Anne Yung Kruglinski (908) 432-5248
(Makeup)

Heidi Kulow (917) 282-9142
(Makeup)

Tina La Spina (917) 388-2573
(Makeup)

Bob Laden (718) 643-6483
(Makeup)

Julia Lallas-Brusilovsky (718) 809-6455
(Makeup)

Ciiauntel Langston (404) 223-6445
(Hair)

Michael Laudati (917) 846-1031
(Makeup)

Sherri Laurence-Berman (323) 253-4676
(Makeup)

Ellin Lavar (212) 724-4492
(Hair) www.lavarhairdesigns.com

Andrew Lavenziano (201) 880-8042
(Hair)

Champagne Lawrence (732) 558-9020
(Hair)

David Lawrence (917) 250-3186
(Hair)

Steven Lawrence (914) 941-2372
(Makeup) (917) 658-6059

Linda Lazar (201) 224-3323
(Makeup)

Nicki Ledermann (917) 912-5240
(Makeup)

Tia Lee (914) 671-6612
(Makeup)

Christine Leiter (212) 496-0935
(Makeup) (646) 831-9113

Stephane Lempire (917) 445-6453
(Hair)

Janelle Leone (917) 617-8160
(Hair)

Anette Lian-Williams (718) 832-5302
(Makeup)

Christina Liberatore-Ciardi (917) 738-5014
(Hair)

Linda Librizzi-Williams (973) 785-4046
(Hair)

Colleen Liddy (212) 561-0420
(Hair)

Craig Lindberg (917) 951-7039
(Makeup)

Nick London (609) 304-7567
(Makeup)

Deborah Long (917) 862-3512
(Hair)

Lanier Long (212) 772-8634
(Makeup)

Renate Long (212) 247-5933
(Makeup)

Angie Lorenzo (914) 576-8035
(Hair)

Karen Lovell (724) 809-9178
(Hair)

Claus Lulla (917) 204-7944
(Makeup)

Craig Lyman (212) 580-0584
(Makeup) (646) 732-4243

Mandy Lyons (917) 670-3223
(Hair)

Joseph Macchia (973) 612-2531
(Makeup)

Ronald Mackiewicz Jr. (718) 442-3823
(Hair)

Mike Maddi (917) 215-0440
(Makeup)

Tinayn Mahler (917) 861-0234
(Makeup)

Maria Maio (646) 894-9661
(Makeup)

Jodi Mancuso (347) 680-1991
(Hair)

Maryann Marchetti (917) 623-9352
(Makeup)

Chantal Mariani (Makeup)	(212) 203-1979	Joel Mendenhall (Makeup)	(917) 309-1358
Christine Marie (Makeup)	(631) 553-6457	Linda Mensching (Makeup)	(973) 772-7647 (201) 390-7099
Eva Marinakis (Hair)	(610) 656-8776	Randy Mercer (Makeup)	(917) 690-6284
Michael Marino (Makeup)	(845) 623-7776	Carol Meredith (Makeup)	(917) 509-0795
Josh Marquette (Hair)	(917) 754-3530	Kimberly Meyerhoff (Hair)	(203) 887-4082
Theresa Marra Siliceo (Hair)	(917) 748-0777	Kathrina Miccio (Makeup)	(917) 975-5496
Tarsha Marshall (Hair)	(516) 983-5228	Andrea Miller (Makeup)	(917) 992-2346
Annie Martin (Hair)	(646) 283-1683	Lisa Miller (Makeup)	(917) 359-5982
Marjorie Martin (Makeup)	(212) 262-3956	Jasia Miszkiel (Makeup)	(917) 673-4391
Eydie Martinez (Makeup)	(914) 263-4909	Jennifer Mooney Bullock (Hair)	(917) 609-0312
Gary Martori (Hair)	(917) 502-1175	Pat Moore-Theis (Makeup)	(917) 414-0899
Geri Mataya (Hair)	(412) 281-5400	Carole Morales (Hair)	(212) 362-4807
Pamela May (Hair)	(917) 804-1607	Maria Morales-Pappas (Hair)	(888) 907-1426
Bernadette Mazur (Makeup)	(914) 391-3520	Clariss Morgan (Hair)	(917) 306-5271
Suzy Mazzarese-Allison (Hair)	(718) 858-4870	Dianne Morgan (Makeup)	(908) 232-4780
Louise McCarthy (Makeup)	(917) 584-1426	Vicki Morgenstern (Makeup)	(617) 367-0103
Stephanie McGee-Glover (Makeup)	(973) 503-0527	Grace Morley (Makeup)	(212) 560-4990
Gail McGuire (Hair)	(347) 582-6330	Heather Morris (Hair)	(917) 667-0404
Christine McInerney (Hair)	(914) 438-8454	Marianne Morrison (Makeup)	(516) 413-1305
Charles McKenna (Hair)	(212) 586-5616	Eve Morrow (Makeup)	(917) 533-7789
Mel McKinney (Hair)	(212) 247-4998 (212) 247-8281	Robert Moulton (Makeup)	(917) 304-9708 www.robertmoultonmakeup.net
Ryan McWilliams (Hair)	(646) 258-7526	Donald Mowat (Makeup)	(310) 467-4152
Milagros Medina-Cerderia (Makeup)	(917) 209-4748	Donna Moyer (Makeup)	(610) 574-6088
Annette Meeks (Makeup)	(646) 724-0768	Mary Mulligan (Hair)	(718) 812-6628
Martha Melendez (Makeup)	(201) 408-4051	Carla Muniz (Hair)	(347) 262-1614
Linda Melo (Makeup)	(212) 246-4008 FAX (646) 296-2463	Tina Murgas (Makeup)	(917) 302-0813
Harold Melvin (Hair)	(212) 724-7700	Sandra Murphy (Hair)	(646) 322-5787

Robin Narvaez (Makeup)	(212) 675-8789
Jenn Nelson (Makeup)	(917) 543-6307
Amy Neswald (Hair)	(917) 330-3550
Merita Neziri (Makeup)	(347) 408-4065
Shpresa Neziri (Hair)	(917) 843-9711
Suzana Neziri (Hair)	(718) 281-2136
Peggy Nicholson	(908) 789-2480 / (908) 868-2826
Evelyne Noraz (Makeup)	(917) 721-7506
Michele O'Callaghan (Makeup)	(914) 815-1328
Karen O'Connell (Hair)	(516) 729-3122
Katherine O'Donnell (Makeup Artist)	(917) 957-7533
Richard Ogden (Makeup)	(212) 696-0318
Rita Ogden (Makeup)	(631) 261-9115
Ann-Marie Oliver (Makeup)	(917) 880-6588
Brendan O'Neal (Hair)	(347) 255-3097
Richard Orton (Hair)	(212) 249-8398
Robin Ostrow (Makeup)	(917) 509-7442
Rachel Pagani (Makeup)	(917) 836-2188
Kyra Panchenko (Makeup)	(201) 388-0802
Stacey Panepinto (Makeup)	(732) 890-4904
Francesca Paris (Hair)	(212) 421-1657 / (917) 539-6788
Joseph Paris (Hair)	(212) 889-4500
Michele Paris (Makeup)	(973) 662-9674
Stephanie Pasicov (Makeup)	(917) 842-2898
Nicky Pattison (Makeup)	(631) 261-9115
Anne Paul (Makeup)	(917) 734-5300
Deborah T. Paulmann (Makeup)	(914) 347-2035 / (914) 396-7687 / FAX (914) 347-6490 / www.deborahtpaulmann.com
Jacqueline Payne (Hair)	(917) 453-3138
Eve Pearl (Makeup)	(917) 757-7525
Pamela Peitzman (Makeup)	(610) 649-1010
Marilyn Peoples (Makeup)	(845) 662-1856
John Perkins (Makeup)	(718) 909-3591
Rebecca Perkins (Makeup)	(914) 450-4843
Tanaj Perry (Makeup)	(646) 725-9073
Julie Petesic (Makeup)	(201) 941-7715
Debra Phillips-Kunkel (Makeup)	(917) 817-1222
Dionne Pitsikoulis (Makeup)	(917) 570-4281
Riva Pizhadze (Makeup)	(212) 863-3206
Kerrie Plant (Makeup)	(917) 279-6870
Thelma Pollard (Hair)	(718) 638-6330
Eva Polywka (Makeup)	(917) 301-9175
Jerry Popolis (Hair)	(917) 319-1445
Bernadet Posey (Makeup)	(201) 871-8797
Bernadette Posey-Wilkms (Makeup)	(201) 463-6412
David Presto (Makeup)	(516) 369-2002
Howard Preston (Hair)	(717) 227-3512
Pearleta Price (Makeup)	(347) 683-7834
Rosanne Puchal (Makeup)	(718) 782-5908
John Quaglia (Hair)	(212) 683-8633
Aaron R. Quarles (Hair)	(917) 617-3305
Sacha Quarles (Hair)	(917) 734-8181
Lyndell Quiyou (Hair)	(917) 623-0018
Anne Michele Radcliff (Hair)	(917) 705-7944

Cassandra Ragusa (Makeup)	(516) 583-5995
Selim Rakib (Hair)	(973) 761-0926
Mark Rampmeyer (Hair)	(917) 548-1989
Carol Ann Ransaw (Makeup)	(917) 292-1440
Kevin Rawlings (Makeup)	(212) 870-5562
Jeffrey Rebelo (Hair)	(212) 928-0208
Patricia Regan (Makeup)	(718) 599-1199
Val Reichenbach (Hair)	(203) 270-9653
Kathleen Reilly (Hair)	(212) 627-1522
Elizabeth Reilly-Davila (Hair)	(917) 574-7513
Susan Reilly-Lehane (Makeup)	(646) 228-5242
Bryant Renfroe (Hair)	(212) 996-3625
Karen Reuter (Makeup)	(973) 762-2989
Lisa Revellese-Mirante (Makeup)	(914) 806-5387
Betsy Reyes (Hair)	(631) 335-0694 www.betsyreyes.com
Tania Ribalow (Makeup)	(917) 363-2415
Linda C. Rice (Hair)	(212) 947-1785
Gina Riggi (Body Painting, Grooming, Hair, Makeup & Special FX Makeup)	(201) 861-0149 (201) 704-7888 FAX (201) 861-0149 www.pixelperfectmakeup.com
Rosalee Riggle (Hair)	(724) 263-0059
Lee Rivera (Makeup)	(201) 337-0158
Sonia Rivera (Hair)	(917) 543-3367
Rob Rivers (Hair)	(860) 434-8197
Kat Robertson (Makeup)	(917) 378-1290
Sajata Robinson (Makeup)	(212) 678-5466
Bettie Rogers (Hair)	(718) 578-9699
Wendi S. Rogers (Makeup)	(516) 767-6631
Barbara Roman (Hair)	(646) 742-7086
Amanda Ross (Makeup)	(908) 294-0677
Elena Roulenko (Hair)	(718) 614-9155
Shazia Saleem (Hair)	(718) 928-4976
Silvie Salle (Hair)	(917) 655-8399
Alba Samperisi (Hair)	(516) 245-1829
Anne Sampogna (Hair)	(914) 490-5957
Wilfredo Sanchez (Hair)	(718) 891-2071
Alessandra Sanitate (Makeup)	(516) 798-2744
David Santana (Hair)	(917) 597-6730
Ray Santoleri	(610) 821-1083
James Sarzotti (Makeup)	(718) 651-3160
Cassandra Saulter (Makeup)	(646) 207-4188
Maria Scali (Makeup)	(212) 206-3676
Elizabeth Scalice (Hair)	(516) 458-2608
Paula Schaffer (Hair)	(212) 740-7617
Vincent Schicchi (Makeup)	(718) 359-8224
Mark Schmidt (Hair)	(201) 914-8407
Charlotte Scott (Hair)	(917) 554-1673
Jennifer Serio (Hair)	(646) 220-6199
Kim Serratore (Hair)	(646) 269-2300
Werner Sherer (Hair)	(212) 243-4607
Ashunta Sheriff-Avery (Makeup)	(718) 862-0631
Brian Sherratt (Hair)	(917) 653-6595
Leslie Shreve (Makeup)	(212) 866-7450
Joyce Sica (Hair)	(718) 645-8453
Diana Sikes (Hair)	(917) 439-3506

Debra Simone (860) 538-2512
(Makeup)

Sharon Sinclair (718) 381-7481
(Makeup)

Bella Sirugo (212) 243-9165
(Makeup)

Nuria Sitja (917) 689-7331
(Makeup)

Petula Skeete (646) 232-5113
(Hair)

Marianne Skiba (917) 887-0501
(Makeup)

Sharon Slattery (917) 686-4828
(Makeup)

Dina Sliwiak (917) 539-6287
(Makeup)

Kerrie Smith (917) 450-4886
(Hair)

Tomasina Smith (201) 886-1816
(Makeup)

Diana Solomon (917) 579-0818
(Makeup)

James Soltis (201) 934-7240
(Makeup)

Donna Soto (914) 562-2961
(Hair)

Nereida Soto (917) 414-7165
(Hair)

Meredith Soupios (212) 969-0707
(Makeup)

Mary Ann Spano (201) 538-7314
(Makeup)

Michele Spooner (201) 874-1090
(Makeup)

Stayc St. Onge (917) 664-9167
www.staycs.com
(Body Painting, Grooming, Hair, Makeup & Special FX Makeup)

Ralph Stanzione (914) 337-2825
(Hair)

Kami Steele (917) 763-0702
(Makeup)

Bradley Stenson (800) 631-2722
(Makeup)

Joanne Stephens (910) 686-3770
(Hair)

Joanna Stewart (773) 425-7839
(Makeup)

Jeffrey Swander (917) 743-9877
(Hair)

Reginald Tackley (212) 929-0354
(Makeup)

Amy Tagliamonti (516) 850-6008
(Makeup)

Elisa Tallerico (917) 887-5042
(Makeup)

Leah Tamburino (212) 249-0560
(Makeup)

Kimberly Taylor (201) 282-4433
(Makeup)

Julie Teel (718) 963-3071
(Makeup)

Daryl Terry (917) 658-9434
(Hair)

Mia Thoen (917) 345-6077
(Makeup)

Diana Thomas (800) 991-0905
(Makeup)

Michael R. Thomas (973) 759-4977
(Makeup) (973) 223-4530
FAX (973) 844-9044
www.make-upartistsatlarge.com

Adele Thorpe (800) 775-4945
(Hair)

Inga Thrasher (201) 944-9515
(Hair)

Marian Torre (516) 851-7968
(Makeup)

Anita Torres (718) 544-0362
(Hair)

Bridget Trama (917) 701-6310
(Makeup)

Nick Troiano (914) 844-7698
(Hair)

Linda Tucker (732) 778-4560
(Hair)

Nicole Tucker (646) 287-2323
(Hair)

Joshua Turi (201) 522-0680
(Special FX)

Michael Van Burger (917) 362-3133
(Hair)

Toy R. Van Lierop (212) 491-4848
(Makeup)

Marina Vance (212) 570-6500
(Makeup) www.marinavance.com

Jorge Vargas (917) 441-8102
(Makeup)

Frank Vazquez (917) 952-3079
(Hair)

Anthony Veader (646) 489-5981
(Hair)

Juliet Veltri (201) 674-6742
(Hair)

Maria Verel (212) 889-4110
(Makeup)

Danielle Vignjevich (917) 816-2403
(Makeup)

Linda Villalobos (917) 282-8507
(Hair)

Vita Viscuso (718) 823-6638
(Hair)

Jovan Vitagliano (Hair)	(917) 886-3185	Sher Williams (Makeup)	(705) 641-8776
Maria Von Torfeld (Makeup)	(212) 223-0905	Taurance Williams (Hair)	(917) 748-2270
Alison Wadsworth (Makeup)	(917) 915-2058	Cheryl Williams-Barnes (Makeup)	(347) 733-8423
Frederic Waggoner (Hair)	(917) 593-5312	Edward J. Wilson (Hair)	(917) 570-9034
Anozine Walker (Hair)	(718) 834-1887	Izear Winfrey	(412) 361-3586
Tracy Warbin (Makeup)	(917) 988-5311	Aleta Wolfe (Makeup)	(845) 612-1010
Thomas Watson (Hair)	(212) 757-3185	Sari Yanishefsky	(917) 797-8063
Karen Weinberg (Makeup)	(232) 889-9092	Matthew Yeandle (Hair)	(917) 754-4239
Kim Weinstein (Makeup)	(917) 794-4000	Mary Kay Yezerski (Makeup)	(212) 740-6444
Allen Weisinger (Makeup)	(201) 960-7135	Tina Ying (Makeup)	(212) 724-2031
Colleen Wheeler (Hair)	(718) 897-3703	Melissa Yonkey (Hair)	(800) 656-7994
Carla White (Makeup)	(917) 359-2917	Jeni Zaharian (Makeup)	(617) 504-0144
Joseph Whitmeyer (Hair)	(201) 675-1406	Louie Zakarian (Makeup)	(718) 986-6818
Cheyenne Williams (Hair)	(973) 785-4046	Ted Zane (Hair)	(212) 420-9498
Mickey Williams (Makeup)	(917) 449-1771	David Zimmerman (Makeup)	(214) 912-3884
Patrece Williams (Makeup)	(917) 318-9529	Daniela Zivkovic (Makeup)	(212) 228-4456
		Rosemarie Zurlo (Makeup)	(212) 645-1423

Hair & Makeup Artists

Mary Aaron (212) 627-4304
(Grooming & Makeup) (917) 701-7762
www.maryaaron.com

Aartist Loft (212) 274-0961
580 Broadway, Ste. 606 FAX (212) 274-0962
(Near W. Houston) www.aartistloft.com
New York, NY 10012
(Reps for Makeup Artists)

Adir Abergel (212) 352-3223
(Hair) www.magnetny.com

Michael Albor (212) 741-3240
(781) 863-1555
www.ennisinc.com

Alejandra (212) 929-7771
(Hair) www.artistsbytimothypriano.com

Michel Aleman (212) 935-0200
(Hair) www.bryanbantry.com

All Crew Agency (818) 206-0144
2920 W. Olive Ave., Ste. 201 FAX (818) 206-0169
Burbank, CA 91505 www.allcrewagency.com
(Reps for Hair and Makeup Artists)

Shirlena Allen (212) 431-8631
(Hair) www.dawn2duskagency.com

Loretta Alston (646) 275-0280
(917) 864-6412
www.llmgmt.com

Lorraine Altamura (914) 907-7725
(914) 969-6007
(Body Painting & Makeup) www.makeupmadesimple.com

Deborah Altizio (646) 453-1585
(Makeup) www.eamgmt.com

Amrita (212) 222-4784
(Makeup)

Helene Andersson (212) 925-1111
(Makeup)

Mark Anthony (646) 453-1585
(Hair) www.eamgmt.com

Jenna Anton (212) 255-2500
(Makeup) www.seemanagement.com

Christopher Ardoff (212) 925-4222
www.art-dept.com

Janet Arena (212) 423-9012
(917) 439-7022
(Makeup)

Art Department (212) 925-4222
48 Greene St., Fourth Fl. FAX (212) 925-4422
(Near Broome St.) www.art-dept.com
New York, NY 10013
(Reps for Hair and Makeup Artists)

Artists by Timothy Priano (212) 929-7771
131 Varick St., Ste. 905 FAX (212) 929-7760
New York, NY 10013 www.artistsbytimothypriano.com
(Reps for Hair and Makeup Artists & Manicurists)

Nicole Artmont (212) 352-3223
(Makeup) www.themagnetagency.com

Jill Astmann (212) 979-0845
(917) 701-3225
(Makeup)

Tom Bachik (212) 352-3223
(Manicurist) www.themagnetagency.com

Elaine Casillo Baez (201) 943-3674
(201) 394-8700
FAX (201) 941-6838

Scott Barnes (917) 270-1521
(Makeup) FAX (310) 300-2901
www.scottbarnes.tv

Carole Barone (212) 586-1953
(917) 862-9167
FAX (212) 586-1953

Nick Barose (646) 453-1585
(Makeup) www.eamgmt.com

Joshua Barrett (212) 929-7771
(Grooming & Hair) www.artistsbytimothypriano.com

Lynn Barron (212) 935-0200
(Makeup) www.bryanbantry.com

Mitch Barry (212) 935-0200
(Hair) www.bryanbantry.com

Tiffany Bartok (212) 802-9221
(Makeup) www.makeupbytiffany.com

Gita Bass (646) 453-1585
(Makeup) www.eamgmt.com

Julie Begin (212) 206-0901
www.halleyresources.com

Young Bek (646) 275-0280
(Makeup) www.llmgmt.com

Nancy Beltrandi (212) 935-0200
(Makeup) www.bryanbantry.com

Stacy Beneke (212) 279-1999
www.markedwardinc.com

Nancy Berg (212) 582-7554
(Makeup)

Maria Berger (516) 770-3007
www.asofttouchbymaria.com

Audrey Berman (212) 741-3240
www.ennisinc.com

Gina Bertolotti (212) 929-7771
(Hair) www.artistsbytimothypriano.com

Sonya Bertolozzi (917) 734-6174
www.sonyamakeup.com

Kate Biscoe (212) 741-0202
(Makeup)

Stephen Bishop (212) 243-4607
(Hair)

Deanna Blackwell (212) 279-1999
(Manicurist) www.markedwardinc.com

Luca Blandi (212) 929-7771
(Hair) www.artistsbytimothypriano.com

Oscar Blandi (212) 929-7771
(Hair) www.artistsbytimothypriano.com

Name	Role	Phone / Web
Jean Block		(212) 967-9470 / (917) 843-4781 / FAX (212) 268-7177 / www.hairtheatrix.com
Jodie Boland	(Makeup)	(212) 255-2500 / www.seemanagement.com
Frederic Boudet	(Hair)	(212) 935-0200 / www.bryanbantry.com
Marissa Bourbonnais	(Makeup)	(212) 431-8631 / www.dawn2duskagency.com
Tobi Britton		(646) 382-8819 / (212) 807-0447 / FAX (212) 727-0975 / www.themakeupshop.com
Dawn Brocco		(310) 458-7800 / www.nyoffice.net
Dawn Broussard	(Makeup)	(212) 352-3223 / www.magnetny.com
Bryan Bantry	(Reps for Hair and Makeup Artists)	(212) 935-0200 / FAX (212) 935-2698 / www.bryanbantry.com
Adam Bryant	(Hair)	(212) 925-4222 / www.art-dept.com
Norman Bryn		(203) 869-5065 / (917) 218-9441 / www.makeup-artist.com
Kristofer Buckle	(Makeup)	(310) 276-0777 / www.thewallgroup.com
Jacqueline Bush	(Hair)	(646) 453-1585 / www.eamgmt.com
Will Carrillo	(Hair)	(310) 246-0446 / (212) 675-6334 / FAX (415) 674-1950 / www.workgroup-ltd.com
Janet Cassidy		(212) 496-8564 / (917) 575-0144
April Chatman-Royce		(212) 643-1736 / www.cec-entertainment.com
Cheyenne		(212) 274-0961 / www.aartistloft.com
Kim Chiu	(Manicurist)	(212) 279-1999 / www.markedwardinc.com
Greg Clark		(212) 206-0901 / www.halleyresources.com
Joanne Cocuzza-Offenhartz	(Hair)	(914) 833-3835
Cohl		(212) 935-0200 / www.bryanbantry.com
James Cola		(718) 457-8887
Chris Colbeck	(Makeup)	(212) 925-4222 / www.art-dept.com
Jonathan Connelly	(Hair)	(212) 925-4222 / www.art-dept.com
Mary Cook	(Hair)	(212) 348-0069 / (917) 287-0909 / www.2thepointpersonalwords.com
Jacqueline Cookson		(212) 242-7050 / www.clickmodel.com/illusions.php
Michael Costain	(Makeup & Wigmaking)	(212) 463-0966 / (212) 866-2059 / www.wigmasterassociates.com
Pauline Coutroulis		(201) 401-0556 / FAX (201) 947-0319
Kumi Craig	(Grooming)	(646) 453-1585 / www.eamgmt.com
Creighton	(Hair)	(646) 453-1585 / www.eamgmt.com
Anthony Cristiano	(Hair)	(212) 929-7771 / www.artistsbytimothypriano.com
Tracy Crystal	(Makeup)	(212) 935-0200 / (646) 785-6407 / www.bryanbantry.com
Alan Cutler	(Makeup)	(917) 301-6235
Michelle Cutler	(Makeup)	(917) 359-0452
John D	(Hair)	(212) 352-3223 / www.themagnetagency.com
Alan D'Angerio	(Hair)	(212) 741-0202
Lisa Davis	(Makeup)	(917) 806-8572
Dawn to Dusk Agency	(Reps for Hair and Makeup Artists)	(212) 431-8631 / (323) 850-6783 / www.dawn2duskagency.com
Charlotte Day	(Makeup)	(212) 255-2500 / www.seemanagement.com
Robin Day	(Hair and Wig Styling)	(917) 856-8256 / (718) 432-5665
Darlene DeBetta	(Manicurist)	(212) 242-7050 / www.clickmodel.com/illusions.php
Mario Dedivanovic		(212) 274-0961 / www.aartistloft.com
Frank De Jesus		(212) 274-0961 / www.aartistloft.com
Silvia Dell' Orto	(Makeup)	(212) 925-4222 / www.art-dept.com
Victor De Nicola Jr.	(Hair)	(718) 886-2907 / (917) 841-9925 / FAX (718) 886-2907
Patrick Dennis	(Makeup)	(212) 929-3921 / (917) 689-1239 / FAX (212) 929-3663
Olaf Derlig	(Grooming, Hair & Makeup)	(646) 453-1585 / www.eamgmt.com
Suzanne DeSimone	(Makeup)	(845) 883-6317 / (914) 456-0229 / FAX (845) 883-9672
Angela Dicarlo		(212) 545-7895 / www.nyoffice.net
Sylvia Dimaki		(212) 206-0901 / www.halleyresources.com
Jake Dingler		(212) 929-7771 / www.artistsbytimothypriano.com

Hair & Makeup Artists

Dion Peronneau Agency (323) 299-4043
(Reps for Hair and Makeup Artists) FAX (323) 299-4269
www.dionperonneau.com

Jane Di Persio (212) 533-0135
(Makeup) (917) 362-8657

Kim Do (917) 709-4381
(Makeup) FAX (212) 721-0604
www.kim-do.com

Christine Domaniecki (973) 223-4529
(Makeup) (973) 759-4977
FAX (973) 844-9044
www.make-upartistsatlarge.com

Naomi Donne (212) 741-0202
(Makeup) FAX (212) 633-6317

Paula Dorf (212) 724-8464
(Makeup)

Paulette Elkind (212) 315-3088
(917) 673-8390

Ennis, Inc. (212) 741-3240
(781) 863-1555
(Reps for Hair and Makeup Artists) FAX (781) 863-1554
www.ennisinc.com

Exclusive Artists Management (646) 453-1585
(646) 453-1583
596 Broadway, Ste. 601 www.eamgmt.com
New York, NY 10012
(Reps for Hair and Makeup Artists)

Jennifer Farhood (610) 970-1205
www.airbrushmakeupartist.com
(Body Painting, Grooming, Hair & Makeup)

Amy Farid (212) 255-2500
(Hair) www.seemanagement.com

Fulvia Farolfi (212) 935-0200
(Makeup) www.bryanbantry.com

Cynthia Faye (908) 654-1381
(Makeup) www.angelfaceinc.com

Martha Fekete (212) 935-0200
(Manicurist) www.bryanbantry.com

Joy Fennell (323) 906-9600
(Hair) www.crystalagency.com

Paolo Ferreira (212) 255-2500
(Hair) www.seemanagement.com

Elisa Ferri (212) 255-2500
(Manicurist) www.seemanagement.com

Therese Flaherty (212) 877-4829

Roxanna Floyd (212) 242-7050
(Makeup) www.clickmodel.com/illusions.php

Filis Forman (212) 580-0687
FAX (212) 580-0422
www.filisforman.com

Marcus Francis (212) 352-3223
(Hair) www.themagnetagency.com

Robin Fredriksz (212) 352-3223
www.magnetny.com

Leslie Fuller (212) 206-7462
(Makeup) (802) 375-2895

Carl Fullerton (201) 767-7690

Kristin Gallegos (212) 935-0200
(Makeup) www.bryanbantry.com

Pam Geiger (212) 935-0200
www.bryanbantry.com

Kay Gelbord (702) 242-4476
(Makeup) (917) 781-5182
FAX (702) 561-4885
www.aprettieryou.com

Heather G. Gerchberg (646) 221-7733

Doreen Gillis (516) 317-2007
(Makeup)

Franco Gobbi (212) 925-4222
(Hair) www.art-dept.com

Jackie Gomez (212) 274-0961
www.aartistloft.com

Rachel Goodwin (212) 352-3223
(Makeup) www.magnetny.com

Elke Gordon (732) 656-0170
(908) 202-3206

Lauren Gott (212) 274-0961
www.aartistloft.com

Coco Grace (212) 741-3240
(781) 863-1555
www.ennisinc.com

Alyson Granaderos (212) 545-7895
www.nyoffice.net

Gloria Grant (212) 874-0387
(Makeup)

Charlie Green (212) 935-0200
(Makeup) www.bryanbantry.com

Gareth Green (212) 242-7050
www.clickmodel.com/illusions.php

Robert Greene (212) 255-2500
(Makeup) www.seemanagement.com

Mary Greenwell (212) 935-0200
(Makeup) www.bryanbantry.com

Italo Gregorio (212) 935-0200
(Hair) www.bryanbantry.com

Linda Grimes (212) 477-3901
(917) 854-3999
(Makeup)

Rodney Groves (212) 925-4222
(Hair) www.art-dept.com

Robin Gurin (908) 832-9421
(Makeup)

Halley Resources (212) 206-0901
231 W. 29th St., Ste. 701 FAX (212) 206-0904
(Near Seventh Ave.) www.halleyresources.com
New York, NY 10001
(Reps for Hair and Makeup Artists)

Marcia Hamilton (323) 299-4043
(Hair) www.dionperonneau.com

Jamal Hammadi (212) 352-3223
(Hair) www.magnetny.com

Danny Hammond	(212) 279-1999 www.markedwardinc.com	Glen Jackson (Makeup)	(212) 255-2500 www.seemanagement.com
Jonathan Joseph Hanousek (Hair)	(646) 453-1585 www.eamgmt.com	Lazarus Jean-Baptiste (Makeup)	(212) 935-0200 www.bryanbantry.com
Lina Hanson (Makeup)	(212) 352-3223 www.themagnetagency.com	Chuck Jensen	(212) 279-1999 www.markedwardinc.com
Tamika Hardy (Manicurist)	(212) 242-7050 www.clickmodel.com/illusions.php	Kathy Jeung (Makeup)	(212) 352-3223 www.themagnetagency.com
Sacha Harford (Grooming, Hair & Makeup)	(212) 274-0961 www.aartistloft.com	Rafael Jiminez (Hair & Men's Grooming)	(212) 242-7050 www.clickmodel.com/illusions.php
Dallas Hartnett (Hair)	(201) 330-0783 (201) 424-0968	Michael Johnson (Hair)	(212) 929-7771 www.artistsbytimothypriano.com
Dawn Haynes	(212) 431-8631 www.dawn2duskagency.com	JSterling	(212) 242-7050 www.clickmodel.com/illusions.php
Justin Henry (Makeup)	(718) 596-2400 www.artmixbeauty.com	Sherri June	(860) 921-7427 (203) 968-9292
Brad Hensler (Hair)	(212) 929-7771 www.artistsbytimothypriano.com	(Makeup) Bethany Karlyn (Makeup)	(212) 741-3240 (781) 863-1555 www.ennisinc.com
Lori Hicks (Makeup)	(718) 768-2922	Devra Kinery (Makeup)	(212) 925-4222 www.art-dept.com
Thomas Hintermeier (Hair)	(212) 925-4222 www.art-dept.com	Harry King	(212) 206-0901 www.halleyresources.com
Keiko Hiramoto (Makeup)	(212) 935-0200 www.bryanbantry.com	Dina Kinion	(212) 673-5509 www.rjbennettrepresents.com
Mary Ann Hogan (Makeup)	(646) 285-6658		
Honey (Manicurist)	(212) 352-3223 www.themagnetagency.com	Todd Kleitsch (Makeup)	(917) 414-1920
Maury Hopson (Hair)	(212) 935-0200 www.bryanbantry.com	Michina Koide (Manicurist)	(212) 925-4222 www.art-dept.com
Daniel Howell (Hair)	(212) 352-3223 www.magnetny.com	Amanda Korfine	(212) 643-1736 www.cec-entertainment.com
Angela Huff	(212) 279-1999 www.markedwardinc.com	Kozmo (Hair)	(212) 935-0200 www.bryanbantry.com
Robert Huitron	(212) 279-1999 www.markedwardinc.com	Marie Josee LaFontaine (Makeup)	(212) 935-0200 www.bryanbantry.com
Nikki Iannelli	(212) 935-0200 www.bryanbantry.com	Mary Ann Lakoseljac (Makeup)	(201) 313-5861
Antoine Ifergan (Hair)	(212) 255-2500 www.seemanagement.com	Barbara Lamelza	(646) 453-1585 www.eamgmt.com
Wendy Iles (Hair)	(212) 925-4222 www.art-dept.com	Dennis Lanni (Hair)	(212) 925-4222 www.art-dept.com
Illusions Management 129 W. 27th St., PH (Near Sixth Ave.) FAX New York, NY 10001 www.clickmodel.com/illusions.php (Reps for Hair and Makeup Artists)	(212) 242-7050 (212) 206-6228	Ellin Lavar (Hair)	(212) 724-4492 www.lavarhairdesigns.com
Francois Ilnseher	(212) 935-0200 www.bryanbantry.com	Steven Lawrence (Makeup)	(914) 941-2372 (917) 658-6059
Danielle Irene (Hair)	(212) 929-7771 www.artistsbytimothypriano.com	Paul Le Blanc (Hair)	(212) 741-0202 FAX (212) 633-6317
Bradley Irion (Hair)	(212) 929-7771 www.artistsbytimothypriano.com	Kate Lee (Makeup)	(212) 352-3223 www.magnetny.com
Anthony Isambert	(212) 206-0901 www.halleyresources.com	Sonia Lee (Grooming, Hair & Makeup)	(646) 453-1585 www.eamgmt.com
Yossi Ivgi (Hair)	(212) 935-0200 www.bryanbantry.com	Catherine Lehtonen (Hair)	(212) 255-2500 www.seemanagement.com

Hair & Makeup Artists

Christine Leiter (212) 496-0935
(646) 831-9113
(Makeup)

Anette Lian-Williams (718) 832-5302
(917) 885-5012
(Makeup)

Amy Lin (212) 279-1999
www.markedwardinc.com

Craig Lindberg (917) 951-7039
(Makeup) FAX (516) 767-2793
www.gmayhem.com

Sandy Linter (212) 935-0200
(Makeup) www.bryanbantry.com

Tina Lipman (212) 935-0200
(Makeup) www.bryanbantry.com

Lisa-Raquel (212) 255-2500
(Hair) www.seemanagement.com

Jeanine Lobell (212) 352-3223
(Makeup) www.magnetny.com

Francky L'Official (212) 274-0961
www.aartistloft.com

Lolita (323) 299-4043
www.dionperonneau.com

Carlo Longo (212) 935-0200
(Makeup) www.bryanbantry.com

Patricia Longo (646) 453-1585
(Grooming, Hair & Makeup) www.eamgmt.com

Vincent Longo (212) 935-0200
(Makeup) www.bryanbantry.com

Leslie Lopez (212) 352-0777
(Makeup) www.thewallgroup.com

Reiko Love (212) 206-0901
www.halleyresources.com

Emma Lovell (212) 352-3223
(Makeup) www.themagnetagency.com

Luna Llena Management, Inc. (646) 275-0280
(917) 864-6412
168 Second Ave., Ste. 254 www.llmgmt.com
New York, NY 10003
(Reps for Hair and Makeup Artists)

Craig Lyman (212) 580-0584
(646) 732-4243
(Makeup) FAX (212) 580-0596

Elie Maalouf (646) 453-1585
(Makeup) www.eamgmt.com

Tyron Machhausen (212) 925-4222
(Makeup) www.art-dept.com

David Maderich (212) 206-0901
www.halleyresources.com

Magnet NY (212) 352-3223
270 Lafayette St., Ste. 901 FAX (212) 941-7471
New York, NY 10012 www.themagnetagency.com
(Reps for Hair and Makeup Artists)

Tre Major (212) 431-8561
(Hair) www.dawn2duskagency.com

Renee Majour (212) 673-5509
www.rjbennettrepresents.com

Donna Malatino (310) 804-7391
(718) 769-9719
www.donnamalatino.com
(Colorist, Grooming, Hair & Makeup)

Didier Malige (212) 935-0200
(Hair) www.bryanbantry.com

Kevin Mancuso (310) 458-7800
(Hair) www.partos.com

Roger Mariani (718) 746-0993
(800) 555-0330

Enrico Mariotti (212) 255-2500
(Hair) www.seemanagement.com

Mark Edward, Inc. (212) 279-1999
325 W. 38th St., Ste. 1011 (Near Eighth Ave.) www.markedwardinc.com
New York, NY 10018
(Reps for Hair and Makeup Artists)

Andie Markoe-Byrne (212) 935-0200
(Makeup) www.bryanbantry.com

Marjorie Martin (212) 631-1175
(Makeup)

Linda Mason (212) 274-0961
www.aartistloft.com

Lauretta McCoy (323) 906-9600
FAX (323) 913-0900
www.crystalagency.com

Mel McKinney (212) 247-8281
(917) 566-6400
FAX (212) 247-8281

Thomas McKiver (212) 929-7771
(Hair) www.artistsbytimothypriano.com

Sam McKnight (212) 935-0200
(Hair) www.bryanbantry.com

Donyale McRae (646) 275-0280
www.llmgmt.com

Linda Melo (212) 246-4008
(Makeup) FAX (646) 296-2463

Patrick Melville (212) 929-7771
www.artistsbytimothypriano.com

Jenna Menard (646) 453-1585
(Makeup) www.eamgmt.com

Linda Mensching (973) 772-7647
(201) 390-7099
(Makeup)

Michaela Michaelanthony (212) 979-5436

Donald Mikula (212) 935-0200
www.bryanbantry.com

Amie Minassian (718) 446-8048
(917) 975-3850
(Makeup) FAX (718) 446-3616

Benoit Moeyaert (212) 925-4222
(Hair) www.art-dept.com

Moiz (212) 925-4222
www.art-dept.com

Laurent Mole (212) 929-7771
(Hair) www.artistsbytimothypriano.com

Montana Artists Agency	(323) 845-4144		Polly Osmond	(212) 925-4222
7715 W. Sunset Blvd., Third Fl.	FAX (323) 845-4155		(Makeup)	www.art-dept.com
Los Angeles, CA 90046	www.montanartists.com			
(Reps for Hair and Makeup Artists)				(917) 692-8053
			Joanne A.A. Ottaviano	(212) 501-9853
	(585) 865-1274			www.joanneottaviano.com
Ann Montesanto	(585) 663-1545			
(Hair)	FAX (585) 663-1185		Kristine Oulman	(212) 673-5509
				www.rjbennettrepresents.com
	(585) 865-1274			
Frank Montesanto	(585) 663-1545		Anthony Palermo	(212) 750-8100
(Makeup)	FAX (585) 663-1185		(Colorist)	FAX (212) 750-8103
				www.anthonyleonardsalon.com
Matthew Monzon	(646) 453-1585			
(Hair)	www.eamgmt.com			(212) 421-1657
			Francesca Paris	(917) 539-6788
James Mooney	(212) 925-4222			
(Hair)	www.art-dept.com		Partos Company	(310) 458-7800
			227 Broadway, Ste. 204	FAX (310) 587-2250
Pat Moore-Theis	(917) 414-0899		Santa Monica, CA 90401	www.partos.com
(Makeup)			(Reps for Hair and Makeup Artists)	
	(212) 741-3240		Anne Paul	(917) 734-5300
Christine Morse	(781) 863-1555		(Makeup)	
	www.ennisinc.com			
			Kristen Paynter	(917) 834-4444
Monifa Mortis	(646) 245-8907			www.kpaynter.com
	www.monifamortis.com			
			Reyna Pecot	(212) 741-3240
Amalia Moscoso	(323) 906-9600			www.ennisinc.com
(Hair)	www.crystalagency.com			
			Aviva Perea	(212) 352-3223
Robert Moulton	(917) 304-9708		(Hair)	www.themagnetagency.com
	www.robertmoultonmakeup.net			
			Shannon Pezatta	(323) 299-4043
Moyra Mulholland	(212) 935-0200		(Makeup)	www.dionperonneau.com
(Makeup)	www.bryanbantry.com			
			Mary Phillips	(212) 352-3223
Munemi	(212) 255-2500		(Makeup)	www.themagnetagency.com
(Makeup)	www.seemanagement.com			
			Benjamin Pinon	(212) 255-2500
	(212) 741-3240		(Hair)	www.seemanagement.com
Cynthia Murphy	(781) 863-1555			
	www.ennisinc.com		Ric Pipino	(212) 935-0200
			(Hair)	www.bryanbantry.com
Roz Music	(212) 352-3223			
	www.magnetny.com		Amoy Pitters	(212) 274-0961
				www.aartistloft.com
	(212) 545-7895			
New York Office	(323) 468-2240		Riva Pizhadze	(212) 863-3206
15 W. 26th St., Fifth Fl.	FAX (212) 545-7941		(Makeup)	
(Near Broadway)	www.nyoffice.net			
New York, NY 10010			Bata Plavsic	(212) 206-0901
(Reps for Hair and Makeup Artists)				www.halleyresources.com
Chris Newburg	(212) 673-5509		Rebecca Plymate	(212) 255-2500
	www.rjbennettrepresents.com			www.seemanagement.com
Bethany Newell	(212) 352-3223		Mike Potter	(212) 255-2500
(Manicurist)	www.themagnetagency.com		(Makeup)	www.seemanagement.com
	(718) 281-2136		Evy Power	(212) 741-3240
Suzana Neziri	(917) 733-7760			www.ennisinc.com
(Hair)				
				(718) 782-5908
Tonya Noland	(212) 279-1999		Rosanne Puchal	(917) 929-9639
	www.markedwardinc.com		(Makeup)	
	(631) 261-9115		Benjamin Puckey	(212) 255-2500
Rita Ogden	(516) 885-7027		(Makeup)	www.seemanagement.com
(Makeup)	FAX (631) 262-7379			
				(908) 469-8277
Timmothy Olan Montgomery	(212) 242-7050		Crystal Nicole Pullen	(908) 868-7418
	www.clickmodel.com/illusions.php		(Makeup)	
Rie Omoto	(212) 255-2500		Gregory Purcell	(212) 279-1999
(Makeup)	www.seemanagement.com		(Hair)	www.markedwardinc.com
One Naked Egg	(212) 925-1111		Q	(212) 242-7050
675 Hudson St., Ste. 4N	FAX (212) 929-6552		(Grooming & Hair)	www.clickmodel.com/illusions.php
(Near 13th St.)	www.onenakedegg.com			
New York, NY 10014			Q Hardy	(323) 299-4043
(Reps for Hair and Makeup Artists)			(Hair)	www.dionperonneau.com

Hair & Makeup Artists

John Quaglia   (212) 683-8633
(Hair)

R.J. Bennett Represents   (212) 673-5509
530 E. 20th St., Ste. 2B   www.rjbennettrepresents.com
(Near First Ave.)
New York, NY 10009
(Reps for Hair and Makeup Artists)

Mikaela Rae   (212) 842-0575 / (917) 312-8641
(Makeup)

Nevio Ragazzini   (212) 242-7050
www.clickmodel.com/illusions.php

Sophie Raimbault   (212) 935-0200
(Hair)   www.bryanbantry.com

Pierre Rakib   (973) 761-0926 / (908) 451-6961
FAX (973) 761-0353

Stephen Ramsey   (212) 929-7771
www.artistsbytimothypriano.com

Rosemary Redlin   (212) 242-7050
(Makeup)   www.clickmodel.com/illusions.php

Jacqueline Reiss   (212) 308-9336
(Makeup)

Bryant Renfroe   (212) 996-3625
(Hair)   www.bryantrenfroe.com

Andrea Richter   (323) 299-4043
(Makeup)   www.dionperonneau.com

Jeannia Robinette   (212) 925-4222
(Makeup)   www.art-dept.com

Sajata Robinson   (212) 678-5466
(Makeup)   www.sajata.net

Ruth Roche   (212) 929-7771
(Hair)   www.artistsbytimothypriano.com

Stephen Rose   (212) 925-4222
(Hair)   www.art-dept.com

Mara Roszak   (212) 352-3223
(Hair)   www.themagnetagency.com

Claire Rothstein   (212) 255-2500
(Hair)   www.seemanagement.com

John Ruidant   (212) 255-2500
(Hair)   www.seemanagement.com

Sue Saccavino   (609) 653-9473
(Makeup)

Alba Samperisi   (516) 245-1829 / (516) 759-0673
(Hair)

Natalia Sandu   (212) 935-0200
(Manicurist)   www.bryanbantry.com

Barbara Sansone   (718) 544-0791 / (917) 273-6521
www.barbarasansone.net

James Sarzotti   (914) 438-3072
(Makeup)

Jaqueline Saulsbery   (212) 279-1999
(Manicurist)   www.markedwardinc.com

Lizz Scalice   (516) 458-2608

See Management   (212) 255-2500
307 Seventh Ave., Ste. 1607   FAX (212) 255-2020
New York, NY 10001   www.seemanagement.com
(Reps for Hair and Makeup Artists)

Jorge Serio   (212) 255-2500
(Makeup)   www.seemanagement.com

Vivian Sevier   (347) 248-4638

Kevin Shapiro   (212) 545-7895
www.nyoffice.net

Shalom Sharon   (212) 529-6712 / (212) 289-2150
www.shalomsharonhair.com

Yvette Shelton   (212) 431-8631
(Hair)   www.dawn2duskagency.com

Werner Sherer   (212) 243-4607
(Hair)

Leslie Shreve   (212) 866-7450
(Makeup)   FAX (212) 932-0191

Joyce Sica   (718) 645-8453
(Hair)

Michael Silva   (212) 274-0961
www.aartistloft.com

Hector Simancas   (212) 255-2500
(Makeup)   www.seemanagement.com

Mili B. Simon   (212) 741-3240 / (781) 863-1555
www.ennisinc.com

Larry Sims   (646) 453-1585
(Hair)   www.eamgmt.com

Roseann Singleton   (212) 925-4222
(Manicurist)   www.art-dept.com

Ben Skervin   (212) 352-3223
(Hair)   www.themagnetagency.com

Lavette Slater   (718) 776-7069

Dina Sliwiak   (212) 545-7895
www.nyoffice.net

Marcos Smith   (212) 925-4222
(Groomer)   www.art-dept.com

Rebecca Sommer   (917) 554-4933 / (212) 343-2331
www.rebeccasommer.com
(Airbrushing, Body Painting, Hair & Makeup)

Jill Spector   (917) 373-0860
(Makeup)

Natalie MacGowan Spencer   (323) 525-0235
(Grooming, Hair & Makeup)   FAX (310) 887-4843
www.macgowanspencer.com

Justin St. Clair   (646) 453-1585
(Grooming, Hair & Makeup)   www.eamgmt.com

Ward Stegerhoek   (212) 935-0200
(Hair)   www.bryanbantry.com

Tate Steinsiek   (212) 643-1736
(Special FX Makeup)   www.cec-entertainment.com

Molly Stern   (212) 352-3223
(Makeup)   www.magnetny.com

Jillayne Stockland (917) 749-4926 / (212) 929-7151
(Makeup)

Debbie Stone (212) 255-2500
(Makeup) www.seemanagement.com

Charles Baker Strahan (212) 929-7771
(Hair) www.artistsbytimothypriano.com

Jo Strettell (212) 352-3223
(Makeup) www.magnetny.com

Amy Strozzi (212) 352-3223
(Makeup) www.themagnetagency.com

Spring Super (212) 741-3240 / (781) 863-1555
www.ennisinc.com

Keiko Takagi (212) 255-2500
(Makeup) www.seemanagement.com

Leah Tamburino (212) 249-0560
(Makeup)

Randall Tang (212) 279-1999
www.markedwardinc.com

Lynn Taylor (212) 545-7895
www.nyoffice.com

Arielle Toelke (212) 643-1736
(Special FX Makeup) www.cec-entertainment.com

Julie Tomlinson (646) 453-1585
(Makeup) www.eamgmt.com

Mark Townsend (212) 352-3223
(Hair) www.magnetny.com

Bridget Trama (917) 701-6310
(Makeup)

Marina Vance (212) 570-6500
www.marinavance.com

Fred Van De Bunt (212) 925-4222
(Hair) www.art-dept.com

Rutger van der Heide (212) 255-2500
(Hair) www.seemanagement.com

Sandrine Van Slee (212) 925-4222
(Makeup) www.art-dept.com

Danny Velasco (212) 673-5509
www.rjbennettrepresents.com

Carlos Vera (212) 279-1999
www.markedwardinc.com

Kim Verbeck (646) 453-1585
(Grooming, Hair & Makeup) www.eamgmt.com

Robert Vetica (212) 352-3223
(Hair) www.magnetny.com

Lona Vigi (212) 352-3223
(Hair) www.magnetny.com

Clark Vincent (323) 906-9600
FAX (323) 913-0900
www.crystalagency.com

Jovan Vitagliano (917) 886-3185
(Hair)

David von Cannon (212) 935-0200
(Hair) www.bryanbantry.com

Ewan Walker (323) 299-4043
(Makeup) www.dionperonneau.com

Ashley Ward (212) 925-4222
(Makeup) www.art-dept.com

Leah Watson (323) 906-9600
FAX (323) 913-0900
www.crystalagency.com

Robin Watson (917) 620-4048
www.robinwatsonmakeup.com

Allen Weisinger (646) 275-0280 / (917) 864-6412
(Makeup) www.llmgmt.com

Heidi Wells (212) 741-3240 / (781) 863-1555
www.ennisinc.com

Reggie Wells (212) 242-7050
(Makeup) www.clickmodel.com/illusions.php

Rheanne White (212) 255-2500
(Hair) www.seemanagement.com

Maranda Widlund (212) 352-3223
(Hair) www.themagnetagency.com

Charlotte Willer (212) 925-4222
(Makeup) www.art-dept.com

Anthony Williams (212) 794-9030

Taurance Williams (646) 824-6859 / (917) 748-2270

Andrea Wilson (646) 275-0280 / (917) 864-6412
(Hair) www.llmgmt.com

Yahaira (212) 274-0961
www.aartistloft.com

Yuki Yamazaki (212) 274-0961
www.aartistloft.com

Nausil Zaheer (212) 279-1999
(Manicurist) www.markedwardinc.com

Louie Zakarian (212) 206-0901
www.halleyresources.com

Hair & Makeup Artists

Lighting Directors

Steve Brill	(212) 685-4940	Gordon Minard	(910) 814-1804
	FAX (212) 685-4927		(910) 890-3428
	www.ldg.com	Chuck Noble	(917) 682-2334
Dave Feldman	(908) 301-9596	Edward Read	(516) 735-3467
	(781) 821-9596		(917) 513-4333
(Local 829 NY)	FAX (908) 301-9597		www.readbroslighting.com
	www.feldmandesigns.com		
Bruce Ferri	(212) 366-4014	Al Rivera	(917) 627-6833
	(917) 682-2333		(718) 389-9800
	FAX (646) 619-4158		FAX (718) 389-9897
			www.alrivera.tv
Michael Haskell	(610) 495-9697	Dennis M. Size	(212) 685-4940
			(917) 887-0876
Deke Hazirjian	(212) 366-9800		FAX (212) 685-4927
	FAX (212) 366-5040		www.ldg.com
Mark Kahn	(212) 595-1570	Philip B. Sorensen	(212) 595-9835
	(917) 579-6938		(917) 887-3432
Jason Licht	(917) 921-5591	Donny Stegall	(732) 742-8222
	(718) 624-6906		(732) 448-1895
	FAX (718) 624-6921		
	home.earthlink.net/~jelicht/lighting/index.html	Michael Stiller	(212) 473-2629
			FAX (212) 473-2629
Daniel McKenrick	(212) 765-0507		www.michaelstiller.com
	FAX (212) 504-8015		
	www.tvld.com	John Viesta	(212) 666-2552
		(Local 829 NY)	
Brian McRae	(212) 643-1736		
	www.cec-entertainment.com		

PRODUCER

*CASTING
*LOCATIONS
*SPECIALIZING IN PRINT

Check out:
www.BranchingOutPro.com
to review portfolio

TRICIA MORAN

Branching Out Productions

(Cell) 516-652-5036
(Office) 516-944-8999
Port Washington, NY

Producers

Gilbert Adler	(310) 273-6700
	www.utaproduction.com
Vincent Agostino	(310) 930-6570
Mark Aji	(212) 206-6365
(Line Producer)	(917) 873-6770
	FAX (212) 206-6891
	www.igniterfilms.com
Andrea Allen	(917) 882-8228
(Line Producer)	
Todd Arnow	(310) 273-6700
	www.unitedtalent.com
Stephanie Austin	(310) 273-6700
	www.utaproduction.com
Sirad Balducci	(212) 643-1736
(Line Producer)	www.cec-entertainment.com
Jane Bartelme	(310) 273-6700
	www.utaproduction.com
Bill Beasley	(310) 273-6700
	www.utaproduction.com
Joan Bennett	(212) 873-9501
Eileen Bernstein	(212) 268-9798
(Line Producer & Producer)	(917) 860-9333
	FAX (212) 268-6648
Janice Biggs	(917) 421-2901
(Line Producer)	
Carrie Bornstein	(212) 627-1040
	(917) 603-5763
Ron Bozman	(310) 273-6700
	www.utaproduction.com
Molly Bradford	(917) 449-6793
Ⓐ Branching Out Productions, Inc.	(516) 944-8999
	(516) 652-5036
(Reps for Producers)	FAX (516) 944-8998
	www.branchingoutpro.com
Ira Brooks	(845) 368-1820
	(917) 861-6084
	FAX (845) 368-1840
Pieter Jan Brugge	(310) 273-6700
	www.unitedtalent.com
Gary Buonanno	(203) 637-3935
Brian David Cange	(718) 788-0070
	(917) 627-1057
	FAX (718) 788-0117
Nancy Cannava	(917) 604-8844
	(212) 334-3374
Carol Cieslinski	(585) 415-3202
David Coatsworth	(310) 273-6700
	www.utaproduction.com
Audrey S. Cohen	(305) 385-2204
	(310) 208-6776
	FAX (310) 208-6776
Gina Contaldi	(516) 763-5110
(Line Producer)	(516) 457-0065
David Crockett	(310) 273-6700
	www.utaproduction.com
Stephen Cubine	(212) 643-1736
(Line Producer)	www.cec-entertainment.com
Amelia Dallis	(917) 859-4445
Patricia Danziger	(203) 222-7217
(Line Producer)	(203) 247-6546
	FAX (203) 222-7137
JD Davison	(917) 319-5123
(Line Producer)	(973) 239-8589
Joe Dea	(818) 990-8993
	www.ambitiousent.com

Daniel Deitchman (Line Producer & Producer)	(201) 362-4737 (646) 688-4424 FAX (212) 428-6711 www.dandeitchman.com	**Callum Greene**	(310) 273-6700 www.utaproduction.com
Sal Del Giudice	(516) 221-1960 (917) 853-6139 www.tangerinefilms.com	**Neil Hallenborg** (Line Producer & Producer)	(609) 914-0311 (609) 351-1952 FAX (609) 914-0233
Margaret M. Denk (Line Producer)	(917) 602-8540	**Todd Hallowell**	(310) 273-6700 www.utaproduction.com
Lynn Descoteau	(212) 875-1507 (917) 754-8843 FAX (212) 875-1507 www.wrenvideo.com	**Daniel Hank** (Line Producer)	(212) 769-4429
		Marilyn A. Harvey (Line Producer)	(718) 721-3011
Kat Dillon	(310) 399-7839	**Jamie Haynes**	(310) 305-7139 FAX (310) 827-7367
Pat Dorfman (Line Producer)	(718) 729-4688	**Eli Heitin**	(212) 475-6310 FAX (212) 473-3748 www.suitespotnyc.com
Janice Doskey (Line Producer)	(914) 261-2267	**Marco Henry** (Line Producer)	(212) 643-1736 www.cec-entertainment.com
Adam Drescher	(212) 475-6310 FAX (212) 473-3748 www.suitespotnyc.com	**Leslie Hirschorn**	(212) 260-4211
James R. Dyer	(310) 273-6700 www.utaproduction.com	**B. Gray Hirshfield**	(516) 944-7864 (516) 455-0851 FAX (516) 944-7852
Lawrence Dzurillay (Line Producer)	(201) 935-0358 FAX (201) 935-3511	**Chip Hourihan** (Line Producer & Producer)	(718) 928-3812 (917) 861-4120
Kate Eisemann (Line Producer)	(917) 873-2256 FAX (203) 259-0124	**Anura Idupuganti**	(917) 916-0554 www.anurafilms.com
George Fares	(917) 544-1839 (917) 388-3951	**Nobuhiro Ikushima** (Line Producer)	(917) 742-1256 FAX (212) 242-8821
Evan Ferrante	(914) 720-8134	**Michael D. Jones** (Line Producer)	(212) 643-1736 www.cec-entertainment.com
John Ficalora (Line Producer)	(914) 591-5238 FAX (914) 591-9603	**Stephen Jones**	(310) 273-6700 www.utaproduction.com
Michael Flynn	(310) 273-6700 www.unitedtalent.com	**John Joseph**	(818) 990-8993 www.ambitiousent.com
Ray Foley	(212) 643-1736 www.cec-entertainment.com	**Adam Kagan** (Line Producer & Producer)	(917) 559-3639 www.kaganfamily.com/adam
Rusty Ford (Line Producer)	(646) 489-8575	**Barbara Kelly**	(310) 273-6700 www.unitedtalent.com
Avenol A. Franco (Line Producer & Producer)	(917) 826-1244	**Ric Kidney**	(310) 273-6700 www.utaproduction.com
Amy Friedman-Norton (Line Producer)	(845) 657-2404	**Erwin Kramer** (Line Producer)	(212) 567-5545 (310) 446-1866 FAX (310) 446-1856 home.earthlink.net/~ekeeeek
Steve Gerbson	(818) 990-8993 www.ambitiousent.com	**Liz Kramer**	(212) 243-7143
Peter Giuliano	(417) 683-6014 (310) 273-6700 www.utaproduction.com	**Liz Kraus** (Line Producer)	(212) 877-5561 FAX (212) 877-5174
Paulette Glassman	(212) 369-3010	**Mark Krumper** 1722 Hiddenwood Court Orlando, FL 32712 (Line Producer)	(407) 353-2099
Preston L. Goddard	(203) 604-8080 (203) 249-4412 FAX (203) 857-4977		
Joanne Golden (Line Producer)	(212) 665-8445	**Steven Levy**	(212) 355-8311 (310) 499-4804 FAX (310) 496-3110 www.stevenjlevy.com
Gregory E. Goodman	(310) 273-6700 www.utaproduction.com		
Robert Graf	(310) 273-6700 www.utaproduction.com		

Kit Liset	(917) 767-6873 / (212) 477-7975
Daniel Lupi	(310) 273-6700 / www.utaproduction.com
Ann Mann	(212) 799-7666
David Marcellino	(212) 929-2519 / (917) 273-0483 / www.davidmarcellino.com
David Marks (Line Producer)	(914) 238-9372 / (917) 767-9269 / FAX (914) 238-9421
Nancy Marks (Line Producer)	(914) 238-9372 / (917) 225-5674 / FAX (914) 238-9421
Karol Marrs	(212) 269-4668 / (917) 854-5029
Adam Merims	(310) 273-6700 / www.utaproduction.com
Mike Michelin (Line Producer & Producer)	(201) 694-0988 / FAX (201) 939-6847
The Mirisch Agency 1925 Century Park East, Ste. 1070 Los Angeles, CA 90067 (Reps for Producers)	(310) 282-9940 / FAX (310) 282-0702 / www.mirisch.com
Montana Artists Agency 7715 W. Sunset Blvd., Third Fl. Los Angeles, CA 90046 (Reps for Producers)	(323) 845-4144 / FAX (323) 845-4155 / www.montanartists.com
Chris Myers	(917) 864-4235
Bob Naud (Line Producer)	(212) 308-8642
David Nelson (Line Producer)	(914) 381-3054 / (914) 282-5693
Alexandra Nevins	(914) 423-6909 / (917) 747-7769 / www.alexnevins.com
David Nicksay	(310) 273-6700 / www.utaproduction.com
Frank Nugent (Line Producer & Producer)	(914) 591-2773 / (914) 582-1565 / FAX (914) 591-3252
Gary Odom	(818) 990-8993 / www.ambitiousent.com
James Parker	(914) 591-5888 / (917) 208-1698
Miriam Patterson	(212) 627-8860
Jennifer Pearlman	(917) 862-9818
Brent Perlman	(212) 580-0226
Maribeth Phillips	(212) 691-1390 / (917) 826-3399 / FAX (212) 691-1390
Jason Pinardo (Line Producer)	(212) 643-1736 / www.cec-entertainment.com
Tom Prince	(310) 822-9113 / www.murthaagency.com
Ellen Rappaport	(212) 737-4992 / (917) 359-6358
Mitje Raschi	(585) 737-3690
Karen Renaudin	(212) 928-1326 / (917) 543-7162 / FAX (212) 928-1328
Nancy Riggs (Line Producer & Producer)	(917) 660-1989 / FAX (212) 842-4619
Kevin Riley	(201) 750-1703 / (201) 403-3183 / FAX (201) 750-1922 / www.rileysight.com
Louise Rosner	(310) 273-6700 / www.utaproduction.com
Ann Ruark	(310) 273-6700 / www.utaproduction.com
Lisa Ruffler	(212) 375-1601 / (917) 439-5170
Kathryn E. Ruopp (Line Producer & Producer)	(718) 840-0718 / (917) 270-4800 / FAX (718) 840-0835
Steven Saeta	(310) 273-6700 / www.unitedtalent.com
Sabine Schenk (Line Producer)	(212) 982-8849 / (917) 650-3535 / FAX (212) 982-7970
John D. Schofield	(310) 273-6700 / www.utaproduction.com
Erica Segal	(917) 913-4617
Prashant Shah (Line Producer & Producer)	(732) 317-3583 / FAX (732) 777-0227 / www.bollywoodhollywood.com
Phillip R. Sheridan	(212) 675-9798
Roger Sherman	(212) 980-5966 / FAX (212) 980-5944 / www.florentinefilms.com/sherman
Nina Shiffman	(718) 858-7858
Marc Sidel (Line Producer)	(212) 477-3675 / (917) 886-7777 / FAX (212) 481-8668
Jeffrey Silver	(310) 273-6700 / www.unitedtalent.com
Scott Sinkler	(917) 446-8977 / www.publiceyeproductions.com
Enzo Sisti	(310) 822-9113 / www.murthaagency.com
Nina Sloan (Line Producer & Producer)	(973) 744-0210 / (201) 259-7818 / FAX (973) 744-6621
Daniel Sollinger	(818) 206-0144 / www.allcrewagency.com
Elizabeth Spinzia	(917) 613-4632 / (845) 876-2808
David Spodak (Line Producer)	(561) 272-8721
Philip Steuer	(310) 273-6700 / www.utaproduction.com

Jennifer Stock (Line Producer)	(516) 569-7759 www.jenstock.com	**Dara Weintraub**	(310) 273-6700 www.utaproduction.com
Kate Sutherland (Line Producer & Producer)	(917) 699-6511	**Llewellyn Wells**	(310) 273-6700 www.utaproduction.com
Mark Tocher (Line Producer & Producer)	(212) 340-1243	**Meredith Welsch**	(917) 405-3427 FAX (201) 928-1057
TRG-RAGAMUFFIN 65 Jay St., Fourth Fl. (Near Front St.) Brooklyn, NY 11201	(212) 213-8824 FAX (212) 202-6373 www.trg-ragamuffin.com	**Shelby Werwa**	(212) 929-4456
Sharon Ullman	(718) 222-9832	**Roni Wheeler**	(917) 974-1397 (201) 291-0215 FAX (201) 291-0216 www.namaste-uth.com
Victoria Vallas-Cullen (Line Producer)	(212) 505-6174 FAX (212) 505-1249	**John Williams**	(347) 489-5343 (631) 968-0050 www.reelworks.org
Richard Vane	(310) 273-6700 www.utaproduction.com	**John Winter** (Line Producer)	(917) 612-2000 (718) 499-1331
Chrisann Verges	(310) 273-6700 www.utaproduction.com	**Stan Wlodkowski**	(310) 273-6700 www.utaproduction.com
Mora Killeen Walker	(805) 493-4469 (805) 341-1689	**Dany Wolf**	(310) 273-6700 www.unitedtalent.com

Production Coordinators (Local 161 NY)

Elizabeth Alton	(917) 855-0626
Alexis Arnold	(917) 501-6058
Leah Katherine Baker	(717) 919-8602
Joane Baptiste-Cummins (Assistant Production Office Coordinator)	(718) 875-4560 (917) 714-1404
Monica D. Barraza (Assistant Production Office Coordinator)	(917) 215-6517
Ashley Bearden (Assistant Production Office Coordinator)	(212) 924-8976 (646) 246-8976
Evan Beier (Assistant Production Office Coordinator)	(864) 650-4015
Laura Benson	(646) 872-0857
Pamela Joan Bertini	(718) 887-8179 (917) 405-1799
Beverly Billin (Assistant Production Office Coordinator)	(917) 446-7698
Brette Billow (Assistant Production Office Coordinators)	(516) 582-0401
Taylor L. Black (Assistant Production Office Coordinator)	(646) 256-4347
Doc Boguski	(610) 449-2560 (610) 613-0565
Michael Boonstra	(212) 260-5094 (917) 657-4784
Erin Borel	(337) 326-2463
Karen Bosma (Assistant Production Office Coordinator)	(904) 631-8938
Faith Brooks	(973) 686-9898 (973) 626-4054
Jamie Buckner (Assistant Production Office Coordinator)	(502) 417-1524
Lauren Butler-Dougherty (Assistant Production Office Coordinator)	(212) 920-8721 (646) 249-0693
Rachel Cates (Assistant Production Office Coordinator)	(509) 998-9779
Sasha Charlemagne (Assistant Production Office Coordinator)	(917) 683-2322
Betty Chin	(212) 772-7198 (917) 375-9462 FAX (212) 717-8977
AmyJoy Clark (Assistant Production Office Coordinator)	(917) 678-2073
Chris Collins	(201) 314-7645
Sarah Connolly (Assistant Production Office Coordinator)	(310) 902-4854
Jennifer Crammer	(917) 287-2084
Colin Cumberbatch	(646) 246-9591
Natalie Marie Damico (Assistant Production Office Coordinator)	(212) 452-1194 (917) 841-6024
Alison Davis (Assistant Production Office Coordinator)	(201) 244-6770 (201) 803-2434
Chrissie Davis	(843) 696-7716
Jason Dean (Assistant Production Office Coordinator)	(718) 501-2649
Barbara DeFina	(845) 534-1244
Elizabeth Ann Dennis	(843) 478-2272
Patricia De Paula	(917) 657-5946
John De Simone	(908) 736-0988 (917) 757-1059
Charlie Dibe (Assistant Production Office Coordinator)	(914) 466-0113
Anna Jane Dobkin (Assistant Production Office Coordinator)	(412) 361-8495 (412) 400-7423
George Doherty	(201) 747-3222
Mary J. Dow	(781) 990-1799 (617) 448-4989
Tanya Doyle (Assistant Production Office Coordinator)	(718) 690-0627
Blake Drummond (Assistant Production Office Coordinator)	(732) 245-0977
Eileen Eichenstein	(212) 865-6140 (212) 678-0999
Margaret Engelhardt	(212) 663-8535 (917) 837-7270
Kimberly Fajen	(646) 284-5351
Erin Feeley (Assistant Production Office Coordinator)	(323) 377-4215
Lindsay Feldman (Assistant Production Office Coordinator)	(215) 680-3099
Kerin Ferallo	(718) 930-1093
Ellen Gannon	(212) 645-8121
Melissa Gelernter	(212) 222-9997 (646) 245-7661
Lawrence Geyer (Assistant Production Office Coordinator)	(412) 816-1388 (412) 638-4589
Anika Gibbons (Assistant Production Office Coordinator)	(917) 312-9489
Erika Goldfarb (Assistant Production Office Coordinator)	(201) 618-0279
Joseph J. Gonzalez	(212) 666-9483

Vanessa Gutin (Assistant Production Office Coordinator)	(856) 889-5257
Leslie Gyson	(917) 671-8966
Mark Hagerman	(631) 757-0430 / (516) 650-1413
Jennifer Haire	(323) 449-6259
Thalia Harithas (Assistant Production Office Coordinator)	(212) 317-2001 / (917) 232-5566
Tanika Fame Holloman (Assistant Production Office Coordinator)	(803) 960-1694
Amy Hong-Man Tung (Assistant Production Office Coordinator)	(212) 491-2563 / (917) 557-0751
Lori Hornung	(617) 803-9300
Thomas Howes	(323) 574-5711
Joshua Huffman	(917) 575-0132
Syndey Huynh (Assistant Production Office Coordinator)	(917) 806-0578
Bradley Jasper (Assistant Production Office Coordinator)	(516) 547-4227
Todd Judson	(917) 509-7747
Erica Kay	(212) 367-9436
Richard Keeshan (Assistant Production Office Coordinator)	(414) 405-8043
Hilary Kehoe	(914) 433-6413
Kate Kelly	(917) 439-3847
Scott Kordish	(718) 596-2993
Mary Kroliczak (Assistant Production Office Coordinator)	(215) 808-6003
Liz Kugle (Assistant Production Office Coordinator)	(917) 304-8050
Terry Ladin	(212) 593-3323 / (917) 593-8652
Gabrielle Lasting (Assistant Production Office Coordinator)	(917) 657-4569
Angela Lee (Assistant Production Office Coordinator)	(646) 602-0293 / (646) 251-6605
Kristina Lee (Assistant Production Office Coordinator)	(717) 413-1285
Mia Lee (Assistant Production Office Coordinator)	(718) 302-5352 / (917) 359-4372
Carrie Leigh (Assistant Production Office Coordinator)	(646) 270-9357
Talia Helena Leone	(763) 442-1003
Amy Lo (Assistant Production Office Coordinator)	(917) 992-3243
Rebecca Locke (Assistant Production Office Coordinator)	(617) 293-2712
Rosemary Lombard	(212) 447-5150 / (917) 748-4649
Jennifer Madeloff	(609) 448-4842 / (609) 577-7060
Gabrielle Mahon	(718) 505-4249 / (917) 825-2915
Francesca Mannix (Assistant Production Office Coordinator)	(401) 864-6506
Gary Martyn (Assistant Production Office Coordinator)	(917) 669-3057
Ryan McDonald (Assistant Production Office Coordinator)	(646) 283-8100
Christian McHenry (Assistant Production Office Coordinator)	(917) 482-8985
Jody Milano (Assistant Production Office Coordinator)	(917) 406-7477
Meredith Mills-Cavalluzzo	(718) 543-5217 / (917) 701-1935
Montez Monroe	(718) 855-6881
Wendy Mooradian	(212) 977-9655
Vincent Morano	(732) 687-0244
Meegan Neeb	(917) 673-2669
Elizabeth Nevin	(646) 263-8161
Maire Ni Rochain	(646) 361-6491
Leda Nornang	(917) 554-7040
Steve Oare	(508) 545-1117 / (617) 549-6273
Matthew O'Brien (Assistant Production Office Coordinator)	(856) 904-9014
Kory O'Donnell	(917) 509-0769
Andrea Denise Pappas	(917) 623-7099
Katrina Joy Parsons	(978) 404-9252
Susan Parsons	(914) 747-0462 / (617) 312-7744
James Pellegrinelli (Assistant Production Office Coordinator)	(917) 517-2960
Elizabeth Pellegrini	(347) 223-4117
Holly Ann Pilch (Assistant Production Office Coordinator)	(917) 817-2017
Ozzie Pisarri (Assistant Production Office Coordinator)	(201) 965-9413
Luke Poling (Assistant Production Office Coordinator)	(617) 469-0021 / (508) 423-3395
Matthew Preston (Assistant Production Office Coordinator)	(305) 538-0168
David Price	(212) 620-9653
Marissa Price	(917) 450-9640
Christine Putnam (Assistant Production Office Coordinator)	(646) 734-6164

Angela Quiles	(718) 625-4581 (917) 576-5865	Karen Sossiadis	(917) 573-8675
Philip A. Ramos	(716) 326-3535 (212) 365-8918	Robin Sprance (Assistant Production Office Coordinator)	(917) 648-8526
David Raynor (Assistant Production Office Coordinator)	(215) 870-4549	Anita Sum	(646) 383-7536 (917) 376-6710
Dawn Murphy Riley	(212) 501-3552	Diane Sunderlin	(412) 477-3841
Blythe Robertson (Assistant Production Office Coordinator)	(617) 290-6335	Lindsay Swartz (Assistant Production Office Coordinator)	(201) 220-1825
Ulises Rodriguez (Assistant Production Office Coordinator)	(917) 359-1080 (212) 744-8838	Nicholas Alfred Thomason (Assistant Production Office Coordinator)	(718) 768-3869 (646) 319-5001
Cassandra Ross Eccles (Assistant Production Office Coordinator)	(412) 828-9664 (412) 980-4444	Victoria Toner	(412) 682-3865 (412) 638-3126
Jonathan Russek (Assistant Production Office Coordinator)	(917) 482-5268	Amy Trachtman (Assistant Production Office Coordinator)	(201) 938-2810
Holly Rymon	(516) 705-0559 (516) 984-6024	Daniel Wagner	(212) 979-6635 (917) 679-9255
Peter Sabat	(917) 374-3653 (212) 228-3816	Sara Webster (Assistant Production Office Coordinator)	(215) 605-4503
Andrew Sarno (Assistant Production Office Coordinator)	(617) 877-1011	Meghan Wicker	(917) 678-9208
		Patricia Willett	(212) 366-1151
Matthew Schneider (Assistant Production Office Coordinator)	(914) 234-6707 (718) 757-5685	Canella Williams	(718) 951-9880 (347) 613-1764
William Sell	(917) 575-7401	Teresa M. Yarbrough	(678) 467-7122
Franses Simonovich	(818) 599-0310	Greer Yeaton	(718) 398-1719
John Stephen Skidmore (Assistant Production Office Coordinator)	(917) 843-4846	Andy Zolot	(646) 623-1138

Production Coordinators

Lynn Appelle	(917) 686-7300	Kim Jackson (Assistant Production Office Coordinator)	(212) 431-9467
Michael Bowes (Production Office Coordinator)	(617) 842-6372	Anne Johns	(212) 643-1736 www.cec-entertainment.com
Branching Out Productions, Inc. (Reps for Production Coordinators) www.branchingoutpro.com	(516) 944-8999 (516) 652-5036 FAX (516) 944-8998	Terry Ladin	(212) 593-3323 (917) 593-8652
Jeremy Crane (Production Office Coordinator)	(646) 331-9012	Ronny Merdinger (Assistant Production Office Coordinator) FAX www.graycatnyc.com	(917) 388-3232 (917) 388-3024
Betsy Davis (Assistant Production Office Coordinator)	(646) 234-8393	Ana Pelaez (Production Office Coordinator)	(347) 228-8022
E. Paul DiMartino Jr. FAX www.milkywaymedia.net	(718) 636-0990 (917) 689-5997 (718) 360-9229	Felice Schachter	(917) 930-5930
		Harriet G. Snyder	(212) 717-9803
Tara Dolack	(973) 931-1016	Eric Trudel www.erictrudel.com	(860) 961-9203
Charles Goon charles.goon.googlepages.com	(917) 692-3229	Susan Vescera FAX	(215) 862-5535 (908) 307-3288 (215) 862-5321

Production Managers

Jim Aleski	(732) 259-0498
	www.349media.com
Richard Baratta	(201) 568-6491
	(917) 797-4750
(UPM)	FAX (201) 568-1932
Bill Blum	(212) 775-7162
(UPM)	
Carrie Bornstein	(212) 627-1040
	(917) 603-5763
Brett M. Botula	(212) 861-8386
(UPM)	
M. Blair Breard	(323) 845-4144
	www.montanartists.com
Jack Briggs	(212) 995-2781
Cornelia Burnham	(718) 387-0728
	(917) 566-3434
(Production Manager & UPM)	
Donald Cager	(212) 741-0698
	(917) 860-2635
Jay Cannold	(212) 755-8560
	(917) 723-0902
Anthony J. Cerbone	(973) 992-4479
	FAX (973) 992-4479
Crew Connection	(800) 352-7397
	(303) 526-4900
(Referral for Production Managers)	FAX (303) 526-4901
	www.crewconnection.com
Amelia Dallis	(917) 859-4445
Eileen Eichenstein	(212) 865-6140
	FAX (212) 678-0999
Rod Elvir	(646) 522-4834
(UPM)	
Andrea Falkenstein	(718) 633-8005
	(917) 670-3576
Scott Ferguson	(212) 245-9060
Avenol A. Franco	(917) 826-1244
(Production Manager & UPM)	
Gary Giudice	(347) 204-1471
	FAX (718) 565-0599
Stephen Andrew Glanzrock	(212) 255-8733
	FAX (320) 205-8733
Julie Goodman	(914) 202-7722
	(917) 602-0420
(UPM)	
Stephanie Haberman	(718) 974-1540
Daniel Hank	(212) 769-4429
Alex Hapsas	(845) 365-3066
Marilyn A. Harvey	(718) 721-3011
Petra Hoebel	(917) 418-5469
(UPM)	FAX (646) 219-0233
Michael Jordan	(845) 236-3566
(UPM)	
Miles Kahn	(718) 274-7651
	(917) 572-3182
	home.earthlink.net/~phisto
Christian Kendrick	(347) 512-1200
Gus Kousoulas	(917) 882-6123
	FAX (718) 504-5203
Steven Levy	(212) 355-8311
	(310) 499-4804
	FAX (310) 496-3110
	www.stevenjlevy.com
Logan Luchsinger	(212) 741-2925
	(917) 929-6169
Adrian Martin	(212) 666-2570
(UPM)	FAX (212) 665-1303
Michelle Menke	(646) 338-6171
Phil Meyerowitz	(917) 453-1570
(UPM)	FAX (732) 494-0628
Charles Miller	(203) 595-0392
	(917) 991-0001
	FAX (203) 595-0397
Chris Myers	(917) 864-4235
P. Claire Pertalion	(917) 554-7677
Cheryl Quarantiello	(732) 223-9731
	(201) 841-7476
	FAX (732) 292-1060
Raymond Quinlan	(631) 513-3327
	(631) 289-7355
Tom Razzano	(201) 569-2377
(UPM)	www.tomrazzano.com
Kathryn E. Ruopp	(718) 840-0718
	(917) 270-4800
	FAX (718) 840-0835
Marc Sidel	(212) 477-3675
	(917) 886-7777
	FAX (212) 481-8668
Michele Stanger	(917) 597-3992
(UPM)	
Will Tatum	(917) 693-5751
	(212) 334-3374
Pamela Thur	(212) 374-0455
	(917) 873-3364
John Trenear	(212) 962-6121
	(917) 536-3481
	FAX (212) 962-6121
Christian von Tippelskirch	(646) 361-4390
(UPM)	FAX (646) 365-3076
	www.cvt-productions.com

Production Stills Photographers (Local 600)

Mikki Ansin	(617) 661-1640
Myles Aronowitz	(310) 702-0076
Jimmy Ayoub	(212) 598-4467 / (917) 847-6514 / FAX (212) 598-4378 / www.jimmyayoub.com
John Baer	(609) 947-7205
K C Bailey	(212) 431-8239
Karen Ballard	(202) 431-3777 / (202) 797-2668
Craig Blankenhorn	(212) 727-2549 / FAX (212) 727-1858 / www.blankenhornphoto.com
James Bridges	(910) 620-6492
Jessica Burstein	(212) 472-1601
Phillip Caruso	(518) 674-0345
John Clifford	(212) 741-0616 / (646) 325-6216
Thomas Concordia	(917) 842-8009
Kent Eanes	(804) 353-0246 / (804) 677-7874
Erin Feinberg	(201) 314-7969 / (212) 874-0655
Claire Folger	(781) 646-5274 / (781) 799-8954
Leah Gallo	(610) 932-5282
Abbot Genser	(212) 675-7435 / (818) 716-1783
David Giesbrecht	(718) 536-0391 / (347) 365-9547 / www.davidgiesbrecht.com
Ali Goldstein	(917) 853-1336
Brian Hamill	(212) 947-2136 / (323) 656-0386
James Hamilton	(212) 475-7087
Patrick Harbron	(917) 494-8828
Will Hart	(917) 691-0849 / www.willhart.net
Kerry Hayes	(416) 698-0245 / (631) 329-5840
Ernest Hayfield	(212) 971-1036
Anne Joyce	(917) 576-9331 / (718) 875-5652
Tom Le Goff	(212) 966-7986
David Lee	(718) 624-3403 / (917) 626-3504
Eric Liebowitz	(212) 477-2899 / (917) 523-7281
Diana Lyn	(412) 668-0122 / (412) 427-7314
Laura Magruder	(787) 655-0903 / (787) 602-0279
Jessica Miglio	(516) 208-8109 / (646) 831-0447
Jeff Neumann	(973) 222-4266 / www.jeffneumannphotos.com
Barbara Nitke	(917) 670-4304 / (212) 725-2335
Fred Norris	(910) 300-3113 / (910) 620-1813
Michael Parmalee (Aerial)	(973) 617-0710
Matt Peyton	(212) 452-3267 / (917) 693-6998
Antony Platt	(757) 627-9729 / www.bluethunderpictures.com
Macall Polay	(917) 744-8065
Donald Rager	(412) 297-3539 / (412) 441-9841
Piotr Redlinski (Aerial)	(917) 327-7853
Nicole Rivelli	(718) 545-0457 / (646) 784-1614 / www.nicolerivelli.com
Javier Rivera Burgos	(787) 407-3498 / (787) 744-5578
Giovanni Rufino (Aerial)	(646) 5227215 / www.giovannirufino.com
David Russell	(917) 922-8332
Paul Schiraldi	(917) 902-9619
Anneke Schoneveld	(804) 687-7244
Andrew Schwartz	(212) 947-0485
Sarah Shatz	(917) 862-8960
Virginia Sherwood	(718) 624-6365
Donald Spiro	(818) 404-9458
Serge Stojiljkovic	(646) 387-6620
Michael Tackett	(910) 545-3281 / (910) 577-7005
Niko Tavernise	(917) 930-9204
Walter Thomson	(646) 554-6683 / (718) 797-3818
Bob Vergara	(845) 406-7670 / (845) 353-1069

Lawrence Watson	(732) 758-1177	Dennis Yeandle	(201) 224-5555
Jonathan Wenk	(888) 311-1617	Peter Zimmern	(646) 729-6868
Barry Wetcher	(212) 349-2498 (917) 509-7675	Tom Zuback	(212) 247-4247 (917) 751-1036 www.tomzuback.com
JoJo Whilden	(917) 601-8945 www.jojowhilden.com		

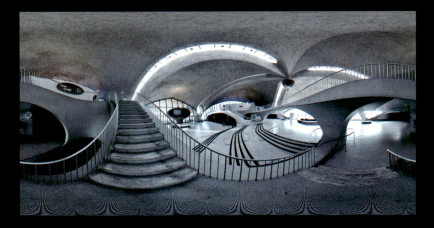

360° Panoramic Photography

HDR Virtual Reality Photography for Web, CGI & Print
Virtual Tours :: QTVR :: Interactive Flash Panoramas
Sam Rohn :: 718.230.3651 :: www.samrohn.com

Production Stills Photographers

ArtMix Photography (718) 596-2400
297 Bond St. (310) 473-0770
Brooklyn, NY 11231 FAX (718) 596-2401
www.artmixphotography.com
(Reps for Stills Photographers)

Dana Belcher (917) 749-8399

Contemporary Photography Services (610) 554-2926
105 Cardinal Dr. (610) 852-2340
Palmerton, PA 18071 FAX (610) 852-2340
www.rjsphoto.com

Roberto D'Este (718) 596-2400
www.artmixphotography.com

Bill Foley (914) 645-4367
(317) 255-0549
www.billfoley.com

Christopher Fragapane (212) 794-9030

Abbot Genser (212) 675-7435

Geoff Green Photography (646) 498-3069
www.geoffgreen.com

Michael Ginsburg (212) 677-0167

Julian Hibbard (212) 925-1111
www.onenakedegg.com

Sheri Lane (917) 837-3645
www.creativehotlist.com/s-lane

Steve Mack (917) 202-4358
FAX (917) 591-1173
www.sdmackpictures.com

Anthony Mandler (718) 596-2400
www.artmixphotography.com

Mary Ellen Matthews (917) 673-5250
(212) 664-6914

Larry Merz (203) 222-1936
(203) 451-2019

One Naked Egg (212) 925-1111
675 Hudson St., Ste. 4N FAX (212) 929-6552
(Near 13th St.)
New York, NY 10014 www.onenakedegg.com
(Reps for Production Still Photographers)

Sebastian Piras (646) 361-9579
www.sebastianpiras.com

Kai Regan (718) 596-2400
www.artmixphotography.com

John Ricard (917) 848-4197
www.johnricard.com

Ⓐ Sam Rohn (718) 230-3651
(917) 771-3651
www.samrohn.com

Gary Sapolin (914) 924-7878

John Seakwood (518) 794-9622

W. Thomson (718) 797-3818

Demmie Todd (518) 854-9704

Matteo Trisolini (646) 678-1654
FAX (212) 741-6648
www.matteotrisolini.com

Props Department (Local 52 NY)

Brett Acker	(215) 284-5120
Robert Ackerman	(646) 239-1131 (212) 724-1311
Troy R. Adee	(201) 995-1228 (800) 225-0256
Walter A. Adee	(718) 721-0731
William C. Adee	(914) 923-4788
Sherri Adler	(212) 541-6141 (917) 797-4845
Gary M. Aharoni	(845) 624-8688
Gregg A. Aharoni	(201) 886-7032 (201) 406-2099
Michael B. Aharoni	(845) 661-8825
Irfan Akdag	(201) 750-9404 (917) 854-7100 FAX (201) 750-9405
Julie Albanese	(845) 735-3294
Jennifer Alex Nickason	(646) 325-4418 (973) 783-9580
Jill Alexander	(718) 596-6494 (646) 523-0540
John Alfredo III	(973) 772-6666 (201) 933-4652
David H. Allen	(508) 362-0069 (917) 620-3096
Pastor Alvarado III	(512) 791-0977
Lawrence Amanuel	(914) 522-9297 (845) 928-3849 FAX (845) 928-3850
James Ansbro	(973) 634-8850
Peter Ansel	(212) 986-0699 (917) 609-4660
James M. Anziano	(518) 865-7909
Dimitri Apletchef	(212) 750-8826
George Apostol	(631) 698-3059 (516) 373-3432
James J. Archer	(908) 522-0437 (908) 447-9446
Ann Armstrong	(631) 669-6651 (917) 864-1181
Brian D. Armstrong	(860) 632-0872
Stephanie Armstrong	(203) 981-5327
Daniel Aronson	(212) 544-0366
John Ashton	(917) 827-6091
Jo Ann Atwood	(212) 353-8886 (917) 750-4312
Joseph Badalucco Jr.	(845) 278-4966 (914) 263-5046
Michael J. Badalucco	(212) 529-3986
Gerald C. Bakal	(201) 475-0328 (201) 218-6145
Melanie J. Baker	(212) 679-5588
Anthony Baldasare	(516) 887-5545
Jasmine Ballou	(347) 726-1445
Shelley Barclay	(212) 741-5036 (917) 922-2710
Kenneth W. Barnes	(610) 543-0889
John T. Barreto	(973) 940-6940 (973) 209-5525
Andrew Baseman	(212) 674-6217
John M. Basile	(732) 830-1155
June Bateman	(212) 925-7951 (917) 806-8200 FAX (212) 925-7951 www.junebateman.com
Shawn Batey	(646) 456-2482
Robert Battaglia	(716) 631-5119 (716) 984-3279
Alayne D. Baxter	(212) 737-1361 (212) 794-1300
Zachary Baylin	(917) 509-7049
Jocelyne Beaudoin	(212) 925-4222 (212) 645-8063 www.art-dept.com
Philip Beck	(917) 806-1990 (917) 570-6013
Susan Beeson-de Havenon	(212) 679-2030
Teri Bella	(917) 512-4975 (917) 701-0191
Charles Bellafiore	(646) 240-5201
Anthony J. Benevento	(631) 345-5707 (631) 806-2177
David S Benninghoff	(203) 629-9135
Russell J. Berg	(718) 857-1488 (917) 974-7501
Andrew Bernard	(212) 586-5139 (212) 545-7895 www.nyoffice.net
Mark Bero	(718) 383-6170
Michael Billig	(914) 837-5803
James Bilz	(212) 724-6794
Stephen J. Binasiewicz	(215) 334-2731 (215) 426-0858

Jaimie Bird	(201) 707-9220
Joseph L. Bird	(201) 444-8356
Joseph R. Bird	(201) 391-8455
Michael Bird	(201) 358-1420 / (201) 522-5992
William J. Bishop	(631) 360-3323 / (516) 426-4502
Kevin E. Blake	(201) 659-0003 / (201) 601-6263
Daniel M. Bleier	(212) 362-1869 / (917) 786-2548
Susan Block	(212) 777-8746
Tara Joy Boccia	(718) 338-4676 / (516) 395-3129
Sheila Bock	(718) 375-2268 / (718) 252-2554
Susan S. Bode-Tyson	(631) 689-0570
Teresa Ann Bolz	(631) 549-7534
James Bono	(718) 951-0685 / (718) 249-7979
Michael Boucher	(201) 599-8153
Shannon R. Bowen	(212) 979-1169 / (917) 568-5835
Paul Bowman	(646) 625-9601
Daniel Boxer	(917) 570-8888
Coburn Boyd	(917) 576-2587
Nancy Boytos	(845) 928-3849 / (914) 522-9297
Wayne T. Brackett	(201) 457-1375 / (917) 567-5615
Joseph J. Bradshaw	(732) 493-6227 / (201) 274-9567
Jack Brandt	(860) 601-1369
Richard L. Brandt (Prop Master)	(860) 567-4674 / (917) 951-4184 / FAX (860) 567-4674
James Branigan (Prop Master)	(917) 686-8167
James M. Breen	(610) 742-4442 / (610) 358-4416
Deirdre Brennan	(212) 308-4092
Steven Brennan	(617) 306-7455
Sarah Bricker	(347) 239-3099 / (718) 545-3013
Edward E. Briggs	(212) 727-2631 / (917) 680-7863
Conrad V. Brink Jr.	(908) 276-5558
Conrad F. Brink Sr.	(908) 241-4712 / (718) 505-9465
Thomas R. Britton	(609) 882-2114
Joan Brockschmidt	(845) 358-1006
Nathanael Brotherhood	(845) 359-0097
Jason A. Brown	(718) 983-0747
D. Eric Bryant	(518) 451-0649
Fred Buchholz	(212) 874-7700
Alexander (Zan) Burnham	(718) 871-4089 / (347) 267-1352
Sarah Jackson Burt	(845) 339-3600
Diana E. Burton	(917) 698-3976 / (718) 622-1510
Jennifer Burton-Akdag	(201) 750-9404 / (917) 539-3910
Rob Buschow	(201) 264-3030
Jeff Butcher (Prop Master)	(718) 930-8092
Brian Buteau	(718) 349-8184 / (646) 359-3480
Anna Butwell	(646) 526-3821
Edwin Caban	(718) 858-4402
Wilfred Caban	(718) 858-1947 / (914) 403-1725
John F. Cahill	(914) 225-3043 / (917) 252-1260
Leni Calas	(718) 850-6352 / (646) 296-0070
Paul Camarro	(973) 875-2092 / (973) 271-0203
Carmen M. Campolo Jr.	(914) 669-5362
Deborah N. Canfield	(914) 804-2158
Kelly T. Canfield	(914) 923-4788 / (914) 879-3308
Philip C. Canfield	(914) 693-8420 / (914) 546-2468
Scott Canfield	(914) 424-8413
Shannon Canfield	(914) 279-6530
Patrice Canfield-Longo	(914) 762-6617 / (914) 551-9323
Jacqueline Canfield-Mahon	(914) 693-7974 / (914) 693-5091
Jacqueline Canto	(212) 580-0851 / (917) 319-5236
Joseph M. Caracciolo Jr.	(212) 577-6255
Jonathan J. Carter	(917) 769-8083
Carolyn Cartwright	(212) 982-1891 / (646) 286-8328
Cristina Casanas	(718) 398-1174 / (917) 400-3601
Stephen Cascarelli	(646) 641-6046

Henry Cespedes	(631) 399-3931
Suzanne E. Cestare	(570) 296-7671 (516) 742-5550
Kimberli Lynne Chapman	(212) 876-6592 (917) 568-5462
Christopher Chenel	(973) 332-6278 (973) 962-1448
Paul Cheponis	(718) 768-0934
Eric Cheripka	(201) 261-5416
Jeffrey Christiano	(718) 343-6619 (516) 328-1991
Lois H. Ciganek-Bernini	(631) 368-4161 (212) 734-7982
Hugo J. Cimmelli	(845) 735-2090 FAX (845) 735-1643
Leah Cimmelli	(845) 735-4693 (845) 735-2090
Joshua Clark	(201) 248-9419
Thomas Coapman	(718) 651-4169 (646) 644-4169
Todd Ian Cole	(303) 882-6041
Douglas E. Coleman	(914) 763-5623
William Comacho	(203) 650-1533
John K. Conway	(516) 921-8107 (917) 954-5719
Joseph T. Conway	(703) 795-0150
Thomas O. Conway	(516) 922-0718
Brandon Cook	(610) 622-5752
Michael J. Cooney	(518) 283-6272
Cory M. Copeland	(917) 312-3928
Joseph A. Coppola	(914) 490-9098
Michael Cory	(646) 287-1909
Damian J. Costa	(914) 698-6923 (518) 827-4255
Edward Cotugno	(518) 221-4049
Erin Cousins	(347) 267-8784
Robert Covelman	(212) 229-2750 (917) 281-1084
Jeffrey A. Cox	(610) 338-0413 (215) 418-1744
Eileen M Coyne-Babich	(631) 790-4282
Karen Coyne-De Luca	(631) 893-3021
Patricia A. Coyne-Rader	(516) 731-2799
Catriona (Cat) Crosby	(718) 389-8243 (917) 407-7491
Abariss Culjak	(718) 501-7611
Lee Cunningham	(310) 277-1900
Robert J. Currie	(845) 351-4439 (917) 674-3432
Joel Custer	(917) 783-4412
Gabriel Camilo S. Dalglish	(646) 351-9881
Roger Danchik	(617) 269-8567
Peter Dancy	(212) 365-0820
James (Bear) Davies	(732) 389-1986 (917) 812-1238
Catherine Davis	(917) 658-0762
Joseph E. Davis	(203) 699-9422
Rena De Angelo	(212) 580-3707 (917) 556-7518
Daniel R. Decelle	(201) 836-9353
William E. Decelle Jr.	(201) 943-2892 (201) 330-4217
Frank De Curtis	(212) 563-5154 (646) 258-1444
Frank De Curtis Jr.	(718) 876-7471 (917) 414-8881
Guido DeCurtis	(917) 797-7774 (914) 457-0985
Louise De Curtis	(917) 656-7351
Peter De Curtis	(718) 777-7293 (917) 853-0758
Paul D. De Filippo	(718) 441-3406 (917) 879-8892
Ruth Ann De Leon	(917) 224-9833
Thomas A. De Lillo	(845) 358-1562 (845) 222-6871
Joseph De Luca	(518) 496-1944
Robert A. De Mar	(718) 384-6797
Mandie Demeskey	(201) 280-3477
Sarah Dennis	(212) 337-0079 (917) 680-9036
Jerry De Rogatis	(732) 261-8615
Joseph V. De Stefano	(845) 746-6882
Beth Ann De Titta	(914) 352-6635
Christopher J. De Titta	(201) 722-0564 (201) 424-0407
Daniel De Titta	(201) 714-0708 (201) 573-1582
Gerald A. De Titta	(201) 261-1743
George M. De Titta Jr.	(201) 573-1582
Patrice De Titta	(914) 638-3401
Nicholas De Titta	(201) 261-1743
Anna De Titta Di Meo	(201) 935-7259
Christopher P. Des Marais	(850) 385-3661

Frank Desmond	(201) 843-5981	Linda T. Ekstrand	(212) 639-9302 (917) 882-7165
Richard Devine	(718) 953-4538 (917) 836-0019	Meredith Elter	(856) 287-9009 (267) 278-6948
Michael T. Dickman	(201) 943-7229 (201) 638-9490	Gregory Embriano	(718) 359-1365
Andrew J. Di Meo	(919) 844-8778	Gerard Engrassia	(516) 369-9015
		Robert Evangelisto	(914) 466-4136
Anthony J. Dimeo	(201) 573-9240 (888) 894-0426	Nicholas M. Evans Jr.	(212) 222-1155 (917) 604-8082
Ruth Di Pasquale	(718) 434-9159 (917) 693-2590	Cindy Anita Fain	(212) 501-9090 (800) 306-1815
John J. (Jack) Dirk	(609) 586-5365	Kathryn Falzarano	(516) 624-7142
Daniel E. Di Tolla	(914) 469-9186	John W. Farraday	(631) 864-8302
Eric Dixon (Prop Master)	(917) 930-0945	Walter J. Fay	(215) 672-2599 FAX (215) 672-5789
Allen G. Doak Jr.	(215) 794-3378 FAX (215) 794-2254	Millacent Fearon	(917) 570-5073
Kathleen M. Dolan	(201) 767-1675	Douglas Fecht	(516) 593-3496 (516) 521-9353
Justine M. Dolan-Cote	(551) 404-4868	Mary E. Fellows	(203) 426-9090
Christine M. Donohue-Pace	(214) 477-2263	Robert Feltman	(347) 409-1781
Natalie N. Dorset	(212) 679-7056	Andrea M. Fenton	(323) 938-8906
Tracy A. Doyle	(253) 851-5716	Carl Ferrara	(201) 424-1956
Robert F. Drago	(610) 970-8866 (215) 588-8088	Nicholas Ferrara	(201) 424-1678 (973) 492-1356
Ana K. Drechsler	(212) 473-7950 (646) 298-8872	Christopher Ferraro	(201) 750-9472 (201) 519-8644
Harry Drennan	(212) 580-0851	Greta Fertik	(212) 877-3468 (917) 873-1662
Neil Driscoll Jr.	(718) 809-2753	Seth Finkin	(518) 581-0049
Edward A. Drohan IV	(914) 793-5292	Stephen Finkin	(518) 581-0049
George Drohan	(914) 715-2945 (914) 965-5625	Joan E. Finlay	(201) 670-8949 (201) 697-9960
Steven Todd Duke	(845) 365-0997 (917) 449-2762	Kenneth H. Finn	(267) 679-5794
Kellen C. Dunbar	(973) 664-1110	Jill D. Finnerty	(718) 738-6449
Maryellen Dunbar	(973) 879-3816 (973) 664-1110	Hulda Fischer	(973) 579-3511
Peter K. Dunbar	(973) 664-1110 (917) 827-2663	Daniel W. Fisher	(845) 268-7688 (917) 954-4151
Julie Duncan	(917) 584-8160	Raymond A. Fisher	(203) 372-4020
Matt Duncan	(917) 804-8177 (212) 582-8052 www.mattduncandesign.com	Yolan Fisher	(718) 744-4821
		Martha Fishkin	(212) 674-2245 (917) 848-1977
Brian Durham	(212) 947-7849 (917) 532-6069	Stephen Foley	(845) 863-3695
Joseph M. Durnin	(518) 692-9528	John R. Ford	(516) 333-2079 (914) 466-4136
William J. Durnin Jr.	(718) 706-9638	Janet Forman	(212) 496-0088
John E. Dwyer	(631) 673-4469 (917) 593-7796	Ernest M. Foster	(860) 927-4087
Ann L. Edgeworth	(212) 633-2839	Katherine Foster	(917) 689-6973

Props Department (Local 52 NY)

Michael Foster	(201) 577-1285 (908) 979-0968	Caroline Ghertler	(718) 768-0012 (917) 951-1004
William J. Foster	(610) 358-3957 (215) 330-7738	Daniel P. Giaquinto III	(609) 218-8889 (609) 464-7748
Edward A. Fountain (Prop Master)	(914) 478-4997 (917) 317-0754	Gary Giffune	(917) 797-6945
		Kley Gilbuena	(484) 390-1083
Janna Fournier	(831) 667-1003	Kathryn Gilliar	(804) 270-1055
Rafael M. Fraguada	(203) 260-3697	Kerri Gilligan	(732) 863-5971 (732) 267-4082
Roberta N. Frankel	(860) 974-1577	Thomas D. Gilligan Jr.	(612) 418-1145
Richard J. Frato	(201) 722-8642	Daniel Gilroy	(610) 449-5894 (484) 889-6780
Michael Frechette	(215) 739-9022 (267) 251-9463	Danielle Giovanniello	(201) 391-4346 (201) 819-0265
Sarah Fredericks	(718) 429-9147 (917) 846-6802	Neil A. Giovanniello	(201) 476-0965 (201) 391-4400
Kathryn Freund	(212) 724-5885 (917) 770-8004	Robyn L. Glaser	(212) 741-8174
Nancy A. Friedman	(212) 242-1564	Ted Glass	(212) 966-3289
Alison Froling	(718) 218-6946 (917) 406-6187	Lane Glisson	(718) 788-0910 (347) 268-1149 FAX (718) 788-0910
Kathryn G. Fundus	(516) 624-7142 (917) 656-2070 FAX (516) 624-0739	Lewis Gluck (Prop Master & Underwater)	(845) 227-6694
Isaac Gabaeff	(718) 383-4061 (917) 859-3465	Brent T. Godek	(718) 545-1357 (917) 859-7922
D. Scott Gagnon	(973) 771-9150 (917) 281-0136	Harvey Goldberg	(516) 781-1174 (516) 359-5143
Paul S. Gaily	(201) 825-4588	Howard Goldstein	(718) 261-5671 (917) 954-4084
Renee Gallo	(732) 607-9047 (917) 885-9270	J. Anthony Gonzalez	(347) 564-0139
Michael T. Galvin	(215) 247-4887 (302) 434-5142	Adam B. Goodnoff-Cernese	(516) 322-8122
Timothy Galvin	(215) 635-1227	Kenneth Goodstein	(516) 578-7300
Anthony S. Gamiello Jr.	(888) 959-4712 (914) 788-8484	Katherine D. Gorman	(609) 466-1336
		Susan M. Goulder	(216) 255-9705
Matthew Gamiello	(718) 539-1353 (347) 256-2738	Christopher Grano	(201) 232-8980 (201) 337-0185
Steven R. Gamiello (Prop Master)	(718) 539-1353 (347) 351-1676	Regina Graves	(212) 706-1718 (917) 748-3567
Christine Gardyasz	(201) 837-0920	Deba Jean Gray	(212) 352-3553 (347) 728-5555
Brian S. Garvey	(215) 336-6976 (215) 796-2802	Greco	(917) 586-1607 www.chocolatecoveredbacon.net
Edward B. Garvey Jr.	(215) 336-6978	Deborah Greene	(646) 522-1125
Ann Gatto-Cimmelli	(914) 735-4693 (914) 735-2090	Roman Greller	(973) 338-6672
Anthony Gentile Sr.	(609) 875-5942 (609) 969-2869	Arthur J. Griffenkranz	(201) 628-1676
Gilbert H. Gertsen	(201) 391-1424	Nancy Griffith	(212) 683-1015 (845) 876-2591
Gordon H. Gertsen	(201) 391-8455	Robert J. Griffon Jr.	(631) 728-9190
Scott Getzinger	(718) 650-9552		

Russ J. Griffon	(516) 367-2114 (917) 658-2650
Timothy M. Grimes	(917) 686-8368
Thomas M. Groody	(609) 597-2792 (800) 374-4434
Bruce L. Gross (Prop Master)	(718) 287-5736 (718) 757-8624 FAX (718) 282-1024
Daniel K. Grosso	(516) 378-1412
Victoria Guariello	(914) 376-8980 (914) 497-1861
Jean-Paul Guirard	(908) 273-5102 (917) 797-7647
David W. Gulick	(617) 492-0031
Judith Gurr	(212) 861-6586 (917) 668-8799
Christine Marie Hackett	(212) 228-2126
Jennifer Ann Halpern	(718) 858-1169 (917) 881-3049
Donna F. Hamilton	(212) 529-2120
Sandy Hamilton	(212) 226-1051 (917) 923-7482
Kevin J. Hammond Jr.	(201) 832-3374
Sandra Handloser	(646) 298-6884
Eric Hanken	(845) 642-1711 (845) 634-2082
Michele Hanken	(845) 634-2082 (917) 682-4406
Edward A. Hansen	(973) 586-0549 (973) 884-2911
James Harbick	(609) 266-7789 (212) 802-9096
Michael D. Harrell	(718) 855-1698 (718) 216-3417
Damien S. Harrer	(267) 249-8444 (215) 467-0282
Mark C. Harrington	(718) 789-5085
Cheryl A. Harrison	(610) 586-1697 (215) 960-2680
Joanna Hartell	(212) 255-1354 (917) 406-6949
Michael H. Hartney	(732) 741-3540 (732) 859-6553
Kelly A. Harvey	(732) 663-0898
Holbrook Hays	(914) 736-0343 (914) 952-8872
Christopher J. Heaps	(201) 825-4653 (201) 248-6328
Steven C. Heaps	(201) 825-2852 (201) 941-0393
Thomas J. Heaps	(201) 825-2852 (201) 409-3122
Andrew Heikkila	(917) 374-5752
Frank Heinemann	(845) 222-2390
William F. Hennessy	(610) 539-3659 (610) 996-0791
Brian T. Hess	(212) 529-4713 (917) 980-2728
Don Hewitt	(914) 726-3320 www.donhhewitt.com
Jery Hewitt	(914) 986-7919
Samantha Higgins	(610) 653-5140
Nicholas Hill	(917) 653-4179
Chryss Hionis	(212) 387-9680 (646) 498-6036
Arlo Hoffman	(518) 524-4749
Ashley Hollister	(718) 625-4302 (917) 270-8429
Robert Holtzman	(215) 423-0794
Linda S. Holtzman-Kenny	(212) 420-1426 (212) 777-4768
Margaret E. Hoppe	(631) 698-2695
Richard Kenneth Hoppe	(631) 764-1662
Thomas (TJ) Horan	(973) 728-6908
Nicholas Houghton	(323) 969-8804
Lee Howard	(917) 853-3359
Jonathan Huggins	(917) 446-5268
Ross Huttick	(718) 461-6346 (917) 670-2927
Laura Hyman	(917) 543-6782
Akeo Ihara	(718) 222-9016 (917) 723-3533
Laura Iler	(212) 727-0640 (917) 373-5625
Colby Ippoliti	(845) 519-9486 (845) 353-2762
Gregory M. Izzo	(914) 320-4467
Kevin Jackson	(516) 546-9045 (516) 351-5818
Tim Jackson	(860) 572-7725
Jacqueline Jacobson	(203) 984-6282
Zachary Jasie	(718) 832-7040 (718) 832-7041
Drew Jiritano	(800) 722-7976 (201) 863-4475 (201) 863-0351 www.djfx.com
Gregory Jiritano	(718) 302-2138
Dale Johnson	(845) 876-8696 (917) 559-8937

Leigh A. Johnson	(310) 392-9816
Lori Johnson-Guirard	(908) 273-5102 / (917) 716-9870
Timothy J. Joliat	(201) 239-1107 / (917) 887-7707
Brian P. Jones	(845) 362-4972 / (845) 224-7846
Glenn W. Jones	(904) 239-9400
Jeffrey Jones	(201) 567-8096 / (718) 241-5607
Chris M. Jordan	(917) 604-5693 / (718) 625-7333
Steven J. Jordan	(201) 762-5841
Michael Jortner	(212) 673-3566 / (917) 673-0664
Vlada J. Joseph	(212) 982-8566 / (917) 812-3525
Kimberly Kachougian	(212) 995-9108 / (917) 951-5660
Jerry Kadar (Prop Master)	(718) 369-1022 / (917) 371-3521
Kenneth Kammerer	(732) 946-4772
Dierdre L. Kane	(718) 626-1303 / (917) 627-6880
Heather D. Kane	(718) 486-6555 / (646) 382-9080
Henry Kaplan	(718) 341-5840 / (516) 793-2910
Ondine Karady	(718) 388-2771 / (917) 445-6079
Barbara A. Kastner	(516) 731-6646 / (516) 241-6492
Frederick D. Kastner	(516) 731-6646
Karen Kates	(212) 246-5443
Erika S. Katz	(215) 627-0187 / (267) 979-8365
Susan Kaufman	(212) 254-3236
John Kelton	(631) 472-3178 / (888) 285-8867
Victor H. Kempster	(213) 878-0881
Kate Kennedy	(917) 834-3922 / www.goodeandplenty.com
Eileen M. Kennedy-Jebrane	(516) 867-0061
Daniel B. Kenney	(212) 233-6542 / (917) 953-5848
James (Jim) Kent	(434) 996-5413
Lisa N. Kent	(212) 877-9142
Robert Keymer	(917) 731-5066
L. Mila Khalevich	(718) 788-6780 / (917) 767-1662
Jon Kim	(212) 631-5864 / (646) 269-1081
Tyler H. Kim	(212) 477-3496
David Kirshoff	(914) 669-8745
Jack Kirshoff	(914) 403-1691 / (914) 669-8745
Steve Kirshoff	(914) 937-9345 / (914) 403-0483 / FAX (914) 937-7274
Clifford F. Klatt	(732) 787-3473 / (732) 939-0947
David Kleinstein	(201) 446-6682
Bradley Klipp	(917) 847-7524
Betsy Klompus	(718) 499-2562 / (917) 439-6242
James Klotsas	(215) 206-5680 / (212) 779-8378
J. Dorothea Klusmann	(718) 384-4708
Jon W. Knoop	(914) 646-0001
Robin Koenig	(973) 429-2075 / (973) 819-3388
William J. Kolpin	(212) 799-9356 / (845) 796-3367
Michael Koval	(518) 584-9952
Paul C. Koval	(518) 587-3980
Fred Kraemer Jr.	(973) 692-0811 / (201) 965-1876
Linda Krantz	(917) 797-2866
Victoria Krasnakevich	(212) 477-5246 / (718) 813-3788
Steven R. Krieger	(845) 735-7674 / (845) 558-0826
Georges N. Krivobok	(718) 522-5944 / (917) 375-1473
Johann Kunz	(917) 689-0603
Beth Kushnick	(212) 502-1147
Kevin C. Ladson	(718) 335-2692
Karl Lake	(917) 476-1757
Eoin Vincent Lambe	(718) 505-3859 / (917) 379-4418
Laura Lambert Andrusko	(917) 836-3630
Edward Landecho	(718) 544-2293
Joseph Landolfi	(917) 734-8860
Martin Lasowitz (Prop Master)	(212) 260-6818 / (646) 522-5841
Ross La Terra (Prop Master)	(908) 770-1987
Todd Latini	(631) 669-1862

Thomas John La Vecchia	(516) 410-0200
Michael Leather	(845) 774-1184 / (917) 895-5580
Anya N. Lebow	(718) 863-3150 / (914) 649-7480
John Lebrecht	(516) 735-4053
Diane Lederman	(212) 414-5462 / (917) 541-8123
Keri Lynn Lederman	(917) 453-2626 / (718) 369-3616
Jonathan B. Lee	(917) 913-1136
Kathleen Leone-Ferraro	(516) 785-9112
Kevin Leonidas	(917) 885-0300 / (212) 586-0440
Edmund Levine	(718) 599-4418 / (646) 345-5455
Gary W. Levitsky	(772) 486-2030 / (516) 223-4896
Peter L. Levitsky	(516) 459-3561
Loren H. Levy	(718) 224-4350 / (718) 344-3987
Rosemarie M. Levy	(800) 784-8242
Theodore J. Lewandowski	(215) 271-1674 / (215) 319-0341
Eric E. Lewin	(201) 224-4515
Kimberley Lieber	(917) 304-7448 / (845) 236-7193
Joyce Lieberman	(212) 533-2222
Richard Liebgold	(646) 220-1610
James Lillis	(914) 665-9756 / (917) 797-4160
Rick Liss	(212) 587-9155 / (917) 439-8966
Victor Littlejohn	(914) 788-5331 / (917) 453-8677
Henry A. Lockwood	(917) 806-8060
Matthew D. Loeb	(212) 730-1770 / (888) 444-9445
Heather Loeffler	(917) 921-2506
Michael Lokensgard	(845) 338-2702
Ana Lombardo	(212) 995-2376 / (917) 847-7754
Robert D. Lopas	(732) 494-5535
Marcie S. Lowy-Wright	(203) 878-3826
Erik R. Lundell	(917) 544-5017
Francis Luskey	(609) 348-8936 / (609) 576-6473
Joan Lynch	(201) 925-7306
Maureen P. Mac Dougall	(973) 347-9368 / (973) 476-8588
Brian P. Madison	(718) 997-9669 / (516) 557-9377
Michael Madison	(516) 783-1917 / (516) 455-5910
Cherish Magennis-Hale	(917) 494-4509
Michael R. Maggi	(973) 839-5374 / (973) 768-1966
Devin Maggio	(914) 774-1707
Daniel Mahon	(631) 661-2458 / (917) 602-5224
Kevin Mahon	(914) 693-7974 / (917) 871-8011
Sarah A. Maine	(718) 937-5958 / (646) 295-6590
Lee B. Malecki (Set Decorator)	(718) 472-2324 / (347) 683-3728
Allen R. Mamet	(845) 987-1965 / (917) 797-9093
Woody Mann	(212) 239-0555 / FAX (240) 250-7108
Brian Mannain	(212) 643-0993 / (917) 826-7021
Janice E. Manser	(610) 269-0712 / (610) 269-0712
Michael D. Marcel	(718) 781-7024
Jeffrey Marchetti	(201) 941-6188 / (917) 899-1772
Lydia Marks-O'Malley	(212) 246-6013 / (917) 673-3872
Cathy Marshall (Prop Master, Prop Stylist, Set Decorator & Underwater)	(973) 625-7472 / (201) 317-8108 / FAX (973) 627-3703
Clinton W. Marshall Jr.	(718) 699-7008
Frank R. Martin	(570) 563-1041 / (570) 563-1019
Joseph Martin	(845) 353-5759
Christopher Maya	(212) 772-2480
Christine Mayer	(212) 688-3837 / (917) 885-3453
Alexandra Mazur	(212) 206-6695 / (917) 882-6201
Vinny Mazzarella	(718) 748-7301 / (917) 886-2232
James R. Mazzola	(718) 945-7494 / (917) 882-3484
Jeff Mazzola (Prop Master)	(347) 242-1830
Matthew Mazzola	(718) 945-7494
Linda Mazzoni	(212) 504-6111 / (718) 234-6864

Robin C. McAllister-Voth	(201) 610-0858 (917) 991-3093
Anthony McCabe	(516) 781-8115 (516) 998-6856
Kevin B. McCarthy	(973) 744-1974 (917) 482-1185
Matthew P. McCarthy	(212) 752-3330
Susannah McCarthy	(215) 887-0008
David McCole	(215) 661-1308 (215) 740-7112
Harold E. McConnell Jr.	(973) 875-8862 (973) 670-2303
Thomas A. McDermott (Prop Master)	(201) 391-7445 (201) 805-1907 FAX (201) 391-7445
James P. McDonagh	(201) 313-5645 (201) 264-5427
John B. McDonnell	(516) 338-4337 (516) 646-0301
Kevin McEntee	(610) 284-3143
Patrick D. McGowan	(516) 984-4040
Ryan T. McGrath	(973) 822-2471 (908) 902-3029
Ann Durnin McKendry	(631) 673-1014
Sarah E. McMillan	(718) 781-2244
Patricia Meere-Abt	(718) 769-6324
Rebecca J. Meis	(212) 929-5266 (917) 721-0212
Daniel Melchiorre	(201) 665-4369
John P. Melendez Jr.	(516) 972-4096
Eugene Melvin Jr.	(862) 200-0105 (973) 749-6316
Darius Menard	(718) 383-0407
Jean-Paul Menard	(631) 261-1596
Ramona Messina	(646) 342-5545 (347) 497-4397
Helayne Messing	(973) 664-1486 (973) 879-9575
Eric Metzger	(908) 789-8540 (908) 230-8299
Timothy Metzger	(908) 789-2284 (908) 305-4920 FAX (908) 789-0155
Nicholas Mevoli	(917) 519-1182
Gifford Meyer	(917) 626-7553
Jeffrey Meyer	(212) 777-1465 (917) 836-7009
Cynthia Michalak	(631) 749-3291
Janine Michelle	(516) 889-3781 (917) 313-4163 FAX (516) 432-5372
Ann Miller (Prop Master)	(917) 903-7192
Catherine Miller	(917) 842-2856
Morgan Miller	(215) 753-0640 (215) 415-4225
Wayne Scott Miller	(516) 382-1916 (516) 488-4447
Laura Lynn Miller-Arpino	(516) 358-4385
Peter Mills	(914) 241-9219 (914) 261-0159
Matthew Milstein	(347) 728-5305
Octavio Molina	(718) 855-8366 (917) 596-3851 FAX (718) 855-8366
Joseph Monaco III	(212) 877-6374
Jeff Monte	(718) 488-0086 (917) 612-0604
Christine A. Montgomery	(914) 963-3011
Christine Moosher	(914) 921-0228 (917) 532-6508
John T. Moran	(203) 981-0441
Kristine Moran	(212) 757-7406 (617) 290-1190
Gregory Morell	(978) 546-9357
Richard Morris	(518) 329-0596 (718) 664-5257
Keith E. Morrissey	(201) 618-2159
Gerard Morrone	(914) 804-1662
Vincent Morsillo	(856) 931-6392
Jack Frank Mortellaro Jr.	(516) 565-6488 (516) 287-4415
Andrew Mortelliti	(914) 267-0194 (917) 269-7882
Deborah Moses	(845) 353-2762 (914) 420-3440
Ruby Moshlak	(718) 591-1199
Molly Rain Moshlak-Barbalat	(212) 517-2505
Anthony G. Munafo	(609) 693-0799 (609) 693-9700
Carol A. Murcko	(860) 447-1034
James P. Murphy	(610) 449-2878 (610) 804-8235
Michael Murphy	(914) 737-4131 (917) 744-0687
Alan Muzeni	(973) 463-1292 (973) 905-7120
Jeff Naparstek	(201) 750-7951 (201) 669-9124
David J. Nash	(661) 252-1811

Carol Nast	(212) 242-7942
Anthony Navarro	(718) 331-5514 / (917) 417-3482
Richard J. Nelson Jr.	(973) 890-0481
Christopher S. Nelson	(201) 261-6806
Daniel Neroda	(732) 382-9177 / (732) 488-9827
Dana C. Neuwirth	(917) 493-8026 / (917) 333-0069
Mark R. Newell	(212) 260-2717 / (917) 501-1181
Marc Newman	(631) 757-9083 / (516) 381-9881
Frazer Newton	(845) 249-1709 / (845) 684-5192
Tom Newton	(845) 679-7604
Thomas Nierenberg	(917) 701-4753
Lynn Marie Nigro	(201) 333-2925 / (917) 922-3593
Lisa K. Nilsson	(914) 764-8435 / (917) 953-5302
Daniel Nisenson	(973) 943-0619
Paul Nisenson	(973) 748-5783 / (646) 265-5656
Valerie Nolan	(212) 375-0302 / (917) 886-4319
Paul D. Normand	(518) 221-6621
Hubert J. Oates	(407) 737-2273
John P. Oates Jr.	(201) 858-6735
Joseph P. Oates	(914) 948-3894
Kevin Oates	(561) 737-2273
Robert J. Oates	(203) 964-5495
Kathleen E. Oates-Frato	(201) 969-8990
Deborah A. Oates-Sparnon	(973) 579-3378
Elaine O'Donnell	(917) 971-6304
Richard L. Oeser	(917) 318-2935
Charles G. Ogle	(609) 854-4817
Susan N. Ogu	(212) 925-8976 / (917) 991-5887
Frank C. Oliva	(203) 339-1226
Frank C. Oliva Jr.	(203) 386-1928
Timothy S. Oravetz	(718) 349-1905 / (917) 701-4156
Dennis O'Reilly	(516) 791-8202 / (516) 263-0726
Donald O'Reilly	(917) 968-2310 / (914) 930-6229
Gavin O'Reilly	(631) 434-4716 / (631) 375-4310
Vincent J. Orofino	(516) 495-4539 / (917) 364-4695
James B. Orr	(215) 928-1506 / (215) 419-4168
Bruce P. Orsino	(732) 270-0923
Lawrence Orvieto	(917) 414-3302
Christopher M. O'Shea	(610) 789-0907
Francis A. O'Shea III	(610) 544-5785 / (610) 734-9302
Jon Oshima	(917) 673-0903 / (718) 832-0351
Benjamin Oshman	(201) 387-1464 / (201) 723-4624
Daniel Pangione	(201) 575-2048
Vincent Pangione	(201) 784-9421 / (201) 694-6303
Debi Prate Panuccio	(516) 735-6065 / (516) 205-0625
Jessica Panuccio	(718) 631-2641 / (917) 466-4458
Gus Papadopoulos	(718) 777-0420 / (914) 589-9674
Marni Papadopoulos	(646) 372-1971
Justin Papp	(201) 674-4048
Richard E. Papp	(201) 825-7623
G. Clark Parkhurst Jr.	(860) 324-0025
Sara Parks	(917) 364-6324
Michael Parmelee	(917) 306-1210
Eric Pastore	(845) 267-8879
Garry Pastore (Prop Master & Set Decorator)	(917) 293-6800
Jane L. Patterson	(718) 721-0731
A. Taylor Pattison	(631) 757-8139
Donna M. Paul	(631) 757-1595 / (516) 835-9332
Jose Pavon	(347) 526-5497 / (347) 365-5845
Mark Peltzer	(973) 783-3121 / (917) 218-1019
Susan Perlman	(212) 262-9820 / (917) 446-2886
James Pesce	(917) 553-9820 / (212) 996-5598
Janine Pesce	(917) 209-5475 / (732) 897-8665
Jamie Lynn Petagna	(732) 566-7226 / (917) 613-9796

Tora Peterson	(917) 309-5126
Joseph Petruccio	(914) 738-6894 / (914) 260-5880
Michael T. Philbin	(860) 568-7124
Graydon Pihlaja	(203) 972-7430
Gerard H. Pineo	(631) 368-6523 / (516) 527-3569
Jane K. Pinkus	(212) 737-0765 / (917) 969-5372
Susan M. Pitocchi	(718) 388-4251
R. Morgan C. Pitts	(212) 929-3115 / (917) 865-7529
Vera Anne Pizzarelli	(917) 804-3110
Michael J. Platarote Jr.	(718) 382-4254 / (347) 693-3489
Michael J. Platarote Sr.	(917) 737-6249
Walter M. Pluff III	(917) 940-8510
Alan G. Polak	(914) 923-7371
Raymond C. Polak	(631) 750-3955
Vincent Polifrone	(732) 615-0252 / (800) 352-4732
Anthony Polizzi	(212) 876-7253 / (917) 992-4208
John H. Pomponio Jr.	(212) 420-5913
Leslie A. Pope	(310) 962-4293
Charles (Chuck) Potter	(910) 367-2675
Andrea Potter-Kirshoff	(914) 669-8745
Sharon L. Potts (Prop Master & Prop Stylist)	(215) 919-0156 / (215) 887-5850 / www.kitschykoo.com
James Power	(914) 669-5808 / (914) 742-0472
Timothy E. Powers	(201) 307-9114
Kathi Prate	(631) 278-9869
Kimberly Prate	(631) 398-9996
Ariana G. Preisner	(914) 739-8687 / (914) 924-4456
Michael Preisner	(212) 307-6227 / (914) 672-7417
Heather Prendergast	(917) 648-5688
Mary Prlain	(917) 412-1392 / web.mac.com/maryprlain/iWeb/Mary%20Prlain/Welcome.html
Joseph F. Proscia	(845) 504-5501 / (845) 598-8082
Michele M. Proscia	(201) 868-1317
Robert Provenzano	(718) 961-7698 / (917) 491-8999
Romano C. Pugliese	(917) 240-1210
Alexander A. Quarles	(917) 714-0114
Thomas Quinn (Prop Master)	(917) 776-4008
Charles C. Radcliffe	(212) 228-9230
John Raffaele	(201) 943-1791 / (201) 545-9384
Susan Raney	(212) 962-5724 / (917) 805-0078
Matthew Ransom	(212) 222-3128 / (646) 345-3343
John Rapp	(516) 425-4746
Michael J. Rattinger	(631) 864-3995 / (917) 944-2561
Shannon L. Rayle-Bourne	(910) 793-9322
Paula Raymond	(212) 595-2587 / (646) 382-3102
Dave Reardon	(201) 433-4458 / (917) 658-0825
Thomas H. Reeve	(212) 245-0555
Peter John Regnier	(518) 578-0566 / (718) 482-8850
Richard M. Regnier Jr.	(518) 374-6299
Richard M. Regnier Sr.	(518) 372-3121
Michael J. Reider	(302) 368-5974
Fr. Michael P. Reilly	(718) 967-3283
Gail-Marie Reilly	(516) 922-5270 / (516) 793-6734
Malicky D. Reilly	(516) 432-8632
William F. Reynolds (Prop Master)	(917) 848-6001
Sarah Riggs	(504) 388-6093
Helen Ripple	(212) 874-4107 / (212) 905-0340
John Roche	(718) 626-1157 / (800) 225-0256
J. Daniel Rodriguez	(973) 277-9222 / (973) 277-9225
Harold Roer	(201) 923-6417
Jason Roer	(201) 845-4206
Louis D. Roer	(201) 845-4206
Stewart B. Roer (Prop Master)	(201) 747-5875
Jeffrey S. Rollins	(914) 232-7217 / (914) 419-1830
Leslie E. Rollins	(860) 487-4919
Debbie A. Romano	(215) 468-4977
Jonathan Rose	(212) 279-0871 / (917) 224-9763

Jesse A. Rosenstock	(516) 764-1663
Jordan Rosenstock	(516) 492-0613 (516) 764-1663
Scott Rosenstock	(516) 764-1663 (917) 301-4779
Briar Rossell	(914) 204-3419
Timothy Rossiter	(917) 570-0058
Beth A. Rubino	(718) 855-7225
Neil Ruddy	(917) 854-2073
Johanna L. Ruhe	(215) 630-3614
James Russo	(631) 567-1254
Lisa Beth Rutledge	(845) 778-3567 (201) 280-5892
Sean F. Ryder	(856) 384-9299
Michael A. Saccio	(212) 588-0133 (917) 407-9806 FAX (212) 937-5270
Michael P. Saccio	(917) 756-8563 (718) 992-0139
Philip B. Saccio Jr.	(718) 317-7377
Philip J. Saccio (Prop Master)	(718) 948-3013 (917) 253-8783
Roseann Saccio	(718) 948-3013
Amy J. Safhay	(914) 736-7344
Rocco Sagarese	(516) 343-9370
Kyle Salvatore	(917) 359-3815
Diana Salzburg	(212) 737-8797 (917) 834-3239
Maria C. Santana	(917) 687-3264
Jennifer Santucci	(646) 246-2670 (212) 420-8851
Joseph F. Sargo	(201) 410-6669 (201) 964-0179
Scott William Sasso	(631) 587-2098 (516) 987-7478
Peter L. Savel	(518) 346-4936
Roy Savoy	(845) 278-7950 (646) 918-2952
John D. Scalzi	(203) 319-9327
Anthony Scalzo Jr.	(718) 442-9371 (917) 586-0078
Bryan R. Scanlon	(201) 970-0660
Paul E. Scanlon	(201) 652-2289 (201) 233-3328
Stephen E. Scanlon	(201) 652-1184 (201) 652-2289
John Scardino Jr.	(716) 834-6372
John C. Schabel	(212) 966-3928
David Schanker	(917) 771-8849
William M. Scheck	(914) 271-4301 (917) 483-4143
Robert H. Schleinig	(781) 784-0105
David Schlesinger	(718) 246-1560 (917) 697-1243
Elizabeth Schlitten	(718) 389-6441
Michelle Schluter Ford	(917) 705-5303 (732) 471-6566
Courtney Schmidt	(347) 282-4970
John M. Schmidt	(310) 408-7455
Matthew Schmidt	(732) 672-7770
Barret D. Schumacher	(718) 549-2894
Debra Schutt	(212) 475-8757
Ari David Schwartz	(845) 573-0152 (845) 729-0082
Robert Schwarze Jr.	(973) 728-0741 (201) 675-0078
Edward P. Scoppa Jr.	(917) 687-4687
Justin Scoppa Jr.	(914) 725-8455
Lisa Scoppa	(917) 582-2322
Nicole Scoppa	(914) 723-1282
Catherine Scorsese	(212) 673-4119 (888) 425-5939
Charles J. Scott	(610) 284-7372 (610) 208-1153
Robert J. Scupp	(732) 721-0186 (800) 430-1692
Alija Sehapovic	(914) 937-7799 (917) 422-0468
Mark Selemon	(914) 478-5565 (917) 453-1055
Theo Sena	(917) 721-5925
Stephen A. Serra	(203) 488-9554
Andrew Shapiro	(919) 225-4382 (718) 434-4653
Janet G. Shaw	(973) 509-9866
Michael D. Shellito	(215) 731-9823 (215) 319-7709
Dylan Sheridan	(718) 237-0932 (917) 776-4306
Matthew Sherwood	(347) 726-1754
Peter (Chevy) Shevlin	(201) 869-2336 (646) 279-1129
Erwin Sholes	(631) 757-5896 (631) 455-2769
Kristy Prate Sicurella	(516) 216-8695
Ruth Ann Siegel	(212) 975-1758 (718) 721-1925

Kenneth Sigler	(201) 750-8504
Carol A. Silverman	(212) 831-0804 / (917) 885-8383
Harlan L. Silverstein	(212) 979-0274 / (732) 489-2651
Mark Simon	(516) 599-0325 / (516) 528-3493
Patricia (Avery) Simons	(718) 885-0762
Charles R. Simunek	(516) 483-2039
William Simunek	(845) 401-3111
Joseph Siwinski	(215) 634-7551 / (800) 917-2371
Todd Siwinski	(215) 739-5244
Mark Skversky	(856) 513-6250 / (609) 828-2960
Kimberly Slosek	(860) 573-6480
Angus Smith	(917) 532-6203
David Smith	(310) 657-8485
Lindsey Smith	(401) 849-5040
R. Vincent Smith	(973) 748-7174 / (973) 303-2580
Gary A. Snyder	(212) 983-0500
Diane Soffian	(718) 891-3182 / (917) 692-6126
Gary Sommers	(845) 794-7740
Anne J. Somoroff	(973) 543-1188 / (917) 782-0628
Kevin R. Sosbe	(860) 799-7299 / (203) 241-3800
John M. Souto	(917) 868-6427
Andrew Spagnoli	(917) 656-8942
Eoin C. Sprott	(212) 371-0521 / (718) 784-1407
Richard Stangarone	(914) 232-8105 / (914) 321-4402
Marc Stankus	(518) 891-1949
Jennifer Starke	(908) 534-5082 / (973) 818-7544
Lisa Ann Stashak	(917) 312-8443
William Stearne	(856) 931-8378 / (856) 901-0558
Kia Steave-Dickerson	(856) 216-9777
Alan R. Steiner	(201) 935-1706
James N. Sten	(718) 204-5539 / (516) 624-7142
Eric H. Stepper	(201) 512-1358 / (201) 788-3550
Rodney T. Sterbenz	(917) 862-1825
Carrie Stewart	(973) 761-7545 / (917) 572-4891
James A. Stidfole	(860) 439-1034
John R. Stifanich	(631) 471-6695 / (800) 797-6739
Ronald C. Stone	(201) 930-9085
Matthew D. Storelli	(201) 391-4317 / (201) 694-0457
Catherine A. Sullivan	(973) 694-4852
Robert B. Sumerfield	(215) 203-1871 / (215) 350-2464
Luke Sutherland	(401) 467-7121
Jonathan B. Swain (Prop Master)	(973) 664-1486 / (973) 879-6755
Bruce E. Swanson	(516) 379-1269 / (516) 312-4437
Lawrence C. Swanson	(516) 781-7412
Stephen Swanson	(917) 567-6903
David Swift	(609) 391-0190
Andrea Swistak	(212) 254-5758 / (917) 817-3203
Christine M. Sysko	(215) 438-5554 / (215) 438-0742
Steve Sysko	(215) 438-5554
Katherine Szilagyi	(212) 475-0511 / (917) 576-6213
Joseph Taglairino	(718) 387-1401 / (917) 644-4228
Jeffrey J. Tanner	(267) 259-2196
Susan Tatom	(201) 222-8947 / (201) 400-1245
Walter Tatro	(201) 262-7660
Hisao Taya	(212) 957-8018
Lisa Taylor	(212) 691-3127
Michael A. Thompson	(201) 746-0110
Richard J. Tice	(516) 365-1168 / (917) 439-5065 / FAX (516) 365-1384
Alexander Toles	(718) 308-1381 / (718) 977-0601
Christina Tonkin	(718) 898-9590 / (917) 488-5910
Kathleen Tonkin	(770) 231-1052
B. Lynn Tonnessen	(631) 298-4483 / (917) 509-7214
Nicholas Torelli	(347) 405-6417 / (951) 522-1740

Angel Torres	(718) 644-2874 (718) 881-2403
Dominick Toto	(718) 796-2333 (917) 816-8371
R. Mitchell Towse	(631) 757-7927 (631) 525-8257
James Traynor	(484) 832-6888
Anthony Trimarchi	(818) 674-1478
Pamela Maiden Turk (Set Decorator)	(212) 964-3675 (917) 647-2020 FAX (212) 964-3675
Jonathan Unger	(201) 315-6703
Anthony Urban Jr.	(856) 939-2555 (215) 419-3632
Victoria Vanasco	(718) 782-2215 (917) 245-9806
Lawrence H. Vande Water	(516) 546-5029
Walter Van Lieu	(908) 995-7919 FAX (908) 995-0589
James Villani	(201) 945-5339 (201) 698-6309
Thomas L. Viviano	(914) 737-8703 (914) 260-3253
Joshua Vogel	(718) 826-3716
Matthew Vogel	(718) 826-3716 FAX (718) 703-4291
Chris M. Vogt	(973) 467-8565 (917) 567-5618
Robert P. Vogt	(917) 468-5809
Peter J. Von Bartheld	(631) 907-1007
Ronald T. von Blomberg	(631) 283-8447 (631) 926-2013
Bryan Walsh	(201) 681-3369
Ginny Walsh	(631) 423-1954 (516) 993-1830
Kevin M. Walsh	(201) 842-8768 (201) 842-0277
Thomas F. (Tom) Watkins	(215) 545-3461 (800) 917-1196
William T. Watkins	(215) 350-3233
Brendan R. Watson	(718) 796-3790 (917) 871-1316
Gary Wattson	(718) 832-8213 (917) 723-8966
Paul R. Weathered	(973) 748-0088 (862) 216-0063
Joel Weaver	(917) 803-5533 (212) 234-6483
Danielle C. Webb	(718) 384-0078 (917) 678-4248
Kerry A. Weeks	(718) 208-6789

David C. Weinman	(914) 472-1924 (917) 567-5616 FAX (914) 472-7119
Jason Weinman	(914) 472-1924
Rachael Weinzimer	(718) 392-8873 (917) 992-6701
Jody Weisenfeld	(415) 731-9021
Alexis Weiss	(510) 295-7036
Peter Weiss (Prop Master)	(845) 878-4391 (914) 645-1118 FAX (845) 878-4391
Anne Wenniger	(212) 460-9631 (917) 848-9634
Andrea J. Werner	(914) 763-6497 (914) 659-7941
Catherine Werner	(908) 281-6057
Lubomyr M. Weselyj	(860) 450-1358
James Wessling (Prop Master)	(914) 523-6347 (914) 741-6315
Laura West	(914) 245-4633
Tom West	(610) 660-9385 (610) 633-2923
Kathryn Westfall-Tharp	(413) 657-7816
Ford Wheeler	(212) 736-0181 (917) 334-5604
James J. Whelan	(201) 860-9676 (201) 424-8706
Diana White	(631) 725-2842 (212) 319-6369
Sharon White	(201) 969-1769 (201) 774-7775
Wendy Whittall	(716) 692-5034
Christine Wick	(215) 514-8371
Michael J. Wiegand	(914) 260-9460
Karin Wiesel	(212) 831-2708
William Wiggins (Prop Master)	(404) 290-1902
James E. Williams	(215) 680-2107
Jim Williams (Prop Master)	(215) 680-2107 (215) 704-7876 FAX (215) 731-0351
Tonero Williams	(718) 832-5416 (718) 578-3401
Michael Wilson	(631) 261-2176 (917) 655-9236
Robert (RJ) Wilson	(732) 671-4373 (732) 979-8388
Robert D. Wilson Jr.	(732) 979-8388
Brian Winkowski	(212) 929-6017 (917) 674-5222

Susan S. Wollock-Spiegel	(718) 984-9512
Bentley Wood	(347) 623-6042
Patrick Woods	(718) 786-5742 / (917) 630-1299
Peter Wright (Prop Master & Underwater)	(718) 791-1254
Sabrina Wright (Prop Master)	(917) 693-2212
Travis K. Wright	(203) 655-2415
Kate Yatsko	(718) 783-3305 / (917) 656-1042
Denis A. Zack	(914) 669-5598 / (646) 773-6217
Kevin Zack	(848) 207-0247
Michael Zadrosny	(718) 624-2280 / (917) 886-0912
Kara Zeigon	(917) 548-5089
Victor J. Zolfo	(323) 876-7783
Harriet Zucker	(718) 643-9401 / (917) 405-0593
Lenore Zydel	(631) 821-7512 / (516) 987-0399
Timothy Zydel	(516) 316-1765 / (631) 821-7512

Props Department

Eddy Alcantara — (212) 279-1999
(Prop Stylist) — www.markedwardinc.com

Christy Alcebo — (212) 279-1999
(Prop Stylist) — www.markedwardinc.com

Richard Alfredo — (212) 279-1999
(Prop Stylist) — www.markedwardinc.com

David H. Allen — (508) 362-0069 / (917) 620-3096
(Prop Master)

Thomas C. Allen — (203) 637-2651 / (203) 273-5894
(Prop Master)

Shawn Patrick Anderson — (212) 925-4222
(Prop Stylist) — www.art-dept.com

Stephen Ang — (212) 206-0901
www.halleyresources.com

Campbell Baird — (212) 633-1953 / (908) 387-1994

Phyllis Evans Baker — (212) 279-1999
(Prop Stylist) — www.markedwardinc.com

David Barnes — (610) 896-8785 / (610) 547-0300 / FAX (303) 474-3130
(Prop Master)

Brenda Barr — (212) 279-1999
(Prop Stylist) — www.markedwardinc.com

Cat Belluschi — (917) 363-0082

David S. Benninghoff — (917) 653-6377 / (206) 232-9646

Kristi Blunt — (212) 255-2500
(Prop Stylist) — www.seemanagement.com

Mark Chandler — (212) 925-4222
www.art-dept.com

Suzanne Cheverie — (212) 741-3240 / (781) 863-1555
www.ennisinc.com

Caroline Colston — (212) 206-0901
www.halleyresources.com

Sarah Conly — (212) 865-3294

Guido DeCurtis — (917) 797-7774 / (914) 457-0985

Dana De Lara — (212) 741-3240
(Prop Stylist) — www.ennisinc.com

Norm Dodge — (212) 289-1092
www.normdodge.com

Michele Faro — (212) 925-4222
www.art-dept.com

Donna Francis — (212) 935-0200
(Prop Stylist) — www.bryanbantry.com

Marissa Gimeno — (212) 206-0901
www.halleyresources.com

Ronald James Groomes — (845) 691-5914 / (845) 417-5300

Halley Resources — (212) 206-0901 / FAX (212) 206-0904
231 W. 29th St., Ste. 701 — www.halleyresources.com
(Near Seventh Ave.)
New York, NY 10001
(Reps for Prop Stylists)

Kris Jensen — (212) 279-1999
(Prop Stylist) — www.markedwardinc.com

Peter Kunz — (845) 687-0400 / FAX (845) 687-0579
www.peterkunzeffects.com

Andy Lassman (Prop Master)	(718) 499-8112	**Alison Scherr** (Prop Stylist)	(212) 279-1999 www.markedwardinc.com
Bill Laughlin (Prop Stylist)	(212) 279-1999 www.markedwardinc.com	**Stephen Shapiro**	(917) 693-4696 FAX (718) 434-4653
Wayne T. Leonard	(407) 322-5299 (917) 312-0255	**James P. Sherman**	(802) 672-4144
Byron Lovelace (Prop Master)	(254) 939-1446 (254) 913-8558	**Chic Silber**	(212) 840-6100 (941) 366-8848 FAX (941) 362-0060
Jeffrey W. Miller	(212) 925-4222 www.art-dept.com	**Ina Slote**	(212) 679-4584 FAX (212) 679-4584
Roger Monaco Sr.	(845) 735-5633	**Norine Smith**	(212) 206-0901 www.halleyresources.com
Julie Morrison (Prop Stylist)	(212) 279-1999 www.markedwardinc.com	**Claire Tedaldi**	(212) 206-0901 www.halleyresources.com
John Ottesen	(607) 336-5009	**Jonathan Tessler** (Prop Master)	(203) 544-8696 (917) 699-4237
Stuart Polasky	(212) 279-1999 www.markedwardinc.com	**Kristy Vant**	(212) 279-1999 www.markedwardinc.com
Lili Abir Regen (Prop Stylist)	(212) 925-4222 www.art-dept.com	**Caroline Woodward**	(212) 741-3240 (781) 863-1555 www.ennisinc.com
Peter John Regnier	(518) 578-0566 (718) 482-8850	**Steven Wright**	(212) 964-3675 (917) 923-9445 FAX (212) 964-3675
Stella Rey	(212) 279-1999 www.markedwardinc.com		

Script Supervisors (Local 161 NY)

Stephanie Angel	(914) 843-1210
Lisa Arnone	(917) 776-7765
Mary Bailey	(212) 571-0930 / (917) 209-4681
Cynthia Balfour	(212) 799-1706 / (917) 913-2772
Kim Berner	(347) 591-6616 / (213) 220-4394
Stephanie A. Bertoni	(412) 953-5551
Katri Billard	(202) 494-2114
Joanie Blum	(212) 642-6250 / (503) 392-3437
Rebecca Breckel	(917) 453-5519 / (718) 638-2086
Renee Foley Burke	(718) 596-4768
Eva Z. Cabrera	(212) 662-7097
George Camarda	(718) 443-9231 / (917) 439-6332
Andrew Cesana	(212) 673-9353 / (917) 743-0444
Rachel Connors	(908) 672-1590
Seth Copans	(917) 453-0447
Claire Cowperthwaite	(212) 714-8368 / (302) 743-4874
Kelly Cronin	(617) 733-9301
Mary Cybulski	(718) 768-5960 / (917) 541-3135
Kellie Cyrus	(310) 801-9570
Judie D'Avolio	(516) 239-3324
Renoir Darrett	(212) 544-9442
Janna Delury	(917) 549-7216
Carolyn De Sousa	(718) 898-5799 / (646) 591-1190
Jodi Domanic-Riccio	(917) 673-5403
Annette Maria Drees	(718) 399-9837 / (646) 250-8763
Dianne Dreyer	(212) 879-6079
Massoumeh Emami	(917) 517-9442
Robert Foglia Jr.	(410) 633-0101 / (410) 493-5595
Andrea Fontaine	(917) 689-3717
Audrey Free	(914) 764-4329 / (914) 420-1050
Mary Gambardella	(917) 846-6354
Joan Ganon	(617) 797-2199
Christine M. Gee	(908) 889-8173 / (908) 591-5605
Rachelle Gibson	(917) 204-5894
Joseph L. Gonzalez	(201) 861-9127 / (201) 926-4024
Catherine Gore	(917) 494-6667
Andrea Greer	(718) 789-9857 / (917) 449-9830
Linda Haftel	(212) 675-2535 / (917) 992-1867 / FAX (212) 675-7467
Valerie Harrington	(718) 789-5085 / (917) 513-6689
Mariana Hellmund	(917) 270-2213
Jane Hershcopf	(917) 817-5396 / (212) 580-8893
Deirdre Horgan	(212) 517-0086 / (917) 721-5580
Diane Hounsell	(212) 861-4796 / (917) 576-0352
Thomas Johnston	(212) 517-6077 / (917) 716-7712
Melissa Kalbfus-Paliocha	(914) 960-3754 / (845) 528-5716
Chiemi Karasawa	(212) 242-3394
Kirsten Kearse	(917) 690-8195
Mary Kelly	(212) 807-0266
Janet Kern	(212) 925-3110 / (845) 744-3813
Stacey Koff	(212) 529-3214 / (914) 262-0943
Simone Lageoles	(917) 747-2157 / FAX (212) 633-8309
Lynn Lewis	(914) 301-5544 / (914) 841-2069
Jessica Lichtner	(212) 749-0978 / (917) 204-5826 / FAX (212) 749-0978
Kimberly A. Ludlow	(212) 929-5453 / (917) 922-4830
Veronica Lupu	(718) 267-2902 / (917) 443-8788
Liz Maas	(914) 693-2645 / (914) 523-3172
Stephanie Ann Marquardt	(718) 728-7928 / (917) 496-1136
Virginia McCarthy	(925) 383-7301
Janet Merwin-Miller	(212) 535-2969 / (609) 204-1992

Robin Meyers	(404) 693-7907	Debra Ronsvalle	(212) 358-5489 (917) 922-7800
Lisa Molinaro	(917) 363-0410	Glenna Ross	(212) 877-1907 (917) 853-4402 FAX (212) 877-1907
Veronica Mulero	(917) 533-5926		
Jennifer Opresnick	(917) 309-0982	Charles Sloan Rowe	(908) 244-5707
Tony Osso	(212) 677-2374 (917) 678-4115	Stacy Lynne Rowe	(908) 489-8202
Sheila Paige	(212) 529-2029	Peggie Shore	(203) 255-9019 (203) 258-3164
Elizabeth Perrin	(718) 383-1687 (310) 993-5612	Carmen Soriano (English, French, Spanish; Visual FX)	(212) 774-7490 (305) 439-9081
Anthony Pettine	(917) 991-7465 (973) 543-5992 FAX (973) 543-0699 www.geocities.com/avpettine	Kara B. Still	(910) 612-2871
		Barbara Stoia	(212) 580-1490 (508) 776-7517
Martha Pinson	(212) 362-1894 (917) 860-1078 FAX (212) 362-1894 www.marthapinson.com	Peggy Sutton	(212) 982-9690
		Melinda Taksen	(954) 232-2858
Daria Price	(212) 683-1266 (917) 579-7259	Lynne Twentyman	(212) 580-0677
		Elisabeth Tyler	(917) 204-7930
Betsy Pritchett Peterson	(908) 459-0084	Holly Unterberger	(718) 789-5117 (917) 202-5237
Joan Puma	(954) 383-1239		
Gail Ragusa	(845) 352-1808 (845) 548-5665	Sharon Watt	(646) 209-5148
Wendy Roberts	(212) 996-0269	Wendy York	(212) 627-8322 (917) 864-3846

Script Supervisors

Joan Bennett	(212) 873-9501	Mel Nelligan	(212) 876-6657 (917) 596-1387 FAX (212) 876-6849
Lisa Bobonis	(718) 956-5626 (323) 377-9866	Nila Neukum	(212) 353-0578 (310) 351-2777
Diane Durant	(310) 641-1302 (310) 989-5082	Philip Ng	(646) 515-6531 (718) 332-6455
Nancy Kaimowitz	(917) 622-4460	Julie Oppenheimer	(212) 229-9882
Lisa Katcher	(212) 447-0497 FAX (212) 447-0497	Jane Slater	(212) 928-0450 (917) 375-7567
Cheryl Malat (Motion Control & Visual FX)	(212) 799-9160 (310) 663-8336	Gretchen Somerfeld (French)	(213) 706-1550 (212) 330-7013 FAX (815) 371-0534
		Karen Wald	(917) 838-8801

Second Assistant Directors (DGA NY)

Alexander Aab	(917) 513-3102
Susan Ackerman	(914) 234-6473
Keith Adams	(917) 841-6820
Ethan Lee Anderson	(917) 445-7793
Arianne Apicelli	(718) 344-3147
David Appelson	(212) 866-6287 / (917) 841-4470 / FAX (917) 591-2868
Adam Aronson	(917) 626-2043
William C. Baker	(201) 819-7384
Daniela Barbosa	(347) 526-5977
Jane Barrer	(917) 509-4674 / (646) 290-7130
Cynthia Bauer-Espinosa	(732) 424-0408
Brian Bennhoff	(212) 727-2934
Adam Bernard	(516) 459-0476
Kristin Bernstein	(347) 697-7403
Lyda Blank	(310) 449-4604
Catherine Bloch	(718) 721-3840 / (917) 232-4993
Cynthia Blount	(203) 227-9607
Arle Bordas	(917) 453-1537
Joan G. Bostwick	(212) 472-8183 / (917) 601-5605
Brett Botula	(212) 861-8386
Stephen Brandt	(917) 297-9949
Cornelia Burnham	(718) 387-0728 / (917) 566-3434
Brian Campe	(518) 466-1715
Patty Carey-Perazzo	(212) 877-5862 / (917) 848-4567
Charles Jefferson Caron	(917) 952-9527
Anne Carroll	(718) 789-0124
David Catalano	(973) 985-4515
Ellen Athena Catsikeas	(917) 608-1385
Pamela Cederquist	(646) 812-2040
David Chambers	(646) 221-7430
Noreen Cheleden	(212) 529-5952
Jean Chien	(917) 826-0691
Katharine Ciric	(917) 692-1845
Paula Cohen	(212) 604-9024
Eddy Collyns	(917) 776-6426
Andrew Cooke	(917) 626-8944
Timothy Cooke	(718) 381-0441 / (917) 686-5706
Peter Cossio	(212) 505-3089 / (917) 225-1028
Jamaine Cripe	(973) 763-2147 / (347) 731-5591
James Czarnecki	(917) 859-2832 / (310) 205-6999
Michael Dister	(718) 933-1303 / (323) 461-1304
Kara Doherty	(917) 568-3782
Janice Doskey	(914) 261-2267
Brian D'Ottillie	(914) 533-6773 / (914) 263-0709
Antoine Douaihy	(917) 881-0141
John J. Egan III	(917) 757-0998
Kate Eisemann	(917) 873-2256 / (212) 222-2196 / FAX (203) 259-0124
Ukeme Emem	(718) 638-1783
Vadim Epstein	(917) 921-4646
Michael Espinosa	(973) 715-1089
Jason Farrar	(646) 522-2471
Nicole Feder	(917) 589-2069
John Fedynich	(973) 338-7746 / (973) 464-2904
Stuart Feldman	(973) 226-8589
Susan Fellows	(917) 445-0604
Jane Ferguson	(718) 599-5483 / (917) 407-5180
Judith Ferguson	(845) 446-7456
Danny Fernandez	(347) 661-5623
Lorri Fischer	(585) 241-0131 / (585) 730-2252
Marta Forns-Escude	(646) 298-7321
Aaron Forste	(201) 613-4306 / (201) 315-6770
Charlie Foster	(917) 922-3374
Betsy Friedman-Palmieri	(718) 648-9738 / (917) 620-5019
Michael Fucci	(718) 676-9918
Marc Garland	(212) 864-1149 / FAX (212) 864-1149 / www.marcgarland.com

Nathan Gendzier	(917) 294-5080
Gregory Gilman	(718) 499-5675
Tg Glazer	(732) 431-4353
Adam Glickman	(516) 295-8670 (516) 295-8671
Preston L. Goddard	(203) 604-8080 (203) 249-4412 FAX (203) 857-4977
Marcos Gonzalez	(646) 342-0518
Damon Michael Gordon	(917) 414-2658
Jason Matthew Graham	(646) 296-5932
Marc Greenberg	(718) 263-9615
Nate Grubb	(917) 309-4416
Joe Guest	(212) 255-9329
John Walker Guss	(912) 398-7515
Cathy Haft	(212) 274-8534
John Hamilton	(301) 585-1073 (202) 270-2081
Jacinta Elizabeth Hayne	(917) 660-7168
Barbara Heller	(212) 229-9757
Regina Heyman	(718) 545-6785 (917) 842-3671
Tracey Hinds	(718) 778-3365
Vanessa Hoffman	(718) 499-5675 (917) 744-6485
Samuel William Hutchins	(917) 864-0156
Anura Idupuganti	(917) 916-0554 www.anurafilms.com
Donna Imbarrato	(631) 537-5077
Jason Ivey	(917) 887-4770 (646) 536-3546
Bear Jackson	(914) 476-2406 (914) 424-4837
Isiah James Jr.	(212) 337-9990
Don Hollis Julien	(917) 584-7858
Shane Nathan Kalman	(516) 448-8189
Karen Kane	(718) 752-9320 (917) 333-4680
Mark William Kaufmann	(917) 674-8475
Takahide Kawakami	(212) 254-4908
Michelle Keiser	(917) 648-7518
Deanna Kelly	(718) 388-9357 (718) 302-9499
Kim Kennedy	(201) 865-2224
Brian Kenyon	(347) 262-4549
Keith Knight	(212) 726-9799
Ronnie Kupferwasser	(917) 302-4118
Matthew Lamb	(212) 722-1721
Ilene Landress	(917) 748-5745 (212) 987-9356
James D. Lee	(917) 509-9217
Thomas Lee	(917) 363-1134
Gina Leonetti	(212) 864-1786
Alexis Li	(213) 400-4141
Kit Liset	(917) 767-6873 (212) 477-7975
Charles Lum	(917) 319-2525 (212) 242-5543
Ian MacGregor	(917) 209-9444
Patrick Mangan	(646) 732-7168
Randy Manion	(917) 509-2140
Jason Manz	(917) 817-0718 FAX (310) 496-1550
Suk Yi Mar	(917) 887-1596
Adrian Martin	(212) 666-2570 FAX (212) 665-1303
Matthew Mason	(646) 418-2299
Alisa Matlovsky	(323) 833-2083
John Mattern	(201) 727-9608 (201) 232-8651
Peter Matthes	(212) 251-0307
Darren Maynard	(201) 222-6828
Leslie McDonough Jr.	(917) 533-5398
Matthew McLoota	(646) 335-5499
Lisa Meier	(808) 295-0551
Eddie Micallef	(201) 224-6135
Mike Michelin	(201) 694-0988 FAX (201) 939-6847
Jamie Miller	(201) 652-1782
Alison Nancy Monico	(914) 763-5325
Paolo Morante	(609) 924-2919
Julia Morgan	(718) 490-2559
Melissa Mugavero	(201) 417-5835
Christie Mullen	(917) 626-6395
Andy Muller	(914) 235-9855 (646) 208-5394
Len Murach	(212) 244-6399 (917) 817-2477
Maggie Murphy	(212) 242-1825 (323) 462-3512

Jim Nickas	(516) 410-5705
Watari Nishida	(917) 374-0140
Murphy Occhino	(201) 766-2033
Jeremy Olsher	(561) 400-3737 / (561) 330-3163
Thomas O'Malley	(203) 642-3474
Caleb Omens	(646) 734-8511
Francisco Ortiz	(917) 453-2626
Genevieve Palmieri	(201) 893-3974
Evan Perazzo	(212) 877-5862 / (917) 923-8475
Brent Perlman	(212) 580-0226
Jill Perno	(203) 645-1319
Tony Phillippe	(718) 606-9740 / (646) 265-8205
Jacqueline Phipps	(917) 749-0412
Michael Pinckney	(917) 721-2016
Lyn Pinezich	(917) 734-5252
Lauri Pitkus	(914) 740-3180 / (914) 929-3102
Matthew Power	(201) 656-1295 / (917) 822-4608
Lynn Powers	(917) 750-3964
Joaquin Diego Prange	(917) 687-9186
Raymond Quinlan	(631) 513-3327 / (631) 289-7355
Santiago Quinones	(212) 353-3258 / (917) 944-0910
Carla Raij	(917) 596-4808
Gary Rake	(917) 304-0086
Ellen Rappaport	(212) 737-4992 / (917) 359-6358
Michelle Regina	(201) 410-6569
Michael Reichman	(212) 721-9626
Demian Resnick	(212) 933-4824
Paul Rosen	(917) 749-0272
Thomas Ross	(212) 475-1330 / (917) 749-4623
Robert Routt	(212) 665-3683 / (917) 951-4741
Kathryn E. Ruopp	(718) 840-0718 / (917) 270-4800 / FAX (718) 840-0835
Holly Rymon	(516) 705-0559
John Saffir	(212) 717-2314
Lawrence Salamone	(212) 247-4478
Drew Santarsiero	(917) 951-1043
Matthew Sauer	(212) 627-8495 / (917) 882-0622
Andrew Saxe	(917) 656-1917 / (973) 325-1815
Beth Schebece	(917) 509-0447
Tibi Scheflow	(212) 375-0172 / (917) 822-2489
Nick Schepisi	(917) 325-2383
Maurice Lincoln Sessoms	(201) 838-8157
Joseph Sevey	(718) 267-8790 / (917) 602-1916
Nina Shiffman	(718) 858-7858
Steven Shore	(212) 545-8500 www.publicdomainny.com
Tim Stacker	(917) 751-6304
Alexandra Steele	(203) 662-1277
Noelle Stehman	(917) 532-3359
Dawn Stewart	(310) 993-4770
Robert Striem	(718) 384-0819
Daniel Strol	(845) 424-3247 / (914) 673-4666
Jermaine Sumra	(212) 234-3203 / (917) 847-1080
Christopher Surgent	(732) 223-8796 / (732) 642-7896
Salvatore Sutera	(201) 370-5784
Cindy Sweeney	(212) 505-5358
David Szani	(201) 372-1172
Michael Tadross Jr.	(212) 219-7500
Annie Tan	(917) 673-3877
April Taylor	(718) 399-0326
Donald Teahan	(718) 634-1569 / (917) 539-2438
Kimberly Anne Thompson	(917) 450-9306
Pamela Thur	(212) 374-0455 / (917) 873-3364
Robert Jerome Tierney	(215) 205-4621
Cristian Trova	(718) 797-3818 / (413) 499-5759
Sasha Tsyrlin	(973) 783-1190 / (718) 768-1761 / FAX (973) 783-4909
Nicholas Vanderpool	(917) 523-8283
Gayle Jennifer Vangrofsky	(646) 523-4592
Christian Vendetti	(201) 757-7314

Michael Vernola	(845) 783-7534 (917) 883-4232	Thomas J. Whelan	(914) 479-0486 (646) 279-4670
Aurora Warfield	(646) 265-9235	Robert Wheway	(203) 877-3071
Patricia Weber Sones	(917) 710-6474	Mark Winter	(212) 787-0516
John Webster	(908) 222-8366 (908) 917-0560	Robin Winter-Young	(917) 698-2507
Matthew Weiner	(212) 967-7298	Deborah Wolpert	(917) 319-0733 (212) 333-5100 FAX (212) 333-5900 www.dvdepot.com
Steven Weisberg	(212) 529-7731		
Adam Weisinger	(718) 503-0794	Andrew Wood	(804) 690-0833
Jane Wells	(917) 969-7117	Greer Yeaton	(718) 393-1719
Laura Wheeler	(917) 821-3470 (212) 726-3371	Edward Yoon	(201) 370-0408
		Mikki Ziska	(917) 656-9788

Second Assistant Directors

Stephen Lawrence Booth (718) 783-5796
www.lockandrollproductions.com

Jamie Haynes (310) 305-7139
(Line Producer) FAX (310) 827-7367

Mary Lew-Goucher (212) 734-2843

Randall Newsome (212) 501-4599

Jenny Peek (401) 331-6949

Ethan Ross (310) 990-1655

John Steinmetz (212) 799-0505
www.dga.org

Set Decorators

Lawrence Amanuel	(914) 522-9297 (845) 928-3849 FAX (845) 928-3850	Sandra Handloser	(646) 298-6884
		Jacqueline Jacobson	(203) 222-1991
Artists by Timothy Priano 131 Varick St., Ste. 905 New York, NY 10013 www.artistsbytimothypriano.com (Reps for Set Decorators)	(212) 929-7771 FAX (212) 929-7760	Lori Johnson-Guirard	(908) 273-5102 (917) 716-9870
David Barnes	(610) 896-8785 (610) 547-0300 FAX (303) 474-3130	Chris M. Jordan	(917) 604-5693 (718) 625-7333
		Susan Kaufman	(212) 254-3236 FAX (212) 254-3236
Andrew Baseman	(212) 674-6217	Christian Kelly	(845) 246-2497 FAX (845) 246-2497
June Bateman	(212) 925-7951 (917) 806-8200 FAX (212) 925-7951 www.junebateman.com	Kate Kennedy	(917) 834-3922 www.goodeandplenty.com
Susan Beeson-de Havenon	(843) 577-3233 (917) 922-3490 FAX (843) 577-3416	Betsy Klompus	(718) 499-2562 (917) 439-6242
		Beth Kushnick	(212) 502-1147
Teri Bella	(917) 512-4975 (917) 701-0191	Laura Lambert-Andrusko	(315) 636-9935 (315) 317-1757
James Branigan	(212) 505-8404 (917) 686-8167 FAX (212) 505-7173	Ross La Terra	(908) 770-1987 (732) 792-3281
Paul Camarro	(973) 875-2092 (973) 271-0203	Lydia Marks	(917) 673-3872 www.lydiamarks.com
Robert W. Carpenter	(212) 223-2298 (203) 253-0458	Cathy Marshall (Prop Master)	(973) 627-1150 (201) 317-8108 FAX (973) 627-3703
Stephanie Carroll	(212) 529-9029 FAX (212) 529-9029		
Carolyn Cartwright	(212) 982-1891 (646) 286-8328	Christina Mayer	(212) 688-3837 (317) 665-5455
Robert Covelman	(212) 229-2750	Alexandra Mazur	(212) 206-6695 (917) 882-6201
George M. De Titta Jr.	(201) 573-1582 (201) 410-1995	Janine Michelle	(516) 889-3781 FAX (516) 432-5372
Norm Dodge	(212) 289-1092 www.normdodge.com	Michael Murphy	(914) 737-4131 (917) 744-0687
Kathleen M. Dolan	(201) 767-1675	Walter M. Pluff III	(917) 940-8510
Thom Driver	(212) 206-0901 www.halleyresources.com	Mary Prlain	(917) 412-1392 www.maryprlain.com
Tim Ebneth	(212) 206-0901 www.halleyresources.com	William F. Reynolds	(917) 848-6001
Christine Gardyasz	(201) 837-0920	Gabrielle Rosenberg	(212) 229-2729 (917) 863-0547 www.changeinc.com
Brian S. Garvey	(215) 336-6976 (215) 625-7558	Sonja Roth	(310) 863-2102 (310) 474-6299
Caroline Ghertler	(718) 768-0012 (917) 951-1004	Jerry Schwartz	(212) 465-9580 FAX (212) 563-1877 www.houseofschwartz.net
Lane Glisson	(718) 788-0910 (347) 268-1149 FAX (718) 788-0910	James P. Sherman	(802) 672-4144
		Ina Slote	(212) 679-4584 FAX (212) 679-4584
Joji Goto	(212) 741-3240 (781) 863-1555 www.ennisinc.com	Dan Toma	(518) 453-2370
Jennifer Ann Halpern	(718) 858-1169 (917) 881-3049	Pamela Maiden Turk	(212) 964-3675 (917) 647-2020 FAX (212) 964-3675

Ronald T. von Blomberg	(631) 283-8447 (631) 926-2013	Alyssa B. Winter	(914) 478-5565 (917) 453-0154 FAX (914) 478-5565
Catherine Werner	(908) 281-6057	Sabrina Wright	(917) 693-2212
Ford Wheeler	(212) 736-0181 (917) 334-5604	Steven Wright	(212) 964-3675 (917) 923-9445 FAX (212) 964-3675
Christine Wick	(215) 514-8371		
Jim Williams	(215) 680-2107 (215) 704-7876 FAX (215) 731-0351	Harriet Zucker	(718) 643-9401 (917) 405-0593

Sound Mixers (Local 52 NY)

Richard Seth Abramson	(914) 337-5232
	FAX (914) 793-0113
Gary Alper	(212) 873-8940
Joshua Anderson	(347) 512-2157
Felix Andrew	(212) 566-8495
	(646) 232-6466
Kandy L. Armstrong	(407) 839-0730
Antonio L. Arroyo	(917) 881-9095
	(212) 862-1871
	FAX (212) 862-1871
Brian W. Bailey	(631) 471-7274
Alexandra Baltarzuk	(718) 965-1506
Steven J. Balzarini (Boom Operator)	(732) 739-0286
	(732) 207-4704
Paul F. Bang	(212) 587-9413
	(917) 414-6341
Scott Bardolf	(914) 355-4078
	(516) 322-0955
Junior Baron	(718) 954-1118
Michael A. Barosky	(212) 787-5735
Michael William Barry	(631) 235-4334
Laurence Basinski	(908) 604-8501
	(201) 268-6056
Melvin M. Becker	(718) 886-6580
Michael A. Bedard	(516) 433-6537
Jason Benjamin	(212) 995-0484
	(917) 538-1480
Brad Bergbom	(718) 935-0430
	(718) 812-2710
Tom Bergin	(201) 659-3944
	(917) 968-5030
Alexander Best III	(718) 677-5514
Tom Biebel	(609) 823-2154
Gioia Birkett-Foa	(720) 261-4804
Neil Bleifeld	(212) 581-3849
John Bolz	(631) 549-7534
	(631) 495-0119
Kevin Bowe	(347) 527-1340
	(917) 340-0906
Timothy R. (T.R.) Boyce Jr.	(212) 627-9619
	(917) 804-6188
Richard Brause	(212) 929-7040
Theodore P. Breen	(718) 646-6890
	(212) 502-3412
Scott M. Breindel	(212) 966-0568
	(917) 748-2470
Laurel Ann Bridges	(212) 222-5019
	(917) 414-2503
Patricia Brolsma	(201) 784-8874
Jerry Bruck	(212) 242-3737
Robert Bryan	(917) 640-0263
Peter Buccellato	(201) 444-7843
John M. Bucher	(212) 866-2115
	(917) 750-1661
Allan Byer	(917) 553-9941
Vincent C. Camuto	(914) 592-7618
	(917) 716-3702
Vincent P. Camuto	(845) 208-3117
	(646) 208-4121
Damian E. Canelos	(917) 699-4765
Andrew C. Capuano	(914) 654-8773
	(914) 261-3270
Thomas Carroll	(914) 271-8734
	(914) 584-5956
Gautam K. Choudhury	(212) 243-8036
	(646) 831-9810
Jon M. Christodoulou	(407) 932-0323
	(877) 623-2157
Frank M. Cianchetta	(718) 727-6910
Paul Ira Cohen	(845) 657-8755
Lucas Corrubia	(800) 673-1328
	(917) 359-7190
Paul Cote	(212) 213-9092
Jerry Cox	(917) 776-3342
Mik Cribben	(800) 235-2713
	(917) 513-3795
	FAX (212) 620-0084
	www.mikcribben.com
Keith Culbertson	(917) 716-3523
David B. Curtin	(201) 222-0790
	(917) 886-7883
John T. Dalton	(941) 598-1793
Bill Daly	(201) 796-8728
	(310) 301-3993
Neil Danziger	(212) 961-6691
Kay Denmark	(917) 846-7072
Stuart C. Deutsch	(718) 383-4144
	(917) 325-7995
Peter J. De Verna	(516) 781-1334
	(516) 639-3705

Frank Di Maulo	(631) 427-6494
Edward Dolan	(845) 226-6462 (845) 223-2723
William P. Drucklieb	(732) 571-3935 (732) 530-1924
Timothy Raul Elder	(646) 335-2428
Robert A. Esposito	(610) 594-2524 (610) 594-7665
Gregg H. Feingold	(888) 380-7077
Victor Filepp	(800) 282-2311
Michael Finamore	(800) 282-2311
Elliott Fisher	(917) 447-5195
Raymond Flynn	(215) 885-8886 (215) 519-3626
Peter C. Fonda	(347) 661-8878
Christopher Fondulas	(860) 705-8358
Michael A. Fortunato	(201) 330-1858 (201) 542-0985
Fritzgerald Francois	(718) 629-1628 (347) 721-8971
Peter W. Freedman	(203) 329-8391
Robert E. Friedman	(212) 753-6847
Frank Fulleda	(718) 381-5976 (917) 570-5294
John K. Fundus	(917) 414-9105
William Gagliano	(845) 988-1729
Joseph Galione	(973) 462-4880
Keith J. Gardner	(212) 866-9537
Chris Gebert	(917) 674-9144
Robert Ghiraldini	(914) 248-7133 (917) 833-6802
Jeanne L. Gilliland	(718) 638-4039 (917) 864-1770
Philip G. Gleason	(212) 222-4957 (917) 822-1436
John D. Gooch	(610) 627-1495 (610) 627-1497
Mark A. Goodermote	(206) 328-3182
Thomas W. Gould	(516) 431-7853 (917) 851-1136
John Grasso	(609) 926-7631
Justin Gray	(267) 974-4565 (718) 768-8067
Frank J. Graziadei	(631) 698-0063 (516) 230-5059
Dennis T. Green	(516) 546-9226
Daniel Glenn Guachione	(860) 983-7674
Anguibe Guindo	(212) 982-3302 (917) 653-5146
Chat Gunter	(646) 602-1090 (917) 859-7194
John Gutierrez	(917) 531-0387
Stephan B. Haas	(516) 569-3237
Franklin R. Haber	(212) 222-8518
Nicholas Hammond	(917) 848-4223
John A. Hampton	(718) 576-2468 (917) 389-2112
Steven M. Hamroff	(212) 873-5081 (917) 994-1011
Leslie Harkness	(716) 876-3487
Christopher Hartnett	(609) 266-1012
Timothy Harvey	(408) 397-6071
Samantha L. Heilweil	(203) 255-6496
Anton F. Higgins	(212) 265-2217
Lawrence Hoff	(845) 365-4046
Joel Holland	(914) 271-3648 (914) 494-6319 www.featurevideo.com
Douglas Holman	(718) 229-4902 (212) 586-3700
Thomas Holman	(718) 423-3856 (917) 797-4202
Jon Hopkins	(631) 667-5361 (516) 662-1614
Claire Houghtalen	(607) 725-4367
Rosa Howell-Thornhil	(973) 761-8829 (973) 761-8828
Herbert Hummel	(516) 623-6072
Charles Hunt	(718) 284-6607 (917) 842-0408
Jack Hutson	(646) 286-5878
Peter A. Ilardi	(718) 225-0260
Anthony R. Inglese	(914) 934-0682
Ken Ishii	(718) 875-4953 (917) 776-3604
Matthew Israel	(917) 279-4134
Abe Jacob	(212) 593-0735
Richard Jacob	(212) 674-1296 (917) 897-2264
Todd Jacobs	(718) 255-4760
Lukasz Janik	(917) 865-4913
Daniel Johnson	(646) 418-1221
Michael L. Jordan	(201) 967-1744
Thomas Jordan	(646) 256-8405

Max Kalmanowicz	(212) 226-4180 / (917) 474-8548
Michael Karas	(973) 744-6450
John C. Kauble	(614) 475-6931
Algis J. Kaupas	(212) 307-1379 / (203) 488-8403
Maryte-Murphy Kavaliauskas	(212) 608-3215
Chris Kellett	(610) 853-6572
Steve C. Kennedy	(845) 353-2292
Giles P. Khan	(212) 729-9425
John E. Kilgore III	(718) 855-3224 / (212) 245-4623
Kathleen King	(718) 858-3532
Ed Kizer	(301) 916-7887
Paul Koronkiewicz	(718) 222-4708
Toussaint Kotright	(917) 929-7193
William Kozy	(212) 560-7273
Andrew (Drew) Kunin	(718) 273-8458
Peter F. Kurland	(615) 665-1855
Richard C. Kuse	(845) 634-4551
James La Farge	(646) 240-3713
Jansen Lambie	(917) 706-6947 / (917) 859-0842
Jane Landis	(710) 499-9064
Ronnie Lantz	(570) 296-5331
Robert Larrea	(917) 287-9430
Alan Lebow	(718) 829-5663 / (917) 499-8298 www.alpdigital.com
Joseph M. Lenihan	(718) 596-4665
George Leong	(718) 507-9383
Bruce Litecky	(610) 566-7229 / (610) 566-8508
Jeffrey Livesey	(212) 414-4331 / (201) 587-3305
Lawrence Loewinger	(917) 902-2219 / (212) 226-2429 FAX (212) 966-7650 www.sohoaudio.com
Dane Lonsdale	(203) 247-6405
R. Michael Lonsdale	(203) 226-9963
Tommy Louie	(718) 465-8871
Yehuda Maayan	(818) 888-9101
Michelle Mader	(718) 545-8470
Dennis L. Maitland II	(412) 231-7547
Kim H. Maitland	(212) 749-3230 / (917) 796-7979
Tod A. Maitland	(212) 777-1823 / (917) 763-7696
Alan R. Manger	(973) 426-9696 / (973) 347-7787
Douglas Martines	(516) 338-7578
Glen M. Marullo	(011) 44 -1275
James Mase	(310) 694-9009
Nicolas Mazet	(917) 686-1060
Gary McCafferty	(201) 939-5557
John D. McCormick	(908) 689-4458 / (917) 742-3694
Daniel McGuire	(516) 621-8836 / (212) 505-5000
Daniel McIntosh	(908) 369-0511 / (908) 625-2422
Charles M. McIntyre	(212) 684-2363 / (917) 774-1698
Teferra McKenzie	(718) 222-2583 / (347) 581-8838
Jan McLaughlin	(973) 778-3488 / (862) 221-5280
John A. McLaughlin	(631) 864-3751
Robert J. McNamara Jr.	(215) 579-0667 / (215) 930-9631
Kevin V. Meehan	(212) 206-1291
Andrew Melnyk	(646) 709-2281
Danny Michael	(914) 478-5810 / (914) 924-8070 FAX (914) 478-5811
Joseph E. Miko	(203) 937-6796
Brian Miksis	(718) 438-1600 / (917) 776-4011
Jeffrey M. Miller	(512) 328-3907
Peter J. Miller	(631) 723-6977
Zachary Moon	(631) 456-9037
Nedenia Moore-Tzouris	(845) 558-5556
Thomas Morse	(914) 362-7301 / (914) 362-7305
David C. Moshlak	(212) 249-3369 / (212) 674-0774
Angel Muniz	(718) 439-8514
John J. Murphy	(917) 783-2882
Richard Murphy	(914) 294-3481 / (845) 346-5143
Bryant Musgrove	(917) 680-4067
Betsy Nagler	(718) 965-1426 / (917) 776-7139

Arthur Nastri	(203) 270-7010	Theresa K.K. Radka	(212) 780-9413 / (917) 864-4104
Kelly Neese	(718) 246-2340	Michael Radow	(212) 662-0770
Thomas Nelson	(845) 365-6505 / (917) 833-6295	David G. Rainey	(610) 490-1865 / (610) 662-9492
Mary Neubig	(718) 822-6486 / (914) 588-4239	David Raphael	(212) 358-8876 / (646) 729-8226
Richard W. Nicholas	(718) 357-8541 / (212) 790-2350	Brenda Ray	(917) 226-3077 / FAX (212) 477-5356
Edward Novick	(310) 836-9901	Schavaria Reeves	(212) 794-1786 / (917) 673-4961
Brendan J. O'Brien	(774) 406-0543		
Terence J. O'Mara	(212) 472-1826	Christopher J. Rennert	(631) 724-3108 / (631) 633-3729
Joseph Origlieri	(201) 709-8253	Gary Rich	(561) 362-9590
Anthony Ortiz	(818) 481-3243	Griffin Richardson	(718) 636-6737
Desiree Ortiz	(718) 638-8148 / (718) 809-4340	Richard Riedel	(631) 968-2879 / (631) 968-2312
Daniel M. Paikin	(646) 602-0226 / (917) 207-6234	Neil Riha	(415) 665-6004
Egor L. Panchenko	(201) 388-7658	Anthony Robinson	(718) 812-2086
Lawrence Panetta	(201) 391-9170 / (201) 441-4039	Robert Roelofs	(718) 578-9362
Tim Pankewicz	(732) 257-9125 / (732) 209-3770	Steven J. Rogers	(718) 983-8185 / (877) 606-4839
Gary M. Parker	(914) 276-4279 / (914) 879-7591	William P. Romanello	(212) 691-7461
David Pastecchi	(516) 495-4855 / (516) 230-4986	Joseph P. Romano	(917) 706-2112
		Brian Ronan	(212) 580-5357
Morning Pastorok	(212) 242-2048	Philip Rosati	(267) 975-8439
Donald S. Perlman	(914) 592-7949	Floyd T. Rose	(202) 544-7244
Sam Perry	(732) 229-0728	Daniel Rosenblum	(212) 777-3589
Roger Phenix	(914) 947-2902	Mark A. Roy	(973) 243-0405
Brian C. Piazza	(845) 838-1038 / (914) 907-1275	Aaron Rudelson	(718) 832-3614 / (917) 279-8272
		Edward F. Ruotolo	(845) 496-7278
Joshua Pitt	(347) 721-3483 / (718) 675-9123	Paul Rusnak	(202) 667-1099
David Platt	(212) 473-7157 / (212) 533-6922	James Sabat Jr.	(212) 439-9727 / (516) 826-9153
David W. Pliskin	(201) 265-6796	James J. Sabat	(516) 826-9153
Paul James Pouthier	(646) 298-4874	Robert A. Sacchetti	(203) 984-9585
David Powers	(212) 777-5529 / (917) 737-2706	Adam J. Sanchez	(215) 386-4345
Mathew Price	(917) 842-4920	Michael F Sanchez	(718) 229-7378 / (917) 359-6313
Michael E. Primmer	(510) 548-4829	Gabriel S. Sanders	(347) 528-7485
Robert Primrose	(917) 685-2805	Dean Sarjeant	(860) 868-9265
Larry Provost	(914) 271-4276	William Sarokin	(914) 666-0233
David Jon Pruger	(212) 580-8690 / (917) 653-6906	Michael Scardino	(716) 691-5021
Jeff Pullman	(732) 651-1933 / (888) 210-9362	Thomas J. Scerbak	(973) 471-2135 / (917) 824-0915

Andrew Schmetterling	(973) 744-3910 / (201) 213-3610
Michael J. Schmidt	(954) 345-3565
William V. Schneiberg	(718) 261-5282
Peter W. Schneider	(212) 255-5716 / (917) 270-2762
Michael H. Scott	(917) 553-0543
Timothia Sellers	(845) 371-1662 / (917) 620-1027
John Sember	(412) 860-7883
Thomas C. Short	(212) 730-1770
Jorge Silva	(914) 937-4717
Gary Silver	(845) 708-0614
Christopher Sloan	(603) 520-8869
Kira Smith	(718) 438-5907 / (347) 432-3373
Wayne E. Smith	(203) 981-7525
Micah (Todd) Solomon	(828) 252-3757
Anthony V. Sozio	(201) 722-5775 / (888) 988-4668
Stefan Springman	(212) 477-2160
Igor Srubshchik	(917) 776-5434 / (718) 256-3076
Julie Stalker-Wilde	(646) 623-7913
Stuart Stanley	(516) 316-9965
Anthony Starbuck	(718) 596-1154
Jason B. Stasium	(646) 245-5910
Scott Stauffer	(718) 636-0419
Jerry Stein	(845) 348-0244 / (917) 750-8667
Franklin D. Stettner	(212) 691-3745
Gregory J. C. Stewart	(917) 476-7640
David Stiegelbauer	(516) 333-8331
Keith P. Stiegelbauer	(516) 257-1666
Rebecca Stone	(718) 325-9514 / (347) 526-3276
Alexander Sullivan	(917) 903-0649 / (718) 643-0922
Orinne J. T. Takagi	(212) 663-3799
Seth Tallman	(917) 439-7709
Martin Talty	(818) 207-5539
Simon T. Tams	(310) 559-5322
Noah V. Timan	(917) 692-6255
David Tirolo	(347) 581-4689
Jose Torres	(917) 721-4506 / (212) 543-2407
Julian L. Townsend	(631) 421-3215 / (516) 380-6078
William Tzouris	(718) 237-9650 / (917) 859-4762 / FAX (845) 818-4200
Michael Urdaneta	(718) 753-6806
Alain Van Achte	(914) 923-0094 / (914) 400-5411
Thomas G. Varga	(914) 591-9675 / (914) 830-3918
Alfredo Viteri	(917) 312-4129
Jerome R. Vitucci	(718) 768-1075
Jerry Wagreich	(914) 734-4490 / (914) 941-5128
Locke E. Wallace III	(718) 834-8169 / (917) 802-5240
Karl G. E. Wasserman	(212) 316-4618 / (646) 418-3484
Steven Watson	(201) 385-6399 / (201) 410-8563
Warren A. Weberg	(617) 901-8313
Mark Weingarten	(323) 839-7550
Daniel H. Wesson	(212) 402-2435 / (888) 381-0205
Jonathan Weston	(212) 989-1987
Joseph White Jr.	(631) 273-3056 / (210) 802-1199
Richard A. Whitfield	(310) 937-1627
Dale Whitman	(914) 271-5507 / (917) 520-0038
Ronald Yoshida	(917) 566-0000 / FAX (212) 691-6961
Jerry H. Yuen	(718) 523-3754 / (917) 218-8488
Thomas Zafian	(212) 228-8718
John Zecca	(908) 832-6956
Ye Zhang	(856) 772-0653 / (610) 999-4592
James J. Zoltowski Jr.	(516) 739-5661 / (888) 778-1419
Andy Zuch	(516) 541-0832 / (917) 213-5549
Bernie Zuch	(516) 364-3189 / (516) 921-4887 / FAX (516) 677-6863
Steven N. Zuch	(631) 367-7112 / (646) 772-0420
Brian Zydel	(631) 266-1938

Sound Mixers

Chris Andersen	(845) 679-8848
	(888) 484-8848
	FAX (845) 679-1208
	www.nevessa.com
Alex Cushman	(860) 673-7341
	(860) 559-0730
Michael Ford	(215) 534-2089
(Boom Operator)	
Matthew Geldof	(917) 628-6200
	www.nysoundmixer.com
Jonathan Jackson	(718) 383-6711
	(646) 872-9564
Mike Keenan	(917) 519-7555
	FAX (212) 979-7462
	www.skywardpictures.com
Martin G.M. Kelly	(845) 591-0881
Jarett Livingston	(917) 533-4903
Margaret Nathans	(213) 304-1605
	www.fortesound.com
David Roche	(718) 768-4882
Peter Rotondo	(212) 414-5153
	(914) 912-6999
David Schumacher	(917) 535-2739
(Boom Operator)	www.magneticmedianyc.com
Anthony Viera	(201) 926-6503
	imdb.com/name/nm0896774/
John Vincent	(845) 758-0478
	(845) 656-2929
	FAX (845) 758-0478

Stage Managers (DGA NY)

Ric Anderson	(212) 967-7639
Dee Bache	(732) 324-5972
Steve Bautista	(732) 614-6397
David Beld	(212) 749-1605
Terence Benson	(212) 724-9302
Robin Bruce-Baron	(845) 680-0398 / (914) 953-7308
Dennis Cameron	(212) 686-5228
Thomas David Citrano	(818) 512-6613
Christine Deluca	(201) 935-1850
Joey Despenzero	(212) 759-0919
Peter Downing	(201) 840-0151 / (201) 723-5751
Leslye Fagin	(908) 866-9030
Andrew Feigin	(631) 423-3855
Lynn Finkel	(973) 425-9287 / (973) 476-5664
Douglas Fogel	(212) 541-9810 / (917) 603-4257
Thomas Gatewood	(973) 661-9257 / (212) 308-8815
Jeffry S. Giller	(212) 255-5299 / (917) 304-7606
Alan Goldfarb	(646) 249-5023
Ginger Gonzalez	(646) 245-7225
Keith Greer	(646) 872-7116
Peter Grimm	(201) 332-2138
Mark Hammond	(201) 533-1835 / (917) 607-3898
Tom Healy	(917) 921-1661
James Henderson Jr.	(212) 975-4321
Steven Hollander	(732) 238-4268 / (212) 664-6053
Brian Jacobs	(201) 833-8944 / (212) 728-2067
Michael Jacobs	(212) 876-6560
Meryl Jaffe	(212) 234-4927
Angela Jensen	(518) 378-0433
Rand Joseph	(914) 946-9087
Cecile Just	(212) 724-2970
Zoya Kachadurian	(212) 864-7762
Howard Kolins	(718) 625-4073 / (718) 625-4073
Arthur Lewis	(718) 222-4044
Peter Liska	(917) 771-3203
Cari Lorberfeld	(914) 261-3143
Ran Lowe	(310) 936-2059
Jeffrey Markowitz	(212) 662-7303 / (212) 662-7635
Michele L. Mayer	(212) 689-3897 / (917) 848-5223
Molly McBride	(917) 470-8553
Bill Miller	(212) 873-9590
Anthony Mirante	(914) 237-3578 / (917) 270-0753
Alan Needleman	(732) 792-3363
James Niforos	(212) 787-5311
Nelson Ortiz	(908) 464-1924
Cyndi Owgang	(917) 412-1522
Jeffrey Pearl	(347) 623-6922
Brandon Phillips	(516) 483-3408 / (516) 770-4241
Susan Reisinger	(914) 282-3867
Rose Riggins	(917) 952-0746
Rosario Roveto Jr.	(914) 248-5155
Emily Rubin	(917) 501-9825
Jonathan Sampson	(845) 641-6120
Lauren Schneider	(212) 956-2366
Susan Schroer	(914) 723-1105
Stephanie Sdanowich	(718) 599-2137
Jim Semmelman	(212) 679-8917
Linda Shiers	(201) 394-0515
Craig Spinney	(203) 866-8244
Michael Spiteri	(917) 720-5541
Paul Tarascio	(860) 227-3874
Bennett Testa	(646) 638-4572
Niclana Tolmasoff	(917) 224-3884
Mark Traub	(914) 764-8435
Edward Valk	(646) 831-9557
Steven James Van Patten	(917) 561-9676
Robert Van Ry	(973) 304-0885 / (904) 471-9494
Ann Vettel	(718) 324-3591
Locke E. Wallace III	(718) 875-0249

Studio Teachers/Welfare Workers

**Bambini Casting & Wrangling/
Michele Avantario** (914) 646-5839
(Baby Wrangler)

Casala, Ltd. (866) 780-7180
(Studio Teachers) FAX (866) 780-8262
www.childreninfilm.com

(516) 624-4944
Leslie Collins, R.N. (516) 428-6447
(Baby Wrangler & Tutor) FAX (516) 624-8026

Lifestyle Resources (212) 947-9792
23 W. 36th St., Ste. 4B FAX (212) 736-9115
(Near Fifth Ave.) www.sterlinglifestyle.com
New York, NY 10018

(973) 857-6244
Pia Mehr-Rose (973) 452-7121
(Baby Wrangler)

(914) 747-2737
🅐 On Location Education (800) 800-3378
400 Columbus Ave., Ste. 7S FAX (914) 747-2750
Valhalla, NY 10595 www.onlocationeducation.com

Missy Simms (619) 405-5050
FAX (619) 226-6220

(646) 331-9456
Janie Teller (310) 820-4522
(Baby Wrangler)

ON LOCATION EDUCATION
It's that simple.

**On-Set Tutoring Services.
We also handle all child permits.**

Tel: 914.666.3664 Fax: 914.666.3810
www.onlocationeducation.com

Stunt Coordinators & Performance Drivers

Ray Abbott	(201) 767-6273
	(201) 707-3331
	FAX (201) 767-8502
	www.rayabbs.com
Aerial Focus/Tom Sanders	(805) 455-3142
	www.aerialfocus.com
(BASE Jumping, Hang Gliding, Skydiving & Ultralight Aircraft)	
Cinema Drivers/	(661) 250-9617
Tom Anthony's Driving Team	(877) 654-9550
	www.cinemadrivers.com
Cinematicstunts.com/	
John-Eric Schuman	(877) 447-8868
41 Kalina Dr.	www.cinematicstunts.com
Saugerties, NY 12477	

Blaise Corrigan	(718) 237-2538
 Drivers East	(800) 803-3992
	www.driverseast.com
Drivers Inc.	(818) 994-4199
620 Resolano Dr.	FAX (310) 459-7374
Pacific Palisades, CA 90272	www.driversinc.com
 Everything Events &	(973) 338-6995
Entertainment, LLC	(323) 230-5527
41 Watchung Plaza, Ste. 236	FAX (973) 200-4291
Montclair, NJ 07042	www.eeande.com

**REAL DRIVERS
REEL RESULTS**

"From Concept to Completion"

Drivers East was formed to meet the needs of the agency/producer who require high performance drivers with outstanding skills developed by years of "on set" experience as stunt drivers and stunt coordinators. We are the only driving team on the east coast who meets and drives as a team on a regular basis at our closed course facility.

1-800-803-3992

or visit us online at www.driverseast.com

Roy Farfel/Stunts East   (732) 449-5885 / (732) 266-1463
www.royfarfel.com

Ⓐ Foy Inventerprises, Inc.   (702) 454-3300
3275 E. Patrick Ln.   www.flybyfoy.com
Las Vegas, NV 89120
(Aerial, Aerial Coordination, Aquatic, Coordination, Extreme Rigging, General Stunts, Hang Gliding, Paragliding, Rigging, Skiing, Skydiving & Skysurfing)

The Geller Agency   (323) 856-3000
1547 Cassil Pl.   FAX (323) 856-3009
Hollywood, CA 90028   www.thegelleragency.com
(Reps for Stunt Coordinators)

Ⓐ GZ Entertainment & Stunts   (201) 675-1118
15 Storig Ave.   www.gzfxandstunts.com
Closter, NJ 07624
(Extreme Rigging, Fencing, General Stunts, Marine Coordination, Rigging, Rope Rescue, Scuba Diving, Skiing, Skysurfing, Stunt Coordination, Sword Fighting, Trampolines & Trick Horseback Riding)

Don Hewitt   (845) 726-3320 / (914) 841-2826
www.donhhewitt.com

Chad Knorr   (610) 587-2673 / (610) 855-8065
FAX (610) 855-0080

GZ ENTERTAINMENT
SPECIAL EFFECTS & STUNTS FOR FILM

WE ARE ACTION !!

- 2nd Unit Direction
- F/X & Stunt Coordinators
- Stunts Players
- Crash Pads/Body Pads

- Pyro/Fire Bars & Rings
- Atmosphere & Mechanical F/X
- Bullet Hits / Explosions / Burns
- Dust & Spark Hits

- Porta-Pits/Air Bag
- Pipe & Rollover Ramps
- Ratches & Rams
- Rigging

WWW.GZFXANDSTUNTS.COM
BRIAN@GZFXANDSTUNTS.COM
BRIAN SCHULEY - (201) 675-1118

Jack McLaughlin	(914) 329-6253	Stunt Specialists/Peter Bucossi	(908) 507-8283
	www.jmstunts.com		FAX (908) 818-1475
			www.stuntspecialists.com
Never Quit, Inc./Brian Smyj	(914) 469-1749		(917) 662-2083
	FAX (201) 485-8244	Stuntworks	(212) 714-5392
	www.neverquitstunts.com		www.stuntworks.biz
	(818) 508-0122		(323) 650-2072
Performance Two, Inc.	(818) 508-7618	Team Hutchinson	(323) 377-2499
5235 Goodland Ave.	FAX (818) 508-0322		FAX (949) 951-7153
North Hollywood, CA 91607	www.performancetwo.com		www.teamhutchinson.com
Ⓐ Stunt Dept., Inc./Chris Barnes	(516) 236-9644	Ⓐ ZFX, Inc.	(502) 637-2500
	FAX (516) 869-0843		FAX (502) 637-7878
	www.stuntdept.com		www.zfxflying.com
		(Aerial, Aerial Coordination, Aerial Rigging & Flying Effects)	

Cinematic Stunts Inc.

Complete Stunt Services
Military Consultation
Police & Military Wardrobe
Licensed Armorer & Weapon Supply
Rescue Diver & Emergency First Responder

877-44 STUNT
www.cinematicstunts.com

STUNT DEPT INC

Stunt Coordination
Film
Television
Print

Performance & Stunt Driving

Marine Coordination
Camera Boats
Water Safety
Divers & More

Chris Barnes 516 236 9644
www.stuntdept.com

Trade Associations/Unions

Advertising Photographers of America/New York
27 W. 20th St., Ste. 601
(Near Fifth Ave.)
New York, NY 10011
(212) 807-0399
FAX (212) 727-8120
www.apany.com

ALSAM/Association of Location Scouts and Managers
www.alsam.net

American Association of Advertising Agencies (AAAA)
405 Lexington Ave., 18th Fl.
(Near E. 42nd St.)
New York, NY 10174
(212) 682-2500
FAX (212) 682-8391
www.aaaa.org

American Federation of TV & Radio Artists (AFTRA)
260 Madison Ave.
New York, NY 10016
(212) 532-0800
FAX (212) 532-2242
www.aftra.org

Association of Independent Commercial Producers (AICP)
Three W. 18th St., Fifth Fl.
(Near Broadway)
New York, NY 10011
(212) 929-3000
FAX (212) 929-3359
www.aicp.com

Association of Independent Creative Editors (AICE)
308 W. 107th St., Ste. 5F
(Near Second Ave.)
New York, NY 10016
(212) 665-2679
www.aice.org

Casting Society of America
311 W. 43rd St., 10th Fl.
New York, NY 10036
(212) 868-1260
FAX (212) 868-1261
www.castingsociety.com

Directors Guild of America (DGA)
110 W. 57th St., Second Fl.
(Near Seventh Ave.)
New York, NY 10019
(212) 581-0370
(800) 356-3754
FAX (212) 581-1441
www.dga.org

IATSE
1430 Broadway, 20th Fl.
(Near W. 44th St.)
New York, NY 10018
(212) 730-1770
FAX (212) 730-7809
www.iatse-intl.org

International Cinematographers Guild (IA Local 600)
80 Eighth Ave., 14th Fl.
(Near W. 14th St.)
New York, NY 10011
(212) 647-7300
FAX (212) 647-7318
www.cameraguild.com

Make-Up Artists & Hair Stylists (IA Local 798)
152 W. 24th St. (Near Seventh Ave.)
New York, NY 10011
(212) 627-0660
FAX (212) 627-0664

A Minor Consideration
14530 Denker Ave.
Gardena, CA 90247
(310) 532-1345
(310) 344-9686
FAX (310) 523-3691
www.minorcon.org

Motion Picture Editors Guild (IA Local 700)
145 Hudson St., Ste. 201
New York, NY 10013
(800) 705-8700
(212) 302-0700
FAX (212) 302-1091
www.editorsguild.com

Motion Picture Studio Mechanics (IA Local 52)
326 W. 48th St. (Near Eighth Ave.)
New York, NY 10036
(212) 399-0980
FAX (212) 315-1073
www.iatselocal52.org

MOTION PICTURE STUDIO MECHANICS
I.A.T.S.E. LOCAL 52
NEW YORK NEW JERSEY PENNSYLVANIA DELAWARE CONNECTICUT

JOHN R. FORD
PRESIDENT

JOHN K. FUNDUS
VICE PRESIDENT

WILLIAM MCGAVIN
SECRETARY/TREASURER

ROBERT STOCKLIN
BUSINESS REPRESENTATIVE

326 WEST 48th STREET   NEW YORK, NY 10036
TEL: (212) 399-0980   **FAX:** (212) 315-1073
WEB: www.iatselocal52.org   **E-MAIL:** ialocal52@msn.com

Craft Service, Electricians, Film Electronics and Computer Technicians, Medics, Grips, Properties and Special Effects, Set Painters, Shop Craftsmen, Sound, Re-Recording, Video, Wardrobe

---

Music Video Production Association (MVPA)
(213) 387-1590
FAX (213) 385-9507
www.mvpa.com

The National Academy of Television Arts & Sciences New York Chapter
(212) 459-3630
FAX (212) 459-9772
www.nyemmys.org
1375 Broadway, Ste. 2103
(Near 37th St.)
New York, NY 10018

New York Production Alliance (NYPA)
(917) 848-2553
www.nypa.org
Six E. 39 St., Ste. 1200
New York, NY 10016

New York Women in Film & Television
(212) 679-0870
FAX (212) 679-0899
www.nywift.org
Six E. 39th St., 12th Fl.
(Near Madison Ave.)
New York, NY 10016

United Scenic Artists
IA Local USA-829

representing

Production Designers
Art Directors
Scenic Artists
Computer Artists
Art Department Coordinators
Costume Designers
Lighting Designers
Scenic Designers

www.usa829.org

Projectionists (IA Local 306) (212) 956-1306
545 W. 45th St., Second Fl. FAX (212) 956-9306
(Near 10th Ave.)
New York, NY 10036

**Radio and Television Broadcast Engineers
(IBEW Local 1212)** (212) 354-6770
225 W. 34th St., Ste. 1120 FAX (212) 819-9517
(Near Eighth Ave.) www.ibew1212.org
New York, NY 10122

Screen Actors Guild (SAG) (212) 944-1030
360 Madison Ave. (Near 45th St.) FAX (212) 944-6774
New York, NY 10017 www.sag.org

**Script Supervisors, Continuity
Coordinators & Production Office
Coordinators (Local 161)** (212) 977-9655
630 Ninth Ave., Ste. 1103 FAX (212) 977-9609
(Near W. 45th St.) www.local161.org
New York, NY 10036

**Script Supervisors/Continuity &
Allied Production Specialists Guild
(IA Local 871)** (818) 509-7871
11519 Chandler Blvd. FAX (818) 506-1555
North Hollywood, CA 91601 www.ialocal871.org

Set Decorators Society of America (818) 255-2425
7100 Tujunga Ave., Ste. A FAX (818) 982-8597
(Near Sherman Way) www.setdecorators.org
North Hollywood, CA 91605

Society of Camera Operators (SOC) (818) 382-7070
P.O. Box 2006 www.soc.org
Toluca Lake, CA 91610

**Society of Motion Picture &
Television Engineers (SMPTE)** (914) 761-1100
Three Barker Ave. FAX (914) 761-3115
White Plains, NY 10601 www.smpte.org

**The Society of Stage Directors &
Choreographers (SSDC)** (212) 391-1070
1501 Broadway, Ste. 1701
(Near W. 43rd St.) FAX (212) 302-6195
New York, NY 10036 www.ssdc.org

Stage Managers' Association (212) 543-9567
P.O. Box 275, Times Square Station FAX (212) 543-9567
New York, NY 10108 www.stagemanagers.org

Steadicam Operators Association (215) 919-4636
Five Waterford Court www.steadicam-ops.com
Monroe Township, NJ 08831

**Theatrical Stage Employees
(IA Local 1)** (212) 333-2500
320 W. 46th St. (Near Eighth Ave.) FAX (212) 586-2437
New York, NY 10036 www.iatselocalone.org

Theatrical Teamsters (Local 817) (516) 365-3470
One Hollow Ln. FAX (516) 365-2609
(Near New Hyde Park Rd.)
New Hyde Park, NY 11042

Theatrical Wardrobe (IA Local 764) (212) 957-3500
545 W. 45th St., Second Fl. FAX (212) 957-3232
(Near 11th Ave.)
New York, NY 10036

United Scenic Artists (IA Local 829) (212) 581-0300
29 W. 38th St., 15th Fl. FAX (212) 977-2011
(Near Fifth Ave.) www.usa829.org
New York, NY 10018

**Writers Guild of America East
(WGAE)** (212) 767-7800
555 W. 57th St., Ste. 1230 (212) 757-4360
(Near 10th Ave.) FAX (212) 582-1909
New York, NY 10019 www.wgaeast.org

Training Centers

3D Training Institute (212) 967-7777
Three E. 28th St., Eighth Fl. FAX (212) 967-7971
New York, NY 10016 www.3dtraining.com

**Center for Design,
Digital Arts and Film - NYU** (212) 992-3370
145 Fourth Ave., Ste. 219 FAX (212) 995-4674
(Near 13th St.) www.scps.nyu.edu/cada
New York, NY 10003
(Digital Media Training)

**David Zema, Inc./
Voice of Success Programs** (212) 675-4978
1123 Broadway, Ste. 1012 www.davidzema.com
(Near 25th St.)
New York, NY 10010
(Speech & Voice)

Maine Media Workshops (207) 236-8581
70 Camden St., P.O. Box 200 FAX (207) 236-2558
Rockport, ME 04856 www.theworkshops.com
(Digital Media, Post Production & Production)

Manhattan Edit Workshop (212) 414-9570
80 Fifth Ave., Ste. 1501 FAX (212) 372-4483
(Near 14th Street) www.mewshop.com
New York, NY 10011
(Apple, Avid & Editing)

New York Film Academy (212) 674-4300
100 E. 17th St. (Near Park Ave. South) FAX (212) 477-1414
New York, NY 10003 www.nyfa.com
(Filmmaking Workshops)

SAFETY FIRST DIVERS, Inc.

KEVIN BRODLEY
(516) 486-5733

MARINE COORDINATORS / SAG DIVERS

SERVING THE NYC FILM & PRODUCTION INDUSTRY FOR OVER 10 YEARS

- U/W MARINE & STUNT CORRDINATION
- U/W PRODUCTION & STUNT PERSONNEL
- U/W SAFETY PERSONNEL
- USCG LICENSED BOAT CAPTAINS
- SCUBA DIVING INSTRUCTION
- LOCATION SCOUTING

- STUNT SAFETY
- SEARCHES
- BOATS
- SURVEYS
- EQUIPMENT
- RECOVERY

NATIONAL TREASURE, FEAR FACTOR, ANALYZE THAT, SEX AND THE CITY, RANSOM, SWIMFAN, HITCH, CSI-NY, LAW & ORDER, THE SOPRANOS, THE MANCHURIAN CANDIDATE, THE BONE COLLECTOR, VISA, COCA-COLA, ROMANCE & CIGARETTES, DON'T SAY A WORD, BUD LIGHT, LOTTO, VERIZON, MYSTIC SEAPORT

CALL OR CHECK OUR WEBSITE FOR A COMPLETE LIST OF SERVICES & CREDITS

WWW.SAFETYFIRSTDIVERS.COM

Underwater Technicians

Captain Mike's Diving/ Michael Carew (718) 885-1588 / (347) 865-4230
530 City Island Ave. FAX (718) 885-2543
City Island, NY 10464 www.captainmikesdiving.com
(Coordination & Safety Training)

Adam Geiger (774) 563-0068 / (508) 645-2849
www.sealightpictures.com
(Director of Photography & Producer)

David Mansfield (212) 875-1507 / (917) 859-1115
FAX (917) 875-1507
www.wrenvideo.com
(Director of Photography)

Miller's Launch (718) 727-7303
Pier 7 1/2 FAX (718) 448-6326
Staten Island, NY 10301 www.millerslaunch.com
(Marine Coordination, Safety/Rescue & Training)

Never Quit, Inc./Brian Smyj (914) 469-1749
FAX (201) 485-8244
www.neverquitstunts.com

Jim Pearson (661) 222-7342 / (877) 877-9605
(Coordination, Safety & Training) FAX (661) 253-3643
www.cinemarineteam.com

Ⓐ Safety First Divers (516) 486-5733
(Marine Coordination & Water Safety)

Stunt Dept., Inc./Chris Barnes (516) 236-9644
(Marine Coordination & Water Safety) FAX (516) 869-0843
www.stuntdept.com

Jason Velez (917) 497-9128
(Electrician/Gaffer)

Unit Production Managers (DGA NY)

Jacob Abraham	(917) 405-2742
Tevin Adelman	(917) 415-7015
Edwin Atkins	(212) 486-9573 / (917) 861-8024
Mark Baker	(845) 638-4302 / (917) 757-6267 / www.montanartists.com
Richard Baratta	(201) 568-6491 / (917) 797-4750
Moshe Bardach	(212) 580-8164
Caroline Baron	(212) 496-9496
Michael Bederman	(516) 697-2496
Laura Benson	(646) 872-0857
Robert Berman	(201) 337-0095
Alysse Bezahler	(212) 242-5081
James Bigwood	(212) 689-6589 / (917) 312-8103
Donna Bloom	(212) 737-1999 / (310) 392-4134
Chris Bongirne	(917) 806-6747
Ron Bozman	(212) 874-3088
M. Blair Breard	(323) 845-4144 / www.montanartists.com
Chris Brigham	(860) 350-9074
Henry Bronchtein	(973) 809-9869
Ira Brooks	(845) 368-1820 / (917) 861-6084 / FAX (917) 861-6084
G. Mac Brown	(310) 273-6700
Jay Cannold	(212) 755-8560 / (917) 723-0902
Gregg Carlesimo	(914) 271-6654 / (646) 725-3800
William Carraro	(914) 333-0348 / (917) 560-6325
William Robert Chase	(212) 724-9418
Cheryl Quarantiello	(732) 223-9731 / (201) 841-7476 / FAX (732) 292-1060
Doug Claybourne	(818) 601-7700
Celia Costas	(212) 721-5277
Jamie Crowell	(917) 750-0664
Carol Cuddy	(732) 291-3380
David Stevens DeClerque	(908) 273-3174
Barbara DeFina	(212) 219-1525
Ged Dickersin	(347) 404-3845
Lori Douglas	(212) 477-1377 / (917) 714-0851
Scott King Ferguson	(646) 280-8994
Jonathan Filley	(845) 677-9201 / (917) 501-6976
Lindsay Ann Fontana	(917) 693-0006
Paulette Glassman	(212) 369-3010
Christopher Giles Goode	(212) 941-7204
Sherry Greenberg	(212) 665-2723 / (917) 309-5893
Robert Allen Halmi Jr.	(212) 977-9001
Daniel Hank	(212) 769-4429
Michael Paul Hausman	(212) 982-1913
Jeffrey Hayes	(212) 222-8595
Amy Herman	(212) 517-6077
Tony Hernandez	(917) 685-4363
William Earl Hewes	(914) 478-5441
Bonnie Hlinomaz	(917) 992-4749
Samuel Hoffman	(212) 529-1707
Joseph Iberti	(212) 477-0433
Nancy Lee Israel	(914) 548-9413
Caroline Jaczko	(917) 991-7410
Kati Johnston	(212) 691-6428 / (917) 971-5787
Mike Jurkovac	(212) 945-7227
Mark Kamine	(973) 464-6354
David Kappes	(718) 884-1919
Anthony Katagas	(917) 903-8356
Jacqueline Kelman	(212) 741-0288
Debra Susan Kent	(323) 462-6447
Ralph Laucella	(917) 754-5067
Paul Lewis	(212) 447-9887
Sophia Lin	(646) 242-8268
James Maniolas	(212) 477-0704
Jason Manz	(917) 817-0718 / FAX (310) 496-1550
Mark McGann	(212) 691-2789
Kathleen McGill	(732) 775-2588

Margo Myers	(212) 633-9208 / (917) 767-9918 / www.montanartists.com
Julius Nasso	(718) 948-0649
George Paaswell	(917) 882-8152
Lydia Pilcher	(212) 625-9608 / (212) 625-3797
Denise Pinckley	(212) 346-7920
Justin Pollock	(718) 855-8646
Howard Potter	(203) 227-7499
James Price	(917) 447-8173
Jane Erica Raab	(212) 463-8936
Thomas A. Reilly	(914) 241-8455
Rebecca Rivo	(718) 783-0997
Dana Robin	(914) 763-1984 / (914) 260-3205
Michael Romero	(917) 449-4252
Richard Schlesinger	(212) 529-8070
Diana Schmidt-O'Brien	(212) 751-2310 / (917) 991-8358
Jenny Schweitzer	(917) 304-4560
Jonathan Shoemaker	(212) 678-5487
Michael Smith	(973) 367-5031 / (917) 328-1085
John Starke	(631) 286-0335 / (631) 275-2598
Jeffery Stolow	(212) 249-3138 / (917) 301-7128
Susan Ann Stover	(917) 224-6249
Michael Stricks	(212) 777-3715 / (917) 282-8047
Bergen Swanson	(917) 405-0842
Robin Sweet	(201) 344-2936
Neri Tannenbaum	(917) 373-1305 / (212) 362-2017
Peter David Thorell	(646) 263-7290
Joan Vitaliano	(914) 469-3198
Anthony Vozza	(917) 991-7899
Victoria Westhead	(718) 797-2211
Mari Jo Winkler	(212) 431-4204
Robin Winter-Young	(917) 698-2507
Dany Wolf	(212) 683-1535
Jonathan David Wolf	(212) 721-8696
Eden Wurmfeld	(212) 627-9898
Charles Zalben	(212) 243-1904 / (917) 678-5690

Andy Zuch
Digital Multi Camera Video Assist
with STORMVISION
Matching • Chroma Key • Wireless
And I Always Bring A Smile!

917.213.5549 cell
516.541.0832
GreenFlagLtd@aol.com

Green Flag, Ltd.

VTR Operators (Local 52 NY)

Andrew Albanese	(845) 735-3294
Rico Omega Alston	(646) 785-4916
Matthew J. Andersen	(516) 333-1257 / (877) 717-0429
Brigette Barnes	(201) 955-1195 / (908) 782-1160
Ronald A. Bernknopf	(732) 830-2113
Alan Buchner	(212) 794-8865 / (917) 070-4709
Clement Canino Jr. (Digital)	(973) 586-9613
Brian Carmichael	(201) 656-4828 / (917) 549-4307
Andrew Cavagnet	(201) 406-6824
Arthur J. Cavallo Jr.	(732) 241-7917 / (908) 712-8813
John Coumarbatch	(718) 565-6194
Gregory Crouser	(845) 255-0353 / (518) 221-4147
David Cugno	(718) 667-1823 / (917) 874-1123
Robert Daraio	(914) 774-2646
James Domorski Jr.	(732) 870-3570
Devin Donegan	(732) 785-9593 / (732) 620-0295
Gregory Edwards	(718) 398-0515
Mc Cord Fitzsimmons	(212) 960-3444
Max E. Frankston	(917) 632-2311 / (212) 661-9300
Nicholas C. Gould	(717) 392-0460 / (717) 380-6064
Peter Grace	(917) 593-5319

FLAT SCREENS · KEYING · WIRELESS
AUSTIN SALISBURY
MULTI-CAM · COLOR PRINTS · AVID

212 777 2121   917 991 4966

ADAM SMELIN enterprises
full-service video assist
914 420 4022

Emily Haddad	(347) 265-9379 (347) 227-8822	David Scott Leibowitz	(201) 836-6712 (917) 949-5848
Michael Hawrylak	(201) 434-7032 (201) 519-5179	Demetrius Lewis	(215) 232-0105 (267) 250-5452
Joel Holland	(914) 271-3648 (914) 494-6319 www.featurevideo.com	William M. Marino	(516) 867-0549
Catherine Isabella	(212) 666-8948	Ⓐ Lionel A. Marks	(845) 638-0961 (914) 843-4030
Stanley F. James	(973) 744-5405 (201) 346-2634	Neida Martinez	(718) 278-1749 (347) 513-5697
Nils Johnson	(201) 576-0758 (917) 935-6758	Kevin McKenna	(914) 693-5861 (914) 924-2064
Brian M. Jordan	(215) 482-3785 (215) 205-2883	Kevin Mosley	(914) 771-6440
Steven Joyce	(973) 652-1530 (201) 392-7710	Christopher M. Murphy	(484) 322-0640 (484) 322-0641
Philippe R. Labeau	(718) 636-1437 (917) 751-8588	James Murphy	(917) 750-0762
Richard Le Fande	(718) 855-7809 (617) 899-0380	Alexander Nobbs	(803) 312-5687 (732) 870-3570
		Reginald Ollen	(917) 612-7604 (718) 398-8155

Lionel Marks
Digital Video Assist
Playback & Effects

845-638-0961
Cell: 914-843-4030

Email: lionmarks@aol.com

VTR Operators (Local 52 NY)

Donna Puntolillo	(212) 595-9564	Igor Srubshchik	(917) 776-5434 / (718) 256-3076
Steven Robinson	(917) 348-4998 / (212) 567-7611 / FAX (212) 567-0941	Roman A. Sypko	(914) 878-7960 / (917) 467-7357
Gustave Roccaforte	(516) 223-5879	Aaron Trammell	(732) 872-1679 / (732) 373-4560
Barry Russo	(201) 871-9697	Joseph E. Trammell	(212) 244-7177 / (212) 244-5495
Darren Ryan	(212) 362-8558 / (732) 768-8380	T. Ray Treece	(646) 319-5790
Ⓐ David A. (Austin) Salisbury Jr.	(212) 777-2121 / (917) 991-4966	Howard Weiner	(212) 864-1408
Daniel R. Salk	(212) 242-4387 / (917) 898-0041	Derrick L. West	(201) 637-6992 / (845) 353-3032
Michael Sime	(973) 332-6425 / (973) 239-3964 / FAX (973) 239-3965 / www.visualalchemy.tv	David Zimmern	(917) 723-6565 / (718) 352-1686
		Ⓐ Andy Zuch	(516) 541-0832 / (917) 213-5549
Ⓐ Adam Smelin	(914) 420-4022	Steven N. Zuch	(631) 367-7112 / (646) 772-0420

VTR Operators

Rhys Carpenter	(212) 781-1375 / (917) 597-1546 / FAX (208) 246-4793	Arturo Lopez	(212) 620-5530 / (917) 800-5057 / FAX (212) 620-5531 / www.playbackny.com
Alex Catcherelli	(661) 312-8674 / www.videorama.com	Kenneth Myers	(866) 322-6039 / (203) 912-4505 / FAX (203) 322-6039
Ⓐ Lee Hopp	(917) 838-3956 / FAX (201) 430-3898 / www.lhvideoservices.com	Nimmers Stern	(917) 332-8293
Peter Kremer	(203) 975-7999	A Video Village, Inc.	(484) 322-0641 / (888) 223-5515 / www.videovillage.com

Wardrobe Stylists/Costume Designers (Local 829 NY)

Marie Abma	(212) 460-5327 / (917) 834-5582 www.thegelleragency.com
Shea Alvarez	(917) 596-6618 www.sheaalvarez.com
Michael Anzalone	(212) 928-9075 / (917) 757-6155
Campbell Baird	(212) 633-1953 / (908) 387-1994
Gail Baldoni	(212) 861-2431
Stacey Battat	(212) 989-1018 / (917) 687-1050
Anna-Alisa Belous	(917) 658-0616 / (212) 923-3720
Suzy Benzinger	(212) 343-2939
Amy C Bradshaw	(718) 833-4723 / (917) 817-9680
Martha Louise Bromelmeier	(718) 727-1082 / (646) 334-2356
Nancy Brous	(212) 924-4591 / (917) 741-7040 www.nancybrous.com
Zack Brown	(718) 832-4677 FAX (718) 832-4679
Astrid Brucker	(212) 995-0246 / (917) 518-5134 www.astrid3d.com
Michael J. Cesario	(212) 787-0075
Patrick M. Chevillot	(212) 724-2123
Marie Anne Chiment	(212) 228-9775 / (314) 779-0153
Michael Clancy	(212) 545-7895 www.nyoffice.net
Amanda (Amy) Clark	(917) 841-9591
Daniel James Cole	(646) 824-5483
Sarah Conly	(212) 865-3294
Virginia Cook	(917) 306-3807
Lucy Corrigan	(917) 312-6134
Laura Crow	(860) 486-1625 / (860) 487-6020 FAX (860) 486-3110
Lynne Curtis	(718) 260-9565 / (917) 373-7848
Vicki R. Davis	(607) 829-3246
Liz Deutsch	(212) 255-0079 / (917) 841-8907
Candice Donnelly	(212) 243-2992 FAX (212) 243-2992
John Dunn	(212) 997-1818 www.gershagency.com
Tina Fagin-Tuttman	(212) 628-0905
Lynn Falconer	(212) 545-7895 www.nyoffice.net
Victoria Farrell	(917) 687-5174
Trayce G. Field	(917) 887-9367
Linda Fisher	(212) 799-4506
Frank Fleming	(323) 845-4144 www.montanartists.com
Jacci Fredenburg	(315) 882-1802
Sue Gandy	(212) 873-8104 FAX (212) 873-8104
Randy Gardell	(718) 383-7684 / (213) 810-8383
Jenny Gering	(212) 545-7895 www.nyoffice.net
A. Christina Giannini	(212) 666-3649 / (917) 690-6958 www.costumebystia.com
Sharon Globerson	(646) 924-6447
Jess Goldstein	(917) 696-6597
Jane Greenwood	(212) 929-2931 FAX (212) 929-9548
Zulema Griffin	(212) 473-0963
Emily Gunshor	(917) 415-7224
Jimm Halliday	(631) 383-1590
Jennifer Halpern	(212) 928-0186 / (917) 657-2635
Bruce Harrow	(212) 673-4289 FAX (212) 260-5131
Gail Cooper Hecht	(212) 475-4836
Sandra Hernandez	(212) 253-6900 www.innovativeartists.com
Thomas Brian Heyer	(212) 868-1050
John Hirsch	(516) 365-7445
Constance Hoffman	(212) 643-2880
Sarah J. Holden	(310) 652-8778 www.lspagency.net
Ann Marie Hould-Ward	(212) 262-7480
Elissa T. Iberti	(212) 477-0433
Daphne E. Javitch	(646) 621-4328
Gary Jones	(310) 273-6700 www.utaproduction.com
Eric Justian	(212) 533-8430
Renee A. Kalfus	(914) 762-9587

Joan Kaufman	(212) 206-9781
Anne Kenney	(917) 826-9089
Karen Hummel Kinsley	(845) 357-4103
Paula Kowalczyk	(212) 242-7284 / (917) 744-6120 / www.paulakowalcyzk.com
Barbra Kravitz	(215) 790-1729 / FAX (215) 790-0120
Whitney Kyles	(212) 281-9183 / (646) 337-4933
Natasha Landau	(212) 753-8490 / (917) 667-9779 / FAX (518) 781-3002 / www.natashalandau.net
Suttirat Larlarb	(323) 845-4144 / www.montanartists.com
Daniel L. Lawson	(973) 783-1953
Karen Ledger	(267) 974-3810
Pilar Limosner	(917) 674-5023
William Ivey Long	(212) 929-7846 / FAX (212) 627-9441
Carol Luiken	(845) 225-5661
Judanna Lynn	(718) 268-7316
Kasia Walicka Maimone	(323) 460-4767 / www.jacobandkoleagency.com
Stephanie Maslansky	(347) 529-4676 / (323) 845-4144
Donna Massimo	(716) 881-4310 / (716) 645-6754
Ingrid Maurer	(212) 406-5080 / (917) 733-9451 / FAX (212) 406-5080 / www.geocities.com/maurer_i
Mimi Maxmen	(212) 260-7712 / (917) 940-3485
Michelle McDonald	(917) 705-1529 / www.dripbook.com/michellemcdonaldsttylist/splash/
Pat Meyers	(212) 366-1434 / (917) 319-2274
Mia Morgan	(212) 935-0200 / FAX (212) 935-2698 / www.miamorgan.com
David Murin	(212) 260-5969 / FAX (212) 358-7610
Kathryn Nixon	(212) 545-7895 / www.nyoffice.net
Catherine F. Norgren	(716) 884-7463 / (716) 570-8479
Carol Oditz	(212) 253-6900 / www.innovativeartists.com
Juliet Ouyoung	(212) 569-5864 / FAX (212) 569-5864 / www.jouyoung.com
Richard Owings	(917) 848-3635 / (212) 534-2153 / FAX (212) 633-8726
Matthew Pachtman	(516) 996-4815 / (516) 763-1107
Devon Painter	(646) 621-3863 / www.devonpainter.com
Robert Perdziola	(212) 366-1815
Juliet Polcsa	(201) 792-3131
Rosemary Ponzo	(212) 463-7971 / (917) 859-6601 / FAX (212) 463-7999 / www.rosemaryponzo.com
Valerie Marcus Ramshur	(917) 449-8668 / www.vmramshur.com
Michele Reisch	(212) 247-5394 / (347) 831-7668
Jennifer Robespierre	(646) 456-8433
David Robinson	(718) 522-5148 / (310) 273-6700 / www.utaproduction.com
Helen E. Rodgers	(201) 946-1657 / (917) 940-7418
Molly Rogers	(646) 246-7200
Hilary Rosenfeld	(914) 763-4633 / (914) 282-3764 / FAX (914) 977-3182
Katherine B. Roth	(212) 255-8536
Isabel Rubio	(718) 797-4353 / (917) 539-7076 / FAX (718) 797-4353
Austin K. Sanderson	(201) 915-0744
Patricia Sarnataro	(917) 701-6271 / FAX (212) 966-5197
Sidney Shane	(917) 586-5340
Moira Shaughnessy	(212) 736-4270 / (917) 664-7454
Elizabeth Shein	(212) 582-8052 / (917) 816-0600
Elizabeth Shelton	(718) 788-3424 / (917) 930-5316
Laurita Shields	(212) 281-8530 / (917) 690-6125
Eduardo Sicangco	(212) 989-3408 / FAX (212) 929-2825
Jessica Sinoway	(718) 263-4178 / (917) 501-6165
Teresa Snider-Stein	(914) 478-4961 / FAX (917) 991-7688
Laura Solin	(212) 529-2177 / (917) 676-5667 / www.nycstylist.com
Theresa Squire	(212) 741-1870 / (917) 783-6972

John Stegmeir	(718) 956-0645	Alejo Vietti	(212) 414-0292 / (917) 701-3438
Debra Stein	(212) 627-3543	Elizabeth Caitlin Ward	(212) 545-7895
			www.nyoffice.net
Steven Stines	(212) 581-4486 / FAX (212) 245-7215 / www.stevenstines.com	Angela Wendt	(212) 533-7112 / FAX (212) 533-7112 / www.angela.wendt.net
Muriel Stockdale	(212) 475-1875 / (646) 522-3819	Amanda Mary Whidden	(718) 788-2011
Catherine Thomas	(323) 845-4144 / www.montanartists.com	Kim Wilcox	(347) 831-3887 / www.kimwilcox.net
David Toser	(212) 942-4283	Gabriela Stanciu Willingham	(917) 721-2177
Mattie Ullrich	(212) 997-1818 / (917) 406-7494 / www.mattieullrich.com	David Woolard	(917) 747-5772
		Antonia Xereas	(212) 274-1855 / (917) 406-2485
Marleen Venantini	(516) 487-7262 / (516) 816-2324	David F. Zambrana	(347) 564-7532 / www.davidfzambrana.com

Wardrobe Stylists/Costume Designers

Aartist Loft (212) 274-0961
580 Broadway, Ste. 606 FAX (212) 274-0962
(Near W. Houston) www.aartistloft.com
New York, NY 10012
(Reps for Wardrobe Stylists/Costume Designers)

Irene Albright (212) 977-7350
www.albrightnyc.com

All Crew Agency (818) 206-0144
2920 W. Olive Ave., Ste. 201 FAX (818) 206-0169
Burbank, CA 91505 www.allcrewagency.com
(Reps for Wardrobe Stylists/Costume Designers)

(212) 741-3240
Manuela Amzallag (781) 863-1555
www.ennisinc.com

Johanna Argan (212) 545-7895
www.nyoffice.net

Art Department (212) 925-4222
48 Greene St., Fourth Fl. FAX (212) 925-4422
(Near Broome St.) www.art-dept.com
New York, NY 10013
(Reps for Wardrobe Stylists)

Artists by Timothy Priano (212) 929-7771
131 Varick St., Ste. 905 FAX (212) 929-7760
New York, NY 10013 www.artistsbytimothypriano.com
(Reps for Wardrobe Stylists)

Andre Austin (212) 545-7895
www.nyoffice.net

Victoria Auth (212) 253-6900
www.innovativeartists.com

Varya Avdyushko (310) 652-8778
www.lspagency.net

B. (212) 643-1736
www.themagnetagency.com

Amela Baksic (212) 643-1736
www.cec-entertainment.com

Britt Bardo (212) 352-3223
www.magnetny.com

Emily Barnes (212) 255-2500
www.seemanagement.com

Brenda Barr (212) 279-1999
www.markedwardinc.com

Shawn Barton (310) 652-8778
www.lspagency.net

Linda Bass (212) 253-6900
www.innovativeartists.com

Monique Bean (212) 352-3223
www.themagnetagency.com

Jenny Beavan (310) 273-6700
www.unitedtalent.com

Sarah Beers (323) 845-4144
www.montanartists.com

Robert Behar (310) 458-7800
www.partos.com

Fifi Bell (323) 299-4043
www.dionperonneau.com

Alycia Belle (323) 460-4767
www.jacobandkoleagency.com

Erin Benach (310) 652-8778
www.lspagency.net

Rebecca Bentjen (212) 997-1818
www.gershagency.com

Rob Bevenger (917) 225-6071

Lois Bewley (212) 752-7573

Anna Bingemann (212) 352-3223
www.magnetny.com

Heidi Bivens (310) 652-8778
www.lspagency.net

Marissa Borsetto (212) 253-6900
www.innovativeartists.com

Penelope Bouklas (212) 206-0901
www.halleyresources.com

Kim Bowen (212) 352-3223
www.magnetny.com

Michael T. Boyd (212) 253-6900
www.innovativeartists.com

(516) 944-8999
Branching Out Productions, Inc. (516) 652-5036
(Reps for Wardrobe Stylists) FAX (516) 944-8998
www.branchingoutpro.com

Mark Bridges (310) 273-6700
www.utaproduction.com

Tom Broecker (212) 997-1818
www.gershagency.com

Stephen Brown (646) 337-7878

(212) 643-1736
Melissa Bruning (323) 377-5353
www.melissabruning.com

Katherine Jane Bryant (323) 856-3000
www.thegelleragency.com

Dana Campbell (310) 652-8778
www.lspagency.net

Candice Carella (310) 458-7800
www.partos.com

Ruth Carter (212) 253-6900
www.innovativeartists.com

Michael J. Cesario (212) 787-0075
FAX (212) 787-0075

Tim Chappel (212) 997-1818
www.gershagency.com

Lulu Chen (212) 935-0200
www.bryanbantry.com

Marie Anne Chiment (212) 228-9775
www.chiment.com

Wendy Chuck (212) 253-6900
www.innovativeartists.com

Stefano Ciocca (212) 242-7050
www.clickmodel.com/illusions.php

Garth Condit (212) 929-7771
www.artistsbytimothypriano.com

Caron Coplan	(212) 288-1009		Wendi Farkas	(585) 461-9711
				FAX (585) 461-9170
				www.farkasproductions.com
James Corry	(212) 366-4888			
	(212) 366-4115		April Ferry	(310) 273-6700
Betsy Cox	(212) 253-6900			www.utaproduction.com
	www.innovativeartists.com			
			Tina Whitney Firestone	(212) 255-4078
Ane Crabtree	(310) 652-8778			(917) 331-9108
	www.lspagency.net			FAX (212) 255-4078
Carol Cutshall	(310) 652-8778			(212) 799-4506
	www.lspagency.net		Linda Fisher	(917) 453-3047
				FAX (212) 799-4506
Jerome Darby	(212) 924-8505			
	www.therighteye.com		Mary Jane Fort	(212) 997-1818
				www.gershagency.com
Dawn to Dusk Agency	(212) 431-8631			
	(323) 850-6783		Leslie Fremar	(212) 352-3223
(Reps for Wardrobe Stylists)	www.dawn2duskagency.com			www.magnetny.com
Tracie Delaney	(310) 458-7800		Louise Frogley	(310) 273-6700
	www.partos.com			www.utaproduction.com
Sophie de Rakoff	(212) 352-3223			(212) 608-2456
	www.themagnetagency.com		Toni Fusco-Wickham	(646) 831-3012
				www.tonifusco.com
Sarah de Sa Rego	(212) 997-1818			
	www.gershagency.com		Amit Gajwani	(212) 279-1999
				www.markedwardinc.com
Melissa Des Rosiers	(310) 458-7800			
	www.partos.com		Pierre-Yves Gayraud	(310) 652-8778
				www.lspagency.net
Marie-Sylvie Deveau	(212) 997-1818			
	www.gershagency.com		The Geller Agency	(323) 856-3000
			1547 Cassil Pl.	FAX (323) 856-3009
Naima DiFranco	(212) 255-2500		Hollywood, CA 90028	www.thegelleragency.com
	www.seemanagement.com		(Reps for Costume Designers)	
			Geren	(212) 352-3223
Dion Peronneau Agency	(323) 299-4043			www.magnetny.com
(Reps for Wardrobe Stylists)	FAX (323) 299-4269			
	www.dionperonneau.com			(212) 997-1818
			The Gersh Agency	(310) 274-6611
Cathy Dixon	(212) 925-4222		41 Madison Ave., 33rd Fl.	FAX (212) 997-1978
	www.art-dept.com		(Near E. 26th St.)	www.gershagency.com
			New York, NY 10010	
Mynka Draper	(212) 997-1818		(Reps for Wardrobe Stylists/Costume Designers)	
	www.gershagency.com			
			Edi Giguere	(914) 834-3295
Tere Duncan	(310) 652-8778			(917) 667-7607
	www.lspagency.net			
			Adam Glassman	(212) 935-0200
Ionia Dunn-Lee	(212) 242-7050			www.bryanbantry.com
	www.clickmodel.com/illusions.php			
			Sharon Globerson	(646) 924-6447
Janet Eiger	(914) 741-6215			
	(914) 523-3387		Elisa Goodkind	(914) 261-6511
Eileen Eisele	(212) 741-3240		Sarah Gore-Reeves	(212) 925-4222
	www.ennisinc.com			www.art-dept.com
Lauri Eisenberg	(646) 453-1585		Gloria Gresham	(310) 273-6700
	www.eamgmt.com			www.utaproduction.com
Gay Morris Empson	(212) 935-0200		Jonas Hallberg	(646) 453-1585
	www.bryanbantry.com			www.eamgmt.com
Nicoletta Ercole	(310) 822-9113		Halley Resources	(212) 206-0901
	www.murthaagency.com		231 W. 29th St., Ste. 701	FAX (212) 206-0904
			(Near Seventh Ave.)	www.halleyresources.com
Leesa Evans	(212) 352-3223		New York, NY 10001	
			(Reps for Wardrobe Stylists/Costume Designers)	
Jennifer Eve	(212) 545-7895			
	www.nyoffice.net		Enid Harris	(323) 856-3000
				www.thegelleragency.com
Exclusive Artists Management	(646) 453-1585			
596 Broadway, Ste. 601	(646) 453-1583		Tiffany Hasbourne	(212) 242-7050
New York, NY 10012	www.eamgmt.com			www.clickmodel.com/illusions.php
(Reps for Wardrobe Stylists)				
			Dawn Haynes	(212) 431-8631
				www.dawn2duskagency.com

Wardrobe Stylists/Costume Designers

Sanja Hays (212) 253-6900
www.innovativeartists.com

Betsy Heimann (310) 273-6700
www.utaproduction.com

Frank Helmer (212) 253-6900
www.innovativeartists.com

Lindy Hemming (310) 273-6700
www.utaproduction.com

Shawnique Hill (973) 614-8582

Erin Hirsh (212) 352-3223
www.themagnetagency.com

Charlett Hobart (212) 673-0186

Cliff Hoppus (646) 453-1585
www.eamgmt.com

Seth Howard (212) 929-7771
www.artistsbytimothypriano.com

Judy Ruskin Howell (941) 809-7286
(310) 652-8778
www.lspagency.net

Susan Hum (917) 855-8791
(718) 852-8345

Beverley Hyde (212) 545-7895
www.nyoffice.net

Illusions Management (212) 242-7050
129 W. 27th St., PH (Near Sixth Ave.) FAX (212) 206-6228
New York, NY 10001 www.clickmodel.com/illusions.php
(Reps for Wardrobe Stylists)

Innovative Artists (212) 253-6900
235 Park Ave. South, Seventh Fl.
New York, NY 10003 www.innovativeartists.com
(Reps for Wardrobe Stylists/Costume Designers)

Arika Itskovich (212) 255-2500
www.seemanagement.com

Francine Jamison-Tanchuck (310) 273-6700
www.utaproduction.com

April Johnson (212) 545-7895
www.nyoffice.net

Carlton Jones (212) 431-8631
www.dawn2duskagency.com

Renee Kalfus (914) 762-9587

Michael Kaplan (310) 273-6700
www.utaproduction.com

Daniell Kays (212) 352-3223
www.magnetny.com

Tad Keil (212) 935-0200
www.bryanbantry.com

Linda Kell (212) 206-0901
www.halleyresources.com

The Kids (212) 352-3223
www.themagnetagency.com

Jill A. Kliber (212) 545-7895
www.nyoffice.net

Michael Kucmeroski (212) 925-4222
www.art-dept.com

Rachel Sage Kunin (212) 253-6900
www.innovativeartists.com

Jeffrey Kurland (310) 273-6700
www.utaproduction.com

Laurent Laborie (212) 206-0901
www.halleyresources.com

Wallace G. (Woody) Lane Jr. (917) 453-6695
(323) 856-3000
www.thegelleragency.com

Alison Lang (646) 275-0280
www.llmgmt.com

Sylvia Lantz (323) 856-3000
www.thegelleragency.com

Tina Latonero (212) 673-5509
www.rjbennettrepresents.com

Christopher Lawrence (212) 253-6900
www.innovativeartists.com

Francine Lecoultre (323) 856-3000
www.thegelleragency.com

Freddie Leiba (212) 935-0200
www.bryanbantry.com

Phyllis Leibowitz (212) 627-1436
(917) 881-3429

Elysha Lenkin (212) 741-3240
www.ennisinc.com

Kevin Lennox (212) 279-1999
www.markedwardinc.com

George Liddle (310) 822-9143
www.murthaagency.com

George L. Little (212) 253-6900
www.innovativeartists.com

Janine Maggiore (212) 741-3240
www.ennisinc.com

Molly Maginnis (212) 253-6900
www.innovativeartists.com

Magnet NY (212) 352-3223
270 Lafayette St., Ste. 901 FAX (212) 941-7441
New York, NY 10012 www.themagnetagency.com
(Reps for Wardrobe Stylists)

Daria Maneche (212) 741-3240
(781) 863-1555
www.ennisinc.com

Bobbie Mannix (310) 995-0803
FAX (661) 251-9321
www.bobbiemannix.com

Maria-Stefania (212) 206-0901
www.halleyresources.com

Rosealee Martinez (212) 741-3240
www.ennisinc.com

Michelle Martini (212) 352-3223
www.magnetny.com

Stephanie Maslansky (917) 846-2318
(323) 845-4144

Evelyn Mason (212) 663-7957

Agata Maszkiewicz (323) 856-3000
www.thegelleragency.com

Maude (212) 352-3223
www.themagnetagency.com

Kelly McDermott	(212) 741-3240 www.ennisinc.com		Lauren Niles	(212) 741-3240 www.ennisinc.com
Robin McGee	(917) 690-4958 www.rlmcgeedesign.com		Patricia Norris	(310) 822-9113 www.murthaagency.com
Roger McKenzie	(212) 926-0477 www.tapestryinc.com		Shelley Norton	(917) 541-9029
Winsome McKoy	(718) 399-2503		Mary-Margaret O'Neill	(212) 643-1736 www.cec-entertainment.com
Deborah McLean	(212) 206-0901 www.halleyresources.com		Kathy O'Rear	(310) 822-9113 www.murthaagency.com
Mimi Melgaard	(212) 253-6900 www.innovativeartists.com		Daniel Orlandi	(310) 273-6700 www.unitedtalent.com
Michele Michel	(310) 652-8778 www.lspagency.net		Eric Orlando	(212) 255-2500 www.seemanagement.com
Roseann Milano	(973) 338-0890 (973) 945-9042		Paradigm 360 Park Ave. South 16th Fl., Ste. 900 (Near Seventh Ave.) New York, NY 10001 (Reps for Costume Designers)	(212) 897-6400 FAX (212) 764-8941 www.paradigmagency.com
Eden Miller	(646) 641-3336 (718) 832-3669 www.edenmiller.com			
Francesca Mills	(212) 935-0200 www.bryanbantry.com		Oneita Parker	(212) 545-7895 www.nyoffice.net
Louise Mingenbach	(310) 273-6700 www.utaproduction.com		Partos Company 227 Broadway, Ste. 204 Santa Monica, CA 90401 (Reps for Wardrobe Stylists)	(310) 458-7800 FAX (310) 587-2250 www.partos.com
The Mirisch Agency 1925 Century Park East, Ste. 1070 Los Angeles, CA 90067 (Reps for Costume Designers)	(310) 282-9940 FAX (310) 282-0702 www.mirisch.com		Beth Pasternak	(212) 997-1818 www.gershagency.com
Elaine Montalvo	(323) 856-3000 www.thegelleragency.com		Beatrix Aruna Pasztor	(212) 997-1818 www.gershagency.com
Montana Artists Agency 7715 W. Sunset Blvd., Third Fl. Los Angeles, CA 90046 (Reps for Wardrobe Stylists/Costume Designers)	(323) 845-4144 FAX (323) 845-4155 www.montanartists.com		Karen Patch	(310) 273-6700 www.utaproduction.com
			Joseph Porro	(212) 997-1818 www.gershagency.com
Vanessa Moore	(212) 925-4222 www.art-dept.com		Stacy Quackenbush	(212) 741-3240 www.ennisinc.com
Lindsay Moremen	(212) 929-7771 www.artistsbytimothypriano.com		Alysia Raycraft	(917) 685-2236 (310) 656-5151 www.alysiaraycraft.com
Beth Morgan	(323) 856-3000 www.thegelleragency.com		Michele Rede	(323) 856-3000 www.thegelleragency.com
Kathryn Morrison	(212) 253-6900 www.innovativeartists.com		The Right Eye 41 Union Square West, Ste. 1004 (Near W. 16th St.) New York, NY 10003 (Reps for Wardrobe Stylists/Costume Designers)	(212) 924-8505 FAX (212) 924-8544 www.therighteye.com
Chrissy Morton	(310) 458-7800 www.partos.com			
Priska Myer	(212) 255-2500 www.seemanagement.com			
			Carrie Robbins	(212) 564-8625 FAX (212) 239-7148 www.peaceablykingdomish.com
Mary Myers	(212) 509-9720 FAX (212) 509-9720			
April Napier	(212) 352-3223 www.magnetny.com		Aggie Rodgers	(323) 460-4767 www.jacobandkoleagency.com
New York Office 15 W. 26th St., Fifth Fl. (Near Broadway) New York, NY 10010 (Reps for Costume Designers)	(212) 545-7895 (323) 468-2240 FAX (212) 545-7941 www.nyoffice.net		Deidre Rodriguez	(212) 673-5509 www.rjbennettrepresents.com
			Jesse Rodriguez	(212) 206-0901 www.halleyresources.com
			Margo Rohan	(212) 206-0901 www.halleyresources.com
Ha Nguyen	(212) 997-1818 www.gershagency.com		Shoshana Rubin	(212) 253-6900 www.innovativeartists.com
Eric Niemand	(212) 929-7771 www.artistsbytimothypriano.com			

Wardrobe Stylists/Costume Designers

Isabel Rubio	(718) 797-4353 (917) 539-7076 FAX (718) 797-4353	Amy Stofsky	(323) 856-3000 www.thegelleragency.com
Rachel M. Rumann	(917) 379-4771 www.nakedstylist.com	Thomas Stokes	(917) 204-0336
Alexa Ryan	(212) 929-7771 www.artistsbytimothypriano.com	Casey Storm	(212) 352-3223 www.magnetny.com
Sharon Ryan	(212) 206-0901 www.halleyresources.com	Francine Tint	(212) 475-3366
		Annabel Tollman	(212) 352-3223 www.magnetny.com
Anita Salerno	(212) 673-5509 www.rjbennettrepresents.com	Michi Tomimatsu	(310) 458-7800 www.partos.com
Bud Santora	(212) 724-8998	Frances Tulk-Hart	(212) 255-2500 www.seemanagement.com
Nicoletta Santoro	(212) 925-4222 www.art-dept.com	Julie Vogel	(917) 520-7490
Peggy Schnitzer	(212) 997-1818 www.gershagency.com	Mary Vogt	(212) 997-1818 www.gershagency.com
Deborah Scott	(212) 997-1818 www.gershagency.com	Keith Wager	(310) 458-7800 www.partos.com
See Management 307 Seventh Ave., Ste. 1607 New York, NY 10001 (Reps for Wardrobe Stylists)	(212) 255-2500 FAX (212) 255-2020 www.seemanagement.com	Mariah Walker	(212) 925-4222 www.art-dept.com
		Ise White	(212) 929-7771 www.artistsbytimothypriano.com
Korey Seney	(212) 741-3240 (781) 863-1555 www.ennisinc.com	Cindy Whitehead	(212) 279-1999 www.markedwardinc.com
Sadia Seymour	(212) 206-0901 www.halleyresources.com	Beth Wickwire	(212) 741-3240 www.ennisinc.com
Laura Jean Shannon	(212) 634-8114 (212) 315-4275 www.partos.com	Stefan Wiklund	(212) 206-0901 www.halleyresources.com
Elizabeth Shelton	(718) 788-3424 (917) 930-3010	Kim Wilcox	(347) 831-3887
Shereese	(323) 299-4043 www.dionperonneau.com	Michael Wilkinson	(310) 273-6700 www.unitedtalent.com
Sara Jane Slotnick	(323) 856-3000 www.thegelleragency.com	Christie Wittenborn	(212) 545-7895 www.nyoffice.net
Katia Stano	(212) 253-6900 www.innovativeartists.com	Anne Wlaysewski	(212) 673-5509 www.rjbennettrepresents.com
Tui Stark	(212) 741-3240 www.ennisinc.com	Johnny Wujek	(212) 352-3223 www.magnetny.com
Jewels Steger	(212) 352-3223 www.themagnetagency.com	Jo Ynocencio	(212) 348-5332
		Nana N. Yoshida	(917) 863-9492 www.yncouture.net
Nancy Steiner	(212) 352-3223 www.magnetny.com	Laura Zanotti	(212) 741-3240 www.ennisinc.com
Eric Stern	(212) 673-5509 www.rjbennettrepresents.com	Mary Zophres	(310) 273-6700 www.utaproduction.com

Wardrobe Supervisors (Local 764 NY)

Pamela L. Aaron	(718) 369-2274 / (484) 213-6752
Arlynn Abseck	(917) 864-8826
Amy Acton	(646) 234-6765
Michael Adkins	(212) 663-2854 / (917) 913-6408
Nanzi Adzima	(732) 826-5709
Mark Agnes	(212) 543-0519
Timothy Alberts	(212) 362-9415
Jennifer Anderson	(212) 595-3699 / (917) 532-9383
Jill Anderson	(914) 762-1694 / (646) 483-8548
Lara Anderson	(516) 320-4727
Denise Andres	(973) 783-4324 / (201) 615-9089
Amelia Andrews	(646) 567-8263
Michael Anzalone	(212) 928-9075 / (917) 757-6155
Natalie Arango	(212) 665-4980 / (646) 436-1674
Jennifer Arnold	(212) 684-0449
Jill Arnold-Pallad	(917) 459-2317
Susan Bakula	(347) 529-5481 / (347) 613-6205
Pattie Barbosa	(917) 723-3494 / (718) 851-6973 / FAX (718) 851-6973
Thomas Beall	(212) 862-8259
Stephanie Biear	(201) 583-9559 / (917) 968-2038
Ghilaine Bouadana	(201) 248-8270
Tommy Boyer	(212) 265-5825 / (917) 841-4913 / FAX (212) 268-1210 / www.wardrobesupplies.com
Micheline Brown	(718) 622-3737 / (917) 650-6835
Jennifer Bryan	(323) 342-0508 / (323) 605-8552
Laurie Buehler	(603) 493-3667 / (603) 670-4208
Amy Burt	(646) 456-9040
Erin Byrne	(973) 715-3895
Gifford Byrne	(917) 586-0465
Danielle Cadorette-Acehan	(646) 257-0725
William Campbell	(718) 852-0525 / (310) 392-6115
Rose Marie Cappelluti	(201) 615-8098
Mary (Mickey) Carleton	(718) 302-4641 / (347) 623-5099
Yolanda Carter	(413) 219-4689
Justine Chevalier	(917) 770-9297
Danajean Cicerchi	(212) 757-6472 / (646) 522-3731
Sonja Cizmazia	(917) 653-2313
Magdalene Clayton	(914) 316-5251
Pashelle Clayton	(212) 932-3493 / (917) 202-4860
Nile Cmylo	(212) 219-2183 / (917) 860-7967
Diana Collins	(718) 796-1913 / (646) 228-6681
Susan Cook	(212) 932-0253
Lorraine Coppin	(718) 777-0720 / (917) 523-0430
John Corbo	(917) 569-3959
Rachel Cottle	(718) 935-9469 / (917) 974-9381
Douglas Couture	(212) 932-8763
Lisa Marzolf Craig	(917) 601-5606
Gerald Crawford	(212) 721-4348 / (212) 501-2948
Charles Crutchfield	(212) 245-4731
Lynne Curtis	(718) 260-9565 / (917) 373-7848
Cara Czekanski	(917) 568-5735
David Davenport	(917) 373-0898
James Deanes	(212) 477-6844 / (646) 418-6576
Mildred Del Rio	(212) 741-0670
Yvens De Thelismond	(917) 273-0322
Tracy Devere	(718) 222-0250 / (917) 374-5140
Michael DiFonzo	(917) 443-2171
Laura Downing	(919) 247-6808
J. Kevin Draves	(212) 581-6167 / (518) 329-3928
Meredith Driscoll	(973) 783-1270 / (917) 375-7064

David Dumais	(718) 832-6247	Deirdra Govan	(917) 771-9796 (212) 678-8747
Debbe Du Perrieu	(212) 399-0004 (646) 418-8904	Jill Graves	(212) 982-1089 (917) 402-0227
Kate Edwards	(212) 620-7445	Nicole Greenbaum	(240) 462-1919
Patricia Eiben	(212) 206-1657	Rachel Greene	(914) 591-9675 (914) 912-7266
Janet Eiger	(914) 741-6315 (914) 523-3387	Rhonney Greene	(202) 412-4485
Anita Ellis	(212) 777-7477	Kelly Gregson	(347) 239-7148
Lisa Emerson Machione	(845) 246-9262 (212) 633-2756	Ulrika Haag	(917) 204-8284
Kendall Errair	(212) 741-0202	Amy Habacker	(917) 673-0897
Nicole Evangelista-Pollini	(917) 907-2591	Thomas Halligan	(973) 669-0955
Kevin P. Faherty	(845) 358-5797	Kenneth Hamilton	(845) 624-6144 (914) 714-3157
Kristin Farley	(845) 634-4705 (917) 749-0892	Kevin Mark Harris	(917) 586-8757
Elizabeth Feldbauer	(908) 245-4343 (908) 447-1105	Paul Hartis	(212) 865-5226 (917) 576-5472
Irene Feldbauer	(908) 789-8785 (908) 612-6124	Barbara J. Hause	(212) 316-0474 FAX (212) 316-0474
Robin Fields	(718) 851-6973 (513) 283-3033	Stacy Havens	(917) 597-3325
Sandi Figueroa	(917) 548-3627	Brian Hemesath	(212) 308-2877 (646) 319-6717
Gail Fitzgibbons	(201) 525-0130	Dan Hicks	(917) 576-6666
Cynthia Flowers	(818) 300-1739	Shawnique Hill	(973) 614-8582
Jill Flowers	(718) 789-9134	Mei Lai Hippisley Coxe	(718) 636-5463 (917) 797-7740
Marta Font	(646) 228-7228	Lynn Hoffman	(617) 277-0745 (917) 821-0167
Careen Fowles	(718) 398-2196		
Jackie Freeman	(646) 283-0663	Barrett Hong	(212) 564-0504 (917) 549-9964
Lisa Frucht	(212) 545-0954	Tonya Huskey	(212) 353-8263 (646) 530-1005
Kate Gaudio	(212) 675-0785 (718) 388-3937	Joni Huth	(931) 796-1070 (917) 670-9874
Catherine George	(718) 789-7158 (917) 482-6286	Jennifer Ingram	(718) 633-8674 (917) 733-6453
Linda Giammarese	(718) 686-0251	Darlene Jackson	(770) 469-9790 (404) 797-4197
Mary C. Gierczak	(516) 632-5454 (516) 428-8548	Askia Jacob	(778) 829-7666
Felicity Gifford	(212) 229-0828 (646) 326-5418	Nina Johnston	(718) 533-7265
Georgette Gogniat	(212) 475-3266	Rochelle Joseph	(713) 526-4282 (917) 217-4064
Eileen Goh	(917) 750-2653	Bernadette Jurkowski	(212) 505-9665 (917) 603-4710
Susan Gomez	(212) 721-5938 (917) 476-5404	Dain Kalas	(718) 619-5416
Elizabeth Goodrum	(718) 676-0723 (917) 439-0509	Suzanne Kelly	(212) 777-4730 (917) 991-4596
Katherine Gordon	(917) 676-1366	Cheryl Kilbourne-Kimpton	(212) 580-5103 (917) 301-1116
Anne Gorman	(703) 942-6515 (443) 388-2393		

Christine Kuhn	(908) 399-6151
June Kushner	(212) 967-7711
Joseph La Corte	(917) 532-7519
Jennifer Lax	(310) 288-3411 / (510) 848-4748
Margo La Zaro	(212) 877-0992 / (917) 520-6874
Iris Horta Lemos	(301) 576-6120
Lucia Lettini	(917) 349-5178
Celeste Livingston	(212) 226-4182 / (646) 456-0013
Cheryl Lovett	(212) 989-4591
Deborah Lucas	(718) 937-4446 / (917) 442-6502
Fionnuala Lynch	(917) 549-9032
Ellen Mahlke	(212) 569-0403 / (917) 449-3650
Vern Malone	(212) 988-4019
Donna Maloney	(610) 599-9921 / (212) 255-5477
Sarah Manowitz	(718) 772-3274
Estella Marie	(718) 726-2019 / (917) 670-4340
Carmia Marshall	(718) 781-0541
Gwyn Martin	(203) 625-0780 / (203) 253-6848
Dorothy Masters	(973) 373-3573 / (917) 880-6811
Bryan Mathison	(917) 406-4039
Barry Mazurek	(516) 521-5685
Alethea McElroy	(646) 391-1232
Mary Joan (MJ) McGrath	(212) 628-8221 / (917) 716-9404
Timothy McKelvey	(212) 228-1263 / (917) 566-2922
Winsome McKoy	(718) 399-2503
Colleen McTigue	(914) 450-2107
Jennifer Michael	(201) 656-6544
Roseann Milano	(973) 338-0890 / (973) 945-9042
Angela Mirabella	(917) 750-9143
Adele (Del) Miskie	(917) 346-1059
Kirsten Mogg	(212) 472-8312 / (646) 522-7058
Jennifer Moore	(917) 687-6880
Colleen Morris	(718) 484-3669 / (917) 570-1083
Elizabeth Muxi	(646) 831-1173
Anne Newton-Harding	(212) 666-5420
Dean Nichols	(212) 315-3029
Janna Notick	(212) 957-7744
Chiara Nuzzi	(845) 267-8805 / (845) 548-5057
Shannon O'Hara	(646) 522-5877
Natalie Opali	(718) 417-0416
Gayle Palmieri	(914) 944-9626 / (914) 282-5553
Alison Parker	(212) 333-5032 / (407) 716-9517
Aissatou Parks	(347) 462-2396 / (917) 653-9016
Marcia Patten	(973) 783-5277
Heather Patton	(323) 337-4165
Virginia Patton	(718) 549-1060 / (917) 439-4547
David Paulin	(212) 714-1549
Suzanne Pettit	(718) 789-7890 / (917) 697-4520
Amy Pickering	(347) 831-0175
Rosemary Ponzo	(212) 463-7971 / (917) 859-6601 / FAX (212) 463-7999 / www.rosemaryponzo.com
Ingrid Price	(212) 567-5882 / (845) 687-0273
Lee Purdy	(212) 995-5385 / (917) 572-5055
Kate Quinlan	(603) 548-5184
Chuck Recar	(917) 539-2509
Francine Ritacco-Sirianni	(973) 761-0331 / (917) 509-1376
Kevin Ritter	(201) 791-3630 / (201) 638-9788
Helen Rodgers	(917) 940-7418 / (201) 946-1657
Laisann Rogovin	(917) 701-8039 / (212) 678-0387
Tiel Roman	(917) 243-1477 / (917) 363-6981
Vernon Ross	(212) 928-2263
Amy Roth	(212) 255-9329 / (917) 579-8873
Brenda Rousseau	(917) 915-3018
David Ruble	(415) 359-7987
Monica Ruiz Ziegler	(212) 665-4070 / (917) 667-1973

Wardrobe Supervisors (Local 764 NY)

Monica Russell	(212) 633-2476 / (917) 660-7464
Chris Sanders	(845) 831-3706 / (516) 426-9231
Patricia Sanftner	(718) 643-9681
Elisa Santiago	(646) 239-4568
Eva Schegulla	(914) 967-2358
Nicole Schinman	(917) 202-8512
Ursula Kiki Schrader	(718) 584-0609
Christine Schultz	(201) 763-7285 / (917) 359-3623
Jonathan Schwartz	(212) 935-0296
Maryann Scinto	(312) 281-0264
Laura Sewrey	(917) 447-9846
Laura Shrewsbury	(646) 591-6356
Stephanie Siegel	(917) 906-4397 / (706) 718-0079
Omar Simmons	(843) 740-3446 / (843) 297-2342
Paul Simmons Jr.	(843) 814-2840
Angielette Smith	(212) 410-0138 / (917) 674-6968
Barnaby Smith Jr.	(407) 702-6444
Jessica Smith	(347) 268-4207
Martha Smith	(???) ??? ???? / (917) 796-6101
Thomas Soluri	(323) 397-9399
Gabriela Stanciu Willingham	(917) 721-2177
Melissa Stanton	(732) 583-7334
Yvette Stapleton	(212) 665-2526 / (917) 202-5979
Laura Steinman	(917) 690-9329
Trillian Stevenson	(917) 573-7787
Thomas Stokes	(917) 204-0336
Abigail Stowe	(212) 265-4311 / (917) 587-6976
D. Barak Stribling	(201) 333-3774
Niki Strippoli	(845) 942-1685 / (917) 751-8466
Joseph Tassone	(212) 315-3029 / (646) 872-6376
D. Hartsell Taylor	(718) 204-5914
Stev Taylor	(212) 206-7413 / (917) 817-5392
Michelle Teague	(718) 622-0710 / (917) 548-7606
Crystal Thompson	(212) 608-3251 / (917) 539-2340
Meg Thornton	(718) 852-1786 / (917) 922-5369
Maryann Towne	(212) 695-7182 / (917) 292-5751
Rose Trimarco Cuervo	(518) 734-5703
Veneda Truesdale	(718) 856-1007
Miriam Wong Tsao	(203) 972-3771
Janet Turner Griffin	(917) 279-8851
Criseida Vargas	(908) 355-8782 / (908) 358-9648
Susan Wachsler	(917) 584-2447
Debra Katz Weber	(845) 651-3758
Laura Wehrman	(917) 861-1490
Rosalie Wells	(212) 988-9228 / (917) 991-7585
Alana West	(973) 762-5468 / (917) 202-8922
Peter White	(212) 799-8910 / (954) 564-5290
Tsiqie White	(212) 246-2140 / (917) 375-0014
Karen Whittaker	(212) 262-4269
Deirdre N. Williams	(212) 206-8161
Benjamin Wilson	(518) 398-6468 / (518) 229-6452
Lynne Wilson	(212) 206-7438 / (646) 842-1121
Jeffrey Wirsing	(212) 673-1762
W. Randall Witherspoon	(718) 789-3048
Michael Woll	(646) 498-1069
Clifford Wray III	(646) 732-7474 / www.cliffordwray.com
Susan J. Wright	(212) 734-9724 / (917) 453-4755
Rosalie Zingales	(212) 989-8363 / (917) 797-5050

NY WORK RULE GRID

NY Union Commercial Work Rules

NY Local:	52 - AICP Agmt Studio Mechanics	161 - AICP NE Corridor Script Supervisors	600 East - AICP NE Corridor Cinematographers	764 - AICP Agmt Theatrical Wardrobe	798 - AICP NE Corridor Makeup & Hair	817 Teamsters	829 Scenic Artists
Term of Contract	2/4/09 - 11/30/11	10/1/07 - 9/30/10	10/1/07 - 9/30/10	10/1/07 - 9/30/10	10/1/07 - 9/30/10	2008	Expired 10/31/08
Contracted Day	10 hours	8 hours, Min. Call 10 hrs	10 hours	8 hours	8 hours, Min. Call 10 hrs	7 hours	8 hours
Contracted Workweek	Any 5 days of 7/ consec.	Any 5 of 7 days	Any 5 of 7 days	Any 5 of 7 days	Any 5 of 7 days	Mon - Fri	Any 5 days of 7/ consec.
Calls Day	Anytime	Anytime	Anytime - On hour or half hour	Anytime	Anytime	8:30am (8am allowed)	Anytime - Photography day (See notes below for non-photo day rules)
Partial Day	No - Except Sun if no shoot (5 hr)	No	No	No	No	No	Sunday Only Scenic Artist on construction day - 4 hrs @ 2x
Night	Anytime	Anytime	Anytime - On hour or half hour	Anytime	Anytime	4:30pm - 4:30am (5 hrs) Special rate: $197.85	Anytime
Calls given at:			End of day/ cannot be changed				Layoff/ change by 2:30pm prior day
Overtime 1.5x (Based on Contracted Day)	11th & 12th hour/ 6th day up to 12 hrs	11th & 12th hr/ 6th day (All OT based on 8 hr rate)	11th & 12th hr/ 6th day	9-12 hr/ 6th day up to 12 (All OT based on 8 hr rate)	11th & 12th hr/ 6th day (All OT based on 8 hr rate)		9th & 10th hrs 6th day up to 12 hrs
2x	After 12th hr/ 7th day/ holiday Sunday if no shoot (5 hr min) 6th day after 12 hrs	13-15th hour/ 7th day/ holiday 6th day after 12 hrs	13-15th hour/ 7th day/ holiday 6th day after 10 hrs	After 12 hrs 7th day/ holiday	13-15th hour 7th day/ holiday 6th day after 10 hrs	Before 8:30am/after 4:30pm > OT on 5 hr call is 2x the 7 hr hourly rate	11th & 12th hours 7th day/ holiday - first 12 hrs
2.5x			Over 15 hrs in day (Excludes meals)	(4x - 7th day after 12 hrs)			13th thru 15th hrs
3x	18+ hrs consec. w/ union perm.	Over 15 hrs in day (Excludes meals)	Over 18 hrs w/ union permission	6th day after 12 hrs	Turnaround		Over 15 hrs w/ written union perm.
Increments	½ hour	½ hour	¼ hour	½ hour	½ hour	1 hour	½ hour
Notes	> Tracking of employees by dept. starts at prelight. Prior by individual. > No employee replaced to avoid OT > Max day 18 hrs w/o union permission > Additional notes on rates page		> Start times for all members must be the same on shooting days > Crew added on premium days for rest of crew get premium pay > Work in excess of 18 hrs must be authorized by union staff > Single production agreements may have different work rules	Per Commercial Prod. Agreement		> Calls later than 8:30am revert to 8:30am > 5 hr calls start when vehicle leaves garage > Driver - Dump day if shoot 3 days or more on location > 5 hr call rate is the premium for Sat, Sun or night calls. OT is not compounded	Wrap Day: Up to 4 hrs ST for Costume Designer/ Stylist to personally return borrowed wardrobe No payments as Ind. Contractors **Non-Photography Day rules (Scenic Artists only)** 8 hrs between 7am and 8pm 8pm - midnight: Extra 10% p/hr of Journey Scenic Artist scale if premium rate not in effect Midnight - 7am: Extra 20% p/hr of Journey Scenic Artist scale if premium rate not in effect Minimum call is 8 hrs Except Sunday - Min is 4 hrs @ 2x Workweek: 7am Mon to 8pm Sat Sat 8pm - midnight @ 1.5x, Sunday all hours @2x
Turnaround: Daily	10 hrs	10 hrs	10 hrs	10 hrs	10 hrs	No	10 hrs
Weekend (5)	54 hrs	54 hrs	54 hrs	54 hrs	54 hrs	No	
Weekend (6)	34 hrs	34 hrs, portal-to-portal	34 hrs, portal-to-portal	34 hrs	34 hrs	No	
Penalty	3x until 10 hr rest period attained	2x the 6th day hourly rate, computed in ½ hr increments	15%/ of 10 hr rate for each ½ hr invaded	3x until 10 hr rest period attained	3x until 10 hr rest period attained		2x for first 2 hrs encroached 3x for hrs encroached beyond 2

NY Union Commercial Work Rules

NY Local:	52 - AICP Agmt Studio Mechanics	161 - AICP NE Corridor Script Supervisors	600 East - AICP NE Corridor Cinematographers	764 - AICP Agmt Theatrical Wardrobe	798 - AICP NE Corridor Makeup & Hair	817 Teamsters	829 Scenic Artists
Meals Intervals	3-6 hrs from call/ 3-6 hrs after	3-6 hrs from call/ 3-6 hrs after	3-6 hrs from call/ 3-6 hrs after	3-6 hrs from call/ 3-6 hrs after	3-6 hrs from call/ 3-6 hrs after	Within 6 hrs of call	1st meal: 4-6 hrs after call 2nd meal: within 6 hrs of previous
Lengths/ Special	1 hour	1 hour	1 hour	1 hour	1 hour	1 hour	1 hour
	---- Allow ½ hr off clock if hot catered ----	---- Allow ½ hr off clock if hot catered ----	DP/Operator not more than ½ hr longer than Asst. Camera		Allow ½ hr off clock if hot catered		Allow ½ hr off clock if hot catered
Penalties: 1st ½ hr	Only 1 meal in 10 hour day						
	$15.00	$15.00	$15.00	$15.00	$15.00		$15.00
2nd ½ hr	$17.50	$17.50	$17.50	$17.50	$17.50		$17.50
3rd ½ hr	$20.00	$20.00	$20.00	$20.00	$20.00		$20.00
4th ½ hr	$20 ea add'l w/ ½ hr break opt.	$25.00 - 1 hr of 3x thereafter	$25.00 - 1 hr of 3x thereafter	$25.00 - 3x thereafter	$25.00 - 3x thereafter		$20 ea add'l w/ ½ hr break option
Location Rules	General Rules - Apply to all	Lodging - 1st Class	Layovers - Non-worked days on location are paid at straight time.				
		Air Trans - Tourist/Coach (L600 Coach or better)	Studio Zone - No travel time - 125th St. to the Battery and designated studios outside Manhattan				
Nearby Location From Columbus Circle	25 mi. See last page	25 miles	25 miles	25 miles	25 miles	50 miles	25 Report To miles
Worktime Provisions		---- Within zone - Starts at location - Travel is off clock ----				Travel is work time	Beyond 25 miles, travel is work time Travel time starts at edge of zone
Travel Time Provisions		---- Company must provide transportation if outside Manhattan below 125th Street ----					Co. provides trans. or reimbursment
Meal Money if meals not provided	B-$6, L-$10, D-$14 B only if call is 7am or earlier		Not in contract - In practice, allows SAG rates: B-$9.30, L-$13.95, D-$25.65			B-$6, L-$7, D-$10 Driver's option to take meal or money	If no meal provided: B-$8, L-$12, D-$25
Distant Location	1x Day's pay for travel days	1x Day's pay for travel days		1x Day's pay for travel days	1x Day's pay for travel days		Travel @ 1x is not to exceed 8 hours Trav/work: 1x for travel portion, but all counted toward OT
	1x Day for unworked day	1x Day for unworked day	1x Day for unworked day	1x Day for unworked day	1x Day for unworked day		
Meal Money if not provided	B- $8, L-$12, D-$25	B-$4.50, L-$7.50, D-$9.50	* See above			B-$6, L-$7, D-$10 as above	B-$8, L-$12, D-$25
Amenities: Laundry, phone, etc.		Producer pays	Producer pays	Producer pays	Producer pays		
Non overnight Dist. Location		---- Travel time paid from studio or producer's office ----					
Other		Air travel ins. - $100K		Travel ins. - $100K	Travel ins. - $100K		
Cancellation of Call	Before 6 hr after start of prior day	By 2:30pm preceding day Penalty - Work Day - 10 hrs pay	By 2:30pm preceding day Penalty - Work Day - 10 hrs pay	Within 6hrs of previous day call By 2:30p non-wk day. Pen: 1 day pay	By 3pm if non-work day End of prior work day		By 2:30pm preceding day
Minimum Staffing	> Keys needed to do job > Snd Mixer & Recordist if sound recorded > To move 4K or larger light requires 2+ Electricians > Moving crane as camera platform req's 3 Grips > L52 Gen Oper. Req. 5KW+	One Script/ Cont. Supervisor Failure to hire penalty = 2x wages that should have been paid	> DP and AC. Operator optional. > Guaranteed 1AC Check On day unless prod'n owns equip. > AC cannot operate camera > One crew for each camera > Only 1 DP needed if multi-camera set > Still Cameraperson if stills not of same set > DP & 1AC req. for Plates, etc.		One Hair-Makeup person to perform covered work Failure to hire penalty = 2x wages that should have been paid	> Drivers for all vehicles carrying prod'n equip. > Helper needed if box over 18 ft except floor load only, or when on distant location > Generator truck driver can function as helper on another truck	No minimum staffing, but all covered work to be done by union members > First Scenic Artist hired at Chargeman rate and supervises > Penalty for non-union hire is 1.5x pay that would have been due > No penalty if union cannot provide qualified personnel, but P&W must still be paid > Non-L829 IATSE members may be hired w/o penalty > May hire Scenic Artists w/o an Art Director/ Designer if that function not performed > Asst Art Dir/ Costume Designers covered if needed for creative function > Art Dept Coord covered if needed and hired
- Additional notes on rates page					As needed		

NY Union Commercial Work Rules

NY Local:	52 - AICP Agmt Studio Mechanics	161 - AICP NE Corridor Script Supervisors	600 East - AICP NE Corridor Cinematographers	764 - AICP Agmt Theatrical Wardrobe	798 - AICP NE Corridor Makeup & Hair	817 Teamsters	829 Scenic Artists
Payment of Wages	Cash at end of week or day (In practice, check by end of week following work)	Consistent w/ state & federal law Penalties if union litigates	Consistent w/ state & federal law Penalties if union litigates	Consistent w/ state & federal law Penalties if union litigates	If terminated, day's pay/ same day, OT next day		
Hazardous Work							
Insurance	$250K Life/Dismemberment & $500 weekly for disability	$100K Life/Dismemberment & $1000 weekly for disability			$100K Life/Dismemberment & weekly disability payment		
Payments	Aerial/Diving etc. $40/ incident Daily max $80	Aerial/Diving etc. $100/ incident	Aerial/Diving etc. $150/ incident Daily max $300		Aerial/Diving etc. $100/incident		
Notes		Prod. provides apparel for cold or wet work			Prod. provides apparel for cold or wet work		
Smoke *prior notification		10 min air change each 60-90 minutes, etc.--------			Air change each 60-90 mins.		
Jurisdiction	NY, NJ, CT, DE, and PA w/ exception of 50-mile radius from center of Pittsburgh. Add'l notes on Zones on rates page	NE Corridor: CT, DE, MD, MA, NJ, NY, PA, DC - these rules. RI, VA, WV, NC, SC, GA, FL - per Commercial Production Agmt	NE Corridor: CT, DE, MD, MA, NJ, NY, PA & DC - these rules. Other areas covered by Com. Prod. Agmt.		NE Corridor: CT, DE, MD, MA, NJ, NY, PA, DC - these rules. RI, VA, WV, NC, SC, GA, FL - per Com. Prod. Agmt.	NY Metro (100 miles)	NY, NJ, CT, PA & DE See "Hiring Rules" in Other below
Pension Health & Welfare	NYC Zone: IAP 5% on Scale for all hrs worked or guaranteed, plus PH&W $10.0870 per hour worked and $.75 per day for accidental death insurance. Phila Zone: $70/day for workers "employed or hired in". Outside NYC & Phil, but within jurisdiction: $55/day workers "hired and employed in"	IAP 5.5% on Scale for all hrs worked or guaranteed, plus $9.3891 per hour worked, as of 1/20/08 See Commercial Prod. Agmt.	IAP 5.5% on Scale for all hrs worked or guaranteed plus $0.75 per day, plus $9.3891 per hour worked, as of 1/20/08 See Commercial Prod. Agmt.	$5.50 per hour H &W $1.80 per hour Pension $12.00 per day	$105 per day, all areas except $70 per day in Baltimore and Wash. DC See Commercial Prod. Agmt.	30% gross wages (17% - Welfare) (11% - Pension) (2% - Scholarship)	$100 per day working in and/or hired in NY Zone; Per Commercial Prod. Agmt if hired outside NY Zone and working outside NY Zone
Holidays	New Year's Day, Pres. Day, Easter Sunday, Memorial Day, July 4th, Labor Day, Columbus Day, Veterans Day, Thanksgiving & day after, Christmas	New Year's Day, MLK Bday, Press Day, Mem. Day, July 4th, Labor Day, Vet's Day, Thanksgiving & day after, Christmas *Observed Fri for Sat, Mon for Sun	New Year's Day, MLK Bday, Presidents Day, Memorial Day, Veterans Day, Thanksgiving & day after, July 4th, Labor Day, Thanksgiving, Christmas *Observed Fri for Sat and Mon for Sun	New Year's Day, MLK Bday, Presidents Day, Memorial Day, July 4th, Labor Day, Thanksgiving, Christmas	New Year's Day, MLK Bday, Presidents Day, Memorial Day, July 4th, Labor Day, Vet's Day, Thanksgiving & day after, Christmas *Observed Fri for Sat and Mon for Sun	New Year's Day, Lincoln's Bday, Presidents Day, Mem. Day, July 4th, Labor Day, Columbus Day, Veterans Day, Election Day, Thanksgiving, Christmas	New Year's Day, Mem. Day, Presidents Day, MLK Bday, 4th, Labor Day, Vet's Day, Thanksgiving & day after, Christmas *Observed Fri for Sat Mon for Sun
Other	Videotaped commercial jurisdiction - See contract No strike clause	Commercials only. Producers to notify before other types of non-theatrical projects to negotiate	> Special rates and rules for gov't work provided > No subleasing of services > Compensation for prep & consult > Quarterly reporting of wages and payments to individuals for rental photographic equipment > Union may require performance bond		> Min $12.50 if materials are provided > For work out of jurisdiction, "flat deals" can be negotiated w/ union approval > Penalty for hiring non-union = 2x day damages		**Hiring Rules:** > "Zone" is 50 mi from Columbus Circle, plus all of Nassau & Suffolk Counties > This contract applies if working in Zone, or hired in Zone and working in Jurisdiction > Com. Prod. Agmt applies if hired outside the Zone > Producer may outsource client and specialized artwork > Multi-sets/ stages for same job with one shooting and other prepping may require Standby Scenic Artist and Asst. Art Director to cover shooting set > Employer must supply materials, tools and brushes

NY Union Commercial Work Rules

NY Local:	52 - AICP Agmt Studio Mechanics	161 - AICP NE Corridor Script Supervisors	600 East - AICP NE Corridor Cinematographers	764 - AICP Agmt Theatrical Wardrobe	798 - AICP NE Corridor Makeup & Hair	817 Teamsters	829 Scenic Artists
Low Budget/Spec/PSA/ Internet Exclusions	PSAs, specs excluded, but may make voluntary P&W contributions Low-budget: In NYC and Philadelphia Zones, wages are negotiable for jobs with daily cost up to $50K and total cost up to $150K	Commercial Prod. Agreement rules apply	Commercial Prod. Agreement rules apply		Commercial Prod. Agreement rules apply		PSAs: Rates and OT may be negotiated; P&W remains the same Spec Comm'l: Same, but full comp if sold
Categories Covered	Props Electricians Grips Sound Video Tape Technician Generator Operator Shop Crafts	Script Supervisors	Director of Photography Camera Operator 1st Camera Assistant 2nd Camera Assistant Still Photographer	Wardrobe Supervisor Wardrobe Assistant Per Commercial Prod Agmt: Key Costumer 2nd Costumer	Make-up Artists Hair Stylists	Drivers Helpers	Art Director/ Scenic Designer Costume Designer/ Stylist Chargeman Scenic Artist Journeyman Scenic Artist Asst. Art Director Asst. Costume Designer/ Stylist Art Department Coordinator Note: Stylist is not a Wardrobe Supervisor
Current Scale Rates - Effective	2/4/09 - 11/30/09	10/1/08 - 9/30/09	10/1/08 - 9/30/09	10/1/08 - 9/30/09	10/1/08 - 9/30/09	2008 Conditions & Rates	10/1/07 - 10/31/08, in negotiation
Contracted Day	10 hours Sound Mixer: $565.75 Video Playback/ Utility: 528.35 VTR Tech.: 665.75 Boom: 528.35 Recordist: 528.35 Dept. Heads: 528.35 2nd Forman: 503.94 3rd Operator: 487.72	8 hours; Min. call 10 hours Min. hourly (0-8): $53.14 Min. hourly (9-10): 79.72 Min. Call: 584.58 6th Day: 87.69/hr 7th Day: 116.92/hr	10 hours Min. Call: D.P.: $1,105.14 Camera Operator: 658.54 1st Camera Assist: 635.85 2nd Camera Assist: 569.68 Still Photographer: 658.54	8 hours Supervisor: $278.55 Assistant: 259.20	8 hours; Min. call 10 hrs Min. hourly (0-8): $53.14 Min. hourly (9-10): 79.72 Min. Call: 584.58 6th Day: 87.69/hr 7th Day: 116.92/hr	7 hours Lead Driver 7 hr call: $264.44 5 hr call: 306.80 OT 2x: 75.56 Driver 7 hr call: $240.40 5 hr call: 280.47 OT 2x: 68.70 Helper 7 hr call: $229.08 5 hr call: 267.15 OT 2x: 65.45	8 hours Art Director: $795.20 Costume Designer/ Stylist: 615.76 Chargeman Scen. Artist: 568.24 Journeyman Scen. Artist: 464.48 Asst. Art Director: Negotiable Asst. CD/ Stylist: Negotiable Art Dept Coord: Negotiable
Union Local Phone #	212-399-0980	212-977-9655	212-647-7300	212-221-1717	212-627-0660	516-365-3470	212-581-0300

NOTE: AICP Agreements apply to AICP member companies who authorize AICP to negotiate on their behalf. All others may be offered other terms and con
Copyright 2009 Media Services. This summary chart is provided for reference purposes only. Decisions regarding application and interpretation of the provisions of any agreement should be made after review of the applicable agreement and, where app
is not responsible for any inaccuracies in the information provided herein.

New York
Steve Bizenov
(646) 829-0702
steve@media-services.com

Los Angeles
Tina Bassir
(310) 471-9369
tina@media-services.com

IATSE (AFL-CIO) Guidelines

Signatory Requirements

Who is the Signatory to a union contract?

A production company producing a bonafide commercial project that wishes to hire union labor should be a signatory to the union. Legally a company is not required to sign a union contract. However, union employees are barred by their union from accepting work offered by a production company that has not signed the union agreement. Some unions have separate agreements for AICP and non-AICP companies.

A production company may become a union signatory in three ways:

Production Company Signs Directly

Commits the production company to observe all aspects of the union contract. DGA, SAG, Local 600 East and the IATSE Commercial Production Agreement require direct signatory. The advertising agency or client is usually the SAG signatory; rarely is the production company a SAG signatory. (SAG signatory issues are covered in greater depth in the introduction to the SAG Contracts.) In certain circumstances, a union might offer the production company a Letter of Adherence (LOA) that covers a single project rather than a Term Agreement, which covers all projects, but this is becoming less common.

The following unions require production companies to sign agreements directly with them:
DGA (if Non-AICP)
IATSE Commercial Production Agreement (Covers L.A. County and rest of U.S. except New York and San Francisco; covers Local 600 Nationwide)
IATSE Local 16 - San Francisco
IATSE Local 52 Studio Mechanics (Non-AICP Independent version)
IATSE Local 600 Cinematographers - Single Production Agreements when available
IATSE Local 829 Set Designers, Scenic Artists & Stylists
Teamsters Local 399 - Separate Driver and Location Scout Agreements (Non-AICP Independent version)

Production Company Signs Via AICP

Association of Independent Commercial Producers member companies are not automatically signatories to any contract. To become a signatory, a company must sign an agreement through the AICP:

DGA (AICP member companies)
IATSE Commercial Production Agreement (Covers L.A. County and rest of U.S. except New York and San Francisco; covers Local 600 Nationwide)
IATSE Local 52 - Studio Mechanics (Must sign Trust Acceptance)
IATSE Local 476 - Chicago (Agreement for locally based companies only)
Teamsters Local 399 - Separate Driver and Location Scout Agreements (AICP version)

New York
Steve Bizenov
(646) 829-0702
steve@media-services.com

MEDIA SERVICES
ENTERTAINMENT ACCOUNTING, PAYROLL & SOFTWARE

Los Angeles
Tina Bassir
(310) 471-9369
tina@media-services.com

Payroll Service Acts as Signatory
In the past, some unions have allowed the payroll service to function as the signatory. This means that the production company need not sign a union contract before hiring union personnel. This is a rare exception.

Union Responsibilities of Production Company
Whichever form of signatory is used, producers are required to follow all terms and conditions of the applicable union contract(s). In general these provisions include, but are not limited to:

Staffing requirements
Wage rates
Overtime
Meal penalties
Turnaround

In general, all employees working in classifications covered by a collective bargaining agreement are entitled to receive the wages, benefits and other terms specified in the collective bargaining agreement regardless of whether they are members of a union.

New York
Steve Bizenov
(646) 829-0702
steve@media-services.com

MEDIA SERVICES
ENTERTAINMENT ACCOUNTING, PAYROLL & SOFTWARE

Los Angeles
Tina Bassir
(310) 471-9369
tina@media-services.com

IATSE Commerical Production Agreement—Jurisdictions

		Prod Centers/Zones	IATSE Local	AICP-CPA	NE Corridor
AK	Alaska	Anchorage		•	
AL	Alabama			•	
AR	Arkansas			•	
AZ	Arizona	Phoenix, Tucson		•	
CA	California	Los Angeles County		•	
		San Francisco	16	L 600 CPA	
		Sacramento, San Diego		•	
CO	Colorado	Denver		•	
CT	Connecticut		52		Local 600/ 161/ 798
DC	District of Columbia	Washington D.C.	487	•	Local 600/ 161/ 798
DE	Delaware	East/West	52/487	52/M-S	Local 600/ 161/ 798
FL	Florida	Miami (Including Palm Beach, Dade & Broward Counties) / Orlando (incl. Winterhaven & Lakeland) / Tampa (St. Petersburg & Clearwater)	477	•	
GA	Georgia	Atlanta		•	
HI	Hawaii	Honolulu		•	
IA	Iowa			•	
ID	Idaho			•	
IL	Illinois	Chicago - Per Contract		•	
IN	Indiana			•	
KS	Kansas			•	
KY	Kentucky			•	
LA	Louisiana	New Orleans	487	•	
MA	Massachusetts	Boston	481	•	Local 600/ 161/ 798
MD	Maryland	Baltimore	487	•	Local 600/ 161/ 798
ME	Maine		481	•	
MI	Michigan	Detroit (Local Co's have local contract)	38, 812	•	
MN	Minnesota	Minneapolis/ St. Paul	490	•	
MO	Missouri	St. Louis	493	•	
MS	Mississippi		492/478	•	
MT	Montana			•	
NC	North Carolina	Charlotte & Wilmington	491	•	
ND	North Dakota			•	
NE	Nebraska			•	
NH	New Hampshire			•	
NJ	New Jersey		52		Local 600/ 161/ 798
NM	New Mexico	Albuquerque & Santa Fe	480	•	
NV	Nevada	Las Vegas		•	
NY	New York	New York - Per Contracts	52, 161, 764, 798		Local 600/ 161/ 798
OH	Ohio	Cleveland	209	•	
OK	Oklahoma			•	
OR	Oregon	Portland	488	•	
PA	Pennsylvania	Pittsburgh (Local 489 - 50 mile radius)	52 (Except Pittsburgh)	Except 52 Area	Local 600/ 161/ 798
RI	Rhode Island			•	600/161/798
SC	South Carolina		491	•	600/161/798
SD	South Dakota			•	
TN	Tennessee	Nashville	492	•	
TX	Texas	Austin, Dallas, Ft. Worth, Houston, San Antonio	484	•	
UT	Utah	Salt Lake City		•	
VA	Virginia	Richmond	487	•	
VT	Vermont		481	•	
WA	Washington	Seattle	488	•	
WI	Wisconsin			•	
WV	West Virginia			•	
WY	Wyoming			•	
PR	Puerto Rico	San Juan	494	•	
VI	U.S. Virgin Islands		494	•	

New York
Steve Bizenov
(646) 829-0702
steve@media-services.com

MEDIA SERVICES
ENTERTAINMENT ACCOUNTING, PAYROLL & SOFTWARE

Los Angeles
Tina Bassir
(310) 471-9369
tina@media-services.com

Work Rules—IATSE Commerical Production Agreement

IATSE COMMERCIAL PRODUCTION AGREEMENT

Working Rules & Conditions

Term of Contract		10/1/07 - 9/30/2010
Contracted Day		8 consecutive hours
Contracted Workweek		Any 5 or 6 consecutive days of 7
Calls	Day/Night	Anytime Time begins at Set Call Time
	Partial Day	No Except Travel Days - Min. 4 hours/ Max. 8 hrs @ 1x
Overtime	1.5x	9-12 hrs, 6th day up to 12 hours
	2x	After 12 hrs, 7th day, Holidays
	3x	6th day after 12 hrs worked
	4x	7th day after 12 hrs worked
	Increments	¼ hr increments
Turnaround	Daily	10 hours (9 hrs overnight location, portal-to-portal. DP/Camera Operator: 10 hrs.)
Penalty	If rest at least 6 hrs	Base or OT rate when released plus 1x for invaded hours
	If rest less than 6 hrs	Base or OT rate when released plus 1x for day until 10 hr rest period provided
Meals	Intervals	6 hr intervals, 1st meal no earlier than 3 hrs
	Lengths	½ hr to 1 hr
	Penalties	1st ½ hr or fraction - $7.50, 2nd ½ hr or fraction - $10, Each additional - $15
	Second Meal	May be deducted if it is outside min call
	Extensions	1st may be extended 15 min to complete setup. 2nd may be extended 30 min to complete setup or wrap
	Walking Meal	Any second meal, excluding NDB, may be a non-deductible walking meal, provided crew is dismissed within 1 hr from time meal was due
Production Zone		Within a circular 30 mile zone from intersection of City Hall for designated production centers
Location Rules		Per Diem allowance and housing or housing allowance to be provided
		Air Transportation: Coach or better
Work Time/ Travel Time Provisions		Overnight locations: Work: Set call to set dismissal. 1 hr allowable travel time. Excess paid as work time.
		Travel Days: Min 4 hrs, Max 8 hrs Straight Time. Mileage at current IRS rate.
Cancellation of Call		By 3pm of prior non-work day; By end of prior work day
		Penalty: Work Day - 8 hrs pay Travel Day - 4 hrs pay
Minimum Staffing		No requirements. Staffing must be consistent with past practices. There is practical interchangeability within the production crafts. Covers classifications traditionally covered by IATSE. Excludes office clerical, PA's and guards. Commercial stylists are not included in the agreement, but Costume Designers and Costumers are.
Payment of Wages		No special provisions. Most states require payment within 2 weeks. CA has severe late payment penalties
Hazardous Work		No special provisions, except in NE Corridor. See NE Corridor Notes page.
Jurisdiction		Throughout U.S., Puerto Rico and U.S. Virgin Islands. See Jurisdiction: Within LA rates page for exceptions.
Pension Health & Welfare		Rates vary geographically. See AICP - IATSE Commercial Production Agreements - PH & W rates page.
		Travel and Idle Days on location: 8 hrs PH & W contribution
Holidays		New Year's Day Martin Luther King Day President's Day Memorial Day
		Independence Day Labor Day Thanksgiving Day Christmas Day
Union Security TV Commercial Roster		Preference of employment: First consideration to those referred by local unions.
		Workers who are not current members of the union may be hired based on advertiser or agency requirements or documented industry experience. All are covered by all of agreement's provisions.
		Marine coordinators, boat handlers & operators covered, if not covered by another union.
Notes		>Outside LA County, NY & Phila Zones, producers must notify LA or NY IA office prior to shoot.
		>Producers must be direct signatory to full agreement. No letters of adherence.
		>Excludes PSAs and spec commercials. P&W contributions optional on PSAs.
		>Excludes traditional low budget commercials w/ single day cost of $75K or less and total cost of $225K or less.
		>Excludes Non-Trad low budget commercials with single day cost of $50K or less and total cost of $750K or less.
		>For ALL low budget, wage rates subject to individual negotiation. P&W normal.
		>IATSE or crew may appoint a Job Steward for each production.
		>Scope of Agreement - Where Employer has no effective control portions of pre and post production not covered. Employers not prevented from subcontracting for services consistent with industry practice.
		>Higher Classification - Two or more hours work in higher classification requires higher rate for day.
		>Recognize jurisdiction over commercials made by traditional means for any medium including Internet.
		>Internet commercials by non-traditional means to be negotiated, all but wages & work rules apply.
Phone numbers		LA IATSE: 818-980-3499, NY: 212-730-1770 LA AICP: 323-960-4763, NY: 212-929-3000

New York
Steve Bizenov
(646) 829-0702
steve@media-services.com

MEDIA SERVICES
ENTERTAINMENT ACCOUNTING, PAYROLL & SOFTWARE

Los Angeles
Tina Bassir
(310) 471-9369
tina@media-services.com

P&W Rules—IATSE Commercial Production Agreement

PH&W Rules & Exceptions - IATSE Commercial Production Agreement

Hired to work in Los Angeles County or hired in Los Angeles County to work anywhere else:
As of 8/3/08: $3.8975 per hr plus 6% of Scale to MPIPHP - Subject to increases in Basic Agreement

Camera department and post-production employees hired and working outside of L.A. County:
As of 8/3/08: $10.0870 per hr plus 6% of Scale to MPIPHP - Subject to increases in Basic Agreement
For NE Corridor, additional $0.75 per day

Hired in New England, Maryland and Washington D.C. (except camera, post-production, Local 798 and Local 161 in CT):
As of 10/22/07: $88 per day to IATSE National Plan; 10/1/08: $93 per day; 10/1/09: $97 per day

Hired in Michigan (except for camera department and post-production employees):
As of 10/22/07: $103 per day to IATSE National Plan; 10/1/08: $108 per day; 10/1/09: $112 per day

Hired in Nevada (except for camera department and post-production employees):
As of 10/22/07: $38.71 per day to IATSE National Plan plus 8% of gross pay to NRA-IATSE Local 720 Joint Trust Fund. As of 10/1/08 $42.71 per day plus 8% gross pay; 10/1/09: $45.71 per day plus 8% gross pay

Hired outside L.A. County, New England (NE Corridor), MD, Wash. D.C., MI, NV, SF (excluding camera, post-production Local 161, Local 798 & Local 784):
As of 10/22/07: $60 per day to IATSE National Plan; 10/1/08: $65 per day; 10/1/09: $69 per day

Exceptions

Local 161: Hired in Delaware, Maryland, Massachusetts, Pennsylvania & Wash. D.C.:
As of 10/22/07: $100 per day to Local 161 Funds; 10/1/08: $105 per day; 10/1/09: $109 per day

Hired in Connecticut, New York & New Jersey:
As of 1/22/07: $9.0416 per hr plus 5.5% of Scale to MPIPHP

Hired in Maine, New Hampshire, Vermont, Rhode Island, Virginia, W. Virginia, N. Carolina, S. Carolina, Georgia & Florida:
As of 10/22/07: $81 per day to IATSE National Plan; 10/1/08: $86 per day; 10/1/09: $90 per day

Locals 798 (Hair & Makeup) & 764 (Wardrobe) Hired in the NE Corridor (CT, DE, MD, MA, NJ, NY & PA):
As of 10/22/07: $105 per day to Local 798 Funds; 10/1/08: $110 per day; 10/1/09: $90 per day

Hired in Baltimore, Wash. D.C., Rhode Island, Virginia, W. Virginia, N. Carolina, S. Carolina, Georgia & Florida:
As of 10/22/07: $81 per day to Local 798 Funds, 10/1/08: $86 per day; 10/1/09: $90 per day

Local 476 & 769 (Wardrobe) - Hired in Illinois:
As of 10/22/07: H&W $5.50 per hr + Pension $1.80 per hr + $12 per day to Local 476 Funds

Local 784 (Wardrobe) Hired in San Francisco:
As of 10/22/07: $81 per day to IATSE National Plan; 10/1/08: $86 per day; 10/1/09: $90 per day

New York
Steve Bizenov
(646) 829-0702
steve@media-services.com

MEDIA SERVICES
ENTERTAINMENT ACCOUNTING, PAYROLL & SOFTWARE

Los Angeles
Tina Bassir
(310) 471-9369
tina@media-services.com

Minimum Wage Rates—Within LA County

IATSE COMMERCIAL PRODUCTION AGREEMENT

L.A. County Minimum Rates 10/1/08 - 9/30/09

Classification	Hourly	8-hour Day	Daily On Call	Weekly On Call
LOCAL 600				
Director of Photography	92.43	739.46		
Camera Operator	56.58	452.62		
First Assistant Cameraman	40.93	327.46		
Second Assistant Camera	37.60	300.76		
Camera Loader/Utility	32.17	257.34		
Digital Imaging Technician	53.38	427.04		
LOCAL 695				
Sound Mixer	63.14	505.11		
Boom Operator	42.62	340.97		
Sound Utility	42.62	340.97		
VTR/Video Playback	42.62	340.97		
LOCAL 80				
Key Grip	39.62	316.99		
2nd Grip	35.48	283.87		
Dolly Grip	36.75	294.00		
Grip	33.87	270.93		
Entry Level Grip	29.64	237.15		
Craft Service	28.72	229.73		
LOCAL 728				
Lighting Gaffer	39.62	316.99		
2nd Electrician	35.48	283.87		
Dimmer Operator	34.65	277.19		
Electrician	33.87	270.93		
Entry Level Electrician	29.64	237.15		
LOCAL 44				
Property Master	39.62	316.99		
2nd Prop	34.65	277.19		
3rd Prop	32.47	259.72		
Propmaker Foreman	39.80	318.39		
Propmaker	34.65	277.19		
Set Decorator (On Call)			570.32	2,407.73
Special Effects Foreperson	39.80	318.39		
Lead Effects	36.75	294.00		
Effects	34.65	277.19		
Lead Set Dresser	34..65	277.19		
Set Dresser	32.47	259.72		
Construction Coordinator (On Call)			554.18	2,342.53
LOCAL 892				
Costume Designer (On Call)			536.08	2,234.13
LOCAL 705				
Key Costumer	37.65	301.17		
2nd Costumer	35.04	280.32		
3rd Costumer	32.75	262.03		
Entry Level Costumer	25.55	204.43		
LOCAL 706				
Key Makeup Artist	45.10	360.83		
2nd Makeup Artist	38.39	307.10		
3rd Makeup Artist	34.79	278.35		
Key Hair Stylist	44.47	357.95		
2nd Hair Stylist	39.24	313.94		
3rd Hair Stylist	33.45	267.64		

New York
Steve Bizenov
(646) 829-0702
steve@media-services.com

MEDIA SERVICES
ENTERTAINMENT ACCOUNTING, PAYROLL & SOFTWARE

Los Angeles
Tina Bassir
(310) 471-9369
tina@media-services.com

Classification	Hourly	8-hour Day	Daily On Call	Weekly On Call
LOCAL 871				
Script Supervisor	33.09	264.75		
LOCAL 767				
First Aid	30.91	247.28		
LOCAL 800				
Art Director (On Call)				3,152.64
Assistant Art Director (On Call)				2,359.45
LOCAL 729				
Paint Foreperson	58.35	466.80		
Painter	34.65	277.19		
LOCAL 800				
Lead Scenic Artist	49.86	398.90		
Scenic Artist	45.09	360.75		
LOCAL 884				
Studio Teacher/Welfare Worker	43.03	344.27		

Five Day Studio "On Call" Rate	
CLASSIFICATION	10/1/08 - 9/30/09
Production Accountant	2,357.10
Production Office Coordinator	1,414.97
Assistant Production Accountant	1,336.35
Assistant Production Office Coordinator	838.54
Art Department Coordinator	838.54

New York		Los Angeles
Steve Bizenov		Tina Bassir
(646) 829-0702		(310) 471-9369
steve@media-services.com	ENTERTAINMENT ACCOUNTING, PAYROLL & SOFTWARE	tina@media-services.com

Minimum Wage Rates—Outside LA County

Outside L.A. County Minimum Rates 10/1/08 - 9/30/09

Classification	Hourly	8-hour Day	Daily On Call	Weekly On Call
LOCAL 600				
Director of Photography	92.43	739.46		
Camera Operator	56.58	452.62		
First Assistant Cameraman	40.93	327.46		
Second Assistant Camera	37.60	300.76		
Camera Loader/Utility	32.17	257.34		
Digital Imaging Technician	53.38	427.04		
LOCAL 695				
Sound Mixer	58.38	467.04		
Boom Operator	39.40	315.18		
Sound Utility	39.40	315.18		
VTR/Video Playback	39.40	315.18		
LOCAL 80				
Key Grip	36.64	293.10		
2nd Grip	32.81	262.44		
Dolly Grip	33.98	271.84		
Grip	31.31	250.50		
Entry Level Grip	27.40	219.18		
Craft Service	26.55	212.43		
LOCAL 728				
Lighting Gaffer	36.64	293.10		
2nd Electrician	32.81	262.44		
Dimmer Operator	32.04	256.35		
Electrician	31.31	250.50		
Entry Level Electrician	27.40	219.18		
LOCAL 44				
Property Master	36.64	293.10		
2nd Prop	32.04	256.35		
3rd Prop	30.01	240.11		
Propmaker Foreman	36.79	294.33		
Propmaker	33.04	256.35		
Set Decorator (On Call)			527.01	2,226.09
Special Effects Foreperson	36.79	294.33		
Lead Effects	33.98	271.84		
Effects	32.04	256.35		
Lead Set Dresser	32.04	256.35		
Set Dresser	30.00	240.03		
Construction Coordinator (On Call)			512.38	2,165.80
LOCAL 892				
Costume Designer (On Call)			495.65	2,065.57
LOCAL 705				
Key Costumer	34.81	278.51		
2nd Costumer	32.40	259.23		
3rd Costumer	30..27	242.17		
Entry Level Costumer	23.64	189.11		
LOCAL 706				
Key Makeup Artist	41.68	333.47		
2nd Makeup Artist	35.49	283.95		
3rd Makeup Artist	32.16	257.25		
Key Hair Stylist	41.36	330.92		
2nd Hair Stylist	36.29	290.30		
3rd Hair Stylist	30.91	247.28		

New York
Steve Bizenov
(646) 829-0702
steve@media-services.com

MEDIA SERVICES
ENTERTAINMENT ACCOUNTING, PAYROLL & SOFTWARE

Los Angeles
Tina Bassir
(310) 471-9369
tina@media-services.com

Classification	Hourly	8-hour Day	Daily On Call	Weekly On Call
LOCAL 871				
Script Supervisor	30.58	244.65		
LOCAL 767				
First Aid	28.58	228.66		
LOCAL 800				
Art Director (On Call)				2,914.79
Assistant Art Director (On Call)				2,170.73
LOCAL 729				
Paint Foreperson	53.95	431.60		
Painter	32.04	256.35		
LOCAL 800				
Lead Scenic Artist	47.48	379.86		
Scenic Artist	42.93	343.44		
LOCAL 884				
Studio Teacher/Welfare Worker	39.79	318.31		

Note: Marine Coordinators, boat handlers and operators are covered, if not covered by another agreement. Wages are negotiable.

New York	Los Angeles
Steve Bizenov	Tina Bassir
(646) 829-0702	(310) 471-9369
steve@media-services.com	tina@media-services.com

Northeast Corridor Agreement—Locals 600, 161 & 798

NORTHEAST CORRIDOR AGREEMENT - LOCALS 600, 161, 798

NE Corridor: Connecticut, Delaware, Maryland, Massachusetts, New Jersey, New York, Pennsylvania and the District of Columbia. **Other areas:** Use Commercial Production Agreement.

LOCAL 600, INTERNATIONAL PHOTOGRAPHERS
Minimum Rates 10/1/08 - 9/30/09 (NE Corridor - AICP)

Classification	Min. Call	6th Day hourly	7th Day hourly
Director of Photography	1,105.14	170.74	227.66
Camera Operator	658.54	98.78	131.71
1st Camera Assistant	635.85	95.38	127.17
2nd Camera Assistant	569.68	85.45	113.94
Still Photographer	658.54	98.78	131.71

Salaries of camerapersons engaged on a temporary basis, for the performance of government work (a Producer under direct contract with the U.S.I.A., or the Army, Air Force or Navy Departments) is 15% less than the above scales.

Overtime
In 1/4 hour units

	1x	1 1/2x	2x	2 1/2x	3x*
First 5 days	10	11-12	> 12	> 15	> 18E
6th day		10	>10	> 15	> 18E
7th day			10	> 15	> 18E
Holidays worked			10	> 15	> 18E

E = Elapsed (meal penalties are *not* deducted from work time during this period)
* With union permission.

LOCAL 161, SCRIPT SUPERVISORS
Minimum Rates 10/1/08 - 9/30/09 (NE Corridor - AICP)

Classification	10 Hr Min. Call	6th Day hourly	7th Day hourly
Script Supervisor	584.58	87.69	116.92

Overtime
In 1/2 hour units

	1x	1 1/2x	2x	2 1/2x
1st 5 days	1-10	11-12	12-15	>15
6th day		1-10	10-15	>15
7th day			1-15	>15
Holidays			1-15	>15

LOCAL 798, HAIR & MAKEUP
Minimum Rates 10/1/08 - 9/30/09 (NE Corridor - AICP)

Classification	10 Hr Min. Call	6th Day hourly	7th Day hourly
Hair & Makeup	584.58	87.69	116.92

Overtime
In 1/2 hour units

	1x	1 1/2x	2x
1st 5 days	1-10	11-12	> 12
6th day		1-10	> 10
7th day			All hours
Holidays			All hours

New York
Steve Bizenov
(646) 829-0702
steve@media-services.com

Los Angeles
Tina Bassir
(310) 471-9369
tina@media-services.com

Local 600 International Photographers Working Rules & Conditions

NORTHEAST CORRIDOR (CONT'D)

Working Rules & Conditions

LOCAL 600 INTERNATIONAL PHOTOGRAPHERS

Term of Contract		10/1/07 - 9/30/2010		
Contracted Day		10 consecutive hours		
Contracted Workweek		Any 5 days of 7		
Calls	Day/Night	Anytime	Time begins at Set Call Time	Dept. on same Call on Shoot Days
	Partial Day	No	Start on hour or half hour	
Overtime	1.5x	Over 10 hrs, 6th day up to 10		
	2x	After 12 hrs, 7th day, 6th day after 10 hrs, Holidays		
	2.5x	Over 15 hrs worked		
	3x	Over 18 consecutive hrs - ONLY with union's permission		
	Increments	¼ hr increments		
Turnaround	Daily	10 hrs, portal to portal		
	Weekly	54 hrs for 5 day week, 34 hrs for 6 day week, portal to portal		
Penalty		15% of 10 hr. rate in 1/2 hr increments for invaded hours.		
Meals	Intervals	No later than 6 hours, no earlier than 3 hours.		
	Lengths	1 hour - 1/2 hr. off clock if hot catered meal provided.		
	Penalties	1st 1/2 hr or fraction - $15.00		
		2nd 1/2 hr. $17.50, 3rd 1/2 hr: $20.00, 4th 1/2 hr: $25.00 and 3X for each 1/2 hr. until a meal break		
		DP meal break may not be more than 1/2 hr. greater than AC		
	Second Meal	No later than 6 hours, no earlier than 3 hours.		
	Extensions	N/A		
	Walking Meal	N/A		
Production Zone		>25 mile radius from Columbus Circle.		
Location Rules		>Per Diem allowance and housing or housing allowance to be provided. >Air Transportation - Coach or better >Employee who lives within 60 miles of location, considered a "Local Hire"		
Work Time/ Travel Time Provisions		In Zone outside Manhattan - If transport provided fr. Col. Circle, travel time is off the clock. Non Overnight Location - Paid travel time computed to/from studio, production or L600 office. Overnight Locations: Time is Portal to Portal. 1X for unworked 6th, 7th or Holiday. Work on 6th day: 1.5x, After 12 hours: 2x. Work on 7th day: 2x all hours.		
Cancellation of Call		Within 6 hours of previous day's call or 2:30pm if non-work day. Call Time by end of prior work day, can't be changed. Penalty - Work Day - 10 hrs pay		
Minimum Staffing		>Dir. Of Photography and 1st Assistant Cameraperson >Cameraperson and Assistant for each standard camera. >AC not allowed to operate camera >Only one DP required for multi-camera filming same set. >Still cameras must be operated by members of Local 600 >Process photography, backgrounds and plates require DP and 1st AC >CPA Art. XVII does not apply. Upgrades continue per past practice.		
Payment of Wages		Consistent with state and federal laws. Not less than semi-monthly. Penalties if union needs to litigate.		
Hazardous Work		$150 per flight or incident. Maximum $300 per day.- See contract for definitions		
Jurisdiction		CT, DE, MD, MA, NY, NJ, PA, DC		
Pension Health & Welfare		As of 1/25/09: $10.0870 per hr. plus 5.5% of Scale plus $.75 per day.		
Holidays		New Year's Day Martin Luther King Day President's Day Memorial Day Independence Day Labor Day Thanksgiving Day Christmas Day Veterans Day Day After Thanksgiving		
Notes		>Guaranteed equipment check out day for AC, unless prod. co. owns or long term leases equipment. >Member's work may not be subleased to another production company. >Consultation, prep and supervision must be compensated at least scale rates. >Union may require Performance Bond. >Excludes PSAs, spec commercials. Excludes low budget commercials with single day production of $75K or less and aggregate cost of $225K or less. Wage rates subject to individual negotiation. P&W normal. >Smoke on Set: Prior notification reqd. Provide appropriate masks and vent for 10 min.every 60-90 min. >Gov't work: On loc. week or more, no pay for layover Sat or Sun. Meal & hotel allowances provided.		
Phone numbers		Local 600 NY: 212-647-7300		AICP LA: 323-960-4763, NY: 212-929-3000

New York
Steve Bizenov
(646) 829-0702
steve@media-services.com

Los Angeles
Tina Bassir
(310) 471-9369
tina@media-services.com

NORTHEAST CORRIDOR (CONT'D)

Working Rules & Conditions

LOCAL 161 SCRIPT SUPERVISORS

Term of Contract		10/1/07 - 9/30/2010
Contracted Day		10 consecutive hours
Contracted Workweek		Any 5 days of 7
Calls	Day/Night	Anytime Time begins at Set Call Time. Start on hour or half hour.
	Partial Day	No Except travel day to/from overnight location - see below.
Overtime (Calculated on 10 hr day rate)	1.5x	11-12th hours, 6th Day
	2x	13-15th hour, 6th day after 10 hrs., 7th day, Holidays
	2.5x	Over 15 work hours.
	Increments	½ hr increments
Turnaround	Daily	10 hrs, portal to portal
	Weekly	54 hrs for 5 day week, 34 hrs for 6 day week, portal to portal
Penalty		2X the 6th Day hourly rate, in ½ hr intervals for invaded hours
Meals	Intervals	6 hour intervals, 1st meal no earlier than 3 hrs
	Lengths	1 hour - 1/2 hr. off clock if hot catered meal provided.
	Penalties	1st 1/2 hr or fraction - $15.00
		2nd 1/2 hr: $17.50, 3rd 1/2 hr: $20.00, 4th 1/2 hr: $25.00 and 3X for each 1/2 hr. until a meal break
		Meal money in lieu of provided meal: Nearby Location: B: $4.00, L: $5.50, D: $9.50
	Extensions	N/A
	Walking Meal	N/A
Production Zone		>25 mile radius from Columbus Circle.
Location Rules		>Per Diem allowance and housing or housing allowance to be provided.
		>Air Transportation - Coach or better
		>Employer must provide $100,000 insurance when traveling by air.
Work Time/ Travel Time Provisions		>In Zone outside Manhattan - If transport provided fr. Col. Circle, travel time is off the clock.
		>Studios are included in the Studio Zone, not the location zone.
		>Non Overnight Location - Paid travel time computed to/from studio, production office.
		>Overnight Locations: 1X for unworked 6th, 7th or Holiday. (Gov't.work: No pay for idle 7th day)
		>Work on 6th day: 1.5X, Work on 7th day: 2X all hours.
		>On overnight location pay 1 day travel unless travel & work in which case all hours are paid as worked.
		>Meal money in lieu of provided meal: Overnight Location: B: $4.50, L: $7.50, D: $9.50. In lieu of hotel $16.00
Cancellation of Call		Determine crew by 2:30pm of previous day. Call time provided by end of prior work day.
		Penalty: Work Day - 10 hrs pay
Minimum Staffing		>One Script/Continuity Supervisor.
		>Failure higher penalty: 2X the wages that should have been paid.
Payment of Wages		Consistent with state and federal laws. Penalties if union needs to litigate.
Hazardous Work		$100 per flight or incident. Employer must provide $100,000 insurance/$1000 per wk for total disability.
Jurisdiction		CT, DE, MD, MA, NY, NJ, PA, DC
Pension Health & Welfare		DE, MD, MA, PA, DC: $105 per day until 9/30/2009
		CT, NY, NJ: As of 1/20/08: $9.3891 per hr. plus 5.5% of Scale
Holidays		New Year's Day Martin Luther King Day President's Day Memorial Day
		Independence Day Labor Day Veterans Day Thanksgiving Day
		Day after Thanksgiving Christmas Day
Notes		>Excludes PSAs, spec commercials. Excludes low budget commercials with single day production of $75K or less and aggregate cost of $225K or less. Wage rates subject to individual negotiation. P&W normal.
		>Employer to provide suitable attire for abnormally cold or wet work.
		>Smoke on Set: Prior notification required. Provide appropriate masks and vent for 10 minutes every 60-90 minutes.
		>Applies to Commercials ONLY. Other types of production must be negotiated.
Phone numbers		Local 161 NY: 212-977-9655 AICP LA: 323-960-4763, NY: 212-929-3000

New York
Steve Bizenov
(646) 829-0702
steve@media-services.com

MEDIA SERVICES
ENTERTAINMENT ACCOUNTING, PAYROLL & SOFTWARE

Los Angeles
Tina Bassir
(310) 471-9369
tina@media-services.com

Local 798 Hair & Makeup Working Rules & Conditions

NORTHEAST CORRIDOR (CONT'D)

Working Rules & Conditions

LOCAL 798 HAIR & MAKEUP

Term of Contract		10/1/07 - 9/30/2010	
Contracted Day		10 consecutive hours	
Contracted Workweek		Any 5 days of 7	
Calls	Day/Night Partial Day	Anytime	Notice by end of previous day
Overtime (Calculated on 10 hr day rate)	1.5x 2x Increments	11-12th hours/ 6th Day Over 12 hrs/ 6th day after 10 hrs/ 7th day/ Holidays ½ hr increments	
Turnaround	Daily Weekly	10 hrs	
Penalty		3X the employee's average hourly rate until 10 hour rest period attained	
Meals	Intervals	6 hour intervals, 1st meal no earlier than 3 hrs	
	Lengths	1 hour - ½ hr. off clock if hot catered meal provided.	
	Penalties	1st ½ hr or fraction - $15.00	
		2nd ½ hr: $17.50, 3rd ½ hr: $20.00, 4th ½ hr: $25.00 and 3X for each ½ hr. until a meal break	
	Extensions	N/A	
	Walking Meal	N/A	
Production Zone		>25 mile radius from Columbus Circle.	
Location Rules		>Per Diem allowance, amenities and first class housing or housing allowance to be provided. >Air Transportation - Coach or better >No obligation to travel L798 member to Distant location. >Employer must provide $100,000 insurance when traveling by air.	
Work Time/ Travel Time Provisions		>In Zone outside Battery-125th St. - Transport to be provided from Col. Circle, travel time is off the clock. >Overnight Locations: 1x for unworked 6th, 7th or Holiday. >Work on 6th day: 1.5x, 2x after 12 hours, Work on 7th day: 2x all hours. >OT in ½ hour intervals.	
Cancellation of Call			
Minimum Staffing		>One Hair-Makeup person to perform covered work. >Failure to hire penalty: 2X the wages that should have been paid.	
Payment of Wages		Upon termination - Same day - OT can be paid the next day.	
Hazardous Work		$100 per flight or incident. Employer must provide $100,000 insurance/$1000 per wk for total disability.	
Jurisdiction		CT, DE, MD, MA, NY, NJ, PA, DC	
Pension Health & Welfare		10/1/08 $86.00 per day in Baltimore, MD and Washington, DC $110.00 per day - All other areas	
Holidays		New Year's Day, Martin Luther King Day, President's Day, Memorial Day Independence Day, Labor Day, Veterans Day, Thanksgiving Day Day after Thanksgiving, Christmas Day	
Notes		>"Flat Deal" contracts may be negotiated with approval of the union. >Penalty for using non-L798 member for covered work: 2X applicable wages plus costs. >Minimum $12.50 per day if member provides materials. >Employer to provide suitable attire for abnormally cold or wet work. Smoke on Set: Employer to give prior notification, provide masks and vent for 10 min. every 60-90 min. >Excludes PSAs & spec commercials. Excludes low budget commercials with 1day production of $75K or less and aggregate cost of $225K or less. Wage rates subject to individual negotiation. P&W normal. >Applies to Commercials ONLY.	
Phone numbers		Local 798 NY: 212-627-0660	AICP LA: 323-960-4763, NY: 212-929-3000

New York		Los Angeles
Steve Bizenov		Tina Bassir
(646) 829-0702	MEDIA SERVICES	(310) 471-9369
steve@media-services.com	ENTERTAINMENT ACCOUNTING, PAYROLL & SOFTWARE	tina@media-services.com

Local 52 Minimum Daily Rates

LOCAL 52, STUDIO MECHANICS

Minimum Daily Rates 2/4/09 - 11/30/11 (AICP)

Rates are for 10 hours work per day.

Category	2/4/09 - 11/30/09
Sound Mixer	$565.75
Video Playback/ Utility	528.35
VTR Tech.	565.75
Boom	528.35
Recordist	528.35
Department Heads	528.35
2nd/ Foreman	503.94
3rd/ Operator	487.72

Overtime
In 1/2 hour units

	1x	1 1/2x	2x	3x
First 5 days	10	>10	>12	>18
6th day		1-12	>12	>18
7th day			1-18	>18

Work in excess of 18 hours per day requires permission from Union.

Pension, Health & Welfare
- NYC Zone: IAP 5% of scale for all hours worked or guaranteed, plus PH&W $10.0870 per hour worked and $.75 per day for accidental death insurance.

- Philadelphia Zone: $70/day for employees "employed in or hired in."

- Outside NYC or Philadelphia: $55/day for employees "hired and employed in."

Zones
New York City: NY rates and conditions apply: Five boroughs, all of Long Island and 75 miles in all directions from Columbus Circle.
Report to Zone: 25 miles from Columbus Circle.

Philadelphia: 30 miles in all directions from center of city. "Report to" within the zone.

Employees hired within NY or Philadelphia zones work under respective zone wages, conditions and benefits wherever employed.

Employees working within New York zone work under NY zone wages, conditions and benefits regardless of where they live or were hired.

Outside zones, but within jurisdiction of Local 52 Commercial Production Agreement, rules and conditions apply except for PH&W rates and with the following additions which apply throughout the jurisdiction:
- No subcontracting of any bargaining unit work
- Application of confidentiality clause

New York	Los Angeles
Steve Bizenov	Tina Bassir
(646) 829-0702	(310) 471-9369
steve@media-services.com	tina@media-services.com

MEDIA SERVICES
ENTERTAINMENT ACCOUNTING, PAYROLL & SOFTWARE

Local 52 Working Rules & Conditions

LOCAL 52 STUDIO MECHANICS (CONT'D)

Working Rules & Conditions

Term of Contract		2/4/09 - 11/30/11
Contracted Day		10 hours
Contracted Workweek		Any 5 days of 7/ consecutive
Calls	Day/Night	Anytime Notice by end of previous day, cannot be changed
	Partial Day	No - Except Sunday if no shoot (5 hr Min.)
Overtime	1.5x	11-12th hours/ 6th Day up to 12
(Calculated on 10 hr day rate)	2x	Over 12 hrs/ 6th day after 12 hrs/ 7th day/ Holidays/ Sunday if no shoot (5 hr Min.)
	3x	18+ consecutive, only with union permission
	Increments	½ hr increments
Turnaround	Daily	10 hrs
	Weekly	54 hrs for 5 day week, 34 hrs for 6 day week
Penalty		3X the employee's average hourly rate until 10 hour rest period attained
Meals	Intervals	6 hour intervals, 1st meal no earlier than 3 hrs. Only 1 meal in 10 hr day.
	Lengths	1 hour - 1/2 hr. off clock if hot catered meal provided.
	Penalties	1st 1/2 hr or fraction - $15.00
		2nd ½ hr: $17.50, 3rd ½ hr: $20.00, Each additional: $20.00 w/ ½ hr break option
	Extensions	N/A
	Walking Meal	N/A
Production Zone		25 mile radius from Columbus Circle, more details on rates page
Location Rules		>Per Diem allowance, amenities and 1st Class housing or housing allowance to be provided.
		>Air Transportation - Coach or better
		>Studio Zone - No Travel Time - 125th Street to Battery and designated studios outside Manhattan
Nearby Location	Work Time	Within zone, starts at location - Travel Time is off the clock
	Travel Time	Company must provide transportation if outside Studio Zone
	Meal money, if not provided	Breakfast - $6, Lunch - $10, Dinner - $14. Breakfast only if call is 7am or earlier.
Distant Location	Travel Days	Paid at Straight Time.
	Non-overnight Dist. Loc.	Travel Time paid from studio or producer's office
	Meal money, if not provided	Breakfast - $8, Lunch - $12, Dinner - $25
Cancellation of Call		Before 6 hrs after start of prior day
Minimum Staffing		>Keys needed to do job.
		>Sound Mixer and Recordist if sound recorded.
		>To move 4K or larger light requires at least 2 Electricians.
		>Moving crane as camera platform requires 3 Grips.
		>Local 52 Generator Operator required for 5KW+
Payment of Wages		Cash at end of week or day. (In practice, check by end of week following work.)
Hazardous Work		>$100 per flight or incident. Employer must provide $250,000 insurance/ $500 per wk for total disability.
		>Aerial/ Diving, etc. - $40/ incident; Daily max $80
Jurisdiction		NY, NJ, CT, DE & PA (except for 50-mile radius from center of Pittsburgh)
Pension Health & Welfare		See notes on rates page
Holidays		New Year's Day / President's Day / Easter Sunday / Memorial Day / Independence Day / Labor Day / Columbus Day / Veterans Day / Thanksgiving Day / Day after Thanksgiving / Christmas Day
Notes		>Videotaped commercial jurisdiction - See contract
		>No strike clause
		>Additional notes on rates page
Phone numbers		Local 52 NY: 212-399-0980 AICP LA: 323-960-4763, NY: 212-929-3000

New York		Los Angeles
Steve Bizenov		Tina Bassir
(646) 829-0702	MEDIA SERVICES	(310) 471-9369
steve@media-services.com	ENTERTAINMENT ACCOUNTING, PAYROLL & SOFTWARE	tina@media-services.com

Local 829 Scenic Artists Minimum Wage Rates

LOCAL 829 SCENIC ARTISTS

Minimum Wage Rates 11/1/07 - 10/31/08*

*Note: New rates in negotiation at time of publication.

	Daily (8 hours)
Art Director	795.20
Costumer Designer/ Stylist	615.76
Charge Scenic Artist	568.24
Journeyman Scenic Artist	464.48
Asst. Art Director	Negotiable
Asst. Costume Designer/ Stylist	Negotiable
Art Dept. Coordinator	Negotiable

Overtime

	1x	1.5x	2x	2.5x	3x
1st 5 days	1-8	9-10	11-12	13-15	>15*
6th Day		1-12		13-15	>15*
7th Day/ Holiday			1-12	13-15	>15*

* No work permitted over 15 hours except with written permission of the union.

New York
Steve Bizenov
(646) 829-0702
steve@media-services.com

MEDIA SERVICES
ENTERTAINMENT ACCOUNTING, PAYROLL & SOFTWARE

Los Angeles
Tina Bassir
(310) 471-9369
tina@media-services.com

Local 829 Scenic Artists Working Rules & Conditions

LOCAL 829 SCENIC ARTISTS (CONT'D)

Working Rules & Conditions

Term of Contract		2/9/06 - 10/31/08
Contracted Day		8 hours
Contracted Workweek		Any 5 days of 7/ consecutive
Calls	Day/Night	Anytime for photography day (see notes below for non-photo day rules)
	Partial Day	Sunday only Scenic Artist on construction day - 4 hrs @ 2x
		Layoff or change by 2:30pm of prior day
Overtime (Based on Contracted Day)	1.5x	9th and 10th hours/ 6th Day up to 12 hrs
	2x	11th and 12th hours/ 7th Day & Holidays up to 12 hrs
	2.5x	13th thru 15th hours
	3x	Over 15 hours with written permission from union
	Increments	½ hr increments
Turnaround	Daily	10 hrs
Penalty		2x for 1st 2 hours encroached, 3x beyond 2 hrs
Meals	Intervals	1st meal: 4-6 hours after call; 2nd meal within 6 hrs of previous
	Lengths	1 hour - ½ hr. off clock if hot catered meal provided
	Penalties	1st ½ hr or fraction - $15.00
		2nd ½ hr: $17.50, 3rd ½ hr: $20.00, Each additional: $20.00 w/ ½ hr break option
Production Zone		25 mile radius from Columbus Circle report to zone
Location Rules		> Per Diem allowance, amenities and 1st Class housing or housing allowance to be provided
		> Air Transportation - Coach or better
		> Studio Zone - No Travel Time - 125th Street to Battery and designated studios outside Manhattan
		> Layovers: Non-worked days on location are paid at straight time
Nearby Location	Work Time	Beyond 25 miles, travel time is work time
	Travel Time	Travel time starts at edge of zone. Company provides transportation or reimbursement.
	Meal money, if not provided	Breakfast - $8, Lunch - $12, Dinner - $25.
Distant Location		Travel time paid at 1x, not to exceed 8 hrs
		Travel/Work: 1x for travel portion, but all time counts toward OT calculation
Cancellation of Call		By 2:30pm preceding day
Minimum Staffing		> No minimum staffing, but all covered work to be performed by union members
		> 1st Scenic Artist hired at Chargeman rate and supervises
		> Penalty for hiring non-union is 1.5x the pay that would have been due
		> No Penalty if union cannot provide qualified personnel, but PH&W must be paid
		> Non-829 IATSE members may be hired without penalty
		> Can hire Scenic Artists without an Art Director/Designer if that function is not performed
		> Asst Art Director/Costume Designers are covered if needed to perform a creative function
		> Art Dept Coordinator covered if needed and hired
Jurisdiction		NY, NJ, CT, DE & PA (see "Hiring Rules" in Notes below)
Pension Health & Welfare		$100 per day working in or hired in NY Zone
		If hired and working outside NY Zone, then go by Commercial Production Agreement
Holidays		New Year's Day, Martin Luther King Day, President's Day, Memorial Day, Independence Day, Labor Day, Veterans Day, Thanksgiving Day, Day after Thanksgiving, Christmas Day

New York
Steve Bizenov
(646) 829-0702
steve@media-services.com

MEDIA SERVICES
ENTERTAINMENT ACCOUNTING, PAYROLL & SOFTWARE

Los Angeles
Tina Bassir
(310) 471-9369
tina@media-services.com

Notes	> Wrap day: Up to 4 hrs 1x for Costume Designer/Stylist to personally return borrowed wardrobe > No payments as independent contractors Hiring Rules "Zone" is 50 miles from Columbus Circle and all of Nassau & Suffolk Counties > This contract applies: Working in Zone or hired in Zone & working in jurisdiction > Commercial Prod. Agreement applies if hired outside Zone > Producer may outsource client and specialized artwork > Multi-sets/stages for same job with one shooting and other prepping may require Standby Scenic Artist and Assistant Art Director to cover shooting set > Employer must supply materials, tools & brushes > Lockers or clean safe place for clothing to be provided in studios Non-Photography Day Rules (Scenic Artists only) > Call is 8 hrs between 7am and 8pm > 8pm - midnight: Extra 10% p/hr of Journey Scenic Artist scale if premium rate not in effect. > Midnight - 7am: Extra 20% p/hr of Journey Scenic Artist scale if premium rate not in effect. > Minimum call is 8 hours, except Sunday: Minimum is 4 hrs at 2x > Workweek: 7am Monday to 8pm Saturday > Saturday: 8pm - midnight at 1.5; Sunday: All hours at 2x
Low Budget/ Spec/ PSAs	PSAs: Rates and OT may be negotiated, but PH&W remains the same Spec Commercial: Same, but full compensation if sold
Phone numbers	Local 829 NY: 212-581-0300 AICP NY: 212-929-3000

New York
Steve Bizenov
(646) 829-0702
steve@media-services.com

MEDIA SERVICES
ENTERTAINMENT ACCOUNTING, PAYROLL & SOFTWARE

Los Angeles
Tina Bassir
(310) 471-9369
tina@media-services.com

Directors Guild of America Commercials Agreement

DGA NATIONAL COMMERCIALS AGREEMENT

Minimum Daily Salaries 11/1/06 - 10/31/09

	11/1/06 - 10/31/07	11/1/07 - 10/31/08	11/1/08 - 10/31/09
Director	1,072	1,126	1,182
UPM	675	675	675
1st Assistant Director	773	796	820
2nd Assistant Director	422	435	448
2nd 2nd Assistant Director	317	326	336
Trainee - 2nd year	139	143	147
Trainee - 1st year	124	128	132

Employer Fringe Benefits

Pension	5.5%	
Health and Welfare	8.5%	
Training Plan and Commercial Qualification Lists Administration	.25	Eastern Region
Vacation Pay	4%	Paid at layoff, dismissal or termination of employment
Unworked Holiday Pay	3.292%	Paid at layoff, dismissal or termination of employment

AICP companies have special pension and health provisions.

New York
Steve Bizenov
(646) 829-0702
steve@media-services.com

Los Angeles
Tina Bassir
(310) 471-9369
tina@media-services.com

Directors Guild of America Work Rules

DGA NATIONAL COMMERCIALS AGREEMENT

Working Rules & Conditions

Term of Contract		11/1/05 - 10/31/09
Contracted Day		12 consecutive hours
Contracted Workweek		Any 5 or 6 consecutive days of 7
Calls	Day/Night	Anytime — 1st & 2nd AD Calls must begin at earliest of cast and crew calls
	Partial Day	No
Overtime (Based on Contracted Day)	13th & 14th hour	1/8 of day rate for each hour invaded
	Over 14 hrs	1/6 of day rate for each hour invaded
	Over 15 hrs	1 day's pay for each 5 hour period; 5 hours computed starting at the 13th hour
	6th day	150% of day rate / 200% on distant location if work is performed
	7th day & holidays	200% of day rate
	Increments	Whole hours
	Additional	Work on 5th day which extends into 6th day before completion of 12 hrs is paid at 2x 1st AD cannot be dismissed prior to crew 2nd AD cannot be dismissed until AD duties are completed Over 18 hrs - Producer must offer 1st class hotel or car service to employee's home or hotel
Turnaround	Daily	8 hrs
Penalty	If short	1 day's pay for each 5 hr period until 8 hr rest is achieved
Meals	Intervals	
	Lengths	Reasonable time provided - Meal time is work time
	Penalties	If no dinner provided by 7:30pm and day started 9am or earlier - $30.00
Location Rules		Lodging - 1st Class Air Transportation - Coach, but 1st or Business Class if over 5 hrs. - Always same class as Director. Layovers - Non-worked days on location are paid at straight time. Members shall not be required to drive transportation vehicles. Producer must provide minimum $100K travel insurance for travel to or from location. Proof must be provided.
Work Time/ Travel Time Provisions		Travel time is work time. Travel to distant loc. on 6th, 7th or holidays is 1x time, if no work performed. Except Report to studios: East - Within 5 Boroughs of NYC ---- West - LA County
Cancellation Fee		One day's pay if Agency cancels or postpones less than 48 hrs prior to call and AD makes best effort to replace work. Use contract for additional rules. Does not apply to work reduced by accelerated schedule or after prod. has started. No PH&W on Fee. Cancellation or termination of job being worked on by 2 PM or owe for the next day.

Minimum Staffing
 	
See AICP Provisions below
		>Director
		>1st AD: Whenever a Director is employed, including screen tests
		>2nd AD: Not less than one shooting day of each commercial
		          When need to control background or crowds
		          When 12 or more persons are photographed.
		>Must include Dir. & 1st AD on all location shoot days when shoot is 4 days or more and cast and crew is 10 or more
		>When Director sent out of U.S., 1st AD must be sent, unless destination country refuses work permit or production subsidy would be lost. (See special AICP Provisions below)
		>UPM shall be hired if UPM duties are being performed, but there is no min. staffing.
		>Southern CA and Third Area qualification lists to be established in addition to current NY list.
		>If 2nd AD member works as Location Scout, must be treated as DGA member. Does not apply in LA County or where other unions have jurisdiction.

Payment of Wages		Per state and federal timely payment requirements
Hazardous Work	Insurance	$500K death and/or dismemberment. $500 per week total disability coverage
	Pay	Pay $150 per incident - Max $300 per day
Jurisdiction		U.S. based companies: Wherever they work.
Pension Health & Welfare		See rates page
Holidays		New Year's Day Martin Luther King Day President's Day Memorial Day Independence Day Labor Day Thanksgiving Day Christmas Day

New York
Steve Bizenov
(646) 829-0702
steve@media-services.com

MEDIA SERVICES
ENTERTAINMENT ACCOUNTING, PAYROLL & SOFTWARE

Los Angeles
Tina Bassir
(310) 471-9369
tina@media-services.com

Notes	>Staffing violations subject to triple damages >1st AD may not be dismissed prior to his/her crew. >Commercial Project Listing Form must be submitted prior to 1st day of production, incl. foreign productions >Minimum 1st AD Prep: 1 day for 1-2 day shoot, 2 days for 3+ day shoot or two or more significantly different or distant locations. >Special provisions for Spec Spots, Internet and Public Service Announcements. - See Contract. >Excludes low budget commercials with single day production of $75K or less and aggregate cost of $225K or less. Wage rates subject to individual negotiation. PH&W based on scale rates. >Signatory Producers may not subcontract to non-signatory producers. >Signatory Producers may be contracted by non-signatory producers, but must notify DGA within 10 days or project will be considered signatory. >DGA will consider requests for signatory employers to provide production services to non-signatory foreign prod. co's producing commercials for non-US/Canada markets. 1st & 2nd ADs must be hired. >Signators are bound to Basic Agmt. and other DGA agreements including production of scripted and reality TV shows, feature films, documentaries, industrials and internet projects. Does not cover music videos.
AICP Special Work Rules	>No 1st AD needed unless crew is more than 6 and cast no more than 1. (Dir. not incl.) >No 1st AD prep day needed if shoot is less than 5 hours. If goes over 5 hrs - 1 AD owed for prep day >No 1st on prep day for 1 day shoot if: Limbo product shots w/no talent or Minor reshoots or >Stop Motion photography or Pick-up shots >No 2nd AD needed for "table top" production, if not required by needs of the production. >UPM shall be hired if UPM duties being handled substantially by one employee, but there is no min. staffing. >No need to travel US 1st AD to foreign countries outside No. America if shoot is 3 or fewer shoot days and is awarded less than 10 bus. days prior to first Shoot day. Local 1st AD to be given preference of employment >Projects in Canada and Mexico require sending of US 1st AD unless destination country refuses work permit or production subsidy would be lost. >Special provisions apply AICP to companies located in the Midwest. Contact DGA for info. >DGA members employed as Location Scouts within 75 miles of Chicago paid as DGA 2nd Ads.
AICP Pension Health & Welfare	Presumed Salaries for P&W Calculation: Principal (Owner) Director: *$150,000* per calendar year (or actual earnings if elected by *1/20* each year). Principal (Owner) or Staff UPM or 1st AD: *$120,000* per calendar year. Staff 2nd AD: $70,000 per calendar year. Other Directors: $7000 per shoot day. Other UPMs or Ads: Actual gross earnings including profits etc.
AICP Director-Deferred Membership	Directors may defer membership not later than 10 shoot days or one year from Director's first shoot day. Applies to director regardless of number of companies worked for. Producers must notify Guild. All other provisions, including PH&W apply.
DGA Office Phone numbers	Los Angeles: 310-289-2000, New York: 212-581-0370, Chicago: 312-644-5050

New York
Steve Bizenov
(646) 829-0702
steve@media-services.com

Los Angeles
Tina Bassir
(310) 471-9369
tina@media-services.com

Directors Guild of America Work Rules

Screen Actors Guild Guidelines

Note: The new SAG/AMPTP agreement was still being negotiated at press time. Please check the SAG website for updated information.

SCREEN ACTORS GUILD
COMMERCIALS CONTRACT DEPARTMENT
5757 Wilshire Blvd., Los Angeles, CA 90036
(323) 549-6858 for commercial queries only
All other questions, call (323) 954-1600 or visit www.sag.org

The following is a brief interpretation of the Screen Actors Guild 2003 Commercials Contract and includes the 2006 Commercials Memorandum Agreement relating to principal performers. This digest is possible due to the generous assistance of the Screen Actors Guild.
For more complete information, LA 411 recommends that the reader review the full text of the 2003 contract, or contact the Screen Actors Guild's Commercials Department.

Auditions

The first two auditions are allowed without compensation if one hour or less. Additional time is paid in 30 minute units @ $35.45 per unit. Third callbacks are $141.80 for the first two hours and $35.45 per half hour thereafter. Fourth callbacks are $283.55 for the first four hours and $35.45 per half hour thereafter.

Bookings & Cancellations

A Performer is booked when:
1. Given written notice of acceptance.
2. A form contract signed by the Producer is delivered to the Performer or when a form contract unsigned by the Producer is delivered to a Performer and is executed by Performer and returned to Producer within 48 hours.
3. A script is delivered to the Performer (does not include delivery for auditions or for the Performer to review for possible employment).
4. Fitted (does not include wardrobe tests).
5. Given a verbal call which he/she accepts.
6. Told he/she will be used but no date is set.
7. Told not to accept an engagement for a spot advertising a competitive product or service.

The Producer shall have the right to cancel any call without payment because of impossibility of production due to "Force Majeure." Postponement of a call to a mutually acceptable date may be made by the Producer upon 24 hours notification (except on Saturdays, Sundays and holidays), as long as the new booking date is made within 15 working days of original date and payment of one half day of the session fee is paid. If production does not take place within 15 days, another half session payment is due and the Performer is thereupon released. None of these payments are creditable toward any session fees payable to the Performer if production should take place at a later date.

(continued)

Employment

1. Session fees must be paid and postmarked within 12 working days.
2. On-camera principals/stunt performers' session fee is $567.10 for an 8-hour day. The voice-over session fee is $426.40 for a 2-hour session.
3. Performer is paid for each commercial shot on the same day. Performer is paid for each day whether or not the commercial is completed. In other words, the Performer is paid a session fee for the number of days or the number of commercials, whichever is greater.
4. If Performer is called in to re-shoot, session fees are due and payable depending on quantity of commercials and number of days.
5. For each tag or dealer identification made beyond one, the voice over rate shall be paid $126.85 . This fee is paid for each tag numbered two through 25. $70.40 is paid for each tag 26 through 50. $38.35 is paid for each tag 51+. If called in for the sole purpose of making tags, a session fee and a specified rate applies for each tag beyond one. (Contact SAG for the specific tier-step rate and whether any other session fee rate is applicable.)
6. Commercials made initially for use on the Internet or in New Media: Producer may bargain freely with Performer and shall pay Performer compensation in such amount as shall be agreed by direct bargaining with the Performer or the Performer's agent.

Work Time

1. All on-camera Principals' sessions are based on an eight-hour day. That does not include their meal periods. Off-camera (voice over) Performers' sessions are based on two-hour engagements.
2. Performer's rate for the ninth and tenth hours of work is time-and-one-half, and the 11th hour of work is paid at double the Performer's hourly rate.
3. Overtime for Principals earning more than 2x the session fee per commercial per day shall be paid 1 1/2 x (instead of double time) after 10 hours.
4. Principle Performers making more than double scale for the session (over $1,134.20 per commercial) shall receive 1 1/2 x their session rate for Saturdays and Sundays. Performers making $1,134.20 or less shall receive double their session rate.
5. Rest periods from time of dismissal to first call thereafter must be 12 hours. Exceptions to this are made when the last shot of the day is an exterior shot on a nearby location and the next day's shooting begins with exterior photography. Then the rest period may be reduced to 10 hours. The reduced rest period pertains only to those performers who are in the respective scenes.

(Contact SAG for other exceptions.)

Night Work

Night work is defined as work between 8 p.m. and 6 a.m., except that a first call for the day at 5 a.m. or thereafter shall not constitute night work.

Except as above provided, the Performer shall receive premium pay for each hour of night work equal to 10% of his/her hourly rate for such hours. In the computation of such premium pay, the hourly rate of the Performer for such hours is first determined, and 10% thereof is added as the night work premium.

Travel Time

1. The Los Angeles Studio Zone is defined as that area within a radius of 30 miles of the intersection of Beverly and La Cienega Boulevards.
2. Travel to and from location when no services are rendered requires a full session fee. There are no half day or hourly rates.
3. Travel time shall be paid as work time if Performer is working. Overtime caused by travel to and from location is paid at straight time in quarterly units.
4. All travel past midnight shall be paid at 1 1/2 x Performer's rate, in quarterly units.
5. If traveling to and from LAX and JFK, add one hour. If traveling to and from La Guardia, add 1/2 hour.

(continued)

Meals & Meal Penalties
1. Meal periods must be within six hours of first call in-studio or on location. Second meal period must be within six hours following completion of first meal period.
2. Meal penalty is $25.00 for first 1/2 hour violation, second 1/2 hour is $25.00, third 1/2 hour and each 1/2 hour thereafter is paid at $50.00.
3. If makeup, wardrobe or hairdress preparation time will disrupt the Performer's normal meal period, the Producer may provide that Performer with a working meal (e.g., coffee, sandwiches) before the Performer's set call if no deduction is made from work time for meal periods.

Mileage & Parking
Mileage based on rate which IRS provides may be paid as a travel expense allowance not reported as income. The Producer shall provide supervised or secured parking.

Travel, Transportation & Accommodations
1. All travel expenses and lodging accommodations shall be furnished by the Producer including first class transportation to and from location for air travel of 1,000 or more air miles. For air travel of less than 1,000 miles, coach service may be provided. Producer shall provide a reasonable single room accommodation.
2. Necessary traveling expenses and meal per diem at breakfast ($10.50), lunch ($15.70), and dinner ($28.95).

Holidays
New Year's Day, Martin Luther King Jr.'s Birthday, Washington's Birthday (Presidents' Day), Memorial Day, July 4, Labor Day, Thanksgiving, Christmas. Holidays that fall on a Sunday will be attributed to the
following Monday.

Principals working on a holiday are entitled to double time for all hours worked

Pension and health contribution is 14.8%.

Visit www.sag.org for more information.